CHINA
4TH EDITION

Where to Stay and Eat
for All Budgets

Must-See Sights
and Local Secrets

Ratings You Can Trust

Fodor's Travel Publications   New York, Toronto, London, Sydney, Auckland
www.fodors.com

FODOR'S CHINA
Editor: David Allan

Editorial Production: Tom Holton
Editorial Contributors: Collin Campbell, Paul Davidson, Charles De Simone, Tracey Furniss, Tom Hilditch, Gregor Irvine-Halliday, Deborah Kaufman, Sandra Lim, Caroline Liou, Keming Liu, Eva Chui Loiterton, Tim Metcalfe, Richard Meyer, Emmanuelle Morgen, Kristin Baird Rattini, Guy Rubin, Douglas Stallings, Sofia A. Suárez, Josie Taylor, Brandon Zatt
Maps: David Lindroth, *cartographer;* Bob Blake and Rebecca Baer, *map editors*
Design: Fabrizio La Rocca, *creative director;* Moon Sun Kim, *cover designer;* Guido Caroti, *art director;* Melanie Marin, *photo editor*
Production/Manufacturing: Colleen Ziemba
Cover Photo (young girl painting parasols in Fuli village near Guilin): Glen Alison Photography/Mira

Fourth Edition

ISBN 1–4000–1326–7

ISSN 1070–6895

SPECIAL SALES

This book is available for special discounts for bulk purchases for sales promotions or premiums. Special editions, including personalized covers, excerpts of existing books, and corporate imprints, can be created in large quantities for special needs. For more information, write to Special Markets/Premium Sales, 1745 Broadway, MD 6-2, New York, New York 10019, or e-mail specialmarkets@randomhouse.com.

AN IMPORTANT TIP & AN INVITATION

Although all prices, opening times, and other details in this book are based on information supplied to us at press time, changes occur all the time in the travel world, and Fodor's cannot accept responsibility for facts that become outdated or for inadvertent errors or omissions. So **always confirm information when it matters,** especially if you're making a detour to visit a specific place. Your experiences—positive and negative—matter to us. If we have missed or misstated something, **please write to us.** We follow up on all suggestions. Contact the China editor at editors@fodors.com or c/o Fodor's at 1745 Broadway, New York, New York 10019.

PRINTED IN THE UNITED STATES OF AMERICA

10 9 8 7 6 5 4 3 2 1

DESTINATION CHINA

The fast-paced bustle of a Beijing market. The slow-motion serenity of a boat trip along the Three Gorges river. The pulsing whirl of a Shanghai nightclub. The austere frozen army of unearthed terra-cotta warriors in Xian. As these experiences demonstrate, China is a land of contradiction. A Communist country on pace to become the world's leading market-driven economy. A nation of vast rural landscape and some of the most crowded industrialized cities on the planet. To travel through China is to embrace a diversity of experience that one book can barely contain. After all, this is a country that invented both paper and movable type, gave birth to two of the world's great religions, and built the Great Wall. To get the most out of your trip in this huge and exciting country, strive to soak in everything it will throw at you. From the Western luxury of Hong Kong, to the European architecture of Shanghai, to the Olympic buzz of Beijing, to the surreal landscape of Everest base camp, these are all shades of China. Have an amazing adventure in China!

Tim Jarrell, Publisher

CONTENTS

Maps

CloseUps

The more you know before you go, the better your trip will be. Shanghai's best restaurant or Hong Kong's best open-air market could be just around the corner from your hotel, but if you don't know it's there, it might as well be on the other side of the globe. That's where this book comes in. It's a great step toward making sure your next trip lives up to your expectations. As you plan, check out the Web as well. Guidebooks have been helping smart travelers find the special places for years; the Web is one more tool. Whatever reference you consult, be savvy about what you read, and always consider the source. Images and language can be massaged to make places appear better than they are. And one traveler's quaint is another's grimy. Here at Fodor's, and at our online arm, Fodors.com, our focus is on providing you with information that's not only useful but accurate and on target. Every day Fodor's editors put enormous effort into getting things right, beginning with the search for the right contributors—people who have objective judgment, broad travel experience, and the writing ability to put their insights into words. There's no substitute for advice from a friend who has just come back from where you're going, but our writers, having seen all corners of China, are the next best thing. They're the kind of people you'd poll for tips yourself if you knew them.

Paul Davidson wrote the Great Itineraries for this edition. He lived in Changsha, China, for several years before moving to Yokohama, Japan. He is also a contributor to *Fodor's Japan*.

Charles De Simone updated the Eastern China chapter. He has worked as a tourism consultant to the Jiangsu Provincial Government and came to China in 2001 on a Harvard-Yenching Fellowship to Nanjing University.

Tracey Furniss, part of our Hong Kong team of writers, has lived in Southeast Asia and Hong Kong for more than 20 years. She started out writing for various magazines in Hong Kong, then went on to work in radio and television, including six years at CNN. She is now an editor for the *Parents' Journal* in Hong Kong and writes for the *South China Morning Post,* as well as covering what's new in Hong Kong for various magazines in the United Kingdom and United States.

British-born journalist **Tom Hilditch** has lived and worked in Hong Kong and China for the past 10 years. He writes for a number of publications including *Time, Asiaweek, South China Morning Post,* and the *Guardian.* He co-updated the Southeastern China chapter with Sandra Lim.

Gregor Irvine-Halliday updated the Mongolias chapter. He worked with CHF International in Mongolia, during which time he repeatedly failed to master horse riding. Previously he completed his MBA at the University of British Columbia and at China Europe International Business School in Shanghai while working with the LUTW Foundation.

A native Californian and graduate of UC Berkeley, **Sandra Lim** moved to China in 2002 to study Mandarin. She is fluent in English and Taiwanese. An avid traveler, she splits her time between the States and Asia. She co-updated the Southeastern China chapter with Tom Hilditch.

Caroline Liou, a former Fodor's production editor, first traveled to China in 1987. She moved to Beijing in 1998 and is currently working for World Wildlife Fund China, the conservation organization. Ms. Liou updated the dining, lodging, shopping, nightlife, and sports sections of the Beijing chapter.

A native of Baoding, **Keming Liu** is a foreign correspondent for *Trends/Bazaar,* a Chinese fashion and lifestyle magazine headquartered in Beijing. She is the coauthor of *Finger Tip Chinese*, a conversational primer for travelers in China. Dr. Liu earned her doctoral degree from Columbia University's Teachers College and is a tenured professor at CUNY. She updated the North Central and South Central chapters.

Born in Hong Kong and raised in Australia, Eva Chui Loiterton returned to her birthplace in 1995. For two years she reported on the city's arts and popular-culture scenes as the entertainment editor for *HK* magazine, a weekly finger on Hong Kong's pulse. Moving to broadcast media, she then spent three years as a producer for Channel V, Asia's No. 1 music-TV station. Currently, she divides her time between writing and working in the television and film industries in Hong Kong. She updated several Hong Kong sections, including Exploring and Nightlife & the Arts.

Tim Metcalfe has been writing, editing, and dining his way around Hong Kong since 1988. The globe-trotting English journalist initially joined the *South China Morning Post* on arrival in the former British colony, and was subsequently assistant editor of the *Hong Kong Standard* for five years. Since 1995 he has freelanced for countless publications, syndication agencies, and organizations in Hong Kong and around the world, specializing in travel, food, and wine. He updated Hong Kong's Where to Eat and Sports & the Outdoors sections for this edition.

Richard Meyer is an American writer who has visited China countless times since 1988 and currently bases himself in Macau. He updated the Southwest China chapter.

Freelance writer Kristin Baird Rattini, who worked on the Shanghai chapter and contributed to the Eastern chapter, has lived in Shanghai since 2002. She remains awed by the city's frenetic pace of change and humbled by the reminder that the current wave of expats flooding into Shanghai is neither the city's first, nor its last. Ms. Rattini is a native of the Chicago area, and she graduated from the University of Missouri School of Journalism. She has contributed travel stories, profiles, and essays to the magazines *Family Circle, National Geographic Kids, People, Sunset, That's Shanghai*, and United Airlines' *Hemispheres*, among other publications.

Guy Rubin, originally from the United Kingdom, has lived in Beijing since 1996. After recovering from spells in industries as disparate as management consultancy and the entertainment industry, in 1999 he cofounded a travel company specializing in luxury tours to China. Mr. Rubin's travel articles have appeared in *City Weekend* and *Capital Views*, two English-language magazines in Beijing; *Citylife Chiangmai*, an English-language magazine in Thailand; and the Web sites cultural-travels.com and chinanow.com. His photographs of China have appeared in several publications in the United States and Italy. Mr. Rubin updated the Exploring section of the Beijing chapter.

Sofia A. Suárez runs her communications company, Fiorini Bassi, in Hong Kong, where she was born and raised. After studying in the U.S. and Italy, the Italian-Filipina moved to New York to work for Fairchild Publications. Sofia now contributes to various newspapers and magazines around the world including the *South China Morning Post*, for whom she writes weekly style and art columns, and *The Peninsula Magazine*. She contributed to the Southeastern China chapter for this edition.

Josie Taylor, divides her time between a live-aboard Chinese junk moored in Hong Kong harbor, a colonial home in Singapore, and a villa in Bali. She travels extensively throughout Asia, by private jet as much as by rickshaw, as part of her day job as regional public relations manager for a multinational company. This gives her ample opportunity to live her secret life as a travel writer. She updated the Tibet chapter.

China-based freelance writer Brandon Zatt updated the Northeastern and North- western China chapters of the book. His other writing specializes in youth and al- ternative culture, ethnic minorities, and border regions. He sells his stories to any- one who will buy them and spends his time roving about the Chinese countryside or tearing up Shanghai's nightclubs.

ABOUT THIS BOOK

The best source for travel advice is a like-minded friend who's just been where you're headed. But with or without that friend, you'll be in great shape to find your way around your destination once you learn to find your way around your Fodor's guide.

SELECTION

Our goal is to cover the best properties, sights, and activities in their category, as well as the most interesting communities to visit. We make a point of including local food-lovers' hot spots as well as neighborhood options, and we avoid all that's touristy unless it's really worth your time. You can go on the assumption that everything in this book is recommended wholeheartedly by our writers and editors. Flip to On the Road with Fodor's to learn more about who they are. It goes without saying that no property pays to be included.

RATINGS

Orange stars ★ denote sights and properties that our editors and writers consider the very best in the area covered by the entire book. These, the best of the best, are listed in the Fodor's Choice section in the front of the book. Black stars ★ highlight the sights and properties we deem Highly Recommended, the don't-miss sights within any region. In cities, sights pinpointed with numbered map bullets ❶ in the margins tend to be more important than those without bullets.

SPECIAL SPOTS

Pleasures & Pastimes focuses on types of experiences that reveal the spirit of the destination. Watch for Off the Beaten Path sights. Some are out of the way, some are quirky, and all are worth your while. If the munchies hit while you're exploring, look for Need a Break? suggestions.

TIME IT RIGHT

Check On the Calendar up front and chapters' Timing sections for weather and crowd overviews and best days and times to visit.

SEE IT ALL

Use Fodor's exclusive Great Itineraries as a model for your trip. Either follow those that begin the book, or mix regional itineraries from several chapters. In cities, Good Walks guide you to important sights in each neighborhood; ▶ indicates the starting points of walks and itineraries in the text and on the map.

BUDGET WELL

Hotel and restaurant price categories from ¢ to $$$$ are defined in the opening pages of each chapter—expect to find a balanced selection for every budget. For attractions, we always give standard adult admission fees; reductions are usually available for children, students, and senior citizens. Look in Discounts & Deals in Smart Travel Tips for information on destination-wide ticket schemes. Want to pay with plastic? AE, D, DC, MC, V following restaurant and hotel listings indicate whether American Express, Diners Club, Master-Card, or Visa are accepted.

BASIC INFO

Smart Travel Tips lists travel essentials for the entire area covered by the book; city- and region-specific basics end each chapter. To find the best way to get around, see the transportation section; see individual modes of travel ("Car Travel," "Train Travel") for details. We assume you'll check Web sites or call for particulars.

ON THE MAPS Maps throughout the book show you what's where and help you find your way around. Black and orange numbered bullets ❶ ❶ in the text correlate to bullets on maps.

BACKGROUND In general, we give background information within the chapters in the course of explaining sights as well as in CloseUp boxes and in Understanding China at the end of the book. To get in the mood, review the suggestions in Books & Movies. The Pronunciation & Vocabulary glossary can be invaluable.

FIND IT FAST Within the book, chapters are arranged in a roughly north-to-south direction starting with Beijing. Chapters are divided into small regions, within which towns are covered in logical geographical order; attractive routes and interesting places between towns are flagged as En Route. Heads at the top of each page help you find what you need within a chapter.

DON'T FORGET Restaurants are open for lunch and dinner daily unless we state otherwise; we mention dress only when there's a specific requirement and reservations only when they're essential or not accepted—it's always best to book ahead. Hotels have private baths, phone, TVs, and air-conditioning and operate on the European Plan (a.k.a. EP, meaning without meals). We always list facilities but not whether you'll be charged extra to use them, so when pricing accommodations, find out what's included.

SYMBOLS

Many Listings
★ Fodor's Choice
★ Highly recommended
⊠ Physical address
✛ Directions
🖈 Mailing address
☎ Telephone
🖷 Fax
⊕ On the Web
✍ E-mail
💷 Admission fee
☉ Open/closed times
► Start of walk/itinerary
Ⓜ Metro stations
▤ Credit cards

Outdoors
🏌 Golf

Hotels & Restaurants
🏨 Hotel
🛏 Number of rooms
♨ Facilities
🍽 Meal plans
✗ Restaurant
🍴 Reservations
👔 Dress code
🚭 Smoking
🍷 BYOB
✗🏨 Hotel with restaurant that warrants a visit

Other
Ⓒ Family-friendly
🕿 Contact information
⇨ See also
⊠ Branch address
☞ Take note

China

KAZAKHSTAN

KIRGHIZSTAN

TAJIKISTAN
AFGHANISTAN

(JAMMU
AND
KASHMIR)

ALTAI MTS.

MONGOLIA

TIEN SHAN

TARIM BASIN

Ürümqi

XINJIANG

TAKLA MAKAN

INNER

GANSU

KUNLUN SHAN

QINGHAI

Xining

PLATEAU OF TIBET

TIBET

SICHUAN

HIMALAYAS

Yarlung Zangbo

Lhasa

Nu (Salween)

Lancang

NEPAL

BHUTAN

BANGLA-
DESH

INDIA

YUNNAN

Kunming

MYANMAR
(BURMA)

Bay of Bengal

THAILAND

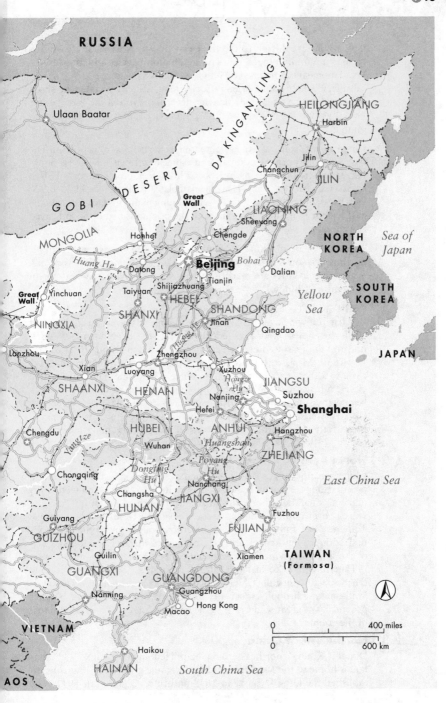

China will reveal itself to the traveler who wants to see it all—snow-capped mountain ranges, cities packed full of bicycles and mopeds, Tibetan monasteries perched on hills, crystal blue rivers, creeks full of raw sewage, markets selling dried rats, charming friendly people who shout hello wherever you go, people who never look you in the face, people who say anything not to lose face. China is a country to be understood on many levels.

China slopes from west to east, creating three general tiers of land. The first tier, in the northwest, incorporates some of the world's highest mountain ranges (the peak being Everest's 29,000 feet, on the border of Tibet and Nepal). Most of China is made up of plateaus of roughly 3,000–6,000 feet, the country's second tier. The remaining plains and lowlands in the east harbor more than two-thirds of the population and the industrial community.

As you navigate in China, remember the Chinese words for directions: north is *bei*; south is *nan*; west is *xi*; east is *dong*; and middle is *zhong*. Street signs in cities are marked in both Chinese characters and pinyin (romanized Chinese).

① Beijing

Red flags blowing over Tiananmen, the Summer Palace at dusk, the Great Wall, the endless steps and red-tile roofs of the Forbidden City—Beijing and the surrounding area are firmly rooted in grandeur. The Liao, Jin, Yuan, Ming, and Qing dynasties all chose it as their capital, for close to 2,000 years of imperial presence. The Chinese view the whole city as a historical and cultural museum, as much of China's past has been demolished elsewhere. Although the wide avenues and huge blocks create a sterile feel, they embody the image those in control want to project; they're laid out so that the individual feels small in comparison to "order."

② North Central China

China's northern treaty ports—Qingdao, Tianjin, and Dalian—offer a counterpoint to nearby Beijing as major cities. Colonial architecture ornaments small neighborhoods in and around these ports. In Qingdao, you can even glimpse a fairly blue ocean past the German villa rooftops. Tianjin, a city full of foreign architecture, boasts one of the country's best antiques markets. The Qing and Song dynasties developed much of the inland provinces, investing cities such as Nanjing and Kaifeng, in Henan, with historical and cultural merit; these cities may be among the most "authentically Chinese" places to visit in the country. The Great Wall snakes through Hebei and Shaanxi provinces as well. Neither province is of great scenic or historic interest, but they do produce most of the country's coal.

③ Northeastern China

Dongbei, China's northeastern region of Heilongjiang, Jilin, and Liaoning, is home to the Manchus. A distinct ethnic group, the Manchus established the Qing Dynasty in 1644 and ruled China until 1911. The region is not as inviting as other provinces because of its cold and barren climate, but Harbin's winter ice festival draws visitors bundled up in −30°C (−22°F) weather to Heilongjiang—China's northernmost province. Just south is Jilin, home to the best Chinese ski resorts as well as China's largest nature reserve, where you can hike through thick forests up into the mountains to stand before a giant crater lake. Dalian, in Liaoning province, is among China's more "green" cities, where many parks and gardens line the colorful streets. The city has a strong colonial past, much of whose architecture survives to this day.

4 **Northwestern China**

The famed Silk Road ran through much of this region, beginning in Shaanxi province in the ancient capital of Xian and ending in Xinjiang's Kashgar, the westernmost city within China. Here you can sip Uighur tea while watching camels carry in goods from across the desert. In Gansu province yaks run aplenty in the charming, ethnically Tibetan town of Xiahe, nestled in the mountains and surrounded by grasslands. Ningxia is home to a large Hui population, beautiful sand dunes, and the Western Xia tombs, which sit among herds of goat and sheep. Qinghai, one of China's most remote provinces, is home to a large Tibetan population, as the region was formerly part of the Tibetan Autonomous Region. Although it is also known to house the country's most severe prisons (*laogai*), Qinghai, like Xinjiang, is a beautiful region full of mountain ranges and sweeping grasslands. At the eastern end of the region, the unforgettable terra-cotta soldiers stand sentinel after 2,000 years in Xian, which has other historic sights and pockets of delightful Muslim character as well.

5 **Shanghai**

Infamous in the 1920s for its gambling, prostitution, gangsters, and opium dens, Shanghai is regaining some of the reputation it lost after the Cultural Revolution. As one of the most Westernized cities in China, excluding Hong Kong, Shanghai is on the cutting edge of China's race for modernization. It's full of underground clubs, high-class restaurants, and upscale boutiques. Almost a quarter of the world's construction cranes stand in this city of 14 million; often it feels like half of those are on the street you happen to be walking down. On the other hand, architectural remnants of a strong colonial past survive along the charming, winding, bustling streets that make this city undeniably and intimately Chinese.

6 **Eastern China**

China's eastern provinces are the most densely populated and industrialized regions in the country. They are also home to some of China's most heavily visited spots. In Jiangsu province, Suzhou, with its meditative gardens, and in Zhejiang province, Hangzhou, with its serene lake, are often paired as "heaven and earth" by the Chinese and have attracted China's most illustrious poets and painters. The old Ming capital of Nanjing, in Jiangsu, is a city full of historic landmarks and Chinese architecture—a requisite stop for the sinologist. The Huangshan range in Anhui is one of China's best-known sacred mountain ranges, with marvelous views as well as an incredible number of people to go with them. Jingdezhen, in Jiangxi, is China's first and main producer of ceramics and porcelain; today it still turns out reproductions of ancient work of astonishingly high quality. Also in Jiangxi, the old hill resort of Lushan is a charming mountain village dotted with 19th-century European-style villas. Fujian's close proximity to Taiwan has created affluent cities, such as Xiamen and Fuzhou, backed by big businesses and industry.

(7) Southeastern China

The Chinese have a saying: In Beijing one talks, in Shanghai one shops, in Guangzhou (Canton) one eats. The infamous Qingping market of Guangzhou demonstrates how well this proverb reflects reality. From insects to dogs to indistinguishable rodents both live and dried, it appears the Cantonese eat anything and everything. The Cantonese tend to associate themselves with neighboring Hong Kong rather than faraway Beijing, sharing the same dialect, food specialties, and money-making ventures. Indeed, Guangzhou and the affluent region of Guangdong province have seriously tested Deng Xiao Ping's 1990 mandate: "To get rich is glorious." A frenzy and chaos define the city, which has a buzz and energy like no other. To the south lies Hainan Island, China's only real resort province. Surprisingly pristine beaches and great seafood dishes make the island province a popular vacation spot for mainlanders.

(8) Hong Kong

When the British handed back Hong Kong to China in July 1997, China acquired one of the world's most prosperous cities. Despite the financial downturn in the late 1990s, Hong Kong remains a city on the move. With all the political hype and foreboding for the future, the city is still intent on landfilling, hotel-expanding, bridge-building, business-dealing, and world-class shopping. Take the tram up to Victoria Peak and witness a city below that can inspire awe the way the Grand Canyon does. Equally spectacular are the blue waters and small islands surrounding the city. Cheung Chau, Lantau, and Lamma islands are speckled with fishing villages and lovely hiking areas. The formerly Portuguese port city of Macau is a delightful anomaly nearby. World-class hotels, Iberian architecture, and Macanese food specialties await the visitor.

(9) South Central China

Looking like sand castles dropped from the sky, the karst rock formations of Guangxi province are among China's most spectacular landscapes. As industry and crowds overtake the city of Guilin, nearby Yangshuo is becoming the more desirable spot for karst mountain viewing. In Guizhou, one of China's more overlooked provinces, are the spectacular Huangguoshu Falls, set in the lush countryside where many of China's minorities make their home. In Hunan the cities of Shaoshan and Changsha—birthplaces of many Communist leaders, including Mao himself—draw steady streams of pilgrims. The industrial city of Wuhan, in Hubei province, is a port on the Three Gorges river cruise.

10 Southwestern China

In Sichuan province from Chengdu to Chongqing, locals gather in tea-houses by day, dine on the spiciest food in China, and play mah-jongg long into the night—a relaxing way of life that has become tradition here. The Three Gorges boat cruise along the Yangzi River originates in Chongqing and shares—with Hubei province—some of the trip's most awesome river scenery. Just north of Vietnam and bordering Burma and Laos lies the ethnically diverse province of Yunnan, home to the Dai, Bai, Yi, and Naxi minorities. Backpackers relax in the ancient town of Dali below spectacular mountains before heading north to Lijiang and hiking past the waterfalls and through the valleys of Tiger Leaping Gorge. Another natural attraction, the Stone Forest, also stands in Yunnan. The Dai minority inhabits the tropical region of Xishuangbanna, where sparkling waters and junglelike flora evoke a bit of Southeast Asia.

11 Inner Mongolia & the Republic of Mongolia

Inner Mongolia, often confused with Mongolia, is an autonomous region of China; here the traditional Mongolian way of life has become mostly nonexistent as modernization hits fast. The Mongols invaded and conquered China on horseback in the 13th century, and today children in the Republic of Mongolia, China's northern neighbor, still learn to ride horses at the age of four or five. Racing, archery, and wrestling make up the annual Naadam Festival in Ulaan Baatar, the country's capital and most heavily populated city, where the surrounding grasslands fill up with riders in brightly colored dress. Bordering Siberia, Mongolia's huge territory (1,550,000 square km [600,000 square mi]) covers diverse geography ranging from the Gobi Desert to the pristine Khovsgol Lake to the Altai Mountain range. Mongolia is home to a variety of cultural and historical museums as well as a few monasteries that survived the Stalinist purge.

12 Tibet

Tibet, hung from the Himalayas, was considered one of the most magical places in the world before the Chinese invasion of 1950. Though the autonomous region still holds a lofty place in Western imagination, Tibet has been largely stripped of its freedom and identity as a thriving Buddhist region. Nevertheless, Tibet remains a land of colorful people strengthened and characterized by the rugged terrain. The Potala Palace, in Lhasa, which only a handful of foreigners laid eyes on before the 1980s, stretches up its 1,000 rooms to the sky.

China Highlights
14 to 21 days

If this is your first or only trip to China, here are all the top spots in one ambitious tour. See China's past in its former capitals of Xian, Hangzhou, and Nanjing. And see where it is headed in its current capital, Beijing, and its economic center, Shanghai. In Suzhou, helped by man's cultivating hand, and in the Three Gorges, left to her own devices, Nature exhibits herself in all her beauty and wonder.

SHANGHAI 2 days. It's worthwhile to make two trips to the Bund for its views—once in the afternoon to the Pudong side of the Huangpu River to get a good look at the art deco buildings dating from the early 20th century, and again after sundown, to the Puxi side of the Huangpu for a look at Shanghai's gaudy, 21st-century skyline. In between visits, check out the Shanghai Museum with its impressive collections of bronzes, plasters, and paintings. On the second day, visit Shanghai's nod to traditional China, Yuyuan, and the nearby French Quarter. In the afternoon, go to Shanghai's strange and nostalgic indoor amusement park, Dashijie, where if you're lucky you might catch a performance by acrobats, musicians, or magicians.

SUZHOU 2 days. You could spend a week or more here and not exhaust all of the gardens and parks in this city, but two days is enough to get a good idea of Suzhou. On Day 1, head over to North Temple Pagoda, which dates back to the Southern Song Dynasty. Afterward, walk or take a cab down the road to Suzhou's biggest garden, the Humble Administrator's Garden, with its large pond areas and many pavilions. In the afternoon, explore Suzhou's canal areas, which encircle the entire city center and give Suzhou its unique charm. On Day 2, go to the exquisite Master of the Nets Garden, Suzhou's most subtle and elegant garden. Blue Wave Pavilion, another garden with a history dating back to the Five Dynasties Period, is nearby and also worth seeing. If you have some extra time and are not sick of Chinese gardens, try either Joyous Garden or Lion's Grove Garden.

HANGZHOU 2 days. The first place you want to visit is West Lake, Hangzhou's signature tourist spot. Take a boat out to the lake's two islands that allow visitors. Santan Yinyue is especially nice. Afterwards, walk or take a bicycle along the two causeways, Sudi and Baidi, and visit some of the parks and temples dotting the waters. On Day 2, go out to the Temple of the Soul's Retreat, with is hundreds of stone Buddhist carvings. In the afternoon, head over to either Running Tiger Dream Spring for forested walks and medicinal waters, or to the Longjing tea fields.

NANJING 2 days. Nanjing's most impressive sites are located in the Purple Mountain park area just east of downtown. Here you'll find Sun Yatsen's grandiose mausoleum, the tomb of the Ming Emperor, and the brick-built Spirit Valley Temple and Pagoda. On Day 2 go to the Confucian Temple and wander around the surrounding streets and alleys with the buildings preserved in Ming and early Qing architectural styles.

THREE GORGES 3 days. Fly to Chongqing from Nanjing. If you have an extra day or two to spare, Chongqing, another Chinese city with a long and colorful history, is worth the time. Otherwise, you can get directly on one of the Three Gorges riverboats and begin your journey through some of China's most stunning scenery. The trip to Wuhan is three days. This is not something to put off for a future trip: in a few years, once the Chinese government floods this channel, much of what now exists will be underwater.

XIAN 3 days. On the first day, go to the Shaanxi History Museum. If you're going to visit only one museum in China, this is the one. Afterward, go see the "forest" of stone stelae at the Xian Forest of Stelae Museum. The next day, go out to the Tomb of Qin Shihuang where thousands of terra-cotta soldiers dating back to the Qin Dynasty were unearthed beginning in 1974. The notorious first emperor of Qin was a tyrant famous for book burnings, inhuming Confucianists, and building the Great Wall. On Day 3, check out the Bell Tower in the center of town and cap it all off by climbing the steps of the 209-foot-high Great Goose Pagoda.

BEIJING 3 days. On the first day go to Tiananmen Square. On the west side on the square is the Chinese Historical Museum and beside it is the Chinese Revolutionary Museum, both worth taking in. Walk across the square and look inside the Great Hall of the People to see where the levers of Chinese government are pulled. Then walk down the square (away from the big picture of Mao) to the Mao Zedong Memorial for a glimpse at the chairman's pasty corpse. If that's a piece of China you're not particularly interested in retaining a memory of, go the opposite direction (toward Mao's picture) to the Forbidden City and then, if the day still has light, to Jingshan Park behind the ancient palace. Plan to spend the next day getting to and walking on, the Great Wall. On the third day, go to the Temple of Heaven and the world's largest imperial garden, the Summer Palace.

By Public Transportation Train travel is best between Shanghai, Suzhou, Hangzhou, and Nanjing. From Nanjing you'll have to fly to Chongqing, the departure point for the Three Gorges river cruise. The cruise ends in Wuhan, from where, unless you fancy an 18-hour train ride, you can take another flight to Xian. The express train from Xian to Beijing takes 20 hours. The flight is 2 hours.

South China
14 to 17 days

This adventurous course will introduce you to some of China's minority (non-Han) peoples, a World Heritage Site, and two of the most scenic places in the country. Midway through your trip you'll eat real Sichuan cooking in Sichuan's capital, Chengdu. This trip across South China offers more variety in landscapes, peoples, and foods than anywhere else in the country.

GUANGZHOU 1 or 2 days. Visit the best preserved example of southern architecture at the Chen Family Temple and then take in the awesome sight of the 184-foot pagoda of the Six Banyan Temple. On Day 2, take a trip over to Orchid Garden with 2,000 species and over 10,000 pots of this treasured flower, or relax at the sprawling and kid-friendly Yuexiu Park.

KUNMING 2 days. While the weather in this city of "eternal spring" is mostly pleasant year-round, what is excellent about Kunming is its relative cleanliness and order. One day should be devoted to Kunming's main attraction, Stone Forest, two hours outside the city. On your second day, go to Lake Dian and visit the several temples and pavilions on the forested hills encircling the water.

DALI 2 days. Take the cable or do the 1½-hour walk up to the lookout on Cangshan Mountain for truly spectacular lookouts of Dali and nearby Erhai Lake. On the way down you can drop by the Three Pagodas, the oldest built in the Tang Dynasty. Take a horse carriage down to the docks of Erhai Lake and hire a boat to visit some of the islands and villages on the opposite shore. On your second day, take a cab or bus to Butterfly Spring for a look at the village of an indigenous, non-Han Chinese people, the Pei tribe.

LIJIANG 1 or 2 days. Old Town Lijiang, the part recorded as a world cultural treasure, is probably China's best preserved ancient city. You can walk the entire town in a few hours. If you have extra time, check out Black Dragon Pool Park just outside the old town. A second day could be spent getting out to and soaking up Tiger Leaping Gorge.

CHENGDU 2 days. As this is Sichuan and home of the giant panda, you'll certainly want to drop by the Giant Panda Breeding Research Base or the Chengdu Zoo to see more of these furry creatures in one place than anywhere else. In the afternoon, go to Du Fu's Cottage, former residence of the Tang Dynasty poet. Or if you have little interest in Chinese poetry, head to Zen Buddhist Zhaojue Temple. On your second day, go out to the architecturally impressive Wenshu Monastery and spend a few hours exploring the surrounding streets and alleys. In the afternoon, visit the Memorial of the Marquis of Wu and the Tomb of Emperor Wang Jian, who ruled the Kingdom of Shu more than 1,000 years ago.

ZHANGJIAJIE 2 days. Arguably China's best national park for its well-preserved and incredible scenery, a trip to this part of China demands a visit to Zhangjiajie National Park, part of the Wulingyuan Nature Reserve. Two days (the time the park sells passes for) are required to see Zhangjiajie, whose mountains and river seem as if right out of a traditional landscape painting.

GUILIN 2 days. The city is charming but the real draw is the nearby Li River and mountains. Spend half a day on the river cruise winding through the gumdrop-shape mountains and alongside riverside villages. Most cruises end in Yangshuo where there are buses to take you back to Guilin. You should spend the night in Guilin and spend the next day exploring some of the nearby villages by bus or bicycle.

XIAMEN **1 or 2 days.** Gulangyu, an island with parks and architectural relics of the former foreign concessions, can be explored in a day. If you stay another day, visit the Wanshi Botanical Garden and the Nanputuo Temple.

Transportation Your best bet is to fly from Guangzhou to Kunming. From Kunming, Dali and Lijiang are easily reached by bus. From Lijiang you can fly to Chengdu or return to Kunming and take the 21-hour train ride. Chengdu has several daily flights to Changsha, from where you can either fly or take the 5-hour train to Zhangjiajie. The train to Guilin passes through Changsha and is about 11 hours. From Guilin you can fly or take the ridiculously slow train to Xiamen.

Silk Road
14 to 17 days

For those who walked this fabled route in the past, the journey took years, if not decades. But car, plane, and train have replaced the camel and human foot, and your trip should be much easier and more relaxed. Centuries of mixing cultures has produced societies unique in themselves—not Chinese, but not exactly something else. See the moon rise over sand dunes, religious devotees' passion painted on cave walls, and the modern-day convergence of diverse people.

XIAN **3 days.** On the first three days follow the Xian recommendations from the China Highlights itinerary.

LANZHOU **2 days.** Use this industrial town with a couple of nice parks and museum as a launching pad toward the caves of the Thousand Buddha Temple and Grottoes, 90 km (56 mi) west of the town. Traveling to and from Lanzhou can take anywhere from 2½ hours to half a day.

JIAYUGUAN **1 day.** You can spend a day walking along the Great Wall's westernmost extremity. The nearby town of the same name is a nice laid-back pause in the itinerary.

DUNHUANG **1 day.** Spend a day or two investigating the Buddhist caves known as the Mogao Grottoes. Then go to the Western Thousand Buddha Caves, dating to the Tang Dynasty.

ÜRÜMQI **2 days.** One place you won't want to miss is Heavenly Lake, a mountainous and forested protected zone, a couple of hours outside the city. If you have extra time and want to see mummies, check out the Xinjiang Museum in town.

TURPAN **2 or 3 days.** You'll want to spend as much time as your schedule allows in this enchanting area. On the first day go out to the Bezeklik Thousand Buddha Caves and nearby tombs. The next day, go to the ancient city of Jiaohe and wander around its ancient ruins. The ancient city of Gaochang, which was formerly a garrison town on the Silk

Road, is another option. If you have a third day go to Grape Valley for a look at local vineyards.

KASHGAR **2 days.** On the first day you'll want to visit Id Kah Emin, one of China's biggest mosques, dating back to 1442. After that, visit the Tomb of Abakh Hoja, with its beautiful green tiled dome roof. Spend the second day strolling the city's markets and making a relaxing side trip to East Lake Park. Try to organize your schedule so that you are in Kashgar for the Sunday Bazaar.

Transportation Unless you have an extra month or so for just traveling, you're better off flying to the more distant parts of Xinjiang and Gansu. Train service is incredibly slow and the distances are great. From Xian to Lanzhou you can fly or take an overnight train (13 hours). The train from Lanzhou to Jiayuguan is about the same amount of time. From Jiayuguan take the 5-hour bus to Dunhuang from where you can take a plane to Ürümqi. Turpan is only 2 hours from Ürümqi by train. For Kashgar, you're best bet is to fly from Ürümqi or take one of the grimy buses from either Ürümqi or Turpan.

Although temperatures can be scorching, summer is the peak tourist season, and hotels and transportation can be very crowded. Book several months in advance if possible for summer travel. The weather is better and the crowds not quite as dense in late spring and early fall, although you need to be prepared for rain. Winter is bitterly cold and not conducive to travel in most of the country. Avoid traveling around Chinese New Year, as much of China shuts down and the Chinese themselves travel, making reservations impossible to get.

Climate

What follows are average daily maximum and minimum temperatures in Beijing and Hong Kong.

🖪 Forecasts **Weather Channel** ⊕ www.weather.com.

BEIJING

Jan	34F	1C	May	81F	27C	Sept.	79F	14
	14	−10		55	13		57	14
Feb.	39F	4C	June	88F	31C	Oct.	68F	20C
	18	−18		64	18		43	6
Mar.	52F	11C	July	88F	31C	Nov.	48F	9C
	30	− 1		70	21		28	− 2
Apr.	70F	21C	Aug.	86F	30C	Dec.	37F	3C
	45	7		68	20		18	− 8

HONG KONG

Jan	67F	19C	May	85F	29C	Sept.	86F	30C
	58	14		75	24		78	26
Feb.	67F	19C	June	86F	30C	Oct.	82F	28C
	58	14		78	26		73	23
Mar.	69F	21C	July	89F	32C	Nov.	75F	24C
	63	17		81	27		67	19
Apr.	77F	25C	Aug.	87F	31C	Dec.	69F	21C
	69	21		78	26		59	15

China has only three official holidays a year: Spring Festival (or Chinese New Year), National Day, and International Labor Day, for a grand total of five days off. These are high travel times for the Chinese, especially during Chinese New Year, and it's best to avoid them if at all possible. The majority of China's holidays and festivals are calculated according to the lunar calendar and can vary by as much as a few weeks from year to year. Check a lunar calendar or with the CITS for dates more specific than those below.

WINTER

December 25, January 1	**Christmas and New Year's Day** are becoming an excuse for the Chinese to exchange cards, buy decorations (made in China), and eat out banquet style. In the big cities Christmas makes itself known by a ubiquitous paper Santa that is taped to almost every store. Some employees get a day off on New Year's.
January & February	**Harbin's Ice Festival,** a tour de force of bigger-than-life ice sculptures of animals, landmarks, and legendary figures, is held from the beginning of January to late February. Although it can be as cold as −30°C (−22°F), many visitors come to Zhaolin Park to check out the best ice festival China has to offer.
February	**Chinese New Year,** China's most celebrated and important holiday follows the lunar calendar and falls in early to mid-February. Also called Spring Festival, it's a time to visit family and relatives, eat special meals, and throw firecrackers to celebrate the respective Chinese zodiac animal. Students and teachers get up to four weeks off. It is a particularly crowded time to travel in China and many offices and services reduce their hours or close altogether.
February & March	Following a lunar calendar, the **Tibetan New Year** is celebrated in Tibet, Gansu, and northern Sichuan provinces with processions, prayer assemblies, and yak butter sculptures and lamps.
February & March	The **Spring Lantern Festival** marks the end of the Chinese New Year on the 15th day of the first moon. Colorful paper lanterns are carried through the streets, sometimes accompanied by dragon dances.

SPRING

April	The Dai minority in Yunnan, celebrate their own Lunar New Year, the **Water Splashing Festival,** usually in mid-April. Minorities in colorful dress come from all over the region to enjoy three days of revelry, with activities ranging from boat races on the river to buffalo slaughter, all part of a symbolic washing away of one's sins of the previous year.
April	The **Third Moon Fair** (from the 15th to the 21st day of the third moon, usually April), attracts people to Dali, Yunnan province, from all

	over the province to celebrate a legendary sighting of the Buddhist goddess of mercy, Guanyin.
May 1	International Labor Day is another busy travel time, especially if the holiday falls near a weekend.
May	In Dali, of Yunnan province, the Three Temples Festival, on the 23rd to the 25th day of the fourth moon, is celebrated with walks to local temples and general merrymaking.

SUMMER

June	The Dragon Boat Festival, on the fifth day of the fifth moon, celebrates the national hero Qu Yuan, who drowned himself in the 3rd century in protest against the corrupt emperor. Legend has it that people attempted to rescue him by throwing rice dumplings wrapped in bamboo leaves into the sea and frightening fish away by beating drums. Today crews in narrow dragon boats race to the beat of heavy drums, and rice wrapped in bamboo leaves is consumed.
July	The Torch Festival is celebrated in the towns of Lijiang and Dali, in Yunnan, on the 24th day of the sixth moon.

FALL

September 8	Confucius's Birthday may be overlooked in other parts of China, but there are celebrations aplenty in Qufu, his birthplace.
October 1	National Day celebrates the founding of the People's Republic of China. Tiananmen Square fills up with flowers, entertainment, and a hefty crowd of visitors on this official holiday.
October	Mid-Autumn Festival is celebrated on the 15th day of the eighth moon, which generally falls in early October. The Chinese spend this time gazing at the full moon and exchanging tasty moon cakes filled with meat, bean paste, sugar, and other delectable surprises.
October & November	For 10 days the Xishuangbanna region of Yunnan shoots off rockets to celebrate the Tan Ta Festival. Special ceremonies take place in local temples in the area.

PLEASURES & PASTIMES

Don't Sleep In   At 6 in the morning, no matter where you are in China, everyone is up and outside buying their daily vegetables, fruits, meats, eggs, and noodles in the local market. Vendors are out steaming, frying, boiling, and selling breakfast snacks to people on their way to work. Men and women practice tai chi in parks, along rivers, and in some unlikely places—the steps of a movie theater, an empty alley, the side entrance of a hotel—whenever the sun rises. Early morning in China is when the cities, towns, and villages come alive and should be experienced as much as possible, as every place has a different way of doing "business."

Eat Your Way Through   Dining in China is best enjoyed in large groups so you can sample a variety of dishes. Usually the menus are divided into appetizers, meats, vegetables, seafood, soups, and so on. It's best to order from each category so you dine in true Chinese style—dishes at your elbows, across the table, in front of you, stacked up, and sometimes even on the ledge behind to make room for the next round. Although each province, indeed each city, in China has a distinctive way of cooking and eating, there are generally four regional categories of food found across the country.

Northern, or Mandarin, cuisine is characterized by fine cutting and pure seasoning, providing dishes with strong garlic, ginger, and onion flavors. Peking duck, served with pancakes and hoisin (spicy soybean sauce), and Mongolian hotpot are also native to this region. An abundance of steamed bread (*mantou*) and flat pancakes are sold on the street and make good snacks.

Southern, or Cantonese, cooking is famous for dim sum, an eating experience found in Hong Kong, Guangdong province, and some larger cities with an overseas contingent. Bite-size dumplings, wonton, rice noodle dishes, sesame seed buns filled with bean paste, and a variety of other tasty snacks are pushed around on carts among patrons. Cantonese cooking tends to be the lightest and least oily of the four categories, though it can be just as exotic, with snake, turtle, monkey, rabbit, and a host of other animal and reptile specialties finding their way onto the menus.

Eastern, most notably Shanghainese, food is notorious for its heavy use of oil, though the freshest seafood, from hairy crabs to snails to shark's fin soup, are served in this region. Chicken and seafood dishes are simmered, boiled, or braised in their own juices, enhancing the natural flavors. Some wonderful *baozis* (steamed white bread filled with either vegetables, pork, or black bean paste) are sold on the streets of most cities and towns scattered throughout the region.

The spiciest of the four categories, Sichuan cooking loves to use the Chinese peppercorn and will keep you slugging back bottles of purified water. Chengdu is famous for its snacks, a variety of small dishes both hot and cold, served all day. Tea-smoked duck, marinated for more than 24 hours, peels right off the bone and melts in the mouth. Sichuan hotpot restaurants have become so popular they are popping up as far away as Beijing.

In some cities restaurants commonly frequented by the locals provide a great enough variety and high enough quality to render them desirable choices—you can see how the populace eats without compromising your own expectations of taste and cleanliness. Other cities have a less-developed dining culture; the local restaurants tend toward a Chinese version of fast food and provide fair to middling quality in a setting not quite up to many visitors' standards. Your best alternatives here usually lie with the city's high-class restaurants and the often excellent food served in the local hotels. Even the fancier venues are often quite affordable by Western standards. Most sizable hotels serving foreigners have a Western as well as a Chinese kitchen.

Go on a Personal Antiques Road Show

Chairman Mao alarm clocks, calligraphy scrolls, porcelain, jade pieces, valuable coins, old Chinese locks, and a great number of fake antiques are spread carefully on tables that line the streets of most Chinese cities on a weekly, sometimes daily, basis. Ask around for the date and time of the antiques market in your area and be mindful of rip-offs when you arrive. If you are seriously searching for antiques, it's best to get a local who speaks English to bargain for you while you wait unseen for the right price.

Ride a Flying Pigeon

Most cities and popular tourist towns offer bicycle rentals for an average of a dollar a day. Mounting a Flying Pigeon and cruising down wide, tree-shaded bike lanes is a quintessential China experience not to be missed.

Strap on Your Boots

Although hiking is unpopular with locals, China rewards the hiker with natural preserves, national parks, and sacred mountains. Songhuahu in Jilin, the Tiger Leaping Gorge, Emeishan, Huangshan, the Guilin-Yangshuo area, Xinjiang—practically every province has something to offer.

Take Time for Tea

Along West Lake in Hangzhou, inside Chengdu's parks, on the fourth floor of a department store, on cobblestone streets, in subway stations, and along China's many rivers—teahouses are to China as cafés are to France. Relax, chat, and meditate over a pot of oolong while sampling dried fruit snacks.

FODOR'S CHOICE

The sights, restaurants, hotels, and other travel experiences listed here are our writers' and editors' top picks—our Fodor's Choices. They're the best of their type in China. You'll find all the details in the chapters that follow.

LODGING

$$$$	**China World,** Beijing. Marble and gold everywhere characterize this luxury hotel on one of Beijing's premier shopping streets. The hotel is part of the China World Trade Center, which includes a mall with 200 stores.
$$$$	**Grand Hyatt,** Shanghai. The world's tallest hotel, the Grand Hyatt offers spectacular views of Shanghai from Pudong, the city's financial district.
$$$$	**Mandarin Oriental,** Hong Kong. Matching convenience with luxury, this is one of the world's great hotels. Celebrities and VIPs agree.
$$$$	**Ritz-Carlton,** Hong Kong. Refined elegance is the name of the game at this luxury hotel with European details.
$$$$	**The St. Regis,** Beijing. Visiting dignitaries and celebrities stay at the St. Regis, where opulence—and prices—know no limits. This is where to go if you really want to splurge.
$$$–$$$$	**Hyatt Regency Hotel,** Xian, Northwest. Great views of the city plus excellent service and proximity to sights and shopping make an unbeatable combination.
$$$–$$$$	**Shangri-La Hotel,** Hangzhou, Eastern China. On the site of a former Buddhist temple, this hotel is surrounded by 40 acres of camphor and bamboo trees. Many of the formal rooms overlook a lake.
$$$–$$$$	**Sheraton Suzhou Hotel & Towers,** Suzhou, Eastern China. A pagoda lobby and traditional-style buildings help this hotel blend in with its surroundings in historic Suzhou.
$$–$$$$	**Sheraton Sanya Resort,** Southeastern China. Sanya's premier resort is an oasis of relaxation and, with its schedule of organized activities, is a great place to brings the kids, too.
$$$	**Island Shangri-La,** Hong Kong. This hotel, which towers above the Pacific Place complex, has spacious rooms and spectacular views of the Peak and Victoria Harbour.
$$$	**Peninsula Palace,** Beijing. With ultramodern facilities, including plasma-screen TVs, and top-notch service, this hotel takes the cake as the classiest hotel in Beijing.

| $$-$$$ | Red Capital Residence, Beijing. This is your chance to stay in an exquisitely restored traditional courtyard home once frequented by red capitalists in the 1950s. |
| $$-$$$ | Shangri-La, Harbin, Northeastern China. Modern facilities deck the stylish rooms of the best hotel to book for a winter visit to Harbin, home of the famous Ice Lantern Festival. |

BUDGET LODGING

$$	Bishop Lei International House, Hong Kong. This simple guesthouse has moderate prices and hotel-style amenities.
$$	Karakorum Ger Camp, Karakorum, Republic of Mongolia. Set in open grassland, this camp offers the chance to stay in a real yurt without having to rough it too much.
$-$$	Ramada Plaza, Shanghai. This classy hotel with a soaring atrium and statues of Greek gods is in the middle of the action on Nanjing Road.
¢-$$	Nanjing Hilton, Eastern China. Mountain views from spacious rooms are the highlight of this elegant hotel a short bike ride from town.
$	Century Swiss-Belhotel, Jilin, Northeastern China. From the Finnish sauna to the Turkish steam bath and with multiple types of massage, this cozy hotel exudes relaxation.
$	Garden View International House, Hong Kong. This small, attractive hotel overlooks the Botanical Gardens and the harbor.
$	Salisbury YMCA, Hong Kong. With excellent fitness facilities and a location next to the famed Peninsula, this "Y" is hardly a spartan affair, and it's worth paying a bit extra for the harbor view, which is four times more expensive across the street.
$	Silk Road Dunhuang Hotel, Dunhuang, Northwestern China. This luxury courtyard-style house is full of Ming reproduction furniture and sits in the middle of an austere desert landscape. Take the hotel-organized sunrise camel ride out to the sand dunes.
¢-$	Victory, Guangzhou, Southeastern China. Composed of former colonial guesthouses, this budget hotel stands on Shamian Island among restored old mansions.
¢	Lüsongyuan, Beijing. A traditional wooden entrance leads to five courtyards, all a part of this excellent hostel, which also has its own restaurant.

RESTAURANTS

| $$$$ | Mei Fu, Beijing. Delicate preparations of Shanghainese cuisine are served on antique wooden tables beside little waterfalls in this lovely restaurant on Houhai Lake. |

$$$$	**Tang Le Gong,** Xian, Shaanxi, Northwestern China. Specializes in Tang Dynasty imperial cuisine.
$$$–$$$$	**The Courtyard,** Beijing. This elegant retreat serves a fusion of Chinese and Continental cuisines before a view of the Forbidden City.
$$$–$$$$	**La Seine,** Guangzhou, Southeastern China. Er Sha Island's premier dining option is the top pretheater option with its menu of classic French fare.
$$$–$$$$	**Red Capital Club,** Beijing. Step back into the days of the Cultural Revolution at this decadent restaurant in a restored courtyard near the homes of former national leaders. Extravagant meals are served banquet-style.
$$–$$$$	**Louwailou Restaurant,** Hangzhou, Eastern China. For more than 150 years this famed restaurant on the banks of West Lake has served succulent pork dishes and the freshest of fish from its private hatchery in the lake.
$$–$$$$	**M on the Bund,** Shanghai. This chic rooftop restaurant serves sophisticated cuisine with hints of Mediterranean and Middle Eastern influences. The view and adjacent lounge draw a hip crowd.
$$–$$$$	**Yung Kee,** Hong Kong. What you expect from Cantonese dining—lightning-fast preparation, high-energy service, and reasonable prices—is what you get at Yung Kee, which is why so many people keep coming back.
$$–$$$	**café TOO,** Hong Kong. This Island Shangri-La takes the international food court to a whole new level of distinction, with made-to-order food from seven different cooking theaters.
$–$$$	**Café Deco Bar & Grill,** Hong Kong. Combining Hong Kong chic and pan-Asian cuisine with panoramic views from atop Victoria Peak, this has become an island favorite.
$–$$$	**Henan Shifu,** Zhengzhou, North Central China. Set in a relaxing courtyard, the menu is an East-meets-West tour de force, renowned for its local and traditional beef pancakes as well as its hamburgers.
$–$$$	**Meilongzhen,** Shanghai. Dating from 1938, Meilongzhen serves outstanding Sichuanese food in traditional surroundings.

BUDGET RESTAURANTS

$–$$	**Baguo Buyi,** Nanjing, Eastern China. Forget the beautiful setting and traditional magic and fire-breathing performances; the best reason to go to Baguo Buyi is to enjoy some of the best authentic Sichuan dishes in the country.
$–$$	**Dingshan Meishi Cheng,** Nanjing, Eastern China. Featuring traditional latticework on the windows and a pleasant atmosphere, this restaurant serves excellent local Hauiyang cuisine.

| $-$$ | **Modern Nomads,** Ulaan Baatar, Republic of Mongolia. This popular upmarket eatery serves Westernized takes on traditional Mongolian dishes, like fried meat dumplings and barbecue. |

| ¢-$$ | **Simply Thai,** Shanghai. First-rate spring rolls, samosas, curries, and fried rice, plus tables on a patio, bring crowds to this low-key restaurant. |

| $ | **Lao Hanzi,** Beijing. Head to this casual restaurant in the Houhai Lake bar area for delicious smoked duck, salt-coated shrimp, and baked fish. |

| ¢-$ | **Baitadaiwei Canting,** Kunming, Southwestern China. Less noisy than many Chinese restaurants, this comfortable restaurant is the top pick for Dai minority–style food, such as pork in banana leaf and deep-fried goat cheese sweetened with sugar. |

| ¢-$ | **EMW Soya,** Shanghai. Candles and strategically placed pillows set the scene for pan-Asian cuisine, including curries, soups, and salads. |

| ¢-$ | **Jiefang Lu Jiaozi Guan,** Xian, Northwestern China. This is the best place for traditional boiled dumplings. With more than 200 different fillings available, no one leaves hungry. |

MAN-MADE WONDERS

Ancient Culture Street, Tianjin, North Central China. Lined with old buildings with carved wooden facades and ornate balconies this street has shops selling antiques, carpets, books, and crafts. It's also a good place to get some dumplings.

The Bund, Shanghai. A waterfront boulevard lined with beautiful art deco buildings and souvenir stands, the Bund is where to get a taste of Shanghai's animated street life.

Dragon Gate Grottoes, Luoyang, North Central China. These caves are filled with thousands of Buddhist figures carved over several centuries.

Evening Sunlight at Thunder Peak Pagoda, Hangzhou, Eastern China. A perfect reproduction of a 10th-century pagoda guards an active archaeological site and numerous treasures, including a miniature silver pagoda containing what is said to be a lock of the Buddha's hair.

Great Wall at Simatai, Beijing. Built by successive dynasties over two millennia, the wall is a collection of many defensive installations that extends some 4,000 km (2,500 mi) from the East China Sea to Central Asia.

Gulangyu, Xiamen, Eastern China. This island of colonial buildings and subtropical gardens is one of the best places to wander and get lost while meandering the island's alleys.

Humble Administrator's Garden, Suzhou, Eastern China. Anything but humble, these elaborate gardens contain a collection of 700 bonsai trees among other botanical marvels.

Lingshan Great Buddha, Wuxi, Eastern China. This bronze statue is the world's largest freestanding figure of the Buddha and is surrounded by displays that demonstrate the feel of contemporary Chinese Buddhism.

Master of the Nets Garden, Suzhou, Eastern China. With ponds, pavilions, and a tiny stone bridge, this perfect little garden offers a serene and beautiful escape.

Mogao Grottoes, Dunhuang, Northwestern China. These extraordinary grottoes are home to caves that were painted by Buddhists from the 4th through the 10th century.

Peace Hotel, Shanghai. This is an art deco masterpiece right on the Bund.

Tomb of Qin Shihuang, Xian, Northwestern China. The tomb of the first Qin emperor, from the 3rd century BC, stands near an army of thousands of life-size terra-cotta soldiers.

Thirteen Ming Tombs, Beijing. The Ming Tombs, in a valley northeast of Beijing, are the final resting place for 13 of the 16 Ming emperors; the approach is along a "spirit way" lined with weeping willow trees and imperial advisers, elephants, camels, horses, and other animals, all carved from stone.

Tiananmen Square, Beijing. The world's largest public square and the scene of several notorious political clashes, Tiananmen Square is at the entrance to the Forbidden City and at the heart of modern China.

Yu Garden, Shanghai. The 16th-century garden creates an atmosphere of peace amid the clamor of the city, with rocks, trees, dragon walls, bridges, and pavilions.

NATURAL WONDERS

Changbaishan Nature Reserve, Jilin province, Northeastern China. This large natural area has mountainous forests, hiking, and hot springs.

Heavenly Lake, Xinjiang province, Northwestern China. One of the prettiest lakes in China, with clear, clear water, is surrounded by mountains.

Hengshang Shan, Hengyang, South Central China. One of China's Five Holy Mountains and a beautiful escape from the cities.

Huangshan, Hefei, Eastern China. The misty pine- and rock-covered mountain, with peaks that have inspired emperors and artists for centuries, is networked with paths and stairways.

Huangguoshu Pubu, Guizhou province, South Central China. Nine waterfalls carve their way through lush countryside that is home to several minority villages.

Li River Cruise, Guilin, South Central China. The Li River is lined with evocative tree-covered karst mountains jutting up above both shores; the cruise to Yangshuo is spectacular.

MacLehose Trail, Hong Kong. You don't have to hike the entire 97-km (60-mi) trail, but tackling the section in Sai Kung Country Park will give you an ideal excuse to see one of Hong Kong's best wilderness areas.

Stone Forest, Kunming, Southwestern China. Limestone karst outcrops formed 270 million years ago give this hilly region its star natural attraction.

Tiger Leaping Gorge, Lijiang, Southwestern China. The source of the Yangzi River, this gorge is one of the deepest in the world and perfect for both hiking and photo opportunities.

Victoria Peak, Hong Kong. Known in Chinese as Tai Ping Shan, or Mountain of Great Peace, on a clear day the peak offers a breathtaking panorama of sea, islands, and city, as well as parklands for walking or hiking.

Wuyi Mountain Natural Reserve, Fujian province, Eastern China. The reserve has dramatic scenery with peaks, waterfalls, bamboo groves, and tea bushes.

Zhangjiajie, Wulingyuan Nature Reserve, South Central China. A popular place to hike trails through a spectacular backdrop of waterfalls, caves, pools, and peaks.

MUSEUMS

Gansu Provincial Museum, Lanzhou, Northwestern China. Though old-fashioned, the museum has some excellent exhibitions on the Silk Road, especially pottery, porcelain, and bronzes.

Hong Kong Museum of Art, Hong Kong. This is the place in town to see ancient Chinese scrolls and sculpture along with the work of the territory's own contemporary masters.

Hong Kong Museum of History, Hong Kong. See what Hong Kong looked like more than 6,000 years ago, when tigers and other animals ranged over the islands. Scenes of Neolithic life, life-size dioramas, military displays, and artifacts trace the territory's development up to the present.

Hubei Provincial Museum, Wuhan, South Central China. The museum contains Mao memorabilia and a fine collection of antiquities from 5th-century BC tombs.

Shaanxi History Museum, Xian, Northwestern China. The museum exhibits artifacts from the Paleolithic Age to 200 BC.

Shanghai Museum, Shanghai. An exquisitely displayed collection of Chinese art and artifacts, the museum houses a world-renowned bronze collection.

Winter Palace Museum of Bogd Khaan, Ulaan Baatar, Republic of Mongolia. This once-glorious palace of the city's former ruler is full of his valuable possessions, religious artifacts, art, taxidermy, and a menagerie of more odd items.

Zhang Residence, Zhouzhuang, Eastern China. This expansive, 15th-century courtyard home is filled with Ming-era furniture, musical instruments, and games. Don't miss the master bedroom upstairs.

Zhongguo Lishi Bowuguan, Beijing. The Museum of Chinese History is one of the world's best troves of Chinese art.

NIGHTLIFE & THE ARTS

Cotton Club, Shanghai. This dark and smoky jazz and blues club is the number one live-music venue in Shanghai.

The Door, Shanghai. Head to the Door for a truly eclectic experience: contemporary interpretations of traditional Chinese music played in a room filled with antique furniture and modern accents.

Felix, Hong Kong. The Peninsula's penthouse bar is your best bet for a drink with a view Kowloon-side. The Philippe Starck–designed room is also beautiful.

Huguang Guildhall, Beijing. Beautifully restored, the city's oldest Peking opera theater still stages traditional performances nightly.

Lan Kwai Fong, Hong Kong. The tiny streets of Central's best nightlife area hide more than 100 restaurants and bars of every description and ethnic orientation, with celebrants often spilling out onto the streets with their drinks. It's a superb way to start, spend, or end an evening.

SHOPPING

Dongtai Lu Antiques Market, Shanghai. Wheelers and dealers peddle antique and reproduction ceramics, jade, furnishings, and curios at this colorful market.

Panjiayuan Market, Beijing. Hundreds of open-air stalls have antiques, bric-a-brac, rugs, jewelry, and clothes for sale.

Shanghai Museum Bookshop, Shanghai. Quality art and gifts, such as pearls, porcelain, and glossy coffee-table books, are sold here.

Silk Alley Market, Beijing. The city's most popular market for clothing, this is where to find designer and knockoff North Face jackets, Esprit sportswear, and cashmere (real and faux) wraps.

TEMPLES, MONASTERIES & PALACES

The **Forbidden City,** Beijing. Home to 24 emperors and two dynasties for 500 years, the 200-acre compound is filled with halls, courtyards, and lesser buildings, all stained imperial vermilion, decorated with gold on the outside, and furnished with exquisite screens, thrones, paintings, and more.

Gandan Monastery, Ulaan Baatar, Republic of Mongolia. Houses a Tibetan Buddhist monastery and temples in buildings covered with golden roofs.

Ganden Namgyeling, Tibet. An enormous monastery established in 1409, it became the foremost center of the Gelugpa sect of Tibetan Buddhism, and draws pilgrims paying homage to its sacred sites and relics.

Jade Buddha Temple, Shanghai. The temple contains a 6½-foot-high statue of Buddha carved from white jade, as well as precious paintings and scriptures.

Jokhang Temple, Lhasa, Tibet. The most sacred building in Tibet is a temple built in the 7th century that continues to attract worshippers.

Labrang Monastery, Xiahe, Northwestern China. One of the two great Lamaist temples outside Tibet, this monastery was founded in 1710 and holds religious festivals several times a year.

Lama Temple, Beijing. Join the monks and pilgrims at this beloved temple decorated with fine scrolls, carvings, and statues.

Po Lin Monastery, Hong Kong. Built on a grander scale than most temple complexes in Hong Kong, Po Lin Monastery is home to Southeast Asia's largest seated, outdoor, bronze Buddha, more than 100 feet high.

Potala Palace, Lhasa, Tibet. Built in the 17th century on the foundation of the 7th-century original, the 11-story palace served as the spiritual and political headquarters of Tibet's theocracy.

Shaolin Monastery, Zhengzhou, North Central China. The legendary home of Chinese martial arts, this place is surrounded by lovely countryside and features both wax martial artist figures in action poses and live performances.

Six Banyan Temple, Guangzhou, Southeastern China. The temple is a landmark in the city with its trompe l'oeil 184-foot-tall pagoda and colorful carved roofs.

Spirit Valley Temple and Pagoda, Nanjing, Eastern China. The Spirit Valley Temple is entered through the 14th-century Beamless Hall, which is made entirely of brick.

Summer Palace, Beijing. Imperial families escaped summer heat in airy pavilions among trees and man-made lakes and aboard a marble boat in this 18th-century garden retreat on the northwest fringe of the city.

Temple of Heaven, Beijing. The Temple of Heaven holds the blue-roof Hall of Prayer for Good Harvests and the round altar where the emperor conducted sacrifices.

Temple of the Soul's Retreat, Hangzhou, Eastern China. Beside this large, 4th-century temple, you can see 338 Buddhist figures carved by monks into the limestone of the mountain.

Thousand Buddha Temple and Grottoes, Gansu, Northwestern China. It's filled with Buddhist wall paintings and statuary from the 10th through 17th century.

Wenshu Monastery, Chengdu, Southwestern China. Dating from the Tang Dynasty, this Buddhist monastery has buildings with exquisite carvings.

SMART TRAVEL TIPS

Finding out about your destination before you leave home means you won't squander time organizing everyday minutiae once you've arrived. You'll be more streetwise when you hit the ground as well, better prepared to explore the aspects of China that drew you here in the first place. The organizations in this section can provide information to supplement this guide; contact them for up-to-the-minute details, and consult the A to Z sections within each chapter for facts on the various topics as they relate to the country's many regions. Happy landings!

ADDRESSES

Street names in China often include pinyin names that are easy to decode to help you with navigation. "Lu" means road, "Jie" means street, "Dalu" is a main road, and "Dajie" is a main street. But those endings are sometimes preceded by the following directions that tell you where you're located on a given road: "Bei" is north, "Dong" is east, "Nan" is South, "Xi" is west, and "Zhong" is middle. So, if you're looking for a street named Beijing Xi Lu, it's the western end of Beijing Road.

AIR TRAVEL

In 2004, transportation officials in China and the United States signed an agreement to expand air service between the two countries, adding 84 passenger flights per week to the existing service over the next six years. Within mainland China all carriers are regional subsidiaries of the Civil Aviation Administration of China (CAAC). Reservations and ticket purchases can be made in the United States through travel Web sites and other agencies. In China you can make reservations through local China International Travel Service (CITS) offices (⇨ Visitor Information) in most cities.

Flying is more expensive in China than it is in the United States, but the standards of service are not as high. You can make reservations for domestic flights at your hotel travel desk, but some routes fill up quickly, so it's best to book in advance.

🚹 Reservations **U.S.-China Travel Service** ☎ 800/332-2831.

BOOKING

When you book, look for nonstop flights and remember that "direct" flights stop at least once. Try to avoid connecting flights, which require a change of plane. Two airlines may operate a connecting flight jointly, so ask whether your airline operates every segment of the trip; you may find that the carrier you prefer flies you only part of the way. To find more booking tips and to check prices and make online flight reservations, log on to www. fodors.com.

CARRIERS

Air Canada has daily flights to Beijing and Shanghai from Vancouver and Montréal. Air China flies nonstop to Beijing and Shanghai from New York and the west coast of the United States. You can choose to stop in Beijing and board a later flight to Shanghai with one single ticket. Cathay Pacific flies to Beijing via Hong Kong. China Eastern and China Southern airlines serve both international and domestic routes. Both airlines fly from China to the west coast of the United States. Japan Airlines and All Nippon fly to Beijing via Tokyo. Northwest and United both have service to Beijing from the United States, and United has a nonstop flight to Shanghai from Chicago.

🚪 To & from China **Air Canada** ☎ 888/247-2262, 800/361-8071 TTY ⊕ www.aircanada.com. **Air China** ☎ 800/982-8802 in New York, 800/986-1985 in San Francisco, 800/882-8122 in Los Angeles ⊕ www.airchina.com. **All Nippon** ☎ 800/235-9262 ⊕ www.fly-ana.com. **Cathay Pacific** ☎ 800/233-2742 ⊕ www.cathaypacific.com. **China Eastern** ☎ 800/200-5118, 626/583-1500, or 310/646-1849 in Los Angeles, 415/982-5115 or 650/875-2367 in San Francisco ⊕ www.ce-air.com. **China Southern** ☎ 888/338-8988 ⊕ www.cs-air.com/en. **Japan Airlines** ☎ 800/525-3663 ⊕ www.japanair.com. **Northwest** ☎ 800/225-2525 ⊕ www.nwa.com. **United** ☎ 800/241-6522 ⊕ www.ual.com.

🚪 Within China **Air China** ☎ 800/982-8802 in New York, 800/986-1985 in San Francisco, 800/882-8122 in Los Angeles ⊕ www.airchina.com. **China Eastern** ☎ 800/200-5118, 626/583-1500, or 310/646-1849 in Los Angeles, 415/982-5115 or 650/875-2367 in San Francisco ⊕ www.ce-air.com. **China Southern** ☎ 888/338-8988 ⊕ www.cs-air.com/en.

China Southwest Airlines ☎ 028/8666-8080 in China ⊕ www.cswa.com/en. **Shanghai Airlines** ☎ 800/620-8888 ⊕ www.shanghai-air.com.

CHECK-IN & BOARDING

Always **find out your carrier's check-in policy.** Plan to arrive at the airport about 2 hours before your scheduled departure time for domestic flights and 2½ to 3 hours before international flights. You may need to arrive earlier if you're flying from one of the busier airports or during peak air-traffic times. To avoid delays at airport-security checkpoints, try not to wear any metal. Jewelry, belt and other buckles, steel-toe shoes, barrettes, and underwire bras are among the items that can set off detectors.

Assuming that not everyone with a ticket will show up, airlines routinely overbook planes. When everyone does, airlines ask for volunteers to give up their seats. In return, these volunteers usually get a several-hundred-dollar flight voucher, which can be used toward the purchase of another ticket, and are rebooked on the next flight out. If there are not enough volunteers, the airline must choose who will be denied boarding. The first to get bumped are passengers who checked in late and those flying on discounted tickets, so get to the gate and check in as early as possible, especially during peak periods.

Always **bring a government-issued photo ID** to the airport; even when it's not required, a passport is best.

Passengers must pay an airport tax of Y90 for international flights and Y50 for domestic flights; passengers with a diplomatic passport, transit passengers who stop over for less than 24 hours, and children under 12 are exempt from the fee.

China's baggage allowances are generally: 40 kilograms (88 pounds) for first-class passengers, 30 kilograms (66 pounds) for business-class, and 20 kilograms (44 pounds) for economy-class.

CUTTING COSTS

The least-expensive airfares to China are priced for round-trip travel and must usually be purchased in advance. Airlines generally allow you to change your return date for a fee; most low-fare tickets, however, are nonrefundable. It's smart to call a number of airlines and check the Internet; when you are quoted a good price, book it on the spot—the same fare may not be available the next day, or even the next hour. Always check different routings and look into using alternate airports. Also, price off-peak flights, which may be significantly less expensive than others. Travel agents, especially low-fare specialists (⇨ Discounts & Deals), are helpful.

Consolidators are another good source. They buy tickets for scheduled flights at reduced rates from the airlines, then sell them at prices that beat the best fare available directly from the airlines. Sometimes you can even get your money back if you need to return the ticket. Carefully read the fine print detailing penalties for changes and cancellations, purchase the ticket with a credit card, and confirm your consolidator reservation with the airline.

When you fly as a courier, you trade your checked-luggage space for a ticket deeply subsidized by a courier service. There are restrictions on when you can book and how long you can stay. Some courier companies list with membership organizations, such as the Air Courier Association and the International Association of Air Travel Couriers; these require you to become a member before you can book a flight.

Many airlines, singly or in collaboration, offer discount air passes that allow foreigners to travel economically in a particular country or region. These visitor passes usually must be reserved and purchased before you leave home. Information about passes often can be found on most airlines' international Web pages, which tend to be aimed at travelers from outside the carrier's home country. Also, try typing the name of the pass into a search engine, or search for "pass" within the carrier's Web site.

🔟 Consolidators **AirlineConsolidator.com** ☎ 888/468-5385 ⊕ www.airlineconsolidator.com; for international tickets. **Best Fares** ☎ 800/880-

1234 or 800/576-8255 ⊕ www.bestfares.com; $59.90 annual membership. **Cheap Tickets** ☎ 800/377-1000 or 800/652-4327 ⊕ www.cheaptickets.com. **Expedia** ☎ 800/397-3342 or 404/728-8787 ⊕ www.expedia.com. **Hotwire** ☎ 866/468-9473 or 920/330-9418 ⊕ www.hotwire.com. **Now Voyager Travel** ✉ 45 W. 21st St., Suite 5A, New York, NY 10010 ☎ 212/459-1616 🖷 212/243-2711 ⊕ www.nowvoyagertravel.com. **Onetravel.com** ⊕ www.onetravel.com. **Orbitz** ☎ 888/656-4546 ⊕ www.orbitz.com. **Priceline. com** ⊕ www.priceline.com. **Travelocity** ☎ 888/709-5983, 877/282-2925 in Canada, 0870/876-3876 in the U.K. ⊕ www.travelocity.com.

🔟 Courier Resources **Air Courier Association/Cheaptrips.com** ☎ 800/280-5973 or 800/282-1202 ⊕ www.aircourier.org or www.cheaptrips.com; $34 annual membership. **International Association of Air Travel Couriers** ☎ 308/632-3273 ⊕ www.courier.org; $45 annual membership. **Now Voyager Travel** ✉ 45 W. 21st St., Suite 5A, New York, NY 10010 ☎ 212/459-1616 🖷 212/243-2711 ⊕ www.nowvoyagertravel.com.

🔟 Discount Passes **All Asia Pass**, Cathay Pacific, ☎ 800/233-2742, 800/268-6868 in Canada ⊕ www.cathay-usa.com or www.cathay.ca.

ENJOYING THE FLIGHT

If you're flying on local carriers while traveling within China, be prepared for less leg room and smaller seats.

State your seat preference when purchasing your ticket, and then repeat it when you confirm and when you check in. For more legroom, you can request one of the few emergency-aisle seats at check-in, if you're capable of moving obstacles comparable in weight to an airplane exit door (usually between 35 pounds and 60 pounds)—a Federal Aviation Administration requirement of passengers in these seats. Seats behind a bulkhead also offer more legroom, but they don't have under-seat storage. Don't sit in the row in front of the emergency aisle or in front of a bulkhead, where seats may not recline.

Ask the airline whether a snack or meal is served on the flight. If you have dietary concerns, request special meals when booking. These can be vegetarian, low-cholesterol, or kosher, for example. It's a good idea to pack some healthful snacks and a small (plastic) bottle of water in your carry-on bag. On long flights, try to maintain a normal routine, to help fight jet lag. At night, get some sleep. By day, eat light meals, drink water (not alcohol), and **move around the cabin** to stretch your legs.

Smoking policies vary from carrier to carrier. Many airlines prohibit smoking on all of their flights; others allow smoking only on certain routes or certain departures. Ask your carrier about its policy.

FLYING TIMES

The flying time to Hong Kong or Beijing is between 20 and 24 hours from New York, including a stopover on the West Coast or in Tokyo; from 17 to 20 hours from Chicago; and 13 hours direct from Los Angeles or San Francisco. With direct flights to China on Air China, there is no stopover or refueling and it cuts flying time from New York to Beijing to 14 to 15 hours.

HOW TO COMPLAIN

If your baggage goes astray or your flight goes awry, complain right away. Most carriers require that you **file a claim immediately.** The Aviation Consumer Protection Division of the Department of Transportation publishes *Fly-Rights,* which discusses airlines and consumer issues and is available online. You can also find articles and information on mytravelrights.com, the Web site of the nonprofit Consumer Travel Rights Center.

⚑ Airline Complaints Aviation Consumer Protection Division ⊠ U.S. Department of Transportation, Office of Aviation Enforcement and Proceedings, C-75, Room 4107, 400 7th St. SW, Washington, DC 20590 ☎ 202/366-2220 ⊕ airconsumer.ost.dot.gov. **Federal Aviation Administration Consumer Hotline** ⊠ for inquiries: FAA, 800 Independence Ave. SW, Washington, DC 20591 ☎ 800/322-7873 ⊕ www.faa.gov.

RECONFIRMING

Check the status of your flight before you leave for the airport. You can do this on your carrier's Web site, by linking to a flight-status checker (many Web booking services offer these), or by calling your car-

rier or travel agent. Always confirm international flights at least 72 hours ahead of the scheduled departure time. When flying within China or departing from China on an international flight, you risk losing your seat if you fail to confirm 72 hours ahead of departure time.

AIRPORTS

China's major airports are Beijing Capital International Airport, Hong Kong International Airport (also known as Chek Lap Kok), Guangzhou International Airport (also known as Baiyun International Airport), Kunming Airport, Shanghai Hongqiao International Airport, Shanghai Pudong Airport, and Xiamen Airport. There is also a new international airport in Guilin. All these airports are centrally located and have easy access to city centers.

⚑ Airport Information Beijing Capital International Airport ☎ 010/6456-3604. **Guangzhou International Airport** ☎ 020/8663-8838. **Guilin International Airport** ☎ 077/3384-3922. **Hong Kong International Airport** ☎ 852/2181-0000. **Kunming Airport** ☎ 0871/312-1220. **Shanghai Hongqiao International Airport** ☎ 021/2153-7764. **Shanghai Pudong International Airport** ☎ 021/6834-1000.

BIKE TRAVEL

Travel by bike is popular around Guilin in Guangxi province and in major cities, but it takes a skilled biker to navigate chaotic city streets and bumpy country alleys. In China, few observe traffic rules. Unlike U.S. cities where vehicles often yield to pedestrians, in China, bikers must yield to motorists and cautiously cross intersections. If you plan to bike between cities, be sure to rent bikes through a travel agency that provides insurance and emergency aids. Large cities such as Beijing, Chengdu, Xian, and Guilin have wide bike lanes on city streets, which makes riding safer.

In some cities, bikes can be rented just about everywhere, although your hotel and CITS are usually the best places to rent or inquire. When renting, you must show ID and pay a deposit. It's also prudent to **park your bike at guarded parking spaces** to avoid theft. Bike-repair shops are common.

Biking around China by yourself is not a good idea, as some areas are off-limits to foreigners without a guide. For organized bike tours check out Backroads and Bike China. Discover China Bicycle Tours is run through GSITS, the Chinese government travel bureau, and was the first group to organize a bike tour for Westerners, starting in 1981.

⑦ Tour Operator Backroads ⊠ 801 Cedar St., Berkeley, CA 94710-1800 ☎ 800/462-2848 ⊕ www.backroads.com. **Bike China** ⊕ www.bikechina.com. **Discover China Bicycle Tours** ⊕ http://trips.discover-china.org.

BIKES IN FLIGHT

Most airlines accommodate bikes as luggage, provided they are dismantled and boxed; check with individual airlines about packing requirements. Some airlines sell bike boxes, which are often free at bike shops, for about $20 (bike bags can be considerably more expensive). International travelers often can substitute a bike for a piece of checked luggage at no charge; otherwise, the cost is about $100. Most U.S. and Canadian airlines charge $40–$80 each way.

BOAT & FERRY TRAVEL

Boat travel is relatively comfortable in China as well as a magnificent means of viewing the countryside, although the bathrooms leave much to be desired. For longer trips, first-class cabins with private bath/shower are available on Chinese boats and mandatory on luxury cruises. Larger boats are also equipped with viewing decks, large cabin windows, and restaurants that serve decent cuisine.

BUS TRAVEL

Long-distance bus travel can be a comfortable and economical means of transport in China, though bus drivers often don't speak English. Depending on the route, roads can be smooth or bumpy, and detours may take you over rocky terrain where roads don't even exist. You may be charged for insurance on more dangerous, mountainous routes. The more expensive bus companies, such as INTAC, are usually safer because drivers are held accountable for accidents by the government. If safety and comfort are a concern, **ask your hotel travel agent or CITS about the reputation of the bus company.** Most buses are equipped with a television (with programs in Chinese, of course). On long trips, drivers stop at concession stands where you can buy food and drink and use the bathroom.

CITS or your hotel can arrange bus tickets and provide bus schedules. You can also buy tickets in advance from the bus station. Unfortunately, bus stations only have schedules in Chinese and rarely have English-speaking staff. Many hotels now have shuttle buses for transport to and from the airport and downtown locations.

CLASSES

China's long-distance bus service offers different seating styles: sleeper, hard seat, and soft seat. Local services are all hard seat.

⑦ Bus Information CITS in any city. Hong Kong Tourist Association (HKTA information hotline) ☎ 852/2807-6177.

BUSINESS HOURS

The majority of business share the same office hours of 8:30 AM to 6 PM. China does not observe different time zones. All businesses are closed on Chinese New Year and other major holidays.

BANKS & OFFICES

Most banks and government offices are open weekdays 9–5, although some close for lunch (sometime between noon and 2). Bank branches and CTS tour desks in hotels often keep longer hours and are usually open Saturday mornings. Many hotel currency-exchange desks stay open 24 hours.

MUSEUMS & SIGHTS

Most temples and parks are open daily 8–6. Museums are generally open 9–4 six days a week, with Monday being the most common closed day. Other tourist sights are typically open daily 9–5.

PHARMACIES

Pharmacies are open daily from 8:30 or 9 AM to 6 or 7 PM. Some large pharmacies stay open until 9 PM or even later.

SHOPS

Shops and department stores are generally open daily 9–7; some stores stay open even later in summer, in popular tourist areas, or during peak tourist season.

CAMERAS & PHOTOGRAPHY

The Chinese love cameras and will be glad to take your picture—some may even want to be in them. However, you should always **ask before taking pictures of people.** Remember that at some sites, like the terra-cotta soldiers in Xian or religious sites, photography is not allowed, and you risk a fine and/or camera seizure if you try to sneak a photo.

The *Kodak Guide to Shooting Great Travel Pictures* (available at bookstores everywhere) is loaded with tips.

▶ Photo Help **Kodak Information Center** ☎ 800/242–2424 ⊕ www.kodak.com.

CUSTOMS

Before departing, **register your foreign-made camera or laptop with U.S. Customs** (⇨ Customs & Duties). If your equipment is U.S.-made, call the consulate of the country you'll be visiting to find out whether the device should be registered with local customs upon arrival.

EQUIPMENT PRECAUTIONS

Don't pack film or equipment in checked luggage, where it is much more susceptible to damage. X-ray machines used to view checked luggage are extremely powerful and therefore are likely to ruin your film. Try to ask for hand inspection of film, which becomes clouded after repeated exposure to airport X-ray machines, and keep videotapes and computer disks away from metal detectors or wrap them in special packing materials to protect them from being damaged. Always keep film, tape, and computer disks out of the sun. Carry an extra supply of batteries, and be prepared to turn on your camera, camcorder, or laptop to prove to airport security personnel that the device is real.

FILM & DEVELOPING

Kodak and Fuji film are available at hotel kiosks, department stores, camera shops, and shopping centers at prices comparable to those in the West. There are one-hour and next-day film-processing outlets in hotels, shopping centers, and film-developing stores.

VIDEOS

China uses the PAL format.

CAR RENTAL

Renting a car in China is not advisable, and in many cases is not possible without a Chinese driver's license. In Beijing or Shanghai, you *can* rent a car, but only for driving within each city. International tourists are forbidden from driving between cities. Because of dangerous driving conditions, difficult parking, a lack of English signage, and the complexity involved in renting a car, it's better to hire a car with a driver for the day. Avis and Hertz rental cars in Beijing and Shanghai come with chauffeurs. The cost for a car and driver is reasonable by Western standards, usually Y500 to Y800 ($60 to $100) per day for an economy vehicle. In China check with your hotel concierge or local CTS office about hiring a car.

In Hong Kong the only major car-rental companies are Avis and Hertz. Rates begin at $100 a day (which includes insurance) and $400 a week for an economy car with unlimited mileage.

▶ Major Agencies **Avis** ☎ 800/331–1084, 800/879–2847 in Canada, 0870/606–0100 in the U.K., 02/9353–9000 in Australia, 09/526–2847 in New Zealand ⊕ www.avis.com. **Hertz** ☎ 800/654–3001, 800/263–0600 in Canada, 0870/844–8844 in the U.K., 02/9669–2444 in Australia, 09/256–8690 in New Zealand ⊕ www.hertz.com.

REQUIREMENTS & RESTRICTIONS

In China your own driver's license is not acceptable. An International Driver's Permit is available from the American or Canadian Automobile Association, or in the United Kingdom, from the Automobile Association or the Royal Automobile Club. Foreigners are forbidden from driving between cities.

CAR TRAVEL

With the exception of Hong Kong, car travel in China, even when you're in the passenger seat, can be frightening. Cars speed to pass one another on one-lane roads, constantly blaring their horns. Taxis and pedicabs pass within inches of each other at intersections. Lanes and traffic rules seem ambiguous to those not accustomed to the Chinese style of driving. Because of these challenges, it is recommended that you hire a car and driver rather than attempt to drive a car yourself.

Taxi driver identification numbers can be used to report bad behavior or bad driving, and thus tend to inspire more care. Many taxi drivers are also held liable for the condition of their vehicles, so they are less likely to take dangerous risks.

GASOLINE

Gasoline stations are easily found in cities and on highways in China. Gas stations often do not accept credit cards and *shouju* (receipts) are handwritten, if at all available.

ROAD CONDITIONS

Road conditions in China, especially in the cities, are usually fine, and the construction of highways and expressways has done much to improve the efficiency and comfort of driving in China. In more rural areas, however, especially in the mountains of western China and the deserts of northwest China, roads can be very poor, narrow, and dangerous. Be sure to look into the conditions of roads before setting off.

RULES OF THE ROAD

Driving is on the right in mainland China. Traffic lights can be sparse but are obeyed. Road signs are also sparse except in cities. Traffic in the cities can move slowly, but pay attention nonetheless. Many street signs are in pinyin as well as Chinese characters. In Hong Kong, in British fashion, people drive on the left. Road signs are in English or pinyin, and speed limits are enforced.

CHILDREN IN CHINA

Cities have parks, zoos, and frequent performances involving acrobats, jugglers, and puppets. Most large international hotels in Hong Kong, Beijing, and Shanghai have baby-sitting services and may even offer special activities, though services may not be on a level with those in the West. In addition, travel can be rugged, familiar foods hard to find, and there are health risks and sanitation problems. It's not advisable to take children on trips outside the major cities.

Check with the CITS office in most cities for activities or tours. In Hong Kong check with the HKTA (⇨ Bus Travel) for scheduled activities for children. *The Great Hong Kong Dragon Adventure,* an illustrated book about a dragon that flies children from place to place, is available at HKTA visitor information centers.

If you are renting a car, don't forget to arrange for a car seat when you reserve. For general advice about traveling with children, consult *Fodor's FYI: Travel with Your Baby* (available in bookstores everywhere).

FLYING

If your children are two or older, ask about children's airfares. As a general rule, infants under two not occupying a seat fly at greatly reduced fares or even for free. But if you want to guarantee a seat for an infant, you have to pay full fare. Consider flying during off-peak days and times; most airlines will grant an infant a seat without a ticket if there are available seats.When booking, confirm carry-on allowances if you're traveling with infants. In general, for babies charged 10% to 50% of the adult fare you are allowed one carry-on bag and a collapsible stroller; if the flight is full, the stroller may have to be checked or you may be limited to less.

Experts agree that it's a good idea to use safety seats aloft for children weighing less than 40 pounds. Airlines set their own policies: if you use a safety seat, U.S. carriers usually require that the child be ticketed, even if he or she is young enough to ride free, because the seats must be strapped into regular seats. And even if you pay the full adult fare for the seat, it may be worth it, especially on longer trips. Do **check your airline's policy about using safety seats during takeoff and landing.**

Safety seats are not allowed everywhere in the plane, so get your seat assignments as early as possible.

When reserving, request children's meals or a freestanding bassinet (not available at all airlines) if you need them. But note that bulkhead seats, where you must sit to use the bassinet, may lack an overhead bin or storage space on the floor.

FOOD

All major tourist areas in China are used to serving children. Aside from the hundreds of familiar American fast-food chains such as McDonald's, Wendy's, or Pizza Hut, Beijing has the following family-friendly restaurants to offer: Texan Bar & Grill (fun Chinese cowboys and cowgirls serve up the best Tex-Mex in town), Xihe Yaju (Cantonese courtyard restaurant with *ayis* or baby-sitting aunties on hand to care for little children while adults dine in peace), Hard Rock Cafe (the music, decor, and American hamburgers, french fries, and fajitas guarantee to keep any Western teenager happy), Sasha's (with a weekend play area for children), and Golden Café (offering a children's menu with Western favorites such as "Donald Burger" and "Hot Doggie," plus a kids' buffet table on weekends).

LODGING

Most hotels in China allow children under a certain age to stay in their parents' room at no extra charge, but others charge for them as extra adults; **be sure to find out the cutoff age for children's discounts.**

PRECAUTIONS

If you're traveling with a child, be sure to take a generous supply of Pepto-Bismol tablets, antibiotics such as Cipro, rehydration salts for diarrhea, motion sickness tablets, Tylenol, and vitamins. Children, like adults, will need some time to adjust to China's food, so be sure all food is thoroughly cooked. Boiled water is fine for children to drink; soybean milk, juices, and mineral water are also available.

SIGHTS & ATTRACTIONS

Places that are especially appealing to children are indicated by a rubber-duckie icon (🐤) in the margin.

SUPPLIES & EQUIPMENT

Formula, baby food, and disposable diapers are readily available in supermarkets.

COMPUTERS ON THE ROAD

Most hotel business centers have computers with up-to-date software and Internet access, but the service can be pricey. High-end hotels that serve foreigners generally have in-room data ports, but be prepared for very slow dial-ups. For your laptop, bring a surge protector and a 220-volt adapter and power converter. **Carry several types of adapters** in case the Asian one (with diagonal prongs slanting inward) doesn't fit.

CONSUMER PROTECTION

Whether you're shopping for gifts or purchasing travel services, **pay with a major credit card** whenever possible, so you can cancel payment or get reimbursed if there's a problem (and you can provide documentation). If you're doing business with a particular company for the first time, contact your local Better Business Bureau and the attorney general's offices in your state and (for U.S. businesses) the company's home state as well. Have any complaints been filed? Finally, if you're buying a package or tour, always consider travel insurance that includes default coverage (⇨ Insurance).

🔊 BBBs **Council of Better Business Bureaus** ✉ 4200 Wilson Blvd., Suite 800, Arlington, VA 22203 ☎ 703/276-0100 🖷 703/525-8277 ⊕ www.bbb.org.

CRUISE TRAVEL

Although cruises are cheaper in China, the boats are not always up to American luxury standards. Overbooking can also take away from your experience. The CITS in Wuhan can provide you with a list of four- and five-star ship models for Yangzi Three Gorges cruises. There are also U.S. companies that offer cruises in China as part of a package.

To learn how to plan, choose, and book a cruise-ship voyage, consult *Fodor's FYI: Plan & Enjoy Your Cruise* (available in bookstores everywhere).

♺ Cruise Operators CHN-Asia Express Tours ✉ 63 W. Prospect, 2nd fl., East Brunswick, NJ 08816 ☎ 800/824–9965 or 732/698–9600 ᕦ 732/698–9380.

University Educational Inc. ✉ 1985 Yosemite Ave., Suite 235, Simi Valley, California 93063 ☎ 800/525–0525 or 805/527–3748 ᕦ 805/527–4219 ⊕ www.uet.com.

CUSTOMS & DUTIES

When shopping abroad, keep receipts for all purchases. Upon reentering the country, **be ready to show customs officials what you've bought.** Pack purchases together in an easily accessible place. If you think a duty is incorrect, appeal the assessment. If you object to the way your clearance was handled, note the inspector's badge number. In either case, first ask to see a supervisor. If the problem isn't resolved, write to the appropriate authorities, beginning with the port director at your point of entry.

IN AUSTRALIA

Australian residents who are 18 or older may bring home A$400 worth of souvenirs and gifts (including jewelry), 250 cigarettes or 250 grams of cigars or other tobacco products, and 1,125 milliliters of alcohol (including wine, beer, and spirits). Residents under 18 may bring back A$200 worth of goods. Members of the same family traveling together may pool their allowances. Prohibited items include meat products. Seeds, plants, and fruits need to be declared upon arrival.

♺ Australian Customs Service ⌂ Regional Director, Box 8, Sydney, NSW 2001 ☎ 02/9213–2000 or 1300/363–263, 02/9364–7222 or 1800/020–504 quarantine-inquiry line ᕦ 02/9213–4043 ⊕ www.customs.gov.au.

IN CANADA

Canadian residents who have been out of Canada for at least seven days may bring in C$750 worth of goods duty-free. If you've been away fewer than seven days

but more than 48 hours, the duty-free allowance drops to C$200. If your trip lasts 24 to 48 hours, the allowance is C$50. You may not pool allowances with family members. Goods claimed under the C$750 exemption may follow you by mail; those claimed under the lesser exemptions must accompany you. Alcohol and tobacco products may be included in the seven-day and 48-hour exemptions but not in the 24-hour exemption. If you meet the age requirements of the province or territory through which you reenter Canada, you may bring in, duty-free, 1.5 liters of wine *or* 1.14 liters (40 imperial ounces) of liquor *or* 24 12-ounce cans or bottles of beer or ale. Also, if you meet the local age requirement for tobacco products, you may bring in, duty-free, 200 cigarettes and 50 cigars. Check ahead of time with the Canada Customs and Revenue Agency or the Department of Agriculture for policies regarding meat products, seeds, plants, and fruits.

You may send an unlimited number of gifts (only one gift per recipient, however) worth up to C$60 each duty-free to Canada. Label the package UNSOLICITED GIFT—VALUE UNDER $60. Alcohol and tobacco are excluded.

♺ Canada Customs and Revenue Agency ✉ 2265 St. Laurent Blvd., Ottawa, Ontario K1G 4K3 ☎ 800/461–9999 in Canada, 204/983–3500, 506/636–5064 ⊕ www.ccra.gc.ca.

IN CHINA

You can generally bring anything into China for personal use that you plan to take away with you when you leave; you should have no trouble bringing in cameras, video recorders, GPS equipment, laptops, and the like. Firearms, drugs, plant materials, animals, and many food items are prohibited. China is very sensitive about printed matter deemed seditious, such as religious, pornographic, and political items, including newspaper articles and books on Tibet. Customs officials are for the most part easygoing, and visitors are rarely searched. It's not necessary to fill in customs declaration forms, but if you carry in a large amount of cash, say several thousand dollars, you should declare it upon arrival.

On leaving, you're not allowed to take out any antiquities dating to before 1795. Antiques from between 1795 and 1949 must have an official red seal attached.

IN NEW ZEALAND

All homeward-bound residents may bring back NZ$700 worth of souvenirs and gifts; passengers may not pool their allowances, and children can claim only the concession on goods intended for their own use. For those 17 or older, the duty-free allowance also includes 4.5 liters of wine or beer; one 1,125-milliliter bottle of spirits; and either 200 cigarettes, 250 grams of tobacco, 50 cigars, *or* a combination of the three up to 250 grams. Meat products, seeds, plants, and fruits must be declared upon arrival to the Agricultural Services Department.

🇳🇿 **New Zealand Customs** ⊠ Head office: The Customhouse, 17–21 Whitmore St., Box 2218, Wellington ☎ 09/300–5399 or 0800/428–786 ⊕ www.customs.govt.nz.

IN THE U.K.

From countries outside the European Union, including China, you may bring home, duty-free, 200 cigarettes, 100 cigarillos, 50 cigars, 100 cigarillos, or 250 grams of tobacco; 1 liter of spirits or 2 liters of fortified or sparkling wine or liqueurs; 2 liters of still table wine; 60 milliliters of perfume; 250 milliliters of toilet water; plus £145 worth of other goods, including gifts and souvenirs. Prohibited items include meat products, seeds, plants, fruits, and dairy products.

🇬🇧 **HM Customs and Excise** ⊠ Portcullis House, 21 Cowbridge Rd. E, Cardiff CF11 9SS ☎ 0845/010–9000 or 0208/929–0152 advice service, 0208/929–6731 or 0208/910–3602 complaints ⊕ www.hmce.gov.uk.

IN THE U.S.

U.S. residents who have been out of the country for at least 48 hours may bring home, for personal use, $800 worth of foreign goods duty-free, as long as they haven't used the $800 allowance or any part of it in the past 30 days. This exemption may include 1 liter of alcohol (for travelers 21 and older), 200 cigarettes, and 100 non-Cuban cigars. Family members from the same household who are traveling together may pool their $800 personal exemptions. For fewer than 48 hours, the duty-free allowance drops to $200, which may include 50 cigarettes, 10 non-Cuban cigars, and 150 milliliters of alcohol (or 150 milliliters of perfume containing alcohol). The $200 allowance cannot be combined with other individuals' exemptions, and if you exceed it, the full value of all the goods will be taxed. Antiques, which U.S. Customs and Border Protection defines as objects more than 100 years old, enter duty-free, as do original works of art done entirely by hand, including paintings, drawings, and sculptures. This doesn't apply to folk art or handicrafts, which are in general dutiable.

You may also send packages home duty-free, with a limit of one parcel per addressee per day (except alcohol or tobacco products or perfume worth more than $5). You can mail up to $200 worth of goods for personal use; label the package PERSONAL USE and attach a list of its contents and their retail value. If the package contains your used personal belongings, mark it AMERICAN GOODS RETURNED to avoid paying duties. You may send up to $100 worth of goods as a gift; mark the package UNSOLICITED GIFT. Mailed items do not affect your duty-free allowance on your return.

To avoid paying duty on foreign-made high-ticket items you already own and will take on your trip, register them with customs before you leave the country. Consider filing a Certificate of Registration for laptops, cameras, watches, and other digital devices identified with serial numbers or other permanent markings; you can keep the certificate for other trips. Otherwise, bring a sales receipt or insurance form to show that you owned the item before you left the United States.

For more about duties, restricted items, and other information about international travel, check out U.S. Customs and Border Protection's online brochure, *Know Before You Go*.

🖪 **U.S. Customs and Border Protection** ⊠ for inquiries and equipment registration, 1300 Pennsylvania Ave. NW, Washington, DC 20229 ⊕ www.cbp. gov ☎ 877/287-8667 or 202/354-1000 ⊠ for complaints, Customer Satisfaction Unit, 1300 Pennsylvania Ave. NW, Room 5.2C, Washington, DC 20229.

DISABILITIES & ACCESSIBILITY

Facilities for people with disabilities are not widespread, but more and more government-run businesses are providing ramps for people who use wheelchairs and "dotted" pavements for people with vision impairments.

Mobility International USA, which has led several group tours to China, can provide information for people with disabilities who wish to visit the country. The Society for Accessible Travel & Hospitality has information on traveling to China, and can refer you to tour operators that specialize in trips for travelers with disabilities.

🖪 Resources **Mobility International USA** ⊠ 45 W. Broadway, Eugene, OR 97405 ☎ 541/343-1284 for phone and TTY ⊕ www.miusa.org. **Society for Accessible Travel & Hospitality** (SATH) ⊠ 347 5th Ave., Suite 610, New York, NY 10016 ☎ 212/447-7284 ⊟ 212/725-8253 ✎ sathtravel@aol.com ⊕ www. sath.org.

RESERVATIONS

When discussing accessibility with an operator or reservations agent, ask hard questions. Are there any stairs, inside *or* out? Are there grab bars next to the toilet *and* in the shower/tub? How wide is the doorway to the room? To the bathroom? For the most extensive facilities meeting the latest legal specifications, opt for newer accommodations. If you reserve through a toll-free number, consider also calling the hotel's local number to confirm the information from the central reservations office. Get confirmation in writing when you can.

TRANSPORTATION

Buses in China do not accommodate people with disabilities, and subway and train stations have long, steep concrete staircases.

🖪 Complaints **Aviation Consumer Protection Division** (⇨ Air Travel) for airline-related problems. **Departmental Office of Civil Rights** ⊠ for general inquiries, U.S. Department of Transportation, S-30, 400 7th St. SW, Room 10215, Washington, DC 20590 ☎ 202/366-4648 ⊟ 202/366-9371 ⊕ www.dot.gov/ost/docr/index.htm. **Disability Rights Section** ⊠ NYAV, U.S. Department of Justice, Civil Rights Division, 950 Pennsylvania Ave. NW, Washington, DC 20530 ☎ 800/514-0301, 800/ 514-0383 TTY, 202/514-0301 ADA information line, 202/514-0383 TTY ⊕ www.ada.gov. **U.S. Department of Transportation Hotline** ☎ 800/778-4838 or 800/455-9880 TTY for disability-related air-travel problems.

TRAVEL AGENCIES

In the United States, the Americans with Disabilities Act requires that travel firms serve the needs of all travelers. Some agencies specialize in working with people with disabilities.

🖪 Travelers with Mobility Problems **Access Adventures/B. Roberts Travel** ⊠ 206 Chestnut Ridge Rd., Scottsville, NY 14624 ☎ 585/889-9096 ✎ dl-travel@prodigy.net ⊕ www.brobertstravel.com, run by a former physical-rehabilitation counselor. **Flying Wheels Travel** ⊠ 143 W. Bridge St., Box 382, Owatonna, MN 55060 ☎ 507/451-5005 ⊟ 507/451-1685 ⊕ www.flyingwheelstravel.com.

DISCOUNTS & DEALS

Be a smart shopper and compare all your options before making decisions. A plane ticket bought with a promotional coupon from travel clubs, coupon books, and direct-mail offers or purchased on the Internet may not be cheaper than the least-expensive fare from a discount ticket agency. And always keep in mind that what you get is just as important as what you save.

DISCOUNT RESERVATIONS

To save money, look into discount reservations services with Web sites and toll-free numbers, which use their buying power to get a better price on hotels, airline tickets (⇨ Air Travel), even car rentals. When booking a room, always **call the hotel's local toll-free number** (if one is available) rather than the central reservations number—you'll often get a better price. Always ask about special packages or corporate rates.

When shopping for the best deal on hotels and car rentals, look for guaranteed exchange rates, which protect you against a falling dollar. With your rate locked in, you won't pay more, even if the price goes up in the local currency.

Airline Tickets **Air 4 Less** ☎ 800/AIR4LESS; low-fare specialist.

Hotel Rooms **Accommodations Express** ☎ 800/444-7666 or 800/277-1064 ⊕ www.acex.net. **Hotels.com** ☎ 800/246-8357 ⊕ www.hotels.com. **Steigenberger Reservation Service** ☎ 800/223-5652 ⊕ www.srs-worldhotels.com. **Turbotrip.com** ☎ 800/473-7829 ⊕ www.turbotrip.com. **Vacation-Land** ☎ 800/245-0050 ⊕ www.vacation-land.com.

PACKAGE DEALS

Don't confuse packages and guided tours. When you buy a package, you travel on your own, just as though you had planned the trip yourself. Fly/drive packages, which combine airfare and car rental, are often a good deal. In cities, ask the local visitor's bureau about hotel and local transportation packages that include tickets to major museum exhibits or other special events.

EATING & DRINKING

In China, chopsticks are the utensil of choice. Be aware that the Chinese like to eat family style, with everyone sitting at a round table (which symbolizes union and perfection), burrowing their chopsticks into a common dish. It's considered bad manners to point or play with your chopsticks, or to place them on top of your rice bowl when you're finished eating (place the chopsticks horizontally on the table or plate). It is appropriate, however, to shovel rice into your mouth, to talk with your mouth full, and to stand up to reach for food across the table from you. Don't hesitate to spit bones directly onto the table: putting your fingers in your mouth is bad manners.

If you're invited to a formal Chinese meal, be prepared for great ceremony, many toasts and speeches, and a grand variety of elaborate dishes. Your host will be seated

at the "head" of the round table, which is the seat that faces the door; it's differentiated from the other seats by a napkin shaped as a crown. The highest guest of honor will be seated to the host's right, the second-highest guest of honor to the host's left. Don't start eating until the host takes the first bite, and then simply serve yourself as the food comes around. Be sure to **always let the food touch your plate before bringing it up to your mouth;** eating directly from the serving dish without briefly resting the food on your plate is considered bad form. It is an honor to be served by the person sitting next to you (though as a guest, you are not expected to do the same).

MEALS & SPECIALTIES

An old saying in China is "food is the first necessity of the people." Color, smell, taste, shape, sound, and serving vessel are all important aspects of the food being served. Vegetables are the main ingredients. Chinese food can be loosely divided into northern and southern styles. Food in northern China is based on wheat products and is often quite oily, with liberal amounts of vinegar and other flavorful spices such as garlic. Meat and vegetable dumplings, noodles, and filled buns are common. The cuisine in southern China is known for its use of fresh ingredients and liberal dosing of hot spices; remember you can always request a dish to be more or less spicy. Rice and rice by-products form the foundation of meals. Do **try as many different kinds of foods as you can;** food is an integral part of Chinese culture. If you're craving Western food, look for American fast-food chains in the major cities. Most higher-end restaurants have a "Western menu," but don't expect it to taste like the food back home.

The restaurants we list in this book are the cream of the crop in each price category.

MEALTIMES

Lunch in China is usually served in restaurants between 11 and 2, dinner from 5 to 10. Unless otherwise noted, the restaurants listed in this guide are open daily for lunch and dinner. Restaurants and bars catering to foreigners may stay open 24 hours or close briefly in the wee hours.

RESERVATIONS & DRESS

Reservations are always a good idea; we mention them only when they're essential or not accepted. Book as far ahead as you can, and reconfirm as soon as you arrive. (Large parties should always call ahead to check the reservations policy.) We mention dress only when men are required to wear a jacket or a jacket and tie.

WINE, BEER & SPIRITS

Among the beers you'll find in China are Tsingtao, China's emperor of beers, and some international brews. Fruit wines, which are quite sweet and at times sparkling, are not commonly served at restaurants, where you're more likely to find spirits and other alcoholic beverages. The most famous brand of Chinese liquor is Moutai, a distilled liquor with an elegant aroma, mellow flavor, and pleasant aftertaste. Always ask for local brands when dining or purchasing liquor in China, as each place has its own local prizewinner. For example, Beijing Erguotou is the most popular white spirit in Beijing due to its affordable price, pure taste, and solid reputation.

ELECTRICITY

The electrical current in China is 220 volts, 50 cycles alternating current (AC); wall outlets come in a variety of configurations to fit two- and three-prong round plugs, as well as two-prong flat sockets. To use electric-powered equipment purchased in the United States or Canada, bring a converter and several types of adapters (the better hotels often supply standard adapters for electrical appliances).

If your appliances are dual-voltage, you'll need only an adapter. Don't use 110-volt outlets marked FOR SHAVERS ONLY for high-wattage appliances such as blow-dryers. Most laptops operate equally well on 110 and 220 volts and so require only an adapter and plug converter. You may also want to bring a power-surge protector.

Although blackouts are not common in Chinese cities, villages occasionally lose power for short periods of time.

EMBASSIES & CONSULATES

Australia **Australian Consulate** ✉ 22F, CITIC Sq., 1168 Nanjing Xi Lu, Jingan District, Shanghai 200041 ☎ 021/5292-5500 🖷 021/5292-5511. **Embassy of Australia** ✉ 21 Dongzhimenwai Dajie, Chaoyang District, Beijing 100600 ☎ 010/6532-2331 🖷 010/6532-6718.

Canada **Canadian Consulate** ✉ Shanghai Center, Tower 4, Suite 604, 1376 Nanjing Xi Lu, Jingan District, Shanghai 200040 ☎ 021/6279-8400 🖷 021/6279-8401. **Canadian Embassy** ✉ 19 Dongzhimenwai Dajie, Chaoyang District, Beijing ☎ 010/6532-3536 🖷 010/6532-4972.

New Zealand **New Zealand Consulate** ✉ Qihua Dasha, 15th fl., 1375 Huaihai Zhong Lu, Xuhui District, Shanghai ☎ 021/6471-1108 🖷 021/6431-0226. **New Zealand Embassy** ✉ 1 Donger Jie, Ritanlu, Chaoyang District, Beijing 100600 ☎ 010/6532-2732 or 010/6532-2733 🖷 010/6532-4317.

United Kingdom **British Consulate** ✉ Shanghai Center, Suite 301, 1376 Nanjing Xi Lu, Jingan District, Shanghai 200040 ☎ 021/6279-7650 🖷 021/6279-7651 ✉ Visa and Consular Sections, Shanghai Center, Suite 715, 1376 Nanjing Xi Lu, Jingan District ☎ 021/6279-8130. **British Embassy** ✉ 11 Guanghua Lu, Chaoyang District, Beijing 100600 ☎ 010/6532-1061 🖷 010/6532-1937.

United States **United States Consulate** ✉ 1469 Huaihai Zhong Lu, Xuhui District, Shanghai 200031 ☎ 021/6433-6880, 021/6433-3936 for after-hours emergencies 🖷 021/6433-1576. **United States Embassy** ✉ 3 Xiushui Bei Jie, Chaoyang District, Beijing 100600 ☎ 010/6532-3431 Ext. 229 or 010/6532-3831 Ext. 264 🖷 010/6532-2483.

EMERGENCIES

If you lose your passport, contact your embassy immediately. Embassy officials can advise you on how to proceed in case of other emergencies. The staff at your hotel may be able to provide a translator if you need to report an emergency or crime to doctors or the police. Most police officers and hospital staff members don't speak English, though you may find one or two people who do. Ambulances generally offer just a means of transport, not medical aid, so take a taxi to the hospital.

Ambulance ☎ 120. **Fire** ☎ 119. **Police** ☎ 110.

ENGLISH-LANGUAGE MEDIA

NEWSPAPERS & MAGAZINES

China's media is by no means independent of government control, although widespread changes have been proposed within the Communist Party to provide greater autonomy. China's main English-language newspaper, a version of the *People's Daily* (⊕ http://english.peopledaily.com.cn) that shares some of the same content but has original articles for the Western readership, is no exception to the rule of heavy government censorship. Its Chinese version is the most influential and authoritative newspaper in China, with a heavy inclination toward voicing the views of the Party. The English version is slightly more open to non-Party news and ideas and tends to be more progressive. The free English-language *City Weekend* (⊕ www.cityweekend.com.cn), *That's Beijing,* and *That's Shanghai*—with information on restaurants, events, and cultural venues—are available in hotel lobbies and at bars. Xianzai (⊕ www.xianzai.com) sends out e-mail newsletters on weekly events and special hotel, flight, and restaurant offers; you can sign up for the Beijing or Shanghai edition on the Web site.

Foreign magazines and newspapers, including *USA Today,* the *International Herald Tribune,* the *South China Morning Post,* and Asian editions of the *Wall Street Journal* and *Newsweek,* are available at kiosks in large international hotels.

RADIO & TELEVISION

Most Western hotels have satellite TV, with CNN, BBC, ESPN, and HBO in addition to the standard Chinese stations. The government-run CCTV has eight channels offering extensive English programming, from international affairs to TV news magazines, sports, and entertainment.

You can listen to music on Beijing Music Radio 97.4 FM and Shanghai East Radio 101.7 FM (with English-language music programs 2 PM–3 PM and 8 PM–9 PM).

Voice of America (www.voanews.com) can be heard in China, but be prepared for interruptions by the government at the slightest political provocation or because of tension between the United States and China.

ETIQUETTE & BEHAVIOR

Be respectful and try not to get upset if things go wrong, especially when reserving tickets and hotel rooms. Be friendly but stern if you are having difficulties—raising your voice and threatening will only embarrass you in front of the Chinese, who feel that "face" is extremely important. It helps to learn a few words of Chinese, even if all you can say is "Thank you" ("shee-yeh, shee-yeh") and "Hello" ("nee how"). If you are stared at, simply smile back or treat it humorously. Playing with chopsticks is a sign of bad manners. Bowing the head and pressing the hands together is a sign of deep gratitude. Handshaking is the common greeting, but don't shake women's hands too firmly. Try to keep an open mind about anything that seems initially appalling, whether it's dog meat or Chinese toilets. The Chinese are generally a gracious people who will reciprocate kindness.

For guidelines on dining etiquette, *see* Eating & Drinking.

BUSINESS ETIQUETTE

For guidelines on business etiquette, *see* the Understand China chapter in the back of the book for a detailed essay titled "Doing Business in China."

GAY & LESBIAN TRAVEL

China is still a conservative country when it comes to outward displays of affection. Although it's not unusual to see Chinese couples walking arm-in-arm in the bigger cities, Western couples, whether heterosexual or homosexual, may want to refrain from even these mild gestures. Homosexuality is not illegal but is considered a perversion or mental illness or, at the very least, improper behavior. There is a growing underground gay scene in Shanghai and other major cities, but discretion is wise. In Hong Kong, *Contacts,* a magazine covering the local gay scene, is available for HK$35 at the boutique Fetish Fashion. Propaganda is the largest gay and lesbian bar in Hong Kong.

Local Resources Fetish Fashion ⊠ Merlin Bldg., 32 Cochrane St., Hong Kong ☎ 852/ 2544-1155. **Propaganda** ⊠ 1 Hollywood Rd., lower ground fl., Hong Kong ☎ 852/2868-1316.

Gay- & Lesbian-Friendly Travel Agencies Different Roads Travel ⊠ 8383 Wilshire Blvd., Suite 520, Beverly Hills, CA 90211 ☎ 800/429-8747 or 323/651-5557 (Ext. 14 for both) ⊟ 323/651-5454 ✉ lgernert@tzell.com. **Kennedy Travel** ⊠ 130 W. 42nd St., Suite 401, New York, NY 10036 ☎ 800/ 237-7433 or 212/840-8659 ⊟ 212/730-2269 ⊕ www.kennedytravel.com. **Now, Voyager** ⊠ 4406 18th St., San Francisco, CA 94114 ☎ 800/ 255-6951 or 415/626-1169 ⊟ 415/626-8626 ⊕ www.nowvoyager.com. **Skylink Travel and Tour/Flying Dutchmen Travel** ⊠ 1455 N. Dutton Ave., Suite A, Santa Rosa, CA 95401 ☎ 800/225-5759 or 707/546-9888 ⊟ 707/636-0951; serving lesbian travelers.

HEALTH

In China you can find an English-speaking doctor in most major cities. The best place to start is with your hotel concierge, then the local Public Security Bureau. The major cities have modern hospitals, but if you become seriously ill or are injured, it is best to try to get flown home, or at least to Hong Kong, as quickly as possible. **Check for medical coverage with your health insurer before you go.**

In Hong Kong, English-speaking doctors are widely available. Hotels have lists of accredited doctors and can arrange for a doctor to visit your hotel room. Otherwise, consult the nearest government hospital. Check the "Government" section of the business telephone directory under "Medical and Health Department" for a list.

Make sure you **take enough of any prescription medication for the duration of your stay.** You should also carry a copy of your prescription with you in case you lose your medicine or are stopped by customs officials. If you wear contact lenses, take a couple of extra pairs along in case you lose or rip a lens. **Wear plenty of sunscreen and a good pair of sunglasses,** even in winter.

Pneumonia and influenza are also common among travelers returning from China; many health professionals recommend inoculations before you leave. Be sure you're well rested and healthy to start with.

As for the breakout of SARS (Severe Acute Respiratory Syndrome) in November of 2002, the threat of the deadly respiratory infection among the general population has fallen to the point of near nonexistence. Temporary travel warnings about traveling to the Guangdong province, where SARS originated, have ended. At the time of writing there have been a few possible SARS cases, but the spread of the infection is believed to be well under control.

According to the National Centers for Disease Control (CDC) there is a limited risk of hepatitis A and B, typhoid, polio, malaria, tuberculosis, dengue fever, tetanus, and rabies in small cities and rural areas. In most urban or easily accessible areas you need not worry. However, if you plan to visit remote regions or stay for more than six weeks, **check with the CDC's International Travelers Hotline.** In areas where malaria and dengue, both of which are carried by mosquitoes, are prevalent, use mosquito nets, wear clothing that covers the body, apply repellent containing DEET, and use spray for flying insects in living and sleeping areas. Also **consider taking antimalarial pills** if you'll be staying in rural areas in warm weather. There is no vaccine that combats dengue.

Do *not* buy prescription drugs in China unless absolutely necessary, as the quality control is unreliable.

FOOD & DRINK

The major health risk in China is traveler's diarrhea, caused by eating contaminated fruit or vegetables or drinking contaminated water. So watch what you eat. Avoid ice, uncooked food, and unpasteurized milk and milk products, and **drink only bottled water,** which is widely available, or water that has been boiled for several minutes. Tap water in major cities like Beijing and Shanghai is safe for brushing teeth.

Mild cases may respond to Imodium (known generically as loperamide) or Pepto-Bismol, both of which can be purchased over the counter. Drink plenty of purified water or tea—chamomile is a good folk remedy. In severe cases, rehydrate yourself with a salt-sugar solution— ½ teaspoon salt and 4 tablespoons sugar per quart of water.

MEDICAL PLANS

No one plans to get sick while traveling, but it happens, so consider signing up with a medical-assistance company. Members get doctor referrals, emergency evacuation or repatriation, hotlines for medical consultation, cash for emergencies, and other assistance.

🚩 **Medical-Assistance Companies International SOS Assistance** ⊕ www.internationalsos.com ✉ 8 Neshaminy Interplex, Suite 207, Trevose, PA 19053 ☎ 800/523-6586 or 215/245-4707 🖷 215/244-9617 ✉ Landmark House, Hammersmith Bridge Rd., 6th fl., London W6 9DP ☎ 20/8762-8008 🖷 20/8748-7744 ✉ 12 Chemin Riantbosson, 1217 Meyrin 1, Geneva, Switzerland ☎ 22/785-6464 🖷 22/785-6424 ✉ 331 N. Bridge Rd., 17-00, Odeon Towers, Singapore 188720 ☎ 6338-7800 🖷 6338-7611.

OVER-THE-COUNTER REMEDIES

Most pharmacies carry over-the-counter Western medicines and traditional Chinese medicines.

SHOTS & MEDICATIONS

While currently no vaccinations are required to travel to China, in summer months malaria is a serious risk in tropical and rural areas, as well as along the Yangzi River. If you'll be staying in cities for the duration of your trip, the risk of contracting malaria is small.

🚩 **Health Warnings National Centers for Disease Control and Prevention** (CDC) ✉ Office of Health Communication, National Center for Infectious Diseases, Division of Quarantine, Travelers' Health, 1600 Clifton Rd. NE, Atlanta, GA 30333 ☎ 800/311-3435 inquiries, 877/394-8747 international travelers' health line, 404/498-1600 Division of Quarantine 🖷 888/232-3299 ⊕ www.cdc.gov/travel. **World Health Organization** (WHO) ⊕ www.who.int.

HOLIDAYS

National holidays include January 1 (New Year's Day), two days in late February–early March (Chinese New Year, also called Spring Festival), March 8 (International Women's Day), May 1 (International Labor Day), May 4 (Youth Day), June 1 (Children's Day), July 1 (anniversary of the founding of the Communist Party of China; in Hong Kong, the anniversary of the establishment of the Special Administrative Region), August 1 (anniversary of the founding of the Chinese People's Liberation Army), and October 1 (National Day—founding of the Peoples Republic of China in 1949) (⇨ Festivals and Seasonal Events *in* Chapter 1).

INSURANCE

The most useful travel-insurance plan is a comprehensive policy that includes coverage for trip cancellation and interruption, default, trip delay, and medical expenses (with a waiver for preexisting conditions).

Without insurance you'll lose all or most of your money if you cancel your trip, regardless of the reason. Default insurance covers you if your tour operator, airline, or cruise line goes out of business—the chances of which have been increasing. Trip-delay covers expenses that arise because of bad weather or mechanical delays. Study the fine print when comparing policies.

If you're traveling internationally, a key component of travel insurance is coverage for medical bills incurred if you get sick on the road. Such expenses aren't generally covered by Medicare or private policies. U.K. residents can buy a travel-insurance policy valid for most vacations taken during the year in which it's purchased (but check preexisting-condition coverage). British and Australian citizens need extra medical coverage when traveling overseas.

Always **buy travel policies directly from the insurance company**; if you buy them from a cruise line, airline, or tour operator that goes out of business you probably won't be covered for the agency or operator's default, a major risk. Before making any purchase, review your existing health and home-owner's policies to find out what they cover away from home.

🚹 Travel Insurers In the United States: **Access America** ✉ 2805 N. Parham Rd., Richmond, VA 23294 ☎ 800/284-8300 🖷 800/346-9265 or 804/ 673-1491 ⊕ www.accessamerica.com. **Travel Guard International** ✉ 1145 Clark St., Stevens Point, WI 54481 ☎ 800/826-1300 or 715/345-0505 🖷 800/ 955-8785 ⊕ www.travelguard.com.

🚹 In Australia: **Insurance Council of Australia** ✉ Insurance Enquiries and Complaints, Level 12, Box 561, Collins St. W, Melbourne, VIC 8007 ☎ 1300/780-808 or 03/9629-4109 🖷 03/9621-2060 ⊕ www.iecltd.com.au.

In Canada: **RBC Insurance** ✉ 6880 Financial Dr., Mississauga, Ontario L5N 7Y5 ☎ 800/668-4342 or 905/816-2400 🖷 905/813-4704 ⊕ www. rbcinsurance.com. In New Zealand: **Insurance Council of New Zealand** ✉ Level 7, 111-115 Customhouse Quay, Box 474, Wellington ☎ 04/472-5230 🖷 04/473-3011 ⊕ www.icnz.org.nz.

In the United Kingdom: **Association of British Insurers** ✉ 51 Gresham St., London EC2V 7HQ ☎ 020/7600-3333 🖷 020/7696-8999 ⊕ www.abi. org.uk.

INTERNET

Although the Internet (*īntèrlái* in pinyin) is still a novel concept for most Chinese outside of metropolitan areas, cybercafés and other types of computer centers are quickly spreading, especially in the large cities. Due to government restrictions, many Chinese still find browsing limited, but many professional Chinese these days do have e-mail addresses. Most major hotels in China have access to the Internet through their business centers, and some even allow you to use it from your room, provided your computer is equipped with the proper tools (modem, 220-volt adapter, outlet converter, Web browser, etc.) Be prepared for very slow dial-ups, and inquire about cost in cybercafés before going online. Consider signing up for a free Internet-based e-mail account before you go.

LANGUAGE

The national language of China is Mandarin, known in China as Putonghua (*pŭtōnghuà*), "common language." Nearly everyone speaks Mandarin, but many also speak local dialects, some of which use the same characters as Mandarin with a very different pronunciation. In Hong Kong the main spoken language is Cantonese, although most people speak English.

All of the Chinese languages are tonal; there are four possible tones for every syllable, in addition to the basic sound of the syllable, and they make up part of a word's pronunciation. Each syllable has a different meaning depending on the pitch or musical inflection the speaker gives it. For example, in Mandarin the syllable *ma* can mean mother, horse, curse, or hemp plant—or, it can be a particle denoting a question—depending on the tone used. Thus, the sentence "Ma ma ma ma" translates as "does mother curse the horse?," a classic example of the complexity of the tonal Chinese language. Additionally, many Chinese characters are homonyms, which makes it difficult if not impossible for the foreign ear to understand what is being said. Since 1949 the government has revamped the teaching of Mandarin, introducing a simplified phonetic system known as pinyin, which uses the Roman alphabet to denote the pronunciations of the myriad Chinese characters (pinyin is taught alongside, and not instead of, ideograms). Names of sites in this book are given in English with pinyin translations, and lists of Chinese place-names in the back of the book provide the names of recommended sites in Chinese characters.

Although Chinese grammar is simple, it is still difficult for foreigners to speak Chinese and even harder to be understood. However, the Chinese will appreciate your making the effort to speak a few phrases understood almost everywhere. Try "Hello"—"*Ní hăo*" (pronounced nee how); "Thank you"—"*Xiè xiè*" (pronounced shee-yeh, shee-yeh); and "Goodbye"—"*Zai jian*" (pronounced dzigh djyan). When pronouncing words written in pinyin, remember that "q" and "x" are pronounced like "ch" and "sh," respectively; "zh" is pronounced like the "j" in "just"; "c" is pronounced like "ts."

You can usually find someone who speaks English in the major cities. There are English signs almost everywhere in Hong Kong, but these are rare in the rest of China (with the exception of the Beijing subway). Fortunately, almost all cities have street signs written in pinyin. It can be difficult to get around China on your own without speaking the language. If you are not planning to go with a tour group, you can go from city to city and hire a local English-speaking guide from the CTS office at each stop.

📕 Language Resource **Business Companion: Chinese,** by Tim Dobbins and Paul Westbrook, Living Language/Random House Inc. ☎ 800/726–0600 ⊕ www.livinglanguage.com. **I Can Read That! A Traveler's Introduction to Chinese Characters,** by Julie Mazel Sussman, China Books and Periodicals, Inc. ☎ 415/282–2994 🖷 415/282–0994 ⊕ www.chinabooks.com. **In the Know in China,** by Jennifer Phillips, Living Language/Random House Inc. ☎ 800/726–0600 ⊕ www.livinglanguage.com.

LODGING

The lodgings we list are the best for each price category, from simple hostels to luxury high-rises owned by international chains. Three-star hotels are common and offer a good value, with air-conditioning, color TV, and private Western-style bathrooms. Many also have Western and Chinese restaurants. Four- and five-star hotels also have swimming pools, business services, and other amenities. One-star hotels always have rooms with private bathrooms, but the toilets are generally just a hole in the floor.

We always list the facilities that are available, but we don't specify whether they cost extra; when pricing accommodations, always ask what's included and what costs extra. Properties are assigned price categories based on rack rates at high season (excluding holidays). A few minutes on the Internet can easily net you discounts up to 50% (⇨ Discounts & Deals). Also be aware that price may have little bearing on quality in China.

APARTMENT & VILLA RENTALS

If you want a home base that's roomy enough for a family and comes with cooking facilities, consider a furnished rental. These can save you money, especially if you're traveling with a group. Home-exchange directories sometimes list rentals as well as exchanges.

Maple Place, owned by King Kok Investment Limited, a consortium of three of Asia's best-known property companies, has well-equipped apartments, villas, and luxury town houses in northeast Beijing on the Wenyun River, aptly named the Beijing Riviera. Maple Place is convenient to Beijing International Airport and guests have access to the Beijing Riviera Country Club. Rentals cost about $500 a week.

Pacific Properties/Pacific Relocations can help you find short-term rental properties in Beijing and Shanghai.

📕 International Agents **Hideaways International** ✉ 767 Islington St., Portsmouth, NH 03801 ☎ 800/843–4433 or 603/430–4433 🖷 603/430–4444 ⊕ www.hideaways.com; annual membership $145. 📕 Local Agents **Maple Place** ✉ 1 Xiang Jiang Bei Lu, Chaoyang District, Beijing 100103 ☎ 010/6517–1275 🖷 010/6510–1368. **Pacific Properties/Pacific Relocations** ✉ Chun Shen Jiang Mansion, Suite 910, 400 Zhe Jiang Zhong Rd., Shanghai 200001 ☎ 021/6351–1503 🖷 021/6351–8213 ✍ shanghai@worthenpacific.com ⊕ www.worthenpacific.com.

HOMESTAYS

Staying with a host family is a unique, inexpensive, and culturally rich experience. Generally your Chinese host family will speak enough English for basic communication, and you'll have the opportunity to experience life off the beaten tourist path. 📕 Organizations **American International Homestays, Inc.** ✆ Box 1754, Nederland, CO 80466 ☎ 800/876–2048 or 303/642–3088 🖷 303/642–3365 ⊕ www.commerce.com/homestays. **ULink Travel Center** ✆ Box 938, He Ping Men, Beijing 100051 ☎ 010/6775–8655 🖷 010/6774–1523.

HOSTELS

No matter what your age, you can save on lodging costs by staying at hostels. In some 4,500 locations in more than 70 countries around the world, Hostelling International (HI), the umbrella group for a number of national youth-hostel associations, offers single-sex, dorm-style beds, and, at many hostels, rooms for couples and family accommodations. Membership in any HI national hostel association, open to travelers of all ages, allows you to stay in HI-affiliated hostels at member rates; one-year membership is about $28 for adults (C$35 for a two-year minimum membership in Canada, £14 in the United Kingdom, A$52 in Australia, and NZ$40 in New Zealand); hostels charge about $10–$30 per night. Members have priority if the hostel is full; they're also eligible for discounts around the world, even on rail and bus travel in some countries.

Organizations **Guangdong Youth Hostel Association of China** ✉ 185 Huanshix Rd., Guangzhou, Guangdong province 510010 ☎ 8620/8666-6889 🖷 8620/8666-5039 ⌨ youthhostel_gd@21cn.com. **Hostelling International–Canada** ✉ 205 Catherine St., Suite 400, Ottawa, Ontario K2P 1C3 ☎ 800/663-5777 or 613/237-7884 🖷 613/237-7868 ⊕ www.hihostels.ca. **Hostelling International–USA** ✉ 8401 Colesville Rd., Suite 600, Silver Spring, MD 20910 ☎ 301/495-1240 🖷 301/495-6697 ⊕ www.hiusa.org.

YHA Australia ✉ 422 Kent St., Sydney, NSW 2001 ☎ 02/9261-1111 🖷 02/9261-1969 ⊕ www.yha.com.au. **YHA England and Wales** ✉ Trevelyan House, Dimple Rd., Matlock, Derbyshire DE4 3YH, U.K. ☎ 0870/870-8808, 0870/770-8868, or 0162/959-2600 🖷 0870/770-6127 ⊕ www.yha.org.uk. **YHA New Zealand** ✉ Level 1, Moorhouse City, 166 Moorhouse Ave., Box 436, Christchurch ☎ 0800/278-299 or 03/379-9970 🖷 03/365-4476 ⊕ www.yha.org.nz.

HOTELS

Major cities in China all have luxury hotels, and a recent wave of hotel construction is the cornerstone of China's new focus on tourism. Except for Hong Kong, Beijing, Shanghai, and Guangzhou, the service even in the best hotels might not measure up to international luxury standards. They will, however, have English speakers on staff, business centers, laundry service, foreign currency exchange, and a concierge who can arrange tours and transportation. Many also have exercise facilities, hairdressers, and restaurants.

Always **bring your passport when checking into a hotel.** The reception desk clerk will have to see it and record the number before you can be given a room. Sometimes unmarried couples are not allowed to stay together in the same room, but simply wearing a band on your left finger is one way to avoid this complication. Friends of the same sex, especially women, shouldn't have a problem getting a room together. There may, however, be regulations about who is allowed in your room, and it's also normal for hotels to post "visitor hours" inside the room.

All hotels listed have private bath unless otherwise noted. Remember that water is a precious resource in China and use accordingly.

Toll-Free Numbers **Best Western** ☎ 800/528-1234 ⊕ www.bestwestern.com. **Choice** ☎ 800/424-6423 ⊕ www.choicehotels.com. **Clarion** ☎ 800/424-6423 ⊕ www.choicehotels.com. **Comfort Inn** ☎ 800/424-6423 ⊕ www.choicehotels.com. **Days Inn** ☎ 800/325-2525 ⊕ www.daysinn.com. **Four Seasons** ☎ 800/332-3442 ⊕ www.fourseasons.com. **Hilton** ☎ 800/445-8667 ⊕ www.hilton.com. **Holiday Inn** ☎ 800/465-4329 ⊕ www.ichotelsgroup.com. **Howard Johnson** ☎ 800/446-4656 ⊕ www.hojo.com. **Hyatt Hotels & Resorts** ☎ 800/233-1234 ⊕ www.hyatt.com. **Inter-Continental** ☎ 800/327-0200 ⊕ www.ichotelsgroup.com. **Marriott** ☎ 800/228-9290 ⊕ www.marriott.com. **Nikko Hotels International** ☎ 800/645-5687 ⊕ www.nikkohotels.com. **Radisson** ☎ 800/333-3333 ⊕ www.radisson.com. **Ramada** ☎ 800/228-2828, 800/854-7854 international reservations ⊕ www.ramada.com or www.ramadahotels.com. **Renaissance Hotels & Resorts** ☎ 800/468-3571 ⊕ www.renaissancehotels.com/. **Ritz-Carlton** ☎ 800/241-3333 ⊕ www.ritzcarlton.com. **Sheraton** ☎ 800/325-3535 ⊕ www.starwood.com/sheraton.

MAIL & SHIPPING

Sending international mail from China is extremely reliable. Letters mailed from China to overseas destinations require 5 to 14 days for delivery. Within China, mail is subject to search so **do not send sensitive materials,** such as religious or political literature, that may cause you or the recipient trouble. Mail your letters from post offices rather than mailboxes. Post offices, which are often crowded, are open 8–6 Monday through Saturday. Large hotels generally have postal services open all day Monday through Saturday and Sunday 8–noon.

You can use the Roman alphabet to write an address. It is customary to organize the address the way the Chinese do, the reverse of the order used in the West, beginning with the country (rather than the individual) and progressing to the province, city or town, followed by the six-digit zip code, street and dwelling number, and finally the individual's name. It's best if you write or ask a local to write the destination country in Chinese characters. Do not use red ink, which has a negative connotation.

OVERNIGHT SERVICES
Major Services in Beijing DHL ☎ 010/6466-5566. FedEx ☎ 010/6462-3183. UPS ☎ 010/6505-5005 ☎ 010/6505-5115.

POSTAL RATES
Overseas postal rates are as follows: postcards Y4.20; letters less than 10 grams Y5.40; letters between 10 and 20 grams Y6.50; air-mail parcels up to 1 kilogram, Y95–Y159 to the United States, Y77–Y162 to the United Kingdom, Y70–Y144 to Australia; express parcels less than 500 grams, Y180–Y240 to the United States, Y220–Y280 to Europe, Y160–Y210 to Australia. Letters and parcels can be registered for a small extra charge. Registration forms and customs-declaration forms are generally available in Chinese and French.

RECEIVING MAIL
Long-term guests can receive mail at their hotels. Otherwise, the best place to receive mail is at the American Express office. Most major Chinese cities have American Express offices with client mail service. Be sure to bring your American Express card, as the staff will not give you the mail without seeing it.

SHIPPING PARCELS
You can ship parcels of purchases made in China at the post office, but the price is very high. Most large stores offer shipping services that include insurance guaranteed in writing. Be prepared for a long negotiation, however. Large antiques stores often offer reliable shipping services that take care of customs in China.

MONEY MATTERS
Museum entrance fees range from Y20 to Y50 and vary according to whether you're a local or a foreigner. A soft drink costs about Y10. A dumpling costs about Y10; a slice of pizza costs about Y50. Newspapers are about Y20.

Prices throughout this guide are given for adults. Substantially reduced fees are almost always available for children, students, and senior citizens. For information on taxes, *see* Taxes.

While in China it's best to **carry currency in several forms** (and in several different places), such as cash, traveler's checks, and an ATM and/or credit card.

ATMS
ATMs using the Cirrus and Plus networks can be found all over Hong Kong, and are increasingly common in larger cities throughout China.

Before leaving home, **make sure your credit cards have been programmed for ATM use in China.** Local bank cards often do not work overseas or may access only your checking account; **ask your bank about a MasterCard/Cirrus or Visa debit card,** which works like a bank card but can be used at any ATM displaying a MasterCard/Cirrus or Visa logo. These cards, too, may tap only your checking account; check with your bank about their policy.

CREDIT CARDS
American Express, MasterCard, and Visa are accepted at most hotels and a growing number of stores and restaurants. Diners Club is accepted at many hotels and some restaurants. Contact your credit card company before you go to inform them of your trip. Credit card companies have

been known to put a hold on an account and send a report to their fraud division upon registering a purchase or cash advance in China. Be sure to copy your credit card numbers on a separate piece of paper, which you should carry in a place separate from your credit cards in case of theft.

Throughout this guide, the following abbreviations are used: **AE,** American Express; **DC,** Diners Club; **MC,** MasterCard; and **V,** Visa.

🚹 Reporting Lost Cards **American Express** ☎ 202/554-2639 [call collect]. **Diners Club** ☎ 303/799-1504 in the U.S. [call collect]. **MasterCard** ☎ 010/800-110-7309 in China. **Visa** ☎ 010/800-110-2911 in China.

CURRENCY

The Chinese currency is officially called the renminbi (RMB), or "People's Money." You can change money at most Bank of China branches, at the front desk of most upscale hotels, or at international airports. **Carry currency in several forms** (and in several different places) while abroad, such as cash, traveler's checks, and an ATM and/or credit card.

The Bank of China issues RMB bills in denominations of 2, 5, 10, 50, 100, 500, and 1,000 yuan. Yuan are commonly referred to as *kuai* (pronounced koowhy), the abbreviation is Y. The exchange rates are approximately Y8.28 = $1 US, Y5.59 = 1C$, Y4.44 = 1$ Australian, Y11.96 = £1, Y3.71 = 1$ New Zealand, Y10.06 = 1€, and Y1.1 = 1 South African rand. At press time, the exchange rates for the Hong Kong dollar (HK$) were HK$8.11 = $1 US, HK$4.25 = 1$ Australian, HK$5.27 = 1C$, HK$3.50 = 1$ New Zealand, $HK9.47 = €1, and HK$1.03 = 1 South African rand.

CURRENCY EXCHANGE

For the most favorable rates, **change money through banks.** Although ATM transaction fees may be higher abroad than at home, ATM rates are excellent because they're based on wholesale rates offered only by major banks. You won't do as well at exchange booths in airports or rail and bus stations, in hotels, in restaurants, or in stores. To avoid lines at airport exchange booths, get a bit of local currency before you leave home.

Certain branches of the Bank of China and other banks can convert your traveler's checks and national currencies to RMB. The rate is fixed by a government agency. Hotel desks also do currency exchanges, usually on a 24-hour basis, at rates as good as or better than the bank's offer. A passport is required. No private offices or kiosks offer currency exchange services.

🚹 Exchange Services **International Currency Express** ✉ 427 N. Camden Dr., Suite F, Beverly Hills, CA 90210 ☎ 888/278-6628 orders 🖷 310/278-6410 ⊕ www.foreignmoney.com. **Travel Ex Currency Services** ☎ 800/287-7362 orders and retail locations ⊕ www.travelex.com.

TRAVELER'S CHECKS

Do you need traveler's checks? It depends on where you're headed. If you're going to rural areas and small towns, go with cash; traveler's checks are best used in cities. Lost or stolen checks can usually be replaced within 24 hours. To ensure a speedy refund, buy your own traveler's checks—don't let someone else pay for them: irregularities like this can cause delays. The person who bought the checks should make the call to request a refund.

PACKING

Informal attire is appropriate for most occasions. Sturdy, comfortable walking shoes are a must. A raincoat, especially a light Gore-Tex one or a fold-up poncho, is useful for an onset of rainy weather. Summers are very hot and winters very cold, so pack accordingly. Avoid bringing clothes that need dry cleaning. You'll find it much easier to get around if you travel light, with no more than two or three changes of clothes, so bring clothes that you can layer should you need extra warmth. Clothes are also inexpensive in China, so you can always buy what you need. Most hotels have reliable overnight laundry, mending, and pressing services, so you can have your clothes washed frequently.

If you're planning a longer trip or will be using local tour guides, bring a few inexpensive items from your home country as gifts. Popular gifts are candy, T-shirts, and small cosmetic items such as lipstick and nail polish. **Do not give American magazines and books as gifts,** as these can be considered propaganda and get your Chinese friends into trouble.

Other useful items to have are a flashlight with extra batteries, English-language books and magazines for your own use, antibacterial hand sanitizer or wipes, and packets of tissues or toilet paper.

In your carry-on luggage, pack an extra pair of eyeglasses or contact lenses and enough of any medication you take to last a few days longer than the entire trip. You may also ask your doctor to write a spare prescription using the drug's generic name, as brand names may vary from country to country. **Never pack prescription drugs, valuables, or undeveloped film** in luggage to be checked. And don't forget to carry with you the addresses of offices that handle refunds of lost traveler's checks.

To avoid customs and security delays, carry medications in their original packaging. Don't pack any sharp objects in your carry-on luggage, including knives of any size or material, scissors, nail clippers, corkscrews, or anything else that might arouse suspicion.

To avoid having your checked luggage chosen for hand inspection, don't cram bags full. The U.S. Transportation Security Administration suggests packing shoes on top and placing personal items you don't want touched in clear plastic bags.

CHECKING LUGGAGE

You're allowed to carry aboard one bag and one personal article, such as a purse or a laptop computer. Your carry-on must fit under your seat or in the overhead bin. Get to the gate early, so you can board as soon as possible, before the overhead bins fill up. If you're flying within China on a local carrier, carry on as little as possible; flights can be very crowded and overhead bin space hard to get.

Domestically, you're officially allowed one checked piece that weighs no more than 44 pounds (20 kilograms). Note that if you have a seat at the back of the plane, you'll probably board first, while the overhead bins are still empty. Be sure to lock your bags—for safety reasons and because some local carriers require that all checked bags be locked.

Baggage allowances vary by carrier, destination, and ticket class. On international flights, you're usually allowed to check two bags weighing up to 70 pounds (32 kilograms) each, although a few airlines allow checked bags of up to 88 pounds pounds (40 kilograms) in first class. Some international carriers don't allow more than 66 pounds (30 kilograms) per bag in business class and 44 pounds (20 kilograms) in economy. Expect to pay a fee for baggage that exceeds weight limits. Check baggage restrictions with your carrier before you pack.

Airline liability for baggage is limited to $2,500 per person on flights within the United States. On international flights it amounts to $9.07 per pound or $20 per kilogram for checked baggage (roughly $640 per 70-pound bag), with a maximum of $634.90 per piece, and $400 per passenger for unchecked baggage. You can buy additional coverage at check-in for about $10 per $1,000 of coverage, but it often excludes a rather extensive list of items, shown on your airline ticket.

Before departure, itemize your bags' contents and their worth, and label the bags with your name, address, and phone number. (If you use your home address, cover it so potential thieves can't see it readily.) Include a label inside each bag and **pack a copy of your itinerary.** At check-in, make sure each bag is correctly tagged with the destination airport's three-letter code. Because some checked bags will be opened for hand inspection, the U.S. Transportation Security Administration recommends that you leave luggage unlocked or use the plastic locks offered at check-in. TSA screeners place an inspection notice inside searched bags, which are resealed with a special lock.

If your bag has been searched and contents are missing or damaged, file a claim with the TSA Consumer Response Center as soon as possible. If your bags arrive damaged or fail to arrive at all, file a written report with the airline before leaving the airport.

🔲 Complaints **U.S. Transportation Security Administration (TSA) Contact Center** ☎ 866/289-9673 ⊕ www.tsa.gov.

PASSPORTS & VISAS

When traveling internationally, carry your passport even if you don't need one (it's always the best form of ID) and **make two photocopies of the data page** (one for someone at home and another for you, carried separately from your passport). If you lose your passport, promptly call the nearest embassy or consulate and the local police.

U.S. passport applications for children under age 14 require consent from both parents or legal guardians; both parents must appear together to sign the application. If only one parent appears, he or she must submit a written statement from the other parent authorizing passport issuance for the child. A parent with sole authority must present evidence of it when applying; acceptable documentation includes the child's certified birth certificate listing only the applying parent, a court order specifically permitting this parent's travel with the child, or a death certificate for the nonapplying parent. Application forms and instructions are available on the Web site of the U.S. State Department's Bureau of Consular Affairs (⊕ travel.state.gov).

ENTERING CHINA

All U.S. citizens, even infants, need a valid passport with a tourist visa stamped in it to enter China for stays of up to 90 days. For Hong Kong you need only a valid passport.

GETTING A VISA

It takes about a week to get a visa in the United States. Travel agents in Hong Kong can issue visas to visit mainland China. Costs range from about $35 for a visa issued within two working days to $50 for a visa issued overnight. **Note:** The visa appli-

cation will ask your occupation. The Chinese do not like journalists or anyone who works in publishing or media. Americans and Canadians in these professions routinely state "teacher" under "Occupation." U.K. passports state the bearer's occupation, and this can be problematic for anyone in the "wrong" line of work. Before you go, contact the consulate of the People's Republic of China to see how strict the current mood is. The Web site www.visatoasia.com/china.html provides up-to-date information on visa application to China.

🔲 In Australia **Chinese Embassy** ☎ 02/6273-4780 Ext. 218 and 258 🖷 02/6273-9615 ⊕ www.chinaembassy.org.au.
🔲 In Canada **Chinese Embassy** ☎ 613/789-3434 🖷 613/789-1911 ⊕ www.chinaembassycanada.org.
🔲 In New Zealand **Chinese Embassy** ☎ 04/472-1382 🖷 04/499-0419 ⊕ www.chinaembassy.org.nz.
🔲 In the U.K. **Chinese Embassy** ☎ 0171/636-2580 🖷 0171/636-2981 ⊕ www.chinese-embassy.org.uk.
🔲 In the U.S. **Chinese Consulate** ✉ Visa Office, 520 12th Ave., New York, NY 10036 ☎ 212/736-9301 automatic answering machine with 24-hr service, 212/502-0271 information desk (open weekdays 2–4) 🖷 212/502-0245 ⊕ www.nyconsulate.prchina.org. **Chinese Embassy** ✉ Room 110, 2201 Wisconsin Ave. NW, Washington, DC 20007 ☎ 202/338-6688 🖷 202/588-9760 ⊕ www.china-embassy.org.

PASSPORT OFFICES

The best time to apply for a passport or to renew is in fall and winter. Before any trip, check your passport's expiration date, and, if necessary, renew it as soon as possible.

🔲 Australian Citizens **Passports Australia** Australian Department of Foreign Affairs and Trade, ☎ 131-232 ⊕ www.passports.gov.au.
🔲 Canadian Citizens **Passport Office** ✉ to mail in applications: 200 Promenade du Portage, Hull, Québec J8X 4B7 ☎ 800/567-6868 or 819/994-3500 ⊕ www.ppt.gc.ca.
🔲 New Zealand Citizens **New Zealand Passports Office** ☎ 0800/225-050 or 04/474-8100 ⊕ www.passports.govt.nz.
🔲 U.K. Citizens **U.K. Passport Service** ☎ 0870/521-0410 ⊕ www.passport.gov.uk.
🔲 U.S. Citizens **National Passport Information Center** ☎ 877/487-2778, 888/874-7793 TDD/TTY ⊕ travel.state.gov.

RESTROOMS

You'll find public restrooms in the streets, parks, restaurants, department stores, and major tourist attractions in major cities (except in Hong Kong where they can be difficult to find), but these are not very clean and seldom provide toilet paper or soap. The restrooms in the newest shopping plazas, fast-food outlets, and deluxe restaurants catering to foreigners are much cleaner and often meet international standards. The public restrooms charge a small fee (usually less than Y1), but seldom provide Western-style facilities or private booths, relying instead on squat toilets, open troughs, and rusty spigots; WC signs at intersections point the way to these facilities. It's a good idea to **carry toilet paper or tissues and antibacterial hand sanitizer or wipes** with you at all times. Using hotel and restaurant bathrooms is the best bet for a clean environment.

SAFETY

There is little violent crime against tourists in China, partly because the penalties are severe for those who are caught—execution is the most common. Use the lockbox in your hotel room to store any valuables, but always carry your passport with you for identification purposes. Be aware that a money belt or a waist pack pegs you as a tourist, and a backpack makes an easy target for thieves in crowded conditions. Be sure to keep your bags in front of you, so that thieves cannot cut them open without your noticing. Distribute your cash and any valuables (including your credit cards and passport) between a deep front pocket, an inside jacket or vest pocket, and a hidden money pouch.

The traffic in major Chinese cities is usually heavy and just as out of control as it looks. Be very careful when crossing streets. Drivers do not give pedestrians the right-of-way; note in particular that drivers seldom stop or look for pedestrians before making a right turn on a red light. Be wary of the countless bicyclists as well as drivers.

Respiratory problems may be aggravated by the severely polluted air in China's cities. Some residents as well as visitors find that wearing a surgical mask, or a scarf or bandana, helps.

LOCAL SCAMS

A general rule of thumb is **don't wear anything that will stand out,** that is, revealing or flashy clothes or expensive jewelry. If nothing else, you may be harassed by people politely asking if you will trade clothes or give them your watch! As a rule, don't exchange money on street corners, even if the rate is favorable. Counterfeit money is rampant on China's black market.

WOMEN IN CHINA

The Chinese do not approve of women wearing revealing clothing so it's best to wear tops that cover most of your torso and shorts that reach your knees in summer. Foreign women rarely face unwanted attention from men, as Chinese custom frowns upon lewd behavior.

If you carry a purse, choose one with a zipper and a thick strap that you can drape across your body; adjust the length so that the purse sits in front of you at or above hip level. Store only enough money in the purse to cover casual spending; distribute the rest of your cash in deep front pockets, inside jacket or vest pockets, and a concealed money pouch.

SENIOR-CITIZEN TRAVEL

To qualify for age-related discounts, mention your senior-citizen status up front when booking hotel reservations (not when checking out) and before you're seated in restaurants (not when paying the bill). Be sure to have identification on hand. When renting a car, ask about promotional car-rental discounts, which can be cheaper than senior-citizen rates.

🎓 Educational Programs **Elderhostel** ⊠ 11 Ave. de Lafayette, Boston, MA 02111-1746 ☎ 877/426-8056, 978/323-4141 international callers, 877/426-2167 TTY ⧉ 877/426-2166 ⊕ www.elderhostel.org. **Folkways Institute** ⊠ 14600 S.E. Aldridge Rd., Portland, OR 97236-6518 ☎ 503/658-6600 ⧉ 503/658-8672. **Interhostel** ⊠ University of New Hampshire, 6 Garrison Ave., Durham, NH 03824 ☎ 800/

733-9753 or 603/862-1147 ⌐ 603/862-1113 ⊕ www. learn.unh.edu.

SHOPPING

Good souvenirs include Chinese medicines, silk, and tea. There are shops specializing in jade, old Chinese porcelain, and antique furniture, but **be alert for forgery when shopping.** Stick to Friendship Stores (formerly emporiums selling luxury goods for foreigners only, now more like an upscale department store chain) and shops attached to international hotels for some assurance of getting what you pay for. When you buy goods in established shops, you first pay the cashier and then present the receipt of sale to the store attendant, who will wrap your purchase. As a word of caution, you should watch your item being wrapped to deter disreputable shops from replacing the item you purchased with an inferior version.

With antiques, an item more than 100 years old will have an official red wax seal attached—but not all items with seals attached are more than 100 years old. The Chinese government has cleared only certain antiques for sale to foreigners. Save the bill of sale to show customs when you leave the country, or the antique will be confiscated. For exports, antiques must have been made after 1795.

China's antiques market exists in state-run tourist sites such as courtyards or gardens. Often, items in these places range from panels ripped off of old house facades to carved headboards. Antiques bought in these places are not old enough to warrant an official seal for customs.

Post offices in hotels usually have interesting Chinese stamps for sale. Ask about designs that were issued during the Cultural Revolution.

SMART SOUVENIRS

Around the tourist centers you'll find street merchants selling an array of cloisonné and jade jewelry, old Chinese coins (usually fake), fans, tea sets, chops (stone stamps that can be carved with your name in Chinese), embroidered silk robes and pillowcases, and other souvenirs. You can often bargain for these items. Areas frequented by tourists also abound with stores and street vendors selling art: scrolls, woodblock prints, paper cuts, and some contemporary oils.

WATCH OUT

In some cities, the open-air markets that line the entrances to major tourist attractions generally charge extravagant prices for poor-quality, mass-produced kitsch and outright fakes. Street-bought pearls and jade are often fake. It's particularly difficult to evaluate jade, but you can trust government-owned factories. Many of these factory showrooms offer free bus services and a glimpse of the production process.

Beware of "student artists" who seek out foreign tourists and persuade them to visit their studios. The artworks in the studios are mass-produced and are marked up way beyond their market value.

Note that expensive fashion items such as silk, batik, and cotton clothes may shrink when dry-cleaned. If you still wish to buy these items, be prepared to hand-wash them in cold water with mild soap. Also keep in mind that some countries, including the United States, prohibit the import of ivory.

Goods are usually not returnable, even with a receipt. Never put down a deposit for a purchase you are still considering; if you decide against the purchase you may not be able to get your deposit back.

STUDENTS IN CHINA

There are abundant and diverse opportunities for students to study in China through programs organized by both U.S. and Chinese universities. Campuses in China have facilities similar to those of their American counterparts, although the quality of Chinese classes varies. Classes are held Monday through Saturday. Dormitories are spartan and visiting rules apply. (If you're staying in a dormitory, it's generally difficult to make arrangements for friends or family to stay with you.) You'll find that relationships between students and teachers are hierarchical and classroom debate is not welcome. However, Chinese teachers generally will be very interested in you—so much so that they may delve into aspects of your life that you may regard as personal.

There are different visas for students staying in China for more than three months. If you're staying up to six months, you'll need an "F" visa; for more than six months but less than a year, an "X" visa; and for a year or longer, a "Z" visa. If for some reason you are issued the wrong visa, you can obtain the correct visa in China for a small fee. China also requires that anyone staying in China for more than a year must get a thorough physical, including a chest X-ray and an HIV test. People who test positive for HIV are prohibited from entering China.

Students in China are entitled to discounts on museum and park fees, as well as 40% discounts on intra-continental air tickets if they have an official Chinese student card issued by their school.

▪ IDs & Services **STA Travel** ✉ 10 Downing St., New York, NY 10014 ☎ 800/777-0112 24-hr service center, 212/627-3111 🖷 212/627-3387 ⊕ www.sta.com. **Travel Cuts** ✉ 187 College St., Toronto, Ontario M5T 1P7, Canada ☎ 800/592-2887 in the U.S., 416/979-2406 or 866/246-9762 in Canada 🖷 416/979-8167 ⊕ www.travelcuts.com.

TAXES

There is no sales tax in China. Hotels charge a 5% tax and sometimes a 10%–15% service fee. Some restaurants charge a 10% service fee.

A departure tax of Y50 (about $6) for domestic flights and Y90 (about $11) for international flights (including flights to Hong Kong and Macau) must be paid in cash in dollars or yuan at the airport. Peoples holding diplomatic passports, passengers in transit who stop over for less than 24 hours, and children under 12 are exempt from the departure tax. There are also taxes for international ferry departures at some ports.

TELEPHONES

AREA & COUNTRY CODES

The country code for China is 86; the city code for Beijing is 10, the city code for Shanghai is 21, and the city code for Hong Kong is 852. To call China from the United States or Canada, dial the international access code (011), followed by the country code (86), the area or city code, and the seven- or eight-digit phone number. When dialing from within China to another city, dial 0 before the city code. To make an international call from within China, dial 00 (the international access code within China) and then the country code, area code, and phone number. The country code is 1 for the United States and Canada, 61 for Australia, 64 for New Zealand, and 44 for the United Kingdom.

Numbers beginning with 800 within China are toll-free. Note that a call from China to a toll-free number in the United States or Hong Kong is a full-tariff international call.

CELL PHONES

Consider renting a cell phone with an SIM card for travel in China, as this allows you to take advantage of low rates. The SIM card, which slips into the cell phone, is prepaid and rechargeable, so you will never receive a phone bill. Try to avoid cell rentals that charge you per-minute rates.

▪ Cell-Phone Rental **Cellular Abroad** ✉ 3019 Pico Blvd., Santa Monica, CA 90405 ☎ 800/287-3020 ⊕ www.cellularabroad.com/chinasg.html.

DIRECTORY & OPERATOR ASSISTANCE

For directory assistance, dial 114. If you want information for other cities, dial the city code followed by 114 (note that this is considered a long-distance call). For example, if you're in Beijing and need directory assistance for a Shanghai number, dial 021–114. The operators do not speak English, so if you don't speak Chinese you're best off asking your hotel for help.

INTERNATIONAL CALLS

In most cities, International direct dialing (IDD) service is provided at hotels, post offices, major shopping centers, and airports. In hotels, an operator will dial the number and place the call for you. Note that it is much cheaper, however, to use a calling card or a rental cell phone.

LOCAL CALLS

You can make local calls from your hotel or any public phone on the street; most public phones use calling cards, which you can purchase at convenience stores, newsstands, post offices, and hotels. For local calls within the same city, omit the city code.

LONG-DISTANCE CALLS

Long-distance rates in China are very low, and hotels are only allowed to add a service charge of up to 15%. To make long-distance calls from a public phone you need an IC card (⇨ Phone Cards). To place a long-distance call, dial 0, the city code, and the eight-digit phone number.

LONG-DISTANCE SERVICES

AT&T, MCI, and Sprint access codes make calling long-distance relatively convenient, but you may find the local access number blocked in many hotel rooms. First ask the hotel operator to connect you. If the hotel operator balks, ask for an international operator, or dial the international operator yourself. One way to improve your odds of getting connected to your long-distance carrier is to travel with more than one company's calling card (a hotel may block Sprint, for example, but not MCI). If all else fails, call from a pay phone.

The local access code in China is 11 for AT&T, 12 for MCI, and 13 for Sprint—dial these numbers after dialing the local operator (108), who will speak English.
🖪 Access Codes **AT&T Direct** ☎ 800/874-4000. **MCI WorldPhone** ☎ 800/444-4444. **Sprint International Access** ☎ 800/793-1153.

PHONE CARDS

There are two main kinds of calling cards in China: the IP card (Internet protocol; *aipi ka*) and the IC card (integrated circuit; *àicei ka*), both of which are available from post offices, convenience stores, and street vendors. The IC card is used for domestic local and long-distance calls on any public phone that has an IC card slot. To make an international long-distance call, you will need to use the IC card to activate a public phone for a dial tone, and then provide the access codes on the IP card to make your call. Both cards' minutes are deducted at the same time, one for local access (IC card) and one for the long-distance call you placed (IP card). You should bargain to pay less than the face value of the card—as little as Y70 for a Y100 card. Instructions are on the back of the cards, but you simply dial the access number, choose English from the menu, and follow the prompts to dial in the number behind a scratch-off panel. Using an IC card for a domestic call, Y50 can give you as much as an hour of talking time. Using the IP card, you can call internationally for a fraction of the cost of a hotel-assisted call.

PUBLIC PHONES

Most hotels have phone booths where you can place domestic and international calls. You pay a deposit of about Y200 and receive a card with the number of the booth. A computer times the call and processes a bill, which you pay at the end. Post offices have telecommunications centers where you can buy cards in denominations of Y20, Y50, and Y100 to make long-distance calls. Standard pay phones accept these cards and coins. The cards tend to be less expensive but only work in the province in which they're purchased.

TIME

The whole of China is 8 hours ahead of London, 13 hours ahead of New York, 14 hours ahead of Chicago, and 16 hours ahead of Los Angeles. There's no daylight saving time, so subtract an hour in summer.

TIPPING

Although tipping is officially forbidden by the government, it's still expected in many cases. Bell hops routinely receive Y5–Y10 per bag, and hairdressers receive 10%. For taxi drivers, you can simply round up the fare. Most restaurants charge a 10% service fee, so there's no need to tip. If this fee has not been added to your bill, leave 10%. Tour guides often expect Y10 from each person for the day.

CTS tour guides are not allowed to accept tips, but you can give them candy, T-shirts, and other small gifts. If you hire a driver and guide independently, the tipping norm is Y80 per day for the guide and Y40 for the driver.

TOURS & PACKAGES

Because everything is prearranged on a prepackaged tour or independent vacation, you spend less time planning—and often get it all at a good price.

BOOKING WITH AN AGENT

Travel agents are excellent resources. But it's a good idea to collect brochures from several agencies, as some agents' suggestions may be influenced by relationships with tour and package firms that reward them for volume sales. If you have a special interest, find an agent with expertise in that area; the American Society of Travel Agents (ASTA; ➪ Travel Agencies) has a database of specialists worldwide. You can log on to the group's Web site to find an ASTA travel agent in your neighborhood.

Make sure your travel agent knows the accommodations and other services of the place being recommended. Ask about the hotel's location, room size, beds, and whether it has a pool, room service, or programs for children, if you care about these. Has your agent been there in person or sent others whom you can contact?

Do some homework on your own, too: local tourism boards can provide information about lesser-known and small-niche operators, some of which may sell only direct.

BUYER BEWARE

Each year consumers are stranded or lose their money when tour operators—even large ones with excellent reputations—go out of business. So check out the operator. Ask several travel agents about its reputation, and try to **book with a company that has a consumer-protection program.** (Look for information in the company's brochure.) In the United States, members of the United States Tour Operators Association are required to set aside funds ($1 million) to help eligible customers cover payments and travel arrangements in the event that the company

defaults. It's also a good idea to choose a company that participates in the American Society of Travel Agents' Tour Operator Program; ASTA will act as mediator in any disputes between you and your tour operator.

Remember that the more your package or tour includes, the better you can predict the ultimate cost of your vacation. Make sure you know exactly what is covered, and beware of hidden costs. Are taxes, tips, and transfers included? Entertainment and excursions? These can add up.

🔢 **Tour-Operator Recommendations American Society of Travel Agents** (➪ Travel Agencies). **Cameron Tours** ✉ 6249 N. Kingston St., McLean, VA 22101 ☎ 800/648-4635 or 703/538-7122 ⊕ www.camerontours.com. **CHN-Asia Express Tours** ✉ 63 W. Prospect, 2nd fl., East Brunswick, NJ 08816 ☎ 800/824-9965 or 732/698-9600 🖷 732/698-9380. **Imperial Tours** ✉ 1802 N. Carson St., Suite 212-2296, Carson City, NV 89701 ☎ 888/296-5306 🖷 800/380-6576 ⊕ www.imperialtours.net. **National Tour Association** (NTA) ✉ 546 E. Main St., Lexington, KY 40508 ☎ 800/682-8886 or 859/226-4444 🖷 859/226-4404 ⊕ www.ntaonline.com. **United States Tour Operators Association** (USTOA) ✉ 275 Madison Ave., Suite 2014, New York, NY 10016 ☎ 212/599-6599 🖷 212/599-6744 ⊕ www.ustoa.com.

TRAIN TRAVEL

Train tickets usually have to be purchased in the city of origin. If you do not speak Mandarin, it will be difficult to negotiate the ticket windows at the train station even though there is a special ticket counter just for foreigners, so buy tickets from the local CTS office or ask your hotel concierge to make the arrangements. Fares are more expensive for foreigners than for the Chinese. Make train reservations at least a day or two in advance, if you can. Boiled water and hot meals are always available on board. Trains are always crowded, overhead luggage space is scarce at times, but you are guaranteed your designated seat. In Hong Kong there will be a queue to get on the train; on the mainland, it's every passenger for him- or herself.

Note that theft on trains is increasing; on overnight trains, sleep with your valuables or else keep them on the inside of the bunk.

CLASSES

The train system offers a glimpse of old-fashioned socialist euphemisms. Instead of first-class and second-class accommodations, you choose hard seat or soft seat, and for overnight journeys, hard sleeper or soft sleeper. The soft sleeper has four compartments with soft beds and is recommended if you're taking a long journey (though it is much more expensive than the hard sleeper).

FARES & SCHEDULES

The tour operator Travel China Guide has an English-language Web site (⊕ www.travelchinaguide.com/china-trains/index.htm) that can help you figure out train schedules and fares.

TRAVEL AGENCIES

A good travel agent puts your needs first. Look for an agency that has been in business at least five years, emphasizes customer service, and has someone on staff who specializes in your destination. In addition, **make sure the agency belongs to a professional trade organization.** The American Society of Travel Agents (ASTA)—the largest and most influential in the field with more than 20,000 members in some 140 countries—maintains and enforces a strict code of ethics and will step in to help mediate any agent-client disputes involving ASTA members if necessary. ASTA (whose motto is "Without a travel agent, you're on your own") also maintains a Web site that includes a directory of agents. (If a travel agency is also acting as your tour operator, ⇨ Buyer Beware *in* Tours & Packages.)

🔢 Local Agent Referrals **American Society of Travel Agents** (ASTA) ✉ 1101 King St., Suite 200, Alexandria, VA 22314 ☎ 800/965-2782 24-hr hotline, 703/739-2782 🖷 703/684-8319 ⊕ www.astanet.com. **Association of British Travel Agents** ✉ 68–71 Newman St., London W1T 3AH ☎ 020/7637-2444 🖷 020/7637-0713 ⊕ www.abta.com. **Association of Canadian Travel Agencies** ✉ 130 Al-

bert St., Suite 1705, Ottawa, Ontario K1P 5G4 ☎ 613/237-3657 🖷 613/237-7052 ⊕ www.acta.ca. **Australian Federation of Travel Agents** ✉ Level 3, 309 Pitt St., Sydney, NSW 2000 ☎ 02/9264-3299 or 1300/363-416 🖷 02/9264-1085 ⊕ www.afta.com.au. **Travel Agents' Association of New Zealand** ✉ Level 5, Tourism and Travel House, 79 Boulcott St., Box 1888, Wellington 6001 ☎ 04/499-0104 🖷 04/499-0786 ⊕ www.taanz.org.nz.

🔢 In Hong Kong In Hong Kong, **Phoenix Travel** ✉ Milton Mansions, 96 Nathan Rd., Room 6B, Tsim Sha Tsui, Kowloon ☎ 852/2722-7378 🖷 852/2369-8884.

VISITOR INFORMATION

Learn more about foreign destinations by checking government-issued travel advisories and country information. For a broader picture, consider information from more than one country.

For general information before you go, including information about tours, insurance, and safety, call or visit the China National Tourist Office in New York City, Los Angeles (Glendale), London, or Sydney.

Within China, China International Travel Service (CITS) and China Travel Service (CTS) are under the same government ministry. Local offices, catering to sightseeing around the area (and to visitors from other mainland cities), are called CTS. CITS offices can book international flights.

🔢 China National Tourist Offices **Australia** ✉ 19th fl., 44 Market St., Sydney, NSW 2000 ☎ 02/9299-4057 🖷 02/9290-1958 ⊕ www.cnto.org.au. **Canada** ✉ 556 W. Broadway, Vancouver, BC V5Z 1E9 ☎ 604/872-8787 🖷 604/873-2823 ⊕ www.citscanada.com. **United Kingdom** ✉ 4 Glentworth St., London NW1 ☎ 0171/935-9427 🖷 0171/487-5842. **United States** ✉ 350 5th Ave., Suite 6413, New York, NY 10118 ☎ 212/760-8218 🖷 212/760-8809 ✉ 333 W. Broadway, Suite 201, Glendale, CA 91204 ☎ 818/545-7504 🖷 818/545-7506 ⊕ www.cnto.org.

🔢 China International Travel Service (CITS) **United States** ✉ 2 Mott St., New York, NY 10002 ☎ 800/899-8618 or 212/608-1212.

🔢 U.S. Government Advisories **Australian Department of Foreign Affairs and Trade** ☎ 300/139-281 travel advice, 02/6261-1299 Consular Travel

Advice Faxback Service ⊕ www.dfat.gov.au. **Consular Affairs Bureau of Canada** ☎ 800/267-6788 or 613/944-6788 ⊕ www.voyage.gc.ca. **New Zealand Ministry of Foreign Affairs and Trade** ☎ 04/439-8000 ⊕ www.mft.govt.nz. **U.K. Foreign and Commonwealth Office** ⊠ Travel Advice Unit, Consular Division, Old Admiralty Bldg., London SW1A 2PA ☎ 0870/606-0290 or 020/7008-1500 ⊕ www.fco.gov.uk/travel. **U.S. Department of State** ⊠ Overseas Citizens Services Office, 2100 Pennsylvania Ave. NW, 4th fl., Washington, DC 20520 ☎ 888/407-4747 or 202/647-5225 interactive hotline ⊕ www.travel.state.gov.

WEB SITES

Do check out the World Wide Web when planning your trip. You'll find everything from weather forecasts to virtual tours of famous cities. Be sure to visit Fodors.com (⊕ www.fodors.com), a complete travel-planning site. You can research prices and book plane tickets, hotel rooms, rental cars, vacation packages, and more. In addition, you can post your pressing questions in the Travel Talk section. Other planning tools include a currency converter and weather reports, and there are loads of links to travel resources.

Government and regional tourist agencies in China sponsor a number of helpful Web sites for travelers to China. Try www.chinatips.net, www.travelchinaguide.com, www.china.com, and www.chinavista.com. The China National Tourism Office is at www.cnto.org. You can also visit CITS at www.chinatravelservice.com or www.citsusa.com.

BEIJING
THE HEART OF THE DRAGON

1

Revised by
Guy Rubin and
Caroline Liou

WIDE-EYED CHINESE TOURISTS converge on Tiananmen Square each day at dawn to watch a military honor guard raise China's flag. As soldiers march forth from the vast Forbidden City, these visitors, who usually number in the hundreds, begin to take pictures. They jockey for spots beneath the fluttering banner. They pose before the vermilion Gate of Heavenly Peace, its huge Chairman Mao portrait gazing benignly from atop the imperial doorway. This same shot, snapped by countless pilgrims, adorns family albums across the Middle Kingdom.

The daily photographic ritual and the giddy throng illustrate Beijing's position—unrivaled to this day—at the center of the Chinese universe. In spite of widespread urban renewal, parts of old Beijing continue to convey an imperial grandeur. But the city is more than a relic or a feudal ghost. Modern temples to communism—the Great Hall of the People, Chairman Mao's mausoleum—hint at the monumental power that still resides within the city's secret courtyards. If China is a dragon, Beijing is its beating heart.

Beijing's 13 million official residents—plus another 2 million migrant workers—are a fascinating mix of old and new. Early morning *taiqi* (tai chi) enthusiasts, bearded old men with caged songbirds, and amateur Peking opera crooners still frequent the city's many charming parks. Cyclists, most pedaling cumbersome, jet black Flying Pigeons, clog the roadways. But few wear padded blue Mao jackets these days, and they all must share the city's broad thoroughfares with China's steadily increasing number of car owners. Beijing traffic has gone from nonexistent to nightmarish in less than a decade, adding auto emissions to the city's winter coal smoke and sparking the newest threat to social order—road rage.

As the seat of China's immense national bureaucracy, Beijing still carries a political charge. The Communist Party, whose self-described goal is "a dictatorship of the proletariat," has yet to relinquish its political monopoly. In 1989 student protesters in Tiananmen Square dared to challenge the party. The government's brutal response, carried live on TV, remains etched in global memory. More than 10 years later, secret police still mingle with tourists and kite fliers on the square, ready to haul away all those so brave or foolish as to distribute a leaflet or unfurl a banner. Mao-style propaganda persists. Slogans that preach unity among China's national minorities, patriotism, and love for the People's Liberation Army (the military arm of the Communist Party) still festoon the city on occasion. Yet as Beijing's already robust economy is boosted even farther by the massive influx of investment prompted by the 2008 Olympics, such campaigns appear increasingly out of touch with the cellphone-primed generation. The result in the streets is an incongruous mixture of new prosperity and throwback politics: socialist slogans adorn shopping centers selling Gucci and Big Macs. Beijing is truly a land of opposites where the ancient and the sparkling new collide.

EXPLORING BEIJING

Be curious. Beijing rewards the explorer. Most temples and palaces have gardens and lesser courtyards that are seldom visited. Even at the

Numbers in the text correspond to numbers in the margin and on the Beijing and Forbidden City maps.

**If you have
1 day**

Begin your day in **Tiananmen Square** ➊ ⌐—you may want to catch the flag-raising ceremony at dawn—to admire the communist icons of modern China. Then, heading north, walk back through time into the **Forbidden City** ➑–⓲. Keep in mind that in 1421, when the imperial palace was built, its structures were the tallest in Asia. You can spend the morning leisurely examining the many palaces, exhibitions, and gardens of the Forbidden City. If this has not exhausted you, head north into **Jingshan Park** ㉑ and climb Coal Hill to get a panoramic view over the entire Forbidden City. Then, jump in a cab and head to Lotus Lane where you can eat lunch overlooking **Qianhai Lake** ㉓.

In the afternoon, take a trip outside the city. Hire a car and driver to take you on the one-hour journey to the **Great Wall at Badaling** ㊶, which is the closest to Beijing. On your way back, consider a stop at either the **Thirteen Ming Tombs** ㊹ or the **Summer Palace** ㊱. The Ming Tombs are en route; the Summer Palace will add an additional half hour to your journey. For both sights, the tickets are sold until one hour before closing time.

**If you have
3 days**

On your first day, visit **Tiananmen Square** ➊ ⌐ and the **Forbidden City** ➑–⓲. Depart through the Gate of Obedience and Purity (the north gate) and walk west to **Beihai Park** ㉒ for lunch at the food stalls. Arrive at the north gate before 1:30 for a half-day hutong tour, a guided pedicab ride through a mazelike neighborhood to the **Drum Tower** ㉕. Have dinner at the ✕ **Quanjude Peking Duck Restaurant,** south of Tiananmen Square.

On Day 2 visit the **Temple of Heaven** ㉝, the **Lama Temple** ㉙, and nearby the **Temple of Confucius** ㉚. Allow time for shopping at **Beijing Curio City, Silk Alley,** and the **Yihong Carpet Factory.** For dinner, eat Sichuanese in the Sanlitun area.

Set aside Day 3 for a trip to the **Thirteen Ming Tombs** ㊹ and the **Great Wall at Mutianyu** ㊷, where a Japanese gondola offers a dramatic ride to the summit. Bring a brown-bag lunch.

---

height of the summer tourist rush, the Forbidden City's peripheral courtyards offer ample breathing room, even seclusion. The Temple of Heaven's vast grounds are a pleasure year-round—and enchanting during a snowstorm.

Although the Forbidden City and Tiananmen Square represent the heart of Beijing from imperial and tourist perspectives, the capital lacks a definitive downtown area in terms of shopping (with the exception, perhaps, of Wangfujing) or business, as commercial and entertainment districts have arisen all over.

When planning your day, keep in mind that Beijing is sprawling. City blocks are very large. To avoid arriving exhausted at sites that appeared deceptively close on the map, ride the subway, rent a bicycle, or hire a taxi to get between sites, saving your legs to walk around once you get there. Ration your foot time for Beijing's intriguing back alleys.

Tiananmen Square to Liulichang Antiques Market

The fame and symbolism of China's heart, Tiananmen, the Gate of Heavenly Peace, have been potent for generations of Chinese, but the events of June 1989 have left it forever etched into world consciousness. South of the square, a district of antiques shops and bookstores shows another side of Chinese culture.

a good walk

Start at the Renmin Yingxiong Jinianbei (Monument to the People's Heroes) in **Tiananmen Square** ❶ ▶. Look to either side of the square for the monuments to the new dynasty—the individual is meant to be dwarfed by their scale. To the west lies the **Great Hall of the People** ❷, home to China's legislative body, the National People's Congress. The equally solid building opposite is host to the important **China National Museum** ❸, which is due to be under renovation until 2007.

Southward, straight ahead, between two banks of heroic sculptures, is the **Mao Zedong Memorial Hall** ❹, housing Chairman Mao's tomb. Beyond it stands **Qianmen** (Front Gate), the colloquial name for the **Facing the Sun Gate** ❺, which affords great views of the city from the top. At street level, the Qianmen area remains as bustling as ever.

Head down Qianmen Dajie, the large road leading south, for about 90 feet before turning right (west) and sharply left (south) down a parallel north–south avenue, Zhu Bao Shi Jie (Jewelry Market Street). The old Beijing Silk Shop, at No. 5, will confirm you are on the right track. Here, in the **Dazhalan Market Area** ❻, amid the silk and fur bargains of the present, continue traditions of commerce and entertainment stretching back to the Ming era.

To escape the bustle into the calm of residential Beijing, take the second alley to your right, Langfang Ertiao; 65 feet in on the left is a three-story house with carved decorative panels. You'll see a number of such former inns and shops as you proceed west past a small alleyway on your left to the Meishijie (Coal Market Street) crossing, where you should head diagonally over to the Qudeng (Fetch Light) Hutong.

Follow Qudeng Hutong past traditional courtyard houses marked by wooden doorways, auspicious couplets, lintel beams, and stone door gods. At its end, veer left, then right and onto Tan'er (Charcoal) Hutong. At its close, turn left again down Yanshou Jie (Long Life Street), and the eastern end of **Liulichang Jie** ❼ (Glazed-Tile Factory Street) will soon be apparent (look for the traditional post office).

TIMING   Allow three hours for the walk, longer if the museums arrest you and if serious antique/curio browsing is anticipated in Liulichang.

Hutong Hikes

Never bypass an intriguing alleyway. Strolls into a *hutong* frequently reveal ancient neighborhoods: mud-and-timber homes; courtyards full of children, laobaixing (ordinary folk), and, in winter, mountains of cabbage and coal; and alleys so narrow that pedestrians can't pass two abreast. This is Old Peking. See it before it vanishes. Make sure you have a Chinese/English map with you so you can be directed somewhere—Tiananmen Square, for example—to regain your bearings.

The "Real" Peking Opera

Pop music has taken root in every Chinese city, but in Beijing it is still possible to see authentic Peking opera. Tragedy, warfare, palace intrigue—this is the stuff of the capital's traditional stage. Operas range from slothful to acrobatic; voices soar to near-shrill heights for female roles and sink to throaty baritones for generals and emperors. Costumes and makeup are without exception extravagant. Shortened performances catering to tourists are held at the Liyuan Juchang Theater. Full operas, and Beijing's enthusiastic opera crowd, can be seen several times each week at a number of theaters, including Chang'an Grand Theater.

Shoppers' Paradise

Numerous "old goods markets" peddle everything from Chairman Mao souvenirs to antique porcelain, jewelry, and furniture—plus a full selection of fakes. The Sunday flea market at Panjiayuan is the first stop for many portable antiques (wood carvings, statues, jade, old tile, and so on) entering Beijing from the countryside. Vendors, especially in the market's open-air rear section, are usually peasants who've journeyed to Beijing to sell items collected in their village. Antique rugs and furniture are perhaps Beijing's best bargain. A few dealers will arrange to ship larger items overseas.

What to See

★ ❸ **China National Museum** (Zhongguo Guojia Bowuguan). On the east side of Tiananmen Square stands a grandiose structure: the forthcoming China National Museum. Until 2003 this iconic building housed both the massive China History Museum and the rather tired Museum of the Chinese Revolution. In honor of the 2008 Beijing Olympics, city authorities have embarked on a renovation and expansion program to create an art institution befitting one of the world's major capitals. The building is scheduled to be closed between April 2005 and December 2007. Prior to that time, visitors may enjoy a reduced but still exquisite collection of bronze, ceramic, and jade pieces, as well as a new waxworks exhibition—a 35-model who's who of Chinese ancient and modern cultural history. Bags must be checked (Y1) before you enter. ⊠ *Central entrance on building on east side of Tiananmen Sq., Chongwen District* ☎ *010/6512–8967* 🎫 *Y30; bag check, Y1* ⊘ *Mar.–June and Sept.–Oct., Mon.–Sun. 8:30–4:30; July–Aug. and Nov.–Feb., Mon.–Sun. 8:30–4; ticket office closes one hour before museum.*

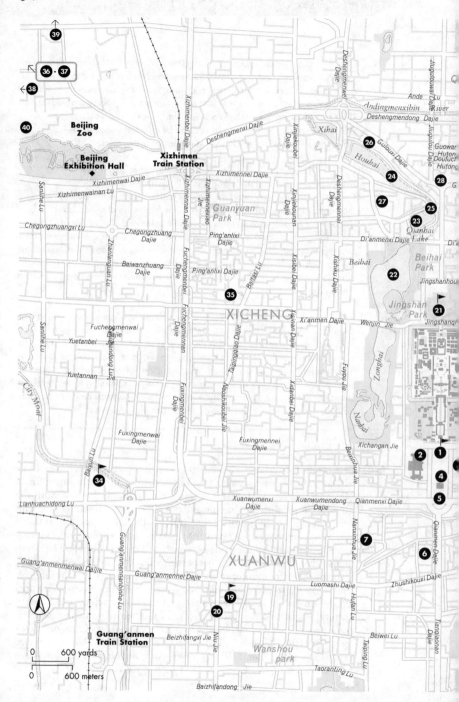

Beijing

❻ Dazhalan Market Area (Large Wicker Gate Market Area). In the Ming era, the Dazhalan gate was lowered each night to enforce a curfew. The area around the gate, known by the same name, is a neighborhood of close-packed lanes crowded with flags and sideboards. It was once filled with a cacophony of merchants, eateries, teahouses, wine shops, theaters, and brothels. Palace officials (and the occasional emperor in disguise) would escape here for a few hours' respite from the suffocating imperial maze. Traditional shops and crowded alleys still make Dazhalan one of Beijing's most interesting commercial areas, especially now that most shopping in the capital is conducted behind the glass screens of glitzy malls. Dazhalan's specialties include clothing, fabric, shoes, Chinese medicine, and Peking opera costumes. ✉ *Zhubaoshi Jie, near Qianmen.*

❺ Facing the Sun Gate (Zhengyangmen). From its top looking south, you can see that Zhengyangmen actually comprised two gates: the **Arrow Tower** (Tian Lou) in front was, until 1915, connected to Zhengyangmen by a defensive half-moon wall. The central gates of both structures opened only for the emperor's biannual ceremonial trips to the Temple of Heaven to the south. Don't miss the evocative photo exhibition of Old Peking. Have some tea atop Zhengyangmen before heading up the Arrow Tower for views of the old Qianmen railway station, now the Railway Workers Cultural Palace. ✉ *Xuanwumen Jie.*

❷ Great Hall of the People (Renmin Dahuitang). This solid edifice owes its Stalinist weight to the last years of the Sino-Soviet pact. Its gargantuan dimensions (205,712 square yards of floor space) exceed that of the Forbidden City. It was built by 14,000 laborers who worked around the clock for eight months. China's legislature meets in the aptly named Ten Thousand People Assembly Hall, beneath a panoply of 500 star lights revolving around a giant red star. Thirty-one reception rooms are distinguished by the arts and crafts of the provinces they represent. Call a day ahead to confirm that it's open. ✉ *West side of Tiananmen Sq., Xuanwu District* ☎ *010/6309–6156* ✎ *Y30* ⏱ *Daily 9 AM–1 PM.*

❼ Liulichang Jie (Glazed-Tile Factory Street). The Ming factory that gave the street its name and the Forbidden City its yellow top was destroyed by the Qing, but renovation has restored the many book, arts, and antiques shops that crowded here in early Qing times. Be sure to visit the **China Bookstore** (Zhongguo Shu Dian; ✉ Opposite No. 115) and the most famous shop on the street, **Rongbaozhai** (✉ 19 Liulichang Xi Jie), which sells paintings, woodblock prints, antiques, and calligraphy materials.

need a break? Old shops line the sides of Liulichang, where high-rises and fancy restaurants are juxtaposed with ancient courtyards and teahouses. You can get a bowl of noodles and a cup of tea upstairs at the **Jiguge teahouse** (✉ 136 Liulichang Dong Jie), next to the stone pedestrian bridge. Employees lunch at the cafeteria in the **Great Hall of the People.** You won't find many English-speakers (or forks) here, but you can order good and inexpensive food (by picture) and get friendly with the locals, with whom you'll share a long table.

Beijing
Subway

Subway Line 5

Xi'ergi

Subway Line 13

Longze Huilongguan Huoying Lishuiqiao

Beiyuan

Shangdi

Wangjing

Wudaokou   Hepingli Xiqiao   Shaoyaoju

Zhichunlu   Hepingli Bei Jie   Guangximen

Drum Tower   Zhangzizhonglu
Dazhong Si   Ji shui tan   An ding men   Liufang   Dong Si
Fuxingmen-Bawangfen   Dengshikou
Subway Line 2   Dongzhimen
              Xizhimen   Beixinqiao

Pingguoyuan   Chegongzhuang   Dongsi shitiao

              Pingguoyuan   Fuchengmen   Chaoyangmen   TO
              Subway Line 1   Jianguomen   TUQIAO →

Fuxingmen Xidan West of Tiananmen East of Tiananmen Wangfu jing Dongdan

Chong wen men

Gu Cheng Station Bajiao Amusement Park Ba bao shan Yu quan Road Wu ke song Wan shou Road Gong zhu fen Military Museum Mu xi di Nan lishi Road

Chang chun jie Xuan wu men Fie ping men Qian men Ciqikou

Yong'an li China World Trade Center Da wang Bridge West Sihui Station East Sihui Station

Tiantandong Men Puhuangyu

Beijing Railway Station

Liujiayao

Songiazhuang

❹ Mao Zedong Memorial Hall (Maozhuxi Jiniantang). Sentries here will assure that your communion with the Great Helmsman is brief. You'll be guided into a spacious lobby dominated by a marble Mao statue and then to the Hall of Reverence, where his embalmed body lies in state, wrapped in the red flag of the Communist Party of China inside a crystal coffin that is lowered each night into a subterranean freezer. In a bid to limit Mao's deification, a second-story museum, dedicated to the former Premier Zhou Enlai, former general Zhu De, and China's Vice Chairman before the Cultural Revolution Liu Shaoqi (whom Mao persecuted to death during the Cultural Revolution), was added in 1983. The hall's builders willfully ignored Tiananmen square's geomancy: the mausoleum faces north, boldly contradicting centuries of imperial ritual. Out back, where reverence turns to tack, hawkers still push "Maomorabilia." For Cultural Revolution souvenirs, wait until Liulichang. ☒ *Tiananmen Sq., Chongwen District* ☎ *010/6513–2277* ☒ *Free* ☉ *Tues. and Thurs. 8:30–11:30 AM and 2–4 PM; Wed. and Fri.–Sun. 8:30 AM–11:30 AM.*

▶ **❶ Tiananmen Square** (Tiananmen Guangchang). The world's largest public
Fodor'sChoice   lic square, and the heart of modern China, it owes little to the grand
★   imperial designs of the Yuan, Ming, and Qing—and everything to the
               successor dynasty of Mao Zedong. Turn your back on the entrance to

A SHORT HISTORY OF BEIJING

D IFFERENT TOWNS OF VARYING SIZE and import have existed at or near the site where Beijing is now since the birth of Chinese civilization. For example, the delicious local beer, Yanjing, refers to a city–kingdom based here 3,000 years ago. With this in mind, it is not unreasonable to describe Beijing's modern history as beginning with the Jin Dynasty, approximately 800 years ago. Led by nine generations of the Jurchen tribe, the Jin Dynasty eventually fell in a war against the Mongol horde expanding their control from the north.

Under the command of the legendary warrior Genghis Khan, few armies between the Mediterranean and the East China Sea had been able to withstand the wild onslaught of the armed Mongol cavalry, the front for the largest land-based empire in the history of humankind. The Jurchen tribe proved no exception, and the magnificent city of the Jin was almost completely destroyed. A few decades later in 1260, when Kublai Khan, the grandson of Genghis Khan, returned to use the city as an operational base for his conquest of southern China, reconstruction was the order of the day. By 1271, Kublai Khan had achieved his goal, declaring himself Emperor of China under the Yuan Dynasty (1271–1368), with Beijing (or Dadu, as it was then known) as its capital.

The new capital was built on a scale befitting the world's then superpower. Its palaces were founded around Zhonghai and Beihai lakes. (Actually, Beijing's Imperial Fangshan Restaurant is located on the site of the former kitchens built for Kublai Khan's palace 700 years ago.) Beijing's current layout still reflects the Mongolian design. The imperial city was protected on four sides by a fortified wall, surrounded by a moat. Within the walls, broad streets connected the main gates and city sections were by alleyways or hutong.

Like today, a limiting factor on Beijing's growth seven centuries ago was its remoteness from water. To ensure an adequate water supply, the famous hydraulic engineer, Guo Shoujing (1231–1316), designed a canal that brought water to the city from the mountains in the west. Then, to improve communications and increase trade, he designed another canal that extended east to the connect with eastern China's Great Canal.

Barely more than 100 years after the Mongolians settled Beijing, they suffered a devastating attack by rebels from the south. Originally nomadic, the Mongolians had softened with the ease of Chinese city life and were easily overwhelmed by the rebel coalition, which drove out the emperor and wrecked Beijing. Thus ended the Yuan Dynasty. The southern roots of the quickly unified Ming Dynasty (1368–1644) deprived Beijing of its capital status for a half century. But in 1405, the third Ming emperor, Yongle, began construction on a magnificent new palace in Beijing, and 16 years later, he relocated his court there. In the interim, the emperor had mobilized 200,000 corvée laborers to build his new palace, an enormous maze of interlinking halls, gates, and courtyard homes, known as the Forbidden City. To the north of the palace, the city was further embellished with the stately Bell and Drum towers. And to the south in 1553, walls were added to encompass an oblong-shape residential suburb.

The Ming also contributed mightily to China's grandest public works project: the Great Wall. The Ming Great Wall linked or reinforced several existing walls, especially near the capital, and traversed seemingly impassable mountains. Most of the most spectacular stretches of the wall that can be visited near Beijing were built by the Ming. But wall-building drained Ming coffers and in the end failed to prevent Manchu horsemen from taking the capital—and China—in 1644.

This foreign dynasty, the Qing, inherited the Ming palaces, built their own retreats (most notably, the Old and New Summer palaces), and perpetuated feudalism in China for another 267 years. In its decline, the Qing proved impotent to stop humiliating foreign encroachment. It lost the first Opium War to Great Britain in 1842 and was forced to cede Hong Kong "in perpetuity" as a result. In 1860 a combined British and French force stormed Beijing and razed the Old Summer Palace, carting away priceless antiquities.

After the Qing crumbled in 1911, its successor, Sun Yat-sen's Nationalist Party, struggled to consolidate power. Beijing became a cauldron of social activism. On May 4, 1919, students marched on Tiananmen Square to protest humiliations in Versailles, where Allied commanders negotiating an end to World War I gave Germany's extraterritorial holdings in China to Japan, not Sun's infant republic. Patriotism intensified. In 1937 Japanese imperial armies stormed across Beijing's Marco Polo Bridge to launch a brutal eight-year occupation. Civil war followed close on the heels of Tokyo's 1945 surrender and raged until the Communist victory. Chairman Mao himself declared the founding of a new nation, the People's Republic of China, from the rostrum atop the Gate of Heavenly Peace on October 1, 1949.

Like Emperor Yongle, Mao built a capital that conformed to his own vision. Soviet-inspired institutions rose up around—and in—Tiananmen Square. Beijing's city wall, the grandest rampart of its kind in China, was demolished to make way for a ring road. Temples were looted, torn down, closed, or turned into factories during the 1966–76 Cultural Revolution. In more recent years old Peking has suffered most, ironically, from prosperity. Many ancient neighborhoods, replete with traditional courtyard homes, have been bulldozed to make room for a new city of fancy apartment blocks and glitzy commercial developments. Preservationism has slowly begun to take hold, but CHAI (to pull down) and QIAN (to move elsewhere) remain common threats to denizens of Beijing's historic neighborhoods.

— Guy Rubin, George Wehrfritz, and Diana Garrett

the Forbidden City, the Gate of Heavenly Peace, and the wonders of feudalism. Looking south, across the proletarian panorama, is the Great Helmsman's tomb. The old Imperial Way once stretched south from the Forbidden City. Where photographers now hustle for customers once stood quarters for the Imperial Guard and rice and wood stores for the imperial kitchen. Fires and demolition resulted in the beginnings of the square during the Republican era. The young protesters who assembled here in the 1919 May Fourth Movement established an honorable tradition of patriotic dissent.

At the square's center stands the tallest monument in China, the **Monument to the People's Heroes** (Renmin Yingxiong Jinianbei), 125 feet of granite obelisk remembering those who died for the revolutionary cause of the Chinese people. Exhortations from Chairman Mao and Premier Zhou Enlai decorate it; eight marble reliefs line the base with scenes of revolution from 1840 to 1949. Constructed from 1952 to 1958, the monument marks the formal passing of Old Peking; once, the outer palace gate of the imperial city stood here.

As you leave the terrace southward, imagine mass Soviet-style parades with 600,000 marchers. At the height of the Cultural Revolution in 1967, hundreds of thousands of Red Guards crowded the square, chanting Mao's name and waving his Little Red Book. In June 1989 the square was the scene of tragedy when hundreds of student demonstrators and bystanders were killed by troops breaking up the pro-democracy protest. Known as "six-four" or "June 4th," the movement became a weight about the Chinese government's neck in regards to human rights and freedom of speech, a traditional point of contention in modern Sino-American relations. Aside from the grand and tragic events here over the last 50 years, Tiananmen is truly a people's square, alive with local kite fliers and wide-eyed tourists from out of town. ⊠ *Bounded by Changan Jie on north and Xuanwumen Jie on south, Chongmen District.*

The Forbidden City

Fodor'sChoice
★
It was from these nearly 200 acres at the heart of the Northern Capital that 24 emperors and two dynasties ruled the Middle Kingdom for more than 500 years. When it was first built, the imperial palace was named the Purple Forbidden City (Zi Jin Cheng), in reference to the North Star, which was also called the purple palace and thought to be at the center of the cosmos. Putting "purple" into the name of the imperial residence strengthened the belief that the emperor, by association with the North Star, was a divine instrument of universal power. Officially and colloquially in China the site is called the Gugong Bowuyuan (the Ancient Palace Museum) or just Gugong.

In imperial times, no buildings were allowed to exceed the height of the palace walls, so the palace towered above old Peking and humbled everything in view. Moats and gigantic timber doors protected the emperor or "son of heaven." Shiny double-eaved roofs, glazed imperial yellow, marked the vast complex as the royal court's exclusive dominion. Ornate interiors displayed China's most exquisite artisanship—ceilings covered with turquoise and blue dragons, walls draped with scrolls holding priceless calligraphy or lined with intricate cloisonné screens, sandalwood thrones padded in delicate silks, floors of ceramic-fired, golden-color bricks. Miraculously, the palace survived fire, war, and imperial China's final collapse.

Equally miraculous is how quickly the Forbidden City rose. The third Ming emperor, Yongle, oversaw 200,000 laborers build the complex in just 14 years, finishing in 1420. Yongle relocated the Ming capital to Beijing to strengthen China's vulnerable northern frontier, and Ming and Qing emperors ruled from inside the palace walls until the dynastic system crumbled in 1911.

The Forbidden City embodies architectural principles first devised three millennia ago in the Shang Dynasty. Each main hall faces south, and looks upon a courtyard flanked by lesser buildings. This symmetry of *taoyuan,* a series of courtyards leading to the main and final courtyard, repeats itself along a north–south axis that bisects the imperial palace. This line is visible in the form of a broad walkway paved in marble and reserved for the emperor's sedan chair. All but the sovereign—even court ministers, the empress, and favored concubines—trod on pathways and passed through doors set to either side of this Imperial Way. ☎ 010/6513–2215 or 010/8511–7311 🖃 Apr.–Oct. Y60; Nov.–Mar. Y40 ☉ Apr.–Oct., daily 8:30–5; Nov.–Mar., daily 8:30–4:30.

a good walk

Enter the Forbidden City through the **Gate of Heavenly Peace** ⑧ ▶, easily identified by its massive Chairman Mao portrait overlooking Tiananmen Square. Northward beyond the **Meridian Gate** ⑨, where military victories were celebrated, stands the outer palace, consisting of three halls used for high public functions. You'll first reach the **Hall of Supreme Harmony** ⑩, once the tallest building in China, then the **Hall of Complete Harmony** ⑪, and after this the **Hall of Preserving Harmony** ⑫. For a change from the Forbidden City's grand central halls, turn right beyond the Hall of Preserving Harmony to visit smaller peripheral palaces—once home to imperial relatives, attendants, and eunuchs, and the scene of much palace intrigue. Next comes the **Hall of Treasures** ⑬. Continue northward to Qianlong's Garden and the Pearl Concubine Well. Return via a narrow north–south passage that runs to the west of these courtyards. On the way is the **Hall of Clocks and Watches** ⑭. Walk northward from the nine-dragon carving and through the **Gate of Heavenly Purity** ⑮ to enter the **Inner Palace** ⑯, where you'll find the private rooms of some imperial families. West of the palace you'll find the entrance to the **Hall of Mental Cultivation** ⑰, where later Qing emperors lived. Heading north, you'll find the rocks, pebbles, and greenery of the **Imperial Gardens** ⑱ just beyond the Inner Palace. Past the gardens is the Forbidden City's northern gate and exit.

TIMING   The walk through main halls, best done by audio tour, takes about two hours. Allow two more hours to explore side halls and gardens.

What to See

▶ ⑧ **Gate of Heavenly Peace** (Tiananmen). This imposing structure was the traditional rostrum for the reading of imperial edicts. The Great Helmsman himself used it to establish the People's Republic of China on October

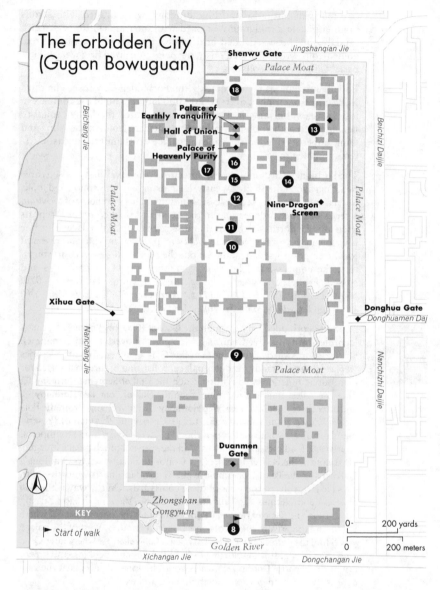

The Forbidden City (Gugon Bowuguan)

Jingshanqian Jie

Shenwu Gate

Palace Moat

Beichang Jie

Palace Moat

Palace of Earthly Tranquility

Hall of Union

Palace of Heavenly Purity

Beichizi Dajie

Palace Moat

Nine-Dragon Screen

Xihua Gate

Nanchang Jie

Donghua Gate
Donghuamen Daj

Nanchizhi Dajie

Palace Moat

Zhongshan
Gongyuan

Golden River

Xichangan Jie

Dongchangan Jie

Duanmen Gate

KEY

► Start of walk

0 – 200 yards

0 – 200 meters

1, 1949, and again to review millions of Red Guards during the Cultural Revolution. Ascend the gate for a dramatic vantage on Tiananmen Square. Bags must be checked prior to entry, and visitors are required to pass through a metal detector. ⊠ *Changan Jie at Tiananmen Guangchang, Forbidden City* ☎ *010/6513–2255* ⊠ *Y30* ⊙ *Daily 8–4:30.*

⑮ Gate of Heavenly Purity (Qianqingmen). Even the emperor's most trusted ministers never passed beyond this gate; by tradition, they gathered outside at dawn, ready to report to their sovereign. ⊠ *Forbidden City.*

need a break? Believe it or not, there's a **Starbucks** (⊠ East of the Gate of Heavenly Purity, Forbidden City) close by! As you descend the marble stairs on the north side of the Hall of Preserving Harmony, look diagonally across the courtyard to your right. Starbucks is in the first pavilion.

⑭ Hall of Clocks and Watches (Zhongbiaoguan). Here you'll find a collection of water clocks and early mechanical timepieces from Europe and China. Clocks astride elephants, implanted in ceramic trees, borne by a herd of goats, and mounted in a pagoda are among this collection's many rewards. Don't miss the temple clock, with its robed monks. ⊠ *Forbidden City* ⊠ *Y5.*

⑪ Hall of Complete Harmony (Zhonghedian). In this more modest building emperors greeted audiences and held banquets. It housed the royal plow, with which the emperor himself would turn a furrow to commence spring planting. ⊠ *Forbidden City.*

⑰ Hall of Mental Cultivation (Yangxindian). West of the Inner Palace, running on a north–south axis, is a group of six courtyard palaces that were reserved for emperors and concubines. The Hall of Mental Cultivation is the most important of these; starting with Emperor Yongzheng, all Qing Dynasty emperors lived and attended to daily state business in this hall. It was here that the last young emperor, Puyi, declared his abdication and formally recognized the Republic of China on February 12, 1912. Those who have prepared for their trip to China by watching Bertolucci's monumental movie, *The Last Emperor,* may recognize the north–south passage outside Yangxindian where the young Puyi is portrayed riding his bicycle in the film. ⊠ *Forbidden City.*

⑫ Hall of Preserving Harmony (Baohedian). The highest civil service examinations, which were personally conducted by the emperor (who possessed superior knowledge of Chinese literature, rhetoric, and politics), were once administered in this hall. Candidates from across China were selected according to merit and, of course, family connections, and those who were successful were assured lives of wealth and power at the imperial court. Behind the hall, a 200-ton marble relief of nine dragons, the palace's most treasured stone carving, adorns the descending staircase. ⊠ *Forbidden City.*

⑩ Hall of Supreme Harmony (Taihedian). The building—used for coronations, royal birthdays, weddings, and Lunar New Year ceremonies—is fronted by a broad flagstone courtyard, the largest open area in the complex. Bronze vats, once kept brimming with water to fight fires, ring this vast expanse. The hall sits atop three stone tiers with an elaborate drainage system that channels rainwater through 1,142 carved dragons. On the top tier outside the hall, bronze cranes symbolize longevity, and an imperial sundial and grain measures invite bumper harvests. Inside, cloisonné cranes flank a massive throne beneath grand timber pillars decorated with golden dragons. Above the imperial chair hangs a heavy bronze ball—put there to crush any pretender to the throne. ⊠ *Forbidden City.*

🄼 **Hall of Treasures** (Zhenbaoguan). Actually a series of halls, it has breathtaking examples of imperial ornamentation. The first room displays imperial candleholders, wine vessels, tea-serving sets, and—in the center—a 5-foot-tall golden pagoda commissioned by Qing emperor Qian Long in honor of his mother. A cabinet on one wall contains the 25 imperial seals, China's equivalent of the crown jewels in their embodiment of royal authority. Jade bracelets and rings, golden hair pins, and ornamental coral fill the second hall; and carved jade landscapes a third. ⊠ *Forbidden City* 🎫 Y5.

🄸 **Imperial Gardens** (Yuhuayuan). Beyond the private palaces at the Forbidden City's northern perimeter stand ancient cypress trees, stone mosaic pathways, and a rock garden. You can exit the palace at the north through the park's **Gate of Obedience and Purity** (Shenwumen). ⊠ *Forbidden City.*

🄼 **Inner Palace** (Nei Ting). Several emperors chose to live in the Inner Palace along with their families. The **Hall of Heavenly Purity** (Qianqinggong) holds another imperial throne; the **Hall of Union** (Jiaotaidian) was the venue for the empress's annual birthday party; and the **Palace of Earthly Peace** (Kunninggong) was the empress's residence and also where royal couples consummated their marriages. ⊠ *Forbidden City.*

🄼 **Meridian Gate** (Wumen). Also known as Five Phoenix Tower (Wufenglou) because of the five towers along its unique U-shape crown, Wumen is the main, southern gate to the Imperial Palace. (Tiananmen is the gate to the Imperial City as opposed to the Palace.) Here, the emperor reviewed his armies and announced yearly planting schedules according to the lunar calendar for the coming year. Before entering, you can buy tickets to the Forbidden City and rent the accompanying Acoustiguide audio tour at the ticket office in the outer courtyard. ⊠ *Forbidden City* 🎫 *Y55; audio tour, Y30* ⊙ *Daily 8:30–4:30.*

> **need a break?** A small snack bar, **Fast Food,** on the north end of vendors' row between the Gate of Heavenly Peace and the Meridian Gate, has instant noodles, tea, and soft drinks.

The Muslim Quarter (Xuanwu District)

Southeast of Liulichang is the lively Niu Jie (Ox Street) and its important mosque. Ethnic Hui—Han Chinese whose ancestors converted to Islam—make up most of the area's faithful. Their enclave, which occupies one of Beijing's oldest neighborhoods, has kept its traditional flavor despite ongoing urban renewal. Nearby is the extensive Buddhist Temple of the Source of Law, buried deep in a quiet hutong that houses a mixture of ancient and modern buildings.

a good walk

Begin at the **Ox Street Mosque** ⑲ ⌐. From the mosque walk south 500 yards along Niu Jie (Ox Street) until you reach a crossroad. Turn left into **Nanheng Xi Jie** ⑳, the center of commerce in the enclave. Continue eastward for 500 yards past a derelict temple on your left and turn left into Jiaozi Hutong just before you reach the massive, five-domed, lime-green building on your left. This is the headquarters of the Chinese Islamic Association (you should spot a red flag fluttering in front of the dome). Turn right immediately into the narrow Fayuan Si Qian Jie, passing new apartments on your left and traditional courtyard houses on your right.

Continue eastward on Fayuan Si Qian Jie until it ends at Qijing Hutong (Seven Well Alley). Turn right, cross Nanheng Xi Lu, and continue southward on Meng'er Hutong. Past a typical stretch of new high-rise apartments, you'll find Wanshou Park on your right. Exit through the south gate and turn right on Baizhifang Dong Jie (White Paper Lane East). Continue westward and turn right at Youannei Dajie, which becomes Niu Jie one block north.

TIMING This walk takes about three hours, allowing for time in the mosque and the temple. Exploring alleys in this neighborhood, especially those running west from Niu Jie, is always rewarding.

What to See

⑳ **Nanheng Xi Jie** (Southern Cross Street West). Nanheng Xi Jie is filled with restaurants and shops catering to both the local Hui Muslims and newcomers from China's distant Xinjiang province. Restaurants serve Muslim dishes, including steamed meat buns, beef noodles, and a variety of baked breads; shops offer tea from across China; and street vendors sell flatbreads, fruit, and snacks. ⊠ *Nanheng Xi Jie, Xuanwu District.*

⌐ ⑲ **Ox Street Mosque** (Niu Jie Qingzhen Si). Built during the Northern Song Dynasty in AD 996, Beijing's oldest and largest mosque sits at the center of the Muslim quarter. Its exterior looks decidedly Chinese, with a traditional tile roof adorning its front gate. The freestanding wall opposite the mosque's main entrance is similarly Chinese rather than Muslim in origin. It is called a spirit wall, and was erected to prevent ghosts, who are believed not to navigate tight corners, from passing into the mosque. Today the main gate to the mosque is kept closed. Enter the mosque from the alley just to the south. Inside, arches and posts are inscribed with Koranic verse, and a Tower for Viewing the Moon allows imams to measure the beginning and end of Ramadan, Islam's month of fasting and prayer. Male visitors must wash themselves in designated bathrooms and remove their shoes before entering the main prayer hall. Women are confined to a rear prayer hall. At the rear of the complex is a minaret from which a muezzin calls the faithful to prayer. All visitors must wear long trousers or skirts and keep their shoulders covered. Women are not permitted to enter some areas. ⊠ *88 Niu Jie, Xuanwu District* ⊡ *Y10* ⊙ *Daily 8–sunset.*

North & East of the Forbidden City

Historic temples, parks, and houses that once lay within the walls of imperial Beijing now provide islands of tranquillity among the busy streets of this modern downtown area, most of which lies in the Dongcheng (East City) District.

a good tour

Start just north of the Forbidden City at the first in a series of parks, **Jing-shan Park** ㉑ ▶. For a panoramic view of the Forbidden City, climb to the five pavilions on the crest of this park's artificial hill. From here you can walk through **Beihai Park** ㉒ around its lake, particularly beautiful during August's lotus season, exiting at the north gate. After crossing the road, and walking a few hundred meters west you will arrive at **Qianhai Lake** ㉓.

Continue north to **Houhai Lake** ㉔, passing the famous Ming Dynasty **Silver Ingot Bridge** ㉕. Following the lake's northern shore, you will arrive at the traditional courtyard of **Soong Ching-ling's Former Residence** ㉖, once the home of Sun Yat-sen's wife. Next, take a cab to **Prince Gong's Palace** ㉗ to see how imperial relatives lived. Walk or take a cab to the **Drum Tower** ㉘ and the nearby bell tower. Take a cab again to the **Lama Temple** ㉙, Beijing's main Tibetan Buddhist temple; then to the **Temple of Confucius** ㉚; and the neighboring **Imperial Academy** ㉛, where Confucian scholars sat imperial examinations.

TIMING   If you want to do this all at once, it will take you a full day. The neighborhood is ideal for bike exploration.

a good tour

A great way to explore Old Peking is by bicycle. The ride between Ditan Park and Coal Hill includes some of the city's most famous sights and finest hutong. Begin at Ditan Park, which contains an altar where emperors once made sacrifices to the earth god, just north of the Second Ring Road on Yonghegong Jie. Park your bike in the lot outside the south gate and take a quick walk. Next, ride south along Yonghegong Jie until you come to the main entrance of **Lama Temple** ㉙. Running west, across the street from the temple's main gate, is Guozijian Jie (Imperial Academy Street). Shops near the intersection sell Buddhist statues, incense, texts (in Chinese), and tapes of traditional Chinese Buddhist music. Browse them before riding west to **Temple of Confucius** ㉚ and the neighboring **Imperial Academy** ㉛. The arches spanning Guozijian Jie are the only ones of their kind remaining in Beijing.

Follow Guozijian Jie west until it empties onto Andingmennei Dajie. Enter this busy road with care (there's no traffic signal) and ride south to Guloudong Dajie, another major thoroughfare. Turn right (west) and ride to the **Drum Tower** ㉘. From here detour through the alleys just north to the Zhonglou. A market of tiny noodle stalls and restaurants links the two landmarks. Retrace your route south to Di'anmenwai Dajie (the road running south from the Drum Tower), turning onto Yandai Jie, the first lane on the right. Makers of long-stem pipes once lined the lane's narrow way (one small pipe shop remains). Sadly, much of the area is slated for redevelopment.

Wind northwest on Yandai Jie past guest houses, bicycle repair shops, tiny restaurants, and crumbling traditional courtyard houses toward

Houhai Park. Turn left onto Xiaoqiaoli Hutong and pass the arched **Silver Ingot Bridge** ㉕, which separates **Houhai** ㉔ and **Qianhai** ㉓ lakes. Before the bridge, follow the trail along Houhai's north shore, traveling west toward **Soong Ching-ling's Former Residence** ㉖. Circle the lake until you arrive at Deshengmennei Dajie. Follow it south to the second alley, turning east (left) onto Yangfang Hutong, which leads back to the arched bridge. Park your bike in the first alley off Yangfang Hutong, Dongming Hutong, and walk toward the lake. At the footpath and market that hugs its banks, turn left and walk about 100 yards to find a tiny lane lined with antiques and curio shops.

After bargain hunting, ride along Yangfang Hutong past the stone bridge and follow Qianhai Lake's west bank. Sip a soda, beer, or tea at the teahouse pavilion on the lake. Continue along the lane to Qianhai Xi Jie, then fork right (northwest) just after a restaurant sign bearing a large heart. Nearby, but difficult to find, is **Prince Gong's Palace** ㉗, 300 yards north of the China Conservatory of Music. Look for the brass plaque.

TIMING   Allow a half day for this ride, longer if you expect to linger at the sights or explore the parks on foot.

What to See

★ ㉒ **Beihai Park** (North Lake Park). Immediately north of Zhongnanhai, the tightly guarded residential compound of China's senior leaders, the park is easily recognized by the white Tibetan pagoda perched on a nearby hill. Near the south gate is the **Round City** (Tuan Cheng). It contains a white-jade Buddha, said to have been sent from Burma to Qing emperor Qian Long, and an enormous jade bowl given to Kublai Khan. Nearby, the well-restored **Temple of Eternal Peace** (Yongan Si) contains a variety of Buddhas and other sacred images. Climb to the pagoda from Yongan Temple. Once there, you can pay an extra Y1 to ascend the Buddha-bedecked **Shangyin Hall** for a view into forbidden Zhongnanhai.

The lake is Beijing's largest and most beautiful public waterway. Amusement park rides line its east edge, and kiosks stock assorted snacks. On summer weekends the lake teems with paddle boats. The **Five Dragon Pavilion** (Wu Long Ting), on Beihai's northwest shore, was built in 1602 by a Ming Dynasty emperor who liked to fish and view the moon. The halls north of it were added later. Among the restaurants in the park is **Fangshan,** an elegant establishment open since the Qing Dynasty. ⊠ *South Gate, Weijin Lu, Xicheng District* ☎ *010/6404–0610* ☞ *Y10; extra fees for some sights* ☉ *Daily 9–dusk.*

★ ㉘ **Drum Tower** (Gulou). Until the late 1920s the 24 drums once housed in this tower were Beijing's timepiece. Sadly, all but one of these huge drums have been destroyed, and the survivor is in serious need of renovation. Kublai Khan built the first drum tower on this site in 1272. You can climb to the top of the present tower, which dates from the Ming Dynasty. Old photos of Beijing's hutong line the walls beyond the drum; there's also a scale model of a traditional courtyard house. The nearby **Bell Tower** (Zhonglou), renovated after a fire in 1747, offers worthwhile views from the top of a long, narrow staircase. The huge 63-ton bronze bell, supported by lacquered wood stanchions, is also worth seeing. ☎ *010/*

6404–1710 ⊠ *North end of Dianmen Dajie, Dongcheng District* ⊠ Y20
⊘ *Daily 9–4:30.*

㉛ Imperial Academy (Guozijian). Once the highest educational institution
in China, this academy was established in 1306 as a rigorous training
ground for high-level government officials. It was notorious, especially
during the early Ming Dynasty era, for the harsh discipline imposed on
scholars perfecting their knowledge of the Confucian classics. ⊠ *Guozijian Lu next to Temple of Confucius, Dongcheng District* ☎ *010/
6406–2418* ⊠ *Y6* ⊘ *Daily 9–5.*

➤ ㉑ Jingshan Park (Prospect Hill Park). This park was built around Coal Hill
(Meishan), a small peak formed from earth excavated for the Forbidden City's moats. The hill was named for an imperial coal supply supposedly buried beneath it. Climb a winding stone staircase past peach
and apple trees to Wanchun Pavilion, the park's highest point. It overlooks the Forbidden City to the south and the Bell and Drum towers to
the north. Chongzhen, the last Ming emperor, is said to have hanged
himself on Coal Hill as his dynasty collapsed in 1644. ⊠ *Jingshanqian
Dajie at Forbidden City, Dongcheng District* ☎ *010/6404–4071 or
010/6403–2244* ⊠ *Y2* ⊘ *Daily 6:30 AM–8 PM.*

㉙ Lama Temple (Yonghegong). This Tibetan Buddhist temple is Beijing's most
visited religious site. Its five main halls and numerous galleries are hung
with finely detailed *thangkhas* (painted cloth scrolls) and decorated with
carved or cast Buddha images—all guarded by young lamas (monks). Originally a palace for Prince Yongzheng, it was transformed into a temple
after he became the Qing's third emperor in 1723. The temple flourished
under Yongzheng's successor, Emperor Qianlong, housing some 500 resident monks. Unlike most "feudal" sites in Beijing, the Lama Temple survived the 1966–76 Cultural Revolution unscathed.

FodorśChoice ★

You'll walk past trinket stands with clattering wind chimes to reach the
temple's five main halls. The Hall of Heavenly Kings has statues of
Maitreya, the future Buddha, and Weitou, China's guardian of Buddhism.
In the courtyard beyond, a pond with a bronze mandala represents a
Buddhist paradise. In the Hall of Harmony sit Buddhas of the Past, Present,
and Future. Note the exquisite silk thangkha of White Tara—the embodiment of compassion—hanging from the west wall. The Hall of Eternal Blessing contains images of the Medicine and Longevity Buddhas.
Beyond, courtyard galleries display numerous statues depicting Tibetan
deities and dharma guardians, some passionately entwined.

A large statue of Tsong Khapa (1357–1419), founder of the Gelug order,
sits in the Hall of the Wheel of Law. Resident monks practice here on
low benches and cushions. A rare sand mandala is preserved under glass
on the west side of the building. The temple's tallest building, the **Pavilion of Ten Thousand Fortunes** (Wanfuge), houses a breathtaking 85-foot
Maitreya Buddha carved from a single sandalwood block. White-and-gold blessing scarves drape the statue, which wears a massive string of
prayer beads. English-speaking guides are available at the temple entrance.
⊠ *12 Yonghegong Dajie, Beixingqiao, Dongcheng District* ☎ *010/
6404–3769 or 010/6404–4499* ⊠ *Y25* ⊘ *Daily 9–4 or 4:30.*

㉗ **Prince Gong's Palace** (Gongwangfu). This grand compound sits in a neighborhood once reserved for imperial relatives. Built during the Ming Dynasty, it fell to Prince Gong, brother of Qing emperor Xianfeng and later an adviser to Empress Dowager Cixi. With nine courtyards joined by covered walkways, it was once one of Beijing's most lavish residences. The largest hall, now a banquet room, offers summer Peking opera and afternoon tea to guests on guided hutong tours. Some literary scholars believe this was the setting of the *Dream of the Red Chamber,* China's best-known classic novel. ⊠ *Xicheng District* ☎ *010/ 6618–0573* 🎫 *Y20* ☉ *Daily 8:30–4:30.*

★ ㉓–㉔ **Qianhai and Houhai Lakes.** These lakes, along with Xihai Lake in the northwest, were together known as *Shichahai,* the Scattered Temples Lake, in reference to the many temples scattered around this historic quarter. Most people come here to stroll casually around the lakes and enjoy the bars and restaurants that perch on their shores. In summer you can boat, swim, fish, and even, on occasion, windsurf on the lakes. In winter sections of the frozen surfaces are fenced off for ice hockey and casual skating. ⊠ *North side of Dianmen Xi Lu, north of Beihai Lake, Xicheng District.*

> **need a break?**
>
> Along **Lotus Lane,** which lines the west side of Qianhai Lake, you'll find several traditional pavilions housing trendy coffeehouses, including **Starbucks,** and juice bars, like **Kosmo.** A few doors down, the restaurant **South Silk Road** is a great place to rest your wearied legs and get a bite to eat.

㉕ **Silver Ingot Bridge** (Yin Ding Qiao). This Ming Dynasty bridge was named for its shape, which is said to resemble a silver ingot turned upside down. Along with the Old Wanning Bridge and the Gold Ingot Bridge, it divides the three rear lakes north of Beihai Park known as Qianhai (Front Lake), Houhai (Rear Lake), and Xihai (Western Lake). These three lakes together are called Shichahai, which means "Lake of the Ten Temples," after the nine monasteries and a nunnery that once graced the lakes' banks. ⊠ *Xicheng District.*

㉖ **Soong Ching-ling's Former Residence** (Song Qing Ling Guju). Soong Ching-ling (1893–1981) was the youngest daughter of the wealthy, American-educated bible publisher, Charles Soong. At the age of eighteen, disregarding her family's strong opposition to the union, she eloped to marry the much older Sun Yat-sen, a then friend of the family. When her husband founded the Republic of China in 1911, Soong Ching-ling became a nationally significant political figure. As early as 1924 she headed the Women's Department of the Nationalist Party. Then in 1949 she became the Vice-President of the People's Republic of China as well as Honorary President of the All-China Women's Federation. Throughout her career she campaigned tirelessly for the emancipation of women. Indeed, the rights of modern-day Chinese women owe a great deal to her participation in the Communist revolution. Though she was hailed a key supporter of the revolution, Soong Ching-ling never actually joined the Communist Party. This former palace was her residence

IMPERIAL SACRIFICES

To understand the significance of the harvest sacrifice at the Temple of Heaven, it is important to keep in mind that the legitimacy of a Chinese emperor's rule depended on what is known as the tian ming, or mandate of heaven, essentially the emperor's relationship with the Gods. A succession of bad harvests, for example, could be interpreted as the emperor losing the favor of Heaven and could be used to justify a change in emperor or even in dynasty. Hence, when the emperor came

to the Temple of Heaven to pray for good harvests and to pay homage to his ancestors, there may have been a good measure of self-interest to his fervor. The sacrifices consisted mainly of animals and fruit placed on altars surrounded by lighted candles. Many Chinese still make sacrifices on special occasions, such as births, deaths, and weddings.

— Guy Rubin

and work place. Even after her death, the Soong Ching-ling Foundation continues to work for her causes. A small museum documents her eventful life and work. Exhibits are labeled in English as well as Chinese. ⊠ *46 Houhai Beiyan, Xicheng District* ☎ *010/6403–5997 or 010/6404–4205* ✆ *Y20* ☉ *Tues.–Sun. 9–4:30.*

★ ㉚ **Temple of Confucius** (Kong Miao). This austere temple to China's great sage has endured close to eight centuries of additions and restorations. Stelae and ancient musical instruments are the temple's main attractions. The Great Accomplishment Hall houses Confucius's funeral tablet and shrine, flanked by copper-color statues depicting China's wisest Confucian scholars. A selection of unique musical instruments are played only on the sage's birthday. A forest of stone stelae, carved in the mid-1700s to record the *Thirteen Classics,* philosophical works attributed to Confucius, lines the west side of the grounds. ⊠ *Guozijian Lu at Yunghegong Lu near Lama Temple, Dongcheng District* ☎ *010/8401–1977* ✆ *Y10* ☉ *Daily 8:30–5.*

The Observatory & the Temple of Heaven

Once among the city's largest structures, these ancient sites, now dwarfed by overpasses and skyscrapers, illustrate the importance of astronomy and astrology to the imperial household. The Temple of Heaven, which rivals the Great Wall as the best-known symbol of Beijing, and the busy park surrounding the temple should not be missed. (The temple and the observatory are actually in different districts, though quite close to one another.)

a good tour

Start at the **Ancient Observatory** ㉜ ☞, where the wide central avenue—called Jiangguonen Dajie here—meets the eastern leg of the Second Ring Road. From the observatory take a taxi, following the Second Ring Road south and then west to Chongwenmenwai Dajie and turning south to Tiantandong Lu and west on Yongdingmen Dajie to the south gate of the **Temple of Heaven** ㉝, one of the most important historic sites in Beijing.

TIMING   Allow three hours for this tour. Weekends or early mornings are better if you want to see Tiantan Park at its best (consider reversing the tour). This is when you will see people enjoying ballroom dancing, qi gong, martial arts, chess, Peking opera, calligraphy, badminton, traditional Yang Ge dancing, and many other activities.

What to See

▶ ㉜ **Ancient Observatory** (Guguanxiangtai). To China's imperial rulers, interpreting the heavens was the better part of keeping power. Celestial phenomena like eclipses and comets were believed to portend change; if left unheeded they might cost an emperor his legitimacy—or Mandate of Heaven. The observatory dates back to the time of Genghis Khan, who believed that his fortunes could be read in the stars. This belief was not new to the Chinese: from laypeople to the emperor, celestial changes played a big part in everyday and political life. In feudal China, the emperor was revered as someone sent from heaven who received order from the supreme ruler there. Heavenly beings were not to be offended; paying attention to celestial changes was one way of safeguarding one's position and power.

The instruments in this ancient observatory, established in 1442 atop the city wall's **Jianguo Gate,** were among an emperor's most valuable possessions. Many of the bronze devices on display were gifts from Jesuit missionaries who arrived in Beijing in 1601 and shortly thereafter ensconced themselves as the Ming court's resident stargazers. Rare documents and a replica of a Ming Dynasty star map are on display inside. ✉ *2 Dongbiaobei Hutong, Jianguomenwai Dajie, Chaoyang District* ☎ *010/6524–2202* 💵 *Y10* ☉ *Mon.–Sun. 9–4.*

㉝ **Temple of Heaven** (Tiantan). Ming emperor Yongle built the Temple of
FodorśChoice   Heaven, one of Beijing's grand attractions, as a site for imperial sacri-
★   fices, which were conducted twice a year, on the 15th day of the first lunar month (in either January or February) and on the winter solstice.

The temple grounds, double the size of the Forbidden City, were designed in strict accordance with numerology and feng shui. The four gates mark the four points on the compass. The park is semicircular on the north end and square on the south—the curve corresponding to heaven's supposed shape, the square to earth's. Audio guides can be rented just inside the south gate for a small fee.

Beyond the south gate rests the **Round Altar** (Huanqiutan), a three-tiered prayer platform. Nearby, the **Imperial Vault of Heaven** (Huangqiong Yu), a round temple that housed tablets commemorating the ancestors of the emperors, is surrounded by the **Echo Wall** (Huiyinbi), where a whisper supposedly can be heard across the courtyard's 213-foot expanse. On the courtyard's step are three echo stones able to rebound hand claps. Extreme quiet is needed to hear the effect.

A raised walkway, the **Red Stairway Bridge** (Danbi Qiao), leads northward to the **Hall of Prayer for Good Harvests** (Qiniandian), the temple's hallmark structure. This magnificent blue-roofed wooden tower, originally built in 1420, burned to the ground in 1889 and was immediately rebuilt using Ming architectural methods (and timber imported from Oregon). The building's design is based on the calendar: four center pillars represent the seasons, the next 12 pillars represent months, and 12 outer pillars signify the parts of a day. Together these 28 poles, which correspond to the 28 constellations of Heaven, support the structure without nails. A carved dragon swirling down from the ceiling represents the emperor, or "son of heaven."

The **Hall of Abstinence** (Zhaigong), on the western edge of the grounds, is not of particular interest. But for Y1 you can climb the bell tower and ring the bell for good luck. Its chimes once served notice that the emperor approached to worship or had completed the rites and would depart. ⊠ *Yongdingmen Dajie (South Gate), Chongwen District* ☎ *010/6702–2617 or 010/6702–8866* 🎫 *Y10; extra Y20 for individual halls; Y30 for audio guide* ⏲ *Daily 8–4:30.*

Western Beijing

Western Beijing, a vast industrial suburb, was once the domain of monks, nuns, and imperial hunting parties. Beijing's oldest temples dot the forested hills just west of the city. The Qing-era summer palace is the city's grandest park.

a good tour

Day 1: This full-day tour takes you to some of Beijing's finest temples and gardens, ending with the majesty of the summer palaces. Hire a car plus driver for a full day, starting from **White Clouds Taoist Temple** 34 ⚑, noted for its tranquil courtyards and rare statuary. Next, head north to the restored **Temple of the White Pagoda** 35, named after its 700-year-old Tibetan-style white stupa.

Head northwest out of the city as far as **Summer Palace** 36, set amid one of China's finest man-made landscapes, complete with lakes, bridges, hills, pavilions, gardens, temples, courtyards, and a Qing shopping street. Nearby the **Old Summer Palace** 37, which once outshone its newer rival, offers quieter walks among splendid ruins. Don't miss the two summer palaces even if you have to skip other sights.

Day 2: If you have another day, there are several more places of interest on this side of town. Start at the 16th-century **Temple of Longevity** 38 on Xisanhuan Bei Lu, slightly north of Zizhuyuan Lu. Next, catch a cab to see the **Big Bell Temple** 39 and then walk south on Baishiqiao Lu to the Indian-style **Five-Pagoda Temple** 40. The Big Bell and Five Pagoda temples are two of the capital's ancient seats of Buddhism. The latter abuts a park, on the other side of which you'll find the Beijing Exhibition Hall, which contains a planetarium.

TIMING There are so many sights in Western Beijing, that you really need two days to take it all in. If you have only one, make the two summer palaces a priority. Both suggested tours will take the better part of a day, so it's best to get an early start. Make arrangements with your hotel to hire the car and driver in advance.

What to See

㊴ Big Bell Temple (Dazhong Si). The two-story bell here is cast with the texts of more than 100 Buddhist scriptures. Believed to date from Emperor Yongle's reign, the 46-ton relic is considered a national treasure. The temple also houses the **Ancient Bell Museum** (Guzhong Bowuguan), a collection of bells from various dynasties and styles. ⊠ *1A Beisanhuanxi Lu, Haidian District* ☎ *010/6255–0843* 🎫 *Y10* ⊗ *Daily 8:30–4:30.*

㊵ Five-Pagoda Temple (Wuta Si). Hidden behind trees and set amid carved stones, the temple's five pagodas reveal obvious Indian influences. Indeed, the Five-Pagoda Temple was built during the Yongle Years of the Ming Dynasty (1403–24), in honor of an Indian Buddhist who came to China and presented a temple blueprint to the emperor. Elaborate carvings of curvaceous female figures, floral patterns, birds, and hundreds of Buddhas decorate the pagodas. Also on the grounds is the **Beijing Art Museum of Stone Carvings** (Beijing Shike Yishu Bowuguan), with its collection of some 1,000 stelae and stone carvings. ⊠ *24 Wuta Si, Baishiqiao, Haidian District* ☎ *010/6217–3836* 🎫 *Y2.5 includes admission to museum and pagodas* ⊗ *Daily 8:30–4:30.*

★ ㊲ Old Summer Palace (Yuanmingyuan). Once a grand collection of palaces, this complex was the emperor's summer retreat from the 15th century to 1860, when it was looted and systematically blown up by British and French soldiers. The Western-style buildings—patterned after Versailles in France—were added during the Qing Dynasty and designed by Jesuits. Catholic missionaries carried the gospel into China in 1583 and settled in Guangdong province (it was on their map that Chinese intellectuals saw their country's position in the world for the first time). In 1597 the missionary Matteo Ricci was appointed director of Jesuit activities in China, and in 1601 he finally achieved his goal of being admitted to Beijing, the capital.

Beijing has chosen to preserve the vast ruin as a "monument to China's national humiliation." Beijing students take frequent field trips to the site and (encouraged by their teachers, no doubt) scrawl patriotic slogans on the rubble. A large lake, ideal for summer boating or winter ice-skating, is in the center of the grounds. ⊠ *Qinghuan Xi Lu, Haidian District* ☎ *010/6255–1488 or 010/6254–3673* 🎫 *Park, Y10; extra 15Y fee for sites* ⊗ *Daily 7–7.*

㊱ Summer Palace (Yiheyuan). This expansive, parklike imperial retreat

FodorśChoice
★

dates from 1153, midway through the Jin Dynasty. Shortly thereafter, under the Yuan Dynasty, engineers channeled in spring water to create a series of man-made lakes. It was not until the Qing that the Summer Palace took on its present form. In 1750 Emperor Qianlong commissioned the retreat for his mother's 60th birthday. Construction of palaces, pavilions, bridges, and numerous covered pathways on the shores of Kunming Lake continued for 15 years. The resort suffered heavy damage when Anglo-French forces plundered, then burned, many of the palaces in 1860. Renovation commenced in 1888 using funds diverted from China's naval budget. Empress Dowager Cixi retired to the Summer Palace in 1889, and nine years later, after the failure of his reform movement, imprisoned her nephew, Emperor Guangxu, on the palace grounds, reclaiming control of the government. Four years later, in 1903, she moved the seat of government from the Forbidden City to Yiheyuan from which she controlled China until her death in 1908.

Enter the palace grounds through the **East Palace Gate** (Donggongmen). Inside, a grand courtyard leads to the **Hall of Benevolent Longevity** (Renshoudian), where Cixi held court. Just beyond, next to the lake, the **Hall of Jade Ripples** (Yulantang) was where Cixi kept the hapless Guangxu under guard while she ran China in his name. Cixi's own residence, the **Hall of Joyful Longevity** (Leshoutang), sits just to the north and affords a fine view of Kunming Lake. The residence is furnished and decorated as Cixi left it. Cixi's private **theater,** just east of the hall, was constructed for her 60th birthday at a cost of 700,000 taels of silver. The **Long Corridor** skirts Kunming Lake's northern shoreline for 2,388 feet until it reaches the **marble boat,** an elaborate two-deck pavilion built of finely carved stone and stained glass. Above the Long Corridor on **Longevity Hill** (Wanshou Shan), intersecting pathways lead to numerous pavilions and several Buddhist prayer halls. Below, Kunming Lake extends southward for 3 km (2 mi), ringed by tree-lined dikes, arched stone bridges, and numerous gazebos. In summer you can explore the lake by paddleboat (inexpensive rentals are available at several spots along the shore). In winter, walk—or skate—on the ice. Although the palace area along Kunming Lake's north shore is usually crowded, the less-traveled southern shore near Humpbacked Bridge is an ideal picnic spot. ⊠ *Yiheyuan Lu and Kunminghu Lu, Haidian District, 12 km (7½ mi) northwest of downtown Beijing* ☎ *010/6288–1144* ⌨ *Y30 additional fees at some exhibits* ⊙ *Apr.–Oct., daily 6:30 AM–6 PM, Nov.–Mar., daily 7 AM–5 PM.*

❸ **Temple of Longevity** (Wanshou Si). A Ming empress built this temple to honor her son in 1578. Qing emperor Qianlong later restored it as a birthday present to his mother. From then until the fall of the Qing, it served as a rest stop for imperial processions traveling by boat to the Summer Palace and Western Hills. Today Wanshou Temple is managed by the Beijing Art Museum and houses a small but exquisite collection of Buddha images. The Buddhas in the main halls include Sakyamuni sitting on a thousand-petal, thousand-Buddha bronze throne and dusty Ming-period Buddhas. ⊠ *Xisanhuan Lu, on the north side of Zizhuqiao Bridge, Haidian District* ☎ *010/6841–3380 or 010/6841–9391* ⌨ *Y20* ⊙ *Tues.–Sun. 9–4.*

❸ **Temple of the White Pagoda** (Baita Si). This 13th-century Tibetan stupa, the largest of its kind in China, dates from Kublai Khan's reign and owes its beauty to a Nepalese architect (name lost to history) who built it to honor Sakyamuni Buddha. Once hidden within the structure were Buddha statues, sacred texts, and other holy relics. Many of the statues are now on display in glass cases in the **Miaoying** temple, at the foot of the stupa. English-language captions on the displays, and explanations of the temples' history and renovations, add to the pleasure of visiting this site. A local qi gong association also runs a traditional clinic on the premises. ✉ *Fuchenmennei Dajie near Zhaodengyu Lu; turn right at first alley east of stupa, Xicheng District* ☎ *010/6616–6099* 🎫 *Y10* ⊙ *Daily 9–4:30.*

▶ ㉞ **White Clouds Taoist Temple** (Baiyunguan). This Taoist temple serves as a center for China's only indigenous religion. Monks wearing blue-cotton coats and black-satin hats roam the grounds in silence. Thirty of them now live at the monastery, which also houses the official All-China Taoist Association. Visitors bow and burn incense to their favorite deities, wander the back gardens in search of a qi gong master, or rub the bellies of the temple's three monkey statues for good fortune.

In the first courtyard, under the span of an arched bridge, hang two large brass bells. Ringing them with a well-tossed coin is said to bring wealth. In the main courtyards, the **Shrine Hall for Seven Perfect Beings** (Laolu Tang) is lined with meditation cushions and low desks. Nearby is a museum of Taoist history (explanations in Chinese). In the western courtyard, the temple's oldest structure is a shrine housing the **60-Year Protector** (Liushi Huajiazi). Here the faithful locate the deity that corresponds to their birth year, bow to it, and light incense, then scribble their names, or even a poem, on the wooden statue's red cloth cloak as a reminder of their dedication. A trinket stall in the front courtyard sells pictures of each protector deity. Also in the west courtyard is a shrine to Taoist sage Wen Ceng, depicted in a 10-foot-tall bronze statue just outside the shrine's main entrance. Students flock here to rub Wen Ceng's belly for good fortune on their college entrance exams. ✉ *Lianhuachidong Lu near Xibianmen Bridge, Xuanwu District* 🎫 *Y5* ⊙ *Daily 9–4:30.*

WHERE TO EAT

China's economic boom has revolutionized dining in Beijing. Gone are shabby state-run restaurants, driven out of business (or into the care of new management) by private establishments that cater to China's emerging middle class. You can now enjoy a hearty Cantonese or Sichuan meal for under $5 per person—or spend $100 or more on a lavish imperial-style banquet. One popular restaurant has commandeered a former palace, while dumpling shops offer dining under the stars in restored courtyard homes. Hamburgers (or sushi, lasagna, and burritos) are available at numerous new eateries that target tourists, expatriates, and Chinese yuppies. While beer is available everywhere in Beijing, wine is usually only available in Western-style restaurants. It is not customary to tip in restaurants (or anywhere else for that matter) in Beijing, and casual attire is acceptable in most restaurants.

WHAT IT COSTS In Yuan				
	$$$$	$$$	$$	$	¢
AT DINNER	over 180	121–180	81–120	40–80	under 40

Prices are for a main course.

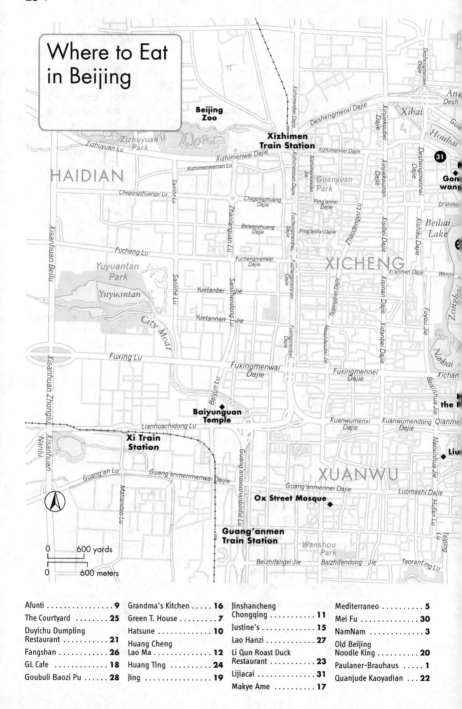

Where to Eat in Beijing

Beijing Zoo

Xizhimen Train Station

HAIDIAN

Guanyuan Park

XICHENG

Beihai Lake

Yuyuantan Park

Yuyuantan

City Moat

Baiyunguan Temple

Xi Train Station

XUANWU

Ox Street Mosque

Guang'anmen Train Station

Wanshou Park

0 — 600 yards
0 — 600 meters

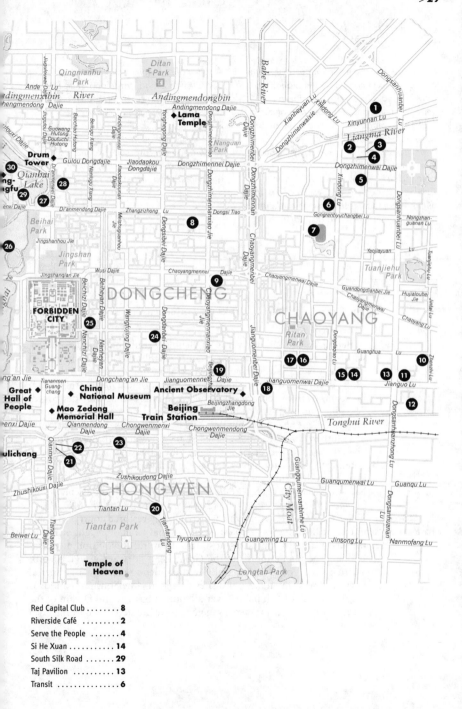

CloseUp

ON THE MENU

Peking duck is the most famous dish of the capital, though it is normally available only in specialist or larger restaurants. Imperial-style banquets offer a contrast to staples like noodles and jiaozi (meat- and vegetable-filled dumplings). New eateries offer regional delights like spicy Sichuan tofu, Cantonese dim sum, Shanghainese steamed fish, Xinjiang kebab—even Tibetan yak penis soup. A slew of fast-food outlets—both Chinese versions and the global franchises—have also taken root.

Against all this competition from inside and outside China, traditional-style Beijing dining is making a comeback. Waiters whisk dishes through crowded, lively restaurants furnished with wooden menu boards and lacquered square tables, while doormen, dressed (like the waiters) in traditional cotton jackets, loudly announce each arrival and departure.

Dongcheng (East City)

The Dongcheng District flanks the Forbidden City to the east.

Chinese

$$$$ ✕ **Huang Ting.** The courtyards of Beijing's traditional noble houses, which are fast facing extinction as entire neighborhoods are demolished to make way for new high-rises, are the theme of Huang Ting. The beautifully decorated walls are constructed from original *hutong* (alleyway) bricks taken from centuries-old courtyard-houses that were destroyed. The pine floorboards and beams are from a large mansion in Suzhou. Huang Ting is also arguably Beijing's best Cantonese restaurant, serving southern favorites like braised shark fin with crab meat; steamed abalone and chicken diced with egg-white cake; and pan-fried cod flavored with yellow tea leaves. Other specialities include sautéed prawns in Sichuan chili sauce, and delicious Peking Duck brought out on a trolley and sliced by a chef. ⊠ *Palace Hotel, 8 Jinyu Hutong, Wangfujing, Dongcheng District* ☎ *010/6512–8899 Ext. 6707* ▤ *AE, MC, V.*

$$$–$$$$
FodorsChoice
★
✕ **Red Capital Club.** Occupying a meticulously restored courtyard home in one of Beijing's few remaining traditional Chinese neighborhoods, the Red Capital Club oozes nostalgia. Cultural Revolution memorabilia and books dating from the Great Leap Forward era (1958–60) adorn every nook. The fancifully written menu reads like an imperial fairy tale, with the names of dishes to match—the South of Clouds is a Yunnan dish of fish baked over a bamboo basket, and Dream of the Red Chamber is a fantastic vegetarian dish cooked according to a

recipe in the classic novel by the same name. ⊠ *66 Dongsi Jiutiao, Dongcheng District* ☎ *010/6402–7150* ⌂ *Reservations essential* ⊟ *AE, DC, MC, V* ☉ *No lunch.*

$$–$$$ ✕**Afunti.** Beijing's largest and best-known Xinjiang Muslim restaurant has become a popular and boisterous dinner-show venue. Uzbek musicians and belly dancers entertain you, and later encourage you to dance on your table! Afunti offers a variety of Xinjiang kebabs, hotpot, baked flat bread, and handmade noodles. ⊠ *166 Chaonei Dajie, Dongcheng District* ☎ *010/6525–1071* ⌂ *Reservations essential* ⊟ *AE, V* ☉ *No lunch.*

★ $$ ✕**Li Qun Roast Duck Restaurant.** If you prefer to stay away from the crowds and commercialism of Quanjude (Beijing's most famous Peking duck restaurant), try this small, casual, family-run restaurant near Qianmen. Juicy, delicious whole ducks roasting in a traditional oven greet you as you enter the simple courtyard house. Li Qun is a good option for the more adventurous at heart, as the restaurant is hidden deep in a hutong neighborhood. It should take you about 10 minutes to walk there, though you may have to stop to ask for directions. The restrooms and dining room are a bit shabby, but the restaurant on the whole is cozy and charming. A menu in English is available. ⊠ *11 Beixiangfeng, Zhengyi Lu, Dongcheng District, northeast of Qianmen* ☎ *010/ 6705–5578* ⌂ *Reservations essential* ⊟ *No credit cards.*

$ ✕**Lao Hanzi.** If you're in the mood for something other than the ubiquitous home-style Beijing or Sichuan fare, try Hakka cuisine. Special-
Fodor'sChoice ties like *sanbei* (smoked) duck, *yanju* (salt-coated) shrimp, and *zhao* fish
★ (baked in aluminum foil) are served at this casual restaurant, which stands in good company among the many watering holes around Houhai Lake. If you're coming in a group, be sure to book one of the private rooms on the second floor with beautiful views over the lake. ⊠ *Shichahai Dongan, Houhai, Dongcheng District, across the street from the north gate of Beihai Park* ☎ *010/6404–2259* ⊟ *No credit cards.*

¢–$ ✕**Si He Xuan.** For homestyle snacks such as dumplings, congee, noodles, and steamed buns, try this cheerful, informal restaurant in the Jinglun Hotel. Wooden gateways separating the dining rooms, and bird cages hanging above the doorways, give it an old Beijing feel. Open until 2 AM, it's also a great place to satisfy the late-night munchies. ⊠ *Jinglun Hotel, 4th floor, 3 Jianguomenwai Dajie, Dongcheng District* ☎ *010/6500–2266 Ext. 8116* ⌂ *Reservations not accepted* ⊟ *AE, MC, V.*

¢ ✕**Goubuli Baozi Pu.** Juicy *baozi* (steamed dumplings) are the specialty of this traditional eatery in a very busy district of Beijing directly north of Tiananmen and Jingshan Park. No trip to China is complete without trying the *goubuli baozi*—dog-doesn't-even-want-to-bother dumpling—filled with meat and scallions and a unique sauce. ⊠ *155 Di'anmenwai Dajie, Dongcheng District, north of Jingshan Park* ☎ *010/ 6404–3097* ⌂ *Reservations not accepted* ⊟ *No credit cards.*

Contemporary

$$$–$$$$
Fodor'sChoice
★

× **The Courtyard.** Beijing's most elegant and upscale restaurant, the Courtyard has its own celebrity chef and an amazing view of the east gate of the Forbidden City. The cuisine showcases a creative fusion of Chinese and Continental styles. You might find steamed sea bass with pickled bell pepper; jumbo shrimp with lemongrass-caramel glacé; and grilled lamb tenderloin with ratatouille. Come here to get away from Beijing's crowded streets, treat yourself to a nice bottle of wine, and perhaps sample a cigar from the cigar den on the second floor. Don't miss the tiny but cutting-edge art gallery in the basement. ☒ *95 Donghuamen Dajie, Dongcheng District* ☎ *010/6526–8883* ⌕ *Reservations essential* ⊟ *AE, DC, MC, V* ⊘ *No lunch.*

$$$–$$$$
× **Jing.** Rated one of the 75 Hottest Tables in the World by *Condé Nast Traveler* in 2003, Jing offers up east-west fusion cuisine in a sleek and ultramodern atmosphere. Signature dishes include the scrumptious duck rolls, the tiger prawns, and the fragrant coconut soup as appetizers; and the fillet of barramundi, and risotto with seared langoustines, as main courses. For dessert, do not miss the mouth-watering warm chocolate cake with almond ice cream. Jing also offers an excellent selection of fine wines from around the world by the glass—a rarity in Beijing. ☒ *Palace Hotel, 8 Jinyu Hutong, Wangfujing, Dongcheng District* ☎ *010/6523–0175 Ext. 6714* ⊟ *AE, DC, MC, V.*

French

$$$–$$$$
× **Justine's.** Classic French cuisine and wine, including foie gras, snails, and Chateau Haut-Brion, are served with the utmost attention at Beijing's best and oldest French restaurant. Justine's also has delicious desserts and tip-top service. Treat yourself to a satisfying brunch here on Sunday. ☒ *Jianguo Hotel, 5 Jianguomenwai Dajie, Dongcheng District* ☎ *010/6500–2233 Ext. 8039* ⊟ *AE, MC, V.*

Chaoyang

The Chaoyang District stretches east from Dongcheng and encompasses Beijing's diplomatic neighborhood, the Sanlitun bar area, and several outdoor markets and upscale shopping malls.

American

$–$$
× **Grandma's Kitchen.** Run by a real American grandma, this is definitely the most authentic American restaurant in Beijing. The country-style checked tablecloths and pastel-colored walls, along with a friendly English-speaking waitstaff, attracts homesick American expats, who indulge in blueberry pancakes, Philly cheesesteak sandwiches, hamburgers with fries, and the best cheesecake in Beijing. ☒ *11A Xiushui Nan Jie, Jianguomenwai, Chaoyang District* ☎ *010/6503–2893* ⊟ *No credit cards.*

Chinese

★ **$$$–$$$$**
× **Green T. House.** Owned by Beijing's "Queen of Style," Jin R., this cutting-edge restaurant rivals any you'd find in New York, Paris, or London. Minimalist and industrial, yet oh-so-elegant, the Green T. is frequented by Beijing's growing population of young nouveaux riches. Dishes are painstakingly prepared and presented, but portions are

dainty, so don't come here too hungry or be prepared to order a lot. The restaurant calls its cuisine neo-classical Chinese, and it's anything but standard Chinese fare—you might have caviar with rose petals, green-tea dumplings, and thin slices of beef or veal covered with black sesame seeds. Tea drinkers should sample one (or more) of the tantalizing teas. ⊠ 6 Gongti Xi Lu, Sanlitun, Chaoyang District ☎ 010/6552–8310 ⚲ Reservations essential ☰ AE, MC, V.

$–$$$ ✕ **Huang Cheng Lao Ma.** If you are visiting Beijing in winter, eating hot-pot is a must. Of Beijing's many hotpot restaurants, Huang Cheng Lao Ma serves the freshest of these popular stews with the widest variety of ingredients, and it has a large, clean, bright, and cheery dining room to boot. Hotpot entails cooking your own raw food in boiling (and spicy!) broths in the center of the table, then dipping them in your choice of sauce before finally putting the tasty morsels in your mouth. ⊠ 39 Nanqingfengzha Houjie Dabeiyao, Chaoyang District (south of China World) ☎ 010/6779–8801 ☰ No credit cards.

¢–$ ✕ **GL Cafe.** Open 24 hours, this popular Hong Kong–style restaurant is fast-paced, slick, and bright. It's a good choice for a quick meal or snack anytime of the day. Stick with the Chinese menu—you might try the soy chicken, roast duck, fried noodles, or congee with fish—and steer clear of the Western menu unless you enjoy the generally bland Hong Kong in-terpretations of Western food. ⊠ 21 Jianguomenwai Dajie, Chaoyang District ☎ 010/6532–8282 ⚲ Reservations not accepted ☰ No credit cards.

Continental

$–$$$ ✕ **Riverside Café.** The owners of Riverside, a friendly Australian cou-ple, have successfully combined a formal restaurant upstairs and a deli, café, and wine shop downstairs. The café offers the best and freshest selection of bread in Beijing, not to mention some of the city's best desserts—try the cheesecake or lemon tart. In summer, the outdoor ve-randah is a nice place to have a leisurely lunch. ⊠ 10 Sanlitun Beixiao Jie, Chaoyang District ☎ 010/6466–1241 ☰ AE, MC, V.

German

$$ ✕ **Paulaner Brauhaus.** Traditional German food is served up in heaping portions at this spacious and bright restaurant in the Kempinski Hotel. Wash it all down with delicious Bavarian beer made right in the restau-rant—try the Maibock served up in genuine German steins. In summer, you can enjoy your meal outdoors in the beer garden. ⊠ Kempinski Hotel, 50 Liangmaqiao Lu, Chaoyang District ☎ 010/6465–3388 ☰ AE, MC, V.

Italian

$$$ ✕ **Mediterraneo.** Summer or winter, this restaurant manages to pack in a full house most nights of the week. Fresh Italian-Mediterranean food served in large portions, a decent wine list, good service, and a conve-nient location on the north end of the Bar Street undoubtedly make up its winning combination. This is also one of the few places in Beijing where you can get a good salad. To start, try the baby-spinach salad with bacon or the warm tomato tart, followed by the slightly sweet pump-kin ravioli or the fresh red snapper pan-fried with rosemary. In summer

there is a large outdoor seating area. ⊠ *1A Sanlitun Bei Jie, Building 8, Chaoyang District* ☎ *010/6415–3691* ▤ *AE, MC, V.*

Indian

$–$$$ ✕ **Taj Pavilion.** Beijing's best Indian restaurant, Taj Pavilion serves up all the classics, including chicken tikka masala, *palak panir* (creamy spinach with cheese), and *rogan josht* (tender lamb in curry sauce). Consistently good service and an informal but slightly upscale atmosphere add to the pleasant dining experience. ⊠ *China World Trade Center, L-1 28 West Wing, 1 Jianguomenwai Dajie, Chaoyang District* ☎ *010/6505–5866* ▤ *AE, MC, V.*

Japanese

$$–$$$$ ✕ **Hatsune.** Owned by a Chinese-American with impeccable taste, this is hands down the best Japanese restaurant in Beijing. The food is delicious and authentic, the interior design is ultra-modern and interesting, and the service is friendly. Try the fresh sashimi, tempura, grilled fish, or one of the many innovative sushi rolls. There's also an extensive sake menu. Hatsune is usually packed for lunch and dinner, so be sure to make a reservation. ⊠ *8 Guanghua Dong Lu, Heqiao Dasha, Building C, 2nd fl., Chaoyang District* ☎ *010/6581–3939* ▤ *AE, MC, V.*

Sichuan

$–$$$ ✕ **Jinshancheng Chongqing.** As Beijing's largest and most popular Sichuan restaurant, this place is always crowded so come prepared to wait in line unless you arrive by 6 PM. When you do finally get seated, you might order the *laziji* (chicken buried under a mound of hot peppers), *ganbian sijidou* (green beans), and *mapou doufu* (spicy tofu). All three are delicious, and even people unaccustomed to spicy food claim to love these dishes. The food is definitely the focus here—don't expect much by way of decor. ⊠ *Zhongfu Mansion, 2nd fl., 99 Jianguo Lu, Chaoyang District, across from the China World Trade Center* ☎ *010/6581–1598* ⌦ *Reservations not accepted* ▤ *No credit cards.*

$ ✕ **Transit.** This little hideaway is a lovely retreat, both quiet and intimate. Come with a date, or book the private room for a small group of friends. The kitchen serves refined versions of fiery Sichuan classics. Traditional-style wooden furniture is complemented by bright, modern murals. This is a good place to unwind and have a long, leisurely dinner followed by a round (or two) of drinks. To get here, go down the alley across the street from the north gate of Worker's Stadium, turn right at the first intersection, and continue about 10 yards. The restaurant is on your left. ⊠ *1 Xingfu Yicun, Sanlitun, Chaoyang District* ☎ *010/6417–6765* ▤ *No credit cards.*

Thai

$–$$ ✕ **Serve the People.** Though it's the favorite of Thais living in Beijing, don't come to this restaurant expecting the kind of light, fresh Thai you'd find in Thailand. The food served here is definitely more of the Chinese–Thai variation. Still, almost everything is tasty. Try the duck salad, pomelo salad, green curry, or one of the many hot-and-spicy soups. ⊠ *1 Xiwujie, Sanlitun, Chaoyang District, across the street from the Spanish embassy* ☎ *010/8454–4580* ▤ *AE, MC, V.*

Tibetan

$ ✕ **Makye Ame.** Tibetan arts and handicrafts decorate this colorful restaurant, and the kitchen serves a range of hearty dishes well beyond the Tibetan staples of yak-butter tea and *tsampa* (barley flour mixed with water and sometimes yak butter to form a dough which is then eaten raw). Try the vegetable *pakoda* (a deep-fried dough pocket filled with vegetables) or the braised beef topped with yak cheese. Heavy wooden tables, dim lighting, and Tibetan textiles make this an especially cozy choice on a chilly winter evening. ⊠ *11 Xiushui Nan Jie, 2nd fl., Chaoyang District* ☎ *010/6506–9616* ▤ *No credit cards.*

Vietnamese

$–$$ ✕ **NamNam.** A sweeping staircase to the second floor, a tiny indoor fish pond, wooden floors, and posters from old Vietnam set the scene in this atmospheric restaurant. The light and delicious cuisine is matched by the speedy service. Try the chicken salad, beef noodle soup, or the raw or deep-fried vegetable or meat spring rolls. The portions are on the small side though, so order plenty. Finish off your meal with a real Vietnamese coffee prepared with a slow-dripping filter and accompanied by sweetened condensed milk. ⊠ *7 Sanlitun Jie, Sanlitun, Chaoyang District* ☎ *010/6468–6053* ▤ *AE, MC, V.*

Xicheng

The Xicheng District extends west and north of the Forbidden City, and includes Beihai Lake.

Chinese

$$$$ ✕ **Lijiacai** (Li Family Restaurant). The restaurant's imperial dishes are prepared and served by members of the Li family in a cozy, informal atmosphere. Li Li established the restaurant in 1985 (after flunking her college entrance exams), using recipes handed down from her great-grandfather, once a steward for the Qing court. The tiny eatery was once in such demand that you had to book a table weeks in advance. Since Beijing's restaurant scene blossomed, however, offering diners many other tantalizing choices, it's been much easier to get into. ⊠ *11 Yangfang Hutong, Denei Dajie, Xicheng District* ☎*010/6618–0107* ⚑*Reservations essential* ▤ *No credit cards.*

$$$$ ✕ **Mei Fu.** In a lavish, restored courtyard on the south bank of Houhai
Fodor'sChoice   Lake, Mei Fu offers an intimate and elegant dining experience. The interior is decorated with antique wooden furniture and velvet curtains,
★   set off by pebbled hallways and little waterfalls. On the walls hang black-and-white photos of Mei Fang, China's most famous Peking opera star. Diners choose from set menus, starting from Y200 per person, that feature dishes typical of Shanghainese cuisine, such as fried shrimp, pineapple salad, and tender leafy green vegetables. ⊠ *24 Daxiangfeng Hutong, south bank of Houhai Lake, Xicheng District* ☎ *010/6612–6845* ⚑ *Reservations essential* ▤ *MC, V.*

$$$–$$$$ ✕ **Fangshan.** In a traditional courtyard villa on the shore of Beihai Lake you can sample China's imperial cuisine. Established in 1925 by three royal chefs, Fangshan serves dishes once prepared for Qing emperors based on recipes garnered from across China. Fangshan is best known

for its filled pastries and steamed breads—traditional snack foods developed to satisfy Empress Dowager Cixi's sweet tooth. To experience Fangshan's exquisite imperial fare, order one of the banquet-style set meals. Be sure to make reservations two or three days in advance. ⊠ *Beihai Park, north of the Forbidden City, Xicheng District (enter through east gate, cross stone bridge, and bear right)* ☎ *010/6401–1879* ⌂ *Reservations essential* ▤ *AE, DC, MC, V.*

$–$$$ ✕ **South Silk Road.** China is an immense country populated with literally hundreds of ethnic minorities that have little in common with the Han majority. If you're curious about the cuisine from a minority group, consider a meal at this trendy restaurant, which serves food from Yunnan province, China's southernmost province bordering Thailand and Laos. Yunnan is home to many of China's minorities as well as a distinctive type of cuisine that you'd be hard pressed to find outside of China. Typical (and delicious) Yunnan specialties include smoked ham, wild mushrooms, and goat cheese. A tasty homemade rice wine is the perfect accompaniment. The two-story glass restaurant, owned by artist Fang Lijun, has plenty of outdoor seating and excellent views over the lake. ⊠ *19A Lotus La., Shichahai, Xicheng District* ☎ *010/6615–5515* ▤ *No credit cards.*

Chongwen

The Chongwen District lies to the southeast of the Forbidden City, south of Dongcheng.

Chinese

$$$ ✕ **Quanjude Kaoyadian.** This establishment has served succulent Peking duck since 1852 and is far and away China's most famous Peking duck restaurant. Nationalized after the 1949 Communist Revolution, it since has opened several branches across Beijing, each more glitzy and commercial than the last. Every branch serves the same traditional feast: cold duck tongue, sautéed webs, sliced livers, and gizzards to start; a main course of roast duck, to be dipped in plum sauce and wrapped with spring onion in a thin pancake; and duck soup to finish. There are several Quanjude branches around the city, with the palatial seven-story Da Ya (Big Duck) the largest with 40 dining rooms seating up to 2,000 people. *Big Duck* ⊠ *14 Qianmen Xi Dajie, Chongwen District* ☎ *010/6301–8833* ▤ *AE, DC, MC, V.*

¢ ✕ **Duyichu Dumpling Restaurant.** History has it that this Shandong-style dumpling house won fame when Qing emperor Qianlong stopped in on his way back to the Forbidden City after a rural inspection tour. A plaque hanging on the wall, supposedly in Qianlong's own hand, attests to the restaurant's flavorful fare. Today the Duyichu's large, raucous dining hall is decidedly proletarian. But the dumplings and assorted Shandong dishes still command applause. Expect to wait for a seat during the dinner rush. Customers share large round tables. ⊠ *36 Qianmen Dajie, Chongwen District* ☎ *010/6511–2093 or 010/6511–2094* ⌂ *Reservations not accepted* ▤ *No credit cards.*

¢ ✕ **Old Beijing Noodle King.** Close to the Temple of Heaven and Hongqiao Pearl market, this restaurant serves traditional-style fast food in a lively

Old Peking atmosphere. Waiters shout across the room to announce customers arriving or leaving. Try the tasty noodles, usually eaten with a thick sesame- and soy-based sauce. Look for the decorative rickshaws parked outside. ⊠ *29 Chongwenmen Dajie, Chongwen District, west side of Chongwenmen, north of Temple of Heaven east gate* ☏ *010/ 6705–6705* ⚱ *Reservations not accepted* ▤ *No credit cards.*

WHERE TO STAY

China's 1949 Communist victory closed the doors on the opulent accommodations once available to visiting foreigners in Beijing and elsewhere. Functional concrete boxes served the needs of the few "fellow travelers" admitted into the People's Republic of China in the 1950s and '60s. By the late '70s China's lack of high-quality hotels had become a distinct embarrassment, and opening the market to foreign investment was the only answer.

Two decades later a multitude of polished marble palaces awaits your dollars with attentive service, improved amenities—such as conference centers, health clubs, and nightclubs—and rising prices. Glitz and Western comfort, rather than history and character, are the main selling points for Beijing's hotels. Some traditional courtyard houses have been converted into small hotels—a quiet alternative to the Western-style establishments. Courtyard hotels usually have a more distinct Chinese character, but those in older buildings may be lacking in the range and standard of facilities. They are often managed by entrepreneurs who bought the courtyard houses from people who once lived there. Given that fewer and fewer old courtyards exist in China, courtyard hotels are often favored by savvy travelers who go to China for its history. Because of the smaller number of rooms in courtyard hotels, reservations are important.

If you're looking for Chinese-style accommodations with gardens and rockeries, consider the Lusongyuan, Haoyuan, Bamboo Garden, and Red Capital Residence guest houses.

As traffic conditions worsen, more business travelers are choosing hotels closer to their interests. However, the more distant hotels, such as the Lido, Friendship, Shangri-La, and Fragrant Hills, do offer shuttle-bus service into the city center. Most hotels will also book restaurants, day tours, taxis, cars with drivers, and travel tickets. Booking rooms in advance is always recommended, but the current glut of accommodations means room availability is rarely a problem, whatever the season.

WHAT IT COSTS In Yuan				
$$$$	**$$$**	**$$**	**$**	**¢**
FOR 2 PEOPLE over 1800	1401–1800	1101–1400	700–1100	under 700

Prices are for two people in a standard double room in high season, excluding 10%–15% service charge.

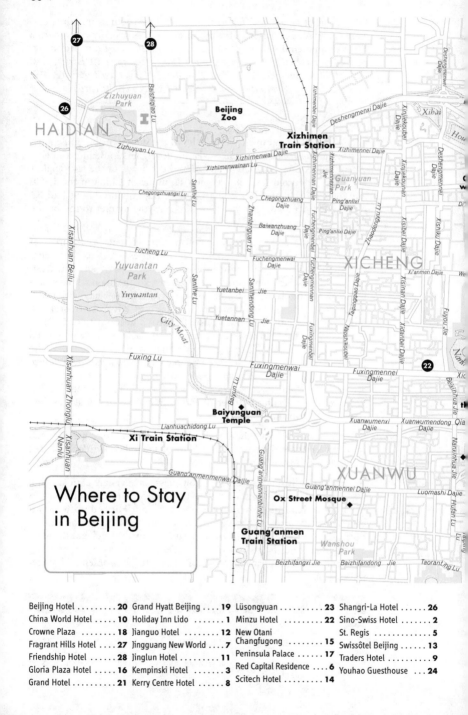

Where to Stay in Beijing

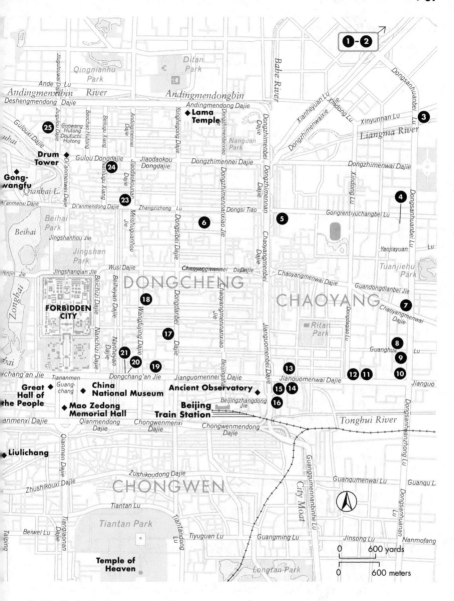

Dongcheng (East City)

The Dongcheng District lies east and north of the Forbidden City and incorporates the city's most important historical sites and temples. The hotels off Dongchang'an Jie and Wangfujing Dajie are within walking distance of Tiananmen Square.

Contemporary Hotels

★ **$$$–$$$$** 🏨 **Grand Hotel.** Standing on the north side of Chang'an Avenue is this luxury hotel whose roof terrace overlooks Beijing's Forbidden City. A former imperial palace, the Grand blends the traditions of China's past with modern comforts and technology. The Red Wall Café, Ming Yuan dining room, Rong Yuan Restaurant, and Old Peking Grill provide a range of cuisines, from Chinese to European. The third floor has a spectacular atrium decorated in marble with Chinese art and antiques. There's a shopping arcade and a fully equipped spa. Even if you don't stay here, try to make it to the rooftop terrace for sunset drinks overlooking the yellow roofs of the Forbidden City. ✉ *35 Dongchang'an Jie, Dongcheng District, 100006* ☎ *010/6513–7788* 🖨 *010/6513–0048* ⊕ *www.grandhotelbeijing.com* 🛏 *217 rooms, 40 suites* ⚑ *6 restaurants, in-room data ports, in-room fax, in-room safes, cable TV, pool, health club, sauna, spa, bicycles, shops, Internet, business services, meeting rooms, car rental* 🖃 *AE, DC, MC, V.*

★ **$$$** 🏨 **Grand Hyatt Beijing.** The impressive Grand Hyatt Beijing, open since 2001, is the centerpiece of Oriental Plaza, a mammoth mall and office complex that dominates Chang'an Avenue. Rooms and suites are decorated in muted tones: beige carpets and curtains, cherry-color wood furnishings, and brown upholstery. The hotel has an Olympic-size swimming pool—the largest in Beijing—surrounded by lush, jungle-like vegetation, waterfalls, statues, and comfortable teak chairs and tables. Over the pool, a "virtual sky" ceiling imitates different weather patterns. The chic Redmoon lounge and restaurant includes a wine bar, a sushi bar, and a cigar bar. The Hyatt is within walking distance of Tiananmen Square and the Forbidden City. ✉ *1 Dongchang'an Jie, Dongcheng District, 100738, corner of Wangfujing* ☎ *010/8518–1234* 🖨 *010/ 8518–0000* ⊕ *www.beijing.grand.hyatt.com* 🛏 *480 rooms, 102 suites* ⚑ *7 restaurants, in-room data ports, cable TV, indoor pool, health club, sauna, spa, steam room, bar, shops, Internet, business services, conference center, airport shuttle, no-smoking floors* 🖃 *AE, DC, MC, V.*

$$$ 🏨 **Peninsula Palace.** The Peninsula Palace Hotel (Beijing Wangfu Fan-
Fodor'sChoice dian) is a beautiful combination of ultramodern facilities and traditional
★ Asian luxury. A waterfall cascades down through the spacious lobby, which is decorated with Chinese antiques. The hotel is in the center of Beijing's business and commercial districts about 10 minutes' walk from the Forbidden City. Rooms have hardwood floors and area rugs, high-quality wood and upholstered furnishings, and 42-inch, flat-screen TVs. A custom bedside control panel lets you adjust the lights, temperature, television, and radio. In the Peninsula arcade you'll find designer stores, including Chanel, Jean Paul Gaultier, and Tiffany & Co. ✉ *8 Dong-danbeidajie, Jinyu Hutong, Dongcheng District, 100006* ☎ *010/ 6559–2888* 🖨 *010/6512–9050* ⊕ *www.beijing.peninsula.com* 🛏 *420*

rooms, 41 suites ⚭ 2 restaurants, room service, snack bar, in-room data ports, some in-room fax machines, in-room safes, minibars, cable TV, tennis court, indoor pool, hair salon, health club, massage, sauna, steam room, bar, lobby lounge, shops, laundry service, business services, conference center, travel services ⊟ *AE, DC, MC, V* ⌾ *BP.*

$$ ⌸ **Beijing Hotel.** The forerunner of them all, the Beijing Hotel is the capital's oldest, born in 1900 as the Hotel de Pekin. Within sight of Tiananmen Square, it has housed countless foreign delegations, missions, and friends of China, such as Field Marshal Montgomery from Britain and the American writer Edgar Snow. Room 1735 still bears a sign indicating where China's longtime premier Zhou Enlai stayed and worked. The central section retains its old-fashioned splendor. The west wing—now the Grand Hotel—was added in 1955 and the east wing in 1974. ⊠ *33 Dongchang'an Jie, off Wangfujing Dajie, Dongcheng District, 100004* ☏ *010/6513–7766* 🖷 *010/6513–7307* ⊕ *www.cbw.com/hotel/beijing* ⤴ *800 rooms, 100 suites ⚭ 5 restaurants, room service, in-room data ports, minibars, cable TV, indoor pool, gym, sauna, bar, Internet, business services, meeting rooms* ⊟ *AE, DC, MC, V.*

$ ⌸ **Crowne Plaza.** A big, contemporary cube, the Crowne Plaza offers some of the best amenities of any downtown hotel. The second floor has an art gallery and a salon, from which Western classical and traditional Chinese music pours forth every evening into the nine-story atrium. The rooms are not large, but they're equipped with the latest facilities, including coffeemakers, hair dryers, and irons; plus they're stocked with two bottles of water daily. The location, near the Wangfujing shopping area, 10 minutes' walk from the Forbidden City, and 15 minutes' walk from Tiananmen Square, is unbeatable. ⊠ *48 Wangfujing Dajie, Dongfeng District, 100006* ☏ *010/6513–3388* 🖷 *010/6513–2513* ⊕ *www.ichotelsgroup.com* ⤴ *332 rooms, 27 suites ⚭ 2 restaurants, room service, in-room data ports, minibars, cable TV, indoor pool, gym, hair salon, gym, sauna, bicycles, bar, shops, baby-sitting, laundry service, business services, free parking, travel services, no-smoking rooms* ⊟ *AE, DC, MC, V.*

Traditional Hotels

$$–$$$ ⌸ **Red Capital Residence.** Beijing's first luxury boutique hotel is in a care-
Fodor'sChoice fully restored, traditional Chinese courtyard in Dongsi, a historic preser-
★ vation district. Five small rooms are differently decorated with original period antiques. The Residence also has a cigar lounge where you can sit on original furnishings used by China's early revolutionary leaders, as well as a wine bar in a Cultural Revolution–era bomb shelter. Special arrangements can also be made for guests to tour Beijing at night in Madame Mao's Red Flag limousine. A second hotel, the Red Capital Ranch, which bills itself as an eco-resort and includes a spa, opened near the Great Wall in the summer of 2004. ⊠ *9 Dongsi Liutiao, Dongcheng District, 100007* ☏ *010/ 6402–7150* 🖷 *010/6402–7153* ⊕ *www.redcapitalclub.com.cn* ⤴ *5 rooms ⚭ Cable TV, bar, laundry service* ⊟ *AE, DC, MC, V* ⌾ *CP.*

¢ ⌸ **Lüsongyuan.** In 1980 China Youth Travel Service set up this delight-
Fodor'sChoice ful courtyard hotel on the site of an old Qing Mandarin's residence, a
★ few lanes south of the Youhao Guesthouse. The traditional wooden en-

trance is guarded by two *menshi* (stone lions). Inside are five courtyards, decorated with pavilions, rockeries, and plants. Rooms are elegant, with large window panels. Though it calls itself an International Youth Hostel, the hotel has no self-service cooking facilities; but it is cheap and has a great Chinese restaurant. ⊠ *22 Banchang Hutong, Kuanjie, Dongcheng District, 100009* ☎ *010/6401–1116* 🖶 *010/6403–0418* 🗪 *38 rooms* ⚭ *Restaurant, bar* ⊟ *No credit cards.*

¢ 🏨 **Youhao Guesthouse.** Behind a high gray wall with a wrought-iron gate, deep in hutong land near the Drum Tower, the Youhao (Friendly) Guesthouse forms a small part of the large traditional compound where Nationalist leader Chiang Kai-shek once stayed. Rooms are basic in the two-story guest house, but have a view of either the spacious front courtyard or the back garden where there are trees, flowers, and Chinese-style corridors. The main building is used for karaoke, but other pleasures remain, such as a Roman-style folly and rockery gates. Beijing's first Japanese restaurant is located here. Though dozens of Japanese restaurants can now be found in Beijing, this is still a good choice for a quiet meal. ⊠ *7 Houyuanensi, Jiaodaokou, Dongcheng District, 100009* ☎ *010/6403–1114* 🖶 *010/6401–4603* 🗪 *30 rooms* ⚭ *2 restaurants* ⊟ *No credit cards.*

★ ¢ 🏨 **Zhuyuan Hotel** (Bamboo Garden Hotel). This charming small hotel was converted from the residence of Sheng Xuanhuai, a high-ranking Qing official, and later, of Mao's henchman Kang Sheng, who lived here after the 1949 Revolution. A powerful and sinister character, responsible for "public security" during the Cultural Revolution, Kang nevertheless had fine taste in art and antiques. The Bamboo Garden cannot compete on comfort and facilities with the high-rise crowd, but its lovely courtyards and gardens bursting with bamboo make it a genuine treasure. ⊠ *24 Xiaoshiqiao Hutong, Jiugulou Dajie, Dongcheng District, 100009* ☎ *010/ 6403–2229* 🖶 *010/6401–2633* 🗪 *40 rooms, 1 suite* ⚭ *Restaurant, hair salon, sauna, bicycles, bar* ⊟ *AE, DC, MC, V.*

Chaoyang

The Chaoyang District extends east of Dongcheng and includes Sanlitun, Beijing's main nightlife area, plus some of the city's best shopping malls and markets. The hotels in this urban district are nearly all modern high-rises and mid-rises.

$$$$ 🏨 **China World Hotel.** One of the finest hotels in Beijing, the China
FodorśChoice World, managed by Shangri-La Hotels & Resorts, is part of the presti-
★ gious China World Trade Center, home to offices, luxury apartments, and premium retail outlets. The lobby, conference center, ballroom, and all the guest rooms, were completely renovated in 2003 to the tune of $30 million. Marble floors and gold accents in the lobby lead to comfortable, contemporary rooms with marble baths. Scene a Cafe is a casual eatery where eight different cuisines are featured, along with chef-entertainers. ⊠ *1 Jianguomenwai Dajie, Chaoyang District, 100004* ☎ *010/6505–2266 or 010/6505–0828* 🖶 *010/6505–3167* ⊕ *www. shangri-la.com* 🗪 *700 rooms, 56 suites* ⚭ *6 restaurants, snack bar, in-room data ports, in-room safes, minibars, cable TV, health club, hair*

salon, massage, 2 bars, dance club, shops, laundry service, Internet, business services, conference center, airport shuttle, travel services, car rental, parking (fee), no-smoking rooms $\rightleftharpoons$ *AE, DC, MC, V.*

$$$$ 🏨 **New Otani Changfugong.** Managed by the New Otani Group from Japan, this hotel combines that country's signature hospitality and attentive service with a premium location in downtown Beijing (near the Friendship Store and the old observatory). The hotel offers authentic Chinese meals that are unforgettable, and the main restaurant serves delicious (and expensive) Japanese food. The hotel is popular with businesspeople and large groups from Japan. It's accessible for people with disabilities. ✉ *26 Jianguomenwai Dajie, Chaoyang District, 100022* ☎ *010/6512–5555* 🖷 *010/6513–9810* ⊕ *www.cfgbj.com* ⤺ *480 rooms, 20 suites* ♻ *2 restaurants, in-room safes, cable TV, tennis court, pool, gym, hair salon, massage, sauna, bicycles, bar, shop, laundry service, concierge, Internet, car rental* $\rightleftharpoons$ *AE, DC, MC, V* ¶⃝ *BP.*

$$$$ 🏨 **St. Regis.** Generally considered to be the best hotel in Beijing, the St.
Fodor'sChoice Regis is a favorite of the foreign business community and visiting dig-
★ nitaries. This is where President Bush stayed during his visit to China, and where Uma Thurman and crew stayed during the filming of Quentin Tarantino's *Kill Bill*. The luxurious interiors combine classical Chinese elegance and fine, modern furnishings—you won't be disappointed. The Press Club Bar, with its grand piano, dark wood, and bookcases, feels like a private club. And the on-site Japanese restaurant has good, moderately priced lunch specials. ✉ *21 Jianguomenwai Dajie, Chaoyang District, 100020* ☎ *010/6460–6688* 🖷 *010/6460–3299* ⊕ *www. stregis.com* ⤺ *137 rooms, 135 suites* ♻ *5 restaurants, in-room data ports, in-room safes, some kitchenettes, cable TV, tennis court, golf privileges, 2 indoor pools, hair salon, health club, hot tub, massage, sauna, spa, steam room, bicycles, badminton, billiards, racquetball, squash, 4 bars, 3 lounges, recreation room, shops, baby-sitting, playground, laundry service, Internet, business services, convention center, airport shuttle, car rental, travel services, parking (fee), no-smoking rooms* $\rightleftharpoons$ *AE, DC, MC, V.*

$$$ 🏨 **Kempinski Hotel.** This fashionable hotel forms part of the Lufthansa Center, together with a luxury department store, offices, and apartments. It's within walking distance of the Sanlitun embassy area and dozens of bars and restaurants. There is an excellent German restaurant with its own micro-brewery, as well as a deli that is frequented by many Beijing expats. The gym and swimming pool are on the 18th floor. ✉ *50 Liangmaqiao Lu, Chaoyang District, 100016* ☎ *010/6465–3388* ⊕ *www. kempinski-beijing.com* 🖷 *010/6465–3366* ⤺ *500 rooms, 114 suites* ♻ *11 restaurants, room service, in-room data ports, in-room safes, cable TV, some minibars, indoor pool, gym, bicycles, 2 bars, shops, laundry service, concierge, business services, conference center, car rental, travel services* $\rightleftharpoons$ *AE, DC, MC, V.*

$$ 🏨 **Holiday Inn Lido.** This enormous Holiday Inn—the largest in the world— is part of Lido Place, a commercial and residential complex northeast of the city center and close to the airport. With a high concentration of international businesses, including retail stores, a deli, and a Starbucks, Lido Place is home to a number of expats, and the Holiday Inn, too, is a haven

CloseUp
KID-FRIENDLY HOTELS IN BEIJING

Many Beijing hotels have special programs and facilities that appeal to children. Holiday Inn Lido, in the Chaoyang District, has an ice-cream parlor, a 20-lane bowling alley, video games, a big swimming pool, and a park next door. Plus, at the hotel's Texan Bar & Grill, Chinese cowpokes serve the best Tex-Mex in town. There's often live entertainment in one of the restaurants or in the lobby, and children under 19 stay free in their parents' room. Kerry Centre Hotel, also in the

Chaoyang District, has two indoor tennis courts, a 25-meter pool, a special splash pool, a play area for kids, and a rooftop outdoor track for in-line skating. Children under 18 stay free in their parents' room. Sino-Swiss Hotel Beijing, near the Capital Airport, has children's programs in summer; among its outdoor facilities are a playground, tennis courts, a volleyball court, an indoor-outdoor swimming pool, and horse stables nearby. Kids under 16 stay free in their parents' room.

for foreigners. The hotel has an Italian restaurant called Pinocchio, a steak restaurant called the Texan Bar & Grill, and a British-style pub called the Pig and Thistle. Key cards let you into your hotel room, and you also need them to turn on the room lights. ⊠ *Jichang Lu at Jiangtai Lu, Chaoyang District, 100004* ☎ *010/6437–6688 or 800/810–0019 in China* 🖷 *010/ 6437–6237* ⊕ *www.beijing-lido.holiday-inn.com* ⤴ *374 rooms, 66 suites* ⚸ *4 restaurants, ice cream parlor, room service, cable TV, indoor pool, hair salon, health club, hot tub, massage, sauna, steam room, bar, lounge, shops, baby-sitting, laundry service, concierge, Internet, business services, meeting rooms, airport shuttle, car rental, travel services, free parking, no-smoking rooms* ⊟ *AE, DC, MC, V.*

$$ 🏨 **Jianguo Hotel.** Despite its 1950s-style name ("build the country"), this is actually a U.S.–China joint venture. Wonderfully central, it is close to the diplomatic compounds and southern embassy area, as well as the Silk Alley Market. Nearly half the rooms have balconies overlooking busy Jianwai Dajie. The Jianguo has maintained its friendly and cozy feel, and Western classical music, including opera, is performed Sunday morning in the lobby. Justine's is the best French restaurant in Beijing. ⊠ *5 Jianguomenwai Dajie, Chaoyang District, 100020* ☎ *010/ 6500–2233* 🖷 *010/6501–0539* ⊕ *www.jianguohotels.com* ⤴ *400 rooms, 68 suites* ⚸ *4 restaurants, in-room safes, cable TV, indoor pool, hair salon, massage, bar, shop, laundry services, concierge, Internet, business services, conference center, no-smoking rooms* ⊟ *AE, DC, MC, V.*

★ $$ 🏨 **Kerry Centre Hotel.** The Shangri-La hotel chain opened this palatial, upscale hotel to much fanfare in 1999. Its ultra-modern interiors and convenient location close to Beijing's embassy and business district make it an excellent choice for business travelers and anyone who wants to be near shopping. The Forbidden City is a 10- to 15-minute drive away. What really distinguishes it from other five-star hotels in Beijing is the amazing health club. With a full-service fitness center and spa, a jogging track, squash and tennis courts, and, of course, a pool, it's *the* health club of choice for expats living in Beijing. ✉ *1 Guang Hua Lu, Chaoyang District, 100020* ☎ *010/6561–8833* 🖷 *010/6561–2626* ⊕ *www.shangri-la.com* ✎ *445 rooms, 42 suites* ⚄ *3 restaurants, in-room data ports, in-room safes, cable TV, minibars, pool, 2 tennis courts, health club, hot tub, massage, sauna, spa, steam room, basketball, billiards, Ping-Pong, squash, bar, shops, playground, Internet* ⊟ *AE, DC, MC, V.*

$$ 🖭 **Swissôtel.** This hotel is a joint venture between Switzerland and the Hong Kong and Macau Affairs Office of the State Council (hence the hotel's Chinese name—Gang'ao Zhongxin—the Hong Kong Macau Center). The Hong Kong connection means Hong Kong Jockey Club members can place bets here. In the large and impressive marble lobby you can enjoy excellent jazz every Friday and Saturday evening. Rooms have high-quality, European-style furnishings in cream and light grey, plus temperature controls and coffeemakers. ✉ *Dongsishiqiao Flyover Junction (2nd Ring Road), Chaoyang District, 100027* ☎ *010/6553–2288* 🖷 *010/6501–2501* ⊕ *www.swissotel-beijing.com* ✎ *362 rooms, 30 suites, 62 apartments* ⚄ *5 restaurants, room service, in-room data ports, some in-room fax machines, in-room safes, minibars, cable TV, indoor pool, gym, hair salon, sauna, bar, baby-sitting, shops, laundry service, concierge, Internet, business services, conference center, car rental, travel services, no-smoking rooms* ⊟ *AE, DC, MC, V.*

$$ 🖭 **Traders Hotel.** Inside the China World Trade center complex, this hotel is connected to its sister property, the China World Hotel, and a shopping mall. The hotel is a favorite of international business travelers, who appreciate its central location, good service, top-notch amenities, and excellent value. Rooms are done in muted colors, such as beige and light green, with queen- or king-size beds. Guests have access to the state-of-the-art health club at the China World Hotel. ✉ *1 Jianguomenwai Dajie, Chaoyang District, 100004* ☎ *010/6505–2277* 🖷 *010/6505–0828* ⊕ *www.shangri-la.com* ✎ *544 rooms, 26 suites* ⚄ *2 restaurants, in-room data ports, in-room safes, minibars, cable TV, massage, bar, shop, baby-sitting, business services, conference center, airport shuttle, car rental, travel services, no-smoking rooms* ⊟ *AE, DC, MC, V.*

$–$$ 🖭 **Scitech Hotel.** This is part of the Scitech complex, which consists of an office tower, a hotel, and a luxury shopping center. The hotel enjoys a good location on busy Jianguomenwai Dajie opposite the Friendship Store. You are greeted by a small fountain in the lobby, which also has a small teahouse off to one side. The rooms are pleasant, if somewhat nondescript, and the service is quite good. ✉ *22 Jianguomenwai Dajie, Chaoyang District, 100004* ☎ *010/6512–3388* 🖷 *010/6512–3542* ⊕ *www.scitechgroup.com* ✎ *262 rooms, 32 suites* ⚄ *4 restaurants, room service, in-room safes, minibars, cable TV, tennis court, indoor pool, gym, hair salon, hot tub, sauna, bar, dance club, shops, baby-sitting, laundry service, business services, conference center, car rental, parking (fee), no-smoking rooms* ⊟ *AE, DC, MC, V* ⏛ *BP.*

$ 🖭 **Gloria Plaza Hotel.** This hotel, built in the late 1990s, is in a commercial area near the Beijing embassy, the New Otani Changfugong, and Scitech. Rooms have good views of the city. The Sports City Cafe broadcasts sports events from around the world and serves up American food along with beer, wine, and cocktails. There's a dance floor and nightly entertainment, such as a DJ or band. ⊠ *2 Jiangguomen Nan Dajie, Chaoyang District, 100022* ☎ *010/6515–8855* 🖷 *010/6515–5273* ⊕ *www.gphbeijing.com* 🛏 *377 rooms, 46 suites* ⚙ *3 restaurants, room service, in-room data ports, cable TV, indoor pool, health club, hot tub, massage, sauna, bar, lobby lounge, laundry service, business services, conference center, airport shuttle, travel services, parking (fee)* ▤ *AE, DC, MC, V.*

$ 🏨 **Jinglun Hotel.** Just 10 minutes' drive from Tiananmen Square, the Jinglun is a well-appointed business and leisure hotel with competitive prices. It's known for its good, fourth-floor, Chinese restaurant, Si He Xuan, and its outdoor café, which serves drinks and barbecue beside a fountain from spring through autumn. Rooms are spacious with standard chain-hotel furnishings in bright blue, pink, and orange. ⊠ *3 Jianguomenwai Dajie, Chaoyang District, 100020* ☎ *010/6500–2266* 🖷 *010/6500–2022* ⊕ *www.jinglunhotel.com* 🛏 *512 rooms, 126 suites* ⚙ *4 restaurants, in-room safes, minibars, refrigerators, cable TV, indoor pool, gym, hair salon, hot tub, massage, sauna, bicycles, bar, shops, baby-sitting, Internet, business services, car rental, travel services* ▤ *AE, DC, MC, V.*

¢ 🏨 **Jingguang New World.** Modern China's obsession with blue glass finds its most monstrous expression in this 53-story building. The Jingguang Center houses the hotel plus offices, shops, and luxury apartments. It's hard to miss on the eastern Third Ring Road, not far from Jianguomenwai Dajie. The restaurants serve Cantonese, Korean, and Western food. ⊠ *Jingguang center, Hujialou, Chaoyang District, 100020* ☎ *010/6597–8888* 🖷 *010/6597–3333* ⊕ *www.newworldhotels.com* 🛏 *426 rooms, 20 suites* ⚙ *3 restaurants, cable TV, pool, hair salon, gym, sauna, massage, 2 bars, shops, Internet, business center, conference center* ▤ *AE, DC, MC, V.*

¢ 🏨 **Zhaolong Youth Hostel.** If partaking in Beijing's lively nightlife scene is on your itinerary, consider this clean and comfortable youth hostel in Sanlitun. The hostel offers clean rooms with two to six beds each, a reading room, a kitchen, and bicycle rentals. The organized hiking trips to the Great Wall (Y90) every other day make this a popular choice for many backpackers. ⊠ *2 Gongti Bei Lu, Sanlitun, Chaoyang District, 100027* ☎ *010/6597–2299 Ext. 6111* 🖷 *010/6597–2288* ⊕ *www. greatdragonhotel.com.cn* 🛏 *20 rooms* ⚙ *Bar, laundry facilities; no room phones, no room TVs* ▤ *AE, MC, V* ⏹ *CP.*

Haidian

The Haidian District is in the far northwestern corner of Beijing, where you'll find the Summer Palace, the city zoo, and numerous parks.

$$ 🏨 **Shangri-La Hotel.** Set in delightful landscaped gardens in the western part of the city, 30 minutes from downtown, this Shangri-La is a wonderful retreat. The lobby and restaurants underwent a major renovation in early 2004, and a new wing, the Horizon Tower, is scheduled for completion in 2006. ⊠ *29 Zizhuyuan Lu, Haidian District, 100084* ☎ *010/ 6841–2211* 🖷 *010/6841–8002* ⊕ *www.shangri-la.com* 🛏 *616 rooms, 19 suites, 15 1- to 3-bedroom apartments* ⚙ *3 restaurants, room service, in-room data ports, in-room safes, some kitchenettes, minibars, cable TV,* *indoor pool, gym, hair salon, health club, massage, sauna, bar, lobby lounge, shops, baby-sitting, laundry service, Internet, business services, conference center, car rental, travel services, parking (fee)* ⊟ *AE, DC, MC, V* ⵔ⃝ *BP.*

¢–$ ⌗ **Friendship Hotel.** The Friendship's name is telling: it was built in 1954 to house foreign experts, mostly Soviet, who had come to help build New China. Beijing Friendship Hotel is one of the largest "garden-style" hotels in Asia. The architecture is Chinese traditional and the public spaces are classic and elegant. Rooms are large with modern, if somewhat outdated, furnishings. With 14 restaurants, an Olympic-size pool, and a driving range, the hotel aims to be a one-stop destination. ⊠ *3 Baishiqiao Lu, Haidian District, 100873* ☎ *010/6849–8888* ▤ *010/6849–8866* ⊕ *www.cbw.com/hotel/friendship* ⤳ *800 rooms, 32 suites* ⌘ *14 restaurants, minibars, cable TV, driving range, tennis courts, 2 pools (1 indoor), gym, massage, sauna, billiards, bowling, bar, dance club, theater, business services, conference center, car rental* ⊟ *AE, DC, MC, V.*

¢ ⌗ **Fragrant Hills Hotel.** This unusual hotel surrounded by gardens—there's a large lake and a miniature stone forest nearby—takes its name from the beautiful park on which it is set. In the western suburbs of Beijing, Fragrant Hills was a favored retreat of emperors through the centuries. The hotel was designed by the Chinese-American architect I. M. Pei and opened in 1983. The lobby forms a traditional courtyard, and rooms extend along a hillside. Each has a balcony overlooking the park. The outdoor swimming pool is covered for year-round use. Despite its lovely surroundings, the hotel is somewhat run-down, and it is a 1½-hour drive from downtown. ⊠ *Fragrant Hills Park, Haidian District, 100093* ☎ *010/6259–1166* ▤ *010/6259–1762* ⊕ ⤳ *200 rooms, 27 suites* ⌘ *3 restaurants, pool, hair salon, massage, sauna, bar, shop, laundry service, business services, parking (fee)* ⊟ *AE, DC, MC, V* ⵔ⃝ *BP.*

Xicheng

The Xicheng District is on the west side of the Forbidden City, opposite Dongcheng. This is where to get lost among Beijing's old hutong alleyways and to take long walks by Qianhai and Houhai lakes.

¢ ⌗ **Minzu Hotel.** At its birth in 1959, the Minzu (Nationalities) Hotel was labeled one of the Ten Great Buildings in Beijing. This paean to the unity of China's different peoples has welcomed many prominent foreign visitors over the years. It's been renovated into yet another shiny pleasuredome but maintains its original appeal. The hotel lies on western Changan Dajie, 10 minutes' ride from Tiananmen Square and next to the Nationalities' Cultural Palace. ⊠ *51 Fuxingmennei Dajie, Xicheng District, 100031* ☎ *010/6601–4466* ▤ *010/6601–4849* ⤳ *600 rooms, 52 suites* ⌘ *4 restaurants, cable TV, hair salon, massage, sauna, bar, shops, business services, conference center, car rental* ⊟ *AE, DC, MC, V.*

Beijing Airport

★ $$ ⌗ **Sino-Swiss Hotel.** This nine-story contemporary hotel near the airport overlooks a gorgeous, enormous outdoor pool surrounded by trees, shrubs, and colorful umbrellas. All the rooms and public areas are completely up-to-date. You'll find large standard rooms with deep-blue carpeting and white bedcovers. The restaurant Mongolian Gher offers barbecue and live entertainment inside a traditional-style felt yurt, while Swiss Chalet serves familiar Continental food to tables on the outdoor terrace. The hotel caters to business travelers with a full-service conference center and duplex business suites. ✉ *Xiao Tianzhu Nan Lu (Box 6913), Beijing Capital Airport, Shunyi County, 100621* ☎ *010/6456–5588* 📠 *010/6456–1588* 🌐 *www.sino-swisshotel.com* ⇆ *408 rooms, 35 suites* ♨ *5 restaurants, in-room safes, minibars, cable TV, 2 tennis courts, 2 pools (1 indoor), gym, hot tub, massage, sauna, bicycles, billiards, Ping-Pong, squash, 2 bars, shop, laundry service, business services, meeting rooms* ▭ *AE, DC, MC, V* 🍽 *BP.*

NIGHTLIFE & THE ARTS

Until the late 1970s the best night out most Beijingers could hope for was dinner at a friend's apartment followed by a sing-along. Since China's more liberal economic policies came into effect, however, countless bars and clubs have opened, many of them hip enough to attract internationally renowned DJs. Just a few years ago much of Beijing's nightlife scene was dominated by Beijing's expat population. Today, the emerging middle-class (not to mention the growing ranks of nouveaux-riches) have breathed real life into the city's entertainment venues. Peking opera, strangled almost to death in the Cultural Revolution (1966–76), has revived just enough to generate some interest among the older generations.

The free magazines *That's Beijing, City Weekend, Beijing Talk,* and *Beijing This Month* (the city's official tourist publication) have useful guides to entertainment, the arts, and expat events in Beijing. The most useful and entertaining of the bunch is *That's Beijing* (🌐 www.thatsbeijing.com), which appears the first week of every month. Pick them up at your hotel or one of the expat bars. Useful maps giving names in both Chinese and English can be bought at many hotels. Chinese name cards for hotels and other destinations are handy for showing taxi drivers.

The Arts

The arts in China took a long time to recover from the Cultural Revolution (1966–76), and political works are still generally avoided. Film and theater reflect an interesting mix of modern and avant-garde Chinese and Western influences. For example, on any given night in Beijing, you might see a drama by the famous Chinese playwright Lao She, a satire by a contemporary Taiwanese playwright, or a Chinese stage version of *Animal Farm.* Although language can be a major barrier for foreigners watching plays, it's much less of a problem for viewers of Peking opera, which involves elaborate costumes and make-up, vocal and instrumental music, and stylized acting. Peking opera was introduced to Qing Emperor Qianlong in 1790 and quickly developed into China's favorite and most sophisticated performing art. Performances were banned during the Cultural Revolution, but they have since resurfaced, albeit with a less significant following. In fact, Chinese people under 60, who grew up in Communist China, are as likely to listen to Western opera as Peking opera; they'll watch performances of the latter only at the Chinese New Year temple fairs.

Your concierge can make recommendations about performances, and the free monthly English-language magazine *That's Beijing,* which you can find in hotels, restaurants, and bars around the city, also lists performances and special events.

Acrobatics

Chaoyang Theater (Chaoyang Juchang). Spectacular individual and team acrobatic displays involving bicycles, seesaws, catapults, swings, and barrels are performed here nightly. Same-day tickets cost between Y50 and Y300. ⊠ *36 Dongsanhuan Bei Lu, Hujialou, Chaoyang District* ☏ *010/6507–2421.*

Universal Theater (Tiandi Juchang). The China Acrobatics Troupe puts on a nightly repertoire of breathtaking, usually flawless stunts. ⊠ *Dongsishi Tiao, Chaoyang District* ☏ *010/6502–3984.*

Music & Variety

Beijing Concert Hall (Beijing Yinyueting). Beijing's main venue for Chinese and Western classical music concerts also hosts folk dancing and singing, and many celebratory events throughout the year. ⊠ *1 Beixinhua Jie, Xicheng District* ☏ *010/6605–5812.*

Forbidden City Concert Hall (Zhongshan Yinyutang). With a seating capacity of 1,400, this is one of Beijing's largest concert halls. It is also one of the most well-appointed, with plush seating and first-class acoustics. Recent performances include classical pieces by the Beijing Symphony Orchestra and the China Philharmonic. ⊠ *In Zhongshan Park, Xichang'an Jie, Xicheng District, on the west side of Tiananmen Square* ☏ *010/6559–8285.*

Poly Theater (Baoli Zhuyuan). One of Beijing's better-known theaters, the Poly, hosts Chinese and international concerts, ballets, and musicals. ⊠ *Poly Plaza, 14 Dongzhimen Nandajie, Dongcheng District* ☏ *010/6506–5343.*

Tianqiao Happy Teahouse (Tianqiao Le Chaguan). In an old, traditional theater, the teahouse hosts Chinese variety shows like those that were so popular before 1949, including Peking opera, acrobatics, cross talk, jugglers, illusionists, and contortionists. ⊠ *113 Tianqiao Shichang, Xuanwu District* ☏ *010/6303–9013.*

Peking Opera

Chang'an Grand Theater (Chang'an Da Xiyuan). At this contemporary theater, like at a cabaret, the audience sits at tables and can eat and drink while watching lively performances of Peking opera. English subtitles appear above the stage. ⊠ *7 Jianguomennei Dajie, Dongcheng District* ☏ *010/6510–1155.*

Fodors Choice
★ **Huguang Guildhall** (Huguang Huiguan). Beijng's oldest Peking opera theater, the Guildhall has staged performances since 1807. The hall has been restored to display its original architecture and appearance, and it's cer-

tainly the most atmospheric place to take in Peking Opera. ⊠ *3 Hu-fangqiao, Xuanwu District* ☏ *010/6351–8284.*

Liyuan Theater (Liyuan Juchang). Popular with tourists, the Liyuan hosts Peking opera with English subtitles as well as acrobatics performances. ⊠ *Qianmen Hotel, 175 Yongan Lu, Chongwen District* ☏ *010/ 6301–6688 Ext. 8860* 🖷 *010/6303–2301.*

Theater

Beijing Exhibition Center Theater (Beijing Zhanlanguan Juchang). Chinese and Western plays, operas, and ballet performances are staged at this theater, in a Soviet-style building that's part of the Exhibition Center complex. ⊠ *135 Xizhimenwai Dajie, Xicheng District* ☏ *010/6835–4455.*

Capital Theater (Shoudu Juchang). This is Beijing's most respected theater, where big-name international and Chinese shows play when in town. ⊠ *22 Wangfujing Dajie, Dongcheng District* ☏ *010/6524–9847.*

☾ **China Puppet Theater** (Zhongguo Mu'ou Juyuan). Shadow and hand-puppet shows about traditional stories provide lively entertainment for children and adults alike. ⊠ *1 Anhuaxili, Chaoyang District* ☏ *010/ 6425–4849.*

Nightlife

A few years ago, nightlife was mainly contained in hotel bars and karaoke lounges, but now you can find everything from dance clubs with internationally known DJs to gay bars to sophisticated jazz lounges. Packed almost every night of the week by Chinese yuppies and expats, Beijing's nightlife scene is sure to satisfy even the most discerning of nightowls.

Beijing has two main nightlife neighborhoods: Sanlitun and Houhai. A third, Dashanzi, an artsy warehouse area, is slowly gaining popularity, but for now it attracts people mainly for special events. Sanlitun's Jiuba Jie, or "Bar Street," has expanded into the surrounding alleyways. Houhai, once a quiet lakeside neighborhood home to Beijing's *laobaixing* (ordinary folk), has in recent years been the site of a flourishing of bars, restaurants, boutiques, and coffee shops—even a Starbucks.

Bars

SANLITUN AREA **Hidden Tree** (Yinbideshu). At the southern end of Bar Street, this is one of Beijing's oldest bars and is popular with working expats as well as locals. In summer you can sit in the outdoor garden. Pizza, salads, and other light meals are also served. ⊠ *12 Dongdaqiao Xie Jie, Sanlitun Nan Jie, Chaoyang District* ☏ *010/6509–3642.*

Poacher's. A predominantly young expat crowd with a thirst for cheap drinks frequents this bar. ⊠ *43 Bei Sanlitun Lu, Chaoyang District* ☏ *010/ 6617–2632 Ext. 8505.*

Suzy Wong (Suxihuang Julebu). This place just west of Chaoyang Park packs in a mixed crowd of expats and locals, especially *xiaojies* (young ladies). Although it's elegant and stylishly decorated in a 1930s Shanghai theme, it has nevertheless earned a reputation as a pick-up bar. Women should expect advances. ✉ *1A Nongzhaguan Lu, Chaoyang District* ☎ *010/6593–6049.*

HOUHAI AREA   **No Name Bar (Bai Feng's).** The first bar to open in Houhai is still the best—the so-called No Name Bar (because it technically has no name, though locals refer to it by the owner's name: Bai Feng) is decorated with plants and wicker furniture, and has a perfect view of the lake. ✉ *3 Qianhai East Bank, Xicheng District* ☎ *010/6401–8541.*

Sanwei Bookstore (Sanwei Shuwu). Here you'll find the traditional Chinese arrangement of a bookstore with an adjacent café. In the past these bookstore–cafés attracted writers who sipped tea while listening to live Peking opera and talking about their work. At Sanwei, there's a popular bar upstairs. Friday is jazz night, and Saturday brings in Chinese classical musicians playing such traditional instruments such as the *pipa* and the *guzheng.* ✉ *60 Fuxingmennei Dajie, Xicheng District* ☎ *010/ 6601–3204.*

Dance Clubs
SANLITUN AREA   **Cloud Nine** (Jiu Yun). This stylish Bar Street spot appeals to Beijng's hippest club-hoppers and is generally considered to be the city's best nightclub. ✉ *Building 7, Sanlitun Bei Jie, Chaoyang District* ☎ *010/6417–8318.*

DASHANZI AREA   **Vibes** (Weibishi). DJs who know their music spin a mix of house, hip-hop, and rock at this cool, little lounge. ✉ *4 Jiuxianqiao Lu, Chaoyang District* ☎ *010/6437–8082.*

SPORTS & THE OUTDOORS

A few years ago, exercise in the capital was mainly limited to bicycling—a major form of transportation—and a few older people doing tai chi in the morning. As personal-car sales have skyrocketed, however, there are fewer and fewer cyclists and more and more (you guessed it) health clubs. Since the late 1990s, dozens of Chinese and foreign health-club companies have opened branches in Beijing, but most of them are only open to members (or hotel guests, if the club is in a hotel).

As in the West, yoga is also hitting it big, and you'll find yoga classes in health clubs and independent studios. Golf has a loyal following in *daquan* (entrepreneurs), and weekend golf outings are often as much for business deal-making as for pleasure.

Biking
Many of Beijing's pleasures are best sampled off the subway and out of taxis. In other words, walk or pedal. Rent bikes (available at many hotels) and take an impromptu sightseeing tour. Beijing is flat, and bike lanes exist on most main roads. Pedaling among the city's cyclists isn't as challenging as it looks: copy the locals—keep it slow and ring your bell often. Punctured tire? Not to worry: curb-side repairmen line most streets. Remember to park your bike (and lock it to something stationary as bike theft is common) only in designated areas. Most bike parking lots have attendants and cost Y20.

CloseUp

PREPARING FOR THE 2008 OLYMPIC GAMES

CCORDING TO NEWSPAPER REPORTS, $22 billion are being invested to host the Olympic games. Whether this figure is accurate or not, there is no doubt that the face and infrastructure of Beijing is undergoing dramatic change as a result of the nation's hosting the Olympics.

Large-scale city planning projects are the most expensive and ambitious undertakings, yet some of these have already been completed. Two new beltways, the city's fifth and sixth, were built in 2004, and a new, seventh, 270-mile ring road is on the way. Of the city's four new rail lines, one was completed in 2003 and two more are scheduled to begin operating in late 2004. At Beijing Airport, a new, $2 billion terminal has been proposed, and another terminal has been completely renovated.

Within the city, a massive refurbishment of the China National Museum is underway and scheduled to be completed in 2007. Meanwhile, ground has been broken at the site reserved for the Olympic Green between the north sections of the fourth and fifth beltways. Apart from the Olympic Village, the Green will contain an 80,000-seat National Stadium and a 17,000-seat National Swimming Center.

In step with these major developments, many Chinese and international hotel chains have secured locations for new hotels, some of which are scheduled to open in late 2005 and 2006. While we must wait until 2008 to witness the achievements of the world's athletes, the Olympics fascinating pre-show is unfolding now, as the sterling efforts of the Beijing Olympics Committee are realized.

–Guy Rubin

CycleChina. This tour company offers guided bike rides around Beijing on weekends. ☎ 1391/188–6524 ⊕ www.cyclechina.com.

Golf

Beijing International Golf Club. Nestled on a hillside above the Ming Tombs, this spectacular 18-hole course is Beijing's finest. Long (par 72), challenging, and meticulously groomed, it has hosted professional tournaments. Facilities include a restaurant, pro shop, and driving range. ✛ 46 km (29 mi) north of Beijing near Changping ☎ 010/6076–2288 ▩ Greens fees: Y650 weekdays, Y1,100 weekends. Caddies (required): Y150. Rental clubs available ⊘ Mar.–Nov., daily 7–5.

Huang Tang International Golf Club. Another excellent golf course in the Beijing area, Huang Tang is loved by expat golfers. You'll find a pro shop, putting green, and driving range. ✛ Yanjiao Development Zone; shuttle bus from the Jingguang Center on weekends ☎ 010/6159–3832 ▩ Greens fees: Y770 weekdays, Y1,500 weekends. ⊘ Mar.–Nov., daily 7–5.

Hiking

Beijing Hikers. This outfitter offers guided hiking trips squarely aimed at expat hikers and tourists. The trips are rated from 1 to 5 in terms of difficulty, and they take you into the hills around Beijing. You might visit a rural village, historic temple, or the Great Wall. Groups depart from the Starbucks in the Lido Hotel. ☎ *1391/002–5516* ⊕ *www. bjhikers.com* ✉ *Y150, including round-trip transportation* ⊙ *Weekends from 8:30 or 9–4:30 or 5.*

Ice Skating

If you are visiting in winter, a nice way to spend an afternoon is skating on Qianhai Lake. A vendor on the lake rents skates on a first-come, first-served basis.

Skiing

Nanshan Ski Resort. Though small with limited runs, Nanshan is Beijing's best resort. The 10 trails are well groomed, and there are two lifts (a two-seater and a four-seater). Beginners and intermediate skiers will find nothing lacking, but experts may be disappointed. ✉ *Shunyi County, 25 mi (40 km) north of Beijing Airport* ☎ *010/6445–0990* ⊕ *www. nanshanski.com* ✉ *Ski rental and lift ticket: Y220 weekdays, Y360 weekends* ⊙ *Dec.–Mar., daily 7–dusk.*

Tai Chi

Chinese Culture Club. Interested in practicing the exercise of choice of traditional Beijingers? This club host regular classes in an opera theater. ✉ *29 Liangmaqiao Lu, Chaoyang District, east of the Kempinski Hotel* ☎ *010/6432–9341* ⊕ *www.chinesecultureclub.org.*

Yoga

Yoga Yard. Owned and operated by two American yoga teachers, this wonderful studio is the perfect place to keep up your yoga practice while in Beijing. ✉ *Yong He Jia Yuan, Building 4, Room 108, Chaoyang District* ☎ *1360/110–3497 or 1361/126–6962* ⊕ *www.yogayard.com* ✉ *Y80 per class.*

SHOPPING

Rapid economic growth and an explosion of commercialism have transformed Beijing into a consumer's paradise. Modern shopping malls, department stores, and boutiques can now be found alongside Beijing's traditional markets. The trend for moving outdoor street markets indoors (such as Yaxiu Market) so far has left the famous Silk Alley Market unscathed, though rumors abound that its days are numbered. For a more traditional flavor—and bargain reproduction antiques—don't miss the marvelous Sunday market at Panjiayuan. The city's main shopping area, along Wangfujing Dajie and its offshoots, remains as popular (and crowded) as ever.

Major Shopping Districts

Dazhalan

Dazhalan is one of Beijing's oldest shopping streets. Many of the shops here are centuries old and sell traditional Chinese goods such as silk, tea, and Chinese medicines. China's most famous traditional Chinese medicine shop, Tongrentang, is on this street and is staffed by specialists who can examine you and make a prescription for you. If you don't speak Chinese, be sure to bring a translator along, as the doctors here don't speak English.

Jianguomenwai Dajie

One of Beijing's most important tourist shopping areas is along this major avenue in Chaoyang District. Jianguomenwai Dajie is lined with big hotels as well as numerous shops, including the Beijing Friendship Store. You'll also find the outdoor Silk Alley Market and the modern China World shopping mall.

Liulichang Jie

The classical architecture on this narrow street, which has been carefully restored to its Ming-era grandeur, is as much an attraction as the art and antiques shops lining it. Artists come here for the selection of brushes, paper, and ink sold in many stores.

Wangfujing Dajie

Beijing's premier shopping street underwent major restoration in the period leading up to Communist China's 50th anniversary in 1999. Joining, and to some extent replacing, the street's tiny shops are shiny, new malls and department stores. If you want to experience how the locals shop, Wangfujing is well worth a browse.

Department Stores

Beijing Department Store. Wangfujing's grand dame continues to attract large crowds with stores selling everything from jewelry to clothing to sports equipment, despite the allure of Sun Dongan and the even bigger Oriental Plaza complex. ⊠ *255 Wangfujing Dajie, Dongcheng District* ☎ *010/6512–6677.*

Beijing Friendship Store. A longtime tourist favorite, the Friendship Store sells the widest range of traditional Chinese goods and handicrafts under one roof, including hand-drawn tablecloths, silk and cashmere goods and clothing, porcelain, watercolor paintings, traditional Chinese medicine, teas, jade and gold jewelry, rugs (both silk and wool), and groceries. ⊠ *17 Jianguomenwai Dajie, Chaoyang District* ☎ *010/6500–3311.*

Lufthansa Center. This top Beijing department store stocks cosmetics, consumer electronics, wool and cashmere clothing, and new rugs; a Western grocery store occupies the basement. ⊠ *52 Liangmaoqiao, Chaoyang District* ☎ *010/6465–1188.*

Malls & Shopping Centers

Malls are gradually replacing markets as the main places to shop and socialize in Beijing. Most malls here have been built since the late 1990s, so they are generally new and shiny, with international chains and independent boutiques, as well as food courts, restrooms, and ATMs.

★ **China World Shopping Mall.** You'll find designer boutiques such as Prada and Ferragamo at this upscale shopping mall. For quality souvenirs, check out **Tian Fu,** a branch of the famous Chinese tea sellers. The teas are of high quality and come in very attractive packaging. **Emperor** sells bedding, tablecloths, and napkins made from Chinese silk. **Zhang's Textiles** is a Chinese crafts store and antique shop; and **Liuligongfang** sells Chinese-style crystal creations and jewelry. ⊠ *1 Jianguomenwai Dajie, Chaoyang District* ☎ *010/6505–2288.*

Malls at Oriental Plaza. This enormous mall is in Beijing's downtown area just east of the Forbidden City. Similar to China World, there are branches of Emperor, Liuligongfang, and Tian Art here. ⊠ *1 Dongchang'an Jie, Dongcheng District* ☎ *010/8518–6363.*

Sun Dongan Plaza. This massive shopping center has dozens of designer shops but makes a concession to Old Peking with a traditional-style shopping street on the second floor. On the fourth floor, **Mu Zhen Liao Chinese Fashion Boutique** sells high-quality, ready-made *qipaos* (Chinese-style dresses) as well as tailor-made ones. The store is especially popular with brides-to-be. ⊠ *138 Wangfujing Dajie, Dongcheng District* ☎ *010/6527–6688.*

Markets

Bargaining is acceptable at all markets. The best way to get what you want at a fair price without becoming overwhelmed by the negotiation process is to decide what you would be willing to pay for an item in advance and pay no more than that. Vendors will sometimes quote a price 10 times what they are willing to sell for, especially if a potential buyer looks wealthy or indecisive, but usually the first quote is two or three times the amount of the final sale.

Beijing Curio City (Beijing Gu'an Chang). This complex has four stories of kitsch and curio shops and a few furniture vendors, some selling authentic antiques. Prices are high (driven by tour groups), so don't be afraid to low-ball. If you are looking for antique furniture, try **Dong Fang Yuan** (⊠ 4th floor, no. 11 ☎ 1352/047–5513) which has a good selection of genuine antiques. ⊠ *Dongsanhuan Nan Lu, Chaoyang District, exit 3rd Ring Road at Panjiayuan Bridge* ☎ *010/6774–7711 or 010/6773–6021 Ext. 63.*

Fodor'sChoice ★ **Panjiayuan Market.** The Panjiayuan Sunday market is Beijing's liveliest and should not be missed. Vendors, many from faraway provinces, fill hundreds of open-air stalls with a dizzying array of collectibles, as well as lots of junk. Old clocks, new porcelain, jade, bronzes, tomb art, wood carvings, Tibetan rugs, "Maomorabilia"—it's all here. The market is grubby, so dress down. Arrive at sunrise to beat the crowds. The market is open Saturdays and Sundays from sunrise to about 3 PM. Be sure to bargain, as many vendors set their first price up to 10 times higher than what they are willing to sell for. ⊠ *Huaweiqiaoxinan Jie, Dongsanhuan, Chaoyang District.*

Fodor'sChoice ★ **Silk Alley Market.** Here, dozens of open-air clothing and accessory stalls sell made-for-export apparel, such as North Face jackets, Esprit sportswear, designer suites, and cashmere shawls. Just be aware that much of the brand-name clothing, and even the cashmere, is fake. Start at the south end of Silk Alley as the north end, which is near to the American embassy, is closed for security reasons. ⊠ *Xiushui Nan Jie and Xiushui Dong Jie, Chaoyang District.*

Zhaojia Chaowai Market. Beijing's best-known venue for affordable antique and reproduction furniture houses scores of independent vendors who sell everything from authentic Qing chests to traditional baskets, ceramics, carpets, and curios. Be sure to bargain; vendors routinely sell items for less than half their starting price. ⊠ *43 Huawei Bei Li, Chaoyang District, two exits south of China World on Dongsanhuan Lu* ☎ *010/6770–6402.*

Specialty Stores

Antiques & Furnishings

Antiques began pouring out of China more than a decade ago despite strict rules banning the export of precious "cultural relics." According to Chinese law, nothing that predates the death of Qing emperor Qianlong (1795) can be legally exported. Also, certain post-1795 imperial porcelains, and any item deemed important to China's Communist Revolution, cannot be taken out of the country. Many antiques—from Tang Dynasty tomb art to priceless Zhou Dynasty bronzes—are smuggled out of China every year, and vendors may try to sell you an antique piece illegally. Buy antiques only from licensed shops (they should have a special customs sticker carrying a Temple of Heaven symbol). Also note that fakes abound in China, so buyer beware. **Tongli Studio** (*see* Malls & Shopping Centers) and **Zhaojia Chaowai Market** (*see* Markets) are good places to shop for home decor items.

Century Arts. This store carries an amazing collection of genuine antique Tibetan cabinets. On display in the shop are only a small fraction of what is available; many more cabinets are at the shop's warehouse. ⊠ *A-6 Gongrentiyuchang Dong Lu, Chaoyang District* ☎ *010/6595–0998.*

Cottage. This charming little boutique sells Chinese giftware and home decor, such as cushion covers, antique-style furniture, table runners, and placemats at reasonable prices. ⊠ *Northeast corner of Ritan Park, Chaoyang District.*

Art Galleries

The international success of contemporary Chinese artists, such as Zhu Wei and Xu Bing, have helped fuel the Beijing art scene. For a real change of pace, spend a day away from the Old Beijing sites to explore the city's contemporary art galleries. The art you'll see offers a glimpse into China's modern culture.

Artists' Village Gallery. If you'd like to see artists in action in their studio spaces (and homes), head out to one of the artists' villages in the suburbs of Beijing. Make an appointment first, and arrange for car service to the village. Most of the art—contemporary watercolors, oil paintings, and sculptures—is for sale. ⊠ *1 Chunbei, Ren Zhuang, Tongxian Songzhuang* ☎ *010/6438–1784.*

China Art & Archives Warehouse. One of the forerunners in the up-and-coming Dashanzi art district, this gallery showcases cutting-edge art in

DVDS IN BEIJING

Digital video discs of current hit movies often hit the streets of Beijing the same week as they open in United States theaters—and sometimes even before. While the sales of these pirated DVDs are illegal (they blatantly disregard international copyright laws), DVD sales take place so openly in Beijing that it doesn't give the impression of being wrong. Prices range from Y7 on the street (such as on Jianguomenwai or in Sanlitun) to Y10 in the shops (such as those at the Friendship Supermarket in Sanlitun).

Most countries, however, including the United States, forbid the importation of pirated DVDs. Those caught carrying DVDs out of China or into another country will likely be fined and the discs will most certainly be confiscated. For more information about U.S. Customs rules and regulations, download the "Know Before You Go" brochure from www.customs.gov.

a variety of mediums, including painting and sculpture. Be sure to call ahead to make sure there's an exhibit, as the space doesn't have regular shows. ✉ *Caochangdi Cun, Jichang Fulu, Chaoyang District, east of Tiedao Bridge, opposite the Nangao Police Station* ☎010/8456–5152.

Red Gate Gallery at the Watch Tower. This gallery, one of the first to open in Beijing, displays and sells modern Chinese paintings and sculpture in a centuries-old Beijing landmark building. ✉ *Dongbianmen Watchtower, 2nd Ring Road at Jianguomen, Chongwen District* ☎ 010/6525–1005 ⊕ *www.redgategallery.com.*

Yan Club Art Centre. Among the best known galleries in Dashanzi is the Yan Club, which has hosted some excellent contemporary art exhibits. ✉ *4 Jiuxianqiao Lu, Chaoyang District, behind Hongyuan Apartments* ☎ 010/8457–3506.

Books

In general China has a very poor selection of English-language books and magazines, thanks to strict censorship authorities. Some hotel kiosks, such as the Kempinski and China World, sell a limited selection of international newspapers and magazines, but rarely do they stock novels. You're best off bringing enough reading material to last your entire trip.

Beijing Friendship Store. The famous department store geared toward tourists has a small bookstore with a good selection of titles on Chinese history and culture. You'll also find foreign news magazines, imported fiction, and a few children's books. ✉ *17 Jianguomenwai Dajie, Chaoyang District* ☎ 010/6500–3311.

Foreign Languages Bookstore. For the most variety, try this four-story shop, which stocks textbooks, tapes, maps, art books, dictionaries, and some foreign-language novels (mainly classics à la Dickens and Austen). ✉ *235 Wangfujing Dajie, Dongcheng District* ☎ 010/6512–6922.

Clothing & Fabric

Beijing's outdoor and indoor markets are some of the best places to find cheap brand-name clothes, though much of the stock is made up of copies of the real designer goods. Among the best markets for clothing are the **Silk Alley Market, Ritan Office Building Market**, and **Yaxiu Market** (*see* Markets). You can also check out the designer boutiques and Chinese and international chain stores in Beijing's malls (*see* Department Stores *and* Malls & Shopping Centers).

Authentic cashmere from Inner Mongolia is one of Beijing's best buys, selling for less than half of what you'd pay at home. As with most things in China, however, look out for unscrupulous dealers trying to pass off synthetic materials as cashmere, as well as poor-quality cashmere. That said, there are some good places to buy real cashmere at bargain prices.

Chinese silk, the best of which comes from Suzhou and Hangzhou in Jiangsu and Zhejiang provinces, can also be purchased for a fraction of what it costs in the United States. The range of colors, designs, and styles available in China are unequalled anywhere in the world. Some of the most popular buys are robes and traditional Chinese dresses and tunics.

Beijing Friendship Store. The city's most popular tourist shop sells a large selection of all things cashmere, from scarves and shawls to sweaters and long underwear. The Friendship Store guarantees authenticity, so rest assured that cashmere items you buy here are the real thing. ⊠ *17 Jianguomenwai Dajie, Chaoyang District* ☎ *010/6500–3311.*

Huan Huan Cashmere Shop. You can find plenty of synthetic "pashminas" in Silk Alley, but the real thing is harder to find. Huan Huan is one of the few stalls that does sell authentic, high-quality men's and women's cashmere sweaters and shawls starting at Y250. There's another Huan Huan stall at **Hongqiao Market** (⊠ Tiantan Lu, between Chongemenwai Lu and Tiyuguan Dajie, 2nd fl. ☎ 010/6711–7630). ⊠ *Silk Alley, Chongwen District* ☎ *010/6773–2866.*

Ruby Cashmere Shop. This small shop sells genuine cashmere sweaters and scarves—often similar stock as in the Friendship Store—at reduced prices. The tailors here can also make copies of cashmere clothing. ⊠ *Ritan Office Building Market, room 1009, 15A Guanghua Lu, southeast corner of Ritan Park, Chaoyang District* ☎ *010/6475–5051.*

Yuanlong Embroidery and Silk Store. Beijing's best yardage shop, Yuanlong has sold silks and yard goods for more than a century. It also offers custom tailoring and shipping. ⊠ *55 Tiantan Lu, Chongwen District, across from north gate of Temple of Heaven Park* ☎ *010/6701–2859.*

Jewelry

Check out **Hongqiao Market** (*see* Markets) for moderately priced freshwater pearls sold from stalls on the third floor.

Shard Box Store (Shendege Gongyipin Shangdian). Many of the silver, jade, coral, and turquoise pieces sold here are one-of-a-kind items from Tibet or Yunnan. The store takes its name from traditional jewelry boxes, which were often made from pottery shards. ⊠ *1 Ritan Bei Lu, Chaoyang District* ☎ *010/8561–3712.*

Things of the Jing. For modern designs inspired by traditional Chinese motifs, try this shop, which carries a beautiful selection of silver earrings, rings, and necklaces at reasonable prices. ⊠ *221 Tongli Studio, Sanlitun, Chaoyang District* ☎ *010/417–2271.*

Rugs

Antique Chinese, Mongolian, Tibetan, and Central Asian rugs are sold in many of Beijing's antiques shops. Many offer shipping services.

Beijing Yihong Carpet Factory (Women's Carpet Cooperative). This back-alley showroom is managed by women from a state-owned carpet factory. You'll find stacks of dusty rugs from Mongolia, Xinjiang, and Tibet. Although it's primarily an outlet for old rugs, new items are on sale as well, and copies of old designs can be made to order, usually within weeks. Cleaning and repairs are free. ⊠ *35 Juzhang Hutong, Chongwen District* ☎ *010/6712–2195.*

Gangchen Carpet of Tibet. This shop in the Kempinski Hotel is the best place to buy new, high-quality, hand-made Tibetan rugs in Beijing. You'll find traditional and modern designs, and the rugs are made according to traditional Tibetan techniques with highland wool, handspun yarn, and hand-dyeing. ⊠ *Kempinski Hotel, 50 Liang Ma Qiao Lu, Chaoyang District* ☎ *010/6465–3388 Ext. 5542.*

Stamps & Coins

Museum of Antique Currency (Gudai Qianbi Zhanlanguan). Collectors buy, sell, and trade old coins and paper currency outside this museum every day. ⊠ *Bei'erhuan Jie, Xicheng District.*

Yuetan Schichang. For old stamps, try the stamp traders' stalls along the west side of Yuetan Park. Coins are sold at many antiques and curio shops in the same area. ⊠ *Yuetan Park, Haidian District.*

SIDE TRIPS FROM BEIJING

The Great Wall

60–120 km (37–74 mi) north and west of Beijing.

Close to Beijing, 9 km (5½ mi) above the giant Juyongguan garrison and an hour by car from downtown, the **Great Wall at Badaling** (Badaling Changcheng) is where visiting dignitaries go for a quick photo-op. Its large sections of restored wall rise steeply to either side of the fort in a rugged landscape. Convenient to the Thirteen Ming Tombs, Badaling is popular with tour groups and is often crowded. People with disabilities find access to the wall at Badaling better than elsewhere in the Beijing area. You can either take the cable car to the top of the wall, or you can walk. ⊠ *Yanqing County, 70 km (43 mi) northwest of Beijing* ☎ *010/6912–1235 or 010/6912–1338* ✉ *Y45; cable car, Y40 one-way, Y60 round-trip* ☉ *Daily 6:30 AM–sunset.*

★ ㊷ A bit farther from downtown Beijing, the **Great Wall at Mutianyu** (Mutianyu Changcheng) is more spectacular and usually less crowded than Badaling. Here, a long section of restored wall is perched on a high ridge

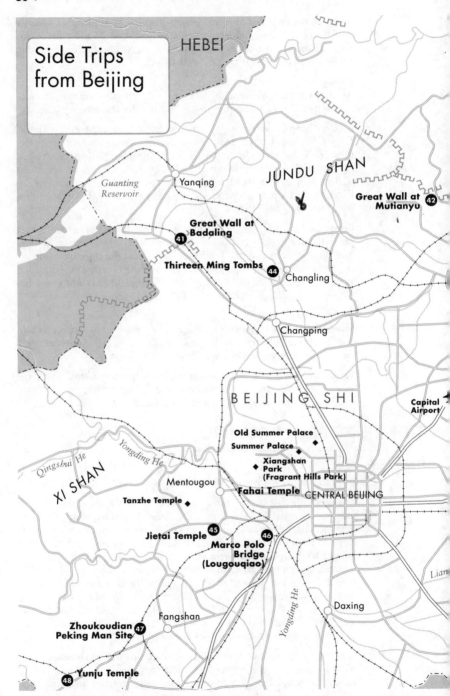

Side Trips
from Beijing

HEBEI

JUNDU SHAN

Guanting
Reservoir

Yanqing

Great Wall at
Mutianyu **42**

Great Wall at
Badaling **41**

Thirteen Ming Tombs **44**

Changling

Changping

BEIJING SHI

Capital
Airport

Old Summer Palace

Summer Palace

Xiangshan
Park
(Fragrant Hills Park)

Qingshui He

Yongding He

XI SHAN

Mentougou

Fahai Temple

CENTRAL BEIJING

Tanzhe Temple

Jietai Temple **45**

Marco Polo
Bridge
(Lougouqiao) **46**

Yongding He

Daxing

Lian

Zhoukoudian
Peking Man Site **47**

Fangshan

Yunju Temple **48**

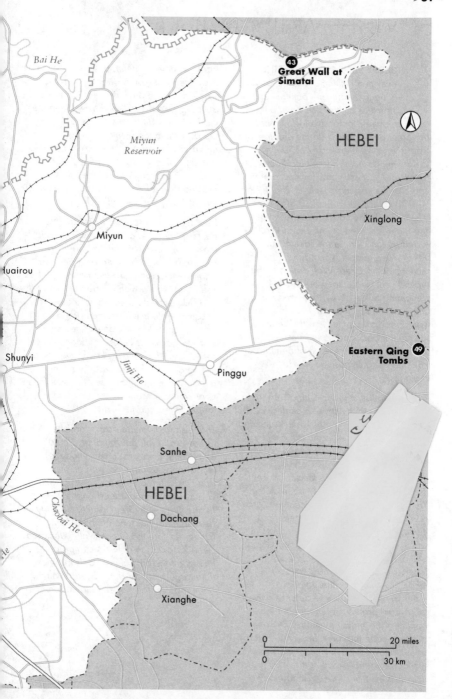

Bai He

Great Wall at Simatai 43

HEBEI

Xinglong

Miyun Reservoir

Miyun

Huairou

Shunyi

Jinji He

Pinggu

Eastern Qing Tombs 49

Sanhe

HEBEI

Chaobai He

Dachang

Xianghe

| 0 | | | | 20 miles |
| 0 | | | 30 km | |

CloseUp

HOW THE WALL WAS BUILT

BUILT BY SUCCESSIVE DYNASTIES over two millennia, the Great Wall (Changcheng) isn't actually one structure built at one time, but a series of layered defensive installations that grew and shrank with the empire. This protective cordon extends 4,000 km (2,480 mi) from the East China Sea west to central Asia; estimates for the combined length of the varying structures range from 10,000 km (6,200 mi) to 20,000 km (12,400 mi). The construction techniques and materials used on the Great Wall varied by location. In the Taklimakan Desert, for example, you can still find sections of the Great Wall dating to the second century BC that were made by combining twigs, straw, rice, and sand. Other sections of the wall from this period were made of rammed earth. The more substantial brick-and-earth ruins that snake across the mountains north of Beijing date from the Ming Dynasty (14th–17th centuries).

The first wall built along China's northern frontier dates to the seventh century BC, but is no longer standing. The oldest surviving section of wall dates to the 5th century BC and is in modern-day Shandong province. These and other sections were built to protect China's northern kingdoms from marauding nomadic tribes, such as the Xiongnu. Over subsequent centuries, more portions of wall were built, creating a motley collection of northern borders. It was the first emperor of a unified China, Qin Shihuang (circa 259–210 BC), founder of the Qin Dynasty in 221 BC, who linked together these various fortifications into a single defense network that would protect the entire northern frontier of his massive empire. By some accounts, Qin mustered nearly a million people, or about a fifth of China's total workforce, a mobilization that claimed countless lives and gave rise to many tragic folktales. (The most famous concerns Lady Meng, a woman whose husband was kidnapped on their wedding night to build the Great Wall. She traveled to the work site to wait for his return, believing her determination would eventually bring him back. In the end, she was turned into a rock, which to this day stands at the head of the Great Wall in the beautiful seaside town of Qinhuangdao, some 480 km [300 mi] east of Beijing.)

Later dynasties repaired existing walls or built new ones. The Ming Dynasty, which took power in 1368, committed vast resources to wall building as a defense against increasingly restive northern tribes. The Ming wall, which is about 26 feet tall and 30 feet wide at its base, could accommodate five horsemen riding abreast on its top. It incorporated small wall-top garrisons linked by beacon towers used for sending smoke signals or setting off fireworks to warn of enemy attack. In the end, however, the wall failed to prevent the Manchu invasion that toppled the Ming in 1644.

That historical failure hasn't tarnished the Great Wall's image. Although China's official line once cast it as a model of feudal oppression—focusing on the brutality suffered by work crews and the vast treasures squandered on the useless fortification—the Great Wall is now touted as a national patriotic symbol. "Love China, Restore the Great Wall," declared Deng Xiaoping in a 1984 campaign that kicked off the official revisionism. Since then large sections of the Great Wall have been repaired and opened to visitors.

above serene wooded canyons. Views from the top of the surrounding landscape are memorable. The lowest point on the wall is a strenuous one-hour climb above the parking lot. As an alternative, you can take a cable car on a breathtaking ride to the highest restored section, from which several hiking trails descend. If you don't plan to hike, phone ahead to make sure the cable car is running. The Mutianyu section is also famed for its toboggan run, which starts three beacon towers east of the cable-car stop and runs all the way down the slope to the site entrance. Look for its reflective steel track snaking down the mountain side. Thrill-seeking teens and adults may want to take a toboggan down (one person at a time), but children under 1.2 meters (4 feet) are not allowed. ⊠ *Huairou County, 90 km (56 mi) northeast of Beijing* ☎ *010/6162–6873 or 010/6162–6506* ⌦ *Y35; cable car, Y35 one-way, Y50 round-trip, Y55 with toboggan descent* ☉ *Daily 7 AM–5 PM.*

43 Remote and largely unrestored, the **Great Wall at Simatai** (Simatai Changcheng) is ideal if you're seeking adventure. Near the frontier garrison at Gubeikou, this section of wall traverses towering peaks and hangs precariously above cliffs. In some places stairways are crumbling and the trail is so steep that the journey is more a crawl than a hike. Be prepared for no-handrails hiking, tough climbs, and unparalleled vistas. Several trails lead to the wall from the parking lot. The hike takes about two hours. A cable car serves a drop-off point about 40 minutes on foot from the wall. If you want a quieter, easier hike, head west from the small lake below the wall, toward the restored Jinshanling section. If you head east, you're in for a good but difficult walk. Eventually you will reach an ascent called the Ladder to Heaven that requires basic rock-climbing skills to scale. After this, the wall narrows to a foot wide with steep vertical drops on either side, sometimes hundreds of yards down. ⊠ *Near Miyun, Miyun County* ☎ *010/6903–5025 or 010/6903–1051* ⌦ *Y20; cable car, Y40 one-way, Y60 round-trip* ☉ *Daily 8–5.*

Fodor'sChoice ★

Thirteen Ming Tombs

44 *48 km (30 mi) north of Beijing.*

Fodor'sChoice ★

A narrow valley just north of Changping is the final resting place for 13 of the Ming Dynasty's 16 emperors (the first Ming emperor was buried in Nanjing, the burial site of the second one is unknown, and the seventh Ming emperor was dethroned and buried in an ordinary tomb in west Beijing). Ming monarchs would journey here each year to kowtow before their clan forefathers and make offerings to their memory. The area's vast scale and imperial grandeur convey the importance attached to ancestor worship in ancient China.

The road to the Thirteen Ming Tombs (Ming Shisanling) begins beneath an imposing stone portico that stands at the valley entrance. Beyond the entrance, a **shendao** (⌦ Y16 ☉ Daily 9–5:30), or spirit way, once reserved for imperial travel, passes through an outer pavilion and between rows of stone sculptures—imperial advisers and huge, serene elephants, lions, horses, and other creatures—on its 7-km (4½-mi) journey to the burial sites.

The spirit way leads to **Changling** (☎ 010/6076–1886 🚌 Y30), the head tomb built for Emperor Yongle in 1427. Architecturally, it matches the design of Yongle's great masterpiece, the Forbidden City, which he built after moving the Ming's imperial capital north to Beijing. The tomb is open daily from 8:30 to 4:30.

Changling and a second tomb, **Dingling** (☎ 010/6076–1424 🚌 Y60 Mar.–June and Sept.–Nov.; Y40 July–Aug. and Dec.–Feb.), were rebuilt in the 1980s and opened to the public. Both complexes suffer from over-restoration and overcrowding, but they're worth visiting if only for the tomb relics on display in the small museums at each site. Dingling is particularly worth seeing because this tomb of Emperor Wanli is the only Ming Dynasty tomb which has been excavated. Unfortunately, this was done in 1956 when China's archaeological skills were sadly lacking, resulting in irrecoverable losses. Nonetheless, it is interesting to compare this underground vault with the tomb of Emperor Qianlong at Qingdongling. Dingling is open daily from 8:30 to 5:30. Allow ample time for a hike or drive northwest from Changling to the six fenced-off **unrestored tombs,** a short distance farther up the valley. Here, crumbling walls conceal vast courtyards shaded by venerable pine trees. At each tomb, a stone altar rests beneath a stela tower and burial mound. In some cases the wall that circles the burial chamber is accessible on steep stone stairways that ascend from either side of the altar. At the valley's terminus (about 5 km [3 mi] northwest of Changling), the **Zhaoling tomb** rests beside a traditional walled village. This thriving hamlet is well worth exploring.

Picnics amid the Ming ruins have been a favorite weekend activity among Beijing-based diplomats for nearly a century. The signs prohibiting this activity are largely ignored; if you do choose to picnic here, though, be sure to carry out all trash. ⊠ *Near Changping, Changping County.*

Jietai Temple

45 *35 km (22 mi) west of Beijing.*

On a wooded hill west of Beijing, Jietai Temple (Jietaisi) is one of China's most famous ancient Buddhist sites. Its four main halls occupy terraces on a gentle slope up to Ma'an Shan (Saddle Hill). Originally built in AD 622, the temple complex expanded over the centuries and grew to its current scale in a major renovation conducted by devotees during the Qing Dynasty (1644–1912). The temple buildings, plus three magnificent bronze Buddhas in the Mahavira Hall, date from this period. To the right of this hall, just above twin pagodas, is the Ordination Terrace, a platform built of white marble and topped with a massive bronze Sakyamuni (Buddha) seated on a lotus flower. Tranquil courtyards, where ornate stelae and well-kept gardens bask beneath the Scholar Tree and other ancient pines, augment the temple's beauty. Many modern devotees from Beijing visit the temple on weekends. ⊠ *Mentougou County* ☎ *010/6980–6611* 🚌 *Y35* ⊙ *Daily 8–5.*

en route Farther along the road past Jietai Temple, **Tanzhe Temple** (Tanzhe Si; ✉ Mentougou County ☎ 010/6086–2500 ✛ 10 km (6 mi) northeast of Jietai Temple, 45 km (28 mi) west of Beijing 🚌 Y35 ⏱ Daily 8–5) is a Buddhist complex nestled in a grove of *zhe* (cudrania) trees. Established around AD 400 and once home to more than 500 monks, Tanzhe was heavily damaged during the Cultural Revolution; it has since been restored. The complex makes an ideal side trip from Jietai Temple or Lugouqiao.

Marco Polo Bridge

46 *16 km (10 mi) southwest of Beijing's Guanganmen Gate.*

Built in 1192 and reconstructed after severe flooding during the Qing Dynasty, this impressive span—known as Marco Polo Bridge (Lugouqiao) because it was praised by the Italian wayfarer—is Beijing's oldest bridge. Its 11 segmented stone arches cross the Yongding River on what was once the imperial highway that linked Beijing with central China. The bridge's marble balustrades support nearly 485 carved stone lions that decorate elaborate handrails. Note the giant stone slabs that comprise the bridge's original roadbed. Carved imperial stelae at either end of the span commemorate the bridge and surrounding scenery.

The Marco Polo Bridge is best remembered in modern times as the spot where invading Japanese armies clashed with Chinese soldiers on June 7, 1937. The assault began Japan's brutal eight-year occupation of eastern China, which ended with Tokyo's surrender at the end of World War II. The bridge has become a popular field-trip destination for Beijing students. On the Beijing side of the span is the **Memorial Hall of the War of Resistance Against Japan** (Kangri Zhanzheng Jinianguan). Below the bridge on the opposite shore, local entrepreneurs rent horses (the asking price is Y120 per hour, but you should bargain) and lead tours of the often-dry riverbed. ✉ *Near Xidaokou, Fengtai District* ☎ *010/8389–3919* 🚌 *Y10* ⏱ *Daily 8:30–6.*

Zhoukoudian Peking Man Site

47 *48 km (30 mi) southwest of Beijing.*

This area of lime mines and craggy foothills ranks among the world's great paleontological sites (and served as the setting for Amy Tan's *The Bonesetter's Daughter*). In 1929 anthropologists, drawn to Zhoukoudian by apparently human "dragon bones" found in a Beijing apothecary, unearthed a complete cranium and other fossils dubbed homo erectus pekinensis, or Peking Man. These early remains, believed to be nearly 700,000 years old, suggest (as do similar homo erectus discoveries in Indonesia) that humankind's most recent ancestor originated in Asia, not Europe (though today some scientists posit that humans evolved in Africa first and migrated to Asia). A large-scale excavation in the early 1930s further unearthed six skullcaps and other hominid remains, stone tools, evidence of fire, plus a multitude of animal bones, many at the bottom of a large sinkhole believed to be a trap for woolly rhinos and other large game. Sadly, the Peking Man fossils disappeared under mysterious circumstances during World War II, leaving researchers only plaster casts to contemplate. Subsequent digs at Zhoukoudian have yielded nothing equivalent to Peking Man, although archaeologists haven't yet abandoned the search. Trails lead to several hillside excavation sites. A small museum showcases a few (dusty) Peking Man statues, a collection of Paleolithic artifacts, two mummies, and some fine animal fossils, including a bear skeleton and a saber-toothed tiger skull. Because of the importance of Peking Man and the potential for other finds in the area, Zhoukoudian is a UNESCO World Heritage Site, but it may not be of much interest to those without a particular inclination for the subject. ⊠ *Zhoukoudian* ☎ *010/6930–1272* 🖅 *Y30* ⊙ *Daily 9:30–5.*

Yunju Temple

48 *75 km (47 mi) southwest of Beijing.*

Yunju Temple (Yunjusi) is best known for its mind-boggling collection of 14,278 minutely carved Buddhist tablets. To protect the Buddhist canon from destruction by Taoist emperors, the devout Tang-era monk Jing Wan carved Buddhist scriptures into stone slabs that he hid in sealed caves in the cliffs of a mountain. Jing Wan spent 30 years creating these tablets until his death in AD 637; his disciples continued his work for the next millennium into the 17th century, thereby compiling one of the most extensive Buddhist libraries in the world. A small pagoda at the center of the temple complex commemorates the remarkable monk. Although the tablets were originally stored inside Shijing Mountain behind the temple, they are now housed in rooms built along the temple's southern perimeter.

Four central prayer halls, arranged along the hillside above the main gate, contain impressive Ming-era bronze Buddhas. The last in this row, the Dabei Hall, displays the spectacular *Thousand-Arm Avalokiteshvara*. This 13-foot-tall bronze sculpture—which actually has 24 arms and five heads and stands in a giant lotus flower—is believed to embody boundless compassion. A group of pagodas, led by the 98-foot-tall Northern Pagoda, is all that remains of the original Tang complex. These pagodas are remarkable for their Buddhist reliefs and ornamental patterns. Heavily damaged during the Japanese occupation and again by Maoist radicals in the 1960s, the temple complex remains under renovation. ⊠ *Off Fangshan Lu, Nanshangle Xiang, Fangshan County* ☎ *010/ 6138–9612* 🖅 *Y30* ⊙ *Daily 8:30–5:30.*

Eastern Qing Tombs

★ **49** *125 km (78 mi) east of Beijing.*

Modeled on the Thirteen Ming Tombs, the Eastern Qing Tombs (Qing Dongling) replicate the Ming spirit ways, walled tomb complexes, and subterranean burial chambers. But they're even more extravagant in their scale and grandeur. The ruins contain the remains of five emperors, 14 empresses, and 136 imperial concubines, all laid to rest in a broad valley chosen by Emperor Shunzhi (1638–61) while on a hunting expedition. By the Qing's collapse in 1911, the tomb complex covered some 18 square mi of farmland and forested hillside, making it the most expansive burial ground in all China.

The Eastern Qing Tombs are in much better repair than their older Ming counterparts. Although several of the tomb complexes have undergone extensive renovation, none is overdone. Peeling paint, grassy courtyards, and numerous stone bridges and pathways convey a sense of the area's original grandeur. Often, visitors are so few that you may feel as if you've stumbled upon an ancient ruin unknown beyond the valley's farming villages.

Of the nine tombs open to the public, two are not to be missed. The first, **Yuling,** is the resting place of the Qing Dynasty's most powerful sovereign, Emperor Qianlong (1711–99), who ruled China for 59 years. Beyond the outer courtyards, Qianlong's burial chamber is accessible from inside Stela Hall, where an entry tunnel descends some 65 feet into the ground and ends at the first of three elaborately carved marble gates. Beyond, exquisite carvings of Buddhist images and sutras rendered in Tibetan adorn the tomb's walls and ceiling. Qianlong was laid to rest, along with his empress and two concubines, in the third and final marble vault, amid priceless offerings looted by warlords early in the 20th century.

Dingdongling was built for the infamous Empress Dowager Cixi (1835–1911). Known for her failure to halt Western imperialist encroachment, Cixi once spent funds allotted to strengthen China's navy on a traditional stone boat for the lake at the Summer Palace. Her burial compound, reputed to have cost 72 tons of silver, is the most elaborate (if not the largest) at the Eastern Qing Tombs. Many of its stone carvings are considered significant because the phoenix, which symbolized the female, is level with, or even above, the imperial (and male) dragon—a feature, ordered, no doubt, by the empress herself. A peripheral hall paneled in gold leaf displays some of the luxuries amassed by Cixi and her entourage, including embroidered gowns, jewelry, a selection of imported cigarettes, and even a coat for one of her dogs. In a bow to tourist kitsch, the compound's main hall contains a wax statue of Cixi sitting Buddha-like on a lotus petal flanked by a chambermaid and a eunuch.

The Eastern Qing Tombs are a two- to three-hour drive from the capital. The rural scenery is dramatic, and the trip is arguably the best full-day excursion outside Beijing. ⊠ *Near Malanguan, Zunhua County* ☎ *0315/694–5348* 🎟 *Y80* ⊙ *Daily 8:30–5.*

BEIJING A TO Z

To research prices, get advice from other travelers, and book travel arrangements, visit www.fodors.com.

AIR TRAVEL

Air China, China Eastern, and China Southern fly from the United States to Beijing and also provide domestic service. Northwest and United have service between Beijing and the United States. Air France, Austrian Airlines, British Airways, and KLM fly to Beijing from Paris,

Vienna, London, and Amsterdam, respectively. Japan Airlines has service to Beijing via Tokyo, and Korean Air via Seoul.

🛪 Carriers **Air China** ☎ 010/6601-7755 ⊕ www.airchina.com. **Air France** ☎ 010/6588-1388 ⊕ www.airfrance.com. **Austrian Airlines** ☎ 010/6462-2161 ⊕ www.austrianair.com. **British Airways** ☎ 010/6512-4070 ⊕ www.ba.com. **China Eastern** ☎ 010/6468-1166 ⊕ www.ce-air.com. **China Southern** ☎ 010/6459-0539 or 010/6459-6490 ⊕ www.cs-air.com/en. **Japan Airlines** ☎ 010/6513-0888 ⊕ www.jal.com. **KLM** ☎ 010/6505-3505 ⊕ www.klm.com. **Korean Air** ☎ 010/6505-0088 ⊕ www.koreanair.com. **Northwest** ☎ 010/6505-3505 ⊕ www.nwa.com. **United** ☎ 010/6463-1111 or 800/810-8282 in China ⊕ www.ual.com.

AIRPORTS
The efficient Beijing Capital International Airport is 27 km (17 mi) northeast of the city center. Departing international passengers must pay a Y90 airport tax before check-in. Passengers on domestic flights must pay Y50. Coupons are sold at booths inside the terminal and collected at the entrance to the main departure hall. After checking in, plan on long lines at immigration if you're flying in from another country, especially in the morning.

🛪 Airport Information **Beijing Capital International Airport (BJS or PEK)** ☎ 010/6456-3604 ⊕ www.bcia.com.cn/en/index.html.

TRANSFERS   The easiest way to get from the airport to Beijing is by taxi. In addition, most major hotels have representatives at the airport able to arrange a car or minivan. When departing from Beijing by plane it's best to pre-book transportation through your hotel.

The taxi line is just outside the terminal beyond a small covered parking area. The (usually long) line moves quickly. Do not accept rides from drivers who try to coax you away from the line. These privateers simply want more cash. At the head of the line, a dispatcher will give you your taxi's number, useful in case of complaints or forgotten luggage. Insist that drivers use their meters, and do not negotiate a fare. If the driver is unwilling to comply, feel free to change taxis. Most of the taxis serving the airport are large-model cars. Flag fall is Y12 (good for 3½ km) plus Y2 per additional kilometer. Passengers are expected to pay the Y10 toll for the airport expressway. If you're caught in rush-hour traffic, expect standing surcharges. A taxi to the eastern district of Beijing (including the toll) costs about Y75; the trip to the center of town costs about Y90. In light traffic it takes about 30 minutes to reach Beijing's eastern district; during rush hour, allow at least 45 minutes. For the city center expect a one-hour cab ride. After 11 PM, taxis impose a 20% late-night surcharge.

The airport bus (Y12) terminal is outside the arrivals area. Buy tickets from the booth, which is easy to spot, before you exit, then cross the road to the buses. There are two routes (A and B), clearly marked in English and Chinese. On board, stops are often announced in English and Chinese (if not, the drivers on these routes speak basic English). Route A runs between the airport and the Beijing railway station, stopping at the airport expressway/Third Ring Road intersection, Lufthansa Center, Kunlun Hotel, Great Wall Sheraton Hotel, Dongzhimen subway station/Second Ring Road, Hong Kong Macau Center (Swissôtel), Chaoyang-men subway station, and one block north of the Beijing train station/ Beijing International Hotel. Route B runs from the airport to the CAAC ticket office on Changan Dajie. It travels west along the Third Ring Road, following it south to Changan Jie. Stops include the SAS Hotel, Asian Games Village, Friendship Hotel, and Shangri-La Hotel.

BIKE TRAVEL

Although in many ways Beijing is made for pedaling, the proliferation of cars has made biking less pleasant and more dangerous. Fortunately, all of the city's main boulevards and many secondary streets have wide, well-defined bike lanes often separated from other traffic by an island with hedges or trees. If a flat tire or sudden brake failure strikes, seek out the nearest street-side mechanic (they're everywhere), easily identi-fied by their bike parts and pumps.

Bikes can be rented just about everywhere in Beijing, although your hotel and CITS (the government tourism office) are the best places from which to rent.

BUS TRAVEL

TO BEIJING Beijing is served by several long-distance bus stations. The main ones are: Beijiao, also called Deshengmen (North); Dongzhimen (Northeast); Haihutun (South); Majuan (East); and Xizhimen (West). Long-distance buses are usually quite basic—much like an old-fashioned school bus—although some overnight buses now have two cramped decks with re-clining seating or bunks.

🚌 **Beijiao** ⊠ Deshengmenwai Dajie, Xicheng District ☎ 010/6204-7096. **Dongzhi-men** ⊠ Dongzhimenwaixie Jie, Chaoyang District ☎ 010/6467-4995 or 010/6460-8131. **Haihutun** ⊠ Yongwai Chezan Lu, Fengtai District ☎ 010/6726-7149 or 010/6722-4641. **Majuan** ⊠ Guangqumenwai Dajie, Chaoyang District ☎ 010/6771-7620 or 010/6771-7622. **Xizhimen** ⊠ 2 Haidian Tou Duicun ☎ 010/6217-6075.

WITHIN BEIJING Getting on or off a Beijing city bus is often, quite literally, a fight. Buses are hot and crowded in summer and cold and crowded in winter. If you choose the bus—and you shouldn't—watch your belongings very care-fully. The Beijing Public Transportation Corporation is the city's largest bus service provider. Fares are Y1 during the day and Y2 at night.
🚌 **Beijing Public Transportation Corporation** ⊕ www.bptc.com.

CAR TRAVEL

It is easy and inexpensive to hire a car and driver for travel and sight-seeing tours in and around Beijing. Most hotels can make arrangements for you, or you can even flag down a taxi and hire the driver for the day at a similar rate, between Y350 and Y600, depending on the type of car. Most drivers do not speak English, however, so be sure to have your destination and hotel names written down in Chinese.

Renting a car and driving yourself is not a good idea—the traffic is ter-rible and it's easy to get lost. American car-rental agencies include mandatory chauffeurs as part of all rental packages. *See* Car Rental *in* Smart Travel Tips.

EMBASSIES

Australia ✉ 21 Dongzhimenwai Dajie, Chaoyang District ☎ 010/6532-2331 🖷 010/6532-6718.

Canada ✉ 19 Dongzhimenwai Dajie, Chaoyang District ☎ 010/6532-3536 🖷 010/6532-4972.

New Zealand ✉ 1 Donger Jie, Ritanlu, Chaoyang District ☎ 010/6532-2732 or 010/6532-2733 🖷 010/6532-4317.

Republic of Ireland ✉ 3 Ritan Dong Lu, Chaoyang District ☎ 010/6532-2691 🖷 010/6532-6857.

South Africa ✉ Suite C801, Lufthansa Center, 50 Liangmaqiao Lu, Chaoyang District ☎ 010/6532-0172 🖷 010/6465-1965.

United Kingdom ✉ 11 Guanghua Lu, Jianguomenwai, Chaoyang District ☎ 010/6532-1961 🖷 010/6532-1937.

United States ✉ 3 Xiushui Bei Jie, Chaoyang District ☎ 010/6532-3431 Ext. 229 or 010/6532-3831 Ext. 264 🖷 010/6532-2483.

EMERGENCIES

In case of an emergency, call your embassy first; embassy staff members are available 24 hours a day to help handle emergencies and facilitate communication with local agencies. Often the police, and fire and medical emergency staff, do not speak much English. Asia Emergency Assistance Center (AEA) has 24-hour emergency and pharmacy assistance. Probably the best place for treatment in Beijing, the Beijing United Family Health Center has 24-hour emergency services. International Medical Clinic (IMC) has 24-hour emergency and pharmacy services, as well as a dental clinic.

Doctors & Dentists Asia Emergency Assistance Center ✉ 2-1-1 Tayuan Diplomatic Office Bldg., 14 Liangmahe Nan Lu, Chaoyang District ☎ 010/6462-9112 during office hrs, 010/6462-9100 after hrs. **Beijing United Family Health Center** ✉ 2 Jiangtai Lu, near Lido Hotel, Chaoyang District ☎ 010/6433-3960, 010/6433-2345 for emergencies. **International Medical Clinic** ✉ Beijing Lufthansa Center, Regis Office Bldg., Room S110, 50 Liagmaoqiao Lu, Chaoyang District ☎ 010/6465-1561 or 010/6465-1562.

Emergency Services Fire ☎ 119. **Police** ☎ 110. **Medical Emergency** ☎ 120. **Traffic Accident** ☎ 122.

ENGLISH-LANGUAGE MEDIA

There are several monthly English-language magazines and newspapers produced for travelers and expatriates, including *Beijing This Month, Metrozine, Beijing Journal,* and *City Weekend.* They're available at hotels and restaurants around town. The Foreign Languages Bookstore and the Friendship Store carry English-language books. Most major hotels sell international newspapers and magazines, plus books about China.

Bookstores Foreign Languages Bookstore ✉ 235 Wangfujing Dajie, Dongcheng District ☎ 010/6512-6922. **Friendship Store** ✉ 17 Jianguomenwai Dajie, Chaoyang District ☎ 010/6500-3311.

PEDICAB TRAVEL

Pedicabs were once the vehicle of choice for Beijingers laden with a week's worth of groceries or tourists eager for a street's-eye city tour. Today many residents are wealthy enough to bundle their purchases into taxis, and the tourist trade has moved on to the tight schedules of air-conditioned buses. But pedicabs still can be hired outside the Friendship Store on Jianguomenwai Dajie and near major tourist sites such as Liulichang and Beihai Park. Be sure to negotiate the fare in advance, clarifying which currency will be used (yuan or dollars), whether the fare is considered a one-way or round-trip (some drivers will demand payment for a round-trip whether or not you use the pedicab for the return journey), and whether it is for one person or two. Fares start at Y10.

SIGHTSEEING TOURS

Every major hotel can arrange guided tours to sights outside Beijing. Among the hotel-based travel agencies are Beijing Panda Tour and China Swan International Tours. China International Travel Service (CITS), the official government agency, can arrange tours. New travel agencies are springing up all the time in Beijing; ask at your hotel about alternatives to CITS.

🎟 Fees & Schedules **Beijing Panda Tour** ✉ Holiday Inn Crowne Plaza, 48 Wangfu-jing Dajie, Dongcheng District ☎ 010/6513-3388 Ext. 1212 ⊕ www.pandatourchina.com. **China International Travel Service** ✉ 28 Jianguomenwai Dajie, Chaoyang District ☎ 010/6515-8565 🖷 010/6515-8603 ⊕ www.citsusa.com. **China Swan International Tours** ✉ Rm. 718, Beijing Capital Times Square, 88 Changan Jie, Xicheng District ☎ 010/8391-3058 ⊕ www.china-swan.com/english.htm.

BIKE TOURS CycleChina leads guided one-day bicycling tours around Beijing and the Great Wall on weekends.

🎟 Fees & Schedules **CycleChina** ☎ 1391/188-6524 ⊕ www.cyclechina.com.

PEDICAB TOURS The Beijing Hutong Tourist Agency offers the only guided pedicab tour of Beijing's back alleys, with glimpses of buildings usually closed to the public. This half-day trip winds its way through what was once Beijing's most prestigious neighborhood (Houhai), stops at the Drum and Bell towers, and finishes with tea at Prince Gong's Palace. Advance reservations are recommended. Tours, which begin on Di'anmen Xidajie near the back entrance of Beihai Park, start at 9 and 2 daily, and cost about Y180 per person.

🎟 Fees & Schedules **Beijing Hutong Tourist Agency** ✉ 26 Di'anmen Xidajie, Dongcheng District ☎ 010/6612-3236 🖷 010/6400-2787.

SUBWAY TRAVEL

The subway is a good way to travel if you want to avoid Beijing's increasingly frequent traffic jams. However, with only two lines, Beijing's subway service is limited. One line circles Beijing beneath the Second Ring Road and the other runs east–west from the city center to the western and eastern suburbs. The lines meet at Fuxingmen. The subway runs from 5 AM to midnight daily. Fares are Y3 per ride for any distance. Stations are marked in both Chinese and English.

TAXIS

There are three classes of taxis in Beijing. The cheapest grade of taxi is the *xiali*, a domestically produced car reminiscent of the first Honda hatchbacks. Tall people find xialis cramped. Flag fall for these taxis is Y10 for the first 4 km (2½ mi) and Y1.2 per kilometer thereafter. The next grade of taxi is similar to the xiali but is generally cleaner and more comfortable; it's often a Citroën or Volkswagen. Flag fall for these taxis is Y10 for the first 4 km (2½ mi) and Y1.6 per kilometer thereafter. At the top end are the sedans found waiting at the airport, major hotels, and large tourist sights. They're clean, comfortable, and still cheap compared with Western cabs. Flag fall is Y12 for the first 3½ km (2 mi) and Y2 per kilometer thereafter, depending on the vehicle. For all taxis, a 20% nighttime surcharge kicks in at 11 PM. Be sure to check that the meter has been engaged to avoid fare negotiations at your destination.

🚹 **Taxi Complaints** ☎ 010/6835-1150 🖶 010/6831-5960.

TRAIN TRAVEL

Beijing is served by four stations: the Beijing Zhan (Main) and Beijing Xi Zhan (West) stations (both of which have International Passenger Booking offices for foreigners), and the Beijing Bei Zhan (North) and Beijing Nan Zhan (South) stations. Most domestic routes depart from the massive Beijing Xi Zhan, Beijing's most modern station. Some major-city routes depart from the Beijing Zhan, as do international routes to Hong Kong or Siberia. Trains are directed to different stations depending on the intricate rail system and not on their travel destinations.

Tickets, which are sold up to five days in advance, can be purchased at all stations for trips that leave from that station, and you can also buy tickets at FESCO Travel Service in the China World Trade Center. Book early to ensure a seat. Ticket office hours are 5:30 AM–7:30 AM, 8 AM–5:30 PM, and 7 PM–12:30 AM.

🚹 Train Information **Beijing Bei Zhan** North Station ✉ 1 Xizhimenwai Beibinhelu, Xicheng District ☎ 010/6223-1003. **Beijing Nan Zhan** South Station ✉ Yongdingmen, Chongwen District ☎ 010/6303-0031. **Beijing Xi Zhan** West Station ✉ Lianhuachi Dong Lu, Haidian District ☎ 010/5182-6253. **Beijing Zhan** Main Station ✉ Beijing Zhan Jie, Dongcheng District ☎ 010/6563-3262. **FESCO Travel Service** ✉ Level 1, China World Trade Center, Jianguimenwai Dajie, Chaoyang District ☎ 010/6461-4441.

VISITOR INFORMATION

China International Travel Service (CITS), an official government agency, maintains offices in many hotels and at some tourist venues. The Beijing Tourism Administration maintains a 24-hour hot line for tourist inquiries and complaints, with operators fluent in English.

🚹 Tourist Information **Beijing Tourism Administration hot line** ☎ 010/6513-0828. **China International Travel Service** ✉ 28 Jianguomenwai Dajie, Chaoyang District ☎ 010/ 6515-8565 🖶 010/6515-8603.

NORTH CENTRAL CHINA
SPIRITUAL & TEMPORAL LEGACIES

2

EXPLORE THE SHOPS AND STALLS
of Tianjin's Ancient Culture Street ⇨*p.81*

CREEP INTO THE BUDDHIST ART CAVES
of the fading Dragon Gate Grottoes ⇨*p.104*

EAT YOUR WAY THROUGH THE DELIGHTS
of Tianjin's eclectic Food Street ⇨*p.81*

STEP INTO THE HOME OF MARTIAL ARTS
at the Buddhist Shaolin Monastery ⇨*p.102*

TOUR THE OLD SONG DYNASTY CAPITAL
of the now-Muslim town of Kaifeng ⇨*p.102*

TRY THE WIENER SCHNITZEL AND BEER
at the international Bader Brauhaus ⇨*p.83*

By David
Murphy
Updated by
Keming Liu

NORTH CENTRAL CHINA IS THE CRADLE OF CHINESE CIVILIZATION, held between the Yellow River in the south and the Great Wall in the north. Many dynasties have made their capitals here and it is the seat of Chinese religion and philosophy. There are ancient Buddhist grottoes at Luoyang and Datong, and the birthplace and mansion of Confucius is at Qufu. On the coast, foreign influences, from the Bavarian architecture in Qingdao to the lovely seaside resort of Beidaihe, established by vacationing diplomats and missionaries at the end of the 19th century, lend the region a cosmopolitan tinge.

Han Chinese civilization originated along the banks of the Yellow River near where the cities of Luoyang and Zhengzhou now stand, in the small but populous province of Henan. The name of the province, which literally translates as "south of the river," is a constant reminder of the river's importance. Traces of what was, 36 centuries ago, the capital of the Shang Dynasty can still be faintly seen in modern-day Zhengzhou, Henan's capital. Archaeological finds suggest that another capital in the same area predated even this early city. The river itself still holds a certain fascination, largely for its potential destructive power.

West of Zhengzhou, Henan harbors the starting point of another aspect of Chinese civilization. Buddhism, brought to China in the 1st century AD, found its first home in White Horse Temple, on the outskirts of present-day Luoyang. The religion, once it was translated and adjusted a bit to Chinese sensibilities, gained enormous popularity, inspiring Henan's extraordinary Dragon Gate Grottoes. In the 6th and 7th centuries AD, artisans carved thousands of Buddhist figures into a stretch of mountain faces near Luoyang. Time has not been kind to these astounding artworks, but despite foreign looting and the ravages of wind and rain, they remain one of the region's most important and impressive sights.

Northward in Shanxi, Datong has its own similarly impressive grottoes. About 50,000 statues were cut into a 1-km (½-mi) length of cliffs in the 5th century, and it is now Shanxi's most important site. This region was the cultural and political center of the state of Qin. As a northern frontier on the Great Wall, it had the important job of defending the state from nomadic tribes of the north. These days Shanxi's strategic importance lies in its coal mines.

Jutting out into the Yellow Sea, the Shandong Peninsula has long been the beneficiary and victim of the Yellow River, which makes the region fertile for farming and susceptible to flooding. The holy Mt. Tai and the birthplace of Confucius, at Qufu, are two of Shandong's sites with deep relevance in Asian history. Across China, Korea, and Japan, the old sage's influential teachings are still clearly evident. Old colonial settlements on the coast brought in the first railroads and missionaries to China. In particular, Qingdao's crumbling Bavarian architecture and seaside strolls are charming.

An industrial powerhouse and trading way station, Tianjin is one of China's new engines of capitalism. But unlike Hong Kong or Shanghai's shiny environs, Tianjin still evokes the more gritty side of enterprise. Even the old neighborhoods that were once European concessions are sooty

The best way to explore North Central China is by train. Overnight sleepers connect Beijing with such destinations as Qingdao and Luoyang. Shorter trips include Beidaihe, Chengde, Datong, and Tianjin.

Numbers in the text correspond to numbers in the margin and on the North Central China map.

2

If you have
3 days

From Beijing head east to **Shanhaiguan** ⑩ ⌐ where you can visit unforgettable structures like the **First Gate Under Heaven,** the eastern tip of the Great Wall, and the legendary **Dragon Head.** Continue to the seaside resort town of **Beidaihe** ⑨ on the second day and finish at the summer resort of **Chengde** ⑧, where you can catch a train back to Beijing.

Alternatively you can travel south to **Luoyang** ㉑ and visit the fantastically carved **Dragon Gate Grottoes,** and if it's spring, get a glimpse of budding peonies before heading back east on a sleeper train to **Mt. Tai** ㉓, one of China's holiest mountains. On your second day take a bus out to visit Confucius's hometown of **Qufu** ㉔. On the final day head east six hours by train to explore **Qingdao** ㉕–㉛, where you can relax on a beach or explore the German-influenced, beer-making port town.

If you have
5 days

Choose either three-day itinerary above. If you take the first route you can extend it another two days by adding on an overnight stay in **Datong** ⑪ and visiting the nearby **Yungang Grottoes** ⑫. If you take the second tour you can extend it by spending the night in **Qingdao** ㉕–㉛ and making a side trip to the sacred Taoist mountain of **Laoshan** ㉜.

If you have
8 or
more
days

To get the full flavor of the region and see all the major sights, combine the two itineraries above. Start by taking the train south to **Luoyang** ㉑ ⌐, making side trips to nearby temples and monasteries and the **Yellow River Park** ⑰ and spending a day and night in the archaeologically rich town of **Zhengzhou** ⑯. Take the train northeast to **Mt. Tai** ㉓ and a bus to **Qufu** ㉔ before heading east to **Qingdao** ㉕–㉛ for another two or three days. From there head north to **Tianjin** ①–⑤ for shopping and city bustle, and on to the more relaxing **Chengde** ⑧. If there's time, take the train west to **Datong** ⑪ and see the grottoes before heading back to Beijing. You could easily spend two weeks or more just visiting all the highlights in North Central China.

and bursting with chaotic storefronts. Tianjin does offer interesting antiques, a great dumpling restaurant, and a quiet riverside stroll.

The southern flatlands of Hebei are crowded with industrial towns. But Chengde, an old imperial retreat in the mountains, has a fantastic collection of Chinese architecture in a variety of styles including Han, Mongol, Qing, Tibetan, and others. On the Bohai Gulf, today's leaders hold Communist Party getaways and policy brainstorming sessions at Beidaihe. Beidaihe also has a number of sanatoriums for locals and a tasteful resort for foreigners. Up the coast at Shanhaiguan, the Great Wall starts west from the sea to climb its first mountain.

Exploring North Central China

North Central China is the breadbasket of China, situated in the heartland near the capital, Beijing. To the northeast are Chengde, the summer resort of top members of the Communist Party, and Beidaihe, where the famed Great Wall juts out into the sea like the head of a dragon. In the southern and southeastern parts of the region lie Tianjin, the bustling industrial port city with its long international heritage; its burgeoning rival port city, Qingdao; Zhengzhou, where China's martial arts originated; and, perhaps most important, Confucius's hometown of Qufu. Hotels are plentiful at a broad spectrum of room rates and the diverse array of restaurants in the region offer local specialties, like baked pancakes covered with sesame seeds and stuffed with mushrooms and beef. Thanks to well-developed highways and railways in the region, it's easy to sample history, culture, great food, and beautiful scenery all in one area.

About the Hotels & Restaurants

Along the coast, seafood predominates on restaurant menus, and you'll often be asked to choose your fare while it's still swimming in the tank. In addition to Chinese, Japanese, and Korean food, the occasional German or Austrian eatery remains in towns like Tianjin and Qingdao, remnants of long-gone colonies and trade concessions.

Most of the large cities have expensive hotels with all the creature comforts and business facilities you might need. Towns like Luoyang, Datong, Chengde, and Shanhaiguan still have good accommodations but are a bit rough on the edges. Luoyang in April, when the peonies are in bloom, is particularly crowded.

WHAT IT COSTS In Yuan					
	$$$$	$$$	$$	$	¢
RESTAURANTS	over 165	100–165	50–99	25–49	under 25
HOTELS	over 1,800	1,400–1,800	1,100–1,399	700–1,099	under 700

Restaurant prices are for a main course, excluding tax and tips. Hotel prices are for a standard double room, including taxes.

Timing

Spring and fall are the best seasons in North Central China. In summer it can be unpleasantly hot, particularly in grimy cities like Tianjin and Zhengzhou. Although this makes the beach most tempting, be warned—Beidaihe in July can be as crowded as a Beijing bus. March and April are good months in Luoyang, famed for its peonies. Aside from museums that close Monday, most other tourist attractions are open daily. Some places, such as the summer resort of Chengde, however, may not be as much fun in winter. The Great Wall, on the other hand, takes on a spectacular splendor when covered in snow.

2

Bottoms Up

China's northern cuisine features hearty red meat and poultry, including the famous Peking duck. But just as essential to a meal is a cold Tsingtao beer or a glass of the local *lao bai gaar* (rice liquor). Each area of North Central China has its own vintage but all sport the name "lao bai gaar," which literally means "old, white, and dry." Chinese custom has it that close friendship is demonstrated by one's generosity in pouring wine and one's willingness to down it, especially at a banquet or large gathering. But pace yourself: the custom could soon put you out of commission. Locals use drinking as a test to help them judge a stranger's character. For example, if your face remains pale after a few glasses, you are considered a Machiavellian schemer. If your face turns red with heat, you are deemed a friend who can be trusted and relied upon. Shandong people are trustworthy because, legend has it, they have yet to find a pale-face drinker there. For an all-out immersion in the great drinking customs (frequently depicted in classical literature), try Qingdao's International Beer Festival, where you are likely to be challenged by the locals to empty your cup. The back-and-forth custom of offering toasts to newcomers is a common reflex of Chinese hospitality.

Get in Gear

A visit to this region wouldn't be complete if at some point you didn't hop on a rental bike and explore the landscape on two wheels, just as many locals do. Glide along the winding path lined with ancient evergreens at the Confucius family mansion in Qufu. Work up an appetite by pedaling around Chengde. And Qingdao's streets are wide and have bicycle lanes so you can pedal out to nearby beaches. Rental bikes are plentiful and inexpensive. In general, the longer you rent a bike, the better deal you get, so ask about daily or multiple-day packages. Aside from a refundable deposit of Y300 to Y400, a half-day rental costs from Y40 to Y50 and a full day costs about Y60 to Y70. For an hour's rental, it costs about Y10. Local CTS and travel agencies can also arrange group bicycle tours with guides.

Pamper Yourself

When visiting North Central China, be sure to make a trip to one of the many natural hot springs around Qingdao and at mountain resorts near Chengde. With increased tourism and the growing wealth of the Chinese people, indoor spas have begun springing up, too. Most are clean and provide professional massage. Spa services at your disposal include toenail clipping, foot reflexology, and neck or whole-body massage. For a two- or three-hour treatment in indoor spa centers, you will receive a whole body scrub, time in a steam room or sauna, a foot reflexology session, or massage (adding milk to your massage is usually an extra Y5). You can often finish up by retiring to a karaoke lounge. The whole package can run anywhere between Y160 and Y350.

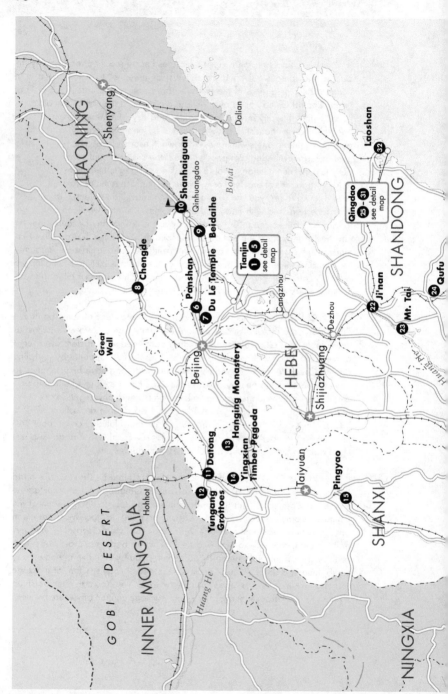

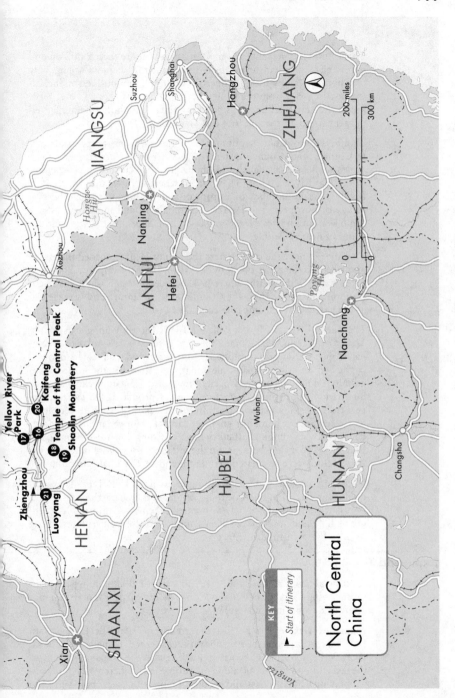

Suzhou

Shanghai

JIANGSU

Hangzhou

ZHEJIANG

Hongze Hu

Nanjing

200 miles

300 km

Kaizhou

ANHUI

Hefei

Poyang Hu

Yellow River
Park

Kaifeng

20

17

16

Nanchang

18 Temple of the Central Peak

19 Shaolin Monastery

Wuhan

Zhengzhou

HENAN

21

Luoyang

HUBEI

HUNAN

Changsha

SHAANXI

Xian

Yangtze

KEY

▶ *Start of itinerary*

North Central China

TIANJIN

The Tianjin municipality has a population of more than 9 million and a thriving seaport with an extensive hinterland that includes Beijing, only two hours away by train. Numerous multinational businesses, including nearly 1,000 from the United States alone, have set up here. Most are in the new satellite city, known as Teda (Tianjin Economic Development Area), to the south of old Tianjin.

Tianjin is one of China's four municipalities, meaning it reports directly to China's State Council instead of to a provincial government. (The others are Beijing, Shanghai, and Chongqing.) The city occupies the banks of the Hai River, 50 km (31 mi) from where it flows into the Gulf of Bohai. A large number of European-style buildings survive here, a legacy of European and Japanese colonialism, and in spring and autumn Tianjin's narrow, leafy streets offer an alternative to the wide avenues of nearby Beijing.

Tianjin signifies "the point where the Son of Heaven forded the river" and refers to the route taken by the Ming Dynasty emperor Yongle to a key battle in the south, where he succeeded in establishing his reign, beginning in 1403. Thereafter Tianjin grew in stature and was viewed as the gateway to the imperial capital of Beijing.

The Second Anglo-Chinese war, in 1858, forced Beijing to sign the Treaty of Tianjin, which made the city a treaty port similar to Shanghai. Concessions were established by the British and the French, followed by the Belgians, the Germans, the Italians, the Russians, the Austro-Hungarians, and the Japanese. The city they called Tientsin became a major international port and manufacturing center, producing the Tientsin carpets that are still a major export. In the first part of the 20th century it was a temporary home for engineer Herbert Hoover in his pre-presidential career. Founding fathers of modern China Sun Yat-sen and Zhou Enlai also spent time here, as did the last emperor, whose parties in the Astor Hotel were re-created here in the movie *The Last Emperor*.

In modern times Tianjin was badly damaged in the 1976 Tangshan earthquake but was rebuilt in time to benefit from the Open-Door policy. Its port is the biggest in northern China, and the new California-like suburb of Teda contains some of China's most successful joint ventures among its 3,000 foreign-funded enterprises.

Exploring Tianjin

An official count reckons there are more than 1,000 buildings in Tianjin surviving from the colonial period. The old quarter is a virtual museum of European architecture.

a good walk

From the Hyatt Regency hotel, at the crossing of Jiefang Bei Lu and Qufu Dao, head north along the riverside promenade, Tai'erzhuang Lu. A block away is the Astor Hotel, worth a quick visit as the occasional home of the last emperor. Continue along the promenade, where you'll find people playing Chinese chess and groups of pigeon fanciers comparing and selling birds. Here you can also stroll by lawns with topiary animals, fountains, and small cafés. The promenade has an inimitable view across the river of surviving 19th-century European-style colonial mansions.

Make a detour on Chengde Dao to see a collection of Chinese art in the city's **Art Museum** ➊ ▶, then continue along the waterfront to Beima Lu. Follow it for a block to reach **Ancient Culture Street** ➋. Explore the shops and the Tianhou Temple, then take the main road, Dongma Lu, south until it becomes Heping Lu. Turn right on Rongji Dajie to **Food Street** ➌, where you can stop for lunch. Return to Heping Lu. In British concession times, this was Cambridge Road, lined with fashionable shops and banks, many of which are still here, albeit with different owners. One classic reminder is the **Quanyechang Department Store** ➍, modeled after Harrod's. Two blocks farther on is Zhongxin Park, with playgrounds and tree-shaded benches surrounded by some grand old buildings. From here you can take the modern avenue Yingkou Dao heading north back to the promenade, or south to **St. Paul's Catholic Church** ➎.

TIMING Assuming you like browsing the museum, Culture Street, and the church, this walk should take about 3½ hours, plus an hour if you include lunch.

What to See

➋ **Ancient Culture Street** (Gu Wenhua Jie). During foreign concession days
Fodor'sChoice the area in the north of the city was a traditional "Chinatown." In the
★ 1980s Tianjin's mayor decided to restore some of the old buildings with their carved wooden facades and ornate balconies hung with silk-banner advertisements. Some contain shops selling antiques, reproductions, carpets, swords, paintings, books, coins, and assorted craft items. Others are restaurants serving such local delicacies as *baozi* (dumplings filled with meat and vegetables) and soup. At one end of the street is the **Tianhou Temple** (Tianhou Gong), dedicated to the mythological goddess of seafarers, with prayer pavilions set in garden courtyards. ⊠ *Beima Lu* ⌦ *Free* ☉ *Daily 9* AM–11 PM.

▶ ➊ **Art Museum** (Yishu Bowuguan). The setting of this collection is itself a prime exhibit, being a restored colonial mansion that recalls the architecture of the belle epoque. Attractively displayed are some fine examples of traditional Chinese paintings and calligraphy on the first floor; folk art, particularly elaborate giant paper kites, on the second; and temporary exhibitions on the third. ⊠ *12 Chengde Dao* ☎ *022/2312–2770* ⌦ *Y5* ☉ *Tues.–Sun. 8:30* AM–11 AM *and 1:30* PM–4 PM.

★ ➌ **Food Street** (Shi Pin Jie). Actually more of a food city, this three-story block contains more than 100 shops selling food and drink from all over China and around the world. The dishes range from donkey meat and burnt rice to pizzas and hamburgers. *Shao mai,* which literally means "burn" and "rice," is a regional specialty that has become popular among many Chinese food connoisseurs. Legend has it that burnt rice has a medicinal effect of helping the digesting system. The complex has pagoda roofs and city-gate-like entrances bearing the characters for "People's lives depend on food." ⊠ *Rongji Dajie* ☉ *Daily 6* AM–*midnight.*

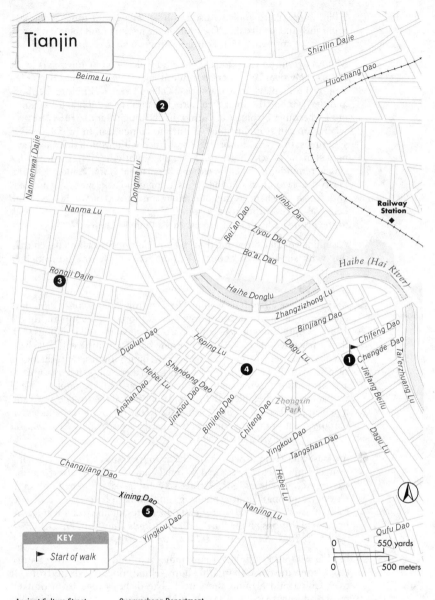

Tianjin

Shizilin Dajie

Beima Lu

Huochang Dao

Nanmenwai Dajie

Dongma Lu

Nanma Lu

Jinbu Dao

Bei'an Dao

Ziyou Dao

Bo'ai Dao

Railway Station ◆

Rongji Dajie ③

Haihe Donglu

Haihe (Hai River)

Zhangzizhong Lu

Binjiang Dao

Chifeng Dao

Chengde Dao

Duolun Dao

Heping Lu

Dagu Lu

① ◄

Tai'erzhuang Lu

Jielang Beilu

Shandong Dao

Hebei Lu

Jinzhou Dao

④

Chifeng Dao

Zhongxin Park

Anshan Dao

Binjiang Dao

Yingkou Dao

Tangshan Dao

Dagu Lu

Changjiang Dao

Hebei Lu

Nanjing Lu

Xining Dao ⑤

Qufu Dao

Yingkou Dao

| 0 | 550 yards |
| 0 | 500 meters |

KEY

► Start of walk

Ancient Culture Street
(Gu Wenhua Jie) **2**

Art Museum
(Yishu Bowuguan) **1**

Food Street
(Shi Pin Jie) **3**

Quanyechang Department
Store (Quanyechang
Baihuoshangchang) **4**

St. Paul's Catholic Church
(Xikai Jiaotang) **5**

❹ Quanyechang Department Store (Quanyechang Baihuoshangchang). Built in the 1920s and modeled after London's Harrod's, this was a landmark of the old British concession. Its handsome facade restored, today it's an upmarket store with imported brand-name fashions, Chinese luxury items, and a selection of arts and crafts. Other grand colonial buildings in the neighborhood that have been renovated include City of London–style banks now used by Chinese financial institutions, uniform tile-paneled apartment blocks, and trading houses filled with the offices of multinational firms. Many have candy-stripe window awnings. ⊠ *Heping Lu at Binjiang Dao* ⊙ *Daily 10–10.*

❺ St. Paul's Catholic Church (Xikai Jiaotang). Built by French Jesuits in 1917, this extraordinary building is a landmark, with its twin domed towers and tan-and-cream brickwork. Amazingly, it survived the Cultural Revolution with no more than a broken window and in recent years has been beautifully restored. It is regularly full for Sunday services and well attended at daily morning mass. ⊠ *Xining Dao* ⊙ *Mon.–Sat. 9 AM–11 AM and 2 PM–4 PM.*

Where to Stay & Eat

Tianjin was once known as the spot where nine rivers flowed together to become the Hai River, so it's not surprising that local specialties include fish, shrimp, and crab. Traditional dishes feature lettuce, shrimp, crab, and shark fins.

★ $$ ✕ **Maobuwen Restaurant.** Famous for its varied types of dumplings, Maobuwen attracts large crowds of both Chinese and foreign dumpling-lovers. These popular Tianjin snacks are made mainly of flour and there are three types: fried, porridge, and sweet food. The stuffed buns, Guifaxiang fried dough twists, and ear-shape fried cakes can be any meal of the day. ⊠ *No. 58, Food Street, Heping District* ☎ *022/2727–0029* ▤ *No credit cards.*

$$ ✕ **Tianjin Kobe Restaurant.** Tianjin is the sister city to Kobe, Japan, and this restaurant combines the names and flavors of both cities. Sushi is served on low kneeling tables with tatami mats for seating. Buckwheat noodle or soba noodle soup in winter is a must, best with tender double-cooked beef or chicken. Smoking is allowed so specify your seating preference upon entry. You can ask for a regular table if you are not comfortable sitting in the lotus position for a whole meal. ⊠ *No. 28, Food Street, Heping District* ☎ *022/2727–0955* ▤ *AE, DC, MC, V.*

★ $–$$ ✕ **Bader Brauhaus.** On the third floor of Kiesslings Bakery (founded in 1911), this tastefully furnished restaurant has wood floors and on the walls hang scenes from old Tianjin. Behind the bar, which occupies the middle of the floor, two large copper vats contain the house's smoky and robust special brew. The menu lists dishes from 10 countries and includes tortillas and Wiener schnitzel. Diners are mostly Chinese who are here to experience something different from the norm. On the floor below is a hotpot restaurant. ⊠ *33 Zhejiang Lu* ☎ *022/2332–1603* ▤ *No credit cards.*

¢–$$ ✕ **Goubili Restaurant.** Tianjin's most famous restaurant is the proud purveyor of the Tianjin-style baozi (steamed dumplings filled with chopped meat and vegetables). The ground floor of the three-story restaurant serves fast food (fast baozi). The second and third floors are a mixture of large dining areas and smaller, more exclusive rooms. Both serve regular Chinese food as well as baozi. ⊠ *77 Shandong Lu* ☎ *022/ 2730–2540* ▤ No credit cards.

$$ ▣ **Crystal Palace.** Another of the city's funky Bauhaus architectural offerings, this upscale hotel looks like two beached cruise ships butted up against Yingbin Lake. Multiple lodging options are available, including office rooms and posh suites. If you are here on business, the all-inclusive facilities will make the trip productive, but if you are simply vacationing it is a bit out of the way from downtown and main local attractions which will necessitate a vehicle or an excellent grasp of the bus system. The hotel also features a wide array of dining options ranging from traditional Chinese to French and Italian. ⊠ *28 You Yi (Friendship) Lu. Hexi District, 300061* ☎ *022/2835–6888* 🖷 *022/2835–8886* 🛏 *346 rooms* ⌂ *3 restaurants, tennis court, gym, bar, business services* ▤ *AE, DC, MC, V.*

$$ ▣ **Sheraton Hotel.** This is one of the better lodging options in town, especially for the price. Located just a 10-minute walk from the hubbub of downtown, it is situated in a rather quiet neighborhood. The spacious rooms exude modern luxury, but maintain a bit of charm with numerous Asian accents. Many rooms feature views of the surrounding lake, so be sure to ask for one. The restaurants serve Japanese, Chinese, and Western food. The World Economy Trade and Exhibition Centre is a quick walk down the road, as is the Water Park, Tianjin's largest park with pavilions, towers, terraces, curved and arch bridges, and dikes lined with weeping willows. ⊠ *Zi Jinshan Lu, 300074* ☎ *022/ 2334–3388* 🖷 *022/2335–8740* ⊕ *www.sheraton.com* 🛏 *230 rooms* ⌂ *3 restaurants, minibars, cable TV, tennis court, pool, gym, bowling, bar, business services* ▤ *AE, DC, MC, V.*

$–$$ ▣ **Astor Hotel.** This charming hotel is the perfect option for anyone wanting to add a bit of history to a vacation. The British erected the colonial-style hotel in 1863 along the Hai River. For an authentic feel for colonial times, ask for room in the old wing which once received dignitaries such as Sun Yat-sen, Herbert Hoover, and Puyi, China's last emperor. The rooms in the new wing are more modern, with roomy and streamlined furnishings. The lobby of the hotel serves as a history museum, with murals, plaques, and interesting relics on display. The restaurants offer Chinese, Italian, and international cuisines. ⊠ *33 Tai'erzhuang Lu, 300040* ☎ *022/2331–1688* 🖷 *022/2331–6282* 🛏 *195 rooms, 28 suites* ⌂ *3 restaurants, minibars, cable TV, gym, bar, business services* ▤ *AE, DC, MC, V.*

$–$$ ▣ **Hyatt Regency Tianjin.** One of the more established high-class hotels in Tianjin, the Hyatt backs onto the Hai River. Old-style green Chinese tiles gird the upper floors of this Hong Kong–managed hotel, making it something of a landmark. Inside is a spacious three-story atrium lobby. Standard rooms are bright, clean, and comfortable and are equipped with a business desk and satellite TV. The restaurants serve Chinese, Japanese, and Western cuisines. ⊠ *219 Jiefang Bei Lu, 300042* ☎ *022/2330–1234* 🖷 *022/2331–1234* ⊕ *www.hyatt.com* 🛏 *428 rooms* ⌂ *5 restaurants, minibars, cable TV, gym, bar, laundry service, business services* ▤ *AE, DC, MC, V.*

$ ▦ **Holiday Inn.** This hotel is exceptionally comfortable, even if the exterior is ugly—two mammoth towers surrounded by an expressway. Once you're inside you won't hear the roar of cars along the riverfront highway just outside the door. Room options include suites with kitchenettes and separate sitting areas. Executive floors are available. The hotel also has numerous dining choices. Tourist attractions like Ancient Culture Street and Da Bei Temple are within walking distance, even though it's situated on the outskirts of downtown. ⊠ *288 Zhongshan Lu, 300141* ☎ *022/2628-8888* 🖷 *022/2628-6666* ⊕ *www.basshotels. com/holiday-inn* ↩ *265 rooms, 21 suites* ⚴ *3 restaurants, pool, gym, bar* ⊟ *AE, DC, MC, V.*

Nightlife

As in all major cities in China, bars, night markets, and karaoke parlors are all over the city. In summer, a walk along the river is most pleasant. The Food Street is alive with raucous crowds, boisterous children, and young lovers strolling the block. Winter warrants an indoor indulgence such as a massage parlor for a session of foot reflexology. These massage parlors are often open 24 hours and some parlors serve wine and snacks. All are equipped with cable TV and karaoke.

Sgt. Pepper's. Even though it's been decades since Sergeant Pepper taught the band to play, this lively bar still honors the music. Nightly live bands amp the atmosphere with popular songs from China and the West, including plenty of Beatles tunes. This ranks as one of Tianjin's most popular clubs with foreign travelers, partly because of its convenient riverside location behind a long row of highbrow hotels. Most drinks average around Y8. ⊠ *62 Jiefang Bei Lu* ☎ *022/2722-1111.*

Shopping

In the early Qing Dynasty, Tianjin's trade developed rapidly and Beidaguan, Heping Lu, and Xiaobailou were the three main commercial areas in the city. As the local economy has developed, some commercial areas have been rebuilt and reinvented while new commercial areas have grown, such as the Ancient Cultural Street. In addition, the city has developed a batch of specialized markets including the Antique Market. Tianjin boasts many unique handicrafts such as Yangliuqing (meaning "everlasting willow green") New Year paintings, colored clay sculptures by the Zhang family, kites by the Wei family, and Tianjin tapestries and carpets. Most of these items can be found on Ancient Cultural Street.

The **Antique Market** is a shopping spectacle of hawking vendors. Some consider this Tianjin at its best. Shoulder-to-shoulder vendors with high-pitched voices stand under umbrellas, extolling the values of vases, scrolls, teapots, ceramics, jades, and Mao memorabilia. Be sure to haggle: the vendors' initial prices are always too high. ⊠ *Shenyang Dao south of Heping Lu* ☎ *022/2835-8812* ⊙ *Daily 9 AM–2 PM.*

Isetan is a mountain of a store, five floors of shopping wonder. Instead of the usual Chinese offerings, it emphasizes Japanese and Western products. All of the latest fashions by big-name designers are well stocked here. You can also find cosmetics, home accessories, and kitchenware. The electronic options are plenty and include DVD players, boom boxes, and video games. You'll find most of these items at home, but not at these prices. ⊠ *209 Nanjing Lu* ☎ *022/2722–1111.*

The **Tianjin Quanyechang Bazaar** is a must-see for any visitor to Tianjin. Situated at the intersection of Binjiang Dao and Heping Lu, Quanyechang is an old commercial establishment built in 1928. A large-scale renovation was carried out in 1994, which expanded the shopping center's business space. The bazaar has 10 floors with one underground. You'll find no shortage of clothes and electronics. Home furnishing goods like prints and paintings (scrolls, small- and large-size canvas paintings, and watercolors on paper) are available as well. Parking can be a hassle, so take a taxi even if you have a car. ⊠ *172 Heping Lu, at Binjiang Dao* ☎ *022/2272–5916.*

Side Trips from Tianjin

❻ Panshan. These magical mountains are one of the area's greatest sites. Five main mountains are the dominant feature, highlighted by Moon Hanging Peak, a sheer wall of vertigo-inducing rock. Thick pine forests, echoing ravines, tumbling waterfalls, and 72 ancient temples and pagodas provide the ultimate backdrop for hiking. Summer's wildflower season and fall's color show are the prime times to visit. ✥ *75 km (46 mi) east of Beijing, 150 km (93 mi) north of Tianjin; trains and buses run from Tianjin daily* ☎ *022/2835–8812.*

★ **❼ Du Le Temple** (Du Le Si). In a nation known for its temples, few, if any, generate as much attention as this National Historic Site dating back to the Tang Dynasty. This complex of art and architecture includes the **Eleven-Faced Guanyin statue** which honors the goddess of mercy, and at 52 feet is one of the largest clay statues in China. Look for the statue stretching three flights to the octagonal ceiling of the Guanyin Pavilion. Colorful Buddhist murals line the interior walls of the pavilion, including portraits of Ming Dynasty guardians with three heads, six arms, and hideously mean eyes. ✥ *3 hrs (100 km (62 mi)) north of Tianjin municipality by train* ☎ *022/2835–8812.*

Tianjin A to Z

To research prices, get advice from other travelers, and book travel arrangements, visit www.fodors.com.

AIRPORT

Tianjin Airport (TSN) is a half hour southeast of the city center. There are regular flights to and from Hong Kong and other major Chinese cities, as well as South Korea.

🚹 **Airport Information Tianjin Airport** ⊠ Southeast of Tianjing near Zhanggui village ☎ 022/2490–2929.

TAXIS

Taxis are the easiest way to get around the city. The meter starts at Y10 for the first 5 km, and Y2 for each kilometer after that.

TRAIN TRAVEL
There are a half dozen departures to and arrivals from Beijing every day. Trains connect Tianjin to Nanjing (14 hrs), Shanghai (18 hrs), Qingdao (8 hrs), and other cities regularly.

🚈 Train Information **Tianjin Beizhan or Tianjin North Train Station** ✉ Intersection of Zhongshan Lu and Zhongshan Bei Lu ☎ 022/2430-6444.

Tianjin Xizhan or Tianjin West Train Station ✉ North end of Dafeng Lu.

VISITOR INFORMATION
🛈 Tourist Information **CITS** ✉ 22 Youyi Lu, opposite Friendship Store ☎ 022/2835-8499 🖷 022/2835-0823.

Tianjin Tourism Bureau ✉ 18 Youyi Lu, Hexi District, 300074 ☎ 022/2835-8812 🖷 022/2835-2324.

HEBEI

The Hebei region wraps itself around the cities of Beijing and Tianjin, with mountains to the north and plains to the south. This was China's old frontier, and the Great Wall wanders among the mountains. There are no major cities of note in the bleak and industrial flatlands but several small towns rich in history, with refreshing clean air, do make excellent short trips from Beijing: Chengde, with its palace and temples, and the seaside resorts of Beidaihe and nearby Shanhaiguan, where the Great Wall meets the sea.

Chengde

 4½ hrs (175 km [109 mi]) by train northeast of Beijing; 7 hrs (470 km [291 mi]) by train southwest of Shenyang.

The city of Chengde, in the Yanshan Mountains, is one of the first ancient cities to be recorded by the government and currently is one of the country's "10 esteemed national-class scenic spots," according to a government source. The town is home to one of the largest intact imperial gardens in China, built in the 17th and 18th centuries as an emblem of national unity. There are several places of interest in and around Chengde, such as the magnificent Mountain Resort and the Eight Outer Monasteries. Aside from its historical sites and cultural relics, Chengde also offers tourists great relaxation havens such as the Qibao Wenquan or Qibao Hot Spring. Tourist trains and buses shuttle between Chengde and Beijing daily.

Mountain Resort (Bishu Shanzhuang). The full Chinese name reflects the utilitarian nature of this place—the Mountain Resort for Escaping the Summer Heat. Now known simply as the Mountain Resort, the site was begun by the Qing emperor Kangxi in the late 17th century. He hoped it would serve as an emblem to encourage minority groups in a newly united China to stay together. Enclosed by a 10-km (6-mi) wall, its interconnected palaces (whose architecture also reflects China's diversity), lakes, and trails sit in a landscape originally manipulated to resemble China's various ecozones. Ideally you could walk from the lakes and lush forests of southern China to the Mongolian steppes in an afternoon. Replicas of famous temples representing China's different religions stand on hillsides surrounding the palace as though paying homage to the court.

Beginning with Kangxi and continuing under his son, construction went on for 89 years. The Mountain Resort gradually became more political as the emperor moved the throne and seat of government to Chengde every summer. At its height the complex had nearly 100 buildings within its walls and 12 temples on the surrounding hillsides. Today numerous buildings remain; some have been restored but many have grass coming up through the cracks. Only eight of the temples are open for visitors (two of the originals were demolished and another two are dilapidated).

Many palace buildings are unpainted wood, reflecting Kangxi's disdain for fame and wealth (although he didn't forgo grand hunting parties and orgies). Various palace rooms have been restored into dioramas, with period furniture, ornaments, and costumed mannequins frozen in time. The surrounding landscape of lakes, open grasslands, and cool forests is lovely for a stroll. Mountains in the northern half of the park and a giant pagoda in the center afford panoramas of the city of Chengde to the south and the temples to the north and east. The Mountain Resort and the temples are so big that even with a massive influx of summer tourists they don't feel crowded. ✤ *Center of town; several entrances* 🎫 Y50 ☯ *Daily 5:30 AM–6:30 PM.*

Viewing Chengde's **Eight Outer Monasteries** from the mountain or from the large pagoda in the summer palace, it looks as though Emperor Kangxi built a Disneyland for China's religions. Originally part of a 12-temple group, each was built to reflect the architectural styles of a different minority group. The glistening gilt tiles and grandiose size show a harmonic combination of designs. The Eight Outer Monasteries were built during the 18th century. These monasteries, together with the Imperial Summer Villa, constitute a UNESCO World Heritage Site. They are grouped on the eastern and northern slopes of the Mountain Resort into two different sections close to the Wulie River. The eastern temples are named Anyuan, Pule, and Puren, and the northern temples are known as Putuozongcheng, Ximifushou, Puning Si, Puyou, and Shuxiang. Only Puning Si is still in active use by monks.

Temple of Universal Peace (Puning Si; ✉ Northeast of Mountain Resort 🎫 Y30 ☯ Daily 8–5), on the western bank of the Wulie River, is the most easterly of the northern temples and occupies an area of over 30,000 square meters (323,000 square feet). It was built in 1755 during the reign of Emperor Qianlong on the model of the Samye Temple, the earliest Buddhist monastery in Tibet. It also contains the largest wooden statue in the world—a 72-foot Avalokitesvara (a popular Buddhist deity) with 42 arms.

Temple of the Potaraka Doctrine (Putuozongcheng Miao; ✤ directly north of the Mountain Resort 🎫 Y20 ☯ Daily 8–6), modeled on the Potala Monastery in Lhasa and known as the Little Potala, is the largest of the eight temples in Chengde. Construction of the temples started in 1767 on a plot of 660,000 square feet. The temple has a tall and imposing entrance gate similar in design to a city gate tower. Inside the gate is a pavilion housing three stelae, the largest one inscribed with "The Record of the Temple of the Potaraka Doctrine" in Han, Manchu, Mongolian, and Tibetan languages. The stela to the east is inscribed with "The Record of Offering Assistance to the Turgot People," also in the four languages of the main stela.

Temple of Universal Happiness (Pule Si; ⚓ east of Mountain Resort, near base of cable car 🎫 Y20 🕗 Daily 8–5:30) was built in 1766 in China's last dynasty, Qing, during which time the imagery of Tibetan and Mongol Buddhism played an important role in the political and cultural arenas, especially in court circles. The architecture of the main building, the Pavilion of the Brilliance of the Rising Sun (Xuguangge) is characteristic of the ancient Chinese court structure and features high, square, box-like ceilings with a wooden Tibetan-style mandala motif. On top of the building's outer walls were eight brilliantly painted pagodas supported by lotus flower stands, only one of which still remains. Traditionally, lotus represents purity and is a common motif in Buddhist temples.

A cable car and a hiking trail lead up to **Club Peak** (Bangzhong Shan), an improbably balanced rock, fatter at the top and skinny at the bottom, that resembles a club standing on end. It juts up from the ridgeline east of the Mountain Resort. 🎫 *Cable car Y35* 🕗 *Daily 8–6.*

Qibao Hot Spring (Qibao Wenquan) lends refuge to your tired feet and muscles. Call for appointments. ☎ *0314/725–0228.*

Where to Stay & Eat

¢–$$ ✕ **Qianlongxing.** Originally an offshoot of a nearby dumpling restaurant, this thriving upscale eatery has become one of the most popular in Chengde. The picture menu carries delicacies ranging from mushrooms with chicken to scorpions and camels' paws. ⌂ *8 Zhongxing Lu* ☎ *0314/203–9766* ▤ *No credit cards.*

¢ ▥ **Huilong Hotel.** Near the train station, this hotel has a grand marble lobby and clean, modern rooms. The restaurant serves Muslim dishes such as lamb kebabs, and karaoke rooms provide entertainment. ⌂ *1 Xinjuzhai, Chezhan Lu, 067000* ☎ *0314/208–5369* 🖷 *0314/208–2404* ▨ *112 rooms* ⚒ *Gym, hair salon, massage, sauna, bowling* ▤ *AE, DC, MC, V.*

¢ ▥ **Mongolian Yurts Holiday Inn.** These concrete "yurts" have beds and TVs but bear no relation to the international Holiday Inn hotel chain. Located inside the Mountain Resort, with its quiet and clean air, this makes for a peaceful and unusual stay. Leave your window open at night to get a constant breeze through your room. ⚓ *Inside Wanshuyuanmen (eastern) entrance to Mountain Resort* ☎ *0314/216–3094* ⚒ *Restaurant; no a/c* ▤ *No credit cards* 🕗 *Closed Dec.–Mar.*

¢ ▥ **Xinhua Hotel.** At this shabby concrete building in the center of town near the bus station the rooms are quiet, airy, and reasonably clean. The hotel is a bit tired, but at least you don't have to go far to refuel: the restaurant downstairs has good regional cooking. ⌂ *4 Xinhua Bei Lu,*

067000 ☎ *0314/206–5880* 🛏 *204 rooms* ⚑ *Restaurant, in-room safes, meeting room, travel services* ▭ *No credit cards.*

¢ 🏨 **Yunshan Hotel.** Modern and clean, this hotel has a few staff members who speak English and can help arrange tours of nearby temples and the Mountain Resort. A good Chinese restaurant, a Western restaurant, a gift shop, and a business center make this one of the choice hotels in Chengde. ✉ *6 Nan Yuan Dong Lu, 067000* ☎ *0314/215–6171* 🖷 *0314/ 215–4551* 🛏 *230 rooms* ⚑ *2 restaurants, in-room safes, hair salon, bar, business services* ▭ *AE, DC, MC, V.*

Beidaihe

❾ *4 hrs (260 km [160 mi]) by express train east of Beijing; 5 hrs (395 km [245 mi]) by train southwest of Shenyang; 1 hr (35 km [22 mi]) by minibus southwest of Shanhaiguan.*

The seaside resort town of Beidaihe with its long beach, cool pine forests, and excellent seafood draws major crowds from July through September. Missionaries and diplomats from European powers first converted what had been a fishing village into a vacation destination, building villas here in the late 19th century to enjoy bathing on the long Mediterranean-style beaches. Now many members of the Communist Party elite have their summer homes here, while the government has built sanatoriums and other facilities for loyal workers to take a break from China's choking cities. The town center is small; it's easy to reach quiet spots along the seashore on foot or by bicycle.

The main attraction in Beidaihe is the **beach.** Walk along it for hours, wiggle your toes in the sand, breathe the clean seaside air, and pinch yourself: this is China, too. At several points along the coast perch pavilions for viewing the sea or rocks shaped like animals.

North of the middle beach is **Lianfeng Hill Park** (Lianfengshan Gongyuan), where quiet paths through pine forest lead to **Guanyin Temple** (Guanyin Si), a quiet place to relax in the woods. There are also good views of the sea from the top of Lianfeng Hill. ✛ *West-central side of town* 🎫 *Y15* ⊗ *Daily 8–5.*

Emperor Qin Shi Huang's Palace (Qinhuang Gong) is a 20th-century replica built in homage to the first Qin Dynasty emperor's inspection of Beidaihe. It contains well-constructed rooms with mannequins in period costumes and donning colorful robes, impressive weapons, and embroideries. ✉ *Near Shan Zhuang village, about 15 min walk from the Beidaihe Wai-jiao Renyuan Binguan hotel (1 Baosan Lu)* 🎫 *Y15* ⊗ *Daily 8–5.*

Where to Stay & Eat

Seafood restaurants line the beach, and you only need point at the most appetizing thing squirming in red buckets for the waiter to serve up a delicious fresh meal. More good seafood restaurants cluster on Haining Lu near the beach.

¢–$$ ✕ **Kiesslings.** This is the only nonstandard Chinese eating place in town. Originally an Austrian restaurant for foreigners, it has good baked goods for breakfast. It's open from May through September, but always call to make sure in advance. ✉ *Dongjing Lu, middle of town, behind Beidaihe Guesthouse for Diplomatic Missions* ☎ *0335/404–1043* ☰ *No credit cards.*

¢–$ 🏨 **Beidaihe Waijiao Renyuan Binguan** (Beidaihe Guesthouse for Diplomatic Missions). Specifically catering to foreigners, the guesthouse has several staff members who speak English remarkably well. The multibuilding complex is set among cypress and pines in a peaceful spot overlooking the sea, not far from Beidaihe's main intersection. Among its accommodations is a "building for distinguished guests," with suites for dignitaries. Rates for more expensive rooms include breakfast. ✉ *1 Baosan Lu, 066100* ☎ *0335/404–1807 in Beidaihe, 010/6532–4336 in Beijing* ⤳ *153 rooms, 12 suites* ⚑ *Restaurant, tennis court* ☰ *No credit cards* ⊙ *Mid-Oct.–Mar.*

¢ 🏨 **Jinshan Hotel.** On a quiet, less-developed section of the beach, this hotel spreads among five large two-story buildings linked by tree-lined paths. The rooms are clean and have two double beds. The CITS office is in the hotel, but the hotel staff's English might not be up to directing you to it. Nevertheless, either can organize tours with English-speaking guides. Few of the hotel's facilities are open outside high season (May through September). ✉ *4 Dongsan Lu, 066100* ☎ *0335/404–1338* 🖷 *0335/404–2478* ⤳ *267 rooms* ⚑ *2 restaurants, gym, nightclub, business services, travel services* ☰ *No credit cards.*

Shopping

Vendors of tourist trinkets will undoubtedly find you, but if you want to run the gauntlet, Haining Lu near the beach has big souvenir shops selling everything from seashell necklaces to water guns to lacquered lobsters.

Shanhaiguan

▶ ❿ *1 hr (35 km [22 mi]) by minibus northeast of Beidaihe; 5 hrs (280 km [174 mi]) by minibus east of Beijing; 5 hrs (360 km [223 mi]) southwest of Shenyang.*

Shanhaiguan is, depending on your point of view, where the Great Wall meets the sea or where it climbs its first mountain. Long, long ago this was China's frontier, and an impressive wall still surrounds the old town, though the warriors on the battlements are now mannequins. The town has myriad narrow, mildly interesting streets, but most of Shanhaiguan's attractions are in the nearby countryside, just a 10- to 15-minute taxi ride away.

The **First Gate Under Heaven** (Tianxiadiyiguan) is the impressive north-facing portal of this fortress-town. It was built in 1381 under the Ming Dynasty and defended China's northern frontier until the Manchus overran it in 1644. The top has views of the town and, through binoculars, of the Great Wall snaking up nearby mountains. ✤ *Northeast side of wall* 🎫 *Y35* ⊙ *Daily 6:30 AM–7 PM.*

The **Great Wall Museum** (Changcheng Bowuguan), housed in a Qing Dynasty–style building past the First Gate Under Heaven, the museum has a good collection of photographs of the wall from across China and cases full of military artifacts. The museum offers a good introduction to the history of the Great Wall and the region, from Neolithic times to the present. ⚓ *Between CITS and Bank of China, south of First Gate Under Heaven* ✉ *Free with admission to First Gate Under Heaven* ⊙ *Daily 7 AM–6 PM.*

Legend has it that the Great Wall once extended all the way into the Bohai Sea, ending with a giant carved dragon head. The original wall fell into such disrepair that the seaside fortress at what today is called **Old Dragon Head** (Lao Long Tou) was reconstructed from archaeological digging and historical records after much difficulty. The final battlement of the Great Wall juts out into the sea, waves smashing at its base. The park's rebuilt army garrisons, lookouts, and beach make for a pleasant stroll. ✉ *Y30* ⊙ *Daily 8–5.*

After tracing a line inland from the sea, connecting with the walled town of Shanhaiguan, and passing through a few kilometers of farmland farther inland, the Great Wall suddenly heads for the sky at **Jiao Mountain** (Jiao Shan). The steep and precipitous section has been thoroughly rebuilt on its lower stretches, but it's a tough hike up on a hot day. As the ridge levels off, the reconstruction has basically ceased, leaving an earthen mound with occasional stretches of intact flagstones. There's a **cable car** (Y10) if you don't want to climb. ⚓ *10-min taxi ride northwest of town.*

Yangsai Hu is a deep blue reservoir with arms jutting in between steep mountains outside town. It has an aviary, a cable car leading up one side of a hill and down the other (if you don't want to follow the tree-lined path around it to the water's edge), and a few pavilions connected by concrete trails dotting the landscape. ⚓ *15-min taxi ride northwest of town* ✉ *Y30.*

Beyond the reservoir is **Longevity Mountain** (Changshou Shan), which has giant characters affirming a long life, elegantly carved and painted onto the rocks. ⚓ *East of Yangsai Hu.*

Down the coast from Dragon Head is **Mengjiangnu Miao,** a shrine commemorating the story of a woman whose husband died in slavery while building the Great Wall. She wept as she searched for his body, and in sympathy the Great Wall is said to have split open before her, revealing the bones of her husband and others buried within. Overcome with grief, she threw herself into the sea. The temple has good views of the mountains and sea, and for some reason houses an old jet-fighter aircraft. ⚓ *10-min taxi ride northeast of town* ✉ *Y30* ⊙ *Daily dawn–dusk.*

Where to Stay & Eat
Shanhaiguan has a street of acceptable restaurants, Dong Da Jie, near the Jingshan Hotel. Beware of the "guides" in this area whose only guidance will be to lead you to the restaurants that employ them.

$–$$ ✕ **Mongolian Hotpot.** This small restaurant with only four tables is sometimes crowded with revelers. The friendly owners will fill you to the hilt on cheap hotpot—thinly sliced meat dipped into boiling broth with an array of sauces and vegetables. ✉ *West side of Nanda Jie, south of main crossroads* ☎ *No phone* 🚫 *No credit cards.*

¢ ⊞ **Jingshan Hotel.** Built to resemble a Qing mansion, this hostelry consisting of gray-brick buildings around courtyards is the cleanest, most comfortable retreat in Shanhaiguan. Conveniently near the First Gate Under Heaven, the hotel is quite shiny on the outside, but the rooms are a little tired. The restaurant is above average; the management doesn't harass customers the way owners do on the nearby street of restaurants. The staff will arrange air and train reservations if you can communicate with them. ⊠ *8 Dong Dajie, 066200* ☎ *0335/505–1130* ↩ *120 rooms* ⌂ *Restaurant, laundry service* ⊟ *No credit cards.*

Hebei A to Z

To research prices, get advice from other travelers, and book travel arrangements, visit www.fodors.com.

AIR TRAVEL
Beidaihe and Shanhaiguan are served by a small airport at the industrial port of Qinhuangdao. There are frequent flights to Dalian and fewer flights to other Chinese cities.

🔲 Airport Information **Qinhuangdao Airport** ⊠ Near Shanhaiguan ☎ 0335/505-1976.

BIKE TRAVEL
Renting bicycles is particularly worthwhile in Beidaihe, given the long coast, but the traffic in Shanhaiguan and Chengde puts you in mortal danger.

BOAT & FERRY TRAVEL
Aboard a boat is certainly the most comfortable way to travel here. Small cruise ships serve the port of Qinhuangdao (between Beidaihe and Shanhaiguan). Overnight boats with comfortable sleepers and good restaurants go to Dalian, Qingdao, Tainjin, and Shanghai. Boat schedules are available at CITS offices; hotels can make reservations for you. Qinhuangdao CITS serves Beidaihe and Shanhaiguan as well as Qinhuangdao.

🔲 Boat & Ferry Information **Qinhuangdao CITS** ⊠ 100 Heping Dajie ☎ 0335/323-1111.

Qinhuangdao Tourism Bureau ⊠ 11 Gangcheng Dajie ☎ 0335/307-6554.

BUS TRAVEL
Long-distance buses are uncomfortable and slow, but they're the only transport linking Chengde with Beidaihe and Shanhaiguan. Several buses a day make this trip, all departing in the early morning.

An excellent minibus service runs between Beidaihe, Qinhuangdao, and Shanhaiguan. Buses leave every 30 minutes and cost Y5 for the somewhat circuitous ride, with frequent stops between Beidaihe and Shanhaiguan. The bus station in Beidaihe is at the intersection of Heishi Lu and Haining Lu, and in Shanhaiguan it is in front of the train station. Buy tickets on the bus.

TAXIS
The half-hour taxi ride between Beidaihe and Shanhaiguan costs about Y100. Within all three towns taxis are cheap and will take you to nearby attractions.

TRAIN TRAVEL

Trains running between Beijing, Tianjin, and Shenyang pass through Beidaihe and Shanhaiguan quite frequently, but not all of them stop. The train station in Beidaihe is somewhat outside town; if you arrive late at night the taxi drivers charge exorbitant rates. The ride from Beijing can take as many as 7 hours or as few as 4½.

Chengde is on a northern rail line between Beijing and Shenyang. Beijing is between 5 and 7 hours away, Shenyang more than 12. No trains run between Chengde and either Beidaihe or Shanhaiguan.

TRANSPORTATION AROUND HEBEI

In general, Chengde, Beidaihe, and Shanhaiguan are all small enough to explore on foot.

VISITOR INFORMATION

For Beidaihe and Shanhaiguan contact CITS in Qinhuangdao, or in the Beidaihe Guesthouse for Diplomatic Missions. In Chengde contact CITS or the Yunshan Hotel.

🚹 Tourist Information **Beidaihe Guesthouse for Diplomatic Missions** ⊠ 1 Baosan Lu, Beidaihe ☎ 0335/404-1287. **Qinhuangdao CITS** ⊠ 100 Heping Dajie, Qinhuangdao ☎ 0335/323-1111.

Qinhuangdao Tourism Bureau ⊠ 11 Gangcheng Dajie, Qinhuangdao ☎ 0335/307-6554.

Yunshan Hotel ⊠ 6 Nan Yuan Dong Lu, Chengde ☎ 0314/215-6171.

SHANXI

Shanxi was at or near the center of Chinese power from about 200 BC until the fall of the Tang Dynasty in the early 10th century. Since then it has remained relatively backward, a frontier area used as a defense against predatory northern neighbors; nevertheless, its very lack of development has allowed a large number of historic sites, such as Datong's grottoes, to survive.

Today trucks and even donkey carts heavily laden with coal dominate the roads of Shanxi, providing a constant reminder that the province produces one-third of China's coal. It wasn't until the Japanese occupation that serious exploitation of the coal reserves began, but the mountainous terrain in Shanxi also worked against the Japanese, providing plenty of cover for Chinese guerrillas fighting the anti-Japanese war.

Datong

⓫ *5 ½ hrs (275 km [170 mi]) by train west of Beijing; 724 km (449 mi) by plane west of Dalian.*

Datong, in the heart of China's coal-mining region, is drab and polluted, but it has some good restaurants and shopping areas, as well as a few historic buildings. The city's most important sites are the nearby grottoes, where China's ancient history is deeply rooted.

In northern Shanxi near the border with Inner Mongolia, Datong lies close to the old Chinese frontier with the Mongolian and Turkic clans who lived beyond the Great Wall. Datong was a heavily defended city, and the countryside around it contained chains of watchtowers where, at the approach of enemy troops, huge bonfires were lighted and the warning passed on, giving defenders time to prepare for attacks.

The old city area, a square within the confines of the still partially surviving city walls, is neatly divided into quarters. The chief areas of interest are within this square.

Originally a screen wall in front of the gate of the palace of the 13th son of the first emperor of the Ming Dynasty, the impressive ceramic tiled **Nine Dragon Screen** (Jiu Long Bi) is about 150 feet long and is decorated with colorful depictions of, well yes, nine dragons. ⊠ *East of Da Dong Jie and Da Bei Jie intersection* ☎ *0352/205–4788* ▩ *Y6* ☉ *Daily 8–6.*

The **Huayan Monastery** (Huayan Si), originally built in the 12th century, is in the western part of the old city. Divided into the Upper monastery and the Lower monastery, it has very-well-preserved statues, frescoes, built-in bookshelves, and ceilings. The main hall of the Upper Monastery is one of the largest Buddhist halls extant in China and houses five gilded Buddha statues seated on lotus thrones. The Bhagavat Storage Hall of the Lower Monastery was used for storing Buddhist scriptures and today houses religious statues. ⊠ *Xiasipo Hutong off Da Xi Jie* ☎ *0352/ 205–3629* ▩ *Y10* ☉ *Daily 8–6.*

The **Shanhua Monastery** (Shanhua Si), situated within Datong's old city walls, dates originally from the Tang Dynasty, but most of the surviving structure is of 12th-century construction. The main hall contains statues of 24 statues of divine generals. ⊠ *Off Da Nan Jie* ☎ *0352/205– 2898* ▩ *Y10* ☉ *Daily 8–6.*

Train spotting is possible only through a CITS tour of the **Datong Locomotive Works** (Datong Jiche Cheliang Chang), which made steam engines until the late 1980s, the last factory in China to do so. These black workhorses, reputedly modeled on a 19th-century British steam locomotive, can still be seen on minor lines or in rail yards away from the boom areas of China. A visit to the works—which now makes diesel engines—includes a ride on one of the old steam engines. ⊠ *Daqing Lu, western suburbs.*

Where to Stay & Eat

¢–$$ ✕ **Hong Ya.** This two-story family-run restaurant has a few specialties, including Peking duck, but don't expect it to live up to Beijing standards. The price is right, however. Waiters speak little to no English so get your pointer finger ready; menus are in English and Chinese. The place can be noisy at times and smoking is de rigueur. ⊠ *1 Yingbin Dong Lu* ☎ *0352/502–5566* ▤ *No credit cards.*

¢–$$ ✕ **Yong He.** Serving the best food in Datong, this restaurant has the same menu on all three floors, but the ground floor—stylish and wood paneled—also serves hotpot, which is what you need to eat if you are in Datong in winter. The regular menu contains a full range of excellent Chinese food, including Peking duck, and seafood, including turtle, crab, and crayfish. A new branch opposite the Yungang hotel serves similar food plus dim sum, but no hotpot. ⊠ *Xiao Nan Jie, at entrance of Shanhua Monastery* ☎ *0352/204–7999* ⚱ *Reservations essential* ▤ *No credit cards* ⊠ *Yong He Hong Qi Meishi Cheng, 8 Yingbin Dong Lu* ☎ *0352/510–1555* ▤ *No credit cards.*

★ ¢–$ ✕ **Grandmother's Bridge** (Wai Po Qiao). Justly renowned as one of the best restaurants in Datong, this fine restaurant is elegantly decorated with traditional furniture and serves surprisingly inexpensive local Datong specialties (listed in an English menu). The excellent local beer is popular with enthusiastic diners. The stewed chicken with wild mushrooms is a good pick. ⊠ *Caochang Cheng Bei Jie* ☎ *0352/603–6608.*

¢ ▦ **Da Tong Hotel.** Among the hotels in the downtown area of this coal-mining city, this is the largest. While it is in the heart of a dusty and bustling town, the hotel offers great service and clean rooms with standard amenities. ⊠ *37 Yingbin Xi Lu, 037006* ☎ *0352/203–2476* 🖷 *0352/ 203–2288* ↝ *221 rooms* ⚱ *Restaurant, minibars, refrigerators, sauna, spa, bar, laundry service, business services* ▤ *AE, DC, MC, V.*

¢ ▦ **Jing Yuan Hotel** Located in the northwest of the city, about 3 km (2 mi) from the downtown area, the hotel provides pleasantly furnished rooms. Bathrooms are spacious with clean and soft towels, and the water pressure is excellent. The hotel garden adds color to an otherwise plain city landscape. The in-house restaurants serve both Western and Chinese food. ⊠ *3A Yongjun Nan Lu, 037001* ☎ *0352/288–0988* ⊕ *www. travelchinaguide.com/hotel/jing-yuan-hotel-datong.htm* ↝ *96 rooms, 7 suites* ⚱ *2 restaurants, cable TV, indoor pool, massage, sauna, bowling, nightclub* ▤ *AE, DC, MC, V.*

¢ ▦ **Yungang.** In the south of the city, this is where most foreigners stay in Datong as it is the top choice among many mediocre ones. Standard rooms are small but adequate. Datong's main CITS office is in the hotel complex. The restaurant serves Chinese food. ⊠ *21 Yingbin Dong Lu, 037008* ☎ *0352/502–1601* 🖷 *0352/502–4927* ↝ *160 rooms* ⚱ *Restaurant, bar, nightclub* ▤ *AE, DC, MC, V.*

Shopping

Although far from any of China's booming coastal regions, Datong's main shopping street, Da Xi Jie, has its share of fashionable clothing chains and department stores. The most modern department store is located elsewhere; the six-story **Hualin Market** (⊠ Xiao Nan Jie ☎ 0352/ 204–4876), which sells groceries and just about every household item you might want, except touristy items.

Side Trips from Datong

★ ⓬ The **Yungang Grottoes** (Yungang Shiku), the oldest Buddhist caves in China, are Datong's most famous site. Built mainly in the latter part of the 5th century, the grotto complex, containing various religious icons, from huge Buddha statues to scores of intricate carvings, stretched over 15 km (9 mi) from east to west. Today only a kilometer of this survives, encompassing 53 major grottoes. Most are now railed off at the front, but visitors can peer in for a better look. ⚁ *16 km (10 mi) west of Datong; take direct bus from railway station* 🚌 *Y30* ⊙ *Daily 9–5.*

⓭ The 1,400-year-old **Hanging Monastery** (Xuankong Si) is attached precariously to the side of a sheer cliff face in the Hengshan Mountains, one of China's five sacred mountain ranges. The all-wooden monastery holds China's three traditional belief systems within its buildings: Taoism, Buddhism, and Confucianism. In one temple there are statues of Laozi, Sakyamuni, and Confucius. ☒ *Near Hunyuan, 75 km (46 mi) south of Datong; take CITS tour bus* 🚌 *Y45* 🕓 *Daily 9:10* AM–*5* PM.

⑭ Built around AD 1100, the octagonal **Yingxian Timber Pagoda** (Yingxian Muta) is thought to be the oldest wooden building in China. Reflecting the dangers of the bad old days in Shanxi, it began life as a watchtower and waited 400 years before being converted into a temple. In something of an architectural trick, the pagoda's 220 feet appear to contain five floors but in fact hold nine. Whatever its construction, it has been strong enough to survive three powerful earthquakes, although most of the statues and relics inside were destroyed by the upheavals of the Cultural Revolution. A notable survivor is the huge statue of Sakyamuni on the ground floor. ☒ *Yingxian, 70 km (43 mi) south of Datong* 🚌 *Y35* 🕓 *Daily 8–7.*

⑮ Billed as the last fortress city in China and declared a World Heritage Site by UNESCO in 1997, the dusty old town of **Pingyao** offers a good sampling of Yuan, Ming, and Qing Dynasty architecture. A visit here is best spent strolling or bicycling through old sections of town viewing wonderfully carved and painted eaves. The top of the city wall affords views of the street layout within and the plains beyond. ✈ *300 km (186 mi) south of Datong—1 hr by plane, 4½ hrs by car, 11 hrs by train southwest of Beijing.*

Shanxi A to Z

To research prices, get advice from other travelers, and book travel arrangements, visit www.fodors.com.

TAXIS
Taking a taxi is the easiest mode of transportation in Datong.

TRAIN TRAVEL
Daily trains link Datong with Beijing (5½ hrs). Datong is also on the route to Inner Mongolia to the north and Lanzhou in the west.
🚄 Train Stations **Datong Train Station** ☒ Zhangqian Jie ☎ 0352/712-2922.

VISITOR INFORMATION
🚄 Tourist Information **Datong Tourism Bureau** ☒ 21 Yingbin Dong Lu ☎ 0352/522-2674. **CITS** ☒ Railway station on Zhangqian Jie ☎ 0352/712-4882 ☒ Yungang hotel, 21 Yingbin Dong Lu ☎ 0352/510-1326 🖷 0352/510-2046.

HENAN

Henan is both a source of pride and a sore point for the nation. The Yellow River (Huang He) area supports the popular conception of China's "5,000-year history," a ubiquitous phrase in any discussion of Chinese culture; but the economy of the current province is in sad shape. The Shang Dynasty, established in the 17th century BC, set its capital in Henan, moving it to several different cities throughout its 600-

year reign. The northern Song Dynasty also returned the capital to this region, occupying Kaifeng. This city, just west of Zhengzhou, remains one of Henan's most enchanting. Threatened by invaders in the 12th century AD, the Song fled south, leaving Kaifeng and the surrounding region to their own devices.

Henan's fertile land supported a growing population, which in the end may have been its downfall. Apart from the periodic flooding of the Yellow River, which wreaks havoc on crops and lives, the steady increase in population has made Henan the home of some of the nation's most impoverished people. Refugees of a sort, fleeing the poverty of their home regions, the majority of China's millions of migrant workers come from Henan and Sichuan.

The area's most famous sight, the Dragon Gate Grottoes (Longmen Shiku), is close to Luoyang; you might start in Luoyang, visit Shaolin Temple on the way from Luoyang to Zhengzhou, spend the night in Zhengzhou, and go on to Kaifeng the next afternoon.

Zhengzhou

⓰ *3 hrs (110 km [68 mi] by train or bus east of Luoyang; 8½ hrs (610 km [378 mi] by train south of Beijing.*

Archaeological finds indicate that the region around this city has been populated since the Neolithic period. It was the Shang Dynasty capital for a time and became an important transportation and economic center under the Sui and Tang dynasties, when canals connecting the Yellow River to the northwest terminated in Zhengzhou's great grain market. When the Song moved their capital east to Kaifeng, the city's importance waned.

In the 20th century Zhengzhou once again became an important transportation center. It was the site of one of the chief railway strikes of the 1920s and, later, of a major wartime disaster. When Chiang Kai-shek's retreating Nationalist army blew up the dams on the Yellow River in a vain attempt to stop Japanese military progress into the country, millions suffered from the ensuing floods. The Nationalists also moved Zhengzhou's industry to avoid its falling into Japanese hands. After 1949 the Communist government rebuilt industry in what was at that point only an administrative and commercial center. The heavy industrialization of recent years has given an otherwise nondescript provincial capital a level of pollution, traffic, and noise befitting a major urban center. Cultural attractions, unfortunately, have not kept pace.

Zhengzhou, along with Luoyang, provides a suitable base for exploring some of China's oldest and best-known sights. The area around Zhengzhou is one of the most important in Chinese ancient history. Sights are organized below in order of their proximity to the central restaurant and hotel district along Jinshui Lu.

If you're lucky, you can catch a glimpse of some city ruins in the far eastern section of **Zijingshan Park** (Zijingshan Gongyuan). The park also has a playground for children, a minimally functional miniature golf course, and several pretty wooden pagodas. It's a worthwhile escape from the noise of the city, especially if you are traveling with children. ✛ *Jinshui Lu between Zijingshan Lu and Chengdong Lu, entrance at intersection of Jinshui Lu and Zijingshan Lu* ▨ *Free* ⊙ *Daily 5 AM–11 PM.*

People's Park (Renmin Gongyuan) provides a relaxing alternative to the city's dusty streets. It contains a small lake with a large island and some aging carnival rides, and provides a favorite dawn and dusk tai chi venue for the local populace. ▨ *Jinshui Lu between Erqi Lu and Minggong Lu, entrance on Erqi Lu south of Jinshui Lu* ▨ *Y2* ⊙ *Daily 8–dusk.*

Zhengzhou's **Henan Provincial Museum** (Henan Bowuguan), housed in a striking and innovative pyramid-shape building, has an excellent collection of archaeological finds from this area as well as others. You can see some of the Neolithic remains found on the Yellow River, Shang bronzes found in and around the city itself, and other ancient artifacts such as earthenware pots and ceramics from various dynasties. ▨ *8 Nongye Lu* ☎ *0371/385–0860* ▨ *Y20* ⊙ *Daily 8:30–6.*

Zhengzhou was the site of one of several important and bloody railway strikes that took place in the early 1920s. On February 7, 1923, striking railway workers halted the busy rail line to Wuhan, angering the regional strongman Wu Peifu as well as the British business community in Wuhan. Wu ended the strike by ordering his troops to fire on a crowd of demonstrators and then publicly executing the strike leaders. Fifty-two people were killed and more than 300 wounded; more than 1,000 workers were fired. The event shook the confidence of the two-year-old Chinese Communist Party and put a damper on the burgeoning Chinese labor movement for the next two years. This early Communist martyrdom is commemorated in the **February 7 Pagoda** (Er Qi Ta), whose fresh colors and distinctive shape ornament a major traffic circle a short way from the train station. Inside, documents and pictures concerning the strike and Communist history in Zhengzhou are on display, but few are labeled in English. ▨ *Junction Erqi Lu, Renmin Lu, and Zhengxing Jie* ☎ *No phone* ▨ *Y5* ⊙ *Daily 8:30–noon and 2–5:30.*

Where to Stay & Eat

$$–$$$$ ✕ **Yuexiu.** Zhengzhou's most famous restaurant, the YX (as it's informally known) caters to its foreign clientele. It offers Western classical music from a string quartet near the bar-and-lounge section, and from a small shop in back it sells not only Chinese books but framed calligraphy scrolls that non-Chinese speakers can also enjoy. Aside from the main dining area there is a selection of themed private rooms, each decorated in a particular Chinese or Western style. It serves up a tasty selection of some favorite Cantonese foods, including more daring specialties like snake gallbladder. ▨ *Renzhai Bei Jie, east section, between Jingqi Lu and Jingba Lu* ☎ *0371/383–7666* 🖷 *0371/393–2222* ▤ *No credit cards.*

$–$$$ ✕ **Henan Shifu.** Among Zhengzhou's many local dining facilities, Henan
FodorsChoice Shifu is one of the best-known places in town. *Shifu,* a Chinese idiom
★ denoting friendliness in daily greetings, connotes a master status when used as the name of an establishment. True to its name, this restaurant offers an authentic local rendering of baked, multilayered sesame *bing*

(pancake with marinated beef inside). The kitchen is also famed for its Zhengzhou hamburger while non–meat eaters can go for the vegetarian tofu casserole with mushrooms and bamboo shoots. Nestled in a traditional courtyard, the restaurant has a soothing atmosphere. English menus and waitstaff are not available, but you probably can't go wrong by guess-ordering in the lingual darkness. ⊠ *22 Renmin Lu* ☎ *0371/ 622–2108* 🖃 *No credit cards.*

★ $–$$ 🏨 **Crowne Plaza Zhengzhou.** At the edge of Zhengzhou's restaurant row, set back from the street behind a tall fountain, this appealing hotel provides everything you would need during a stay in Zhengzhou. Every room has modern furnishings and good lighting. The Shang Palace restaurant, on the first floor, tends toward formality and serves a variety of excellent Chinese dishes in a tasteful and quiet environment. Mama Mia's Pizzeria claims actual American-style oven-baked pizzas, and the downstairs Patisserie serves fine coffee and a variety of cakes and cookies. Geared toward foreign business travelers, the hotel has a friendly staff whose English tends to be quite good. ⊠ *115 Jinshui Lu, 450003* ☎ *0371/595–0055* 🖷 *0371/599–0770* ✒ *hicpzz@public.zz.ha.cn* ⚟ *177 rooms, 44 suites* ⚏ *3 restaurants, patisserie, pizzeria, in-room safes, minibars, cable TV, pool, gym, bar, nightclub, business services, meeting room, travel services* 🖃 *AE, DC, MC, V.*

¢ 🏨 **Asia Hotel.** The hotel is located at the bustling city center, on the west side of Er Qi Square, within easy distance to city attractions. Rooms are large, on average, and sport modern facilities. Bathrooms are in good condition. ⊠ *165 Jiefang Xi Lu, 450000* ☎ *0663/836–4700* ⚟ *187 rooms* ⚏ *Restaurant, room service, sauna, laundry facilities, business services, car rental, travel services, free parking* 🖃 *AE, DC, MC, V.*

¢ 🏨 **Red Coral.** This hotel, close to the railway station, caters mainly to a business clientele that values its convenient location. It is tastefully decorated and offers an excellent range of facilities including a newly expanded fitness center. The in-house restaurant offers a full international menu. Rooms on the 15th and 16th floors were most recently refurbished. ⊠ *20 Er Ma Lu, 450003* ☎ *0371/698–6688* 🖷 *0371/699–3222* ⊕ *www. redcoralhotel.com* ⚟ *155 rooms, 12 suites* ⚏ *2 restaurants, refrigerators, cable TV, pool, bowling, dance club, business services, travel services* 🖃 *AE, DC, MC, V.*

¢ 🏨 **Tianquan Dajiudian.** Conveniently located right next to the railway station, this hotel offers relatively clean accommodations at reasonable prices. Guest rooms are a little dark, with forgettable furnishings, but are otherwise quite comfortable. Bathrooms are acceptably clean, if a little old. Be sure to ask for a room in the back, as the honking from taxis in the front of the square can be a rude surprise at 3 AM. The staff makes an effort to be helpful. ⊠ *1 Xi Datong Lu* ☎ *0371/698–6888* 🖷 *0371/696–9877* ⚟ *214 units* ⚏ *Restaurant, bar, nightclub, laundry service, business services* 🖃 *AE, DC, MC, V.*

¢ 🏨 **Zhong Du Hotel.** Located near the entrance to the expressway linking Zhengzhou City and the airport, the Zhong Du Hotel offers easy access for those wishing to get away. Among the five in-house restaurants, one serves a Western buffet dinner and the rest feature a variety of Chinese cuisine, including southern and northern dishes. Ask about discount room rates when booking. A taxi ride to the center of town will cost you about Y15. ⊠ *99 Hanghai Lu, 450005* ☎ *0371/878–1665* ↩ *300 rooms ৬ 5 restaurants, in-room safes, minibars, cable TV, bar, lounge, nightclub, baby-sitting, laundry service, business services, convention center* ⊟ *AE, DC, MC, V.*

Nightlife

In Zhengzhou the few bars that spring up now and then tend to have a short and uncertain life span. **Cola Planet** (⊠ Fazhan Bldg., 1st fl., 105 Jian Kang Lu ☎ No phone) serves coffee by day and transforms into a bar and disco by night. For a relaxed evening check out the **Target Bar** (⊠ 10 Jing Liu Lu ☎ No phone), which serenades customers with jazz through the week and rap on weekends. In recent years, a new bar scene took shape in Zhengzhou for the health conscious and for overworked entrepreneurs. The "fruit bar," with individually partitioned cubicles and minimal decoration with books and paintings, serves mainly fruit platters and freshly squeezed juice and a range of fruit drinks. For more detailed information about Zhengzhou's night scene, contact the local CITS (⊠ Yubo Bldg., West Tower, 16th fl., No. 1 Nongye Lu ☎ 0371/585–2310) or Henan Tourism Bureau (⊠ 16 Jinshui Lu, Zhengzhou ☎ 0371/595–5026)

Shopping

Zhengzhou has several night markets where the local Muslims set up food stands and local merchants peddle wares. You can find anything from baby clothes to the most recent publications here, but the main attraction is usually the people. The **Erqi Area Night Market** (⊠ Along small side streets off Minzhu Lu, 1 block west of Erqi Lu) starts doing business around 7 PM and keeps going until the crowd gets tired—usually around 10 PM.

The best shopping for regional crafts and reproductions of famous archaeological finds can be found at the sights outside Zhengzhou. The local **Friendship Store** (⊠ 96 Erqi Bei Lu ☎ 0371/622–0082) sells prints and antiques. The **Henan Museum Shop** (⊠ Nongye Lu in Henan Provincial Museum ☎ No phone) sells local art, reproductions of its own exhibits, carved jewelry, and the like. The **Jin Bo Da Shopping Center** (⊠ 200 Erqi Lu ☎ 0371/624–8054) is the best department store in town. The **Shaolin Monastery** is surrounded by stands selling everything from art reproductions to little martial arts figurines.

Side Trips from Zhengzhou

❶⑦ A short ride from the city, the clean and relaxing **Yellow River Park** (Huang He Youlan Qu) offers an impressive view of the river. Exhibits document the importance of the river as both the origin of ancient civilization and a major destructive force in recent times. Its flooding has claimed millions of lives over the years. Several dams now harness the river's power for hydroelectric use. To get to the park, catch a minibus from outside the train station or ask at your hotel travel or information desk about rides. ✥ *30 km (19 mi) northwest of Zhengzhou* 🚋 *Y10* ⊙ *Daily 8:30–dusk.*

❶⑧ One of the lesser-known attractions in this area, **Temple of the Central Peak** (Zhongyue Si) stands amid beautiful mountains. Officially, it is the local Taoist temple, but China has a long tradition of intermingling religions. Like most temples of its kind, Zhongyue in fact bears as much significance to Buddhists as to Taoists: locals come to pray, and who they pray to is completely up to them. You can stop in on the way to or from Shaolin Monastery. *60 km (37 mi) southwest of Zhengzhou; accessible by minibus or hired car* *Y10* *Daily 8:30–dusk.*

19 Fodor's Choice ★ If you like martial arts, you'll want to see where it started in China—at **Shaolin Monastery** (Shaolin Si). Chinese combat martial art is thought to have been invented here by Buddhist monks who needed some diversion from their meditation. Amid gorgeous hills checkered with large patches of farmed land, the site actually extends up and down a fairly long street, including far more than just the temple. The large temple has a bamboo grove surrounded by stone stelae and a pavilion illustrated with scenes from the Confucian *Classic of Filial Piety.* Across the street, something resembling a wax museum portrays famous martial artists in various fighting positions and battle arrays. Children tend to enjoy this bit. The martial arts school at the temple often has performances and competitions, so you may get to see actual monks and other students showing off their skills. Farther up the hill, famous monks of the past are commemorated in the **Forest of Pagodas.** *70 km (43 mi) southwest of Zhengzhou; accessible by minibus or hired car* *Y60 (ticket buys entry to all sights)* *Daily 8:30–5:30.*

★ 20 Once the capital of the Song Dynasty, **Kaifeng,** east of Zhengzhou, was abandoned by the court in the 12th century when northern invaders forced the Song south to Hangzhou. Amazingly, it has managed to retain many of its attractions, as well as large chunks of its city wall, without having been turned into a heavy industrial center or a tourist trap. It's a relatively quiet, friendly city that has preserved its neighborhood feel. The Muslim population has a strong influence, and two mosques in white-and-green tile, complete with Middle Eastern onion domes, have been built in the last few years. Older, Chinese-style mosques, as well as Buddhist temples, dot the side streets. The Muslims also run one of the busiest food and wares markets in Zhengzhou.

The city's most famous sight stands near Tieta Lake (Tieta Hu). The **Iron Pagoda** (Tie Ta) is not made of iron but of brick covered with tiles that look like iron. You can climb to the top on a narrow pitch-black staircase that leads to several small windows. You can also see the lake and wander around the pretty surroundings. *Northeast corner of town near No. 3 bus terminus* *Park Y20, pagoda Y5* *Daylight hrs.*

Dragon Pavilion Park (Longting Gongyuan), Kaifeng's major park, includes three lakes and a pavilion. It is a favorite family outing spot. *North end of Zhongshan Lu* *Y10* *Daily 8–5.*

The **Xiangguo Temple** (Xiangguo Si), originally built in the 6th century, was most recently rebuilt in the 18th century and houses some old artifacts. A food and souvenirs market has sprung up around it. *Ziyou Lu* *Y20* *Daily 8–5.*

Near the middle of town, the **Yangqing Taoist Temple** (Yangqing Guan) is a two-story structure with a strikingly ornate exterior around an unusually bare interior. A shop displays some calligraphy scrolls. ✉ *Off Yingbin Lu* 🚇 *Y10* ◔ *Daily 8:30–5:30.*

Luoyang

▶ *3½ hrs (430 km [267 mi]) by train west of Zhengzhou; 7 hrs (320 km [198 mi]) by train northeast of Xian.*

First established by the Zhou in the 12th century BC, Luoyang became the dynastic capital in 771 BC. Although well known as one of the "ancient capitals," Luoyang became more important for its religious and artistic history. Not only did it serve as capital to 10 successive dynasties, it also welcomed and built a temple for the first monk to bring Buddhism to the Middle Kingdom. Under instructions from the emperor of the northern Wei Dynasty, cave temples were constructed slightly south of the city. These temples are now regarded as some of the most important monuments to Buddhist art. Buddhism's incorporation into indigenous beliefs and everyday lives was so complete that even restrictions and periodic purges by various dynasties as well as by modern governments have not kept people from praying to the arhats. In fact, with increased government openness—fueled perhaps partly by a desire to attract tourists, particularly those from Taiwan, Hong Kong, and Singapore—Buddhism seems to be on the rise again today.

The art that Buddhism fostered once adorned Luoyang's many temples and monasteries, but the city reached its cultural apex centuries ago, and for hundreds of years its symbolic importance as a name associated with religious and dynastic powers carried more weight than the fact of its existence. Nowadays it is a growing industrial center. The city itself holds few important sights, but you'll need about a day to see the chief places of interest around Luoyang. If you can get here in April, you should give yourself an afternoon to see the blooming peonies that are Luoyang's pride, second only to the Buddhist grottoes. All sights except Wangcheng Park lie outside the city proper.

☙ Spring means peonies in Luoyang. Stroll through the peony show in **Park of the Royal Town** (Wangcheng Gongyuan) during the third week of April every year, when Luoyang is crowded with visitors from the region. Families come out to enjoy the sight, and college students skip class and take the seven-hour train ride from Xian to participate. At other times of year, the park is a restful if unremarkable recreation area. It has a small zoo in the back, as well as a playground for kids. ⊕ *Northwest of Zhongzhou Zhong Lu and Wangcheng Lu* ☎ *No phone* 🚇 *Y3; Y15 during peony show* ◔ *Daily 8:30–dusk.*

The **Ancient Tombs Museum** (Gumu Bowuguan) stands north of the city atop Mangshan Mountain, which was viewed as an auspicious site. The museum displays 22 of the thousands of ancient tombs found in the area. The underground tombs come from dynasties from the Han to the Song. ⊕ *4 km (2½ mi) north of city; accessible by tour or minibus* 🚇 *Y15* ◔ *Daily 8:30–6.*

East of town is the site of the first Buddhist temple in China, dating back to the Han Dynasty. **White Horse Temple** (Baima Si)—named for the white horses believed to have carried the first scriptures from India to China—became a focal point for China's powerful fascination with this imported religion. The temple has been destroyed several times over, and the buildings we see now date from the Ming and Qing dynasties. Statues of white horses stand to either side behind the central hall as emblems of its origins. ✛ *13 km (8 mi) east of city; accessible by minibus or hired car* ▨ *Y25* ⊙ *Daily 8:30–6.*

South of the city lies the **Grove of Guan** (Guanlin), a large enclosure with tree-lined paths between its many prayer halls. Not far from the Dragon Gate Grottoes, it provides a peaceful setting for an afternoon walk as well as a glimpse of contemporary Buddhist practice. ✛ *7½ km (4½ mi) south of town; accessible by minibus or hired car* ☎ *No phone* ▨ *Y15* ⊙ *Daily 8:30–6.*

Fodor'sChoice
★
To the southeast, the **Dragon Gate Grottoes** (Longmen Shiku) are a tribute to Buddhism's immense force in the Chinese past. Carved during two successive dynasties over several centuries, these thousands of Buddhist figures are ranged along the mountainside overlooking the Luo River. Although some of the grottoes are labeled in English, you rarely get more than a dynasty name and an uninformative blurb. The Chinese blurbs are not much better. The atmosphere of the site is part artwork, part ruins—exposure to the elements has done its bit to wear away the intricacy of the work. The real damage was done by the English and other Western enthusiasts of the 19th century who decided to take some of the artwork home with them. Many figures now stand headless, their faces decorating European museums or private collectors' shelves. You can visit the caves on your own or take one of numerous guided tours offered by CITS and the local hotels. ✛ *16 km (10 mi) southeast of town; accessible by taxi, Buses 53, 60, and 81, and private minibuses with same numbers* ▨ *Y50* ⊙ *Daily 8–6.*

Where to Stay & Eat

$–$$ ✕ **Zhen Butong.** The name means "truly different" and not surprisingly it is the only restaurant around that specializes in real "Luoyang flavor." The house specialty is a "water banquet," named for the rapidity of each successive course, but perhaps also referring to the soupy sauces in which each dish swims. These include both spicy entrées and a soothing dessert that tastes something like a Middle Eastern version of rice pudding. You don't have to order a whole banquet to enjoy some of its component parts. ✉ *369 Zhongzhou Dong Lu, Old District* ☎ *0379/ 395–5787* ▤ *No credit cards.*

$ ✕ **Churrascaria Do Brasil.** This Chinese-style Brazilian barbecue offers all-you-can-eat lunch and dinner buffets. Choose from any number of meats, including beefsteak, lamb, chicken wings, cuttlefish, and even spicy vegetarian chicken made of tofu. Chefs will deliver the grilled skewers right to your table, accompanied by a variety of cold Chinese dishes, dim sum, dumplings, and fruit. ✉ *278 Jinghua Lu* ☎ *0379/492–2839* ▤ *No credit cards.*

¢ ▥ **Luoyang Friendship Guest House.** A joint venture, the Friendship has tasteful amenities and a lovely courtyard out back whose artificial lake, curved bridge, and rock arrangement are inspired by the gardens of

Suzhou. Rooms are very clean. ⊠ *6 Xiyuan Lu, Jianxi District, 471003* ☎ *0379/491–2780* 🖷 *0379/491–3808* 🖙 *125 rooms, 13 suites* ♻ *2 restaurants, food court, in-room safes, pool, hair salon, sauna, business services* ⊟ *AE, DC, MC, V.*

¢ 🏨 **Luoyang Peony Hotel** (Luoyang Mudan Dajiudian). This joint-venture hotel lies a short walk from Wangcheng Park, home of Luoyang's peony festival. Its rooms are clean and its small restaurant serves fairly good Western food and some excellent Chinese dishes. More than half its guests are foreign tourists and businesspeople. The staff is friendly and the atmosphere is tasteful and quiet. ⊠ *15 Zhongzhou Xi Lu, 471003* 🖷🖷 *0379/ 485–6699* 🖙 *188 rooms, 6 suites* ♻ *Restaurant, in-room safes, minibars, cable TV, bar, travel services* ⊟ *AE, DC, MC, V.*

¢ 🏨 **New Friendship Hotel** (Xin Youyi Binguan). Located in the western part of town, this newer annex (renovated in 2000) to the old Friendship Hotel has pleasant modern rooms. Units come with the usual nondescript brown furniture but beds have clean linens and are comfortable. Bathrooms are small but clean. The hotel also has a Western restaurant, part of its entertainment center that includes a pool table, coffee bar, and shuffleboard. ⊠ *6 Xiyuan Xi Lu, 471003* ☎ *0379/491–3770* 🖷 *0379/491– 2328* 🖙 *120 rooms* ♻ *2 restaurants, refrigerators, cable TV, sauna, bar, lounge, concierge, business services* ⊟ *AE, DC, MC, V.*

¢ 🏨 **Peony Plaza Hotel Luoyang** (Mudan Cheng Binguan). Although this towering edifice was obviously built to cater to business travelers and upscale tourists, it also offers some great weekend deals and tour prices. The hotel is clean and has a professional and energetic staff. Guest rooms are cozy enough but the furniture is showing some wear. Bathrooms are a good size and come with scales to measure your dim sum intake. A revolving rooftop restaurant on the 25th floor offers great views of the city. A Western buffet breakfast is served. ⊠ *2 Nanchang Lu, Jianxi, 471000* ☎ *0379/468–1111* 🖷 *0379/493–0303* 🖙 *143 rooms, 20 suites.* ♻ *3 restaurants, minibars, cable TV, indoor pool, gym, sauna, bar, lounge, shops, concierge, dry cleaning, laundry service, business services* ⊟ *AE, DC, MC, V.*

Nightlife

Locals head to the outdoor market that springs up between Jingxuan Lu and Kaixuan Lu and bustle around the shopping district on Zhongzhou Dong Lu in the old city. For dancing, drinking, and entertainment, you're best off staying in your hotel.

Shopping

The tricolor pottery associated with the Tang Dynasty developed in Luoyang. The lot in back of the Longmen Grottoes has many Tang-style figurines. The Ru ceramics of the Song Dynasty are also local; the greenish glaze has a distinctive thick, opaque quality. Reproductions of these creations are sold at hotel shops and specialty stores. For everyday goods, try the **Luoyang Department Store** (⊠ 21 Zhongzhou Zhong Lu ☎ 0379/323–3531). The **Meitao Cheng** (⊠ Jian Dong Lu ☎ 0379/393– 1817) carries regional products. **Wenwu Shangdian** (⊠ Zhongzhou Dong Lu ☎ No phone) specializes in antiques, including calligraphy, pottery, and jewelry.

Henan A to Z

To research prices, get advice from other travelers, and book travel arrangements, visit www.fodors.com.

AIR TRAVEL

Luoyang is not as convenient to reach by plane as Zhengzhou. There are flights to Xian on weekdays and to major cities several times a week. Book through the travel offices in the Luoyang Peony Hotel or in the Friendship hotels or through CAAC at the Luoyang Airport.

Zhengzhou Airport is about 40 minutes' ride from town and offers daily flights to major Chinese cities. Tickets can be purchased at the central CAAC office or at CAAC outlets in the major hotels.

🖪 Airlines & Contacts **Central CAAC office, Luoyang** ⊠ Daobei Lu 🕾 0379/231-0121. **Central CAAC office, Zhengzhou** ⊠ 3 Jinshui Lu 🕾 0371/696-4789.

BUS TRAVEL BETWEEN CITIES IN HENAN

From the long-distance bus station in Kaifeng (just south of Baogong Lake on Yingbin Lu; take Bus 4, 6, 10, 12, or 13) buses run daily to Zhengzhou every hour on the half hour until 6:30 PM. An hourly service is available to Luoyang.

The Luoyang Bus Station is right across from the train station and provides buses to Zhengzhou (every 20 minutes), 3 hours away, and to Shaolin Temple, about 1½ hours away.

The long-distance bus station in Zhengzhou is directly across from the train station and offers buses to just about everywhere in China. The easiest places to reach by bus are Luoyang (every 20 minutes) and Kaifeng (every hour).

🖪 Bus Depot **Zhengzhou long-distance bus station** 🕾 0371/696-6107.

BUS TRAVEL WITHIN CITIES IN HENAN

Kaifeng's bus system covers all points of interest in the city. Bus 4 goes from the effective center of town at Gulou to the long-distance bus station.

A number of buses run the route down Luoyang's main drags, Zhongzhou Xi Lu and Zhongzhou Dong Lu; these are crowded at rush hour but are otherwise not bad. Public buses go out to the Buddhist grottoes and to White Horse Temple, but private minibuses are usually more comfortable.

Zhengzhou is a rather sprawling metropolis, and buses are a convenient way of getting around it. Public buses do not run to the out-of-town sights, but you can catch minibuses at the train station, or ask at your hotel information desk—many hotels run their own services.

CAR TRAVEL

It may be convenient to hire a car for a tour of the sights surrounding Zhengzhou and Luoyang. Check with a major hotel for hiring information. Kaifeng is smaller and best handled by bus or on foot.

EMERGENCIES

In Luoyang and Zhengzhou it is best to contact the police and hospitals through your hotel.

Hospitals Henan People's Hospital ⊠ Weiwu Lu, Zhengzhou ☎ 0371/558-0114. **Second People's Hospital of Luoyang** ⊠ 288 Zhongzhou Zhong Lu ☎ 0379/326-4500.

TAXIS

Kaifeng's friendly drivers have red taxis and pedicabs. Luoyang has vans and four-door cars that congregate mostly on Zhongzhou Lu, east and west. These are easy to flag down and aren't expensive. Unless you know how much a ride should cost, it is usually to your advantage to make sure the driver follows the meter, rather than agreeing on a price beforehand. Canary-yellow minivans and dark-red four-door cars roam the streets of Zhengzhou, particularly around the hotel and restaurant strip of Jinshui Lu.

TOURS

In Kaifeng the sights are within the city proper and don't require minibus hauls out of town. You're best off just getting a map and exploring the sights on your own.

Hotels in Luoyang offer minibus service out to the Longmen Grottoes and White Horse Temple. Other guided tours of the area can be arranged with CITS and include Mangshan Mountain and the ancient tombs.

Most hotels in Zhengzhou offer their own buses to Shaolin Temple and the Yellow River, and some will create custom tours if you want to see more of what lies between Zhengzhou and Luoyang. There are no guided city tours.

TRAIN TRAVEL

Kaifeng is easily accessible by rail: any train going east out of Zhengzhou will pass through here. Getting out is harder: the train station can't guarantee seats, and the place is often crowded and unruly. Leaving Kaifeng, it's best to take a bus.

Luoyang is on the rail line between Xian (six to seven hours) and Zhengzhou (about three hours). Trains run often to and from these destinations. The double-decker "tourist trains" are the most comfortable option.

Zhengzhou is one of the best-connected cities in China, lying on the intersection of both north–south and east–west lines. You can buy tickets to most major Chinese cities. Foreigners are encouraged to go to ticket window Number 1 or 2; you can also go to the advance booking office to avoid the crowds. Some hotels will book tickets for you.

Train Information Advance booking office ⊠ 193 Erqi Lu, Zhengzhou ☎ 0371/835-2222 or 0371/697-1920.

TRAVEL AGENCIES

In Zhengzhou, it's best to stick with the hotel travel agencies—every major hotel has one.

Local Agent Referrals CITS ⊠99 Dayuankengyan Jie, Kaifeng ☎0378/595-5743 ⊠Jiudu Xi Lu, Luoyang ☎ 0379/431-3701 ⊠ 50 Jingqi Lu, Zhengzhou ☎0371/595-2072.

Haitian Hotel ✉ 288 Chengdong Lu, north section, 8th fl., Zhengzhou ☎ 0379/595–9988. **Peony Hotel** ✉ 15 Zhongzhou Xi Lu, Luoyang ☎ 0379/485–6699.

Tourism Administration ✉ 14 Yingbin Lu, Kaifeng ☎ 0378/595–4370 ✉ Tourism Bldg., Jiudu Xi Lu, Jianxi District, Luoyang ☎ 0379/491–3824 ✉ 233 Zhongyuan Xi Lu, Zhengzhou ☎ 0371/744–8357 or 0371/595–5026.

VISITOR INFORMATION
Hotels, the CITS offices, and local tourist bureaus are the best sources of visitor information in all three cities.

SHANDONG

As the birthplace of Confucius (born in Qufu) and site of two of China's holy mountains (Taishan and Laoshan), Shandong is home to some of China's most important cultural sights. Along with the city of Qingdao, these are among the province's highlights. It is also the *laojia* (old home) of many current inhabitants of the northeastern provinces of Liaoning, Jilin, and Heilongjiang who escaped from poverty and war into Shandong in the decades after 1911 or colonized the area in Mao Zedong's postrevolutionary China.

The Yellow River, hard hit by drought in recent years, enters the Yellow Sea on the Shandong coastline. To the north lies the Bohai Gulf, and on land Shandong is bordered by Hebei, Henan, Anhui, and Jiangsu provinces. Shandong is one of the most populous provinces in China (population 87 million), and although Qingdao is relatively prosperous, many cities and much of the countryside are still very poor.

Ji'nan

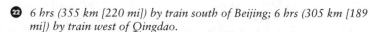

㉒ *6 hrs (355 km [220 mi]) by train south of Beijing; 6 hrs (305 km [189 mi]) by train west of Qingdao.*

The old city of Ji'nan was given a new lease on life about a hundred years ago by the construction of a railway line linking it to the port city of Qingdao. German, English, and Japanese concessions operated here, and a good number of buildings in the downtown area survive from this era. Ji'nan is a pleasant city, and the locals are friendly—something for which Shandong people in general enjoy a good reputation.

Today's city center, the most interesting part of Ji'nan, where European influence lingers, is laid out in a grid to the south of the railway station. An exploration of the city should begin here.

Sun Yat-sen Park (Zhongshan Gongyuan) is a quiet retreat from the city traffic. Early in the morning small groups of elderly people gather here to do tai chi, watched over by birds in cages the people hang on nearby trees while they exercise. ✉ *138 Jing San Lu* 🚇 *Y2* ☉ *Daily 6 AM–8 PM.*

need a break?

Shandong Elite Teahouse (✉ 9 Qianfoshan Lu ☎ No phone) makes for a lovely break any time of day. The teahouse serves many varieties of tea at polished dark wooden tables. The exquisite traditional Chinese teahouse setting is decorated with lattice wooden paneling, vases, and musical instruments.

Thousand Buddha Mountain (Qianfoshan), on the southern outskirts of the city, is still the focus of religious festivals, though most of the Buddhas have been lost to the ravages of time and the Cultural Revolution. The mountain does offer a good view of Ji'nan—air quality permitting. ⊠ *18 Jing Shiyi Lu, off Qianfoshan Lu beside Qilu Binguan hotel* 🕾 *Y15* 🕓 *Daily 6 AM–7 PM.*

One interesting architectural legacy of the foreign occupation is an imposing redbrick **Protestant church**, with its landmark twin towers. Built in 1927, it is still in use. ⊠ *425 Jing Si Lu.*

Where to Stay & Eat

$–$$ ✕ **Jinsanbei.** Customers here choose their meals in a novel way: ingredients—meat, fish, vegetables, and so on—are stocked in open coolers off the lobby, and live fish are in nearby tanks. After you take your pick, the staff carries it to the kitchen while you retire to the large wood-paneled dining room to wait for the meal. ⊠ *5 Qianfoshan Lu* 🕾 *0531/296–1616* 🖃 *No credit cards.*

¢–$$ ✕**A Fun Ti Hometown Music Restaurant.** This delightful Xinjiang-style restaurant serves up a culinary and audio feast. Customers can sample Muslim-influenced dishes from China's western regions while listening to live music also of central-Asian origin. In the late evening tables are cleared aside and eating gives way to dancing. ⊠ *18 Chaoshan Jie* 🕾 *0531/612–7228* 🖃 *No credit cards.*

¢–$$ ✕ **Luneng Shaoezai.** This Mongolian barbecue–style restaurant is very popular with locals. It presents a vast buffet of fresh seafood, meat, vegetables, and seasonings for customers to combine as they please and deliver to the kitchen for cooking. ⊠ *Jing Si Lu in Linxiang Dasha complex* 🕾 *0531/601–1888* 🖃 *No credit cards.*

¢–$$ ✕ **Shandong Danlian Seafood Restaurant.** At this simple open-plan restaurant specializing in seafood, customers can choose their meal from the selection of live (in tanks) and frozen seafood displayed in the lobby. ⊠ *86 Jing Ba Lu* 🕾 *0531/290–1618* 🖃 *No credit cards.*

$ 🏨 **Hotel Sofitel.** In the center of town, this modern 49-story edifice incorporates classical European elements in its decor, from chandeliers and thick columns in the lobby to traditional furniture in the rooms. Guest rooms are spacious and offer impeccable luxury and comfort, high above Ji'nan. The marble bathrooms, which come with separate tub and shower, are on the small side. The hotel is a tightly run operation with friendly and obliging staff. Among its six restaurants, be sure to try the Silver Sky Revolving Restaurant on the roof for a panoramic view of the city and a hearty buffet dinner, all while being entertained with a live music performance. ⊠ *66 Luoyuan Dajie, 250063* 🕾 *0531/606–8888* 🖷 *0531/606–6666* ⊕ *www.accorhotels.com/asia* 🛏 *432 rooms* ⚭ *6 restaurants, minibars, cable TV, pool, gym, bar, business services* 🖃 *AE, DC, MC, V.*

¢ 🏨 **Guidu.** In the heart of town, this hotel offers modest accommodations at reasonable prices. Rooms in the south tower, renovated in 2002, are elegant and have modern furniture and comfortable beds with pristine white comforters. The marble bathrooms are on the small side, but are bright and clean. North-tower rooms are large though the furniture and carpets are worn. Service is adequate and some staff members speak a little English. ⊠ *2 Nanmen Dajie* ☎ *0531/692–1911* 🖷 *0531/692– 3187* 🛏 *400 units* ⚑ *2 restaurants, minibars, cable TV, massage, sauna, bar, lounge, nightclub, shops, dry cleaning, concierge, business center* ▭ *AE, DC, MC, V.*

¢ ⌸ **Qilu Binguan.** This hotel, located on fringes of the city near Thousand Buddha Mountain, is a decent option. The hotel lobby, decorated in dark woods, is quite elegant. Guest rooms are average, aged with faded pink carpets, but otherwise functional and clean, as are the clashing yellow-and-green marble bathrooms. The restaurants serve Chinese, Japanese, and Western food. ⊠ *Qianfoshan Lu, 250014* ☎ *0531/296–6888* 🖷 *0531/296–7676* 🛏 *255 units* ⚑ *3 restaurants, in-room safes, minibars, cable TV, massage, sauna, bowling, bar, lounge, shops, dry cleaning, concierge, business services, airport shuttle* ▭ *AE, DC, MC, V.*

Nightlife

There is little in the way of conventional nightlife in Ji'nan. What exists is concentrated in a short strip near the Qilu Binguan hotel.

The popular **Boiling Point Bar** (⊠ 9 Qianfoshan Lu ☎ No phone) is furnished in timber and has a dance floor in the middle, a dartboard on the wall, and a cooler full of imported beers.

Shopping

The best department store in Ji'nan is the **Yin Zuo** (Silver Plaza; ⊠ Luo Yuan Dajie), with seven shiny floors of everything from domestic appliances to cosmetics, plus a basement supermarket and Chinese fast-food outlets. There's not much in terms of typical tourist items.

Side Trips from Ji'nan

㉓ The top of **Mt. Tai** (Taishan), reaching 5,067 feet above sea level, is one of China's five holy Taoist mountains. The walk up—on cut-stone steps—by open mountainside, steep crags, and pine woods takes three to four hours. Some people stay overnight to watch the sun rise, but the classic sunrise over cloud-hugged mountainside seen in photos is actually a rare sight. Confucius is said to have climbed the mountain and commented from its height: "The world is very small." Much later Mao Zedong climbed it and even more famously said: "The East is red." At the foot of the mountain is the unremarkable town of Taian. ⊠ *About 50 km (30 mi) south of Ji'nan.*

㉔ **Qufu** is the birthplace of the great sage himself. A good percentage of Qufu's population claim to be descendants of Confucius. The **Confucius Temple, Confucius Family Mansion,** and the **Family Graveyard** are the focus of today's visitors. Confucius has been honored in Qufu almost consistently since his own time 2,500 years ago. Money was regularly sent from Beijing by the emperors to augment and keep up the extensive buildings devoted to his memory. Regular buses run trips from Ji'nan to Qufu. The Qufu Bus Station is located south of the town center at the intersection of Shen Dao and Jingxuan Lu. ⌖ *3 hrs by car or bus (110 km [68 mi]) south of Ji'nan.*

Qingdao

12 hrs (540 km [335 mi]) by train or 2 hrs by plane southeast of Beijing; 6 hrs by train (310 km [192 mi]) east of Ji'nan.

Qingdao was a sleepy fishing village until the end of the 19th century, at which point Germans, using the killing of two German missionaries in the vicinity as a pretext, set up another European colony on the coastal fringe of China. The German presence lasted only until 1914, but the city continued to build in the German style, and large parts of the old town make visitors feel as if they have stumbled into southern Germany. Today it is one of China's most charming cities and home to the country's best-known brewery, Tsingtao (the old-style Romanization of Qingdao), founded in 1903. East of the main harbor, Tsingtao still does a fair impression of a good German lager and produces a sweet black Island stout as well. The city is also nursery to a growing wine industry.

As one of the fastest-growing cities in China, Qingdao is rapidly evolving into a leading economic port city with foreign investment exceeding billions of dollars. With a mild climate and seaside-town beauty, Qingdao provides an ideal venue for golfing and other sports such as cycling and mountain climbing.

Qingdao, with its seafront promenades, winding colonial streets, parks, and red-tile roofs, is made for strolling. The main shopping areas are around Zhongshan Lu; nearby is the city's landmark building, a twin-spired Catholic church. Don't miss the fascinating wholesale fresh seafood markets along the edge of the city's smaller harbor.

㉕ A landmark in Qingdao is the **Catholic church** (Tianzhu Jiaotang), with its towering 200-foot twin steeples and red-tile roof. Originally named St. Emil Church, it was built by the Germans in 1934. ⊠ *15 Zhejiang Lu* 🚋 *Y5* ⊙ *Mon.–Sat. 8–5, Sun. 9–5.*

㉖ Qingdao's **Protestant church** (Jidu Jiaotang) has a bell tower with a clock. It was built in 1910 at the southwest entrance of Xinhao Hill Park. ⊠ *15 Jiangsu Lu* 🚋 *Y3* ⊙ *Daily 8:30–4:30.*

> **need a break?**
>
> The **Mingtian Coffee Language** (⊠ 82 Hong Kong Central Rd. ☎ 0532/592–3101 ⊟ No credit cards) is an elegant and comfortable coffee shop decorated entirely with materials imported from Taiwan, and specializes in the flavored milk teas so popular on the island. Chinese snacks and set meals are also served, but no alcohol is permitted.

㉗ One of the best views of old Qingdao is from the three red, mushroom-shape towers on the top of Xinhao Shan in **Xinhao Hill Park** (Xinhao Shan Gongyuan). ⊠ *Off Daxue Lu* 🚋 *Park Y2, towers Y12.*

㉘ The old **German governor's residence** (Qingdao Ying Binguan) was a public hotel until 1996 when it became a museum. Built in 1903 as the official residence of the governor-general of the then-German colony of Qingdao, it is set on a hill in mature gardens overlooking the old city.

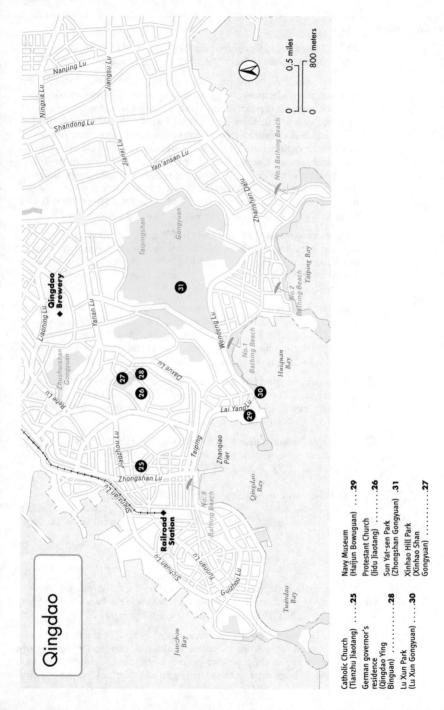

Qingdao

The interior is warm, with wood paneling and a wide staircase leading from the ground-floor foyer to the guest rooms. Among the famous leaders who stayed here were Mao Zedong; his wife, Jiang Qing; Zhou Enlai; Deng Xiaoping; and Cambodia's Prince Sihanouk. ⊠ *26 Longshan Lu, below Xinhao Hill Park* ⌚ *Y10* ⊙ *Daily 8:30–4:30.*

㉙ In the upper yard of the **Navy Museum** (Haijun Bowuguan) is an indoor exhibition documenting the history of the Chinese navy and displaying an extensive collection of uniforms and plaques presented by visiting navies. Outside in the lower yard stands a range of military equipment, including Russian-made fighter aircraft, fixed-turret and anti-aircraft naval guns, rockets, tanks, ground artillery, naval vessels (including three moored in the adjacent harbor), and even an old biplane. ⊠ *8 Lai Yang Lu* ☎ *0532/286–6784* ⌚ *Y20* ⊙ *Daily 8:30–7:30.*

㉚ **Lu Xun Park** (Lu Xun Gongyuan), built in 1929, faces onto Huiquan Bay, combining traditional Chinese garden art with the rocky coastline. In 1950 it was named for the distinguished Chinese writer and commentator Lu Xun. ⊠ *West end of No. 1 Bathing Beach* ⌚ *Y2.*

Ⓒ **㉛** **Sun Yat-sen Park** (Zhongshan Gongyuan), named for Dr. Sun Yat-sen, is the largest park in the city. Its Oriental cherry path, osmanthus garden, and other exotic plant gardens are best visited in spring. The park is also home to the Qingdao Zoo. ⊠ *28 Wendeng Lu, north of Huiquan Dynasty hotel* ⌚ *Y5* ⊙ *Daily 5 AM–9 PM.*

Where to Stay & Eat

$–$$ ✕ **Chunhe Lou.** This venerable, generations-old culinary mecca is housed in a two-story corner building in the German concession. Reserved for more formal gatherings, the second floor is furnished with large tables for big parties and private dining vestibules for private business meals. The first floor entertains daily diners who come in for a quick and hearty meal. Tourist groups are often led up to the second floor where courses are presented in a sequence of appetizers followed by meat, vegetables, seafood, and soup. House specials include Shandong delicacies such as *you-bao hailuo* (snails stir-fried with traditional bean sauce), or crispy tender chicken in the style of Peking duck. ⊠ *146 Zhongshan Lu* ☎ *0532/282–4346* ▤ *No credit cards.*

¢–$$ ✕ **Dou Lia Shun.** This seafood restaurant across from the Catholic church has big fish tanks and a courteous staff. A new interior and high ceilings make it airy and quiet. Dark and pale beers are brewed on-site. ⊠ *26 Zhejiang Lu* ☎ *0532/288–1717* ▤ *No credit cards.*

¢–$$ ✕ **Yiqinglou.** Immensely popular with locals, this restaurant requires diners to choose live seafood from tanks, or from a huge array of demonstration plates of mixed meat, vegetables, and fish. An identical meal is then prepared by the chefs and presented at the table. ⊠ *90 Xiang Gang Zhong Lu* ☎ *0532/588–3388* ▤ *No credit cards.*

¢–$ ✕ **Tudali.** Next to the Shangri-La hotel is this Korean barbecue restaurant open until late at night. It has a comfortable and familiar feel to it, evidenced by the walls covered with grateful patrons' messages. Like the outdoor Mongolian barbecue, the barbecued lamb or beef and vegetables attract most diners. Authentic Korean kimchi and stir-fried noodles make tasty side dishes. ⊠ *52 Xiang Gang Xi Lu* ☎ *0532/322–9720* ▤ *No credit cards.*

$$$ 🏨 **Shangri-La.** This top-class hotel opened in late 1997 with standard Shangri-La facilities. Though situated in a commercial rather than a tourist district, it is nevertheless only a block from the scenic coastline, and close to some of the best shopping and eating in town. Rooms are well equipped with modern amenities, including two sofa chairs. Bed sheets are crisp and clean. ⊠ *9 Xiang Gang Zhong Lu, 266071* ☎ *0532/388–3838* 🖷 *0532/388–6868* ⊕ *www.shangri-la.com* ⌘ *402 rooms* ♨ *2 restaurants, in-room data ports, in-room fax, minibars, refrigerators, cable TV, tennis court, pool, gym, bar, business services* ▤ *AE, DC, MC, V.*

$$–$$$ 🏨 **Grand Regency.** Extravagantly modern, the hotel has a huge foyer and an immense ballroom made with materials imported from Italy, England, and South Africa. Rooms are tastefully decorated and spacious. The only drawback is the relatively poor view due to the hotel's location in the industrial and commercial district. All rooms offer in-house movie channels and satellite TV. The restaurants serve Cantonese, French, Japanese, and international fare. ⊠ *1 Taiwan Lu, 266071* ☎ *0532/588–1818* 🖷 *0532/588–1888* ⊕ *www.grh-ohm.com* ⌘ *448 rooms* ♨ *4 restaurants, in-room safes, minibars, cable TV, tennis court, pool, gym, 2 bars, nightclub, business services* ▤ *AE, DC, MC, V.*

$$ 🏨 **Haitian.** Having gone multiple renovations, this hotel now has state-of-the-art amenities in clean, modern rooms with good coastal views overlooking Qingdao's Number 3 Bathing Beach. The restaurants serve Chinese, Japanese, Korean, and Western fare. When weather permits, barbecue is served outside. ⊠ *48 Xiang Gang Xi Lu, 266071* ☎ *0532/387–1888* 🖷 *0532/387–1777* ⊕ *www.hai-tian-hotel.com* ⌘ *608 rooms* ♨ *4 restaurants, minibars, cable TV, pool, gym, bar, business services* ▤ *AE, DC, MC, V.*

☾ $–$$ 🏨 **Huiquan Dynasty.** This modern hotel overlooks the Number 1 Bathing Beach and the sea east of the downtown area. In the newest part, a high-rise tower, every guest room has a private balcony overlooking the Yellow Sea. The revolving restaurant—serving Chinese and Western breakfast and evening meals—on the 25th floor affords views of the beautiful old city of Qingdao. Spacious and comfortable standard rooms come with color TV with in-house movies. The restaurants serve Chinese, Japanese, and Western cuisine. ⊠ *9 Nanhai Lu, 266003* ☎ *0532/288–6688* 🖷 *0532/287–1122* ⊕ *http://qingdao-cn.hotels-x.net/Huiquan-dynasty-hotel.html* ⌘ *409 rooms* ♨ *4 restaurants, in-room safes, minibars, miniature golf, tennis court, pool, gym, sauna, bar, nightclub, baby-sitting, business services* ▤ *AE, DC, MC, V.*

¢–$ 🏨 **Dongfang.** Located in the university area within walking distance of downtown, this hotel has good views of colonial Qingdao from its comfortable guest rooms. All are equipped with modern facilities. The restaurants serve Chinese and Western food. ⊠ *4 Daxue Lu, 266003* ☎ *0532/286–5888* 🖷 *0532/286–2741* ⊕ *www.hotel-dongfang.com* ⌘ *145 rooms* ♨ *2 restaurants, in-room safes, minibars, cable TV, tennis court, gym, bar, nightclub, business services* ▤ *AE, DC, MC, V.*

¢–$ 🏨 **Oceanwide Elite.** This modern, elegant hotel built in a semi-German style sits right on the seafront promenade. Rooms range from the elegant wood-paneled Presidential Bedroom to a standard, simply furnished, spic-and-span room. All rooms come with satellite TV, Internet access, and hair dryers. ⊠ *29 Taiping Lu, 266001* ☎ *0532/288–6699* 🖷 *0532/289–1388* 🖅 *82 rooms, 8 suites, 30 no-smoking rooms, 8 rooms for people with disabilities* ⚭ *2 restaurants, minibars, cable TV, gym, nightclub* ⊟ *AE, DC, MC, V.*

Nightlife & the Arts

The **International Beer Festival,** in August, is Qingdao's biggest event of the year, with fireworks and gallons of beer for tasting. There are also several **harvest festivals,** including the **Taidong Radish Festival** and the **Sugar-Coated Haws Festival** (a *haw* is a type of sour fruit, about the size of a cherry with hard pits inside; haws are dipped in caramel, with 5 to 10 on a stick, as a regional specialty), both in January. The **Cherry Festival** takes place in April and May. In early September the **Mt. Daze Grape Festival** celebrates the fruit of the vine.

Sports

Many new golf clubs are open to all visitors and provide numerous standard courses and practice areas. Three good options are Qingdao International Golf Club (⊠ Gaozhi Lu in Hightech Park ☎ 0532/789–1133), International Golf Country Club (⊠ Huanshan, Jimo City ☎ 0532/456–1190), and Surf Plaza Golf Club (⊠ Qingdao Shilaoren National Resort ☎ 0532/889–7718).

Shopping

The north end of Zhongshan Lu has a cluster of antiques and cultural artifacts shops. The **Ju Bao Zhai Art Shop** (⊠ 169 Zhongshan Lu ☎ 0532/282–4184) offers a selection of porcelain, metal, and stone wares. The largest antique shop on the street is the **Qingdao Art and Craft Store** (⊠ 212 Zhongshan Lu ☎ 0532/281–7948), with four floors of porcelain, scroll paintings, silk, gold, jade, and other stones.

Department stores include **Fada Mansion** (⊠ Junction of Zhongshan Lu and Hunan Lu ☎ 0532/296–1818) and **Parkson** (⊠ 46 Zhongshan Lu ☎ 0532/202–1085). The Japanese-owned **JUSCO** (⊠ 72 Xiang Gang Zhong Lu ☎ 0532/571–9600) has the best supermarket and mall in town.

Side Trips from Qingdao

32 The holy **Laoshan,** which rivals Shandong's other famous mountain, Taishan, rises to a height of more than 3,280 feet above sea level. A repository of Taoism, during its heyday it had nine palaces, eight temples, and 72 convents. With sheer cliffs and cascading waterfalls, the beautiful mountain is widely recognized in China as a source of the country's best-known mineral water. The mountain area covers 400 square km (154 square mi), but paths to Laoshan proper lead from the Song Dynasty Taiqing Palace. Tourist buses to Laoshan leave from the main pier in Qingdao. Contact the local CITS (⊠ Block A, Yuyuan Bldg., 73 Xiang Gang Xi Lu, Qingdao, 266071 ☎ 0532/389–3028) or the Qingdao Tourism Administration (⊠ 16 1st Guanhai Lu, Qingdao ☎ 0532/288–2420) for bus schedule and price range. ⊠ *40 km (25 mi) east of Qingdao.*

Near Laoshan, **Huadong Winery,** Shandong's best winery, is not yet as famous as the province's brewery but has already won a string of prizes. The winery's equipment comes from France and the United States, and the vines were bought from France in the mid-1980s. The chardonnay is on a par with any good American wine, perhaps because the wine-growing area of Shandong is on the same latitude as California's Napa Valley. Tours are only available through CITS.

Shandong A to Z

To research prices, get advice from other travelers, and book travel arrangements, visit www.fodors.com.

AIR TRAVEL

Regular flights link Ji'nan Yiao Qiang Airport with Hong Kong and other major Chinese cities. The airport is 70 km (43 mi) northeast of Ji'nan.

Qingdao Liu Ting Airport is 30 km (19 mi) from the city center. Direct flights link Qingdao with Osaka and Seoul, as well as Hong Kong and other major Chinese cities. Flights can be booked through hotels or at CAAC.
🚹 Airport Information Ji'nan Airport ⊠ Near Yiao Qiang Village ☎ 0531/694-9400. Qingdao Airport ⊠ Near Liu Ting Village ☎ 0532/471-5139.
🚹 Airlines & Contacts Qingdao CAAC ⊠ 29 Zhongshan Lu ☎ 0532/289-5577 📠 0532/287-0747.

BOAT & FERRY TRAVEL

In summer several boats a week link Qingdao with Shanghai. Ask at CITS or buy tickets at the passenger ferry terminal.
🚹 Boat & Ferry Information CITS ⊠ 9 Nanhai Lu, Qingdao ☎ 0532/288-0390. Ferry Terminal ⊠ Xinjiang Jie near the Friendship Store , Qingdao.

BUS TRAVEL

Regular buses link Qufu with Ji'nan, three hours away, and Taian, two hours away. Taian is about an hour from Ji'nan by bus. Buses ply the route between Qingdao and Ji'nan every 20 minutes, taking four to five hours. The bus terminals in Qingdao and Taian are opposite the respective train stations.
🚹 Bus Depot Qufu Bus Station ⊠ South of town center at intersection of Shen Dao and Jingxuan Lu ☎ 0543/7441-2554.

TRAIN TRAVEL

Ji'nan Station is on the Beijing–Shanghai rail line and the Beijing–Qingdao line, so there is no shortage of trains. The trip to Beijing takes about 5½ hours. Taian Station is on the main Beijing–Shanghai rail line with onward connections in either direction.

Direct trains link Qingdao with Beijing (10 hrs), Shanghai (19 hrs), Shenyang (24 hrs), Yantai (4 hrs), Xian (22 hrs), and Lanzhou (31 hrs).
🚹 Train Information Ji'nan Station ⊠ Chezhanjie or Chezhan Ave. ☎ 0531/242-8862. Taian Station ⊠ Yingzhe Dajie ☎ 0538/824-6222.

NORTHEASTERN CHINA
INDUSTRY & WILDERNESS

3

By David
Murphy
Updated by
George
Vaughton

NORTHEASTERN CHINA HAS THE HUGE URBAN CENTERS OF MODERN CHINA—some booming, some going bust—and a giant wilderness contiguous with Siberia. The region, also known as Manchuria, has witnessed the rise of the Manchu Dynasty, Russian adventurism, Japanese invasion, Chinese resistance, and Cold War hostility. Yet it retains the architectural stamps of each. From Harbin's Ice Lantern Festival to the port of Dalian ("Hong Kong of the north") to the wilderness outside the cities, northeastern China rewards travelers with a surprising diversity, if you're willing to leave the tourist trail.

The Northeast—what the Chinese call Dongbei—consists of the provinces of Liaoning, Jilin, and Heilongjiang. This land was home to China's last imperial house, the Qing, who conquered Beijing in 1644 and ruled China until the 1911 Republican revolution. The Qing were Manchus, who still survive as a distinct ethnic group in the Northeast.

Until 1911 Han were forbidden to settle in Manchuria, and the area, though agriculturally rich, was sparsely inhabited. In the 1920s, driven by war and poverty, people flocked from neighboring Shandong across the Bohai Gulf to work as farmers or in the many Japanese factories that had been established in the puppet state of Manchukuo. After the 1949 Communist Revolution, China's new leader, Mao Zedong, encouraged people to fill the empty parts of China. This created another massive flood of settlers, again mostly from Shandong. As a result, many in these three northeastern provinces claim Shandong as their *laojia* (ancestral home). Most outsiders who come here are on business. Tourism facilities are not as plentiful as they are in other parts of the country, but the resulting peace and quiet can be a blessing.

Exploring Northeastern China

China's vast Northeast sprawls between Inner Mongolia, Russia, and the Korean peninsula. While much of Heilongjiang is a wilderness of Siberian forest and icy rivers, Jilin is separated from North Korea by the Changbaishan, home to the Heavenly Lake and, allegedly, China's own version of the Loch Ness Monster. Relatively more developed, the southern area of Liaoning has beaches and golf courses near Dalian and ancient tombs in Shenyang. On the whole Dongbei's forested western and mountainous eastern extremes are remote and difficult to reach. The central heartland, providing most of China's domestic wheat crop, is well crisscrossed by railroads and highways linking up the major population centers. Though well connected, the region is huge and hitting all the towns could leave you staring out the window for days on end as golden wheat fields roll by.

About the Restaurants
Visitors arriving from southern China will be shocked by the enormity of northeastern portions. The people here tend to be the biggest in China and so do their appetites. Wheat replaces rice as the staple grain and restaurants are more likely to feature steaming platters of noodles, dumplings, and bread rather than the ubiquitous rice bowl. While northern tastes tend to be gamier, often serving deer and wild boar, the south-

The itineraries below are based on train journeys, but a combination of rail and flight is possible on any tour of this region.

Numbers in the margin correspond to points of interest on the Northeastern China and Dalian maps.

If you have 3 days

3

Dalian ⑩–⑬ ⌐, a former colonial center and currently one of China's smartest cities, makes an excellent weekend trip from Beijing. Comfortable overnight sleeper trains are available from Beijing, departing at nightfall. Spend your days here in pure relaxation—having a round of golf, lounging on the beach, or taking a stroll along the coast roads. At night indulge in the seafood extravaganza that is dining in Dalian.

On the first day, take in morning tai chi with the locals in **Sun Yat-sen Square** ⑩ and stroll the city's quiet, tree-lined streets viewing local life amid old-colonial architecture. Sample some quality, inexpensive Korean food for lunch before striking out on any seaside road to view port activity, the local fishermen, and the sea. Try the Japanese food or the local seafood for dinner and consult your hotel staff for the hottest nightspots as these change regularly. On your second day, head out to the **Golden Stone Beach** and spend the day hiking trails along the cliff sides or relaxing in secluded lagoons. Make sure to sample the local seafood before heading back to town. On your third day squeeze in a round at the **Dalian Golden Pebble Golf Course** if there's time, or simply cruise the Laodong Park and stock up on souvenirs before heading back to Beijing.

If you have 5 days

After spending a few days in Dalian, following the three-day itinerary, take the train to **Changchun** ③ (about eight hours) and spend a day here exploring the history of the Japanese occupation of the area. On the way back take a look at **Shenyang** ⑧, one of China's great industrial cities. The historical heritage in Shenyang is of an older vintage, and the palace, pagodas, and tombs easily make for a day or two of sightseeing.

If you have 8 or more days

Begin by spending a couple of days in **Harbin** ❶ ⌐, a border town with an intriguing blend of cultures which, even when the Ice Lantern Festival is not happening, has a rich architecture tradition, a picturesque shopping district, and some interesting markets. In winter, spend a day on the slopes at the **Yabuli International Ski Resort** ❷ outside of Harbin or head south to **Jilin City** ❺ and take a few turns at **Beidahu Ski Resort** ❻. Alternatively, in summer, use either **Changchun** ③ or Jilin City as a launch pad into the wilds of the **Changbaishan Nature Reserve** ❹.

A couple of days in the mountains or forest may have you craving creature comforts, so head for Changchun and **Shenyang** ⑧, where you can spend a day or two in each exploring China's rich Manchurian history, as in the five-day itinerary. On the sixth day, arrive in **Dalian** ⑩–⑬, the up-and-coming coastal resort and typical eastern China boomtown located on the tip of the Liaodong peninsula.

ern coastal city of Dalian has some of the best seafood in China. Throughout the region, hotpot is a favorite, a delicious option that allows you to choose from any number of ingredients and spices and cook food at your own table. Northern appetites can be fierce and don't always stop with food; locals can quaff the local firewater, called *baijiu*, morning, noon, and night. Ranging from 80 to 128 proof, this rice "wine" is not for the faint of heart, or liver.

If you want to take a break from Chinese food, you'll find Korean and Japanese street-front and hotel restaurants in many cities. For Western food, it's better to stick to the restaurants in leading foreign-managed or joint-venture hotels, which often have excellent-value Western-style buffet lunches.

About the Hotels

China's tourism industry has taken off in the past few years and, albeit slowly, the Northeast's hotels are responding. Every major city seems to be gaining a few "luxury" Western-, Hong Kong–, or Singapore-managed hotels each year. State-run hotels, known for their musty rooms, poor service, and inadequate facilities, may keep their shabby facades, but competition has forced many to privatize, renovate, lower prices, and include things like in-room Internet access and complimentary breakfast. That said, no matter what you're told at the front desk, it's always wise to check the hot water or air-conditioning in your room before moving in.

Occupancy is as low as 30% in some top-class hotels, and special deals are available; fax ahead to request the hotel's best rate or reserve directly on Web sites like www.sinohotel.com. As elsewhere in China, the holidays during the first weeks of October and May and the Chinese New Year (usually between mid-January and mid-February) are the busiest times of the year, when discounts are scarce and hotels fill up fast. Additionally, those seeking rooms with a view for Harbin's Ice Lantern Festival in early January should make reservations several months in advance.

WHAT IT COSTS In Yuan					
	$$$$	**$$$**	**$$**	**$**	**¢**
RESTAURANTS	over 165	100–165	50–99	25–49	under 25
HOTELS	over 1,800	1,400–1,800	1,100–1,399	7001,099	under 700

Restaurant prices are for a main course, excluding tax and tips. Hotel prices are for a standard double room, including taxes.

Timing

Late April and May are the best times to visit the region; the emergence of natural colors in spring is a relief from the unrelenting grayness of winter. Melting snow and ice swell the rivers, causing wildflowers to blossom and birds to sing. Spring, however, is the dry season and a series of especially destructive forest fires in 2003 has led to outdoor smoking bans in certain areas.

3

I Like the Nightlife

Typical Dongbei nightlife once consisted solely of the holy trinity of dinner, karaoke, and sauna, but times are changing fast and Northeast China is rapidly embracing the bar-and-nightclub culture already popular in China's major cities. With its Russian colonial influence, Harbin tends to favor mass quantities of drink while hipper Dalian has sleek new bars and nightclubs opening every week. On weekends, local bands rotate gigs at certain nightspots while local ex-pats belly up to the bar to drink away their frustrations with weekday life in the factories. Be warned: the karaoke plague is still widespread.

Ice Ice Baby

Winter sets this part of China apart from all the rest of the country. The giant icicles hanging from trees and eaves and a blanket of snow stretching as far as the eye can see make a somewhat forsaken land seem clean and pure. Whereas people in other regions begin to complain when the mercury drops, Northeasterners truly come into their own. Much of the region spends at least half the year under snow and ice, and the locals make the best of it. For sheer spectacle, nothing can surpass Harbin's Ice Lantern Festival, where frozen sculptures arise in the snow, so intricate and grand that they draw visitors from all over Asia and the world. A cacophony of light erupts through the ice, turning the park into a virtual kaleidoscope. Contests are held and judges take their job very seriously.

Other winter festivities don't take on such a grand scale. Ice fishing yields some of the biggest and best catches of the year. Ice-skating is also a local activity of choice. Walk down to any frozen lake or river and find skate rental stands set up. If that action is too flat, head for the hills where skiing, China's newest sport is taking off with the newly rich. The two best resorts (and that relatively speaking, of course) are Yabuli and Beidahu. The bravest winter revelers, however, test their mettle by swimming in the not-yet-frozen or recently thawed rivers. Saunas and public baths abound should you lose circulation. For true winter buffs, Dongbei should not be missed.

The Manchurian Candidate

Dongbei is a history buff's dreams come true. It's sometimes hard to imagine that so many nations would have fought over a land so bitterly cold but the palaces, ruins, and tombs have all lived to tell the tale. From Russian churches and Japanese temples to Manchurian palaces and the last remnants of China's imperial system, Dongbei provides a fascinating window onto the vicissitudes of Northeast China's enduring relationships with it neighbors.

The Russian-built churches and cathedrals of Harbin give a rich flavor of the forces shaping Northeast China's pre-Communist modern history. Shenyang's pagodas, particularly the Sheli Pagoda and the Northern Pagoda are must-sees for lovers of ancient Chinese history, while the Imperial Palace is a fascinating homage to the empire builders of the region. The Puppet Emperor's Palace in Changchun proves a poignant reminder that, sooner or later, all empires witness the setting of their own sun.

From late September to early November the countryside takes on rich natural hues, ripe wheat fills the fields with rolling gold, the climate remains comfortable, and high-pressure systems often clear the pollution from the skies. Beware though: old man winter comes on fast and anyone visiting in November should bring an extra set of precautionary long johns.

Though spring and autumn may be the most comfortable times to visit, any local will tell you that winter is the time to see Dongbei's true colors. Whether it's a winter wonderland or a frozen hell is a question of perspective. The area has a number of winter attractions, primarily the outstanding Ice Lantern Festival in Harbin, the ice-covered trees of Jilin, and several emerging ski resorts. Locals take to frozen rivers and lakes to ice-skate and ice fish while unfrozen rivers abound with people partaking in China's latest health craze: winter swimming. In many cities, restaurants and other service- or visitor-oriented businesses close early in winter.

Summer is the rainy season and can be hot and humid—climate and mosquitoes keep many visitors away. While good hotels have air-conditioning, many taxis and offices do not. For travelers hoping to visit the Changbaishan Nature Reserve along the North Korean border, however, summer is the only reasonable time to make the trip, as frozen roads the rest of the year make the park inaccessible. As you head farther north, daylight hours noticeably increase.

HEILONGJIANG

With a relatively small population and an area of nearly 470,000 square km (181,500 square mi), Heilongjiang (literally Black Dragon River) is making a name for itself as an outdoor destination, with an emphasis on fishing and bird-watching. It was one of the points where imperial European expansion (in this case czarist Russia) met imperial China in the 19th century. Heilongjiang belonged to the vast swath of empty territory in eastern Asia that was colonized in the 20th century by European Russians and Han Chinese. Native tribes that survived in the Heilongjiang, for example the Oroqen, are now happy modern citizens of the People's Republic of China (PRC), according to the official press at least. The province is renowned for its rich black soil and is a major producer of grain. The Heilong River (Heilongjiang), known to the Russians as the Amur, provides the boundary between the province and Russia, though even today the border is not fully delineated.

Harbin

 16 hrs (1,000 km [621 mi]) northeast of Beijing by train or just over 2 hrs by plane.

Harbin, on the banks of the Songhua River, takes its name from the Manchu word *alejin,* suggesting fame and reputation. It's the capital of the province and was once a Russian railway terminus for the line to

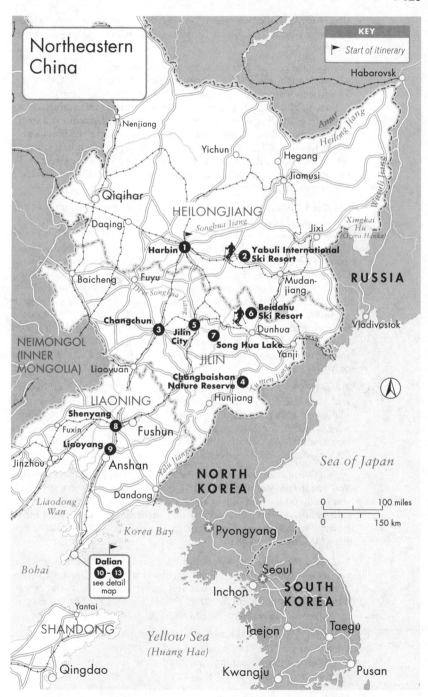

Northeastern China

Habarovsk

Nenjiang

Yichun

Hegang

Jiamusi

Qiqihar

HEILONGJIANG

Songhua Jiang

Daqing

Jixi

Xingkai Hu (Ozero Hanka)

Baicheng

Fuyu

Harbin ❶

❷ Yabuli International Ski Resort

Mudan-jiang

RUSSIA

Dise Songhua Jiang

Changchun

❸

❺

Jilin City

❼

Song Hua Lake

❻ Beidahu Ski Resort

Dunhua

Vladivostok

NEIMONGOL (INNER MONGOLIA)

Liaoyuan

JILIN

Yanji

Changbaishan Nature Reserve

❹

Tu men Jiang

LIAONING

Hunjiang

Shenyang

❽

Fushun

Fuxin

Liaoyang ❾

Jinzhou

Anshan

Yalu Jiang

Dandong

NORTH KOREA

Sea of Japan

Liaodong Wan

Korea Bay

0		100 miles
0		150 km

Bohai

Dalian ❿ – ⓭ see detail map

Yantai

⭐ Pyongyang

⭐ Seoul

SOUTH KOREA

SHANDONG

Yellow Sea (Huang Hae)

Inchon

Taejon

Taegu

Qingdao

Kwangju

Pusan

Vladivostok. The city bounced between the Russians and the Japanese until after World War II. Today Russians are again on the scene—as tourists and traders.

Winters are cold in Harbin temperatures average close to −20°C (−4°F) in January, the coldest month, and can plunge to −38°C (−36°F). The frozen waters of the Songhua River in winter are bringing a bit of fame to Harbin, in the form of ever more intricate ice carvings. Massive blocks of ice are taken from the river by mechanical excavators and transported to Zhaolin Park, where artists carve the blocks into more than 1,000 fantastic ice sculptures, many with colored lanterns placed inside. Exhibitions regularly include versions of the Great Wall, famous pagodas, and the Xian terra-cotta warriors. The festival usually begins on January 5.

The **Daoli** District contains numerous buildings dating from the era of Russian domination in Harbin. Many have been restored in recent years, along with the cobblestone streets. The area centered on **Zhongyang Dajie** has been revitalized as a commercial district. A good stroll is down Zhongyang Dajie to the river embankment and the huge **Flood Control Monument** (Fanghong Jinian Ta), a column commemorating the construction of a flood-control embankment along the banks of the river. People practice tai chi here in the morning and *yang ge* (a rhythmic traditional dance) in the evenings. You can turn right down the **esplanade** (a favorite kite-flying spot) on the banks of the Songhua or left through the **night market** (mostly clothes), which runs parallel to the river and then winds around to Tongjiang Jie and the junction of Youyi Lu.

Ⓒ **Zhaolin Park** (Zhaolin Gongyuan) is where the bulk of Harbin's ice sculptures are displayed during the Ice Lantern Festival. At other times of the year it's a pleasant place to stroll—you can barely hear the honking horns from here. Its weekend outdoor amusement park includes a Ferris wheel. ⊠ *Youyi Lu and Shangzhi Dajie, Daoli District* 🖃 *Y2* ⊙ *May–Sept., daily 7 AM–9 PM; Oct.–Apr., daily 8–7.*

About five minutes' walk east of the Flood Control Monument, the **Dao Wai Street Fish Market** (Dao Wai Jie Yu Shi Chang) is not very well stocked in winter, but during the rest of the year a wide range of tropical fish (in jam jars and trays) is on sale here, as well as caged birds, flowers, teapots, raw tobacco, and much more. ⊠ *Dao Wai Jie, east of Flood Control Monument.*

Ⓒ **Youle Park** (Youle Yuan) has kiddie rides, an indoor children's playground, and a large roller coaster. The pavements around it are lined with stalls selling Buddhist tokens, trinkets, and joss sticks for use in the nearby temples. ⊠ *Dongda Zhi Jie* 🖃 *Y2 (Y5 during the Ice Lantern Festival)* ⊙ *May–Sept., daily 8 AM–9 PM; Oct.–Apr., daily 8–5.*

★ Ⓒ In winter, Harbinites build snow sculptures at **Taiyang Dao.** The area is home to a small military museum and an amusement park. It is a favorite walking and jogging spot for locals. ✦ *North of city, across river, to right-hand side of bridge.*

need a
break?
One of the nicest cafés in northern China, **Russia** (☒ 57 Xitou Dajie,
Daoli District ☎ 0451/456–3202) is the ideal spot to defrost after a
day on the ice. Housed in a Russian-era building near the north end
of Zhongyang Dajie, it serves perfect coffee and crepes in an old-
world setting.

Harbin has quite a few surviving Christian **churches,** many of them architectural as well as cultural novelties. Several of the establishments listed
below are active places of worship, and although they charge no entry
fee they are officially open only during service times. However, you may
be able to talk the caretakers into letting you look around at other times.
The **Russian Orthodox church** (☒ 268 Dongda Zhi Jie ⊙ Sat. 2 PM service), built of red brick with cupolas, stands in its own square, a reminder
of the time when Russians dominated Harbin. Across the street from
the Russian Orthodox church is a rather unimpressive, but active,
Catholic church (☒ 211 Dongda Zhi Jie). Farther up the road, also in
its own grounds, the busy **Protestant church** (☒ 252 Dongda Zhi Jie
⊙ Wed., weekends, service times vary), built in 1910 by German missionaries, is a thriving center for the Harbin Protestant community. The
elaborate Catholic **Wuhao Siguan Church** (☒ 47 Sheke Jie, Nangang District) was built in 1922 and reopened in 1980 following a pause for the
Cultural Revolution.

★ The most impressive church in Harbin is the 1907-built **St. Sofia's
Cathedral** (☒ Zhaolin Jie ☒ Y10), which until the 1960s served the more
than 100 Russian residents of Harbin. The cathedral was closed down
when the Russians were forced to leave China during the Cultural Revolution. The building's huge green onion dome atop a redbrick nave is
striking in its incongruity with its surroundings. Until recently the cathedral was contained by a tight square of old six-story workers' apartments and a timber yard; but these have now been cleared away, and
the cathedral stands resplendent in the center of a paved square. Despite the attention the physical structure has received, it no longer functions as a religious building. It's actually the Harbin Architecture Arts
Center, housing an exhibition of photographs documenting the city's turbulent 20th-century history.

Where to Stay & Eat

In Harbin particularly—though the practice can be seen elsewhere in
the Northeast—red lanterns are hung outside Chinese restaurants to denote cost and quality. The greater the number—the maximum is usually five—the higher the cost and quality. Blue lanterns denote Hui (a
Muslim minority) restaurants.

★ $$–$$$ ✕ **Million Land House Restaurant.** This large open-plan restaurant is one
of the best in Harbin. It serves some excellent seafood, including pearl
fish cooked in a light batter and dipped in salt; scallops; and North Pole
shrimp which is first cooked and then frozen before being served. Also
on the menu are hotpot and frozen tofu. ☒ 169 Zhongshan Lu, Nangang District ☎ 0451/261–1111 ☐ No credit cards.

$$–$$$ ✕ **Portman Western Restaurant.** This is Harbin's latest entrant in the
competition to serve good European cuisine. The interior is cozy, with

ON THE MENU

THE CLOSEST THING MANY CHINESE HAVE TO RELIGION IS FOOD. While the Northeast may lack many of the cultural advancements gained in China's wealthier cities, its extremely varied cuisine provides a chance to sample some of the diverse flavors that make China culturally rich. Good meals need not cost much and often the best culinary treats come from the least-expected places.

The northern latitude provides fresh excellent seafood all along Liaoning's coast while the icy rivers of Jilin and Heilongjiang yield flaky, meaty cold-water fish. Since China shares a border with Korea, kimchi and other spicy pickled vegetables abound and the barbecue in this area is cheaper than in South Korea and just as good. In addition, the region's proximity to Japan yields China's greatest variety of raw food consumption.

For those with more adventurous tastes, the wild game from Heilongjiang, such as deer, elk, rabbit, wild duck, wild boar, and pheasant, gives plenty of opportunities to try something new. China's northernmost provinces' proximity to Russia also means that no hankering for goulash will go unfulfilled. Though vodka occasionally rears its head, the region still seems to prefer the strong Chinese rice wine, baijiu.

A curious restaurant custom found in this province and nowhere else in China is the practice of hanging red lanterns out front to denote quality and price. Hence, the more lanterns, the bigger the bill. The Northeast also has a large ethnic-Muslim population and their restaurants are set apart, curiously, by blue lanterns.

comfortable upholstered chairs and dark wooden fittings. The menu has mainly Russian dishes, with an emphasis on river and lake fish, and the international drinks list is extensive. A live pianist plays weekend evenings. ⊠ *63 Xiqi Dajie, off Zhongyang Dajie* ☎ *0451/468–6888* ⊟ *No credit cards.*

★ **$–$$** ✕ **Huamei Restaurant.** Built in the 1920s by Russian expatriates, the second floor of this three-story restaurant features wooden floors and high, ornate ceilings supported by Greek-style columns. The walls are hung with pastoral Russian scenes. Cold dishes include caviar, sour cucumber, and thick slabs of white bread and jam. Chicken and fish au gratin, braised mutton chops, and *shashlik à la russe* (a type of mutton kebab) make up the main courses. Huamei is also open as a café between meals, with inexpensive (Y2) coffee served thick, sweet, and with enough sugar to keep you buzzing for a week. ⊠ *112 Zhongyang Dajie, Daoli District* ☎ *0451/467–5574* ⊟ *No credit cards.*

$–$$ ✕ **Shun Feng.** This 24-hour restaurant, immensely popular with locals, is plainly furnished with wooden tables and chairs. It has a glossy picture menu and specializes in beef hotpot, although plenty of other meats, vegetables, and seafood are available. ⊠ *107 Wen Chang Jie, Nangang District* ☎ *0451/268–8888* ⊟ *No credit cards.*

¢ ✕ **Lao Du Yi Chu.** This time-honored restaurant has been serving *jiaozi* (dumplings) to the people of Harbin since 1929, and many locals claim it is still the best place to go if you want the real thing. Look for the big "1" sign outside. ⊠ *25 Xi Shisan Dajie, off Zhaoyang Dajie* ☎ *0451/ 461–5895* ▤ *No credit cards.*

$$–$$$ ▣ **Shangri-La.** Ideally situated for a winter trip to Harbin, this luxuri-
Fodor$Choice   ous hotel overlooks the stretch of the Songhua River on which a large
★   portion of the Ice Lantern Festival takes place. The stylish green and gold rooms come complete with electronic safe, color TV, IDD phone, and Internet/fax lines. ⊠ *555 Youyi Lu, Daoli District, 150018* ☎ *0451/ 485–8888* ⊟ *0451/462–1777* ⊕ *www.shangri-la.com* ▨ *300 rooms, 46 suites* ⚭ *2 restaurants, minibars, tennis court, indoor pool, gym, bar* ▤ *AE, DC, MC, V.*

$–$$ ▣ **Holiday Inn.** At this modern hotel in the Daoli District standard rooms are a little dark but otherwise comfortable. They are equipped with a color TV with movie channels. The restaurants serve Chinese and Western food. ⊠ *90 Jingwei Jie, Daoli District, 150010* ☎ *0451/422– 6666* ⊟ *0451/422–1661* ⊕ *www.holiday-inn.com/harbincn* ▨ *143 rooms* ⚭ *2 restaurants, minibars, gym, bar, nightclub, business services* ▤ *AE, DC, MC, V.*

$ ▣ **Gloria Inn.** Large and modern, this hotel near the Flood Control Monument occupies an impressive building constructed in the old neo-classical European style. Standard rooms are bright and comfortable and are equipped with satellite TV. There is a Cantonese restaurant and a coffee shop serving Western and Asian food. ⊠ *257 Zhongyang Dajie, Daoli District, 150010* ☎ *0451/463–8855* ⊟ *0451/463–8533* ⊕ *www. giharbin.com* ▨ *304 rooms* ⚭ *2 restaurants, minibars, refrigerators, nightclub, business services* ▤ *AE, DC, MC, V.*

¢   ▣ **Hong Kong Palace Hotel.** Overlooking Zhaolin Park, this friendly hotel has clean and bright rooms with satellite TV. The restaurant serves Chinese food, and the café offers Western and Southeast Asian food. ⊠ *212 Shangzhi Jie, 150010* ☎ *0451/469–1388* ⊟ *0451/461–0894* ▨ *106 rooms* ⚭ *2 restaurants, minibars, business services* ▤ *MC, V.*

¢   ▣ **Lungmen Hotel.** An excellent value, the Lungmen is directly opposite the main railway station. The rooms are clean and quiet and have In-ternet connections and satellite TV. Rooms in the newer building are nicer, though more expensive, than those in the original structure. ⊠ *85 Hongjun Jie, 150001* ☎ *0451/642–6810* ⊟ *0451/363–9700* ⊕ *www. lmhotel.com.cn.* ▨ *252 rooms* ⚭ *2 restaurants, minibars, gym, bar, busi-ness services* ▤ *AE, MC, V.*

¢   ▣ **Modern Hotel.** The rooms in this Russian-era hotel are comfortable, with high ceilings and drapes suspended to create a four-poster effect on the beds. Try to get a room overlooking fashionable Zhongyang Dajie (unless you are a light sleeper). There are also cheaper rooms that are more simply furnished. ⊠ *89 Zhongyang Dajie, 150010* ☎ *0451/461– 5846* ⊟ *0451/461–4997* ▨ *133 rooms* ⚭ *2 restaurants, bar, business services* ▤ *AE, DC, MC, V.*

Nightlife

Harbin nightlife is fairly quiet. One place that's worth a visit is the **Log Cabin Bar** (⊠ 24 Zhongxuan Jie, Nangang District ☎ 0451/264–9797), which is tastefully decorated, has good beer and pool tables—and no karaoke facility. Local musicians playing various styles (country and western, rock) provide the entertainment.

Shopping

Besides the area around Zhongyang Dajie and the night market near the Flood Control Monument, a couple of other places in Harbin have some interesting shopping. The outdoor **Minmao Market** (Minmao Shi Chang) deals mostly in clothes but also sells souvenirs, antiques, fishing rods, and an inordinate number of binoculars, telescopes, and hand-held periscopes. Soviet-era stamps, Russian babushka dolls, watches, ginseng, and dried penises in several varieties (they're traditional medicine, mind you)—are also available. The market is busiest on the weekends, and many Russians come from the border city of Khabarovsk to buy goods for resale at home. The touts and money changers speak Russian to foreigners.

A massive bomb shelter built at a time of high tension in Sino-Soviet relations is now home to a booming shopping center in the **Nangang District** (⊠ Dongda Zhi Jie), where clothes, leather, and household goods are available.

Side Trips from Harbin

② **Yabuli International Ski Resort** is China's premier winter alpine destination, but serious skiers shouldn't expect the Alps. Yabuli was once the Qing Dynasty's royal hunting grounds. In 1996 it hosted the Asian Winter Games and since then has steadily pushed to increase its lift service and terrain. It now boasts 13 trails and 9 lifts, with a vertical drop of 1,870 feet. The resort claims to have terrain suited to every kind of skier but don't expect mind-bending chutes or stunning bowls. Skiing in China is still in its infancy so be happy if half the lifts run. A ski school and equipment rentals are available. New lodges and restaurants are opening continuously. For more information, call the nearby Windmill Hotel (☎ 0451/339–0088). ⊠ *Yabuli, 200 km (125 mi) east of Harbin.*

Heilongjiang A to Z

To research prices, get advice from other travelers, and book travel arrangements, visit www.fodors.com.

AIR TRAVEL

Regular flights link Harbin with major Chinese cities including Beijing and Shanghai.

🚹 China Northern Airlines ☎ 0451/231-1888. Harbin Airport Ticket Office ☎ 0451/8289-4219.

TAXIS

Taxis are the easiest way to get around Harbin. Flag fall is Y10, and all the cabs have meters. In the Daoli District going by foot gives you more time to appreciate the area's unique architecture.

TRAIN TRAVEL

There are regular rail connections between Harbin and Changchun (4 hrs) and points south, including Shenyang, Dalian (12 hrs), and Beijing (14 hrs). Keep in mind that no one at the general inquiries line is likely to speak English; travelers generally buy tickets through hotels and travel agents, which charge a commission.

⚡ Rail Inquiries ☎ 0451/642-0115.

VISITOR INFORMATION

📋 Tourist Information CITS ✉ Hushi Bldg., 2 Tielu Jie, 11th fl., Nangang District, south of train station entrance, Harbin ☎ 0451/367-2074 🖷 0451/367-1789.

JILIN

The smallest of the three provinces making up China's Dongbei is Jilin. Its capital, Changchun, was the birthplace of China's film industry. Heavy influences from North Korea show up not only in the spicy local cuisine but also in the sauna culture, widespread throughout the province. Bordering North Korea to the southeast, the Changbaishan Mountain range separates the two countries with its Martian landscape and provides the most dramatic setting in all the Northeast. Jilin has a population of about 27 million, the bulk of whom are Han; many ethnic Koreans live in the Korean border area.

Changchun

❸ *12 hrs (850 km [527 mi]) by train or 1½ hrs by plane northeast from Beijing.*

Changchun (literally, Long Spring) is a name based more on hope than reality, given the long cold winters of China's Northeast. Under Japanese rule from 1931 to 1945, Changchun was renamed Xinjing (New Capital) when it was made capital of the puppet state of Manchukuo. It's now the provincial capital of Jilin. After the 1949 Communist Revolution Changchun was established as China's very own motor city—home to First Auto Works (FAW), and more recently FAW's large joint-venture Volkswagen plant (joint ventures are one of the few ways foreign companies are allowed to operate in China), which dominate industry here. China's former president Jiang Zemin worked here as a factory director in the late 1950s. Today the pleasant city of some 6.8 million has wide avenues, lined with evergreen trees, which make for pleasant walks, notably in the areas around Xinfa Lu and Renmin Guangchang.

The **Puppet Emperor's Palace** (Weihuanggong) belonged to Puyi, China's last emperor before the 1911 revolution. It was set up by Japan to be the nominal head of the state of Manchukuo. Appropriately, the palace of the puppet emperor has a puppet feel to it. The buildings are more suited to a wealthy merchant than to the successor to a nearly 300-year-old dynasty. The building offers no sense that power resided here. Puyi's former house is now a museum documenting his life from childhood through his role as a pawn of the Japanese, and then it traces his conversion as a citizen of the new China after the 1949 revolution. Photos are on display in an adjacent courtyard house—one shows Hitler and the Manchukuo economic minister shaking hands during the latter's trip to Europe. Some torture instruments, including a bed of nails, depict the savagery of the Japanese war in China. There are also details on the notorious Camp 731, where crude experiments were carried out on prisoners of war. ☒ *5 Guangfu Bei Lu* ☎ *0431/566–7139* ⚏ *Y20* ⊙ *May–Sept., daily 8:30–5; Oct.–Apr., daily 8:30–4:30.*

The **Changchun Film Studio** (Changchundianying Zhipianchang), home to a large slice of China's movie industry, contains props of palaces, castles, and scenery. If you're lucky you may even get to see scenes being filmed. ☒ *28 Huxi Lu, Chaoyang District* ☎ *0431/762–8737* ⚏ *Y20* ⊙ *Daily 8–4.*

☺ **Changchun Film City** (Changchun Dianying Cheng) is a glitzier theme park version of the Film Studio. It's divided into thematic areas, including a huge indoor "undersea world" aquarium, traditional Chinese and European architecture zones, a dinosaur world, and a children's cartoon park. ☒ *92 Zhengyang Jie, Luyuan District* ☎ *0431/595–3511* ⚏ *Y80 all-inclusive, or Y15 for park entry plus Y15–Y30 per attraction* ⊙ *Daily 8:30–5.*

Bethune First Medical University (Bai Quan Di Yi Ke Daxue) is named for Canadian surgeon Norman Bethune, who was with the Republicans in 1930s Spain before working with the Communists at their base in Yanan in Shaanxi province. Built between 1933 and 1936, the university was modeled on Tokyo's parliament building; during the Japanese occupation it housed the Manchukuo Parliament. The fourth floor houses a small museum dedicated to this regime, but all captions are in Chinese. The ground-floor shop stocks a range of ginseng and medicinal products. The prize of the tour is on the first floor, where a collection of specimens of human body parts, in row upon row of formaldehyde jars, is stored. It's interesting, though not for the squeamish. ☒ *2 Xin Min Dajie, next to Wenhua Guangchang and opposite Bethune Hospital* ⚏ *Free; Y8 for the museum* ⊙ *Daily 9–7.*

Banruo Monastery (Banruo Si) was established in 1921, turned into a cardboard-box factory in 1966 at the beginning of the Cultural Revolution, and restored to its role as a monastery after 1982. Forty Buddhist monks now live here. The Grand Hall occupies the center of a courtyard complex that includes the reception, meditation, dining, and head monk's halls. In the Great Hall you can write down a prayer, strike a bell, and hope your prayer is answered. Inside the main gate are two drum towers. The drums are sounded on the arrival of an important visitor. ☒ *Changchun Lu, Nanguan District* ⊙ *Daily 8–3.*

A monument in the center of **People's Square** (Renmin Guangchang)—actually a circular green area—commemorates the Soviet liberation of Changchun from the Japanese in 1945. It's a great place for people-watching in the evening or early morning. ☒ *Bounded by Renmin Lu, Changchun Lu, Minkang Lu, and Xian Lu.*

Around **Xinfa Lu**, on pleasant tree-lined avenues—good for strolling—are a number of buildings dating from the Japanese era, now occupied by the current provincial government.

Where to Stay & Eat

$–$$$$ ✕**Tongda Restaurant.** Marked by garish plastic greenery draped from ceiling beams, this restaurant nevertheless serves good northeastern cuisine, including stewed pork, and such southern imports as spareribs steamed in lotus leaves. A specialty of the house is braised ginseng root and deer penis. ⊠ *60 Tongzhi Jie, Chaoyang District, 130021* ☎ *0431/563–2682* ⊟ *No credit cards.*

★ **$–$$$** ✕**Ben Tu Feng.** One of a growing number of Japanese eateries in town, this charmingly decorated little restaurant offers a range of authentic sushi, sashimi, tempura, and udon noodles, all served by Japanese exchange students from the city's universities. ⊠ *4 Ming De Lu* ☎ *0431/566–2899* ⊟ *No credit cards.*

¢–$$$ ✕**Tai Shan Hotel Korean Restaurant.** On the ground floor of the Tai Shan Hotel this dimly lighted open-plan restaurant serves familiar Korean food, including spring onion pancakes and ginseng chicken soup. ⊠ *35 Tongzhi Jie, Chaoyang District, 130021* ☎ *0431/563–4991* ⊟ *AE, DC, MC, V.*

¢–$$ ✕**Eastern King of Dumpling Restaurant.** Walk the length of this unpretentious restaurant, which has several sections, to see the chefs rolling the dough and preparing the fillings for the thousands of tasty jiaozi served here daily. You can mix your own dip with mustard, garlic, chili, soy sauce, and vinegar. Prepare to be amazed at the accuracy and flourish with which waiters refill your tea from a pot with a 3-foot spout. ⊠ *59 Gongnong Lu* ☎ *0431/560–2847* ⊟ *No credit cards.*

★ **$$** ▥ **Shangri-La.** Changchun's best hotel is modern, centrally located, stylish, and charming throughout. The wood paneling in the public areas and the friendly staff give it a slightly old-fashioned feel. All rooms have a full-size executive desk and fax, phone, and computer outlets. There are both Chinese and Western restaurants. ⊠ *9 Xian Dalu, 130061* ☎ *0431/898–1818* 🖷 *0431/898–1919* ⊕ *www.shangri-la.com* ⤶ *458 rooms* ♻ *3 restaurants, room service, minibars, refrigerators, room TVs with movies, tennis court, pool, gym, bowling, bar, business services* ⊟ *AE, MC, V.*

$ ▥ **Changchun Nobel.** This 25-floor hotel is the only one in northeastern China that has a Thai restaurant. The lobby gleams with its polished stone floor and pillars. The rooms offer sweeping views of the city, comfy beds, and elegant wood furniture. ⊠ *135 Renmin Lu, 130021* ☎ *0431/562–2888* 🖷 *0431/566–5522* ⤶ *300 rooms* ♻ *3 restaurants, room service, room TVs with movies, pool, gym, bowling, bar, business services* ⊟ *AE, DC, MC, V.*

$ ▥ **Swiss Belhotel.** Standard rooms are spacious and well furnished. The hotel's revolving hotpot restaurant is worth a visit for the view it offers of the city. ⊠ *39 Chuang Ye Da Jie, 130011* ☎ *0431/598–8888* 🖷 *0431/598–9999* ⊕ *www.swiss-belhotel.com* ⤶ *230 rooms* ♻ *2 restaurants, minibars, refrigerators, room TVs with movies, tennis court, pool, gym, bar, business services* ⊟ *AE, DC, MC, V.*

¢   ⌣ **Changchun Overseas Chinese Hotel.** Overlooking South Lake, this hotel offers views to take away the big-city blues. Though not luxurious, the rooms are comfortable and tastefully appointed. There are both Western and Chinese restaurants. The service attitude at both the hotel and restaurant has improved in recent years. ⌂ *1 Hubin Lu, 130022* ☎ *0431/538–8719* 🖶 *0431/538–6099* ⇘ *170 rooms* ⌂ *3 restaurants, minibars, bar, business services* ▤ *AE, MC, V.*

¢   ⌣ **South Lake Hotel.** This post-revolution hotel has high ceilings and the musty smell of Chinese state-run hostelries. The rooms are average, but the hotel is set in huge wooded grounds peppered with guest buildings and villas, which you can also rent. Many of the villas are occupied by Volkswagen staff from the FAW factory. Top leaders stay here when they come to Changchun. ⌂ *2 Nanhu Dalu, 130022* ☎ *0431/568–3571* 🖶 *0431/568–2559* ⇘ *250 rooms* ⌂ *Restaurant, hair salon, travel services* ▤ *AE, DC, MC, V.*

Nightlife & the Arts

The **Cultural and Entertainment Center** (⌂ Near junction of Renmin Lu and Jiefang Lu) frequently puts on plays (in Chinese).

A number of bars in Changchun have live music. Be warned, though, that establishments here can close down as suddenly as they appear. The **Happy Hour Bar** (⌂ 19 Longli Lu, behind Changchun Nobel Hotel ☎ 0431/567–2769) sees a lively crowd of Chinese, Koreans, and Westerners mix at its bars and small dance floor. Many of the Happy Hour clientele head to the **New Millennium Club** (⌂ 34 Guilin Lu ☎ 0431/566–4409) disco later in the evening, where African DJs (mainly exchange students) keep the show going well into the early hours. **Second Home** (⌖ Across from Shangri-La hotel ☎ 0543/896–9086 ⊘ Daily 7 PM–10 PM) is a favorite for foreigners; on weekends you'll see a crowd of German autoworkers ordering Johnny Walker Black by the bottle and singing Bayern Munich football songs.

Sports & the Outdoors

Changchun is home to the **Jilin Tigers** (⌂ Changchun Renmin Dajie), one of the stars of the CNBA (China National Basketball Alliance); they compete against the likes of the Beijing Lions, Guangzhou Rams, and Shanghai Nanyang. The season runs from November through March, and games are played two or three evenings a week.

Shopping

DEPARTMENT   The most modern department store in Changchun, **Changchun Mall**
STORES   (⌂ 2 Liaoning Lu ☎ 0431/271–1601 ⊘ Daily 9–8:30), is opposite the railway station. The upscale **Charter Shopping Center** (⌂ 99 Chongqing Lu, next to Shangri-La hotel ☎ 0431/896–3423) stocks everything from brand-name perfumes to imported electronic goods. The **Friendship Store** (⌂ Ziyou Lu ☎ 0431/569–9278) sells Chinese paintings and furniture.

MARKETS   Markets are fun to explore and curios may take your fancy, so give yourself a little time for treasure hunting. Bargaining is advisable at all stalls and is even possible in many stores.

The best place for souvenirs in Changchun is the **Jilin antiques market** (Jilin Guwu Cheng; ⊠ Heping Da Shijie Bldg., 15 Chongqing Lu, 2nd fl.). The entire floor is taken up with stamps and phone cards, metal and ceramic badges from the Cultural Revolution, coins, banknotes, and secondhand cameras. There are also paintings, calligraphy posters, carved jade, wood and walnut carvings, wall clocks, phonographs, and a whole shop dedicated to Mao paraphernalia.

Guilin Road Market (Guilin Lu Shichang; ⊠ Guilin Lu, Chaoyang District) is a large indoor market for one-stop shopping. Meat, fruit, and vegetables are displayed in open stalls, as are fish (from Dalian), cigarettes, spices, alcohol, canned foods, and household hardware. In the Guangfu Lu vicinity is **Pifa Shichang,** a large indoor wholesale market selling everything from household furniture to Pepsi, which is made locally. The streets nearby are lined with stalls.

need a break?

Need to get off your feet after bargain hunting at the Guilin Road Market? The **French Bakery** (⊠ 33 Guilin Lu ☎ 0431/562–3994) is the answer to your prayers. The café makes a range of good breads, pizza, and fruit tarts. Take away, or eat in with a coffee.

off the beaten path

Clear Moon Lake (Jingyue Hu). Built by the Japanese as a reservoir to serve Changchun, the lake lies in a large pine-wooded area where horseback riding and boating facilities are available. A hotel and villas are concentrated near the entrance to the area; on the far side of the lake is a practice ski slope and one larger, steeper snowfield. A two-hour ski pass and equipment rental costs Y60. A cheap all-day rate could be achieved through bargaining but there's probably not enough terrain to make it worthwhile. ⊹ *20 mins southeast of Changchun city center by car.*

Changbaishan Nature Reserve

❹ *10 hrs (300 km [186 mi]) by train and bus southeast of Changchun.*

Fodor'sChoice
★

The main attraction in this huge forest reserve is **Heavenly Pool** (Tianchi), a lake in the crater of a now-extinct volcano, on the China–North Korea border. Sacred to Korean culture, it draws thousands of South Korean visitors every year and has spectacular views, particularly in autumn and winter. The area is part of the Yanbian Korean Autonomous Prefecture and is home to large numbers of ethnic Koreans. (Certain areas in China with a high percentage of ethnic minorities are granted "autonomous" status, meaning they have [limited] powers to decide on local issues independently of the central government.) The lower slopes are densely wooded, but vegetation becomes sparse higher up. Bathing in hot springs and hiking are just two of the activities possible here. Three-day CITS tours are available from Changchun or Jilin between early June and early September. Alternately, there's a bus from Changchun leaving daily at 9 AM but be prepared for a long and grueling ride. Trains are also available to Baihe but, once again, local transport can be unpredictable and slow. You can also hire a car, or take a shared minivan from Baihe, the small town nearest Changbaishan. In summer accommodations are available in the reserve (expensive) or in Baihe (cheaper), but the reserve is open year-round, as long as the road isn't iced over.

Jilin City

⑤ *2½ hrs (95 km [59 mi]) by car or train east of Changchun.*

Jilin City, on the banks of the winding Songhua River, is the second-largest city in the province (but small by Chinese standards). Although it's an industrial center, local authorities are making a determined effort to draw tourists by promoting winter activities. Ski resorts around the city, an ice festival, and the phenomenon of ice-rimmed trees are all being peddled as worthy attractions.

The city is set in picturesque lake and mountain scenery, like the kind found in the city's **North Mountain Park** (Bei Shan Gongyuan). On the south side of the park's lake are a number of pavilions. The main attraction here is the **Guan Emperor Temple** (Guan Di Si), founded in 1701 and named 50 years later by the emperor Qian Long for one of his predecessors. Among several lesser temples nearby are the **Three Kings Temple** (San Wang Miao) and the **King of Medicine Temple** *(Yao Wang Miao)* ✛ *West side of city behind Beishan railway station* ☎ *0432/484–3283* 🎫 *Y5.*

Jilin has made a virtue out of ugly industrial development in the form of its **rime trees.** A hydroelectric plant, which supplies power to Jilin's industries, takes in cold water from the Songhua River and expels warm water. The vapor, which rises from the river as it flows along in the depths of winter, freezes on the trees overhanging the riverbank, resulting in the sort of picturesque scene beloved by Japanese, Korean, and Chinese tourists. ✛ *Take Bus 9 from roundabout north of Xiguan Hotel on Songjiang Lu to hydroelectric plant.*

The twin spires of the Gothic-style **Catholic Church** reach nearly 150 feet. Catholics first arrived in Jilin in 1898 and began construction of the church in 1917. Its doors opened in 1926, and it still serves the local Catholic community, who come in large numbers for the main Christian festivals. ✉ *3 Song Jiang Lu* ☎ *0432/202–5142.*

Where to Stay & Eat

¢–$$$$ ✕ **Yang Guang Yan Yuan.** The ground floor of this establishment—one of the most popular in town—serves snacks and quick meals, while upstairs is a more formal dining room. Hundreds of plates of ingredients and tankfuls of live seafood are displayed, complete with prices, for you to select and send off to the kitchen. ✉ *1 Yangguang Lu* ☎ *0432/253–0888* 🚫 *No credit cards.*

¢–$$ ✕ **Dong Sheng Xing Islamic Restaurant.** This two-story restaurant is decorated with Arabic calligraphy, pictures of people dancing to traditional music, and a poster of Mecca. Serving traditional Hui and Uighur cuisine like stewed chicken, roast lamb, and hand-pulled noodles, this restaurant mostly caters to Jilin City's Muslim population. ✉ *Tianjin Lu (opposite Xin Hua Theater)* ☎ *0432/243–1016* 🚫 *No credit cards.*

¢–$ ✕ **Xin Xing Yuan Dumpling Restaurant.** Jiaozi and northeastern dishes are the specialty in this white two-story restaurant. Try the entire banquet of dumplings, which include many unusual shapes and fillings. ⊠ *115 He Nan Jie* ☎ *0432/202–4393* ▤ *No credit cards.*

$ ▦ **Century Swiss-Belhotel.** The most upscale hotel in Jilin offers sumptuous accommodation just south of the town center. Cozy rooms and a whole suite of relaxation facilities—including a Finnish sauna and Turkish steam bath; Thai, Korean, Chinese, and Japanese shiatsu massage; and a 100-foot indoor heated swimming pool—make for a very comfortable stay (especially after working it on the nightclub's dance floor). ⊠ *77 Jilin Dajie, 132013* ☎ *0432/464–9888* 🖷 *0432/464–9000* ⊕ *www. swiss-belhotel.com* ↦ *245 rooms* ⌂ *3 restaurants, pool, gym, squash, bar, nightclub, business services* ▤ *AE, DC, MC, V.*

Fodor'sChoice
★

$ ▦ **Jilin Crystal Hotel** (Rime Hotel). On the banks of the Songhua River and near the foot of scenic Longtan Mountain, this seven-story hotel has a short, sloping roof. Views from certain rooms, though by no means from all, provide a pleasant contrast to a relatively plain-looking city. Rooms have snazzy new furnishings, though the beds can be a bit hard. ⊠ *29 Longtan Dajie, 132021* ☎ *0432/398–6200* 🖷 *0432/398–6501* ↦ *113 rooms* ⌂ *3 restaurants, minibars, pool, gym, bowling, bar* ▤ *AE, DC, MC, V.*

¢ ▦ **Jiangcheng Hotel.** This seven-story hotel has the huge gleaming lobby common in China's newer hotels. Standing beside Qingnian Park on the banks of the Songhua River, it enjoys one of the best locations in the city. Though the decor is a bit drab, the beds are comfortable enough for budget accommodations. ⊠ *4 Jiangwan Lu, 132001* ☎ *0432/245–7721* 🖷 *0432/245–8973* ↦ *157 rooms* ⌂ *Restaurant, gym, business services* ▤ *AE, DC, MC, V.*

¢ ▦ **Yinhe Hotel.** The lobby in this Hong Kong joint-venture hotel is all bright lights and gleaming surfaces. Rooms, equipped with satellite TV, are small and not exceptionally smart. Both Western and Chinese food is available. ⊠ *79 Songjiang Lu, 132011* ☎ *0432/484–1780* 🖷 *0432/ 484–1621* ↦ *169 rooms* ⌂ *2 restaurants, business services* ▤ *AE, DC, MC, V.*

Shopping

East Shopping Building (⊠ 131 Henan Lu ☎ 0432/202–4831) is an all-purpose shopping center with an emphasis on domestic appliances and clothing. **Jilin Department Store** (⊠ 179 Jilin Dajie ☎ 0432/245–5489) has four floors of household goods and food.

Side Trips from Jilin City

❻ **Beidahu Ski Resort,** China's second-largest ski resort, 65 km (40 mi) from Jilin City, is reachable by bus, taxi, or hired car. With six runs, six lifts, and a vertical drop of 1,150 feet, those who come expecting ideal conditions may be seriously disappointed. Though it claims terrain for all levels of skiers, the most perilous aspect may be avoiding the "yard sales" (where all your gear is unintentionally spread out around a fall) of beginning skiers. That said, Beidahu does have one off-piste area that may have some decent powder after a big snowfall. Equipment rental is available for both skiers and boarders. Ski instruction is generally in Chinese, though English is sometimes available upon request. Lift ticket and gear begin at around Y160 per day and can increase during holiday times. Snow stays on the ground from December to mid-March. The resort has a small hotel and restaurants that serve Chinese, Western, and Hui food. ⊠ *Wu Li He Town, Yong Ji County* ☎ *0432/420–2222.*

❼ The Songhua River flows from the Changbaishan Mountains into long, narrow **Song Hua Lake** (Song Hua Hu) before continuing on its way about 24 km (15 mi) southeast of the city center. It was built as a reservoir between 1937 and 1943. Boating facilities are available on the lake amid beautiful natural surroundings. Tours are available through CITS.

Jilin A to Z

To research prices, get advice from other travelers, and book travel arrangements, visit www.fodors.com.

AIR TRAVEL

Changchun Airport is 10 km (6 mi) west of the city center. Regular flights link it with Beijing, Shanghai, Guangzhou, Shenzhen, and, less frequently, Hong Kong and Irkutsk, in Siberia. Jilin City airport is 25 km (15 mi) outside the city and has scheduled flights to Beijing, Shanghai, and Guangzhou, as well as to Shenyang, Dalian, and Harbin.

🚹 Airport Information **Changchun Airport** ⊠ Dafangshen Feijichang ☎ 0431/798-7841. **Jilin City Airport** ⊠ Yaoqiang Feijichang ☎ 0432/351-3000.

BUS TRAVEL

Express buses link the Linjiang long-distance bus station (west of the Yinhe Hotel) in Jilin with Changchun's long-distance bus station (south of Weixing Square, at the southern extreme of Renmin Dajie) every half hour. The trip costs Y30 and takes around 90 minutes. Both Changchun and Jilin City are linked by bus to numerous other towns and cities, both inside and outside of Jilin province, like Harbin, Shenyang, and Dalian.

🚹 Bus Depots **Changchun Bus Station** ☎ 0431/279-2544. **Jilin City Bus Station** ☎ 0432/255-5401.

EMERGENCIES

Dial 120 to call the hospital and 110 to call the police in Changchun or Jilin City. Changchun's Public Security Bureau (PSB) is located at the southwestern corner of the People's Square, near the main Bank of China. Jilin City's PSB is located at 10 Beijing Lu. In Changchun or Jilin you can find medicines at the state-owned medicine shop, which is open 24 hours and stocks Chinese-style Western medicines, or at the lobby shop of the Shangri-La hotel, which stocks some Western medicines. In a medical emergency, consult your hotel; most operators at emergency numbers cannot speak English.

🚹 **Changchun Hospital emergency line** ☎ 120. **Jilin City Hospital emergency line** ☎ 120. **Lobby shop** ⊠ Shangri-La hotel, 9 Xian Dalu, Changchun. **Medicine shop** ⊠ Tongzhi Jie, Changchun.

TAXIS

In both Changchun and Jilin taxis are inexpensive and the most convenient means of transportation. For longer trips outside the cities, check with the hotels or tour operators.

TRAIN TRAVEL

The Changchun railway station is about 15 minutes north of downtown. Trains link it with Harbin, Jilin, Shenyang, Dalian, and Beijing regularly. The Jilin City train station is served by trains from Beijing, Shenyang, Dalian, Harbin, and Changchun.

Train Information **Changchun train station** ☏ 0431/612-2222. **Jilin City train station** ✉ Off Yanan Yu ☏ 0432/454-529.

VISITOR INFORMATION

Tourist Information **CITS** ✉ Yinmao Dasha Bldg., 14 Xinmin Dajie, 7th fl., Changchun ☏ 0431/560-9039 ✉ Jiangcheng Hotel, 4 Jiangwan Lu, 4th fl., Jilin City ☏ 0432/243-6810 🖷 0432/243-6811.

LIAONING

Home to China's last imperial dynasty, the Qing, Liaoning was the seat of power for all of Manchuria. Today, though plagued by unemployment and failed industry, the northeast region still looks to Liaoning and its capital Shenyang, China's fourth-largest city, for leadership. Liaoning fared better than most during the post-revolution period, when steel mills and manufacturing industries were set up prior to the decline of state-owned industries. Ruins, both industrial and ancient, dot the countryside while the city of Shenyang is itself rich in historical sites. In recent years, the North Korean border area has seen a surge in China's tourists and cross-border trade. In summer, revelers flock to Liaoning's beaches and its major port city, Dalian. Blessed by natural and administrative advantages—among them a port and preferential tax breaks—Dalian hopes to be the light at the end of Liaoning's tunnel.

Shenyang

8 *2 hours (280 km [174 mi]) by express train southwest of Changchun; 9 hrs (600 km [372 mi]) by express train northeast of Beijing.*

The modern provincial capital, Shenyang (formerly Mukden) became the capital of Manchuria under the warrior king Nurhachi in the 16th century. In 1644 when the Manchus took Beijing and founded the Qing Dynasty, which ruled China until the 1911 revolution, Manchuria remained a place apart from the rest of China, and Mukden remained its capital. Mao Zedong's new China added to the industry the Japanese had established here, and Shenyang was a key city in the industrial drive of the 1950s and '60s. With the switch to market reforms Shenyang lost its edge to the busy coastal cities. Today it is a place of high unemployment and industrial decay.

Although not a particularly beautiful place, Shenyang has something to offer in the way of imperial tombs, pagodas, and the old Imperial Palace, a predecessor of Beijing's Forbidden City.

The **Imperial Palace** (Gugong) was home to the Manchu emperors before they conquered the rest of China and established themselves in Beijing. Dating from the early 17th century, it is very similar to the capital's Forbidden City, but smaller, less crowded, and of greater architectural variety. ☒ *171 Shenyang Lu* ☎ *024/2484–4192* ✆ *Y35* ☉ *Daily 8:30–5:30.*

Sun Yat-sen Square (Zhongshan Guangchang) makes for a great after-dinner stroll, weather permitting. It's overlooked by a huge fiberglass statue of the late Chairman Mao surrounded by heroic workers, peasants, and soldiers. Mao's majestic wave is interpreted by the local kids as the Chairman trying to flag down a taxi. ☒ *Nanjing Jie and Zhongshan Lu.*

The sight of stern, gray Gothic-style **Nanguan Catholic Church of the Sacred Heart of Jesus,** set amid the apartment blocks and *hutongs* (alleys) of urban China, is arresting. Built in 1878, it burned during the Boxer Rebellion in 1900. Its spires rise 120 feet into Shenyang's gray sky. ☒ *40 Nan Le Jiao Lu, Xiao Nan Da Jie, Shenhe District* ☎ *024/2484–3986* ☉ *About 5:30 AM–about 6 PM.*

The courtyard of the **Loving Kindness Buddhist Temple** (Ci En Fozhao Si) has seen a lot. Founded during the Tang Dynasty, it was rebuilt in the Qing, and then during the Cultural Revolution it was converted into a factory. The reforms of the 11th Party Congress in 1977 paved the way for its restoration, though the factory did not finally pull out until 10 years later. Monks now live in this pleasant temple, and worshippers burn incense in bronze containers and bow to the Buddhist statues in the halls. The alleys around the monastery are lined with stalls selling Buddha statues, trinkets, and incense. ☒ *Ci En Si Hutong, Da Nan Jie* ☉ *Daily 7–4* ✆ *Free.*

The old city of Shenyang was ringed by **pagodas,** which are now well within the urban area. Although they're in various stages of disrepair, they provide oases of calm and architectural delight among the modern industrial chaos. Beautifully secluded in the northeast of the city is the **Sheli Pagoda** (Sheli Ta; ☒ Hutong 45, Tawan Jie ✆ Y4 ☉ Daily 8:30–4:30), a thousand-year-old Buddhist tower and temple courtyard. (Chinese temples generally take the form of a large rectangular courtyard, within which are various halls, gateways, and gardens.) Side buildings house a photographic exhibition of Chinese pagodas and stupas, which is interesting despite the Chinese-only captions. The **Northern Pagoda** (Beita Pagoda; ☒ 27 Beita Jie, off Chongshan Dong Lu ✆ Y5 ☉ Daily 8–5) is one of the best preserved of the lot, and has a small museum with an impressive model of the ancient city of Shenyang.

Set in parkland in the north of the city, the **North Tomb** (Beiling) is the burial place of Huang Taiji (1592–1643), founder of the Qing Dynasty. Inside the entrance a short avenue is lined with stone animals surrounded by pine trees—good feng shui tokens. The burial mound is at the rear of the complex and can be viewed from the top of the wall that encircles the two large central courtyards. Some of the outer buildings house souvenir shops, while another contains the 400-year-old bodies of a government official and his wife on open display. ⊠ *Taishan Lu, north side of city* 🎫 *Y3 for park, Y10 for tomb area.*

Where to Stay & Eat

¢–$$ ✕ **Dong Lai Shun.** Cook your own beef, squid, shellfish, rice noodles, green vegetables, or a host of other dainties in a copper hotpot of constantly boiling water placed on your table in this clean, reasonably priced restaurant. Hotpot is a winter favorite in the north of China, though it is eaten year-round. You can also choose cold plates and enjoy the sesame sauce, soy, chili, bean curd sauce, and sour mustard dips that come with the hotpot. ⊠ *23 Huanghe Nan Dajie, Heping District* 🕾 *024/8685–5555* ▭ *No credit cards.*

¢–$$ ✕ **Lao Bian Dumpling Restaurant.** In business for 170 years and now in the hands of the fourth generation of the founding family, this spartan two-story restaurant is famous in Shenyang for its jiaozi. While the quality of the dumpling filling falls suspect in many restaurants, Lao Bian has built its reputation on using only the freshest meat and vegetables and by paying careful attention to the wrapping. Its poor service seems to only make people like it more. ⊠ *57 Beishi Yi Lu, Heping District* 🕾 *024/2272–1819* ▭ *No credit cards.*

¢–$$ ✕ **Na Jia Guan.** This local specialty restaurant, just west of the Gugong, serves up dishes such as cold noodles, Mutton Hot Pot, smoked meat flat bread, and dumplings, all traditional cuisine of the Manchu people, the original inhabitants of northeastern China. Selections tend to be hearty and meat-based, with plenty of pickles and stewed dishes. ⊠ *90 Shenyang Lu, Shenhe District* 🕾 *024/2485-7761* ▭ *No credit cards.*

★ $$ 🏨 **Shenyang Marriott Hotel.** The first luxury hotel to open in Shenyang, the Marriott overlooks the Yun River, not far from the U.S. Consulate. Tasteful and classically appointed rooms feature soft, comfortable beds and pleasant vistas of the city. ⊠ *388 Qing Nian Dajie, Shenhe District, 110003* 🕾 *042/2388–3456* 🖷 *024/2388–0677* ⊕ *www.marriotthotels. com* ⤵ *435 rooms, 43 suites* ⚭ *2 restaurants, room service, in-room safes, minibars, tennis court, pool, gym, bar, baby-sitting, laundry service, business services, travel services* ▭ *AE, DC, MC, V.*

$$ 🏨 **Traders Shenyang Hotel.** Part of the rapidly growing Shangri-La hotel chain, the Traders Shenyang is modern and centrally located. The spacious lobby gives access to restaurants, a bar, and a airy lounge. Comfortable, tastefully furnished standard rooms are equipped with executive desks and satellite TVs. ⊠ *68 Zhong Hua Lu, Heping District, 110001* 🕾 *024/2341–2288* 🖷 *024/2341–1988* ⊕ *www.shangri-la.com* ⤵ *92 rooms* ⚭ *2 restaurants, minibars, refrigerators, gym, spa, bar, nightclub, business services* ▭ *AE, DC, MC, V.*

$ 🏨 **Gloria Plaza.** This modern hotel stands opposite the North Railway Station in Shenyang's commercial district, just 10 minutes from the Imperial Palace. Standard rooms are bright and comfortable, and all are equipped with satellite TV. The restaurants serve Chinese food; a café serves Western dishes. ⊠ *32 Yingbin Jie, Shenhe District, 110013* 🕾 *024/2252–8885* 🖷 *024/2252–8533* ⊕ *www.gloriahotels.com* ⤵ *289 rooms* ⚭ *2 restaurants, minibars, refrigerators, gym, business services* ▭ *AE, DC, MC, V.*

$ ▦ **Liaoning Guesthouse.** This hotel possess real character. Built by the Japanese in 1927 to a European design, the lobby and dining room interiors have wood paneling, tiled and wooden floors, high ceilings, and the style of 18th-century Europe. Japanese visitors like it for its good feng shui. The hotel restaurants serve Shandong, Liaoning, and Western food. ✉ *97 Zhongshan Lu, on Zhongshan Sq., Heping District, 110001* ☎ *024/2383–9166* 🖷 *024/2383–9103* 🖢 *79 rooms* ♨ *3 restaurants, tennis court, exercise equipment, billiards* 🖃 *AE, DC, MC, V.*

Shopping

Five Loaves Wholesale Market (Wu Ai Shichang; ✉ Re Nao Lu, Shenhe District ⊙ 3 AM–1 PM) is a great place to see the free market in operation. It contains acres of stalls—mostly clothes but also shoes and light consumer goods. Most things are made locally.

Tai Yuan Jie Market (✉ Next to Traders Shenyang Hotel) mainly sells clothing, some electronic goods, and CDs. The **Gong Yi Meishu Shangdian** (✉ Taiyuan Jie) has crafts and artworks—scroll paintings, tea sets, vases, small and large pieces of jade, and other tourist pieces—on the fourth and fifth floors. The **Cashmere Building** (✉ 67 Sanjing Jie, Shenhe District ☎ 024/2284–6759) carries a reasonable collection of cashmere garments.

Side Trips from Shenyang

The road out of Shenyang in the direction of Dalian puts you on the first highway in China, built in the early 1980s. Along it, in the town **❾** of **Liaoyang**, the **White Tower** (Baita) is worth a look. Built in the time of the local Liao Kingdom during China's Song Dynasty about AD 1000, the White Tower is an impressive octagonal structure with a tier of 13 eaves and Buddhist statues and reliefs carved around it. Repaired several times since it was first built, it was last restored in 1986 but does not bear the kitschy new look of so much restoration in China. To get here, contact CITS for a price quote (which will run on the high side) and then hire a taxi for a little less; you can ask the driver to use the meter. The cheapest option is to go by bus, which leaves from the long-distance bus station south of the Wu Ai Shichang. ⊹ *Road to Dalian, 30 km (18 mi) south of Shenyang.*

Dalian

▶ *4 hrs (350 km [217 mi]) by train south of Shenyang; 12 hrs (450 km [279 mi]) by train, 1 hr by plane east of Beijing.*

Dalian is easily one of the most charming cities in China. Lying at the tip of the Liaodong peninsula between the Yellow Sea and the Bohai Sea, this small city is at once a postcard from China's past and a signpost to the country's future. In the 19th century, Russia, seeking an ice-free port, established a trading center here but lost it to Japan in their 1904–05 war. Other Europeans traded here later on, and the resulting combination of Russian, Japanese, and Western European architecture that survives in public buildings and houses gives Dalian a unique atmosphere. After the 1949 revolution the Soviet Union continued to wield enormous influence in China and retained control of Dalian and Port Arthur,

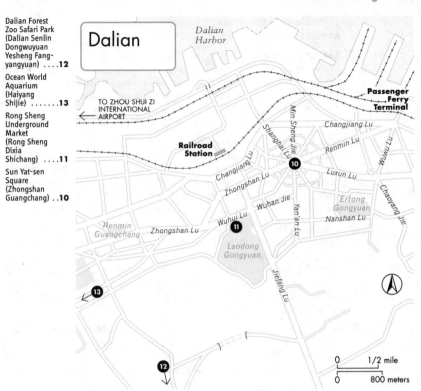

which they had taken over when the Japanese surrendered at the end of World War II (strategically the Russians have always been hampered by the lack of an ice-free port in the east). When Stalin died in 1955, much of the pressure on China was relaxed, and these two cities were returned to the Chinese.

Dalian is a great city for walking. Its wide colonial-era streets and public squares and parks, including Zhongshan Square, Renmin Square, and Laodong Park, are its most striking features. With the sea on three sides, it has something else that is rare in a Chinese city—relatively clean air.

But more tangible than history are the present economic boom and rising wealth that give Dalian the sort of sophistication for which Shanghai is frequently noted. Many of the large colonial buildings have been renovated, new hotels are springing up, and Japanese and Korean fashions dominate the streets. The city's special economic status (a package of tax and investment breaks to attract foreign companies) and general economic health are often attributed to the charismatic and politically savvy former mayor Bo Xilai, son of Long March veteran Bo Yibo. The source of the area's economic boom is its good port facilities (Dalian is also China's biggest shipbuilding center) and the Dalian Economic and

Trade Development Zone, 25 minutes from the city, where Japanese, Korean, European, and U.S. companies are based.

⑩ Sun Yat-sen Square (Zhongshan Guangchang) is actually a large circle at the center of Dalian where (in good weather) locals gather in the evenings to practice genteel ballroom dancing and the lazy version of badminton that is common throughout China. Scenes from the movie *The Last Emperor* were filmed in the square, which is encircled by stately colonial-era buildings, most of which are now occupied by banks.

⑪ Rong Sheng Underground Market (Rong Sheng Dixia Shichang) has everything from flatfish to salmon steaks, plus shrimp, octopus, sea cucumber, turtle, tortoise, lobster, crab, eels, barnacles, and scallops, as well as stalls of fresh fruit and canned goods. The upper part of the two-level underground complex is dedicated to household furniture. ⊠ *Wuhui Lu, east of the north entrance to Laodong Park* ⊙ *Daily 9–6.*

☾ **⑫** The **Dalian Forest Zoo Safari Park** (Dalian Senlin Dongwuyuan Yesheng Fangyangyuan) is where Dalian proudly shows off its Siberian tigers in natural surroundings, together with around 4,000 other animals of over 60 species. The park occupies an expansive parkland setting with some areas accessible by foot, others by safari bus only. ⊹ *Between city center and beach (main entrance on Bin Hai Lu)* ☎ *0411/249–5072* ▨ *Y40* ⊙ *Daily 7:30–4.*

☾ **⑬** Next to a small beach in Xinghai Park, **Ocean World Aquarium** (Haiyang Shijie) has a 380-foot Plexiglas walk-through tunnel where you can get a full view of the more than 200 varieties of resident fish. ⊠ *508 Zhongshan Lu* ☎ *0411/468–5136* ▨ *Y35* ⊙ *May–Sept., daily 9–4; Oct.–Apr., daily 8–6.*

Where to Stay & Eat

Fresh seafood in Dalian can be found anywhere from high-end chains to local dives. For the widest selection, visit the Rong Sheng Underground Market, choose your fresh catch from the tanks of local fisherman, take it to any number of restaurants across the street, and get it cooked to order.

★ **$–$$$$** ✕ **Tian Tian Yu Gang.** This is one of the best in a chain of nine restaurants around the city serving excellent Dalian seafood. They offer sea cucumber sautéed and served with asparagus, carrots, and cucumber; abalone, raw or braised; and prawn and crab. The entrance is guarded by fish tanks and basins from which you can choose your meal. There's an open dining area on the ground floor, and upstairs are a half dozen private dining rooms. ⊠ *10 Renmin Lu* ☎ *0411/280–1122* ▤ *No credit cards.*

$$–$$$ ✕ **Market Place.** On the first floor of the Holiday Inn, overlooking busy Chang Jiang Lu, this restaurant has a German chef and serves the best Western food in town. It runs special theme menus, such as traditional Italian, New Zealand lamb, or barbecue. ⊠ *18 Shengli Guangchang* ☎ *0411/280–8888* ▤ *AE, DC, MC, V.*

★ **$–$$$** ✕ **Le Café Igosso.** This offbeat Japanese-owned Italian restaurant is decorated in cream colors and serves pizza, pasta, and cappuccino. There's jazz at night and outdoor seating on a veranda in summer. The manager plays saxophone and his partner, who runs the kitchen, plays bass. ⊠ *45 Nanshan Lu* ☎ *0411/265–6453* ▤ *AE, DC, MC, V.*

★ ¢–$$ ✕**Sorabol.** The staff here prepares delicious Korean food right at your table. Among the offerings are the traditional *boolgogi* (marinated beef and vegetables barbecued at the table) and *boolgahlbi* (marinated beef served on and off the bone). The restaurant has both private rooms and open booths. Wooden floors and surroundings and friendly service give the place a warm feel. ⊠ *18 Qiyi Jie* ☎ *0411/263–1460* ▤ *AE, DC, MC, V.*

¢–$$ ✕**Taiyang Cheng.** For reasonable late-night food, try the restaurants here. Like many Chinese restaurants, the ground floor serves fast food and cheap eats, while upstairs is a more upscale dining room. Order from the menu, or choose your own live seafood from tanks. ⊠ *109 Youhao Lu* ☎ *0411/264–3232* ▤ *DC, MC, V.*

★ $$$ ▦ **Shangri-La Dalian.** Rooms at this modern high-rise are tastefully decorated and comfortable. Several floors are given over to the Horizon Club, which has its own business center and offers complimentary breakfast, cocktails, and express check-in and checkout. The restaurants offer Chinese, Japanese, and Western food. ⊠ *66 Renmin Lu, 116001* ☎ *0411/252–5000* 🖷 *0411/252–5050* ⊕ *www.shangri-la.com* ⤴ *563 rooms ⚫ 3 restaurants, snack bar, in-room fax, minibars, refrigerators, room TVs with movies, tennis court, indoor pool, gym, hot tub, bar, shops, baby-sitting, business services, airport shuttle, car rental* ▤ *AE, DC, MC, V.*

$$–$$$ ▦ **Furama Hotel.** Next door to the Shangri-La, the Furama has executive-floor rooms, offices, apartments, and suites. Its massive atrium lobby decked out in marble links its two towers. The rooms are spacious and comfortably furnished. The restaurants serve Chinese, Western, and Japanese cuisines. ⊠ *60 Renmin Lu, 116001* ☎ *0411/263–0888* 🖷 *0411/280–4455* ⊕ *www.furama.com.cn* ⤴ *832 rooms, 28 suites ⚫ 6 restaurants, minibars, room TVs with movies, tennis court, pool, gym, squash, 3 bars, business services* ▤ *AE, DC, MC, V.*

$$ ▦ **Holiday Inn.** Just a two-minute walk from the railway station, this hotel is among the best lodging values in Dalian. The red-front 23-story building was one of the first high-rises in the city when it was built in 1988. All rooms come with soft, comfortable beds and bathrooms with good water pressure. Standard in Holiday Inns, the hotel restaurant serves up standard Western fare and a large breakfast buffet. ⊠ *18 Shengli Guangchang, 116001* ☎ *0411/280–8888* 🖷 *0411/280–9704* ⊕ *www. holiday-inn.com* ⤴ *405 rooms, 26 suites ⚫ 3 restaurants, minibars, cable TV, pool, exercise equipment, hair salon, sauna, 2 bars, shop, baby-sitting, dry cleaning, concierge, business services, car rental* ▤ *AE, DC, MC, V.*

¢–$ ▦ **Grand Hotel.** This modern hotel houses the Dalian International Exhibition Center, which hosts trade fairs. Located in Zhongshan Square, the Grand gives prime access to the heart of Dalian's commercial district. Some of the plain, red-carpeted rooms have a view of the harbor, so be sure to ask. ⊠ *1 Jiefang Jie, 116001* ☎ *0411/280–6161* 🖷 *0411/ 280–6980* ⤴ *248 rooms ⚫ Restaurant, gym, massage, 2 bars, business services, airport shuttle* ▤ *AE, DC, MC, V.*

Nightlife & the Arts

THE ARTS The **Children's Palace** (Er Tong Le Yuan; ✉ Renmin Guangchang) hosts occasional photographic and painting exhibitions. The eight-story **Dalian Culture and Art Mansion** (Dalian Wenhua He Meishu Guan; ✉ Shidao Nan Jie) is home to the city's dance and theater ensembles.

Spring Festival (part of the Chinese New Year celebrations in January or February) is the big annual holiday; traditional festivities include a fireworks display. An ice lantern and **ice sculpting** show takes place in Dalian and Bingyugou (2½ hours drive northeast of Dalian) over the Chinese New Year. **Acacia Flower Festival** (last week in May) culminates with a song-and-dance performance in Laodong Park in celebration of the blooming lotus.

NIGHTLIFE **Nawei Senlin Bar** (✉Renmin Lu, west of Furama Hotel ☎0411/281–2329), a bar by night and a tea shop by day, is frequented by young Chinese and some foreigners. The **Dalian New Friendship Nightclub** (✉ 6 Renmin Lu, 10th fl. ☎0411/282–5888 Ext. 385) has singers with a backup band (Western and Chinese rock music) and a dancing show. The strobe-lighted dance floor of **JJ's** (✉ 4 Wuwu Jie ☎ 0411/270–5518), with a capacity of about 1,200, is packed on weekends with young Chinese rocking to a DJ.

Sports

The 36-hole **Dalian Golden Pebble Golf Course** (✉ Dalian Jin Shitan State Tourist and Vacation Zone ☎ 0411/790–0543), on the coast, a half hour northeast of the city center, is open to the public, but you must make reservations in advance.

Shopping

The **Dalian Friendship Shopping Center** (✉ 6–8 Renmin Lu) is a modern department store stocking a wide range of men's and women's clothing, cosmetics, and luxury goods.

Five minutes' walk from the Holiday Inn lies the commercial district around **Qingni Jie,** where you'll find department stores, markets, and fast-food outlets.

The **Ti Yu Chang outdoor market** (Xigang District) sells food, clothes, and electronic goods and is busiest on weekends. **Wenwu Zongdian Shop** (✉ 229 Tianjin Jie ☎ 0411/263–4955) sells quality Chinese wood carvings, scrolls, pottery, and interesting lamps and lamp shades; you can bargain here.

Side Trips from Dalian

The 32-km-long (20-mi-long) road that winds south of Dalian along the peninsula has some attractive views and a number of good beaches, including Lao Hu and Fujiazhuang. Local couples drive out here following their marriage ceremony to use the coastline and sea as backdrops for wedding photographs.

☾ **Golden Stone Beach** (Jin Shi Tan), a series of small coves strung along the coast, is near the Dalian Golden Pebble Golf Course. A visit here makes a wonderful day's outing. Besides seaside cliffs and rock formations, its distance from the city make the beaches here some of China's most pristine. As if that wasn't enough, there's a nearby amusement park.

Buses leave regularly from the square in front of the Dalian train station. ✛ *1 hr (60 km [37 mi]) northeast of Dalian.*

Liaoning A to Z

To research prices, get advice from other travelers, and book travel arrangements, visit www.fodors.com.

AIR TRAVEL
Dalian airport is 30 minutes northwest of the city center. There are regular flights to Beijing, Shanghai, Guangzhou, Hong Kong, and Tokyo.

AIRPORTS
🚹 Airport Information **Dalian airport** ✉ Dalian Guoji Feijichang ☎ 0411/364-5892 or 0411/362-6151 for international ☎ 0411/364-5892 or 0411/362-6151 for domestic.

BOAT & FERRY TRAVEL
Frequent passenger service links Dalian with Yantai (in Shandong), Tianjin, and Shanghai.
🚹 Boat & Ferry Information **Dalian Marine Co.** ☎ 0411/462-3064.

CONSULATE
🚹 United States **U.S. Consulate** ✉ 52 Shisi Wei Lu, Heping District, Shenyang 110003 ☎ 024/2322-1198 🖷 024/2322-2374.

EMERGENCIES
The below emergency contact numbers are for the cities of both Shenyang and Dalian.
🚹 **Ambulance** ☎ 119. **Hospital** ☎ 120. **Police** ☎ 110.

TAXIS
The most convenient mode of transport in Dalian is taxi. Flag fall is Y10, though you may have to ask that the meter be used. You can negotiate a price for longer trips outside the city. There are three tram lines (5 mao [50¢] flat fare, equivalent to Y0.50).

The easiest way to get around Shenyang is by taxi. Flag fall is Y8.

TRAIN TRAVEL
From Dalian station the overnight train to and from Beijing has two-berth sleeper cabins and four-berth hard sleepers, making it more comfortable than most other trains in China. Regular services link Dalian with Shenyang (5 hrs) and beyond.

Shenyang has two train stations: Bei Huo Che Zhan (North Railway Station) and Nan Huo Che Zhan (South Railway Station).
🚹 Train Information **Bei Huo Che Zhan** (North Railway Station) ☎ 024/2204-3522. **Dalian station** ✉ Shengli Guangchang, Zhongshan District ☎ 0411/254-2993.

Nan Huo Che Zhan (South Railway Station) ☎ 024/2206-3222.

VISITOR INFORMATION
🚹 Tourist Information **CITS** ✉ 1 Changtong Jie, Dalian 116011 ☎ 0411/369-1165 🖷 0411/368-7868 ✉ 113 Huanghe Nan Dajie, Shenyang ☎ 024/8680-9383 🖷 024/8680-6986.

NORTHWESTERN CHINA
TERRA-COTTA SOLDIERS & THE SILK ROAD

4

By Jan
Alexander,
Anya
Bernstein,
Christopher
Knowles

Updated and
revised by
Brandon Zatt

THE NATION'S MOST HAUNTING AND MEMORABLE SITES are found in northwestern China, including a vast, life-size army of soldiers built to outlast death, and the fabled Silk Road. The legendary East–West trade artery brought silks, spices, and other precious goods from the nation's great ancient capital of Chang'an to Rome more than two millennia ago. Today China's ancient Silk Road provides a living, unfolding lesson in geography, history, and culture and an excellent route for exploring China's Wild West.

The provinces of Shaanxi, Gansu, Ningxia, Qinghai, and Xinjiang extend more than 1,600 km (1,000 mi), starting in the nation's heartland abundant in fertile farmland, then winding west past barren mountains and eerily desolate grasslands to the "wild west" of China's dusty frontier reaches. It is a territory rich in history and paradoxes, including magnificent Buddhist lamaseries in two of the poorest provinces in the nation and seething ethnic unrest in the troubled but wildly colorful border region of Xinjiang.

The Silk Road starts in Xian (formerly Chang'an), capital of Shaanxi province and the seat of Chinese imperial power for more than a millennium. Heir to some of the oldest civilizations known to man, Chang'an birthed 12 dynasties, including the reign of China's first emperor, Qin Shihuang, and the illustrious Tang Dynasty, from the 7th to the 9th century—the most hallowed era of the nation's history. During this Chinese renaissance, travel along the Silk Road flourished, bringing Persians, Arabs, Japanese, Mongols, Greeks, and other foreigners in great numbers to the most cosmopolitan city of the ancient world. Turkish costumes swept the city, birds from tributary countries fluttered about court aviaries, Chinese women rode horses, and polo was all the rage.

After the collapse of the Tang in the 9th century, Chang'an steadily declined in importance until the city became little more than a dusty provincial metropolis in the 20th century, overshadowed by tales of its former glory. In 1974 all this changed, when local peasants accidentally unearthed one of the greatest archaeological finds of the 20th century—the terra-cotta army of Qin Shihuang—with rich treasures still unexcavated in Qin's nearby booby-trapped tomb. Today an infusion of foreign capital and glitzy hotels has transformed Xian into the most modern city on the old Silk Road.

Shaanxi is also home to the Communist pilgrimage site of Yanan, 260 km (161 mi) north of Xian, where Mao's Communists camped for a decade at the height of their civil war in the 1930s and '40s against the Nationalists.

Going westward, the caravans of the Silk Road wound their way through the largely barren strip of Gansu province, historically the last frontier of the nation, where the Great Wall ends. During the Han Dynasty, horsemen patrolled the borders of this natural corridor, which provided an essential military and communications link between China and the fiercely contested northwestern territories. Tibetans, Mongols, Han Chinese, Kazakhs, and the Xiongnu tribes poured through in ensuing centuries, battling for control of shifting territory. Today the province's population still comprises more than a dozen different ethnicities. Bordered by mountains and dominated by bleak deserts, however, Gansu continues to be one of the most impoverished regions of China despite recent attempts by the government to industrialize it. But the province is also heir to some of the most stunning religious sites of the Silk Road, including the oasis town of Dunhuang, which has the world's richest repository of Buddhist shrines, and the famed Labrang Monastery in the tiny town of Xiahe, where Tibetan Buddhist pilgrims come to pray.

To the north, nestled in between Shaanxi and Gansu, lies Ningxia, the quietest of China's five autonomous regions. Once the capital of the 11th-century Kingdom of the Xia, Ningxia has never played a terribly significant political or geographic role in China's history, having been passed back and forth between various administrative regions. Today the province, with a large Muslim Hui population, is a pleasant place that remains largely untrafficked by tourists. The Silk Road wound through the southern part of present-day Ningxia, en route from Chang'an to Lanzhou, the capital of Gansu.

Southwest of Gansu, on the northeast border of Tibet, lies Qinghai, a province of grasslands and desert locked in by mountains and pitted with strange moonlike craters. Historically this was a part of Tibet, until the 18th century when a Qing Dynasty emperor lopped it off and claimed it as Chinese terrain. Too remote to experience any major Silk Road traffic, even today, despite an influx of Han Chinese into its metropolises, much of the province remains unpopulated.

Since 1949 Qinghai's desolate beauty has had a shadow cast over it by its notorious political role as the nation's Siberia. Intellectuals and political prisoners were sent here in droves in a whole series of Communist crackdowns, including the Hundred Flowers campaign in the late 1950s, the Cultural Revolution, and present-day incarcerations. But the province is much more than a forbidding series of prisons and *laogais* (the word literally means "reform through labor" and, accordingly, many inmates are forced to work in factories without pay to make goods for export). Home to one of the six renowned temples of the Tibetan Buddhist Yellow Hat sect, Qinghai continues to share a strong cultural heritage with Tibet. Away from the industrializing cities, under an epic sky and vast open plains, seminomadic herders clad in brown robes slashed with fluorescent pink sashes still roam the grasslands, herding yak and goats the way their ancestors did for centuries before them—on horseback.

From Gansu the Silk Road crosses into Xinjiang (literally, New Dominion), an immense territory half the size of India, divided in ancient times into 36 different kingdoms. Xinjiang now comprises a sixth of China's total area. Here, in a province populated by at least 13 different ethnic groups—including Uighurs, Mongols, Kazakhs, Uzbeks, and Tatars—you may feel you've crossed over into another land. It is a region of extremes—stunning mountain ranges, sapphire-blue lakes, blasted terrain, and the deadly sweep of the Taklamakan Desert. Positioned in an area of strategic importance to the Chinese, Xinjiang has always been politically volatile as well.

A pared-down list of must-see sites on the Silk Road would have to include the terra-cotta warriors in Xian, Dunhuang's Mogao Grottoes, the lost city of Jiaohe, and other Silk Road sites outside Turpan. The Thousand Buddha Temple and Grottoes outside Lanzhou are also well worth the trip.

Numbers in the text correspond to numbers in the margin and on the Northwestern China, Xian, and Lanzhou maps.

4

If you have 3 days

Begin with a flight to ⊞ **Xian** ①–⑨ ► to see the terra-cotta warriors, the Great Mosque, and the Ming Dynasty city walls. The next day, fly to ⊞ **Dunhuang** ⑰ and hire a car to visit the Mogao Grottoes outside the city. At sunset head to Singing Sand Mountain to see the most spectacular sand dune vistas on the Silk Road. On the following day return to Xian. If time permits, visit the Shaanxi History Museum and take a walking tour of the city to catch the **Great Goose Pagoda** ⑨, **Small Goose Pagoda** ⑦, **Xian Forest of Stone Stelae Museum** ④, the **Bell Tower** ③, and the **Drum Tower** ②.

As an alternative, if the Wild West of China attracts you, head to Xinjiang to see the buried cities of the Silk Road. Arrive in ⊞ **Ürümqi** ㉚ and visit the Xinjiang Museum and the Erdaoqiao Market. At night stop by the Wuyi night market to sample the smoky lamb kebabs and spicy hotpot of Uighur cuisine. The next day go to **Turpan** ㉞ in the morning by bus or hired car; in the afternoon visit the ruins at the **City of Jiaohe Ruins** ㊳. On the last day visit the Flaming Mountains, **Bezeklik Thousand Buddha Caves** ㉟, **Atsana-Karakhoja Tombs** ㊱, the ruins of the **City of Gaochang Ruins** ㊲, Karez Irrigation Tunnels, and Emin Ta. Return to Ürümqi in the evening.

If you have 5 days

Arrive in ⊞ **Xian** ①–⑨ ► and follow the itinerary for the first two days, above. On the third day fly into ⊞ **Ürümqi** ㉚ and follow the alternative three-day itinerary above for Ürümqi. Another option is to start with the three-day itinerary above for Ürümqi. On the fourth day take a bus or hire a car to **Heavenly Lake** ㉛, return in the afternoon to Ürümqi, and take the train out to the border town of **Yinying** ㉜ and see nearby **Sayram Lake** ㉝ on the last day.

If you have 10 or more days

Spend the first two days in ⊞ **Xian** ①–⑨ ►, seeing the terra-cotta warriors and the sights on the walking tour of the city. On Day 3 fly to ⊞ **Xining** ㉕ and see the **Ta'Er Monastery** ㉖. On Day 4 hire a car to visit Qinghai Lake and **Bird Island** ㉙. In the morning of day five take the four-hour train ride to ⊞ **Lanzhou** ⑲–㉑ and visit the **Gansu Provincial Museum** ⑳. On Day 6 hire a car to see the **Thousand Buddha Temple and Grottoes** ㉒ outside Lanzhou, and return to town in the evening. On Day 7 fly to ⊞ **Dunhuang** ⑰ and visit the Mogao Grottoes and Singing Sand Mountain. On the following day fly to **Ürümqi** ㉚ to visit the museum and market. The next day take the bus to ⊞ **Turpan** ㉞. Spend the next two days visiting the ancient city of Jiaohe, Flaming Mountains, **Bezeklik Thousand Buddha Caves** ㉟, **Atsana-Karakhoja Tombs** ㊱, the **City of Gaochang Ruins** ㊲, Karez Irrigation Tunnels, and Emin Ta.

China's influence first extended to Xinjiang in the 1st century AD under the Han Dynasty, when the opening of the Silk Road thrust the territory to the forefront of the nation's economic and military concerns. As the dynasty waned, local warlords and kings reasserted sovereignty over their former terrain. This pattern of Chinese conquest followed by loss of military control occurred again in the Tang and Qing dynasties. In 1884 Xinjiang was officially declared a Chinese province by the Qing government, but when the Qing fell in 1911, the area was once again left to local warlords. In 1945 a Kazakh named Osman established an independent state—the Turkestan Republic—but it was short-lived, and in 1949 the Communist army moved in and claimed the territory as its own.

Since the 1950s the Chinese government has flooded the area with Han Chinese in an attempt to dilute the minority populations and quell ethnic dissent. But many Uighurs, who comprise a majority of Xinjiang's populace, still consider the Chinese to be invaders. Over the past few decades, most recently in the late 1990s, Uighur separatists have increasingly resorted to violent means, including gun trafficking, bus bombings, riots, and even assassination, to make their point. A swift crackdown by the Chinese military, however, ensures that the territory, despite rising tensions, remains under Chinese control. The discovery of valuable oil deposits in Xinjiang, notably near Turpan and in the Taklamakan Desert, has only cemented China's resolve to hold on to the vast region.

Nowadays many cities in Xinjiang, notably the capital, Ürümqi, and even the small city of Yining, in the northwest, are quickly "catching up" with modern China, with the attendant slapped-together buildings, traffic, and air pollution. Still, religion and tradition continue to play crucial roles in the inhabitants' lives. Special festivals, ethnic music, cuisine, and traditional costumes—far from disappearing—have become a source of ethnic pride. Xinjiang also has the spectacular Karakorum Highway, where ancient caravans wound their way over three mountain ranges and through the Valley of Blood into present-day Pakistan. Outside the city of Turpan, abandoned oasis cities of the Silk Road such as Kharakhoja and Yarkhoto can be explored. At the Sunday Bazaar in Kashgar—a bustling city rich with color and traditions—veiled women in resplendent colors bargain over bolts of cloth and old Uighur men squat by the roadside, haggling for hours over the price of sheep.

Exploring Northwestern China

Northwestern China and the Silk Road start at the classical Chinese province of Shaanxi in the geographical heart of the nation and stretch across some of the country's most beautiful and undeveloped regions to China's culturally Central-Asian western borders. Northwestern China is a long way from anywhere else and merits a stay of two weeks at the very least, but even a few days can be rewarding if you plan wisely. As you move west from Shaanxi towards Xinjiang, the culture slowly morphs from Han Chinese to Central Asian, the landscape changes from farms to desert to mountains, and transport becomes less predictable. The entire region is vast so weather conditions in one province, or even a part of one province, can be totally different from those next door.

4

Goin' to a Party

At the Labrang Monastery in Xiahe, the Great Prayer Festival (Monlam) is held on the 13th, 14th, and 15th days of the first month of the Tibetan New Year which usually falls around February 1, though it changes every year. Monks assemble to hold philosophical debates, and Tibetan pilgrims flock in droves to the monastery to celebrate Tibet's most important religious ceremony. The same festival is celebrated at the Ta'Er Monastery, outside Xining in Qinghai. Remarkable sculptures are carved out of frozen yak butter as part of the festivities. There are also many ethnic festivals at both places, especially in summer. Traditional ethnic music and dancing take place then, as well as special events, often including contests on horseback.

Dates for holidays based on the Muslim calendar vary slightly from year to year. The Rozi Festival (in February) ends the monthlong fast of Ramadan, the Muslim New Year. The Kazakh Nawiriz Festival (mid-March) has special events on horseback—horse races, lambskin tussling, and contests in which young men chase young women on horseback. The Korban Festival (mid-April; 70th day after the Rozi Festival on the Muslim calendar) is the Sacrifice Festival, to mark the time when Allah asked the prophet Abraham to sacrifice his son as a test of loyalty; Muslim families slaughter sheep and have a feast. The Mongolian Naadam Fair (July or August), at Sayram Lake, includes horse races, competitions in archery and wrestling, dancing, and music. At the height of the grape harvest season, Turpan stages the 10-day-long Grape Festival (end of August), with traditional Uighur music and dancing nightly around the city.

Nature Loving

Outside Shaanxi, the northwestern region is a nature-lover's paradise. Stunning mountain ranges, vast grasslands, and the harsh but desolate beauty of the Taklamakan Desert offer the chance to experience a region that has never been tamed by humankind, even at the beginning of the 21st century. The Karakorum Highway scenery, exploring the area around Lake Karakul, climbing the sand dunes outside of Dunhuang, and bird-watching on Qinghai Lake are all highlights. CITS and a number of foreign travel outfitters now organize intriguing adventure trips: biking, mountain climbing, horseback riding in the lake areas, rafting down rivers on inflatable goatskin rafts, and riding camels through the desert. Some of the mountains have the potential to develop skiing trails, but there are no lifts as of yet.

The Road Most Traveled

One of the best things about traveling the Old Silk Road is that it still maintains a sense of adventure. Though it may not be as forbidden as it was to explorers at the beginning of the 20th century, the 21st finds it brilliantly alive with cultures still largely unknown to Westerners. Incredible ruins of ancient civilizations and a stunning range of landscapes that continually take your breath away are accessible for even the least ambitious of today's visitors.

Whether you're heading west from Xian or east from the border town of Kashgar, ruined cities half covered by encroaching desert abound, decaying sections of the Great Wall line farm plots, and mountain passes, once crucial stages for caravans plying the Silk Road, await you. Though ravaged by both Western explorers and Red Guard soldiers, Buddhist cave art still flourishes, especially in the regions of Maijishan, Dunhuang, and Turpan. Traveling the region by bus, train, or car readily evokes images of ancient caravans, their camels and horses laden with silk, carpets, spices, and gems. Furthermore, China's most western reaches are like a vivid mosaic of culture, religion, architecture, clothing, and food, all meeting at one of the world's most ancient crossroads.

Though modern China is often criticized for diluting the Old Silk Road's ancient culture, one could view the changes as simply another phase of the famous route. The Silk Road was never a fixed road, nor even a fixed phenomena, but existed throughout centuries of shifting empires, marauding conquerors, trade missions, truces, and cultural exchanges. It is, in a sense, an earnest expression of the need, between different cultures—a need for contact, trade and philosophical exchange. The Silk Road found by today's travelers is simply the newest incarnation of an age-old way.

To foster a deeper appreciation for this region, predeparture recommended readings include: *The Great Game* and *Foreign Devils on the Silk Road* by Peter Hopkirk, *Life along the Silk Road* by Susan Whitfield, and *The Mummies of Ürümqi* by Elizabeth Wayland Barber.

China has extended its trains to its westernmost extremity, Kashgar, and roads in this area can be washed away by summer snowmelt or covered by spring sandstorms. On the whole, trains usually run on time and are often immune to the climatic changes that can wreak havoc on the open roads. Despite the obstacles, overland transport in this part of the world reveals the changes in culture, architecture, and landscape that are missed by flying, and the journey gives the traveler a chance to relive the ancient Silk Road. If you're short on time, however, the region's great distances are more efficiently traversed by plane.

Xian, Lanzhou, and Ürümqi are all reasonable bases from which to explore the surrounding sites. Private cars abound and deals can often be struck with drivers to include several days touring in air-conditioned comfort. Drivers can also often arrange homestays and meals with local families, an ideal way to appreciate the local color. Drivers often wait around tourist sites, hotels, and backpacker cafés. They are numerous, so choose carefully to find one you like.

About the Restaurants

Fine dining in China's Northwest is found, almost exclusively, in the larger cities and upscale hotels. The vast majority of restaurants, however, are either small family-run joints or moderate-size chains. Except for a few restaurants in Xian and Ürümqi, the entire region is decidedly casual and in most places, reservations are unheard of.

In Xinjiang, the locals eat according to Xinjiang time (two hours ahead of Beijing) while most Han settlers keep to their Beijing time-oriented schedules, which can make dining schedules a bit confusing. Travel in this region reveals another interesting dining dichotomy: pork. Although most of the Northwest is traditionally Muslim and focuses on dishes of mutton, beef, and chicken, increasing Han settlement has brought with it an array of Sichuan restaurants serving, among other things, pork, which is not on a strict Muslim's diet.

About the Hotels

The major capital cities (Xian, Lanzhou, and Ürümqi) generally have the best hotels in the region, with comfortable and well-appointed rooms in the more upscale establishments. Some hotels in lower price categories also offer good service and accommodations, though others can be downright grubby. Outside Xian, an English-speaking staff is a rarity.

Aside from the capital cities, hotels in the western provinces tend to be fairly run-down, not the cleanest, and subject to plumbing problems such as brown water, lack of hot water, or lack of any water. Despite these realities, prices are no longer rock-bottom, except for dorm rooms. The situation is gradually improving as the Silk Road becomes more popular and a rush of new hotels spurs competition.

If you're staying in the mountains or near a lake between May and October, nomadic families may offer inexpensive accommodations in a yurt. There is rarely plumbing but plenty of ambience. Expect to pay about Y20 per person per night, plus a few yuan extra for meals.

WHAT IT COSTS In Yuan					
	$$$$	$$$	$$	$	¢
RESTAURANTS	over 165	100–165	50–99	25–49	under 25
HOTELS	over 1,800	1,400–1,800	1,100–1,399	700–1,099	under 700

Restaurant prices are for a main course, excluding tax and tips. Hotel prices are for a standard double room, including taxes.

Timing

The best time to visit the region is from early May to late October, when the weather is warm. This is also the high tourist season, when many festivals take place and the land is in bloom with grasses and flowers.

Spring is a double-edged sword. At no other time of the year (and in no other part of China) do wildflowers make such a colorful, riotous appearance on the mountain meadows, rolling grasslands, and lush valleys. That said, much of northwest China is desert and spring is when warm winds whip across the land causing dust devils and sandstorms. By May most of the fury has died down.

Dry sunny summers provide blue skies and long days, optimal for exploring and photographing the region. Lunchtime, however, can be insufferably hot and most tourists follow the locals' lead in taking midday siestas. If you plan to explore mountain areas, summer gives the most access and fluctuates between chilly nights and warm bright days.

Clear skies last well into fall, usually through October. The changing leaves explode into a symphony of yellow, orange, and red, once again

Northwestern China

KAZAKHSTAN

Lake Balkhash

Alakol

Altay

Karamay

33 Sayram Lake

32 Yining

Changji

Grape
Valley **39**

Shihezi

Heavenly
Lake

KYRGYZSTAN

Ysyk-Kol

Ürümqi **30** **31**

Bezeklik
Thousand
Buddha
Caves

Turpan **34**

35

Aksu

City of
Jiaohe Ruins **38**

36

Atsana-
Karakho
Tombs

Artux   Sugun

Korla

Kashgar

Mor Ta

37

Lop
Nor

TADZHIKISTAN

Tashkurgan

City of
Gaochang
Ruins

XINJIANG

Hotan

Qiemo

K   U   N   L   U   N   S   H

Karakorum
Shankou

PAKISTAN

A   HOH XIL
                                              SHAN
                                                        N

H
 I
  M
   A
    L
     A
      Y
       A

XIZANG ZIZHIQU
(TIBET AUTONOMOUS REGION)

Tanggula
Mountain
Pass

INDIA

Q I N G S H A N   G A O Y U A N
(PLATEAU OF TIBET)

TANGGULA SH

creating ideal opportunities for the shutterbug. Cold weather, however, can come quickly and unannounced. If you visit in fall, bring an extra set of warm clothes.

Winter brings freezing temperatures, and a noticeable dearth of tourists and travelers. Although solitude may have its own charms, many interesting sights close for the off-season, making it the least desirable time to visit.

SHAANXI

One of the oldest habitations of Chinese people, Shaanxi was also home of the first unifier of China, Qin Shihuang—first (and penultimate) emperor of the Qin Dynasty. Because of the prestige of its capital city, then called Chang'an, the province grew in importance until it reached new heights of prosperity and artistic productivity during the Tang Dynasty. The great trade caravans of the Silk Road set off from here, and as a locus of Asian trading routes, the city prospered. At the same time, the Muslim, Buddhist, and, to a lesser extent, Christian influences from the West added to the vibrant diverse culture encouraged during the Tang.

In subsequent centuries China's focus turned inward, the outside seemed to grow more distant, and the capital was moved east. With less trade and a clampdown on religious and cultural diversity, Shaanxi's assets became its losses. Minority Muslim unrest caused major rebellions in the 14th and 17th centuries, and the harsh repression of uprisings caused thousands of deaths during the late Qing Dynasty. The complex web of irrigation canals that sustained the populace fell into disrepair, and the province was ravaged by famine. These cultural conflicts and natural disasters ensured that it would never again reach the heights it had known in the 10th century.

The late 19th and early 20th centuries saw poverty and famine sweep this once-prosperous area; millions died as the country was wracked by military unrest and, finally, civil war. In the late 1920s the young Communist Party started a countrywide effort to win over Chinese peasants; the state of disaffection and despair in this province gained them enthusiastic recruits. When the embattled Communists embarked on their Long March in 1934, it was from Shaanxi that they chose to emerge. They set up a camp in Yanan that would last them for more than 10 years of intermittent Japanese and Guomindang (GMD) conflict. It was here where much party theory was first hammered out and where Mao Zedong consolidated his power over the party. In 1947 the Communists were finally routed by the GMD and fled the province, only to return in triumph two years later.

Xian

▶ *7 hrs by train southwest of Luoyang; approximately 2 hrs by plane northwest of Nanjing.*

Haunting in sweep, artistry, and scale, the magnificent life-size terracotta army of China's first emperor is justly considered one of the 20th century's greatest archaeological finds. The emperor Qin, acceding to the throne in 221 BC at the age of 38, ruled China with an iron hand until his death just 11 years later. He not only ruled it, he created it. At the time of his accession, the lands we now call China were splintered into numerous small kingdoms. Qin took it upon himself to "unite"—that is, to conquer—a huge territory during his lifetime. He imposed military unity and instigated a series of bureaucratic reforms to centralize the country's governmental systems as well. He standardized money and measurements, divided the country into administrative units under central control, started construction on the Great Wall, and burned any books he could find that challenged state decrees—including many of the ancient classics. His son inherited the throne, but the dynasty crumbled four years after Qin's death. Nevertheless, his conquered lands and his administrative ideas formed the foundation of what China would become.

The area met with changing fates for the next millennium. The Han Dynasty, which overthrew the Qin, established its capital just northwest of modern-day Xian, but when in AD 23 the Eastern Han moved its capital to Luoyang, the region's prestige declined. In the 6th century the Sui Dynasty returned to Xian—then called Chang'an, meaning "eternal peace." Over the next centuries, under the Tang Dynasty, Chang'an became one of the largest and most cultured cities in the world. A complex web of communication systems united the capital with the rest of the country. It also became an important center for what is considered China's most cultured and artistic dynasty. Not surprisingly, the Silk Road flourished during this period as well, bringing Turkish fashions to court, rare birds to royal aviaries, and foreigners from as far as Persia and even Rome to the city. The name Xian, which translates as "western peace," was given during the Ming Dynasty, a less idealistic time. Much of the city lies on a grid that focuses on what used to be its exact center, where the Bell Tower stands.

More recently, in 1936, Xian "hosted" Chiang Kai-shek when his own general, Zhang Xueliang, had him arrested. Zhang used the arrest to convince Chiang to join the Communist Party in opposing the Japanese invasion of China. Chiang agreed—although Zhang later paid heavily for the betrayal; accused by Chiang of treason, Zhang was eventually confined to house arrest for decades. Today Xian contains a wealth of cultural artifacts and architecture, chiefly concentrated in the southeastern and western quarters.

a good walk

Start at the **Great Mosque** ① ↑. The Muslim neighborhood around the mosque is also a great place to wander and shop. Head east and south to pass under the **Drum Tower** ②. Next, follow Xida Jie east to the **Bell Tower** ③, which stands in the exact center of Xian, where Dongda Jie turns into Xida Jie and the north–south axis street of Nanda Jie (south) and Bei Da Jie (north) comes into view. From here you can go south on Nanda Jie and east to the **Xian Forest of Stone Stelae Museum** ④. Exit and turn west (right) onto Sanxue Jie, which will quickly lead you to **Calligraphy Yard** ⑤, a small pedestrians-only street with old-fashioned architecture where shops sell calligraphy brushes, imitation terra-cotta soldiers, and other esoterica. At the crossing with Nanda Jie, notice the impressive Ming Dynasty **South Gate** ⑥ on your left. This gate is one of the city wall's access points. Here you can climb up on the top and stroll along the 32-foot-wide walls. You can even take a minibus along the top if you don't feel like walking. Just south of the South Gate is the pleasant **Small Goose Pagoda** ⑦. Farther south and east, the excellent **Shaanxi History Museum** ⑧ contains terra-cotta warriors from the Qin tomb farther outside town, among other important dynastic relics. Southeast of the museum, you can visit the **Great Goose Pagoda** ⑨, one of the best-known pagodas in the country.

The chief places of interest in the Xian vicinity—**Banpo Neolithic village, Huaqing hot spring,** the **Imperial Tombs,** several **temples (sí)**, and, especially, the **Tomb of Qin Shihuang** and the **Museum of Qin Terra-cotta Warriors**—lie outside the city and can be visited on tours or by minibus.

What to See

★ **Banpo Neolithic Village** (Banpo Bowuguan). Accidentally unearthed in 1953, this settlement 6 km (3½ mi) east of the city holds the remains of the earliest Yangshao culture yet discovered. The matriarchal village of 200–300 people was populated from around 4500 BC to 3750 BC, and though villagers survived mainly by fishing, hunting, and gathering, there is evidence of animal domestication (pigs and dogs, and perhaps cattle or sheep) as well as farming in the surrounding areas.

This was also one of China's earliest pottery sites, with kilns reaching temperatures of 1,000°C (1,800°F) to produce cooking ware as well as ceremonial containers, many of which are decorated with animal designs. Five pottery kilns were unearthed here, along with more than 40 dwellings and more than 200 graves. Banpo is part village, part museum: an attempt has been made to re-create the conditions of the ancient village to give a sense of the past. Unfortunately, the re-created "village" seems to boast little if any historical value. The Disneyfied section to the side of the dig is fronted by a modern reddish-clay hut with two unmistakable breasts protruding out of the side wall. Inside, there's not much, other than locals paid to dress up in traditional garments and play musical instruments. The museum displays actual archaeological finds, including 6,000-year-old bone needles and stone axes. ✉ *139 Banpo Lu, off Changdong Dong Lu, 6 km (3½ mi) east of city; Bus 11 from train station* ☎ *029/8353–2482* 💴 *Y15* 🕐 *Daily 8–6:30.*

❸ **Bell Tower** (Zhonglou). The Bell Tower was first built in the late 14th century to mark the center of the city. Subsequent changes in city organization have displaced it from this prominent position, but the city still revolves around it. Despite its lack of centrality, it marks the point where Xida Jie (West Main Street) becomes Dongda Jie (East Main Street) and Bei Dajie (North Main Street) becomes Nanda Jie (South Main Street). To reach the tower, which stands in the middle of a traffic circle, go through an underground passage from the north side of the street and climb up. You'll see its centuries-old pillars and roofs, as well as an art exhibition on its upper floor. The tower was renovated in the Qing Dynasty and was being renovated at the time of writing. The large iron bell that gives

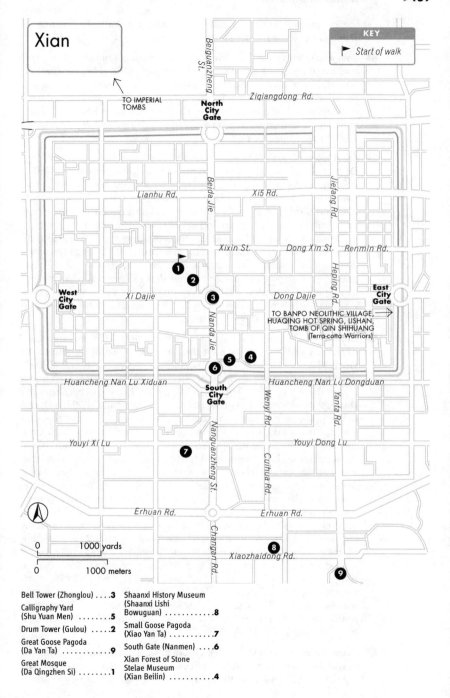

Xian

the tower its name is rung at 8 AM and 6 PM daily. ⊠ *Junction of Dongda Jie, Xida Jie, Bei Dajie, and Nanda Jie* ▨ *Y15* ⊘ *Daily 7–7.*

❺ Calligraphy Yard (Shu Yuan Men). The government renovated this walkway for tourism in 2000; it's now also known as Wen Hua Jie (Cultural Street). The houses on the lively bustling pedestrian street are built in a traditional style. A good place to buy gifts, the sides of the road have peddlers and shops selling various wares—calligraphy brushes and artworks including scrolls and watercolors. ⊹ *2 blocks north of Nanmen; look for traditional red archway.*

❷ Drum Tower (Gulou). Originally built in 1380, this 111-foot-high Ming Dynasty building, which used to hold the alarm drums for the imperial city, marks the southern end of the Muslim Quarter. The tower was renovated during the Qing Dynasty and again in the 1950s. The second and third floors hold exhibits of calligraphy and peasant paintings (brightly colored folk paintings of rural subjects). Both the street on which the tower is located and the side street running left directly after the tower are restored market streets on which ubiquitous peddlers offer anything from Chinese Muslim–style clothing to seals engraved on the spot, in Chinese or English, by old men bent over their metal picks. The drum in the tower sounds twice a day, at 8 AM and 6 PM, after the bell in the tower is rung. ⊠ *Bei Yuan Jie* ☎ *029/8727–4580* ▨ *Y12* ⊘ *Daily 8–7.*

❾ Great Goose Pagoda (Da Yan Ta). Four kilometers (2½ mi) southeast of the city wall's south gate, on the former grounds of the Temple of Great Maternal Grace (Da Ci'En Si), this impressive 209-foot-high Buddhist pagoda was originally constructed in the 7th century AD but was rebuilt during the Qing Dynasty, in Ming style. Parts have been restored since 1949. Here the Tang Dynasty monk Xuan Zang (600–664), one of the best-known travelers of the Silk Road, spent 11 years translating more than 600 Buddhist scriptures that he had brought back from India. In 652 he asked the emperor that a stone stupa be built to house the scriptures. The emperor partly obliged, with a five-story brick-and-wood edifice, originally called the Scripture Pagoda. It was directly connected to the imperial palace during the Tang and in fact houses the tumulus of the emperor Qin Shihuang. In 703, five more stories were added to the pagoda; a fire later burned down three stories. Inside the pagoda, statues of Buddhist figures in Chinese history line the various chambers. The pagoda also houses the **Tang Dynasty Arts Museum,** on the eastern side of the temple grounds, which collects originals and reproductions from that era of high artistic production. Walk behind the pagoda to see a courtyard of pavilions, erected in 1999, commemorating Xuan Zang's trip. In 2001, the entranceway to the pagoda was extended; the new square is graced with a statue of the eminent monk. ⊠ *Yanta Lu* ☎ *029/8525–5141* ▨ *Y20; additional Y15 to enter the pagoda* ⊘ *Daily 8:30–6.*

▶ **❶ Great Mosque** (Da Qingzhen Si). This lushly gardened mosque with four graceful courtyards may have been established as early as AD 742, during the Tang Dynasty, but the remaining buildings date mostly from the

18th century. Amazingly, it was left standing during the Cultural Revolution and has been significantly restored since then. Stone tablets mark the various pavilions, often bearing inscriptions in both Chinese and Arabic. Be sure to look above the doors and gates: there are some remarkable designs here, including 3-D Arabic script that makes the stone look as malleable as cake frosting. The northern lecture hall holds a handwritten Koran from the Ming Dynasty. Non-Muslims are not allowed in the prayer hall, as the mosque is still an active place of worship. The bustling **Muslim Quarter,** in the small side streets surrounding the mosque, is the center of the city's Muslim community, with shops and a lively market. In the alleyway called Hua Jue Xiang leading to the mosque, crowded tourist stands sell everything from prayer beads to jade paperweights; it's a fine place to pick up souvenirs. A few blocks west, the bustling Islamic market street **Da Mai Shi Jie** has peddlers hawking a pointillistic array of dried fruits and candies, as well as tiny noodle and kebab stalls. Look for the seaweed-green Islamic archway on the north side of Xida Jie, one block west of Da Xue Xi Jie. ⊠ *30 Hua Jue Xiang, off Beiguangji Jie, 5 mins north of Gulou, small side street on left with sign in English: Great Mosque* ☎ *029/8727–2541* ✉ *Y12* ⊙ *May–Sept., daily 8–7; Oct.–Apr., daily 8–6:30.*

Huaqing Hot Spring (Huaqing Chi). The Tang Dynasty equivalent of a Beverly Hills spa, this spring once provided natural hot water for 60 pools, as well as private baths. It stands amid elegant gardens east of the city overlooked by Li Shan (Black Horse Mountain). Unfortunately, it has almost run dry, save for two fountains from which a trickle of water is siphoned out to allow tourists to bathe their hands and face (Y5). The imperial history of the spring is said to extend back to the 8th century BC, when the Zhou rulers first discovered the pleasures of warm water. Later rulers, notably China's first emperor, Qin Shihuang, also came to bathe. The site is most famously linked, however, to Tang emperor Xuanzang, who built a walled palace here for his favorite concubine, Yang Guifei, in AD 747. Standing in front of a lake, a voluptuous white statue of Yang is a magnet for Chinese tourists who like to pose before it for photos.

In 1936 the "Xian Incident" occurred here, when Guomindang leader Chiang Kai-shek was taken prisoner by his subordinate Zhang Yueliang, known as the "Young Marshal." Zhang was deeply troubled by the Japanese military threat to China and Chiang's preoccupation with his civil war with the Communists. At dawn on December 12, his army stormed Chiang's headquarters at the hot springs where Chiang was sleeping. After a brief chase into the hillside, they captured the shivering, barefoot, and pajama-clad generalissimo, who purportedly didn't even have time to put in his dentures. On the orders of Stalin himself, Zhang released Chiang on Christmas Day. Chiang angrily court-martialed Zhang and sentenced him to 10 years in prison (later changed to house arrest, which he served for decades). The incident nevertheless eventually prompted Chiang's Nationalists to work more closely with Mao's Communists until the end of World War II.

Chiang's threadbare headquarters and the bedroom from which he fled are in the buildings to the side of the hot spring. The spot on the hill where he was captured is marked as well. ✚ *Northern foothills of Li Shan, 30 km (19 mi) east of Xian* ☎ *029/8381–2004* 🎫 *Y40* 🕐 *May–Sept., daily 7–7; Oct.–Apr., daily 7:30–6.*

Imperial Tombs. This series of tombs north and west of the city can be seen most conveniently on a day tour organized by a travel agency or hotel. The **Qian Tomb** (Qian Ling) is the burial place of the Tang emperor Gao Zong and his wife, Empress Wu, whose 21-year reign after his death was marked by an effective acquisition of power through such age-old means as political intrigue and murder. **Prince Zhang Huai and Princess Yong Tai's Tombs** (Zhang Huai Mu and Yong Tai Gongzhu Mu), near Qian Tomb, hold murals and engravings, although the ones with the princess have stood the test of time better than the prince's. Both of these royals—he, the second son of Empress Wu; she, Emperor Gao Zong's granddaughter—fell out of favor with the empress. The princess was killed and the prince exiled; both were posthumously rehabilitated and their remains returned to Xian. ✚ *85 km (53 mi) northwest of Xian.*

Many of the most important artifacts in the **Zhao Tomb** (Zhao Ling) have been transported to other sites, notably the Philadelphia and Xian museums, but the tomb itself, built for the second Tang emperor, is still a sight to see. Tai Zong died in AD 649 and was buried surrounded by his retainers and relatives. A small museum holds murals and examples of tricolor Tang pottery. ✉ *70 km (43 mi) northwest of Xian.*

The largest Han Dynasty tomb around—about 154 feet high—the **Mao Tomb** (Mao Ling) was built for the Han's strongest leader, Emperor Wu. The emperor was interred with retainers and horses, clad in a burial garment of jade and gold. None of these treasures are on display, however. Only the gate ruins can be seen. ✚ *40 km (25 mi) west of Xian.*

off the beaten path

LISHAN – This small mountain east of the city has several pavilions along its paths, as well as the local Taoist temple and Han Dynasty beacons. It's an inviting stroll if your tour stops at Huaqing Hot Springs and you want to get away from the crowds. A cable car at the bottom provides easy access to the summit. ✚ *30 km (19 mi) east of Xian.*

❽ **Shaanxi History Museum** (Shaanxi Lishi Bowuguan). The works in this
Fodor'sChoice imposing two-story museum, built in Tang Dynasty style, are arranged
★ chronologically. Included are artifacts from the Paleolithic and New Stone ages, later Zhou Dynasty bronzes and burial objects, and several terracotta warriors taken from the tombs outside town. This is the closest you can get to these statues, which are displayed behind glass. The exhibits, which have English labels, also show Han, Wei, and northern Zhou Dynasty relics, ending with more recent technological displays from the Sui, Tang, Ming, and Qing, as well as impressive bronze and jade artworks and religious statues. Look for the tricolor ceramic Tang Dynasty horses. Unlike most ancient Chinese relics which tend toward subdued earth tones, these are painted with all the colors of the Silk Road. Foreigners enter through a door to the left of the main gate. ✉ *91 Xiaozai Dong Lu* ☎ *029/8525–4727* 🎫 *Y35* 🕐 *Daily 8:30–6.*

★ ❼ **Small Goose Pagoda** (Xiao Yan Ta). Once part of the 7th-century AD Da Jianfu Temple and Monastery, this 15-tier pagoda south of the city's south gate was built by Empress Wu Zetian in 707 to honor her deceased predecessor, Emperor Gao Zong. The pagoda housed Buddhist texts brought back from India by the pilgrim Yiqing in the 8th century. A tremendous 16th-century earthquake lopped off the top two stories of the original pagoda, but they were rebuilt. The other buildings were actually constructed during the Ming Dynasty and have also been rebuilt at various times. The grounds are pleasant, and the pavilions are a good place to relax and stroll. Near the entrance a pavilion houses a small arts shop that sells local imitations of ancient styles as well as more modern paintings that still bear the marks of their Chinese origin. There are some excellent reproductions here at reasonable prices. ⊠ *Youyi Xilu, west of Nanguan Zhengjie* ☎ *029/8525–3455* 🎫 *Y10* ⊙ *Daily 8:30–6.*

❻ **South Gate** (Nanmen). This is the most impressive access point of Xian's 39-foot-high Ming Dynasty city walls. The south gate of the city wall hosts a small market during the day. This is also one of the points at which the city wall can be climbed; take a stroll along this ancient structure for a panoramic view of the old city of Xian inside and of the new city sprawling outside. The walls mark the original site of Tang Dynasty walls; the present ones were built at the beginning of the Ming and renovated in the 1980s. Enterprising locals have started a minibus service (Y10) that zips you to the far end of the south wall and back. Although many city walls in China were torn down during the 20th century, these remained standing. During the Japanese invasion small caves were hollowed out in them and used as storage and protection areas. ⊠ *South end of Nanda Jie* 🎫 *Y10* ⊙ *Daily 8–6.*

Temples (si). A number of temples near Xian are worth a visit. To the south, **Daxingshan, Caotang, Huayan, Xiangji,** and **Xingjiao** were all built to house Buddhist scriptures or to commemorate famous monks. Several schools of Buddhism begun in this area grew to renown and popularity throughout Asia. To the northwest, **Famen Temple** (Famen Si; 🎫 Y20 ⊙ Daily 8–6), originally built in the 3rd century AD, was renovated in 1981. It held a crypt that housed thousands of coins and various sacrificial objects of jade, gold, and silver. These can be viewed at the museum on the temple grounds. All these temples are best seen on an organized tour. Located 115 km (71 mi) northwest of Xian, tours can be organized through CITS. Alternatively, from Xian you can bus to Fufeng and hire local transport from there.

FodorsChoice ★ **Tomb of Qin Shihuang** (Qin Shihuang Ling). The first Qin emperor started construction on his enormous, richly endowed tomb, said to be booby-trapped with automatic crossbows, almost as soon as he took the throne. According to ancient records, this underground palace with 100 rivers flowing with mercury took 36 years and 700,000 workers to build. Though the tomb was rediscovered to the east of the city in the 1970s, the government cordoned it off without touching it due to lack of sophisticated machinery—and reportedly executed any local foolish enough to attempt a treasure-seeking foray. In 1999 a team of archaeologists finally began initial excavations in honor of the nation's 50th anniversary, and—as anticipated—unearthed some fabulous treasures. Just a mile away from Qin's tomb, the **Bing Ma Yong,** an army of thousands of man-made, life-size terra-cotta warriors was buried. Complete with weapons and horses, they were to be Qin's garrison in the afterlife. Each of the thousands of soldiers has individual facial features, including different moustaches, beards, and hairstyles. After the fall of the Qin to the Han—during which the soldiers were damaged—the terra-cotta army was forgotten, only to be found again in 1974, when some farmers digging a well unexpectedly came up with a piece of sculpture. Only a part of the entire area has been excavated, and the process of unearthing more warriors continues. In fact, no one is sure just how many warriors there are or how far their "tomb" extends beyond the 700-foot-by-200-foot section being excavated.

You can see what they've dug up so far in three vaults—at the impressive **Museum of Qin Terra-cotta Warriors** (Qin Shihuang Bing Ma Yong Bowuguan)—about a mile from Qin's tomb. The government has spared no expense to make Xian's star attraction a modern one, and new touch-screen computer displays and other exhibits installed in 1999 make this museum one of the nation's finest. The first vault holds about 6,000 warriors, though only 1,000 have been painstakingly pieced together by archaeologists. The warriors stand in their original pits and can only be seen from the walkways erected around the digs. Those in the front ranks are well shaped and fully outfitted except for their weapons, whose wooden handles had decayed over the centuries (the bronze blades were still sharp upon excavation). Be sure to walk around the entire pit: in the back, a less fully excavated section dramatically displays half-formed figures, some headless or limbless, emerging from the hard earth. Pit 2 offers a glimpse of Chinese archaeologists still working on excavating an estimated 1,000 soldiers. In 1999, they discovered the first tricolor figures of the site here: look closely and you can still see pink on the soldiers' faces and patches of dark red on their armor. Vault 3 has 68 warriors and a chariot.

Nearby, an imposing sand-color pavilion, also erected in 1999, now houses two miniature **bronze chariots** unearthed in the western section of the tomb. Found in 1980, these chariots have intricate detail on their finely crafted surfaces. In the atrium leading to the bronze chariots, look for the massive bronze urn—it's one of the treasures unearthed by archaeologists in their May 1999 excavation of an accessory pit near Qin Shihuang's mausoleum. On the second floor, rotating exhibits are held as well.

Photographs and videos are now allowed inside the vaults, a change from previous years when guards brusquely confiscated your film if they noticed your camera. There is also a 360-degree movie on the making of the terra-cotta warriors. Postcards and other souvenirs are available in the shops outside the vaults and the movie, or from hawkers outside the main gates, who sell them for under half the museum's price. CITS and practically every hotel arrange tour buses out, or you can go solo on public Bus 306 or 307, which leave from the train station. ✛ *30 km*

(19 mi) east of Xian ☎ *029/8391–1954* 🎟 *Y90 (includes movie)* ⊙ *May–Sept., daily 7:30–6; Oct.–Apr., daily 8–5.*

★ ❹ **Xian Forest of Stone Stelae Museum** (Xian Beilin). The first thing you see as you walk through the mammoth pagoda-style entranceway here is the impressive Forest of Stone Stelae, in a quiet courtyard shaded with trees. As the name suggests, there is no shortage here of historical stone tablets, on which imperial edicts and poems were engraved, starting as early as the Han Dynasty. More than 1,000 stelae bear inscriptions ranging from descriptions of administrative projects to artistic renditions of landscape, portraiture, and even calligraphy. One of the world's first dictionaries and a number of Tang Dynasty classics are housed here. One, known as the **Popular Stela**, dates from AD 781. It records the interaction between the emperor and a traveling Nestorian priest, Raban. After presenting the empire with translated Nestorian Christian texts, Raban was allowed to open a church in Xian. The rest of the museum holds Silk Road artifacts, including stone sculptures from the Tang Dynasty. ⊠ *15 Sanxue Jie, west of Duanlu Men* ☎ *029/8721–0764* 🎟 *Y30* ⊙ *May–Sept., daily 8:15–6; Oct.–Apr., daily 8:15–5:15.*

need a break? In the southeast corner of the city, outside the walls, **Xingqingsong Park** is the perfect place to rest on a busy sightseeing day. Although it can sometimes be hard to find proper shade in the busy, urban area inside the walls, this small oasis merits a visit on a nice day. Alternatively, two smaller parks, **Lianhu Park** and **Geming Park**, in the north-central and northeast parts of the walled city, also make nice places to take a break.

Where to Stay & Eat

$$$$ ✕ **Tang Le Gong.** Using recipes preserved from ancient times, Tang Le

FodorsChoice Gong specializes in Tang Dynasty imperial cuisine—a taste you're not

★ likely to find back home at your local Chinese restaurant. The prawns sautéed with caramelized pecans are a treat. Book in advance for an unusual evening of entertainment: a full-length imperial banquet, complete with Tang Dynasty singing and dancing. Dinner begins at 7, and the performance at 8:30. ⊠ *75 Changan Bei Lu* ☎ *029/8526–1633* ⌂ *Reservations essential* 🖃 *AE, MC, V.*

★ ¢–$$ ✕ **De Fa Chang Restaurant.** If you think dumplings are just occasional snack food, think again. De Fa Chang, one of Xian's fanciest and most famous restaurants, first opened in 1936. With red lanterns hanging outside and neon lighting at night, this four-story behemoth attracts large groups of locals, who sometimes exit singing. Its claim to fame is its dumpling banquet, which former President Jiang Zemin has sampled. The restaurant also serves a tempting hotpot, which comes out flaming in an intricate brass pot, or try an array of tiny dessert dumplings, stuffed with everything from minced carrots to crushed sweetened walnuts. ⊠ *Bei Dajie, north side of Zhonglou Guangchang* ☎ *029/8721–4060* 🖃 *No credit cards.*

★ ¢–$$ ✕ **Xian Muslim Restaurant** (Laosun Jia). This traditional, family-run affair, crowned by a green dome and crescent moon, serves some of the best local Islamic specialties in lamb and beef. The first floor has a snack

CloseUp

ON THE MENU

MUCH OF THE CUISINE—like much of the population—is Muslim, though good Chinese cooking can also be found all across the northwestern region. The particular dishes vary from city to city but invariably include grilled mutton kebabs, lamian (hand-pulled noodles sprinkled with diced tomatoes, green peppers, and chili peppers), and different types of naan (flat breads).

Another common dish is Mongolian hotpot. The price is usually reasonable, and the buffet has ingredients to suit every palate: meat, seafood, chicken, bean curd, mushrooms, vegetables, and noodles. You pick the ingredients, add them yourself to a simmering pot filled with a spicy stew, and mix your own seasonings. You can make a satisfying meatless meal out of hotpot (though the soup is invariably a meat-based one unless you specifically request that it not be); otherwise, it is often difficult to stick to a vegetarian diet in western China, unless you frequent Chinese restaurants.

Of all the cities in this region, Xian unquestionably offers the best and most exciting variety of foods, both Chinese and Muslim. Shaanxi province doesn't have its own regional cuisine, but restaurants tend to focus on noodles and jiaozis (dumplings) rather than rice, and they serve a colossal number of meat-based dishes. Still, vegetables and fresh fruit are also available. A Xian Muslim specialty is yangroù paomo, a spicy lamb soup poured over broken pieces of naan. Other popular Muslim street foods are heletiao (buckwheat noodles marinated in soy sauce and garlic) and roùjiamo (pita bread filled with beef or pork and topped with cumin and green peppers).

Outside Xian, the farther west you go, the less variety there is. Gansu, Ningxia, and Xinjiang don't offer much in the way of culinary surprises, but in Xinjiang, where temperatures can reach scorching levels, you'll find a variety of local ices, ice cream, and bingshui (a refreshing apricot or peach juice mixed with water). In Kashgar a popular drink for locals is an iced sour yogurt drink ladled from huge basins. The outdoor food stalls near the Sunday market are also worth checking out, where a lush display of tomatoes, red and green peppers, and other food items all piled together rises majestically from a boulder of solid ice. Fruit in Xinjiang is plentiful as well. Grapes from Turpan and melons from the oasis town of Hami are famous throughout China.

In Qinghai the many Tibetan restaurants serve such traditional staples as yak butter tea, yak meat, and stemba, a dough made by combining yak butter, yak cheese, sugar, boiling water, and barley flour; it's eaten with the fingers. Yak penis is a delicacy served when available.

Dress is casual everywhere except in the luxury hotel restaurants in Ürümqi. Unless otherwise indicated, reservations are not necessary. Tipping is not necessary, although diners may consider adding a 10% tip in higher-priced restaurants.

bar; the second floor has a more formal atmosphere and friendly service. The decor isn't special, but two more branches have opened up around town, evidence that the food is worth the lackluster view. ⊠ *364 Dongda Jie, southeast corner of Dongda Jie and Duanlumen* ☎ *029/ 8724–0936* ▤ *No credit cards.*

¢–$$ ✕ **Xian Fanzhuang.** The oldest and largest restaurant in the city, the Xian specializes in local foods with a Muslim flavor as well as "small eats"— street food spruced up for the visitor. Suited businessmen and T-shirt-clad college students alike head to the bustling first-floor cafeteria for quick service. The second floor is a proper restaurant, where more intricate dishes—from fresh steamed carp to roasted duck—are prepared. The private rooms on the third floor host banquets. ⊠ *298 Dongda Jie* ☎ *029/8727–3821 (ask for restaurant)* ▤ *No credit cards.*

¢–$ ✕ **Jiefang Lu Jiaozi Guan.** *Jiaozi* generally refers to boiled dumplings with
Fodor'sChoice meat fillings. This restaurant, which makes large succulent jiaozis with
★ more than 200 different fillings at low prices, has become so popular for its handmade delights that it's opened up five more branches around town. Service is friendly and prompt. The restaurant offers a couple of nonmeat dumplings. ⊠ *302 Jiefang Lu* ☎ *029/8744–2132* ⌦ *Reservations essential* ▤ *No credit cards.*

$$$–$$$$ 🏨 **Hyatt Regency Hotel.** Former presidential couple Bill and Hillary Clin-
Fodor'sChoice ton stayed here when they visited Xian in 1998. The deluxe establish-
★ ment, a few steps away from the town's chicest boutiques and bars, provides excellent service and high-quality Chinese food, as well as data ports in all rooms. The beds are super-comfortable and large windows provide great views of the city. It's a short ride from the best Xian sights, as well as within walking distance of the East Gate of the city wall. ⊠ *158 Dongda Jie, 710001* ☎ *029/8723–1234* 🖷 *029/8721–6799* ⊕ *www.hyatt.com* ⇘ *382 rooms, 22 suites* ⌂ *2 restaurants, café, tennis court, gym, bar, nightclub, dry cleaning, laundry service, business services, meeting room, airport shuttle* ▤ *AE, MC, V.*

★ $$$–$$$$ 🏨 **Shangri-La Golden Flower Xian.** Its golden glassy veneer shields a well-lighted property with excellent service and facilities. One of the most imposing and upscale hotels in the city, the Shangri-La maintains the chain's usual strict quality. The hotel offers bicycle rentals and tours of the area. Its only disadvantage is its location outside the old city walls, a 10-minute cab ride from the city center (without traffic). ⊠ *8 Changle Xi Lu, 710032* ☎ *029/8323–2981, 800/8942–5050 in the U.S.* 🖷 *029/ 8323–5477* ⊕ *www.shangri-la.com/eng/hotel/15/* ⇘ *389 rooms, 57 suites* ⌂ *2 restaurants, indoor pool, gym, 2 bars, nightclub, business services, meeting room* ▤ *AE, MC, V.*

$$$ 🏨 **Sheraton.** Never mind the dusty blue-glass facade: this is a joint venture with high-quality standards and well-appointed rooms. Unfortunately, it's some distance from town (staying here adds roughly 30 to 40 minutes to a terra-cotta warriors excursion), but it has the convenience of a CITS branch on site. ⊠ *12 Fenghao Dong Lu, 710001* ☎ *029/8426–1888* 🖷 *029/8426–2188* ⇘ *438 rooms, 17 suites* ⌂ *4 restaurants, pool, gym, bar, business services, travel services* ▤ *AE, MC, V.*

$$ 🏨 **ANA Grand Castle Hotel.** Right outside the old city's south gates, this classy hotel—with its white walls and black-tipped pavilion roof mod-

eled after the Great Goose Pagoda—is luxurious and less expensive than its competitors. Decorated in a tasteful modern classic Chinese style, the comfortable, well-appointed rooms give a taste of ancient China while providing all the modern amenities. It's a good base for touring the old city. ⊠ *12 Xi Duan Huan Cheng Nan Lu, 710068* ☎ *029/8723–1800* 🖷 *029/8723–1500* ⊕ *www.anahotels.com* 📮 *293 rooms, 18 suites* 🛆 *3 restaurants, gym, hair salon, business services, travel services* ⊟ *AE, MC, V.*

★ **$–$$** 🏨 **Bell Tower Hotel.** Relatively inexpensive compared to other hotels in its class, the Bell Tower has spacious airy rooms with views over looking some of downtown Xian's most impressive sights. Managed by the Holiday Inn group and now enjoying renovations completed in 2003, this hotel provides all the Western creature comforts while maintaining its posh Chinese flair. Located directly across from the Bell Tower, this hotel has the most desirable address in the city. Upstairs there's a branch of CITS and the Golden Gate Travel Service. You can rent bicycles here or set up tours of the area, and the hotel is home to some of Xian's best Western food. ⊠ *110 Nanda Jie, 710001* ☎ *029/8760–0000* 🖷 *029/ 8727–1217* 📧 *belltower@ihw.com.cn* 📮 *309 rooms, 11 suites* 🛆 *2 restaurants, bar, baby-sitting, dry cleaning, laundry service, business services, meeting room, travel services* ⊟ *AE, MC, V.*

$–$$ 🏨 **Grand New World.** This luxurious hotel benefits from its proximity to an access point in the city wall as well as from its association with the Xian Cultural Center, which holds performances of plays and Xian-style operas in the hotel's theater. The courtyard, with statues of historic figures, is an escape from the busy street outside. Though not extremely spacious the rooms are comfortable and well lighted. This may all be changing as the vast majority of the hotel was being renovated at the time of writing. Besides cultural events, guests also benefit from the hotel's full gym and indoor pool. Several bus routes run on Lianhu Lu going to more central parts of town. ⊠ *48 Lianhu Lu, 710002* ☎ *029/ 8721–6868* 🖷 *029/8721–9754* ⊕ *www.newworldhotels.com/sianw* 📮 *469 rooms, 22 suites* 🛆 *3 restaurants, tennis court, indoor pool, gym, business services, travel services* ⊟ *AE, MC, V.*

$ 🏨 **Royal Xian.** This Japanese-owned hotel, with its rectangular modernist facade and splashing fountains in front, has reasonable service and standard amenities. Conveniently located in one of Xian's most prosperous commercial districts, clean rooms and standard amenities make it a prime choice for a business traveler on a budget. A bit cheaper than other hotels in its class, it's a solid choice. As a Nikko Hotel, it often caters to Asian tour groups. ⊠ *334 Dongda Jie, 710001* ☎ *029/ 8723–5311* 🖷 *029/8723–5887* ⊕ *www.nikkohotels.com* 📮 *420 rooms, 29 suites* 🛆 *2 restaurants, driving range, gym, bar, nightclub, laundry service, business services, meeting room, travel services* ⊟ *AE, MC, V.*

¢ 🏨 **Jiefang.** Across from the railway station, the Jiefang is a standard Chinese hotel that caters mostly to Chinese guests, with relatively clean if small rooms. Its service is lackadaisical at best, but it's very convenient if you're coming in late at night or want to be at the hub of Xian excursion possibilities. CITS has a ticketing office upstairs. ⊠ *181 Jiefang Lu, 710005* ☎ *029/8766–8888* 🖷 *029/8766–6666* 📮 *313 rooms, 8* *suites* ♨ *3 restaurants, hair salon, massage, sauna, laundry service, business services, travel services* 🖃 *No credit cards.*

¢ 🏨 **Liging.** The Liging is probably the best choice for a hotel in its price range. Rooms are relatively clean and comfortable, and the service is friendly. Its trump card is its location, just a stone's throw from the Bell Tower. ✉ *6 Xida Jie, 710002* 🕾 *029/8728–8731 or 029/8721–8895* 🛏 *100 rooms, 3 suites* ♨ *Restaurant, business services, travel services* 🖃 *No credit cards.*

Nightlife & the Arts

The **Shaanxi Provincial Dance and Song Assembly** (✉ 5 Wenyi Bei Lu 🕾 029/8785–2664) stages traditional performances in colorful ethnic regalia; check with CITS for times. The **Shaanxi Provincial Drama Assembly** (✉ 59 Bei Dajie 🕾 029/8727–1515) has periodic performances of regional-style traditional opera and plays.

One of the busiest parts of town in the evening is the **Muslim Quarter,** where crowds converge to shop, stroll, and eat virtually every night of the week. This is a top spot in town to check out the local color by night. Street-side chefs fire up the stoves and whip up tasty dishes, vendors ply the crowded lanes peddling their wares, and locals and tourists alike jostle in the frenetic pace. If you want to have a great night without spending a lot of money, this is the place.

In the late 1990s a spurt of Western-style bars and discos hit Xian, mainly grouped in a strip on Dongda Jie, between the Hyatt Regency and the Royal Xian hotel. Although many went under after a 2000 nationwide crackdown on nightspots, prostitution, and gambling, the most chic and sleekest club in town is still the metal-sheathed **Bar 1+1** (✉ 285 Dongda Jie 🕾 029/8721–6265 or 029/8726–3128), which is a magnet for beautiful people. Hordes, bathed in red neon laser lights, pack the dance floor even on weekdays to vogue to Japanese techno. Kitsch mixes with cool at Xian's other popular hangout, **China City** (✉ Corner of Nan Dajie and Fen Xiang Lu, 4th fl., entrance on Fen Xiang Lu 🕾 029/8721–0215 or 029/8721–4395), where local singers croon soft-pop standards.

If you're looking for quieter haunts to while away the afternoon or evening, Xian's **De Fu Xiang Café Street** is another popular choice among locals. Here, over a dozen almost-identical Western-style cafés offer your choice of tea or cappuccino in comfortable surroundings with pinewood floors. To find De Fu Xiang, walk south on Nanda Jie and take a right at Fen Xiang. After five minutes or so, you'll see the café street, marked by a neon-lighted archway on the left-hand side. One of the street's more popular cafés is the pleasant **Touch Café** (Jie Chu Ta Chi; ✉ 22 De Fu Xiang 🕾 029/8721–8019), where you can drink Colombian coffee or one of a variety of teas while tinkering with an assortment of puzzles and brainteasers.

Shopping

Predictably, Xian is overloaded with terra-cotta references in various flavors and styles: aside from postcards and picture books, you can get imitation terra-cotta warriors at virtually every tourist site in town. Made with detail that resembles the originals, these range from palm-size to actual size. Bigger terra-cotta warriors can be shipped home for you.

But there is more to buy here than Qin reminders. The **Art Carving Factory** (⊠ 8 Nanxin Jie ☎ 029/8721–7332) carries local art wares. All kinds of crafts and souvenirs can be bought at the **Friendship Store** (Youyi Shang Dian; ⊠ 1A Nanxin Jie ☎ 029/8721–0551). The **Jade Carving Factory** (⊠ 173 Xi Yi Lu ☎ 029/8745–2570) sells sculptures by local jade workers. The **Overseas Chinese Department Store** (⊠ 297 Dongda Jie ☎ 029/8721–7673) has two floors of local artists' wares. Xian also has a number of market streets where peddlers sell foods, replica antiques, and more. You can sometimes find lovely souvenirs here. The **Dajue Xiang market** (⊠ Hua Jue Xiang), on the alley that leads into the entrance of the Great Mosque, is one of the best places to find souvenirs. Expect the antique dagger or beautiful porcelain bowl you're eyeing to be fake, however, no matter how hard the vendor insists your find is "genuine Ming Dynasty." **Fangu Jie** and the area around the **North Gate** also have antiques sellers. One of the liveliest food markets is the covered **Nan Shi Jie,** off Dongda Jie, where everything from fresh fruit to turtles and monkey testicles is sold.

Side Trip from Xian

A few hours east by train from Xian lies one of China's Five Sacred Mountains, **Huashan** (☞ Y60). The 7,218-foot mountain has some lovely scenery, including tall, sloping pines whose distinctive tufts of green are reminiscent of a Dr. Seuss creation and sheer granite walls that rise shockingly out of the surrounding flatter lands. This is not a trip for the fainthearted: hiking the main trail takes a good seven to nine hours one-way, some of it along narrow passes on sheer cliffs. For the less athletically inclined, there is a cable car ride to North Peak three-quarters up the main trail (Y55 one-way, Y100 round-trip); frequent minibuses (Y10) run from Huashan Village to the cable car station, located just a few kilometers southeast of the village. From Xian, you can take a train (1¾–3 hours, Y10) to Huashan Village, at the base of the mountain. Note: the Huashan Train Station is confusingly located 15 km (9 mi) outside Huashan Village, in the neighboring town of Mengyuan; frequent minibuses (Y3) link both places. Alternatively, buses (2 hours, Y12) run direct to Huashan Village hourly from the Xian Bus Station. A decent budget option with relatively clean and comfortable rooms is the **Xiyue Fandian** (⊠ Yuquan Lu ☎ 0913/436–3145).

Shaanxi A to Z

To research prices, get advice from other travelers, and book travel arrangements, visit www.fodors.com.

AIR TRAVEL

You can book tickets at CAAC, through CITS, or at your hotel travel desk. For Hong Kong flights you can take the domestic carrier or Dragonair.
🚄 Airlines & Contacts **CAAC** ☎ 029/870-8486. **CITS** ⊠ 32 Changan Bei Lu ☎ 029/727-9200 Ext. 2842 🖷 029/526-1454. **Dragonair** ⊠ 12 Fenghao Dong Lu, in Sheraton hotel ☎ 029/426-2988.

AIRPORTS

Around 40 km (25 mi) northwest of town, Xian's Xiguan Airport has daily or almost daily service to Beijing, Shanghai, Guangzhou, Chengdu, and Ürümqi, and several flights a week to Hong Kong and Macau. It's also connected internationally, with daily flights to Japan.

Taxis to and from the airport should cost Y120–Y160. China Northwest Airlines also runs a regular shuttle-bus service (Y15) between the airport and its booking office 5 AM–8 PM daily.

⏭ Airport Information Xian Xiguan Airport ☎ 029/8870–8450. **China Northwest Airlines shuttle service** ✉ 296 Laodong Nan Lu ☎ 029/8870–2299.

BIKE TRAVEL

Many Xian hotels rent bicycles for a song. In good weather this is a great way to see the city—all the sights within the city walls are close enough to get there by bike.

BUS TRAVEL

Xian's bus center stands directly south of the Bell Tower; just about every bus in the city passes through here. City maps show bus routes and numbers. From here you can also catch convenient, and less crowded, buses to out-of-town sights. Buses run frequently and traverse the city, but they're very crowded, and the driving tends to be a little fast and loose. It's best to stick to the cabs, which are plentiful, cheap, and easily hailed.

The long-distance bus station, across from the train station on Jiefang Lu, has buses to Huashan every hour 6 AM–4 PM daily (2 hours, Y12) and other Shaanxi destinations, as well as Henan stops.

CAR TRAVEL

Because so many of the sights lie outside the city proper, hiring a taxi or hotel car with a driver is convenient and allows you the freedom to leave when you like instead of waiting for the rest of the tour. Ask for a rental car at your hotel; major hotels provide car services.

EMERGENCIES

In case of an emergency, contact your hotel manager for assistance. If you speak Chinese (or are traveling with someone who does), the following numbers may prove useful: **Police** (☎ 110), the **fire department** (☎ 119), and the **first-aid hotline** (☎ 120).

⏭ Xian Medical University Affiliated Hospital No. 1 ✉ 1 Jiankang Lu ☎ 029/522–7604.

INTERNET SERVICES

Most major hotels in town provide free broadband Internet service in the rooms. If you still hanker for an Internet café, however, there are numerous choices. The most centrally located place is Internet Club 169, where you can pay Y12 for an hour. Cheaper Internet places have also sprung up on Dongda Jie, including the popular and crowded Mu Wei Jiu Ba, where going online is Y3 an hour; and Internet 169 Bar, where surfing the Web costs Y10 an hour. Nanda Jie south of the old city walls (Nan Guan Zheng Jie) has a number of Internet cafés. If you have your own laptop, you can also get online with a public access Internet number. The telephone number, user name, and password is 163; all you pay for is the phone time.

🚹 **Internet Club 169** ✉ China Telecom Bldg., 2nd fl., Bell Tower Sq. ☎ 029/723-2017 🖷 029/723-2047. **Internet 169 Bar** ✉ 213 Dongda Jie ☎ 029/728-1449. **Mu Wei Jiu Ba** ✉ 341 Dongda Jie, 2nd fl. ☎ 029/721-1245.

TOURS

Every hotel offers its own guided tours of the area, usually dividing them into eastern area, western area, and city tours. More upscale hotels have special English-language tour guides, but their availability often depends on the number of people in your group. You don't have to stay at the hotel to participate in a tour. CITS arranges similar tours.

🚹 Tour-Operator Recommendations **CITS** ✉ 32 Changan Bei Lu ☎ 029/727-9200 Ext. 2842 🖷 029/526-1454.

TRAIN TRAVEL

SCHEDULES The train station, Xian Zhan, lies on the same rail line as Lanzhou (10 hrs), the next major stop on the Silk Road; Dunhuang (24 hrs); and Ürümqi (35 hrs). Off the Silk Road, other major stops are Beijing (13½ hrs), Shanghai (17 hrs), Guangzhou (28 hrs), Chengdu (15 hrs), and Kunming (36 hrs). Going east you can also connect to Luoyang (6½ hrs), Zhengzhou (8 hrs), and Nanjing (14 hrs). The main Huashan stop is about an hour out of Xian on the train. The foreigners' ticket window upstairs above the main ticket office is open daily 8:30–11:30 and 2:30–5:30. First order your destination at one of the windows on the far left, then take the receipt and line up on the other side of the room. CITS will book tickets for a fee, as will Golden Bridge Travel Agency (⇨ Travel Agencies); both need three days' notice.

🚹 Train Information **Xian Zhan** ✉ Huancheng Bei Lu Dong Duan and Jiefang Lu ☎ 029/727-6076.

TRAVEL AGENCIES

CITS offers good basic tours of the area all year, and books hotels, train, and plane tickets. Across the hall from CITS, Golden Bridge Travel Agency has similar services and can book hotels for a discount, but be prepared to bargain hard for lower prices.

🚹 Local Agent Referrals **Golden Bridge Travel Agency** ✉ Bell Tower Hotel, 227 Nanda Jie, 2nd fl. ☎ 029/725-7275 🖷 029/725-8863. **Xijing Travel Agency** ✉ North Bldg., 77 Qingnian Lu, 3rd fl. ☎ 029/721-7951.

VISITOR INFORMATION

🚹 Tourist Information **CITS** ✉ 32 Changan Bei Lu ☎ 029/727-9200 Ext. 2842 🖷 029/526-1454.

NINGXIA

The smallest of China's five autonomous regions is something of an enigma, with little known about it outside its own borders. With an area of 66,400 square km (25,600 square mi) and a population of a mere 6.3 million, it is surrounded by the provinces of Gansu and Shaanxi and the huge autonomous region of Inner Mongolia. A third of the population is composed of minorities, most of them Hui (Muslim Han), but also significant numbers of Mongols and Manchurians.

An arid region traditionally inhabited by nomads, most of Ningxia is high, flat plateau, and the rest lowland plain along which the Yellow River flows, providing water for the network of canals that have been in use for many hundreds of years. The climate of Ningxia is continental, characterized by very cold winters and warm summers that are rarely excessively hot. The annual rainfall is less than 8 inches.

With the exception of a couple of comparatively brief periods, the region has been under Chinese control since the Qin Dynasty. Ningxia was part of various administrative regions until 1928, when it became a province. In 1958 the government turned the area into the Autonomous Region of Ningxia Huizu Zizhiqu.

Ningxia's capital, Yinchuan, is quite lively. The remoter areas offer insight into the lesser-known aspects of Chinese life—ancient waterwheels are still used for irrigation, and in some areas leather rafts, once used to transport goods over distances of up to 2,000 km (1,240 mi), are still in use.

Yinchuan

⑪ *10 hrs (540 km [335 mi]) by train southwest of Hohhot; 20½ hrs (850 km [530 mi]) by train southwest of Beijing.*

Once the capital of the 11th-century Western Xia Dynasty, Yinchuan stands amid a network of irrigation canals thought to have been in constant use since the Han Dynasty. It's close to the Yellow River to the east and the Helan Mountains to the west. The town is actually divided in two: the New Town, site of the railway station, and the Old Town, about 5 km (3 mi) southwest.

All ancient Chinese cities had their drum and bell towers, which were used to announce the beginning and end of the hours of curfew. Yinchuan's **Drum Tower** (Gulou), having survived the destructive phases of Chinese history, stands on the main street not far from the post office. Of interest to history buffs may be the black-and-white photography exhibition of Communist history on show here in four rooms: amid the pictures of Ningxia Communist Party members, there are some fine photos, including a haunting one of Deng Xiaoping in his youth and one of Chiang Kai-shek and his wife. ⌧ *Gulou Jie* ☎ *0951/602–4652* 🚌 *Y3* ⊙ *May–Sept., daily 8–noon and 3–6; Oct.–Apr., daily 8–noon and 2:30–6 (If there is no one at the entrance, go to Yuhuang Pavilion, and ask the ticket attendant to open the door.).*

Close to the Drum Tower, the **Yuhuang Pavilion** (Yuhuang Ge) is a restored 400-year-old house containing a small museum. On the first floor is an exhibition of contemporary landscape paintings; head upstairs to look at artifacts from the New Stone Age to the Qing Dynasty, including coins, sculptures, pottery, and brassware. ⌧ *2 Yuhuang Ge Bei Jie* ☎ *0951/602–4652* 🚌 *Y5* ⊙ *May–Sept., daily 8:30–noon and 3–6:30; Oct.–Apr., daily 8:30–noon and 2:30–6.*

In the northern suburbs is a pagoda that has stood here since the 5th century. The current **Treasure Pagoda** (Haibao Ta), also called **North Pagoda** (Bei Ta) dates from 1771, when it replaced an earlier one destroyed by an earthquake in 1739. Forming part of a temple complex, it has 11 stories and is 177 feet high, offering fine views across the town to the Yellow River. Although actually rectangular in shape, it has niches designed to create the illusion that it's 12-sided. Walk to the back of the pagoda for a visit with the large golden reclining Buddha. ☒ *Jinning Jie* ☎ *0951/503–8045* 🖃 *Y5* ☯ *Daily 8–6.*

In a former monastery, **Ningxia Museum** (Ningxia Bowuguan) houses a fine collection of Western Xia and Zhou Dynasty artifacts, ceramics, and sculptures, as well as materials illustrating Hui Muslim culture, some Stone Age petroglyphs from the Helan Mountains, and a collection of Ming and Qing paintings. Not to be missed are the spectacular antique carpets from the Qing Dynasty's Qian Long Period. Of the monastery itself the most obvious remaining part is the towering pagoda, known as the **West Pagoda** (Xi Ta), with its glazed-tile roof. It was built around 1050 during the Western Xia Dynasty. The museum offers car service to the Western Xia Tombs and Helanshan Petroglyphs at some of the cheapest rates in town. ☒ *32 Jinning Nan Jie* ☎ *0951/503–6497* 🖃 *Y22* ☯ *Daily 9–noon and 2–5.*

The modern, busy **Nanguan Mosque** (Nanguan Si) is interesting for its purely Arabic architectural style. Yinchuan's main mosque, Nanguan, is an active place of worship and proper etiquette for mosque visits is required. ☒ *South of Nanguancheng Lu* ☎ *0951/410–6714* 🖃 *Y8* ☯ *Daily 8–8.*

The restored red **South Gate** (Nanmen), built in classical Chinese style, is all that remains of the city wall. ☒ *Zhongshan Jie* 🖃 *Y2* ☯ *Daily 8–8.*

Where to Stay & Eat

You can eat tolerably well in the hotel restaurants, but in Yinchuan you're almost better off eating at the smaller places on the street. A great food alley to try is Zhong Xin Xiang, between Jiefang Xi Jie and Xinhua Dong Lu, near the Yuanheng Hotel. The local food is essentially Islamic, with lamb and beef dishes, dumplings and pastries, and blended teas. But regional specialties include several tasty cold vegetarian dishes as well: try the *zhima bocai* (sesame spinach) or *kuku cai* (bitter greens marinated in vinegar and spiced with garlic and red peppers). *Hongshao ji yu* ("red-cooked" river fish) is another popular dish, made with fish caught from the Yellow River.

¢–$ ✕ **Shaojigong.** This restaurant specializes in a cook-it-yourself sort of chicken hotpot. The spicy chicken stew is brought to your table in a sizzling cauldron to which you can add an assortment of vegetables, noodles, and spices. One serving is usually enough for two people and it makes a fun dinner meal that can easily stretch late into the night. ☒ *Jiefang Dong Jie and Limin Jie* ☎ *No phone* ▤ *No credit cards.*

¢–$ ✕ **Yingbinlou Islamic Restaurant.** (Yingbinlou Qingzhen Fanzhuang). A popular local venue for Muslim dining, this place is often packed with families and friends eating and drinking beer. The second-floor restaurant has good kebabs, *plov* (rice with chunks of mutton and carrot), and noodle dishes while the first floor serves yogurt and ice cream, making it an excellent midday stop. ⊠ *Jiefang Dong Jie and Minzu Bei Jie* ☎ *No phone* ▤ *No credit cards.*

¢ ✕ **Muslim Spicy Beef Noodle Restaurant** (Qingzhen Niurou Lamian). Specializing in beef noodles and mutton dumplings, the noodles come in a blazing red broth and the fragrant dumplings are filling and cheap. Stop here for lunch and a quick fix of the local flavor. ⊠ *Intersection of Zhongshan Nan Jie and Nanxun Dong Lu* ☎ *No phone* ▤ *No credit cards.*

¢ ▦ **Ningfeng Hotel.** This good, modern hotel boasting a cozy white-marble lobby has comfortable rooms and reasonable facilities. ⊠ *236 Jiefang Dong Jie, 750004* ☎ *0951/602–8898* 🖷 *0951/602–7224* ⚑ *132 rooms, 11 suites* ⚖ *3 restaurants, hair salon, massage, bar, shop* ▤ *No credit cards.*

¢ ▦ **Rainbow Bridge Hotel** (Hongqiao Da Jiu Dian). Centrally located, the Hongqiao Da Jiu Dian is possibly the best hotel of its price category in town. The resplendent gold-trimmed lobby has subtle touches of white marble and rose, the staff is friendly, and the rooms are comfortable and well priced. ⊠ *16 Jiefang Xi Jie, 750001* ☎ *0951/691–8888* 🖷 *0951/ 691–8788* ⚑ *142 rooms, 12 suites* ⚖ *3 restaurants, miniature golf, sauna, business services* ▤ *AE, MC, V.*

Shopping

For centuries, Ningxia produced China's finest wool carpets, many of which were solely for the Emperor's use. Though true antique Ningxia carpets are quite hard to find these days, if you have a good eye it is worth browsing along the main shopping street, Gulou Jie, as well as around the shops near the Nanguan Mosque and the Provincial Museum. Ningxia also produces the best tea in northwestern China so it may be wise to stock up before continuing your travels.

Side Trips from Yinchuan

★ ⓬ Lying at the foot of the Helan Mountains 35 km (22 mi) west of Yinchuan, the **Western Xia Tombs** (Xixia Wangling) have a certain dramatic appeal. Because this dynasty, which lasted 189 years (1038–1227) before being exterminated by the Mongols, was not included in the imperial annals, little is known about many aspects of it, including the occupants of the tombs. Despite the shortness of its history, however, the dynasty invented its own written language (similar to Chinese), minted new currency, possessed a strong military, and developed a flourishing culture and new artistic style. Stunning artifacts unearthed from the tombs—including horse and cow sculptures, gold masks, patterned tiles, and simple but striking glazed ceramics, as well as several dioramas of the surrounding region—are housed in the impressive yellow-pavilion Xixia Museum on site; unfortunately, there are no English captions. In a wing opposite the museum, plaster sculptures depicting well-known scenes from Xixia history have been erected; avoid these if you can, and head over to the tombs. The founder of the dynasty, Li Yuanhao, is believed to have built 72 tombs for himself and his relatives. Only one of the circular brick mounds is open to the public; to gain entry, you have to book a tour with a travel agency. ⚓ *Hire a taxi,* *book a CITS tour or a car from Ningxia Museum, or take Bus 17 from bus station to terminus, then taxi* 🚕 *Y45* 🕐 *Daily 8–5.*

⑬ Helankou Yanhua are also called Helanshan Yanhua (Petroglyphs of the Helan Mountains). Etchings of goggling human masks, fleet-footed deer, crouching tigers, sexual intercourse, and even a witch draining energy from a human captive appear in these New Stone Age petroglyphs, chiseled into the rocks at the base of the Helan Mountains between 3,000 and 10,000 years ago. The site opened to the public in 2000 after an international conference was convened by local archaeologists to call attention to the historic value of the petroglyphs; no paved road to the site existed before this. Over 3,200 petroglyphs have been discovered here so far, as well as a Qing Dynasty inscription commemorating the renovation of the Helanshan Pass by soldiers. Go, if only for the breathtaking scenery: steps have been carved into the slopes of the mountains, and as you wind past overhanging shrubbery to gaze down at the barren white plain of rocks at the base of the mountains, mountain goats occasionally cross the path. ✚ *70 km (44 mi) northwest of Yinchuan, via hired taxi or car from Ningxia Museum or a CITS tour* 📞 *0139/ 9519–2603* 🚕 *Y30* 🕐 *Daily 8–6.*

Qingtongxia Zhen

⑭ *1–1½ hrs (80 km [50 mi]) by train south of Yinchuan.*

Qingtongxia Zhen (Old Qingtongxia) is an ancient town that contains one of the most famous sites in Ningxia, that of a group of **108 Dagobas.** Aligned in 12 rows forming a giant triangle on the shores of a lake in the middle of arid semidesert land, these Tibetan-style sacred pagodas were built in the Yuan (Mongol) Dynasty. Nobody knows why they were placed here: maybe in celebration of some great event or as thanks for the water of the lake.

Zhongwei

⑮ *2½–3 hrs (160 km [100 mi]) by train southwest of Yinchuan.*

A market town on the fringes of the desert, Zhongwei is close to the Yellow River. Here the **Gao Temple** (Gao Si), entrance Y5, was originally built in the 15th century and has been rebuilt and expanded several times since. Essentially constructed of wood, it was designed to cater to all the main religions and beliefs of China, with chapels and shrines to Buddhism, Confucianism, and Taoism.

Outside the town it's possible to see relics of ancient ways of life. As in other parts of China, irrigation techniques using waterwheels have been in operation since the Han Dynasty. They have become largely obsolete, but examples can still be found close to the village of **Xiaheye,** on the far side of the Yellow River. With luck you will be able to make the crossing using a leather raft, a traditional form of transportation made from sheep or cow skin wrapped around a wooden frame.

Shapotou

🐾 ⑯ *1 hr (21 km [13 mi]) by bus west of Zhongwei.*

Shapotou lies on the edge of the Tengger Desert, where several thousand acres of green fields have been reclaimed from drifting sand dunes. The site was first founded in 1956 around the Shapotou Desert Research Center, when researchers were looking for a way to keep sand dunes from covering the railway line; they solved the problem by planting straw checkerboard bales into the sand. Since the late 1990s, Shapotou has been turned into the region's main tourist attraction. Inside a sprawling complex of a Chinese amusement park, lined with lush fields and trees amid desert scenery, you can ride camels and horses, sail down the Yellow River on an animal-skin raft or motorboat (followed by a camel ride back to the park), or sled down a golden mountain of sand, amid other carnival attractions. Near Shapotou, shimmering rice paddies and muddy plots dot the landscape: among the peasant laborers, mules, and oxen working the land, you may see the occasional camel plowing the fields as well. Quite popular with Chinese tourists as a fun desert oasis, most Western tourists tend to brush it off as "kitsch." Independent minibuses leave from the Zhongwei Bus Station about every half hour, 7–5 daily. The trip takes about an hour and costs Y3.5. ☎ *0953/701–2961* 🌐 *Y30; additional fees for some attractions* ⊙ *Daily 24 hrs.*

Ningxia A to Z

To research prices, get advice from other travelers, and book travel arrangements, visit www.fodors.com.

AIR TRAVEL
Direct flights link Yinchuan daily to Beijing and Xian, and several times a week to Shanghai, Chengdu, Nanjing, Lanzhou, Ürümqi, Xiamen, and Guangzhou.

AIRPORTS
CAAC runs a shuttle-bus service (Y15) to the airport, which is 21 km (13 mi) outside the city.
🛈 Airport Information **CAAC** ⊠ Ming Hang Bldg., 93 Jiefang Dong Ji, Nan Men Sq., Yinchuan ☎ 0951/609-3722 or 0951/691-3456.

BUS TRAVEL
SCHEDULES From Yinchuan buses go daily to Lanzhou and Xian every 20 minutes as well as to the other towns in the province, such as Zhongwei (3½ hours). The bus station is in the south of town.
🛈 Bus Information **Yinchuan Bus Station** ⊠ Zhongshan Jie, near Nan Men Sq. ☎ 0951/603-1571.

CAR RENTAL
Cars with drivers can be hired through CITS.
🛈 **CITS** ⊠ 116 Jiefang Xi Jie, 3rd fl., Yinchuan 750001 ☎ 0951/504-8006 🖷 0951/504-3466.

MONEY MATTERS

CURRENCY   In Yinchuan you can change money in the major hotels or at the Bank
EXCHANGE   of China.

🚹 Exchange Services **Bank of China** ⊠ 80 Jiefang Xi Jie, Yinchuan ☎ 0951/504-1115.

TOURS

In Zhongwei, Sha Po Tou Travel Agency has some intriguing tours, including camel riding in the Tengger Desert and camping by the Ming Dynasty Great Wall, as well as sheepskin rafting down the Yellow River.

🚹 Tour-Operator Recommendations **Sha Po Tou Travel Agency** ⊠ Zhongwei Binguan, 33 Gulou Xi Jie, 1st fl., Zhongwei ☎ 0953/701-2961 🖷 0953/701-8841.

TRAIN TRAVEL

SCHEDULES   Direct trains link Yinchuan with Datong (15 hrs), Hohhot (10 hrs), Lanzhou (8 hrs), Beijing (20½ hrs), Shanghai (39 hrs), Xian (13 hrs), and Xining (11 hrs). From Yinchuan station there are several trains a day to Qingtongxia Zhen (1½ hrs) and Zhongwei (2½ hrs). Direct trains link Zhongwei to Shanghai (36 hrs), Beijing (23 hrs), Lanzhou (5½ hours), Jiayuguan (12 hrs), Hohhot (12½ hrs), Xian (11 hrs), and Yinchuan (1 hr).

🚹 Train Information **Yinchuan Station** ⊠ Xingzhou Lu, eastern part of New Town ☎ 0953/504-6271.

TRANSPORTATION AROUND NINGXIA

Buses and minibuses around Yinchuan link the old and new towns, running along Jiefang Jie and continuing on to the train station in the new city, for the low price of Y1. Alternatively, privately operated minibuses charge Y3. Taxis are widely available with the flag falling at Y5 for the older vehicles, Y6 for newer ones. To ride from the train station to the old city, expect to spend about Y25.

VISITOR INFORMATION

🚹 Tourist Information **CITS** ⊠ 116 Jiefang Xi Jie, 3rd fl., Yinchuan 750001 ☎ 0951/504-8006 🖷 0951/504-3466.

GANSU

Gansu is the long narrow corridor province that links central China with the desert regions of the Northwest. It has an area of 451,000 square km (174,130 square mi) and a population consisting of Hui, Mongol, Kazakh, and Tibetan peoples.

Despite its length, the geography of Gansu is not as variable as you might expect. It has an average altitude of between 3,300 feet and 9,900 feet, with the highest peak reaching 19,000 feet. The eastern part of the province is a loess area through which flows the Yellow River, and much of the south and west is steppe land. What has long been the poorest province in China is essentially rugged and barren. The climate is of the continental kind, with cold and dry winters and hot summers.

Historically Gansu has been a vital conduit between China and the Western world because it was the beginning of the Silk Road. For centuries merchants transported their wares through this region, until shifting power and maritime trade rendered it obsolete. Gansu first became part of China proper in the Qin Dynasty (221–206 BC). Buddhism made its way into China through here as early as the 1st century BC. The oasis towns that were strung along the desert areas became the provision stations for pilgrim and merchant alike—as the merchants made their fortunes from silk and other luxuries, so the oasis towns became significant shrines.

Gansu became the edge of China, the last link with the Middle Kingdom and therefore with civilization. The Great Wall, the most solid representation of ancient Chinese opinion of the outside world, passed through Gansu to the great fortress at Jiayuguan, beyond which lay Dunhuang, and then perdition. And yet Gansu has never been the most compliant of provinces. The influence of Islam was considerable here, and 19th-century rebellions were savagely put down. The decline of the Silk Road brought terrible suffering and poverty, from which the area has only very recently begun to recover as tourism boosts the local economy.

There has also been considerable industrial and mining expansion. Agriculture is important, but conditions are difficult, despite irrigation. Horses are reared here as well as sheep, pigs, and cattle; wheat, melons, cotton, and millet are important crops. Still, outside of its major cities, Gansu remains one of China's most impoverished and undeveloped provinces.

Dunhuang

⓱ *16 hrs (900 km [558 mi]) by bus northwest of Lanzhou.*

Dunhuang, a small oasis town, was in many ways and for many centuries the most important Buddhist destination on the Silk Road. Here, just outside of town, you can see an extraordinary array of wall paintings in caves that form part of Mogao Grottoes, considered the richest repository of Buddhist shrines in the world.

Dunhuang (literally "Blazing Beacon") was made a prefecture in 117 BC, during the Han Dynasty. At that time it was at the very edge of the Chinese empire, on the fringes of "barbarian" desert country. Its earthen "beacons" were a sort of extension of the Great Wall, used for sending signals between garrisons.

Buddhism entered China via the Silk Road in the century prior to the spread of Christianity. As Dunhuang was the point of entry to the Chinese world, it was not long before a temple was established here. By AD 366 the first caves were being carved at the Mogao oasis. The carving continued until the 10th century; the works were subsequently left undisturbed for nearly a thousand years until adventurers from Europe and America began to plunder the area at the end of the 19th century. The paintings' and carvings' miraculous state of preservation is due to the dry desert conditions.

Dunhuang remained an important center until the end of the Tang Dynasty. Wars sparked by the power vacuum left after the demise of the Tang, along with a trend away from overland shipping, brought an end to the Silk Road and to centuries of creative energy. Dunhuang became known as Shazhou (Sand Town). Yet, the paintings survived, and even more astounding was the discovery by Sir Aurel Stein in 1907 of one cave (seemingly deliberately sealed by departing priests at this period of decline) that revealed a stack of early Buddhist sutras. One was written on paper and dated AD 406, many centuries before paper was in use elsewhere, making it one of the earliest printed documents. You can see this document, the Diamond Sutra of 868, in London's British Museum. The discovered papers were not only religious, there were also many items relating to local administration (though today there are next to no documents to be seen at Dunhuang). The murals and statuary are all still in place. Modern Dunhuang still exudes the sleepy air of a dusty frontier town, although it has begun to change with the influx of tourists.

The surprisingly small **Dunhuang Museum** (Dunhuang Bowuguan), with a pink tri-camel sculpture in front, has three sections. One displays the items discovered in Cave 17 by Stein and his French colleague Paul Pelliot. Another focuses on more practical items found in the region (silks and old textiles), while the third is devoted to sacrificial and funeral items. The museum sometimes closes without warning for staff weddings and other events. ⊠ *8 Yangguan Dong Lu* ☎ *0937/882–2985* 🖙 *Y10* ⊙ *Daily 8–6:30.*

Across the Donghe River, west of town, the elegant but solitary-looking nine-tiered **White Horse Dagoba** (Bai Ma Ta) was established in AD 384 during the Northern Wei Dynasty by a Kuchean monk to commemorate the death of his brave white horse. In the back corner of the lot that encloses the dagoba, look for a rusted iron door that leads to the remains of the ancient city walls of Shazhou. Unfortunately, there's nothing but fields of dirt left to see now: the ancient city walls were knocked down by the Red Guards during the Cultural Revolution, as was the temple that surrounded Bai Ma Ta. ✛ *3 km (2 mi) west of the city center* 🖙 *Y13* ⊙ *Daily 9–6.*

South of Dunhuang, the oasis gives way to desert. Here, among the gorgeous sweep of sand dunes known as **Singing Sand Mountain** (Ming Sha Shan) is nestled **Crescent Moon Lake** (Yueyaquan), a lovely crescent-shape pool of water that by some freak of the prevailing winds never silts up. The dunes themselves are the main attraction, named for the light rattling sound that the sand makes when wind blows across the surface—"rumbling sands," noted Marco Polo. Forty kilometers (25 mi) in length and 20 km (12 mi) wide, the tallest peak of the dunes is 5,600 feet above sea level. The half-hour climb to the summit is hard work but worth it for the views, particularly at sunset. Camel rides are available for Y30–Y40, sleds can be rented for Y10 a ride, and a paraglide can launch you off a dune's steep face for Y30. ✛ *Take Dingzi Lu, continue about 5 km (3 mi) south of town* 🖙 *Y50.*

FodorśChoice
★
The magnificent Buddhist **Mogao Grottoes** (Mogao Ku) lie southeast of Dunhuang. At least 40 caves are open to the public, the earliest dating from the Northern Wei period (AD 386–534: Caves 246, 257, 259); followed by the Western Wei (AD 535–556: Cave 249); the Sui (AD 581–618:

Caves 244, 420, 427); Tang (AD 618–907: Caves 17, 96, 130, 148, 172, 209, 323, 329); and Five Dynasties (AD 907–960: Caves 16, 98). These are just a selection of some of the most interesting—there are plenty of others. Which caves are open on a given day depends on the local authorities. If a particular cave is closed, you can request that it be opened; whether that will happen is another matter. Don't miss Caves 96 and 130—usually included on the regular tour—with stunning statues of a 108-foot- and a 78-foot-high Buddha. A flashlight is a useful item for your visit.

In creating the paintings, the artists plastered the surfaces of the cave walls first with mud and then with layers of dung, straw or hair, and still more mud. The final surface was prepared with china clay, and mineral paints were applied (to both walls and statues), the colors of which have changed as they oxidized over the centuries. The monks who worshipped in these grottoes lived in small unadorned caves in the cliff to the right of the painted caves as you look at them. The whole of the cliff was carved out eventually, so several of the caves were painted over in later dynasties. The art is definitely under threat, as the extra oxidation from huge numbers of tourists is fading the colors. A fine museum on-site funded by a Japanese preservation organization contains reproductions of eight of the caves, where the art can be studied in full light. A smaller auxiliary exhibition space opposite the real caves has excellent rotating exhibitions on the history and art of individual caves. English-speaking guides are usually only available in the morning. ✛ *25 km (15 mi) southeast of town; take minibus or taxi (Y50–Y80 round-trip)* ☎ *0937/886–9056* 🎟 *Y80 for tour of 10 caves, exhibition space, and museum; additional Y20 for English-speaking guide* ⊙ *Guided tours only, daily 9–5.*

Southwest of Dunhuang are the **Western Thousand Buddha Caves** (Xi Qian-fodong). Considered to be of less importance than those at Mogao, they do nonetheless contain paintings from the Northern Wei and Tang dynasties. ⊠ *30 km (18 mi) southwest of town; take a taxi (Y30)* 🎟 *Y30* ⊙ *Daily 9–noon and 2–5.*

★ ⑱ The once-impressive old fort of **Jiayuguan,** 5 km (3 mi) outside the town of the same name, and some 280 km (174 mi) southeast of Dun-huang, stands in a dramatic spot guarding a pass between two mountain ranges. It was the westernmost point of the Great Wall during the Ming Dynasty. The fort was built in 1372 with 33-foot-high walls and a circumference of well over 770 yards. In the vicinity of Jiayuguan you can visit (reconstructed and new-looking) parts of the Great Wall, rock paintings from the Warring States period, and tombs in the desert. History aside, it's only worth a day trip here if you're en route to or from Dunhuang by rail. On the other hand, the city itself is laid back, and the silver light of the sun flooding down from an immense sky can be transcendental. ⊠ *Jiayuguan* 🎟 *Y60* ⊙ *Daily 8–6.*

Where to Stay & Eat

Aside from the hotel dining rooms, the night market just off Yangguan Dong Lu—though less exciting than night markets in Xinjiang—is worth a visit for spicy hotpot, cold beer, and charred but flavorful lamb kebabs. Near the bus station, enterprising individuals have started a few small restaurants around Dingzi Lu with Western backpacker fare and a number of small Chinese restaurants.

¢–$ ✕ **John's Information Café.** Cool off after a full day of sightseeing on John's trellised patio and sip fresh fruit juice. Another option is to come before you start your day for a delicious Western-style breakfast and a cup of joe. ⊠ *Mingshan Lu, on grounds of the Lanzhou Legend hotel* ☎ *No phone* ⊟ *No credit cards.*

¢   ✕ **Charlie Johng's Café.** This friendly café caters to a mainly backpacker crowd and serves an assortment of comfort food like banana pancakes and chocolate milk shakes. ⊠ *Mingshan Lu* ☎ *No phone* ⊟ *No credit cards.*

¢   ✕ **Shirley's Café.** Shirley is the sister of Charlie (of Charlie Johng's Café) and has gone into business for herself, taking with her the closely guarded family recipes for backpacker fare. ⊠ *Mingshan Lu* ☎ *No phone* ⊟ *No credit cards.*

$ ▦ **Silk Road Dunhuang Hotel.** Outside town, a half mile from the desert, Fodor'sChoice this stone fortress of a Hong Kong joint-venture hotel, with its enormous grounds, is the most luxurious place to stay in Dunhuang, and ★ one of the most elegant hotels on the entire Silk Road. Designed in the manner of a traditional *siheyuan* or Chinese courtyard house, it has desert rock gardens, stone tiles, and light-wood ceilings. The large, spacious rooms have historical touches like Ming reproduction furniture and traditional wooden shower buckets. The hotel arranges some great tours, including a camel ride to the sand dunes of Singing Sand Mountain at sunrise, followed by breakfast. ⊠ *West side of Dunyue Lu, 736200* ☎ *0937/888–2088* 🖷 *0937/888–2086* ⊕ *www.the-silk-road.com/hotel/ dunhuanghotel* ⤳ *294 rooms, 6 suites* ⚴ *2 restaurants, gym, shops, business services, travel services* ⊟ *AE, MC, V.*

¢   ▦ **Dunhuang Binguan.** The first hotel built to cater to the influx of foreigners after 1976, this mid-range hotel is aging but provides reasonable comfort and facilities in a good location. The professional staff speaks decent English, and there's a travel agency on the first floor. ⊠ *14 Yangguan Dong Lu, 736200* ☎ *0937/882–2538* 🖷 *0937/882–2195* ⤳ *145 rooms, 15 suites* ⚴ *4 restaurants, gym, hair salon, shops, business services, travel services* ⊟ *MC, V.*

¢   ▦ **Dunhuang International Hotel.** At the southern edge of town, this towering white monolith with black-speckled marble floors is a Hong Kong joint-venture, with pleasant and clean rooms at a good value, though bathrooms tend to be on the smallish side. ⊠ *28 Mingshan Lu, 736200* ☎ *0937/882–8638* 🖷 *0937/882–1821* ⤳ *170 rooms, 6 suites* ⚴ *2 restaurants, gym, hair salon, shops, business services* ⊟ *V.*

¢   ▦ **Grand Sun Hotel Dunhuang.** Don't be put off by the gaudy metallic sun motif glitzing up this hotel's shiny white-marble lobby. The rooms here are spacious and well appointed, with all the modern conveniences. The older wing, once a separate hotel, was annexed when the new 12-story Grand Sun building was constructed in 1997. ⊠ *5 Shazhou Bei Lu, 736200* ☎ *0937/882–9998* 🖷 *0937/882–2019* ⤳ *220 rooms, 22* *suites ⑤ 4 restaurants, gym, hair salon, massage, sauna, billiards, bar, shops, business services, travel services* ▤ *AE, MC, V.*

Nightlife & the Arts

There isn't exactly a rockin' night scene in Dunhuang. The cafés on Dingzi Lu, which are often open past midnight, draw backpackers eager to check their e-mail or just hang out. However, these are open only in high tourist season. There is also the occasional performance of song or dance at various hotels. Check with CITS.

The Outdoors

You can hire a bicycle easily from any of several outlets and bike around town or to the sand dunes to watch the sunset.

Lanzhou

(900 km [558 mi]) southeast of Dunhuang; (450 km [279 mi]) northwest of Xian.

Built on the banks of the Yellow River, the capital of Gansu extends along the base of a narrow gorge whose walls rise to 5,000 feet. A city with a long history, Lanzhou has been nearly ruined by rampant industrialization and is now one of the most polluted urban areas in the world—a pity, as the locals are unusually friendly and many of the streets are wide and graciously shaded by trees.

Founded more than 2,000 years ago, Lanzhou was already a substantial town by the middle of the Han Dynasty, soon developing into one of the most important centers along the Silk Road. Following the decline of the Han, Lanzhou became the capital of a series of tribal kingdoms. In a narrow corridor between mountains, its strategic location, through which all traffic heading northwest or southeast must pass, has continued to invest it with considerable importance. After 1949 Lanzhou became the second-largest city in the region as the Chinese government turned it into an important industrial center. It is also a key railway junction linking the northwest with central, north, and northeastern China.

⑲ Wuquan Shan (Five Spring Mountain), named for the springs at its foot in the south of the city, rises to 5,250 feet. On it, from **Five Spring Park** (Wuquanshan Gongyuan), you can see impressive views of the city below, though the five springs have dwindled to only a trickle. In the park are a number of monuments. The **Temple of Reverent Solemnity** (Chongqing) dates from 1372. In it is a large bronze bell, 10 feet high and weighing 5 tons, that dates from 1202. A 16-foot bronze Buddha, dated at 1370, commands the main hall. Behind Wuquan Shan is another peak, Lanshan, towering over 6,600 feet and accessible by chairlift. ✤ *Bus 8 from Jiuquan Lu in town center* 🎫 *Y5* ⊙ *Daily 8–6.*

⑳ The old-fashioned but nonetheless excellent **Gansu Provincial Museum** (Gansu Sheng Bowuguan) has exhibits on three floors, including a perfectly reconstructed 26-foot-long prehistoric elephant on the first floor, and relics from the Silk Road on the second. Among the most memorable in the collection are the 7,000-year-old pottery shards from the Dadiwan culture (the earliest Neolithic site so far discovered in China)

FodorśChoice
★

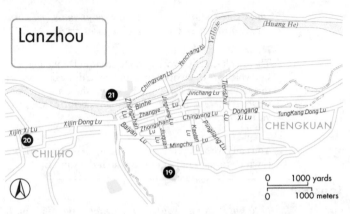

Lanzhou

decorated with what are probably the earliest pictograms. There are also examples of decorated wares that indicate contact between China and Rome at least as far back as 2,200 years ago, as well as early textiles and magnificent tricolor Tang porcelain. The most famous item is the elegant bronze "Flying Horse," considered a masterpiece of ancient Chinese art, and found in an Eastern Han tomb at Wuwei (a city in Gansu). With its hoof delicately poised on the wings of a bird, its image is much used as a symbol of the area. Among the other items on display are collections of early Yangshao pottery, Zhou bronzes, a Chinese minorities exhibition, and a Han Dynasty tomb reconstruction. ⊠ *3 Xijin Xi Lu* ☎ *0931/233–3346* 💰 *Y30* ✆ *Tues.–Sun. 9–4.*

㉑ The **Mountain of the White Pagoda Park** (Baitashan Gongyuan), a public park laid out in 1958, covers the slopes on the Yellow River's north bank close to the ancient crossing place used by merchants and travelers for centuries. The park is named for the white dagoba that was built at the summit of the hill during the Yuan Dynasty (1271–1368) and rebuilt in the 15th century. In the pleasant park are some interesting pavilions and terraces. ⊠ *Entrance at Zhongshan Qiao, the bridge extending over the Yellow River from Zhongshan Lu* 💰 *Y10* ✆ *Daily 7–7.*

Where to Stay & Eat

The best restaurants in Lanzhou are in the hotels; a good one to try is the elegant Chinese restaurant in the Lanzhou Hotel. One of Lanzhou's best food streets is along Nongmin Xiang to the north of the Lanzhou Hotel, where by night crowds of locals and tourist alike throng the busy lane lined with lively vendors hawking their cuisine. This is a great place to try the *roùjiamo*, a local specialty of onion, chili, and flash-fried lamb or beef stuffed in a pita.

$$ ✕ **Wan He Huo Guo Lou.** If you're a fan of hotpot, head here: locals tout Wan He Huo Guo Lou as the best in town. Despite curt service and flotsam on the floors, hordes of diners crowd the place nightly. Red-suited waiters run to tables with huge pots of freshwater fish simmered with red chili peppers and other spices, all extraordinarily flavorful and succulent due to the eatery's secret recipe. The traditional hotpot meal fol-

lows. Prices are low. Unfortunately there are no English menus. ✉ *118 Gaolan Lu, 2nd fl.* ☎ *0931/872–2170* ▤ *No credit cards.*

¢ ✕▦ **Lanzhou Hotel.** Once just another concrete Sino-Stalinist block in the center of town, this fan-shape hotel, built in 1956, has been extensively remodeled and now has a black-marble lobby, pleasant service, and clean, standard-size rooms that are good value; an older wing houses shabbier rooms with worn red carpets for half the price. At the renowned Chinese restaurant, Zhong Hua Yuan, you can sample the best of local cuisine, from hand-rolled dumplings and roasted lamb shank (served with a side of spices and raw garlic bulbs) to more esoteric entrées like camel's feet soup. ✉ *434 Donggang Xi Lu, 730000* ☎ *0931/841–6321* 🖷 *0931/ 841–8608* 🖅 *476 rooms, 50 suites* ⬧ *5 restaurants, massage, sauna, shops, business services, travel services* ▤ *MC, V.*

¢–$ ▦ **Lanzhou Legend.** Also known as the Feitian Hotel, the Legend is plush and expensive, with service to match the high prices. The rooms are well furnished, though on the small side. It is right in downtown Lanzhou. ✉ *599 Tianshui Lu, 730000* ☎ *0931/853–2888* 🖅 *384 rooms, 22 suites* ⬧ *2 restaurants, massage, sauna, billiards, bar, shop* ▤ *AE, MC, V.*

¢ ▦ **Lanzhou Friendship Hotel.** Off the beaten path in the western part of the city (near the Lanzhou Museum), this hotel, sporting a pagoda-style roof complete with flying eaves and splashing fountains, was originally built in the 1950s and has been extensively renovated. Don't be deterred by the red-neon "KTV" (advertising the karaoke) sign as you walk in: the spacious rooms have been tastefully modernized, and there is a tennis court and a garden with a miniature golf course. ✉ *16 Xijin Xi Lu, 730000* ☎ *0931/268–9999* 🖷 *0931/233–0304* 🖅 *400 rooms, 46 suites* ⬧ *5 restaurants, miniature golf, tennis court, bar, shops, business services, travel services* ▤ *V.*

★ ¢ ▦ **Ningwozhuang Guesthouse.** Before tourism took off, the best accommodations in cities like Lanzhou were villa-style guest houses set in beautiful gardens. This is one of those—old-fashioned, now veering toward the shabbier side of gentility, but still gracious and secluded. Once reserved only for visiting cadres, the rooms in the old building are solidly furnished; the newer VIP building has spacious and more modern rooms in pale green, with a touch of glitz. ✉ *366 Tianshui Lu, north of Nanchang Lu, 730000* ☎ *0931/826–5888* 🖷 *0931/827–8639* 🖅 *200 rooms, 33 suites* ⬧ *5 restaurants, tennis court, pool, hair salon, massage, sauna, bowling, bar, shops, laundry service, business services* ▤ *AE, MC, V.*

Nightlife & the Arts

Ask CITS (⇨ Gansu A to Z) or your hotel about opera or acrobatics performances. There are a few karaoke parlors scattered around the center; but the booming bar/café scene on Zhongshan Lu is where the city's trendy now head for dates. A cozy little place to try is **Impression: Sunrise** (✉ 191 Zhongshan Lu ☎ 0931/330–3520 ☾ Noon–1 AM), which serves imported Carlsberg and Corona beer for Y15–Y20, as well as a variety of teas and coffee. Next door, Da Shanghai is popular with locals as well.

Thousand Buddha Temple and Grottoes

㉒   *3 hrs (90 km [56 mi]) by train west of Lanzhou.*

FodorsChoice
★

Near Yongjing, the Thousand Buddha Temple and Grottoes (Bingling Si Shiku) site, filled with Buddhist wall paintings and statuary—including one impressive 89-foot-tall Buddha carved into a cliff face—is Lanzhou's most important sight. It is definitely worth the trip, despite a lengthy boat ride upstream from the Liujiaxia Dam to the Yellow River to get here. Though the art is disappointing compared to the Mogao Grottoes at Dunhuang, the 200-foot-high canyon is stunning, dominated by spectacular cliff formations of porous rock. The caves were first decorated in AD 420, but the best work, as at Dunhuang, was executed during the later Song and Tang dynasties. It became a Tibetan monastery during the Yuan (Mongolian) Dynasty. There are more than 700 statues and several hundred square yards of wall painting; the finest paintings are in Caves 3, 4, 11, 70, 82, and 114, where the largest Buddha (Maitreya, the Buddha of the Future) sits. To see all the locked caves, including Caves 169 (the oldest cave) and 172 (considered the most magnificent), the entrance fee of Y300 will gain entrance and include a guided tour.

The canyon is located along one side of the Yellow River; seasonal rains occasionally flood the river, prohibiting access to the caves, but when water levels are low, the journey through a gorge lined by water-sculpted rocks and capped by rising peaks and an immense sky is spectacular. When the canyon is dry you can travel 2½ km (1½ mi) up to see the small community of Tibetan lamas at the Upper Temple of Bingling. The temple itself is run-down and nothing special, but the twists and turns of the upper gorge are breathtaking, and the monks are friendly. If the walk is too arduous, catch a jeep ride on the dry riverbed for Y5 (or a boat ride, if there is water) from enterprising locals. Travel agencies also sell all-inclusive round-trip ferry ride plus entrance fee, Y150 (speedboat trip plus entrance fee, Y230) at the Liujiaxia boat dock. ✤ *CITS or private travel agent; or local bus from Lanzhou's West Bus Station, 7:30 or 8:30 AM, then ferry at Liujiaxia boat dock; fast boat, Y80, 3 hrs; slow boat, Y30, 8 hrs* ▨ *Y20* ☉ *Daily 8–5 (subject to water level).*

Xiahe

㉓   *5–6 hrs (250 km [155 mi]) by bus southwest of Lanzhou.*

FodorsChoice
★

This tiny town blessed with an extraordinary clarity of light is nestled amid hills downed with light-green grass—one of the most interesting excursions possible from Lanzhou. Xiahe is home to the **Labrang Monastery** (Laboleng Si), one of the most important Tibetan institutions. A member of the Gelupka (Yellow Hat) sect, it is one of two great Lamaist temples outside Tibet (the other being the Ta'Er Monastery in Qinghai). Founded in 1710, it once had as many as 4,000 monks, a number now much depleted due in large part to the Cultural Revolution, when monks were forced to return home and temples were destroyed. Though the monastery reopened in 1980, the government's policy of restricted enrollment has kept the number of monks down to about 1,500.

Since the late 1990s, Xiahe has experienced a dizzying rise in the number of backpackers and tourists. Even monks clad in traditional fuchsia robes now watch TV, play basketball, and listen to pop music, and the town's one main street is crowded with cafés flaunting English-language menu signs. Despite these signs of encroaching modernity, Xiahe is still a place of tremendous atmosphere, attracting large numbers of Tibetan pilgrims who come to study and to spin the 1,147 prayer wheels of the monastery daily, swathed in their distinctive costume of heavy woolen robes slashed with brightly colored sashes.

Although partly gutted by fire in 1985, the temple looks much as it always has. It's divided into a number of institutes of learning (including law and medicine), as well as the **Gongtang Pagoda** (Gongtang Baota), the **Prayer Hall** (Qi Dao Tang), and the **Golden Temple** (Ser Kung Si).

Apart from the religious festivals during the Tibetan New Year and the month after, when pilgrims and nomads congregate by the thousands, a daily highlight (a feature of most Tibetan monasteries) is the gathering of monks on a lawn for religious debate, when fine points of theology are discussed in the liveliest fashion. Soft-drink bottles are thrown into the air, the monks charge at each other in groups, hissing good-naturedly, and the older monks supervise everyone, including the Tibetan pilgrims gathering to watch, with a benevolent air. The debate takes place after lunch in the afternoons; ask at the ticket office for times. ⊠ *2 km (1 mi) west of long-distance bus station* ⛨ *Free; Y25 for guided tours* ⊙ *Daily 8–7.*

Maijishan Grottoes

★ ㉔ *8 hrs (300 km [186 mi]) by train or bus southeast of Lanzhou.*

The **Corn Rick Mountain Grottoes** (Maijishan Shiku) are among the four largest Buddhist caves in China. The site is dramatic, a steep outcrop of rock into which have been carved several dozen grottoes dating from the 4th century onward. The caves, between 100 and 230 feet above the foot of the mountain, are reached by wooden steps. An earthquake in the 8th century split the site in two, east and west. The western caves are the best preserved, having been left untouched since the Song Dynasty. Early Western influences are seen in some of the work (for example in Cave 100), while the finest work is generally considered to be that in Cave 133, which has engravings dating from the Wei and Zhou periods. The eastern caves are less well preserved, but there is fine work here, too, most notably in Caves 4, 7, 13, 102, and 191. A flashlight is essential. You should either join a tour or obtain a private guide in order to get the best out of the visit. The caves are best reached by train (seven hours, Y26–Y52) to Tianshui and then bus (45 minutes, Y25 roundtrip) the remaining 30 km (19 mi). ⊠ *Due east of Tianshui* ⛨ *Door ticket Y50, English-language tour Y70* ⊙ *Daily 8–6.*

Gansu A to Z

To research prices, get advice from other travelers, and book travel arrangements, visit www.fodors.com.

AIR TRAVEL

There are daily flights from Dunhuang to Jiayuguan, Lanzhou, Beijing, Ürümqi, and Xian.

From Lanzhou, there are flights daily to Beijing, Guangzhou, Shanghai, Chengdu, Ürümqi, and Xian. Within Gansu, there are flights twice daily to Dunhuang and three times a week to Jiayuguan.

AIRPORTS

Dunhuang's airport is 13 km (8 mi) east of town. The CAAC office, open daily 8–11:30 and 3–6, is in town. CAAC runs a shuttle bus service (Y6) to and from the airport; a taxi ride costs Y20–Y30.

Lanzhou's airport is about 90 km (56 mi) north of the city. The CAAC office runs a shuttle bus to and from the airport (Y25) if there are enough passengers.

🚹 Airport Information **Dunhuang CAAC** ✉ 12 Yangguan Dong Lu ☎ 0937/882-2389. **Lanzhou CAAC** ✉ 520 Donggang Xi Lu ☎ 0931/888-9666.

BUS TRAVEL

Dunhuang's long-distance bus station is in the south of town. Buses go to Jiayuguan (7 hours) and other local destinations.

Buses leave Lanzhou's East Bus Station every afternoon for Yinchuan (12 hours) and Xian (15 hours). From the West Bus Station in the northwest part of the city, buses go to Jiayuguan (16 hours) in the afternoon. Buses for Xiahe (5–6 hours) leave twice a day; the slow bus is at 7:30 AM and the fast bus is at 8:30 AM.

🚹 Bus Information **Dunhuang Bus Station** ✉ Dingzi Lu ☎ 0937/882-2174. **Lanzhou East Bus Station** ✉ Ping Yuang Lu (next to Jiaotong Fandian) ☎ 0931/841-8411. **Lanzhou West Bus Station** ✉ 458 Xijin Dong Lu ☎ 0931/233-3285.

CAR RENTAL

Cars with drivers can be hired through CITS (⇨ Tours).

🚹 **Dunhuang PSB** ✉ Xi Dajie ☎ 0937/882-2425. **Lanzhou PSB** ✉ 310 Wudu Lu ☎ 0931/846-2851.

MONEY MATTERS

🚹 Currency Exchange **Bank of China** ✉ 90 Dongda Jie, Dunhuang ☎ 0937/261-4812 ✉ 589 Tianshui Lu, Lanzhou ☎ 0931/883-1988.

TOURS

In Dunhuang, CITS can arrange multiday tours to both the northern and southern Silk Road, as well as day tours of Mogao Grottoes and Singing Sand Mountain. The Dunhuang Tourist Agency also arranges tours, and books train and plane tickets. If you want to ride a camel to watch the sunset at Singing Sand Mountain, sand-sled, or sand-bathe, head to the Silk Road Dunhuang Hotel where the hotel's English-speaking staff can help you with your arrangements. Numerous guides and tour providers hang out outside the cafés and around the tourist sites and will also help you (for a small commission) but the hotel may be your less confusing option.

CITS in Lanzhou can arrange trips to Bingling Si and Xiahe; the friendly Western Travel Agency offers similar tours.

🎫 Tour-Operator Recommendations **Dunhuang Tourist Agency** ✉ Dunhuang Bin-guan, 1st fl. ☎ 0937/882-2195. **Silk Road Dunhuang Hotel** ✉ Dunyue Lu ☎ 0937/882-5388.

Western Travel Agency ✉ Lanzhou Hotel, 434 Donggang Xi Lu, 1st fl. ☎ 0931/841-6321.

TRAIN TRAVEL

The railway station serving Dunhuang is in the small town of Liuyuan, 130 km (81 mi) away. Don't be fooled by the name of the train station, which was changed to "Dunhuang Station" to attract more tourists. There are trains to Jiayuguan (3 hours) and Lanzhou (12½ hours), as well as Chengdu (46 hours), Beijing (37 hours), Shanghai (41 hours), Turpan (8 hours), Ürümqi (10 hours), and Xian (24 hours). Buses leave regularly for Dunhuang (about every hour 8 AM–4 PM, though drivers often wait until all the seats are filled. Once on the road, the journey takes 2–3 hours.

Lanzhou's train station is fairly central, toward the southwest of the city. Trains go to Beijing (24 hours), Shanghai (27 hours), Xian (10 hours), Chengdu (26 hours), Ürümqi (24 hours), Guangzhou (42 hours), Ho-hhot (17½ hours), Qingdao (37 hours), and Xining (4 hours). Within Gansu, trains go northwest to Jiayuguan (10 hours) and Liuyuan (for Dunhuang; 12½ hours). CITS books tickets three days in advance for trains out of Lanzhou and Dunhuang; otherwise, buy the tickets at the train station.

🚆 Train Information **Lanzhou Train Station** ✉ Houche Zhan Dong Jian ☎ 0931/492-2222. **Liuyuan Train Station** ✉ Liuyuan Huoche Zhan ☎ 0937/557-2307.

TRANSPORTATION AROUND GANSU

For getting around in the immediate vicinity of Dunhuang, you should rent a bicycle, the best way to navigate the town. If the desert sun gets too hot for you, taxis, easily hailed, will cost you Y10 for the first 10 km (6 mi). The alternative is to use minibuses, which leave (when full) for various places around and outside town.

In Lanzhou taxis are readily available. Otherwise, the public bus system is good—you can get maps at CITS, railway and bus stations, and bookshops—though, as always in China, be wary of pickpockets or bag-slashers in crowded buses.

VISITOR INFORMATION

ℹ Tourist Information **CITS** ✉ 32 Mingshan Lu, Dunhuang ☎ 0937/882-2474 ✉ 18 Nongmin Xiang, Lanzhou ☎ 0931/881-3222.

QINGHAI

A remote province on the northeast border of Tibet with sweeping grasslands locked in by mountain ranges, Qinghai is known to the rest of China mostly as the nation's Siberia, a center for prisons and work camps. Yet the province shares much of the majestic scenery of Xinjiang, combined with the rich legends and culture of Tibet. With the exception of the eastern area around Xining, Qinghai, formerly known as Amdo, was part of Tibet until the early 18th century. The mountains and forests of Qinghai are home to wild deer, wild yaks, and the endangered snow leopard.

Qinghai's relative isolation from the rest of the mainland may change in the next decade, however, with the central government's planned construction of the highest railway in the world—the multibillion-dollar Qinghai–Tibet railway—to be laid along the world's highest plateau at an elevation of higher than 12,000 feet. The project to connect the "roof of the world" to Qinghai was attempted before, but the government abandoned its effort in 1984 after savage weather and the icy terrain made construction efforts near impossible. The new rail initiative, announced in 2000, is part of the Communist Party's ambitious campaign to develop China's Northwest and encourage foreign investment. Officials have already admitted that construction of the railway will have a "devastating impact" on the surrounding environment, but they claim they are seeking ways to minimize the damage. The project is currently underway and officials hope to complete it by 2006. When completed it will span over 1,700 km (1,100 mi), and end in Lhasa.

For now, the province continues to be sparsely populated, with a little more than 5 million people, not counting prisoners. About 57% of the population are Han Chinese, and about 21% are Tibetan. The rest are Mongolian, Hui, and Salar (the two latter are Muslim ethnic minorities). The 14th Dalai Lama himself was born in the northeastern part of Qinghai, in a mountainous peasant village a day trip away from Xining.

Xining

❷⑤ *4 hrs (225 km [140 mi]) by train west of Lanzhou; 28 hrs (1,370 km [849 mi]) by train southeast of Ürümqi.*

Qinghai's capital, Xining (literally, Western Peace), started out as a remote Chinese military garrison in the 16th century, guarding the western borders. It was also an important center for trade between China and Tibet. A small city by Chinese standards, with a population slightly more than 1 million, today's Xining is no longer cut off from the rest of China. An airport and rail links to Beijing, Shanghai, Xian, and Lanzhou ensure that the population now has a steady diet of Coca-Cola and Ritz crackers. Modernization has hit hard. In fact, the city is an industrial vision straight out of Dickens—heavy gridlock, black clouds of smoke, workers toting shovels, and stripped-down anti-quated tractors clanking noisily down side streets. Glitzy office towers and Hong Kong–style boutiques are starting to spring up alongside faded Communist billboards glorifying policemen and soldiers, but the city remains at heart a desolate mix of the curiously old and curiously new, a frontier town revving up for the future but without the capital to pull it off.

Xining is not without its occasional charms, of course: green-domed mosques rise gracefully from clusters of modern tiled buildings—evidence of the city's ample population of Hui and Uighurs. Still, Xining functions most frequently as a convenient stopping-off point for visits to the important Ta'Er Monastery, just outside the city, and the stunning bird sanctuary of Bird Island, 350 km (217 mi) away on the shores of China's largest saltwater lake, Qinghai Hu (Green Lake).

Xining lies on the Tibetan plateau at an altitude of nearly 7,000 feet. It's not high enough to cause serious altitude sickness, but you may feel light-headed during your first day or two here. Eating light and getting plenty of rest and water will help ease altitude discomfort. The weather is moderate in the city, with cool summers and very little rainfall. In winter the temperature averages around –1°C (30°F), with sunshine. Winter can be very cold in the surrounding mountains.

Start your visit early in the morning with a walk or taxi ride to the **North Mountain Temple** (Beishan Si), at the northwest end of town. The modern Buddhist temple, which is still in use, sits at the top of a hill and offers a sweeping view of town. ✤ *North of intersection of Qilian Lu and Chanjiang Lu* ☉ *Dawn–dusk.*

> **need a break?**
>
> If you could go for a rest and a spot of tea, duck into **Zheng Pai Ming Ren Yu Cha** (⊠ 6 Bei Da Jie ☎ 0971/824–7075 ▤ No credit cards). With red lanterns and a log-lined facade, this cozy 24-hour two-decker teahouse is one of the nicest spots in town to relax. The interior is highlighted by hardwood floors, small, intimate dark corners, and an eager-to-please staff. Regular green and oolong teas start at Y10–Y20 a pot and climb to a dizzying Y180 for the name brands. Walk to the north end of Bei Da Jie and make a left.

From Chanjiang Lu and Xi Jie you can stroll through the **market stalls** starting at Xi Jie, as it crosses the South River (Nan Chuan). Vendors hawk everything from goldfish to socks alongside the river promenade, but the once-picturesque cityscape has largely been engulfed by a modern plaza boasting kebab stands and various construction projects.

If you've ever wanted to see what the outside of a laogai (prison factory) looks like, here is your chance. Follow Nanshan Lu east to Nantan Jiedao (South Beach District). After about 300 yards watch for a road turning to the right. You'll see two grim-looking compounds on the left, both laogai. Pass the gate of the second one, **Qinghai Hide and Garment Factory** (Qinghai Pimao Beifu Chang). Right next door to the entrance gate is another door leading to the factory shop, where the goods made by inmates of this prison are displayed for sale. You can walk or take a taxi back along Nanshan Lu to the Qinghai Guest House. ⊠ *40 Nanshan Lu* ☎ *0971/824–7342.*

Where to Stay & Eat

In and around the Qinghai Guest House are a number of restaurants where you can stop for lunch. ✦ *On western side of river, walk south about 15 mins from where Xi Jie crosses Huanghe Lu.*

$ ✕ **The Cafe.** In a huge hall with large round tables, Chinese style, this spot serves an excellent Mongolian hotpot buffet—all you can eat for Y45. ⊠ *Xining Hotel, 348 Qi Yi Lu* ☎ *0971/823–8701* ▤ *No credit cards.*

¢–$ ✕ **Shang Yi Da Xia.** This popular Muslim restaurant is in downtown Xining, a few doors east of the Bank of China tower. It has a small, crowded dining room, but excellent hotpot and kebabs. ⊠ *190 Dongguan Lu* ☎ *No phone* ▤ *No credit cards.*

¢   ✕ **Tibetan Restaurant.** The aroma of yak butter permeates this small bare-bones restaurant with orange tablecloths, where a big bowl of noodles can be had for just Y3. It's down the street from the Xining Hotel. ⊠ *348–29 Qi Yi Lu* ☎ *0971/823–8701* ▤ *No credit cards.*

¢   ⊡ **Jian Yin Hotel.** A handsome, pink-marble foyer entrance greets you at this hotel, opened by the China Construction Bank. Not surprisingly, given its origins, everything shouts money here: from the silver-and-chrome facade to the tan leather couches down to the marble ball revolving inside the lobby's rock-lined pool. The rooms are about the same as everywhere else in town, but with an extra layer of shininess and glitz. ⊠ *55 Xida Jie, 810000* ☎ *0971/826–1885* 🖷 *0971/826–1551* ➹ *160 rooms, 20 suites* ♨ *2 restaurants, hair salon, massage, sauna, bowling, shops, laundry service, business services, meeting room, travel services* ▤ *No credit cards.*

¢   ⊡ **Qinghai Guest House** (Qinghai Minzu Binguan). This centrally located hotel with its white marble facade and friendly staff is a good value. The fixtures generally work in the clean bathrooms, and the standard rooms exude a cheerful air despite the shabbiness of the yellow curtains and worn red rugs. A friendly branch of China Youth Travel Service (CYTS) is in the back of the hotel on the first floor; there is also a medical clinic here. ⊠ *1 Huayuan Bei Jie, at Dongda Jie* ☎ *0971/822–5951* 🖷 *0971/ 822–5892* ➹ *96 rooms, 8 suites* ♨ *2 restaurants, business services, travel services* ▤ *No credit cards.*

¢   ⊡ **Qinghai Hotel.** A gigantic pink box of a hotel, the Qinghai has shiny marble floors and a somewhat impersonal feel, with rooms that are a tad more expensive than those at the Xining Hotel, but no cleaner or more comfortable. The hotel has a shopping arcade, a small Bank of China branch, and a CITS office. ⊠ *158 Huanghe Lu, 810001* ☎ *0971/ 614–4888* 🖷 *0971/614–4145* ➹ *330 rooms, 62 suites* ♨ *4 restaurants, gym, hair salon, massage, bowling, laundry service, business services, meeting room, travel services* ▤ *No credit cards.*

¢   ⊡ **Xining Hotel.** In contrast to Xining's often gray monotony, the Xining Hotel has a charming garden and teahouse that provides much-needed respite from the urban malaise. The rooms are fairly inexpensive, clean, and decently furnished but on the downside it's set a bit outside the city center. With all the amenities of its more expensive neighbors, the Xining Hotel is a good bargain. At the very least, the garden oasis is a welcome place to relax after a long, hard day sightseeing. ⊠ *348 Qiyi Lu, 810001* ☎ *0971/845–8701* ⇘ *270 rooms, 32 suites* ♦ *Restaurant, gym, hair salon, massage, bowling, laundry service, business services, meeting room, travel services* ⊟ *No credit cards.*

Shopping
Xining is a good place to find Tibetan and Chinese crafts at reasonable prices. **Native Arts and Crafts** (⊠ Qinghai Hotel, 158 Huanghe Lu, 2nd-fl. arcade) has vests, hats, and toys in designs using the techniques of traditional Tibetan folk embroidery; brass gongs; jewelry; and some Chinese jade and porcelain objects. **Ba Chang Ge** (⊠ 30 Bei Dajie) has Chinese antique porcelain, jade figurines from the region, and Tibetan folk embroidery.

Side Trips from Xining
Trips can be arranged through various travel agencies, including CITS (⇨ Visitor Information) at the Qinghai Hotel. The government travel agency has something of a monopoly on transportation of tourists to the scenic spots outside Xining, and traveling with CITS or one of its offshoots seems to be the surest way to get around without being turned away by the police for entering an area without clearance.

★ ㉖ The magnificent **Ta'Er Monastery** (Ta'Er Si), also known as Pagoda Lamasery or Kum Bum, is southwest of Xining. Built in 1560, it is one of the six great monasteries of the Tibetan Buddhist sect known as Yellow Lamaism—now the dominant sect in Tibet—and reputedly the birthplace of the sect's founder, Tsong-Kha-pa, as well. A great reformer who lived in the early 1400s, Tsong-Kha-pa formulated a striking new doctrine at a time of great religious Tibetan strife; his reform movement (known as the Dge-lugs-pa, literally "virtuous") stressed a return to monastic discipline, strict celibacy, and moral and philosophical thought over magic and mysticism. Tsong's followers were easily identified by their hats: hence the name Yellow Hat Sect. Still a magnet for Tibetan pilgrims, Ta'Er Si boasts a dozen prayer halls, an exhibition hall, 20,000 religious paintings and embroideries, and the monks' quarters, all in a complex that covers nearly a quarter of a square mile. The **Kumbum Festival,** a religious fair at which monks perform 500-year-old songs and activities—including the Devil Dance to purge bad spirits—is held five times a year at the monastery, in February, May, July, November, and December. In winter frozen yak butter is carved into extraordinary Buddhist scenes and exhibited on the 15th day of the lunar New Year. Shops right outside the main gate of the monastery sell beads, prayer scarves, brass gongs, and even some sacrificial yak skulls. ⚑ *Huangzhong, 26 km (16 mi) southwest of Xining. Minibuses (Y3–Y4) leave from left side of Xining Gymnasium on Xi Dajie, west of Ximen (West Gate) every 10–20 mins for the 45-min trip; cars can also be hired through CITS* ☒ *Y21.*

㉗ Dek Tser, a peasant village in Ping'an County, is the birthplace of the 14th Dalai Lama, the current exiled spiritual leader of Tibetan Buddhism. The long, winding, and rocky road up to the high mountain village is not for the fainthearted. Behind the wooden door next to the old Hong Ya School (which is still marked in Chinese characters) live two great-nieces of the Dalai Lama. One teaches at the school. Across the road, just up the hill, a wall encloses a temple painted in bright colors, where the Dalai Lama first practiced Buddhism. If you knock on the great-nieces' door, they'll let you in to see the temple, past a yard filled with pigs, chickens, donkeys, sheep, and cows. ⊕ *32 km (20 mi) east of Ta'Er Si.*

㉘ Riyue Shan (Sun Moon Mountain), in Huangyuan County, has two pagodas—the Sun and the Moon—on adjoining peaks, each with friezes depicting the story of a 7th-century Chinese princess, Wen Cheng: she married the Tibetan emperor against her will as a result of the wiles of Ludong Zan, the Tibetan prime minister. The site is nice enough, amid grasslands and gently rolling mountains with a desolate beauty, but not worth a visit on its own. It's often a stop on the Qinghai Lake trip. Yak rides are available here (Y5). ⊕ *11 km (7 mi) west of Xining.*

★ **㉙ Bird Island** (Niao Dao) is the main draw at **Green Lake** (Qinghai Hu), China's largest inland saltwater lake, which lies in the northeastern part of Qinghai province and the Tibetan Plateau. The eerily electric-blue lake has a circumference of 360 km (223 mi) and is surrounded by four mountain ranges. From late spring to early fall, the grasslands and rolling hills surrounding the lake are green and covered with yellow rapeseed flowers. Wild yaks roam here. Beyond the hills the area is ringed with snow-capped mountains. An estimated 100,000 birds flock in spring and summer to breed at Niao Dao, on the western side of the lake. Egrets, speckle-headed geese, cormorants, gulls, and black-neck cranes are among the birds that settle on the various shores and fill the air with clucks, coos, squawks, and screeches. You can see the breeding birds only from a couple of special viewing areas cordoned off from the sites themselves—but the sight is nevertheless astounding. The best times to view the birds are May and June. The name Bird Island is a bit misleading: the site was once an island, until the lake receded and made the shore part of the mainland. ⊕ *7- to 8-hr drive, about 350 km (217 mi) northwest of Xining* ⌂ *Y60.*

WHERE TO   Several small restaurants line the main road beside Qinghai Hu. The restau-
STAY & EAT   rants serve Qinghai Lake's only fish, *wulin huangyu* (naked carp), as well as yak meat and other local delicacies. Lunch costs about Y25–Y30 per person.

¢ ✕⌂ **Birds' Islet Hotel.** Decent and relatively clean accommodations with 24-hour hot water can be had in this generic white hotel with blue-glass windows. There are no private baths. The second-floor restaurant (¢–$) serves very good food, including Qinghai Lake's naked carp, fresh vegetables, and other local delicacies. ✉ *51 Bayi Xi Lu, Bird Island, about 20-min walk from Bird Island observation sites* ☎ *0971/812–5416*

27 rooms, 20 dorm rooms & *Restaurant* = *No credit cards* ⊘ *Closed Sept.–Mar.*

Qinghai A to Z

To research prices, get advice from other travelers, and book travel arrangements, visit www.fodors.com.

AIR TRAVEL
Several flights a week link Xining with Beijing, Shanghai, Guangzhou, Xian, and Ürümqi, and three flights a week go to Lhasa (Y1,290, not including travel permit).

AIRPORTS
The Xining airport (Xining Jichang), 30 km (19 mi) southeast of Xining, takes about a half hour to reach by taxi.

BUS TRAVEL
Purchase bus tickets for Lhasa from CITS in Golmud; the buses (26–28 hours if the bus doesn't break down) officially run each day, if weather conditions permit, departing from the Tibet Bus Station at around 4 PM.
🚌 Bus Information **Tibet Bus Station** ⊠ Xizang Lu 📞 No phone. **Xining Main Bus Station** ⊠ Jianguo Lu (across river from train station) 📞 0971/814–9506.

EMERGENCIES
🚑 **Qinghai People's Hospital** ⊠ 2 Gonghe Lu, Xining east side of town 📞 0971/817–7911. **Xining Number 2 People's Hospital** ⊠ 29 Tongren Lu, Xining, northwest end of town 📞 0971/614–3314.

TOURS
Qinghai's CITS runs 10-day tours to the source of the Yellow River and 12-day hikes in the 20,000-foot-high Anyemaqen Mountains (sacred to the Tibetans), 800 km (500 mi) southwest of Xining. These trips are not for the faint of heart and should only be done through a tour. For more information on these area you may want to consult Galen Rowell's book *Mountains of Tibet and the Middle Kingdom*.
🚩 Tour-Operator Recommendations **CITS** ⊠ 156 Huanghe Lu Xining, next to Qinghai Minzu Binguan 📞 0971/614–4888 Ext. 2439 or 0971/614–3711.

TRAIN TRAVEL
Daily trains link Xining with Lanzhou (4 hours), Xian (14 hours), and Shanghai (40 hours). Every other day, trains run between Xining and Beijing (33½ hours) and Qingdao (41 hours). Tickets can be purchased in Xining from CITS or at the railway station.
🚆 Train Information **Xining Railway Station** ⊹ east of town beyond Qilian Lu 📞 0971/814–9793.

TRANSPORTATION AROUND QINGHAI
The best ways to get around Xining is on foot or by taxi. For day trips, catch a taxi in town and negotiate the fare to your destination in advance, or hire a car and driver from CITS.

VISITOR INFORMATION
To arrange travel permits for Tibet, head to CITS (open daily 8:30–12:30 and 2–6); permits can be processed within 24 hours. The agency also arranges tours to Lhasa.

i Tourist Information **China Youth Travel Service Qinghai** ✉ 136 Huzhu Xilu, Xining ☎☎ 0971/817–8096. **CITS** ✉ 156 Huanghe Lu, 300 feet north of Qinghai Minzu Binguan, Xining ☎ 0971/614–4888 Ext. 2439 ✉ 14 Jianguo Lu, Xining ☎ 0971/817–8814.

XINJIANG

The vast Xinjiang Uighur Autonomous Region, covering more than 966,000 square km (375,000 square mi), or half the size of India, is the largest province in China and one of the most resource rich and ethnically diversified. It borders Mongolia, Kazakhstan, Kirghizstan, Tadzhikstan, Afghanistan, and Kashmir. About 40% of Xinjiang's 19.25 million people are Han Chinese, about 47% are Uighur (a people of Central Turkic origin), and the remainder are Kirghis, Kazakhs, Tajiks, Uzbeks, Hui, Mongols, Manchus, Tatars, Daur, and Russians.

Historians believe the area was first settled by nomadic Turkic tribes in the 3rd century BC. In the 1980s archaeologists discovered dozens of tombs in various parts of Xinjiang, with bodies that had been buried about 3,000 years before yet remained remarkably preserved, thanks to the arid desert climate. Many of the mummies, believed to be forefathers of the Uighurs, had northern European features, including fair hair and skin. The theory is that they intermarried with other peoples and gradually evolved into a tribe of mostly dark-haired people. Even today fair coloring and blue or green eyes are not uncommon among Uighurs.

In the Qin and Han dynasties (221 BC–AD 220) Xinjiang was inhabited by a variety of tribes, with anywhere from 36 to 50 walled states. Chinggis (Genghis) Khaan's troops conquered part of the region in 1218. By the time the Qing Dynasty came to power in 1644, the area was under constant dispute among four different Mongol tribes that roamed the areas north of the Tian Shan (Heavenly Mountains), while the areas south of the mountains were inhabited by the Uighur people, ruled by descendants of the Mongol khans. The Muslims declared independence during the Tang Dynasty (AD 618–970) and held on to it until the 19th century.

Although territorial wars continued throughout most of Xinjiang's history, and climatic conditions on the vast desert were not always hospitable to travelers, the region nevertheless became one of the most important crossroads for trade between China, Europe, and the ancient Persian empire.

In the 20th century the Uighurs continued to resist Chinese rule. In 1933 they succeeded briefly, seizing power from a warlord governor and claiming the land as a separate republic, which they named East Turkistan. China tightened its grip after the revolution, however, encouraging Han settlers to emigrate to the province to dilute the Uighur population. In 1949, the entire province was home to only 6% Han; today the capital, Ürümqi, is about 73% Han. The Uighurs live mostly in the less-industrialized areas, and many complain that business and government are dominated by the Han Chinese. Since the breakup of the Soviet Union, the Uighurs have seen their Muslim neighbors in the Central-Asian countries gain independence and have renewed their own efforts, sometimes resorting to violent means, only to be repressed in a series of crackdowns that have resulted in countless arrests and a few hundred executions.

Throughout the 1990s, as the insurgency continued to grow, the government aggressively stepped up religious persecution, banned Islamic publications, sentenced scores of Uighurs to life imprisonment after forced confessions, and arbitrarily executed prisoners accused of being terrorists or separatists. The most explosive clashes between separatists and authorities occurred in 1997, when hundreds of Uighurs in Yining City rioted against Chinese rule for two days. Bombs exploded aboard buses in both Ürümqi and Beijing. The new millennium, however, brought a new tune as post–9/11 tensions caused the United States to withdraw their support for Uighur insurgency and, instead, back China's Communist Party in their crackdowns and "anti-terrorist" efforts. Compared to the explosive late-1990s, the early 2000s have been rather quiet in Xinjiang.

Xinjiang is currently the region in China where the greatest number of political prisoners have been executed in recent years. The party is hoping that its new "Develop the West" campaign will pour money into the local economy, encourage even more Han immigration to the region, and sap ethnic tensions. In recent years Beijing has spent billions of dollars on some 70 major infrastructure projects in Xinjiang.

Although the territorial dispute may never be resolved, today much of Xinjiang is wide open to foreign visitors. And even in years of violence, tourists have never been a target or fallen victim. The roads are bumpy, but the landscapes are magnificent. The Uighurs and other so-called minority groups are generally eager to introduce foreigners to their traditional music, cuisine, and celebrations.

One quirky side effect of China's rule is that Xinjiang is officially in the same time zone as Beijing. Clocks run on "Beijing time," so in winter it's almost 9 AM when the sun rises. Hours stated here are Beijing time. Unofficially, clocks run on "Xinjiang time," which is an hour earlier than Beijing time.

The majority of the people in Xinjiang speak Mandarin, but the predominant language is Uighur, a Turkic-derived language. Little English is spoken. A few Uighur words to remember: Hello: *Yahshimu siz* (yah-shee-moo siz). Thank you: *Rachmad* (rak-*mad*). How much?: *Kanche pul?* (kan-che *poll*). Market: *Bazargha* (ba-*zaar*-ga). Goodbye: *Heri hosh* (her-*ee* hosh).

Xinjiang has a desert climate, with very little rainfall. It gets very cold in winter and very hot in summer, especially in the Turpan Basin, although the temperature can drop by as much as 20 degrees at night. Xinjiang's average annual rainfall is only 6 inches. Winter lasts from around November through April. The sun is strong all year, so pack sunglasses, sun hats, and sunscreen.

Ürümqi

30 *2 days (2,250 km [1,400 mi]) by train northwest of Beijing.*

Xinjiang's capital and largest city, Ürümqi has the distinction of being the most landlocked city in the world—the nearest sea is 2,240 km (1,389 mi) away. It is a new city by Chinese standards, built on pastureland in 1763. Originally the city was little more than barracks for Qing Dynasty troops. The Qing emperors called the city Dihua (meaning both Enlightening and Civilizing). In 1884, when the Chinese declared the region a province and named it Xinjiang (New Territories), Dihua became the capital. In 1954, five years after the Revolution, the city was renamed Ürümqi, or "beautiful pastures" in Mongolian.

A sleepy and dusty trading post for light industrial goods and farm produce in the mid-1980s, Ürümqi has grown to a modern city, with a population of just over 2 million, and new buildings constantly under construction. Nevertheless, the occasional peasant does walk a sheep along its downtown streets. About 3 km (2 mi) from the center of town is the Erdaoqiao District, an Uighur area where some residents still live in adobe huts and drive donkey carts.

Exploring Ürümqi

Start your tour of Ürümqi with a 15-minute walk up a stone path to the top of **Red Mountain** (Hong Shan), a hill about a half mile above sea level that offers a panoramic view of the city. At the top is an array of incongruously grouped objects, including a Big Buddha and the **Zhenglong Pagoda** (Zhenglong Ta), built by the emperor in 1788 to suppress an evil dragon. There's also an entire **amusement park,** including bumper cars, gondolas, and a Ferris wheel, but the rides aren't included in the regular admission price. ⊠ *North end of Xinhua Bei Lu, 45-min walk or 10-min taxi ride from center; entrance halfway up hill, on east side* 🎟 *Y10* ⊙ *Sunrise–sunset.*

In the Uighur section south of the center of town is the **Erdaoqiao Market** (Erdaoqiao Shichang). Once the streets here were lined with adobe dwellings and full of donkey carts, flocks of sheep, men in embroidered skullcaps, and women in heavy brown wool veils and leggings. With modernization, the area has sprouted several tiled buildings, but the rakish, laid-back atmosphere remains. The main market is in a covered alleyway. You can bargain for Uighur crafts, such as embroidered caps and vests or decorated knives. Farther down the passageway are several shops selling carpets, animal pelts, and fur hats, as well as food vendors. ✤ *About 5 km (3 mi) south of center, ½ block north of Tuan Jie Lu, between Xinhua Nan Lu and Jiefang Lu.*

Don't miss the exhibition of nearly a dozen 3,000-year-old mummies at the superb **Xinjiang Museum** (Xinjiang Bowuguan). The mummies were excavated from tombs in various parts of Xinjiang, including those from the ancient Silk Road cities of Loulan, Hami, and Cherchen, and the Atsana graves in Turpan. In addition, the museum has intriguing fragments of silk brocade, wool rugs, pottery, and even hemp-cloth documents discovered in the tombs along with the corpses. There are also some fine examples of minority costumes, crafts, musical instruments, and architecture, including a few yurts and stuffed sheep and yaks. The museum shops have fairly good selections of carpets, Chinese jewelry, porcelain, and Uighur musical instruments (cash only). ⊠ *59 Xibei Lu* ☎ *0991/453–6436* 🖅 *Y25* ⊙ *Weekdays 9:30–5:30, weekends 10:30–5:30.*

Where to Stay & Eat

Ürümqi is a fine place to try both Uighur and Chinese cuisine. The row of restaurants on Hongqi Lu, in the boutique district serves everything from Beijing-style dumplings to the traditional Uighur specialties of grilled lamb and vegetable kebabs, flat bread, *lamian* (pulled noodles seasoned with tomatoes, green peppers, and red chili peppers), and spicy hotpot. Farther north, the cluster of restaurants on Jianshe Lu is also worth checking out. To get the real flavor of Ürümqi nightlife, head to the bustling night market on Wu Yi Lu near the Hong Fu Da Jiu Dian hotel; among the dazzling variety of foods and fruits there are heaps of fresh seafood, crabs, and dark little escargots marinated in chilies (piled beside the Mongolian hotpot stands). There's also a night market just outside the Renmin Hotel. Unless otherwise stated, restaurants are open daily noon–3 and 6:30–9.

★ ¢–$$$ ✕ **Xi Wang Mu.** A memorable Chinese restaurant, it serves a number of regional specialties from around the country. Try the Shanghai-style fish (a whole poached fish with ginger slivers) and chicken with Sichuan black-bean sauce. There's also a delicious shark's-fin soup. ⊠ *Holiday Inn, 168 Xinhua Bei Lu, 2nd fl.* ☎ *0991/281–8788* 🖢 *Reservations essential* 🖃 *AE, MC, V.*

$$ ✕ **Shang Jian Jiu.** Instantly recognizable by the Jaeger Beer sign out front, this is a noisy, friendly place with an excellent all-you-can-eat Mongolian hotpot buffet for lunch and dinner. ⊠ *Luoyang House, 18 Jianshe Lu* ☎ *0991/481–5690* 🖃 *No credit cards.*

¢–$$ ✕ **Hotpot Place.** This unassuming but clean hotpot restaurant with a cheerful staff is a quick and convenient pit stop for lunch. Ordering is easy: just point at the mushrooms, lamb chunks, and other ingredients already pre-skewered on kebab sticks. ⊠ *18 Jianzhu Xi Lu, off side street near Holiday Inn* ☎ *0991/230–2295* 🖃 *No credit cards.*

★ ¢–$$ ✕ **Kashgari's.** Decorated with Uighur tapestries and other ornaments, this hotel restaurant has background music that evokes images of snake charmers. The Uighur cuisine is prepared with an imaginative flourish, using local ingredients such as Turpan raisins. ⊠ *Holiday Inn, 168 Xinhua Bei Lu, ground fl.* ☎ *0991/281–8788* 🖃 *AE, MC, V.*

¢–$$ ✕ **Pearl Palace.** A bit out of the way, this Chinese seafood restaurant, complete with tanks full of fresh catches that are flown in daily, is worth the trip. Private rooms are available for large parties. Try the special fresh-baked *mianbao* (slightly sweet bread filled with a paste of nuts and mushrooms). ⊠ *World Plaza hotel, 2 Beijing Nan Lu* ☎ *0991/383–6400 Ext. 3138* 🖢 *Reservations essential* 🖃 *AE, MC, V.*

¢ ✕ **Da Han San Guan.** This is one of the cleaner choices on a little street known as Restaurant Alley. The noodles are tasty, and there are fresh-roasted sunflower seeds to munch on while you wait for your food. ⊠ *33 Jian Shi Lu* ☎ *No phone* 🖃 *No credit cards.*

¢–$$$ ⊞ **Hong Fu Da Jiu Dian.** Owned by the nearby China Telecom, the dusty-rose–marble Hong Fu is an upscale hotel offering spacious elegant rooms with beautiful mahogany furniture and touch-sensitive light switches, all in a good location. The night market on Wuyi Lu is just steps from the hotel entrance. ⊠ *26 Huanghe Lu, 830000* ☎ *0991/588–1588* 🖷 *0991/582–3188* ↩ *343 rooms, 18 suites* ♨ *6 restaurants, gym, massage, sauna, laundry service, business services, meeting room* ▤ *AE, MC, V.*

$$ ⊞ **Holiday Inn.** The first foreign-owned hotel in all of western China, the Holiday Inn continues to be one of the leading hotels in Ürümqi—and a very reasonable rate. It has the usual luxuries, good restaurants, nicely appointed rooms, and an English-speaking staff, though some fixtures are aging. Silks, the disco, is popular with both visitors and locals, as is the lobby bar, Unicorns, which has live entertainment nightly. ⊠ *168 Xinhua Bei Lu, 830002* ☎ *0991/281–8788* 🖷 *0991/281–7422* ⌨ *holiday@mail.wl.xj.cn* ↩ *360 rooms, 22 suites* ♨ *3 restaurants, snack bar, refrigerators, indoor pool, gym, hair salon, billiards, bar, shops, dry cleaning, laundry service, business services, meeting room, airport shuttle, travel services* ▤ *AE, MC, V.*

$–$$ ⊞ **Hoi Tak Hotel Xinjiang** (Hai De Dajiudian). One of Ürümqi's newest luxury hotels, the Hoi Tak is a good deal and well located in the commercial heart of the town. This Hong Kong–managed hotel supports a gleaming white tower offering first-rate views of the snowcapped Tian Shan Mountains. The sparkling marble lobby leads to several restaurants and lounges and an indoor pool and gym complete the amenities. Standard rooms, though not huge, are tastefully appointed with comfortable beds and ample closet space. ⊠ *1 Dongfeng Lu, 830000* ☎ *0991/232–2828* ⌨ *hthxjbc@mail.wl.xj.cninfo.net* ↩ *346 rooms, 38 suites* ♨ *3 restaurants, indoor pool, tennis courts, miniature golf, gym, hair salon, massage, sauna, billiards, nightclub, baby-sitting, laundry service, business services, meeting room, travel services* ▤ *AE, MC, V.*

$ ⊞ **Tunhe Hotel** (Tunhe Da Jiu Dian). A bright-yellow sign splashed across the front of a tall white tower greets visitors at the centrally located Tunhe, which opened in 2000. The lobby here is elegant, and spacious light-color rooms offer all the standard amenities, including Internet outlet ports. There is also an in-house medical clinic. ⊠ *52 Chanjiang Lu, 830000* ☎ *0991/587–6688* 🖷 *0991/587–6689* ⌨ *thdjd@mail.xj.cninfo.net* ↩ *277 rooms, 20 suites* ♨ *3 restaurants, gym, hair salon, massage, sauna, billiards, nightclub, baby-sitting, laundry service, business services, meeting room, travel services* ▤ *AE, MC, V.*

$ ⊞ **World Plaza.** A huge high-rise built near the airport in the early 1990s, the World Plaza looks old for its age. Inside, though, it's perfectly comfortable, with an eager-to-please staff and tasteful rooms decorated with gray satin-striped comforters. The second floor has a spacious and classy Internet café (Y10 per hour), with high-speed connection. Drinks and sandwiches are also available. Note that the hotel is about a 1-mi trek from the city center. ⊠ *2 Beijing Nan Lu, 830011* ☎ *0991/383–6400* 🖷 *0991/383–6399* ↩ *352 rooms, 32 suites* ♨ *3 restaurants, café, refrigerators, indoor pool, gym, hair salon, massage, billiards, dry cleaning, laundry service, airport shuttle, travel services* ▤ *AE, MC, V.*

¢   ▦ **Silk Road Hotel.** This friendly hotel is at the south end of town, about 10 km (6 mi) from downtown Ürümqi—a 10-minute walk from Erdaoqiao Market. It's a pleasant place to stay if you want to get away from the hustle-and-bustle of the city center, rooms are clean and comfortable, and the staff is professional. ⊠ *52-1 Yanan Lu, 830001* ☎ *0991/255–8899* 🖶 *0991/255–7788* ⚡ *98 rooms, 9 suites* ⚫ *3 restaurants, tennis court, pool, massage, sauna, basketball, billiards, bowling, bar, business services* ▤ *AE, MC, V.*

¢   ▦ **Xinjiang Hotel.** Near the train station, this hotel, with its dark lobby and fluorescent lighting, is underwhelming, but it has clean rooms for moderate prices, and the staff is usually amiable. With dark-wood furnishings and slightly hard beds, the rooms are nothing special but they are spacious, with high ceilings, and offer decent views. The Chinese restaurant here is popular with locals for its roast duck. To the left of the hotel entrance, the inexpensive self-serve Chinese fast-food eatery has a range of tasty street food, noodles, and vegetable dishes. ⊠ *107 Chanjiang Lu, 830002* ☎ *0991/585–2511* 🖶 *0991/581–1354* ⚡ *55 rooms, 12 suites* ⚫ *3 restaurants, business services, travel services* ▤ *No credit cards.*

Nightlife

Karaoke is the most popular form of nighttime entertainment in China's cities, and Ürümqi is no exception. The bars seem to come and go every few months, scattered all over the downtown area. The action doesn't begin until after 10 PM.

The **Rock & Roll Café** (⊠ 1–108 Xinhua Bei Lu) plays rock music until the wee hours and tries to look like a Hard Rock Cafe.

Silks Disco (⊠ Holiday Inn, 168 Xinhua Bei Lu) starts jumping after about 10 PM, especially from Thursday through Sunday, with strobe lights and Western disco recordings.

Shopping

Stores are open 10–6 daily.

An extensive **outdoor food market** sells local fruits, nuts, bread, and small cakes, along with handmade noodles and kebabs, in the alley beside the **Xinjiang Jinxin Hotel** (⊠ Renmin Lu, east of Xinhua Nan Lu at Jiefang Nan Lu), a lodging that doesn't admit foreigners.

Ürümqi is not known for its Uighur handicrafts in the way that Kashgar and Turpan are, but the **Erdaoqiao Market** (⇨ Exploring Ürümqi) has a good selection of handicraft items, fruit (fresh and dried), and carpets brought in from other parts of Xinjiang.

Ürümqi Carpet Factory (⊠ 40 Jin Er Lu ☎ 0991/581–3338) sells carpets made in the factory workshop based on Central-Asian patterns. You can tour the factory any time during the day, after which a guide will usher you into the showroom and try to talk you into buying something. You can arrange shipment at an extra charge. **Xinjiang Antique Store** (⊠ 325 Jiefang Nan Lu ☎ 0991/281–5284) has a good selection of Uighur handicrafts and Chinese bric-a-brac, including jade, jewelry, carpets, ink brushes, bronze ware, and porcelain.

Heavenly Lake

③ *2–3 hrs (115 km [71 mi]) by bus northeast of Ürümqi.*

Fodor'sChoice
★

About a three-hour ride from Ürümqi is the not-to-be-missed Heavenly Lake (Tianchi Hu), possibly the prettiest lake in China, surrounded by snow-sprinkled mountains. The water is crystal clear with a sapphire tint. Taiwanese tourists come here to commune with the Buddhist goddess of mercy. Others come for the hiking and horseback riding, or simply to spend a day enjoying nature. In summer white flowers dot the hillsides. Though tourism has been leaving its ugly footprint here with increasing depth over the years, a ferry (Y20) allows you to tour the area without contributing to the growth of other tourist services. For a better dose of escapism give yourself an afternoon to hike up into the hills and around the lake.

Kazakh families still set up traditional yurts along the shores of Heavenly Lake from early May to late October, bringing their horses, sheep, and cashmere goats. The Kazakh people have a long history as horse breeders and are known as skilled riders. Most of the yurt dwellers are able to furnish horses—and a guide—for a day of riding around the lake. The more business-minded ones are erecting clusters of yurts to cater to tour groups. From Ürümqi, buses (Y25 round-trip) to Heavenly Lake leave at 9 in the morning from both the north and south gates of Renmin Gongyuan (People's Park) in summer; add Y15 if you want to stay overnight.

Where to Stay & Eat

There are some excellent small **restaurants** without names along the western shore, near the hotels, that will prepare whatever they have on hand for lunch and dinner and produce a fresh and delicious array of stir-fried meat, vegetables, and noodles. Ask to move your table outside, and you can enjoy the view while you eat. Prices for dinner for two will be Y30–Y50. Only cash is accepted.

There is a cluster of **hotels** at the western shore of the lake. You will not find any luxury accommodations here. Showers and toilet are shared, and some hotels have dorm beds only.

You can also stay in a **yurt** for about Y20 per person per night, Y40 for lodging and three meals (soup made mostly from flour, hard-as-rock sheep cheese, and tea with either salt or fried flour in it; if you bring your own tea bags, your host will provide plain boiled water). The sleeping quarters are communal, and there's no plumbing. However, you'll have a rewarding glimpse into the way your Kazakh hosts live. Yurts are made from hides or canvas stretched over a wooden frame. The interior is colorfully decorated with handmade rugs and blankets, neatly hung along the walls and lining the floor. There is usually a wood-burning stove in the center, for cooking and keeping the yurt warm at night. Most accommodate four people.

¢ 🏨 **Shui Shou Shan Zhuang.** This group of yurts and cabins, run by the water-management company, offers sterile-looking but clean accommodations set off from the rest of the pack at the southeastern side of the lake. Due to increasing tourism demands, the cabins have been up-graded and now feature hot water and showers. To cater to karaoke-crazed guests, some yurts are even equipped with a fully functional karaoke (KTV) lounge in a common room sheathed with yellow satin, which can make sleeping difficult. The toilets are communal but clean; there are sinks and showers. ✛ *Southeastern side of lake, 15–20-min trek from bus stop on paved road* ☎ *0994/325–1007* ⚑ *6 cabins, 5 yurts* ⚭ *Restaurant; no a/c, no room phones, no room TVs* ▭ *No credit cards.*

¢ ▦ **Shui Xin Hotel.** The Shui Xin has private guest rooms (with shared baths) and a restaurant open for lunch and dinner. ✛ *Western shore of lake, near stop for bus from Ürümqi* ☎ *0994/325–1103* ⚑ *12 rooms* ⚭ *Restaurant; no a/c* ▭ *No credit cards.*

Yining

㉜ *1 day (700 km [434 mi]) by bus west of Ürümqi.*

The city of Yining is the main stop in Ili Prefecture, a rich farming val-ley in northern Xinjiang near the border of Kazakhstan. Yining itself is too industrialized to be charming, but all around the city are the apple orchards for which Ili is famous, and in summer local Uighurs and Kaza-khs perform traditional folk dances in the orchards. The countryside on the outskirts of Yining is a pleasant area to explore. Take a taxi to the Yili River bridge, 6 km (4 mi) from the town center, then walk or take a horse carriage over the bridge. Just across the river is a rustic vil-lage where the dirt roads are lined with birch trees. The houses have blue-painted doors that open into courtyards filled with grapevines.

㉝ From Yining you can take a three-hour bus ride to **Sayram Lake** (Sayram Hu), in nearby Bole Prefecture. In summer you can circle the lake on horseback with a guide (about Y60 a day). It's a pretty ride, with the grasslands in bloom and the snowcapped mountains in the distance. In July or early August, Sayram Lake's shore swarms with Kazakhs gath-ering for the **Naadam Fair.** They sell handicrafts, perform traditional music and dance, and stage a number of games and races on horseback. "Sheep polo" is a popular spectator sport. Here the men from the vil-lage slaughter and skin a sheep, then race around a ring on horseback, each contestant trying to grab the sheepskin from whoever has it and ride a complete circle around the ring with it. The game can go on for hours. In another version of the game, known as the "girl chase," vil-lage men try to capture women on horseback.

Where to Stay

A yurt is the preferred place to stay at Sayram Lake. Yurts cost about Y20 a night per person, with accommodations similar to those at Heav-enly Lake.

¢ ▦ **Friendship Hotel** (Youyi Binguan). The Youyi has renovated its rooms in recent years, and most rooms now offer clean bathrooms, 24-hour hot water, and air-conditioners. It's a popular choice among back-packers. ✉ *7 Sidaling Jie, Lane 3, 835000, south of bus station* ☎ *0999/ 802–3901* 🖶 *0999/802–4631* ⚑ *155 rooms, 6 suites* ⚭ *Restaurant, hair salon, massage, laundry service, travel services* ▭ *No credit cards.*

¢ ⌂ **Huacheng Hotel.** Once just a backpacker accommodation close to the bus station, the Huacheng now boasts renovated doubles with 24-hour hot water, bathrooms, and air-conditioners. The dorm rooms, however, continue to be dark and poorly ventilated with fans instead of air-conditioning. A long way from the center of town, you can eat at the hotel's 24-hour Chinese restaurant. ⊠ *5 Ahe Mai Ti Jiang Jie, No. 7 Alley, 835000, south of bus station* ☎ *0999/812–5050* 🖷 *0999/812–1640* 🗪 *158 rooms, 10 suites* ⌕ *3 restaurants, hair salon, sauna, business services, travel services; no a/c in some rooms* 🖃 *No credit cards.*

¢ ⌂ **Yili Guest House** (Yili Binguan). Located in a lushly gardened complex, the Yili has modest and rather sterile-looking rooms in the main building. Newer rooms in the west wing come with more amenities, including spacious bathrooms and great views. ⊠ *22 Ying Bin Lu, 835000* ☎ *0999/802–3799* 🖷 *0999/802–4964* 🗪 *200 rooms* ⌕ *2 restaurants, hair salon, massage, business services, travel services* 🖃 *No credit cards.*

Turpan

❸❹ *2½–3 hrs (184 km [114 mi]) by bus southeast of Ürümqi.*

Turpan lies in a desert basin at the southern foot of the Heavenly Mountains. Part of the basin, called the Turpan Depression, lies 505 feet below sea level, the hottest and lowest spot in China and the second-lowest point in the world, after the Dead Sea. Temperatures have been known to soar to more than 43°C (110°F), and the sunshine is relentless.

The oasis town of Turpan has a population of just under a quarter of a million people; 70% are minorities, mostly Uighur, though this demographic is constantly shifting as, along with neighboring Hami, Beijing continues to support (through tax breaks and land grants) Han migration to Xinjiang. It's surrounded by mountains and some of the richest farmland in Xinjiang; its fruit orchards and vineyards support a few small wineries. Late summer, when the grapes are ripe, is Turpan's busiest tourist season. Unfortunately, the city has been infected by the tourist bug of late; a 2001 city government poster proclaimed, "One hand grabs grapes, the other tourism." Accordingly, new roads to star attractions outside the city have been paved, cutting down on travel times, but new Disneyfied Buddhist caves and other simulacra are also popping up alongside ancient sites. September 11 and then SARS slowed down the inevitable boom, thus buying Turpan at least a few more years. Make a note of the sites you definitely want to visit before approaching taxi drivers, as they will attempt to bring you to some of the new attractions.

Walk about 10 minutes west on Laocheng Zhong Lu, which separates the two main hotels on the Qingnian Lu pedestrian walkway, to the **bazaar**, behind an ornate green gate. Some crafts are available here, as well as plenty of local fruit and nuts piled up in huge sacks. For a real treat, hit the food stands on the side of the bazaar adjacent to the main road for local Turpan ice cream. Made from shaved ice, fresh cream, sugar, and sweet rice wine, this snack will chase away the midday lethargy and leave you feeling refreshed and cool. ⊠ *Laocheng Xi Lu near Gao Jiang Nan Lu, past Bank of China, opposite bus station.*

West on Laocheng stands the picturesque **City Mosque** (Qingzhen Si), the most active of the group of mosques in the district, about 3 km (2 mi) from the center of town. Out here in a predominantly Uighur neighborhood are sod huts and donkey carts, as well as family-run restaurants where cooks bake naan in deep, open ovens. ⊠ *Laocheng Lu ☺ In between prayers.*

need a break? The heat of summer can be a bit much if you're walking through Turpan. Some suggestions: if you start early in the morning and stop frequently at the outdoor stands for cold drinks, you can keep cool. Grapevine-covered canopies provide welcome shade over many of the city sidewalks. And instead of walking you may want to rent a bike or take a taxi, many of which have air-conditioning.

East on Laocheng Zhong Lu, the side street Qiu Nian Zhong Lu leads to **Sugong Tower** (Emin Ta), also called the Tower for Showing Gratitude to Eminhojaat, at the southeast end of town. The Emin Tower and adjoining **mosque** were built in 1777 in the Afghani style to commemorate a military commander who suppressed a rebellion by a group of aristocrats. The 141-foot tower is simple and elegantly spare, built in the shape of a cone, with bricks arranged in 15 patterns and a spiral staircase. The sunbaked roof of the mosque, which is cracking in places, can be scaled for a view of the surrounding lush vineyards. Renovations in 2001 added structural extensions and a large square at the entrance for "antiques" vendors. ✛ *From east end of Laocheng Dong Lu, turn right on last paved road before farmland, walk south to tower* ☎ *0995/856–7158* 🎫 *Y20 ☺ May–Sept., daily 8–8; Oct.–Apr., daily 8–6.*

The remarkable 2,000-year-old **Karez Irrigation Tunnels** (Kanerjing) allowed the desert cities of the Silk Road to survive and even flourish despite an unrelentingly arid environment. In the oasis cities of Turpan and Hami, more than 1,000 wells linked to more than 1,600 km (1,000 mi) of underground tunnels brought water, moved only by gravity, from melting snow at the base of the Bogdashan Mountains to the cities. You can view the Karez Tunnels in Turpan from several sites, some without an admission fee. Most bus or cab drivers take visitors to the largely educational Karez Irrigation Museum, opened in 2000 by a Sino-Japanese joint venture that also has a hotel next to the site. The admission fee here includes entry to the tunnel next to the museum, which has been widened into a pleasant underground pathway that extends for a few hundred yards. Bring good walking shoes, as you may need to pick your way over dead branches or dirt piles. ⊠ *888 Xincheng Lu, on western outskirts of city* 🎫 *Y20 ☺ May–Sept., daily dawn–dusk; Oct.–Apr., daily 8–8.*

Where to Stay & Eat

Some of the best and safest dining, as in the rest of Xinjiang, is in the hotel restaurants, but a cluster of small cafés with outdoor seating and English-language menus offers cheap, filling meals along Laocheng Lu (between Qingnian Lu and Gaochang Lu). The lively night market, with rows of kebab and spicy hotpot stands, on Gaochang Lu just next to the huge public square, is also worth visiting.

¢–$$ ✕ **Muslim Restaurant.** Like most hotel restaurants in the region, this one is poorly lighted and lacks ambience, but it does have a hearty variety of standard Uighur dishes—lamb, noodles, and vegetables. ⊠ *Turpan Guesthouse, 2 Qingnian Nan Lu* ☏ *0995/852–2301* ▤ *No credit cards.*

¢–$ ✕ **Chipu Café.** The most popular of the little cafés that cater to foreigners on a strip around the junction of Qingnian Lu and Laocheng Lu serves a variety of Chinese dishes, posted on the outdoor blackboard in English. ⊠ *Qingnian Lu above Laocheng Lu* ☏ *No phone* ▤ *No credit cards* ☾ *No dinner.*

¢ ✕ **Tian Shan Bai Huo Shang Chang.** It's easy to go numb on noodle dishes after you've been subject to a steady diet of Xinjiang fare, but this relatively clean hole-in-the-wall with pink tabletops creatively hammered out of linoleum serves up an especially tasty lamian (pulled noodles). ⊠ *21 Laocheng Lu, opposite bus station* ☏ *0995/852–2313* ▤ *No credit cards.*

¢ ▦ **Oasis Hotel.** The Oasis, with a professional staff dolled up in traditional Uighur costume, is one of the town's two main hotels. It has spacious, comfortable, and clean air-conditioned rooms, friendly service, and a pleasant grapevine-lined courtyard. The Turpan branch of CITS is on the grounds, next door to the hotel. The Oasis Café on the first floor has a good American-style breakfast. ⊠ *41 Qingnian Bei Lu* ☏ *0995/852–2491* ☒ *0995/852–3348* ⇖ *180 rooms, 10 suites* ⌂ *3 restaurants, bicycles, bar, laundry service, business services, travel services* ▤ *No credit cards.*

¢ ▦ **Turpan Guesthouse** (Turpan Binguan). In the grapevine-trellis-covered courtyard here, you can get fruit juices and beer in summer. The rooms are nothing to write home about but are relatively clean and large, especially those in the newer wing. The Muslim restaurant is quite good, and the gift shop is one exception to Turpan's status as a shopping nonentity. ⊠ *2 Qingnian Nan Lu, off Laocheng Lu* ☏ *0995/852–2301* ☒ *0995/852–3262* ⇖ *200 rooms, 6 suites* ⌂ *3 restaurants, shops, laundry service* ▤ *V.*

Nightlife & the Arts

Every summer evening there are Uighur musical performances in the courtyards of both Turpan's Oasis Hotel and the Turpan Guesthouse.

The cafés in the center of town are open late, and much of the nightlife, Turpan-style, consists of drinking beer and kicking back at the outdoor tables. Many locals head to the night market on Gaochang Lu, at the west end of the public Tour and Culture (Luyou Wenhua Guangchang) square.

Side Trips from Turpan

About 47 km (29 mi) east of Turpan, in the middle of the Turpan Depression, the red-clay **Flaming Mountains** (Huo Yan Shan), a branch range of the Heavenly Mountains, are named for the vibrant color and the way they seem to glow at sunset. The range is 100 km (62 mi) long and 10 km (6 mi) wide; the ground temperature here has been recorded at a scorching 43°C (110°F). In 1923 a scientific expedition unearthed the first dinosaur eggs discovered in modern times at the base of the cliffs, as well as a host of fossils and other Stone Age relics. Nowadays, drivers generally only stop at the Flaming Mountains upon request and, due to the heat, prefer to view them en route as buses head for the Bezeklik Caves.

★ ㉟ The **Bezeklik Thousand Buddha Caves** (Bozikeli Qianfo Dong), in a breathtaking valley nestled against the Flaming Mountains, are an ancient temple and monastery built between the 5th and 9th century AD by slaves whose entire lives went into the construction. Many of the fine examples of Buddhist sculpture and wall frescoes were destroyed after Islam came to the region in the 13th century. Other sculptures and fragments of frescoes, including several whole murals of Buddhist monks, all in excellent condition, were taken by 20th-century archaeologists like German Albert von Le Coq, who shipped his finds back to Berlin, where many of them were destroyed in World War II bombing. Though they remain a feat of early engineering, and some of the 77 grottoes have partially restored frescoes, the caves are really in atrocious condition. Go just to see the site itself, which is magnificent. A new Buddha Cave was constructed in 1980 by a local artist a few hundred yards in front of the Thousand Buddha Caves. Cab drivers sometimes stop at this entrance, but the new site, with its garish colors and artificial atmosphere, isn't worth the separate Y20 ticket price. ⊕ *Northwestern side of Huo Yan Shan* 🎫 *Y20* ☯ *Daily 9–6.*

㊱ The ancient **Atsana-Karakhoja Tombs** (Atsana-Karakhoja Mu) southeast of Turpan are where the imperial dead of the city of Gaochang were once buried. Though the site was discovered by Western archaeologists in the early 1900s, extensive Chinese excavations were undertaken only in the early 1970s. These have unearthed more than 400 graves, which contain mummies and artifacts dating to the 3rd century AD. Many of the relics and mummies were relocated to the Xinjiang Museum in Ürümqi. At present, three tombs here are open to visitors. The tomb of Minister Feng Changqing, a Tang Dynasty governor, contains a fresco depicting the governor's life stages, from innocent child to wise Buddha-like old age. Apart from the murals, the tombs contain three fairly well-preserved mummies. ⊕ *40 km (25 mi) southeast of Turpan* ☎ *0995/869–2202* 🎫 *Y20* ☯ *May–Sept., daily dawn–dusk; Oct.–Apr., daily 9–5:30.*

★ ㊲ The ruins of the **City of Gaochang Ruins** (Gaochang Gucheng) lie in the valley south of the Flaming Mountains. At the entrance to the ancient city are donkey-driven carts to take you around the ruins. Legend has it that a group of soldiers stopped here in the 1st century BC on their way to Afghanistan, found that water was plentiful, and decided to stay. By the 7th century the city was the flourishing capital of the Kingdom of Gaochang that ruled over 21 other towns, and by the 9th century the Uighurs had moved into the area from Mongolia, establishing the Kingdom of Kharakojam. In the 14th century Mongols conquered and destroyed the kingdom, leaving only the remains of walls and buildings that are here today. Despite repeated plundering of the site by local farmers and Muslim religious militants, in the early 1900s German archaeologists von Le Coq and A. Grunwedel were still able to unearth ancient manuscripts, statues, and frescoes in superb condition. Nowadays, only the city walls and a partially preserved monastery surrounded by muted, almost unrecognizable shapes remain, an eerie and haunting excursion into the pages of history. ✛ *5 km (3 mi) southeast of Atsana-Karakhoja Tombs* 🖼 *Y20* ☯ *May–Sept., daily dawn–dusk; Oct.–Apr., daily 9–5:30.*

★ ㊳ The impressive ruins of the **City of Jiaohe Ruins** (Jiaohe Gucheng) lie in the Yarnaz Valley west of Turpan, on an island at the confluence of two rivers. The city, established as a garrison during the Han Dynasty, was built on a high plateau, protected by the natural fortification of cliffs rising 98 feet above the rivers, rather than by walls. Jiaohe was governed from the 2nd to the 7th century by the Kingdom of Gaochang and occupied later by Tibetans. Despite destruction in the 13th century by Mongol hordes, large fragments of actual streets and buildings remain, including a Buddhist monastery and Buddhist statues, a row of bleached pagodas, a 29-foot observation tower, government centers, and a prison. ✛ *8 km (5 mi) west of Turpan* 🖼 *Y30* ☯ *May–Sept., daily dawn–dusk; Oct.–Apr., daily 9–5:30.*

㊴ **Grape Valley** (Putao Gou), at the western end of the Flaming Mountains, is lush and green in stark contrast to the blasted, gravel-strewn desert all around. Grapes were first introduced to the area more than 2,000 years ago. Pleasant pathways lead among trellises hanging with grapevines to a winery and a restaurant. ✛ *19 km (12 mi) northeast of Turpan* 🖼 *Y20.*

Xinjiang A to Z

To research prices, get advice from other travelers, and book travel arrangements, visit www.fodors.com.

AIR TRAVEL

Daily flights link Ürümqi with most major Chinese cities, including Beijing, Guangzhou, Shanghai, Xian, Lanzhou, and Chengdu. There are also weekly flights between Ürümqi and Hong Kong. International destinations include Almaty (Kazakhstan), Bishkek (Kyrgyzstan), Islamabad, Kabul, Novosobirsk, and Moscow.

Flights from Ürümqi to Yining run six days a week. As with the buses, return flights are frequently delayed or canceled.
🚹Carriers **Xinjiang Airlines** ✉China Construction Bank Bldg., 2 Ximin Lu, 1st fl. ☎0991/264-1862.

BIKE TRAVEL

Few people ride bicycles in Ürümqi due to the heavy traffic and dusty roads. The Oasis Hotel in Turpan has bike rentals, as does John's Information & Café. Present a photocopy of your passport to be held as identification.

BUS TRAVEL

Buses (Y22 round-trip) leave for Heavenly Lake (Tianchi Hu) at 9 AM and 9:15 AM from the north and south gates of Renmin Park and return at 4 PM or 4:30 PM and takes 2–3 hrs.

City buses in Ürümqi (Y1–Y3) are generally crowded, and there have been reports of pickpocketing. It's been a few years since there has been a bus bombing.

FARES &
SCHEDULES
Daily buses link Ürümqi with Turpan (2½–3 hours) and Yining (1 day, with a stop at Sayram Lake). The return bus schedules for Yining are sporadic and unreliable.

Buses from Turpan go to Ürümqi (2½–3 hours) every 2 hours.
🚌 Bus Information **Turpan Bus Depot** ✉ 27 Laocheng Lu ☎ 0995/852-2325.

BUSINESS HOURS

BANKS & OFFICES
Government offices are open Monday through Saturday 9–noon and 4–8.

SHOPS
Uighur-run stores in Xinjiang generally operate on Xinjiang time, two hours ahead of Beijing.

CAR TRAVEL

Contact CITS in Ürümqi for round-trip car transportation to Yining and/or Sayram Lake (Y2,000 a day for two people to stop at both destinations).

DINING

MEALTIMES
Restaurants and Uighur-run stores in Xinjiang generally operate on local time. This means that meals are often served late; for instance, lunch is typically served from 1 to 3 Beijing time, and dinner starts at 7 Beijing time.

EMERGENCIES

🚔 Police **Ürümqi PSB** ✉ Guangmin Lu, just northeast of Renmin Sq.; ask hotel to phone PSB.
🏥 Hospitals **Chinese Medicine Hospital of Ürümqi** ✉ 60 Youhau Nan Lu, Ürümqi ☎ 0991/242-0963. **People's Hospital** ✉ 4 Gaochang Lu, Turpan ☎ 0995/852-2461.

INTERNET SERVICES

In Turpan, 168 Internet Bar opened by China Telecom has Internet access for Y12 an hour. The bar is next to the 168 Binguan hotel. Major hotels in Ürümqi usually have Internet access; for a lower rate, head to China Telecom, which charges Y3 per hour.
🌐 **China Telecom** ✉ 28 Huanghe Lu, Ürümqi ☎ 0991/231-2012. **168 Internet Bar** ✉ 32 Gaochang Lu, at Luzhou Lu, Turpan ☎ 0995/853-5044.

TIME

Airline, train and bus schedules, banks, offices, government departments, museums, and police stations run on Beijing time. Many local residents, however, set their watches by local time, one hour behind Beijing time. When you make appointments, make sure to establish the designated hour as local time or Beijing time.

TOURS

CITS can arrange multiday large group tours in Turpan following the ancient silk routes.

The Ürümqi CITS offers a range of pricey but interesting tours, including horseback riding by Sayram Lake, adventure trekking into the Taklamakan Desert and Kunlun Mountains, and a 25-day tour to find the buried ruins of the kingdom of Loulan, located near Lop Nor Lake.
🚌 Tour-Operator Recommendations **John's Information & Café** ✉ Seman Lu, opposite Seman Hotel ☎ 0998/282-4186. **New Century** ✉ 243 Seman Lu ☎🖷 0998/282-4500.

TRAIN TRAVEL

SCHEDULES Daily trains run between Ürümqi and Beijing (2 days), Shanghai (2¼ days), Chengdu (50 hours), Xian (1½ days), and Lanzhou (1 day). A train departs Ürümqi for Turpan (2 hours) twice a day, though the rail station for Turpan is inconveniently located 58 km (36 mi) south of the city at Daheyan (making the bus quicker and more convenient).

TRANSPORTATION AROUND XINJIANG

BY DONKEY CART On the outskirts of Turpan you can hire a donkey cart (Y2 per 1 km [½ mi]). This is a very informal process: if you see a donkey cart, just flag him down and jump on!

BY HIRED CAR In Ürümqi, CITS (⇨ Tours) can provide a car with driver at about Y200 per day for driving within the city. Trips outside the city can be arranged for higher fees.

BY TAXI The best way to get around Ürümqi and Turpan is by taxi (seat belts, though useful, tend to be very dusty and may leave marks on clothing). Ask your hotel desk attendant to write down your destination in Chinese for the driver, as well as the hotel's name for the return trip. For shorter distances, walking is fine, and the dry sunny weather is almost always conducive to a stroll.

The best way to see the sights, which lie scattered all around Turpan, is to rent a taxi for the whole day (Y250–Y500). As an alternative, you can take a daily bus (Y36) that visits all the sights, departing from the bus station at 9 and returning at 6.

VISITOR INFORMATION

🗐 Tourist Information **CITS** ⊠ Oasis Hotel, 41 Qingnian Bei Lu, 2nd fl., back entrance, Turpan ☎ 0995/852-3215 🖷 0995/852-3706 ⊠ Luyou Hotel, 51 Xinhua Bei Lu, 1st fl., Ürümqi ☎ 0991/282-1428 🖷 0991/281-0689 ⊕ www.xinjiangtour.com ⊠ 88 Xinhua Xi Lu, Yining ☎ 0999/804-3722.

SHANGHAI
THE HEAD OF THE DRAGON

5

Kristin Baird
Rattini

SHANGHAI, THE MOST NOTORIOUS OF CHINESE CITIES, once known as the Paris of the East, now calls itself the Pearl of the Orient. No other city can better capture the urgency and excitement of China's economic reform, understandably because Shanghai is at the center of it.

A port city, lying at the mouth of Asia's longest and most important river, Shanghai is famous as a place where internationalism has thrived. Opened to the world as a treaty port in 1842, Shanghai for decades was not one city but a divided territory. The British, French, and Americans each claimed their own concessions, neighborhoods where their laws and culture—rather than China's—were the rule.

By the 1920s and '30s, Shanghai was a place of sepia-lighted nightclubs, French villas, and opium dens. Here rich taipans walked the same streets as gamblers, prostitutes, and beggars, and Jews fleeing persecution in Russia lived alongside Chinese intellectuals and revolutionaries.

But now Shanghai draws more parallels to New York City than Paris. A true city, it is laid out on a grid (unlike sprawling Beijing), and with a population of 16 million, it is one of the world's most crowded urban areas. The Shanghainese have a reputation for being sharp, open-minded, glamorous, sophisticated, and business-oriented, and they're convinced they have the motivation and attitude to achieve their place as China's powerhouse. Far away from Beijing's watchful political eyes, yet supported by state officials who call Shanghai their hometown, the people have a freedom to grow that their counterparts in the capital don't enjoy. That ambition can be witnessed firsthand across Shanghai's Huangpu River, which joins the Yangzi at the northern outskirts of the city. Here lies Shanghai's most important building project—Pudong New Area, China's 21st-century financial, economic, and commercial center. Pudong, literally "the east side of the river," is home to Shanghai's stock market building, the tallest hotel in the world, the city's international airport, and the world's first commercial maglev (magnetic levitation) train. Rising from land that just a few years ago was dominated by farm fields is the city's pride and joy, the Oriental Pearl Tower—a gaudy, flashing, spaceshiplike pillar, the tallest in Asia. As Shanghai prepares to host the 2010 World Expo, Pudong is again immersed in a decade-long round of construction.

Puxi, the west side of the river and the city center, has also gone through staggering change. Charming old houses are making way for shiny high-rises. The population is moving from alley housing in the city center to spanking-new apartments in the suburbs. Architecturally spectacular museums and theaters are catching the world's attention. Malls are popping up on every corner. In 1987 there were about 150 high-rise buildings in the city. Today there are more than 3,000, and the number continues to grow. Shanghai is reputed to be home to one-fifth of all the world's construction cranes.

Shanghai's open policy has also made the city a magnet for foreign investors. As millions of dollars pour in, especially to Pudong, Shanghai has again become home to tens of thousands of expatriates. Foreign influence has made today's Shanghai a consumer heaven. Domestic stores rub shoulders with the boutiques of Louis Vuitton, Christian Dior, and Ralph

Numbers in the text correspond to numbers in the margin and on the Shanghai map.

If you have 3 days

Start with a trip to **Yu Garden** ① ⌐, sip some tea, and take a walk around the surrounding old Chinese city and its antiques markets. Afterward, work your way over to **the Bund** ④ for a leisurely stroll, take a quick look at the historic **Peace Hotel** ⑧, and walk down **Nanjing Lu** to experience Shanghai's busiest street. For dinner, the exceptional M on the Bund offers good views of the river and the Bund lit up at night.

The next day take a cab north to **Jade Buddha Temple** ⑳. Afterward, head back to Nanjing Lu if you didn't finish its sights the day before. Spend the afternoon people-watching at **People's Square** ⑪, taking in China's ancient treasures at **Shanghai Museum** ⑬, and swinging over to the nearby **Bird and Flower Market** ⑮.

Day 3 can be spent walking in the French Concession, particularly around Huaihai Lu, for a view of old Shanghai and the city's new chic stores. Here you can also tour **Sun Yat-sen's former residence** ㉓ and the **First Chinese Communist Party Congress site** ㉑ ⌐. The evenings of Days 2 and 3 can be spent catching a show of the Shanghai acrobats, relaxing on a night cruise of the Huangpu River, or experiencing Shanghai's happening nightlife.

If you have 5 days

Follow the three-day itinerary and on the fourth day make a trip to Pudong and go to the top of the **Oriental Pearl Tower** ㉝ or the spectacular **Jinmao Tower** ㉜—or both—for a bird's-eye view of the city. On Day 5 go to the Hongkou District to stroll around the old houses and **Ohel Moishe Synagogue and Huoshan Park** ㊳, and spend some time on **Duolun Lu** ㊱. Fill any spare time with visits to Shanghai's antiques markets, antique-furniture warehouses, and arts and crafts stores.

5

Lauren. Newly made businessmen battle rush-hour traffic in their Mercedes and Lexus cars. Young people keep the city up until the wee hours as they dance the night away in clubs blasting techno music. And everyone walks around with a cell phone. It's not surprising that the Shanghainese enjoy one of the highest living standards in China. Higher salaries and higher buildings, more business and more entertainment—they all define the fast-paced lives of China's most cosmopolitan and open people.

EXPLORING SHANGHAI

Shanghai as a whole encompasses a huge area. However, the city center is a relatively small district in Puxi (west of the river). On the east side lies what many think is Shanghai's future—Pudong (east of the river). Shanghai's main east–west roads are named for Chinese cities, while some north–south streets are named for Chinese provinces.

The city was once delineated by its foreign concessions, and to some extent, the former borders still define the city. The old Chinese city is now surrounded by the Zhonghua Lu–Renmin Lu circle. North of the city, the International Settlement—run by the British, Americans, Europeans, and Japanese—was the area between the Huangpu River and Huashan Lu, and bordered by Suzhou Creek to the north and Yanan Lu to the south. The former French Concession lies south of Yanan Lu, north of Zhaojiabang Lu. The southwest corner of the Concession lies at Xujiahui, from which point it runs all the way east to the Bund, with the exception of the northern half of the old Chinese city.

Although technically most Shanghainese consider the city center to be whatever lies within the Ring Road, the heart of the city is found on its chief east–west streets—Nanjing Lu, Huaihai Lu, and Yanan Lu—cut off in the west approximately at Wulumuqi Lu and in the east by the Bund. At one time, the closer you got to the Bund, the stronger the heartbeat became, but with the city's constant construction, demographics are also changing, and the heart of Shanghai seems to beat ever outward.

To the east and west of city center lie Shanghai's new development areas. In Hongqiao, the area outside the Ring Road to the west, are office and commercial buildings for foreign and domestic business and the residential area of Gubei. Rising from countryside across the Huangpu River to the east is Pudong, the new concrete behemoth that Deng Xiaoping designated as China's future financial, economic, and commercial center. It's quickly fulfilling its destiny.

Shanghai is very much a walking city, so parts of it are easily explored on foot, and taxis are readily available. In compact central Shanghai, cab rides would be short if not for the outrageous traffic. Water towns outside Shanghai offer getaways from the city's urban chaos, and with ever-improving roads and public transportation, day trips to Suzhou, Zhouzhuang, and Hangzhou are possible.

The Old City & the Bund

When Shanghai was carved up by foreign powers, one part of the central city remained under Chinese law and administration. These old winding back alleys eventually became notorious as a gangster- and opium-filled slum. Today the narrow meandering lanes and a dwindling number of tiny pre-1949 houses are still standing (though the vices have disappeared for the most part). A walk through the Old City gives an idea of how most Shanghainese once lived and many still do. The city's most important sightseeing spot, the Bund, on Shanghai's waterfront, has outstanding foreign buildings from pre-1949 times.

a good walk

Start at **Yu Garden** ❶ ▐▔. Stroll through the garden, check out the bazaar surrounding it, and stop at the teahouse for a serene rest. Just outside the bazaar, meander through the **Cang Bao Antiques Building** ❷ on Fangbang Lu. You can also wander the small alleys of the Old City, which lies inside the Renmin Lu–Zhonghua Lu circle. Within these alleys is a bustle of activity. Follow Dajing Lu west from Henan Lu and you can watch how locals shop for groceries at a wet market. A bit farther, south-

Raiders of the Lost Architecture

Shanghai's history is eclectic, and so is its architecture. Although significant portions of the city are making way for skyscrapers, some of what has defined its original charm still exists. From the neoclassicism of the Bund to the art deco of the French Concession to the quaint Chinese alleys of the old city, a walk through town can evoke memories of romantic old Shanghai. But hurry: as you read this, old buildings are being torn down. The high points, literally, of new architecture are the skyscraping Jinmao Tower and Oriental Pearl Tower in Pudong, both of which have opened sky-high observatories.

Shoppers' Port of Call

Because of Shanghai's commercial status as China's most open port city, it has the widest variety of goods to be found in the nation after Hong Kong. Ritzy chrome shopping malls stand alongside dingy state-run stores and around the corner from local markets, inundating the consumer with both foreign name brands and domestic goods. Take some time to browse the curio stands and stores around Yu Garden and to do some window-shopping on Nanjing Xi Lu, China's premier shopping street for designer and luxury goods.

---

west of the intersection of Dajing Lu and Xizang Lu, lies **Dongtai Lu Antiques Market** ❸, several blocks lined with antique vendors' stalls.

From the Old City, you can take a taxi or walk east along Jinling Lu to **the Bund** ❹, which begins along the river. A raised concrete promenade borders the side of the street nearest the river. At the intersection of Zhongshan Dong Lu and Jinling Lu, marked by a pedestrian overpass, you'll see the observation tower that houses the **Bund Museum** ❺. If you're feeling adventurous, you can jump on a ferry boat and start a tour of Pudong here. The Huangpu River Cruises dock is also nearby. Or walk north and mingle with the crowds of strolling families, lovers walking hand in hand, and camera-snapping tourists.

If you continue walking north, historic buildings begin appearing on the west side of the street facing the river. Just north of Yanan Dong Lu, in the former Union Assurance Company Building, is the high-profile **Three On The Bund** ❻, a dining, shopping, and art complex. Farther along is the **Former Hongkong and Shanghai Bank Building** ❼. At Shanghai's main thoroughfare, Nanjing Lu, you'll see one of the city's most famous monuments: the **Peace Hotel** ❽ consists of the two buildings on the corner of the Bund and Nanjing Lu. Just north of the Peace Hotel is the **Bank of China** ❾, the main bank in the city.

Across the street on the river at the junction of the Bund and Beijing Dong Lu lies the **Bund History Museum** ❿. Across the old Waibaidu Bridge on Suzhou Creek there are more pre-1949 buildings: the art deco Shanghai Dasha (Shanghai Mansions, now called Broadway Mansions)

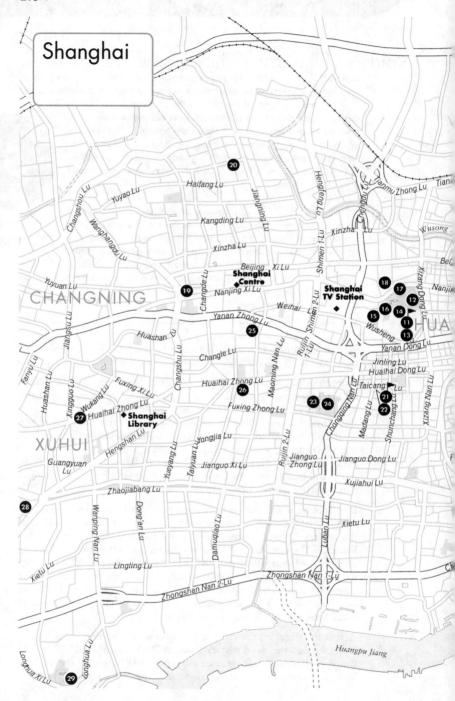

Shanghai

KEY

36 37

▶ Start of walk

is in front of you to the left, and the former Shanghai Stock Exchange and the Russian Consulate are to the right. All these old buildings face the modern skyline of Pudong, which lies on the other side of the river, with the **Oriental Pearl Tower** and the **Jinmao Tower** rising above the water. The Bund provides a good vantage point for viewing both pre-revolutionary and postopening Shanghai.

TIMING It can take about two hours to stroll casually without stopping at any sights. Allow another two hours to wander through the Yu Garden, bazaar, and teahouse, which are almost always crowded, and especially so on weekends. Plan on another hour if you go to Dajing Ge and the Dong-tai Lu antique market. Access to many of the Bund's old buildings is not allowed, but if you go inside the ones that are open to visitors, you should allow 15 minutes per building. Note that the Bund gets crowded on weekends, but isn't too bad on weekdays. For a cruise on the Huangpu River, count on one to three hours.

On National Day (October 1) and Labor Day (May 1), the Bund is closed to bicycle and automobile traffic, and the roads are choked with people. On those days a fireworks show is usually put on over the water.

What to See

9 Bank of China (Zhongguo Yinhang). Here, old Shanghai's Western architecture (British art deco in this case) mixes with Chinese elements. In 1937 it was designed to be the highest building in the city and surpassed the neighboring Cathay Hotel (now the Peace Hotel) by a hair, except for the green tower on the Cathay's roof. ✉ *23 The Bund (Zhongshan Dong Yi Lu), Huangpu District* ☎ *021/6329–1979.*

4 The Bund (Waitan). Shanghai's waterfront boulevard best shows both the city's pre-1949 past and its focus on the future. The district's name is derived from the Anglo-Indian and literally means "muddy embankment." In the early 1920s the Bund became the city's foreign street: Americans, British, Japanese, French, Russians, Germans, and other Europeans built banks, trading houses, clubs, consulates, and hotels in styles from neoclassical to art deco. As Shanghai grew to be a bustling trading center in the Yangzi Delta, the Bund's warehouses and ports became the heart of the action. With the Communist victory, the foreigners left Shanghai, and the Chinese government moved its own banks and offices here.

Fodors Choice
★

Today the municipal government has renovated the old buildings of this most foreign face of the city, highlighting them as tourist attractions, and even tried for a while to sell them back to the very owners it forced out after 1949.

On the riverfront side of the Bund, Shanghai's street life is in full force. The city rebuilt the promenade, making it an ideal gathering place for both tourists and residents. In the mornings just after dawn, the Bund is full of people ballroom dancing, doing aerobics, and practicing kung fu, *qi gong,* and tai chi. The rest of the day people walk the embankment, snapping photos of the Oriental Pearl Tower, the Huangpu River, and each other. Be prepared for the aggressive souvenir hawkers; while you can't completely avoid them, try ignoring them or telling them *"bu yao,"* which means "Don't want." In the evenings lovers come out for romantic walks amid the floodlit buildings and tower. ⊠ *5 blocks of Zhongshan Dong Yi Lu between Jinling Lu and Suzhou Creek, Huangpu District.*

⑩ Bund History Museum (Waitan Chenlieshi). The photo gallery here chronicles the role of the Bund in Shanghai's history: as an architectural showcase, as a commercial hub, and as a stage for the political upheaval of the 1920s to the '40s. ⊠ *1 Zhongshan Dongyi Lu, Huangpu District* ☎ *021/6321–6542* ⊠ *Free* ☉ *Daily 10 AM–2 AM.*

❺ Bund Museum (Waitan Bowuguan). The white and red observation tower has held watch over the weather and the Huangpu River since 1884. The base, now home to this tiny museum, was built 19 years earlier. Photos along the walls present a round-up of the Bund's most famous buildings, both past and present. ⊠ *Unit A, 1 Zhongshan Er Lu (The Bund), Huangpu District* ☎ *No phone* ⊠ *Free* ☉ *Daily 9–5.*

❷ Cang Bao Antiques Building (Cang Bao Lou). This market, formerly on Fuyou Lu, occupies the four-story Cang Bao Antiques Building, a warehouse just west of Yu Garden. During the week, you can browse permanent booths selling everything from Mao paraphernalia to crossbows to real and fake porcelain. (It's difficult to distinguish the two; real porcelain will appear transparent when held against a light.) On Sunday, the action begins before sunrise, a time when, according to a popular saying, only ghosts should be awake—hence the market's nickname of the Ghost Market. Hawkers from the provinces arrive early to display their goods on the sidewalk or inside on the fourth floor. Ivory, jade, and wood carvings are among the many goods sold here, at prices that are always negotiable. ⊠ *457 Fangbang Zhong Lu, Huangpu District* ☉ *Weekdays 9–6, weekends 5 AM–6 PM.*

❸ Dongtai Lu Antiques Market (Dongtai Lu Gudai Chang). A few blocks west of the Old City, antiques dealers' stalls line the street. You'll find porcelain, Victrolas, jade, and anything else worth hawking or buying. The same bowls and vases pop up in multiple stalls, so if your first bargaining attempt isn't successful, you'll likely have another opportunity a few stores down. Prices have shot up over the years, and fakes abound, so be careful what you buy. ⊠ *Off Xizang Lu, Huangpu District* ☉ *Daily 9–dusk.*

FodorśChoice
★

❼ Former Hongkong and Shanghai Bank Building (Pudong Fazhan Yinhang). One of the Bund's most impressive buildings—some say it's the area's pièce de résistance—the domed structure was built by the British in 1921–23, when it was the second-largest bank building in the world. After 1949 the building was turned into Communist Party offices and City Hall; now it is used by the Pudong Development Bank. In 1997 the bank made the news when it uncovered a beautiful 1920s Italian-tile mosaic in the building's dome. In the 1950s the mosaic was deemed too extravagant for a Communist government office, so it was covered by white paint, which, ironically, protected it from being found by the Red Guards during the Cultural Revolution. It was then forgotten until the Pudong Development Bank renovated the building. If you walk into the bank, look up, and you'll see the circular mosaic in the dome—an outer circle painted with scenes of the cities where the Hongkong & Shanghai Bank had branches at the time: London, Paris, New York, Bangkok, Tokyo, Calcutta, Hong Kong, and Shanghai; a middle circle made up of the 12 signs of the zodiac; and the center painted with a large sun and Ceres, the Roman goddess of abundance. ⌧ *12 The Bund (Zhongshan Dong Yi Lu), Huangpu District* ☎ *021/6329–6188* ▧ *Free* ☉ *Daily 9–6.*

❽ Peace Hotel (Heping Fandian). This hotel at the corner of the Bund and Nanjing Lu is among Shanghai's most treasured old buildings. If any establishment will give you a sense of Shanghai's past, it's this one. Its high ceilings, ornate woodwork, and art deco fixtures are still intact, and the ballroom evokes old Shanghai cabarets and gala parties.

FodorśChoice
★

The south building was formerly the Palace Hotel. Built in 1906, it is the oldest building on the Bund. The north building, formerly the Cathay Hotel, built in 1929, is more famous historically. It was known as the private playroom of its owner, Victor Sassoon, a wealthy landowner who invested in the opium trade. The Cathay was actually part of a complete office and hotel structure collectively called Sassoon House. Victor Sassoon himself lived and entertained his guests in the green penthouse. The hotel was rated on a par with the likes of Raffles in Singapore and The Peninsula in Hong Kong. It was *the* place to stay in old Shanghai; Noel Coward wrote *Private Lives* here. In the evenings, the famous Peace Hotel Old Jazz Band plays in the German-style pub on the first floor. ⌧ *20 Nanjing Dong Lu, Huangpu District* ☎ *021/6321–6888* ⊕ *www.shanghaipeacehotel.com.*

> **need a break?**
>
> **The Peace Hotel's Shanghai Night Bar** offers a memorable view by taking the hotel's middle elevators to the top floor of the north building and then climb the last two flights of stairs to the roof. There's an outdoor bar and café, from which you can see Sassoon's former penthouse and the action on the streets and river below. There is a Y50 admission charge (not always imposed), but it includes a soft drink or tea.

❻ Three On The Bund (Waitan San Hao). The renovation of this stunning, seven-story, post-Renaissance-style building has garnered more headlines than any other building project on the Bund. Built in 1916 as the Union Assurance Company Building, it was the first in China to use a structural steel frame. It was given a second life in the hands of famed architect Michael Graves, who, between 2002 and 2004, transformed the 140,000 square feet of space into Three On The Bund, an upscale dining, shopping, spa, and art complex. ⌧ *3 The Bund (Zhongshan Dong Yi Lu), Huangpu District* ☎ *021/6323–3355* ⊕ *www.threeonthebund.com.*

▶ ❶ Yu Garden (Yuyuan). Since the 18th century, this complex, with its traditional red walls and upturned tile roofs, has been a marketplace and social center where local residents gather, shop, and practice *qi gong* in the evenings. Although not as impressive as the ancient palace gardens of Beijing and accused of being overly touristed, Yu Garden is a piece of Shanghai's past, one of the few old sights left in the city.

FodorśChoice
★

Surrounding the garden is a touristy bazaar of stores that sell traditional Chinese arts and crafts, medicine, and souvenirs. Over the past few years, the bazaar has become more of a mall, with chain stores replacing many mom-and-pop stalls, and Western fast food outlets—McDonald's, KFC, Subway—popping up alongside noodle shops. A basement antiques market with somewhat inflated prices is in the Huabao Building.

At the southeast end of the bazaar lies the **Chenghuang Miao** (Temple of the City God). The temple was built during the early part of the Ming Dynasty but was later destroyed. In 1926 the main hall was rebuilt and has been renovated many times over the years. Inside are gleaming gold figures, and atop the roof you'll see statues of crusading warriors, flags raised, arrows drawn.

To get to the garden itself, you must wind your way through the bazaar. The ticket booth is just north of the lake and the pleasant **Huxingting Chashi** (teahouse). The garden was commissioned by the Ming Dynasty official Pan Yunduan in 1559 and built by the renowned architect, Zhang Nanyang, over 19 years. When it was finally finished it won international praise as "the best garden in southeastern China," an accolade that would be hard to defend today, especially when compared with the beautiful gardens of Suzhou. In the mid-1800s the Society of Small Swords used the garden as a gathering place for meetings. It was here that they planned their uprising with the Taiping rebels against the French colonialists. The French destroyed the garden during the first Opium War, but the area was later rebuilt and renovated.

Winding walkways and corridors bring you over stone bridges and carp-filled ponds and through bamboo stands and rock gardens. Within the park are an **old opera stage,** a **museum** dedicated to the Society of Small Swords rebellion, and an **exhibition hall,** opened in 2003, of Chinese calligraphy and paintings. One caveat: the park is almost always thronged with Chinese tour groups, especially on weekends. As with most sights in Shanghai, don't expect a tranquil time alone. ⊠ *218 Anren Lu, Bordered by Fuyou Lu, Jiujiaochang Lu, Fangbang Lu, and Anren Lu, Huangpu District ☎ 021/6326–0830 or 021/6328–3251 ▧ Garden, Y30; Temple, Y5 ☉ Gardens, daily 8:30–5; Temple, 8:30–4:30.*

need a break?

The **Midlake Pavilion Teahouse** (Huxingting Chashi; ⊠ 257 Yuyuan Lu, Huangpu District ☎ 021/6373–6950 downstairs, 021/6355–8270 upstairs), Shanghai's oldest, opened in 1856 and stands on a small man-made lake in the middle of the Yu Garden and Bazaar, at the center of the Bridge of the Nine Turnings. Although tea is cheaper on the first floor, be sure to sit on the top floor by a window overlooking the lake. Upstairs, a bottomless cup of tea comes with Chinese snacks. Every night from 8:30 PM to 10 PM a traditional tea ceremony is performed. An ensemble with *erhu, pipa,* and other traditional instruments performs Monday from 2 to 5 PM and Friday through Sunday from 6:30 to 9 PM.

On the west side of the central man-made lake in Yu Garden is **Nanxiang Steamed Bun Restaurant** (✉ 85 Yuyuan Lu, Huangpu District ☎ 021/6355–4206), a great dumpling house famed for its *xiao long bao* (steamed pork dumplings). You'll spot it by the long line of people outside, but you can shorten your wait by heading to the upstairs dining room.

Nanjing Lu & the City Center

The city's *zhongxin*, or center, is primarily in the Huangpu and Jing'an districts. These two areas make up most of what was known in imperial and republican times as the International Settlement. Nanjing Lu, Shanghai's main thoroughfare, crosses east–west through these two districts. You can spot it at night by its neon extravaganza and in daytime by the sheer volume of business going on. Hordes of pedestrians compete with bicycles and one another, and cars move at a snail's pace in traffic jams.

a good walk

The following long walk can also become a series of cab rides. Go west on the shopping street Nanjing Lu from the Heping Fandian, meandering among the crowds and stores. The first blocks of Nanjing Dong Lu are shorter and still have some of Old Shanghai's architecture. On the blocks north and south of the street you can also sense the atmosphere of the place in the 1920s. The portion of Nanjing Lu between Henan Lu and Xizang Lu is a pedestrian walkway, so no need to worry about the road's infamous traffic here, just the throngs of Chinese tourists. For Y2, you can take a tram ride along the walkway. At the start of Nanjing Xi Lu, turn left (south) on Xizang Lu, and in a block you'll arrive at the city's huge social and cultural center, **People's Square** ⑪ ▶. At this former dog track–turned–public square you'll find the **Shanghai Urban Planning Exhibition Center** ⑫, the wonderful **Shanghai Museum** ⑬, and the impressive **Grand Theater** ⑭.

On their western side, the Grand Theater and People's Square are bordered by Huangpi Bei Lu. Turn right (north) on Huangpi Bei Lu, past the **Bird and Flower Market** ⑮, and to your right will be the **Shanghai Art Museum** ⑯, at the corner of Nanjing Lu. Adjacent the museum is the west gate of **People's Park** ⑰, Shanghai's largest and most important, though not necessarily the nicest. Opposite the park, on the north side of Nanjing Xi Lu, is the historic **Park Hotel** ⑱.

Continue west on Nanjing Lu. Once you pass Chengdu Lu, the street of the overhead Ring Road, the Shanghai Television Station and Broadcasting Building is on the left, with a very large TV screen in front. About a mile down, after the intersection of Xikang Lu, and two blocks west on Nanjing Lu, on the corner of Huashan Lu, is the **Jingan Temple** ⑲. From here or from the Shanghai Center, jump into a cab to the important **Jade Buddha Temple** ⑳, which lies several blocks north of Nanjing Lu.

TIMING   The above walk is fairly long and doesn't have to be done all at once. You can hop a cab between sights, which is especially recommended for the trip to Jade Buddha Temple. The distance from the Bund to Jing'an

Temple is about 4 km (2½ mi). The whole walk without stopping will probably take you 1½ to 2 hours. The Shanghai Museum is worth at least three hours of your time, and you may want to return another day. If you go to the Jing'an Temple, the Bird and Flower Market, or Jade Buddha Temple, block off half an hour for each of these sights. The rest you can walk through or by very quickly.

Nanjing Lu and the People's Square are both most crowded and most exciting on weekends. You may have to fight the hordes, but you'll get a good idea of what life is like in Shanghai.

What to See

⑮ Bird and Flower Market (Hua Niao Shichang). Just a block off the tourist track of Nanjing Road, winding Jiangyin Lu gives you a good slice of Shanghai life. A fair number of vendors decamped to the Xizang Nan Lu market as the neighboring JW Marriott was built. But the street is still home to hawkers selling fish and birds, orchids, and bonsai trees. You can see women airing out their bed linens on sunny days and students racing out the iron gate of a school building with traditional up-turned eaves. ⊠ *Jiangyin Lu, off Huangpi Bei Lu between Nanjing Lu and Weihai Lu, Huangpu District* ⊙ *Daily 9–dusk.*

⑭ Grand Theater (Da Ju Yuan). The spectacular front wall of glass shines as brightly as the star power within this magnificent theater. Its three stages host the best domestic and international performances, including the debut of *Les Miserables* in China in 2002 and *Cats* in 2003. The dramatic curved roof atop a square base is meant to invoke the Chinese traditional saying, "the earth is square and the sky is round." See it at night. ⊠ *190 Huangpi Bei Lu, Huangpu District* 🕾 *021/6318–4478* 🎫 *Tour, Y40* ⊙ *Tours daily 9–11 and 1–4, depending on performance schedule.*

⑳ Jade Buddha Temple (Yufo Si). Completed in 1918, this temple is fairly new by Chinese standards. During the Cultural Revolution, in order to save the temple when the Red Guards came to destroy it, the monks pasted portraits of Mao Zedong on the outside walls so the Guards couldn't tear them down without destroying Mao's face as well. The temple is built in the style of the Song Dynasty, with symmetrical halls and courtyards, up-turned eaves, and bright yellow walls. The temple's great treasure is its 6½-foot-high, 455-pound seated Buddha made of white jade with a robe of precious gems, originally brought to Shanghai from Burma. Other Buddhas, statues, and frightening guardian gods of the temple populate the halls, as well as a collection of Buddhist scriptures and paintings. The 100 monks who live and work here can sometimes be seen worshiping. There's a vegetarian restaurant on the temple grounds. ⊠ *170 Anyuan Lu, Putuo District* 🕾 *021/6266–3668* 🎫 *Y10* ⊙ *Daily 8–4:30.*

Fodor's Choice ★

⑲ Jingan Temple (Jingan Si). Originally built about AD 300, the Jingan Temple has been rebuilt and renovated numerous times, including at present. The sound of power tools often drowns out the monks' chanting. The temple's Southern-style halls, which face a central courtyard, gleam with new wood carvings of elephants and lotus flowers, but the hall interiors have stark, new concrete walls and feel generally antiseptic. The temple's main draw is its copper Hongwu bell, cast in 1183 and weighing in at 3.5 tons. ✉ *1686 Nanjing Xi Lu, next to the Jingan Si subway entrance, Jing'an District* ☎ *021/6256–6366* ✉ *Y5* ☉ *Daily 7:30–5.*

⑱ Park Hotel (Guoji Fandian). This art deco structure overlooking People's Park was originally the tallest hotel in Shanghai. Completed in 1934, it had luxury rooms, a nightclub, and chic restaurants. Today it's more subdued, with the lobby the most vivid reminder of its glorious past. ✉ *170 Nanjing Xi Lu, Huangpu District* ☎ *021/6327–5225.*

⑰ People's Park (Renmin Gongyuan). In colonial days, this park was the northern half of the city's racetrack. Today the 30 acres of flower beds, lotus ponds, and trees, plus a small amusement park (which is rarely open), are crisscrossed by a large number of paved paths. The park is widely known for its English corner, where locals gather to practice their language skills. ✉ *231 Nanjing Xi Lu, Huangpu District* ☎ *021/6327–1333* ✉ *Y2* ☉ *Daily 6–6.*

★ ▶ **⑪ People's Square** (Renmin Guang Chang). Shanghai's main square, once the southern half of the city's racetrack, has become a social and cultural center. The Shanghai Museum, Municipal Offices, Grand Theater, and Urban Planning Exhibition Center surround it. During the day, visitors and residents stroll, fly kites, and take their children to feed the pigeons. In the evening, kids roller-skate, ballroom dancers hold group lessons, and families relax together. Weekends here are especially busy. ✤ *Bordered by Weihai Lu on south, Xizang Lu on east, Huangpi Bei Lu on west, and Fuzhou Lu on north.*

⑯ Shanghai Art Museum (Shanghai Meishu Guan). At the northwest corner of People's Park, the former site of the Shanghai Library was once a clubhouse for old Shanghai's sports groups, including the Shanghai Race Club. The building is now the home of the state-run Shanghai Art Museum. Its permanent collection includes paintings, calligraphy, and sculpture, but its rotating exhibitions have favored modern artwork. There's a museum store, café, and a rooftop restaurant. ✉ *325 Nanjing Xi Lu (at Huangpi Bei Lu), Huangpu District* ☎ *021/6327–2829* 🖷 *021/6327–2425* ✉ *Varies, depending on exhibition* ☉ *Daily 9–5.*

⑬ Shanghai Museum (Shanghai Bowuguan). Truly one of Shanghai's treasures, this museum has the country's premier collection of relics and artifacts. Eleven state-of-the-art galleries exhibit Chinese artistry in all its forms: paintings, bronzes, sculpture, ceramics, calligraphy, jade, Ming and Qing Dynasty furniture, coins, seals, and art by indigenous populations. Its bronze collection is among the best in the world, and its gallery of minority dress showcases intricate handiwork from several of China's 52 minority groups. If you opt not to rent the excellent acoustic guide, information is well presented in English. You can relax in the museum's pleasant tearoom or buy postcards, crafts, and reproductions of the artwork in the stellar bookshop. Students are admitted to the museum for free on Saturday from 5 to 7 PM. ✉ *201 Renmin Da Dao, Huangpu District* ☎ *021/6372–3500* ⊕ *www.shanghaimuseum.net* ✉ *Y20, Y60 with acoustic guide* ☉ *Sun.–Fri. 9–5, Sat. 9–8, last ticket sold one hour before closing.*

Fodor'sChoice ★

⑫ **Shanghai Urban Planning Exhibition Center** (Shanghai Chengshi Guihua Zhanianguan). To understand the true scale of Shanghai and its ongoing building boom, visit the Master Plan Hall of this museum. Sprawled out on the third floor is a 6,400-square-foot planning model of Shanghai—the largest model of its kind in the world—showing the metropolis as city planners expect it to look in 2020. You'll find familiar existing landmarks like the Pearl Tower and Shanghai Center as well as future sites like the so-called Flower Bridge, an esplanade over the Huangpu River to be built for Expo 2010. ⊠ *100 Renmin Dadao, Huangpu District* ☎ *021/6372–2077* 🎫 *Y25* ⊙ *Mon.–Thurs. 9–5, Fri.–Sun. 9–6, last ticket sold 1 hr before closing.*

need a break? A hip café below street level in CITIC Square, **Wagas** (⊠ 1168 Nanjing Xi Lu, Jing'an District ☎ 021/5292–5228), has a menu for all your moods. Illy espresso, fruit juices, and smoothies, freshly made soups, sandwiches, salads, and quiches are all reasonably priced. Enjoy exhaust-fume-free alfresco dining or grab a table inside.

The Old French Concession

The former French Concession is in the Luwan and Xuhui districts. Once populated primarily by White Russians, the area is today a charming historic district known for its atmosphere and beautiful old architecture, as well as its shopping, and bars and cafés. Most of the action centers on the main east–west thoroughfare, the tree-lined Huaihai Lu, a relaxed, upscale, international shopping street. Many of the old consulates and French buildings still line it.

a good walk You can start your walk at the **First Chinese Communist Party Congress Site** ㉑ ▶, on Xingye Lu and Huangpi Lu. Once you exit, you're already at **Xintiandi** ㉒, a restaurant and shopping complex that's given a second life to an area of traditional Shikumen houses. The **Wulixiang Shikumen Museum** shows you what the houses were like in days long before Starbucks became one of the tenants. From here take a cab or walk 15 to 20 minutes to **Sun Yat-sen's Former Residence** ㉓. If you walk, go south on Huangpi Lu until you reach Fuxing Lu, where you turn right. On the corner of Chongqing Nan Lu and Fuxing Lu is **Fuxing Park** ㉔. Across the way, on the southeast corner of the intersection, is a beautiful old arrowhead-shape apartment building that was once American journalist and Communist sympathizer Agnes Smedley's residence. If you continue west on Fuxing Lu, turn right at the first corner (Sinan Lu); Sun Yat-sen's Former Residence is just ahead on your right, at Xiangshan Lu. From here, head north on Sinan Lu. At Huaihai Lu, the main street of the old French Concession, take a left. This middle stretch of the shopping street Huaihai Zhong Lu is the heart of the Concession. State-run and foreign shops, boutiques, and department stores dominate the area.

Continue down a couple of blocks on Huaihai and turn right on Maoming Lu at the old Cathay Cinema. At the intersection with Changle Lu stand the historic Jinjiang and Garden hotels. On the northeast corner is the old Lyceum Theatre. If you're really into looking at old architecture, you can walk one block west and one block north to the corner of Shaanxi Nan Lu and Julu Lu. Here, you can view and stroll around the grounds of the dollhouselike **Heng Shan Moller Villa** ㉕. Another out-of-the-way old villa complex lies farther south on Maoming Lu, at what is now the Ruijin Hotel.

Back at Huaihai Lu and Maoming Nan Lu, continue west. As you pass Shaanxi Nan Lu, you'll enter the fray surrounding **Xiangyang Market** ㉖ and be inundated with hawkers asking you "DVD? CD? Bag? Watch?" A block past the market, turn left on Fenyang Lu. If you return to Huaihai Lu and continue westward, the shopping district will give way to the consulate area. You can end your walk anywhere between Fenyang Lu and Wulumuqi Lu. If you decide to continue walking, eventually you'll pass the Shanghai Library, on your left (south) side past Wulumuqi Lu. Farther down the street at the corner of Xingguo Lu is **Soong Chingling's Former Residence** ㉗. You can take a cab here.

Besides walking down Huaihai Lu, an excellent way of seeing the French part of town is to hop on Bus No. 911, a double-decker bus that runs up and down the thoroughfare. If you sit on the upper level, you can sneak a good view of the old homes that are otherwise hidden by compound walls.

Farther away in Xuhui District is the **Xujiahui Cathedral** ㉘. From Huaihai Lu, go south on Hengshan Lu, which will end in Xujiahui. The church is on the west side of Caoxi Bei Lu. You'll need to take a taxi to **Longhua Temple** ㉙ to end your tour.

TIMING   Huaihai Lu, like Shanghai's other main thoroughfares, is most crowded on the weekends, when hordes of shoppers enjoy their weekly outings. Allow yourself at least two hours just to walk the above itinerary without stopping at any shops or taking a look around at the old houses. Allow about a half hour to an hour for each of the more major sights, such as Sun Yat-sen's former residence, Soong Chingling's former residence, and the site of the First National Party Congress. You can walk through some of the historic buildings, while others involve only a short look from the outside.

What to See

need a break?   As implied by the name **1931** (✉ 112 Maoming Nan Lu, Luwan District ☎ 021/6472–5264), this café exudes an Old Shanghai atmosphere, down to the cute little tables, working Victrola, and the waitstaff clad in *qipao* (traditional Chinese dresses). The café serves simple drinks, coffee, and tea, and excellent home-style Shanghai cooking, with some Japanese selections, too.

One of the premier estates of old Shanghai, the **Morriss Estate** (✉ 118 Ruijin Er Lu, Luwan District), now the Ruijin Hotel, was built by a Western newspaper magnate. Today the estate's three huge houses, standing among green lawns and trees, have also become home to such exceptional foreign restaurants as Lan Na Thai and

Hazara. They share the north mansion with **Face**, one of Shanghai's most popular bars. Stop in here for a drink or Thai appetizer, or sip a cup of tea in the **View Cafe Bar** overlooking the main mansion's south lawn. Stroll around the estate to view its ornate details, such as a stained-glass scene in Old House No. 3 that shows a tiger crouched beside a tropical stream.

▶ ㉑ **First Chinese Communist Party Congress Site** (Zhonggong Yidahuizhi; short for Zhongguo Gongchangdang Di Yi Ci Quanguo Daibiao Dahui Huizhi Jinian Guan). The secret meeting on July 31, 1921, that marked the first National Congress was held at the Bo Wen Girls' School, where 13 delegates from Marxist, communist, and socialist groups gathered from around the country. Today, ironically, the site is surrounded by Xintiandi, Shanghai's center of conspicuous consumption. The upstairs of this restored shikumen is a well-curated museum explaining the rise of communism in China. Downstairs lies the very room where the first delegates worked. It remains frozen in time, the table set with matches and tea cups. ⊠ *374 Huangpi Nan Lu* ☎ *021/5382–2171* 💴 *Y3* ☉ *Daily 9–5, last ticket sold at 4.*

㉔ **Fuxing Park** (Fuxing Gongyuan). The grounds of this European-style park—known as French Park before 1949—provide a bit of greenery in crowded Shanghai. Here you'll find people practicing tai chi and lovers strolling hand in hand. ⊠ *2 Gaolan Lu, Luwan District* ☎ *021/ 6372–0662* 💴 *Y2* ☉ *Daily 6–6.*

need a break?
One example of Shanghai's cultural resurgence is the **Yandan Lu Pedestrian Street** (✛ Yandan Lu between Huaihai Zhong Lu and Nanchang Lu). Luwan District heads repaved one block of Yandan Lu with tile, lined it with classic lampposts, threw out all the traffic and run-down stores, and replaced them with pedestrians and quaint cafés.

㉕ **Heng Shan Moller Villa** (Heng Shan Ma Le Bie Shu Fandian). With its colorful details, gingerbread–like brickwork, and pointy roof, this Shanghai mansion is part dollhouse, part castle. British businessman Eric Moller built the Norwegian–style house to resemble a castle his daughter once envisioned in a dream. Construction took 10 years and was completed in 1936. The family fled the invading Japanese in 1941, and after 1949 the house served as the Communist Youth League's headquarters. It's now a boutique hotel. Check out the lobby's ornately carved ceilings and stairwells and vast landscape painting, or rest in the Bonomi Café in the house's south garden. ⊠ *30 Shaanxi Nan Lu, just north of Julu Lu, Xuhui District* ☎ *021/6247–8881* ⊕ *www.mollervilla.com.*

need a break?
The Promenade (⊠ 4 Hengshan Lu) lies across from the small ivy-covered International Cathedral and is part of the popular bar and restaurant stretch of Hengshan Road. There are several Western and Asian restaurants as well as a coffee house and, if you're in need of a trim, a hair salon favored by expats.

★ ㉙ **Longhua Temple** (Longhua Si). Shanghai's largest and most active temple has as its centerpiece a seven-story, eight-sided pagoda. Although the temple is thought to have been built in the 3rd century, the pagoda dates from the 10th century; it's not open to visitors. Near the front entrance of the temple stands a three-story bell tower, where a 3.3-ton bronze bell is rung at midnight every New Year's Eve. Along the side corridors of the temple you'll find the Longhua Hotel, a vegetarian restaurant, and a room filled seven rows deep with small golden statues. The third hall is the most impressive. Its three giant Buddhas sit beneath a swirled red and gold dome. The monks gather here each day from 8 to 11 AM and from 1 to 3 PM to pray for the souls of the deceased, whose photos top the altar. You can watch this moving ceremony from the sidelines. ✉ *2853 Longhua Lu, Xuhui District* ☎ *021/6456–6085 or 021/ 6457–6327* ✍ *Y5* ⊘ *Daily 7–4:30.*

㉗ **Soong Chingling's Former Residence** (Song Qingling Guju). While she first came to national attention as the wife of Dr. Sun Yat-sen, Soong Chingling became revered in her own right for her dedication to the Communist party. Indeed, many mainland Chinese regard her as the "Mother of China." (On the other hand, Soong's sister, Meiling, married Chiang Kai-shek, who was the head of the Nationalist government from 1927 to 1949, at which point the couple fled to Taiwan.) This three-story house, built in 1920 by a German ship owner, was Soong's primary residence from 1948 to 1963. It has been preserved as it was during her lifetime: her 4,000 books in the study, furniture in the bedroom that her parents gave as her dowry. The small museum next door has some nice displays from Soong Chingling and Sun Yat-sen's life, including wedding pictures from their 1915 wedding in Tokyo. ✉ *1843 Huaihai Zhong Lu, Xuhui District* ☎ *021/6431–4965* ✍ *Y8* ⊘ *Daily 9–4:30.*

㉓ **Sun Yat-sen's Former Residence** (Sun Zhongshan Guju). Dr. Sun Yat-sen, the father of the Chinese republic, lived in this two-story house for six years, from 1919 to 1924. His wife, Soong Chingling, continued to live here after his death until 1937. Today it's been turned into a museum, and you can tour the grounds. ✉ *7 Xiangshan Lu, Luwan District* ☎ *021/ 6437–2954* ✍ *Y8* ⊘ *Daily 9–4:30.*

off the beaten path

OLD CHINA HAND READING ROOM – To learn more about all the beautiful architecture you're seeing in Shanghai, have a cup of coffee at the Old China Hand Reading Room. Part library, part bookstore, part café, it's the brainchild of Shanghainese photographer Erh Dongqiang (also known as Deke Erh), who has partnered with author Tess Johnston on a series of coffee-table books about Shanghai. ✉ *27 Shaoxing Lu, off Ruijin Er Lu, Luwan District* ☎ *021/6473–2526.*

㉖ **Xiangyang Market** (Xiangyang Shichang). The most infamous of Shanghai's markets, Xiangyang Market is where tourists go to buy knock-off Rolexes, Prada bags, North Face jackets, Mont Blanc pens, and anything else that's been copyright-infringed. While the official market is about four blocks square, just as much business goes on in the dilapidated apartment blocks bordering the market, where many vendors have their showrooms of illicit goods. ✉ *999 Huaihai Zhong Lu, Xuhui District, Bordered by Xiangyang Lu, Huaihai Zhong Lu, Fenyang Lu, Shaanxi Nan Lu, and Nanchang Lu* ☯ *Daily 9–9.*

㉒ Xintiandi. At one time, 70% of Shanghai's residents lived in *shikumens,* or "stone gate" houses. Most have been razed in the name of progress, but this 8-acre collection of stone houses was renovated into an upscale shopping and dining complex and renamed Xintiandi, or "New Heaven on Earth." The restaurants are busy from lunchtime until past midnight, especially those with patios for watching the passing parade of shoppers and camera-toting tourists. Just off the main thoroughfare is the visitor center and the **Wulixiang Shikumen Museum** (✉ House 25, North Block, 181 Taicang Lu, Luwan District ☎ 021/3307–0337), a shikumen restored to 1920s style and filled with furniture and artifacts collected from nearby houses. Exhibits explain the European influence on shikumen design, the history of the Xintiandi renovation, as well as future plans for the entire 128-acre project. ✉ *181 Taicang Lu, Luwan District, Bordered by Taicang Lu, Madang Lu, Zizhong Lu, and Huangpi Nan Lu* ☎ *021/6311–2288* ⊕ *www.xintiandi.com* ✉ *Museum Y20* ☯ *Museum, daily 10–10.*

㉘ Xujiahui Cathedral (Xujiahui Dajiaotang). Built by the Jesuits in 1848, this Gothic-style cathedral still holds regular masses in Chinese. Stained-glass artist Wo Ye is in the midst of a five-year project to design and install new windows for the entire cathedral. ✉ *158 Puxi Lu, Xuhui District* ☎ *021/6469–0930.*

Pudong New Area

If you're traveling to Shanghai on business, you'll probably spend at least part of your time in Pudong. And even if you're in Shanghai for pleasure, the high-rises and energy in Pudong are sure to draw you to the other, eastern side of the Huangpu River. Here, where before 1990 you'd find farm fields, is an urban experiment that is swiftly becoming the financial, economic, and commercial center of Asia. Many of the big international companies with a presence in China have their factories or headquarters here. Although much of Pudong is still empty, and its sterility can't match the pockets of charm in Puxi, it does give you an idea of where Shanghai is heading. You'll find superlatives of all sorts in Pudong—the tallest tower in China, the highest hotel in the world, the first commercial maglev (magnetic levitation) train. Among the district's wonders are the Yangpu and Nanpu bridges (supposedly the second and third longest in the world) connecting Pudong to Puxi, the architecturally absurd International Exhibition Center, the Jinmao Tower, and, of course, the Oriental Pearl Tower.

a good walk

Start by crossing underneath the Huangpu River on the **Bund Tourist Tunnel** ㉚ ⌐. As you exit on the Pudong side, you'll see the unmistakable crown of the Bund Center to the west. Walk toward the crown and the **Riverside Promenade** ㉛. From here you can see the most beautiful views of the Bund. Standing above Riverside Promenade is the **Shangri-La Hotel,** where you can get a drink and a somewhat higher vantage point over the Bund.

A SHORT HISTORY OF SHANGHAI

SHANGHAI, which literally means the "City on the Sea," lies on the Yangzi River delta where China's main waterway completes its 5,500-km (3,400-mi) journey to the Pacific. Until 1842 Shanghai's location made it merely a small fishing village. After the first Opium War, however, the British named Shanghai a treaty port, opening the city to foreign involvement.

The village was soon turned into a city carved up into autonomous concessions administered concurrently by the British, French, and Americans, all independent of Chinese law. Each colonial presence brought with it its particular culture, architecture, and society. Although Shanghai had its own walled Chinese city, many native residents still chose to live in the foreign settlements. Thus began a mixing of cultures that shaped Shanghai's openness to Western influence. Shanghai became an important industrial center and trading port that attracted foreign businesspeople (60,000 by the 1930s) and Chinese migrants from other parts of the country.

In its heyday, Shanghai was the place to be—it had the best art, the greatest architecture, and the strongest business in Asia. With dance halls, brothels, glitzy restaurants, international clubs, and even a foreign-run racetrack, Shanghai was a city that catered to every whim of the rich. But poverty ran alongside opulence, and many of the lower-class Chinese provided the cheap labor that kept the city running.

The Paris of the East became known as a place of vice and indulgence. Amid this glamour and degradation the Communist Party held its first meeting in 1921. In the 1930s and '40s, the city weathered raids, invasions, then outright occupation by the Japanese. The party was over. By 1943, at the height of World War II, most foreigners had fled and the concessions had been ceded to the Japanese, bringing Shanghai's 101 years as a treaty port to a close. Despite the war's end, fighting continued as Nationalists and Communists fought a three-year civil war for control of China. The Communists declared victory in 1949 and established the People's Republic of China, after which the few remaining foreigners left the country. Closed off from the outside world with which it had become so comfortable, Shanghai fell into a deep sleep. Fashion, music, and romance gave way to uniformity and starkness of Communism.

The decades from 1950 to 1980 passed by with one Five Year Plan after another, marked by periods of extreme famine and drought, reform and suppression. Shanghai's industries soldiered on during these years; the city remained the largest contributor of tax revenue to the central government. Its political contribution, however, had far greater ramifications: the city was the powder keg for the Cultural Revolution and the base of operations for the infamous Gang of Four, led by Mao Zedong's wife, Jiang Qing. The so-called January Storm of 1967 purged many of Shanghai's leaders, and

Red Guards in Shanghai fervently carried out their destruction of the "Four Olds": old ways of idea, living, traditions, and thought.

Yet, in 1972, with the Cultural Revolution still raging, Shanghai hosted the historic meeting that would help lay the groundwork for the China of today. Premier Zhou Enlai and U.S. president Richard Nixon signed the Shanghai Communiqué, which enabled the two countries to normalize relations and encouraged China to open talks with the rest of the world. Twenty years later, the 14th Party Congress endorsed the concept of a socialist market economy, opening the door ever wider to foreign investment.

Today Shanghai has once again become one of China's most open cities ideologically, socially, culturally, and economically, striving to return to the internationalism that defined it before the Revolution. Shanghai's path to this renewed prominence began in 1990 when China's leader, Deng Xiaoping, chose it as the engine of the country's commercial renaissance, aiming to rival Hong Kong by 2010. If China is a dragon, he said, Shanghai is its head. Indeed the city is once again all about business. Having embraced competition and a market-driven economy in just a few years, it now hosts the nation's stock market, accounts for approximately one-fifth of the country's gross national product, and serves as the most important industrial base in the nation.

Today, beauty and charm coexist with kitsch and commercialism. From the colonial architecture of the former French Concession to the forest of cranes and the neon-lighted high-rises jutting above the city, Shanghai is a city of paradox and change.

From the Shangri-La's front entrance on Fucheng Lu, cross the street and head left one block to Century Boulevard (Shi Ji Da Dao). Keep to the right on Century Boulevard, heading southeast away from the water, and you'll be facing the skyscrapers of Lujiazui, the central financial area, or Wall Street, of Pudong. Continue walking toward the tallest highrise in front of you, the beautiful industrial pagoda **Jinmao Tower** ㉜. Go up to the 88th-floor observation deck for a great view, or take a sky-high coffee break at the Grand Hyatt, which occupies the Jinmao's 53rd through 87th floors.

From the base of the Jinmao Tower head back northwest toward the water and the **Oriental Pearl Tower** ㉝. You'll see it towering in its gargantuan grandeur at the northwest end of Century Boulevard. You can take a ride to the top for yet another 360-degree view of Shanghai. The **Shanghai History Museum** ㉞ is in the bottom of the tower.

If you'd like to call it day, take a cab or hop on the subway back to Puxi. (Board the train on the side that says ZHONGSHAN PARK.) If you'd like to continue exploring, take the metro east three stops to the exceptional **Shanghai Science and Technology Museum** ㉟.

TIMING   The tourist tunnel ride takes just five minutes. You can take a leisurely stroll on the Bingjiang Dadao. Then allow about 15 minutes to walk to the Jinmao from the Shangri-La and another 15 to get to the Pearl Tower from the Jinmao, or take a short taxi ride. You can spend a half-hour to an hour at the observatory decks and at the Shanghai History Museum. If lines are long, you may have to wait a while to get to the top. Allow an hour at the Ocean Aquarium. It takes less than 10 minutes by subway to reach the Science and Technology Museum, where you'll need an hour or two to explore.

What to See

▶ ㉚ **Bund Tourist Tunnel** (Waitan Guanguan Shuidao). For a look at Shanghai kitsch at its worst, you can take a trip across—actually, under—the Huangpu in plastic, capsular cars. The accompanying light show is part Disney, part psychedelia, complete with flashing strobes, blowing tinsel, and swirling hallucinogenic images projected on the concrete walls. The tackiest futuristic film of the 1960s couldn't have topped this. The five-minute ride will have your head spinning and you wondering if the Chinese central government isn't giving Shanghai just a little too much money. ⊠ *Entrances are on the Bund at Nanjing Dong Lu and in Pudong near the Riverside Promenade* ☎ *021/5888–6000* 💲 *Y30 one-way, Y40 round-trip* ⊗ *May–Oct., daily 8 AM–10:30 PM; Nov.–Apr., daily 8 AM–10 PM.*

★ ㉜ **Jinmao Tower** (Jinmao Dasha). This gorgeous 88-floor (8 being the Chinese number implying wealth and prosperity) industrial art deco pagoda is among the five tallest buildings in the world and the tallest in China. In it is also the highest hotel in the world—the Grand Hyatt Shanghai takes up the 53rd to 87th floors. The lower floors are taken up by office space, an entertainment center, and a neighboring exhibition center. The 88th-floor observation deck, reached in 45 seconds by two high-speed elevators, offers a 360-degree view of the city. The Jinmao, designed by Chicago's Skidmore Owings & Merrill, is both ancient and modern, Eastern and Western—the tapering tower combines the classic 13-tier Buddhist pagoda design with postmodern steel and glass. Check out the Hyatt's dramatic 33-story atrium. ⊠ *88 Shiji Dadao, Pudong* ☎ *021/5047–5101* ⌦ *Observation deck Y50* ⊙ *Daily 8:30 AM–9 PM.*

★ ㉝ **Oriental Pearl Tower** (Dongfang Mingzhu). The tallest tower in Asia (1,535 feet) has become the pride and joy of the city, a symbol of the brashness and glitz of today's Shanghai. This UFO-like structure is especially kitschy at night, against the classic beauty of the Bund. Its three spheres are supposed to represent pearls (as in "Shanghai, Pearl of the Orient"). An elevator takes you to observation decks in the tower's three spheres. Go to the top sphere for a 360-degree bird's-eye view of the city or grab a bite in the Tower's revolving restaurant. On the bottom floor is the ⇨ **Shanghai History Museum.** ⊠ *1 Shiji Da Dao, Pudong* ☎ *021/5879–1888* ⌦ *Y100, all three spheres plus museum; Y50 second sphere* ⊙ *Daily 8 AM–9:30 PM.*

㉛ **Riverside Promenade** (Bingjiang Da Dao). Although the park that runs 2,750 yards along the Huangpu River is sugary-sterile in its experimental suburbia, it still offers the most beautiful views of the Bund. You can stroll the grass and concrete and view a perspective of Puxi unavailable from the west side. If you're here in the summer, you can "enjoy wading," as a sign indicates, in the chocolate-color Huangpu River from the park's wave platform. ⊠ *Bingjiang Dadao* ⌦ *Free.*

need a break? With its curving glass facade and large patio along the Riverside Promenade, **Red Dot** (⊠ Binjiang Dadao, Fu Du Duan, Pudong ☎ 021/5887–1818) serves up great views of the Bund with its fair Western fare.

★ ㉞ **Shanghai History Museum** (Shanghai Lishi Bowuguan). This impressive museum in the base of the Pearl Tower recalls Shanghai's pre-1949 history. Inside you can stroll down a re-created Shanghai street circa 1900 or check out a street car that used to operate in the concessions. Dioramas depict battle scenes from the Opium Wars, shops found in a typical turn-of-the-20th-century Shanghai neighborhood, and grand French Concession buildings of yesteryear. ⊠ *1 Shiji Dadao, Pudong* ☎ *021/ 5879–1888* ⌦ *Y35* ⊙ *Daily 9–9:30.*

☙ ㉟ **Shanghai Science and Technology Museum** (Shanghai Kexue Bowuguan). This museum, a favorite attraction for kids in Shanghai, has more than 100 hands-on exhibits in its six main galleries. Earth Exploration takes you through fossil layers to the earth's core for a lesson in plate tectonics. Spectrum of Life introduces you to the animal and plant kingdoms within its simulated rainforest. Light of Wisdom explains basic principles of light and sound through interactive exhibits, and simulators in AV Paradise put you in a plane cockpit and on television. Children's Technoland has a voice-activated fountain and miniature construction site. And in Cradle of Designers, you can record a CD or assemble a souvenir. Two IMAX theaters and an IWERKS 4D theater show larger-than-life movies. All signs are in English; the best times to visit are weekday afternoons. ✉ *2000 Shiji Dadao, Pudong* ☎ *021/6854–2000* 💰 *Y60 adults, Y20 children* ☉ *Tues.–Sun. 9–5, last ticket sold at 3:30.*

Hongkou District

On the west side of the river north of Suzhou Creek are the northeastern districts of Hongkou and Yangpu. At the turn of the 20th century Shanghai was not only an international port but also an open one, where anyone could enter regardless of nationality. As the century wore on and the world became riddled with war, Jews, first fleeing the Russian Revolution and then escaping Hitler, arrived in Shanghai from Germany, Austria, Poland, and Russia. From 1937 to 1941 Shanghai became a haven for tens of thousands of Jewish refugees. In 1943 invading Japanese troops forced all the city's Jews into the "Designated Area for Stateless Refugees" in Hongkou District, where they lived until the end of the war. Today you can still see evidence of their lives in the buildings and narrow streets of the area.

a good walk

Start with a stroll through **Duolun Lu** 36 ⌐ which begins at the archway on Sichuan Bei Lu. Take your time along this pedestrian street to browse the antiques shops and art galleries, especially the **Shanghai Duolun Museum of Modern Art** 37. Continue east one more block to where Duolun Lu rejoins Sichuan Bei Lu to hail a taxi for the short ride to **Ohel Moishe Synagogue and Huoshan Park** 38.

What to See

⌐ 36 **Duolun Lu.** Designated Shanghai's "Cultural Street," Duolun Road takes you back in time to the 1930s, when the half-mile–long lane was a favorite haunt of writer Lu Xun and fellow social activists. Bronze statues of those literary luminaries dot the lawns between the well-preserved villas and row houses, whose first floors are now home to antiques shops, cafés, and art galleries. As the street takes a 90° turn, its architecture shifts 180° with the seven-story stark gray ⇨ **Shanghai Duolun Museum of Modern Art.** ✉ *Off Sichuan Bei Lu, Hongkou District.*

need a break?

Old Film Café (✉ 123 Duolun Lu, Hongkou District ☎ 021/ 5696–4763) shares the 1920s feel of its Duolun Lu surroundings but eschews Chinese culture for Hollywood. Pictures of Marilyn Monroe and Humphrey Bogart preside over the subdued café. Stick to the drink menu, which includes teas, coffee, wine, and other spirits.

38 **Ohel Moishe Synagogue and Huoshan Park** (Moxi Huitang and Huoshan Gongyuan). Now called the Jewish Refugee Memorial Hall of Shanghai, the Ohel Moishe Synagogue served as the spiritual heart of Shanghai's Jewish ghetto in the 1930s and '40s. In this sanctuary-turned-museum, the lively 85-year-old narrator Wang Faliang provides colorful commentary for the black-and-white photo collection depicting daily life for the 30,000 Jews—academics, writers, doctors, musicians—who flooded into the Hongkou District from Europe.

An attic bedroom is frozen in time, with photos and a menorah left behind by residents who moved on after World War II. Around the corner, down a lane just as well preserved, Huoshan Park bears a memorial tablet in the immigrants' honor. The museum's art gallery best conveys the refugees' lasting gratitude to their Chinese hosts, a bond made most clear by a crystal Star of David, engraved with Chinese characters. ✉ *62 Changyang Lu, Hongkou District* ☎ *021/6541–5008* 🖷 *021/ 6512–0229* ⊕ *www.moishe.sh.cn* 🎫 *Y50* ⊗ *Mon.–Sat. 9 AM–4 PM.*

🔟 **Shanghai Duolun Museum of Modern Art** (Shanghai Duolun Xiandai Meishu Guan). Opened in December 2003, this is Shanghai's first official venue for modern art. The six-story museum's 14,400 square feet of exhibition space include a café and a metal spiral staircase that's a work of art in itself. A video installation roars to life underfoot as you step off on the second floor. The exhibitions, which change frequently, are cutting edge for Shanghai. They've showcased electronic art from American artists, examined gender issues among Chinese and featured musical performances ranging from Chinese electronica to the *dombra,* a traditional Kazak stringed instrument. ✉ *27 Duolun Lu, Hongkou District* ☎ *021/6587–2530* 🖷 *021/6587–6902* ⊕ *www.duolunart.org* 🎫 *Y20* ⊗ *Daily 9–5.*

WHERE TO EAT

You'll notice most Chinese restaurants in Shanghai have large, round tables. The reason will become clear the first time you eat a late dinner at a local restaurant and are surrounded by jovial, loud, laughing groups of people toasting and topping off from communal bottles of beer, sharing cigarettes, and spinning the lazy Susan loaded with food. Dining out with friends and family isn't just a favorite social activity; it's ritual. Whether feting guests or demonstrating their growing wealth, hosts will order massive spreads, for the more dishes, the more honor. While takeaway boxes for leftovers are starting to become popular, proud hosts wouldn't deign to use them.

Besides Chinese restaurants and food stands, Shanghai has hundreds of restaurants representing cuisines from around the globe, a diversity befitting an international center. Brazilian *churrascaria* joints, all-you-can-eat Japanese teppanyaki restaurants, and tapas bars have proliferated over the past few years. Popular restaurant chains like Indian Kitchen, South Beauty, and Simply Thai have opened additional branches to satisfy demand, while respected restaurateurs Steve Baker and Eduardo Vargas have expanded their empires with the sophisticated Mesa and Azul/ Viva, respectively. The Xintiandi complex and the Hengshan Road area remain dining hotspots, but all eyes have been on the Bund as well, where the venerable M on the Bund faces competition from its new neighbor, the Three on the Bund complex and its four high-profile restaurants: Jean Georges, Laris, New Heights, and Whampoa Club.

Most restaurants in Shanghai offer set lunches, multi-course feasts at a fraction of the usual price. It's the best dining deal going, allowing you to eat at local Chinese restaurants for Y25 or less and at such places at M on the Bund without completely blowing your budget. Also, check out the "Restaurant Events" section of *That's Shanghai,* which lists dining discounts and promotions around town.

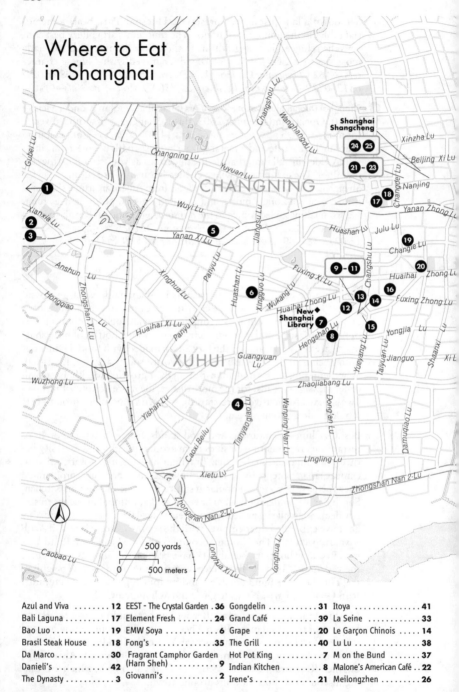

Where to Eat in Shanghai

CHANGNING

XUHUI

New Shanghai Library

Shanghai Shangcheng

0   500 yards
0   500 meters

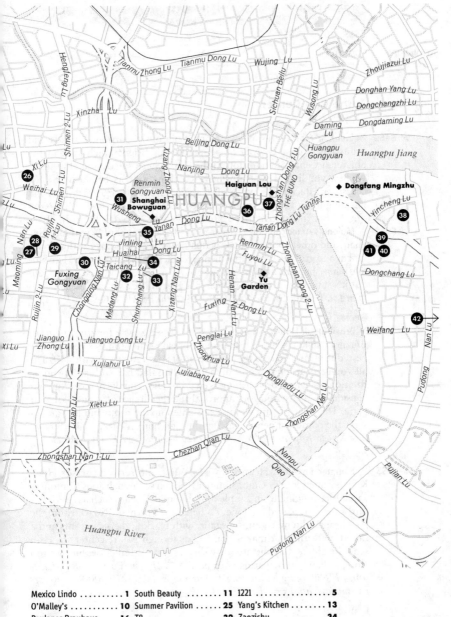

WHAT IT COSTS	In Yuan			
$$$$	**$$$**	**$$**	**$**	**¢**
AT DINNER	over 180	121–180	81–120	40–80	under 40

Prices are for a main course.

Nanjing Lu & the City Center

American

★ **$–$$** ✕ **Element Fresh.** Freshly made and generously portioned salads and sandwiches draw crowds of people to this bright lunch spot in the Shanghai Center. In addition to the usual chef's salads and club sandwiches, you'll find such inventive combinations as bacon with blue cheese, and duck breast with grilled apple. An equally creative drink menu has long lists of juices and smoothies. ⊠ *Shanghai Center, 1376 Nanjing Xi Lu, Jing'an District* ☎ *021/6279–8682* ⊟ *AE, DC, MC, V.*

$–$$ ✕ **Malone's American Café.** Larger-than-life caricatures of Wayne Gretzky, Shaq, and other sports legends watch over the proceedings at this popular bar and grill. Its substantial menu includes American favorites like buffalo wings, burgers, and pizza, as well as Asian dishes. The food isn't superb but it's satisfying as a casual meal in a cheerful bar setting. ⊠ *255 Tongren Lu, Jing'an District* ☎ *021/6247–2400* ⊟ *AE, DC, MC, V.*

Brazilian

$ ✕ **Brasil Steak House.** Shanghai has developed a taste for *churrascarias,* Brazilian-style barbecue restaurants. Brasil Steak House is perhaps the best, due in large part to the percentage of South Americans on staff. The all-you-can-eat lunches and dinners pair a salad bar with an unending rotation of waiters brandishing skewers of juicy chunks of meat for your consideration; just nod your approval and they'll slice off a piece for your plate. The large picture windows brighten up the room and let you observe the parade of people passing through Jing'an Park. ⊠ *1649 Nanjing Xi Lu, Jing'an District* ☎ *021/6255–9898* ⊟ *AE, DC, MC, V.*

Cantonese

$$–$$$$ ✕ **Summer Pavilion.** Helmed by Ho Wing, the former chef of Hong Kong's famed Jockey Club, Summer Pavilion serves delicious Cantonese specialties ranging from simple dim sum to delicacies such as shark fin, bird's nest soup, and abalone. As befits the Portman Ritz-Carlton, the restaurant's dining room is elegant, with black and gold accents and a raised platform that makes you feel as though you're center stage—a sense heightened by the attentive servers, who stand close, but not too close, at hand, anticipating your needs. ⊠ *2F, The Portman Ritz-Carlton, 1376 Nanjing Xi Lu, Jing'an District* ☎ *021/6279–8888* ⚑ *Reservations essential* ⊟ *AE, DC, MC, V.*

Chinese

$–$$$ ✕ **Meilongzhen.** Probably Shanghai's most famous restaurant, Meilongzhen is one of the oldest dining establishments in town, dating from 1938. The building served as the Communist Party headquarters in the 1930s, and the traditional Chinese dining rooms still have their

FodorsChoice
★

ON THE MENU IN SHANGHAI

Shanghai's dining scene reflects the city's standing as China's most international city. You'll find restaurants representing not only every regional Chinese fare but also a world of other cuisines. Shanghainese food itself tends to be sweet and oily and is known for its own style of dim sum, especially xiao long bao (steamed pork dumplings). River fish is often the highlight (and most expensive part) of the meal, and hairy crab is a seasonal delicacy.

The city's increasingly sophisticated dining scene means you can enjoy jiaotzi (Shanghai-style dumplings) for breakfast, foie gras for lunch, and Kobe beef teppanyaki for dinner. When eating out, it's traditional to order several dishes, plus rice, to share among your party.

Shanghai's street snacks are the city's main culinary claim to fame. You'll see countless sidewalk stands selling the famed xiao long bao, as well as shuijiao, (Chinese ravioli) and mantou (steamed dumplings without any filling).

intricate woodwork, and mahogany and marble furniture. The exhaustive menu features more than 80 seafood options, including such traditional Shanghainese fare as Mandarin fish, as well as dishes with a Sichuan flair, like shredded spicy eel and prawns in chili sauce. Since this is a stop for most tour buses, expect a wait if you don't book ahead. ⊠ *No. 22, 1081 Nanjing Xi Lu, Jing'an District* ☎ *021/6253–5353* ⌂ *Reservations essential* ▤ *AE, DC, MC, V.*

Chinese Vegetarian

¢–$ ✕ **Gongdelin.** A two-story gold engraving of Buddha pays tribute to the origins of the inventive vegetarian dishes this restaurant has served for 80 years. Chefs transform tofu into such surprising and tasty creations as mock duck, eel, and pork. The interior is just as inspired, with Ming-style, wood-and-marble tables; metal latticework; and a soothing fountain. Tables fill up quickly after 6 PM, so either arrive early or buy some goodies to go at the take-out counter. ⊠ *445 Nanjing Xi Lu, Huangpu District* ☎ *021/6327–0218* ▤ *AE, DC, MC, V.*

Indonesian

$–$$ ✕ **Bali Laguna.** Overlooking the lily pond in Jing'an Park, with interior and alfresco dining, Bali Laguna is a popular choice for couples. Balinese music piped along the statue- and palm-lined walkway sets the mood even before the sarong-clad hostess welcomes you inside the traditional, three-story, Indonesian-style house or to a pond-side table. The menu is heavy on seafood, such as grilled fish cakes and chili crab, which captures the fire of Indonesian cuisine. Quench it with a Nusa Dua Sunset or other Bali-inspired cocktail. ⊠ *Jing'an Park, 189 Huashan Lu, Jing'an District* ☎ *021/6248–6970* ⌂ *Reservations essential* ▤ *AE, DC, MC, V.*

Mexican

¢ ✕ **Taco Popo.** The tiny Taco Popo is packed around the clock with customers craving its Mexican fast-food fare. The dozen seats along the diner counter fill up the quickest—especially right after the bars have closed—but there's more seating upstairs. The menu is short but solid—tacos, burritos, enchiladas, and quesadillas. Throw in another Y5 to Y10 for extras like sour cream or tortilla chips. ⊠ *265 Tongren Lu, Jing'an District* ☎*021/6279–4820* ⚑*Reservations not accepted* ▤*No credit cards.*

Shanghainese

★ ¢–$$$ ✕ **1221.** This stylish but casual eatery is a favorite of hip Chinese and expatriate regulars. The dining room is streamlined chic, its crisp white tablecloths contrasting the warm golden walls. Shanghainese food is the mainstay, with a few Sichuan dishes as well. From the extensive 26-page menu (in English, pinyin, and Chinese), you can order dishes like sliced *you tiao* (fried bread sticks) with shredded beef, a whole chicken in a green-onion soy sauce, and *shaguo shizi tou,* or Lion's Head pork meatballs. ⊠ *1221 Yanan Xi Lu, Changning District* ☎ *021/6213–6585 or 021/6213–2441* ⚑ *Reservations essential* ▤ *AE, DC, MC, V.*

Thai

$–$$$ ✕ **Irene's.** This traditional Thai teak house certainly stands out from its neighbors on Tongren Lu. The inside is just as distinctive, with pink and purple textiles, golden statues, and a platform with low tables and cushions on the floor. The food is good but not as inspired as the surroundings and somewhat overpriced. Spring rolls, pineapple rice, and papaya salad are among the best choices. Consider going on a Monday or Friday, when a Y150 all-you-can-eat special lets you sample across the menu. ⊠ *263 Tongren Lu, Jing'an District* ☎ *021/6247–3579* ⚑ *Reservations essential* ▤ *AE, DC, MC, V.*

Old Town and the Bund

Contemporary

$$–$$$$ ✕ **M on the Bund.** Espousing Shanghai's return to glamour, M does
Fodor'sChoice   everything with flair. Its seasonal menus of Mediterranean- and Mid-
★   dle Eastern–influenced cuisine draw on the freshest of ingredients and the creative minds of owner Michelle Garnaut and executive chefs Julie and Michael Roper. Its rooftop location in the 1920s Nissin Shipping Building provides unparalleled views of the Bund, Huangpu River, and the Pudong skyline beyond. Consider lunch on the terrace; three course "simple lunches" run Y118, about half the typical dinner tab. Or stop for a drink in the adjoining **Glamour Bar,** a luxurious lounge with impeccable service that's popular among networking business types. ⊠ *7F, 20 Guangdong Lu, Huangpu District* ☎ *021/6350–9988* ⚑ *Reservations essential* ▤ *AE, DC, MC, V* ⊗ *No lunch Mon.*

Japanese

$$–$$$$ ✕ **EEST–The Crystal Garden.** This impressive three-in-one venue has full Japanese, Cantonese, and Thai menus, all perfectly prepared. While the

WHERE TO REFUEL AROUND TOWN

For those times when all you want is a quick, inexpensive bite, look for these local chains. They all have English menus and branches in Shanghai's tourist areas.

Bi Feng Tang: *Dim sum is the sum of the menu, from chickens' feet to less exotic items such as shrimp wontons and barbecue pork pastries.*

Sumo Sushi: *Sit along the carousel and watch the chefs slice and dice fresh made-*

to-order sushi. You can order set lunches, à la carte, or all you can eat.

Gino Café: *The inexpensive Italian fare at this café chain includes pizza, pasta, sandwiches, and good desserts.*

Manabe: *This Japanese coffee house chain serves Western fast food, such as club sandwiches and breakfast fare, as well as Japanese snacks and a long list of teas.*

sushi bar and teppanyaki grill make it easy to zero in on the Japanese offerings, sampling across the menus is the best approach. Shark-fin dumpling, pomelo salad, and rice with green tea and crab meat are among the treasures buried in the pages of possibilities. This sunny glass-roofed garden of a restaurant has retracting overhead shades, which cool you during the day and allow you to stargaze at night. ⊠ *The Westin Shanghai, 88 Henan Zhong Lu, Huangpu District* ☎ *021/6335–1888* ⊟ *AE, DC, MC, V.*

The Old French Concession

American

¢–$ ✕ **Rendezvous Café.** With its inexpensive menu of juicy hamburgers and bacon-and-eggs breakfasts, Rendezvous Café is as close to an American diner as you'll find in Shanghai. Owner Richard Soo ran its namesake and predecessor in San Francisco before pulling up stakes for Taiwan, then Shanghai. The café's coffee selections are equally satisfying, which is no surprise considering that Soo also owns a nearby coffee shop. While its location behind Metro City shopping mall can be difficult to find, Rendezvous Café is definitely worth seeking out. ⊠ *#1-29, 1111 Zhaojiabang Lu, off of Tianyaoqiao Lu, Xuhui District* ☎ *021/ 6426–7152* ⊟ *MC, V.*

Beijing

$–$$ ✕ **Quan Ju De.** The original Beijing branch of this restaurant has been *the* place to get Peking duck since 1864, though the Shanghai location only opened in 1998. The elevator doors open on a traditional Chinese restaurant: big and noisy, with red and gold columns, painted ceilings, and dangling lanterns whose tassels resemble the imperial-style headdresses worn by the hostesses. The roast duck is worthy of its hype, but be sure to order several other dishes—such as vegetables, crystal shrimp, or spicy peanuts—to offset its greasiness. ⊠ *4F, 786 Huaihai Zhong Lu, Luwan District* ☎ *021/5404–5799* ▤ *AE, DC, MC, V* ⚛ *Reservations essential.*

Chinese

★ ¢–$ ✕ **Grape.** Entry-level Chinese food at inexpensive prices has been the Grape's calling card since the mid-1980s. This cheerful two-story restaurant remains a favorite among expatriates and travelers who've wandered north a few blocks from Xiangyang Market. The English and photo menu includes such recognizable fare as sweet and sour pork and lemon chicken as well as delicious dishes like garlic shrimp and *jiachang doufu* (home-style bean curd), all of which are served with a smile. ⊠ *55 Xinle Lu, Luwan District* ☎ *021/5404–0486* ▤ *No credit cards.*

Chinese Hotpot

¢–$ ✕ **Hot Pot King.** *Huo guo,* or hotpot, is a popular Chinese ritual of at-the-table cooking, in which you simmer fresh ingredients in a broth. Hot Pot King reigns over the hotpot scene in Shanghai because of its extensive menu as well as its refined setting. The most popular of the 17 broths is the *yin-yang,* half spicy red, half basic white pork-bone broth. Add in a mixture of veggies, seafood, meat, and dumplings for a well-rounded pot, then dip each morsel in the sauces mixed tableside by your waiter. The minimalist white and gray interior has glass-enclosed booths and well-spaced tables, a nice change from the usual crowded, noisy, hotpot joints. ⊠ *2F, 10 Hengshan Lu, Xuhui District* ☎ *021/6474–6545* ▤ *AE, DC, MC, V.*

Contemporary

★ $$$–$$$$ ✕ **T8.** A favorite haunt for celebrities, T8 has garnered its share of headlines for its stunning interior and inspired contemporary cuisine. The restaurant occupies a traditional shikumen, or stone gate, house within Xintiandi and has modernized the space with raw stone floors, carved-wood screens, and imaginative lighting that transforms shelves full of glasses into a modern-art sculpture. The show kitchen turns out such Thai- and Chinese-inspired dishes as a slow-cooked, Sichuan-flavored lamb pie, and nori-wrapped sashimi-grade tuna. Like the clientele, the wine list is exclusive, with many labels unavailable elsewhere in Shanghai. ⊠ *House 8, North Block, Xintiandi, 181 Taicang Lu,, Luwan District* ☎ *021/6355–8999* ⚛ *Reservations essential* ▤ *AE, DC, MC, V* ☺ *No lunch Tues.*

★ $$–$$$ ✕ **Azul and Viva.** In creating his continent-hopping New World cuisine, owner Eduardo Vargas drew upon his globe-trotting childhood and seven years as a restaurant consultant in Asia. As a result, the menus in Azul, the tapas bar downstairs, and Viva, the restaurant upstairs, feature a delicious, delicate balance of flavors that should please any palate. Classics like beef carpaccio contrast cutting-edge dishes like coffee-glazed pork. Lunch and weekend brunch specials provide lower-priced options.

The relaxed, romantic interior—dim lighting, plush pillows, splashes of color against muted backdrops—invites you to take your time on your culinary world tour. ⊠ *18 Dongping Lu, Xuhui District* ☎ *021/ 6433–1172* ▤ *AE, DC, MC, V.*

Continental

¢–$$ ✕ **Fragrant Camphor Garden** (Harn Sheh). Given Harn Sheh's desirable Hengshan Lu address, its budget prices come as a surprise. The 16-page menu, divided equally between Eastern and Western fare, ranges from curry to hotpot to pasta; drinks alone include 14 teas and 19 smoothies. Many dishes include salad, soup, and fruit. As Harn Sheh is considered a teahouse, you're welcome to linger, browse magazines from the towering rack, and gaze out the large windows at the hustle and bustle of Hengshan Road. ⊠ *2A Hengshan Lu, Xuhui District* ☎ *021/ 6433–4385* ▤ *MC, V.*

French

★ $–$$$ ✕ **La Seine.** Its stylish dining room and authentic contemporary fare make La Seine a perfect place to savor and contemplate the intricacies of French cuisine. Royal purple reigns, in the linens, flower arrangements, suede chairs, and the throw pillows on the generously sized booths. The artfully presented dishes range from the expected escargot and foie gras to delicate seafood like tilapia in mustard–cream sauce. The weekday lunch semi-buffet (pairing an entrée with salad and dessert bar), weekend brunch buffet, and dinner prix-fixe menus are the best deals. Be sure to stop in the patisserie, where the heavenly scent will inspire you to buy some truffles and croissants for the way home. ⊠ *8 Jinan Lu, Luwan District* ☎ *021/6384–3722* ⚞ *Reservations essential* ▤ *AE, DC, MC, V.*

German

$$–$$$$ ✕ **Paulaner Brauhaus.** There's a shortage of good German food in Shanghai. Paulaner Brauhaus does its best to fill the void with a menu of classic German dishes—Wiener schnitzel, bratwurst, apple strudel—accompanied by the house-brewed lager. The Fenyang Lu location is more laid-back, with a courtyard beer garden in the summer. The Xintiandi branch, open for lunch, is great for people-watching. ⊠ *150 Fenyang Lu, Xuhui District* ☎ *021/6474–5700* ☉ *No lunch* ⊠ *House 19-20, North Block Xintiandi, 181 Taicang Lu, Luwan District* ☎ *021/ 6320–3935* ▤ *AE, DC, MC, V.*

Indian

★ $–$$$ ✕ **The Tandoor.** Don't miss the unbelievable *murgh malei kebab* (tandoori chicken marinated in cheese and yogurt mixture) or try some vegetable curries—*palak aloo* (spinach with peas) or *dal makhani* (lentil). Decorated with mirrors, Indian artwork, and Chinese characters dangling from the ceiling, the restaurant is ingeniously designed to show the route of Buddhism from India to China. The management and staff, all from India, remain close at hand throughout the meal to answer questions and attend to your needs. ⊠ *Jinjiang Hotel, South Building, 59 Maoming Nan Lu, Luwan District* ☎ *021/6472–5494* ⚞ *Reservations essential* ▤ *AE, DC, MC, V.*

¢ ✕ **Indian Kitchen.** The Indian chefs working their magic in the show kitchen provide the entertainment while you wait for a table at this tremendously popular restaurant. Delicious butter chicken marsala and tandoor-cooked chicken tikka taste as good as they look in the picture menu, which is packed with classic Indian dishes. The 36 bread selections include melt-in-your-mouth spring onion *parotas* (fried flat bread). Two blocks from the Hengshan Lu metro station and bar district, Indian Kitchen is a convenient dining spot and the perfect start to an evening out on the town. ✉ *572 Yongjia Lu, Xuhui District* ☎ *021/6473–1517* ⌂ *Reservations essential* ▭ *AE, DC, MC, V* ✉ *House 8, 3911 Hongmei Lu, Changning District* ☎ *021/ 6261–0377* ⌂ *Reservations essential* ▭ *AE, DC, MC, V.*

Irish

$–$$$ ✕ **O'Malley's.** With a fire in the hearth, a super-friendly Irish staff, and a band playing traditional tunes from the balcony, O'Malley's feels every bit like an authentic Irish pub. The old French mansion has lots of dark, cozy corners, while the huge outdoor patio is packed to capacity during broadcasts of European football (soccer) and rugby matches. The requisite Guinness and Kilkenny are on tap and complement the meat-and-potatoes menu, but all come with rather steep price tags. ✉ *42 Taojiang Lu, Xuhui District* ☎ *021/6437–0667* ▭ *AE, DC, MC, V.*

Italian

$–$$$ ✕ **Da Marco.** Its reasonably priced authentic Italian fare makes Da Marco a universal favorite in Shanghai. The original location on Dong Zhu An Bang Lu is a magnet for Italian expats in search of a late dinner, while the Yandang Lu location attracts a mix of locals, expats, and tourists. Lasagna, ravioli, Caprese salad, and pizza (11 types) are among the classic dishes on the menu. The wine list includes many selections under Y200. Three-course set lunches—with tiramisu for dessert—ring up at only Y68. You can choose alfresco dining under the bright orange awning or a comfy seat on the banquette in the sunshine-yellow dining room. ✉ *62 Yandang Lu, Luwan District* ☎ *021/6385–5998* ⌂ *Reservations essential* ▭ *AE, DC, MC, V.*

Japanese

$–$$$ ✕ **Tairyo.** After indulging in the Y150 all-you-can-eat teppanyaki special at Tairyo, you might feel as big as the three sumo wrestlers in the restaurant's wall-sized mural. While locals seem to prefer the cheaper à la carte menu, Westerners come here for the endless delicious servings of sashimi, scallops, lemon prawns, and some of the best beef in town. Beer, sake, wine, and plum wine are included in the price, too. ✉ *139 Ruijin Yi Lu, Luwan District* ☎ *021/5382–8818* ⌂ *Reservations essential* ▭ *AE, DC, MC, V.*

Pan-Asian

★ ¢–$ ✕ **EMW Soya.** The EMW stands for East Meets West, an apt description of the nine-page menu in this fashionable yet reasonably priced restaurant. Singaporean and Indonesian influences enhance such classics as lobster bisque and Caesar salad and are in full form in the curries and "Asian delights" selections. Mocha suede benches with purple, green, and orange throw pillows ring the periphery while dark wood tables fill the center of the bright, airy upstairs rooms. The first floor is a more romantic space, with candlelight flickering off the mango-colored gauze panels that drape down from the ceiling. ⌧ *380 Xingguo Lu, Xuhui District* ☎ *021/6280–8399* ▤ *AE, DC, MC, V.*

Shanghainese

¢–$$$ ✕ **Yang's Kitchen.** Traditional Shanghainese food without the usual *renao* (hot and noisy atmosphere) draws customers down the narrow laneway to the restored villa that's now home to Yang's Kitchen. The 19-page menu includes familiar dishes like mandarin fish, the obligatory *xiao long bao* (steamed pork dumplings), as well as 22 soups. An apricot-and-white side dining room with small tables spaced widely for privacy is popular among couples and solo diners seeking a quiet and inexpensive meal. ⌧ *No. 3, 9 Hengshan Lu, Xuhui District* ☎ *021/6445–8418* ▤ *AE, DC, MC, V.*

¢–$ ✕ **Bao Luo.** While its English menu caters to tourists, Bao Luo is Chinese dining as the Chinese enjoy it, a fact confirmed by the usual long wait for a table. The freshness of the ingredients comes through in every dish, from perfectly steamed broccoli to tender stewed crab and pork meatballs. Tables are packed tightly in this small two-story restaurant, and the light-wood interior merely serves as backdrop to the can't-miss cuisine. However, look closely for the red scroll neon sign with a tiny "BL," or you may miss the restaurant altogether. ⌧ *271 Fumin Lu, by Changle Lu, Jing'an District* ☎ *021/5403–7239* ⌆ *Reservations essential* ▤ *No credit cards.*

Sichuanese

★ $–$$$ ✕ **South Beauty.** The elegant interior and spicy fare are both worth beholding at South Beauty. As the sliding glass front door opens—revealing a walkway between two cascading walls of water—it splits the restaurant's trademark red Chinese opera mask in two. Likewise, the menu is split down the middle between cooler Cantonese cuisine and sizzling hot Sichuan fare. Don't be fooled: even dishes with a one-pepper rating, like sautéed baby lobster, will singe your sinuses. ⌧ *28 Taojiang Lu, Xuhui District* ☎ *021/6445–2581* ⌆ *Reservations essential* ▤ *AE, DC, MC, V* ⌧ *10F, Super Brand Mall 168 Lujiazui Lu, Pudong* ☎ *021/5047–1817* ▤ *AE, DC, MC, V.*

Spanish

$$ ✕ **Le Garçon Chinois.** This dimly lit restaurant in an old French villa is a favorite spot for couples on a date. The walls are painted in warm hues, the art deco fittings are tasteful, and large windows frame surrounding trees and old mansions. Run by a Japanese–European couple, the restaurant presents a predominantly Spanish menu, with several tapas and paella selections. ⌧ *No. 3, Lane 9, Hengshan Lu, Xuhui District* ☎ *021/ 6445–7970* ⌆ *Reservations essential* ▤ *AE, DC, MC, V* ⊘ *No lunch.*

Thai

¢–$$ ✕ **Simply Thai.** Unpretentious Thai fare at moderate prices has earned FodorsChoice this restaurant a loyal expat clientele. Customers flock to the tree-★ shaded patio to savor such favorites as green and red curries (on the spicy side) and stir fried rice noodles with chicken (on the tame side). The appetizers are all first-rate, especially the crispy spring rolls and samosas. The wine list includes a half-dozen bottles under Y200 ($25), a rarity in Shanghai. The branch in Xintiandi is a bit noisier but features the same great food and prices. ⊠ *5C Dongping Rd., Xuhui District* ☎ *021/6445–9551* ⌂ *Reservations essential* ☰ *AE, DC, MC, V.*

Vegetarian

¢ ✕ **Zaozishu.** Calling itself a "vegetarian lifestyle" restaurant, Zaozishu is perhaps the only place in Shanghai where you can get real vegetarian food, not just endless variations of tofu. You'll find hotpot and clay pot, dim sum, and desserts, plus 12 teas "for the health" formulated by a doctor from the Shanghai Xiangshan Chinese Medicine Hospital. ⊠ *77 Songshan Lu, Luwan District* ☎ *021/6384–8000* ☰ *No credit cards.*

Vietnamese

$–$$ ✕ **Fong's.** Don't be deterred by Fong's location in an office plaza. Inside, chirping birds, gauze curtains, bamboo furniture, and hostesses wearing *ao dai* (long Vietnamese dress with side slits worn over pants) set a romanticized scene for Fong's excellent French-style Vietnamese cuisine. The English and photo menu focuses on traditional dishes like spring rolls and a wonderfully smoky fried vermicelli with seafood, but it also includes bouillabaisse and other French specialties. Waiters are friendly but may not always hear you over the din in this busy and justifiably popular restaurant. ⊠ *2F, Lippo Plaza 222 Huaihai Zhong Lu, Luwan District* ☎ *021/6387–7228* ☰ *AE, DC, MC, V.*

Hongqiao Development Zone

Cantonese

$–$$$ ✕ **The Dynasty.** Although its cuisine is mostly Cantonese, Dynasty has expanded its reign to include other regional fare, such as first-rate Peking duck and Sichuan-influenced hot-and-sour soup. The Cantonese seafood dishes, especially the prawns and lobster, are particularly good, and the shrimp *jiaozi* (dumplings) are delicious. Keyhole cutouts in the subdued pewter walls showcase Chinese vases and artifacts. Thick carpets mute any hotel noise, but the prices quickly remind you this is indeed a hotel restaurant. ⊠ *Renaissance Yangtze Hotel, 2099 Yanan Xi Lu, Changning District* ☎ *021/6275–0000* ⌂ *Reservations essential* ☰ *AE, DC, MC, V.*

Italian

$$–$$$$ ✕ **Giovanni's.** Its Italian courtyard with a penthouse view provides a wonderful backdrop for Giovanni's traditional Italian fare. The antipasta and calamari are delicious, the pastas served perfectly al dente. Seasonal promotions add a taste of Tuscany and other regions to the menu. ⊠ *Sheraton Grand Tai Ping Yang, 27th floor, 5 Zunyi Nan Lu, Changning District* ☎ *021/6275–8888* ⌂ *Reservations essential* ☰ *AE, DC, MC, V.*

Mexican

$$–$$$ ✕ **Mexico Lindo.** Fiery fare in a south-of-the-border setting has made Mexico Lindo Cantina & Grill the best entry on Shanghai's limited Mexican dining scene. This Spanish-style casa is hidden off Hongmei Lu, down a tiny alley that's evolved into a well-respected restaurant row. In ad-

dition to tacos, fajitas, and quesadillas, the menu includes spicy prawns—rated three peppers—and a tasty one-pepper carnita pork burrito. A stairway mural depicts farm workers as well as fiesta revelers, whose ranks you can join with the eight margaritas and eight tequilas on the drink menu. ⊠ *Villa 1, 3911 Hongmei Lu, Changning District* ☎ *021/6262-2797* ⚔ *Reservations essential* ▤ *AE, DC, MC, V.*

Pudong New Area

Continental

$$$-$$$$ ✕ **Grand Café.** Two of the Grand Hyatt's restaurants (the other is the Grill) present Continental cuisine while offering absolutely spectacular views of Shanghai (unless the building is shrouded in fog). The sophisticated 24-hour restaurant Grand Café touts its "show kitchen"—a buffet that includes appetizers, daily specials, fresh seafood, and desserts. ⊠ *Grand Hyatt, 88 Shiji Dadao, Pudong* ☎ *021/5049-1234* ⚔ *Reservations essential* ▤ *AE, DC, MC, V.*

$$$-$$$$ ✕ **The Grill.** Part of the Hyatt's three-in-one, open-kitchen restaurant concept, the Grill shares the 56th floor with two other restaurants (serving Japanese and Italian cuisine). At the Grill you can feast on a great seafood platter or unbelievably tender steak. ⊠ *Grand Hyatt, 88 Shiji Dadao, Pudong* ☎ *021/5049-1234* ⚔ *Reservations essential* ▤ *AE, DC, MC, V.*

Italian

★ **$$-$$$$** ✕ **Danieli's.** The show kitchen in Danieli's reveals the magic of its prodigy of an executive chef, Luca Cesarini. His creations are, quite simply, the most inventive Italian fare in Shanghai. Seasonal menus include such dishes as tomato and onion soup, and pumpkin and amaretto ravioli. Pastry chef Brian Tan Beng Tai's desserts are equally divine and inspired: dark chocolate mousse is shaped like a coffee cup, with a delicate chocolate handle. On the 39th floor of the St. Regis, Danieli's lives up to the hotel's exacting standards of elegance and excellence. ⊠ *The St. Regis Shanghai, 889 Dongfang Lu, Pudong* ☎ *021/5050-4567* ⚔ *Reservations essential* ▤ *AE, DC, MC, V.*

Japanese

$-$$$ ✕ **Itoya.** The waitstaff's precision teamwork makes dining at Itoya a pleasure. Servers pause to greet all guests in unison. You're handed a hot towel upon sitting down and instantly after finishing your meal. The menu sticks to traditional Japanese fare: tempura, sushi, sashimi. In line with its location directly across from the Grand Hyatt's entrance, the restaurant also has several budget-busting items such as Kobe beef and lobster sashimi. Another location in the Kerry Center on Nanjing Xi Lu in Puxi is also a popular spot with businessmen in the city center. ⊠ *178 Huayuan Shiqiao Lu, Pudong* ☎ *021/5882-9679* ▤ *AE, DC, MC, V.*

Shanghainese

$-$$$ ✕ **Lu Lu.** With its widely spaced round tables, black and gold color scheme, and tasteful paintings, Lu Lu resembles an executive dining room. Fitting, given its main clients are the businessmen from the nearby office buildings. The menu focuses on traditional Shanghainese dishes such as sliced beef in black pepper sauce and sautéed bean curd with crab meat. Service is polite but not attentive, reacting to requests rather than anticipating them. ✉ *2–3F, 161 Lujiazui Dong Lu, Pudong* ☎ *021/ 5882–6679* ✎ *Reservations essential* ▤ *AE, DC, MC, V.*

WHERE TO STAY

Shanghai's hotels cater mostly to business travelers and can be divided into two categories: modern Western-style hotels that are elegant and nicely appointed, or hotels built in the city's glory days that became state-run after 1949. The latter may lack great service, modern fixings, and convenient facilities, but they often make up for it in charm, tradition, history, and value.

Hotels in China often have a "soft opening," a trial period to work out the kinks before the official ribbon-cutting ceremony. Judging by the number of five-star and Western chain hotels now in Shanghai, the city has surpassed the soft stage and proven just how grandly it has opened to the outside world. The Grand Hyatt, JW Marriott, Portman Ritz-Carlton, and St. Regis aren't merely hotels; they're landmarks on the Shanghai skyline and standard-bearers for all lodgings in town. Even the historic properties that make up the other half of Shanghai's hotel market feel the pressure to update their rooms and facilities. The increasing competition means there are bargains to be had, especially during the low season of November through March. Avoid traveling during the three national holidays—Chinese New Year (mid-January to mid-February), Labor Day (May 1), and National Day (October 1)—when rooms and prices will be at a premium.

Thanks to Shanghai's excellent subway system and cheap, plentiful taxis, no one neighborhood has a distinct advantage as a base for exploring the city. As Pudong and Hongqiao have developed into business destinations in their own right, they've attracted some of the city's finest hotels. The Bund is home to the most budget properties. The Old French Concession and City Center have the broadest selection of hotels and many popular tourist sites within their districts.

WHAT IT COSTS In Yuan				
	$$$$	$$$	$$	$	¢
FOR 2 PEOPLE	over 1800	1401–1800	1101–1400	700–1100	under 700

Prices are for two people in a standard double room in high season, excluding 10%–15% service charge.

Nanjing Lu & the Bund

$$$$ ▦ **The Four Seasons.** With palm trees, fountains, and golden-hued marble as warm as sunshine, the lobby of the Four Seasons establishes the hotel's theme as an elegant oasis in bustling downtown Puxi. Opened in 2002, this 37-story luxury hotel caters to its largely business clientele with impeccable service and its 24-hour business center, gym, and

butler service. The 439 spacious rooms—just 12 to 15 per floor—include a safe big enough for a laptop and a separate marble shower and tub. Nanjing Road and the Shanghai Museum are within a 10-minute walk, but the full-service spa, Jazz 37 club, and exceptional Si Ji Xuan Cantonese restaurant provide convincing reasons to stay in. ⊠ *500 Weihai Lu, Jing'an District, 200041* ☎ *021/6256–8888 or 800/819–5053* 🖷 *021/6256–5678* ⊕ *www.fourseasons.com* 🛏 *360 rooms, 79 suites* ⚭ *4 restaurants, room service, some in-room fax, in-room data ports, in-room safes, minibars, cable TV, in-room VCRs, pool, gym, hair salon, hot tub, spa, steam room, bar, lounge, shop, baby-sitting, dry cleaning, laundry services, concierge, concierge floor, Internet, business services, convention center, travel services, some free parking, no-smoking floors* 🖃 *AE, DC, MC, V.*

$$$$ 🏨 **JW Marriott.** The JW Marriott's futuristic 60-story tower turns heads with its 90-degree twist, which divides the executive apartments below from the 22-story hotel above and creates 360-degree views of the Puxi skyline. The interior follows classic lines with subtle Chinese accents. Celadon vases, wedding boxes, and ornamental jades complement the soft green-and-yellow palette and warm fiddleback wood in the spacious rooms. The largely business clientele appreciates the one-touch "At Your Service" call button, while the hotel's Mandara Spa, excellent restaurants, and JW Lounge—which has 50-plus martinis—are big draws for leisure travelers. ⊠ *399 Nanjing Xi Lu, Huangpu District, 200003* ☎ *021/5359–4969 or 888/236–2427* 🖷 *021/6375–5988* ⊕ *www. marriotthotels.com/shajw* 🛏 *305 rooms, 37 suites* ⚭ *3 restaurants, coffee shop, room service, in-room data ports, in-room safes, some in-room fax, minibars, cable TV, indoor pool, outdoor pool, health club, hot tub, sauna, steam room, spa, lobby lounge, lounge, library, piano, shops, baby-sitting, dry cleaning, laundry service, concierge, concierge floor, Internet, business services, convention center, travel services, parking (fee), no-smoking rooms, no-smoking floor* 🖃 *AE, DC, MC, V.*

★ **$$$$** 🏨 **The Portman Ritz-Carlton.** Outstanding facilities, gold standard service, and a high-profile location in the Shanghai Center make the Portman Ritz-Carlton one of the city's top attractions. The 50-story hotel devotes three floors solely to its fitness center, another four to its executive club rooms. The two-story lobby—a popular networking spot—exudes cool refinement with its ebony, marble, and chrome touches, while the guest rooms are gradually adopting a warmer peach and salmon palette. In addition to the Shanghai Center's surrounding shops, banks, airline offices, and restaurants, the hotel has its own deli and four top-notch restaurants. Its consistent rankings as one of the best employers and hotels in Asia translates into content employees and even happier customers. ⊠ *1376 Nanjing Xi Lu, Jing'an District, 200040* ☎ *021/6279–8888 or 800/241–3333* 🖷 *021/6279–8887* ⊕ *www.ritzcarlton.com* 🛏 *510 rooms, 68 suites* ⚭ *4 restaurants, deli, room service, in-room data ports, in-room safes, minibars, cable TV, tennis court, indoor-outdoor pool, health club, hair salon, hot tub, massage, sauna, steam room, squash, racquetball, 2 bars, shops, baby-sitting, dry cleaning, laundry service, concierge, concierge floor, Internet, business services, convention center, helipad, parking (fee), no-smoking rooms* 🖃 *AE, DC, MC, V.*

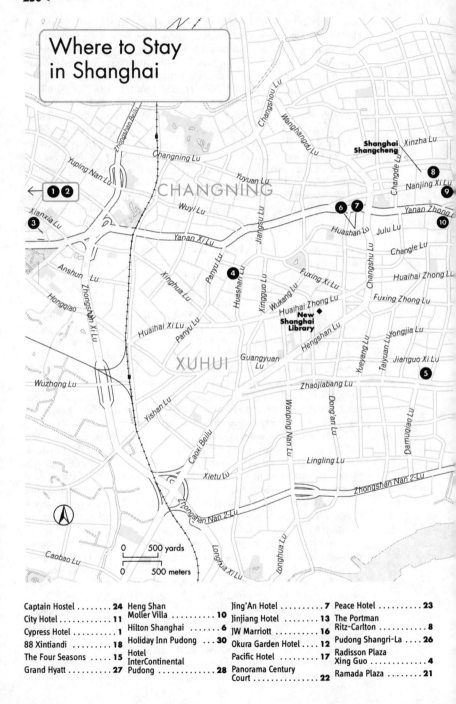

Where to Stay in Shanghai

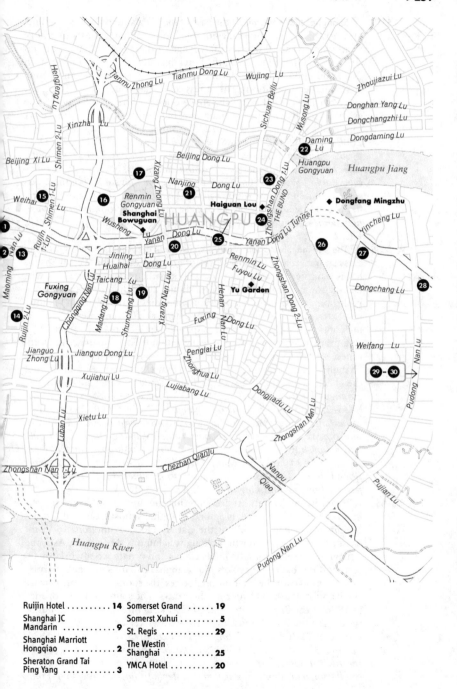

$$$$ ⊞ **Shanghai JC Mandarin.** At the base of the JC Mandarin's 30-story blue-glass towers lies the most memorable lobby in Shanghai. Its five-story hand-painted mural depicts the voyage of the Ming Dynasty admiral Zheng Ho. Opened in 1991, the hotel overhauled most public areas in 2003 and 2004. The Mandarin Club Lounge now occupies an inviting space on the second floor. The fitness center has added a spa. The Cuba cigar bar has carved a stylish lounge out of a former storeroom. The spacious rooms are due for an update, but are comfortable with earthy tones and natural wood. ⊠ *1225 Nanjing Xi Lu, Jing'an District, 200040* ☎ *021/6279–1888 or 800/338–8355* ⌂ *021/6279–1822* ⊕ *www.jcmandarin.com* ↴ *475 rooms, 35 suites* ⌂ *4 restaurants, café, patisserie, room service, in-room data ports, in-room safes, mini-bars, cable TV, tennis court, indoor pool, gym, hair salon, hot tub, massage, sauna, spa, steam room, squash, 2 bars, piano, shops, baby-sitting, dry cleaning, laundry service, concierge, concierge floor, Internet, business services, conference center, parking (fee), no-smoking floors* ⊟ *AE, DC, MC, V.*

★ **$$$$**   ⊞ **The Westin Shanghai.** With its distinctive room layouts, glittering glass staircase, and 90-plus works of art on display, the Westin Shanghai is a masterpiece, fittingly located near the majestic Bund. Crowne Deluxe rooms are miniature suites; sliding doors divide the sitting area, bathroom, and bedroom. Luxurious amenities include rainforest showers, extra deep tubs, and Westin's trademark Heavenly Beds. Pampering continues at the Banyan Tree spa—China's first—and stellar EEST restaurant, a sunny three-in-one venue with full Thai, Japanese, and Cantonese menus. Sunday brunch at the Stage restaurant is considered Shanghai's best. Service is so attentive that extra staff stand in front of the check-in counter to assist. ⊠ *Bund Center, 88 Henan Zhong Lu, Huangpu District, 200002* ☎ *021/6335–1888 or 888/625–5144* ⌂ *021/6335–2888* ⊕ *www.westin.com/shanghai* ↴ *276 rooms, 25 suites* ⌂ *3 restaurants, grocery, patisserie, juice bar, room service, in-room data ports, in-room fax, in-room safes, minibars, cable TV, indoor pool, health club, hair salon, hot tub, sauna, spa, steam room, bar, lobby lounge, piano, shops, baby-sitting, dry cleaning, laundry service, concierge, concierge floor, Internet, business services, convention center, travel services, some free parking, no-smoking floors* ⊟ *AE, DC, MC, V.*

★ **$$–$$$**   ⊞ **Peace Hotel.** With its art deco interior and unmistakable green pyramid roof, the Peace Hotel is among Shanghai's most treasured historic buildings. Opened in 1929 as the Cathay Hotel by millionaire Victor Sassoon, the 11-story north building was famous throughout Asia and a magnet for celebrities. Its high ceilings and ornate woodwork are intact, and the ballroom evokes old Shanghai cabarets and gala parties. However, save for the international suites, the rooms tend more toward small and stuffy than glamorous these days. The south building, opened in 1906 as the Palace Hotel, is the oldest structure on the Bund, but its rooms are the hotel's most modern, with larger bathrooms and nicer furniture. ⊠ *20 Nanjing Dong Lu, Huangpu District, 200002* ☎ *021/6321–6888* ⌂ *021/6329–0300* ⊕ *www.shanghaipeacehotel.com* ↴ *411 rooms, 9 suites* ⌂ *2 restaurants, room service, in-room safes, minibars, small gym, hair salon, massage, sauna, steam room, billiards, Ping-Pong,*

2 bars, lobby lounge, shops, baby-sitting, small playground, concierge, concierge floor, convention center, travel services, free parking, no-smoking rooms ▤ *AE, DC, MC, V.*

$–$$
Fodor'sChoice
★

▦ **Ramada Plaza.** With its ornate lobby resembling a European opera house, the Ramada Plaza Shanghai brings a touch of grandeur to the Nanjing Road pedestrian walkway. Statues of Greek gods reign from atop intricate inlaid tables. Soaring marble columns direct the eye skyward toward a stained-glass skylight. The fair-size rooms contrast dark woods with beige walls and upholstery, and they face in toward a dramatic atrium, topped by yet another courtyard and the executive lounge. Given the lush setting and ace location, the Ramada Plaza is a good value for the money, and you can usually get a room for less than the rack rate. ⊠ *719 Nanjing Dong Lu, Huangpu District, 200001* ☎ *021/6350–0000 or 800/854–7854* 🖷 *021/6350–6666* ⊕ *www.ramadainternational.com* ⤳ *333 rooms, 36 suites* ⚭ *4 restaurants, patisserie, room service, in-room data ports, in-room safes, minibars, cable TV, gym, hair salon, massage, sauna, steam room, billiards, lobby lounge, nightclub, shops, baby-sitting, dry cleaning, laundry service, concierge, concierge floor, Internet, business services, convention center, travel services, parking (fee), no-smoking floors* ▤ *AE, DC, MC, V.*

$
▦ **Pacific Hotel.** This 1926 property has done an admirable job of preserving its charm. In the original Italian-style front building, sixth- and seventh-floor rooms have wood floors, ornate molded ceilings, and great views of People's Park. (Bathrooms, though, are rather institutional.) The formal lobby has coffered ceilings and imposing columns. The smaller rooms in the rear building lack the fine detail and views but are still comfortable. Amenities fall short, and soundproofing could be better, but the hotel's proud history, prime location, and prices make it an appealing choice. ⊠ *108 Nanjing Xi Lu, Huangpu District, 200003* ☎ *021/6327–6226* 🖷 *021/6372–3634* ⊕ *www.jjusa.com* ⤳ *161 rooms, 5 suites* ⚭ *2 restaurants, room service, in-room data ports, minibars, cable TV, lobby lounge, shop, laundry service, Internet, business services, meeting rooms, travel services* ▤ *AE, DC, MC, V.*

$
▦ **Panorama Century Court.** In a part of town dominated by historic properties, Panorama Century Court stands out for its modern facilities, competitive prices, and great Bund views from across the Waibaidu Bridge. Opened in 2000, the 32-story Accor-owned hotel attracts European tourists familiar with the brand as well as business travelers. One- to three-bedroom suites all include living rooms and tiny kitchens, but you'll have to request utensils. Standard rooms have thoughtfully designed bathrooms with handy shelves for toiletries. The well-equipped gym has one of the best views in Shanghai. ⊠ *53 Huangpu Lu, Hongkou District, 200080* ☎ *021/5393–0008* 🖷 *021/5393–0009* ⊕ *www.panorama-sh.com* ⤳ *62 rooms, 92 suites* ⚭ *1 restaurant, room service, in-room data ports, in-room safes, kitchens, minibars, microwaves, refrigerators, cable TV, gym, sauna, steam room, lobby lounge, library, piano, laundry facilities, laundry service, concierge, Internet, business services, meeting rooms, parking (fee)* ▤ *AE, DC, MC, V.*

¢
▦ **Captain Hostel.** Backpackers choose Captain Hostel as much for its roof-top bar and restaurant as for its clean, bright rooms and conve-

nient location a half-block west of the Bund. The hopping Noah's Bar on the sixth floor has views of the Pudong skyline that rival those from much pricier lodgings. The dormitories accommodate 5 to 10 people per room in bunks resembling ship's berths, in keeping with the overall nautical theme in this 1920s hotel. The 20 first-class rooms are tired but fair-sized, with TVs and private bathrooms. Bunk rooms must be paid for in cash. ⊠ *37 Fuzhou Lu, Huangpu District, 200002* ☏ *021/6323–5053* 🖷 *021/6321–9331* ⊕ *www.captainhostel.com.cn* ⤴ *20 rooms, 85 rooms with shared bath* ⚂ *1 restaurant, cable TV in some rooms, bar, laundry facilities, Internet, meeting rooms, no-smoking rooms; no phones in some rooms* ▤ *MC, V.*

¢ 🏨 **YMCA Hotel.** Its central location—within a 15-minute walk of People's Square, Xintiandi, and the Bund—makes the YMCA Hotel a top destination for budget travelers. Built in 1929 as an actual YMCA, the 11-story brick building retains some of its original features: a temple-like exterior, painted ceiling beams on the second floor. A 2003 makeover gave the small rooms an apricot-and-beige color scheme and lighter furniture. The four dormitory rooms have single beds, rather than bunks. ⊠ *123 Xizang Nan Lu, Huangpu District, 200021* ☏ *021/6326–1040* 🖷 *021/6320–1957* ⊕ *www.ymcahotel.com* ⤴ *140 rooms, 6 suites, 4 rooms with shared bath* ⚂ *2 restaurants, coffee shop, small grocery, room service, some in-room safes, minibars, cable TV, gym (fee), hair salon, massage, billiards, Ping-Pong, recreation room, shops, laundry service, Internet, business services, meeting rooms, airport shuttle, travel services* ▤ *AE, DC, MC, V.*

Old French Concession

$$$$ 🏨 **Okura Garden Hotel.** Its park-like setting in the heart of the French Concession makes the 33-story Garden Hotel a favorite Shanghai retreat, especially for Japanese travelers familiar with the Okura Group name. The first three floors, which were once old Shanghai's French Club, have been restored, with cascading chandeliers, frescoes, and art deco details at every turn. Average-size rooms are simply furnished with silk wallpaper and European-style furniture. The romantic third-floor terrace bar overlooks the 2-acre garden, and the Japanese and French restaurants serve excellent but high-priced food. ⊠ *58 Maoming Nan Lu, Luwan District, 200020* ☏ *021/6415–1111* 🖷 *021/6415–8866* ⊕ *www.gardenhotelshanghai.com* ⤴ *478 rooms, 22 suites* ⚂ *5 restaurants, room service, in-room data ports, in-room safes, some in-room fax, minibars, cable TV, 2 tennis courts, indoor-outdoor pool, health club, hair salon, hot tub, massage, sauna, 3 bars, lobby lounge, shops, dry cleaning, laundry service, concierge, concierge floor, Internet, business services, convention center, airport shuttle, travel services, some free parking, no-smoking floors* ▤ *AE, DC, MC, V.*

$$$$ 🏨 **Radisson Plaza Xing Guo.** This quiet garden property was once the government-owned Xing Guo Hotel, a villa complex where Chairman Mao frequently stayed. The modern 16-story Radisson Plaza sprouted up in 2002, its garden-view rooms overlooking the central lawn and Mao's legendary Villa No. 1. The comfortable beige-tone rooms have ample work space, with two club chairs and a large desk. The Clark Hatch

Fitness Center has top-name equipment, an aerobics room, and an elevated pool. However, the hotel's location in the consular district is far from the subway and most attractions. ⊠ *78 Xingguo Lu, Changning District, 200052* ☎ *021/6212–9998* 🖨 *021/6212–9996 or 888/201–1718* ⊕ *www.radissonasiapacific.com* ⋧ *150 rooms, 40 suites* ⚫ *2 restaurants, café, room service, in-room data ports, some in-room fax, in-room safes, minibars, cable TV, golf simulator, health club, indoor pool, hair salon, hot tub, massage, sauna, steam room, bowling, Ping-Pong, squash, bar, lobby lounge, library, shops, baby-sitting, dry cleaning, laundry service, concierge, concierge floor, Internet, business services, meeting rooms, airport shuttle, travel services, some free parking, no-smoking rooms* ▤ *AE, DC, MC, V.*

$$$–$$$$ ▦ **88 Xintiandi.** Although it targets business travelers, 88 Xintiandi is a shopper's and gourmand's delight. The 53-room boutique hotel is in the heart of Xintiandi, its balconies overlooking the top-dollar shops and restaurants below. The rooms, all mini- or full-size suites with kitchens, are likewise upscale. Beds are elevated on a central, gauze-curtained platform; sitting areas have large TVs and DVD players. Stylish wood screens accent the rooms and common areas. Deluxe rooms and the executive lounge overlook man-made Lake Taipingqiao, and guests have access to the comprehensive Alexander City Club gym next door. ⊠ *380 Huangpi Nan Lu, Luwan District, 200021* ☎ *021/5383–8833* 🖨 *021/5353–8877* ⊕ *www.88xintiandi.com* ⋧ *12 suites, 41 rooms* ⚫ *1 restaurant, room service, in-room data ports, some in-room fax, in-room safes, kitchens, minibars, microwaves, refrigerators, cable TV, in-room VCRs, indoor pool, gym, bar, baby-sitting, laundry service, concierge, business services, parking (fee), no-smoking floors* ▤ *AE, DC, MC, V.*

$$$–$$$$ ▦ **Hilton Shanghai.** Opened in 1988 as Shanghai's first five-star hotel, the Hilton remains a local favorite among businessmen and airline crews. The 43-story triangular building is lower-keyed than its younger competitors, with an understated sand-tone color scheme and comfortable but not cutting-edge rooms. The delectable Gourmet Corner now occupies a large storefront in the front lobby, while in the rear lies the much-lauded Italian restaurant Leonardo's and the sunlit 24-hour Atrium Café, which resembles a quiet Chinese garden. On the top floors, the conference center, Penthouse Bar, and stellar Sichuan Court restaurant all have stunning views of the ever-expanding Puxi skyline. ⊠ *250 Huashan Lu, Jing'an District, 200040* ☎ *021/6248–0000 or 800/445–8667* 🖨 *021/6248–3848* ⊕ *www.shanghai.hilton.com* ⋧ *692 rooms, 28 suites* ⚫ *6 restaurants, café, coffee shop, grill, room service, in-room data ports, some in-room fax, minibars, cable TV, tennis court, indoor pool, health club, hair salon, hot tub, spa, sauna, Japanese baths, steam room, squash, 3 bars, lobby lounge, shops, baby-sitting, dry cleaning, laundry service, concierge, concierge floor, Internet, business services, convention center, airport shuttle, travel services, some free parking, no-smoking floors* ▤ *AE, DC, MC, V.*

$$–$$$ ▦ **City Hotel.** The joint-venture City Hotel almost matches the facilities but definitely lacks the polish of its brand-name competitors. Compact standard rooms have cream linens with baby-blue and pink stripes and small all-white marble bathrooms. Larger executive rooms, on the 21st through 23rd floors, have double closets, and more modern furniture and fixtures. The comprehensive City Club fitness center includes a full spa, and there's an indoor playroom for kids. Reasonably close to Huai-hai Lu shops and metro line 1, the hotel has equal appeal for business and leisure travelers. ⊠ *5–7 Shaanxi Nan Lu, Luwan District, 200020* ☎ *021/6255–1133* 🖷 *021/6255–0211* ⊕ *www.cityhotelshanghai.com* ↩ *274 rooms, 10 suites ☖ 3 restaurants, café, room service, in-room data ports, some in-room safes, minibars, cable TV, indoor pool, health club, hair salon, sauna, spa, steam room, billiards, 2 bars, lobby lounge, piano bar, shop, baby-sitting, laundry service, Internet, business services, convention center, travel services, parking (fee), no-smoking rooms* ▤ *AE, DC, MC, V.*

$$–$$$ 🏨 **Somerset Grand.** Designed as serviced apartments for expatriates, the Somerset Grand's suites are great for families wanting extra space plus the usual hotel amenities. The twin 34-story towers have 334 one-to three-bedroom suites, ranging from 890 to 2,500 square feet. (One-bedroom suites have only king beds.) The units feel homey, with blue-and-pink floral comforters and rugs and a small kitchen. Kids can burn off steam at the pool and play room. There's a great French restaurant and coffee shop on the grounds, plus the hotel is two blocks from the restaurants, shops, and movie theater at Xintiandi and 10 minutes to the subway. ⊠ *8 Jinan Lu, Luwan District, 200021* ☎ *021/6385–6888* 🖷 *021/6384–8988* ⊕ *www.the-ascott.com* ↩ *334 suites ☖ In-room data ports, in-room safes, kitchen, minibars, refrigerators, cable TV, 2 tennis courts, indoor pool, health club, hair salon, hot tub, massage, sauna, steam room, billiards, library, baby-sitting, playground, dry cleaning, laundry facilities, laundry service, concierge, Internet, business services, meeting rooms, travel services, parking (fee), no-smoking rooms* ▤ *AE, DC, MC, V.*

$–$$$ 🏨 **Jinjiang Hotel.** The former Cathay Mansions, Grosvenor Gardens, and Grosvenor House, now known collectively as the Jinjiang Hotel, are among the few art deco buildings left standing in the city. It's here that President Nixon and Premier Zhou Enlai signed the Shanghai Communique in 1972. Luxury suites in the Grosvenor House start at $800 nightly. The 193 rooms in the 1929 Cathay Building are plain but fair-sized with separate showers and tubs. Deluxe rooms are more stylish. The Jin Nan Building will reopen in summer 2005 with 120 renovated budget-price standard rooms. ⊠ *59 Maoming Nan Lu, Luwan District, 200020* ☎ *021/6258–2582* 🖷 *021/6472–5588* ⊕ *www. jinjianghotelshanghai.com* ↩ *328 rooms, 33 suites ☖ 5 restaurants, room service, in-room data ports, in-room safes, minibars, cable TV, indoor pool, health club, hair salon, sauna, bowling, 2 bars, lobby lounge, shops, baby-sitting, Internet, business services, convention center, airport shuttle, travel services, free parking, no-smoking rooms, no-smoking floors* ▤ *AE, DC, MC, V.*

$$ 🏨 **Jing'An Hotel.** The weekly chamber music concert in its lobby is just one example of how the Jing'An Hotel has retained its elegance and charm after 70 years. In a 1.5-acre garden, the Spanish-style main building carries the garden theme throughout its rooms. Mauve upholstery and cream wallpaper bloom with delicate floral patterns. Elab-

KID-FRIENDLY HOTELS IN SHANGHAI

Several hotels have good amenities for families with children. The **Somerset Grand,** in the old French Concession, is the best option, with fully equipped kitchens in large apartment-like suites. The hotel has a play room and a pool, and it's within walking distance of the shops and movie theater at Xintiandi. The **City Hotel,** also in the old French Concession, has smallish, somewhat tired rooms but there's an indoor playroom for kids. Rooms on the executive floors are larger and more up-to-date. Suites with kitchens at competitive rates are the main draw at the **Somerset Xuhui,** between the French Concession and Xujiahui. It's a bit far from the action on Nanjing Lu, but there's an indoor playroom and a sizeable pool.

orately carved wooden door frames and lintels direct the eye upward toward the 10-foot ceilings. Facilities are lacking, but the hotel's proximity to the subway line and its French Concession setting make this oft-overlooked property a winner. ⊠ *370 Huashan Lu, Jing'an District, 200040* ☎ *021/6248–0088* 🖷 *021/6249–6100* ⊕ *www.jinganhotel. net* ↩ *210 rooms, 17 suites* ⚴ *2 restaurants, coffee shop, room service, in-room data ports, in-room safes, minibars, cable TV, gym, hair salon, massage, sauna, chess room, lobby lounge, piano bar, shops, babysitting, dry cleaning, laundry service, concierge, Internet, business services, meeting rooms, airport shuttle, travel services, parking (fee), no-smoking rooms* ⊟ *AE, DC, MC, V.*

$–$$ 🏨 **Ruijin Hotel.** Formerly the Morriss Estate, the Ruijin Hotel showcases how opulently *taipans* (expatriate millionaire businessmen) lived in Shanghai's heyday of the 1930s. Rooms within the two preserved villas—No. 1 and Old No. 3—are rich with detail: high ceilings, ornate plaster molding, bamboo-etched glass. The two other buildings are significantly shorter on charm but still overlook the verdant grounds, which are shared with several top-notch restaurants. A hotel tower slated to open in 2006 will add 150 rooms and much-needed amenities; however, it will also result in the conversion of Villa No. 1 into a VIP villa, so reserve these rooms while you can. ⊠ *118 Ruijin Er Lu, Luwan District, 200020* ☎ *021/6472–5222* 🖷 *021/6473–2277* ⊕ *www. shedi.net.cn/outedi/ruijin* ↩ *62 rooms, 20 suites* ⚴ *Restaurant, coffee shop, room service, in-room safes, minibars, cable TV, hair salon, 2 bars, lobby lounge, shops, laundry service, Internet, business services, convention center, parking (fee), no-smoking rooms* ⊟ *AE, DC, MC, V.*

$–$$ 🏨 **Somerset Xuhui.** The family-focused facilities of the all-suites Somerset Xuhui help compensate for its location: off the subway line, halfway between Xujiahui's shops and French Concession attractions. An indoor playroom, sizeable pool, and fitness center overlooking Zhaojiabang Road provide diversion for children and adults—as does the

Starbucks downstairs. There are no restaurants, just small en suite kitchens. Units range from one to three bedrooms, the latter having twin beds for kids. Cozy living rooms and huge closets help make this hotel a good spot for families in Shanghai. ⊠ *888 Shaanxi Nan Lu, Xuhui District, 200031* ☎ *021/6466–0888* 🖷 *021/6466–4646* ⊕ *www. the-ascott.com* 🖙 *167 suites* ⧫ *In-room safes, in-room data ports, kitchens, minibars, microwaves, refrigerators, cable TV, 2 tennis courts, indoor pool, health club, hot tub, massage, sauna, steam room, billiards, Ping-Pong, library, baby-sitting, playground, dry cleaning, laundry facilities, laundry service, concierge, Internet, business services, meeting rooms, travel services, parking (fee), no-smoking rooms* ➯ *AE, DC, MC, V.*

$ 🏠 **Heng Shan Moller Villa.** Part gingerbread dollhouse, part castle, the Heng Shan Moller Villa has been one of Shanghai's most enchanting properties since its completion in 1936. British businessman Eric Moller built the villa to resemble a castle his daughter envisioned in a dream. The family fled Shanghai in 1941, and after 1949 the house was the Communist Youth League's headquarters. Opened as a boutique hotel in 2002, the original villa has 11 deluxe rooms and has been lushly restored with parquet floors, chandeliers, and ornately carved stairwells. Standard rooms in Building No. 2, however, are disappointingly plain. Guests have access to the neighboring Shanghai Grand Club's excellent fitness center. ⊠ *30 Shaanxi Nan Lu, Jing'an District, 200040* ☎ *021/6247–8881 Ext. 607* 🖷 *021/6289–1020* ⊕ *www.mollervilla.com* 🖙 *40 rooms, 5 suites* ⧫ *6 restaurants, coffee shop, in-room data ports, some in-room safes, minibars, cable TV, hair salon, shop, laundry service, Internet, business services, meeting rooms, free parking* ➯ *AE, DC, MC, V.*

Hongqiao Development Zone

$$$$ 🏠 **Shanghai Marriott Hongqiao.** With only eight stories and 325 rooms, the Marriott Hongqiao feels like a boutique hotel compared to its soaring competitors in Hongqiao. Opened in 2000, the hotel transformed its top two floors into executive floors in 2003. The hotel is quiet; inside twin rooms have balconies overlooking the third-floor pool-side courtyard. Porcelain vases and Ming-influenced furniture add some Chinese flair to the generous-size rooms. The Manhattan Steakhouse serves tender, juicy steaks, while the Marriott Café has an excellent Sunday brunch. ⊠ *2270 Hongqiao Lu, Changning District, 200336* ☎ *021/ 6237–6000 or 800/228–9290* 🖷 *021/6237–6222* ⊕ *www.marriott. com* 🖙 *312 rooms, 13 suites* ⧫ *4 restaurants, patisserie, room service, in-room data ports, in-room safes, minibars, cable TV, some in-room VCRs, 1 tennis court, indoor pool, health club, hair salon, hot tub, massage, sauna, steam room, 2 bars, lobby lounge, sports bar, baby-sitting, dry cleaning, laundry service, concierge, concierge floor, Internet, business services, convention center, airport shuttle, travel services, parking (fee), no-smoking floors* ➯ *AE, DC, MC, V.*

★ $$$$ 🏠 **Sheraton Grand Tai Ping Yang.** Business travelers value the Sheraton Grand for its conscientious service and its location, 15 minutes from Hongqiao Airport and adjacent to Shanghai Mart and INTEX. Formerly the Westin, this Japanese-managed property has four club floors, one-

A MASSAGE FOR EVERYONE

N CHINA, a massage isn't an indulgence; it's what the doctor orders. According to the tenets of traditional Chinese medicine, massage can help the body's qi, or energy, flow freely and remain in balance.

Of course, where you choose to have your massage can tip the scale toward indulgence. Around Shanghai are hundreds of blind massage parlors, inexpensive no-frills salons whose blind masseurs are closely attuned to the body's soft and sore spots. At the other end of the spectrum lie the hotel spas, luxurious retreats where pampering is at a premium. Here are just a few of the massage outlets in Shanghai that can attend to your needs.

The **Banyan Tree Spa** (⌷ 3F, the Westin Shanghai, 88 Henan Zhong Lu, Huangpu District ☎ 021/6335–1888), the first China outpost of this ultra-luxurious spa chain, occupies the third floor of the Westin Shanghai. The spa's 13 chambers as well as its treatments are designed to reflect wu xing, the five elemental energies of Chinese philosophy: earth, gold, water, wood, and fire. Relax and enjoy one of 10 massages (Y450–Y720), facials, body scrubs, or indulgent packages that combine all three.

With instructions clearly spelled out in English, **Double Rainbow Massage House** (⌷ 47 Yongjia Lu, Luwan District ☎ 021/ 6473–4000) provides a cheap (Y35–Y50), non-threatening introduction to traditional Chinese massage. Choose a masseur, state your preference for soft, medium, or hard massage, then keep your clothes on for a 45- to 60-minute massage. There's no ambience, just a clean room with nine massage tables.

Dragonfly (⌷ 20 Donghu Lu, Xuhui District ☎ 021/5405–0008) is a therapeutic retreat center that has claimed the middle ground between expensive hotel spas and workmanlike blindman massage parlors. Don the suede-soft treatment robes for traditional Chinese massage (Y120), or take them off for an aromatic oil massage (Y200).

The Three on the Bund complex includes the first **Evian Spa** (⌷ 3, The Bund [Zhongshan Dong Yi Lu], Huangpu District ☎ 021/6321–6622) outside of France. Its 14 theme rooms offer treatments from head to toe and nine different massages, including an Indian head massage (Y600) or a hot stone aromatherapy massage (Y900).

With its exposed wood beams, unpolished bricks and soothing fountains, the **Mandara Spa** (⌷ 399 Nanjing Xi Lu, Huangpu District ☎ 021/5359–4969) in the JW Marriott resembles a traditional Chinese water town. Face, beauty, and body treatments include the spa's signature Mandara massage (Y960), a 90-minute treatment in which two therapists administer a blend of five massage styles: Shiatsu, Thai, Lomi Lomi, Swedish, and Balinese.

Ming Massage (⌷ 298 Wulumuqi Nan Lu, Xuhui District ☎ 021/5465–2501) is a Japanese-style salon that caters to women, who receive a 20-percent discount daily from 11 to 2. Cross over the foot bridge to one of five small treatment rooms for a foot, body, or combination "Ming" massage (Y178).

touch service by phone, and golf privileges at Shanghai International Golf Club. Spacious standard rooms include large desks and ergonomic chairs, while plush grand rooms have oriental carpets and overstuffed chairs in the separate bed and sitting rooms. A grand staircase sweeps you from the formal lobby up to the second floor and the exceptional Bauernstube deli. Giovanni's serves Italian food as impressive as its views from the atop the 27th floor. ⊠ *5 Zunyi Nan Lu, Changning District, 200336* ☎ *021/6275–8888 or 888/625–5144* 🖷 *021/6275–5420* ⊕ *www.sheratongrand-shanghai.com* ✍ *474 rooms, 22 suites* ➘ *5 restaurants, café, coffee shop, in-room data ports, in-room safes, minibars, cable TV, golf privileges, pool, gym, hair salon, massage, sauna, steam room, 2 bars, lobby lounge, piano, shops, baby-sitting, dry cleaning, laundry service, concierge, concierge floor, Internet, business services, convention center, travel services, parking (fee), no-smoking floors* 🚭 *AE, DC, MC, V.*

$$–$$$ 🏨 **Cypress Hotel.** Once part of tycoon Victor Sassoon's estate, the Cypress Hotel's shaded, stream-laced grounds remain a tranquil retreat in noisy Shanghai. From the hotel's 149 rooms, you can look out over the garden and actually hear birdsong rather than car horns. The comfortable, moderate-size rooms have, appropriately, a garden-green color scheme. Expansion plans will likely close the extensive health club in 2005, but you'll still be able to drop a line in the fishing pond and take a stroll over the bridges and through the woods. ⊠ *2419 Hongqiao Lu, Changning District, 200335* ☎ *021/6268–8868* 🖷 *021/6268–1878* ✍ *141 rooms, 8 suites* ➘ *2 restaurants, room service, in-room data ports, in-room safes, minibars, cable TV, driving range, putting green, 3 tennis courts, indoor pool, gym, hair salon, massage, sauna, steam room, fishing, basketball, billiards, bowling, Ping-Pong, squash, bar, shop, baby-sitting, dry cleaning, laundry service, Internet, business services, meeting rooms, airport shuttle, travel services, parking (fee), no-smoking rooms* 🚭 *AE, DC, MC, V.*

Pudong New Area

$$$$ 🏨 **Grand Hyatt.** Occupying floors 53 through 87 of the spectacular Jin-
FodorśChoice mao Tower, the Grand Hyatt is the world's highest hotel. A combina-
★ tion of traditional and postmodern design, the Hyatt's interior is defined by art deco lines juxtaposed with space-age grillwork and sleek furnishings and textures. The 33-story central atrium is a marvel in itself—a seemingly endless cylinder with an outer-space aura. Room amenities are space age as well: CAT 5 optical lines for laptop use, Internet connections on the TV through a cordless keyboard, and three high-pressure water heads in the shower. Views from the rooms are spectacular; corner rooms have two walls of pure glass for endless panoramas of the Oriental Pearl Tower, majesty of the Bund, and expanse of the city below. ⊠ *Jinmao Dasha, 88 Shiji Dadao, Pudong 200121* ☎ *021/5049–1234 or 800/233–1234* 🖷 *021/5049–1111* ⊕ *www.shanghai.grand.hyatt.com* ✍ *510 rooms, 45 suites* ➘ *5 restaurants, café, coffee shop, food court, room service, in-room data ports, in-room safes, minibars, cable TV, indoor pool, health club, hair salon, spa, sauna, steam room, 3 bars, nightclub, piano bar, lobby lounge, shops, dry cleaning, laundry service, concierge, concierge*

floor, Internet, business services, convention center, parking (fee), some free parking ▤ *AE, DC, MC, V.*

★ **$$$$** ▦ **Pudong Shangri-La.** The Shangri-La occupies one of the most prized locations in Shanghai: overlooking the Huangpu River, opposite the Bund, near the Pearl Tower in Lujiazui. The hotel's breathtaking water's-edge views, white-glove service, and spacious rooms attract a mix of business and leisure travelers. Standard rooms alone are almost 400 square feet, with large closets and marble bathrooms. A 36-story addition scheduled for opening in spring 2005 will boost the number of rooms to nearly 1,000 and provide a more regal setting for the chain's signature Shang Palace Chinese restaurant. ⊠ *33 Fucheng Lu, Pudong 200120* ☎ *021/6882–8888 or 800/942–5050* ᐰ *021/6882–6688* ⊕ *www.shangri-la.com* ⇗ *575 rooms, 31 suites* ⌂ *4 restaurants, patisserie, in-room data ports, in-room safes, minibars, cable TV, tennis court, indoor pool, gym, hair salon, hot tub, massage, sauna, steam room, lobby lounge, nightclub, shops, baby-sitting, dry cleaning, laundry service, concierge, concierge floor, Internet, business services, convention center, travel services, parking (fee), no-smoking floors* ▤ *AE, DC, MC, V.*

★ **$$$$** ▦ **St. Regis.** The amphitheater-like lobby of the St. Regis sets the stage for the most indulgent hotel experience in Shanghai. The 318 rooms in this 40-story red granite tower—its design lauded by *Architectural Digest*—spare no expense, with Bose wave radios, Herman Miller Aeron chairs, and rainforest showers that give you the feeling of being under a waterfall. At 500 square feet, standard rooms compare to other hotels' suites and set the bar in Shanghai. Its two women-only floors are unique in Shanghai. Butlers address all your needs, from in-room check-in to room service. The location—15 minutes from the riverfront—is a drawback, but the fitness center and remarkable Danieli's Italian restaurant add to this pampering property's appeal. ⊠ *889 Dongfang Lu, Pudong 200122* ☎ *021/5050–4567 or 800/325–3589* ᐰ *021/6875–6789* ⊕ *www.starwood.com/stregis/index.html* ⇗ *270 rooms, 48 suites* ⌂ *3 restaurants, room service, in-room data ports, some in-room fax, in-room safes, minibars, cable TV, tennis court, indoor pool, health club, hair salon, hot tub, sauna, spa, steam room, 2 bars, lounge, shops, baby-sitting, dry cleaning, laundry service, concierge, Internet, business services, convention center, travel services, parking (fee), no-smoking floors* ▤ *AE, DC, MC, V.*

$$$–$$$$ ▦ **Hotel InterContinental Pudong.** The *pièce de résistance* of the 24-story Intercontinental is a nearly 200-foot-high Italian Renaissance–inspired atrium that brings in natural light to the 19 guest floors, six of which are executive floors. A vivid coat of red livens up the hallways and spacious guest rooms, which all have separate tub and shower. The restaurants cater to a wide range of tastes: Japanese, Cantonese, Shanghainese, Chaozhou, Continental. The open kitchen of Level One restaurant turns out a great lunch buffet with samples of all those cuisines. ⊠ *777 Zhangyang Lu, Pudong 200120* ☎ *021/5831–8888 or 800/327–0200* ᐰ *021/5831–7777* ⊕ *www.shanghai.intercontinental.com* ⇗ *317 rooms, 78 suites* ⌂ *4 restaurants, coffee shop, patisserie, room service, in-room data ports, in-room safes, minibars, cable TV, indoor pool, gym, hair salon, sauna, billiards, bar, piano, shops, baby-*

sitting, dry cleaning, laundry service, concierge, concierge floor, Internet, business services, convention center, parking (fee), no-smoking floors ⊟ *AE, DC, MC, V.*

$$$ ⊞ **Holiday Inn Pudong.** In the commercial district of Pudong, this Holiday Inn is well-situated for travelers with business in the area and just a four-block walk from metro line 2 into Puxi. Rooms are simply decorated—beige walls, bird's-eye maple furniture—but provide plenty of room to spread out your suitcases. The gym and indoor pool are quite large. For entertainment, there's a KTV (karaoke) club, a lobby piano bar and an Irish pub with Guinness and Kilkenny on tap. ⊠ *899 Dongfang Lu, Pudong 200122* ☎ *021/5830–6666 or 800/465–4329* ⊟ *021/ 5830–5555* ⊕ *www.ichotelsgroup.com* ⌫ *285 rooms, 30 suites* ⌷ *3 restaurants, coffee shop, patisserie, in-room safes, minibars, cable TV, indoor pool, gym, hair salon, massage, sauna, steam room, billiards, 2 bars, piano bar, pub, baby-sitting, dry cleaning, laundry service, concierge, concierge floor, Internet, business services, convention center, travel services, parking (fee), no-smoking floors* ⊟ *AE, DC, MC, V.*

NIGHTLIFE & THE ARTS

For up-to-date information about what's going on in the city, check out *That's Shanghai* and *City Weekend*, monthly and biweekly expatriate magazines available at Western bars, restaurants, and hotels throughout town; or *Shanghai Daily*, the English-language newspaper.

The Arts

Acrobatics

Shanghai Acrobatics Troupe. Considered China's best, the Shanghai Acrobatics Troupe performs remarkable gravity-defying stunts. The troupe holds court at both the Shanghai Center Theater and Shanghai Circus World, a glittering gold and green dome that seats more than 1,600 people. (⊠ Shanghai Center Theater, 1376 Nanjing Xi Lu, Jing'an District ☎ 021/6279–8945 ⊙ Daily 7:30 PM ⊠ Y50–Y100 ⊠ Shanghai Circus World, 2266 Gong He Xin Lu, Zhabei District ☎ 021/6652–7750 ⊠ Y50–Y150).

Chinese Opera

Kunju Opera Troupe. Kun opera, or Kunju, originated in Jiangsu province more than 400 years ago. Because of the profound influence it exerted on other Chinese opera styles, it's often called the mother of Chinese local opera. This troupe holds matinee performances every Saturday at 1:30 PM. Tickets cost Y20–Y50. ⊠ *9 Shaoxing Lu, Luwan District* ☎ *021/6437–1012.*

Yifu Theatre. Not only Peking opera, but also China's other regional operas, such as Huju, Kunju, and Shaoxing, are performed regularly at this theater. Considered the marquee theater for opera in Shanghai, it's just a block off People's Square. Call the box office for schedule and ticket information. ⊠ *701 Fuzhou Lu, Huangpu District* ☎ *021/6351–4668.*

Dance & Music

Jing'An Hotel. Every Sunday, the Shanghai Symphony Orchestra performs chamber music in the lobby of the Jing'An Hotel. Past concerts have included pieces by Bach, Ravel, and Chinese composer Huang Yongxi. ⊠ *San Diego Hall, Jing'An Hotel, 370 Huashan Lu, Jing'an District* ☎ *021/6248–1888 Ext. 687* ▧ *Y20.*

Majestic Theatre. Asian and Western performers from the Shaolin Warriors to the Wiggles have graced this stage in Shanghai's city center. ⊠ *66 Jiangning Lu, Jing'an District* ☎ *021/6217–4409.*

Shanghai Center Theater. One of the chief venues in town for quality performances, this stage serves as a home to the **Shanghai Acrobatic Troupe** and has hosted performers such as the Israel Contemporary Dance Group. The building's distinct bowed front was designed to resemble the Marriott Marquis Theater in New York's Times Square. ⊠ *Shanghai Center, 1376 Nanjing Xi Lu, Jing'an District* ☎ *021/6279–8663.*

Shanghai Concert Hall. City officials spent $6 million in 2003 to move this 73-year-old hall two blocks and turn the stage 180 degrees. It's the home of the Shanghai Symphony Orchestra and also hosts top-level classical musicians from around the world. ⊠ *523 Yanan Dong Lu, Luwan District* ☎ *021/6386–9153.*

Shanghai Conservatory of Music. A renovation in 2003 boosted the stature of this 780-seat hall as a top venue for acoustic performances. The hall showcases the conservatory's talented students and occasionally hosts visiting Asian and Western musicians. ⊠ *20 Fenyang Lu, Xuhui District* ☎ *021/6431–8756.*

Shanghai Grand Stage. Built in 1975, this 12,000-seat arena usually hosts rock concerts. In 2004 the venue got a multi-million dollar facelift thanks to the return of favorite son Yao Ming in an NBA exhibition match. ⊠*1111 Caoxi Bei Lu, inside Shanghai Stadium, Xuhui District* ☎*021/6473–0940.*

Shanghai Grand Theatre. The premier venue in town, this spectacular stage hosts top-billed domestic and international music and dance performances. In 2003 the theater hosted *Riverdance* and the Vienna Boys' Choir. ⊠ *300 Renmin Dadao, Huangpu District* ☎ *021/6372–8701, 021/6372–8702, or 021/6372–3833.*

Shanghai Oriental Art Center. Designed to resemble a white magnolia in full bloom, the glass-shrouded Shanghai Oriental Art Center represents the blossoming of Pudong's art scene. This $94 million center is intended to rival the Shanghai Grand Theater and includes a 2,000-seat symphony hall, 1,100-seat theater, and 300-seat auditorium. ⊠ *Shiji Da Dao at Jinxiu Lu, Pudong.*

Theater

Shanghai Dramatic Arts Center. In the budding theater district along Anfu Lu, this venue presents performances of Chinese plays, as well as foreign plays in Chinese translation, such as the Royal Shakespeare Theatre Company's production of the *Merchant of Venice* in 2002. ⊠ *288 Anfu Lu, Xuhui District* ☎ *021/6473–4567.*

Shanghai Grand Theater. As the premier stage in town, the Shanghai Grand Theater hosts top national and international performances. When Broadway shows come to Shanghai—as *Cats* did in 2003 and *Sound of Music* did in 2004—they play here. ✉ *300 Renmin Dadao, Huangpu District* ☎ *021/6372–8701, 021/6372–8702, or 021/6372–3833.*

Shanghai Theatre Academy. The academy's performance hall presents a full schedule of student and professional works. ✉ *670 Huashan Lu, Jing'an District* ☎ *021/6248–2920 Ext. 3040.*

Nightlife

Other cities in China may close down after dinner, but Shanghai never sleeps. In the wee hours of the morning, clubbers are still bar-hopping by cab between Hengshan Lu and Fuxing Park and all the hip spots in between. In the past, most partiers stopped at some point at the infamous Maoming Lu bar strip, whose seedy reputation was well deserved. But in summer 2004, city officials called off the party by imposing noise restrictions that forced many of the Maoming bars out of business or to move elsewhere. As a result, several bars listed below were in transition at press time; check the *that's Shanghai* bar listings to confirm current addresses.

Despite the recent upheaval, you'll find that Shanghai's nightlife scene still adheres to certain formulas. If there's live music, it's probably a Filipino cover band. Hotel bars will likely have jazz and cigars, with optional skyline views. Gay bars will be merely hinted at, never boldly promoted. And drink prices will strike you as expensive, especially if you've been coerced into buying one for one of Shanghai's countless "drinking girls." So grab your wallet, and *ganbei!* (bottoms up!).

Bars

★ **Amber.** If you prefer a mellow evening, Amber shines as a refined, low-key lounge. A comfy white banquette rims the downstairs room, while upstairs the glow-in-the-dark tables add splashes of color to the minimalist setting. The bar's known for its creative drink specials, such as deducting your taxi fare from the cost of your first drink. ✉ *184 Maoming Nan Lu, Luwan District* ☎ *021/6466–5224.*

Arch Bar and Café. For the artsy and intellectual crowd, head to Arch. Its location in Shanghai's only Flatiron building attracts architects and design professionals as well as people with an appreciation for this one-of-a-kind venue. ✉ *439 Wukang Lu, Xuhui District* ☎ *021/6466–0807.*

The Blarney Stone. The friendly Irish bartenders and lively chatter make the Blarney Stone one of the best places for drinking alone in Shanghai. ✉ *5A Dongping Lu, Xuhui District* ☎ *021/6415–7496.*

Blue Frog. A Maoming Lu survivor, the Blue Frog has hopped over to the burgeoning new bar strip along Tongren Lu, near the Shanghai Center. Popular among Westerners, this chummy chill-out pad serves up more than 100 shots, well-mixed cocktails, and decent Western pub food. ✉ *Tongren Lu, near Nanjing Xi Lu, Jing'an District* ☎ *021/ 6445–6634.*

FodorśChoice **Cotton Club.** A dark and smoky jazz and blues club, the Cotton Club
★ is an institution in Shanghai and considered *the* place for live music.
The house band is a mix of Chinese and foreign musicians with a sound
akin to Blues Traveler. ⊠ *8 Fuxing Xi Lu, Xuhui District* ☎ *021/
6437–7110.*

FodorśChoice **The Door.** The stunningly extravagant interior of the Door inspires ad-
★ miration and distracts from the bar's overpriced drinks. Take in the
soaring wood-beam ceilings, sliding doors, and museum's worth of antiques as you listen to the eclectic house band, which plays modern,
funky riffs on Chinese music on the *erhu, pipa,* and other traditional
instruments. ⊠ *4F, 1468 Hongqiao Lu, Changning District* ☎ *021/
6295–3737.*

Dublin Exchange. If you find yourself in Pudong, the Dublin Exchange
is a great place for a pint. Its upmarket Irish banker's club ambience
caters to the growing Wall Street that is Lujiazui. ⊠ *2F, HSBC Bldg.,
101 Yincheng Dong Lu, Pudong* ☎ *021/6841–2052.*

★ **Face.** The see-and-be-seen circuit in Shanghai starts at Face. Candlelighted
tables outside and a four-poster bed inside are the most vied-for spots
in this colonial villa with Indonesian furnishings. ⊠ *Bldg. 4, Ruijin Hotel,
118 Ruijin Er Lu, Luwan District* ☎ *021/6466–4328.*

Glamour Bar. For a beautiful view as well as beautiful people, go to the
Glamour Bar. As the lounge for the city's top restaurant, **M on the Bund,**
it enjoys the same prestige and panorama of the Bund and Pudong skyline. ⊠ *7F, 20 Guangdong Lu, Huangpu District* ☎ *021/6350–9988.*

Guandii. Opened by several Hong Kong celebrities, Guandii's minimalist low-slung bar attracts hopeful star-watchers as well as flush Chinese
who flash their wealth by ordering bottles of one of the 30 champagnes
on the drink menu. ⊠ *Fuxing Park, 2 Gaolan Lu, Luwan District*
☎ *021/5383–6020.*

Long Bar. In the Shanghai Center, the narrow, horseshoe-shape Long Bar
has a loyal expat-businessman clientele. Rousing rounds of liar's dice,
a big-screen TV, and chest-thumping conversations among executives
provide the entertainment. ⊠ *1376 Nanjing Xi Lu, Jing'an District*
☎ *021/6279–8268.*

Malone's American Café. A magnet for Western expats and travelers, Malone's is always packed. The fun Filipino cover band, Art-7, belts out
pitch-perfect versions of Van Morisson and No Doubt. TVs broadcast
sporting events, and pool tables draw people upstairs to the second floor.
The Shanghai Comedy Club brings in comedians one weekend each month
to the makeshift third-floor stage. ⊠ *255 Tongren Lu, Jing'an District*
☎ *021/6247–2400.*

★ **O'Malley's.** The most beloved of Shanghai's Irish pubs, O'Malley's, has
the requisite Guinness on tap and live Irish music. Its outdoor beer garden packs in the crowds in the summer and during broadcasts of European soccer and rugby matches. ⊠ *42 Taojiang Lu, Xuhui District*
☎ *021/6474–4533.*

Dance Clubs

California Club. Celebrity guest DJs play everything from tribal to disco for the bold and beautiful crowd at this hip establishment. The club is part of the Lan Kwai Fong complex at Park 97, which also includes Baci and Tokio Joe's restaurants and ShanghART gallery. ✉ *Park 97, 2A Gaolan Lu, Luwan District* ☎ *021/5383–2328.*

Judy's Too. A veteran on the club scene, Judy's Too is infamous for its hard-partying, meat-market crowd. The club grew in notoriety after being memorialized in Wei Hui's racy novel *Shanghai Baby*. ✉ *Tongren Lu, near Nanjing Xi Lu, Jing'an District* ☎ *021/6473–1417.*

Rojam. A three-level techno behemoth, Rojam is like a never-ending rave that bulges with boogiers and underground lounge lizards from the under-30 set. ✉ *4/F, Hong Kong Plaza, 283 Huaihai Zhong Lu, Luwan District* ☎ *021/6390–7181.*

Hotel Bars

B.A.T.S. (Bar At The Shangri-La). Tucked away in the basement of the Shangri-La, B.A.T.S. is perhaps the best dance club in Pudong. However, the crowd ebbs and flows depending on the quality of the band. The cave-like brick-walled space has diner-style booths arranged around a large central bar. ✉ *Pudong Shangri-La, 33 Fucheng Lu, Pudong* ☎ *021/6882–8888.*

★ **Cloud 9.** Perched on the 87th floor of the Grand Hyatt, Cloud 9 is the highest bar in the world. It has unparalleled views of Shanghai from among—and often above—the clouds. The sky-high views come with sky-high prices; there's a spending minimum of Y95 per person. If you're lucky, maybe the Chinese fortune teller who makes nightly rounds of the candlelit tables will tell you that wealth is in your future. ✉ *Grand Hyatt, 88 Shiji Dadao, Pudong* ☎ *021/5049–1234.*

★ **Jazz 37.** The Four Seasons' jazz bar matches its penthouse view with a stylish interior. Grab a canary-yellow leather chair by the white grand piano for some top-quality live jazz. ✉ *The Four Seasons, 500 Weihai Lu, Jing'an District* ☎ *021/6256–8888.*

Patio Bar. No skyline views here, just a dazzling, dizzying view of the Grand Hyatt's soaring 33-story atrium. It's an expensive, but impressive, stop for a pre- or post-dinner drink. ✉ *Grand Hyatt, 88 Shiji Dadao, Pudong* ☎ *021/5049–1234.*

Karaoke

Karaoke is ubiquitous in Shanghai; most nights, the private rooms at KTV (Karaoke TV) establishments are packed with Shanghainese crooning away with their friends. Many KTV bars employ "KTV girls" who sing along with (male) guests and serve cognac and expensive snacks. (At some establishments, KTV girls are also prostitutes.) That said, karaoke is largely a legitimate, and fun, pastime in town.

Cash Box (Party World). This giant establishment is one of Shanghai's most popular KTV bars. Its warren of rooms is packed nightly. ✉ *457 Wulumuqi Lu, Xuhui District* ☎ *021/6374–1111* ✉ *208 Chongqing Nan Lu, inside Fuxing Park, Luwan District* ☎ *021/5306–3888.*

Maya. Shanghai's well-heeled hipsters favor the deluxe KTV rooms at Maya over its dance floor. Its super-stiff cocktails will turn even the meekest performer into a microphone hog. ✉ *4–5F, Yunhai Bldg., 1333 Huaihai Zhong Lu, Xuhui District* ☎ *021/6415–2281.*

SPORTS & THE OUTDOORS

Auto-Racing
Shanghai International Circuit. Shanghai made its debut on the Formula 1 circuit in 2004 with the opening of this circuit. ✉ *Anting District* ☎ *021/ 6330–5555.*

Go-Carting
DISC Kart. This is definitely not your father's go-cart. A lap on a 160cc cart around the tight indoor track can, at times, seem more like a demolition derby. ✉ *326 Aomen Lu, Jing'an District* ☎ *021/6277–5641.*

Shanghai Hauge Racing Car Club. Races are a bit more civilized at this club. You are required to wear a helmet while racing its 50cc to 200cc carts around its large outdoor track. ✉ *880 Zhongshan Bei Yi Lu, Hongkou District* ☎ *021/6531–6800.*

Golf
With its own international tournament—the Volvo China Open—and several courses designed by prestige names, Shanghai is making its mark on the golf scene. Approximately 20 clubs dot the countryside within a two-hour arc of downtown. All clubs and driving ranges run on a membership basis, but most allow nonmembers to play when accompanied by a member. A few even welcome the public. Most clubs are outside the city, in the suburbs and outlying counties of Shanghai.

Grand Shanghai International Golf and Country Club. This club has a Ronald Fream–designed 18-hole championship course and driving range. ✉ *18 Yangcheng Zhong Lu, Yangcheng Lake Holiday Zone, Kunshan City, Jiangsu province* ☎ *0512/5789–1999.*

Shanghai Binhai Golf Club. Peter Thomson designed the Scottish links-style, 27-hole course at this club in Pudong. Another 27 holes are on the books. ✉ *Binhai Resort, Baiyulan Dadao, Nanhui County, Pudong* ☎ *021/5805–8888.*

Shanghai Silport Golf Club. This club hosts the Volvo China Open. Its 27-hole course on Dianshan Lake was designed by Bobby J. Martin; a new nine holes designed by Roger Packard opened in 2004. ✉ *1 Xubao Lu Dianshan Lake Town, Kunshan City, Jiangsu province* ☎ *0512/ 5748–1111.*

Shanghai Sun Island International Club. You'll find a 27-hole course designed by Nelson & Haworth plus an excellent driving range at this club. ✉ *2588 Shantai Lu, Zhu Jia Jiao, Qingpu District* ☎ *021/5983–0888 Ext. 8033.*

Tianma Country Club. Tianma is the most accessible course to the public. Its 18 holes have lovely views of Sheshan Mountain. ✉ *3958 Zhaokun Lu, Tianma Town, Songjiang District* ☎ *021/5766–1666.*

Tomson Shanghai Pudong Golf Club. The closest course to the city center, Tomson has 18 holes and a driving range designed by Shunsuke Kato. Robert Trent Jones II has inked a deal to develop the club's second course. ✉ *1 Longdong Dadao, Pudong* ☎ *021/5833–8888.*

Health Clubs, Swimming Pools & Tennis

Most of the best health clubs and pools are at the Western-style hotels. Fees are charged for those who are not hotel guests. A few facilities outside of hotels offer day passes for Y100 to Y200.

Fitness First. This independent club is popular among the younger expats and locals. Cardio training is its strength. ✉ *Plaza 66, 1266 Nanjing Xi Lu, Jing'an District* ☎ *021/6288–0152.*

Grand Hyatt. In Pudong, the Hyatt's Club Oasis has the workout room with the best view in town, from the 57th floor of the Jin Mao. Nonmembers and nonguests must pay a Y300 day rate. ✉ *Jin Mao Dasha, 88 Shiji Dadao, Pudong* ☎ *021/5047–1234 Ext. 8938.*

Kerry Center. Fitness fanatics in town favor the gym at the Kerry Center. There are extensive classes and personal training options, well-equipped weight rooms, a swimming pool, and even a rotating rock-climbing wall. ✉ *1515 Nanjing Xi Lu, Jing'an District* ☎ *021/6279–4625.*

Radisson Plaza Xing Guo. The Clark Hatch gym at the Radisson is run by an American manager and has top-name equipment, an aerobics studio, a pool, even a bowling alley. Nonmembers and nonguests pay a Y200 day rate. ✉ *78 Xingguo Lu, Changning District* ☎ *021/6212–9998.*

Shanghai Hilton. The Spa here has an elevated swimming pool; weight room; tennis, racquetball, and squash courts; and a full schedule of aerobics, yoga, and other classes. The day rate for nonguests and nonmembers is a prohibitive Y480. ✉ *250 Huashan Lu, Jing'an District* ☎ *021/6248–0000.*

The St. Regis. This hotel has a complete, well-designed fitness center, with a curtain of water surrounding its pool for privacy. The day rate for nonmembers is Y180. ✉ *889 Dongfang Lu, Pudong* ☎ *021/5050–4567 Ext. 6652.*

Skiing

Shanghai Yin Qi Xing Indoor Skiing Site. This innovative indoor venue brings winter fun to Shanghai's tropical climes. The world's second largest indoor ski run, the gentle 4,100-foot slope is good for beginners, who can take snowboarding or skiing lessons in Chinese or Japanese. ✉ *1835 Qixing Lu, Minhang District* ☎ *021/6478–8666.*

Soccer

Shanghai Stadium. The overwhelmingly grandiose, UFO-like Shanghai Stadium seats 80,000 spectators and holds athletic events, especially soccer matches, regularly. ✉ *666–800 Tianyaoqiao Lu, Xuhui District* ☎ *021/6426–6888 Ext. 8268.*

SHOPPING

You can accomplish most of your souvenir shopping in Shanghai at two stops. The shops around Yu Garden are convenient for traditional Chinese gifts: chopsticks, name chops (seals with your name engraved in Chinese and English), painted bottles, silk, pearls, and teapots. Xiangyang Market is knockoff central, with watches, bags, shoes, and clothes galore. The clothing sold here is made for export, so you're more likely to find items that fit. Most department stores don't carry Western-sized clothing, and those that do will likely hand you an XXXL to try on, so prepare your ego for the bruising.

While prices are fixed at government-owned stores and most malls, never accept the first price (or even the first counteroffer) at markets and small stores. Bargaining is a full-contact sport in Shanghai, with as many bluffs, blitzes, and strategies as an NFL playbook. Decide what your desired final price is, then start negotiations at 15% to 25% of the asking price. If the vendor's not budging, walk away; he'll likely call you back.

Major Shopping Districts

Huaihai Zhong Lu

Huaihai Zhong Lu in Puxi is shopping for the middle-class masses. Retail stores for such Asian brands as Baleno dominate the seemingly endless strip mall.

Nanjing Dong Lu

Shanghai No. 1 Department Store anchors the row of Chinese department stores along the Nanjing Dong Lu pedestrian walkway, which stretches from just east of People's Square to a few blocks west of the Bund.

Nanjing Xi Lu

Nanjing Xi Lu, around the Shanghai Center in Puxi's city center, is Shanghai's equivalent of New York's Fifth Avenue. Plaza 66, CITIC Square, and Westgate Mall are home to the big-name brands—Prada, Burberry, and Versace—copied shamelessly at Xiangyang Market.

Taikang Lu

Taikang Lu in Puxi has become Shanghai's Soho. International designers and artists have settled into the lofts and lanes along this short stretch of street.

Xujiahui

The megamall corner at Xujiahui in Puxi looks straight out of Tokyo. The cavernous domed Grand Gateway holds center court, flanked by Metro City, Oriental Shopping Center, and Huijin Department Store.

Other Shopping Districts

Even outside the malls, Shanghai's shopkeepers of a feather tend to flock together. Shanghai's book street, **Fuzhou Lu,** is a few blocks south of and parallel to the Nanjing Dong Lu pedestrian walkway in Puxi. For furniture warehouses, wander **Wuzhou Lu,** in western Puxi. For greatly discounted children's clothing and shoes, hit the underground mall at **10 Puan Lu**, a few blocks north of Xintiandi in Puxi. You'll find *qipao* (traditional Chinese dress) shops aplenty on **Changle Lu** between Maoming Nan Lu and Shaanxi Nan Lu, two streets that also are home to dozens of tiny boutiques in the blocks just north and south of Huaihai Lu.

Department Stores & Malls

Grand Gateway. Look for the dome; beneath you'll find more than 1.4 million square feet of shopping and entertainment, including a theater, restaurants, and floor after floor of clothing stores. ⌂ *1 Hongqiao Lu, Xuhui District* ☎ *021/6407–0115.*

Plaza 66. Home of the elite brands that are copied so shamelessly at Xianyang Market, Plaza 66 is where you can buy real Prada, Piaget, and Versace. Most of the mall's customers are strictly window shoppers. ⌂ *1266 Nanjing Xi Lu, Jing'an District* ☎ *021/5306–8888.*

Super Brand Mall. The 10-story Super Brand Mall has promise in the underdeveloped Pudong shopping scene. You'll find a movie theater, a huge Lotus Supermarket in the basement, a substantial food court, and outlets for several of Shanghai's popular restaurants, such as **South Beauty.** ⌂ *168 Lujiazui Lu, Pudong* ☎ *021/6887–7888.*

Westgate Mall. Quality Chinese restaurants and a movie theater help make Westgate a well-rounded mall. Its anchor store is **Isetan**, a fashionable Japanese-run department store that carries such brands as Lancôme, Clinique, Benetton, Esprit, and Episode. ⌂ *1038 Nanjing Xi Lu, Jing'an District* ☎ *021/6322–3344.*

Markets

Bargaining is an inescapable part of the sales ritual in markets. Remember that vendors inflate their first offers, expecting to negotiate. Don't be afraid to counter-offer a price less than half the amount of the first offer. And shop around, many vendors stock identical items.

Antiques Market of Shanghai Old Town God Temple (Huabao Building). Tucked in the basement of this cornerstone building at Yu Garden, this market is a convenient, albeit higher priced, stop for antiques. You'll find 250 booths selling ivory, jade, porcelain, and other collectibles, all at negotiable prices. ⌂ *Yu Garden, 265 Fangbang Zhong Lu, Huangpu District* ☎ *021/6355–9999.*

Cang Bao Antiques Building (Cang Bao Lou). During the week, you can browse four floors of booths that sell everything from Mao paraphernalia to real and fake antique porcelain. On Sunday, the action starts far before sunrise when, according to a local saying, only ghosts should be awake, hence the market's nickname: "ghost market." Hawkers from the provinces arrive early to lay out their goods on the sidewalk or inside on the fourth floor. Ivory, jade, and wood carvings are among the many goods sold here, all at negotiable prices. ⌂ *457 Fangbang Zhong Lu, Huangpu District.*

★ **Dongjiadu Lu Fabric Market.** You'll find everything you need to make a garment: buttons, Chinese knots, even the tailors themselves. (Try Shirly at stall 220.) More than 250 vendors sell fabrics from cashmere to leather to silk of all kinds. There's Thai silk at stall 154, double-sided cashmere in winter and linen in summer at stall 164. All prices are negotiable. Try to shop here in the morning, before the temperatures and crowds become unbearable. ⊠ *118 Dongjiadu Lu, by Zhongshan Nan Lu, Huangpu District* ⊙ *Daily 9–5.*

Fodor'sChoice **Dongtai Lu Antiques Market.** Outside antiques stalls line six blocks and
★ sell everything from Buddha statues to Mao posters to Victrolas. While the chances of finding a real antique among the reproductions are slim, it's fun scavenging among the shelves to see what you can unearth. You'll see the same "jade" bowls and porcelain vases in multiple stalls, so if your first bargaining attempt isn't successful, you'll have another opportunity a few stores down. Prices have shot up over the years and fakes abound, so bargain hard and with the knowledge you're likely getting a curio rather than a true collectible. ⊠ *Off Xizang Lu, Huangpu District.*

Pearl City. Several dozen vendors sell and repair pearl jewelry at this market in the heart of the Nanjing Road pedestrian walkway. ⊠ *2nd and 3rd floors, 558 Nanjing Dong Lu, Huangpu District.*

★ **Xiangyang Market** Shanghai's headquarters for knockoff items, Xiangyang Market sells it all. In addition to souvenir T-shirts and silk duds, you'll find designer-label purses, jackets, watches, and clothing. Some are real—seconds or swiped from the factory in China—but most are copies, so check all purchases carefully for flaws before agreeing on a price. ⊠ *999 Huaihai Zhong Lu, bordered by Huaihai Zhong Lu, Fenyang Lu, Shaanxi Nan Lu and Nanchang Lu, Xuhui District.*

Specialty Stores

Antiques & Furniture

Antiques markets, shops, and furniture warehouses abound in Shanghai, as increasing numbers of foreigners, lured by news of great deals, flock to the city. Great deals, however, are gradually becoming only good deals. Note that fake antiques are often hidden among real treasures and vice versa. Also be aware of age: the majority of pieces date from the late Qing Dynasty (1644–1911); technically, only items dated after 1795 can be legally exported. When buying antique furniture, it helps to know age, of course, and also what kind of wood was used. Although the most commonly used was elm, woods ranging from camphor to mahogany can be found in Chinese antiques. All shops will renovate any pieces you buy, and most can arrange international shipping.

Henry Antique Warehouse. This company has the unique honor of being a Chinese antique furniture research, teaching, and training institute for Tongji University. Part of the showroom often serves as an exhibition hall for the modern designs created jointly by students and the warehouse's 50 craftsmen. On average, the showroom has 2,000 pieces on display, ranging from altar tables to 1920s art deco bedroom furniture.

✉ *3F, Building 2, 389 Hongzhong Lu, off Wuzhong Lu, Minhang District* ☎ *021/6401–0831.*

★ **Hu & Hu Antiques.** Co-owner Marybelle Hu worked at Taipei's National Palace Museum as well as Sotheby's in Los Angeles before opening this shop with sister-in-law, Lin, in 1998. Their bright, airy showroom contains not only such furniture as Tibetan chests but also a large selection of accessories, from lanterns to moon-cake molds. Their prices are a bit higher than their competitors, but so is their standard of service. ✉ *1685 Wuzhong Lu, Minhang District* ☎ *021/6405–1212.*

Madame Mao's Dowry. From Depression-era glass to Cultural Revolution propaganda posters, this boutique's eclectic collection chronicles the past century of Shanghai's turbulent history. ✉ *70 Fuxing Xi Lu, Xuhui District* ☎ *021/6437–1255.*

Arts & Crafts/Galleries

Art Scene. A 1930s French Concession villa serves as a beautiful, albeit contrasting, backdrop for this gallery's contemporary Chinese artwork. Like the established and emerging artists it represents, the gallery is making a name for itself internationally, having participated in Art Chicago and the San Francisco International Art Exposition. ✉ *No. 8, Lane 37, Fuxing Xi Lu, Xuhui District* ☎ *021/6437–0631.*

Arts and Crafts Research Institute. Shanghai artisans create pieces of traditional Chinese arts and crafts right before your eyes at this institute. You can purchase everything from paper cuts to snuff bottles, although at prices higher than you'll pay at the stalls around Yu Garden. ✉ *79 Fenyang Lu, Xuhui District* ☎ *021/6437–0509* 🖭 *Y8.*

Eddy Tam's Gallery. Inexpensive picture framing is one of Shanghai's best-kept shopping secrets. While its frame selection is somewhat limited, this skilled shop does attractive, inexpensive custom framing work. It also sells original peasant paintings, shadowboxed Chinese mementos, and other artwork. ✉ *20 Maoming Nan Lu, Luwan District* ☎ *021/ 6253–6715.*

Elegance Art Studio. David Yang's beautiful silk photo albums, CD cases, and notebooks are sold at many of Shanghai's five-star hotels and in American boutiques. You can buy from him directly at his home studio at discounted prices. Call ahead for an appointment. ✉ *Building 10, Suite 201, 350 Guiping Lu, Minhang District* ☎ *021/6485–8720.*

Friendship Store. This state-owned chain for foreigners started in major Chinese cities as a sign of friendship when China first opened to the outside world. It's touristy but a good quick source of Chinese silk clothes, snuff bottles, carpets, calligraphy, jade, porcelain, and other traditional items that are certified as authentic, and therefore priced accordingly. The current location, opened in late 2003, is half the original's size but includes a mix of domestic and imported food products—including Starbucks, which has a kiosk on the first floor. There's no bargaining, but there are occasional sales. ✉ *65 Jingling Xi Lu, Huangpu District* ☎ *021/6337–3555.*

Shanghai Museum Bookshop. In the museum's comprehensive gift shop, you'll find everything from postcards and pearls to reproductions of the museum's porcelains. Its large book section has coffee table books as well as titles on Chinese art and culture. ⊠ *Shanghai Museum, 201 Renmin Dadao, Huangpu District* ☎ *021/6372–3500.*

ShanghART. The city's first modern art gallery, ShanghART is *the* place to check out the work of art-world movers and shakers such as Ding Yi, Xue Song, and Shen Fan. Here you can familiarize yourself with Shanghai's young contemporary avant-garde artists, who are garnering increasing international attention. ⊠ *Park 97, 2 Gaolan Lu, Luwan District* ☎ *021/6359–3923* 🖷 *021/6359–3923.*

Simply Life. Dress up your table with Simply Life's tasteful Asian-influenced tableware and silk accessories (many of which are copied and sold cheaper at the local markets). You'll find gold and red lacquerware, hand-painted bone china, Thai silverware, and silk placemats. ⊠ *1–2F, Xintiandi South Block, Building 5, 123 Xingye Lu, Luwan District* ☎ *021/6387–5100.*

Carpets
Beijing has always been a better place to buy Chinese rugs, but Shanghai has a few shops that sell silk and wool carpets.

Tom's Gallery. The carpet gallery at the back of this antiques store sells three varieties of carpets: high-quality silk carpets from Henan province, wool carpets from Xinjiang, and lower-priced fashion rugs from Qinghai. ⊠ *325-1 Huashan Lu, Jing'an District* ☎ *021/6209–9058.*

Chinese Medicine
Shanghai No. 1 Dispensary. Claiming to be China's largest pharmacy, the state-run No. 1 Dispensary has 12 locations in Shanghai. Its flagship store on Nanjing Dong Lu carries Eastern and Western medicines from ginseng to hairy antler, aspirin to acupuncture needles. ⊠ *616 Nanjing Dong Lu, Huangpu District* ☎ *021/6322–4567.*

Clothing
Feel. The qipao may be a traditional Chinese dress, but Feel proves with its original designs that it's a style for modern times as well. The staff will alter its styles to fit your frame. ⊠ *No. 2, Lane 210, Taikang Lu, Luwan District* ☎ *021/5465–4519.*

Shanghai Tang. This trés chic expensive boutique started in Hong Kong and opened its Shanghai branch in late 2003. Its trademark neon-colored silks come in every form, style, and size: *qipaos* and bags for the ladies, jackets for the men, plus accessories and home furnishings. ⊠ *Promenade, Shop E, 59 Maoming Nan Lu, Luwan District* ☎ *021/5466–3006.*

Supermarkets & Drug Stores
City Supermarket. The city's premier import grocery store, City Supermarket, can be counted on for products you can't find anywhere else—at sky-high prices you won't see elsewhere. You'll find surprises on every aisle: nylons, laundry detergent, corkscrews, even baby food. ⊠ *Shang-*

hai Center, 1376 Nanjing Xi Lu, Jing'an District ☎*021/6279–8018* ✉*BF,*
Hong Kong New World Department Store, 939 Huaihai Zhong Lu, by
Shaanxi Nan Lu, Luwan District ☎ *021/6474–1260.*

Watson's. The Walgreens of China, Watson's has everyday health and
beauty items: shampoo, soap, nail polish remover. ✉ *787–789 Huaihai Zhong Lu, Luwan District* ☎ *021/6431–8650.*

Fabrics & Tailors

China is famous for its silk, but some unscrupulous vendors will try to
pass off synthetics at silk prices. Ask the shopkeeper to burn a small scrap
from the bolt you're considering. If the burnt threads bead up and smell
like plastic, the fabric is synthetic. If the threads turn into ash and smell
like burnt hair, the fabric is real silk. (The same goes for wool.) For brocade silk, fair market prices range from Y30 to Y40 a meter; for synthetics, Y10 to Y28. You'll pay more in retail shops.

Tailors usually charge a flat fee and require a deposit, with the balance
paid upon satisfactory completion of the garment. If you can, bring in a
picture of what you want made or an existing garment for them to copy.
Try to allow enough time for an initial and follow-up fitting. Tailors are
accustomed to working with Chinese bodies and may need to adjust the
garment a bit more to achieve a proper fit on larger Western frames.

Dave's Custom Tailoring. Its English-speaking staff and skilled tailoring
make Dave's a favorite among expat and visiting businessmen. The shop
specializes in men's dress shirts and wool suits, which require 10 days
and two fittings to complete. The store moved from its popular Shanghai Center location in 2004; although another tailor has filled the space,
the original Dave—owner Dave K. C. Shiung—can only be found at the
shop on Wuyuan Lu. ✉ *No. 6, 288 Wuyuan Lu, Xuhui District* ☎ *021/
5404–0001.*

Hanyi. A well-respected qipao shop, Hanyi has a book of styles that its
tailors can make in three days or more complex, finely embroidered patterns that require a month for proper fitting. Prices range from Y1,000
to Y1,800. ✉ *217–221 Changle Lu, Luwan District* ☎ *021/5404–4727.*

Silk King (Shanghai Silk Commercial Company). Silk King is respected
for its quality silk and wool. Prices start at Y68 per meter. Staff tailors
can transform that silk into qipaos for Y500 to Y700. ✉ *139 Tianping
Lu, Xuhui District* ☎ *021/6282–5013* ✉ *590 Huaihai Zhong Lu,
Luwan District* ☎ *021/6372–0561* ✉ *1226 Huaihai Zhong Lu, Xuhui
District* ☎ *021/6437–3370.*

Jewelry

Many freshwater pearls sold in Shanghai are grown in nearby Suzhou;
seawater pearls come from Japan or the South Seas. The price of a strand
of pearls depends on several factors. The longer the strand and bigger
the pearl, the higher the price. High quality pearls have a shiny, clear
luster and are uniform in size, color, and roundness on the strand. Real
pearls are cool to the touch and feel gritty if you bite them. In most shops,
you can bargain down the price 15% to 50%, with the clasp often negotiated separately.

★ **Amy's Pearls and Jewelry.** Friendly owner Amy Lin has sold pearls to European first ladies and American presidents but treats all her customers like royalty. Her shop just outside the west gate of Xiangyang Market has inexpensive trinket bracelets, strings of seed pearls, and stunning Australian seawater pearl necklaces. ⊠ *77 Xiangyang Nan Lu, Xuhui District* ☎ *021/5403–9673.*

Lilli's. Perhaps the best jewelry designer in town, Lilli's is known for refashioning old pieces into new styles. You'll find pearls, dainty silver bracelets with Chinese characters, and mah johngg tile bracelets. There's a pricey selection of swank silk photo albums and purses. ⊠ *Suite 1D, Maosheng Mansion, 1051 Xinzha Lu,, Jing'an District* ☎ *021/6215–5031* ⊠ *Suite 605, Shanghai Center, 1376 Nanjing Xi Lu, Jing'an District* ☎ *021/6279–8987* ⊠ *The Gatehouse, Dong Hu Villas, 1985 Hongqiao Lu, Changning District* ☎ *021/6270–1585.*

Ling Ling Pearls & Jewelry. Ling Ling sells traditional pearl necklaces at every price point; bargaining can net you 40% to 50% off the price. Its inexpensive fashion jewelry stands out for being hipper than the competition. ⊠ *2F, Pearl City, 558 Nanjing Dong Lu, Huangpu District* ☎ *021/6322–9299.*

Tea

Shanghai Huangshan Tea Company. Its nine shops around Shanghai sell traditional Yixing tea pots as well as a huge selection of China's best teas by weight. The higher the price, the better the tea. ⊠ *853 Huaihai Zhong Lu* ☎ *021/6545–4919.*

Tianshan Tea City. More than 300 vendors occupy the three floors of Tianshan Tea City. You can buy such specialties as West Lake dragon well tea and Wuyi red robe tea as well as a porcelain tea set to serve it in. ⊠ *518 Zhongshan Xi Lu, Changning District* ☎ *021/6259–9999.*

SHANGHAI A TO Z

To research prices, get advice from other travelers, and book travel arrangements, visit www.fodors.com.

ADDRESSES

Shanghai is loosely laid out on a grid. Major east–west roads divide the city into *bei* (north), *zhong* (middle), and *nan* (south) sections, and north–south roads divide the city into *dong* (east), *zhong* (middle), and *xi* (west) segments. Xizang Lu, Beijing Lu, and Yanan Lu are the demarcation points for most surface streets in the city center. Puxi's main east–west roads are named for Chinese cities; some north–south streets are named for Chinese provinces.

AIR TRAVEL

Many offices of international carriers are represented in the Shanghai Center and Shanghai's western hotels. Major foreign airlines that serve Shanghai are: Aeroflot, Air Canada, Air France, Asiana, Dragon Airlines, Japan Airlines, Lufthansa, Malaysian Airlines, Northwest Airlines, Qantas, Singapore Airlines, Thai Airways, and Virgin Atlantic Airways.

Domestic carriers that connect international destinations to Shanghai include Air China and China Eastern Airlines.

Although several regional carriers serve Shanghai—Shanghai Airlines, China Southern, Shenzhen Airlines—China Eastern Airlines dwarfs them all. It's the main Chinese carrier connecting Shanghai to the rest of China. Beijing is by far the most popular destination, with 35 flights daily, the majority out of Hongqiao International Airport.

🗐 Carriers **Aeroflot** ✉ Shanghai Center, 1376 Nanjing Xi Lu, Jing'an District ☎ 021/6279-8033. **Air Canada** ✉ United Plaza, 1468 Nanjing Xi Lu, Jing'an District ☎ 021/6279-2999. **Air China** ✉ 600 Huashan Lu, Jing'an District ☎ 021/5239-7227 or 021/6269-2999. **Air France** ✉ Novel Plaza, 128 Nanjing Xi Lu, Huangpu District ☎ 021/6380-6688. **Asiana** ✉ Rainbow Hotel, 2000 Yanan Xi Lu, Changning District ☎ 021/6219-4000. **China Eastern Airlines** ✉ 200 Yanan Xi Lu, Jing'an District ☎ 021/6247-5953 domestic, 021/6247-2255 international or 95108. **China Southern Airlines** ✉ 227 Jiangsu Lu, Changning District ☎ 021/6226-2299. **Dragon Airlines** ✉ Shanghai Plaza, 138 Huaihai Zhong Lu, Luwan District ☎ 021/6375-6375. **Japan Airlines** ✉ Plaza 66, 1266 Nanjing Xi Lu, Jing'an District ☎ 021/6288-3000. **Lufthansa** ✉ Puxiang Plaza, 1600 Shiji Dadao, Pudong ☎ 021/5831-4400. **Malaysian Airlines** ✉ Shanghai Center, 1376 Nanjing Xi Lu, Jing'an District ☎ 021/6279-8607. **Northwest Airlines** ✉ Shanghai Center, 1376 Nanjing Xi Lu, Jing'an District ☎ 021/6884-6884. **Qantas** ✉ Shanghai Center, 1376 Nanjing Xi Lu, Jing'an District ☎ 021/6279-8660. **Shanghai Airlines** ✉ 212 Jiangning Lu, Jing'an District ☎ 021/6255-8888. **Shenzhen Airlines** ✉ Suite 1107, 2088 Huashan Lu, Xuhui District ☎ 021/5298-0092. **Singapore Airlines** ✉ Kerry Center, 1515 Nanjing Xi Lu, Jing'an District ☎ 021/6289-1000. **Thai Airways** ✉ Kerry Center, 1515 Nanjing Xi Lu, Jing'an District ☎ 021/5298-5555. **United Airlines** ✉ Room 3301-3317, 33F, Shanghai Central Plaza, 381 Huaihai Zhong Lu, Luwan District ☎ 021/3311-4567. **Virgin Atlantic Airways** ✉ 12 The Bund [Zhongshan Dong Yi Lu], Huangpu District ☎ 021/5353-4600.

AIRPORTS

Most international flights and larger airplanes serving Beijing and other major Chinese cities are routed through the ultramodern Pudong International Airport (PVG), which is across the river east of the city center. Hongqiao International Airport (SHA), in western Shanghai about 15 km (9 mi) from the city center, receives most domestic flights, especially those to smaller city airports. A taxi ride between the two airports will cost you about Y250 and take approximately 90 minutes. Shuttle buses between the airports cost Y30 and take much longer.

🗐 Airport Information **Hongqiao International Airport** ☎ 021/6268-8918 Ext. 2 for 24-hr airport information. **Pudong International Airport** ☎ 021/3848-4500 Ext. 2.

TRANSFERS　Depending on the traffic, the trip between Hongqiao International Airport and the city center can take anywhere from 30 minutes to an hour. Pudong International Airport is 60 to 90 minutes from the city center.

Plenty of taxis are available at the lines right outside both the international and domestic terminals of both airports. Don't ride with drivers who tout their services at the terminal entrances; their cars don't have meters, and they'll try to charge you exorbitant rates. Taxis from Pudong to the city center cost Y120–Y150. From Hongqiao to the city center, it should cost Y50–Y70, plus a Y15 toll for the Yanan Elevated Road.

Pudong Airport Shuttle Buses link the airport with a number of hotels and major sites in the city center. The trip takes about 1½ hours and costs about Y19–Y30, depending on the destination. A shuttle also runs between Pudong and Hongqiao airports and costs Y30. From Hongqiao, Bus 925 runs to People's Square, but there's little room for luggage. It costs Y4. Many hotels have shuttle or car transfers available as well.

The high-speed maglev train, the city's showpiece, covers the 30 km (19 mi) between Pudong International Airport and Longyang Lu subway station in a mere eight minutes. The entrance to the platform is on the airport's second floor. Tickets cost Y50 one-way. The train operates weekdays 8:30 AM–12:30 PM, and weekends 8:30 AM–5:30 PM.

Dazhong Taxi Company ☎ 021/82222. **Jinjiang Taxi** ☎ 021/6275–8800. **Maglev Train** ✉ Longyang Lu Station, 2100 Longyang Lu ☎ 021/2890–7777. **Pudong Airport Shuttle Buses** ☎ 021/6834–6612. **Qiangsheng Taxi** ☎ 021/6258–0000.

BIKE TRAVEL

Shanghai's frenzied traffic is not for the faint-of-heart cyclist. If you wish to explore the city on wheels, consider a ride through the old lanes of the French Concession, with its marvelous 1930s houses that have managed thus far to escape the wrecking ball. Pudong roads have far less traffic but also less scenery.

Rental options are few in Shanghai; the going rental rate is Y150 per day. It's not much more expensive to buy yourself a bike, but local laws, not always enforced, require all bikes to be registered and licensed.

Bike Rentals **Bohdi Bikes** ✉ Room 406, No. 59, 710 Dingxi Lu, Changning District ☎ 021/3226–0000 ⊕ www.bohdi.com.cn.

BOAT & FERRY TRAVEL

There are more than 20 ferry lines between Pudong and Puxi. The most convenient ferry for tourists runs daily between the Bund in Puxi and Pudong's terminal just south of the Riverside Promenade. There are no seats, merely an empty lower deck that welcomes the masses with their bikes and scooters. The per-person fare is Y0.5 (5 *jiao* or 50 *fen*) each way. The ferries leave the dock every 10 minutes, 24 hours a day.

The Shanghai Ferry Company runs a weekly ferry between Shanghai and Osaka, Japan. The ferry, which has restaurants, a game room, and even karaoke on board, leaves from Waihongqiao Harbor every Tuesday at 11 AM and arrives in Osaka at 9 AM the following Thursday. Tickets can be booked through the company or through China International Travel Service (CITS), the government tourism office. The China-Japan International Ferry Company also launches one ship from Shanghai's Waihongqiao Harbor every Saturday, alternating between Osaka and Kobe in Japan. The journey takes approximately two days. Tickets can be booked through the company or through CITS.

Most domestic boats leave from the Shiliupu Passenger Terminal for such destinations on the Yangzi River (Changjiang) as Wuhan and Chongqing; coastal cities such as Nantong, Dalian, and Ningbo; and the outlying island of Putuoshan. All domestic tickets can be purchased through CITS.

There's a wide range of boats, although most domestic boats are not luxurious. They do, however, have different levels of berths, the most comfortable being first class.

📌 Boat & Ferry Information **China-Japan International Ferry Company** ✉ 908 Dongdaming Lu, Hongkou District ☎ 021/6595-7988. **CITS** ✉ 1277 Beijing Xi Lu, Jing'an District ☎ 021/6289-8899. **Ferry passenger information** ☎ 021/6326-3560. **Pudong-Puxi ferry** ✉ Puxi dock, the Bund at Jinling Lu, Huangpu District ✉ Pudong dock, 1 Dongchang Lu, south of Binjiang Da Dao, Pudong ☎ 021/6321-6547. **Shanghai Ferry Company** ✉ 908 Dongdaming Lu, Hongkou District ☎ 021/6537-5111. **Shiliupu Passenger Terminal/boat information** ✉ Zhongshan Dong Lu south of the Bund, Huangpu District ☎ 021/6326-0050. **Waihongqiao Harbor/boat information** ✉ 100 Yangshupu Lu, Hongkou District ☎ 021/6595-9529.

BUS TRAVEL

TO SHANGHAI

Getting to and from Shanghai by bus is usually less convenient than by train. Be sure to compare train fares and schedules before taking the bus. Regular buses, most of which are uncomfortable, run from the long-distance bus stations and are acceptable for shorter trips to places such as Hangzhou and Suzhou (there are hourly departures) and other destinations in Jiangsu and Zhejiang provinces. With several stations scattered around town, it can be difficult to know which buses leave from where. Things should be simpler once a four-story bus terminal opens in 2005 adjacent to the Shanghai Railway Station, replacing many smaller terminals. In conjunction, the city also plans to open more than 200 bus-ticket kiosks around the city. Among the existing stations, the main one is on Hengfeng Lu near the Railway Station.

📌 Bus Information **Bus hotline (operators speak Chinese only)** ☎ 021/96850 or 021/5631-0327. **Long-distance bus stations** ✉ High Speed Passenger Transport, 270 Hengfeng Lu, Zhabei District ☎ 021/6317-3912 ✉ North Bus Station, 80 Gongxin Lu, Zhabei District ☎ 021/5663-0230 ✉ Renmin Lu Station, 31 Renmin Nan Lu, Huangpu District ☎ 021/5782-0748.

WITHIN
SHANGHAI

Many Shanghai buses have air-conditioning and plenty of seats. Much of the fleet, though, is still very old and uncomfortable, primarily standing-room only, and extremely inconvenient. Although the network canvasses the whole town, you'll often have to change buses several times to reach your destination. During busy traffic hours the buses are unbelievably crowded, and in the frenzy you may get carried past your stop.

One exception to the above is Bus 911, a double-decker bus running down Huaihai Lu through the old French Concession. It's a pleasant ride, as the vehicles on this line are imported from Hong Kong and have many seats. From the top deck, you have a great view over the compound walls of the beautiful old Shanghai buildings that line the thoroughfare. Fares on this bus line will run you a few yuan, depending on how far you take it. The line starts at the Laoshi Men (Old City Gate) on Renmin Lu, just north of Yu Garden.

FARES &
SCHEDULES

On most buses the fare for any stop on the line is Y2 for air-conditioned buses, Y1 for those without air-conditioning. Most buses run from 5 or 5:30 AM to 11 PM.

📌 Local Bus Information **Passenger hotline** ☎ 021/96900.

CAR TRAVEL

Highways connect Shanghai to neighboring cities such as Suzhou and Nanjing in the west, and Hangzhou in the south. However, due to government restrictions, it's virtually impossible for nonresidents of China to drive. You can, however, hire a car and driver through your hotel's transportation service or through Hertz or Avis, both of which have several locations throughout the city.

🚗 **Avis** ☎ 021/6241-0215. **Hertz** ☎ 021/6252-2200.

CONSULATES

🚗 Australia **Australian Consulate** ✉ 22F, CITIC Square, 1168 Nanjing Xi Lu, Jing'an District ☎ 021/5292-5500 🖷 021/5292-5511.

🚗 Canada **Canadian Consulate** ✉ Tower 4, Suite 604, Shanghai Center, 1376 Nanjing Xi Lu, Jing'an District ☎ 021/6279-8400 🖷 021/6279-8401.

🚗 New Zealand **New Zealand Consulate** ✉ Qihua Dasha, 15th fl., 1375 Huaihai Zhong Lu, Xuhui District ☎ 021/6471-1108.

🚗 United Kingdom **British Consulate** ✉ Suite 301, Shanghai Center, 1376 Nanjing Xi Lu, Jing'an District ☎ 021/ 6279-7650 🖷 Visa and Consular Sections, Suite 715, Shanghai Center, 1376 Nanjing Xi Lu, Jing'an District ☎ 021/6279-8130.

🚗 United States **United States Consulate** ✉ 1469 Huaihai Zhong Lu, Xuhui District ☎ 021/6433-6880, 021/6433-3936 for after-hours emergencies 🖷 021/6433-1576 🖷 Citizen Services Section, Westgate Mall, 8th fl., 1038 Nanjing Xi Lu, Jing'an District ☎ 021/ 3217-4650.

DISCOUNTS & DEALS

For Y70 (a saving of Y15), you can buy a combined ticket for the Shanghai Museum, Shanghai Grand Theater, and Shanghai Urban Planning Exhibition Center; the pass is available at any of the three sites. The Y280 Enjoy card, available through the Enjoy Web site, entitles you to discounts at participating restaurants, bars, and shops around town.

🚗 **Enjoy** ☎ 021/6431-6764 ⊕ www.enjoyshanghai.com.

EMERGENCIES

In a medical emergency don't call for an ambulance. The Shanghai Ambulance Service is merely a transport system that takes you to the closest hospital, not the hospital of your choice. If possible, take a taxi to the hospital; you'll get there faster.

International SOS 24-hour Alarm Center has information on emergency evacuations. Lifeline, a nonprofit support group for expatriates, operates a counseling hotline daily noon–8 PM.

The clinics and hospitals listed below have a limited number of English-speaking doctors on hand. At most hospitals, few staff members will speak English.

🚗 Dentists **Cidi Dental Clinic** ✉ 821 Yanan Zhong Lu, Jing'an District ☎ 021/6247-0709. **DDS Dental Care** ✉ 1 Taojiang Lu, Xuhui District ☎ 021/6466-0928. **Orthodontics Asia** ✉ 3F, Ciro's Plaza, 388 Nanjing Xi Lu, Huangpu District ☎ 021/6473-7733. **World Link Dental Center** ✉ Mandarin City, 1F, Unit 30, 788 Hongxu Lu, Minhang District ☎ 021/ 6405-5788.

🚗 Doctors **World Link Medical Center** ✉ Room 203, West Tower, Shanghai Center, 1376 Nanjing Xi Lu, Jing'an District ☎ 021/6279-7688 🖷 Hongqiao Clinic ✉ Mandarin

City, 1F, Unit 30, 788 Hongxu Lu, Minhang District ☎ 021/6405-5788 ✉ Specialty and Inpatient Center, 3F, 170 Danshui Lu, Luwan District ☎ 021/6385-9889.

🖪 Emergency Services **Fire** ☎ 119. **International SOS 24-hour Alarm Center** ☎ 021/6295-0099. **Police** ☎ 110 or 021/6357-6666 (English). **Shanghai Ambulance Service** ☎ 120.

🖪 Hospitals **Huadong Hospital** ✉ Foreigners' Clinic, 2F, 221 Yanan Xi Lu, Jing'an District ☎ 021/6248-3180 Ext. 30106. **Huashan Hospital** ✉ Foreigners' Clinic, 15F, 12 Wulumuqi Zhong Lu, Jing'an District ☎ 021/6248-3986, 021/6248-9999 Ext. 2531 for 24-hour hotline. **Shanghai East International Medical Center** ✉ 551 Pudong Nan Lu, near Pudong Dadao, Pudong ☎021/5879-9999. **Shanghai United Family Hospital** ✉1111 Xianxia Lu, Changning District ☎ 021/6291-1635.

🖪 Hot Line **Lifeline** ☎ 021/6279-8990.

🖪 24-Hour Pharmacy **Shanghai Wu Yao Pharmacy** ✉ Celebrity Garden, 201 Lianhua Lu, Changning District ☎ 021/6294-1403.

ENGLISH-LANGUAGE MEDIA

English-language city magazines such as the biweekly *City Weekend* and monthly *That's Shanghai* are the most widely available independent publications in town, distributed through local bars, restaurants, and shops; they provide information on restaurants, cultural venues, and events. The state-owned *Shanghai Daily* publishes world, national, and business news, while the weekly *Shanghai Star* is more feature-heavy. English-language books and periodicals are harder to come by; you can buy them at the Foreign Language Bookstore (also known as Shanghai Book Traders), Shanghai City of Books (also known as the Shanghai Book Mall), City Supermarket, and the high-end Western hotels.

🖪 English-Language Bookstores **City Supermarket** ✉ Shanghai Center, 1376 Nanjing Xi Lu, Jing'an District ☎021/6279-8018. **Foreign Language Bookstore** ✉390 Fuzhou Lu, Huangpu District ☎ 021/6322-3200 ⊕ www.sbt.com.cn. **Shanghai City of Books** ✉ 465 Fuzhou Lu, Huangpu District ☎ 021/6391-4848.

RADIO & TELEVISION Most Western hotels have satellite TV, with CNN, BBC, and HBO in addition to the standard Chinese stations. As for radio, there's an English-language music program on 101.7 FM two times daily: 2 PM–3 PM and 8 PM–9 PM.

MAIL & SHIPPING

Shanghai's main post office is at 276 Sichuan Bei Lu, but there are branches all over town. Look for the green English CHINA POST signs. The Shanghai Center branch has the best English service; the Xintiandi location even has a small postal museum.

Most major hotels have in-room Internet access, and there are numerous Internet cafés around town. Eastday Bar is the largest chain, with approximately 240 Internet cafés.

🖪 Post offices **Main post office** ✉ 276 Sichuan Bei Lu, Hongkou District ☎ 021/6306-0438. **Post office information** ☎ 021/6393-6666 Ext. 00. **Shanghai Center post office** ✉ Shanghai Center, 1376 Nanjing Xi Lu, Jing'an District ☎ 021/6281-7434. **Xintiandi post office** ✉ 123 Xinye Lu, Huangpu District ☎ 021/6385-7449.

MONEY MATTERS

The best places to convert your money into yuan are at your hotel's front desk or a branch of a major bank, such as Bank of China, CITIC, or HSBC. You'll need to present your passport to do so.

ATMs are widespread, but not always reliable. Although you'll incur an extra fee, run a balance inquiry first; if the connection goes through, then make your withdrawal.

🚩 Currency Exchange **Bank of China** ⊠ 23 The Bund (Zhongshan Yi Lu), Huangpu District ☎ 021/6329-1979. **HSBC** ⊠ Shanghai Center, 1376 Nanjing Xi Lu, Jing'an District ☎ 021/6279-8582.

PASSPORTS & VISAS

To extend your visa or ask for information about your status as an alien in China, stop by the Public Security Bureau Division for Aliens, which is open weekdays 9 to 11:30 and 1:30 to 4:30. The office is extremely bureaucratic, and the visa officers can be difficult. Most of them can speak English. It's usually no problem to get a month's extension on a tourist visa. You'll need to bring in your passport and your registration of temporary residency from the hotel at which you're staying. If you are trying to extend a business visa, you'll need the above items as well as a letter from the business that originally invited you to China saying it would like to extend your stay for work reasons. Rules are always changing, so you will probably need to go to the office at least twice to get all your papers in order.

🚩 **Public Security Bureau Division for Aliens** ⊠ 333 Wusong Lu, Huangpu District ☎ 021/6357-6666.

SIGHTSEEING TOURS

BOAT TOURS A boat tour on the Huangpu River affords a great view of the Pudong skyline and the Bund. Huangpu River Cruises launches several small boats for one-hour daytime cruises as well as its unmistakable dragon boat for two night cruises. The company also runs a 3½-hour trip up and down the Huangpu River between the Bund and Wusong, the point where the Huangpu meets the Yangzi River. You'll see barges, bridges, and factories, but not much scenery. All tours depart from the Bund at 239 Zhongshan Dong Lu. You can purchase all tickets at the dock or through CITS; prices range Y35–Y90.

Shanghai Oriental Leisure Company runs 40-minute boat tours along the Bund from the Pearl Tower's cruise dock in Pudong. Daytime cruises cost Y40, nighttime Y50. Follow the brown signs from the Pearl Tower to the dock.

🚩 Fees & Schedules **CITS** ⊠ 1277 Beijing Xi Lu, Jing'an District ☎ 021/6289-8899. **Huangpu River Cruises** ⊠ 239 Zhongshan Dong Er Lu (the Bund), Huangpu District ☎ 021/6374-4461. **Shanghai Oriental Leisure Company** ⊠ Oriental Pearl Cruise Dock, 1 Shiji Dadao, Pudong ☎ 021/5879-1888 Ext. 80435.

BUS TOURS Grayline Tours has escorted half- and full-day coach tours of Shanghai as well as one-day trips to Suzhou, Hangzhou, and other nearby waterside towns. Prices range from Y289 to Y1,323.

Jinjiang Tours runs a full-day bus tour of Shanghai that includes the French Concession, People's Square, Jade Buddha Temple, Yu Garden, the Bund, and Pudong. Tickets cost Y250 and include lunch. Small groups can arrange for a tour by car with an English-speaking guide.

The Shanghai Sightseeing Bus Center has more than 50 routes, including 10 tour routes that make a circuit of Shanghai's main tourist attractions. There are also one-stop itineraries and weekend overnight trips to sights in Zhejiang and Jiangsu provinces. One-day trips range from Y30 to Y200; overnight trips cost as much as Y400. You can buy tickets up to a week in advance. The main ticket office and station, beneath Staircase No. 5 at Shanghai Stadium, has plenty of English signage to help you through the ticketing process.

🚩 Fees & Schedules **Grayline Tours** ✉ 2 Hengshan Lu, Xuhui District ☎ 135/1216–9650 ⊕ www.grayline.com. **Jinjiang Tours** ✉ 161 Chang Le Lu, Luwan District ☎ 021/ 6415–1188. **Shanghai Sightseeing Bus Center** ✉ No. 5 Staircase, Gate 12, Shanghai Stadium, 666 Tianyaoqiao Lu, Xuhui District ☎ 021/6426–5555.

SUBWAY TRAVEL

The Shanghai subway is constantly being expanded. So far, three lines are fully operational and nine more are planned. With Shanghai's traffic-choked streets, it is by far the quickest way to get to most places. Stations are clean and fairly well signed in English, although not all exit signs list their corresponding streets. In-car announcements for each station are given in both Chinese and English. The subway is not too crowded, except at rush hour.

Pick up a subway or city map at your hotel; at most stations, you won't find an English-language route map until after you've bought your ticket and cleared the turnstile. Ticket machines have instructions in English; press the button for the fare you want (Y2–Y4), then insert your coins. You can get change at the adjacent booth. Keep your ticket handy; you'll need to insert it into a second turnstile as you exit at your destination.

Line One travels between Xinzhuang and the Shanghai Railway Station, with stops in the French Concession at Hengshan Lu, Changshu Lu, Shaanxi Nan Lu, and Huangpi Lu. It intersects with Line Two at People's Square, a labyrinth of a station with two levels and 20 exits. Line Two, which will eventually link Hongqiao International Airport with Pudong International Airport, currently runs from Zhongshan Gongyuan in Puxi to Zhangjiang Station in Pudong. Stops in the city center include Jing'an Temple and Shimen Yilu, with the Henan Zhong Lu station right at the entrance to the Nanjing Dong Lu pedestrian walkway. A light rail line, called the Pearl Line, will eventually circle the city, with twin tunnels under the Huangpu River. For now, it runs from the South Railway Station to Jiangwan Town.

FARES & SCHEDULES

Trains run regularly, with three to six minutes between trains on average. Service on Line One begins at around 5:20 AM and ends at about 11:30 PM. Line Two opens at 6:30 AM and closes just before 11 PM. The Pearl Line operates from around 6:20 AM to 10:15 PM. Tickets cost Y2–Y6, and there's no charge to change trains.

🚩 **Passenger information** ☎ 021/6318–9000.

TAXIS

Taxis are plentiful, easy to spot, and by far the most comfortable way to get around Shanghai. Almost all are Volkswagen Santanas or Passats, and they come in a rainbow of colors: teal, green, yellow, red, dark blue, and white. They are all metered. You can spot the available ones by looking in the front window for a small lit-up sign glowing on the passenger side. The fare starts at Y10 for the first 2 km (1 mi), with each kilometer thereafter costing Y1. After 11 PM, the base fare is Y13, with each kilometer thereafter costing Y2.6; the price per kilometer jumps to Y3.9 after you've gone 10 km (6 mi). You also pay for waiting time in traffic.

Cabs can be hailed on the street or called for by phone. If you're choosing a cab from a queue, peek at the driver's license on the dashboard. The lower the license number, the more experienced the driver. Drivers with a number below 200,000 (out of a possible 260,000) can usually get you where you're going. Stars on the license are awarded for professional or courteous service.

Most cab drivers don't speak English, so it's best to give them a piece of paper with your destination written in Chinese. (Keep a card with the name of your hotel on it handy for the return trip.) Hotel doormen can also help you tell the driver where you're going. It's a good idea to study a map and have some idea where you are, as some drivers will take you for a ride—a much longer one—if they think they can get away with it.

🚕 Taxi Companies **Dazhong Taxi Company** ☎ 021/82222. **Jinjiang Taxi** ☎ 021/6275-8800. **Qiangsheng Taxi** ☎ 021/6258-0000.

TELEPHONES

🚕 **Local directory assistance** ☎ 114. **Time** ☎ 117. **Weather** ☎ 121.

TRAIN TRAVEL

Shanghai is connected to many destinations in China by direct train. The Shanghai Railway Station is in the northern part of the city; a second key station will open in southwest Shanghai, in Xuhui District, in spring 2006. Currently, several trains a day run from the railway station to Suzhou, Hangzhou, Nanjing, and other nearby destinations. The best train to catch to Beijing is the overnight express that leaves around 6 PM and arrives in Beijing the next morning. The express train for Hong Kong departs around noon and arrives at the Kowloon station 24 hours later.

You can buy train tickets at CITS, but a service fee is charged. Same-day, next-day, and sometimes third-day tickets can also be easily purchased at the ticket office on the first floor of the Longmen Hotel, on the western side of the train station.

🚆 Train Information **Shanghai Railway Station** ✉ 303 Moling Lu, Zhabei District ☎ 021/6317-9090. **Ticket office** ✉ 777 Hengfeng Lu, Zhabei District ☎ 021/6356-0051.

TRAVEL AGENCIES

The agencies below are accustomed to dealing with expatriates and English-speaking visitors; they can arrange both domestic and international travel. For additional agents, check out the travel section of *That's Shanghai*.

📋 Agencies **American Express** ✉ Shanghai Center, 1376 Nanjing Xi Lu, Jing'an District ☎ 021/6279-8082. **China International Travel Service (CITS)** ✉ 1277 Beijing Xi Lu, Jing'an District ☎ 021/6289-8899. **Great West Travel** ✉ Room 660, East Tower, Shanghai Center, 1376 Nanjing Xi Lu, Jing'an District ☎ 021/6279-8489 ⊕ www.greatwest-travel.com. **Huating Overseas Tourist Company** ✉ 4F, 501 Wulumuqi Bei Lu, Jing'an District ☎ 021/6249-1234. **Polo Air** ✉ Suite 4107A, Plaza 66, 1266 Nanjing Xi Lu, Jing'an District ☎ 021/6288-1555.

VISITOR INFORMATION

📋 Community Organizations **American Chamber of Commerce** ☎ 021/6279-7119. **Australia Chamber of Commerce** ☎ 021/6248-8301. **British Chamber of Commerce** ☎ 021/6218-5022. **Canadian Business Forum** ☎ 021/6279-8400. **Hong Kong Chamber of Commerce** ☎ 021/5306-9533. **Jewish Community of Shanghai** ☎ 021/6278-0225.

📋 Tourist Information **China International Travel Service** ✉ 1277 Beijing Xi Lu, Jing'an District ☎ 021/6279-8899. **Shanghai Tourist Information Services** ✉ Yu Garden, 159 Jiujiaochang Lu, Huangpu District ☎ 021/5355-5032 ✉ Hongqiao International Airport ☎ 021/6268-8899. **Spring Travel Service** ☎ 021/6252-0000 Ext. 0. **Tourist Hotline** ☎ 021/6439-0630 or 021/6439-8947.

EASTERN CHINA
WATERWAYS, GARDENS, WORKERS' MOVEMENTS, HIP CITIES

6

By Anya
Bernstein and
Christopher
Knowles
Updated by
Charles De
Simone

A MICROCOSM OF THE FORCES AT PLAY IN CONTEMPORARY CHINA is presented in the provinces that make up the eastern section of the country. Here the rich legacy of the past and the challenges and aspirations for China's future combine in a present that is dizzying in its variation and speed of transformation. Jiangsu, Zhejiang, and Fujian for centuries have been some of the most affluent provinces in China, well known for their fine silks, handicrafts, and teas, and today are enjoying renewed prosperity. The poorer interior provinces of Anhui and Jiangxi are better known for natural beauty, material hardships, peasant revolts, and the birth of Mao's Communist forces.

In the northeast, Jiangsu and Zhejiang have long been wealthy centers of culture, learning, and commerce. These cities, with their elegant gardens, elaborate temples, and fine crafts, evoke the sophisticated and refined world of classical China's literati. Described by Marco Polo as the finest and noblest city in the world, Hangzhou is famous for Xihu, or West Lake, which has inspired poets, painters, and other artists for more than 700 years. The largest artificial waterway in the world, the Grand Canal, extending from Beijing to Hangzhou, secured Hangzhou's importance as an early commercial and cultural center. Nearby Suzhou is famous for its many well-preserved gardens. Originally commissioned by wealthy intellectuals, these beautifully designed artificial landscapes demonstrate a cultivated sense of artistic design as well as respect for the beauty of the natural forms of small trees and strangely gnarled rocks. Many of the gardens are set among quiet lanes of traditional whitewashed houses with black-tile roofs and alongside its many narrow canals, so that walking between the gardens seems like a stroll through the China of centuries ago.

Nanjing, an imperial capital during the Ming Dynasty until 1421 and later twice the national capital of the Republic of China, is home to a rich cultural heritage and a splendid array of national monuments that illustrate the diversity of China's history. For example, on the slopes of Purple Mountain the tomb of the founder of the Ming Dynasty is neighbor to the tomb of Sun Yat-sen, who led the revolution that toppled the dynastic system.

Since the Southern Song Dynasty (1127–79), large numbers of Fujianese have emigrated around Southeast Asia. As a result, Fujian province has strong historic ties with overseas Chinese. In 1979 Fujian was allowed to form the first special economic zone (SEZ)—a testing ground for capitalist market-economy ideas—at Xiamen. Today Xiamen is a pleasant city with a vibrant economy. Its numerous seafood restaurants appeal to both the palate and the pocketbook. The former colonial settlement on the peaceful, traffic-free island of Gulangyu is a charming place to stroll and explore quiet streets lined with old colonial mansions. The Wuyi Mountain range, in the north of the province, has peaks that reach 6,000 feet. Protected as a nature preserve, these mountains are spectacular to look at and to hike.

Classic scenery can also be found at Huangshan, one of China's traditional Five Famous Mountains, in Anhui province. The mountain's peaks

6

Eastern China is one of the country's most diverse and varied sections, with imposing mountains, tranquil countryside, storied traditional towns, and thriving modern cities. A visitor to the region can either try to sample it all, or just focus on one theme, like classical gardens, for example. Transportation varies by province, but is fairly good for the most part. With some of the richer provinces in China, this region's buses and trains are generally comfortable, and the roads are well maintained. Getting around Jiangsu and northern Zhejiang is remarkably convenient—dozens of buses and trains travel the area's web of roads and rails each day.

Numbers in the text correspond to numbers in the margin and on the Eastern China, Nanjing, Suzhou, and Fuzhou maps.

If you have 3 days

Fly into **Nanjing** ❶–❺ ➤ and spend a day checking out the city's historic sights before taking an evening train for the short ride to spend the night in **Suzhou** ❿–❸❶, where you can spend the second day wandering, exploring gardens, and shopping for silk, Suzhou's specialty. An overnight ferry down the Grand Canal gets into **Hangzhou** ❸❷ in the morning, and you can spend a day here exploring. It's a short bus or train ride back to Nanjing.

If you have 5 days

For a look at the scenery that has inspired Chinese art, follow the three-day itinerary to **Hangzhou** ❸❷, then catch a plane to **Xiamen** ❹❻ and spend an afternoon wandering through the peaceful streets of Gulangyu as you enjoy the colonial architecture. If there is time, you should check out some other attractions on the mainland before settling down to a fresh seafood dinner on Gulangyu or in town. The following day, arrange a day trip to **Quanzhou** ❹❺ or **Meizhou** ❹❸, or simply continue on to **Fuzhou** ❸❺–❹❷ in order to go to **Wuyi Mountain Natural Reserve** ❹❹. Fly back to Shanghai either in the evening or the next morning.

If you have 8 or more days

Flying into **Nanjing** ❶–❺ ➤, spend a day exploring the city—Zijinshan is particularly pleasant, and the Fuzi Miao area is a good evening hangout spot. The next day catch a morning train or bus into **Zhenjiang** ❻. The trip takes only an hour, so you will have plenty of time to stroll around this small city before heading off that evening or the next morning to **Wuxi** ❼. Then go to **Suzhou** ❿–❸❶ and the gardens, taking the overnight Grand Canal ferry down to **Hangzhou** ❸❷ before continuing on to **Huangshan** ❸❹ for a couple of days of climbing.

For a smorgasbord of ancient and revolutionary China, as well as a taste of the urban and the rural, start by spending a few days in **Xiamen** ❹❻. Then catch an overnight train from Xiamen to **Nanchang** ❹❼ to check out the revolutionary sights and shop at the markets near Tengwang Pavilion. If you have time, you can easily take a day trip to **Lushan** ❹❾ or the kilns at **Jingdezhen** ❹❽. From Nanchang fly or take a train to Hangzhou before returning to Nanjing.

rising from the mist have inspired whole schools of Chinese painting. The rest of Anhui is better known for harshness—many of its streams and rivers flood seasonally, which in the past led to periodic peasant uprisings against unconcerned local governments. Although much of the flooding has been controlled by irrigation projects implemented since 1949, the province is still one of the least developed in all of China.

A reputation for hardship spills over into Jiangxi, the province rimmed by hills and mountains directly to the south. Here in the early 1930s Mao Zedong and Zhu De organized peasants, forming their own independent government. In 1933 Jiangxi witnessed violent struggles between the Nationalists and the Communists. The famous Long March began from the revolutionary stronghold at Jinggangshan. Jiangxi is also well known for its porcelain industry at Jingdezhen, which dates from the 11th century.

Exploring Eastern China

The wealthy and cultured cities of the lower Yangzi River delta in Jiangsu and Zhejiang are almost a region unto themselves—during the Qing Dynasty they actually formed a single province. The prosperity of the region has funded an excellent network of modern freeways and rail lines that cut through the flat delta farmland, making transportation between these cities and Shanghai fast and convenient. Beyond this area the landscape grows more rugged as roads wind through rural valleys dotted with peasant villages. The main cities of Anhui and Jiangxi lie on a single snaking rail line. Several areas of the mountains are famed for their scenic beauty: Huangshan in Anhui; Jinggangshan in the far south of the province; and Jiangxi Lushan near Nanchang. These are perhaps the best places to get a sense of what much of China was like during imperial—as well as revolutionary—China. The wealthy coastal cities of Fujian are convenient to each other, but the province's mountainous interior make them a long train trip away from the rest of the region.

About the Restaurants

Eastern China's rich heritage and booming economy have fueled a restaurant boom. To meet the tastes of the rising middle class, there is an abundance of pleasantly appointed restaurants serving both local cuisines and authentic specialties from around China. These are often reasonably priced, with most dishes in the Y20–Y40 range, with well-trained and friendly staff willing to help out the unexpected foreign diner.

Reservations are rarely necessary for regular tables, but if you need a private room it's worth calling ahead. Although most major hotels include restaurants, they're often not as good and are somewhat more expensive than private restaurants. Of course there are also the innumerable small restaurants, stir-fry joints, and street-side snack restaurants. Most larger cities also have a few Western-style restaurants, serving both homesick expats and curious locals. The standard Western fast-food chains litter most downtowns and are always popular with young people, who linger to enjoy the air-conditioning. Most restaurants are usually open for lunch 11:30 AM–1:30 PM, closed for the afternoon, and reopen around 5, serving until 8 or 9.

All Hands on Deck Jiangsu and Zhejiang are laced with countless small canals connecting China's two main water transit arteries, the Yangzi River and the Grand Canal. Although today much of the traffic on these waterways consists of humble barges carrying exciting things like cement and fertilizer, the canals pass through a pastoral countryside of rice paddies and duck ponds, and connect many of the region's cities. Some foreign travel agents arrange group tours around the region that travel the canals on comfortable boats, docking at different towns for sightseeing. For shorter trips, a regular ferry runs between Suzhou and Hangzhou as well as between the water towns outside Suzhou. Afternoon boat tours are a great way to experience the beauty of Lake Taihu in Wuxi and Hangzhou's West Lake, as well as see some of their quieter islands. On West Lake you can rent your own boat and explore at your leisure. Foreign tour groups in Wuxi often arrange to use the traditional seven-masted fishing junks on Taihu for cruises, often including a meal of fish and shrimp from the lake served on board. There is also a beautiful cruise along the mouth of the Min River in Fuzhou, as well as trips out to Ping Tan Islands offshore. Hotel travel desks and CITS, as well as other private travel agencies, can arrange tickets.

Stuff Your Suitcase Eastern China is a great region to pick up traditional Chinese crafts and art objects. Many of the items that Western merchants originally came to China to buy—silk, top quality tea, porcelain, carved jade, lacquer, fans, and embroidery—are all from the region and still widely produced and affordable. Suzhou boasts workshops producing silks, fine silk embroidery, and hand-carved and painted fans. The city also produces the lightly sweet Bi Luo Chun green tea. Wuxi has its own famous clay figurines as well as Yixing ceramic teapots, supposedly the best vessel for brewing tea. Nanjing still produces silk brocade using the same methods once used to weave the robes of emperors, and its Fuzi Miao market sells craft items from all over the province. Hangzhou is another center for silk, and its Longjing (Dragon Well) tea is justly renowned. When buying silk in any of these cities, you can either buy it ready made, by the bolt, or have it tailored in either traditional Chinese styles or in Western cuts. In the south and east the items of choice are porcelain and carvings. The kilns of Jingdezhen, in Jiangxi, have been churning out pottery since the 11th century; today these wares can be found stocking the shelves in Nanchang and other towns. In Fujian, Shaoshan stone carvings and Hui'an carvings are the things to keep an eye out for. All over these areas tea and tea paraphernalia are good buys. Friendship stores sell local arts products as well as some antiques, and major tourist sites are surrounded by peddlers selling souvenirs. Small-trades people occupying endless stands sell handmade trinkets ranging from the charming and well crafted to the amusingly tacky. Bargaining is de rigueur in the outdoor markets, while prices are taken somewhat more seriously at bona fide stores.

Outdoor markets provide locals with an opportunity to gather socially but you can bargain-hunt as well. The markets in Nanjing, Suzhou, and Hangzhou are well known for their variety of products, ranging from silk scarves and clothing to ceramic teapots to Cultural Revolution memorabilia. Xiamen, and Jiangxi, as well as smaller towns, all have some version of the night market, especially in summer when urban residents take to the streets to escape their cramped hot rooms. Street food, also a main part of these markets, is a cuisine unto itself.

Take a Hike The mountain ranges of the region offer everything from leisurely one- or two-hour hikes to longer overnight excursions. Some mountains are sacred religious sites, while others are more historically significant or set aside as nature preserves. Depending on the day, time of year, and location, you may find yourself in the company of any number of Chinese tourists out in small groups. Most hikes are on well-worn paths. On all of them you are certain to happen upon temples, small shrines, or pavilions honoring famous individuals or beliefs. Gushan, in Fuzhou, and Nanjing's Purple Mountain are great for short afternoon hikes—the trails are easily accessible from the city, and often lead to ancient temples and tombs. For one- or two-day getaways, Lushan in Jiangxi and Huangshan in Anhui are great options—both are convenient to get to, offer decent hotels, and have first-rate scenery praised by everyone from classical poets and painters to the Communist Party's top brass. Wuyi Mountain Natural Reserve, in Fujian, is excellent for longer excursions. Lodging and dining in these areas tend toward the simple and basic; the views, the fresh air, and the peaceful surroundings make up for that.

About the Hotels

Visitors to Eastern China are spoiled for choice when it comes to hotels. Most of the major cities boast at least one four- or five-star (according to official Chinese ratings) Western chain hotel. Competition and exposure to international management means that many of the more high-end Chinese hotels offer comfort and service comparable to international standards, and often at lower prices than foreign-managed hotels of the same quality. Many domestic tourists and business travelers also support an array of mid-price hotels, most of which are quite comfortable. The push of competition means that hotels often offer promotions and discounts—if you comparison shop or even ask for a discount you're likely to find a lower price. Air-conditioning and TV are standard in all but the cheapest hotels. Reservations are strongly advised at major tourist spots like Huangshan at any time of year. Hangzhou and Suzhou are also popular tourist destinations in spring and autumn; you should make reservations in both cities during these seasons.

WHAT IT COSTS In Yuan					
	$$$$	**$$$**	**$$**	**$**	**¢**
RESTAURANTS	over 165	100–165	50–99	25–49	under 25
HOTELS	over 1,800	1,400–1,800	1,100–1,399	700–1,099	under 700

Restaurant prices are for a main course, excluding tax and tips. Hotel prices are for a standard double room, including taxes.

Timing

Fall and spring are the ideal times to visit the region. Spring in Jiangsu and Zhejiang, especially April and May, have very comfortable temperatures and the trees and flowers are in full bloom, making the region's many gardens even more appealing. Hot and muggy summer is not the best time to visit—Nanjing is known as one of the "Three Furnaces of China" and many other cities are also uncomfortable from mid-June though August. The region has a long and very pleasant fall season—moderate weather and clear skies lasting well into early December. Chinese tourists flood in during the two "Golden Week" holidays at the start of May and October, so try to avoid those two weeks. Many visitors come in early March to see the cherry and plum blossoms in the many traditional gardens, and if you are around in mid-June you can catch the thriving Dragon Boat competition in Nanjing. Almost all of the region's sights are open daily.

Autumn is the best time to climb Huangshan, with clear weather and pleasant temperatures. The mountain is drenched with rain in spring, and climbing is not as much fun in the summer heat. Although the steps are more treacherous in winter, snow and ice give the mountain a unique atmosphere. Fujian has pleasant weather most of the year, though it is noted for its heavy rains that give the landscape its tropical flavor. To avoid most of the rains, visit in early spring or late autumn.

JIANGSU

Beijing and Xian showcase China's ancient splendor and imperial majesty, but Jiangsu sights and traditions are a testament to the sophisticated and cultured world that local literati, scholars, and merchants created. One of China's richest provinces and home to some of its most arable land, Jiangsu has long been an economic and political center. Refugees fleeing the barbarian invasions of the 5th and 6th centuries made the region thrive, and several short-lived dynasties were based here. The construction of the Grand Canal in the 7th century allowed merchants to ship the province's plentiful rice, vegetables, and tea to the north. It was given province status under the Ming Dynasty (1368–1644), which brought the capital to Nanjing for a time before moving it back north to Beijing. Nanjing and Jiangsu retained their nationwide importance, owing partly to the Grand Canal, which cuts southward through the province. Throughout these centuries, many of the country's top scholars in the imperial examinations came from the wealthy and cultured cities of Jiangsu. After the early-19th-century Opium Wars, the region was opened to Western trade. For a decade the messianic Taiping Rebellion controlled much of the province, but after its suppression the province returned to prosperity as foreign trade blossomed. After the 1911 revolution the province once again hosted the nation's capital, in Nanjing. The last 20 years since the reform and opening policies have again made Jiangsu one of China's richest and most modern provinces.

These centuries of culture and wealth have left many of Jiangsu's cities with a rich cultural heritage and many fascinating sights. Nanjing's many

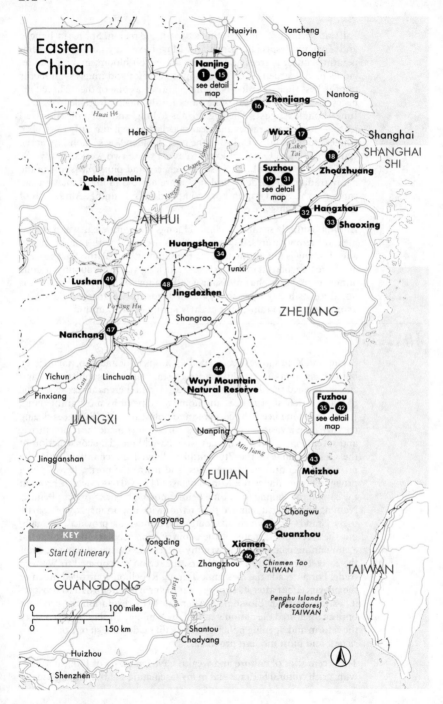

Eastern China

KEY

▶ Start of itinerary

0 ——— 100 miles
0 ——— 150 km

monuments are an impressive testament to the diversity of China's long history, while the gardens of Suzhou are a showcase of Chinese artistry and tradition. Planning a trip in the province is remarkably easy—the cities are quite close together, and connected by many buses and trains. Autumn tends to be warm and dry here, with ideal walking temperatures; spring can be rainy and windy, but it also brings the blooms to Nanjing's Plum Blossom Hill and Zhenjiang's Nanshan Park. Summers are oppressively hot and humid; January and February have mild temperatures but are often rainy.

Nanjing

▶ *2½ hrs (309 km [192 mi]) by "tourist train" west of Shanghai; 4½ hrs by normal train.*

Known as the "Capital of Six Dynasties," Nanjing has long been one of China's great cultural, political, and economic centers. It first rose to prominence as the capital of several of the short-lived dynasties that ruled China after the fall of the Han empire, and has remained a major trade and intellectual cultural center since. Many of the city's grand historic sights, including its massive city walls, were built under the rule of the first Ming emperor, who relocated the imperial court here in 1356. Although his son returned the capital to Beijing, Nanjing has retained a special place in Chinese history. The messianic Christian Taiping Rebellion established its capital here in the mid-19th century, and from here ruled a large portion of southern China with its promises of egalitarianism, morality, and wealth—not to mention its significant armies. The Ming tombs on Zijinshan Hill are a reminder of the city's glorious dynastic past, as the Sun Yat-sen mausoleum, nearby, is a reminder of more recent honors. Sun Yat-sen harked back to the indigenous Ming Dynasty in his determination that Nanjing should be the capital of the new Republic, not Beijing, which had housed the non-Chinese Qing Dynasty until 1912. The city served as the republican capital from 1927 to 1937, a time known as the "Nanjing decade," and again as the Nationalist Party (Guomindang or GMD) capital during the civil war, from 1945 to 1949.

Nanjing was also the scene of some of the first unequal treaties, which forcibly opened Chinese ports to the West after the Opium Wars. The treaties and the European encroachment on Chinese sovereignty have been a sore point for more than 100 years. In the 1930s Japan occupied the area. The hundreds of thousands of civilians killed during the atrocities committed in what became known as the "Rape of Nanjing" in 1937 are commemorated at the Nanjing Massacre Memorial.

This rich and diverse history has endowed Nanjing with a unique range of historic sights. Grand tomb complexes, temples, traditional markets, and imposing Communist monuments still stand. One such wonder is found in sections and gates of the 33-km (20-mi) Ming wall built around Nanjing in the 14th century. Many of the main streets and business districts are lined with gleaming new skyscrapers, but head down the side streets and you'll enter the traditional world of low-rise buildings and

ON THE MENU

JIANGSU, ANHUI, ZHEJIANG, FUJIAN, and Jiangxi cover a lot of culinary ground. Although the same basic dishes—cooked with greater or lesser success—can be found at cheap sit-down eateries pretty much everywhere in China, both the more serious specialty restaurants and the ubiquitous street foods here are different from those elsewhere in the country. Many of the region's special dishes use fish and other seafood, often fresh from the two major rivers and the ocean coast, as well as from numerous lakes. Dishes often tend to have lighter and more mild flavors, relying more on the taste of the ingredients and using much less chili than in Hunan and Sichuan farther up the Yangzi.

The cuisine of Fujian is considered by some to have its own characteristics and by others to form part of the Eastern tradition, one of the four major styles of Chinese cooking. Spareribs are a specialty, as are soups and stews using a soy and rice-wine stock. The coastal cities of Fujian offer a wonderful range of seafood, including shark's fin soup, a great delicacy usually served—contrary to custom with other soups—at the beginning of the meal rather than at the end. Other dishes to look for are river eel with leeks, fried jumbo prawns, and steamed crab. Jiangxi, never noted for its cooking, has tended to absorb the traditions of the provinces that surround it. However, there are a few specialties to try—five-flower pork (slices of pork cooked in spice), sautéed frog, and soy-braised chicken.

The cuisine of Jiangsu tends to have lighter flavors—Nanjing is famous for its salty duck, Zhenjiang cuisine relies on the city's famous vinegar, and Wuxi cooking uses the fish and shrimp of Lake Taihu. The cooking of Anhui is well known for stewed or braised dishes that use thick sauces with a touch of spice. Zhejiang dishes, in contrast, are more often steamed or roasted and have a more subtle, salty flavor; specialties include yellow croaker with Chinese cabbage, sea eel, drunken chicken (chicken soused in Shaoxing wine), and stewed chicken. Zhejiang is also justly famous for its huang jiu, a mellow yellowish-red wine brewed from rice. Many of the region's most famous dishes, such as su dongpo pork, are cooked in the wine. In Shaoxing locals traditionally start the day by downing a bowl or three of huang jiu—the true breakfast of champions. Shaoxing's most famous dish is its deep-fried chou dofu, or stinky tofu. Despite the unappealing name, it's actually delicious, especially with a touch of the local chili sauce.

Dress is usually casual by Western standards in even the more upscale places, but tends to be more formal in the hotel restaurants, especially the Western sections. Reservations are almost never necessary; in fact, many restaurants are loath to give out their phone numbers at all.

street life. You can see a slice of traditional neighborhood life, and you'll often be greeted with a curious smile.

The rural areas under Nanjing's administrative control supply the city with most of its food. Vegetables, fresh meat, and fish fill huge lively markets held daily in every neighborhood. Nanjing University, a quiet, green, tastefully constructed campus, now ranks as China's number-two educational institution, second only to Beijing University.

a good walk

The best place for a long stroll in Nanjing actually lies just outside the city proper, on Purple Mountain. People come to this delightful area to escape the noise and traffic of the city, particularly in spring and autumn. A wealth of historic sites dots the mountain. Take a taxi to Mingling Lu, or take Bus 20 to its penultimate stop, ending up by **Plum Blossom Hill and Middle Mountain (Sun Yat-sen) Botanical Gardens ❶** ▶, both just east of the road. After a stroll on the hill and in the gardens, head west again to the **Ming Tomb ❷**, where the founder of the Ming Dynasty is buried. Continue on uphill. In warm weather shuttle buses run to the **Sun Yat-sen Memorial ❸**. Also in warm weather, a cable car plies up the mountain. Otherwise, keep on going west to **Spirit Valley Temple and Pagoda ❹**. Catch the shuttle back and walk or ride south along Lingyuan Lu to stop by the **Meiling Palace ❺**, Chiang Kai-shek's weekend house. From the sights on Purple Mountain, the **Nanjing Museum ❻** is a short cab ride, or you can walk south from Zhongshan Ling before heading west through Zhongshan Men (Gate).

A bit farther south, just outside the Zijinshan scenic area, you reach the city wall at the **South Gate of City Wall ❼**. Not far down the street is the **Rain Flower Terrace and Martyrs Memorial ❽**, a memorial dedicated to Communist martyrs. Backtrack on Zhongshan Nan Lu north and turn right on Jiankang Lu. A short way down the street is the **Confucian Temple ❾**, sitting in the midst of a shopping and entertainment district. Northward just west of Zhongshan Lu is the **Drum Tower ❿**. Farther north, east of Zhongshan Lu, you can take in the lakes of **Xuanwu Lake Park ⓫**. Hop on Bus 8 and take it to its final stop, on the banks of the Yangzi, where the lovely **Sparrow's Rock ⓬** overlooks the river. From Yanzi Ji, a taxi ride will take you across the **Yangzi River Bridge ⓭**, to the northwest of the city. From here head a short way east to the **Yuejiang Lou Tower ⓮** for views over the river and the sprawling city. Take a bus or cab across the Qinhuai River southwest of the city to visit the **Nanjing Massacre Memorial ⓯**, commemorating those killed during the Japanese occupation of the city.

TIMING The above walk should be done over two days. An entire day alone is ideal for exploring the Purple Mountain area.

What to See

❾ **Confucian Temple** (Fuzimiao). The traditional-style temple on the banks of the Qinhuai, a tributary of the Yangzi, sits in the midst of the city's busiest shopping and entertainment district. A replica of the original statue of Confucius has been moved to the side of the temple. Here the master presides over children in bumper cars and arcades, and shopkeepers sell everything imaginable. The back alleys behind the temple were once home to China's most famous district of courtesans. The women of easy virtue have gone but they have been replaced by some excellent curio shops. The entire neighborhood has been restored with traditional-style buildings and is one of China's most famous bazaars for souvenirs and crafts. ⊠ *Zhongshan Lu and Jiankang Lu* 🚋 *Y15* ⊘ *Daily 8:30–5:30.*

❿ Drum Tower (Gulou). The traditional center of ancient Chinese cities, the tower housed the drums used to signal events to the populace, from the changing of the guard to an enemy attack or a fire. Nanjing's tower, constructed in 1382, still has a certain centrality although it now holds only one drum. Its first floor is an exhibition hall for local art. ⊠ *1 Dafang Kiang* 🕿 *025/8663–1059* 🚋 *Y2* ⊘ *Daily 8 AM–11 PM.*

❺ Meiling Palace (Meiling Gong). Chiang Kai-shek built this house as a vacation and weekend retreat for himself and his wife, Song Meiling, who was a sister of Sun Yat-sen's wife, Soong Ching-ling. The house, with its photographs, portraits, and historical blurbs, is mostly interesting as an artifact of modern Chinese views of this period's history. Although it is supposedly furnished with original furniture, it's well known that the place was looted several times over. ⊠ *Lingyuan Lu, eastern suburbs* 🚋 *Y15* ⊘ *Daily 8:30–5.*

❷ Ming Tomb (Ming Xiaoling). Zhu Yangzhang—the Emperor Hong Wu, founder of the Ming Dynasty—ordered 100,000 men to construct this elaborate burial ground. Laid out in the shape of the Dipper constellation, a long avenue leads through the **Spirit Way** (Shen Dao), lined by massive Ming Dynasty stone statues of guardian animals. Ranging from mythical Ki-Riin unicorns and fearsome lions to more humble elephants and camels, the pairs of animals represent the virtues of the emperor. Beyond them, colossal statues of civil and military statues stand as a silent guard of honor. Behind a grand red gate are the ceremonial buildings used for rituals and sacrifices. Although they were damaged during civil wars, their scale and elegant carvings convey the splendor of the site. The emperor and his wife are buried under an unexcavated tumulus, so large it looks like a forested hill. ⊠ *Mingling Lu, eastern suburbs* 🚋 *Y30* ⊘ *Daily 8:30–5.*

⓯ Nanjing Massacre Memorial (Datusha Jinianguan). In the winter of 1937, Japanese forces occupied Nanjing and, in the space of a few days, thousands of Chinese were killed in the chaos, which became commonly known as the "Rape of Nanjing." This monument commemorates the victims, many of whom were buried in a mass grave on this site. Be advised, however: this is not for the squeamish. Skeletons have been exhumed from the "Grave of Ten Thousand" and are displayed with gruesomely detailed explanations as to how each victim lost his or her life. The memorial also displays artifacts from the Sino-Japanese reconciliation after World War II, which ended the conflict between the two countries on a less strident, more hopeful note. ⊠ *195 Chating Dong Jie, take Bus 7* 🕿 *025/8650–1033* 🚋 *Y8* ⊘ *Daily 8:30–5.*

❻ Nanjing Museum (Nanjing Bowuyuan). Nanjing's museum has one of the largest and most impressive collections in China, dating from when it

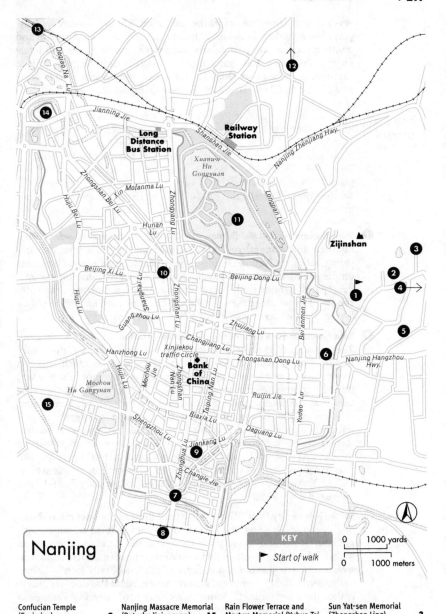

Nanjing

was a national museum before the revolution. The artifacts are well displayed in a modern building with English captions. The porcelain and painting sections are particularly impressive, and there are also interesting collections of folk crafts, furniture, and elaborate lacquer and jade carvings. ⊠ *Zhongshan Dong Lu inside Zhongshan Gate, next to Nanjing Hilton* ☎ *025/8480–2119* ⊕ *www.njmuseum.com/english.*

need a break?

Since the late 1990s downtown Nanjing has been taken over by a vibrant late-night coffee and tea culture. New coffee shops are being built almost overnight and seem to be filled up just as quickly by Nanjing's well-dressed nouveaux riches. **City Garden Coffee Shop** (⊠ 87 Guanjiaqiao ☎ 025/8471–3515) draws a lively crowd that plays cards and chats while fielding cell-phone calls and pagers. **Danfengyulu Coffee Shop** (⊠ 14-6 Anren Jie ☎ 025/8335–6085) is usually packed at night with cardplayers and people socializing.

▶ ❶ **Plum Blossom Hill and Middle Mountain (Sun Yat-sen) Botanical Gardens** (Meihuashan and Zhongshan Zhiwuyuan). Plum Hill is a favorite early spring outing for Nanjing residents, who delight in the myriad blossoms on the rolling hill. Several pavilions and running streams line the gardens' paths. Around the hill is the botanical garden, with more than 300 species of plants along the walkways. ⊠ *Taiping Men Lu in Zhongshan Scenic Area, eastern suburbs* ▨ *Y10 (Y20 in spring)* ⊙ *Daily 7:30–5.*

❽ **Rain Flower Terrace and Martyrs Memorial** (Yuhua Tai Lieshi Lingyuan). The terrace gets its name from the legend of Yunzhang, a 15th-century Buddhist monk who supposedly pleased the gods so much with his recitation of a sutra that they rained flowers on this spot. The site was turned into a more grim purpose in the 1930s when the Nationalists used it as a detention and execution grounds for their left-wing political enemies. The site was rebuilt after the revolution into a grand memorial park in monumental Socialist Realist style, complete with massive statues of heroic martyrs, memorial obelisks, flower arrangements of the hammer and sickle, and a moving museum that uses personal objects to convey the lives and personalities of some of those executed here. ⊠ *215 Yuhua Lu, south of the city* ▨ *Y10* ⊙ *Park daily 7 AM–10 PM, memorial daily 8–5:30.*

Ⓒ ❼ **South Gate of City Wall** (Zhonghua Men). Built as the linchpin of Nanjing's defenses, it's less of a gate than a complete fortress, with multiple courtyards and tunnels where several thousands soldiers could withstand a siege. It was in fact never taken or even attacked; aggressive armies wisely avoided it in favor of the less heavily fortified areas to the north. Today bonsai enthusiasts have gardens and displays in several of the courtyards. ⊠ *South side of city wall at end of Zhonghua Lu, near Fuzi Miao* ▨ *Y10* ⊙ *Daily 8–6.*

⓬ **Sparrow's Rock** (Yanzi Ji). North of the city, overlooking the Yangzi, this small park is worth the extra effort it takes to get here. Paths wind up the hill to several lookout points for what may be Nanjing's best—and most pleasant—view of this great river. The park's name comes from the massive boulder that beetles over the water; it supposedly resembles a sparrow (you decide). A stone, appropriately named "Wine Barrel Rock," at the park's highest point, commemorates the visit of the Tang poet Li Bai who got drunk on the rock and wrote verse. ⊠ *North of city on Yangzi, Bus 8 to last stop* 🖅 *Y6* ⊙ *Daily 7:30–6.*

❹ Spirit Valley Temple and Pagoda (Linggu Si and Linggu Ta). Away from

FodorśChoice the hordes at Sun Yat-sen's mausoleum and set against forested hills,

★ several fascinating historic sights are connected by trails through the woods. The beautiful 14th-century **Beamless Hall** (Wuliang Dian)—made entirely of brick—leads you into the temple, which has a hall with relics and altars dedicated to Xuan Zang, the monk who brought Buddhist scriptures back from India. (A piece of the monk's skull is on display as well.) At the rear of the park stands the 200-foot-tall pagoda, constructed in 1929. Climb the spiral staircase for spectacular views of Purple Mountain. ⊠ *Ta Lu, eastern suburbs* 🕾 *025/8444–6111* 🖅 *Pagoda Y10, temple Y3* ⊙ *Daily 8:30–5.*

❸ Sun Yat-sen Memorial (Zhongshan Ling). Both the Communists and the Nationalist Party recognize Sun Yat-sen as the father of the Chinese revolution; he is widely admired and honored on the mainland today. Sun always insisted that the capital of China should lie in Nanjing, and after his death in 1925, this mausoleum was erected in his honor. The enormous stairway echoes the ascent to ancient emperors' tombs. Several bronzes stand in the middle and at the top of the stairway—some of these bear bullet marks incurred during the war with Japan. The ceiling of the first room of the mausoleum itself bears Sun's design for the flag; although it was used as the Nationalist Party flag, the Communist government has not covered it out of respect for the dead leader. The second room houses Dr. Sun's coffin with a marble sarcophagus carved in his likeness. On the ceiling is a beautiful blue-and-white-tile mosaic representing the sky and sun. Zhongshan Ling is one of China's most popular tourist spots and always crowded. Try to visit on a weekday. ⊠ *Lingyuan Lu, eastern suburbs* 🖅 *Y25* ⊙ *Daily 8:30–5.*

⓫ Xuanwu Lake Park (Xuanwu Hu Gongyuan). A favorite local getaway, this area offers more lake than park. The monumental Ming Dynasty city wall runs along the south and west shore, the Purple Mountain rises on the east, and the glittering skyscrapers of modern Nanjing reflect in the calm water. Causeways lined with trees and benches connect several large islands in the lake. ⊠ *Off Hunan Lu eastbound or north of Beijing Dong Lu* 🖅 *Y10* ⊙ *Daily 8–8.*

⓭ Yangzi River Bridge (Changjiang Daqiao). The second bridge ever to span the Yangzi, it was the first built without foreign aid (after relations between China and the Soviet Union soured). Completed in 1968 at the height of the Cultural Revolution, the bridge is decorated in stirring Socialist Realist style. Huge stylized flags made of red glass rise from the bridge's piers, and groups of giant-sized peasants, workers, and soldiers stride forward heroically. Look closely and you'll even see one African— a reminder of Mao's support for revolutionaries around the world. The Great Bridge Park lies on the south side or Nanjing side—and you can take an elevator from the park up to a small museum. ✛ *Northwest side of city* 🖅 *Free* ⊙ *Daily 9–5.*

⑭ **Yuejiang Lou Tower.** This massive tower complex, built in Ming Dynasty style, perches on a hill in the northeast of the city, looking out over a broad sweep of the Yangzi River. The Ming founder decided to have a tower built here where he could view the river, and wrote a poem explaining his plans for the building. But other imperial business got in the way and for several centuries his well-known poem described a building that hadn't been built. The grand tower and its surrounding buildings were recently built in a historically accurate style, and are an impressive sight and a fine scenic viewpoint over the river and Nanjing. ⊠ *202 Jianning Lu* ☎ *025/8880–3977* ⊕ *www.yuejiangtower.com* ▤ *Y30* ☾ *Daily 8–6.*

Where to Stay & Eat

For more information on bars and restaurants in Nanjing, pick up a copy of the local bilingual *Map Magazine* at your hotel. It has listings and reviews of many popular spots in the city, as well as upcoming cultural events.

★ **$$–$$$** ✕ **Dingshan Meishi Cheng.** Run by the Dingshan hotel and in the Fuzi Miao area, this is one of Nanjing's finest upscale restaurants. Built in traditional Chinese style, it has wooden latticework on the windows. The cuisine is the local Hauiyang (farther up the Yangzi River), which is not as spicy as Sichuan nor as sweet as Shanghai (farther down the Yangzi) cuisine. ⊠ *5 Zhangyuan Lu* ☎ *025/8662–7555* ▤ *AE, MC, V.*

$–$$ ✕ **Baguo Buyi.** One of the best places to try authentic Sichuan food, the
Fodor'sChoice award-winning Baguo Buyi offers not only first-rate cuisine, but serves
★ it in a beautiful setting, decorated with traditional wood carvings and antique furniture. The spicy stew of beef and yellow tofu is delicious, and their delicately flavored soups feature regional vegetables airfreighted from Sichuan. Every evening there are performances of traditional magic and fire-breathing. ⊠ *211 Longpan Zhong Lu* ☎ *025/8460–8801* ▤ *No credit cards.*

$–$$ ✕ **Hong Ni Restaurant.** It's hard to miss the Hong Ni—its facade lights up the neighborhood with a three-story, psychotropic, neon water-wall extravaganza. Although the exterior is pure Vegas, the cuisine is excellent Yangzi Delta food at reasonable prices, served in a sleek dining room. It's conveniently located downtown, near the Xinjiekou traffic circle, and many of the staff speak English. ⊠ *23 Hongwu Lu* ☎ *025/8689–9777* ▤ *No credit cards* ☾ *Kitchen closes at 8:30.*

$–$$ ✕ **Jimingsi Vegetarian Restaurant.** This establishment cooks up excellent Chinese fare with absolutely no meat. The food is not the only draw, however—the restaurant is inside the Jiming Si Temple and provides a lovely view of the grounds as well as access to the Ming Dynasty wall, which runs directly to the north of the park. The wall in this area has been restored, and from here you can climb up to get a closer look at the structure as well as the parks surrounding it. ⊠ *Inside Jiming Si Temple off Beijing Dong Lu, south of Xuanwu Lake* ☎ *025/8771–3690* ▤ *No credit cards* ☾ *No dinner.*

★ **$–$$** ✕ **Tiandi Restaurant.** This charming restaurant standing on old temple grounds is surrounded by a small wood on a little hill off the road. Seating is in pavilions. Outdoor seating near a stone wall with a stream and pond provides a quiet setting from which to view the pavilions. The staff speaks a little English and will be happy to guide you through the restaurant's Jiangsu specialties and other Chinese cuisine. ✉ *179 Huju Lu* ☎ *025/8372–0088* 🖶 *No credit cards.*

$$$–$$$$ 🏨 **Jinling Hotel.** Nanjing's best-known hotel, the Jinling stands in the city's busy center. It's a huge modern building with an excellent staff. The hotel is connected to a shopping center, and the travel agency on its first floor provides friendly and efficient service. On the second floor is the freshest and most authentic Japanese food in town. Rooms have every comfort. ✉ *2 Xinjiekou, 210005* ☎ *025/8471–1888 or 025/8471–1999* 🖶 *025/8471–1666* 🛏 *570 rooms, 30 suites* ⚂ *7 restaurants, 2 cafés, gym, hair salon, billiards, bar, dance club, business services, meeting room* 🖶 *AE, MC, V.*

$$–$$$ 🏨 **Sheraton Nanjing Kingsley Hotel and Towers.** This beautiful hotel has a good location in the center of the city. Top-rate facilities make this a favorite among business travelers, but if you're not on an expense account, the prices are a bit steep. It's also home to Nanjing's only Irish pub, Danny's, with Guinness on tap and a group of expat regulars. ✉ *169 Hanzhong Lu, 210029* ☎ *025/8666–8888* 🖶 *025/8666–9999* ⊕ *www.sheraton.com* 🛏 *350 rooms* ⚂ *2 restaurants, tennis courts, indoor pool, gym, 3 bars, business services, meeting rooms, no-smoking rooms* 🖶 *AE, DC, MC, V.*

$–$$ 🏨 **Mandarin Garden Hotel.** Contrary to the impersonal bent of most hotels of its caliber, this well-appointed establishment is warm and friendly. Its setting on the north side of the Confucian Temple lets you view the city center while keeping the noise out of your room. The excellent rooftop bar-lounge on the eighth floor affords a good view of the Fuzi Miao District. The Huicui Ting (Galaxy Restaurant), on the second floor, serves Cantonese food. Guests are treated to a free and excellent breakfast buffet. ✉ *9 Zhuang Yuan Jing, Fuzi Miao 210001* ☎ *0258/220–2555 or 0258/220–2988* 🖶 *0258/220–1876* ⊕ *www.mandaringarden-hotel.com* 🛏 *500 rooms, 24 suites* ⚂ *12 restaurants, miniature golf, indoor pool, gym, hair salon, sauna, squash, bar, business services, meeting room, no-smoking floor* 🖶 *AE, MC, V.*

¢–$$ 🏨 **Grand Hotel.** This large elliptical building in the center of town is a good base for seeing the sights around Nanjing. Along with standard amenities, it has a classical Chinese roof garden looking over the modern city. ✉ *208 Guangzhou Lu, 210024* ☎ *025/8331–1999* 🖶 *025/8331–9498* 🛏 *294 rooms, 11 suites* ⚂ *Tennis court, pool, gym, hair salon, sauna, bar, meeting room, travel services* 🖶 *AE, DC, MC, V.*

¢–$$
FodorśChoice
★
🏨 **Nanjing Hilton.** Everything here, from the glass-enclosed lobby to the rooms, is spacious and comfortable. Rooms with northern exposure afford beautiful views of Zijinshan, but the hotel is less central than others. Rental bicycles are available for rides up into the park or around town. Be sure to ask about weekend rates. ✉ *319 Zhongshan Dong Lu, 210016* ☎ *025/8480–8888* 🖶 *025/8480–9999* ⊕ *www.hilton.com* 🛏 *490 rooms, 30 suites* ⚂ *5 restaurants, tennis court, gym, hair salon, bicycles, business services, meeting room* 🖶 *AE, MC, V.*

¢–$ 🏨 **Central Hotel.** The Central caters to foreign guests by arranging day tours of Nanjing and having 24-hour travel services. Modern rooms are stylish and reasonably priced, and the sleekly decorated sauna and beautiful star-shape courtyard pool are very inviting after a long day of sightseeing. ✉ *75 Zhongshan Lu, off Xinjiekou traffic circle, 210005* ☎ *025/8473–3666* 🖷 *025/8473–3999* 🖙 *354 rooms, 22 suites* ♨ *2 restaurants, coffee shop, pool, gym, sauna, bar, dance club, shops, business services, meeting room* 🖃 *AE, MC, V.*

¢–$ 🖭 **Xuanwu Hotel.** Across the street from Xuanwu Park, the hotel has a 20th-floor restaurant serving excellent Jiangsu cuisine (including frog ovaries—no kidding). From the modern and comfortable rooms you can get excellent views of Nanjing and the park. The gym has an unusual feature: it offers lessons in basic *qi gong*—a traditional healing practice related to tai chi—and examination by a trained specialist in traditional Chinese medicine. ✉ *193 Zhongyang Lu, 210009* ☎ *025/8335–8888* 🖷 *025/8336–6777* 🖙 *408 rooms, 161 suites* ♨ *6 restaurants, gym, massage, sauna, bar, business services, meeting room* 🖃 *AE, MC, V.*

¢ 🖭 **Nanjing Hotel.** Originally built in 1936, the hotel is set back from the road, surrounded by lawns and trees that seem pleasantly out of place in such a busy area of town. The staff is well trained and friendly. A separate section has rooms that are older and mustier, but they are half the standard rate. ✉ *259 Zhongshan Bei Lu, 210003* ☎ *025/8341–1888* 🖷 *025/8342–2261* 🖙 *307 rooms, 14 suites* ♨ *14 restaurants, gym, hair salon, massage, sauna, business services, meeting room* 🖃 *AE, MC, V.*

Nightlife

BARS & DANCE CLUBS
From classical guitar to Chinese punk, **The Answer** (✉ Jinyin Jie ☎ 025/8360–2486) is one of the few venues in Nanjing for live music.

Just north of the Drum Tower, **Castle Bar** (✉ 6 Zhongyang Lu ☎ 025/836–19190) is a favorite among young foreigners and locals who come for the friendly atmosphere, inexpensive drinks, and predictable Western music.

Located in the heart of the Xinjiekou area, **Next To Paradise** (✉ Nanjing Bookmall Bldg., 21st fl., 18 Zhongshan Dong Lu ☎ 025/8471–5730) is a friendly meeting place for Nanjing's young white-collar professionals, with reasonable drinks and beautiful views of the night skyline.

Orgies (✉ 202 Zhongshan Lu ☎ 025/8341–9991) may not live up to its Neronian name, but it its lively bar and small dance floor attract a mix of locals and expats.

A perennially popular bar, **Scarlet** (✉ 34-1 Hubei Lu, near Drum Tower ☎ 025/8335–1916) reincarnates itself as a buzzing disco after 11, drawing lots of twentysomething Chinese, foreign students, and aging expats on the prowl.

Shopping

The best place to buy traditional crafts, arts, and souvenirs is the warren of small shops in the Fuzi Miao area. For more conventional goods, the main shopping districts center on Zhongshan Bei Lu and Shaanxi Lu traffic circle in the northern section of town, the Xinjiekou traffic circle in midtown, and the Confucian Temple in the south. For silks, both off the roll and tailored, go to the **SoHo Silk Market** in Fuzi Miao, just west of the main temple square, for high quality and fixed, fair prices. The lavish embroidered robes once worn by the emperors were traditionally produced in Nanjing, and the **Brocade Research Institute** (⌧ 240 Chating Dong Jie, behind Nanjing Massacre Memorial ☎ 025/ 8651–8580) has a fascinating museum and workshop where the brocades are still produced using massive traditional looms. Their gift shop sells beautiful examples of traditional brocade.

Nanjing is a convenient place to pick up many of the traditional crafts of Jiangsu—Yixing teapots, silks, carvings, and folk paper cuttings. You have to bargain for goods, but at markets like Fuzi Miao prices are much lower and the selection is better than at many stores. The **Nanjing Arts & Crafts Company** (⌧ 31 Beijing Dong Lu ☎ 025/8771–1193) has a range of items, from jade and lacquerware to silk *qipaos* (traditional Chinese dresses) and tapestries; they also will carve seals from stone and draw calligraphy to order.

The **Shaanxi Lu night market** has all sorts of odd items and some good finds waiting to be unearthed by savvy shoppers. In the courtyard of the Confucian Temple, the **Chaotian Gong Antique Market** (⌧ Wangfu Dajie) has an array of curios, ranging from genuine antiques to fakes of varying quality. Vendors' opening prices can border on the ludicrous, especially with foreign customers, but some good-natured bargaining can yield good buys. The market is open every day, but is liveliest on weekend mornings. For the latest in Chinese fashion, try the **Golden Eagle department store** (⌧ Hanzhong Lu and Tieguan Xiang ☎ 025/8470–8899) or the **Xinjiekou department store** (⌧ Xinjiekou traffic circle ☎ 025/ 8471–5188).

Side Trip to Zhenjiang

16 *1 hr (71 km [44 mi]) by train east from Nanjing on Shanghai–Nanjing rail line; 1 hr by long-distance bus.*

Zhenjiang was once a city of great administrative and economic importance, a vital grain shipping point as well as a tax-collection center at the junction of the Grand Canal and the Yangzi River. Several major Buddhist temples thrived along the shores of the river, and still draw visitors and pilgrims from all over Asia. After the Opium Wars the city was opened to foreign trade, and around the old British consulate many of the streets are lined with buildings from this era. Quiet and relaxed, Zhenjiang is a great place to spend a day exploring. But the sights aside, for most Chinese, Zhenjiang is most famous as the home of the country's best-known vinegar, a richly flavored black brew that is the best complement to a bowl of dumplings or wontons.

A little west of the city center and along the Yangzi River floodplains is **Gold Hill** (Jinshan). The Tang Dynasty Zen monk, Fa Hai, supposedly gave it its name when he stumbled on a vein of gold that allowed him to fund the construction of a new monastery. Inside the park are several temples and pavilions, most importantly **Gold Hill Temple** (Jinshan Si) and **Heroes Palace** (Daxiong Baodian), with its elaborate ornamentation. The temple draws Chinese devotees from around the world, and they keep the many souvenir stands in business. This has created a commercial feel to the site, but it has a fine location, especially on clear days when the top pagoda has views over the city and river. Also on the mountain are several interesting caves. Most notable of these is **White Dragon Cave** (Bailong Dong). According to legend, a huge venomous snake lived here, until Ling Tan, a Zen monk, came here and drove it out to sea with his magical powers. ⊠ *62 Jinshan Xi Lu* ⌦ *Y20* ⊘ *Daily 8–5:30.*

The neighborhood around the **Zhenjiang Museum** (Zhenjiang Bowuguan) is a fascinating area, with turn-of-the-20th-century buildings and huge trees shading the quiet streets. A century ago the museum was the British Consulate (if you look closely you can see Queen Victoria's initials decorating the masonry), and the neighborhood around it was a thriving commercial district. The Western-inspired buildings and traditional Chinese architecture have been incorporated into the fabric of the neighborhood, with soft-drink vendors perched between the columned entrance way of an old trading house. Behind the museum are much older streets, including one where the narrow path is covered by a small Buddhist stupa built into an arch. The museum itself has a small but interesting collection of paintings, ceramics, and a Tang Dynasty drinking game based on the Confucian classics. ⊠ *95 Boxian Lu* ☎ *0511/527–7143* ⌦ *Y5* ⊘ *Daily 9–11 and 2–5.*

On the banks of the Yangzi, **Beigushan Park** (Beigushan Gongyuan) houses the **Temple of Sweet Dew** (Ganlu Si) and its Tang Dynasty pagoda. Two rival warlords swore allegiance here during the Three Kingdoms Period (3rd century AD), supposedly slashing one of the garden's rocks with their swords to show their commitment. ⊠ *Dongwu Lu* ⌦ *Y8 park, Y1 pagoda* ⊘ *Daily 8–5:30.*

In the middle of town, the restored **Dream Spring Garden** (Mengxi Yuan) provides pleasant walkways and rock formations in the Jiangsu garden style. It was originally the home of Chinese politician and writer Pan Kuo; today a large statue of him stands on the grounds. ⊠ *21 Mengxi Yuan Xiang, off Huancheng Lu* ⌦ *Y5* ⊘ *Daily 8–5.*

East of the city, on a small forested island in the Yangzi, **Jiao Hill Park** (Jiaoshan Gongyuan) is home to the **Dinghui Temple** (Dinghui Si), a much more interesting temple than the touristy Gold Hill Temple. Monks practice their calligraphy in the quiet halls, inspired by the masterpieces next door in the **Jiaoshan Forest of Stelae** (Jiaoshan Beilin). This museum of classical calligraphy is housed in a quiet traditional garden, the calligraphy carved into sheets of gray stone and set into the whitewashed walls. Some of the pieces are by China's most renowned calligraphers, and one dates back more than 1,500 years. Trails lead from here through the woods to the ruins of several old forts, while other paths lead up to the pagoda on the crest of the hill and its views over the river. It's an interesting place to explore, with several facets of China's cultural heritage, a quiet wooded setting, and the great Yangzi flowing past. Take the free ferry or a cable car (Y20) to get to the island. ⊠ *Southern end of Dongwu Lu* ⌦ *Y30* ⊘ *Daily 7–5:30.*

WHERE TO   Zhenjiang's local vinegar and sundry pickled delicacies add a splash of
STAY & EAT   spunk to the town's countless small noodle and dumpling restaurants.

For a classic Chinese experience, head for the local noodle shops on the old streets around the Zhenjiang Museum where locals while away the hours playing cards. Local hotels also offer decent restaurant options.

¢ ✕ **Yanchun Restaurant.** More formal than street cafés, this classic restaurant has been steaming up tasty dumplings since the 1920s. ⊠ *17 Renmin Jie* ☎ *0511/527–1615* ▤ *No credit cards.*

¢–$ ⌷ **Zhenjiang International Hotel.** This is the best and biggest hotel in Zhenjiang. It caters mostly to businessmen and is located in the downtown area, with comfortable standard rooms. The restaurant serves decent Jiangnsu food. ⊠ *218 Jiefang Lu, 212001* ☎ *0511/502–1888* ⊟ *0511/502–1777* ☜ *408 rooms* ⚬ *Restaurant, gym, bar, business services.*

¢ ⌷ **Zhenjiang Hotel.** Near the train station, this hotel is a convenient place to stay the night. The hotel is divided into two wings; both offer the same standard facilities but the rooms in the cheaper wing are more worn yet still clean and comfortable. ⊠ *92 Zhongshan Xi Lu, 212004* ☎ *0511/523–3888* ⊟ *0511/523–1055* ☜ *186 rooms, 10 suites* ⚬ *Restaurant, gym, hair salon, bar, business services* ▤ *AE, MC, V.*

SHOPPING Along with the standard tourist markets outside the Jinshan Temple the streets around the Zhenjiang Museum have several small stores and vendors selling antiques and curios. The **Arts and Crafts Store** (⊠ 191 Jiefang Lu) sells wares such as porcelain, jade, and carved stone seals.

Wuxi

⑰ *2¾ hrs (183 km [114 mi]) by train southeast of Nanjing; 1¾ hrs (112 km [70 mi]) by train southeast of Zhenjiang; 40 mins (52 km [32 mi]) by train northwest of Suzhou.*

Wuxi has a talent for reinventing itself, always keeping its place among the most prosperous of China's cities. Originally a tin-mining town more than 2,000 years ago, the mines eventually ran out (Wuxi literally means "without tin") and the city became a transport hub, shipping the bounty of the surrounding countryside on the Grand Canal. At the turn of the 20th century local entrepreneurs rode the wave of industrialization, creating textile factories to export around the world. Today, Wuxi is booming again, drawing foreign investment and business. Each of these incarnations has given the city distinctive sights, and the city's talent for innovation turned the quiet shores of nearby Lake Taihu into a major tourist draw with its many gardens and the world's largest statue of the Buddha.

The canal passes by the northeast edge of Wuxi's **Lake Tai.** Taihu covers more than 2,200 square km (850 square mi) and is dotted with 48 islands; its fish provide much of the local cuisine.

Jutting into the southern part of the lake, **Turtle Head Peninsula** (Yuantouzhu) is a rocky peninsula developed into a series of lakeside gardens by wealthy Wuxi industrialists at the turn of the 20th century. Carefully arranged groves and bridges complement the natural scenery, while tucked away in the woods are several historic buildings. **Broad Happiness Temple** (Guangfu Si), originally built in the 6th century, stands on the site of a nunnery, and **Clear Ripples Hall** (Chenglan), a well-preserved prayer hall, now holds a teahouse. The park by the lake is laid out in four sections, each with its own pavilions and artistic remnants. A 20-minute ferry ride from Turtle Head Peninsula are the wooded **Three Hills Isles** (San Shan Dao) dotted with old temples, a huge stone statue of Lao-tzu (the founder of Taoism), and teahouses, where you can look out over the lake scenery. ⊠ *End of Hubin Lu, southeast of city* ⌦ *Y35 (including ferry)* ⊗ *Daily 7–5:30.*

★ Just outside the city, **Xihui Park** (Xihui Gongyuan) is home to the two hills that are the symbol of Wuxi. But the real highlight of the park is the intricate classical **Jichang Garden** built by a Qing Dynasty official who retired in disgust at the corruption and pettiness of the bureaucracy. He devoted his energies to creating this elegant garden complex and family mansion, which climbs up the slopes of one of the park's hills. The Emperor Qianlong so admired it he had a copy built for his palace in Beijing. The garden was designed to incorporate views of the landscape of the park outside to complement the garden's groves, rockeries, and pavilions. Well restored and immaculately maintained, the garden is a glimpse into the elegant world of China's literati. The garden connects to the **Number Two Spring Under Heaven** (Di'Er Quan), once famed for its pure waters ideal for brewing tea, but now looking unappealingly murky. ⊠ *Renmin Xi Lu and Hehui Lu, west side of city* ⌦ *Y15* ⊗ *Daily 8:30–5.*

The **Plum Garden** (Mei Yuan) is famed for its thousands of spring plum trees, which come in more than 30 varieties. Several pavilions provide views of the garden and the surrounding scenery. Early March, when the trees bloom, is the ideal time to visit. ⊕ *7 km (4 mi) west of city, near Bus 2 terminal* ⌦ *Y10* ⊗ *Daily 8:30–5:30.*

Fodor'sChoice   Looming over Lake Tai, the **Lingshan Great Buddha** is currently the world's
★   largest freestanding statue of the Buddha, a towering 288 feet tall, not including its lotus flower pedestal, making it higher than the Statue of Liberty. Built in 2001 and made of cast bronze, the statue is undeniably impressive, especially when you stand between its huge toes, where the folds of the Buddhas robes soar upward in great waves of bronze. Around the statue are several other attractions, including a large bronze statue of the grinning and obese Buddha of the Future with babies frolicking on his body (and doing some excavations in his navel), a water fountain extravaganza worthy of Las Vegas, bronze reliefs showing the Buddhist afterlife, and the "Number One Hand Under Heaven"—a full-scale replica of the giant statue's hand, which became an impromptu spot for devotions when it was waiting to be attached to the main statue. The scene may be a bit kitschy, but the Great Buddha is breathtaking, and the park provides an insight into contemporary China's form of popular Buddhism. ⊠ *Lingshan Lu outside town near lake.*

Where to Stay & Eat

★ $$–$$$$ ✕ **Wuxi Roast Duck Restaurant.** As its name implies, this restaurant specializes in Wuxi-style roast duck (a sweeter, leaner cousin of Peking duck). Most nights diners pack its 28 banquet rooms. The restaurant's excellent English menu has a photo of every one of its many other delicious Chinese dishes, from dumplings to Lake Tai fish. ⊠ *222 Zhongshan Lu* ☎ *0510/270–8222* ⊟ *No credit cards.*

$–$$$ ✕ **Lake Tai Jumbo Restaurant.** From the outside this restaurant looks like a smaller version of the Jumbo floating restaurant in Hong Kong. Inside, the dining rooms, with good views of Lake Tai, are clean and spacious. English menus list a wide variety of local fare. ⊠ *Liyuan Garden on shore of Lake Tai near Hubin Hotel* ☎ *0510/510–1888* ⊟ *No credit cards.*

$–$$ ✕ **Drunken Moon Restaurant** (Zuiyue Lou). The Drunken Moon has a selection of Wuxi specialties, snacks, and cold dishes. The furnishings are nothing special, and the place has seen better days, but it remains one of Wuxi's better-known venues. ⊠ *73 Tongyun Lu* ☎ *0510/272–0423* ⊟ *No credit cards.*

$$ 🏨 **Sheraton Wuxi.** The first of three Sheratons in Jiangsu province, this is the finest hotel in Wuxi and provides the dependable service of the Sheraton chain. It stands in the downtown district and offers some of the best food in Wuxi in its Western and Chinese restaurants. ⊠ *443 Zhongshan Lu, 214001* ☎ *0510/272–1888* 🖷 *0510/275–2781* ⊕ *www.sheraton.com* ⇖ *396 rooms, 15 suites* ⚭ *4 restaurants, pool, gym, sauna, travel services* ⊟ *AE, MC, V.*

$–$$ 🏨 **Pan Pacific Wuxi.** Between the center of Wuxi and Lake Tai, this hotel is comfortable with standard, international business–style rooms and facilities. ⊠ *11 Liangqing Lu, 214000* ☎ *0510/580–6789* 🖷 *0510/270–0991* ⊕ *www.panpac.com* ⇖ *325 rooms, 36 suites* ⚭ *4 restaurants, no-smoking floor* ⊟ *AE, MC, V.*

¢ 🏨 **Shuixiu Hotel and Hubin Hotel.** Next door and connected to one another, these hotels share management and service facilities; the Hubin is much more upscale than the economically priced Shuixiu. They lie close to the lake in a peaceful area next to the Liyuan Garden. Rooms in the hotels' three cozy lake villas are also available. ⊠ *Off Hubin Lu, 214000* ☎ *0510/510–1888* 🖷 *0510/510–2637* ⇖ *Hubin: 202 rooms, 18 suites; Shuixiu: 106 rooms, 2 suites* ⚭ *4 restaurants* ⊟ *AE, MC, V.*

Nightlife & the Arts

Wuxi has several song-and-dance ensembles, as well as its own style of Chinese opera. Several local theaters occasionally host performances; ask your hotel for current info and ticketing info. All show similar types of shows, ranging from traditional opera to stylized folk dances and occasional performances by students at local conservatories. The **Dazhong Theater** (⊠ 90 Renmin Lu ☎ No phone) has performances. The **Jiefang Theater** (⊠ People's Bazaar No. 13, Beitang District ☎ No phone) is another option.

The **Renmin Theater** (⊠ 134 Gongyuan Lu ☎ No phone) also has periodic shows.

Shopping

Some of Wuxi's most famous traditional products are its brightly painted folk-style Huishan clay figures. Derived from peasant designs, they often show pudgy smiling babies holding flowers, fish, or other allegorical symbols evoking health, wealth, and happiness. They are sold outside many tourist sights and at major stores, but the best place to buy them is at the **Wuxi Clay Figurine Research Institute** (⊠ 8-1 Xihui Xia He Lu, near Xihui Park ☎ 0510/370–7925), where you can watch master artisans shape and paint them with fine brushes, see examples of their development over the centuries, and buy top-quality but reasonably priced figurines.

Wuxi is also famous for the brown ceramic teapots from nearby Yixing county. Prized by tea connoisseurs throughout China, their special clay and firing techniques brew a much finer tea than glass or porcelain. In addition, you can find embroidery, carved seals, and jade carvings in many of the shops lining the streets near the city center at the intersection of Zhongshan Lu and Renmin Lu. Try the **Friendship Store** (⊠ 297 Zhongshan Lu ☎ 0510/286–8414) for Chinese crafts in a non-overpriced environment. The **Wuxi Arts and Crafts Store** (⊠ 192 Renmin Lu ☎ 0510/272–8783) is another major emporium.

ZHOUZHUANG

⑱ *90 mins (49 km [30 mi]) by bus west of Shanghai; 45 mins (26 km [16 mi]) by bus southeast of Suzhou.*

More than 2.5 million visitors head to the water village of Zhouzhuang each year to catch a glimpse of the China that was. Its 14 arched stone bridges, crisscrossing canals, narrow lanes, and centuries-old houses evoke the quaint river life depicted in traditional Chinese paintings throughout the ages. The town dates to the 12th century when Shen Wansan, a wealthy bureaucrat, diverted water from the Baixian River to create its canals. Two-thirds of the town's tile-roof wooden houses skirting the canals date to the Ming (1368–1644) and Qing (1644–1911) dynasties, when they were built as mansions for the rich.

Today, the ramshackle houses are occupied by poorer folk, for whom Zhouzhuang's development into a tourist destination has been a mixed blessing. Many were forced from their homes to make way for the hundreds of restaurants and shops occupying the ½ square km (⅕ square mi) that makes up the old town. But you'll hear others singing the town's official song, "New Zhouzhuang is Good," as they steer tourists in gondolas along the town's canals.

Most tour buses drop you at the main parking lot a mile from the main gate. English signs point the way to Zhouzhuang's landmarks, so you can hoof it through the new Zhouzhuang (which utterly lacks the charm of its predecessor) or haggle for a ride on a pedicab. One of the first things you'll pass on the way to the old town is an "ancient memorial archway"—which is actually modern. Beside this arch is a **ticket window,** where you can purchase a pass that covers all of the major sights of the old town. ⊠ *Quanfu Lu* ☎ *0512/5721–7213 ticket office, 0512/ 5721–1654 general information* ⊕ *www.zhouzhuang.net* ☒ *Y60 for pass for Zhouzhuang's sights* ⊙ *Daily 7 AM–6:30 PM.*

Full Fortune Pagoda (Quanfu Ta), a five-story, 100-foot-tall tower, serves as a symbol of the old town, but it's surprisingly new: it was built in 1987. It's one of the first landmarks you'll pass on the way to the old town from new Zhouzhuang. Unfortunately, you can only admire it from the outside. ⊠ *Quanfu Lu.*

The **Museum of Zhouzhuang** (Zhouzhuang Bowuguan) is worth a stop for its long scroll painting, a 100-foot-long landscape of Zhouzhuang completed over six months by 30 artists in 1998. Another noteworthy exhibit is a collection of 5,000-year-old artifacts unearthed from nearby Lake Taihu. The museum is to the right of the white-marble carving of Zhouzhuang that marks the entrance to the first canal. ✉ *Laopai Lu at Quanfu Lu.*

Zhouzhuang is known for its ancient stone bridges, particularly the **Double Bridge** (Shuang Qiao), which consists of two arched bridges—Shi De and Yong An—that resemble an ancient Chinese key. It was built between 1513 and 1619. Artist Chen Yifei painted the bridge in a work called "Memory of Hometown," which was purchased by industrialist Armand Hammer and presented to China's then-leader, Deng Xiaoping, in 1985. The donation put Zhouzhuang in the national—and world—spotlight.

Fodor'sChoice
★ Built between 1436 and 1449, the **Zhang Residence** (Zhang Ting), also called Jade Swallow Hall (Yuyan), is the oldest building in Zhouzhuang open to the public. The 18,000-square-foot property comprises six courtyards and 70 rooms. The Big Chamber is noteworthy for its wooden drum foundation, a rare surviving example of a traditional Ming architectural style. But this chamber is formal and cold in comparison to the dark rosewood recreation room, where tea tables, a zither, and a mah-jongg table speak of past amusements. The study room is lovely, too, with latticed windows overlooking a rear courtyard through which the Ruojing River runs. Today, this small canal and a turnabout pond are used more by geese than by boats. For a separate Y10 fee, you can tour the **Roundabout Building,** the upstairs personal chambers of the Zhang Residence. The master bedroom is the grandest, with a red-and-gold wooden bed chamber covered with elaborate tapestries and carved panels of fish, vases, and gods. ✉ *Beishi Jie south of Double Bridge.*

An antiquer's dream, the **Folk Collection Hall** (Tianxiaode) is bursting at the seams with more than 200,000 items assembled over 30 years. Han Dynasty coins, ivory chopsticks, porcelain, opium pipes, embroidered slippers, and much, much more pack dozens of display cases in the warren of rooms. ✉ *Chenhuangdi Jie north of Fu'an Bridge.*

Just inside the **Shen Residence** (Shen Ting) is a framed work of calligraphy by architect I. M. Pei that reads "Zhouzhuang is a national treasure." The Shen Residence is a town treasure, dating to 1742. Most visitors overlook the estate's true front entrance; it's not the tearoom but the water gate along the canal, with a wharf for docking barges. Among the more than 100 rooms, **Song Mao Hall** is the most glorious, with phoenix, crane, and dragon carvings on its beams and a full suite of oversize Qing-style furniture. Look for the faded but elegant poems and landscape paintings on the door panels in the Big Chamber. ✉ *Nanshi Jie southeast of Fu'an Bridge.*

★ Zhouzhuang is named for Zhou Digong, a devout Buddhist who in 1086 donated his 32 acres to the **Full Fortune Temple** (Quanfu Si). Here, 21 gold Buddhas, plus a 15-foot-tall bronze one, watch over the lovely temple grounds, which circle a large pond. An arch bridge and zigzag corridors connect the halls and gazebos that stand as islands. It's a tranquil spot to sit and listen to birds chirping or admire the flowers in **Nanhu Garden**. (⊠ Off Nanhu Jie, south end of town)

A **gondola ride**, available at the **Boat Hall** (Chuan Matou), is a must in Zhouzhuang. The price is Y80 per boat, regardless of the number of passengers, and the ride is worth the fee. Blue-smocked women serenade you as they steer the long tillers mounted on the stern. After passing under the Double Bridge and several other stone bridges, the boat drops you off at the Museum of Zhouzhuang. ⊠ *Xiwan Lu south of Fu'an Bridge* 🖭 *Y80* ⊙ *Daily 8–5:30.*

Where to Stay & Eat

Most people visit Zhouzhuang as a day trip, but there are a few budget hotels in the area. Restaurants are largely mom-and-pop operations—some of them on floating barges—with a live tank of fish, a few tables, and a view of the canal. Zhouzhuang's culinary specialties are pickled vegetables, three-flavor meatballs, and Wansan pork tendon, a crispy glazed-pork hindquarter for sale at dozens of stores throughout town.

¢–$$ ✕ **Shenting Restaurant.** Don't let the "steamed bad-smelling bean curd" on the menu stop you from eating at Shenting, also known as Shen House Restaurant. It serves Zhouzhuang classics like Wansan pork as well as a good selection of seafood and cold dishes. ⊠ *Beishi Jie north of Fu'an Bridge* 🕾 *0512/5721–7203* 🖳 *Reservations not accepted* 🖃 *No credit cards.*

¢–$$ ✕ **Wanxian Restaurant.** Founded in the late 19th century, Wanxian is a landmark in Zhouzhuang. Steamed seafood—eel, turtle, fish, shrimp—dominates the menu. Tables beside the open latticed windows on the second floor provide a good perch for people-watching. ⊠ *Xiwan Jie south of Fu'an Bridge* 🕾 *0512/5721–2315* 🖳 *Reservations not accepted* 🖃 *No credit cards.*

¢ 🏨 **Zhouzhuang Hotel.** Among Zhouzhuang's limited lodging options, this hotel has the highest standards and best facilities. There are two restaurants, one serving Chinese and the other Western food, plus a tiny gym. Fair-size rooms are simple but clean, with robes for lounging. The hotel is just a two-block walk from the old town's main gate. ⊠ *108 Quanfu Lu, Kunshan City 215325* 🕾 *0512/5721–6666* 🖷 *0512/5721–6698* ⊕ *www.zhouzhuanghotel.com* ⇥ *97 rooms, 11 suites* ♨ *2 restaurants, grocery, in-room data ports, minibars, cable TV with movies, gym, hair salon, sauna, Ping-Pong, bar, shop, laundry service, business center, meeting rooms* 🖃 *MC, V.*

Suzhou

Approximately 3½ hrs (225 km [140 mi]) by train on Nanjing–Shanghai rail line southeast of Nanjing, or 1 hr (84 km [52 mi]) by train west of Shanghai.

Suzhou has long been renowned as a place of culture, beauty, and sophistication. It produced scores of artists, writers, and politicians over the centuries, and it developed a local culture based on refinement and taste. Famous around the world for its carefully designed classical gardens, Suzhou's elegance extends even to its local dialect—Chinese often say that two people arguing in the Suzhou dialect sounds more pleasant than lovers talking in standard Chinese. If the renowned gardens of Suzhou form a thriving monument to the city's past, the passages leading up to them speak of a time of transition. Entire blocks of old-style houses still line some of the city's canals. Decorated gates and doorways from centuries ago catch the eye, but they now lead into shops selling silk and cashmere in Chinese and Western styles. The small whitewashed houses from past eras border on tall office buildings and shiny new hotels. And the sloping, tiled roofs often sit atop structures built in the last few years, the result of urban planning regulations that preserved much of the city's traditional feel. This mixture of old styles with new makes Suzhou's central districts a pleasure to explore.

Suzhou is threaded by a network of narrow canals, which gave rise to its moniker as the "Venice of the Orient." The canals were once the main arteries of the city and the surrounding countryside, choked with countless small boats ferrying goods between the city's merchants, and connecting to Imperial China's main artery, the **Grand Canal** (Da Yunhe), which passes through the outskirts of town. Just 5 km (3 mi) south of the city is the **Precious Belt Bridge** (Baodai Qiao), one of the most famous and grandiose bridges on the canal. Although today the canals have been superceded by roads, they still weave through the city's traditional neighborhoods, lined with trees and stone walkways where locals dry laundry, wash clothes, and while away the evening hours. The section of the Grand Canal south of Suzhou is still navigable and navigated; you can take an **overnight boat** (⊠ CITS, 115 Shiquan Lu ☎ 0512/522–2401) to explore the canal more thoroughly.

Suzhou's main claim to fame is its fabulous array of gardens, which set a style and standard for gardens throughout the country. They were originally created by retired officials or unaffiliated literati as places in which to read and write poetry and philosophy, to stroll and drink with their friends, and to meditate and spend quiet hours. The attraction of these gardens goes beyond the mazes of bizarre rock formations or the thoughtfully arranged vegetation; rather, each garden is meant to be enjoyed for its overall atmosphere, as well as for its unique style and layout. Sit in a teahouse near the pond and feel the peaceful breeze as you watch it ruffle the water, carrying fragrances with it. Pathways lead to an artfully planted tree winding its way up the garden wall, a glimpse of lake from a small man-made cave, a pavilion displaying Qing Dynasty tree-root furniture. Every plant, rock, bit of water, piece of furniture, wall, and even fish has been carefully created or chosen for its individual shape, color, shadow, and other characteristics and for the way each blends with the whole at different times of the day and year. Although spring is considered prime viewing time, each season works its own magic.

a good walk

Starting where Renmin Lu meets Xibei Jie in the northern section of town, check out the tall **North Temple Pagoda** ⑲ ▶, with views of the city. Walk east along the restored street with its traditional-style fronts and shops until you come to the **Suzhou Arts and Crafts Museum** ⑳, then continue on to the **Humble Administrator's Garden** ㉑, the largest of Suzhou's gardens. Then turn south along Yuan Lin Lu, checking out the silk shops that line the street. **Lion's Grove Garden** ㉒, filled with caves, will be on your right about halfway down the short street. At the end of the street turn right and then left onto Lindun Lu; follow that south to Guanqian Lu and turn right to reach the **Temple of Mystery** ㉓, an ancient temple in a market square. On Renmin Lu, just north of Guanqian Lu, stop to visit a newer garden, **Joyous Garden** ㉔. Make your way down to Fenghuang Jie and head south to Shiquan Jie, turning left for the small exquisite **Master of the Nets Garden** ㉕. From here go left on Shiquan Jie to Renmin Lu, turn left again and follow it to the **Blue Wave Pavilion** ㉖, a large garden off the street to the left. From here, walk south or catch a taxi to see the ancient city gate, the **Pan Gate** ㉗. Take a bus or taxi north and west across the city moat and a branch of the Grand Canal to the large, well-designed **Lingering Garden** ㉘. Just to the west, at the end of Liuyuan Lu, is the Buddhist **West Garden Temple** ㉙. From West Garden Temple, catch a taxi to **Hanshan Temple** ㉚. From the West Garden Temple or Lingering Garden you can take another taxi or Bus 5 to **Tiger Hill** ㉛, a large park north of the city with a leaning pagoda.

TIMING   The most leisurely way to do this walk is to spread it out over two days.

What to See

㉖ **Blue Wave Pavilion** (Canglang Ting). First built in 1045, the Blue Wave Pavilion is the oldest existing garden in Suzhou. Of the four components of Suzhou-style gardens, it relies most heavily on rocks and structures for its charm. A maze of oddly shaped doorways circles a central rocky hill. From atop the hill you can see the adjacent canal. A path here leads down through a human-made cave to a small stone picnic table. The **Pure Fragrance Pavilion** showcases Qing Dynasty furniture at its most extreme; the entire suite is created from gnarled Fujian banyan root. ⊠ *Off Renmin Lu between Shiquan Jie and Xinshi Lu* ⌑ *Y10* ☼ *Daily 8–5.*

㉚ **Hanshan Temple** (Hanshan Si). One of Suzhou's most ancient temples, it's best known as a subject of one of the Tang Dynasty's most famous poems, which described the sound of its massive bell at midnight. The poem is canonical in Japan, and scores of Japanese tourists visit the temple. At the end of the Ming Dynasty, Japanese pirates, apparently with a penchant for poetry, decided to raid Suzhou and steal the bell mentioned in the poem. The current bell was donated by a Buddhist association in Japan to make amends for the literature-inspired larceny. Just north of the temple, down a lane lined with souvenir shops, is an ivy-draped fortified bridge, built in the Ming Period as a defense against bell-stealing Japanese pirates and other thieves. ⊠ *24 Hanshan Si Nong* ☎ *0512/6533–6634* ⊕ *www.hanshansi.org* ⌑ *Y15* ☼ *Daily 8–5.*

㉑ **Humble Administrator's Garden** (Zhuo Zheng Yuan). This 10-acre gar-
FodorśChoice   den, Suzhou's largest, was built in 1509 by Wang Xianjun, an official
★   dismissed from the imperial court. He chose the garden's name from a line in a Tang Dynasty rhapsody. The line of poetry, reading "humble people govern," seems like a clever bit of sarcasm when considered in conjunction with the grand scale of this private garden—perhaps explaining Wang's unsuitability for public life. East and west sections (the

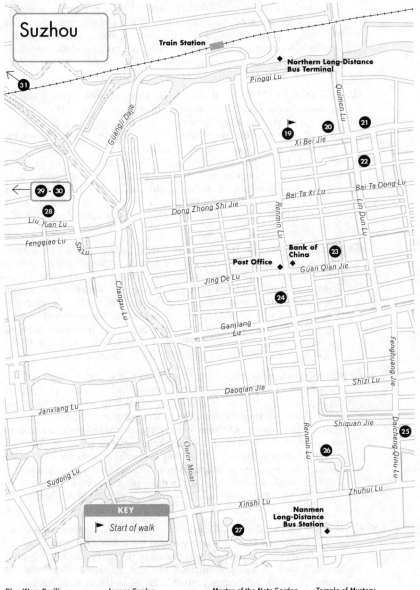

Suzhou

Train Station

Northern Long-Distance
Bus Terminal

Pingqi Lu

Quimen Lu

Xi Bei Jie

19 **20** **21**

22

Bai Ta Xi Lu

Bai Ta Dong Lu

Guangji Dajie

Dong Zhong Shi Jie

Renmin Lu

Lin Dun Lu

29 · 30

28

Liu Yuan Lu

Fengqiao Lu

Shi Lu

Changxu Lu

Bank of
China

Post Office

Guan Qian Jie

23

Jing De Lu

24

Ganjiang
Lu

Daoqian Jie

Fenghuang Jie

Shizi Lu

Janxiang Lu

Shiquan Jie

25

Outer Moat

Renmin Lu

26

Daicheng Qinu Lu

Sudong Lu

Zhuhui Lu

Xinshi Lu

Nanmen
Long-Distance
Bus Station

KEY

▶ Start of walk

27

Blue Wave Pavilion (Canglang Ting) **26**	Joyous Garden (Yi Yuan) **24**	Master of the Nets Garden (Wangshi Yuan) **25**	Temple of Mystery (Xuanmiao Guan) **23**
Hanshan Temple (Hanshan Si) **30**	Lingering Garden (Liu Yuan) **28**	North Temple Pagoda (Beisi Ta) **19**	Tiger Hill (Huqiu) **31**
Humble Administrator's Garden (Zhuo Zheng Yuan) **21**	Lion's Grove Garden (Shizi Lin) **22**	Pan Gate (Pan Men) . . . **27**	West Garden Temple (Xi Yuan Si) **29**
		Suzhou Arts and Crafts Museum **20**	

latter with a collection of 700 bonsai trees) flank the garden's centerpiece: its central pond. Lily pads float on the surface, forsythias skirt the edge, walkways zigzag across the corners, and a series of open-air pavilions perfectly frame the scene, which retains a timeless tranquility despite the throngs passing through the tableau. ⊠ *178 Dongbei Jie* ☎ *0512/6751–0286* 🎫 *Y70* ⊘ *Daily 7:30–5.*

② Joyous Garden (Yi Yuan). Built in 1874, Joyous Garden is the youngest garden in Suzhou, and it pleasantly blends pavilion and rockery, courtyard and pond. An on-site nursery shelters fledgling blooms. The most unusual feature among the many corridors in the garden is an oversize mirror. Inspired by a tale of Bodhidharma (founder of Zen Buddhism), who stared at a wall for years to find enlightenment, the garden's founder hung the mirror opposite a pavilion, so that the building could contemplate its reflection. At night, the garden doubles as a popular teahouse. ⊠ *343 Renmin Lu* ☎ *0512/6524–9317* 🎫 *Y15, 7:30 AM–5 PM; Y20, 5 PM–2 AM, Y45 with tea (only in evening April–Oct)* ⊘ *Daily 7:30 AM–2 AM.*

② Lingering Garden (Liu Yuan). Created during the Ming Dynasty, Liu Yuan has since become one of Suzhou's most famous gardens. True to its name, the 5-acre garden has many pavilions and courtyards in which visitors linger. The **Mandarin Duck Hall** is particularly impressive, with a lovely moon gate engraved with vines and flowers. Follow the zigzag corridors and walkways inlaid with stone cranes and flowers to the back of the garden to view the garden's centerpiece: the nearly 70-foot-tall rock that is said to have come from Lake Taihu. ⊠ *80 Liuyuan Lu* ☎ *0512/6533–7903* 🎫 *Y40* ⊘ *Daily 7:30–5:30 (last ticket sold at 5).*

★ **② Lion's Grove Garden** (Shizi Lin). This garden uses countless gnarled rocks from nearby Lake Taihu to create a surreal landscape. A labyrinth of man-made caves surrounds a small scenic lake. Its wall is divided and its pavilions are sited to make the garden seem more spacious than it really is. The illusions of space are expertly created here, and the bridges on the lake provide many a couple with a romantic photo op. You can get a wide view of the garden walking the paths around the lake, while the cave maze brings your attention to minute landscaping details. A tearoom on the second floor of the main pavilion overlooks the lake. ⊠ *23 Yuanlin Lu* ☎ *0512/6727–8316* 🎫 *Y20* ⊘ *Mar.–Oct., daily 7:30–5:30; Nov.–Feb., daily 8–5.*

★ **② Master of the Nets Garden** (Wangshi Yuan). Despite its comparatively small size and subdued beauty, this is perhaps the finest garden in a city famous for its gardens. All of the elements of the Suzhou style are here—artificial rock hills, an abundance of flora, pavilions overlooking a central pond—in seemingly perfect balance, as if this were the culmination of the art of garden design. The park was originally constructed in the 12th century, and reworked in the 18th. The former living quarters now house exhibits of Qing Dynasty tree-root furniture and some fine pieces of traditional ink painting and calligraphy. One placard announces that the **Spring Cottage** (Dianchun Yi) was reproduced for an exhibition in the Metropolitan Museum of Art in New York. From May to October, the garden hosts traditional musical performances in the evenings. ✉ *Shiquan Jie* ☎ *0512/6529–3190* 💰 *Y30; Y60 for evening performances* ⊙ *Daily 7:30–5 (last ticket sold at 4:30); evening performances mid-Mar.–mid-Nov., daily 7:30 AM–10 PM.*

▶ ⓳ **North Temple Pagoda** (Beisi Ta). One of the symbols of ancient Suzhou, this temple towers over the old city. This complex has a 1,700-year history, dating to the Three Kingdoms Period. The wooden pagoda has been renovated several times and stands nine stories, or approximately 2,500 feet high, with windows and balconies on each floor. You can climb as high as the eighth floor to get what might be the best view of Suzhou. Within the grounds are also the Copper Buddha Hall and Plum Garden, which, built in 1985, lacks the history and the complexity of Suzhou's other gardens. ✉ *Xibei Jie and Renmin Lu* ☎ *0512/6753–1197* 💰 *Y15* ⊙ *Mar.–Oct., daily 7:45–6; Nov.–Feb., daily 7:45–5:30.*

ⓔ **Pan Gate** (Pan Men). With traffic into old Suzhou coming both by road and canals, the city's gates were designed to control access by both land and water. The Pan Men Gate, more of a small fortress than a simple gate, is the only one remaining. In addition to the imposing wooden gates on land, a double sluice gate can be used to seal off the canal and prevent boats from entering. The gate connects to a section of the old city wall running along a canal, with interesting views down into the inner courtyards of traditional neighborhoods and over the beautifully arched Wumen Qiao Bridge. Admission also includes the **Ruiguang Pagoda**, a tall, slender spire originally built more than a thousand years ago. ✉ *1 Dong Dajie* ☎ *0512/5426–0004* ⊕ *www.szpmjq.com* 💰 *Y20* ⊙ *Daily 8–5:30.*

⓴ **Suzhou Arts and Crafts Museum.** Dedicated to showcasing Suzhou's long tradition of fine craft products, the highlight of this museum are the studios where you can watch masters practicing their crafts. Along with jade carving, hand cutting latticework fans from thin sheets of sandalwood, and making traditional brushes, the most amazing craft is the fine needlework and attention to detail of the women making elaborate silk embroidery. Housed in a traditional mansion compound, other halls showcase masterpieces of wood carving and embroidery. The attached shop is a good place to pick up quality products. ✉ *274 Jingde Lu* 💰 *Y10* ⊙ *Daily 8–5.*

ⓤ **Temple of Mystery** (Xuanmiao Guan). One of the most well-preserved old-style temples, the Temple of Mystery backs a large market square, which used to be temple grounds. Founded in the 3rd century, the Taoist temple has undergone fewer restorations than most its age, still retaining parts from the 12th century. The main building, Sanqing Dian, is one of the largest wooden structures in China. Fortunately, it suffered very little damage in the Cultural Revolution. The ceiling is the most splendid feature, its carefully arranged beams and braces still painted in their original colors. ✉ *Guanqian Jie* 💰 *Y5; additional fees for different temples* ⊙ *Daily 7:30–5.*

ⓔ **Tiger Hill** (Huqiu). Five kilometers (3 mi) northwest of the city center stands this park, home of the tomb of Helu, the supposed founder of the city. At the base of the hill, the trees open onto sheets of flat rock, some decorated with huge calligraphy by China's ancient masters. The dark waters of a man-made pool in one corner slope mysteriously downward to conceal the king's tomb. Farther up the hill, the massive **Leaning Pagoda** (Xia Ta), Suzhou's version of the Leaning Tower of Pisa, tilting at a 15-degree angle, has loomed over the scene for over a thousand years. A helpful audio guide explains many of the parks legends. ⊠ *Huqiu Lu north of city* ☞ *Y25* ☉ *Daily 7:30–5:30.*

㉙ West Garden Temple (Xi Yuan Si). This Buddhist temple was originally constructed in the Yuan Dynasty, although the current building dates from the 19th century (Qing Dynasty). Behind the main temple is the Xihua garden, a large open area with several ponds. Of particular interest is the **Hall of 500 Arhats** (Wubai Luohan Tang), which houses 500 gold-painted statues of arhats, each with its own peculiar expression. ⊠ *8 Xiwan Lu, down street from Liu Yuan* ☞ *Y6* ☉ *Daily 7–5.*

Where to Stay & Eat

In addition to the restaurants below, Shiquan Jie is quickly becoming one of the city's restaurant hubs, with both Suzhou-style restaurants and Chinese regional cuisine from Xinjiang to Yunnan. Many offer English menus, and are popular with both locals and guests at nearby hotels.

★ $–$$$ ✕ **Deyuelou.** This restaurant which has served Suzhou-style food for more than 400 years has a wide array of fish dishes, local-style dim sum, and a particularly tasty *deyue tongji* (braised chicken). It also specializes in an attractive type of food presentation, the ancient art of "garden foods"—an assortment of dim sum specialties arranged to resemble various sorts of gardens, with foods portraying flowers, trees, and rocks. ⊠ *27 Taijian Nong* ☎ *0512/6523–8940* ▤ *AE, MC, V.*

★ $–$$ ✕ **Pine and Crane** (Songhelou). With more than two centuries of history, the Pine and Crane is one of Suzhou's most famous restaurants. It serves Suzhou specialties and catches from the river that in the old days were actually eaten on riverboats during banquet cruises—hence their popular designation as "boat food." The recommended dish here is the songshu guiyu, or "squirrel-shape Mandarin fish" (don't let the English translation turn you off). The restaurant has nine dining halls decorated with Suzhou regional arts and calligraphy. ⊠ *18 Taijian Nong* ☎ *0512/6523–3270* ▤ *AE, MC, V.*

¢   ✕ **Huangtianyuan.** Here the specialty is the local favorite of *mifen* (rice gluten), made by pounding rice to a fine paste. In business since 1821, it has different seasonal menus, serving the foods traditionally considered most appropriate for specific times of year. Other house specialties include *babao fan* (syrupy rice with various sweets, nuts, and fruit bits) and *tang tuan* (a kind of dim sum, the skin made of mifen). These come in a variety of sizes and with both meaty and sweet fillings. ⊠ *86 Guanqian Jie* ☎ *0512/6727–7033* ▤ *No credit cards.*

$$$–$$$$ ▨ **Sheraton Suzhou Hotel & Towers.** With its three-story pagoda lobby, **Fodor's**Choice   beautiful garden grounds, and traditional-style white buildings with up- ★   turned eaves, the Sheraton is a landmark in itself that seamlessly matches its surroundings. The two-story stone entrance is modeled after the city's Pan Gate, which lies just behind the hotel. The large rooms have plush beds and separate showers and tubs; you can order an aromatherapy bath to be drawn. The fitness center includes a stunning indoor Roman pool, its fiery red-and-gold-tile waterfall sharply contrasting with the turquoise-glazed pool. The Garden Brasserie has a great Asian buffet, and high tea is served on weekends. ⊠ *388 Xinshi Lu, 215007* ☎ *0512/6510–3388* 🖷 *0512/6510–0888* ⊕ *www.sheraton-suzhou.com* 🛏 *370 rooms, 30 suites* ⚖ *3 restaurants, patisserie, room service, in-room data ports, some in-room faxes, minibars, cable TV, golf privileges, tennis court, indoor-outdoor pool, gym, hot tub, massage, sauna, steam room, bicycles, bar, lobby lounge, piano, shop, baby-sitting, dry cleaning, laundry service, concierge, concierge floor, Internet, business services, convention center, travel services, no-smoking rooms, no-smoking floors* 🖃 *AE, DC, MC, V.*

★ **$–$$$** 🏨 **Gloria Plaza Hotel Suzhou.** From the watercolor paintings lining the halls to the cascading waterfall windows of its Sampan Restaurant, the Gloria Plaza Hotel stands out as an inviting property. The large standard rooms dwarf the furniture inside; rooms on the Plaza floor fill the space better by adding a valet and pull-out couch. The service is attentive. The hotel is a five-minute walk from Guanqian Jie's shops and restaurants. ⊠ *535 Ganjiang Dong Lu, 215006* ☎ *0512/6521–8855* 🖷 *0512/6521–8533* ⊕ *www.gphsuzhou.com* 🛏 *281 rooms, 13 suites* ⚖ *2 restaurants, room service, in-room data ports, in-room safes, minibars, cable TV, some in-room VCRs, putting green, gym, hair salon, massage, sauna, steam room, Ping-Pong, lobby lounge, shops, baby-sitting, laundry service, concierge, concierge floor, Internet, business services, convention center, travel services, no-smoking rooms* 🖃 *AE, DC, MC, V.*

$–$$ 🏨 **Lidu (Jasper) Hotel Suzhou.** The jasper in this hotel's name applies to its color scheme: bright-green headboards and chairs add a splash of color to the well-maintained, comfortably sized rooms. Deep green carpets mute the sound in the lobby and halls. The hotel's lengthy list of recreation and business facilities makes it a destination for both leisure and corporate travelers. The well-meaning staff tries its best but doesn't always succeed when working with English-speaking guests. ⊠ *168 Ganjiang Xi Lu, 215002* ☎ *0512/6511–9358* 🖷 *0512/6511–3172* ⊕ *www.lidu-h.com* 🛏 *122 rooms, 7 suites* ⚖ *2 restaurants, coffee shop, room service, in-room data ports, in-room safes, minibars, cable TV, tennis court, gym, hair salon, massage, sauna, billiards, bowling, Ping-Pong, lobby lounge, shops, baby-sitting, dry cleaning, laundry service, Internet, business services, meeting rooms, travel services, no-smoking rooms* 🖃 *AE, DC, MC, V.*

$–$$ 🏨 **Ramada Plaza Bamboo Grove Hotel.** A modern hotel that caters to international guests, the Bamboo Grove offers many amenities but not the best location—it's southeast of the main tourist track. The three-story open lobby, Suzhou-style garden courtyard, and vast Emerald Place restaurant are attractive spaces. Rooms are bland but comfortable; ask for one of the third- or fourth-floor rooms, which have newer furniture and carpets. The hotel's bamboo logo pops up everywhere, from chair-backs to the cute cotton robes hanging in room closets. ⊠ *168 Zhuhui Lu, 215006* ☎ *0512/6520–5601* 🖷 *0512/6520–8778* ⊕ *www.bg-hotel.com/eindex.htm* 🛏 *314 rooms, 42 suites* ⚖ *2 restaurants, patisserie, room service, in-room data ports, in-room safes, minibars, cable TV, 2* *tennis courts, indoor pool, gym, hair salon, massage, sauna, steam room, billiards, lobby lounge, piano, shops, baby-sitting, dry cleaning, laundry service, concierge, concierge floor, Internet, business center, meeting rooms, no-smoking rooms* ⊟ *AE, DC, MC, V.*

¢–$ ⌂ **Nanyuan Guest House.** Its 10 acres off Shiquan Jie make the Nanyuan a garden in itself, but the guesthouse's greater selling point is its location two blocks from Suzhou's famous Master of the Nets Garden. The apricot-and-mauve rooms, which are scattered among six buildings, show their age, with worn carpets and trim; bathrooms are a bit brighter with silver and pearl wallpaper. At this writing the Nanyuan was undergoing significant renovations to add a gym and 200 new rooms. ⊠ *249 Shiquan Jie, 215006* 🕾*0512/6519–7661 Ext. 3101* 🖶*0512/6519–8806* ⋺*93 rooms, 7 suites* ⌂ *2 restaurants, coffee shop, room service, minibars, cable TV, hair salon, massage, sauna, bar, shops, laundry service, Internet, business services, meeting rooms, travel services* ⊟ *AE, DC, MC, V.*

¢–$ ⌂ **Suzhou Hotel.** Its location—15 acres on Shiquan Jie—is the main attraction of the Suzhou Hotel. It's a short walk from the Master of the Nets Garden and a stretch of restaurants and silk and cashmere stores along Shiquan Jie. Creams and grays decorate the fair-size but tired standard rooms. In the Chinese-style suites, a moon gate separates the beds from the sitting area. This spot is popular with Chinese tour groups. At this writing the hotel was undergoing a substantial renovation of its facilities. ⊠ *115 Shiquan Jie, 215006* 🕾 *0512/6520–4646* 🖶 *0512/6520–4015* ⊕ *www.suzhou-hotel.com* ⋺ *283 rooms, 23 suites* ⌂ *16 restaurants, room service, minibars, cable TV, gym, hair salon, massage, sauna, Ping-Pong, lobby lounge, piano, shops, playground, dry cleaning, laundry service, business services, convention center, free parking, no-smoking floors* ⊟ *AE, MC, V.*

¢ ⌂ **Lexiang Hotel.** Catering mainly to Chinese guests, this budget option is more basic in its approach than the hotels on fashionable Shiquan Jie. It does have a fine location, just down the street from the Joyous Garden and a block from the beautiful Temple of Mystery, near Guanqian Jie's restaurants. ⊠ *18 Dajingxiang, 215005* 🕾 *0512/6* 🖶 *0512/6524–4165* ⋺ *38 rooms, 2 suites* ⌂ *2 restaurants, gym, hair salon, bar, business services, meeting room* ⊟ *AE, MC, V.*

¢ ⌂ **Nanlin Hotel.** Although its sprawling lobby and spiral marble staircase make a grand first impression, the Nanlin Hotel is definitely a budget hotel. Rooms are plain, with dated furnishings. It's within walking distance of the Master of the Nets Garden and Blue Wave Pavilion, yet the hotel is off the tourist track, down a hard-to-find lane, which makes this a fairly quiet property. ⊠ *20 Gunxiu Fang, at Shiquan Jie, 215006* 🕾 *0512/6519–4641* 🖶 *0512/6519–1028* ⊕ *www.nanlinhotel.com.cn* ⋺ *252 rooms, 5 suites* ⌂ *Restaurant, coffee shop, room service, cable TV, indoor pool, gym, hair salon, massage, sauna, Ping-Pong, lobby lounge, shops, dry cleaning, laundry service, Internet, business services, meeting rooms, no-smoking rooms* ⊟ *AE, DC, MC, V.*

Nightlife & the Arts

At night, Shiquan Jie between the Suzhou Hotel and Renmin Lu is home to a thriving and expanding range of bars and nightclubs, ranging from mellow places to have a few beers to lively dance clubs.

Mid-March to mid-November, the Master of the Nets Garden has **traditional opera and music performances** (✉ Shiquan Jie ☎ 0512/6826–7737) every night from 7:30 to 10; the cost is Y60. The show presents a taste of various scenes from opera, as well as an opportunity to hear classical Chinese instruments. It can be a bit crowded during the peak tourist season. The beautiful location, however, makes the performance a uniquely enjoyable experience. Check at the entrance gate of the garden or with CITS (the tourism office, at 18 Dajingxiang) about times and tickets.

Wuyuegong Restaurant Theater stages a **show of Wu culture** (✉ Suzhou Hotel, 115 Shiquan Jie ☎ 0512/6519–2556) every evening at 6:30. The hour-long song-and-dance program features local "Kun " opera, acrobatics, and a river-village dance. Tickets range from Y80, which includes tea, to Y150, which includes a dinner of traditional Suzhou "boat food."

Shopping

Districts around the gardens and temples teem with silk shops and outdoor markets. The city's long history of wealth and culture have encouraged a tradition of elegant and finely worked craft objects. One of the best known is double-sided embroidery, where the designs are carefully stitched on both sides of a sheet of silk. The city is also famous for its finely latticed sandalwood fans. Both are available at the **Suzhou Arts and Crafts Museum.** The area outside the gate of the Master of the Nets Garden has dozens of small stalls selling curios and inexpensive but interesting souvenirs. Shiquan Jie also has a range of craft and antique shops.

The **Friendship Store** (✉ 504 Renmin Lu ☎ 0512/6523–6165) has a selection of local products in silk, wood, and jade. Since 1956 the **Suzhou Antiques Store** (✉ 328 Renmin Lu, near Leqiao Bridge ☎ 0512/6522–8368) has been selling antiques, calligraphy, jades, and other "cultural products." You can get jewelry and carvings at the **Suzhou Jade Carving Factory** (✉ 33 Baita Xi Lu ☎ 0512/6727–1224). The **Suzhou Silk Museum Shop** (✉ 661 Renmin Lu ☎ 0512/6753–4941) is really the reason to come to the Silk Museum in the first place. For local artworks and calligraphy, visit the **Wumen Artstore** (✉ 105 Liuyuan Lu ☎ 0512/6533–4808).

Jiangsu A to Z

To research prices, get advice from other travelers, and book travel arrangements, visit www.fodors.com.

AIR TRAVEL

Most international flights from Europe or North America go through Shanghai or Beijing before continuing on to Nanjing's Lukou Airport, but there are direct flights from Nanjing to Asian hubs like Seoul, Nagoya, Singapore, and Bangkok. From Nanjing several flights leave daily for Shanghai, Beijing, Guangzhou, Xiamen, Wuhan, and Hong Kong; flights leave daily for Xian and Chengdu; and several flights leave weekly for Zhengzhou and Hangzhou.

You can buy tickets at any travel agency, at major hotels like the Jinling, or at CITS. Dragonair, which also has a desk in the Jinling Hotel, has daily flights to Hong Kong. In Wuxi and Suzhou CITS can arrange plane tickets through the Shanghai or Nanjing airports for you, or you can get in touch with China Eastern Airlines in Suzhou.

🛈 Airport Information **Lukou Airport** ☎ 025/248-0063 🖶 025/248-0025🛈 **Airlines & Contacts CAAC (Air China)** ✉ 52 Ruijin Lu, Nanjing ☎ 025/8449-9378. **China Eastern Airlines** ✉ 192 Renmin Lu, Suzhou ☎ 0512/6522-2788. **CITS** ✉ 202/1 Zhongshan Bei Lu, Nanjing ☎ 025/8342-8999. **Dragonair** ✉ 208 Guangzhou Lu, Room 810, Nanjing ☎ 025/8331-1999 Ext. 810. **Jinling Hotel** ✉ Xinjiekou, Nanjing ☎ 025/8471-1888.

TRANSFERS   Taxis from Nanjing Airport to the center of town should take about 20 minutes and cost around Y170. There is also a bus from the airport to downtown Nanjing near the Sheraton for Y25.

BOAT & FERRY TRAVEL

The Yangzi is a wide and impressive river, and getting out in the middle of it on a boat really conveys its immense sweep. Ferries cross the Yangzi at Nanjing, and head to several rural islands. Sometime river cruises are available in Nanjing, passing by the two main bridges, the Yanzi Ji and the Yuejiang Lou. Many passenger boats also ply the Yangzi from Nanjing. But those heading upriver towards Wuhan and Chongqing are mostly popular with rural migrant workers, and therefore often quite crowded and not very fast. A short trip down the Yangzi to Shanghai is a better idea; the trip is scenic enough, and boats leave every morning and three afternoons a week from the dock in the northwest side of town. You can get to Nanjing via boat by starting an eastbound Yangzi River cruise in Wuhan. Most passenger boats leave from the Zhongshan Dock (Matou) in the northwest of Nanjing, at the northwest end of Zhongshan Bei Lu.

The overnight ride from Suzhou to Hangzhou along the Grand Canal takes you through some great countryside scenery between these two of China's prettiest cities. Tickets can be purchased through your hotel or a travel agent. The Suzhou Ferry Terminal is on the south side of the city near the old city gate.

🛈 Boat & Ferry Information **Nanjing City's Zhongshan Matou (Ferry Terminal)** ✉ Zhonghshan Lu,, connected to downtown by Bus 10 ☎ 025/5880-5405.

Suzhou Ferry Terminal ✉ 2 Renmin Lu ☎ 0512/6520-6681.

BUS TRAVEL

Frequent bus service runs between Nanjing, Zhenjiang, Wuxi, and Suzhou, with connections or direct lines to Shanghai as well. Some routes have modern tourist buses with air-conditioning. Nanjing's bus station lies west of the railway station at Zhongyang Men. The direct air-conditioned coach to Shanghai takes about 3½ hours.

In Zhenjiang the station is in the southeast corner of the city center. Direct buses run frequently to Nanjing, Suzhou, and Wuxi. In Wuxi the station is right across from the railway station. The Suzhou Bus Station offers trips to other Jiangsu destinations. For all of these, it's best to have the name of your destination written in Chinese to avoid misunderstanding. Buses are the most convenient choice for short trips like Nanjing–Zhenjiang and Wuxi–Suzhou. Otherwise, trains are more comfortable.

🛈 Bus Information **Nanjing Bus Station** ✉ Jianing Lu and Zhongyang Lu ☎ 025/8550-3672. **Suzhou Bus Station** ✉ Southern tip of Renmin Lu ☎ 0512/6520-4867. **Wuxi**

Bus Station ✉ Tonghui Dong Lu ☎ 0510/230-0751. **Zhenjiang Bus Station** ✉ Jiefang Lu ☎ 0511/501-3270.

EMERGENCIES
All of the establishments below are open 24 hours.
🚹 **First Aid Station** ✉ 231 Zhongshan Lu, Nanjing ☎ 025/8330-4392, 025/8663-3858, 110 for emergencies. **People's Hospital No. 1** ✉ 111 Renmin Zhong Lu, Wuxi ☎ 0510/270-0778. **People's Hospital No. 2** ✉ 26 Daoqian Jie, Suzhou ☎ 0512/6522-3691. **Wuxi People's Hospital No. 3** ✉ 320 Tonghui Dong Lu, Wuxi ☎ 0510/270-7391.

TOURS
Major hotels will often arrange a tour guide for a group, as will CITS. Individuals may offer you day tours; just make sure the price is set and the guide's English is good enough to make it worthwhile. Because the major sights in Jiangsu lie inside the cities, they are generally quite accessible to individual travelers.

TRAIN TRAVEL
Nanjing, Zhenjiang, Wuxi, and Suzhou are all on the same rail line, which continues on to Shanghai. Two comfortable air-conditioned "tourist trains" run daily between Nanjing, Wuxi, Suzhou, and Shanghai, leaving Nanjing at 9 AM and 5 PM, reaching Wuxi in about an hour, Suzhou in about 2 hours, and Shanghai in about 2¾ hours. Other trains between all these destinations leave quite frequently. Several daily trains from Nanjing will take you on a day trip to Zhenjiang in about an hour, and several from Suzhou will take you on a day trip to Wuxi in about 40 minutes. Tickets can be purchased either through your hotel or at the stations.

TRANSPORTATION AROUND JIANGSU
Taxis are plentiful and quite inexpensive in all these cities and are a better bet than the crowded and confusing bus systems. Motor tricycles are inexpensive and convenient if you have only a couple of people.

In Nanjing, the Y series of buses connects tourist sights like the Confucian Temple and Sun Yat-sen Memorial. These buses are green, and more comfortable than the standard city buses. Zhenjiang's buses are relatively easy to handle. Bus 4 travels east to the Yangzi, where you can catch a ferry to Jiaoshan. Buses 6 and 21 go south. Bus 2 takes you out to Jinshan Park. If you cannot read Chinese, ask the driver exactly where the bus goes and stops before getting on. A bilingual map is handy.

VISITOR INFORMATION
Hotels are the chief source of tourist information in Zhenjiang and Wuxi. It's best to do any planning you need in Nanjing or Suzhou, where both hotels and special agencies tend to be much better informed.
🚹 Tourist Information **CITS** ✉ 202/1 Zhongshan Bei Lu, Nanjing ☎ 025/8342-8999 ✉ 115 Shiquan Lu, Suzhou ☎ 0512/6522-3783. **Jiangsu Jinling Business International Travel Service** ✉ Jinling Hotel basement, Nanjing ☎ 025/8470-4149. **Suzhou International Travel Service** ✉ Fenghuang Jie, Dinghuishi Xiangkou, Suzhou ☎ 0512/6511-4339. **Suzhou Taihu International Travel Service** ✉ 105 Renmin Nan Lu, Suzhou ☎ 0512/6510-4522.

ZHEJIANG

One of China's wealthiest provinces, Zhejiang has always been a favorite of travelers (including Marco Polo), classical scholars, and countless tourists, many of whom are struck by its combination of charming scenery, refinement, and cultural heritage. Zhejiang is home to Hangzhou, one of China's two "heavens on earth," a city sitting along the shores of the beautiful West Lake. Another jewel in the province's treasure chest is the fascinating small town of Shaoxing, the hometown of a surprising number of China's intellectuals and scholars, with a trove of well-preserved traditional architecture threaded by narrow lanes and canals.

The river basin area to the north is countered by mountains in the south, and cultivated greenery is everywhere. The province was dynastically important starting in the 12th century, when Hangzhou was the capital of the Southern Song Dynasty. It continued in importance even when the capital was moved away, largely because of its grain production and its scenic and cultural attractions. Zhejiang's farms are among the most prosperous in the country, producing tea, rice, wheat, barley, corn, and sweet potatoes. This province also provides one-third of China's silk. Foreign investment and local entrepreneurship have turned the province into one of China's wealthiest. It's famous for its crafts and wares, including fine porcelain, silk products, embroideries, lace, wood and stone carvings, and sculptures. Zhejiang is also home to Putuoshan, a sacred Buddhist island.

Hangzhou

 3 hrs (200 km [124 mi]) by train or express bus southwest of Shanghai.

Hangzhou has long been renowned as a prosperous city on the shores of West Lake, a setting that became a byword for natural beauty in China. The southern terminus of the Grand Canal, Hangzhou was destined for greatness as an economic center from the canal's completion in AD 609. In 1126 the Song Dynasty fled south from Kaifeng to Hangzhou to escape the Jurchen invaders. The era that ensued, later known as the Southern Song, witnessed the rise of Hangzhou's cultural and administrative importance. Its proximity not only to the canal but to river and ocean, as well as the unusual fertility of its environs, made Hangzhou the hub of southern Chinese culture. By the 13th century the city had a population of between 1 and 1.5 million people. From 1861 to 1863 it was occupied by the Taiping forces, and in the ensuing battles with the imperial forces, the city, along with its cultural artifacts and monuments, was somewhat damaged. The Cultural Revolution took a further toll on the city.

Over the last 20 years Hangzhou has emerged as one of China's most vibrant cities. The thriving local economy has provided ample funds to repair or rebuild many of the city's monuments, and the gardens around West Lake, which lend Hangzhou much of its romantic beauty, are once again lovingly maintained. A little way outside the city you can visit the plantations that produce the area's famous Longjing tea, or stroll in forested hills to take in the views of the surrounding area. The lake and its historic sights lie alongside the modern downtown, creating an atmosphere rarely found in modern Chinese cities.

To explore Hangzhou's sights, you can start at the lake, which is the effective center of town. From the lake you can go on to visit the city proper and then move out to the less populous region to the southwest.

Hangzhou culture revolves around **West Lake** (Xihu). The lake was originally a lagoon, cut off from the nearby river, until the local government began taking steps to clear the lake's waters. A few years back they began pumping water from the nearby Qiantang River into the lake, and with the periodic dredging of the lake floor and the daily skimmings of its surface, the lake is clearer and cleaner than it's been in centuries. The lake is crossed by two pedestrian causeways: the **Baidi** (named for the famed Tang Dynasty poet, Bai Juyi) and the **Sudi** (named for the Song poet, Su Dongpo). Both walkways are lined with willow and peach trees, flowers, and benches, and closed to automobiles, making them ideal for strolling or bicycle riding.

Officially run multiseat boats leave every half hour or so from near the **Hangzhou Overseas Chinese Hotel** (⊠ 15 Hubin Lu) to the lake's islands, and a slew of smaller private boats are moored around the lake. If you want your own boat with no rower you can rent a skiff from the Hubin Lu park near the start of the Baidi Causeway, or a rather goofy-looking paddleboat from Gushan Island.

Gushan Island, in the middle of Baidi Causeway, is the lake's largest island. Inside is **Zhongshan Gongyuan,** a small but lovely park, centered on a pond and several pavilions. From here, you can follow the path up the hill to the **Seal Engraver's Society** (Xileng Yinshe). This was once the headquarters of a professional seal-carving operation. There are several small buildings with examples of carvings and calligraphy, including an engraved monument dating from nearly 2,000 years ago. The trip up the hill to the society is worth it, even for those who aren't interested in Chinese stamps. A beautiful garden in front of the society's buildings has the best views of West Lake in all of Hangzhou. Gushan Island is also home to the **Zhejiang Provincial Museum** (Zhejiang Bowuguan; ☎ 0571/8797–1177 ⊠ Free ☉ Weekdays 8:45–4:45). The museum has a good collection of archaeological finds, especially finely carved jades and ancient bronzes as well as galleries for ceramics, classical furniture, and contemporary art. ⊠ *Free* ☉ *Daily 8–dusk.*

need a break?

On the crest of the hill inside the Seal Engraver's society is a small **souvenir shop** where you can drink local teas. Order a cup and have a seat on the hilltop veranda. The view, especially at sunset, will explain why Chinese have loved this place for centuries.

Just off the banks of Gushan is the small man-made island of **Three Pools Reflecting the Moon** (Santan Yinyue). On the island are numerous ponds connected by small bridges and dotted with pavilions. Off the island's southern shore are three stone pagodas. During the autumn moon (August), fires are lighted in the pagodas. The moonlight reflects three golden disks into the water, hence the name. Official multiseat boats travel to the island from Solitary Hill Island. ✉ *Y20, boats from Solitary Hill Island Y35 (includes admission).*

Parks and a paved waterfront-walkway ring most of West Lake. Hubin Lu, where the city meets the lake, has recently been turned into a beautiful pedestrian park. Farther along is the **Orioles Singing in the Willow Waves** (Liulang Wenying). This is a nice place to relax on a bench or in the grass and watch boats and windsurfers on the lake. Orioles still sing here, though not in the "willow waves." Rather, they cry from the large aviary that cages them near the water.

On the southeastern shore of West Lake, the **Evening Sunlight at Thunder Peak Pagoda** (Leifeng Xizhao), completed in 2002, has arisen like a phoenix from atop the crumbled remains of its predecessor, which collapsed in 1924. The foundation dates to AD 976 and is an active archaeological site, where scientists uncovered a miniature silver pagoda containing what is said to be a lock of the Buddha's hair; it's on display in a separate hall. You can watch the dig before climbing (or riding an elevator part way) up five stories, each with remarkable paintings and carvings. Most noteworthy is a vast carved tableau from the Chinese opera *White Snake*, whose heroine was imprisoned in the pagoda. The view of the lake is breathtaking, particularly, as the name suggests, at sunset. ✉ *15 Nanshan Lu* ☎ *0571/8796–4515* ⊕ *www.leifengta.com. cn* ✉ *Y40* ☺ *May–Oct., daily 8 AM–10 PM; Apr. and Nov., daily 8 AM–9 PM; Dec.–Mar., daily 8–5:30; last admission 30 mins before closing.*

☺ **Hangzhou Aquarium** (Hangzhou Haidi Shijie), or Underwater World, on West Lake's eastern shore, is a small but well-designed aquarium with a walk-through glass tunnel in its main tank and several hands-on exhibits. ✉ *49 Nanshan Lu* ☎ *0571/8706–9500* ✉ *Y50* ☺ *Daily 8:30–5.*

✓ **Precious Stone Hill** (Baoshi Shan), with its famous pagoda, **Protecting Chu Pagoda** (Baochu Ta), can be seen on the north side of West Lake from just about anywhere on the lake. Numerous paths lead from the lakeside up to the hilltop, from where you can see not only all of West Lake, but also a good part of Hangzhou. The original pagoda was built about AD 970; the present structure dates from 1933. Both paved and unpaved paths cover the mountain which you can easy spend a pleasant morning or afternoon exploring. Precious Stone Hill is dotted with Buddhist and Taoist shrines and temples—some impressive, others not so—as well as some mysterious caves. In summer, locals often gather in the bigger caves for picnics or cards to escape the heat.

On the back side of Precious Stone Hill is a well-kept park, also with a cave. **Yellow Dragon Cave** (Huanglong Dong) is famous for its (purportedly) never-ending stream of water spurting from the head of a yellow dragon into a pond several meters below. Above the fountain on the hillside is another yellow dragon's head, standing as the entrance to the cave. Below, near the lower entrance, lies a stage, where several times a day traditional Yue opera performances are given. There is also a bamboo groove with rare "square bamboo." A bronze statue of two dragon angels stands before the grove. As the placard to the statue says, be sure to "touch the buttocks" of these cherublike imps for good luck. ⊠ *Shuguang Lu* ☎ *0571/8798–5860* 🖭 *Y15* ⏱ *Daily 7:30–5:30.*

Near Gushan stands the **Yue Fei Mausoleum** (Yue Fei Mu), a temple built to honor the Song general Yue Fei (1103–42), a commander against the Jurchen invaders. When he was young, his mother tattooed his back with the exhortation to "Repay the nation with your loyalty." At the height of his success, a jealous courtier convinced the emperor that the loyal Yue Fei was a traitor, and the emperor ordered him executed. Twenty years later he was rehabilitated and deified and is now one of China's national heroes, a symbol of patriotic duty. The tombs of Yue Fei and his son stand within a quiet grove, flanked by ancient stone statues of horses and officials. It is said that if you trip on the steep bridge leading to the tombs, as Yue Fei's slanderers supposedly once did, you have a guilty conscience. The temple wall replicates the tattooed inscription, while a statue of the traitorous courtier kneels in shame nearby. Traditionally, you're supposed to spit on statues of traitors, but a recent sign near the statue asks visitors to refrain. ⊠ *Beishan Lu west of Gushan* 🖭 *Y25* ⏱ *Daily 7–6.*

A short ride southwest of the lake takes you to the **Dragon Well Tea Park** (Longjing Wencha), where you can buy the local Longjing green tea from people who are serious about quality. This park, set in the middle of some tea plantations, is the site of the well from which water for the best tea comes. Tea sellers may invite prospective buyers to taste the tea, often at the seller's house. The prices seem ridiculous until you take a sip: there really is a difference. However, be sure to bargain for a good price. Note: In recent years the tea park has gotten a bit touristy and commercialized. If you are a fan of tea you may want to skip the buying and go to the superb China Tea Museum instead. ⊠ *South on Longjing Lu.*

√ ★ The fascinating and well-presented **China Tea Museum** (Zhongguo Chaye Bowuguan) explores all the facets of China's tea culture, from galleries on the development of tea drinking styles and ancient tea utensils to exhibits explaining the differences between varieties of tea and tips on how to brew each type of tea perfectly. The excellent and small museum has extensive and informative English explanations and is located a short bus ride away from the lake, among lovely, quiet tea plantations. ⊠ *Just off Long Jing Lu west of lake. Take Tourist Bus 3 from lake, get off at "Shuang Feng" stop, walk west a few minutes, turn right on first road, turn right again at T-intersection. Museum is down this road* 🖭 *Free* ⏱ *Daily 8–4:20.*

Almost directly south of the lake, about 15 minutes by bus, the **Running Tiger Dream Spring** (Hupao Meng Quan) has a temple built on a dream. According to legend, Qi Gong, a traveling monk, decided this setting would be perfect for a temple but as there was no stream or other water in the place, he couldn't build one. Sleeping on the ground, he dreamed that two tigers came and ripped up the earth around him. When he awoke, he was lying next to the stream the dream tigers had dug for him. He duly built the temple. The grounds have a bamboo grove, a nondescript teahouse, a modern statue of the dreamer with his tigers, and an intriguing "dripping wall." This cutout part of the mountainside is so porous and moist that it exudes water from its surface. Locals always come here to fill their water jugs, believing the water has special qualities—and it does. If you don't believe it, ask one of the people working in the temple souvenir shop to float a coin on the surface of the water to prove it. ✉ *Hupao Lu south of West Lake* 🎫 *Y15* ⊙ *Daily 6:45 AM–6 PM.*

The **Temple of the Soul's Retreat** (Lingyin Si) was founded in AD 326 by Hui Li, a Buddhist monk from India (Hui Li was his Chinese name). Reportedly, he looked at the mountains surrounding the site of the current temple and exclaimed, "This is the place where the souls of immortals retreat," hence the name. Perhaps even more than the temple itself, this site is famous for the Buddhist figures carved into the limestone of the mountain—named the **Peak That Flew from Afar** (Feilai Feng)—that faces the temple. From the 10th to the 14th century, monks and artists carved 338 stone iconographical images on the mountain's face and in caves. Unfortunately, the destruction wrought by the Red Guards in Hangzhou during the Cultural Revolution is nowhere more evident than here, even though admirable attempts have been made to restore much that was damaged.

The temple itself, across from the Buddhist carvings, is one of China's 10 large Zen (Chan) Buddhist temples and is definitely worth visiting. However, as one of Hangzhou's most popular attractions, the temple is always crowded. Avoid the place on weekends and holidays if possible. ✉ *Lingyin Si Lu west of city* 🕿 *0571/8796–9691* 🎫 *Park Y25, temple Y20* ⊙ *Park daily 5:30 AM–6 PM, temple daily 7–5.*

At the **China National Silk Museum** (Zhongguo Sichou Bowuguan), well-curated galleries, signed in Chinese and English, explore the history of the "queen of fibers." On display are weaves and samples—some replicas, some real—of Chinese silk clothing worn during different dynasties. Upstairs there's an art gallery. The first-floor shop sells clothing and silk by the meter. The museum is south of West Lake, on the road to Jade Emperor Hill. ✉ *73-1 Yuhuangshan Lu* 🕿 *0571/8706–2129* 🎫 *Free* ⊙ *Daily 8–6.*

A few miles outside the city, atop **Moon Mountain** (Yuelin Shan) and overlooking the banks of the Qiantang River, stands the impressive **Pagoda of Six Harmonies** (Liuhe Ta). Great views are rewarded to those who climb to the top of the seven-story pagoda. On the 18th day of the eighth lunar month, the pagoda is packed with people, all wanting the best seat for "Qiantang Reversal." On this day the flow of the river reverses itself, creating large waves that for centuries have delighted observers. Behind the pagoda in an extensive park with a pagoda exhibition: expert re-creations of a hundred or so miniature pagodas, representing every Chinese style, are on permanent display here. ✉ *Fuxing Jie south of city* 🎫 *Y15* ⊙ *Daily 6–6:30.*

Where to Stay & Eat

At this writing, several hotels were under construction as a result of the selection of Hangzhou to host the 2006 World Leisure Expo. The added competition has put pressure on existing hotels to upgrade facilities or drop prices—meaning there are bargains to be had, especially among the older Chinese hotels whose facilities can't match the newcomers.

The city's dining scene, likewise, is on the rise. Along the eastern shore of West Lake lies Xihu Tiandi (West Lake Heaven on Earth)—an upscale dining and shopping complex patterned on Shanghai's Xintiandi. Along the surrounding Nanshan Lu bar and restaurant district, you'll find good Indian, Italian, Thai, and Continental fare.

$$–$$$$
Fodor'sChoice
★

✕ **Louwailou Restaurant.** Founded in 1848, this restaurant on the banks of West Lake is Hangzhou's most famous. It has impressed everyone from the famous writer Lu Xun and Premier Zhou Enlai to flocks of less-illustrious tourists with its delicious Hangzhou cuisine. A highlight is the classic *su dongpo* pork, stewed in yellow rice wine until it's so tender you can eat it with a spoon. The fish dishes are made with fish raised in a small sectioned-off area of West Lake in front of the restaurant. ⊠ *30 Gushan Lu* ☎ *0571/8796–9682* ▤ *AE, MC, V.*

¢–$$$

✕ **Zhiweiguan Restaurant.** The first floor here is a pay-as-you-go dim sum cafeteria. With no English menus you'll need to rely on body language to order a bamboo steamer of their famous dumplings. The second and fourth floors offer a much more pleasant dining experience (with English menus). The third floor hosts private parties. Try the peaceful dining room just off the banquet room on the fourth floor. ⊠ *83 Renhe Lu* ☎ *0571/8706–6933* ▤ No credit cards.

$$

✕ **Haveli.** Haveli brings an authentic taste of India to Hangzhou, with a short but solid list of classic dishes: samosas, lamb vindaloo, and chicken *makhni* (chicken cooked with butter), plus fantastic mango lassis. The artful use of gauze curtains as dividers among the candlelighted tables makes the restaurant feel intimate rather than small; a high peaked ceiling with exposed wood beams also opens up the room. A large patio handles the overflow, but if you dine outdoors you'll miss the belly dancer who performs nightly. ⊠ *77 Nanshan Lu* ☎ *0571/8707–9677* ⌂ *Reservations essential* ▤ *AE, DC, MC, V.*

$–$$

✕ **Lingyin Si Vegetarian Restaurant.** This restaurant has turned the Buddhist restriction against preparing meat into an opportunity to invent a range of deliciously unique vegetarian dishes using soy to replicate traditionally meaty meals. ⊠ *Inside Temple of the Soul's Retreat* ▤ No credit cards ⊙ *No dinner.*

$$$–$$$$
Fodor'sChoice
★

🏠 **Shangri-La Hotel Hangzhou.** The best hotel in Hangzhou, the Shangri-La, once the site of the Feng Lin Temple, is a scenic and historic landmark. The hotel's 40 hillside acres of camphor and bamboo trees merge seamlessly into the nearby gardens and walkways surrounding West Lake and Solitary Hill Island. Spread over two wings, the large rooms have a formal air, with high ceilings and heavy damask couches and bedspreads. Request a room overlooking the lake; the Horizon Club's patio has the best views. The gym and restaurants are all top caliber. ⊠ *78 Beishan Lu, 310007* ☎ *0571/8797–7951* ⊟ *0571/8707–3545* ⊕ *www.shangri-la.com* ⇔ *355 rooms, 28 suites* ⌂ *3 restaurants, room service, in-room data ports, in-room safes, minibars, cable TV, tennis court, indoor pool, gym, hair salon, hot tub, massage, sauna, steam room, bicycles, billiards,* *bar, lobby lounge, shops, baby-sitting, dry cleaning, laundry service, concierge, concierge floor, Internet, business services, convention center, airport shuttle, travel services, no-smoking rooms* ⊟ *AE, DC, MC, V.*

★ **$$–$$$** ⊞ **Sofitel Westlake Hangzhou.** A stone's throw from West Lake and Xihu Tiandi, the Sofitel has made waves on the lodging scene since quietly opening in late 2003. Brown-gauze curtains and etched-glass-and-wood columns divide the distinctive lobby, with its gold-and-black mural of three Hangzhou landmarks: Pagoda of Six Harmonies, Protecting Chu Pagoda, and Evening Sunlight at Thunder Peak Pagoda. The rooms—most of which have lake views—are thoughtfully designed, with sleek oval desks, gauze-covered headboards, and a glass privacy screen in the bathroom. The roman-style pool overcomes its drab basement location. ⊠ *333 Xihu Dadao, 310002* ☎ *0571/8707–5858* 🖷 *0571/8707–8383* ⊕ *www.accor.com* ⊃ *186 rooms, 15 suites* ⚴ *4 restaurants, room service, in-room data ports, in-room safes, minibars, cable TV with movies, indoor pool, gym, hair salon, massage, sauna, spa, bar, lobby lounge, piano, shops, dry cleaning, laundry service, concierge, concierge floor, Internet, business services, convention center, airport shuttle, no-smoking rooms* ⊟ *AE, DC, MC, V.*

$–$$$ ⊞ **Dragon Hotel.** Within walking distance of Precious Stone Hill and the Yellow Dragon Cave, this hotel stands in relatively peaceful and attractive surroundings. It's a large hotel, but seems smaller because the buildings are spread around peaceful courtyards with ponds, a waterfall, and a gazebo. Two towers house the fair-size guest rooms, which are decorated in pale greens and blues; the cream wallpaper is peeling in places. Although it has plenty of facilities, the hotel lacks the polish of its Western competitors and the next-door World Trade Center Grand Hotel Zhejiang. ⊠ *120 Shuguang Lu, 310007* ☎ *0571/8799–8833* 🖷 *0571/8799–8090* ⊕ *www.dragon-hotel.com* ⊃ *468 rooms, 28 suites* ⚴ *3 restaurants, room service, in-room data ports, in-room safes, minibars, cable TV, tennis court, pool, gym, hair salon, hot tub, massage, sauna, bicycles, lobby lounge, shops, baby-sitting, dry cleaning, laundry service, concierge, Internet, business services, convention center, travel services, no-smoking rooms, no-smoking floors* ⊟ *AE, DC, MC, V.*

$$ ⊞ **Wanghu Hotel.** A couple minutes' walk from the lake, the Wanghu is oriented toward business travelers. It offers a special "business club" service with a 24-hour business center and meeting rooms as well as translation services and PCs. The hotel also serves complimentary breakfasts and teas to give business travelers a chance to meet. ⊠ *2 Huancheng Xi Lu, 310006* ☎ *0571/8707–1024* 🖷 *0571/8707–1350* ⊕ *www.wanghuhotel.com* ⊃ *406 rooms, 14 suites* ⚴ *2 restaurants, pool, gym, hair salon, sauna, bar, business services, meeting room* ⊟ *AE, MC, V.*

$–$$ ⊞ **Lakeview Hotel.** True to its name, the Lakeview Hotel has good views of West Lake from its corner at the lake's northeastern shore. The top-floor Solmer Restaurant, in particular, is a great vantage point for watching the sun set over the lake. A blue-and-gray color scheme decorates the rooms, and the furniture has some nice inlaid detailing. The hotel is popular with domestic and Japanese travelers, for whom state-of-the-art, heated Japanese toilets have been installed in the bathrooms. The staff's English is shaky, but the hotel is marketing itself more toward

Westerners. ⊠ *2 Huancheng Xi Lu, 310006* ☎ *0571/8707–8888* 🖷 *0571/8707–1350* ⊕ *www.lakeviewhotelhz.com* ⤶ *347 rooms, 14 suites* ⚿ *3 restaurants, room service, in-room data ports, in-room safes, minibars, cable TV, indoor pool, gym, hair salon, massage, sauna, bicycles, billiards, lobby lounge, piano, shops, baby-sitting, dry cleaning, laundry service, concierge, meeting rooms, travel services, no-smoking rooms* ▤ *AE, DC, MC, V.*

$ ▦ **Dragon New World Hotel Hangzhou.** In the hilly area around Yellow Dragon Cave and Dragon Well Tea Park, the Dragon New World stands in relatively peaceful and attractive surroundings. It makes a good starting point for walking tours of the city: you can reach the Protecting Chu Pagoda and the lake on foot. ⊠ *7 Shuguang Lu, 310007* ☎ *0571/ 8799–8833* 🖷 *0571/8799–8090* ⤶ *476 rooms, 31 suites* ⚿ *3 restaurants, tennis court, pool, gym, hair salon, massage, sauna, bicycles, baby-sitting, business services, meeting room, travel services* ▤ *AE, MC, V.*

¢ ▦ **Dong Po Hotel.** This budget business hotel is clean and comfortable. The smaller rooms are a bit spartan, but its prime location in the center of town—two blocks from the lake and two blocks from the night market—makes it a good pick. ⊠ *52 Renhe Lu, 310000* ☎ *0571/ 8702–4220* ⤶ *80 rooms, 3 suites* ⚿ *Restaurant, business services* ▤ *MC, V.*

¢ ▦ **Hangzhou Overseas Chinese Hotel.** In spite of its name, this budget hotel welcomes visitors of any origin, although the staff's English skills are shaky. Its location is the main draw, just steps from West Lake and the Hubin Lu pedestrian walkway. Rooms on the fifth floor have the best lake views. Modern beige wallpaper and carpeting help brighten the fairly large rooms but can't hide the cracked walls and scratched woodwork in this older state-owned hotel. You can hire a car and driver here to tour the outlying area. ⊠ *39 Hubin Lu, 310006* ☎ *0571/8707–4401* 🖷 *0571/8707–4978* ⤶ *218 rooms, 21 suites* ⚿ *2 restaurants, in-room safes, minibars, hair salon, massage, sauna, 2 bars, shops, baby-sitting, laundry service, business services, meeting rooms, travel services* ▤ *AE, DC, MC, V.*

Nightlife & the Arts

Nanshan Lu is the epicenter of Hangzhou's nightlife scene. The laidback **Kana Pub** (⊠ 152 Nanshan Lu ☎ 0571/8706–3228) is the highlight of the strip and an expat favorite for its well-mixed cocktails, live music, and the hospitality of its owner. The warm, muted, brown-and-yellow interior of **Paradise Rock** (⊠ 39 Hubin Lu, next to Hangzhou Overseas Chinese Hotel ☎ 0571/8707–4401), a British-style pub, is perfect for light drinks and conversation. The friendly staff at the **Shamrock** (⊠ 70 Zhongshan Zhong Lu ☎ 0571/8702–8760), Hangzhou's first Irish pub, serves Guinness and Kilkenny pints, bottled-beer specials, and great food.

Yue opera performances take place daily from 8:45 AM to 11:45 AM and 1:45 PM to 4:45 PM at the **Huanglong Dong Yuanyuan Mingshu Yuan Theater** (⊠ 16 Shuguang Lu ☎ 0571/8798–5860), at the Yellow Dragon Cave. The performances are free, but you must pay the Y15 park admission.

Shopping

The best souvenirs to buy in Hangzhou are green tea and silk, but all sorts of wooden crafts, silk fans and umbrellas, and antiques are available in small shops sprinkled around town. For the best Longjing tea, head to the tea plantations at Dragon Well Tea Park. Around town, especially along Yanan Lu, you can spot the small tea shops by the large woklike tea roasters at each store's entrance.

China Silk City (Zhongguo Sichou Cheng; ✉ 253 Xinhua Lu, between Fengqi Lu and Tiyuchang Lu ☎ 0571/8515–2901) sells silk ties, pajamas, and shirts, plus silk straight off the bolt. The **Xihu Longjing Tea Company** (✉ 602 Fengqi Lu ☎ 0571/8510–3878) has a nice selection of Longjing tea.

Although it has been relocated several times, Hangzhou's **night market** (✉ Renhe Lu east of Huansha Lu) is still thriving. Merchants sell silk clothing and accessories of every kind—ties, scarves, pillow covers—as well as knockoff purses, silver jewelry, and alleged antiques. You'll find the same items at multiple stalls, so don't hesitate to walk away if the price isn't right. It's open nightly 6 PM–10:30 PM.

Shaoxing

★ ㉝ *1 hr (65 km [40 mi]) by bus or train east from Hangzhou.*

The small, well-preserved town of Shaoxing is perhaps the best place to experience the historic atmosphere of a traditional Yangzi Delta town. For centuries it was a center of regional trade—thanks especially to the city's famous rice wine—and scholarship, but much of the region's development of the last 50 years has passed it by, leaving a town mostly made up of low stone houses interlaced with canals and narrow streets, where neighbors chat as they wash their laundry next to one of the town's centuries-old stone bridges.

Much of the charm of Shaoxing comes from exploring its narrow alleys lined with traditional houses, crisscrossed with narrow canals and arching stone bridges. In the early part of the 20th century, a surprising number of the city's residents went on to become famous political and cultural figures, including Communist China's first premier Zhou Enlai. Family homes have become museums, fascinating to visit even if you have no special interest in their former residents. Well preserved and decorated with antique or reproduction furniture, these homes are a great way to experience the city's wealth of traditional architecture, and to imagine what Shaoxing was like in the days of Old China.

Lu Xun Family Home (Lu Xun Gu Ju) was once the stomping grounds of literary giant Lu Xun. This family complex is a great way to explore a traditional Shaoxing home and see some beautiful antique furniture. A series of courtyards housed the extended Lu family. Nearby is the local school where Lu honed his writing skills. ✉ 398 Lu Xun Zhong Lu 🖭 Y30 ☉ Daily 8–4:45.

Shaoxing is dotted with old bridges, and the **Bazi Qiao Bridge** (Number 8 Character Bridge) is the city's finest and best known. Its long sloping slides rising to a flat crest make it look much like the auspicious Chinese number 8, giving the bridge its name. The current bridge dates from the Southern Song Dynasty, more than 800 years ago, and is draped with a thick beard of ivy and vines. It sits an a quiet area of old stone houses, while on the canal-side terraces you can see neighbors wash clothes and chat.

Just before the bridge is the city's **Catholic Church of St. Joseph** (⊠ Bazi Qiao Jie), painted bright pink and dating from the turn of the 20th century. The Italian-inspired interior is decorated with Chinese calligraphy of passages from the Bible. To get to the bridge and the church, turn left on Bazi Qiao Zhi Jie from Renmin Zhong Lu in the center of town.

The area in the north of the city, north of Shengli Lu and east of Jiefang Lu, is especially atmospheric for wandering, and is dotted with several historic homes and temples, now preserved as museums. Quiet, atmospheric, and little visited, they have richer historic atmosphere than the more popular sights. The largest is the **Cai Yuanpei's House** (⊠ On alley north of Xiaoshan Lu, which runs east from Jiefang Lu ⌨ Y5 ⊘ Daily 8–5). Cai was a famous educator during the Republic and his family's large compound is decorated with antique furniture. From his home, head east on Maojia Qiao, and you'll come to a picturesque crossroad with an ancient bridge, near a quiet temple facing old stone houses surrounding a small stone pool. From here you can follow Jishan Jie south back to Shengli Lu. Head south on Jiefang Zhong Lu one block, and turn left on Laodong Lu to reach the **Zhou Enlai Family Home** (⊠ Laodong Lu ⌨ Y5 ⊘ Daily 8–5). The beloved first premier of Communist China was from a family of prosperous Shaoxing merchants. The compound, a showcase of traditional architecture, has been preserved and houses exhibits on Zhou's life, ranging from his high school essays to vacation snapshots with his wife.

The narrow **East Lake** (Dong Hu) runs along the base of a phantasmagorical-shape rocky bluff rising up from the rice paddies of Zhejiang. The cliffs were used as a rock quarry over the centuries, and today their sheer gray faces billow in and out like huge sails or sheets of steel. You can hire a local boatman to take you along the base of the cliffs in a traditional black awning boat for Y30, one-way. Bus 1 from Jiefang Lu runs here, or it's a Y10 taxi ride from Lu Xun Lu. ⊠ *Yundong Lu outside the city center* ⌨ *Y25* ⊘ *Daily 7:30 AM–9 PM.*

Where to Stay & Eat

Two of Shaoxing's local products have entered China's culinary pantheon, and no visit to the city is complete without trying the local *chou dofu* ("stinky tofu") and drinking some yellow rice wine. Stinky tofu is a local Shaoxing snack now poplar around China. Although the name isn't so appealing, the tofu is actually quite tasty, and not as smelly as you might expect. It's made from slightly fermented tofu which is deep-fried. Dip it in the local chili sauce and you'll be a convert, too. The city's famed rice wine, *huang jiu* (meaning yellow wine), is more reddish brown than yellow, and slightly sweet and mellow. Its flavor is similar to sweet sherry and it's lovely when served warm on a cool rainy evening. Locals supposedly drink prodigious quantities of the wine, with men even downing some for breakfast. It's often stored in huge ceramic jugs like ancient Greek amphoras, and then ladled out for customers.

¢–$ ✕ **Sanwei Jiulou.** This tasty restaurant serves up local specialties, all washed down with warm local rice wine, served in Shaoxing's distinctive tin kettles. Relaxed and atmospheric, it's located in a restored old building and appointed with simple, traditional wood furniture. The second story looks out over the street below. ⊠ *2 Lu Xun Lu* ☎ *0575/893–5578* ▤ *No credit cards.*

¢ ✕ **Xianheng Winehouse** (Xianheng Jiudian). This is Shaoxing's most famous restaurant, although the locals who hang out here with the out-of-towners don't seem to care. Order a plate of the delicious chou dofu at the counter and get a bowl of the rice wine. One of Lu Xun's short stories led to the literary apotheosis of this small café. ⊠ *179 Lu Xun Zhong Lu* ☎ *0575/511–6666* ▤ *No credit cards.*

¢–$ ▦ **Shaoxing Xianheng Hotel.** Conveniently located along the traditional Lu Xun Lu near many of the city's restaurants, the Xianheng hotel offers modern comfortable rooms and good service. ⊠ *680 Jiefang Nan Lu , 312000* ☎ *0575/806–8688* ⇴ *235 rooms, 4 suites* ⚁ *2 restaurants, bar, business services* ▤ *MC, V.*

¢ ▦ **Shaoxing International Hotel** (Shaoxing Guoji Dajiudian). Surrounded by pleasant gardens, this hotel offers bright, well-appointed rooms and a range of facilities. ⊠ *100 Fushan Xi Lu, 312000* ☎ *0575/516–6788* ▤ *0575/516–6778* ⇴ *308 rooms* ⚁ *2 restaurants, tennis courts, pool, sauna, business services* ▤ *AE, DC, MC, V.*

Shopping

Shaoxing has some interesting local crafts, mainly related to calligraphy and rice wine—its two main preoccupations. The most convenient place to buy souvenirs is Lu Xun Zhong Lu, the restored old street near the Lu Xun sights. In addition to calligraphy brushes, fans, and scrolls decorated with calligraphy, look for shops selling the local tin wine pots. The traditional way of serving Shaoxing's yellow rice wine, the pots can be left on the stove to heat up wine for a cold winter night. You might also want to get yourself a traditional boatmen's hat—waterproof and made of thick black felt.

Zhejiang A to Z

To research prices, get advice from other travelers, and book travel arrangements, visit www.fodors.com.

AIR TRAVEL

Hangzhou International Airport has flights to most major cities around China. You can travel between Hong Kong and Hangzhou daily on Dragonair. There are regular flights to all other major Chinese cities, often daily, depending on the season.

🖈 Airport Information **Hangzhou International Airport** ☎ 0571/8666-1236 🖈 Airlines & Contacts **CAAC** ⊠ 390 Tiyuchang Lu Hangzhou ☎ 0571/8515-4259. **Dragonair** ⊠ Shuguang Lu Hangzhou ☎ 0571/8799-8833 Ext. 6061.

TRANSFERS Major hotels offer limo service to the airport. Taxis to the airport cost around Y80. A bus leaves from the **Minhang Ticket Office** (✉ 395 Tiyuchang Lu Hangzhou) every 40 minutes during the day for about Y25.

BIKE TRAVEL

Bikes are a great way to get around the West Lake area—it's a very pleasant ride, shaded by trees, and makes getting between the sights much quicker. The two causeways, Baidi and Sudi, are closed to automobile traffic and perfect for cycling. Major hotels have bike rentals, as does the Liulang Wenying park, south of the Children's Park (Ertong Gongyuan). The rental rate is usually about Y10 per hour, though a deposit of several hundred yuan or a form of identification is usually required.

📌 Bike Rentals **Liulang Wenying Park** ✉ Nanshan Lu Hangzhou, on east side of lake.

BOAT & FERRY TRAVEL

You can travel overnight between Hangzhou and Suzhou by ferry up and down the Grand Canal. Tickets are available through CITS or at the dock. The boat leaves daily from Hangzhou at 5:30 PM and arrives in Suzhou the next morning at 7.

One of the best ways to experience the charm of West Lake is on one of the many boats that cross the water. Ferries charge Y35 for trips between the two causeways and the main islands in the lake, and leave when there are enough passengers, usually around every half hour. Small private boats charge a set Y80 for up to four people, and you can choose your own route. If you have sea legs yourself you can head out on your own boat for Y20 for two hours, although with these small boats it's not possible to dock at the islands.

📌 Boat & Ferry Information **CITS** ✉ Huancheng Bei Lu Hangzhou ☎ 0571/8515-3360.

BUS TRAVEL TO & FROM ZHEJIANG

The bus hub of the province is Hangzhou, which has four stations in town. The West Bus Station (Xi Zhan) has several buses daily to Huangshan, in Anhui, as well as to Nanjing. The East Bus Station (*Dong Zhan*) is the town's biggest, with several hundred departures per day to destinations like Shaoxing (1 hr), Suzhou (2 ½ hrs), and Shanghai (3 hrs). A bus connects these two bus stations. The other two stations service small residential hamlets. Make sure you check with your hotel or travel agent which bus station you need to use.

📌 Bus Information **East Bus Station** ✉ 215 Liangshan Xi Lu, Hangzhou. **West Bus Station** ✉ 60 Tianmushan Lu, Hangzhou.

BUS TRAVEL WITHIN ZHEJIANG

In Hangzhou, in addition to regular city buses, a series of modern airconditioned buses connect most major tourist sights. They loop around the shores of the lake and are an easy way to get to more isolated sights. Bus Y1 connects the east shore of the lake, Yue Fei Mausoleum, and the Temple of the Soul's Retreat, while Bus Y3 runs to the Longjing area and the China Tea Museum. Hangzhou's East Bus Station has dozens of buses to Shaoxing from morning until around 7:30 PM. Buses from Shaoxing to Hangzhou leave from the main bus station in the north of town, at the intersection of Jiefang Bei Lu and Huan Cheng Bei Lu, near a colossal sculpture modeled on ancient bronzes. Buses run every hour before 7 PM to Hangzhou's East Bus Station, and cost around Y15. Ask at your hotel desk, at the Xinhua Bookstore in downtown Hangzhou, or at newspaper stands about English-language bus maps.

EMERGENCIES

As one of China's wealthier cities, the standard of medical care in Hangzhou is reasonably high, and for major emergencies nearby Shanghai's hospitals are also an option.

🚹 **Hangzhou Red Cross Hospital** ✉ 38 Huancheng Dong Lu ☎ 0571/8518-6042 or 0571/8518-3137. **Zhejiang Medical University Affiliated Hospital No. 1** ✉ 261 Qingchun Lu Hangzhou ☎ 0571/8707-2524.

TAXIS

Hangzhou's taxi fleet is among the most modern and comfortable in China, and makes it easy getting from the banks of West Lake to farther-away sights like the Temple of the Soul's Retreat and the China Tea Museum and tea plantations. Although Shaoxing is small enough that walking is an easy way to get between many sights, Shaoxing's small red taxis are remarkably inexpensive. Most trips within the city are only Y5.

TOURS

Hotels can set up tours for interested groups, and CITS can also make arrangements, for a fee. Hawkers or taxi drivers at the train station or in front of your hotel may offer tours. Although these can be as good as official ones, their English is often minimal.

🚹 **CITS** ✉ 1 Shihan Lu Hangzhou ☎ 0571/8515-2888.

TRAIN TRAVEL

Travel between Shanghai and Hangzhou is quick and convenient: normal trains take about three hours; the newer "tourist train" takes only two. The train station is crowded and difficult to manage, but hotel travel desks can often book tickets for you for a small fee. Trains also run to Nanjing, Huangshan, and most cities in Fujian and Jiangxi. Trains run to Shaoxing from Hangzhou but buses depart much more frequently. The Shaoxing Train Station is just north of the bus station, where you can catch trains to Hangzhou several times a day.

🚹 Train Information **Hangzhou Train Station** ✉ Jiang Cheng Lu, in western part of city.

TRAVEL AGENCIES

Most hotels have their own agencies, as well as visitor information, and there is always CITS.

🚹 Local Agent Referrals **Zhejiang Comfort Travel** ✉ In Shangri-La Hotel Hangzhou, 78 Beishan Lu, Hangzhou ☎ 0571/8796-5005. **Zhejiang Women's International Travel Service** ✉ 1 Huancheng Xi Lu Hangzhou ☎ 0571/8702-9348.

VISITOR INFORMATION

🚹 Tourist Information **Hangzhou Travel and Tourism Bureau** ✉ 484 Yanan Lu ☎ 0571/8515-2645. **Zhejiang CITS** ✉ 1 Shihan Lu Hangzhou ☎ 0571/8516-0877.

ANHUI

One of Eastern China's most mountainous and rural provinces, Anhui is also home to one of China's greatest natural wonders, the Huangshan Mountain, a truly breathtaking landscape that seems even more unbelievable than the peaks and spires of Chinese landscape painting. Its rugged mountain landscape and difficult transportation kept Anhui a fairly poor place for much of its history—the 19th and 20th centuries were not kind to Anhui, but with increasing control over the Yellow River and growing industrial production, the province seems to be pulling itself up. In 1850 the Yellow River flooded and changed course, causing major famine and destruction. Widespread disenchantment and government indifference led to peasant revolts. The revolts, put down by imperial forces, led to further famine and destruction. In 1938 the province suffered another flood, this one caused by Chinese military forces attempting to hold off the Japanese. Despite its efforts, Anhui was occupied by Japanese troops during World War II, before the Nationalist Party reoccupied it in 1946. Until the Communists took it in 1949, Anhui was considered the most backward province in Eastern China. It is still one of the poorest.

The Yangzi River runs from Nanjing west through the southern half of Anhui, and the province's best sights are defined by this natural boundary. North of the river are flatlands and the pleasant if dull provincial capital, Hefei. Between the river and Anhui's southern border lies one of China's most famous mountain ranges. In the popular consciousness, Huangshan is one of the five great mountains of China. These mountains undeniably present some of the most spectacular scenery in the country, perhaps in the world. The mountains have drawn a steady influx of visitors for hundreds of years, from Tang Dynasty emperors to modern families on vacation. If you have extra time to explore, the villages around Shexian near Huangshan are first-rate examples of Ming Dynasty architecture.

Huangshan (Yellow Mountain)

34 *5½ hrs (250 km [155 mi]) by train west of Nanjing; 3½ hrs by long-distance bus.*

FodorsChoice
★

By far the most important attraction in Anhui is Huangshan, also known as Huangshan Scenic Area (Huangshan Fengjing Qu). A favorite retreat of emperors and poets of old, its peaks have inspired some of China's most outstanding artworks and literary endeavors. They were so beguiling, in fact, that years of labor went into their paths, which are actual stone steps rising up—sometimes gradually into the forest, sometimes sharply through a stone tunnel and into the mist above. The mountain is known particularly for three common sights. Colloquially they are known as: "grotesque pines" twisted by the winds, "unusual rock formations" coming in animal shapes, and the "sea of mist" that sweeps in and out of the upper reaches of the peaks. What you must see, though, is the sunrise from the top of the mountain. Hundreds of people gather to observe the stunning sight before walking sleepily back down for some breakfast.

There are two routes up the mountain—the Eastern and Western steps. The Eastern Steps are a fairly straightforward hike through woods, with views of the main peaks rising up behind, while the Western Steps wind up, around, and over a dizzy landscape of vertiginous peaks and narrow ridges. If you have the stamina, it's best to make the trip up the Western Steps, where you can admire the amazing scenery before you get dead tired (if you climb down this way, you'll be too busy watching your feet to take in much of the landscape). If you spend the night, you can make a leisurely trip up the western route, explore the peak area the next morning, and come down the Eastern Steps in time for mid-afternoon trains or buses onward. If thousands of stone steps seem a bit too intimidating, there are also several cable car routes up the mountain (Y50–Y110).

Climbing up the western route, the trail winds upwards toward **Mid-Mountain Temple** (Banshan Si), after which Huangshan's breathtaking splendor comes on in full. A cable car (Y40) here cuts up to **Yuping Lou**, a complex of buildings farther up the mountain. If you're feeling energetic and not afraid of vertigo, a side trail loops around to **Heavenly Capital Peak** and the **Crucian Carp's Back,** where sheer cliffs drop thousands of feet on either side of a ridge barely a meter wide. Otherwise, the main trail climbs up to Yuping Lou and the nearby **Welcoming Guest Pine,** a beautifully arched lone pine standing at the edge of a cliff, with a particularly spectacular mountain landscape as its backdrop. The pine has become a symbol of Huangshan, and has even inspired its own brands of cigarettes and beer. From here you can choose to climb **Lotus Peak,** the highest point of the mountain and a truly vertiginous experience. The peak rises up like a monolith, and the stairs upward are cut into the rock, wrapping upward before emerging on the bare summit with the dozens of smaller crests spread out below. After Lotus Peak, the trail becomes more mild before reaching the weather station that marks the start of the peak area. Unlike the rest of the mountain, the top of Huangshan is actually fairly flat and wooded, with several small lakes and guesthouses among the trees. If you have extra time, a trail leads west from the **Haixin Ting Pavilion** into a section of trails less overrun by tour groups. This route has a much more natural feel and eventually reaches the **Immortal's Walk Bridge** (Buxian Qiao), a small arched bridge crossing over the misty abyss below to reach a small terrace on the side of one of the mountain's spires. A huge landscape spreads out beneath, without a single Chinese tour group in sight.

The Eastern Steps are less spectacular, and are a fairly straight shot down the mountain, taking only a few hours to reach the base. You can have a rest exactly where Deng Xiaoping did—the spot is marked with a huge billboard of Deng, well, resting. If you feel like exploring more, there are several waterfalls near the base of the Eastern Steps, as well as thick groves of bamboo on the lower slopes.

There are many options for getting to Huangshan. Sleeper trains leave from Hangzhou, Nanjing, and Shanghai in the evening, arriving in the morning to allow for a full day's hiking. Buses also connect the area to most cities in neighboring provinces. Most transport and all trains arrive in **Tunxi,** a small town near the mountain. Dozens of minibuses and cabs loiter outside the train and bus stations waiting to ferry tourists to Tangkou, where the trail heading up the mountain actually begins. The trip from Tunxi to Tangkou takes under an hour. A nearby airport also connects the region to many other cities in China, although it is mainly used by Chinese package tours. The bus route from Jiangsu or Zhejiang to Tangkou follows mountain passes to reveal a patchwork of small, sloping, graded fields traversed by thin irrigation canals. You'll get a glimpse of peasant life in the hills as you pass farmers dipping long-handled wooden ladles into the canals to water their crops, or working with sickles and other hand tools to set their lands in order. You could also go to Huangshan by bus from Wuhu or Guichi, towns on the Yangzi River at which the Wuhan–Shanghai ferry stops.

Where to Stay

Reservations are essential for any hotel in the Huangshan area, as this is one of China's major tourist spots. The mountaintop hotels tend to be overpriced; you pay more for Huangshan than for the facilities provided (Tunxi hotels are less expensive). Food in the area tends to be less than amazing, but after a day of hard climbing and breathtaking scenery, you probably won't care.

$ ⊞ **Xihai Hotel.** This joint venture is ideally situated at the top of the mountain, providing a convenient site for sunrise-watching as well as for comfortable living. It's not a luxury hotel, but it is one of the best lodgings around. ⊠ *Huangshan Scenic Area, 242709* ☎ *0559/556–2132* 📠 *0559/556–2988* 🛏 *121 rooms, 5 suites* ♨ *Restaurant, bar* ▤ *AE, MC, V.*

¢–$ ⊞ **Beihai Hotel.** This is one of the three mountaintop hotels that accept foreigners. Deng Xiaoping stayed here, and the top man chose one of the best bets on the mountain. Considering it's somewhat overpriced, he's probably glad he wasn't footing the bill, but it is clean and has a few extras—like a massage service and saunas—that might be a welcome end to a day of hiking. The hotel's rooms and villas are picturesquely sited. ⊠ *Huangshan Scenic Area, 242709* ☎ *0559/556–2555* 📠 *0559/556–2996* 🛏 *137 rooms, 2 suites* ♨ *Restaurant, massage, sauna, bar* ▤ *AE, MC, V.*

¢   ⊞ **Peach Blossom Hotel.** A winding road takes you over a bridge and past a waterfall to this enchanted-looking resort between the main gate of the mountain park and the beginning of the Western Steps. The Peach Blossom has the best food (both Chinese and Western) of the three mountain hotels. You'll have to hustle to catch the sunrise if you stay here, but the hot springs next door are great to come back to after a day of hiking. ⊠ *Huangshan Scenic Area, 242709* ☎ *0559/556–2666* 📠 *0559/556–2888* 🛏 *110 rooms, 4 suites* ♨ *Restaurant, bar* ▤ *AE, MC, V.*

Anhui A to Z

To research prices, get advice from other travelers, and book travel arrangements, visit www.fodors.com.

AIR TRAVEL

🛂 Airlines & Contacts **China Eastern Airlines** ⊠ 246 Jinzhai Lu, Hefei ☎ 0559/282-2357.

AIRPORTS

Tourists flying to Huangshan fly to the Huangshan City airport near Tunxi, and is connected to the train and bus stations by local buses. It's probably best to buy both legs of your trip from your starting point, since a flight can be unexpectedly booked by tour groups. It has daily flights to the western town of Hefei, as well as flights to Beijing and Guangzhou several times a week, Shanghai almost daily, Xian once a week, and Hong Kong twice a week. If you don't get an advance ticket it's best to buy tickets at your hotel.

🚹 Airport Information **Huangshan City airport** ☎ 0559/2934–1113.

BUS TRAVEL TO & FROM ANHUI

Buses are a convenient way of getting to Huangshan from Zhejiang, Jiangsu, and even Shanghai. Although buses from Hangzhou (9 hours) go through some gorgeous scenery, they often do not provide the most comfortable ride. You can try going to or from Hangzhou by bus and traveling the other direction by train or plane—the views from the bus really are worth the ride. Buses from Huangshan to Nanjing take much less time—around 5 hours.

TAXIS

Minibuses and taxis from Tunxi to Tangkou congregate around the train station and will take you to the Huangshan main gate at the bottom of the mountain or up to the actual entrance to the climbing section for about Y20.

TOURS

At both the train station in Tunxi and at the main gates of Huangshan, peddlers will offer you guided tours of the area, including transportation to various gates. These are usually reasonably priced; however, the guides' English tends to be minimal. You are usually better off just buying a map and hiring a taxi or taking a minibus up to the East Gate.

TRAIN TRAVEL

Trains to Huangshan stop in Tunxi, from where you can catch a minivan or cab to the Huangshan gates. The ride takes about an hour. It's best to arrive early in the day as many drivers are not eager to traverse the winding road in the dark.

TRAVEL AGENCIES

China Travel Service (CTS) in Tunxi at the base of Huangshan can help set up tickets onward and arrange a place to stay on the mountain, and also has info on getting out and exploring the surrounding countryside. CTS (✉ 12 Qianyuan Bei Lu, Tunxi ☎ 0559/211–5832).

VISITOR INFORMATION

The best bet for tourist info is Tunxi's CTS.

🚹 Tourist Information **CTS** ✉ 12 Qianyuan Bei Lu, Tunxi ☎ 0559/211–5832.

FUJIAN

Fujian has a long and distinctive recorded history, dating back at least as far as the Warring States Period (475–221 BC). At that time the state of Yue—which ruled the area that covers today's provinces of Jiangsu and Zhejiang—moved southward to an area that included Fujian after being defeated by the neighboring state of Chu. Under the Qin Dynasty, the first to rule over a united China, what is now Fujian became a prefecture known as Min, a name that even now is sometimes used as an abbreviation for Fujian.

Evidence of early civilizations that predated the Warring States Period has been found in abundance. The strange so-called boat coffins from Wuyi almost certainly date from the mysterious Xia Dynasty that, it is thought, flourished between 2100 and 1600 BC. Carved pictographs have also been discovered here from the earliest dynasty known to have existed, the Shang (about 1600–1100 BC).

Although very clearly part of mainstream—or Han—China, Fujian is home to a surprising number of non-Han ethnic groups. The Ding and the Guo, in the southern part of the province, are the descendants of Arabs and Persians who traded here in the Tang and Song dynasties, and the Dan people are thought to descend from the Mongols who settled here during the Yuan Dynasty. Best known are the Hakka, with their distinctive fringed hats, who migrated to Fujian from Henan many centuries ago.

Hilly, rural Fujian is particularly associated with the massive waves of emigration that took place from China during the 19th century, when war and a decadent government caused widespread poverty here. Its most famous agricultural product is tea, some of which is considered among the very best in China. (Wuyi Rock Tea is said to be an essential traditional drink for the British royal family.)

Fujian's main attractions are the principal cities of Fuzhou and Xiamen, which have become bustling paradigms of the new entrepreneurial China, and the scenic area of Wuyi Mountain Natural Reserve in the northeast. Food is distinctive and good in the coastal cities, and for the shopper Fujian is a famed provider of soapstone, much of which is used in the production of chops (traditional seals). Other crafts typical of the region include lacquerware, puppet heads from Quanzhou, and porcelain from Dehua.

Fuzhou

6 hrs (200 km [124 mi] by bus northeast of Xiamen; 32 hrs (1,500 km [930 mi]) by train southeast of Beijing; 22 hrs (700 km [434 mi]) by train northeast of Hong Kong.

The capital of Fujian, lying about 40 km (25 mi) upstream from the Min River estuary, Fuzhou dates from the 3rd century BC, when it was well known as a center of ore smelting. Subsequently it became the capital of the independent and small kingdom of Minyue, when it was known as Minzhou. In the 8th century, when it was absorbed into the Chinese empire during the Tang Dynasty, Fuzhou acquired its present name, which means "fortunate city." The name may derive from its splendid location close to the Fu Mountains on a green subtropical plain. It became an important commercial port specializing in the export of tea, growing extremely wealthy in the process.

As a major port city, it was the home base for the voyages of the Ming eunuch, admiral-explorer Zheng He. This status as a major port also attracted Western powers in the mid-19th century, making it one of the first ports opened to foreign traders and residents following the signing of the Treaty of Nanking in 1842.

Marco Polo is supposed to have passed through in the 13th century, referring to Fuzhou as a "veritable marvel." It cannot be described as such any longer; on the whole, despite its proliferation of banyan trees planted during the Song Dynasty, it is a rather gray town in the modern Chinese idiom. It is, nevertheless, an important city—the home of Fujian University and several industries, including tea production and the making of stone handicrafts—with some sites of historical significance. It is also a good base for visits to other places of interest in the province. Getting around this sprawling city on foot is difficult—pedicabs or taxis are more efficient.

a good tour

Begin on Gutian Lu in the center of town. After returning a salute to the statue of Mao, head for the **Yu Mountain Scenic Area** ㉟ ▶ and its White Pagoda, a 16th-century brick-and-wood tower modeled on the 10th-century original. Walk up the paved path to the Fuzhou City Museum and learn a bit about the city's history. Farther up, stop and have a cup of tea or soda in the relaxing orchid garden and take in the city views. **Black Hill** ㊱, another mountain park, is a 10-minute walk along Gutian Lu (though the name changes to Wushan Lu). Buy some incense and say a prayer in the Taoist temple at the top of the hill. From here walk or take a taxi to Aomen Lu, on the north side of Wushan, and the **Tomb of Lin Zexu** ㊲ for a history lesson of the Opium Wars. Wander through **Three Lanes and Seven Alleys** ㊳ for a look at old Fuzhou. Another 15-minute walk up Bayiqi Lu will bring you to **Kaiyuan Temple** ㊴, where you can check out the bronze Buddha. If you arrive at lunchtime (11:30, sharp) the monks may invite you to eat a vegetarian meal with them. From here grab a taxi or the bus and head north to **West Lake** ㊵. Spend some time wandering around the lakeside park, perhaps visiting the zoo or prefectural museum. A taxi ride to the western suburbs will bring you to **Western Chan Temple** ㊶, Fuzhou's most important Zen (Chan) Buddhist temple. Finally, take a taxi east to the city's most famous sightseeing spot, **Gushan** ㊷. The best time to visit Gushan is early in the morning, before the crowds and city smog from Fuzhou invade the place.

TIMING You'll probably enjoy the sights more if you spread the tour across two days. It would be a shame to not spend at least a half day—an entire day would be ideal—exploring Gushan.

What to See

㊱ **Black Hill** (Wushan). In the center of the city, the slopes of Black Hill are covered in stone inscriptions, among them an example of the work of the famous Tang calligrapher Li Yangbing and records of the duties of Ming eunuchs, who were put to work in the shipyards. Historically, Wushan was known as a place for Taoists to gather for ascetic training. A small active temple rests on the summit. At the bottom of the hill is the black granite **Black Pagoda** (Wu Ta). This 115-foot-high pagoda was originally built in 799 and is covered with fine carving work. ✉ *Wushan Lu.*

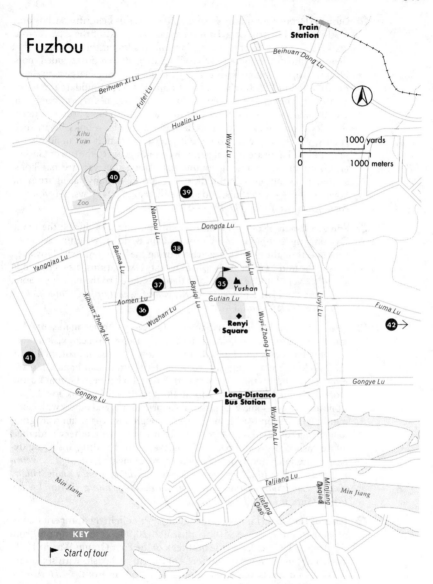

Fuzhou

Train Station

Beihuan Dong Lu

Beihuan Xi Lu

Fufei Lu

Hualin Lu

Wuyi Lu

Xihu Yuan

Zoo

0   1000 yards

0   1000 meters

Nanhou Lu

Dongda Lu

Baima Lu

Yangqiao Lu

Xihuan Zhong Lu

Aomen Lu

Wushan Lu

Bayiqi Lu

Gutian Lu

Wuyi Lu

Yushan

Liuyi Lu

Fuma Lu

Renyi Square

Wuyi Zhong Lu

Gongye Lu

Gongye Lu

Long-Distance Bus Station

Wuyi Nan Lu

Min Jiang

Taijiang Lu

Jiefang Qiao

Minjiang Daqiao

Min Jiang

KEY

▶ Start of tour

42 Gushan (Drum Mountain). Rising 3,200 feet, this beautiful park is only a 20-minute bus trip or a 10-minute taxi ride east of the city. A stone walkway goes up to the more important places on the mountain, but there are also dozens of unpaved trails leading off to more secluded spots. Near the top is **Surging Spring Temple** (Yongquan Si), a large active temple founded in 908 by the Duke of Fujian to accommodate the monk Shen Yan. The temple is home to an outstanding library of more than 10,000 Buddhist sutras, some of which are said to have been written in the blood of disciples. Every afternoon at 4, the monks begin their chants, which you're welcome to listen to and watch for an admission price of Y6. There are several paths that continue up to the top of Gushan and onto the surrounding mountains. Along the way are pavilions, stones, and grottoes with Buddhist inscriptions—many dating from the Song Dynasty—waterfalls, and above all, marvelous views. ⊠ *Fuma Lu east of city* 🚌 *Y15* ⊗ *Daily 8–4:30.*

39 Kaiyuan Temple (Kaiyuan Si). Originally built in 548 during the Liang Dynasty, the temple is known for its iron Buddha, weighing some 40 tons and thought to have been cast during the Tang Dynasty. However, during the mid-16th-century Qing Dynasty restorations, a silver pagoda was discovered under the Buddha that was dated to the Northern Song Period, in the 11th century. ⊠ *17 Kaiyuan Lu, east of Jing Dalu* 🚌 *Free* ⊗ *Daily 8–11:30 and 3–5.*

★ **38 Three Lanes and Seven Alleys** (San Fang Qi Xiang). To get an idea of what much of Fuzhou looked like until the early 1980s, you can visit a number of small alleys and lanes that up to now have been protected from the wrecking ball of Chinese urban modernization. San Fang Qi Xiang refers to the streets that intersect with Bayiqi Lu between Gutian Lu and Dongda Jie just west of Yu Mountain. On Bayiqi Lu look for the old stone archways—some with classical Chinese motifs and others with Communist hammer-and-sickle insignias. Although some of the lanes are gradually being squeezed out of existence by urban growth, others, with their whitewashed walls and peaceful courtyards of the Ming and Qing dynasties, are still home to old men playing mah-jongg. ✥ *Guang Lu, Wenru Lu, and Yijin Lu; Jibi Xiang, Gong Xiang, Ta Xiang, Anmin Xiang, Huang Xiang, Langguan Xiang, and Yangqiao Xiang; along Bayiqi Lu between Gutian Lu and Dongda Jie.*

37 Tomb of Lin Zexu (Linzexu Jinianguan). An enlightened imperial commissioner, Lin (1785–1850), confiscated 20,000 cases of opium from the British. This act led to the outbreak of the First Opium War, in 1840. The tomb, in the northern suburbs of the city, is lavish, with six chambers on four levels and a pair of guardian lions in front. ⊠ *16 Aomen Lu, on Jinshishan* 🚌 *Y3* ⊗ *Daily 8–5:30.*

need a break?

Near **Water and Cloud Pavilion** (Shuiyun Ting), next to a trickling waterfall and overlooking the valley and the Min River, is a small and inexpensive teahouse where for Y15–Y25 you can drink locally produced Wulong tea and enjoy the pleasant scenery. The tearoom also serves snacks.

⚓ ❹ **West Lake** (Xihu). Dug in AD 282 to irrigate the surrounding countryside, West Lake has been used as a park ever since the Min Kingdom (from the 8th century). On his return to Fuzhou toward the middle of the 19th century, after his time as an imperial official, Lin Zexu, a native of Fuzhou, had the lake cleared and some of the Tang pavilions restored. They eventually fell into disrepair but were restored in 1985 to commemorate the 200th anniversary of Lin's birth. A prefectural museum, with artifacts and art from Fuzhou, and the Fuzhou Zoo are also here. ⊠ *Xihu Yuan, east end of Hualin Lu in northwest part of town* 🎫 *Park Y5, museum Y10, zoo Y10* ☉ *Daily 7 AM–8 PM, zoo 7–6.*

❹ **Western Chan Temple** (Xichan Si). Ancient Fuzhou had four Zen (Chan) Buddhist temples laid out along the four points of the compass—one each in the northern, southern, eastern, and western quarters of the city. Western Chan is the only temple of the four to survive. It was originally built in the Sui Dynasty, but most of the current buildings were constructed during the Qing. The incredible amount of recent construction financed by overseas donations is evidence of the growing vibrancy of Buddhism on the mainland. The beautiful giant brass statue of Guanyin— the bodhisattva of mercy and compassion—in the small pavilion **Guanyin Ge** was financed by a devout Singaporean businessman. It was cast in Shanghai and brought down by train in the early 1990s. The 15-story **Pagoda of Declaring Grace** (Baoen Ta), also built with foreign donations, affords a beautiful view of the temple. The spacious temple grounds are perfect for walking. ⊠ *45 Gongye Lu* 🎫 *Y3; additional Y1 for the pagoda* ☉ *Daily 7–7.*

▶ ❸ **Yu Mountain Scenic Area** (Yushan Fengjing Qu). Downtown Fuzhou has two nice parks, both situated on small mountains, covered with banyan trees and flowers and within walking distance of each other. Yushan Fengjing Qu is the larger and more central of the two, rising across the street from **Renyi Square** (Renyi Guangchang) and behind the large, alabaster statue of Chairman Mao. At the bottom of Yushan stands the **White Pagoda** (Baita), an unspectacular pagoda, dating from 1548, whose main claim to fame are its inscriptions, some dating from the Song Dynasty (Y10). For those interested in local history, check out the **Fuzhou City Museum** (Fuzhou Shi Bowuguan), halfway up the Yushan (Y5). Closer to the top is an nice orchid garden with a tea patio. ⊠ *Gutian Lu* 🎫 *Y3* ☉ *Daily 8–6, museum and pagoda, daily 8:30–5.*

Where to Stay & Eat

For inexpensive food, the area around the train station abounds in street restaurants selling noodles and dumplings. The hotels in this area are also some of the cheapest (and grimiest) in town. The better places are all closer to downtown. Fuzhou is also famous for two different dishes, at opposite ends of the price scale. At the more modest end is *fuzhou yanpi,* which looks like long sheets of parchment but is actually cooked pork that's been pounded incessantly until it become the texture of paper. At the more luxurious end is *fotiao qiang,* a pot of shark's fin, fish heads, squid, sea cucumber, and pork tripe. The name of the dish literally means "Buddha Jumped Over the Wall," referring to a legend that the rich aroma of the dish caused a Buddhist monk to forget his vows of vegetarianism to leap over a wall in his eagerness to get at the tasty dish. Your wallet may be more of an obstacle than that monks' wall: the dish isn't cheap but many say its worth the splurge.

$$–$$$$ ⤬ **Beijing Restaurant.** Here crowds feast on Peking duck, beef kebabs, and Mongolian hotpot while the waitstaff and dishwashers rush to keep up. The decor is simple because the food is the main attraction. Come early or ask someone from your hotel staff to reserve a table for you. ⊠ *92 Dong Jie* ☎ *0591/753–5922* ▤ *No credit cards.*

★ **$–$$$$** ⤬ **Fuzhou Restaurant.** At this comfortable restaurant you'll find local dishes, especially fish and fried oysters. The master chef, Qiang Mugen, is famous for his fotiao qiang, which he prepared for Ronald Reagan during the president's visit to China in the 1980s. The dish arrives in a large pot sealed in a red ribbon. ⊠ *18 Dongda Lu, 5th fl.* ☎ *0591/753–5777* ▤ *No credit cards.*

★ **$–$$$$** ⤬ **Juchunyuan.** Founded in 1877, this esteemed restaurant has a very cozy dining room and well-trained waitstaff. It specializes in seafood and the ever-popular fotiao qiang. ⊠ *2 Bayiqi Bei Lu, 3rd fl.* ☎ *0591/753–3604* ▤ *AE, MC, V.*

$–$$$$ ⤬ **Nantai Lezhuang.** The cuisine is local here, and although the atmosphere is unsophisticated, the dishes—which include fresh fish, when available, and subtly flavored soups such as shark's fin—are usually reliable. ⊠ *Guohuo Nan Lu* ☎ *0591/753–2034* ▤ *No credit cards.*

$–$$ ⤬ **Xichan Si Sucai Guan.** On the grounds of the Western Chan Temple, this restaurant cooks up excellent vegetarian fare. The menu is in Chinese, but fortunately most of the offerings are set meals. To order, simply select the number of people and the price range you would like. ⊠ *Western Chan Temple, Gongye Lu* ☎ *No phone* ▤ *No credit cards.*

¢–$ ▦ **Hot Spring Hotel.** One of the first upscale hotels in Fuzhou, this one is still counted among the best. It's in the northern part of the city near the airport. ⊠ *218 Wusi Lu, 350003* ☎ *0591/785–1818* ▦ *0591/783–5150* ⇒ *303 rooms* ⚭ *2 restaurants, pool, hair salon, sauna, bowling, business services* ▤ *AE, V.*

★ **¢** ▦ **Foreign Trade Centre Hotel.** This hotel in the middle of the commercial district is the spot for creature comforts. There are two wings; the newer has larger rooms and more modern decoration, but the older wing still offers all standard amenities. The hotel has an excellent Western restaurant. ⊠ *73 Wusi Lu, 350001* ☎ *0591/752–3388* ▦ *0591/755–0358* ⇒ *343 rooms, 54 suites* ⚭ *4 restaurants, tennis court, pool, gym, sauna, business services* ▤ *AE, MC, V.*

¢ ▦ **Fuzhou Hotel.** This hotel is sparklingly clean, and the staff is eager to please. The location is ideal—in the center of town just south of Yushan. The complimentary breakfast buffet is enough to fuel you up for a day of excursions around Fuzhou. ⊠ *103 Bayiqi Lu, 350005* ☎ *0591/333–3333* ▦ *0591/332–9833* ⊕ *www.fuzhouhotel.com* ⇒ *255 rooms, 53 suites* ⚭ *2 restaurants, gym, hair salon, nightclub, business services* ▤ *AE, MC, V.*

¢ ▦ **Fuzhou Lakeside Hotel.** Located slightly outside the city center, the hotel has a pleasant location beside the lake, with all the comforts and range of services of a major hotel. Some rooms have lake views. ⊠ *158 Hubin Lu, 350003* ☎ *0591/783–9888* ▦ *0591/783–9752*

' *info@lakeside-hotel.com* 📞 *526 rooms* 🛎 *2 restaurants, pool, business services* 🖭 *AE, V.*

¢ 🏨 **Yushan Hotel.** Centrally located by the Yushan park and between two of Fuzhou's pagodas, the Yushan Hotel is a good base for sightseeing, with standard rooms at a reasonable price. ✉ *10 Yushan Lu, 350005* ☎ *0591/335–1668* 📠 *0591/335–7694* 📞 *99 rooms* 🛎 *2 restaurants, business services* 🖭 *AE, MC, V.*

Nightlife & the Arts

There are no specific venues for the performing arts, but there are often concerts both of traditional music and of the local version of Chinese **opera.** Opera is often performed during the day in parks by local enthusiasts. Check with **CITS** (✉ 107 Jing Dalu ☎ 0591/750–2794) for locations and times.

As well as the standard hotel bars and discos, there are a decent number of bars and discos around Fuzhou. One popular place is the **No Nationality Popular Club** (✉ 56 Qingcheng Lu, 2nd fl. ☎ 0591/750–4128) which draws a regular crowd of foreign residents. **Karaoke** parlors are all over the city—look for neon signs with the letters OK included in them.

The Outdoors

★ Through CITS you can arrange **boat trips** along the Min River, 40 km (25 mi) downstream to the sea. The scenery is attractive—you pass Gushan as you go—and the various craft on the river make it an absorbing ride. Ticket prices start at around Y60.

You can rent a **bicycle** through CITS. The best **swimming pools** are in hotels, where nonresidents must pay a fee. There are also **beaches** at Meizhou. For **hiking** try the scenic area of Wuyi Mountain Natural Reserve or Gushan.

Shopping

Among the local specialties are Shoushan stone carving, made with a form of alabaster; porcelain from Dehua; lacquerware; and lacquer painting. Tea is also a good buy in this part of China. For arts and crafts try the **Fuzhou Cultural Products Center** and other stores along Gutian Lu just south of Yushan.

Among street markets, the most interesting is the **Flower and Bird Market** (✉ Liuyi Zhong Lu), which stocks ornamental fish, miniature trees, rock gardens, and exotic pets such as monkeys.

Meizhou

43 *2½ hrs (110 km [68 mi]) east by express bus from Fuzhou via Putian and Wenjia; 4 hrs (165 km [103 mi]) north by bus from Xiamen via Putian and Wenjia.*

A rocky offshore island ringed by beaches and small fishing villages, Meizhou is well known for its rugged beauty. According to Taoists it is the birthplace of Mazu, goddess of the sea. The **Meizhou Mazu Temple** (Meizhou Mazu Si), a short walk from the ferry pier, is the main center of activity on the island. The temple is actually a complex of dozens of structures filled with burning incense and hawkers selling cheap souvenirs. Stone paths lead up to a small peak where a huge statue of Mazu looks out over the ocean.

Mazu's original name was Lin Mo. She was born in AD 930 in Zhongmen to a prominent Fujian family. According to legend, as a child she never cried and was exceptionally intelligent. At the age of 13 she was adopted by a Taoist priest and devoted the rest of her life to scientific, spiritual, and charitable pursuits. In 987, deciding that she had had enough of temporal life, the legend goes, Lin Mo climbed Mt. Meifeng and sailed away on the clouds. Thereafter she was often sighted at sea at times of danger and acquired the name *Mazu* (ancestral mother).

Since numerous tour groups invade the island during the day, the temple is best visited in the morning before the people arrive or in the evening after they go. On the far side of the island are several nice fishing villages and secluded beaches worth exploring. The water is, however, a bit chilly.

The busiest days on the island are Mazu's birthday, on the 23rd day of the 3rd lunar month in April or May, and the anniversary of her death, on the 9th day of the 9th lunar month, in September or October. Puxian opera is performed on these days and all the halls are brightly illuminated.

You can reach the island by taking a bus from Fuzhou's main terminal to the city of Putian, and then a ferry from the pier at Wenjia. The fare is Y15 for a one-way ferry ride plus Y40 admission to the island.

Where to Stay

¢ ⚂ **Meizhou Hotel.** This hotel is quiet and sleepy except at the peak of the tourist season. The rooms are clean and simple but small and a bit musty from the moist ocean air. ⊠ *12 Jiang Bian Lu, 351154* ☎ *0594/509–4510* 🖷 *0594/509–4602* ⟿ *47 rooms, 3 suites* ♨ *Restaurant, hair salon, sauna* ⊟ *No credit cards.*

Wuyi Mountain Natural Reserve

④④ ½ *hr (210 km [130 mi]) northwest by air from Fuzhou; 7 hrs by long-*
FodorsChoice *distance bus or train from Fuzhou.*
★

In the north of Fujian province, Wuyi Mountain Natural Reserve (Wuyi Shan Fengjingqu) is known for its spectacular scenery. Magnificent peaks covered in waterfalls (most notably the Shuilian), bamboo groves, and tea bushes rise from the banks of the **Nine Meanders or Nine Bends Creek** (Jiuqu Xi). You can enjoy the scenery on boats that wend their way up and down stream, or climb the mountains for the views or to visit the pavilions and temples that stand on the slopes of some—for example, Tianyou Feng.

The cliffs along the river were once used for "boat burials," in which wooden boat-shape coffins were placed in niches some 160 feet above the river. Some date as far back as 3,000 years but little is known about how and why these burials took place. From Fuzhou, you can fly or take a train to Nanping and then continue on by bus.

Where to Stay

¢ ▣ **Wuyi Shan Villa Hotel.** This is one of the nicer and more reasonably priced hotels in the area, and it's at the base of the mountain. Rooms are comfortable, and it's convenient to get into the hills. ⊠ *Wuyi Mountain, 354302* ☎ *0599/525–1888* 🔢 *0599/525–2567* ✆ *203 rooms, 16 suites* ♨ *2 restaurants, sauna, bar, dance club, business services* ▤ *AE, MC, V.*

Quanzhou

45 *1½ hrs (80 km [50 mi]) by express bus north of Xiamen; 2½ hrs (155 km [96 mi]) by express bus south of Fuzhou.*

Quanzhou is an ancient port on the Jin River. During the Song and Yuan dynasties it was the foremost port in China, sometimes described as the starting point of the Maritime Silk Road. As a result, it had a considerable Muslim population, which has bequeathed to the city what is probably the most interesting mosque in China. To Arabs, Quanzhou was called "Zaiton," from which the English word *satin* is derived.

The Quanzhou of reform-era China made a valiant effort to resist the shapeless, drab architectural malaise that has stricken most Chinese cities. The local answer was to combine selective demolition with renovation to re-create a Minan (southern Chinese)-style downtown area. It looks clean and colorful, but the effect is closer to a suburban strip mall than to a classical Chinese architectural style. Although the downtown area has been artificially re-created, throughout Quanzhou, the growth of a number of temples indicates a revival of a more natural kind. Any visit to Quanzhou should include a visit to some or all of these temples.

The mosque **Qingjing Mosque** (Qingjing Si) was built in 1009, enlarged in 1309, and restored in 1350 and 1609. Unlike other ancient mosques in China, which were heavily influenced by Chinese styles, this one is mainly in the purely Islamic architectural idiom. Partially ruined, it still retains some impressive features, particularly the entrance, which is 66 feet high. ⊠ *174 Tumen Jie* ▣ *Y3* ⊙ *Daily 8–5:30.*

★ The **Kaiyuan Temple** (Kaiyuan Si) was founded in AD 686, is flanked by two pagodas that have some fine bas-relief carving on the niches of each story. The style is a Sino-Indian mix; following the death of the Chinese monk who had initiated the carving, an Indian monk was placed in charge of the work. In the temple's Mahavira Hall, among the roof timbers, are some marvelous carvings of *apsaras* (Buddhist angels). ⊠ *Xi Jie* ▣ *Y6* ⊙ *Daily 6:30–6.*

Three kilometers (2 mi) north of Quanzhou, the scenic **Qingyuanshan** area has a huge 700-year-old **statue of Lao-tze,** the founder of Taoism. Also close to the town are two stone bridges built in the Song Dynasty to help with the endless flow of goods into the port—the **Luoyang Bridge** (Luoyang Qiao) and the **Anping Bridge** (Anping Qiao), which is 2½ km (1½ mi) long.

Where to Stay

¢ ▣ **Overseas Chinese Mansion.** The "mansion" in the name is surely ironic. But what the hotel lacks in elegance it makes up in its price (which often runs cheaper than quoted). The rooms are clean and fairly comfortable. ✉ *Wenling Lu , 361003, north of bus station* ☎ *0595/228–2192* 🖷 *0595/228–4612* 📞 *234 rooms, 13 suites* ♨ *3 restaurants, sauna, nightclub, business services* ▤ *AE, MC, V.*

¢ 🖼 **Quanzhou Hotel.** At the best hotel in Quanzhou the staff seems to be concerned about things other than prompt service. The rooms are, however, comfortable. Due to strict traffic rules city taxis are not allowed to drive up to the hotel doors. For door-to-door service you'll need to call ahead; the hotel will arrange a driver. ✉ *22 Zhuangfu Lu, 362000* ☎ *0595/228–9958* 🖷 *0595/218–2128* 📞 *271 rooms, 22 suites* ♨ *2 restaurants, pool, sauna, bowling, business services* ▤ *AE, MC, V.*

Xiamen

46 *3 hrs (200 km [124 mi]) by bus southwest of Fuzhou; (500 km [310 mi]) by ferry northeast of Hong Kong.*

Known as Amoy to the foreign traders who made the town on these two islands their home from the middle of the 19th century on, Xiamen, with a total population of about 1 million, is one of the most pleasant cities in China, with some interesting corners to explore. By Chinese standards Xiamen is a new town, founded only in 1394 during the Ming Dynasty as a defense against pirate attacks. It has remained important ever since, with its well-located natural harbor, as a center of coastal trade. Many of the city's most charming corners date from the 19th and early 20th centuries, when it was opened to foreign trade after the Opium Wars and foreign traders and local Chinese merchants turned the city into an entrepôt shipping Fujian's tea around the world. The heritage of this period is most obvious on the small island of Gulangyu, once the preferred neighborhood of foreign residents and still covered with their villas and churches. Many of the side streets of the main city preserve the feel of what Old Hong Kong must have been like, with romantic narrow alleys of three-story wooden houses with balconies.

At the end of the Ming era it became the stronghold of the Ming loyalist Zheng Chenggong, better known as Koxinga, who held out with some success against the Manchus. Born in Japan to a Chinese father and a Japanese mother, he went to China and became a favorite of the court during the final years of the Ming Dynasty. When China was overrun by the Qing, he built up a fleet of more than 7,000 junks and a force of some three-quarters of a million men, including pirates. In 1661 he succeeded in driving the Dutch from Taiwan and went on to try to extend his power to the Philippines. He murdered both his cousin and his uncle for their ineptitude, and killed himself in 1662 on Taiwan as his rebellion collapsed.

Although the Communist revolution and anxieties over nearby Taiwan cooled off the city's prosperity, when Deng Xiaoping liberalized the economy, Xiamen was one of the first cities opened to foreign trade, and the money rushed back in, especially from Taiwanese businessman whose families had fled a few decades before. Xiamen is today one of the most prosperous cities in China, with many pleasant parks and waterfront promenades to complement its historic architecture. Only a few miles farther out to sea are other small islands that still belong to Taiwan.

The city consists of two islands: Xiamen, linked to the mainland by a causeway built in the 1950s, and Gulangyu. The main street on Xiamen, leading down to the port, is Zhongshan Lu.

The most interesting part of the city—and also the most attractive to the eye—is **Gulangyu** (Island of Drumming Waves), where foreign communities were established after 1842. The colonial buildings on Gulangyu, mostly dating from the late 19th and early 20th centuries, are surprisingly large, considering that in 1912 there were only 250 foreign residents. The villas are built in a range of different styles and shaded by rich subtropical gardens. Although the sights below are the island's highlights, the best way to experience Gulangyu's charm is to explore the meandering streets, away from the tourists, stumbling across a particularly distinctive old mansion or the weathered graves of missionaries and merchants. These quiet back alleys are fascinating to wander, with the atmosphere of a quiet Mediterranean city, punctuated by touches of calligraphy or the click of mah-jongg tiles to remind you where you really are. You can get to the island by the **ferry** (💴 Y3; return trip is free ☺ Daily 5:45 AM–12:30 AM) that leaves every 15 minutes from Xiamen Island. Gulangyu is closed to automobile traffic, but the island is small enough to explore on foot without exhausting yourself. Golf carts with drivers, which you can rent by the hour, are also available at the tourist spots if you don't want to walk.

off the
beaten
path

JINMEN – This Taiwanese island lies only a few miles off the coast of Xiamen. Chinese tourist boats leave regularly from the Xiamen quay, carrying mainlanders interested in seeing the land of their estranged countrymen. Although the boats do not actually land on either Jinmen or any of the smaller rocks belonging to Taiwan, you can get close enough to see the faces of the Taiwanese guards patrolling the shores or call out to the Taiwanese fisherman netting the waters. The boat (💴 Y43 ☺ Daily 8–5) leaves several times a day from the dock next to the Gulangyu ferry.

Most of the interesting sights of Xiamen Island are along the Bus 2 route passing by the ferry terminal. There are several nice parks here, all on the southern half of the island. From the ferry turn left and follow the ocean-side street until you come to **Bright Moon Garden** (Haoyue Yuan). The garden is both a seaside memorial to Koxinga and a peacock "garden," creating the rather odd scene of its massive stone statue of Koxinga staring menacingly at Taiwan while large flocks of peacocks mill about his feet (💴 Y15 ☺ Daily 8–7). On the way, you'll pass some quaint Western villas.

Continuing along Tianwei Lu, the waterfront road, and you'll come to **Shuzhuang Garden** (Shuzhuang Huayuan). The grounds were originally private, before the owner donated them to the state in 1956. The garden is immaculately kept—something that cannot be said about too many parks in China—and dotted with pavilions and bridges, some extending out to rocks just off shore. 🚻 *Y40.*

The island's highest point is part of **Sunlight Rock** (Riguang Yan), which rises 300 feet from its summit. The views include Gulangyu and the Xiamen waterfront, and, on clear days, the Taiwanese island of Jinmen. Inside is a large aviary full of birds from around the world. Although not as spectacular as Sunlight Rock, the narrow streets of the northeastern side of the island lead up to a quiet (and free) park with views over the harbor to the skyscrapers of the mainland. 🚻 *Y65, Y20 after 5 PM* ⊘ *Daily 8 AM–9 PM.*

Nanputuo Temple (Nanputuo Si), on Xiamen Island in the southern suburbs of the city, dates from the Tang Dynasty. It has been restored many times, most recently in the 1980s. Built in the exuberant southern Chinese style, the roofs are decorated with brightly painted swirling flourishes of clustered flowers, serpents, and mythical beasts. Pavilions on either side of the main hall contain tablets commemorating the suppression of secret societies by the Qing emperors. As the most important temple remaining in Xiamen, it is nearly always the center of a great deal of activity as monks and local believers mix with tour groups. Behind the temple a rocky path threads its way past a series of stone inscriptions, leading up to views over the ocean. At the height of summer the lakes in front of the temple are covered with lotus flowers. Attached to the temple complex is an excellent vegetarian restaurant (⇨ Dining, *below*). ⊠ *Siming Nan Lu, take Bus 1 or 2 from port* 🚻 *Y3* ⊘ *Daily 7:30 AM–6:30 PM.*

Housed in a fascinating mix of local Minan-style and colonial-style buildings close to the Nanputuo Temple, **Xiamen University** (Xiamen Daxue) was founded in the 1920s with the help of overseas Chinese donations. The **Museum of Anthropology** (Renlei Bowuguan; 🚻*Y1* ⊘Daily 8:30–11 and 3–5), dedicated to the study of Neolithic southern China as well as local ethnology, is also here. It has a very good collection of fossils, ceramics, paintings, and ornaments. ⊠ *Xiamen Daxue, Siming Nan Lu.*

Southeast of the university at the end of the Bus 2 line is the **Huli Cannon.** Made in Germany by the Krupp Company and placed here in 1891, at a cost of 60,000 silver taels, the cannon weighs 60 tons and measures 45 feet in length. It sits along with other smaller armaments on the bare bones of an old fortress, overlooking the sea. It is the only well-preserved coastal cannon left in China, a strange relic from the end of the declining Qing Dynasty. A portion of the fortress has been converted into a museum that displays an exceptional collection of ancient weaponry, including swords, cannons, and 18th-century flintlocks. You can also see the "Bacon Rock," a rock that looks remarkably like, well, a slab of bacon. Just beneath the ramparts is a quite and clean sandy beach, which is a convenient (and free) place for a swim or some sunbathing. ⊠ *Off Daxue Lu, in southeast of city, about 20-min walk from university* 🚻 *Y25* ⊘ *Daily 7:30–7:30.*

In the southern part of the city, the **Overseas Chinese Museum** (Huaqiao Bowuguan) is an institution founded by the wealthy industrialist Tan Kah-kee. Three halls illustrate, by means of pictures and documents, personal items and relics associated with the great waves of emigration from southeastern China during the 19th century. One section of the museum re-creates the small shops, plantation barracks, and backstreets of Southeast Asia where the Chinese émigrées got their start on their road to fortune. ⊠ *Off Siming Nan Lu, at foot of Fengzhao Shan* ☑ *Y5* ☉ *Tues.–Sun. 8:30–11:30 and 2–5:30.*

The undulating **Wanshi Botanical Garden** (Wanshi Zhiwuyuan) has a fine collection of more than 4,000 species of tropical and subtropical flora, a pretty lake, strangely shaped rocks and caves, and several pavilions, of which the most interesting are those forming the **Temple of the Kingdom of Heaven** (Tianjie Si). Close to the lake is a large gray stone marking the spot where Koxinga killed his cousin and then took command of the troops to fight the Qing. The garden specializes in the flora of southern China and of Southeast Asia, including the varieties of eucalyptus that originated in Australia but have been widely planted throughout the south of China. ⊠ *Huyuan Lu off Wenyuan Lu, in eastern part of city* ☑ *Y10* ☉ *Daily 8–6.*

Where to Stay & Eat

Seafood is on the menu everywhere in Xiamen. The lanes of Gulangyu are lined with tanks, tubs, and buckets of just about anything that swims or crawls in the ocean—just point to what you want. One warning: make sure the price is established before you send your meal to the kitchen.

$$–$$$$ ✕ **Shuyou Seafood Restaurant.** Shuyou means "close friend," and that is how you're treated at this upscale dining establishment. Fresh seafood and a more friendly waitstaff than you know what to do with produce excellent dining. It may be the best-known restaurant in Xiamen. ⊠ *Hubin Bei Lu* ☎ *0592/509–8888* ▤ *AE, MC, V.*

$–$$$$ ✕ **Jili Seafood Restaurant.** Tanks of fresh seafood line the walls of this restaurant, which serves southern-style dishes. Top-notch service, a beautiful skylighted dining room, and 19 private rooms means you can get dressed up for a meal here. There are English menus. ⊠ *819 Hubin Nan Lu, 4th fl.* ☎ *0592/516–9999* ▤ *AE, MC, V.*

$$–$$$ ✕ **Guan Hai Canting.** Located on the rooftop terrace of the waterfront Lujiang Hotel, the beautiful views over the bay are a reminder of where your tasty seafood dinner would rather be swimming. With delicious seafood main dishes as well as a range of fishy snacks and appetizers, the food and panorama are equally satisfying. ⊠ *14 Huyuan Lu* ☎ *0592/ 202–2922* ▤ *No credit cards.*

¢–$$ ✕ **Puzhaolou Vegetarian Restaurant.** The comings and goings of monks add to the atmosphere of this Buddhist vegetarian restaurant adjacent to the Nanputuo Temple. Two buildings offer different price ranges—the white building is more upscale, and therefore more expensive, but both offer the same delicious food. There are no English menus; just choose the set menu you want at the "Meal Booking Office" and you'll be served a multidish set menu. ⊠ *Nanputuo Temple, Siming Nan Lu* ☎ *0592/ 208–5908* ▤ *No credit cards.*

¢ ✕ **Huangzehe Peanut Soup Shop.** Peanuts hold center stage at this popular snack restaurant located near the waterfront. Tasty peanut soup, peanut sweets, and even peanut dumplings show off the culinary potential of the humble goober. ⊠ *24 Zhongshan Lu* ☎ *0592/212–5825* ▤ *No credit cards.*

$$ 🏨 **Holiday Inn Crowne Plaza Harbourview.** This modern hotel has an excellent location overlooking the harbor. Rooms are comfortable in the usual reliable Holiday Inn style. There is a medical clinic on the premises. ⊠ *12 Zhenhai Lu, 361001* ☎ *0592/202–3333* 🖶 *0592/203–6666* ⊕ *www.holiday-inn.com* ➷ *334 rooms, 7 suites* ⚴ *4 restaurants, pool, business services* ▤ *AE, MC, V.*

$$ 🏨 **Marco Polo Xiamen.** Situated between the older sections of town and the commercial district, the hotel is convenient to transportation if not to sights. The occasional barbecue is held for guests in summer at the beautiful swimming pool, which is surrounded with lush greenery. Rooms are comfortable and well appointed. ⊠ *8 Jianye Lu, 361004* ☎ *0592/509–1888* 🖶 *0592/509–2888* ⊕ *www.marcopolohotels.com* ➷ *246 rooms, 38 suites* ⚴ *3 restaurants, pool, gym, sauna, business services, no-smoking rooms* ▤ *AE, MC, V.*

¢–$ 🏨 **Lujiang Hotel.** In a refurbished prerevolutionary building, this hotel has an ideal location opposite the ferry pier and next to Zhongshan Lu and the waterfront boulevard. Many of the rooms have ocean views along with standard amenities, while a rooftop terrace restaurant looks over the straits. ⊠ *54 Lujiang Lu, 361001* ☎ *0592/202–2922* 🖶 *0592/202–4644* ➷ *153 rooms, 18 suites* ⚴ *4 restaurants, bar, business services* ▤ *AE, MC, V.*

¢–$ 🏨 **Xiamen Hotel.** Fairly close to the center of town, this hotel has a good range of facilities. The rooms are comfortable and well appointed. ⊠ *16 Huyuan Lu, 361003* ☎ *0592/202–2265* 🖶 *0592/204–9960* ➷ *264 rooms, 22 suites* ⚴ *Pool, gym, business services* ▤ *AE, MC, V.*

¢ 🏨 **Gulangyu Villa Hotel.** On the west side of Gulangyu and near the Fujian Arts and Crafts School, this is about the most peaceful hotel you're going to find in Xiamen. The rooms are clean but simple and the staff is friendly enough. There is a decent Chinese restaurant on the premises. ⊠ *14 Gusheng Lu* ☎ *0592/206–0160 or 0592/206–3280* 🖶 *0592/206–0165* ➷ *75 rooms* ⚴ *Restaurant, business services* ▤ *No credit cards.*

¢ 🏨 **Luzhou Hotel.** Near the ferry terminal on Gulangyu, this hotel is simple in its services, but its location, on an island with no automobiles, makes it very restful. Rooms with ocean views are available, and rooms are generally comfortable, if not luxurious. ⊠ *Gulangyu, 361002* ☎☎ *0592/206–5390* ➷ *34 rooms, 5 suites* ⚴ *Restaurant* ▤ *No credit cards.*

Nightlife & the Arts

Much of the nightlife in Xiamen centers on the strip of Zhongshan Lu that extends from the Gulangyu ferry pier to Siming Lu. The charm of the waterfront esplanade looking out over the bright city lights reflected in the lapping waves brings out locals for their evening stroll. Trawling this area and some of the side streets will turn up a vibrant mix of small tea shops, bars, fashionable stores, and locals out for evening strolls. There are some Western-style bars on the street **Bailu Zhou,** off Huzhong Lu. A particularly nice, and relatively inexpensive, one is the **Bailuzhou Yidian Yuan** (⊠ Hubin Zhong Lu ☎ 0592/889–8931), which is in a wooden lodge on the shore of the river that divides the city. For a break from Chinese nightlife, try the **Londoner** which offers an authentic friendly pub atmosphere and Western snacks, run by an English expat. ✉ *Guan Ren Lu behind Marco Polo Xiamen hotel* ☎ *0571/8508–9783.*

Most Xiamenites in search of evening entertainment seek out one of the many karaoke parlors that dot the area (usually distinguished by the letters OK); they are of varying standard, with some offering "hostesses" that you should avoid. One of the more outstanding discos in town is **XO-2** (✉ Junction of Hubin Nan Lu and Hubin Zhong Lu).

In spring and fall there are often performances of **traditional music, local opera, and acrobatics** by visiting troupes. CITS is likely to be the best source of information.

The Outdoors

Xiamen has some of China's best beaches, and **swimming** is a popular pastime. The southwest shore of Gulangyu has a well-maintained beach with changing rooms and showers where you can rent chairs, umbrellas, and blankets. Next to the Huli Cannon on the main island, just behind Xiamen University is a long public beach that is kept quite clean and is popular with locals, although the facilities are less posh than those on Gulangyu. **Jogging** is also a pleasant option on Gulangyu Island, where there is no traffic. On Xiamen Island the area around the university is reasonably quiet and good for jogging as well.

Shopping

Shops along Zhongshan Lu have squeezed out residential buildings, and in the balmy evenings locals stroll along the arcades and window-shop. There is a rather large **night market** that runs parallel to Zhongshan Lu near the ferry pier. Look for the few interesting items mixed in among stall after stall of tacky clothing printed with unintelligible English phrases. Local specialties include: tea, Hui'an stone carving (of tablets and of products for ornamental and daily use), puppet heads, silk figurines, wood carving, and lacquerware. Fujian black tea is traditionally brewed in the *gongfu* style, which uses an array of delicate pots and small glasses, and tea shops often sell beautiful ceramic or porcelain sets. The **Friendship Store** (✉ Si Ming Bei Lu) doesn't have as wide a selection as its counterparts in other cities. The widest selection and the best prices in Xiamen, however, are found in the narrow winding lanes of Gulangyu.

Fujian A to Z

To research prices, get advice from other travelers, and book travel arrangements, visit www.fodors.com.

AIR TRAVEL

The local branch of CAAC is Xiamen Airlines. There are domestic flights all over China and international flights to Jakarta, Manila, Penang, and Singapore. Other airlines with offices in Xiamen include Dragonair and Philippine Airlines.

▪ Airlines & Contacts **CAAC office** ✉ Wuyi Lu, Fuzhou ☎ 0591/334–5988. **Dragonair** ✉ Seaside Bldg., Jiang Dao Lu, Xiamen ☎ 0592/202–5433. **Philippine Airlines** ✉ Holiday Inn, 12 Zhenhai Lu, Xiamen ☎ 0592/202–3333 Ext. 6742. **Xiamen Airlines** ☎ 0592/602–2961.

AIRPORTS

Fuzhou Airport is 12 km (7 mi) from the city center. It has flights to all the other major cities in China, including Hong Kong, as well as to Wuyi Mountain Natural Reserve. There are buses between the main CAAC office and the airport. Xiamen Airport, one of the largest and busiest in China, lies about 12 km (7 mi) northeast of the city.

▓ Airport Information **Fuzhou Airport** ☎ 0591/801-3249. **Xiamen airport** ☎ 0592/602-0017.

BOAT & FERRY TRAVEL

Ferries for Meizhou leave from the pier at Wenjia, at the tip of a small peninsula along the coast between Fuzhou and Xiamen. Approaches to Wenjia are all made via the port of Putian City, a half hour away. Putian is about 2 hours south of Fuzhou and 3½ hours north of Xiamen by express bus. The Jimei Hao ferry travels once a week between Xiamen and Hong Kong. The trip is about 18 hours and costs around US$45. To check times call the Jimei Hao information line.

▓ Boat & Ferry Information **Jimei Hao information** ☎ 0592/202-2913.

BUS TRAVEL BETWEEN THE CITIES OF FUJIAN

There are three long-distance bus stations in Fuzhou, one in the north of the city near the train station, serving mostly destinations to the north, another in the south of the city, serving destinations to the south, and one next to the Minjiang Hotel, also serving southern destinations. From Fuzhou you can travel to most of the major coastal cities of the region, including Xiamen (6 hrs) and Quanzhou (2½ hrs) and as far as Guangzhou (20 hrs). There are also air-conditioned overnight buses to some more distant destinations.

Xiamen has service to Quanzhou and all the main cities along the coast as far as Guangzhou and Shanghai from the long-distance bus station. Private companies also run air-conditioned long-distance buses from offices around the town.

▓ Bus Information **Long-distance bus station** ✉ 56 Hubin Nan Lu, Xiamen. **North Bus Station** ✉ 371 Hualin Lu, Fuzhou. **South Bus Station** ✉ 195 Wuyi Lu, Fuzhou.

BUS TRAVEL WITHIN THE CITIES OF FUJIAN

Like most cities in China, Fuzhou has a comprehensive and cheap public bus system. Buses can also be slow and very crowded. Route maps are available from hotels, from CITS, or from the railway station.

Maps for the comprehensive bus service around Xiamen are available from the railway station, CITS, and hotels. Much of interest in Xiamen (for example, the port area) can be explored on foot. Bus 1 runs from the station to the university area and the park that houses Huli Cannon.

CAR RENTAL

There is no self-drive car rental in Fuzhou or Xiamen. Cars with drivers can be hired on a daily basis through CITS or through hotels.

EMERGENCIES

▓ **Public Security Bureau or PSB** (Gonganju) ✉ Xian Ta Lu, Fuzhou ✉ Off Zhongshan Lu near Xinqiao Hotel, Xiamen.

MONEY MATTERS

Most major hotels in Fuzhou and Xiamen have foreign exchange counters that are open during the day (possibly closing for lunch).

American Express ✉ Holiday Inn, 12 Zhenhai Lu, Xiamen ☎ 0592/212-0268. **Bank of China** ✉ 10 Zhongshan Lu, Xiamen.

TAXIS

In Fuzhou, your best bets for getting around are taxis or pedicabs, which are comfortable and reasonably cheap. They are easily hailed in the street or from outside hotels. In Xiamen taxis can also be found around hotels or on the streets; they're good for visiting the sights on the edge of town.

TRAIN TRAVEL

The Fuzhou Train Station is on the northern edge of the city, about 6 km (4 mi) from the river. From Fuzhou there are direct trains to Guangzhou (26 hrs), Shanghai (16 hrs), and Beijing (32 hrs). Part of the journey to Wuyi Mountain Natural Reserve can also be undertaken by train as far as Nanping.

Rail travel to and from Xiamen is not very convenient. Many journeys will involve a change. There are, however, direct links to Shanghai and also to Fuzhou (a long journey better undertaken by bus). The railway station is about 3 km (2 mi) northeast of the port; bus service between the two is frequent.

Train Information Fuzhou Train Station ✉ Liuyi Bei Lu. **Xiamen Train Station** ✉ Xiahe Lu.

VISITOR INFORMATION

Tourist Information CITS ✉ 107 Jing Da Lu, Fuzhou ☎ 0591/750-2794. **CITS** ✉ Hubin Bei Lu, Zhenxing Daxia, 15th fl., Xiamen ☎ 0592/505-1822.

JIANGXI

This inland province (the name means "west river") to the northwest of Fujian has been part of mainstream China since the Qin Dynasty. It remained thinly populated until the 3rd century, when Han Chinese arrived, fleeing the steppe peoples beyond the Great Wall, who were threatening to invade. From the 7th century onward the construction of the Grand Canal channeled trade to the southeastern regions and brought more immigrants from the northern regions into what was still a sparsely populated area. At first most of those who came were poor peasants, but as silver mining and tea cultivation took hold, a wealthy merchant class developed. By the time of the Ming Dynasty the province had acquired its present boundaries. After 19th-century coastal shipping ate into the canal trade, Jiangxi became one of the poorest Chinese provinces, which may explain why it was an important guerrilla stronghold for the Communists during the civil war.

Running south to north through the center of the 166,000-square-km (64,000-square-mi) province is a river known as the Ganjiang. One of the largest freshwater lakes in China, Poyang Hu, is also here. Much of

Jiangxi is flat, but to the east, west, and south it is fringed by mountains that reach 6,500 feet.

Nanchang

47 *17 hrs (400 km [248 mi]) by train northwest of Fuzhou; 13 hrs (750 km [465 mi]) by train northeast of Hong Kong; 17 hrs (1,200 km [744 mi]) by train south of Beijing.*

With its wide avenues and relative absence of tall buildings, Nanchang looks like much of China before the 1990s, and the city's various grand Communist monuments are a blast from the ideological past. The capital of Jiangxi is experiencing the changes of China's reform era but to a much lesser degree than China's wealthier coastal provinces. The city can be toured in an afternoon and is a useful stepping-off point for more interesting places in the region.

Nanchang has existed under a variety of names since the Han Dynasty, when it became well known as a city of merchants and alchemists. Its current name means "to flourish from the south." It was often used as a transit point for the ceramics made in the imperial kilns at Jingdezhen; indeed, the son of the founder of the Ming Dynasty was made ruler of the area. Matteo Ricci, the Jesuit missionary who was the first European to gain access to the Chinese court, reportedly visited Nanchang in the 16th century.

Nanchang is best known for events in the early part of the 20th century. On August 1, 1927, there was an uprising in the city, in protest of Chiang Kai-shek's attack on the Shanghai Commune in April of the same year. Several eminent Communists, officers in the Nationalist army—among them Zhou Enlai and Zhu De—were serving in the area of Nanchang. They decided to take the city, and with a force of 30,000 they succeeded in holding out for three days before the Nationalists retook it. The defeated soldiers fled to the mountains and later regrouped to form what was to become the Red Army. It was from this moment that Mao began to diverge from Soviet orthodoxy by concentrating on the rural peasantry instead of urban workers. The uprising is still celebrated nationally on August 1, known as Army Day. In 1986 the central government named Nanchang a national cultural heritage city.

The building housing the **Former Headquarters of the Nanchang Uprising and Revolutionary Museum** (Bayi Jinianguan; ✉ Zhongshan Lu 💰 Y10 ☉ Daily 8–5:30) was a hotel until it was taken over for use as the headquarters of the leaders of the Communist uprising of August 1, 1927. The somewhat esoteric exhibits consist of furniture of the period and photographs of the protagonists. The marble-and-granite **Memorial to the Nanchang Uprising** (Bayi Jinianta; ✉ Renmin Guangchang) was erected in 1977. The **Memorial Hall to the Martyrs of the Revolution** (Geming Lieshi Jinian Tang; ✉ 399 Bayi Dadao 💰 Y6 ☉ Daily 8:30–11:30 and 2:30–5) details the lives of hundreds of local revolutionaries from the early part of the 20th century. The **Residence of Zhou Enlai and Zhu De** (Zhou En Lai, Zhu De Guju; 💰 Y12 each ☉ Daily 8:30–5)on Minde Lu, reveals how the leaders lived.

In the suburbs about 10 km (6 mi) south of the center is the country house Qingyun Pu (Blue Cloud Garden), where Zhu Da (sometimes known as Badashanren—"man of the eight great mountains") lived from 1626 to 1705. It has been preserved as a **Memorial to Badashanren** (Badashanren Jinian Tang). The retreat has a long history; by the 4th century it had already found favor with Taoists. The rooms have been preserved, with reproductions of Master Zhu's works on the walls (the originals are mostly in the Shanghai Museum) and a number of items dating from the Ming Dynasty. Zhu was a kinsman of the Ming imperial household, and when the Ming collapsed in 1637 he sequestered himself in a temple for the remainder of his life and devoted himself to painting, creating highly spirited and individualistic paintings and calligraphy. ⚓ *Near Dingshan Qiao (Dingshan Bridge); best reached by taxi or bus from Bayi Dadao near Renmin Guangchang* ☎ *0791/521– 2565* 💷 *Y15* ⏱ *Daily 8:30–5.*

The huge **Tengwang Pavilion** (Tengwang Ge), on the banks of the Fu River, is the foremost sight in Nanchang. Reconstructed in 1989 on the site of a building that has known some 28 incarnations—the first during the Tang Dynasty in AD 653—the pavilion is now part of a sprawling complex of shops, teahouses, and exhibits. Made of granite and nine stories high, it reflects the architectural styles of the Tang and Song dynasties. Performances of traditional Chinese music are given here throughout the day. ✉ *Yanjiang Lu* 💷 *Y30* ⏱ *Daily 7:30–5:45.*

Youmin Temple (Youmin Si), founded in the 6th century, is the largest and most active temple in Nanchang. It is notable for its 18-ton bell cast in 967 by order of a Tang Dynasty general. There is also a large bronze Buddha in the rear hall and a bronze bell cast during the Ming Period. ✉ *Huanhu Lu* 💷 *Y5* ⏱ *Daily 7–5:30.*

Where to Stay & Eat

Other than those in the hotels, there are very few restaurants of particular note in Nanchang. However, there is no shortage of choice along the main streets and around the railway station, where small, cheap restaurants sell dumplings and other local specialties like river snails.

$–$$ ✕ **Far East Restaurant.** This is one of the best places to eat in Nanchang. The large dining room gets a little noisy, but the excellent selection of southern-style Chinese and Cantonese foods will satisfy. No need to worry about a menu; just walk into the small room near the entrance to peruse refrigerated sample dishes. Point at what looks good, and the chefs will prepare a dish like it for your table. ✉ *95 Fuzhou Lu* ☎ *0791/622– 3688* 🚫 *No credit cards.*

¢–$$ 🏨 **Jiangxi Hotel.** The Jiangxi's exterior is vintage proletarian 1950s, but fortunately the interior has been completely renovated to a higher standard of bourgeois comfort. The hotel's location smack in the middle of town is perfect for walking. ✉ *368 Baiyi Dadao, 330006* ☎ *0791/620– 6666* 🖨 *0791/620–6996* 🛏 *243 rooms, 48 suites* ⚹ *4 restaurants, bar* 💳 *AE, MC, V.*

¢–$ 🏨 **Gloria Plaza Hotel.** This Hong Kong–managed hotel is next to Tengwang Pavilion. The entire hotel is done in a beautiful tropical forest motif, with imported furniture that has a 1960s retro feel to it. The rooms have river views. ⊠ *88 Yan Jiang Bei Lu, 330008* ☎ *0791/673–8855* 🖷 *0791/ 673–8533* ✆ *328 rooms, 30 suites* ☖ *2 restaurants, pool, gym, sauna, bar, shops, business services* ▤ *AE, DC, MC, V.*

¢ 🖭 **Nanchang Hotel.** Although not a luxury hotel, Nanchang's inexpensive rooms provide standard amenities like air-conditioning. It's in a small garden located between the train and bus station in one of the main business districts. ⊠ *16 Baiyi Dadao, 330006* ☎ *0791/885–9999* 🖷 *0791/ 622-3193* ✆ *228 rooms* ☖ *Restaurant, shops* ▤ *No credit cards.*

Nightlife & the Arts

Although there is the occasional opera or acrobatics performance, the odd bar or karaoke parlor, the main interest is ordinary Chinese life—the occasional **night market,** or a visit to the cinema are your best bets. Ask at the CITS or your hotel about **performances.**

The Outdoors

Ask at your hotel for **bike** rentals. Renmin Park and Bayi Park are good for **jogging.** The best place for **hiking** in this area is at the hill resort of Lushan.

Shopping

The chief item in this region is **porcelain.** Jingdezhen is the best place to buy, but it's also widely available in Nanchang and elsewhere. New shops, privately owned, are appearing all the time, and some are selling very good quality wares, especially reproductions of classical porcelain. Otherwise, try the **Nanchang Porcelain-ware Store** (⊠ Minde Lu). The area right around the entrance to Tengwang Pavilion is home to dozens of small privately owned shops that sell a smattering of everything: antiques, old coins, jade objects, and especially porcelain. Keep an eye out for porcelain statues from the Cultural Revolution, when the kilns of Jingdezhen churned out statues of Mao and members of the Red Guards. Bargaining is expected at these shops.

Jingdezhen

★ ❹ *4½ hrs (230 km [143 mi]) northeast by train or long-distance bus from Nanchang.*

Jingdezhen is synonymous with porcelain—for centuries emperors and wealthy merchants ordered their finest ceramics from the city's kilns, using the particularly high-quality clays found in the hills outside town. From these high-profile clients, the city's potters began turning out huge volumes of porcelain and sending it to eager buyers around the world. Jingdezhen ceramics were popular with European aristocrats and the emirs of Egypt and Syria alike. The industry continues to thrive today—the characters for Jingdezhen are stamped on most Chinese porcelain sold in the West. The city is a great place to learn about ceramics, at its museums, factory tours, and kilns that still produce it using the methods of Imperial China. Of course this is also the best place to purchase top-quality porcelain at cheap prices (even if you have to sift through a pile of tacky pieces on the way).

There were kilns in operation here from as early as the Eastern Han Dynasty, using the region's rich deposits of kaolin clay, which can produce especially light and fine ceramics. From the 4th century the rulers of a dynasty based in Nanjing commissioned pottery wares for use in their palaces. At that time Jingdezhen produced mostly white ware with a transparent or pale blue glaze. As manufacturing methods were perfected, a finer porcelain, using kaolin clay, was created by firing at higher temperatures.

Beginning with the Song Dynasty, the imperial court, compelled to move southward to Hangzhou, began to place orders on a serious scale, partly to satisfy the widespread demand for vessels from which to drink tea but also because metal was in shorter supply. In fact it is from this era that the town, formerly known as Xinping, acquired its current name: one period (1004–07) of the Song was known as the Jingde, at which time all pieces of porcelain made for the court had to be marked accordingly. Both the custom and the name stuck.

In later centuries, during the Yuan and Ming dynasties, Jingdezhen became famous for its blue underglaze porcelain (the classic Ming blue and white), which was widely exported to the rest of Asia and to Europe. Much of the export material was fussy and overdecorated—classic porcelain was much simpler.

Although mass production is the norm now, this type of output is not an entirely a modern phenomenon. Most of the finest artistic ware was made by special order, such as when the paintings of an artist favored at court were copied onto porcelain. But most production was on a considerable scale—certainly it was by the 18th century, when European travelers described the methods used. It is clear that much depended on organization, with certain workers responsible for certain roles in the creative process, just as in the modern-day assembly line.

The pottery ovens here are known as dragon kilns. They have several chambers and are fueled with wood. Many among the population of the town are involved in porcelain production, manufacturing some 400 million pieces each year. Although parts of Jingdezhen resemble a dreary Victorian manufacturing town that Charles Dickens would have relished describing, it is a fascinating place to visit.

Off the main streets, Zhushan Lu and Zhongshan Lu, older, narrower streets close to the river have considerable character. You can get a comprehensive tour of the porcelain works at the **Art Porcelain Factory** (Yishu Taocichang). The **Porcelain Sculpture Factory** (Meidiao Taocichang) also has tours, by arrangement with **CITS** (⊠8 Lianhuating Lu ☎0798/822–2293).

The **Museum of Ceramic History** (Gu Taoci Lishi Bowuguan) shows items found among the ancient kiln sites and has workshops demonstrating porcelain techniques of the Ming and Qing dynasties. ⊠ *Off Cidu Dadao* 🖭 *Y10* 🕙 *Daily 8:30–5.*

In the vicinity of Jingdezhen are a number of **ancient kilns** including **Liujia Wan** is 20 km (12 mi) outside the town, and **Baihu Wan** is 9 km (6 mi) out on the road to Jingwu. Buses from downtown run to both places. A taxi ride to Liujia Wan will cost about Y40, to Baihu Wan, about Y25.

Where to Stay

¢ ▦ **Hezi Hotel.** One of Jingdezhen's more upmarket hotels, its standard rooms are reasonably priced. Prices vary according to the size of the room, and suites are also available. ⊠ *Fengjing Lu , 333000* ☎ *0798/822–5015* 🖷 *0798/822–6416* 🛏 *141 rooms, 5 suites* ⟑ *2 restaurants, gym, sauna, business services* ▤ *MC, V.*

¢ ▦ **Jinsheng Hotel.** Conveniently located in the commercial district, the clean, standard rooms are a definite steal, with a friendly staff to boot. Cheaper rooms are somewhat smaller, but with the same facilities. ⊠ *29 Zhushan Lu* ☎ *0798/827–1818* 🖷 *0798/827–1158* 🛏 *65 rooms* ⟑ *Restaurant, business services* ▤ *No credit cards.*

Lushan

49 *1¼ hrs (29 km [18 mi]) by bus southwest from Jiujiang; 2½ hrs (126 km [78 mi]) north by bus direct return to Nanchang.*

Lushan is intimately associated with many facets of Chinese history— art and poetry, Western colonialism, conferences of Communist Party heavyweights, and green tea. The rolling hills have been admired by scholars and painters for centuries, not least because their moist slopes were excellent for growing the green tea that fueled their paintings, calligraphy, and poetic musings. Foreign diplomats and merchants used the hills as an escape from the sweltering summer heat of Wuhan and Nanchang, and they built dozens of Western-style villas for their holidays. After the 1949 revolution, Communist bigwigs grabbed the prime real estate, and Lushan has often been used for significant Party conferences, notably the one in 1959 after the catastrophe of the Great Leap Forward, a meeting that attempted to sideline Mao and, some argue, indirectly led to the Cultural Revolution. In 1970 it was the scene of a bitter argument between Mao and his defense minister, Lin Biao, who died the following year in a plane that went down over Mongolia under mysterious circumstances.

This historically significant mountain resort is a relaxing place to pass a couple of days if you can escape the crowds of Chinese tourists who flock here in summer. The whole area is a massif of 90 peaks, which reach a height of 4,836 feet, liberally sprinkled with turn-of-the-20th-century Western villas, rocks, waterfalls, temples (mostly destroyed), and springs that have charmed visitors for more than 2,000 years. Entrance to the National Park Area is Y50; buses will stop at the main gate en route to allow nonlocals to purchase admission tickets.

The lush vegetation and famous waterfalls and clouds, which often cover the mountain slopes in the mornings and evenings, have drawn painters and poets here for centuries. The natural beauty of the Lushan area, as well as its historical importance, led to its being designated a World Heritage Site by UNESCO in 1996.

The focal point of the Lushan region is the town of **Guling,** well known because eminent politicians, including Chiang Kai-shek, have had villas here and because it is home, in the Hanbokou Valley, to the Lushan Botanical Garden. Many villas here are European in style, having originally been built for Westerners working on the plains below. Like those in Shanghai, they are a fascinating mix of various styles of architecture from the early 20th century. Unfortunately, because of local regulations forbidding construction of any kind—including renovation—many houses, slouching with age in the moist mountain air, are making the transition from mature structures to run-down old buildings.

Guling is 3,838 feet above sea level; once you're here, most things of interest can be reached on foot. The **Meilu Villa** (Meilu Bieshu), built in 1903 by a British expatriate, was the summer home of Chiang Kai-shek from 1933 to 1948. Although the old wooden house has not weathered very well, there is an interesting photo exhibit here on Lushan in the 20th century. Tea and other drinks are served on the second-floor balcony. ⊠ *Hexi Lu* 🎫 *Y15* ⊙ *Daily 7:30–6.*

About 4 km (2½ mi) south of the village is Lulin Lake (Lulin Hu), beside which is the **Former Residence of Mao Zedong** (Mao Zedong Guju), which also houses the **Lushan Museum** (Lushan Bowuguan). The building was used as a retreat for the late chairman and still contains his huge bed. Here you can also see an exhibition on local geology and natural history, as well as photographs commemorating important events in Lushan and items relating to the observations made about the area by various poets and scholars. ⊠ *Near Lulin Lu* 🎫 *Y10* ⊙ *Daily 8–6.*

The **Botanical Garden** (Zhiwuyuan) lies about 2 km (1 mi) east of the lake and has a collection of alpine and tropical plants, as well as a cactus display. ✤ *Southeast of Lulin Hu* 🎫 *Y10* ⊙ *Daily 9–5.*

About 2½ km (1½ mi) west of Guling is **Ruqin Lake** (Ruqin Hu). You can take a walk beyond it to **Xianren Cave** (Xianren Dong) and **Dragon Head Cliff** (Longshouya) which perches on the edge of a dizzying drop of several hundred feet.

Where to Stay

¢ 🏨 **Lushan Guest House.** This old hotel of some character is well managed. It has comfortable modern rooms and an excellent restaurant. There are two sections, varying considerably in price and comfort—you get what you pay for. ⊠ *446 Hexi Lu, Guling 332900* 🕾 *0792/828–2060* 🖷 *792/828–2843* 🛏 *56 rooms, 1 suite* ⚒ *Restaurant, bar, shops* ▤ *AE, MC, V.*

¢ 🏨 **Lushan Villa Hotel.** This hotel actually consists of nearly two dozen villas of various comfort and size, all nestled among picturesque pines and bamboo groves. Some of the villas here were once the country homes of political bigwigs. ⊠ *179 Zhihong Lu, Guling 332900* 🕾 *0792/828–2525* 🛏 *39 rooms, 8 suites* ⚒ *Restaurant* ▤ *No credit cards.*

Jiangxi A to Z

To research prices, get advice from other travelers, and book travel arrangements, visit www.fodors.com.

AIR TRAVEL

The airport lies 40 km (25 mi) south of Nanchang. There are flights to most of the main cities in China on regional carrier China Eastern Air.
🛫 **China Eastern Air** ☎ 0791/623-1351.

BOAT & FERRY TRAVEL

Between Nanchang and Jingdezhen, you can take a ferry from Bayi Bridge in Nanchang across Lake Boyang to Boyang and then continue by bus. Speed and prices vary depending on the boat.
🚢 **Ferry information** ☎ 0791/681-2515.

BUS TRAVEL

From the Nanchang long-distance bus station, buses leave several times daily for Changsha (Y110; 9 hrs), Jiujiang (Y40; 2½ hrs), and Jingdezhen (Y60; 4½ hrs). There is also regular service to Lushan (Y40; 1½ hrs).
🚌 Bus Information **Jingdezhen Bus Station** ✉ Tongzhan Lu ☎ 0798/822-5159.

Nanchang Bus Station ✉ Bayi Dadao ☎ 0791/624-3217.

CAR RENTAL

Driving a rental car yourself is not possible, but cars with drivers can be arranged through CITS.

EMERGENCIES

🚨 In case of medical problems or other emergencies, contact the Public Security Bureau in Nanchang **PSB** ✉ Shengli Lu, Nanchang ☎ 0791/677-2115.

MONEY MATTERS

🏦 Banks **Bank of China** ✉ Cidu Dadao, Jingdezhen. **Bank of China** ✉ 1 Zhanqian Xi Lu, Nanchang.

TRAIN TRAVEL

Nanchang is a major rail hub, and trains head to many destinations around the country. Major routes include Nanjing (Y60–Y200; 18 hours), Shanghai (Y110; 14 hours), Guangzhou (Y85–Y360; 19 hours), and Xiamen (Y60–Y310; 12 hours).
🚆 Train Information **Jingdezhen Train Station** ✉ Tongzhan Lu, east of city center. **Nanchang Train Station** ✉ End of Zhanqian Lu, in southeast part of city.

TRANSPORTATION AROUND THE CITIES OF JIANGXI

Nanchang has both buses and trolley buses. Maps for the system are sold at the train and bus stations. Pedicabs and taxis can be hailed on the streets or outside hotels and at the railway and bus stations.

Many, if not most, sights in Lushan, Jingdezhen, and Jiujiang can be visited on foot.

VISITOR INFORMATION

ℹ️ Tourist Information **CITS** ✉ 8 Lianhuating Lu, Jingdezhen ☎ 0798/822-2293 ✉ Nanhu Guest House, 28 Nan Hu Lu, Jiujiang ✉ Jiangxi Hotel, Nanchang ☎ 0791/621-9711.

SOUTHEASTERN CHINA

FAR FROM THE EMPEROR

7

By Tom Hilditch
& Sandra Lim

THE CHINESE HAVE A SAYING: "Heaven is high, and the emperor is far away." Perhaps nowhere in China does this saying apply more than the Southeast, a booming area synonymous with distance from the political center and a relationship with the West. Over the past decade no Chinese region has rushed more enthusiastically to capitalism.

Earth-at-night satellite photos give a telling view of Southeast Asia. Tokyo, Seoul, and Taiwan glow strongly. But it is Guangdong province with its boomtown cities clustering along the Pearl River delta that burns brightest. The region is an economic supernova. Remote from Beijing's authority, with its own distinct culture and language and a long history of contact with the West, Guangdong has taken advantage of China's Open Door Policy to reinvent itself as the workshop of the modern world. Its exports exceed that of Thailand, Vietnam, and the Philippines combined. It is China's most affluent and fastest-growing region, with an emerging shopping, bar, and restaurant culture to match.

History enthusiasts will want to head to Guangzhou, Guangdong province's ancient capital and the historic center of Cantonese culture. The rest of the region—particularly the area around the Pearl River delta—is focused on the future. Growth has been spectacular. In the last 15 years some 10,000 bridges have been built over the Pearl River. Rice paddies have sprouted skyscrapers. Rolling hills have been scraped flat for landfill. Shenzhen, Zhuhai, Dongguan, Zhongshan, and Foshan were just small agricultural townships until the late 1980s when paramount leader Deng Xiaoping famously announced that "to get rich is glorious" and designated these towns as centers of free trade. Flying into these brand-new, aggressively capitalist cities today, you often descend through a gray cloud of building site dust. And your first view is of a meandering urban sprawl of building sites, oily-gray rivers, and gleaming skyscrapers draped with neon. The scale is both exhilarating and alienating.

Some 20 million workers have arrived from other parts of China to seek their fortune in Guangdong—one of the largest human migrations anywhere in the modern world. Many have made it and enjoy lifestyles that two decades ago would have been unimaginable, sparking a property boom throughout the coastal cities. For some the display of wealth seems to be a competitive sport. In the streets of Guangdong's cities you will find dealerships for Rolls-Royces, Porsches, even Humvees. In Shenzhen's most opulent Chinese restaurants you can have gold-leaf sprinkled into your food just to increase the size of the bill. Many more migrants, of course, are still struggling. Begging is big problem in the major cities. Prostitution is widespread.

There is a sense that when it is finished the Pearl River delta region will be China's great 21st-century statement: a future-world of big bridges, bullet trains, skyscrapers, golf courses, seaside villas, and fantastically short commutes. For now, however, what you see is a work in progress.

Hainan Island, which until recently was governed from Guangdong province, is also rapidly changing. Once the dreaded destination for banished imperial politicians, it is now an increasingly well-managed vacation spot for those who want to get away from it all. The

Numbers in the text correspond to numbers in the margin and on the Southeastern China, Guangzhou, and Guangdong maps.

If you have 3 days

Three days in southeastern China are best spent at the same hotel in **Guangzhou** ① – ⑰ ⌐. Mixing taxi trips with long leisurely walks adds optimal balance to a three-day stay here. Follow neighborhhod itineraries to fill your three days with all the yop attractions in town. If you are eager to get out of Guangzhou, a taxi ride to **Foshan** ⑱ makes an excellent day trip. With Guangzhou's wealth of good restaurants, it's tempting to stop for leisurely lunches, but not advisable, as museums and temples close at 5. Save the big meal for dinnertime.

If you have 6 days

Option A: Guangzhou and Shenzhen. After three days in **Guangzhou** ① – ⑰ ⌐, another option would be to explore Shenzhen for Days 4–6. On Day 4, take an air-conditioned express bus or train to **Shenzhen** ㉔ to explore its wide variety of entertainment. After checking into your hotel, spend the afternoon shopping at Lo Wu Commercial City. Start Day 5 by taking a bus or taxi to Splendid China to view the miniatures of Chinese historical sites. Have lunch, and then head over to Happy Kingdom in the same theme-park area. On Day 6 you can either cross the border into Hong Kong or return to Guangzhou.

Option B: Guangzhou and Hainan Island. For a more relaxing six days, stay two days in Guangzhou itinerary and then fly to **Hainan Island** ㉚ – ㉜ to spend Days 3–6 kicking back on China's finest white-sand beaches or play golf and relax in the hot springs of resorts in the **Boao Scenic Zone** ㉛. On the third day, take a morning flight to **Haikou** ㉚, and spend the afternoon sightseeing at the Temple of the Five Lords. After dinner, stroll through the downtown streets and take a look at the night markets on Haidian Island. On the fourth day, visit Xiuying Fort in the morning and then take an air-conditioned express bus down the coast to **Sanya** ㉜. You should arrive just in time to enjoy sunset from the peak at Luhuitou Park. On the fifth day you can spend the morning visiting Tianya Haijiao and Nanshan Temple, a 45-minute taxi ride one-way. It will take about four hours to visit both sights and return to your resort. After lunch you can spend the afternoon participating in resort-arranged activities such as scuba diving, glass-bottom boating, or paragliding. For dinner, try heading to Dadonghai Beach where you can indulge in cheap barbecued seafood under the open sky. End your journey on the sixth day by flying directly from Sanya to Guangzhou or to Hong Kong.

If you have 10 days

If you have 10 days, spend three days in **Guangzhou** ① – ⑰ ⌐, three in **Shenzhen** ㉔, and four on **Hainan Island** ㉚ – ㉜. On the sixth day, fly from Shenzhen to **Haikou** ㉚. For Days 7–10, see the Hainan itinerary of Option C in the six-day itinerary section.

self-administered area is carefully developing family and romantic get-away resorts for every income level (particularly China's fast-growing middle class), and has aspirations to rival Bali and Phuket. With great beaches, a jungle hinterland, and fine weather all year, it certainly has the potential.

Exploring Southeastern China

Southeastern China divides into two distinct regions: the industrial powerhouse of Guangdong province and the tropical resort island of Hainan. The major cities of Guangdong—Shenzhen, Zhuhai, Foshan, Dongguan, Zhongshan, and its capital Guangzhou—are all on the Pearl River delta, China's commercial link to Hong Kong, Macau and, ultimately, the global market. A comfortable tour of the region could start in Hong Kong and arc through Shenzhen, Guangzhou, Foshan, Zhongshan, Zhuhai, and Macau, and then back to Hong Kong by one-hour hydrofoil. Guangzhou, the region's capital and the center of Cantonese cuisine and culture, is worth exploring over a few days. An idea might be to base yourself on the city's colonial-era Shamian Island, and make occasional day trips to the surrounding cities.

Hainan, China's only tropical island and the country's southernmost point, is fast becoming the country's choice holiday destination. The best way to get there is to fly. Both Sanya and Haikou have busy airports and several daily flights to Guangzhou, Shenzhen, Zhuhai, Hong Kong, and Macau. Hainan has three major destinations: Haikou, its rather run-down capital city; Boao, an upscale west-island resort designated for conventions; and Sanya, the island's most popular destination and China's southernmost point.

About the Restaurants

Few cultures relish their food with as much gusto as the Cantonese. Restaurants and food stalls are everywhere. Guangzhou alone has 150,000 at last estimate, ranging from simple street-side barbecues with wobbly plastic tables to cavernous multistory emporiums capable of seating 10,000 diners a day. These often garish places are not just restaurants but vast, noisy theaters of Cantonese life. While they can be intimidating at first, once you get the hang of them—and get used to pointing at dishes you like—they can be fun and fascinating places to eat.

Dim sum ("little heart," in Cantonese), in particular, is a meal that should not be missed. Traditionally it is a Sunday-lunch family affair (although many Cantonese restaurants serve it all day, every day) and peak hours are 11 AM–2 PM. The dishes, steamed in bamboo baskets, are snack size and stacked onto trolleys wheeled around the restaurant by old ladies. As one passes by, flag her down and check her wares. On average each dish costs between Y3 and Y8, so it is worth taking a risk on a mystery dish. If the restaurant is busy you will probably be expected to share a table with other patrons. This can be fun. Someone will invariably take you under their wing and make sure you get some great dishes. Don't worry about table manners: Cantonese eating etiquette requires only that you enjoy your meal.

Sand Between Your Toes

The white-sand beaches along Hainan's southern coast are China's best. Particularly notable is the private 7-km (4-mi) stretch of white-sand beach along Yalong Bay, the upscale resort area in eastern Sanya. Each resort has its own section along this sandy bar, and portions are shark-netted to protect swimmers. There are dozens of beach activities to indulge in, including scuba diving, Jet Ski rental, and paragliding. Most resorts have beachside lounges and umbrellas for sunbathers. For quality public beaches, try heading over to Dadonghai Beach in southern Sanya. There is a lively boardwalk lined with hotels, dive operators, and restaurants. Because it is public, it may be difficult or impossible to find a quiet spot. Groups of local Chinese tourists revel in the sea and sand, playing badminton, Frisbee, or paddleball. The beaches of Boao and Haikou are not as nearly refined as their southern counterparts. Nonetheless, they are still great places to park your towel and catch some strong rays.

See You at the Clubhouse

Golf is China's fastest-growing sport, and 70% of the country's courses are in Guangdong. Before the Zhongshan Hot Springs course was built in 1983, there were no decent greens in all China. Now there are 200 international courses, driving ranges at every turn, and China wants to be first to host the sport as an Olympic event. The sport's popularity may just say something about southern China's appetite for conspicuous consumption. After all, in densely populated China, nothing screams money as loudly as open space. Just how much money southeastern China spends on the sport became apparent when Tiger Woods was listed as Shenzhen's biggest taxpayer after paying $500,000 in taxes on his appearance fee at Mission Hills Golf Club (where corporate membership starts at $300,000 but trades privately for much more). Woods had played for just one weekend.

Shop 'Til You Drop

The days when you could impress a Chinese friend with foreign-bought luxuries are long gone. Just about every mass-market must-have, particularly toys, sports shoes, DVDs, clothes, electrical goods, and fashion accessories, is made in the Pearl River delta region. This makes the area excellent for shopping. You never know when you will run into a stall selling original items that somehow never made it to the United States or Europe, for a tenth of their rack price. One place to try is Mouse Street in Guangzhou, another is the Lo Wu Commercial City in Shenzhen. But be warned: the average Chinese shopper is not particularly discerning, and for every genuine product that somehow lost its way, there are thousands of poor-quality fakes with misspelled brand names. Some of these fakes are so awful—Nuke baseball caps and Chris Dior socks—they actually make pretty good joke gifts.

During southeastern China's balmy summer evenings, open-air street restaurants are a great nighttime eating option. In Guangdong you tend to find them around markets, riversides, and bar areas. In Hainan they are usually set up on the streets surrounding the beach. Look for sprawls of plastic chairs and tables after about 9 PM. Find yourself a table, explore the stalls, point, and smile. Most vendors specialize in just one or two dishes and cook them right in front of you, so the food is likely to be fresh and very tasty. A delicious and complete meal for one can be had for Y15–Y20. A large bottle of cold beer (from the corner shop) should cost between Y4 and Y6.

Chinese restaurant banquet dining is more expensive and complicated. Dishes are shared among everyone in a communal, family-style way (it makes more sense if you have a large dinner party, so everyone can try different dishes). If you order seafood, be prepared to pay per *jin* (pound) and to make your selections from an aquarium. If you are the host of the meal, you are expected to pick up the entire tab. If you are an invitee, graciously thank your host or make some show of trying to get the bill. Dinner for four can range from Y80 to Y400.

Another option might be to eat at Chinese or Hong Kong chain restaurants, such as Café de Coral, which often have picture or English menus. As with Western chain restaurants, you can expect to pay Y20–Y30 per person for a meal.

About the Hotels

Southeastern China is currently experiencing its second major hotel building boom. It is a buyer's market and a great time to travel. The first boom—back in the early 1990s—saw a plethora of four-star business hotels developed by local Chinese firms. These tended to be opulent, glitzy affairs, featuring marble lobbies and revolving restaurants. This time around international chain hotels are the ones fueling the boom. Groups like Shangri-La, Holiday Inn, and Sofitel are vastly expanding their portfolios of hotels across South China. Most hotels open in stages, so be sure to inquire about current construction projects in order to avoid a room that has a hammer sounding all morning long.

In Hainan, lush tropical scenery enhances the beautiful interiors and excellent service of some world-class resort hotels. Most hotels here will have at least one outdoor swimming pool, and a choice of daytime sporting activities. Air-conditioning is offered at all the hotels listed in this guidebook unless otherwise noted. Mosquitoes are not a problem if you make sure to close your windows and turn on the air-conditioner at night.

Most hotels listed in this chapter offer business services and most have in-room broadband connection (be sure to check if there is a nominal fee). Many also have gyms and some form of evening entertainment, the most popular being karaoke. The general trend is that major hotel chains, such as Sheraton, Shangri-La, and Holiday Inn, will offer staff who speak better English.

Always inquire about discounts on published rates. It is not unusual to have a discount of 40%–50% during the low season (March to November) or on weekends. However, expect prices to double from their published rates during trade fair periods in Guangzhou, held April and October annually. Be sure to book early during these periods or you may find yourself with little options. Chinese New Year, usually in late January or early February, is also a bad time to travel, as hotels will be full priced and booked.

Don't forget to check the Internet for weekend specials on some of the higher-end hotels.

WHAT IT COSTS In Yuan					
	$$$$	$$$	$$	$	¢
RESTAURANTS	over 165	100–165	50–99	25–49	under 25
HOTELS	over 1,800	1,400–1,800	1,100–1,399	700–1,099	under 700

Restaurant prices are for a main course, excluding tax and tips. Hotel prices are for a standard double room, including taxes.

Timing

Try to avoid Guangzhou during the city's twice-annual trade fairs, usually in the last two weeks of April and October every year. Each fair attracts an average of 25,000 visitors so hotels are booked solid and prices rocket. If you are attending the fair, book your hotel room well in advance and be prepared to pay twice the listed rates.

Hainan, at the southernmost tip of China, is on the same latitude as Hawaii and is bikini-warm even when the rest of China is freezing in its thermals. Hainan's hotels are especially full around Christmas. Typhoons dog the tropical island between May and October, impeding transport, communications, and travelers' itineraries. The island has some fun festivals you might want to keep in mind, particularly the Sanya International Wedding Festival held November 18–21 every year.

Avoid travel anywhere in China during Spring Festival when the entire country shuts down and takes a one-week holiday. The lunar calendar dictates the dates of the annual Spring Festival, but it tends to fall in late January, or early to mid-February. Expect trains to be packed, hotels to be booked, and prices to soar.

GUANGZHOU

Guangzhou (also known as Canton), the capital of Guangdong province, is both a modern boomtown and an ancient port city. As the administrative heart of the Pearl River delta, this metropolis of over 7 million people has all the expected accoutrements of a competitive, modern Chinese city: thickets of skyscrapers (including the country's second tallest), a shiny new airport (China's biggest and busiest), a new convention hall (Asia's largest), an efficient underground train system, new railway stations, expressways, and so on.

Unlike so many cities in the region, however, Guangzhou is quite old. Records show a city has continuously existed on this particular bend of

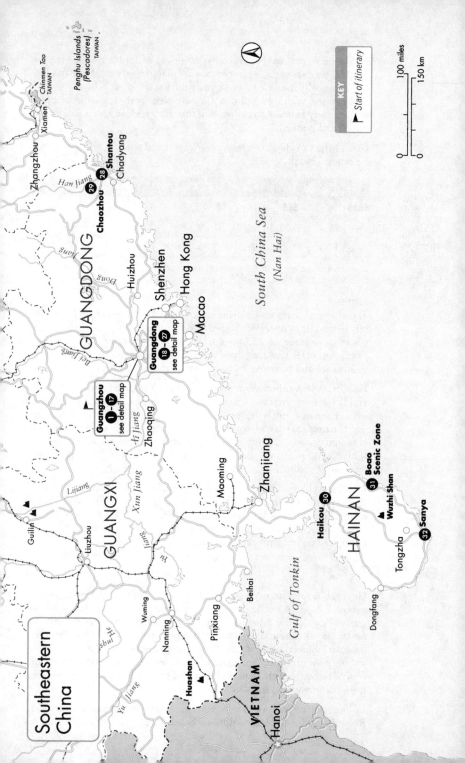

Southeastern China

GUANGDONG

GUANGXI

HAINAN

VIETNAM

Penghu Islands
(Pescadores)
TAIWAN

Chinmen Tao
TAIWAN

Xiamen
Zhangzhou

Chaozhou
Shantou
Chadyang

Han Jiang

Huizhou
Shenzhen
Hong Kong
Macao

South China Sea
(Nan Hai)

Guangdong
18 – 27
see detail map

Guangzhou
1 – 17
see detail map

Zhaoqing

Bei Jiang

Xi Jiang

Lijiang

Guilin

Liuzhou

Xun Jiang

Yi Jiang

Maoming

Zhanjiang

Beihai

Gulf of Tonkin

Dongfang

Haikou
30

HAINAN

Boao
Scenic Zone
31

Wuzhi Shan

Tongzha

Sanya
32

Wuming

Nanning

Pinxiang

Huashan

Hanoi

Yu Jiang

He

Long Shui He

KEY

▶ Start of itinerary

100 miles

150 km

the Pearl River since at least 214 BC. Exploring its riverfront, parks, temples, and markets, one is constantly reminded of the city's long history and the inordinate impact its irrepressible culture, language, and cuisine has made on the world.

The story of Guangzhou is the story of China's interaction with the West, beginning with the Silk Road trade routes. Some merchants—all too aware of the hazards of the long overland journey westward—chose to take their caravans south and transport silk and other luxuries by sea. The sheltered port of Guangzhou was a natural choice. By the end of the Han Dynasty (206 BC–AD 220) the city was a major port. Han Dynasty records reveal that traders from as far away as Rome arrived to buy silk and spices at semiannual festivals (foreshadowing today's Canton Export Commodities Fairs). The majority of Guangzhou's foreign visitors, however, were from Arabia. The first Islamic mosque was built in the city in the 7th century.

The Cantonese talent and enthusiasm for business was as keen then as now, so the city's inhabitants welcomed the Portuguese explorer-merchants who arrived in the 16th century looking for a trading post. Attempts by the Ming court in Beijing to ban all foreign trade had little impact in Guangzhou. As the saying goes, "the emperor is far away." On their own initiative the local mandarins allowed the Portuguese to settle in Macau to act as middlemen for the Cantonese merchants' trade with Japan and the West.

The trade was dominated by Japanese silver; Chinese silk, porcelain, and tea; Indian muslin; Persian damascene; African ivory; and European manufactured goods, and flourished for a century, until Japan closed itself off to the outside world. The Portuguese lost their sea lanes and cargoes to the newly mercantile nations of Europe, led by Britain, which used Macau as a base for doing business in Guangzhou. The British called Guangzhou "Canton," an anglicized version of the Portuguese *cantão*.

From the late 18th century, Western merchants set up trading houses in Guangzhou where they negotiated the purchase of tea. The beverage became so important to Britain that the British East India Company had to find an import to match it in value. China didn't want more European manufactured goods or woolen cloth, but the British were able to create a market for opium. The British colonial government took control of the Bengal opium market, and private British companies were soon making fortunes from the opium trade.

Attempts by the Chinese authorities to stop the sale of opium in 1839 resulted in the first of the Opium Wars, with naval battles in the Zhujiang (Pearl River) estuary. Defeated, the Chinese were forced to cede the island of Hong Kong to Britain and open treaty ports like Shanghai to foreign trade and influence.

Guangzhou lost its pivotal importance as an international trading hub and went into decline. In the 19th century tens of thousands of Guangzhou people left in search of a better life. Among the scholars who found an education overseas was Dr. Sun Yat-sen, who was born a few miles north of the Macau border. He led the movement to overthrow the Manchus that culminated in the 1911 Revolution.

Guangzhou later became a hotbed of revolutionary zeal and a battleground between Nationalists and Communists. Chiang Kai-shek founded the Whampoa Academy for military instruction, and Mao Zedong taught at the Peasant Movement Institute, as did Zhou Enlai.

Following the 1949 Revolution, Guangzhou reinstituted its biannual trade fairs (April and October) and welcomed foreign business, but it wasn't until the open-door policy of Deng Xiaoping in 1979 that the port city was able to resume its role as a commercial gateway to China. Since then the city has become an economic dynamo and the population has increased dramatically (7.2 million in 2001).

Rapid modernization during the 1980s and '90s has taken its toll not just on the environment but also on the pace of city life. On bad days the clouds of building site dust, aggressive driving, shop touts, and persistent beggars can be a bit much. But in Guangzhou's parks, temples, winding old quarter backstreets, restaurants, river islets, and museums, the old city and a more refined way of life is never far away.

Exploring Guangzhou

Guangzhou can be roughly divided into six districts, each with unique sights to see and walks to take. Because of the logistics and time involved in moving from place to place around the city, it is best to concentrate on a neighborhood at a time. Colonial Canton consists of the area on and around Shamian Island and the Pearl River. The part of the city that was formerly encircled by the city wall comprises Ancestral Guangzhou. To the north of the former walled city is the Station District, and even farther north is the airport area. On the eastern edge of the formerly walled city are sights related to Chinese revolutions, and farther east, Tianhe District and the Eastern Suburbs.

Colonial Canton

To recapture the days of Canton as it looked to the foreign merchants in the latter half of the 19th century and first part of the 20th, stroll around Shamian Island and have lunch within sight and sound of the Pearl River traffic, which once included tea clippers and opium ships. Cross the small bridge to visit the antiques shops of Qingping.

a good walk

Start from the White Swan hotel, leaving by the rear entrance. Follow the three streets that run parallel along the length of **Shamian Island ❶ ▶**. Here you can see restored buildings and watch the locals at leisure in the small central park. Then cross the north bridge to visit **Qingping Market ❷**.

TIMING   This walk can be done in three hours, but lunch and shopping can add another two to three hours.

What to See

❷ **Qingping Market** (Qingping Shichang). Across the short bridge from the north shore of Shamian is the bustling, noisy complex of alleys packed with shops and market stalls. The Qingping Market caters to a wide variety of shoppers. The central alley contains herbalists, spice sellers, and fruit and vegetable stalls. To the left is the infamous meat market, with dogs, cats, and various endangered species on sale. If you have any qualms at all about seeing animals slaughtered, don't go here. Turn right on Dishipu Lu, and on the left is a collection of jade shops, along with stores selling reproduction antiques, old watches and jewelry, Mao memorabilia, and other collectibles. Farther north, on Daihe Lu, is the private **antiques market,** where you'll find plenty of old furniture, porcelain, jade, and banknotes. ⊠ *Dishipu Lu and Daihe Lu.*

▶ ❶ **Shamian Island.** More than a century ago the mandarins of Guangzhou designated a 44-acre sandbank outside the city walls in the Pearl River as an enclave for foreign merchants. The foreigners had previously lived and done business in a row of houses known as the Thirteen Factories, near the present Shamian, but local resentment after the Opium Wars—sometimes leading to murderous attacks—made it prudent to confine them to a protected area, which was linked to the city by two bridges that were closed at 10 every night.

The island rapidly became a bustling township, as trading companies from Britain, the United States, France, Holland, Italy, Germany, Portugal, and Japan built stone mansions along the waterfront. With spacious gardens and private wharves, these served as homes, offices, and warehouses. There were churches for Catholics and Protestants, banks, a yacht club, football grounds, a cricket field, and the Victory hotel.

Shamian was attacked in the 1920s but survived until the 1949 Revolution, when its mansions became government offices or apartment houses and the churches were turned into factories. In recent years, however, the island has resumed much of its old character. Many colonial buildings have been restored, and both churches have been beautifully renovated and reopened to worshippers. **Our Lady of Lourdes Catholic Church** (⊠ Shamian Dajie at Yijie), with its cream-and-white neo-Gothic tower, is particularly attractive. A park with shady walks and benches has been created in the center of the island, where local residents come to chat with friends, walk around with their caged birds, or practice tai chi.

Ancestral Guangzhou

To explore what used to be the walled city of Guangzhou takes a full day. The major attractions are scattered, and the narrow streets are invariably congested with human and vehicular traffic. Nevertheless, it's interesting to cover some of the itinerary on foot to experience the dynamism of Cantonese city life.

a good walk

Start with a taxi ride to the **Huaisheng Mosque** ❸ ▶, except on Friday, when it is closed to non-Muslims. You can walk from here to the **Six Banyan Temple** ❹ and on to the nearby **Bright Filial Piety Temple** ❺. After lunch take a taxi to the **Chen Family Temple** ❻ and end the day with a stroll in **Liuhua Park** ❼.

Timing. This itinerary should take six to seven hours, depending on how much walking you do and how long you take for lunch.

Guangzhou

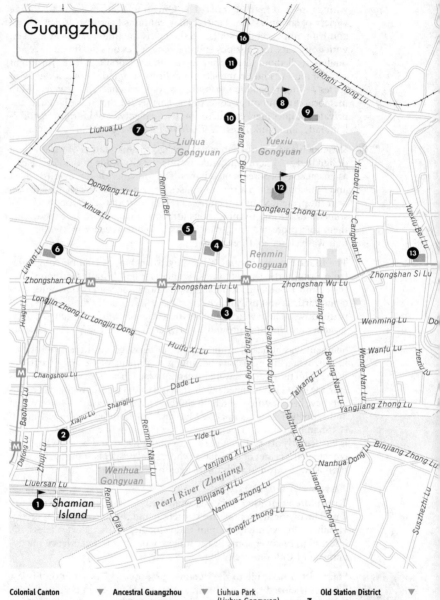

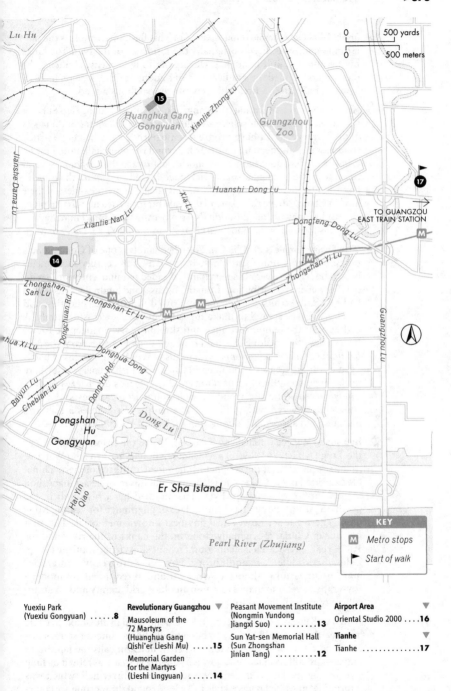

What to See

❺ Bright Filial Piety Temple (Guangxiao Si). This Buddhist temple is the oldest in Guangzhou. It was originally the residence of the Nan Yue kings but became a temple in AD 401. During the Tang Dynasty, Huineng, the monk who founded the southern sect of Buddhism, studied here. In 1629 it was rebuilt after a fire, with new prayer pavilions added.

Among the most charming of Guangzhou's temples, Guangxiao Si has a warm, welcoming atmosphere. A gilded wooden Laughing Buddha sits at the entrance, and a huge bronze incense burner, wreathed in joss-stick smoke, stands in the main courtyard. Beyond the main hall, noted for its ceiling of red-lacquer timbers, is another courtyard that contains several treasures, among them a small brick pagoda said to contain the tonsure hair of Huineng, and a couple of iron pagodas that are the oldest of their kind in China. Above them spread the leafy branches of a myrobalan plum tree and a banyan called Buddha's Tree because it is said Huineng was given his tonsure in its shade. ⊠ *Guangxiao Lu* 🚇 *Y2* 🕐 *Daily 6:30–5.*

❻ Chen Family Temple (Chen Jia Ci). The Chen family is one of Guangdong's oldest and most numerous clans. In the late 19th century local members, who had prospered as merchants, decided to build a memorial temple. They invited contributions from the Chens—and kindred Chans—who had emigrated overseas. The money flowed in from 72 countries, and no expense was spared to make this a tribute to a successful family. A highlight of the temple is a huge and skillfully carved ridgepole frieze. It stretches 90 feet along the main roof and depicts scenes from the epic *Romance of Three Kingdoms,* with thousands of figures against a backdrop of ornate houses, monumental gates, and lush scenery. Elsewhere in the huge compound of pavilions and courtyards are friezes of delicately carved stone and wood, as well as fine iron castings and a dazzling altar covered with gold leaf. The temple also houses a folk arts museum and shop. ⊠ *7 Zhongshan Qi Lu* 🚇 *Y4* 🕐 *Daily 8:30–5.*

▶ ❸ Huaisheng Mosque (Huaisheng Si Guang Ta). In the cosmopolitan era of the Tang Dynasty (618–907) a Muslim missionary named Abu Wangus, said to be an uncle of the prophet Mohammed, came to southern China. He converted many Chinese to Islam and built this mosque in Guangzhou as their house of worship. Ever since he died here, his tomb in the northern part of the city has been a place of pilgrimage for visiting Muslims. The mosque, however, is his best-known memorial. The first mosque in China, it originally stood on the banks of the river and for 1,300 years provided a beacon for merchant ships from Southeast Asia, India, the Middle East, and Europe. Following progressive land reclamations, it is now almost downtown and surrounded by modern skyscrapers, yet it manages to retain an old-world dignity and an atmosphere of peaceful devotion.

A high wall encloses the mosque, which is dominated by the smooth, white minaret. Rising to 108 feet, it can be climbed using an interior spiral staircase, and the views from the top—where a muezzin calls the faithful to prayer—are still spectacular. Below is a gate-tower that was rebuilt in Tang style during the late 17th century, and the main prayer hall, which was refurbished in Ming Dynasty style in 1936. Around the mosque are courtyards and gardens where local Muslims and visitors can rest and meditate. ⊠ *Guangta Lu* 🎫 *Free* ☉ *Sat.–Thurs. 8–5, except special holy days.*

7 **Liuhua Park** (Liuhua Gongyuan). Next to the trade fair hall, this park is ideal for relaxation, people-watching, and dining. It has a serpentine lake, groves of trees, flower beds, and plenty of benches. You can sit and watch men gather to compare the talents of their pet songbirds, finches that are kept in exquisite bamboo cages fitted with porcelain feeding bowls and decorated with pieces of jade. In late afternoon the scene changes as young lovers come in search of secluded benches. As for dining, the glittering white palace in the lake is the Sun Kwong restaurant. ⊠ *Dongfeng Xi Lu and Renmin Bei Lu* 🎫 *Y3* ☉ *Daily 11–6.*

4 **Six Banyan Temple** (Liu Rong Si Hua Ta). Look at any ancient scroll painting or lithograph by early Western travelers, and you will see two landmarks rising above old Guangzhou. One is the minaret of the mosque; the other is the 184-foot pagoda of the Six Banyan Temple. Still providing an excellent lookout, the pagoda appears to have nine stories, each with doorways and encircling balconies. Inside, however, there are 17 levels. Thanks to its arrangement of colored, carved roofs, it is popularly known as the Flowery Pagoda.

Fodor'sChoice
★

The temple was founded in the 5th century, but following a series of fires, most of the existing buildings date from the 11th century. It was built by the Zen master Tanyu and is still a very active place of worship, with a community of monks and regular attendance by Zen Buddhists. It was originally called Purificatory Wisdom Temple but changed its name after a visit by the Song Dynasty poet Su Dongpo, who was so delighted by six banyan trees growing in the courtyard that he left an inscription with the characters for six banyans.

The trees are no longer to be found, but the stone bearing his calligraphy can be seen in the temple, along with tablets telling the history of the place and a 1,000-year-old bronze statue of Zen master Huineng. In one prayer hall there are also three statues of Buddha—each weighing 5 tons—and one of the goddess of mercy, all made of brass and cast in 1663. ⊠ *Haizhu Bei Lu* 🎫 *Y6* ☉ *Daily 8–5.*

Old Station District

The area around the old railway station and exhibition hall offers an agreeable combination of ancient and natural history. Dominated by the Zhenhai Tower, Yuexiu Park is Guangzhou's answer to New York's Central Park, while the Guangzhou Museum and Tomb of the Southern Yue Kings uncover an extraordinary era in the city's past, and the Orchid Garden proves you can find peace and quiet in the busiest part of town.

a good walk

Begin at **Yuexiu Park** **8** ▶, strolling to pay respects to the Five Celestial Rams before visiting the **Guangzhou Museum** **9**, housed in the 14th-century Zhenhai Tower. Have lunch in the park, then cross Jiefang Bei Lu to the **Tomb of the Southern Yue Kings** **10**. End the day with a stroll through the **Orchid Garden** **11**, where you can stop for tea in a classic tea pavilion.

Timing. This walk, including lunch, should take about 5½ hours.

What to See

❾ Guangzhou Museum (Guangzhou Bowuguan). Dominating Yuexiu Park is the five-story, 92-foot **Tower Controlling the Sea** (Zhenhai Lou), built in 1380. Three centuries later it was converted into a watchtower overlooking the old port. Today its entrance is still guarded by a dozen old cannons and three Krupp guns, but it now it houses the municipal museum, whose displays outline the history of the city from prehistoric times to the present. On the first floor is a huge anchor from the Ming Dynasty, which was found in the river mud, and a bas-relief model of Guangzhou as it was projected to look in the 21st century.

On the second floor are the remains of pottery from a Han Dynasty (206 BC–AD 220) tomb; Han bronzes; and examples of early trade goods such as rhinoceros horns, hawksbill turtle shells, and precious stones. The third floor is devoted to Guangzhou's experience of the Western world. Here is the original clock face from the Roman Catholic cathedral, bibles, export-ware porcelain, models of the first railway car and first plane used in Guangzhou, pictures of the foreign factories on Shamian, and a bas-relief of the city in the 19th century.

Guangzhou after the Opium Wars is the focus of exhibits on the fourth floor. There are pictures of the first brewery, the first sugar refinery, and early sewing machines, along with displays of an old fire engine, telephone, radio, household implements, and a sedan chair. On the top floor are shops selling antiques, tea, jade, cheongsams (high-neck, split-skirt Chinese dresses), and such local specialties as snake wine. Tea, beer, soft drinks, and snacks are served at tables on the balcony, which affords marvelous views of the park. ⊠ *Yuexiu Gongyuan, Jiefang Bei Lu* ☎ *020/8355–0627* ⌦ *Y6* ☉ *Daily 9–5.*

★ **⓫ Orchid Garden** (Lanpu). This garden offers a wonderfully convenient retreat from the noise and crowds of the city. It's spread over 20 acres, with paths that wind through groves of bamboo and tropical trees, beside carp-filled ponds, to a series of classic teahouses. Here you can sit and enjoy a wide variety of Chinese teas, brewed the traditional way. There are tables inside and on terraces that overlook the ponds. As for the orchids, there are 10,000 pots with more than 2,000 species of the flower, which present a magical sight when they bloom (peak time is May and June). ⊠ *Jiefang Bei Lu* ⌦ *Y5* ☉ *Daily 8:30 AM–11 PM.*

★ **❿ Tomb of the Southern Yue Kings** (Nan Yue Wang Mu). Until quite recently only specialist historians realized that Guangzhou had once been a royal capital. In 1983 bulldozers clearing ground to build the China Hotel uncovered the intact tomb of Emperor Wen Di, who ruled Nan Yue (southern China) from 137 BC to 122 BC. The tomb was faithfully restored and its treasures placed in the adjoining **Nan Yue Museum.**

The tomb contained the skeletons of the king and 15 courtiers—guards, cooks, concubines, and a musician—who were buried alive to attend him in death. Also buried were several thousand funerary objects, clearly designed to show off the extraordinary accomplishments of the southern empire. Now attractively displayed in the museum, with intelligent labeling in Chinese and English, they include jade armor, gem-encrusted swords and crossbows, gold jewelry, lacquer boxes, pearl pillows, 139 pi-discs used in pottery, 1,000 bronze and iron cooking pots, and an orchestra of bronze and stone chimes that are still in tune.

The tomb itself—built entirely of stone slabs—is behind the museum and is remarkable for its compact size. Divided into two parts, it is 66 feet deep, 40 feet wide, and 35 feet long. The emperor was buried in the central chamber, while six smaller adjoining rooms were packed from floor to ceiling with the funeral objects and the courtiers.

On the second floor an incomparable collection of 200 ceramic pillows—from the Tang, Song, Jin, and Yuan dynasties—was donated by Hong Kong industrialist Yeung Wing Tak and his wife. ⊠ *867 Jiefang Bei Lu* ☏ *Y12* ☉ *Daily 9:30–5:30.*

★ ▶ ☺ ❽ **Yuexiu Park** (Yuexiu Gongyuan). To take a break from business or get away from the bustle, residents and visitors alike adjourn to Yuexiu Park in the heart of town. The park's wide range of attractions and facilities covers 247 acres and includes Yuexiu Hill and six hillocks, landscaped gardens, man-made lakes, and recreational areas. Kids can enjoy fish-feeding ponds and playgrounds, while adults can appreciate the bamboo garden or exercise in the municipal gym.

The best-known sight in Yuexiu Park is the **Five Rams Statue** (Wuyang Suxiang), which celebrates the legend of the five celestials who came to Guangzhou riding on goats to bring grains to the people. Today Guangzhou families take each other's photo in front of the statue before setting off to enjoy the park. They hire boats on the three man-made lakes, which contain islands also accessible by humpbacked bridges, or they stroll along paths lined with flowering bushes, bamboo groves, and small forests of pine, cypress, and kapok.

For a different kind of enjoyment, the park has a stadium for soccer matches and other sports, a Journey to the West theme park (with a giant wooden cockerel that crows at the entrance), and a children's playground with fairground rides. ⊠ *Jiefang Bei Lu* ☏ *Y5* ☉ *Daily 6 AM–9 PM.*

Revolutionary Guangzhou

In the center of the city are memorials to people who changed Chinese history in the 20th century, using Guangzhou as a base of operations. The most famous were local boy Dr. Sun Yat-sen, who led the overthrow of the Qing Dynasty, and Communist Party founders Mao Zedong and Zhou Enlai. There were many others, among them thousands who died in the struggles. All are recalled in different ways.

a good walk

Start with a taxi ride to the **Sun Yat-sen Memorial Hall** ⑫ ▶, visit the hall and its grounds, then walk or take a taxi to the **Peasant Movement Institute** ⑬ to recapture the days when youthful revolutionaries Mao and Zhou taught their followers how to organize a peasant revolt. Walk on to the **Memorial Garden for the Martyrs** ⑭ and Revolutionary Museum and finish with a cab ride to the **Mausoleum of the 72 Martyrs** ⑮.

Timing. This itinerary should take three to four hours.

What to See

⑮ Mausoleum of the 72 Martyrs (Huanghua Gang Qishi'er Lieshi Mu). In a prelude to the successful revolution of 1911 a group of 88 revolutionaries staged the Guangzhou armed uprising, only to be defeated and executed by the authorities. Of those killed, 72 were buried here. Their memorial, built in 1918, incorporates a mixture of international symbols of freedom and democracy, including replicas of the Statue of Liberty. ⊠ *Xianlie Zhong Lu* 🚇 *Y8* ⊙ *Daily 6 AM–8:30 PM.*

⑭ Memorial Garden for the Martyrs (Lieshi Lingyuan). Built in 1957, this garden has been planted around a tumulus that contains the remains of 5,000 revolutionaries killed in the 1927 destruction of the Guangzhou Commune by the Nationalists. This was the execution site of many victims. On the grounds is the **Revolutionary Museum,** which displays pictures and memorabilia of Guangdong's 20th-century rebellions. ⊠ *Zhongshan San Lu* 🚇 *Y3* ⊙ *Daily 6 AM–9 PM.*

⑬ Peasant Movement Institute (Nongmin Yundong Jiangxi Suo). Today the atmosphere of the institute—with its quiet courtyards and empty cells—recalls its origin as a 14th-century Confucian temple, but it doesn't take long to detect the ghostly presence of the young idealists who came here in the early 1920s to learn how to create a new China based on equality and justice.

The institute was established in 1924 by some of the founders of the Chinese Communist Party, who had set up a Guangzhou Commune modeled on the 19th-century Parisian example. Young people came from all over the country to listen to party leaders. In 1926 Mao Zedong became director of the school, and Zhou Enlai was a staff member. They and their colleagues lectured on "the problem of the Chinese peasantry," "rural education," and geography to students who were then sent to the countryside to educate the peasants.

The venture proved short-lived, as it soon became obvious that the Nationalists under Chiang Kai-shek were planning to drive the Communists from the city. The institute was closed in late 1927, just before the Commune was crushed and 5,000 revolutionaries killed. In 1953 the Beijing government restored the buildings and made them a museum. The result is very evocative. The main lecture hall, with desks arranged in front of a blackboard, looks as if the students might return any minute. Instead they can be seen in photographs displayed along the corridors: keen young men and women, bright-eyed with expectation, but in most cases doomed. As the captions reveal, a majority were captured and killed by the Nationalists. As for their leader, Mao is recalled in a re-creation of his room: a simple cell with a metal-frame bed, desk, and bookcase. ⊠ *42 Zhongshan Si Lu* 🚇 *Y2* ⊙ *Daily 10–6.*

▶ ⑫ Sun Yat-sen Memorial Hall (Sun Zhongshan Jinian Tang). By the end of the 19th century the Qing Dynasty was in its last throes. The moribund court and its corrupt mandarins were powerless to control the Westerners who had taken over much of China's trade or the warlords who kept the peasantry in feudal misery. Dissent was widespread, but it was

Guangzhou that became a center for rebellion. The leader was Sun Yat-sen, a young doctor from a village in the Pearl River delta who had studied in Honolulu and graduated from Hong Kong's medical college. Inspired by democratic ideals, he set up the Revive China Society in Guangzhou in 1892 and petitioned the emperor, demanding equality and justice. In return, a price was put on his head, and he was forced to spend the next years as an exile in Japan, the United States, and Europe.

Everywhere he went he gathered supporters and funds for a revolution, which finally took place in 1911, when he returned to Guangzhou to be proclaimed "Father of the Revolution" and provisional president. However, Dr. Sun was no politician and soon lost Nationalist leadership to Chiang Kai-shek. He spent his last years in Shanghai and died in Beijing in 1925, but he remains a favorite son of Guangzhou.

Dr. Sun's Memorial Hall is a handsome pavilion that stands in an attractively landscaped garden behind a bronze statue of the leader. Built in 1929–31 with funds mostly from overseas Chinese, the building is a classic octagon, with sweeping roofs of blue tiles over carved wooden eaves and verandas of red-lacquer columns. Inside is an auditorium with seating for 5,000 and a stage for plays, concerts, and ceremonial occasions. ⊠ *Dongfeng Zhong Lu* 🎫 *Y10* ⊙ *Daily 8–5:30.*

Airport Area

One of the newest entertainments of Guangzhou is a reproduction film studio where you can get a close-up view of the action taken from kung fu and Shanghai gangster films. The studio is in the northern suburbs, next to Baiyun Airport. You can reach it by taxi in 10 minutes from the China Hotel.

🕐 ⑯ **Oriental Studio 2000.** Modeled on Hollywood's Universal Studios, this entertainment complex has two movie sets dedicated to the best-known genres of Chinese moviemaking: the kung fu epic and the good old bad days of Shanghai. The "Shanghai in the Roaring '30s" set has a chorus line of scantily clad girls, slick-haired gangsters, motorcycles, and machine guns. The "traditional Chinese courtyard" set, with stables and workshops, features a battle between "lion" armies whose warriors leap high into the air and perform breathtaking acrobatics.

The studio opened in 1996 in the **Dongfang Amusement Park** (Dong Fang Leyuan). The two shows utilize all the equipment to be found in local film studios, so there are overhead wires for "flying," facades that "collapse," mats that become springboards, and blowers to provide a snowfall or smoke. The introductions are in Chinese, and there's no program, but that does nothing to detract from this totally visual experience. The shows last 15 minutes, with three performances a day.

Along with the sets, the park has restaurants, some modeled on old films, serving Chinese and Western food; shopping arcades with souvenirs; staged folk dancing; acrobatics; and street performances by conjurers, magicians, and *qi gong* (traditional Chinese exercise said to release the inner power or *qi* of the spirit) experts. In the main part of the vast amusement park there are a huge Ferris wheel, a roller coaster, and other fairground rides, plus a lake with pleasure boats. ⊠ *Dajing Zhonglu in Dong Fang Leyuan* ☎ *020/8662–8628 Ext. 316* 🎫 *Y80* ⊘ *Daily 9–5.*

Tianhe District & Eastern Suburbs

The Tianhe District is Guangzhou's new designated business and up-market residential area. It is the site of the new Guangzhou East Railway Station, the terminus for Hong Kong trains, a world-class sports stadium, and a growing number of office/apartment skyscrapers.

Take a taxi to the Guangzhou East Railway Station, look inside, and from here stroll around **Tianhe** ⑰ ▶. See the handsome sports stadium and some attractive modern statuary, then take a look at the eclectic architecture of the city's newest skyscrapers, which combine Doric-column courtyards, neo-Gothic archways, colored glass–clad facades, and traditional Chinese roofs. Drop by the multistory bookshop and the newest shopping arcades of Teem Plaza.

Timing. An hour and a half is enough to see the highlights of Tianhe, unless there is a special event in the stadium.

What to See

▶ ⑰ **Tianhe,** Guangzhou's bright new business area, bristles with skyscrapers. Among the buildings is the 80-story **GITIC Plaza** which soars 1,300 feet and is China's second-tallest building. Tianhe's new railway station, **Guangzhou East Railway Station** (⊠ Linhe Lu), is light, airy, and very spacious, with a vast entrance hall.

Tianhe is designed to be a hub of sports activity. The two outdoor and indoor arenas of the **Tianhe Stadium Complex** (⊠ Huanshi Dong Lu, East Guangzhou) are equipped for international soccer matches, track and field, and athletics competitions, as well as pop concerts and large-scale ceremonies. Around the stadiums is a pleasant landscaped park, with outdoor cafés and tree-shaded benches. The park surrounding the complex also contains a bowling center with 38 lanes and video games.

Already the upmarket district is drawing shoppers. The **Guangzhou Book Center** (⊠ Huanshi Dong Lu, East Guangzhou ☎ 020/8759–4208) has seven floors with space for books on every subject (including some bargain-priced art books in English), from software to literature. Across the street is **Teem Plaza,** a vast complex of shops and supermarkets.

Where to Eat

The biggest dining problem in Guangzhou is choosing from the extraordinary range of restaurants (some 150,000 at last estimate). The following selection includes tried-and-true favorites for Chinese and Western meals. Unless specified otherwise, all restaurants are open daily for lunch and dinner, with most Chinese establishments also serving a traditional breakfast of rice porridge and dim sum snacks. Reservations are usually not necessary except in Western restaurants during the fair periods. Chinese banquets are part of all business deals here; you can organize a meal for local colleagues by contacting the restaurant at least a day in advance and either choosing the menu (if you're very familiar

ON THE MENU

THE INCREDIBLY DIVERSE and ingenious Cantonese cuisine has developed from both abundance and scarcity. Guangdong province has some of the most fertile land in China, thanks to silt brought down by the Pearl River into its extensive delta. The area has two crops of rice per year, vegetable and animal farms, and a rich supply of seafood. The Cantonese are infamous for their creative uses of all parts of an animal. Nothing is spared or wasted.

One famous cuisine from the region is dim sum (or "yum cha," in Cantonese dialect). Dim sum literally means "drink tea," and consists of small appetizers served with a pot of tea. Usually, having dim sum is a social event, where friends and family gather together to chat and recap the week's events. Popular dishes are shrimp dumplings, barbecue pork spareribs, and steamed buns filled with pork or vegetables. More adventurous

souls may want to try chicken feet or pork innards.

Guangdong province is also home to **Chiu Chow cuisine.** Many Chiu Chow dishes are fried, including such favorites as chicken wings stuffed with glutinous rice, shrimp, and mushrooms or xinxing beef balls—a mixture of beef, shrimp, and fish. Chiu Chow often combines sweet and salty tastes. One dish wraps the yolk of a salted duck egg with sweetened rice in thin sheets of bean curd. Another dish is cooked goose with mango, served with garlic and vinegar. No account of Chiu Chow cuisine would be complete without a mention of Iron Buddha tea, also known as kungfu tea because of its strength. The oolong is brewed three times in an elaborate ceremony and served in tiny white bowls. It is tossed back in one gulp for full effect.

with banquet dishes) or specifying the number of guests—to fill each table with 12—and price range and leaving it in the restaurant's experienced hands.

$$$$ ✕**Chiu Chou City.** One of the best places for authentic food from the Shantou area is this restaurant in the Landmark Canton hotel. It has a large main room and several private rooms, which are invariably packed for lunch and dinner. The house special is Chiu Chou goose, served as cold cuts or cooked in its own blood and dipped into a sauce of white vinegar and chopped garlic. ⊠ *Landmark Canton hotel, 8 Qiao Guang Lu, Colonial Canton* ☎ *020/8335–5988* ▬ *AE, DC, MC, V.*

$$$$ ✕**Connoisseur.** The Garden Hotel's premier restaurant feels like Regency France with its arched columns with gilded capitals, gold-framed mirrors, lustrous drapes, and immaculate table settings. The resident French chef specializes in lamb and steak dishes. ⊠ *Garden Hotel, 368 Huanshi Dong Lu, 3rd fl., Ancestral Guangzhou* ☎ *020/8333–8989 Ext. 3964* ▬ *AE, DC, MC, V* ☉ *No lunch.*

$$$$ ✕**The Roof.** The China Hotel's fine-dining restaurant sits in understated splendor on the 18th floor, with panoramic views of Guangzhou. The menu offers seasonal specialties and classic staples, such as saddle of

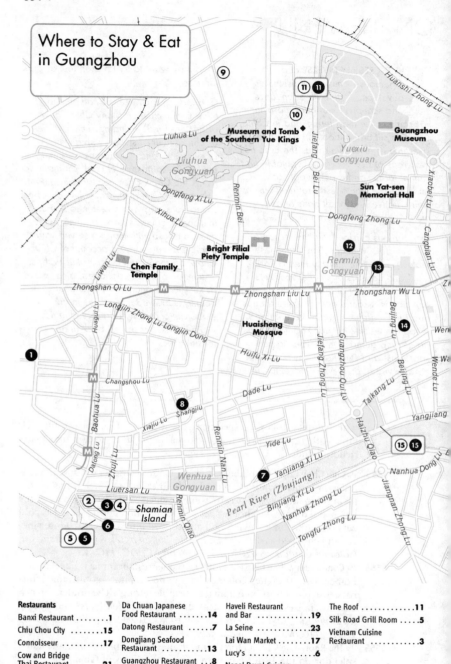

Where to Stay & Eat
in Guangzhou

Restaurants ▼

Banxi Restaurant	1
Chiu Chou City	15
Connoisseur	17
Cow and Bridge Thai Restaurant	21
Da Chuan Japanese Food Restaurant	14
Datong Restaurant	7
Dongjiang Seafood Restaurant	13
Guangzhou Restaurant	8
Haveli Restaurant and Bar	19
La Seine	23
Lai Wan Market	17
Lucy's	6
Nepal Royal Cuisine Restaurant and Bar	12
The Roof	11
Silk Road Grill Room	5
Vietnam Cuisine Restaurant	3

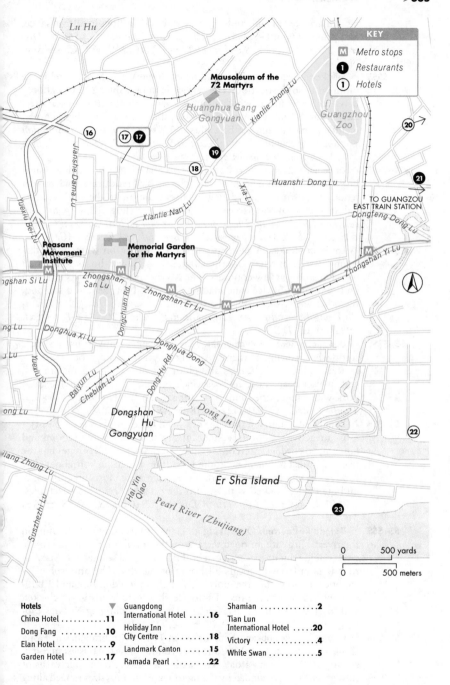

KEY

- Ⓜ Metro stops
- ❶ Restaurants
- ① Hotels

Lu Hu

Mausoleum of the 72 Martyrs

Huanghua Gang Gongyuan

Xianlie Zhong Lu

Guangzhou Zoo

⑳ →

⑯

⑰ ❶⑰

⑲

⑱

Jianshe Dama Lu

Huanshi Dong Lu

Xia Lu

㉑

TO GUANGZOU EAST TRAIN STATION

Yuexiu Bei Lu

Xianlie Nan Lu

Dongfeng Dong Lu

Peasant Movement Institute

Memorial Garden for the Martyrs

Ⓜ

ngshan Si Lu

Zhongshan San Lu

Ⓜ

Zhongshan Er Lu

Ⓜ

Ⓜ

Ⓜ

Zhongshan Yi Lu

Dongchuan Rd.

ng Lu

Donghua Xi Lu

Yuexiu Lu

Bayun Lu

Chebian Lu

Donghua Dong

Dong Hu Rd.

Dongshan Hu Gongyuan

Dong Lu

㉒

iang Zhong Lu

Suszhezhi Lu

Hai Yin Qiao

Er Sha Island

㉓

Pearl River (Zhujiang)

| 0 | 500 yards |
| 0 | 500 meters |

Hotels ▼

China Hotel	**11**
Dong Fang	**10**
Elan Hotel	**9**
Garden Hotel	**17**
Guangdong International Hotel	**16**
Holiday Inn City Centre	**18**
Landmark Canton	**15**
Ramada Pearl	**22**
Shamian	**2**
Tian Lun International Hotel	**20**
Victory	**4**
White Swan	**5**

lamb marinated in mint and yogurt, fettuccine, scallops in saffron sauce, and prime cuts of U.S. beef. ⊠ *China Hotel, Liuhua Lu, Station District* ☎ *020/8666–6888 Ext. 71892* ▤ *AE, DC, MC, V* ⊗ *Closed Sun. No lunch.*

$$$$ ✕ **Silk Road Grill Room.** This grill room in the White Swan hotel is the ultimate in sophistication. The service is impeccable. You can choose between the set menu, which includes appetizer, cold dish, soup, entrée, dessert, and drink (excluding wine), and à la carte. Highlight entrées include prime rib and sea bass fillet. ⊠ *White Swan hotel, Yi Shamian Lu, Shamian Island, Colonial Canton* ☎ *020/8188–6968* ▤ *AE, DC, MC, V* ⌂ *Reservations essential* ⊗ *No lunch.*

$$$–$$$$ ✕ **La Seine.** This upscale restaurant on Er Sha Island offers a daily lunch
Fodor'sChoice buffet. Dinner highlights include all the classic French fare, such as beef
★ tenderloin, escargot, and foie gras. Located close to the city's concert hall it is an ideal place to eat before or after a show. ⊠ *Xinghai Concert Hall, 33 Qing Bo Lu, ground fl., Er Sha Island, Colonial Canton* ☎ *020/8735–2531* ⌂ *Reservations essential* ▤ *AE, DC, MC, V.*

$$$–$$$$ ✕ **Lai Wan Market.** A re-creation of the old Canton waterfront, this theme restaurant has booths shaped like flower boats and small wooden stools at low counters. The Market is known for its dim sum and two kinds of rice, one made with pork, beef, fish, and seafood, the other with fish, beef, and pork liver. ⊠ *Garden Hotel, 368 Huanshi Dong Lu, 2nd fl., Ancestral Guangzhou* ☎ *020/8333–8989 Ext. 3922* ▤ *AE, DC, MC, V.*

$$–$$$$ ✕ **Dongjiang Seafood Restaurant.** This city-center stalwart has a simple setting but a brilliant menu. Among the favorites are braised duck stuffed with eight delicacies and glutinous rice, stuffed giant prawns, crab in black bean sauce, salt-roast chicken, stuffed bean curd, and steamed pork with salted, dried mustard cabbage. ⊠ *276 Huanshi Zhong Lu, Tianhe District* ☎ *020/8322–9188* ▤ *AE, DC, MC, V.*

$$–$$$ ✕ **Banxi Restaurant.** On the edge of Liwan Lake, this is one of the city's most attractive traditional restaurants. Its series of teahouse rooms and landscaped gardens interconnected by zigzag paths and bridges has the feel of a Taoist temple. One room is built on a floating houseboat. The food is as tasty as it looks, with dishes such as scallop and crab soup, and quail eggs cooked with shrimp roe on a bed of green vegetables. ⊠ *151 Longjin Xi Lu, Station District* ☎ *020/8181–5718* ▤ *AE, MC, V.*

$$–$$$ ✕ **Datong Restaurant.** Occupying all eight stories of an old building on the riverfront, with an open terrace on the top floor, this is one of the city's veteran dining places. It can be difficult to find seating as the restaurant is popular with locals all hours of the day. The atmosphere is chaotic and noisy, but the morning and afternoon dim sum and 1,000-dish menu is worth the fuss. Famous dishes include crisp-skin chicken and roasted Xishi duck. ⊠ *Nanfang Dasha, 63 Yanjiang Xi Lu, Colonial Canton* ☎ *020/8188–8988* ▤ *AE, DC, MC, V.*

$$–$$$ ✕ **Guangzhou Restaurant.** Established in 1936, with branches in Hong Kong and Los Angeles, this Cantonese restaurant is the busiest in town, serving 10,000 diners a day. The setting is classic, with courtyards of flowery bushes surrounded by dining rooms of various sizes ranged along arcaded corridors. The house specialties are abalone sprinkled with 24-carat gold flakes; Eight Treasures—including game, chicken, ham, and mushrooms—served in winter melons carved to make a bowl; duck feet stuffed with shrimp; and roast sliced goose. ⊠ *2 Wenchang Nan Lu, Ancestral Guangzhou* ☎ *020/8138–0439* ⊟ *AE, DC, MC, V.*

$–$$ ✕ **Cow and Bridge Thai Restaurant.** Walking into this restaurant, the first thing you will notice is the sleek bar and the handsome gold Thai writing on the walls. The clientele is white collar, twenty- to thirtysomethings. The menu impresses with over 300 selections, including *tom yum* (spicy Thai soup), seafood, curries, and fresh ice-blended juices. The staff isn't particularly helpful, but for the price, this restaurant is a good value. ⊠ *Xianglong Huayuan, 175–181 Tianhe Bei Rd., 2nd fl., Tianhe District* ☎ *020/8525–0693* 📠 *020/8525–0693* ⊟ *No credit cards.*

$–$$ ✕ **Haveli Restaurant and Bar.** This inexpensive Indian restaurant near the Holiday Inn is a favorite of Guangzhou's sizable South Asian community, thanks to its tree-shaded garden and great tandoor-oven serving up chicken, king prawn, and lamb specialties. ⊠ *2 Aiguo Lu, opposite Holiday Inn, Ancestral Guangzhou* ☎ *020/8359–4533* ⊟ *No credit cards.*

$–$$ ✕ **Lucy's.** Shamian Island's most eclectic restaurant has a good mix of dishes at very reasonable prices. The main menu lists Asian curries, mixed grills, Tex-Mex dishes, fish-and-chips, noodles, burgers, sandwiches, and much more. There is an outdoor dining area and take-out service. ⊠ *3 Shamian Nan Jie, Shamian, Colonial Canton* ☎ *020/8121–5106* ⊟ *No credit cards.*

$ ✕ **Da Chuan Japanese Food Restaurant.** This local eatery is conveniently located in a busy shopping area on Beijing Road. Prices are much lower than what you would pay at a five-star hotel restaurant, and the quality of the sashimi shows it. The best value is a sushi set meal, or you can dive into à la carte dishes plucked straight off the rotating sushi bar. ⊠ *294 Beijing Rd., 4th fl., Colonial Canton* ☎ *020/8319–0283* ⊟ *No credit cards.*

$ ✕ **Nepal Royal Cuisine Restaurant and Bar.** Next to the People's Park is this colorful restaurant serving traditional Nepalese food. The restaurant is tastefully decorated with Nepali art and press clippings. Entrées include Himalayan rabbit with rice, and curry lamb chops. There is also a wide selection of coffee drinks. ⊠ *21 Lianxin Lu, Ancestral Guangzhou* ☎ *020/8338–3409* ⊟ *No credit cards.*

¢–$ ✕ **Vietnam Cuisine Restaurant.** This small and elegantly decorated eatery near the Victory hotel on Shamian Island is popular with resident expatriates due to its low prices, helpful English-speaking staff, and fresh food. Recommended dishes include raw beef noodle soup (*pho*), Vietnamese spring rolls, and curry beef. ⊠ *54 Shamian Lu, next to Victory hotel, Colonial Canton* ☎ *020/8121–5795* ⊟ *AE, MC, V.*

Where to Stay

The purpose of your visit to Guangzhou is likely to determine your choice of hotel. Businesspeople increasingly choose the upcoming Tianhe District, close to Guangzhou East Railway Station and the city's growing thicket of office skyscrapers. Tourists are more likely to choose a hotel on beautiful Shamian Island at the heart of the city, but away from the hubbub. Moving around the city is much easier than in recent years. Recently completed expressways and a growing underground train system have vastly reduced cross-city travel time.

$$–$$$$ 🏨 **China Hotel.** This hotel is part of a multicomplex that includes office and apartment blocks, a shopping mall, and restaurants. Opposite the Trade Fair Exhibition Hall—with bridge links over the road—the hotel is a favorite of fair participants and year-round business travelers. The 66-room Executive Floor has spacious private lounges. In the basement is Catwalk, an entertainment center with bar, disco, and karaoke areas. ⊠ *Liuhua Lu, Station District, 510015* ☎ *020/8666–6888* 🖷 *020/8667–7014* 🛏 *1,013 rooms, 74 suites* 🍴 *4 restaurants, tennis court, pool, gym, nightclub, shops, business services, meeting room* ▤ *AE, DC, MC, V.*

$$–$$$$ 🏨 **Holiday Inn City Centre.** Next to the Guangzhou World Trade Center, the hotel is a good, reliable place to stay for business travelers. You can expect typical Holiday Inn management and the standard plethora of restaurants. One new addition is the add-on service for women travelers: for an added Y80, the room includes extras such as cushions and essence oil. For an additional Y150 you can enjoy in-room massages. Discounts of 50% are the norm during the off-season. ⊠ *28 Guangming Lu, Overseas Chinese Village, Huanshi Dong Lu, Ancestral Guangzhou, 510095* ☎ *020/6128–6868* 🖷 *020/8775–3126* 🛏 *430 rooms, 38 suites* 🍴 *4 restaurants, pool, gym, lounge, cinema, business services, meeting rooms, car rental, travel services* ▤ *AE, DC, MC, V* ⊕ *www.guangzhou.holiday-inn.com.*

$$–$$$$ 🏨 **White Swan.** Built in 1983, China's first joint-venture international hotel occupies a marvelous site on historic Shamian Island beside the Pearl River. The huge luxury complex has landscaped gardens, two pools, a jogging track, and a separate gym and spa. Its restaurants are second to none; the windows of the elegant lobby bar and coffee shop frame the panorama of river traffic. All the rooms have been fitted with broadband Internet connection. Even if you don't stay here, visit the lobby and take a look at the spectacular indoor waterfall. ⊠ *Yi Shamian Lu, Shamian Island, Colonial Canton, 510133* ☎ *020/8188–6968, 852/2524–0192 in Hong Kong* 🖷 *020/8186–1188, 852/2877–0811 in Hong Kong* ⊕ *www.whiteswanhotel.com* 🛏 *843 rooms, 92 suites* 🍴 *9 restaurants, 2 pools, gym, bar, shops, business services, meeting rooms, travel services* ▤ *AE, DC, MC, V.*

$$–$$$ 🏨 **Garden Hotel.** In the northern business suburbs, this huge, aging hotel is famous for its spectacular garden that includes an artificial hill, a waterfall, and pavilions. The cavernous lobby, decorated with enormous murals, has a bar lounge set in an ornamental pool. Great restaurants and an Irish-style pub round out the offerings. ⊠ *368 Huanshi Dong Lu, Ancestral Guangzhou, 510064* ☎ *020/8333–8989* 🖷 *020/8335–0467* 🛏 *1,028 rooms, 63 suites* 🍴 *7 restaurants, 2 tennis courts, pool, gym, squash, lounge, pub, shops, business services, convention center* ▤ *AE, DC, MC, V* ⊕ *www.thegardenhotel.com.cn.*

$–$$$ 🏨 **Guangdong International Hotel.** Part of a spectacular complex, the hotel occupies the top floors of an 80-story tower, along with restaurants, banquet halls, and a large shopping mall with fashion boutiques. There are also extensive recreation facilities in an indoor-outdoor gym. Discounts of up to 50% are the norm in the off-season. ⊠ *339 Huanshi Dong Lu, Ancestral Guangzhou, 510098* ☎ *020/8331–1888* 🖷 *020/8331–3490* 🖙 *603 rooms, 200 suites* ⌂ *3 restaurants, tennis court, pool, gym, bar, shops, business services* ▤ *AE, DC, MC, V.*

$–$$ 🏨 **Dong Fang.** Across from Liuhua Park and the trade fair headquarters, this vast luxury complex is built around a 22½-acre garden with pavilions, carp-filled pools, rock gardens, and trees. Amenities include a large fitness club and complete spa. The shopping concourse holds an interesting selection of Chinese antiques and carpets. The hotel has recently added a 86,000-square-foot convention center. Discounts of up to 30% are not unheard of. ⊠ *120 Liuhua Lu, Station District, 510016* ☎ *020/8666–9900, 852/2528–0555 in Hong Kong* 🖷 *020/8666–2775, 852/2520–0991 in Hong Kong* ⊕ *www.dongfanghotel-gz.com* 🖙 *772 rooms, 114 suites* ⌂ *6 restaurants, gym, hair salon, spa, recreation room, shops, business services, meeting room* ▤ *AE, DC, MC, V.*

¢–$ 🏨 **Landmark Canton.** Towering above Haizhu Square and the main bridge across the river, this hotel is in the heart of central Guangzhou. It is managed by China Travel Service of Hong Kong and gets much of its business from there. Most of the guest rooms have great views of the river or city. ⊠ *8 Qiao Guang Lu, Colonial Canton, 510115* ☎ *020/ 8335–5988* 🖷 *020/8333–6197* 🖙 *688 rooms, 103 suites* ⌂ *3 restaurants, pool, gym, bar, dance club, shops, business services, meeting room* ▤ *AE, DC, MC, V.*

¢–$ 🏨 **Ramada Pearl.** Located 10 minutes from Guangzhou East Railway Station, this international hotel on the Pearl River has interesting views of the river traffic, a two-story gym, and a children's playground. Ask for a room overlooking the river. ⊠ *9 Ming Yue Yi Lu, Colonial Canton, 510600* ☎ *020/8737–2988* 🖷 *020/8737–7481* 🖙 *323 rooms, 42 suites* ⌂ *3 restaurants, tennis court, 2 pools, gym, pub, business services, meeting rooms* ▤ *AE, DC, MC, V.*

¢–$ 🏨 **Tian Lun International Hotel.** Located next to Guangzhou East Railway Station, this business hotel opened in 2003 and offers large luxury rooms with a sleek edge. The colors are kept to soft blacks, grays, and beige. The buffet in the second-floor café is beautifully arranged around a centerpiece of coral, and the tall ceilings lend an air of sophistication. Many rooms have a great view of the train concourse garden. Don't worry: outside traffic noise does not permeate into the rooms. ⊠ *172 Linhe Lu Central, Tianhe District, 510610* ☎ *020/ 8393–6388* 🖷 *020/3882–4162* ⊕ *www.tianlun-hotel.com* 🖙 *400 rooms, 8 suites, 20 apartment units* ⌂ *2 restaurants, lounge, business services* ▤ *AE, DC, MC, V.*

¢–$ 🏨 **Victory.** This hotel on Shamian Island has two wings, both originally
FodorsChoice colonial guesthouses that have been superbly renovated. The main
★ building has a pink-and-white facade, an imposing portico, and twin domes on the roof, where you will also find the pool. Nevertheless, it is basically for budget travelers, with small rooms and inexpensive dining rooms. The setting among restored old mansions is priceless. ⊠ *53 Yi Shamian Lu, Shamian Island, Colonial Canton, 510130* ☎ *020/ 8121–6688* 🖷 *020/8121–9889* ⊕ *www.gd-victory-hotel.com* 🖙 *328*

rooms ∴*4 restaurants, pool, gym, business services, meeting rooms* *AE, DC, MC, V.*

¢ ☐ **Elan Hotel.** If you like cheap, funky, and hip little hotels, this is the spot for you. In Guangzhou's first attempt at a boutique hotel, the Elan offers compact Ikea-inspired rooms with bold color palettes and clean lines. Celine Dion muzak wafting through the hallways can be an annoyance, but the warm, cozy bed guarantees restful sleep. The small first-floor restaurant serves cheap Northeast Chinese food that is as authentic and tasty as the cuisine gets but the service is patchy. ✉ *32 Zhan Qian Heng Rd., Station District, 510010* ✆*020/8622–1788* *020/8622–3376* ⊕ *www.hotel-elan.com* ↪ *76 rooms, 8 suites* ∴ *Restaurant, business services; no a/c*  *AE, DC, MC, V.*

¢ ☐ **Shamian.** This is a great hotel for tourists on a budget. Its rooms are a little spartan and the lobby cramped, but it is clean and friendly and the location—right in the middle of Shamian Island—is second to none. ✉ *52 Shamian Nan Jie, Shamian Island, 510130* ✆ *020/8121–8288*  *020/8121–8628* ⊕ *www.gdshamianhotel.com* ↪ *58 rooms, 20 suites*  *No credit cards.*

Nightlife & the Arts

The Arts

Cantonese opera is a traditional form of art, which can still be enjoyed today in Guangzhou theaters. If this option does not suit your fancy, try catching a Western classical music concert or a live puppet show. Comic-dialogue shows and ballets are also evening entertainment options. Please check the monthly *That's Guangzhou* magazine, under Music and Stage Events, or call the following theaters for schedules. Ticket prices for Cantonese opera range from Y15 to Y50. Prices for Western classical concerts are a little higher, ranging from Y80 to Y380.

Friendship Theatre (✉ 698 Ren Min Bei Lu ✆ 020/8666–8991) is host to song and dance troupes, ballets, and Cantonese opera. Check the schedule of the **Nan Fang Theatre** (✉ 80 Jiao Yu Lu ✆ 020/8335–2871) if you want to see comedy or the ubiquitous Cantonese opera. **Guang Ming Theatre** (✉ 293 Nan Hua Zhong Lu ✆ 020/8449–9721) is another good place to catch live Cantonese opera. **Guangdong Puppet Art Centre** (✉ 21 Fenyuan St. ✆ 020/8431–0227) hosts live puppet shows every Saturday and Sunday at 10:30 AM and 3. **Xinghai Concert Hall** (✉ 33 Qing Bo Lu, Er Sha Island ✆ 020/8735–2222 Ext. 312 for English ⊕ www.concerthall.com.cn) is a good place to catch classical, both Western- and Asian-style, music concerts. Check the schedule for international orchestras that come through town.

Nightlife

No longer the preserve of businessmen and rented karaoke "companions," Guangzhou's nightlife is finally flourishing. These days Western-style clubs vie for an increasingly hip and knowledgeable crowd and invest serious money on international DJs and design. Pubs, sports bars, coffee shops, and cafés have also sprung up. Bars tend to stay open until 2 AM; clubs continue to 5 AM.

CANTONESE OPERA

A FORM OF CHINESE OPERA *began as early as the mid-16th century, as evidenced from the Ten Thousand Blessings Stage (Wanfutai) in Foshan. Built in 1658, it is the oldest surviving wooden stage in China. In the early 18th century one of the great men of Chinese theater, Master Zhang, moved to Foshan from the capital and set about establishing a distinctive Cantonese operatic tradition.*

The performers belonged to acting families, learning by example and tradition all the rules of the stage. The music, adapted from folk melodies, was sung according to the role. Everyone in the audience knew the plots, which could be from classics such as Journey to the West, the Romance of Three Kingdoms, Dream of the Red Chamber, or any of the action-packed epics of the Qing Dynasty. It wasn't what was being sung but rather how it was sung that mattered, so actors

and actresses had to put all their energy into a performance without breaking traditional rules.

Cantonese audiences remain dedicated, as can be seen at regular evening opera performances in Guangzhou's Culture Park. For the uninitiated, however, the art form needs some preparation. The music sounds cacophonous to Western ears, and the stylized movements seem strange at first. The costumes are brilliant and fantastic. Makeup is equally exotic, with colors to emphasize the character of the role. White means sinister, green cruel, and black obedient; yellow symbolizes nobility and purple royalty.

It is very much up to the actors to hold the stage. Cantonese audiences do not particularly like to sit in rapt attention, preferring to stroll around, chat with friends, or have a snack.

BARS All the leading hotels have bars, where it's pleasant to relax after a hard day's work or sightseeing. **Bai e Dan** (⊠ South of Shamian Island, across the Pearl River) is the newest hip street for decent but indistinct bars. The popular **Café Lounge** (⊠ China Hotel, lobby ☎ 020/8666–6888) has big comfortable bar stools, quiet tables for two, live music on weekends, and a fine selection of cigars. The big attraction of the **Hare & Moon** (⊠ White Swan hotel, Yi Shamian Lu, Shamian Island ☎ 020/8188–6968) is the panorama of the Pearl River as it flows past the picture windows.

DANCE CLUBS **Baby Face** (⊠ 83 Changdi Da Ma Lu ☎ 020/8335–5771 ⊟ No credit cards ⊠ Y20) is where the stylish go to strike a pose. It fills up quickly on weekends with most tables reserved. Arrive early and be prepared to spend. **Club Tang** (⊠ 1 Jianshe Liu Ma Lu ☎ 020/8384–1638 ⊟ No credit cards ⊠ Y40) has a stylish club lounge on the first floor and a karaoke maze upstairs. Bottle-spinning bartenders serve up beers at Y45 and strong Long Island ice teas for Y38. **F4** (⊠ TP Plaza, 109 Linhua Lu, 1st fl. ☎ 020/8666–8070 ⊟ No credit cards ⊠ Y30) is where the young and beautiful spend their time under spotlights. A bottle of Jack Daniels is Y600 (green tea to mix is extra), and to sit at a table you need to drop a minimum of Y1,200. A live band takes the stage between sets from resident and international DJs.

PUBS   **Café Elles** (✉ Huaxin Dasha, 2 Shuiyin Lu, 2nd fl. ☎ 020/8761–2939) caters to French expatriates and Francophiles with French music and food and a small dance floor.

The **Hard Rock Café** (✉ China Hotel, basement ☎ 020/8666–6888 Ext. 2050) has Elton John's trousers, Tina Turner's black dress, and stained-glass pictures of rock icons such as John Lennon and Michael Jackson; there's live and taped rock music and a choice of hamburgers and Chinese dishes.

Opened in 1996 by a Canadian-Chinese, **Kathleen's** (✉ 60 Taojin Lu ☎ 020/8359–8045) is a popular expatriate meeting point and where you find can often find out what's going on in Guangzhou.

L'Africain (✉ Zi Dong Hua Bldg., 707 Dongfeng Zhong Lu, 2nd fl. ☎ 020/8762–3336) is the place for late-night dancing to reggae, African, Spanish, and American pop music.

1920 Restaurant (✉ 183 Yanjiang Zhong Lu ☎ 020/8333–6156 ▤ No credit cards) is popular with foreigners and locals alike. It serves up Bavarian food and imported wheat beers on an outdoor patio. Meals start from Y30, beers from Y28.

Sportsman's American Bar and Restaurant (✉ 28 Taojin Jie ☎ 020/8359–1509 ▤ No credit cards) is where locals catch the game (their satellite captures everything from American baseball to Australian rugby) over a steak and beer. The Hash House Harriers running club sets off from here every Saturday at 2 PM.

Shopping

It's no surprise that the world's busiest manufacturing city has fantastic shopping options with new malls and street markets opening all the time. But beware: genuine brand-name products, electronic items, and perfume are cheaper and more likely to be the real thing in Hong Kong. Shops are usually open from 9 AM or 10 AM until late into the evening. Street markets tend to close at sunset.

Antiques & Traditional Arts & Crafts

On Shamian Island, the area between the White Swan and Victory hotels has a number of small family-owned shops that sell paintings, carvings, pottery, knickknacks, and antiques. **Guangzhou Arts Centre** (✉ 698 Renmin Bei Lu ☎ 020/8667–9898) has a fine selection of painted scrolls. **Guangzhou Ji Ya Zhai** (✉ 7 Xinwen Lu, Zhongshan Wulu ☎ 020/8333–0079) is a specialist in Chinese calligraphy and painting. The **South Jade Carving Factory** (✉ 15 Xia Jiu Lu ☎ 020/8138–8040) offers a wide variety of jade and jadeite products at reasonable prices. On the second floor visitors can watch jade being carved.

Bookstores

Guangzhou Books Center (✉ 123 Tianhe Lu ☎ 020/3886–4208) is a chain with seven floors of books on every subject, including some bargain-priced art books in English. **Xinhua Bookstore** (✉ 276 Beijing Rd. ☎ 020/8333–2636) sells an extensive catalog of books on a wide range of subjects at very affordable prices.

Department Stores

The **Friendship Store** (✉ 369 Huanshi Dong Lu) occupies a five-story building with departments selling a wide range of designer wear, children's wear, luggage, and household appliances. **Guangzhou Merchandising Building** (✉ 295 Beijing Rd.) has 11 departments on its six floors, selling watches, women's and men's garments, shoes and leather goods, children's wear, cosmetics, household appliances, and daily necessities.

Malls

Beijing Road is Guangzhou's frenzied, neon-draped answer to Beijing's Wangfujing Street or Shanghai's Nanjing Street. Pedestrianized and open from around 10 AM until 10 PM, this is where city teenagers buy sensible, mid-range Hong Kong clothes and increasingly garish local brands. Noisy and fun, the street is lined with cheap eats stalls, cafés, and the ubiquitous fast-food chains like KFC and McDonald's. **GITIC Plaza Arcade** (✉ Huanshi Dong Lu) has stores in the mid- to upmarket range. Some are contained in the Monte Carlo Shopping Center, where women's and men's fashions, accessories, cosmetics, and stationery are sold. More clothing boutiques, jade shops, and Chinese arts and crafts are found here as well. The spacious arcade is busy from 8 AM to 9 PM. **La Perle** (✉ 367 Huanshi Dong Lu) offers 100% genuine upscale designer clothes at expensive rates, with shops such as Versace, Louis Vuitton, Polo, and Prada. Open 10–10. **Mouse Street** (Lao Shu Jie; ✉ North of China Plaza, Zhong Shan Lu) is also known as "women's street" (Nu Ren Jie) and is where Guangzhou's modern misses hit the rails. Hundreds of tiny stores sell locally produced, Japanese-brand clothes, shoes, and accessories. It's cheaper than Beijing Road, but more crowded. Bargaining is essential. Open 10–6. The **White Swan Arcade** (✉ White Swan hotel, Yi Shamian Lu, Shamian Island) has some of the city's finest upmarket specialty shops. They sell genuine Chinese antiques, traditional craft items, works of modern and classical art, Japanese kimonos and swords, jewelry, cameras, and books published in and about China.

Yi Jin Yuan Toys and Crafts Centre (✉ Haizhu Sq., north of Haizhu Bridge, Haizhu Guangchang Metro, exit D) is really a souvenir wholesale market, but you can purchase individual items such as Chinese dresses, cushion covers, "antique" chests, toys, and sculptures. Reflecting Guangzhou's preeminence as a manufacturing center, it even sells African souvenirs destined for South Africa and Kenya. Make sure to bargain hard. Open 10–6.

Sports & the Outdoors

Bowling

Ten-pin bowling is one of China's fastest-growing indoor sports. **Baiyun Bowling Center** (✉ Yungang Hotel, Jichang Lu ☎ 020/8612–8034) is the place to bowl if you are in the airport area. Call for prices. Guangzhou's newest and best bowling alley is **Top Bowl** (⊠ 102 Liuhua Lu, next to Guangzhou Trade Fair ☎ 020/3623–7033), where you can rent shoes and lanes at a nominal charge.

Golf

The **Guangzhou Luhu Golf & Country Club** (☎ 020/8350–7777) has 18 holes spread over 180 acres of Luhu Park, 20 minutes from the Guangzhou Railway Station and 30 minutes from Baiyun Airport. The 6,820-yard, par-72 course was designed by world-renowned course architect Dave Thomas. The club also offers a 75-bay driving range and a clubhouse with restaurants, pro shop, and a gym. Members' guests and those from affiliated clubs pay Y637 in greens fees on weekdays, Y1,274 on weekends. Nonmembers pay Y849 and Y1,486, respectively. These prices include a caddie. Clubs can be rented for Y265. The club is a member of the International Associate Club network. **White Swan Hotel Golf Practice Center** (⊠ White Swan hotel, Yi Shamian Lu ☎ 020/8188–6968) is a good driving range on Shamian Island if you are pressed for time or don't want to leave the city. Admission is Y70, a rental of one club is Y30, and a box of 20 balls is Y10.

Guangzhou A to Z

To research prices, get advice from other travelers, and book travel arrangements, visit www.fodors.com.

AIR TRAVEL

Guangzhou's new $2.4 billion international Baiyun Airport in Huada city opened in August 2004 and is expected to establish Guangzhou as a regional air hub connecting the city to 40 international destinations by 2007. The airport currently offers 10 flights per day to both Hong Kong (Y670) and Beijing (Y1,240) between 9 AM and 9 PM. It has direct flights to Paris, Los Angeles, Singapore, Bangkok, Sydney, Jakarta, and Phnom Penh, and Northwest Airlines even plans to run direct flights to Detroit. The airport also serves 107 domestic flights to 77 Chinese cities. International airport tax is Y90, domestic departure tax is Y50.

🚩 Airline & Contacts **Civil Aviation Administration of China, CAAC represented by China Southern** ☎ 020/8668–2000, 24-hr hotline ⊠ 181 Huanshi Lu, on left as you exit Guangzhou Railway Station.

BOAT & FERRY TRAVEL

The Turbojet Company runs daily ferries connecting Guangzhou's East River Ferry Terminal and China Hong Kong City Ferry Terminal. The trip takes one hour.

🚩 Boat & Ferry Lines **Turbojet Company** ☎ 852/2921–6688.

BUS TRAVEL

Bus services in Guangzhou are plentiful. Citybus, which charges Y143 from Hong Kong and Y160 from Guangzhou, has five round-trips a day between Hong Kong and Guangzhou using new vehicles that have toilets, individual air-conditioning, and personal lighting controls. The trip takes 3½ hours, and buses leave from China Hong Kong City Ferry

Terminal and Shatin City One shopping mall in Hong Kong, and the Garden Hotel in Guangzhou. Among other bus services, China Travel Service (Y180) has 11 round-trips a day, with pickup and drop-off at major Guangzhou hotels. You can purchase your tickets at the concierge desks of these hotels.

Air-conditioned express buses, run by myriad private companies, link Guangzhou with just about every town in the region. Direct buses to Macau, via Zhuhai, (2½ hours, Y70) leave from the China and Garden hotels, as well as from Jinhan bus station. Air-conditioned buses to Shenzhen (2½ hours, Y60) depart every half hour from several bus stations including Jinhan, Liuhua (in front of Guangzhou Railway Station) and the long-distance bus station (Sheng Qi Che Zhan), west of Guangzhou Railway Station on Huanshi Xi Lu. From Liuhua bus station, you can also take buses to Guilin that are equipped with air-conditioning, reclining seats, and toilets (13 hours, Y100), Haikou (16 hours, Y180), Shantou (8 hours, Y90), Foshan (45 minutes, Y18), Zhongshan (2½ hours, Y35), and many other cities.

🚌 Bus Depots **Guangdong Provincial Bus Station** ✉ 145 Huanshi Xi Lu ☎ 020/8666-1297. **Guangzhou Bus Station** ✉ 158 Huanshi Xi Lu ☎ 020/8668-4259. **Tianhe Bus Station** ✉ Yuangang, Tianhe District ☎ 020/8774-1083.

🚌 **Citybus Hong Kong Office** ✉ Canton Road, Tsimshatsui, Kowloon, Hong Kong ☎ 852/2873-0818.

CONSULATES

🚌 Australia **Australian Consulate** ✉ Guangdong International Hotel, 339 Huanshi Dong Lu, Room 1509 ☎ 020/8335-0909.

🚌 Canada **Canadian Consulate** ✉ China Hotel, Wing C, Room 801, Liuhua Lu ☎ 020/8666-0569 Ext. 0.

🚌 United Kingdom **British Consulate** ✉ Guangdong International Hotel, 339 Huanshi Dong Lu, 2nd fl. ☎ 020/8335-1354.

🚌 United States **U.S. Consulate** ✉ White Swan hotel annex, 1 Yi Shamian Nan Lu, Shamian Island ☎ 020/8121-8000.

EMERGENCIES

🚌 **Can-Am International Medical Centre** ✉ Garden Tower, 368 Huanshi Dong Lu, 5th fl. ☎ 020/8121-8000. **Guangzhou Emergency Treatment Centre** ☎ 120. **Guangzhou Red Cross** ☎ 020/8444-6411. **Public Security Bureau** ☎ 110. **Tourist Hotline** ☎ 020/8668-4112 or 020/8669-6882.

MONEY MATTERS

Foreign currency is easily changed at hotels and banks in Guangdong; the Hong Kong dollar is accepted at larger department stores. Counterfeit Y100 and Y50 bills, identified by poor-quality paper, can be a problem.

SUBWAY TRAVEL

Guangzhou's clean and efficient underground Metro currently has two lines connecting 36 stations, including the new East and old Central railway stations. Tickets range from Y2 to Y7.

🚌 **Metro** ☎ 020/8310-6622 for information in English or 020/8310-6666.

TAXIS

Taxis are easy to find but few drivers speak English, so you need your destination written in Chinese. Better still: carry a cell phone, call someone at your destination, and hand the phone to the driver. The initial charge is Y7 with Y2.60 increments per kilometer. After 10 PM taxi prices increase 30% by law.

TOURS

Four-day circular tours (Y2,675) of the region (departing Hong Kong Tuesday, Thursday, and Saturday), available through CITS and other agencies, begin with a fast ferry to Macau. This is followed by a visit to Cuiheng, an overnight stay in Shi, a day in Foshan, a night in Zhaoqing, and a night and day in Guangzhou before a return by train to Hong Kong.

TRAIN TRAVEL

Five express trains (Y234 first class, Y190 second class) depart daily for Guangzhou East Railway Station from Hong Kong's Kowloon Station. The trip takes about 1¾ hours. The last train back to Hong Kong leaves at 5:25 PM. Trains between Shenzhen's Lo Wu Railway Station and Guangzhou East Railway Station run every hour and cost between Y80 and Y100. Guangzhou East Railway Station, located north of the city, is the terminus for daily express trains from Beijing. Free luggage carts are available at the newer Guangzhou East Railway Station, but the walk between trains and immigration is long.

The best way to buy train tickets is either direct at the station, through your concierge, or through local travel agents.

▉ Train Stations **Guangzhou East Railway Station** ✉ Lin Hezhong Rd, Tianhe District ☎ 020/6134-6222. **Guangzhou Railway Station** ✉ Huanshi Lu ☎ 020/6135-7222. **Kowloon Station** ✉ Hong Chong Rd., Tsim Sha Tsui East, Hong Kong.

TRAVEL AGENCIES

Travel agencies are the best way to book train and plane tickets. Increasingly deregulated and competitive, they often sell tickets cheaper than train stations or airline companies. If you're coming from Hong Kong, China Travel Service (CTS) is the most convenient place to book tickets to Guangzhou and the Pearl River delta area, although they add a small service charge, usually Y50.

▉ Agencies **Guang Zhi Lu Agency** ☎ 020/8633-8888. **Guangdong CITS** ✉ 179 Huanshi Lu ☎ 020/8666-6889 Ext. 222 🖷 020/8666-8859. **Guangdong CTS** ✉ 10 Qiaoguang Lu ☎ 020/8639-3308 🖷 020/8630-4308. **Guangdong International Travel** ✉ 120 Liuhua Lu, Dong Fang hotel, 2nd fl. ☎ 020/8666-1646 🖷 020/8668-8921.

Hong Kong China Travel Service (CTS) ☎ 852/2853-3533.

Yan Yang Tian Agency ☎ 020/8326-4292.

VISITOR INFORMATION

Check out English-language listings magazine *That's Guangzhou* for the latest on club, pub, and dining events. It is free and available in coffee shops, bars, and hotel lobbies throughout the city. The small-ads section is a great way to find apartments, language teachers, translators, and so on. Ads can be placed in advance of your visit via their Web site. Tourist maps are available at street kiosks and the city's numerous 7-11s for around Y15. The Guangzhou Tourist Board produces a free map with landmark drawings and useful phone numbers—ask a hotel concierge. Other good sources of information are consulates, hotel concierges, and, for business advice, the Hong Kong Trade Development Council.

🔃 Tourist Information **English Language Directory Inquiries** ☎ 114 **Hong Kong Trade Development Council** ✉ GITIC Plaza Offices, 339 Huanshi Dong Lu, 23rd fl. ☎ 020/8331-2889. **That's Guangzhou** ⊕ www.thatsmagazine.com. **Trade fair information** ☎ 020/8332-8829.

GUANGDONG

Far from the political center of Beijing and historically in close contact with areas outside China, Guangdong has found itself at the confluence of unique historical events. Next to the economic powerhouses of the Hong Kong Special Administrative Region (SAR) and Shenzhen Special Economic Zone (SEZ) as well as home to one of China's largest cities, Guangzhou, Guangdong is almost a kingdom unto itself. Indeed, since the mid-1980s scholars in the West have written about the possibility of Guangdong splitting from the rest of China. Although such a split is unlikely, it is clear that there is a strong regional culture in Guangdong.

The economic boom that in the space of 10 years transformed Shenzhen from rice paddies to a metropolis and Zhuhai from a village to a thriving city with one of China's highest standards of living has had a huge effect on the rest of Guangdong province as well. Knit together by an expanding communication and transportation network, the Pearl River delta region has become wealthy, the destination for international businesses, upwardly mobile Chinese, and hundreds of thousands of migrant laborers from inland provinces.

Guangdong has few exotic sights, but the temples, shrines, and other markers of a more ancient China still exist in pockets. Most older structures have, however, been "developed" into high-rises or bulldozed for superhighways. Guangdong's phenomenal growth is itself a subject of interest.

Foshan

🔞 *1 hr (17 km [10 mi]) by bus, 45 mins by taxi southwest of Guangzhou.*

The history of Foshan (Buddha Mountain), a city on the main circuit of the delta region, goes back 1,200 years. At one time it was an important religious center with a population of a million. Today, after centuries of obscurity, it is again a prosperous town with numerous joint enterprises involving overseas cousins.

Happily, this prosperity has encouraged residents to maintain the legacy of their past, dramatically in the city's **Ancestral Temple** (Zu Miao). It dates from the building of a Taoist temple on this spot during the Song Dynasty (960–1279). Rebuilt during the Ming Dynasty, without the use of nails, the main prayer hall is a masterpiece of art and architecture.

Its wooden roof with interlocking beams has a ridgepole crowded with porcelain figurines depicting the epic story of the *Romance of Three Kingdoms*. This is possibly the greatest example of porcelain tableaux art, which was developed by the potters of the nearby town of **Shiwan**, also known as Shekwan, where the art continues to flourish. You can visit workshops to see the artisans at work and buy their wares.

Inside the temple is a gilded altar table carved with scenes of Chinese defeating long-nosed foreign invaders. On the altar is a bronze statue of the Northern Emperor, cast in the Ming era and weighing 5,500 pounds. On either side are examples of old spears, swords, and other weapons, plus gongs and an Iron Cloud Board, which were carried by a mandarin's entourage.

In the courtyard outside is the **Ten Thousand Blessings Stage** (Wanfutai) built in 1658, it's the oldest surviving wooden stage in China. A great roof sweeps over the large platform, and gilt carvings and colored glass decorate the walls. Behind the stage is a display of old theater masks.

The vibrant artistic heritage of Foshan is not confined to historic buildings, however. At the **Renshou Temple** (Renshou Si) Folk Art Center craftsmen make intricate paper cutouts, huge paper lanterns, butterfly kites, and heads for lion dances. Shops display calligraphy, scroll paintings, and carvings of jade, wood, and bone. In addition, there are many examples of Shiwan pottery, including a set depicting Bruce Lee in different kung fu postures. All are for sale at very reasonable prices. ⊠ *Renmin Lu at Aumiao Lu* ⊗ *Daily 8–6.*

Where to Stay

$ ⌁ **Foshan Hotel.** This four-star, L-shape hotel is conveniently located in the downtown region. The rooms are decorated in coral-color carpeting and wood trim. There may not be anything spectacular about the hotel, but it is clean and in a handy location. The Milky Way Nightclub located in the hotel offers excellent karaoke facilities. Discounts of 30% are available. ⊠ *75 S. Fenjiang Rd., 528000* ☎ *0757/335–3338* 🖷 *0757/ 335–2347* ⇥ *395 rooms* ☖ *2 restaurants, pool, gym, sauna, nightclub, business services* ▤ *AE, DC, MC, V.*

⑲ The Pearl River delta town of **Zhaoqing** has drawn visitors for hundreds of years with its photogenic limestone **Seven Star Crags** and the beautiful landscape of mist-shrouded **Dinghu Shan mountains,** with its waterfalls, rivers, and temples. The area resembles a miniature Guilin in South Central China. The town itself is worth a stop as well. Although it's undergoing rapid industrial growth, Zhaoqing's modern shops are juxtaposed with sections of the city's 800-year-old walls. (*3 hrs by long-distance bus west of Guangzhou.*)

Zhongshan County

2½ hrs (60 km [37 mi]) by long-distance bus southwest of Guangzhou.

Zhongshan County, with a total population of about 5 million, is a conurbation of six light industrial townships sprawling over 1,780 square km (690 square mi) of the Pearl River delta. Zhongshan City (Zhongshan Shi) is its administrative center. Formerly called Heungshan (Fragrant Mountain), the area was renamed Zhongshan (Central Mountain) in honor of locally born hero Sun Yat-sen (1866–1925). Dr. Sun, who is considered the founder of modern China, used Zhongshan as his nom de guerre.

Zhongshan's six townships each specialize in a particular light industry. Guzhen, for example, produces some 80% of all China's lighting fittings. With 500 clothing manufacturers and a turnover of Y36 billion in 2003, the township of Shanxi is justified in calling itself the "Casualwear Capital of China."

This unfettered commerce has been brutal to local ecology. The city's professional promoters constantly trumpet apparent environmental awards, but the reality is different. Zhongshan's local river is oily black, its air quality is poor (you will want to keep taxi windows shut tight), and much of the county's once famously gentle undulating farmland has been flattened for landfill and rebuilt as an endless suburban sprawl of cheap second homes and "holiday villas" for Hong Kong investors. Despite these obvious problems the city constantly trumpets itself as the National Garden City.

❷⓪ Cuiheng (1½ hours by long-distance bus southeast of Guangzhou, 1 hour north of Macau) is the village where Sun Yat-sen was born in 1866. The **Sun Yat-sen Museum** (Sun Yat-sen Bowuguan) costs Y10 and is open daily 9–5. Its rooms are arranged around a patio, each showing the life and times of Sun as a man and a revolutionary. Next to the museum is the **Sun Yat-sen Guju,** the house that Sun built for his parents during a visit in 1892. It is a fine example of China coast architecture, with European-style verandas facing west. Bad geomancy for traditional Chinese, it underscored Sun's reputation for rebellion. The interior, however, is traditional, with high-ceilinged rooms, ancestral plaques, gilded carvings, and heavy black-wood furniture that includes a roofed Chinese marriage bed. Nearby is the **Sun Yat-sen Memorial High School,** free and open to tour (though not the classrooms) daily 9–5. Built in 1934 with splendid blue-tile roofs and a traditional Chinese gateway, it has about 700 students today.

❷⓵ Zhongshan City (2½ hours by bus southwest of Guangzhou) is the capital of Zhongshan County, and for 800 years it has been an important market center and inland port. It's about 78 km (48 mi) from Guangzhou and 61 km (38 mi) northwest of Macau. Until recently it was a picturesque port, where a cantilever bridge over the Qi River was raised twice a day to allow small freighters to pass, but the old town has been all but obliterated by modern high-rises, and farms that used to surround it are now covered with factories. Nevertheless, you can still join the throngs that stroll along the riverbanks in the evening. The **Sun Yat-sen Memorial Hall** (Sun Zhongshan Jinian Tang; ⌨ Y10 ☉ Daily 8–4:50) on Sunwen Zhong Lu and the **Xishan Temple** (✉ Xishan Park ⌨ Y5 ☉ Daily 8–5), restored in 1994, are also worth a visit.

Where to Stay & Eat

¢–$$ ✕ **No. 1 Chicken Seaport Restaurant.** Actually one restaurant with two kitchens, patrons can choose from a restaurant offering low-priced chicken and duck specialties such as Zhongshan-style 14-day pigeon, or from a restaurant selling fresh seafood by the jin (pound). Offerings include crab, shrimp, clams, and fish. ✉ *Food St., Zhang Jian Bian District* ☎ *0760/559–3038* ▤ *No credit cards.*

$–$$ ✕▦ **Shangri-La Zhongshan.** Opened in 2004, this is the first five-star international hotel in Zhongshan County and an oasis for business travelers. The rooms are tastefully decorated, as expected from a member of the Shangri-La chain. The views are not a draw but the beds are extremely comfortable. It has the city's only truly first-class Western restaurant ($–$$$$), a fully fitted spa, indoor pool, impeccable service and, thanks to its Austrian head chef, South East China's best homemade pastries. ✉ *16 Qi Wan Rd. N, Eastern Area, 528403* ☎ *0760/838–6888* 🖷 *0760/833–2905* 🌐 *www.shangri-la.com* ✏ *423 rooms, 40 suites* ⚲ *2 restaurants, 2 tennis courts, indoor pool, gym, spa, business services, meeting rooms* ▤ *AE, DC, MC, V.*

¢–$$ ▦ **Fuhua Hotel.** Located downtown near Walking Street, this business hotel has a certain 1980s charm. Its revolving Western restaurant offers Y99 "romantic dinners," 1970s-era airport carpets, and views of the city. Other hotel features include a foot bath center, karaoke, and sauna rooms. The staff is friendly. ⊠ *1 Fuhua Rd., Zhongshan City* ☎ *0760/863–8888* 🖷 *0760/861–1862* ⊕ *www.fuhuahotel.com.cn* 🖙 *400 rooms, 30 suites* ♤ *4 restaurants, hair salon, sauna, billiards, business services, meeting rooms* ▤ *AE, DC, MC, V.*

¢ 🏨 **Zhong Shan Hot Springs Resort.** This vast recreational complex built in 1980 by Hong Kong tycoon Henry Fok was China's first joint-venture hotel. Like its sister hotel, the White Swan in Guangzhou, it succeeds by excess. It has over 30 indoor hot springs, a swimming pool, a traditional Chinese garden, villa rooms with pagoda roofs, and two 72-par golf courses, one of them designed and tested by Arnold Palmer. Its English-speaking staff is helpful, and there is a large Chinese restaurant and a smaller Western restaurant. ⊠ *Yong Mo village, Zhongshan, San Xiang County, 528430, 24 km (15 mi) from Macau* ☎ *0760/668–3888* 🖷 *0760/668–3333* 🖙 *300 rooms, 14 villas* ♤ *2 restaurants, 2 18-hole golf courses, 2 tennis courts, pool, shops* ▤ *AE, MC, V.*

¢ 🏨 **Zhongshan International Hotel.** This 20-story tower, topped with a revolving restaurant, is a landmark of downtown Zhongshan City. This bargain hotel has rooms that have seen better days and tend to smell of cigarettes. Most of the guests are Chinese businessmen. Chinese, Japanese, and Western cuisines are served its three restaurants. Be warned: English is not easily understood. ⊠ *142 Zhongshan Yi Lu, Zhongshan City 528400* ☎ *0760/863–3388* 🖷 *0760/863–3368* ⊕ *www.interhotel-zs.com* 🖙 *350 rooms, 20 suites* ♤ *3 restaurants, pool, sauna, billiards, gym, nightclub* ▤ *AE, DC, MC, V.*

Sports & the Outdoors

㉒ The **Zhong Shan Hot Springs Resort** was the first, and is still considered one of the best, golf club in China. Designed by Arnold Palmer's company, it opened in 1984, with Palmer among the first to try it out. It's a par-72, 6,552-yard course of rolling hills, streams, and tricky sand traps. A second 18-hole course, designed by Jack Nicklaus, was added in the early 1990s. The elegant clubhouse, with mahogany paneling and rattan furniture, has a bar, restaurant, sauna, pool, and pro shop. Greens fees for visitors are Y550 for 18 holes on weekdays, Y1,320 on weekends. Caddies cost Y176, and club rentals cost Y121–Y198. Carts are Y220. Open 6:30 AM–8 PM (last tee time is at 3). ⊠ *Yong Mo village, Zhongshan City, San Xiang County* ☎ *0760/669–0055.*

Agile Golf & Country Club offers an 18-hole, par-72, 7,022-yard course next to the second-largest reservoir of Guangdong, the Changjiang Reservoir. The clubhouse consists of deluxe suites, a business center, two restaurants, tennis courts, a swimming pool, snooker, bowling alleys, a hair salon, and a pro shop. Greens fees for visitors are Y600 during the week, and Y1,400 on weekends. Caddies are Y140 and golf carts Y240. First tee time is 6 AM, last tee time is 5 PM. Nonmembers must reserve at least one day in advance via phone. ⊠ *Changjiang Tourist Spot, Eastern District of Zhongshan City* ☎ *0760/833–2868* 🖷 *0760/830–5938.*

Zhuhai

❷❸ *1½ hrs (99 km [62 mi]) by express bus south from Guangzhou; across border from Macau.*

Zhuhai, set up in 1980, was one of China's first four Special Economic Zones with liberal laws to encourage foreign investment. The zone has been extended from its original 13 square km (8 square mi) to 121 square km (74 square mi), complete with a long coastline and many small off-shore islands.

Zhuhai's million-plus residents have one of China's highest standards of living, and several major universities have campuses here. It is also one of China's most congenial and cleanest areas, thanks to its high-tech industrial base. Zhuhai produces electronics (Canon has its manufacturing headquarters here), textiles, shoes, DVD players, mobile handsets, and computer discs—products which all somehow find their way into the city's busy cut-rate shopping malls. Zhuhai also functions as a supply town for Macau. Every day thousands cross the border to work in the booming casino enclave. Mainland tourists use the city as a cheap base. But with an increasing number of golf courses, a hot spring, theme parks, and the biennial Asian Air Show, Zhuhai is becoming a destination in its own right.

Where to Stay & Eat

¢–$ ✕⚏ **Zhuhai Hotel.** This is a delightful reproduction of a Qing Dynasty courtyard mansion. The Jade City restaurant ($$–$$$) serves excellent Cantonese and Hunanese food in both common and private dining rooms. ⊠ *177 Jingshan Lu, 519015* ☎ *0756/333–3718* 🖷 *0756/333–2339* ⊕ *www.zh-hotel.com* ⬐ *312 rooms, 18 suites* ⚏ *2 restaurants, 2 tennis courts, pool, gym, bar, business services, meeting rooms* ⊟ *AE, DC, MC, V.*

$–$$$ ⚏ **Holiday Inn Zhuhai.** Opened in 2002, this Holiday Inn is a great value with excellent service and spacious, well-designed rooms. There are three restaurants, including Italian, Chinese, and Western cuisine, and a pub. The health center is comprehensive, with a large pool, steam room, and sauna. Friendly staff are quick, efficient, and speak excellent English. ⊠ *188 Jingshan Lu, Jida, 519015* ☎ *0756/322–8888* 🖷 *0756/ 322–8866* ⊕ *www.holidayinn-zhuhai.com* ⬐ *229 rooms, 39 suites* ⚏ *3 restaurants, pool, gym, sauna, steam room, billiards, pub, business services, meeting rooms* ⊟ *AE, DC, MC, V.*

¢–$$$ ⚏ **Paradise Hill.** Looking like a belle epoque palace on the French Riviera, this hotel has a stunning white-and-cream stone facade with balconies overlooking a garden terraced around fountains. To one side are swimming pools beside a lake, and at the back are three villas and a tennis court. Inside, the atrium lobby centers on a marble grand staircase. The restaurants, serving Chinese, Western, and Japanese meals, are equally opulent, and the health center is state-of-the-art. Discounts of up to 50% are possible. ⊠ *193 Jingshan Lu, 519015* ☎ *0756/333–7388* 🖷 *0756/333–3508* ⬐ *195 rooms, 45 suites, 3 villas* ⚏ *3 restaurants, tennis court, pool, gym, hair salon* ⊟ *AE, DC, MC, V.*

$ ⌦ **Grand Bay View.** This handsome hotel stands on the bay between the Macau border and the Zhuhai Ferry Terminal. Many rooms overlook the water and at night it's possible to see the lights of Macau. There are three restaurants, including a Western-style buffet and a nightclub, Club de Pearl. Imaginative meeting rooms include French windows overlooking the water and Macau. ✉ *245 Shui Wan Rd., Gongbei District, 519020* ☎ *0756/887–7998* 🖷 *0756/887–8668* ⊕ *www.gbvh.com* ↝ *273 rooms, 19 suites* ⌂ *3 restaurants, pool, gym, billiards, bar, nightclub, meeting rooms, business services* ▤ *AE, DC, MC, V.*

¢–$ ⌦ **Jinye Hotel.** This hotel is directly opposite the Macau border and bus station, on a busy shopping street. A nice, clean option for travelers who do not mind forgoing some amenities for a lower price. Discounts of up to 50% are possible. ✉ *1011 Yinbin S Rd., Gongbei District, 519020* ☎ *0756/813–2668* 🖷 *0756/888–2788* ⊕ *www.zhjinye.com* ↝ *165 rooms, 14 suites* ⌂ *Restaurant, business services* ▤ *MC, V.*

Shopping

Near the Macau border across from the bus station is **Yinbin Street,** a popular shopping area. Cheap seafood restaurants in the surrounding lanes stay open well after midnight and, thanks to a variety of hawkers, street musicians, and food stalls, it makes for a fascinating, if slightly earthy, evening stroll.

Sports & the Outdoors

In Zhuhai, the **Lakewood Golf Club,** about 20 minutes from the Zhuhai Ferry Terminal, is the most popular of the city's five golf clubs. It opened its Mountain Course and clubhouse at the end of 1995 and the Lake Course in 1997. Visitor packages, including greens fees and a caddy, are Y420 for weekdays and Y820 weekends. Golf carts cost Y200. ✉ *Da'-nan Mountain, Jinding District* ☎ *0756/338–3666* 🖷 *0756/338–0452.*

Shenzhen/Shekou

1 hr by express train, 2½ hrs by express bus (112 km [70 mi]) from Guangzhou. Walk across border from Hong Kong's Lo Wu KCR (Kowloon-Canton Railway) train station.

㉔ In 1980 **Shenzhen** was a small farming town of 20,000 people, then Deng Xiaoping made it one of China's first Special Economic Zones. Today it is the country's most liberal, Westernized, and densely populated city, a metropolis of almost 6 million energetic hopefuls whose average age is just 29.

Bordering Hong Kong, Shenzhen was long characterized as the former British colony's dark and twisted sister: an imposter city, full of theme parks, Vegas-style neon, sleazy karaoke bars, fake-brand shopping malls, and plastic-surgery parlors. It was where Hong Kong businessmen played golf and parked their "second wives." But as ambitious railway, road, and underground projects come to fruition, Shenzhen is emerging as an increasingly livable and (especially in suburban towns like Shekou), green, and pleasant city. In 2001, Shenzhen's gross domestic production per capita became the highest of all Chinese cities. It has 130 star-level hotels, two stock exchanges, an airport 35 km (20 mi) from the city center, and the country's busiest port. No wonder grateful locals hang portraits of Deng Xiaoping everywhere. For a city with no past, Shenzhen has a great future.

㉕ Shekou came into being in 1978 as the company city of China Merchants, a mainland shipping and trading conglomerate with headquarters in Hong Kong. The company recognized the potential of Shekou's location, at the entrance to the Pearl River estuary and next door to Hong Kong, not only as a new port but as a base for oil-exploration firms. Since then all the big oil companies have made their regional headquarters here, and it shows. There are spacious California-style suburbs, with balconied villas and swimming pools. Nearby are supermarkets (there's even a Wal-Mart), high-rise office blocks, and a row of trendy bars and Western restaurants. The streets are clean and the beach immaculate. There's virtually no crime and certainly no unemployment.

Most foreign visitors come to Shekou by sleek, Norwegian-made catamaran ferries, which commute in 50 minutes from Hong Kong, but the opening of new expressways between Lo Wu Railway Station and Shekou has made the port city readily accessible from Shenzhen City, a half-hour's drive away, and Guangzhou, less than two hours away. A new underground train system connecting Lo Wu Railway Station at the Hong Kong border and Shekou, due to open in 2005, will further improve links.

Shenzhen has many theme parks. Its four largest—Windows of the World, Splendid China, China Folk Culture Villages, and Happy Kingdom—are grouped at Overseas Chinese Town and connected by an elevated monorail which costs Y20.

㉖ Splendid China (Jin Xiu Zhong Hua) is China's 74 best-known historical and geographical sights collected and miniaturized to 1:15 scale. Built in 1991 and popularized by Deng Xiaoping (who stopped in for a photo-op on his famous 1992 journey south promoting free enterprise), it is still a big draw with the patriotic camera-wielding masses, and not a few Westerners "doing China" in a day. The 74-acre site includes a waist-high Great Wall, a fun-size Forbidden City, and little Potala Palace—all in a "splendid," illogical proximity. ⊠ *Shenzhen Bay, Shenzhen* ☎ *0755/2660–0626* 🎫 *Y120* ☾ *Daily 10–10.*

☾ **Windows of the World** (Shijie Zhi Chuang) gives a similar miniature makeover to 130 of the world's most famous landmarks and is China's biggest and busiest homegrown theme park. Divided into eight geographical areas interconnected by winding paths and a full-size monorail, it includes randomly scaled Taj Mahal, Mount Rushmore, Sydney Harbor Opera House, and a 328-feet-high Eiffel Tower that can be seen miles away. There is an evening "extravaganza" show every night and plans to add rides and roller coasters in 2005. It's surreal fun and extremely popular with Chinese couples waiting for that world holiday. ⊠ *Overseas Chinese Town, Nan Shan District, Shenzhen* ☎ *0755/ 2660–8000* ⊕ *www.szwwco.com* 🎫 *Y120* ☾ *Daily 9 AM–10 PM.*

27 **China Folk Culture Villages** (Zhong Hua Minzu Wen Hua Cun) recreates 21 Chinese ethnic villages along with typical scenery. Here "professional" natives wearing traditional costume perform dances, sing folk songs, and produce handicrafts for sale at the gift shop. Another popular activity is a dine-around-China tour, on which you can sample regional dishes made by locals using local ingredients. ✉ *Chinese Overseas Town, Nan Shan District, Shenzhen* ☎ *0755/2660–0626* ⊕ *www.happyvally.com. cn* ⌨ *Y85* ☺ *Daily 10–10.*

☺ **Happy Kingdom** is for those who find Shenzhen's other theme parks "too cultural." Huge, noisy, trashy, and great fun, it's Disneyland minus copyrighted characters. Imported Western attractions include roller coasters, water chutes, and the stomach-squeezing "Space Shot," which launches you into the air for a thrilling vertical fall. Junk food and tacky souvenirs abound. This is the perfect place for single-child families to let loose their "Little Emperors." ✉ *Overseas Chinese Town, Nan Shan District, Shenzhen* ☎ *0755/2694–9168* ⌨ *Y120* ☺ *Daily 10–10.*

Where to Stay & Eat

$–$$$ ✕ **Seagull Restaurant.** This well-serviced Western-style restaurant and pub has outside tables overlooking the beach. The food is consistent and the staff speaks some English. Entrées include baked salmon and sirloin steak, as well as Asian favorites. ✉ *Haibin Yu Chang Nei, next to Hai Shang Shi Jie, Shekou, on the beach* ☎ *0755/2682–0768* ▭ *No credit cards.*

¢–$ ✕▤ **Landmark Shenzhen.** This handsome hotel in downtown Shenzhen looks and feels European. Its lobby is like a foyer, with informal check-in counters, and the central Piazza Café is really like an Italian square, with a skylight roof, overhanging balconies, striped canopies, and tables set out as in a sidewalk café. The Landmark is also popular for its Chinese restaurant, Artisan Court ($$), which serves Chiu Chow and Cantonese cuisine. The hotel also features a jazz club, BJ's, on the third floor, which hosts live performances every night except Monday. ✉ *3018 Nanhu Lu, Shenzhen 518001* ☎ *0755/8217–2288* 🖷 *0755/8229–0473* 🖢 *351 rooms, 34 suites* ⌂ *3 restaurants, driving range, pool, gym, bar, shops, business services, meeting rooms* ▭ *AE, DC, MC, V.*

★ $$$ ▤ **Shangri-La Shenzhen.** This international hotel has become a city landmark and it is conveniently situated opposite the Hong Kong border. The top floor's (no longer revolving) restaurant has a 360-degree view that is one-half dense skyscraper thicket and one-half empty green hills of the Hong Kong border. Rooms are first class and the hospitality is excellent. The gym has marbled spa facilities. On the second floor is a Henry J. Bean's American Grill. The concierge team—the city's busiest and best—relish a challenge. ✉ *1002 Jianshe Lu, Shenzhen 518001* ☎*0755/8233–0888* 🖷*0755/8233–9878* ⊕*www.shangri-la.com* 🖢*553 rooms, 30 suites* ⌂ *6 restaurants, pool, gym, hair salon, bar, shops, business services, meeting rooms* ▭ *AE, DC, MC, V.*

$–$$$ ▤ **Marina Ming Wah Convention Center Hotel.** This 25-story multipurpose high-tech commercial complex has large, irregularly shaped rooms, many with private terraces. Serviced apartments are available at double the price and hardly worth it. The complex has Cantonese, Japanese, and Western restaurants, as well as the popular Marina Tavern and an Asian buffet, Spice Market. You can ask for discounts of up to 40%. ⊠ *8 Gui Shan Lu, Shenzhen 518067* ☎ *0755/2668–9968* 🖷 *0755/ 2667–9615* 📞 *265 rooms, 50 suites, 126 serviced apartments* ⚭ *4 restaurants, pool, gym, bowling, bar, dance club, business services, convention center* 🖃 *AE, DC, MC, V.*

¢–$$$ 🖸 **Sunshine.** Although it looks like an average Shenzhen multipurpose building from the outside, this is one of the most attractive hotels in the region. The beige-colored rooms are clean and spacious; even the smallest are roomy. The grand lobby flows from the entrance, through the lounge and bar, past the white-marble staircase, to the executive wing. Here you find the Sunshine City Health Club, with a vast indoor pool, a golf putting green and simulator, a fully equipped gym, and a TV-aerobics room. ⊠ *1 Jiabin Lu, Shenzhen 518005* ☎ *0755/8223–3888* 🖷 *0755/8222–6719* ⊕ *www.sunshinehotel.com* 📞 *374 rooms, 42 suites* ⚭ *3 restaurants, putting green, tennis court, pool, gym, hair salon, squash, bar, lounge, dance club, shops, business services, meeting rooms* 🖃 *AE, DC, MC, V.*

¢–$ 🖸 **Nan Hai.** Shenzhen's first luxury hotel, designed for international oil company demands, is starting to show its age. However, the rooms are large and expensively furnished, and all have terraces. The hotel has extensive resort facilities and a great location right next to Shekou's ferry to Hong Kong. ⊠ *1 Gongye Yilu, Shekou 518069* ☎ *0755/2669–2888* 🖷 *0755/2669–2440* ⊕ *www.nanhai-hotel.com* 📞 *358 rooms, 86 suites* ⚭ *5 restaurants, 2 tennis courts, pool, hair salon, billiards, bar, dance club, shops, meeting rooms* 🖃 *AE, DC, MC, V.*

Shopping

Shenzhen, with its wealthy and young population, is emerging as a major shopping city. Some 7,000 Hong Kongers cross into the city every day for bargain clothes, food, and electrical goods. For detailed information on where to shop, try Ellen McNally's excellent guidebook *Shopping in Shenzhen,* on the Web at www.shopinshenzhen.com.

GITIC Plaza (⊠ 1095 Shennan Rd., across from Government Bldg., Shenzhen ☎ 0755/2594–1502) offers upscale shopping for the time-conscious business traveler. Shops include Japanese department stores Seibu and Jusco, Louis Vuitton, Polo, and Tommy Hilfiger. Open 10:30–10 daily.

Lo Wu Commercial City (⊠ Follow the Hong Kong hoards left out of Lo Wu Railway Station, Shenzhen ☎ No phone). This five-story mall infamously sells phony versions of just about every name brand, especially "LV" handbags, "Prada" shoes, "Polo" shirts, and a near infinite selection of DVD knockoffs at Y10 each. The fifth floor even sells counterfeit Picasso paintings. Quality varies, but it is always fun for a browse. The third floor has excellent made-to-measure curtains. Elephant Restaurant on the fourth floor serves great dim sum. When you are exhausted, drop into one of the many foot massage parlors for a pedicure (Y30). Open 10–10.

Sports

Mission Hills Golf Club (⊠ Nan Shan, Da Wei, Sha He, Shenzhen ☎ 0755/ 2690–9999) hosted the World Cup of Golf in 1995. In addition to an 18-hole course, it has a spectacular clubhouse and an adjoining 20-room hotel, a tennis court, two restaurants, and an outdoor pool. The greens fees are Y600 weekdays and Y1,000 weekends; caddies are Y150. Open 6–9:30.

The **Sand River Golf Club** (⊠ 1 Baishi Lu, Shenzhen Bay, near Window of the World, Shenzhen ☎ 0755/2690–0111) offers two courses—one is 9 holes and floodlighted—designed by Gary Player. Other facilities include a large driving range, a lake, and various resort amenities. Visitor fees for 9-hole greens fees are Y330 weekdays and Y550 weekends. Fees for 18 holes are Y660 weekdays and Y1,100 weekends. Caddies are Y160–Y180. Open 7–9.

Shantou/Chaozhou

28–**29** *5 hrs (240 km [149 mi]) by express bus or 45 mins by air northeast of Guangzhou; 6 hrs by long-distance bus.*

The ancestral homeland of the Chaozhou people—better known outside China by the Cantonese pronunciation *Chiu Chow*—is the region on the east coast of Guangdong province between the port of Shantou (formerly written Swatow) and the historic capital of Chaozhou.

Although there was a settlement here from the 2nd century BC, the original Chiu Chow arrived in the 4th century, fleeing war-torn central China. They developed a distinctive dialect, cuisine, and operatic style, as well as a talent for business, which was conducted through Chaozhou. Silting of the Han River forced business downstream to Shantou, which in 1858 became one of the ports opened up to foreigners by the Treaty of Tianjin.

Companies like Jardine Matheson and British American Tobacco set up shop, but Shantou remained a minor-league treaty port compared with Shanghai. Nevertheless, the local lace and porcelain became world famous. Meanwhile, droughts and warlords spurred the Chiu Chow people to emigrate on a mass scale to Southeast Asia and beyond.

Today there are an estimated 6 million overseas Chiu Chow, half of them in Thailand, 1.2 million in Hong Kong, and large numbers in Taiwan, Malaysia, and North America. An amazing number have made their fortunes in their new homes, but they don't forget their roots, which is why Shantou was chosen in 1980 as a Special Economic Zone for investment from abroad.

The results have exceeded every expectation, with vast sums flowing in to build a new port and new highways, hospitals, and schools, as well as office buildings and homes. Today the picturesque port of old Shantou lies on 30 international and domestic shipping routes; modern vessels far outnumber the traditional fishing boats. Gleaming high-rises have replaced all but a handful of the Victorian houses and offices, with their neoclassical facades and colonnaded verandas. The best of the survivors is the former British consulate in Jiaoshi Scenic Park, which now houses government offices.

The waterfront **Xidi Park** (Xidi Gongyuan), with its parade of beautifully sculpted stone animals and people alongside tree-shaded benches and open-sided pavilions, is where locals play Chinese chess and read newspapers. From here you have intimate views of the busy harbor with its fleets of fishing boats, ferries, and freighters, which somehow steer clear of oyster farms that produce the key ingredient for delicious oyster pancakes.

Where to Stay & Eat

Although Chiu Chow food ranks as one of China's great cuisines, it is not easy to sample the authentic dishes without a local contact. There are, of course, plenty of restaurants around Shantou and Chaozhou, but virtually none has an English menu or English-speaking staff, and in most cases even the name is in Chinese only. Restaurants in the major hotels serve what are often less-inspired versions of authentic Chiu Chow meals, have English menus, and usually keep at least one English speaker on staff.

$–$$$ ✕⌂ **Golden Gulf Hotel.** Sophisticated elegance aptly describes this luxury hotel. Guest rooms occupy a white semicircular tower. The pool terrace and tennis courts are laid out on an open podium, and the lobby is a circular courtyard with a globe-shape fountain as a centerpiece and a glass-domed ceiling. Restaurants and shops are arranged around the colonnaded gallery. The decor is stylish throughout. There are four restaurants to choose from. Chiu Chow, Cantonese, Japanese, and Western cuisines are all represented but the best is the Chiu Chow option, Magnificent Palace ($$$$), which serves elaborate banquet dishes. The food is as good as the settings are beautiful. ⊠ *96 Jingshan Lu, Shantou 515041* ☎ *0754/826–3263* 🖷 *0754/826–5162* ⇖ *400 rooms, 23 suites* ♨ *4 restaurants, tennis court, pool, gym, bar, dance club, business services, meeting rooms* ▤ *AE, DC, MC, V.*

$–$$ ✕⌂ **Shantou International Hotel.** When it opened in 1988, this was the first international-class hotel in East Guangdong, and it remains a major landmark, with its zigzag facade and revolving restaurant, Palace Revolve ($$$$), serving Western and Chinese buffet breakfast in the morning, and Western food throughout the day. The Han Jiang Chun restaurant cooks up good Chiu Chow and Western options. In the elaborately traditional Tea House, you prepare your own "kung fu tea" around a carved wooden cabinet. The hotel rooms are large and comfortable. Ask for discounts. ⊠ *52 Jingshan Lu, Shantou 515041* ☎ *0754/825–1212* 🖷 *0754/825–2250* ⇖ *273 rooms, 16 suites* ♨ *3 restaurants, gym, bar, dance club, business services, meeting rooms* ▤ *AE, DC, MC, V.*

¢   ✕⌂ **Shantou Harbour View.** Overlooking the harborside park, a block or so from the International Ferry Terminal, this smartly modern hotel has marvelous views of the busy port. It has a nautical theme, with a blue-and-white color scheme and a tower of rooms that suggests a giant sail. Rooms are attractively decorated; each garden suite has a private terrace. The Harbor View Restaurant is a superior coffee shop, serving

Western and Chinese food against a backdrop panorama of the port. For fine dining Chiu Chow and Cantonese style there is the Palace Restaurant ($$$$). Discounts of over 50% are the norm. ⊠ *Haibin Lu, Zhongduan, Shantou 515041* ☎ *0754/854–3838* 📠 *0754/855–0280* 🛏 *112 rooms, 17 suites* ⚭ *2 restaurants, bar, business services, meeting rooms* ▤ *AE, DC, MC, V.*

Shopping

All kinds of locally made porcelain are available in Shantou shops and roadside stores in **Fungxi,** a village on the outskirts of Chaozhou, where family factories produce customized dinnerware and commemorative mugs, openwork Chinese stools, and waist-high jars encrusted with brightly colored and gilded figures. Most are produced for export around the world but are sold here for the best prices. Most shops pack and ship overseas. Lace is very cheap and abundant in shops in Shantou and Chaozhou. If you're lucky, you also might find some of the local three-dimensional wood carvings.

Side Trip from Shantou

The best reason for visiting Shantou is to make the 50-minute drive inland to **Chaozhou.** During the Tang and Song dynasties it thrived as an inland port with its own sophisticated cultural style. The port succumbed to river silt, but Chaozhou preserved much of its heritage. Thanks to the fine local clay and traditional craftsmen, it continues to produce all kinds of Chinese porcelain in workshops that welcome visitors. One company still makes Chaozhou wood carvings, and there are factories producing lace, but the distinctive sculpted embroidery is no longer made, for lack of skilled needle workers.

The **Kaiyuan Temple** (Kaiyuan Si), built in AD 738 as one of the 10 major temples in China, is a Chaozhou treasury that contains three huge gilt statues of Buddha, a 3,300-pound Song Dynasty bronze bell, and a stone incense burner said to have been carved from a meteorite. Its prayer pavilions have ridgepole decorations of multicolor porcelain birds and flowers in exuberant swirling patterns.

Not much is left of the old **Ming Dynasty wall,** except for two carved wooden gates that have been attractively restored. There were also plans to restore the original bridge built over the Han in the 12th century. It once rested on 18 wooden boats in a traditional "floating gate," which swung with the tide, a device to overcome the problem of building foundations in the then swiftly flowing river; they have since been replaced by concrete piers.

Guangdong A to Z

To research prices, get advice from other travelers, and book travel arrangements, visit www.fodors.com.

AIR TRAVEL

Shenzhen Airport is very busy, with flights to 50 cities. There is commuter service by catamaran ferries and buses between the airport and Hong Kong. Bus service links the Shenzhen Railway Station, via Huaren

Dasha, direct to Shenzhen Airport for Y25 (one-way). Zhuhai International Airport, the largest in size in China, despite its name operates only domestically, to 24 cities.

🚹 Airport Information **Shenzhen Airport** ☎ 0755/2777-7821. **Zhuhai International Airport** ☎ 0756/889-5494.

BOAT & FERRY TRAVEL

Fast modern catamaran ferries (Y251 first class, Y224 second, Y208 third) make six round-trips daily to the pier at Jiuzhou (on the coast of Zhuhai, just north of Macau) from China Hong Kong City Ferry Terminal (CHKC) and six round-trips from the Macau Ferry Terminal. The trip takes 70 min from either destination.

Catamarans (Y266 first class, Y245 second, Y235 third) make seven daily trips between Hong Kong and Zhongshan Harbor, close to Zhongshan, leaving from the CHKC Terminal. The trip takes approximately 90 min from either destination.

Comfortable double-deck catamaran ferries (Y154 first class, Y117 economy) make the pleasant 50-minute trip between Macau and Shekou (passing under the new Tsing Ma Bridge), with five departures daily from the Macau Ferry Terminal.

Tickets for an overnight ferry to Hainan can also be purchased at the Shekou pier.

🚹 Boat & Ferry Information **Jiuzhou CHKC** ✉ Canton Rd., Kowloon. **Macau Ferry Terminal** ✉ Shun Tak Centre, Connaught Rd., Central ☎ 853/2546-3528.

BUS TRAVEL

Citybus buses make eight round-trips daily between Hong Kong and Shenzhen, with six continuing on to Shenzhen Bay theme parks. Buses depart from Hong Kong's Admiralty Station and CHKC Terminal (Shenzhen City: Y69 one-way weekdays, Y90 weekends; Shenzhen Bay: Y80 one-way weekdays, Y101 weekends).

Air-conditioned express buses crisscross most of the Pearl River delta region. These buses are reasonably priced and have many departures each day. Most areas can be reached in only a few hours. Ask at your hotel for the closest bus station.

🚹 Bus Information **Citybus** ☎ 852/2873-0818.

TOURS

By far the most popular tour is from Hong Kong to Zhongshan via Macau, which provides a full and interestingly diverse, if rather tiring, daylong outing. All one-day Zhongshan tours include a bus transfer from Macau to the border at Gongbei District in the Zhuhai Special Economic Zone, a trip to Cuiheng Village for Sun Yat-sen sites, a six-course lunch, a visit to a "typical" farming village kept traditional for tourists, and return to Hong Kong via Zhongshan Harbor.

The other established one-day China trip takes in the Shenzhen Special Economic Zone, immediately across the border from Hong Kong, to visit either Splendid China or the adjoining theme park, China Folk Culture

Villages, as well as a Hakka village, a kindergarten, and a market. Purchase tickets for either tour from any travel agent in Hong Kong.

TRAIN TRAVEL
There is a rail route from Beijing to Hong Kong via Shenzhen, and Shenzhen can easily be reached from Hong Kong by taking the KCR light railway from Hong Kong's Kowloon Tong KCR station to Lo Wu Railway Station and then crossing over to Shenzhen on foot. Trains depart from Lo Wu to Hong Kong every five minutes.

VISITOR INFORMATION
Most travel can be easily arranged in Guangzhou. In other areas CITS may be of assistance.

Tourist Information **CITS** ✉ 8 Jinlong Lu, Shantou ☎ 0754/824–0557 🖷 0754/862–5653 ✉ 6 Yenhe Nan Lu, near east exit of Shenzhen Station, Shenzhen ☎ 0755/233–8822 🖷 0755/232–9832 ✉ 142 Zhongshan Yilu, Zhongshan ☎ 0760/861–1888 🖷 0760/861–7064 ✉ Next to Zhuhai Hotel, Zhuhai ☎ 0756/333–3859 🖷 0756/333–6718.

HAINAN

Hainan is a large subtropical island and China's southernmost point. It has long white-sand beaches, lilting palm trees, natural hot springs, cheap seafood, and warm weather all year round. It was administered by the government of Guangdong until 1988, when it became a self-administering Special Economic Zone. After a shaky start, it has finally begun to emerge as China's main domestic holiday destination with something for every budget—including a string of impressive five-star international resorts.

The island, which at 33,900 square km (13,100 square mi) is a little smaller than Taiwan, is less crowded and more laid-back than the rest of southeastern China. There is no heavy industry or pollution and with more than half of the island forested, the air is fresh and clean. About 1 million of its 7 million population is made up of Li, Hui, and Miao minorities, whose traditional agricultural lifestyles continue inland and are well worth the trek. The rest are Han Chinese. Historically, Hainan was a place of exile. Su Shi, the Song Dynasty writer, was banished here. So was Li Deyu, a prime minister of the Tang Dynasty, who dubbed the island "the gates of hell." These days, however, most Han immigrants, especially cabdrivers and hotel staff who tend to be recent arrivals from the freezing north, seem to be delighted to be here. The island has an easygoing and relaxed atmosphere, noticeably different from the mainland.

Hainan's chief businesses are tourism and agriculture, its principle export being the coconut. Back in the early 1990s, as Hainan got used to its Special Economic Zone status, there was a period of free-market madness as the island attempted to turn itself into a "little Hong Kong." This effort stoked a property boom that stalled badly. Today growth is more steady and focused. In the capital, Haikou, and at resorts Boao and Sanya, the cranes are turning again. But this time the investors are major international hotel chains buying into China's huge and increasingly affluent tourism market. Almost 14 million people visited the island in 2003, and, thanks to a huge national publicity campaign and Sanya's hosting of the Miss World Beauty Pageant Final in 2003 and 2004, that number is increasing each year. In 2001, Hainan gained more notorious fame after a U.S. Navy plane was forced to make an emergency landing there and China refused to return the "spy plane" or release its crew for 11 days.

Haikou

➌ *1 hr (520 km [322 mi]) by plane southwest of Guangzhou; 1 hr (480 km [298 mi]) by plane southwest of Hong Kong.*

Haikou (literally, "Mouth of the Sea") is Hainan's capital, and with a population of around 540,000, its largest city as well. It is on the northern coast of the island directly across the Hainan Strait, 18 km (11 mi) from the southern coast of Guangdong province, surrounded by water on three sides. It is the commercial and transportation hub of the island—nearly everything coming in and out of Hainan makes its way through Haikou—but the moist tropical breezes, palm tree–lined streets, and sunlight make even afternoon traffic in Haikou seem somehow less irritating. The city has more than 100 hotels and 4,000 taxis, so finding a place to stay and getting around is not a problem. Chinese settlements in and around the Haikou area since at least the Tang Dynasty have left behind some interesting sites.

The **Temple of the Five Lords** (Wugong Ci), in the southeastern part of the city, is a complex of buildings devoted to five officials who were exiled to Hainan during the Tang and Song dynasties. The first building was constructed by a local official in 1889 on the site of two ancient springs dug in 1097 during the Song. The **Fu Su Springs** (Fu Su Quan) have been flowing for more than 1,000 years. Outside the complex, across a small, arched bridge, is the **Five Lords Exhibition Hall** (Wugong Ci Zhanlan Guan), which has a number of good exhibits on the history of the Chinese in Hainan. ⊠ *169 Haifu Lu* ☎ *No phone* 💰 *Y10* ☉ *Daily 7–6.*

Hai Rui's Tomb (Hai Rui Mu) was built in 1589 to honor Hai Rui (1514–87), a prominent Ming Dynasty official who gave up his post for the good of the empire. Criticism, written in the spring of 1966, of a play about this prominent historical figure was one of the opening salvos in the Cultural Revolution. The walkway of stone figures near the grave exhibits a heavy Southeast Asian influence. ⊠ *Sugang Lu* ☎ *No phone* 💰 *Y5* ☉ *Daily 8–6.*

In the northern part of the city near the coast is the well-preserved **Xiuying Fort** (Xiuying Paotai), one of a number of coastal forts that once ringed Hainan. Built in 1891 at the end of the Qing Dynasty by the Krupp Company, the fort is one of five still in existence in China. Inside are a network of underground passages and a museum of weaponry. ⊠ *Off Jingmao Dong Lu* ☎ *No phone* 💰 *Y15* ☉ *Daily 7:30–6:30.*

For a fine walk, stroll Haikou's **old town.** Meander the narrow streets, which, happily, are less jam-packed than in larger cities. Here you'll find a number of beautiful older buildings in the Portuguese-Chinese style so common in Southeast Asia. You'll often see curving arches and tiles from Portugal, with red Chinese script written on the signs hanging out front. ⊠ *Xinhua Lu and Zhongshan Lu.*

Wanlu Park (Wanluyuan), a vast expanse of green in the northeast part of the city near the shore, would be a great place to let children run, play games, or jog.

The most famous of Haikou's parks is **Golden Ox Park** (Jinniuling Gongyuan). The park is named after a legendary golden ox that was sent to Hainan by the Jade Emperor to aid the people of Hainan after a volcanic eruption devastated the land. When the ox landed, four streams sprung from its hooves and brought water to the island's impoverished inhabitants. A statue of the ox stands near the entrance to the park. The park also has the **Golden Ox Zoo** (Jinniuling Dongwuyuan). The zoo's fascinating exhibits of local animal life, including macaques, would be more enjoyable if the animals had better living conditions. ⊠ *Western part of city* ☎ *No phone* 🎟 *Y2 park, Y15 park and zoo* ⊙ *Park, daily 6:30 AM–7:30 PM; zoo, daily 8–5.*

Lending some credence to legends of golden ox and volcanic eruptions, **Volcano Mouth Park** (Huoshankou Gongyuan), 15 km (9 mi) inland southwest of Haikou, is an ancient volcanic cone encrusted with tropical growth. The volcano is the highest point in the northern maritime plain and affords fantastic views of Haikou, the Hainan Strait, and far-off Guangdong province. At the edge of the crater is the **Tablet of the Three Gods** (Sanshen Bei), which honors the gods who have the responsibility for putting out mountain fires, ensuring abundant crops, and protecting the indigenous Li people. ⊠ *Qiongshan City* 🎟 *Y15* ⊙ *Daily 24 hrs.*

Along the coast to the west of Haikou, about 25 minutes by taxi, is **Holiday Beach** (Jiari Haitan). The place is packed on weekends, when hordes of people from the city descend on it. During the week, however, the beach is a fine place to sunbathe or walk and enjoy the scenery of the Hainan Strait. You don't want to go swimming here, however, unless you don't mind pollution and sharks.

Where to Stay & Eat

Besides hotel dining, the best bet for good food is along Jinlong Lu, Haikou's **Street of Beautiful Chinese Flavors** (Zhonghua Fengwei Meishi Jie), which is lined with restaurants that offer various regional styles of Chinese cooking. It may be difficult to find menus in English, so be prepared to point.

A cheaper and less touristy option is **Haidian Island,** just north of downtown Haikou. There are plenty of late-night, lively street food stalls, offering fresh BBQ oysters for Y1 each, piquant lamb kebabs, and other local specialties. On **Haidian 3 East Road** (Haidian San Dong Lu), also known as "bar street," rows of plastic tables and chairs line the streets, similar to Beijing's San Li Tun. Touts try vigorously to entice you to drink at their establishment, though there is little difference between them. Non-alcoholic beverages are about Y10, beers Y10, and cocktails start at Y25. Live entertainment starts at 10 on most nights.

$$$$ ✕ **Heyou Seafood Restaurant.** This well-known restaurant earned its reputation for serving the freshest seafood to military officials. Now, however, it is open to the general public with only a red star in the middle of the dining room ceiling as a token of its former status. There are no English menus, so you'll have to point. ⊠ *28 Haixiu Lu* ☎ *0898/6671–1002* ▤ *No credit cards.*

¢–$ ✕ **Aiwanting Restaurant.** This popular chain restaurant, serving spicy Hunanese cuisine, is one of the key draws on Haikou's Street of Beautiful Chinese Flavors. There is a sister branch in Shanghai. ⊠ *61 Jinlong Lu* ☎ *0898/6853–8699* ▤ *No credit cards.*

$$–$$$$ ▥ **Golden Coast Lawton.** A grand hotel on the northern island of Haidian, the Golden Coast has a number of beautiful architectural flourishes, such as trim around the windows and brass fixtures in the more expensive rooms. The lobby is a vast open space tastefully decorated with dark wood and Chinese antiques. ⊠ *68 Renmin Dadao, Haidian Island 570208* ☎ *0898/6625–9888* 🖷 *0898/6625–8889* ⊕ *www.golden.com.cn* ⇥ *354 rooms, 32 suites* ⚭ *6 restaurants, 2 tennis courts, pool, gym, hair salon, dance club, shops, business services, meeting rooms* ▤ *AE, MC, V.*

$$$ ▥ **Crowne Plaza Hainan Spa & Beach Resort.** Located 20 minutes by car from downtown Haikou, this resort-spa offers a chance for peaceful relaxation. Modeled like a French château, the hotel actually consists of three buildings. In the middle of the outdoor area, next to the beach, is a grand pool, with two waterslides in the children's area and a swim-up bar. All rooms have garden or sea views and a huge bathroom with a bay window. The hotel's Tea Tree Spa, in a separate building, claims to be the world's largest indoor hot spring. The traditional Chinese body massage is a great option. ⊠ *1 Qiongshan Ave., East Riverside, 571100* ☎ *0898/6596–6888* 🖷 *0898/6596–0666* ⊕ *www.crowneplazahainan.com* ⇥ *314 rooms, 337 suites* ⚭ *4 restaurants, pool, gym, spa, 3 bars, business services, meeting rooms* ▤ *AE, DC, MC, V.*

$–$$$ ▥ **Baohua Harbourview.** This huge complex on the shore directly across from the vast green expanse of Wanlu Park has beautiful views of the Hainan Strait. The smallish rooms are clean and comfortable and have great ocean views. There is a shopping arcade on the first floor. One of the four restaurants serves good Thai food, a rarity in this area. Discounts of 50% on rooms are the norm. ⊠ *69 Bin Hai Lu, 570105* ☎ *0898/6853–6699* 🖷 *0898/6853–5358* ⊕ *www.hibaohua.hotel.com* ⇥ *417 rooms, 35 suites* ⚭ *4 restaurants, gym, hair salon, bar, dance club, shops, business services* ▤ *AE, DC, MC, V.*

$$ ▥ **Haikou Mandarin.** As a member of the Meritus Hotel chain, you can expect excellent service. Located in the center of the financial district, this was the diplomatic hotel of choice during 2001's U.S. "spy plane" crisis. A large U.S. negotiating team and more than 100 foreign journalists stayed here while the crisis was resolved. The incident firmed up the hotel's reputation as the most comfortable business hotel in Haikou.

✉ *18 Wenhua Lu, 570105* ☎ *0898/6854–8888* 🖷 *0898/6854–0453* ⊕ *www.meritus-hotels.com* ➦ *318 rooms, 22 suites* ⚭ *3 restaurants, 2 pools, gym, hair salon, shops, business services, meeting rooms* ▤ AE, DC, MC, V.

¢ 🏨 **Haikou.** Although it is showing its age, this hotel in the center of town makes an excellent base for exploring Haikou on foot. ✉ *4 Haifu Lu, 570203* ☎ *0898/6535–0221* 🖷 *0898/6535–0232* ➦ *196 rooms, 8 suites* ⚭ *Restaurant, shops, business services, meeting rooms* ▤ AE, MC, V.

Nightlife

Haikou, once infamous for its "wild-east" boomtown sleaze, has cleaned up considerably. There are still plenty of neon-encrusted karaoke bars, saunas, and discos, as in any Chinese city. The best bet for evening entertainment is to stroll the streets. There are two interesting night markets just off of Jichang Lu south of Haixiu Lu.

Shopping

The area around the intersection of Haixiu Lu and Jichang Lu has a large number of small shops selling everything from coconut carvings to minority costumes. Hainan is a major exporter of pearls. Stores are usually open 9 AM–10 PM. The main shopping complex in Haikou, **DC Department Store** (✉ Haixiu Lu at Jichang Lu ☎ 0898/677–4312), has a wide assortment of sundries as well as local art. Fangsai Lu is also a good place to buy suntan lotion **Hongsheng Jewelry** (✉ 6 Wahai Lu ☎ 0898/672–2091) has a wide assortment of fine pearls, silver, and jade.

Boao Scenic Zone

㉛ *1½ hrs (86 km [53 mi]) by air-conditioned bus south from Haikou; 2 hrs (170 km [106 mi]) by air-conditioned bus northeast from Sanya.*

Boao Scenic Zone, on the eastern side of Hainan, is China's newest international resort and convention area. Some 85 km (53 mi) from Haikou Airport, it is a group of three small islands at the junction of the Wanqung River and the ocean—a naturally secure area. Since 2002 it has been the permanent site of the Boao Forum for Asia, an annual gathering of the region's political leaders. The majority of the area's hotels are clustered around a new convention center on Dongyu, the largest of the three connected islands off Hainan. Jade Belt Beach, at the mouth of the river, is unusual; it has seawater on one side and freshwater on the other. The old town of Boao, about 5 km (3 mi) away, is quiet but useful for basic shopping. The nearest city, Qionghai, is 16 km (10 mi) away.

Where to Stay

★ $$$$ 🏨 **Sofitel Boao.** Opened in 2003, this upmarket resort hotel was built to host top-tier guests at China's annual Boao Forum for Asia conference and already boasts a guest list including presidents George H. W. Bush, Pervez Musharraf, and Fidel Ramos. The service and facilities are excellent and the opulence includes a lobby with a six-tier crystal chandelier and two sprawling pools that encircle the entire hotel. Each spacious and luxuriously decorated room includes a freestanding bathtub, balconies, and teak floors. Nighttime hot springs are a treat under the stars. Three restaurants, serving Chinese, Japanese, and Western cuisines, are quite good. ⊠ *Dongyu Island, Boao 571434* ☎ *0898/6296–6888* 🖷 *0898/6296–6999* ⊕ *www.sofitel.com* ↝ *403 rooms, 34 suites* ⚿ *5 restaurants, 3 pools, gym, 3 bars, lounge, business center, convention center* ▤ *AE, DC, MC, V.*

$$–$$$ 🖼 **Gold Coast Hot Spring Hotel.** Built at the mouth of the Wanquan River, this upmarket Chinese resort is aimed at convention center attendees and China's growing middle-class leisure demographic. The hotel's pool and hot springs are huge, and a nicely designed lobby has great views of the ocean and river. ⊠ *8 Golden Coast Ave., Boao 571533* ☎ *0898/ 6277–8888* 🖷 *0898/6277–8899* ↝ *420 rooms, 36 suites* ⚿ *6 restaurants, tennis courts, pool, gym, massage, sauna, business services* ▤ *AE, DC, MC, V.*

Sports

Boao Golf & Country Club. At the mouth of the Wanquan River, this golf course offers two 18-hole, par-72 courses. The 7,019-yard tournament-quality course was designed by top international designers and continues to attract celebrity players, such as the former prime ministers of Australia and Japan. Greens fee are Y700 and caddies are Y120. ⊠ *Shapo Island, Boao* ☎ *0898/6277–7307* 🖷 *0898/6277–7315.*

Sanya

㉜ *3 hrs (256 km [159 mi]) south on express bus from Haikou.*

Sanya, the country's southernmost city, is China at its most laid back. The beaches are long and white, the weather averages 23°C (73°F), and the ocean is clear. With 3 million tourists annually heading to its three very different resort areas, there is much to see and something for every budget. You can hide away at a world-class international spa resort or join Chinese package tourists at industrial-size attractions.

Arguably China's capital of kitsch, Sanya was the host city of the 2003 and 2004 Miss World beauty pageants. It is also hosts the International Wedding Festival November 18–21 each year—a bizarre swarming of hundreds of Chinese couples reliving their big day.

The town itself does not have much to see, beyond a pleasant ocean boardwalk (where sunset falls bull's-eye among the fishing boats) and a photogenic dock. The three main beach resort areas are Yalong Bay, Dadonghai, and Sanya Bay.

★ **Yalong Bay National Resort,** 25 km (15½ mi) east of Sanya, is the focus of the current upscale building boom. It has a 7-km (4-mi) stretch of white-sand beach, perfect for sunbathers and beach-sports fanatics. There are nine resort hotels currently operating, and another six international-brand resorts nearing completion. The bay is privately owned and operated so you'll find a pristine but eerily quiet area with no local nonhotel restaurants or bars. To avoid cabin fever, guests always have the option of taking a taxi to downtown Sanya for about Y50 one-way.

Dadonghai Beach has more than 50 locally owned and operated hotels, catering mostly to Chinese and Russian tour groups. It is a long curved bay with a busy public beach, dotted with rented chairs and beach-loving tourists. Shark nets are set up to help alleviate swimmers' fears. Just up the beach on the boardwalk is a restaurant area serving seafood, with large tables catering to noisy, hungry tour groups.

Sanya Bay is a 15-km (9-mi) stretch of beach, catering mostly to Chinese groups on cheap package tours. There are no international hotels and the majority of quality English-speaking staff have been lured away to upmarket Yalong Bay. Still, this beach is a great place to walk, particular in the evening when old fishing junk boats and fishermen move into place among picture-postcard sunsets. After dark there is a nice boardwalk for strolling or people-watching. Seat yourself at a cheap seafood restaurant for fresh, just-caught fish, crab, or clams. For more evening entertainment, try slipping into a pair of matching Hawaiian-print shorts and T-shirt, and joining the locals in mass-synchronized disco-dancing.

For a quiet walk and beautiful scenery away from the crowds, take a five-minute cab ride to the Luhuitou Peninsula. **Luhuitou Park** (Luhuitou Gongyuan) has lush tropical flora, and from the peak there are fabulous views of the city and the ocean. ✛ *On rise just east of downtown Sanya* 🎫 *Y60* ⊙ *Daily 7 AM–11:30 PM.*

Where to Stay & Eat

$$–$$$$ ✕🏨 **Sheraton Sanya Resort.** The official "home of Miss World," where **Fodor'sChoice** the contestants stay each December, this is Sanya's premier resort. The ★ landscaping is beautiful and the open-air teak lobby has sliding wall-to-ceiling windows. Outside, three pristine pools are set along the shoreline. This is a great place to bring the family as the hotel offers daytime sports activities for kids and adults. Wireless broadband Internet connection allows business travelers to stay connected poolside. There are two good dining options here, the first-floor Lotus Café has indoor and outdoor seating, and kids may enjoy feeding the koi in the restaurant's fishpond. The Bai Yun Chinese Restaurant ($$–$$$) is a solid choice, offering highlights of Chinese dishes from the various provinces and specializing in seafood. ✉ *Yalong Bay National Resort, Sanya 572000* 🕾 *0898/8855–8866* ⊕ *www.sheraton.com/sanya* 🛏 *462 rooms, 49 suites* ⚴ *4 restaurants, 2 tennis courts, 3 pools, gym, spa, 2 bars, babysitting, business services* ▤ *AE, DC, MC, V.*

$$$–$$$$ 🏨 **Gloria Resort.** Yalong Bay's first five-star resort lacks the impact of its ritzy new neighbors. Still, its rooms are clean and spacious, with great views. The hotel's private white-sand beach is still among China's best. ✉ *Yalong Bay National Resort, Sanya 572000* 🕾 *0898/8856–8855* 🕾 *0898/8856–8533* ⊕ *www.gloriaresort.com* 🛏 *404 rooms, 18 suites* ⚴ *3 restaurants, 2 pools, business services* ▤ *AE, DC, MC, V.*

$$–$$$$ 🏨 **Holiday Inn Resort.** This well-kept hotel makes the most of its location in the middle of idyllic Yalong Bay. The lobby and coffee shop's huge open windows frame panoramic views of the ocean and surrounding islands. English is spoken at the front desk, and discounts of 40% are available. ✉ *Yalong Bay National Resort, Sanya 572016*

☎ 0898/8856–5666 🖷 0898/8856–5688 ⊕ www.ichotelsgroup.com
📞 358 rooms, 53 suites ♨ 3 restaurants, 2 pools, gym, spa, 2 bars, nightclub, baby-sitting, business services ▤ AE, DC, MC, V.

$$–$$$$ 🖭 **Resort Intime.** The hotel, popular with Russian tour groups, was ren-
ovated in 2003 to give it a funky, modern feel. Green glass pillars out-
fit the two-story lobby, making the hotel easy to see from the main
boardwalk. Most rooms have balconies, and the suites on the top floor
offer 270-degree views of the ocean. Discounts of 40% are possible.
✉ Donghai Lu, Dadonghai Bay, Sanya 572021 ☎ 0898/8821–0888
🖷 0898/8821–1088 ⊕ www.resortintime.com 📞 370 rooms, 46 suites
♨ 3 restaurants, tennis court, 3 pools, nightclub, business services
▤ AE, DC, MC, V.

$–$$ 🖭 **Pearl River Garden Hotel.** From the outside, this hotel resembles a cruise
ship with lighted decks and the layout is a unique wave shape. There is
a round two-story restaurant in the front, and an ornately golden lobby
mural. The clientele is mostly Chinese tourists. ✉ Donghai Lu, Dadonghai, Sanya 572000 ☎ 0898/8821–1888 🖷 0898/8821–1999 ⊕ www.
prgardenhotel.comm.cn 📞 235 rooms, 13 suites ♨ 2 restaurants, pool,
business services ▤ AE, DC, MC, V.

$–$$ 🖭 **Sanya Shanhaitian.** This hotel's name literally means "mountain, sea,
sky," as it's nestled up against a mountain overlooking Dadonghai
Beach and the blue skies of southern Hainan. The hotel is by far the
most luxurious in the area. Many rooms, decorated in peaceful pastels,
have sunrise views. ✉ Luling Lu, Dadonghai, Sanya 572021 ☎ 0898/
8821–1688 🖷 0898/8821–1988 📞 180 rooms, 21 suites ♨ 4 restaurants, pool, hair salon, sauna, bowling, bar, nightclub, business services
▤ AE, MC, V.

¢ 🖭 **Cactus Resort.** Set well back from the beach, and occupied mostly by
tour groups, this hotel is among Yalong Bay's cheapest. An Aztec theme
keeps the setting surreal; there are cactus motifs everywhere and a huge
pyramid (the stage for occasional evening shows) dominates the sprawling shallow pool. Spacious rooms are cheerful and clean with all modern conveniences. Smiling staff struggle with English, but try very hard.
One large restaurant serves passable Western and Chinese food. ✉ Yalong Bay National Resort, Sanya 572016 ☎ 0898/8856–8866 🖷 0898/
8856–8867 ⊕ www.cactusresort.com 📞 600 rooms ♨ Restaurant, 2
tennis courts, pool, massage, billiards ▤ AE, DC, MC, V.

¢ 🖭 **Palm Beach Resorts and Spa.** This clean and competitively priced hotel
is one of the few resorts located on Sanya Bay. There are two free-form
pools, a Jacuzzi, and plenty of sports activities from which to choose.
The restaurants serve Cantonese and Hainanese cuisines, specializing
in seafood dishes. ✉ Haipo Development Area, Sanya 572023 ☎ 0898/
8833–1888 🖷 0898/8833–0001 📞 340 rooms, 24 suites ♨ 3 restaurants, bar, 2 pools, tennis court, business services, meeting rooms ▤ AE,
DC, MC, V.

Nightlife & the Arts

Nightlife, such as it exists in Sanya, is centered along **Dadonghai Beach.**
Most of the action is on **Yuhai Lu,** where there are rows of seafood restaurants and beachside bars. Some of the beachside hotels have barbecues
and various types of musical performances (both Western and Chinese).

A fun sightseeing option is to cruise the boardwalk and surrounding streets in one of the many motorcycle and sidecar taxis.

Shopping

The stores along **Dadonghai main boardwalk** (⊠ Donghai Lu, Dadonghai) sell the must-have Hawaiian print beachwear, carved coconuts, shells, and T-shirts. Although Sanya does not offer the shopping choices of Guangzhou or Hong Kong, it does have a lively local market scene. **Second Market** (⊠ Jiefang Er Lu, Sanya) is one such market, offering everything from fruit to dried seafood and local-quality clothing.

Sports & the Outdoors

Yalong Bay Golf Course. Located in Yalong Bay National Resort are two 18-hole, par-72 golf courses. The 7,000-plus-yard courses were conceived by American designer Robert Jones Jr. and are set among waterfalls, coconut palms, and year-round sunshine. Facilities include restaurants and a tropical-style clubhouse. Greens fees are Y850, caddies Y145. ⊠ *Opposite Sheraton Sanya Resort, Yalong Bay, Sanya* ☎ *0898/8856–5039* 🖷 *0898/8856–5055.*

Sanya Jiu Hao Driving Range. For those who want to hit some balls, this driving range in the middle of Sanya is the place. The range extends over 200 yards and is lighted at night. It costs Y25 for a basket of 50 balls and Y10 for one club rental. Open 8:30–10. ⊠ *Er Huan Rd. between Chaojian and Xinfeng bridges, Sanya* ☎ *No phone.*

Check your resort for afternoon beach activities. You can rent speedboats, Jet Skis, kayaks, scuba diving equipment, or banana boats. A half day of scuba diving costs about Y400–Y600. The best white-sand beach for chilling out is Yalong Bay, followed by Dadonghai and Sanya Bay. All beaches are excellent for sunbathers, swimmers, and joggers. Sunset is a nice time to stroll along any of the beaches.

Side Trips from Sanya

☙ **Butterfly Valley** is an interesting place to bring the kids for an afternoon. More than 500 species of the 650 indigenous species of butterflies are represented here. ⊠ *Opposite Cactus Resort, Yalong Bay, Sanya* 🖭 *Y23.*

Nanshan Temple is touted as a cultural theme park for Buddhists. Its major attraction is a 354-foot-high bodhisattva statue which is being constructed on a small island 100 feet out into the sea. The purpose of this spiritual skyscraper appears to be squeezing cash out of tourists (a common Chinese mix of religion and consumerism). Having paid a hefty entrance fee, the devout masses must also pay Y20 extra to view special temples and Y15 for the sightseeing cart. ✛ *1-hr drive along west coast of Sanya* 🖭 *Y65* ⊙ *Daily 9–5.*

A major attraction for Chinese tourists is **Tianya Haijiao** (literally, "edge of the sky and rim of the sea"), a beach famous for its rock formations and Chinese calligraphy. The location is beautiful: the site is portrayed on the back of the Chinese two-yuan bill. Swimming is not allowed. Sightseeing carts are an additional Y10 per person. ✛ *45-min drive along west coast of Sanya* 🖭 *Y65 adults* ⊙ *Daily 9–5.*

Five Fingers Mountain (Wuzhi Shan) is, at 6,125 feet, Hainan's highest peak. For the adventurous, it is a good three- to four-hour hike to reach the top. ✛ *65 km (40 mi) northeast of Tongzha, accessible by bus or taxi.*

off the beaten path

TONGZHA – Hainan's third-largest city and the former administrative center from the island's Li and Miao (Hmong) autonomous prefecture, is also a good base from which to explore real minority villages, as opposed to the commercial theme park–like "villages" that are highly touted in tour packages. You probably won't see any tourists here so bringing along a guide is wise. ✛ *2½-hr (88 km [55 mi]) drive from Sanya, 5½-hr (223 km [139 mi]) drive from Haikou.*

WHERE TO STAY | Although not known for exciting cuisine, you can find small restaurants along any street in Tongzha. Better yet is to eat at food stalls on the street as you can see how fresh the ingredients are.

¢ 🏨 **Tongzha Resort Hotel.** Nestled against a mountain at the top edge of the city, this hotel provides good views of the urban scene below. Though not a luxury hotel as the name suggests, it is comfortable and clean. ⊠ *38 Shanzhuang Lu, Tongzha 572200* ☎ *0899/8662–3188* 🖷 *0899/ 8662–2201* 🖥 *103 rooms, 3 suites* ⚭ *Restaurant, hair salon, bar, business services* 🖃 *AE, MC, V.*

Hainan A to Z

To research prices, get advice from other travelers, and book travel arrangements, visit www.fodors.com.

AIR TRAVEL

Both Haikou's Meilan Airport and Sanya's Phoenix Airport have daily flights to most major Chinese cities. The three main airline carriers that service all of Hainan Island include Hainan Airlines, China Southern Airlines, and Air China. Flights to Haikou leave from: Hong Kong twice on Monday and Thursday and once a day on all other days; Guangzhou 12 flights daily; Shanghai 7 flights daily; Beijing 8 flights daily; and Shenzhen 16 flights daily. Flights to Sanya leave from: Hong Kong once on Wednesday, Friday, and Sunday and twice daily on all other days; Guangzhou 9 flights daily; Shanghai 5 flights daily; Beijing 3 flights daily; and Shenzhen 5 flights daily.

🛦 Airlines & Contacts **Air China** ⊠ 6 Nan Tian Rd., 1st fl., Nan Tian Bin Guan, Haikou ☎ 0898/6678–0099 ⊕ www.airchina.com. **China Southern Airlines** ⊠ 53 Long Kun Rd., Haikou ☎ 0898/6670–0803 ⊕ www.cs-air.com. **Hainan Airlines** ⊠ Hai Xiang Rd., Hai Hang Fa Zhan Bldg., Haikou ☎ 0898/6671–0274, 800/876–8999 in U.S. ⊕ www. hnair.com.

🛦 Airport Information **Meilan Airport** ⊠ Haikou ☎ 0898/6575–1333 or 0898/657–0114. **Phoenix Airport** ⊠ Sanya ☎ 0898/8828–9389.

BOAT & FERRY TRAVEL

Haikou's Xiuying Port offers ferry services to Guangzhou. Boats sail every Monday, Wednesday, and Friday, once a day, departing at 4 PM, arriving at 10 AM the following morning. Tickets cost between Y147 and Y453, depending on class of service. The boats are comfortable but they are not cruise ships.

🚢 Boat & Ferry Lines **Xiuying Port** ✉ Haikou ☎ 0898/6865-3315.

BUS TRAVEL

Buses are the fastest way to get anywhere in Hainan. Comfortable express buses with air-conditioning and toilets run regularly between Haikou and Sanya (3 hours; Y70) on the Eastern Highway. Buses depart Haikou from the East Bus Station. Buses depart Sanya from the bus station in town, but tickets can also be purchased from nearly every small shop along the highway near Dadonghai. There is also bus service to Boao from both Haikou (leaving every 1½ hours; Y42) and Sanya (leaving every 20 minutes; Y22). Most bus station phone operators do not speak English. If you need assistance, contact your hotel concierge.

🚌 Bus Station Information **Haikou East Bus Station** ✉ Hai Fu Rd. ☎ 0898/6534-0753. **Sanya Bus Station** ✉ Corner of Gangmen Rd. and northern end of Jiefang Lu ☎ 0898/8827-2440.

CAR RENTAL

Car rental is available from Haikou, and requires either a Chinese driver's license, class C, or an International Driver's License.

🚗 **Hainan Car Company** ✉ West door of passenger transport center, Xiu Ying port, Binghia Rd., Haikou ☎ 0898/6864-4930. **San Jiu Car Company** ✉ Ou Ba Ai He Travel Rent Co., Zhonghua Bldg., 1st fl., Sanya ☎ 0898/8866-5199.

EMERGENCIES

In an emergency, call the **police** (☎ 110) or the nearest local hospital. English may not be understood, however, so you may want to call the nearest upscale hotel where an English speaker is usually available if that is the case.

🏥 **Boao Hospital** ✉ Bin Hai Lu, Boao ☎ 0898/6277-8255. **Haikou City Hospital** ✉ 43 Ren Min Dalu, Haikou ☎ 0898/6618-9675. **Sanya Hospital** ✉ Jiefang San Lu, Sanya ☎ 0898/8825-8884.

TRAIN TRAVEL

Hainan only offers cargo service on trains.

TRANSPORTATION AROUND HAINAN

For city travel in Hainan, taxis (car or motorcycle) are your best bet for getting around. If riding a motorcycle taxi, be sure to negotiate the price in advance: Y5–Y8 should get you just about anywhere in any city. For longer-distance car taxi rides, it is usually to your advantage to negotiate a flat fee rather than use the meter. Off-meter, negotiated car taxi fares are: Haikou downtown to Meilan Airport (Y40); Haikou downtown to East Haikou (Y40); Sanya downtown to Yalong Bay (Y40–Y50); Sanya downtown to Nanshan Temple–End of Earth Monument (Y120); Yalong Bay to Phoenix Airport (Y80–Y100).

TRAVEL AGENCIES

In Haikou and Sanya, China International Travel Service (CITS) and China Travel Service (CTS) can assist with booking air tickets as well as arranging other transportation. They also have a number of package tours and driving tours available.

🚩 Local Agency Referrals **Haikou CITS** ⊠ Nantian Hotel, 1st fl., Lantian Rd., Haikou ☎ 0898/6671-0998 🖷 0898/6670-8009. **Haikou CTS** ⊠ CTS Mansion, Datong Rd., Haikou ☎ 0898/6672-6661 Ext. 2. **Sanya CITS** ⊠ Gold Bay Hotel, W. Guangming Rd., Sanya ☎ 0898/8895-8220 🖷 0898/8895-8221. **Sanya CTS** ⊠ Re Hai Guang Chang, Dadonghai, Sanya ☎ 0898/8821-0055.

VISITOR INFORMATION

In tourist information in Haikou or Sanya, inquire at your hotel or call the Hainan Tourist Board. The Hainan Tourism Administration has set up Tourist Complaint Hotlines in Haikou and Sanya.

🚩 Tourist Information **Complaint Hotline** ☎ 0898/6625-0780. **Hainan Tourist Board** ☎ 0898/6674-0005.

HONG KONG
FINANCE, COMMERCE & HIGH STYLE

8

FLOAT AROUND THE CITY
on the top level of the Star Ferry ⇨ *p.435*

SOAK IN A BIT OF HIGH CULTURE
at the Hong Kong Museum of Art ⇨ *p.439*

ELEVATE YOURSELF TO NEW HEIGHTS
on the fun and steep Peak Tram ⇨ *p.435*

SAVOR THE CRISPIEST ROAST GOOSE
at the vast Yung Kee restaurant ⇨ *p.449*

TAKE IN A VIEW THAT JUST WON'T QUIT
at the Café Deco Bar & Grill ⇨ *p.448*

GET THE BEST IN OLD-WORLD STYLE
inside the Peninsula Hong Kong ⇨ *p.460*

SAVE MONEY WITHOUT LOSING COMFORT
at Garden View International House ⇨ *p.458*

Updated by
Eva Chui
Loiterton

TO STAND ON THE TIP OF KOWLOON PENINSULA and look out across the harbor to the full expanse of the Hong Kong island skyline—as awesome in height as Manhattan's, but only a few blocks deep and strung along the entire north coast—is to see the triumph of ambition over fate. Whereas it took Paris and London 10 to 20 generations to build the spectacular cities seen today, and New York 6, Hong Kong built almost everything you see before you in the time since today's young investment bankers were born. It is easy to perceive this tremendous creation of wealth as an inevitable result of Hong Kong's strategic position, but at any point in the territory's history things might have happened slightly differently, and the island would have found itself on the margins of world trade rather than at the center.

When the 78-square-km (30-square-mi) island of Hong Kong was ceded to the British after the Opium War of 1841, it consisted, in the infamous words of the British minister at the time, of "barren rock" whose only redeeming feature was the adjacent deep-water harbor. For the British, though, it served another purpose: Hong Kong guarded the eastern edge of the Pearl River delta, and with it access to Guangzhou (Canton), which in the mid-19th century was China's main trading port. By controlling Hong Kong, Britain came to control the export of Chinese products such as silk and tea, and to corner the Chinese market for Western-manufactured goods and opium. The scheme proved highly profitable.

If British trade were all Hong Kong had going for it, however, its prosperity would have faded with the rest of the empire. No, the real story of Hong Kong began in the 1920s, when the first wave of Chinese refugees settled here to avoid civil unrest at home. They were followed in the '30s and '40s by refugees fleeing the advance of the invading Japanese army. But the biggest throngs of all came after the 1949 Communist revolution in China—mostly from the neighboring province of Guangdong, but also from Fujian, Shanghai, and elsewhere. Many of these mainland arrivals came from humble farming backgrounds, but many others had been rich and had seen their wealth and businesses stripped away by the revolutionaries. They came to Hong Kong poorer than their families had been in generations, yet by virtue of their labor, their descendants are the wealthiest generation yet.

Hong Kong has always lived and breathed commerce, and it is the territory's shrines to Mammon that will make the strongest impression when you first arrive. The Central district has long been thick with skyscrapers bearing the names of banks and conglomerates, and yet more continue to be built, squeezed into irregular plots of land that would seem insufficient for buildings half the size. When that doesn't work, the city simply reclaims more land from the harbor and builds on it almost before it dries. For a few years it will be obvious which land is reclaimed and which is old as the ground is turned and foundations laid, but soon enough the two will meld into one, just as they have before: you now have to walk four blocks from the Star Ferry Terminal, through streets shaded by office towers, to reach Queen's Road Central, the former waterfront. You may well ask what one can know for sure in this world if

8

Numbers in the text correspond to numbers in the margin and on the Hong Kong map.

If you have 3 days

Spend the first day exploring Hong Kong Island, starting with a ride on the **Star Ferry Pier** ❶ ►. Walk through the territory's Central business district, which includes the headquarters of **Hongkong & Shanghai Bank** ❹ and the **Bank of China Tower** ❸, then on to the antiques stores along **Wyndham Street** ❺ and **Hollywood Road** ❼. Proceed on to **Man Mo Temple** ❽ and then take a taxi to the **Peak Tram** ⑫, which runs up a near-vertical cliff to **Victoria Peak** ⑬, where there are views of the harbor. Late afternoon and evening is a good time to spend on the south side of the island shopping in **Stanley Village** or strolling around **Shek O** ⑮.

On Day 2 you can discover Kowloon, starting with the **Space Museum** ⑰ and **Hong Kong Museum of Art** ⑱ along the waterfront near the Star Ferry pier. Stop at the colonial-style **Peninsula Hotel** ⑲ for tea, then wander up **Nathan Road** ⑳, one of the most densely packed shopping streets on earth. Proceed to the **Jade Market** ㉓ or the **Bird Garden** ㉕, then end the day with the **Temple Street night market.**

The final day should be spent on one of the outer islands like **Lantau,** where you can take a bus to the **Po Lin Monastery** ㉛ and visit the **Giant Buddha.** Also on the island are the fishing villages of **Tai O** ㉜ and **Mui Wo,** now somewhat modernized but still sedate compared to Central.

If you have 6 days

With more time you can add a second day for exploring Hong Kong Island, visiting the bustling department store district of **Causeway Bay.** Spend the afternoon in the dried foods and traditional herbal medicine shops in the **Western district,** and come nightfall, you can meander through the back alleys of **Wanchai** looking for the dens of iniquity that were once so legendary among sailors of the Pacific.

Your last two days provide an opportunity to visit the old Chinese villages of the **New Territories** (best done on a tour as the sights are so spread out) and the charming East/West hybrid of neighboring **Macau,** the former Portuguese colony just an hour away by boat.

If you have 8 days

Follow the six-day itinerary above, then stay overnight in Macau and give yourself time to discover a hidden gem of a town, one underrated even by many in Hong Kong. Best known for its casinos and fantastic food, Macau also has pastel-color baroque churches, traditional Chinese gardens, and even a black-sand beach. You can also take a day to visit either **Lamma** or **Cheung Chau Island** to see a slower-paced side of Hong Kong life and try fresh-caught seafood cooked Cantonese style.

not where the earth ends and the oceans begin, but Hong Kongers have gotten used to such vagaries.

Watching young investment bankers out on a Friday night in Hong Kong's nightspot haven of Lan Kwai Fong, reveling in their outrageous good fortune at being in this place at this time in history, you can't help but wonder whether this can possibly last. There's a heady, end-of-an-era exuberance to it all—a decadence that portends doom ahead. Yet visitors to Hong Kong have felt this same sentiment for almost a century and a half and, save for the rare economic downturn, the day of reckoning has not come. One of those rare exceptions came within a month after Hong Kong's handover back to China. But the change of sovereignty was not the issue which many expected to be the source of problems. Rather, it was the Asian crisis which took almost everyone by surprise. For a moment during these uncertain times, it seemed Hong Kongers would have to permanently scale back their ambitions. But then the moment passed and the usual breakneck growth returned.

Rapid change has not been limited to Hong Kong Island or the crowded Kowloon Peninsula, but extends up through the "new towns" of the New Territories. Some of these, like Sha Tin, were rice paddies 20 years ago and now form thriving cities of a half million people. The most ambitious project of all is the one you see on arrival: the leveling of Chek Lap Kok, an uninhabited island of rock and scrub, that made way for Hong Kong's stylish, ultraefficient international airport, the final legacy of British-ruled Hong Kong. Arriving in Hong Kong may now lack the rooftop-grazing shock of flying into the old Kai Tak, but you're whisked through the airport in no time and can then zip into Central in just 23 minutes on the Airport Express train. In a fairly short time, Lantau Island will be the location of the new Disneyland Hong Kong, which is scheduled at this writing to open by late 2005 or 2006; this will no doubt make the island an important destination for tourists from Hong Kong, the rest of China, and the rest of the world.

Amid all the change it can be easy (even for residents) to forget that most of Hong Kong has nothing to do with business or skyscrapers: three-quarters of it is actually rural land and wilderness. A bird's-eye view reveals the 236 islands that make up the lesser-known parts of Hong Kong; most are nothing but jagged peaks and tropical scrub, just as Hong Kong Island itself once was. Others are time capsules of ancestral China, with tiny temples, fishing villages, and small vegetable farms. Even Hong Kong Island, so relentlessly urban on its north coast, consists mostly of rolling green hills and sheltered bays on its south side. So whether you're looking for the hectic Hong Kong or the relaxed one, both are easy enough to find—indeed, sometimes only a few minutes apart.

EXPLORING HONG KONG

Just 78 square km (30 square mi), **Hong Kong Island** is where the action is, from high finance to nightlife to luxury shopping. As a result—even though Kowloon is just a short ride away—many residents feel little reason to ever leave the island. One of Hong Kong's unexpected pleasures

8

Beach Bummin'

Surprising as it may seem, splendid beaches are all over Hong Kong. Repulse Bay is a sort of Chinese Coney Island. Around the corner is the smaller and less crowded Deep Water Bay; Turtle Cove is isolated and beautiful; Shek O's Big Wave Bay has a Mediterranean feel; and in the New Territories you can catch a sampan from the Sai Kung waterfront to several idyllic island beaches, including Hap Mun (Half Moon) Bay.

Tops for Shops

Hong Kong has some of the best shopping in the world, if you work at it. Although the thought of crowded streets and mind-boggling choices can be daunting, no place makes big spending easier than this center of international commerce. Every major designer label is here, including their bargain-priced factory overruns. Computers and software are famously good value in Sham Shui Po's many computer stores. Novelties and T-shirts galore are best sought at Temple Street Night Market. Chinese antiques and paintings, handicrafts from all over Asia, electronic goods, and luxury accessories—you name it, Hong Kong sells it. Just as remarkable is the physical array of places to shop, from sophisticated boutique-lined malls to open-air markets and shadowy alleyways.

Yin & Yang in Action

There are so many ways of absorbing Chinese culture. Even on public transport or in the street, you will be amazed by how polite and courteous people are obliged to behave as they move around a crowded city. This necessity to "get along" and respect an individual's personal space keeps Hong Kong one of the safest cities in the world to walk around, either by day or night. But there's probably no better way of pondering the culture than in the early morning, at any park, at the tai chi ritual. The calmness amid frenetic life beyond reflects the philosophy of yin and yang balance that essentially underlies what it means to be Chinese. This philosophy extends beyond exercising to eating, conversation, and meeting people for the first time, where such a simple matter as exchanging name cards assumes its own polite ritual. Appreciate this side of Hong Kong and you will go a long way to understanding why so many people, both Chinese and foreigners, fall in love with the city.

---

is that, despite what sometimes feels like unrelenting urbanity, property development has actually been restricted to a few small areas. As a result, a 20-minute taxi ride from downtown Central can have you breathing fresh air and seeing only lush green vegetation.

Hong Kong has few historical landmarks (largely because soaring property values have long since caused most older buildings to be torn down and replaced) and no more than a handful of cultural sights, but it pulses with an extraordinarily dynamic contemporary life. In general, the commercial and shopping districts are on the island's north coast, interspersed with the ubiquitous apartment blocks, while the towns on the rest of

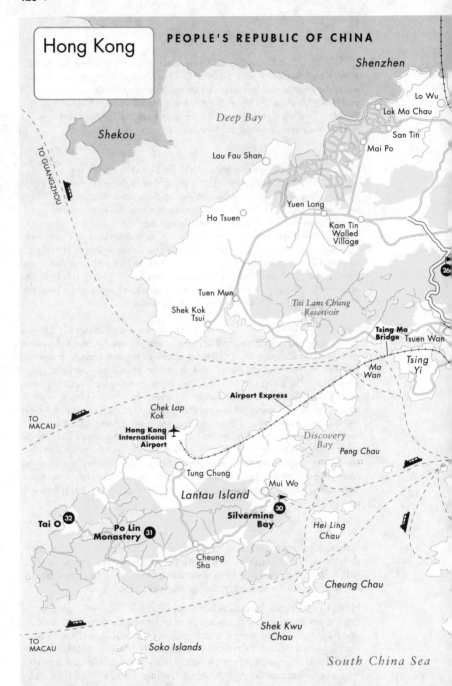

Hong Kong

PEOPLE'S REPUBLIC OF CHINA

Shenzhen

Lo Wu

Lok Ma Chau

Deep Bay

San Tin

Shekou

Mai Po

Lau Fau Shan

Yuen Long

Ha Tsuen

Kam Tin Walled Village

TO GUANGZHOU

Tuen Mun

Shek Kok Tsui

Tai Lam Chung Reservoir

Tsing Ma Bridge Tsuen Wan

Tsing Yi

Ma Wan

Airport Express

Chek Lap Kok

TO MACAU

Hong Kong International Airport

Discovery Bay

Peng Chau

Tung Chung

Mui Wo

Lantau Island

Silvermine Bay

Tai O **32**

Po Lin Monastery **31**

30

Hei Ling Chau

Cheung Sha

Cheung Chau

TO MACAU

Shek Kwu Chau

Soko Islands

South China Sea

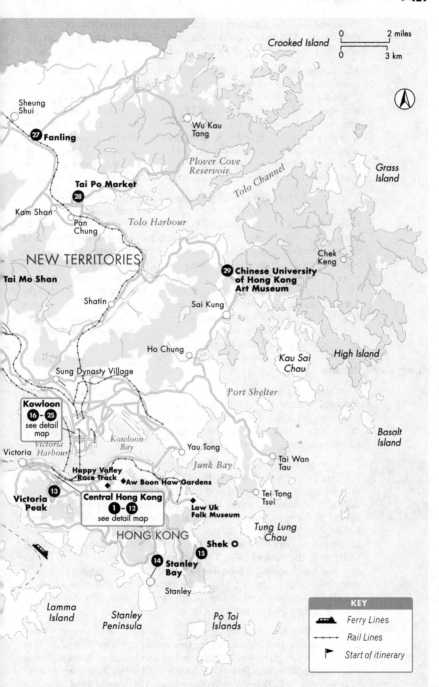

Crooked Island

0   2 miles

0   3 km

Sheung Shui

27 Fanling

Wu Kau Tang

Plover Cove Reservoir

Tolo Channel

Grass Island

Tai Po Market

28

Kam Shan

Pan Chung

Tolo Harbour

Chek Keng

NEW TERRITORIES

Tai Mo Shan

29 Chinese University of Hong Kong Art Museum

Shatin

Sai Kung

Ho Chung

Kau Sai Chau

High Island

Sung Dynasty Village

Port Shelter

Basalt Island

Kowloon 16 – 25 see detail map

Kowloon Bay

Yau Tong

Junk Bay

Tai Wan Tau

Victoria

Victoria Harbour

Happy Valley Race Track

◆ Aw Boon Haw Gardens

Tei Tong Tsui

Victoria Peak

13

Central Hong Kong 1 – 12 see detail map

◆ Law Uk Folk Museum

Tung Lung Chau

HONG KONG

Shek O

15

14 Stanley Bay

Stanley

Lamma Island

Stanley Peninsula

Po Toi Islands

KEY	
🚢	*Ferry Lines*
┼┼┼	*Rail Lines*
⚑	*Start of itinerary*

the island tend to be more residential. Each district has a name (and the name of its MTR stop usually corresponds) and a slightly distinct character, but the borders tend to blur together.

The **Kowloon** peninsula lies just across the harbor from Central and is bounded in the north by the string of mountains that give Kowloon— a word derived from *gau lung,* or "nine dragons"—its poetic name. Kowloon is closer to China than Hong Kong in more ways than just geography: although the island is home to international finance and glittering modern skyscrapers, Kowloon's urban fabric is more densely woven. Nevertheless, Kowloon has many of the territory's best hotels as well as a mind-boggling range of shopping options, and no visit is complete without taking on the commercial chaos of Nathan Road.

The expansive **New Territories** lies between Kowloon and the Chinese border and feels far removed from the congestion and urban rigors of the rest of the region. Lush parks and therapeutic nature walks are spread out across its 200 square mi. You can also get a glimpse of the precolonial culture of ethnic groups like the Hakka by visiting some of the temples and villages that preserve a traditional way of life—or at least as close as you can get to it in this modern age. But the New Territories is not all ancient: over the last few decades public housing projects throughout the area have led to the creation of new towns like Sha Tin and Tsuen Mun, some of which are now home to a half million people. They may lack the sights of interest to visitors, but they represent real life for a large percentage of Hong Kong's residents.

Hong Kong Island

Most districts on the island are best explored on foot, but taxis are so plentiful (except during typhoons, when you really need them) that it is easy to get a ride farther afield. The best strolling weather is in the dry season from late September to mid-December; the rest of the year you should carry a folding umbrella.

a good tour

For more than a century, the natural starting point for any walk through this area has been the **Star Ferry Pier** ❶ ► in Central. Follow the awnings to the right of the terminal and go straight through the underground walkway to come to Statue Square. The intriguing Victorian/Chinese hybrid building on the east side of the square is the **Legislative Council Building** ❷. Along the southern end of the square are the buildings of the three note-issuing banks in Hong Kong: the art deco former headquarters of the **Bank of China Tower** ❸, the spectacular strut-and-ladder facade of the **Hongkong & Shanghai Bank (HSBC)** ❹, and, pressing up against it, the rose-color wedge of Standard Chartered Bank. You can walk under the HSBC building, looking up into the atrium through a curved glass floor, and then exit on the south side.

A little farther ahead on the right, at the intersection of Queen's Road Central and Pedder Street, lies the **Landmark** ❺, the mother of all luxury shopping centers, but by turning left and heading up the hill, you will run into **Wyndham Street** ❻, which is lined with Chinese art and antiques stores. Wyndham eventually turns into **Hollywood Road** ❼, which

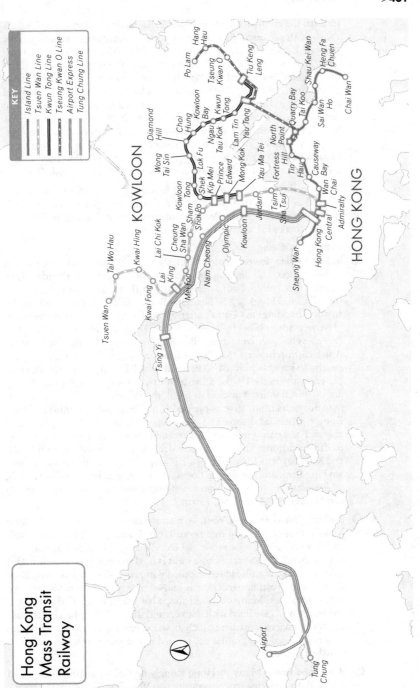

Hong Kong Mass Transit Railway

KEY
- Island Line
- Tsuen Wan Line
- Kwun Tong Line
- Tseung Kwan O Line
- Airport Express
- Tung Chung Line

KOWLOON

HONG KONG

leads to the colorful **Man Mo Temple** ⑧. To reach the curios and trinkets shops of **Upper Lascar Row** ⑨, also known as **Cat Street,** walk down the steps of Ladder Street, just across from Man Mo Temple. By walking straight down the hill and continuing toward the waterfront, you'll run into **Bonham Strand East and West** ⑩, which has many traditional shops selling dried seafood. When you're just about ready to turn back, head toward the harbor and follow Connaught Road east until you come to the cream-and-brown **Western Market** ⑪, which dates from 1906 and has been lovingly restored. From there it's an easy tram ride back to Central, or you can take a taxi to the **Peak Tram** ⑫ terminal and ride up to **Victoria Peak** ⑬. From the peak you can take a taxi to the south side of the island to visit **Stanley Bay** ⑭ or the seaside village of **Shek O** ⑮.

TIMING This is a difficult tour to complete in a day; two would be ideal. The Central and Western districts walk will take about four hours, and it's worth leaving time at the Peak for coffee or a meal. The trip to the south side can make for a day's outing on its own.

Sights to See

❸ **Bank of China Tower.** In the politics of Hong Kong architecture, the stylish art deco building that served as the old **Bank of China headquarters** was the first trump: built after World War II, it was 20 feet higher than the adjacent Hongkong & Shanghai Bank (HSBC). It is now one of the smallest buildings in Central, utterly dwarfed by the imposing steel-and-glass structure HSBC finished in 1985. The Bank of China refused to take this challenge lying down, however, and commissioned the Chinese-American architect I. M. Pei to build a bigger, better headquarters nearby to supersede HSBC. The result: the Bank of China Tower, completed in the early 1990s, a masterful twisting spire of replicating triangles and the first building to break the ridgeline of Victoria Peak. It may not be as innovative as the HSBC building, but it dominates Hong Kong's urban landscape and embodies the post-handover balance of power. For a panoramic, and uncrowded, viewing spot of Central, head to the 43rd floor. The observation deck is open weekdays from 9 to 5 and Saturday 9 to 1; and best of all, it's free. The old building now houses Sin Hua Bank and, on the top floors, David Tang's exclusive China Club, which manages to be both postmodern and nostalgic for pre-Communist Shanghai. ⊠ *Bank St., Central.*

★ ❿ **Bonham Strand East and West.** A major thoroughfare in one of Hong Kong's most charmingly traditional areas, Bonham Strand is lined with shops selling goods that evoke the old China Coast trade merchants. A few shops sell live snakes, whose meat is used in winter soups to ward off colds and whose gallbladders reputedly improve vigor and virility. Bonham Strand West, in particular, is known for its Chinese medicines and herbal remedies. Many of its old shops have their original facades, and inside, the walls are lined with drawers and shelves of jars filled with hundreds of pungent ingredients such as wood barks and insects. These are consumed dried and ground up, infused in hot water or tea, or taken as powders or pills.

❼ **Hollywood Road.** Many of Hong Kong's best antiques, furniture, and classical-art galleries are concentrated on Wyndham Street, at the road's

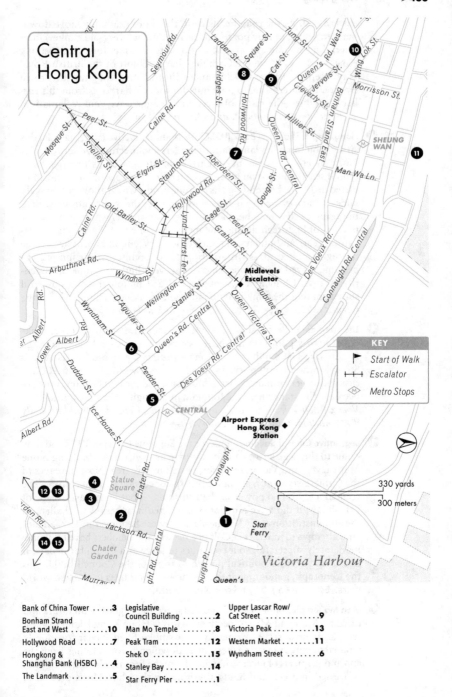

Central Hong Kong

Seymour Rd.

Mosque St.
Peel St.
Shelley St.
Caine Rd.
Ladder St.
Square St.
Tung St.
Bridges St.
Hollywood Rd.
Cat St.
Queen's Rd. West
Jervois St.
Cleverly St.
Bonham Strand
Wing Lok St.
Morrisson St.

⑧
⑨
⑩

Caine Rd.
Peel St.
Elgin St.
Staunton St.
Aberdeen St.
Hollywood Rd.
Gough St.
Queen's Rd. Central
Hillier St.
Queen's Rd. Central

⑦

SHEUNG WAN
Ⓜ
Man Wa Ln.
⑪

Caine Rd.
Old Bailey St.
Hollywood Rd.
Gage St.
Peel St.
Graham St.
Des Voeux Rd.

Arbuthnot Rd.
Wyndham St.
Lyndhurst Ter.
Midlevels Escalator
Jubilee St.
Connaught Rd. Central

... Rd.
Albert
Lower Albert
Wyndham St.
D'Aguilar St.
Wellington St.
Stanley St.
Queen Victoria St.
Queen's Rd. Central

⑥
Queen's Rd. Central
Des Voeux Rd. Central

Duddell St.
Pedder St.
⑤
Ⓜ CENTRAL

Airport Express Hong Kong Station ◆

Ice House St.
Albert Rd.
Connaught Pl.

KEY

⚑ Start of Walk
┝┿┥ Escalator
Ⓜ Metro Stops

⑫ ⑬
④
Statue Square
Chater Rd.

③
②
Jackson Rd.

0   330 yards
0   300 meters

⑭ ⑮
Chater Garden
...den Rd.
Queen's Rd. Central
burgh Pl.

①
Star Ferry

Murray ...
Queen's

Victoria Harbour

eastern end. As the road heads west, the shops gradually move down-market, selling mostly porcelain, curios, and not-very-old trinkets masquerading as ancient artifacts. Look to the left for a sign saying POSSESSION STREET, where Captain Charles Elliott of the British Royal Navy stepped ashore in 1841 and claimed Hong Kong for the British empire. It's interesting to note how far today's harbor is from this earlier shoreline—the result of a century of aggressive land reclamation. ⊠ *Between Wyndham St. and Queen's Rd. W.*

★ ➍ **Hongkong & Shanghai Bank (HSBC).** With its distinctive ladder facade, this striking building is a landmark of modern architecture. Designed by Sir Norman Foster as the headquarters of Hong Kong's premier bank (you'll see it depicted on most of the territory's paper money) and completed in 1985, the building sits on four props, which allow you to walk under it and look up through its glass belly into the soaring atrium within. Imposing as that may be, the building is most interesting for its sensitive use of high-tech details: the mechanics of everything from the elevators' gears and pulleys to the electric signs' circuit boards are visible through smoked glass. In addition to its architectural triumph, the building served a symbolic function as well: built at a time of insecurity vis-à-vis China at a cost of almost US\$1 billion, it was a powerful statement that the bank had no intention of taking its money out of the territory. ⊠ *1 Queen's Rd., across from Statue Sq., Central.*

➎ **The Landmark.** Few fashion designers, watch craftsmen, or other makers of luxury goods do not have—or do not crave—a boutique in the Landmark. The building is no longer the city's poshest, but its Pedder Street location is still priceless, and it has its own MTR entrance. Classical music performances, art exhibitions, and the odd fashion show are occasionally staged near the fountain in the high-ceiling atrium. ⊠ *Des Voeux Rd. between Ice House and Pedder Sts., Central* ☉ *Building, daily 9 AM–midnight; most shops, daily 10–6.*

➋ **Legislative Council Building.** Built for the Supreme Court in 1912 and now home to the Legislative Council (known as LegCo), this building is one of the few grand Victorian structures left in this area. Note the eaves of the Chinese-style roof, a modest British concession to local culture. The council had no real power in the British days, but in the last decade of British law, it did have a majority of elected members who challenged the administration every Wednesday. Since the handover in 1997, mainland attempts to muzzle LegCo's pro-democracy members have been only moderately successful, so it continues to serve as a forum for debate, if not as an organ of political power. In front of the Council Building is the **Cenotaph,** a monument to all who lost their lives in the two world wars. ⊠ *Statue Sq. at Jackson Rd., Central.*

➑ **Man Mo Temple.** Built in 1847 and dedicated to the gods of literature and of war—Man and Mo, respectively—this is Hong Kong Island's oldest temple. It now serves primarily as a smoke-filled haven for elderly women paying respects; ashes flutter down onto your clothes from the enormous spirals of incense hanging from the beams. The statue of Man is dressed in green and holds a writing brush, while Mo is dressed in red and holds a sword. To their left is a shrine to Pao Kung, god of justice, whose face is painted black; to the right is Shing Wong, god of the city. The temple bell, cast in Canton in 1847, and the drum next to it are sounded to attract the gods' attention when a prayer is being offered. To check your fortune, stand in front of the altar, take one of the small bamboo cylinders available there, and shake it until one of the sticks falls out. The number on the stick corresponds to a written fortune. The English translation of said fortune is in a book that the temple will happily sell you. ⊠ *Hollywood Rd. at Ladder St., Central* ⊙ *Daily 8–6.*

★ ☾ ⑫ **Peak Tram.** Housed in the Lower Peak Tram Terminus is the world's steepest funicular railway. It passes five intermediate stations on its way to the upper terminal, 1,805 feet above sea level. The tram was opened in 1880 to transport people to the top of Victoria Peak, the highest hill overlooking Hong Kong Harbour. Before the tram, the only way to get to the top was to walk or take a bumpy ride up the steep steps in a sedan chair. The tram has two 72-seat cars, which are hauled up the hill by cables attached to electric motors. Bus 15C, an antique double-decker, shuttles you to the Peak Tram Terminal from Edinburgh Place, next to City Hall. ⊠ *Between Garden Rd. and Cotton Tree Dr., Central* ☎ *852/ 2522–0922* ⊕ *www.thepeak.com.hk* 🎫 *HK$20 one way, HK$30 round-trip* ⊙ *Daily every 15 mins 7 AM–midnight.*

⑮ **Shek O.** The easternmost village on the south side of Hong Kong Island is a popular weekend retreat. It's filled with old houses, great mansions, a superb golf course and club, a few simple restaurants, a pretty beach, and fine views, albeit marred by some ugly modern housing developments. Leave the town square, full of small shops selling inflatable toys and other beach gear, and take the curving path across a footbridge to the "island" of **Tai Tau Chau,** really a large rock with a lookout for scanning the South China Sea. Little more than a century ago, this open water was ruled by pirates. You can hike through **Shek O Country Park** (⊠ Southeast side of Hong Kong Island) in less than two hours. Look here for birds that are hard to find in Hong Kong, such as Kentish plovers, reef egrets, and black-headed gulls, as well as the colorful rufus-backed shrike and the ubiquitous, chatty bulbul.

★ ⑭ **Stanley Bay.** The town became notorious as the home of the largest World War II prisoner-of-war camps that the Japanese ran in Hong Kong. Today Stanley is known for its picturesque beaches and its market, where casual clothing and tourist knickknacks are sold at wholesale prices. You can also visit the old police station, which was built in 1859 and now houses a restaurant. Past the market, on Stanley Main Street, a strip of restaurants and pubs faces the bay. On the other side of the bay is a Tin Hau Temple, wedged in among giant new housing estates. ⊠ *Southern tip of Hong Kong Island, 40 mins from Central via Bus 6, 6X, 64, or 260.*

★ ⚑ ☾ ❶ **Star Ferry Pier.** Since 1898 the ferry pier has been the gateway to the island for commuters and travelers coming from Kowloon. First-time visitors are all but required to cross the harbor on the Star Ferry at least once and ride around Hong Kong Island on a double-deck tram. In front of the pier you will usually see a few red rickshaws; once numbering in the thousands, these two-wheel man-powered taxis are all but gone. You'll have a choice between buying a first-class or second-class ticket for the ferry ride: first class is the upper deck of the ferry and has air-conditioned compartments, while second class is the lower deck and tends to be noisy due to the proximity to the engine room. ☒ *Enter pier through tunnel next to Mandarin Hotel, Connaught Rd. and Connaught Pl., Central* ☎ *1st class HK$2.20, 2nd class HK$1.70* ☉ *Daily 6 AM–midnight.*

off the beaten path

HONG KONG DOLPHIN WATCH – The Chinese white dolphin (actually from pink to dark gray, and found in waters from South Africa to Australia) is on its way to extinction in the South China Sea, mainly because of the dredging to create the Chek Lap Kok airport. Hong Kong Dolphin Watch sponsors a Dolphin Discovery Cruise three times a week (Wednesday, Friday, and Sunday), weather permitting—there's no guarantee, but on most trips you'll catch one or two dolphins playing in the water. They claim a 96% success rate in spotting dolphins, and if you don't see a dolphin, you get to go again for free. Tours leave from Tung Chung New Pier on North Lantau, but you get there by coach, departing from central points on Hong Kong Island or Kowloon: at 8:30 AM from the east lobby entrance of the Mandarin Oriental Hotel in Central, or at 9 AM from the Kowloon Hotel in Tsim Sha Tsui. The trip makes for an enjoyable half day at sea, and tickets help raise money to build a sanctuary that will ensure the dolphins' survival. Try to reserve at least two weeks in advance, but also be aware that you must pay in advance—either in cash or by credit card—in person at the Dolphin Watch office; no payments are accepted on the day of the tour. ☒ *1528A Star House, 3 Salisbury Rd., Tsim Sha Tsui* ☎ *852/2984–1414* 📠 *852/2984–7799* ⊕ *www.hkdolphinwatch.com* ☎ *HK$280* ☉ *Wed., Fri., Sun.*

❾ Upper Lascar Row. Cat Street, as Upper Lascar Row is often called, is a vast flea market. You won't find Ming vases here—or anything else of significant value—but you may come across an old Mao badge or an antique pot or tea kettle. It's marvelous to wander here and watch the bargaining going on, but be careful if you venture into the negotiating game: these vendors wrote the book.

Victoria Peak. Known in Chinese as Tai Ping Shan, or Mountain of Great Peace, the Peak is Hong Kong's one truly essential sight. On a clear day, nothing rivals the view of the dense, glittering string of skyscrapers that line Hong Kong's north coast and the carpet of buildings that extend to the eight mountains of Kowloon. It's well worth timing your visit to see the view both by day and at night, perhaps by taking in a meal at one of the restaurants near the upper terminus. The Peak is more than just a view, however; it also contains extensive parkland, perfect for a picnic or a long walk.

FodorsChoice ★

With the opening of the **Peak Tower** (☒ Peak Rd., The Peak ☎ 852/2849–7654) the commercial complex of shops, restaurants, and diversions up top, the site's developers have tried to re-brand a visit to the Peak, spectacular enough in the old days, as "the Peak Experience," complete with shopping, amusements, and restaurants. This has been a mixed success, but children might enjoy some of the activities: the Peak Explorer is a virtual-reality ride through outer space, while the Rise of the Dragon takes you on a railcar through a series of animated scenes from Hong Kong's history, including a frighteningly accurate rendition of the 1907 typhoon that devastated the territory. There's also a branch of Ripley's Believe It or Not! Odditorium. The tower is open daily from 7 AM to midnight.

At the top of Victoria Peak, in the Peak Tower complex is a **Madame Tussaud's** wax museum with lifelike wax figures of famous Asian celebrities including Jackie Chan and Michelle Yeoh; and, not to be upstaged, a replica of Chinese President Jiang Zemin. ⊠ *128 Peak Tower, Peak Rd., level 2 The Peak* ☎*852/2849–6966* 💰*HK$95* ⊙ *Daily 10–10.*

⑪ Western Market. Erected in 1906, this is the only surviving segment of a larger market building built in 1858. It functioned as a produce market for 83 years and included living quarters for coolies and inspectors in the four corner towers. Threatened with demolition, it was exquisitely restored and turned into a unique shopping outlet. Alas, they've never gotten the retail mix quite right, filling the place with souvenir and trinket shops on the ground floor, fabrics on the middle floor, and a Chinese restaurant on the top floor. The building, however, gorgeously decorated with Chinese bunting, is worth a trip. ⊠ *323 Connaught Rd. W, Sheung Wan* ⊙ *Daily 10 AM–11:45 PM.*

★ **❻ Wyndham Street.** The galleries that pack the curving block of Wyndham Street from the Fringe Club to where Wyndham becomes Hollywood Road can be approached more as a collection of miniature museums than as mere shops. Their showrooms hold some spectacular antique furniture, art, and artifacts (albeit perhaps smuggled out of their countries of origin) at prices that, while not cheap by any means, are a fraction of what they would be outside the region. Most stores are open daily from 10 to 7, though some have shorter hours or close altogether on Sunday. ⊠ *Wyndham St. at Glenealy and Lower Albert Rds.*

Kowloon

Kowloon Peninsula is on the Chinese mainland just across the harbor from Central, bounded in the north by the string of mountains that give Kowloon its poetic name: *gau lung,* "nine dragons" (there are actually eight mountains, the ninth represented the emperor who named them). Kowloon is closer to China than Hong Kong in more ways than just geography: although the island's glittering skyscrapers are suffused with international commerce, Kowloon's urban fabric is even denser but has an older look to it. The proximity of the old Kai Tak airport kept building heights down (though landings still made you feel like you were scraping Kowloon's rooftops), but with the opening of Chek Lap Kok airport on Lamma Island, Kowloon will no doubt rival the physical heights of Hong Kong at some point. The peninsula has many of the territory's best hotels as well as a mind-boggling selection of shopping options; and no visit to Hong Kong is complete without taking in the commercial chaos of Nathan Road.

The southernmost part of Kowloon is called Tsim Sha Tsui, where such landmarks as the Star Ferry Pier and the elegant Peninsula Hotel stand proudly. A series of cultural buildings lines the waterfront, including the bold parabolic curves of the Cultural Centre and the golf ball–shape Space Museum. North of Tsim Sha Tsui is the market districts of Mong Kok, where you can buy everything from pirated videos to electronics to name-brand clothes at fire-sale prices. A 75-meter Observation Wheel, which is being built atop the Ocean Terminal Mall, is expected to open in 2006; the wheel will be much like the London Eye, with self-rotating capsules that carry about a dozen people for magnificent views of the harbor.

Tsim Sha Tsui is best reached by the Star Ferry from Central or Wan-chai, while the rest of Kowloon is easily accessible by MTR or taxi.

Numbers in the text correspond to numbers in the margin and on the Kowloon map.

a good walk

The Star Ferry pier on the Kowloon side is a 10-minute ferry ride from the pier on the Hong Kong side; the ferry ride is the most romantic way to see the harbor, day or night. East of the pier is a long promenade along Salisbury Road, where you can visit the **Hong Kong Cultural Centre** ⑯ ▶, **Hong Kong Space Museum** ⑰, and the **Hong Kong Museum of Art** ⑱. The luxurious **Peninsula Hotel** ⑲ is across the street, on the corner of Salis-bury and Nathan Road. Walk north on **Nathan Road** ⑳ to experience one of the territory's most famous (and congested) shopping districts, then on to Haiphong Road to get to **Kowloon Park** ㉑. Continue north on Nathan Road three blocks to Jordan Road; make a left and then a right onto **Temple Street** ㉒. Follow Temple Street north to the **Kansu Street Jade Market** ㉓, to the west. From here take a taxi to **Wong Tai Sin Temple** ㉔ or the newly relocated and renamed **Bird Garden** ㉕.

Sights to See

★ ☾ ㉕ **Bird Garden.** On Yuen Po Street, 10 minutes from the Prince Edward MTR station, this garden replaced the old Bird Market, whose narrow streets of bird shops have been redeveloped. What the garden lacks in spontaneous tumult it makes up for with an attractive outdoor setting in the shadow of the Kowloon–Canton Railway (KCR) railroad tracks—and the rumble of each passing train sends the birds into a frenzy. The garden is composed of various courtyards filled with trees and sur-rounded by 70 stalls selling birds, cages, and such accoutrements as tiny porcelain feeders and fresh grasshoppers. Plenty of free birds also swoop in to gorge on spilled food and commiserate with their imprisoned brethren. If you walk from the MTR, you'll enjoy an aromatic ap-proach through the flower market. Take the Police Station exit, walk east along Prince Edward Road for three short blocks, then turn left onto Sai Yee Street, and then right onto Flower Market Road. The bird gar-den is at the end of this flower market street. ⊠ *Yuen Po St., Prince Ed-ward* ⊑ *Free* ☾ *Daily 7 AM–8 PM.*

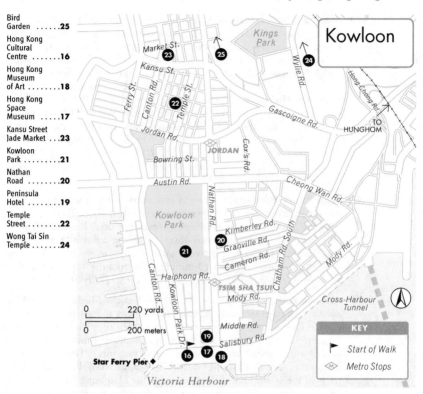

16 Hong Kong Cultural Centre. This stark, architecturally controversial building (which looks better by its flattering nighttime lighting than by day) has tile walls inside and out, sloped roofs, and no windows—an irony, since the view of the harbor would be superb. Its concert hall and two theaters host almost every major artist who performs in the territory. Exhibits are occasionally mounted in the atrium, which has its own three-story metallic mural by Van Lau called *The Meeting of Yin and Yang*. In front of the center is a long, two-level promenade with plenty of seating and a view of the entire north coast of Hong Kong. The center is a few minutes' walk from either the Star Ferry or Tsim Sha Tsui MTR stop. ⊠ *10 Salisbury Rd., Tsim Sha Tsui* ☎ *852/2734–2010* ⊕ *www. hkculturalcentre.gov.hk.*

18 Hong Kong Museum of Art. The exterior is unimaginative, but inside are five floors of innovatively designed galleries. One is devoted to historic photographs, prints, and artifacts of Hong Kong, Macau, and other parts of the Pearl River delta; other galleries highlight Chinese antiquities, fine art, and visiting exhibits. The museum is a few minutes' walk from either the Star Ferry or Tsim Sha Tsui MTR stop. ⊠ *10 Salisbury Rd., Tsim Sha Tsui* ☎ *852/2721–0116* ⊕ *www.lcsd.gov.hk* ☎ *HK$10, or included in Museum Tour pass; free Wed.* ☉ *Fri.–Wed. 10–6.*

FodorśChoice
★

⏱ ⑰ Hong Kong Space Museum. Across from the Peninsula Hotel, this dome-shape museum houses one of the most advanced planetariums in Asia. Interactive models help to explain basic aspects of space exploration (though some of these are less than lucid); fly wires let you experience weightlessness and such. It also contains the **Hall of Solar Science,** whose solar telescope permits you to take a close look at the sun, and the **Space Theatre** (seven shows daily from 11:10 to 9:25), with Omni-imax movies on space travel, sports, and natural wonders. Children under three are not admitted. It's a few minutes' walk from either the Star Ferry or Tsim Sha Tsui MTR stop. ⊠ *10 Salisbury Rd., Tsim Sha Tsui* ☎ *852/ 2734–2722* ⊕ *www.lcsd.gov.hk* ⊠ *HK$10, or included in Museum Tour pass; free Wed.; Omnimax and Sky shows HK$24–HK$32* ⊙ *Mon. and Wed.–Fri. 1–9, weekends 10–9.*

㉓ Kansu Street Jade Market. The old jade market was a sea of pavement trading, but this more orderly market has 450 stalls, selling everything from priceless ornaments to fake pendants. If you don't know much about jade, take along someone who does or you might pay a lot more than you should. Try to come between 10 and noon, as many traders close shop early. The market is a 10-minute walk from the Yau Ma Tei MTR stop. ⊠ *Kansu and Battery Sts., Yau Ma Tei* ⊙ *Daily 10–3:30.*

⏱ ㉑ Kowloon Park. The former site of the Whitfield Military Barracks is now a restful, green oasis. Signs point the way to gardens with different landscaping themes—the sculpture garden is particularly interesting, and the Chinese Garden has a lotus pond, streams, a lake, and a nearby aviary with a colorful collection of rare birds. Take the Mosque exit of the Tsim Sha Tsui MTR stop. The **Jamia Masjid & Islamic Centre** is in the south end of the park, near the Haiphong Road entrance. This is Hong Kong's principal mosque, albeit not its most graceful; built in 1984, it has four minarets, decorative arches, and a marble dome. It is not open to visitors. At the northern end of the park sits an extraordinary **public swimming complex** built, like so much else in the city, by the Hong Kong Jockey Club with revenues from the races. Admission is HK$19, and it's open year-round. ⊠ *Just off Nathan Rd., Tsim Sha Tsui* ☎ *852/2724–3344 park, 852/2724–3846 swimming complex* ⊕ *www.lcsd.gov.hk* ⊠ *Free* ⊙ *Park daily 6 AM–midnight; pool Apr.–Oct., daily 6:30 AM–noon, 1 to 5 PM, and 6–10 PM; call to determine winter opening schedule.*

⑳ Nathan Road. The densest shopping street in town, the so-called Golden Mile runs for several miles north from Salisbury Road in Tsim Sha Tsui and is filled with hotels, restaurants, and shops of every description. To the left and right are mazes of narrow streets lined with even more shops crammed with every possible type of merchandise—jewelry, electronics, clothes, souvenirs, cosmetics, and so on. Expect to be besieged with street hawkers trying to sell you cheap "Rolexes." ⊠ *North from Kowloon waterfront.*

⑲ Peninsula Hotel. The grande dame of Hong Kong hotels, the Peninsula is a local institution. The exterior of this sumptuous hotel is lined with a fleet of Rolls-Royce taxis and doormen in white uniforms, while the huge colonnaded lobby has charm, grandeur, string quartets, and the sedate air of excessive wealth tastefully enjoyed. Even if you're not staying here, stop inside to browse the upscale shopping arcade, partake of high tea, or just marvel at the architecture. ⊠ *Salisbury Rd., Tsim Sha Tsui* ☎ *852/2920–2888* 🖷 *852/2722–4170* ⊕ *www.peninsula.com.*

> **need a break?**
>
> Tsim Sha Tsui is short on quiet cafés, but the **Peninsula Hotel** serves high tea—the perfect way to rest your shopping feet in style. Nibble on a majestic selection of scones and pastries in the grand lobby (for HK$180 per person, a bargain considering all you get) daily from 2 to 7. Or settle down for à la carte tea in the Verandah restaurant Friday through Sunday 3 to 5. You can't make reservations for tea, so arrive early if you don't want to stand in line.

★ ㉒ **Temple Street.** The heart of a busy shopping area, Temple Street is ideal for wandering and people-watching. By day you'll find market stalls with plenty of kitsch and plenty of bargains in clothing, handbags, accessories, tapes, and CDs, so it's worth it to stroll through if you visit the nearby Kansu Street Jade Market, but the best time to come is after 8 PM, when the streets become an open-air bazaar of fortune-tellers, prostitutes, street doctors offering cures for almost any complaint, and occasionally Chinese opera.

Such nearby lanes as **Shanghai Street** and **Canton Road** are also worth a peek for their shops and stalls selling everything from herbal remedies to jade and ivory. **Ning Po Street** is known for its paper kites and for the colorful paper and bamboo models of worldly possessions (boats, cars, houses) that are burned at Chinese funerals. ⊠ *North from Austin Rd. to Kansu St.*

★ ㉔ **Wong Tai Sin Temple.** Have your fortune told at this large vivid compound, whose Buddhist shrine is dedicated to a shepherd boy who was said to have magic healing powers. In addition to the main altar, the pavilions, and the arcade—where soothsayers and palm readers are happy to interpret Wong Tai Sin's predictions for a small fee—there are two lovely Chinese gardens and a Confucian Hall. The temple is in front of the Wong Tai Sin MTR stop. ⊠ *2 Chuk Yuen Village, Wong Tai Sin* ☎ *852/ 2327–8141* 🖷 *Small donation expected* ☉ *Daily 7–5:30.*

New Territories

Until a generation ago, the expansive New Territories consisted almost exclusively of farmland and traditional walled villages. Today, following a government housing program that created "new towns" such as Sha Tin and Tuen Mun with up to 500,000 residents, parts of the New Territories are beginning to feel more like the rest of Hong Kong. Within its expansive 518 square km (200 square mi), however, you'll still feel far removed from the congestion and urban rigors of Hong Kong Island and Kowloon. It's here you'll find many of the area's lushest parks and therapeutic nature walks. In addition, you'll be able to sneak glimpses of traditional rural life in the restored walled villages and ancestral clan halls scattered throughout the area.

The New Territories got their name when the British acquired this area. Whereas Hong Kong Island and Kowloon were taken outright following the Opium War of 1841, the land that now constitutes the New Territories was handed over much later on a 99-year lease. It was this lease that expired in 1997 and was the catalyst for the return of the entire colony to China. Because of its size, the New Territories can be difficult to explore without a car, but between the bus, MTR, and the Kowloon–Canton Railway, you can at least get close to many sights.

Because of its size, the New Territories can be difficult to explore without a car, although between the bus, MTR, and the Kowloon–Canton Railway you can get close to many sights by relying on public transport. Perhaps the best way to see smaller villages is one of the the **Hong Kong Tourist Board**'s organized tours—even if you don't think you're a tour kind of person—which do a loop through the region. Book through your hotel tour desk or an **HKTB Visitor Information Centre** (⊠ Ground floor, The Center, 99 Queen's Rd. Central, Hong Kong ⊠ Star Ferry Concourse, Kowloon).

a good drive

A typical HKTB package tour takes you to **Tai Mo Shan** ㉖ ⌐, Hong Kong's tallest mountain; **Fanling** ㉗, a local market; a country park, **Tai Po Market** ㉘; and the **Chinese University of Hong Kong Art Museum** ㉙.

TIMING   Set aside a full day for the tour.

Sights to See

㉙ **Chinese University of Hong Kong Art Museum.** The Art Museum in the Institute of Chinese Studies Building is well worth a visit for its large exhibits of paintings and calligraphy from the Ming period to modern times. There are also important collections of bronze seals, carved jade flowers, and ceramics from South China. Take the KCR to University station, then a campus bus or taxi. ⊠ *Tai Po Rd., Sha Tin* ☎ *852/ 2609-7416* ⊕ *www.cuhk.edu.hk/ics/amm* ⊡ *Free* ☉ *Mon.–Sat. 10–4:45, Sun. 12:30–5:30.*

need a break?

Across from the Chinese University campus is the popular restaurant **Yucca de Lac** (⊠ Tai Po Rd., Ma Liu Shui Village, Sha Tin ☎ 852/ 2691–1630), which serves Chinese meals outdoors in the green hills along Tolo Harbour, affording a pleasant view of the university.

off the beaten path

TAP MUN ISLAND – About a 15-minute walk from the Chinese University along Tai Po Road is the Ma Liu Shui Ferry Pier, the starting point for a ferry tour of the harbor and Tap Mun Island. The ferry makes many stops, and if you take the 8:30 AM trip you'll have time to hike around Tap Mun Island and still turn back by late afternoon. The last ferry returning from the island is at 5:30 PM. Tap Mun has a small village with a few Chinese restaurants, but you can also bring a picnic lunch. This trip is better by far in sunny weather. The New Fisherman's Village, on the southern tip of the island, is populated mainly by Hakka fisherwomen. About 1 km (½ mi) north, near the western shore, is the ancient village of Tap Mun, where you'll see old women playing mah-jongg. The huge Tin Hau Temple, dedicated to the goddess of the sea, is one of the oldest temples in Hong Kong and is less than ½ km (¼ mi) north of the village. It sits at the top of a flight of steps that leads down into the water of the harbor; inside are old model junks and, of course, a veiled figure of the goddess herself. Go to the east side of the island to see the Tap Mun Cave and some of the best-kept beaches in the territory. ☎ *852/2527–2513 for Tsui Wah Ferry schedule ☒ Round-trip ferry: HK$32 weekdays, HK$50 weekends.*

㉗ Fanling. Although this town has the rather spare functional feel of many of the "new towns" and may be of little interest to you, the nearby **Luen Wo Market** is one of the territory's most impressive and well worth a look. A grid of small stalls selling everything from T-shirts to pigs' lungs and the bustle and pungent aromas prove that local merchants can quickly make even a relatively new marketplace feel traditional. ☒ *North-central part of New Territories, 2 towns below Chinese border on KCR line.*

▶ **㉖ Tai Mo Shan.** Rising 3,230 feet above sea level, Tai Mo Shan—which translates as Big Hat Mountain—is Hong Kong's highest peak, which has been cordoned off as a country park. Access is via a former military road (you can see the old British barracks, now occupied by the People's Liberation Army, en route), and a lookout about two-thirds of the way up gives you a chance to see both sides of the territory: rolling green hills in the foreground and dense urban development in the distance. On a clear day you can even see the spire of the Bank of China Tower in Central. Take the MTR to Tsuen Wan and exit the station at Shiu Wo Street, then catch Minibus 82.

㉘ Tai Po Market. *Tai po* means "shopping place," and the town more than lives up to its name. In the heart of the region's breadbasket, Tai Po is fast becoming a utilitarian "new town," but its main open-air market is a feast for the eyes, with baskets of lush green vegetables, freshly cut meat hanging from great racks overhead, fish swimming in tanks awaiting selection, and all types of baked and steamed treats. Adjacent to the Tai Po market is the 100-year-old **Man Mo Temple**; you'll smell the incense offered by worshippers. The temple is open daily from 9 to 6. To reach the village, take the KCR to the Tai Po Market stop.

off the
beaten
path

SAI KUNG PENINSULA – To the east of Sha Tin, Sai Kung Peninsula has a few small towns and Hong Kong's most beloved nature preserve. The hikes through the hills surrounding High Island Reservoir are spectacular, and the beaches are among the territory's cleanest, largely because they are sheltered from the Pearl River delta effluence. A number of open-air seafood restaurants dot the area as well. (If you choose to eat in a seafood restaurant, note that physicians caution against eating raw shellfish here because of hepatitis outbreaks.) Take the MTR to Choi Hung and then Bus 92 or 96R, or Minibus 1 to Sai Kung Town. Instead of taking the bus,

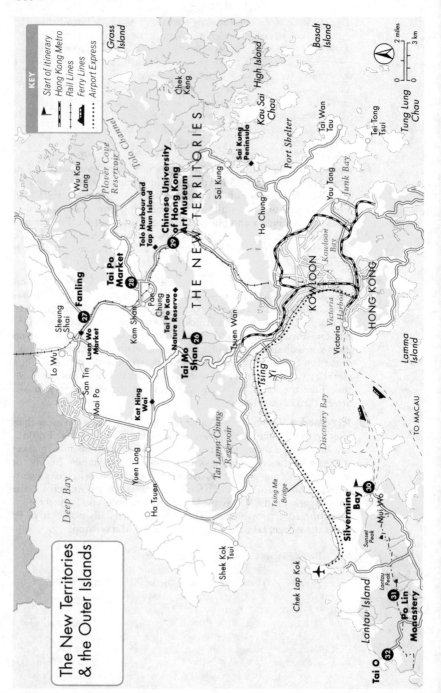

The New Territories
& the Outer Islands

KEY

▲ Start of itinerary
Hong Kong Metro
Rail Lines
Ferry Lines
Airport Express

0   2 miles
0   3 km

Grass
Island

Wu Kau
Lang

Plover Cove
Reservoir

Tolo Channel

Chek
Keng

Basalt
Island

Kau Sai
Chau High Island

Sai Kung
Peninsula ◆

Port Shelter

Tai Wan
Tau

Lo Wu

Sheung
Shai

Fanling **27**

Luen Wo
Market

Tai Po
Market **28**

Tolo Harbour and
Tap Mun Island

Chinese University
of Hong Kong
Art Museum **29**

Sai Kung

Ho Chung

Yau
Kong

Junk Bay

Tei Tong
Tsui

Tung Lung
Chau

San Tin

Mai Po

Kam Sheung

Pan
Chung

Tai Po Kau
Nature Reserve ◆

THE NEW TERRITORIES

Tai Mo
Shan ◆ **26**

Tsuen Wan

KOWLOON

Kowloon
Bay

Victoria
Harbour

HONG KONG

Lamma
Island

Yuen Long

Kat Hing
Wai

Tai Lam Chung
Reservoir

Tsing
Yi

Tsing Ma
Bridge

Discovery Bay

Victoria

TO MACAU

Ha Tsuen

Deep Bay

Shek Kok
Tsui

Chek Lap Kok

Silvermine
Bay **30**

Mui Wo

Lantau Island

Sunset
Peak

Lantau
Peak

Tai O **32**

Po Lin
Monastery **31**

you can also catch a taxi along **Clearwater Bay Road,** which will take you into forested areas and land that is only partially developed, with Spanish-style villas overlooking the sea. To cruise around the harbor, rent a *kaido* (pronounced "guy-doe"; one of the small boats run by private operators for about HK$130 round-trip), and stop at tiny **Yim Tin Tsai Island,** which has a rustic Catholic mission church built in 1890. **Sai Kung Country Park** has several hiking trails that wind through majestic hills overlooking the water. This excursion will take a full day, and you should go only in sunny weather.

The Outer Islands

It's easy to forget that Hong Kong is not the only island in these parts. But for residents, the Outer Islands are a popular and important chance to escape the city and enjoy the waterfront, good seafood, and a little peace and quiet. The islands' villages are very much up to speed (and, to the regret of many, cellular phones still work here), but they run at a more humane pace. For maximum relaxation, try to come on a weekday, as the Hong Kong weekenders often come in large numbers and bring their stresses with them.

In addition to Hong Kong Island and the mainland sections of Kowloon and the New Territories, 235 islands were under the control of the British until the handover back to China. The largest, Lantau, is bigger than Hong Kong Island; the smallest is just a few square feet of rock. Most are un-inhabited. Others are gradually being developed, but at nowhere near the pace of the main urban areas. A few of the outlying islands are off-limits, occupied by prisons or military bases. The four that are most easily accessible by ferry—Lantau, Lamma, Cheung Chau, and Peng Chau—have become popular residential areas and welcome visitors.

You can reach the islands by scheduled ferry services operated by the **New World First Ferry.** The ferries are easy to recognize by the large letters HKF on their funnels. For most destinations you'll leave from the Outlying Districts Services Pier, in Central, on the land reclamation area just west of the Star Ferry Terminal. Boats to Discovery Bay on Lantau leave from the Star Ferry Terminal itself.

The island of **Lantau** lies due west of Hong Kong. At 143 square km (55 square mi), it is almost twice the size of Hong Kong Island. Hong Kong's impressive airport Chek Lap Kok is on Lantau, and the island will someday have Disneyland Hong Kong, which is currently under construction at Penny's Bay and due for completion in late 2005 or 2006. In early 2006, another development will likely increase tourism to Lantau. A 5.7-km cable car is being constructed at this writing between the town of Tung Ching and Po Lin Monastery; travelers will be whisked along to the monastery in about 15 minutes. The latter may eventually change the face of Lantau, but for the time being the island is sparsely populated and makes a nice getaway from the city.

RELIGIONS & TRADITIONS

BUDDHISM, TAOISM, CONFUCIANISM— the three great strands of Chinese religious thought are at work everywhere in Hong Kong.

Buddhism. There are more than 400 Buddhist temples in Hong Kong, from the large Po Lin Monastery in Lantau, with its giant seated Buddha, to the small smoky shrine covered with incense in a dead-end street near Lan Kwai Fong. Lord Buddha's birthday, the eighth day of the fourth moon, is a public holiday in Hong Kong. Buddhist devotees give offerings to the gods in return for luck, health, and of course, prosperity. One of the most popular gods is Tin Hau, Queen of Heaven and Protector of all Seafarers. The territory's maritime history has given her an important place in Hong Kong, and her birthday is celebrated on the 23rd day of the third month of the lunar calendar when fishermen colorfully decorate their boats and pray at temples for good catches in the coming year.

Taoism. Tai chi, or "shadow boxing" is a graceful series of exercises that combines thought and action and is believed to stimulate the central nervous system, lower blood pressure, relieve stress, and gently tone muscles without strain. The rhythmic movements also massage internal organs and improve their functionality. The essence of tai chi is a combination of control and balance, which embodies Taoist thought. Walking through any part of Hong Kong in the early morning, you'll no doubt encounter groups or individuals performing this ancient Chinese martial art. One of the best known Taoist gods is Kwan Tai, the God of War and the patron of the Hong Kong police, and, ironically, of the Triads as well. Tai was a historical figure who lived during the Three Kingdoms period (AD 220–AD 265) and who was later deified as a Taoist symbol of loyalty and integrity. At the 19th-century

Man Mo Temple on Hollywood Road, an ever-burning lamp stands before his statue. Sung Dynasty general Che Kung is another god who was elevated to a Taoist deity. Legend has it that he saved the inhabitants of Sha Tin Valley from the plague centuries ago. Now, believers gather at his major temple in Sha Tin on his birthday, the third day of the lunar New Year.

Confucianism. The fundamental concerns of the Confucian tradition are learning to be human and filial devotion. Respecting elders is considered one of the most important values in families, and this is reflected in the Ching Ming Festival or "Remembrance of Ancestors Day," when families visit cemeteries to sweep their ancestors' graves and clean headstones in a sign of respect. The importance of the family gathering on Chinese New Year's Eve is equivalent to Christmas in the West. It is a time for celebrations and a huge feast. Traditionally, lai see, or red pockets, with tokens of cash, are handed out from the elders to the young, and are considered lucky money. The period leading up to New Year's Day is very busy, too, with superstitious families taking steps to avoid any chance of bad luck in the coming year. It's believed that you must not wash your hair in the first few days of the new year, otherwise your life span will be shortened. Also, sweeping the floors during this same time is considered unlucky, because all the money and good fortune will be swept out the door.

— Eva Chui Loiterton

a good
tour

The ferry will take you to the town of Mui Wo on **Silvermine Bay** ㉚ ▶, which is being developed as a commuter suburb of Hong Kong Island. The island is very mountainous, so for a tour of the outlying villages, plan to hike or take a bus. From Mui Wo, the island's private bus services head out to **Po Lin Monastery** ㉛, home of a giant Buddha; and **Tai O** ㉜, an ancient fishing village.

TIMING Take an entire day to tour the island.

Sights to See

㉛ **Po Lin Monastery.** Within the Po Lin, or "Precious Lotus," Monastery in
Fodor'sChoice Lantau's mountainous interior, is the world's tallest outdoor bronze statue
★ of Buddha, the **Tin Tan Buddha**—measuring more than 100 feet high and weighing 275½ tons. The statue is all the more impressive for its situation at the peak of a hill, which essentially forces pilgrims to stare up at it as they ascend. The adjacent monastery, gaudy and exuberantly commercial, is known for the vegetarian meals served in the temple refectory. Take the bus marked PO LIN MONASTERY from Mui Wo and ask the driver to let you off at the monastery stop, from which you follow signs. A new cable-car connection to the monastery is expected, at this writing, to open in early 2006. ⊠ *Po Lin, Lantau Island* ⊡ *Free* ⊙ *Daily dawn–dusk.*

▶ ㉚ **Silvermine Bay.** This area is being developed as a commuters' suburb of Hong Kong Island, but right now the area is still surrounded by terraced fields. You can rent bicycles in front of the **Silvermine Beach Hotel** (⊠ Silvermine Bay, Mui Wo, Lantau Island ☎ 852/2984–8295) to ride around the village of Mui Wo.

㉜ **Tai O.** Divided into two parts connected by a modern drawbridge, the village still has many waterfront stilt houses and fishing shanties. However, a fire that devastated part of the old village subsequently raised concerns about the safety of the traditional stilt houses. The fires reportedly spread quickly throughout the homes because of inadequate safety measures when they were built. Today there are plans to rebuild homes under modern safety guidelines, while the dwellings that were spared from the fire are a reminder of earlier village life. Visit the local temple dedicated to Kuanti, the god of war, and taste the local catch at one of Tai O's seafood restaurants. To reach the town, take the bus marked TAI O from the village of Mui Wo.

WHERE TO EAT

Wherever you go in Hong Kong, you're bound to see a restaurant sign. Establishments that sell prepared food are as old as Chinese culture itself, and because most people live in small apartments and have little space to entertain at home, restaurants are usually the chosen venues for special occasions and family gatherings. Cooking may be more varied in Hong Kong than anywhere else in the world. Cantonese cuisine, for which Hong Kong is famous since most residents trace their roots to Guangdong (Canton) province, has been long regarded by Chinese gourmands as the most intricate and sophisticated in Asia. However, the

Cantonese are noted for cooking foods you might not think edible; as one saying goes, if it has four legs and isn't a table, the Cantonese will steam, stir-fry, or boil it. Specialties include pigeon, bird's nest soup, shark's-fin soup, and abalone.

The deeply rooted Chinese love of good food also extends here to French, Italian, Portuguese, British, Spanish, Australian, Japanese, Indian, Thai, Vietnamese, Korean, Mexican, and specialty American fare. It's likely you will be able to find something from almost every culinary region on earth. Note: Restaurants in Hong Kong tend to change menus as often as people change their clothes, following the season and the clientele's tastes. Don't be surprised if your favorite dish is no longer on the list the second time you visit.

WHAT IT COSTS In HK$				
$$$$	**$$$**	**$$**	**$**	**¢**
AT DINNER over 300	201–300	101–200	60–100	under 60

Prices are per person for a main course at dinner and do not include the customary 10% service charge.

Hong Kong Island

Asian

$$–$$$$ ✕ **ToTT's Asian Grill & Bar.** The funky decor, which includes zebra-stripe chairs, a central oval bar, and designer tableware, is matched by the East-meets-West cuisine at this restaurant that sits atop the Excelsior hotel looking down on Causeway Bay and the marina. Caesar salad with tandoori chicken is a good example of the culinary collision as is the red-crab bisque served in a baby papaya. The grilled rare tuna steak is another long-standing favorite, and the sampler platter of desserts is a grand finale. Live music kicks in late during the evening, offering a chance to burn a few calories on the dance floor. ⊠ *Excelsior hotel, 281 Gloucester Rd., Causeway Bay* ☎ *852/2837–6786* ▤ *AE, DC, MC, V.*

☾ **$–$$$** ✕ **Café Deco Bar & Grill.** If you're in Hong Kong on a clear day, take
FodorsChoice   the Peak Tram to the top and dine at this 1930s-inspired art deco
★   restaurant overlooking the city. The views are stunning. The menu—which includes Chinese, Thai, Indian, Italian, Mexican, and Japanese cuisine as well as Angus beef steaks from the grill and gourmet pizzas—is prepared by chefs in open kitchens; a culinary theater to rival the magnificent panorama. Food festivals are regularly staged here, and nightly live jazz transforms the venue into a swinging supper club. ⊠ *1st level, Peak Galleria, 118 Peak Rd., The Peak* ☎ *852/2849–5111* ▤ *AE, DC, MC, V.*

★ **$–$$$** ✕ **Indochine 1929.** This stunningly successful restaurant resembles a French plantation veranda in colonial Indochina. The food is as tasty as it is authentic; in fact, most of the ingredients are imported from Vietnam. Highlights include soft-shell crab, fried beef and tomato, stir-fried fillet of pork, and fried fish Hanoi style (using northern spices). This is not the cheapest Vietnamese food in town, but it's arguably the best. The staff's traditional costumes—*ao dais,* straight, elegant silk gowns worn over flowing pants—and the surrounding old maps and antique fans and lamps add to the authentic atmosphere. ⊠ *2/F, California Tower, 30–32 D'Aguilar St., Lan Kwai Fong* ☎ *852/2869–7399* ▭ *AE, DC, MC, V* ⊗ *No lunch Sun.*

British

★ **$$** ✕ **SoHo SoHo.** Modern British cuisine is creating culinary waves, and this smart little restaurant is a prime representative in Hong Kong. SoHo SoHo takes traditional dishes, combines them with eclectic ingredients, and transforms them into modern classics. The roast cod with white beans, chorizo, and garlic aioli is Mediterranean-influenced, while the lamb shank shepherd's pie with parsnip carrot topping is a more traditionally British culinary highlight. Don't miss the sticky toffee and the bread-and-butter puddings. The crowds testify to a winning formula of high-quality and delicious food, helpful service, and value for money. ⊠ *43 Lyndhurst Terr., Central* ☎ *2147–2618* ▭ *AE, DC, MC, V* ⊗ *Closed Sun.*

Chinese

★ **$$–$$$$** ✕ **Dynasty.** The haute Cantonese cuisine with panoramic views over Victoria Harbor from the highest Chinese restaurant in Hong Kong makes this a memorable experience. Award-winning Tam Sek Lun comes from a long line of chefs and is famed for adapting family-style recipes into works of art. Lunchtime dim sum is recommended. The menu changes, as it should, with the seasons and heavily leans towards fresh seafood, plus top-end temptations like bird's nest soup, abalone, and shark's fin. Try the signature dessert of chilled sago cream with mango and grapefruit to finish. ⊠ *3/F, Renaissance Harbour View, 1 Harbour Rd., Wanchai* ☎ *852/2802–8888* ▭ *AE, DC, MC, V.*

$$–$$$$ ✕ **Lao Ching Hing.** One of the oldest Shanghainese restaurants in Hong Kong (open since 1955), Lao Ching Hing has earned its good name over the years. From simple stuff such as the Shanghainese noodles to deluxe abalone, you're bound to find something intriguing on the menu. Chicken in wine sauce and sautéed river shrimp are popular choices. Also check out the Shanghainese dumplings and buns. For a real adventure, investigate the braised sea cucumber in brown sauce for its distinct texture and strong sauce. Try the freshwater crab if you're here in September or October. ⊠ *Novotel Century Hong Kong Hotel, 238 Jaffe Rd., basement, Wanchai* ☎ *852/2598–6080* ▭ *AE, MC, V.*

$$–$$$$ ✕ **Yung Kee.** Since 1950 this massive eatery has served Cantonese food FodorsChoice amid riotous decor and writhing gold dragons. Convenient to both hotels and businesses, Yung Kee specializes in roast goose with beautifully ★ crisp skin. More adventurous palates may wish to check out the famous thousand-year-old eggs with ginger, which melt in your mouth. Among the good seafood offerings are sautéed fillet of pomfret with chili and black-bean sauce or braised garoupa. ⊠ *32–40 Wellington St., Central* ☎ *852/2522–1624* ▭ *AE, DC, MC, V.*

$$–$$$ ✕ **Forum.** The name of this prestigious restaurant connotes two things: chef Yeung Koon Yat and his special abalone. Yeung has earned an international reputation with his Ah Yat abalone. The price is steep, but if you want to experience this luxurious Asian ingredient, you really

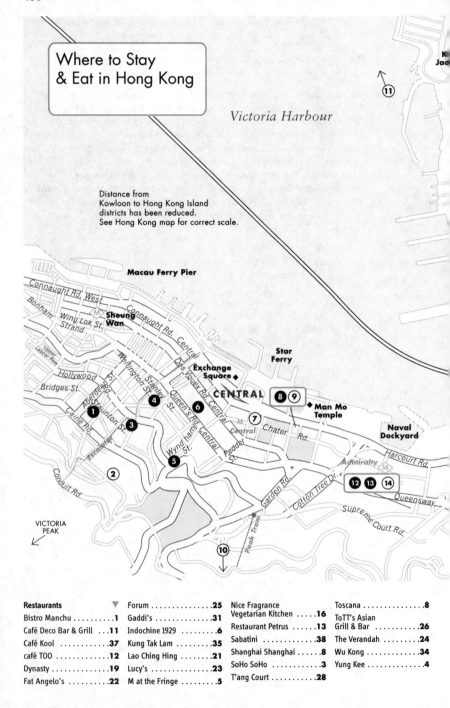

Where to Stay & Eat in Hong Kong

Victoria Harbour

Distance from
Kowloon to Hong Kong Island
districts has been reduced.
See Hong Kong map for correct scale.

Macau Ferry Pier

Connaught Rd. West

Bonham
Strand
Wing Lok St.

Connaught Rd. Central

Sheung Wan

Star Ferry

Upper Lascar Row

Hollywood

Bridges St.

Exchange Square ◆

Des Voeux Rd. Central

Wellington St.

Stanley St.

Queen's Rd. Central

CENTRAL

⑧ ⑨

◆ **Man Mo Temple**

Aberdeen St.

Staunton St.

①

③

Peel St.

④

⑥

⑦

M
Central

Chater Rd.

Naval Dockyard

Wyndham St.

⑤

Pedder St.

Harcourt Rd.

Caine Rd.

②

Conduit Rd.

Garden Rd.

Admiralty M

⑫ ⑬ ⑭

Cotton Tree Dr.

Queensway

VICTORIA PEAK ↙

⑩

Peak Tram

Supreme Court Rd.

⑪

K Jad

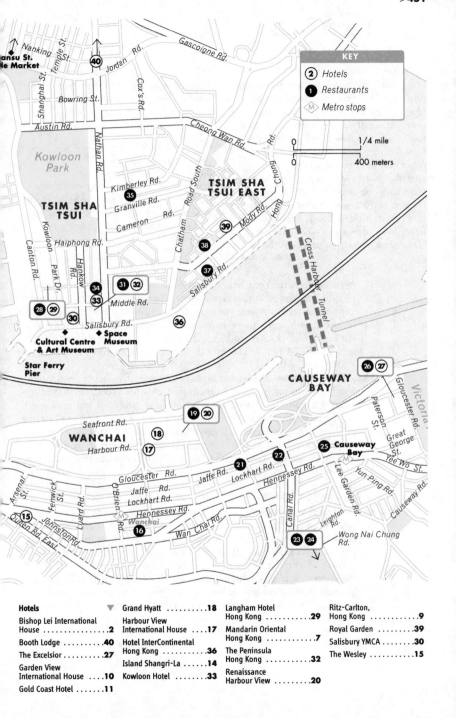

ON THE MENU

No other city in the world, aside from New York, can match the distinct variety and integrity of cuisines in Hong Kong. One of the most exciting aspects is eating a variety of authentic Chinese food—which you will find far different from Chinatowns in the West. Expect a puzzled response if you request something like chop suey, chow mein, or fortune cookies, all of which were created in the United States. They just don't exist in Hong Kong. Subtlety and freshness of flavor are what count in Cantonese dishes, regarded as the

prince of Chinese cuisine, although visitors frequently find themselves more familiar with the menus in the numerous Szechuan, Shanghainese, Peking, and Chiu Chow restaurants.

At the same time, at a cultural crossroads like Hong Kong, the aromatic flavors of pan-Asian cuisine are another unique culinary opportunity, along with every style of international cuisine from Cajun to Cambodian, Lebanese to Moroccan, and Korean to Mexican. There's even an authentic New York deli.

must come here. Your beautiful abalone is boiled and braised to perfection and served with a rich brown sauce—one of the most extravagant dishes in Cantonese cooking. If you want to leave with some cash in hand, you can choose from several more affordable choices, including boiled chicken and a noodle broth that lures regulars back time and again. ⊠ *485 Lockhart Rd., Causeway Bay* ☎ *852/2891–2516* ▤ *AE, DC, MC, V.*

$–$$$ ✕ **Bistro Manchu.** This smart and cozy little bistro serves up warming, soothing, stomach-filling Manchurian cuisine. Noodles, dumplings, vegetables, and meat are mainstays of these rarely encountered northern Chinese specialties. The vegetable stew is a large bowl full of eggplant, potato, cabbage, and green beans in a clear broth. Other menu staples include smoked chicken, cumin lamb, refreshing *lapi* salad (potato noodles and thinly sliced bean curd in sesame dressing), and handmade sorghum noodles. To complement the hearty dishes savor from the vast array of Chinese teas or sweet Harbin beer. ⊠ *33 Elgin St., SoHo* ☎ *852/2536–9218 or 852/2536–9996* ▤ *AE, DC, MC, V.*

★ ¢–$$ ✕ **Shanghai Shanghai.** This retro-Chinese restaurant with art deco touches, stained glass, discreet private rooms, and wooden booths captures the atmosphere of 1930s Shanghai. The menu ranges from simple Shanghainese midnight snacks and cold appetizers, such as mock goose and smoked fish, to pricey delicacies such as abalone. After 9 PM the lights dim and a chanteuse croons favorites requested by diners. This intimate restaurant has become a hot spot for affluent Chinese reminiscing about the good old days. ⊠ *Ritz-Carlton Hotel, 3 Connaught*

Rd., basement, Central ☎ 852/2869–0328 ⚑ Reservations essential ⊟ AE, DC, MC, V ☉ Closed Sun.

European

★ **$$$** ✕ **The Verandah.** Step into another era here with antique fans, champagne-cocktail trolleys, cool, granite-tile floors, and palm trees waving through the arched teak windows. Tuxedoed waiters attend to your every whim at this unashamed celebration of the halcyon days of colonial rule, which also serves an excellent Sunday brunch and daily afternoon tea. It comes into its own at night, however, when the chef whips up an impressive array of Continental dishes, from lobster to rack of lamb. The soufflé is reputedly the finest "this side of Suez." ✉ *The Repulse Bay, 109 Repulse Bay Rd., Repulse Bay* ☎ 852/2812–2722 ⊟ *AE, DC, MC, V.*

★ **$–$$$** ✕ **M at the Fringe.** M is consistently hailed as Hong Kong's best restaurant by magazine food critics and polls alike, and deservedly so. Michelle Garnaut, the founder, sets herself above the rest with a menu and style that defies categorization, embracing French, European, Turkish, Lebanese, and Italian cuisines. The common denominator is, she says, "simple, good, down-to-earth food that I like to eat and cook," from rabbit, homemade sausages, and her trademark slow-cooked lamb to antipasto or meze platters, suckling pig, and creamy fish pie. Her pavlova is legendary, but try it amid her grand dessert platter of eight bite-size desserts (HK$198 for two). ✉ *1/F, South Block, 2 Lower Albert Rd., Central* ☎ 852/2877–4000 ⚑ *Reservations essential* ⊟ *AE, MC, V* ☉ *No lunch Sun.*

French

★ **$$$$** ✕ **Restaurant Petrus.** Commanding breathtaking views atop the Island Shangri-La Hotel, Restaurant Petrus is as prestigious as it gets. Considered by many to be one of the best French restaurants in the world, it attracts the finest chefs and features a premium collection of Petrus wine and 900 celebrated vintages. Signature dishes include foie gras and roast-braised suckling pig. À la carte dining is pricey, but lunch menus are an affordable HK$290–HK$340, while the five-course Menu Gourmand dinner is HK$750. ✉ *56/F, Island Shangri-La, Pacific Place, Supreme Court Rd., Admiralty* ☎ 852/2820–8590 ⚑ *Reservations essential* ⚏ *Jacket required* ⊟ *AE, DC, MC, V.*

★ **$$** ✕ **Lucy's.** The lighting is low, the decor warm, and the waiters friendly and casual. Laid-back and intimate, Lucy's draws regulars back again and again. The food is fresh, lovingly presented, and unpretentious. Stilton, spinach, and walnuts in phyllo pastry is a perfect starter. Veal with polenta and crispy Parma ham is delicate but powerful in taste; sea bass with pumpkin mash is delightfully light. Leave room for Lucy's quintessential chocolate cake for dessert. ✉ *64 Stanley Main St., Stanley* ☎ 852/2813–9055 ⊟ *MC, V.*

International

⏱ **$$–$$$**   ✕ **café TOO.** The innovative café TOO introduces all-day dining and drama
Fodor'sChoice   with seven separate cooking "theaters" and a brigade of 30 chefs. Take
★   your pick from seafood, sushi, and sashimi; Peking duck and dim sum;
a carving station for roasts, poultry, and game; noodles and pastas; and
pizzas, curries, tandooris, antipasto, cured meats, salads, or sandwiches—all made to order and all exceptionally good. Finish with a choice
of hot and cold desserts. Try lunch (HK$235), dinner (HK$308), or even
a late-night snack from 10:30 AM to midnight, priced at just HK$128
with two-for-one drinks. ⊠ *7/F, Island Shangri-La, Pacific Place,
Supreme Court Rd., Admiralty* ☎ *852/2820–8571* ▤ *AE, DC, MC, V.*

Italian

★ **$$$–$$$$**   ✕ **Toscana.** One of the best Italian restaurants in Asia, Toscana is clas-
sical dining at its finest; sumptuous, elegant, and relaxed—equally ideal
for an impressive business lunch or a romantic dinner. The opulent
atmosphere is matched by chef Umberto Bombana's cuisine, hand-
picked wines, and friendly service. Signature dishes include braised veal
shank, pigeon served with foie gras, rack of lamb, and sea bass—all pre-
pared with outstanding originality. A roasted mango, banana, and wild
berry tart is a perfect finale. The three-course executive lunch is a bar-
gain treat at HK$338. ⊠ *Ritz-Carlton, 3 Connaught Rd., Central*
☎ *852/2532–2062* ▤ *AE, DC, MC, V* ☉ *Closed Sun.*

$$ ✕ **Fat Angelo's.** Diners cram into this place—partly for the lively atmosphere, but mostly for the huge portions. Fat Angelo's is an Italian-Amer-
ican–style diner, with green-checked tablecloths and wooden chairs.
Portions come in "big" (serving five–eight) and "not so big" (serving
two–four). Favorites are mounds of steamed green-lipped mussels in
tomato sauce, massive meatballs, roast chicken with rosemary, and pastas of every kind. Linguine with pesto is hearty and filling. Meals come
with a salad and a bread basket. Wine is served in water glasses. The
branches in SoHo and Tsim Sha Tsui are equally as fun. ⊠ *414 Jaffe
Rd., Causeway Bay* ☎ *852/2574–6263* ▤ *AE, DC, MC, V.*

Vegetarian

¢–$$ ✕ **Nice Fragrance Vegetarian Kitchen.** Simple bean curd, mushrooms,
and taro are whipped into unexpected and delicious forms here. Don't
be surprised to see a whole fish on the next table: taro paste, molded
into a fish shape and deep-fried, is one of the most popular dishes in
Chinese vegetarian cooking. Crispy on the outside and succulent inside,
the "fish" is served with a tangy sweet-and-sour sauce. Vegetarian dim
sum and a snack counter at the door round out the offerings. You must
spend a minimum of HK$200 to use your credit card. ⊠ *105–107
Thomson Rd., Wanchai* ☎ *852/2838–3608 or 852/2838–3067* ▤ *AE,
DC, MC, V.*

Kowloon

Chinese

★ **$$–$$$$**   ✕ **T'ang Court.** Bedecked with golden silk curtains, T'ang Court is one
of Hong Kong's most elegant Cantonese restaurants—impressive for a
lunch with either business associates or Chinese friends. The dining room

covers two floors connected by a spiral staircase. The cuisine is faithfully traditional yet creatively original—from home-style Cantonese soups and baked oysters with port as appetizers, to baked salty chicken with crispy skin for a main course. Desserts are irresistible: try the steamed pumpkin dumplings with egg-yolk cream. ✉ *Langham Hong Kong, 8 Peking Rd., Tsim Sha Tsui* ☎ *852/2375–1133 Ext. 2250* ▭ *AE, DC, MC, V.*

¢–$$ ✕ **Wu Kong.** At the intersection of Nathan Road and Peking Road, this big basement dining room serves first-rate Shanghainese fare at reasonable prices. Pigeon in wine sauce is an excellent appetizer. Goose wrapped in crispy bean curd skin is delicious and authentic, as is the fish smothered in a sweet-and-sour sauce. The Shanghai-style doughnut on the dessert menu is a deep-fried sweet ball whipped up with fluffy egg whites and stuffed with red bean and banana. ✉ *Alpha House, 23–33 Nathan Rd., basement (entrance on Peking Rd.), Tsim Sha Tsui* ☎ *852/2366–7244* ▭ *AE, DC, MC, V.*

French

$$$$ ✕ **Gaddi's.** With exemplary service, world-class French cuisine, and a magnificent wine list, the Peninsula's flagship restaurant is a world of neoclassical elegance unto itself. With British chef Philip Sedgwick at the helm, the dress code has been relaxed and prices have been brought down: set lunches start at HK$340, set dinner menus at HK$650. Braised veal shank is an eternally popular signature dish, and twice-cooked suckling pig is remarkable. For dessert, the lightly caramelized lemon tart will melt in your mouth. For a gourmet treat, dine at the Gaddi's Chefs' Table in the kitchen (HK$688 for lunch, HK$1,188 for dinner). ✉ *Peninsula Hong Kong, Salisbury Rd., Tsim Sha Tsui* ☎ *852/2315–3171 or 852/2366–6251 Ext. 3989* ⚑ *Reservations essential* 🏛 *Jacket and tie* ▭ *AE, DC, MC, V.*

International

☺ $–$$$ ✕ **Café Kool.** This 300-seat international food court has something fun for the whole family, with entertainment by chefs in six "show kitchens" focusing on cuisines from around the world. Take your pick from the salad counter; a seafood station; pasta, paella, risotto, and carvery from the Western kitchen; favorites from all over Asia; tandoories and curries from the Indian counter; and fresh soufflés, crepes, and even liquid chocolate from Hong Kong's only chocolate fountain at the dessert station. Good-value, all-you-can-eat buffets are served up to midnight for HK$188 to HK$338. A deli sells take-out food and gourmet gifts. ✉ *Kowloon Shangri-La, 64 Mody Rd., Tsim Sha Tsui East* ☎ *852/ 2733–8753* ▭ *AE, DC, MC, V.*

Italian

★ $$–$$$ ✕ **Sabatini.** Run by the Sabatini family, who also have restaurants in Rome, Japan, and Singapore, this small corner of Italy with sponge-painted walls and wooden furnishings is in the Royal Garden's atrium. It has a cult following among those who crave authentic Italian cuisine. Linguine Sabatini, the house specialty, is prepared according to the original Roman recipe in a fresh-tomato-and-garlic marinara sauce, served with an array of luscious seafood. For dessert, try homemade tiramisu or refreshing wild-berry pudding. ⊠ *3/F, Royal Garden, 69 Mody Rd., Tsim Sha Tsui East* ☎ *852/2733–2000* ⌒ *Reservations essential* ⊟ *AE, DC, MC, V.*

Vegetarian

¢–$ ✕ **Kung Tak Lam.** Health-conscious diners will appreciate this simple Shanghainese vegetarian food. Don't turn your back when you see the no-frills interior; it's the food that makes this place so popular. Try the cold noodle plates, which come with an array of sauces to mix and match for as sweet or sour a flavor as you want. The bean curd ravioli also gets a big thumbs up. Set-price meals are incredibly cheap. ⊠ *1/F, 45–47 Carnarvon Rd., Tsim Sha Tsui* ☎ *852/2367–7881* ⊟ *AE, DC, V.*

WHERE TO STAY

Considering its size, Hong Kong has more than its fair share of upscale hotels, and more often than not these have magnificent views over Victoria Harbour from either the Hong Kong or the Kowloon side. As they focus increasingly on the business traveler with an expense account, most hotels charge at least US$150 (HK$1,170) a night for rooms of a normal international standard. These may not be in prime locations, but they offer basic and reliable facilities—color TV, radio, telephone, same-day valet laundry service, room service, safe-deposit box, refrigerator and minibars, air-conditioning, and business services. Most hotels also have at least one restaurant and bar, a travel desk, and limousine or car rental. If you pay the full rate, many hotels will offer perks such as limousine pickup at the airport.

The **Hong Kong Tourist Board** publishes the *Hotel Guide,* which lists rates, services, and facilities for all of its members. The HKTB does not make hotel reservations. The Hong Kong Hotel Association (HKHA) does, and at no extra charge, but only through its reservations office at Hong Kong International Airport.

WHAT IT COSTS In HK$				
	$$$$	**$$$**	**$$**	**$**	**¢**
FOR 2 PEOPLE	over 3,000	2,101–3,000	1,101–2,100	700–1,100	under 700

Prices are for two people in a standard double room in high season.

Hong Kong Island

Admiralty & Central

$$$$ ⊞ **Mandarin Oriental Hong Kong.** A legend worldwide, the Mandarin
Fodor'sChoice   has served the international elite since 1963, and many world travel-
★   ers wouldn't consider staying anywhere else in Hong Kong. Eastern antiques adorn the lobby; the comfortable and luxurious guest rooms have antique maps and prints, traditional wooden furnishings, Eastern knickknacks, and glamorous black and gold accents. The top floor houses Vong, a trendy French-Asian fusion restaurant. A harpist plays during high tea in the Clipper Lounge, and a live band performs in the Captains Bar in the evening. ⊠ *5 Connaught Rd., Central* ☎ *852/2522–0111*

852/2810–6190 ⊕ *www.mandarin-oriental.com* ⇔ *486 rooms, 55 suites ⚹ 4 restaurants, room service, in-room data ports, in-room safes, minibars, cable TV with movies, indoor pool, gym, health club, hair salon, hot tub, sauna, spa, 3 bars, dry cleaning, laundry service, concierge, Internet, business services, meeting rooms, no-smoking floors* ▤ *AE, DC, MC, V.*

⚝ **$$$$** ▦ **Ritz-Carlton, Hong Kong.** Refined elegance and superb hospitality
FodorśChoice are signatures of the Ritz-Carlton. Gilt-frame mirrors and crystal chan-
★ deliers reflect a homey European and Asian blend of furnishings, lush
carpeting, and period oil paintings. In your room, complimentary flowers and fruit baskets are replenished daily; you'll also receive a morning newspaper. Other comforts include a bath menu, which includes
bath essences for kids, romantics, ladies, or gentlemen brought to your
room by the bath butler; there is also a tea and coffee cabinet. Rooms
have either harbor or garden views. The upper club floors have a private concierge, lounge, and complimentary refreshments as added services. The main restaurant, Toscana, serves northern Italian cuisine. ⊠ *3
Connaught Rd., Central* ☎ *852/2877–6666, 800/241–3333 in the
U.S.* 🖷 *852/2877–6778* ⊕ *www.ritzcarlton.com* ⇔ *187 rooms, 29 suites
⚹ 5 restaurants, room service, in-room data ports, in-room safes,
minibars, cable TV with movies, pool, gym, health club, hot tub, massage, sauna, bar, lounge, shop, baby-sitting, dry cleaning, laundry service, concierge, Internet, business services, meeting rooms, no-smoking
floors* ▤ *AE, DC, MC, V.*

$$$ ▦ **Island Shangri-La.** The lobby of this deluxe hotel sparkles with more
FodorśChoice than 780 dazzling Austrian crystal chandeliers hanging from high ceil-
★ ings and huge, sunlit windows. A 16-story glass-topped atrium houses
the world's largest Chinese landscape painting, *The Great Motherland
of China.* Take the elevator up from the 39th floor and see the main-
land's misty mountains drift by. Rooms are the largest on Hong Kong
Island and have magnificent views; all have large desks and all-in-one
bedside control panels. Service is friendly and efficient. For very upscale
dining there's the French eatery Petrus, or for Chinese food, the Sum-
mer Palace. ⊠ *Supreme Court Rd., 2 Pacific Place, Central* ☎ *852/
2877–3838, 800/942–5050 in the U.S.* 🖷 *852/2521–8742* ⊕ *www.
shangri-la.com* ⇔ *531 rooms, 34 suites ⚹ 4 restaurants, room service,
in-room data ports, in-room safes, minibars, cable TV with movies, pool,
gym, health club, hair salon, hot tub, massage, sauna, spa, steam room,
bar, lounge, shops, baby-sitting, dry cleaning, laundry service, con-
cierge, Internet, business services, meeting rooms, no-smoking floors*
▤ *AE, DC, MC, V.*

Midlevels

$$ ▦ **Bishop Lei International House.** Owned and operated by the Catholic
FodorśChoice diocese of Hong Kong, this guesthouse is up the Midlevels Escalator
★ at the top of SoHo. Rooms are small but clean and functional, and
half have harbor views. Although it's economically priced, there are
a fully equipped business center, a workout room, a pool, and a restaurant serving Chinese and Western meals. ⊠ *4 Robinson Rd., Midlevels*
☎ *852/2868–0828* 🖷 *852/2868–1551* ⊕ *www.bishopleihtl.com.hk*
⇔ *104 rooms, 101 suites ⚹ Restaurant, in-room data ports, in-room*

safes, minibars, cable TV, pool, exercise equipment, gym, baby-sitting, laundry service, Internet, business services, no-smoking floors ▤ *AE, DC, MC, V.*

$ ⏱

Fodor'sChoice

★

▦ **Garden View International House.** Run by the YWCA, this attractive cylindrical guesthouse on a hill overlooks the botanical gardens and harbor. Its well-designed rooms make excellent use of small irregular shapes and emphasize each room's picture windows. If you want to do your own cooking, ask for a room with a kitchenette (which will include a microwave oven); if not, the coffee shop serves European and Asian food. You can also use the renovated swimming pool and gymnasium in the adjacent YWCA. Garden View is a five-minute drive (Bus 12A or Minibus 1A) from Central and just a few minutes from the Peak tram station. ✉ *1 MacDonnell Rd., Midlevels* ☎ *852/2877–3737* 📠 *852/ 2845–6263* ⊕ *www.ywca.org.hk* ⤴ *130 rooms* ⏱ *Coffee shop, in-room data ports, some kitchenettes, minibars, cable TV, pool, gym, laundry service, Internet, business services, no-smoking floors* ▤ *AE, DC, MC, V.*

Wanchai

★ ⏱ $$$$

▦ **Grand Hyatt.** A ceiling hand-painted by Italian artist Paola Dindo tops the Hyatt's art deco–style lobby, and black-and-white photographs of classic Chinese scenes accent the modern but rather bland corridors and rooms. Rooms have sweeping harbor views as well as large interactive TVs with cordless keyboards; all meeting rooms have ethernet and video-conference facilities. Grissini restaurant and the Cantonese One Harbour Road are notable—as is J J's nightclub—and the ground-floor breakfast buffet is a decadent feast. The new Plateau spa is grand indeed, and suffused with a zen-like calm; extensive outdoor facilities are shared with the Renaissance Harbour View hotel. ✉ *1 Harbour Rd., Wanchai* ☎ *852/2588–1234* 📠 *852/2802–0677* ⊕ *www.hongkong. grand.hyatt.com* ⤴ *519 rooms, 51 suites* ⏱ *4 restaurants, room service, in-room data ports, in-room safes, minibars, cable TV with movies, driving range, 2 tennis courts, pool, exercise equipment, gym, health club, hair salon, spa, bar, lounge, nightclub, baby-sitting, dry cleaning, laundry service, concierge, Internet, business services, meeting rooms, no-smoking floors* ▤ *AE, DC, MC, V.*

★ ⏱ $$$

▦ **Renaissance Harbour View.** Sharing the Hong Kong Convention & Exhibition Centre complex with the Grand Hyatt is this more modest but equally attractive hotel. Guest rooms are medium size with plenty of beveled-glass mirrors that reflect the modern decor. Many rooms have good harbor views and all have high-speed Internet access. Grounds are extensive and include the largest outdoor hotel pool in town, plus gardens, a playground, and jogging trails, which makes this hotel a good place to stay if you are with children; these facilities are shared with the Grand Hyatt. The lobby lounge has a live jazz band in the evening and is a popular rendezvous spot for locals and visiting businesspeople. ✉ *1 Harbour Rd., Wanchai* ☎ *852/2802–8888* 📠 *852/2802–8833* ⊕ *www.renaissancehotels.com* ⤴ *807 rooms, 53 suites* ⏱ *4 restaurants, room service, in-room data ports, in-room fax, in-room safes, minibars, cable TV with movies, driving range, 2 tennis courts, pool, gym, health club, hair salon, sauna, 2 bars, shops, baby-sitting, playground, dry clean-*

ing, laundry service, concierge, Internet, business services, meeting rooms, no-smoking floors ▤ *AE, DC, MC, V.*

$$ ▦ **Harbour View International House.** This waterfront YMCA property has small but clean—and relatively inexpensive—rooms near the Wanchai Star Ferry Pier. The best rooms face the harbor. The hotel is well placed if you want to attend cultural events in the evening: both the Arts Centre and the Academy for Performing Arts are next door. Opposite Harbour View is the Hong Kong Convention & Exhibition Centre. The 16-story hostel provides free shuttle service to Causeway Bay and the Central Star Ferry. You can use the superb YMCA Kowloon facilities, just a short ferry ride away, for a small fee. ⊠ *4 Harbour Rd., Wanchai* ☎ *852/2802–0111* ⊞ *852/2802–9063* ⊕ *www.hvih.com.hk* ⤴ *320 rooms* ⚹ *Restaurant, room service, in-room data ports, minibars, cable TV, baby-sitting, laundry service, concierge, Internet, business services, meeting rooms, no-smoking floor* ▤ *AE, DC, MC, V.*

$$ ▦ **The Wesley.** Built on the site of the old Soldiers & Sailors Home, this 21-story reasonably priced hotel is a short walk from the Hong Kong Convention & Exhibition Centre, the Academy for Performing Arts, and the MTR. Rooms are small but pleasantly furnished, and the more spacious corner "suites" have alcove work areas. No health center or pool is on the premises, but long-stay guests can use the facilities at the Grand Plaza Apartments in Quarry Bay for a discounted fee. A tram stop is right outside the door, and Pacific Place and the bars of Wanchai are close by. ⊠ *22 Hennessy Rd., Wanchai* ☎ *852/2866–6688* ⊞ *852/2866–6613* ⊕ *www.grandhotel.com.hk* ⤴ *251 rooms* ⚹ *Restaurant, coffee shop, minibars, cable TV, laundry service, concierge, Internet, business services, no-smoking floor* ▤ *AE, DC, MC, V.*

Causeway Bay

★ ⏱ $$$ ▦ **The Excelsior.** This hotel opened in 1973 and remains perennially popular with travelers due in part to its high standard of service. Most rooms are spacious and enjoy splendid sea views, including the yachts and boats moored at the Hong Kong Yacht Club; other rooms have street views. The location is ideal for shopping and dining and is adjacent to Victoria Park. ToTT's Asian Grill & Bar, on the top floor, has East-meets-West cuisine and live music. On a historical note, the hotel sits on the first plot of land auctioned by the British government when Hong Kong became a colony in 1841. ⊠ *281 Gloucester Rd., Causeway Bay* ☎ *852/2894–8888* ⊞ *852/2895–6459* ⊕ *www.excelsiorhongkong.com* ⤴ *866 rooms, 21 suites* ⚹ *4 restaurants, room service, in-room data ports, in-room safes, minibars, cable TV with movies, 2 tennis courts, health club, hair salon, spa, 2 bars, lounge, shop, dry cleaning, laundry service, concierge, Internet, business services, meeting rooms, no-smoking floors* ▤ *AE, DC, MC, V.*

Kowloon

Tsim Sha Tsui

★ $$$$ ▦ **Hotel InterContinental Hong Kong.** You'll have spectacular harbor views at this luxury hotel formerly known as the Regent. The spacious and modern guest rooms include 24-hour butler service, Italian marble bathrooms with sunken tubs and separate shower stalls, and a TV-based Internet service in all rooms. Suites have harbor views, and some have private terraces with outdoor hot tubs. The spa, open to the public, has luxurious private rooms, each with Jacuzzi, sauna, and steam shower and specialty treatments such as Jet Lag Relief and Oriental Healing. Dining options are top-rate and include Yü for seafood, Yan Toh Heen for Cantonese food, and the Steak House Bar & Grill. ⊠ *18 Salisbury Rd., Tsim Sha Tsui* ☎ *852/2721–1211, 800/327–0200 in the U.S.* 🖷 *852/2739–4546* ⊕ *www.ichotelsgroup.com* ⇨ *422 rooms, 92 suites* ⌂ *4 restaurants, in-room data ports, minibars, cable TV with movies, pool, gym, health club, hot tub, sauna, spa, steam room, shop, baby-sitting, dry cleaning, laundry service, concierge, Internet, business services, meeting rooms, no-smoking floors* ▤ *AE, DC, MC, V.*

★ **$$$$** ▦ **The Peninsula Hong Kong.** Established in 1928, the Pen is known worldwide for its impeccable taste and old-world style evidenced in its colonial architecture, columned and gilt-corniced lobby, and fleet of Rolls-Royces. Service is attentive and discreet. Spacious rooms, decorated with plush fabrics and Chinese prints, have bedside remotes that operate everything from the lights to the curtains. Sumptuous corner suites have Jacuzzis with views of the skyline. Helicopter transfers and private sightseeing tours take off from the rooftop helipad. Restaurants include Gaddi's, Chinese Spring Moon, and the trendy rooftop Felix. ⊠ *Salisbury Rd., Tsim Sha Tsui* ☎ *852/2366–6251* 🖷 *852/2722–4170* ⊕ *www. peninsula.com* ⇨ *246 rooms, 54 suites* ⌂ *7 restaurants, room service, in-room data ports, in-room fax, in-room safes, minibars, cable TV with movies, in-room VCRs, pool, gym, health club, hair salon, hot tub, spa, bar, shops, baby-sitting, dry cleaning, laundry service, concierge, Internet, business services, meeting rooms, helipad, no-smoking floors* ▤ *AE, DC, MC, V.*

$$$ ▦ **Langham Hotel Hong Kong.** Formerly the Great Eagle Hotel, this luxury hotel's new name aligns it with its sister property in London, the Langham Hilton. The sophisticated lobby has glowing back-lighted onyx pillars reaching up to beautifully painted ceiling murals. On the rooftop is a gym and poolside oasis. Stylish guest rooms mix comfort and elegance with classic European touches. Harbor views, however, are blocked by a high-rise. The Main Street Deli is the only genuine New York deli in town; Asian-attuned palates will love the innovative and delicately presented Chinese dishes at T'ang Court. ⊠ *8 Peking Rd., Tsim Sha Tsui* ☎ *852/2375–1133* 🖷 *852/2375–6611* ⊕ *www.langhamhotels. com* ⇨ *461 rooms, 25 suites* ⌂ *5 restaurants, room service, in-room data ports, some in-room faxes, in-room safes, minibars, cable TV with movies, pool, gym, sauna, spa, bar, lounge, shop, dry cleaning, laundry service, concierge, Internet, business services, meeting rooms, no-smoking floors* ▤ *AE, DC, MC, V.*

$$$ ▦ **Royal Garden.** A garden atrium with lush greenery and whispering running water rises from the ground floor to the Royal Garden's rooftop. Glass elevators, live classical music, trailing greenery, and trickling streams create a sense of serenity. The spacious comfortable rooms surround the atrium. Rooftop health facilities include an indoor-outdoor pool fashioned after an ancient Roman bath with fountains, a colorful sun mosaic, and underwater music. Its Sabatini restaurant is the sister to the famous Rome dining establishment. ⊠ *69 Mody Rd., Tsim Sha Tsui East* ☎ *852/2721–5215* 🖷 *852/2369–9976* ⊕ *www. theroyalgardenhotel.com.hk* ⇋ *374 rooms, 48 suites* ⚴ *4 restaurants, room service, in-room data ports, in-room safes, minibars, cable TV with movies, tennis court, indoor-outdoor pool, gym, health club, hair salon, sauna, spa, bar, pub, dance club, shop, baby-sitting, dry cleaning, laundry service, concierge, Internet, business services, meeting rooms, no-smoking floor* ⊟ *AE, DC, MC, V.*

$$ 🏨 **Kowloon Hotel.** The mirrored exterior and the chrome, glass, and marble lobby reflect the hotel's high-tech orientation. Kowloon means "nine dragons" in Cantonese and is the theme here. Triangular windows and a pointed lobby ceiling, made from hundreds of handblown Venetian-glass pyramids, represent dragons' teeth. The Kowloon is the lesser sibling to the adjacent Peninsula hotel, so you can sign for services at the Pen and charge them to your room account here; similarly, all the luxurious facilities of the Peninsula are open to you. Rooms are small, but each has a computer with free Internet service and fax. Airline information is displayed in the lobby *and* in each room. ⊠ *19–21 Nathan Rd., Tsim Sha Tsui* ☎ *852/2929–2888* 🖷 *852/2739–9811* ⊕ *www.peninsula.com* ⇋ *719 rooms, 17 suites* ⚴ *3 restaurants, room service, in-room data ports, in-room fax, minibars, cable TV with movies, hair salon, shop, baby-sitting, dry cleaning, laundry service, Internet, business services, meeting room, no-smoking floors* ⊟ *AE, DC, MC, V.*

⚙ $ 🏨 **Salisbury YMCA.** This upscale YMCA is Hong Kong's most popular
FodorśChoice and is great value for your money. Next to the Peninsula and opposite
★ the Cultural Centre, Space Museum, and Art Museum, it's in an excellent location for theater, art, and concert crawls. The clean, pastel-color rooms have harbor views and data ports. The Y also has a chapel, a garden, a conference room with a built-in stage, a children's library, and excellent health facilities, which include a dance studio and even a climbing wall. Restaurants here are both cheap and good. The shops are also affordable. ⊠ *41 Salisbury Rd., Tsim Sha Tsui* ☎ *852/2369–2211* 🖷 *852/2739–9315* ⊕ *www.ymcahk.org.hk* ⇋ *303 rooms, 62 suites* ⚴ *2 restaurants, room service, in-room data ports, in-room safes, minibars, cable TV with movies, indoor pool, gym, health club, hair salon, spa, squash, lounge, shops, baby-sitting, laundry facilities, business services, meeting room, no-smoking floors* ⊟ *AE, DC, MC, V.*

★ ¢ 🏨 **Booth Lodge.** This pleasant contemporary retreat, which is down a dead-end side street near the Jade Market, is operated by the Salvation Army. But contrary to the image that might conjure up for you, everything in this renovated lodge is clean, bright, and new, from freshly painted walls to starched sheets on the double beds. The lobby is a study in minimalism and may resemble an office, but the Booth is a good value. The coffee shop serves mainly buffets, with a small outdoor balcony offering nice views. The Yau Ma Tei MTR is nearby. ⊠ *11 Wing Sing La., Yau Ma Tei* ☎ *852/2771–9266* 🖷 *852/2385–1140* ⇋ *54 rooms* ⚴ *Restaurant, coffee shop, cable TV, laundry service* ⊟ *AE, MC, V.*

New Territories

☾ $$ ⊞ **Gold Coast Hotel.** The Gold Coast is Hong Kong's only conference resort, and it can accommodate more than 1,000 people, so check before booking if you want a quiet weekend away. Its vast complex on Kowloon's western harbor front is well connected to the city by public bus, and the hotel runs shuttle buses to the Tsuen Wan MTR and the airport. It is extravagantly decorated inside with acres of marble, miles of wrought-iron balustrades, and several palm-court atriums. All guest rooms are spacious and face the sea. The extensive facilities include a children's play area, a water-sports area, and volleyball and soccer fields. ⊠ *1 Castle Peak Rd., Tuen Mun* ☎ *852/2452–8888* 🖷 *852/ 2440–7368* ⊕ *www.goldcoasthotel.com.hk* ⇗ *440 rooms, 10 suites* ☾ *4 restaurants, room service, in-room data ports, minibars, cable TV with movies, putting green, 2 tennis courts, pool, health club, hair salon, spa, beach, boating, archery, soccer, squash, volleyball, bar, baby-sitting, playground, laundry service, Internet, business services, meeting rooms* ▤ *AE, DC, MC, V.*

NIGHTLIFE & THE ARTS

Nightlife

The most comprehensive nightlife listings are in *HK Magazine,* a free weekly newspaper distributed each Friday to many restaurants, stores, and bars. The nightlife coverage in *BC Magazine* is almost as extensive. Another good source of nightlife information is the *South China Morning Post.*

Think twice before succumbing to the city's raunchier hideaways. If you stumble into one, check out cover and hostess charges *before* you get too comfortable. Pay for each round of drinks as it's served (by cash rather than credit card), and never sign any blank checks. Hong Kong is a surprisingly safe place, but as in every tourist destination, the art of the tourist rip-off is well practiced to some degree. If you're unsure, visit spots that are sign-carrying members of the Hong Kong Tourist Board (HKTB). You can pick up its free membership listing (including approved restaurants and nightspots) at any HKTB Visitor Information Centre.

Bars & Pubs

FodorsChoice   Most Westerners and a growing number of locals meet in crowded
★   comfort in the **Lan Kwai Fong area,** a hillside section around Central's D'Aguilar Street that has many appetizing bistros and a large selection of bars. When people tire of Lan Kwai Fong itself, there are plenty more bars just around the corner.

Alibi. Sophisticated guys and dolls flock to this cool bar (with fine dining upstairs) that's wall to wall with bodies most nights. If there's one place to dress to impress, this is it. ⊠ *73 Wyndham St., Central* ☎ *852/ 2167–8989.*

Bahama Mama's. You'll find tropical rhythms at the Caribbean-inspired bar, where world music plays and the kitsch props include a surfboard over the bar and the silhouette of a curvaceous woman showering behind a screen over the restroom entrance. ✉ *4–5 Knutsford Terr., Tsim Sha Tsui* ☎ *852/2368–2121.*

Balalaika. Vodka is served in a minus -20°C (-36°F) room at this Russian-theme bar, but don't be alarmed at the freezing temperature—they provide you with fur coats and traditional Russian fur hats. Take your pick from the 15 varieties of vodka from five different countries. ✉ *2/F, 10 Knutsford Terr., Tsim Sha Tsui* ☎ *852/2312–6222.*

★ **California.** Singles mix happily at the ultramodern bar, which stays open late most nights and after several years as a trendsetter is still one of the hottest places to be seen. ✉ *32–34 D'Aguilar St., Lan Kwai Fong* ☎ *852/2521–1345.*

Club 64. Writers, artists, travelers, and the occasional banker gravitate toward the unpretentious environs of this bar, where you can get a reasonably priced drink in a humble and cozy, if a little run-down, setting. ✉ *12–14 Wing Wah La., Lan Kwai Fong* ☎ *852/2523–2801.*

★ **Delaney's.** Both branches of the pioneer of Hong Kong Irish pubs have interiors that were made in Ireland and shipped to Hong Kong, and the mood is as authentic as the furnishings. There are Guinness and Delaney's ale (a specialty microbrew) on tap, corner snugs (small private rooms), and a menu of Irish specialties, plus a happy hour that runs from 5 to 9 PM daily. ✉ *71–77 Peking Rd., basement, Tsim Sha Tsui* ☎ *852/2301–3980* ✉ *G/F, 1 Capital Pl., 18 Luard Rd., Wanchai* ☎ *852/2804–2880.*

Dickens Bar. For a reasonably priced hotel drinking hole, try the Excelsior's basement pub, which offers live music and football games via satellite TV. ✉ *281 Gloucester Rd., basement, Causeway Bay* ☎ *852/2837–6782.*

Dublin Jack. Drink Guinness and Irish ales while watching the latest football games. This pub just off the Midlevels outdoor escalators stands out with a fetching, bright-red exterior. ✉ *37 Cochrine St., Central* ☎ *852/2543–0081.*

D'Apartment. Step into the library, lounge room, or even bedroom in the ultrahip basement "apartment," which opened in early 2004. The tiny library is dimly lighted and stacked with real books, but there's no chance of dozing off with the music blaring in the next "room." The bedroom has a lush bedlike sofa to laze on, and, don't worry, there are no neighbors to complain about the loud racket. ✉ *California Entertainment Bldg., 34–36 D'Aguilar St., basement, Lan Kwai Fong* ☎ *852/2523–2002.*

★ **Felix.** This bar, high up in the Peninsula hotel, is a must for visitors; it not only has a brilliant view of the island, but the impressive bar and disco were designed by the visionary Philippe Starck. Don't forget to check out the padded disco room. ✉ *28/F, The Peninsula Hong Kong, Salisbury Rd., Tsim Sha Tsui* ☎ *852/2920–2888.*

★ **Fringe Club.** The arts-minded mingle in a historic redbrick building that also houses the members-only Foreign Correspondents Club. The Club is the headquarters for Hong Kong's alternative arts scene and normally stages live music twice a week. ✉ *2 Lower Albert Rd., Central* ☎ *852/2521–7251.*

Just "M." The guess is that this curiously named pub stands for either "men" (but don't mistake it for a gay bar) or "money," but the owners playfully refuse to give up the goods. The minimalist industrial design gives it a laid-back feel, and the small mezzanine level has large black couches to sink into. ⊠ *Shop 5, Podium Plaza, 5 Hanoi Rd., Tsim Sha Tsui* ☎ *852/2311–9188.*

La Dolce Vita. The tiny bar—beneath its sister restaurant **Post 97** and next to its other sibling **Club 97**—often spills onto the pavement. With a sleek interior and a crowd to match, this chic haven for the name-dropping masses is a place to be seen. ⊠ *9 Lan Kwai Fong, Lan Kwai Fong* ☎ *852/ 2810–9333.*

Ned Kelly's Last Stand. An institution, Ned Kelly's has Aussie-style beer tucker (pub grub), and rollicking live jazz in the evening. ⊠ *11A Ashley Rd., Tsim Sha Tsui* ☎ *852/2376–0562.*

Old China Hand Hand. This pub has been here since time immemorial, and the interior suffers accordingly, but the authentic vibe is intact. It's something of an institution for those wishing to sober up with greasy grub after a long night out. ⊠ *104 Lockhart Rd., Wanchai* ☎ *852/2865–4378.*

★ **1/5.** Walk upstairs through the narrow, mirrored ceiling corridor to enter a large, dimly lighted bar with triple-height ceilings and brown velour lounge areas. Located in the hip Star Street area, this bar is the location of choice for those who want an alternative to Lan Kwai Fong and SoHo. ⊠ *1/F, Starcrest Bldg., 9 Star St., Wanchai* ☎ *852/2520–2515.*

Rick's Cafe. A local hangout, this restaurant-pub is decorated à la *Casablanca*, with potted palms, ceiling fans, and posters of Bogie and Bergman. ⊠ *53–59 Kimberly Rd., Luna Ct., Tsim Sha Tsui* ☎ *852/ 2311–2255.*

Sky Lounge. Ride the bubble elevator to this bar high up in the Sheraton in time for sunset, and you won't be disappointed. ⊠ *18/F, Sheraton Hong Kong Hotel & Towers, 20 Nathan Rd., Tsim Sha Tsui* ☎ *852/ 2369–1111.*

Staunton's Wine Bar & Cafe. Adjacent to Hong Kong's famous outdoor escalator is this hip bistro-style café and bar. Partly alfresco, it's the perfect place to people-watch; it attracts crowds at night to drink and by day to sip coffee or take in a meal. It's also a Sunday-morning favorite for nursing hangovers over brunch. ⊠ *10–12 Staunton St., SoHo* ☎ *852/ 2973–6611.*

Talk of the Town. At the Excelsior's bar, also known as ToTT's, you're treated to a 270-degree vista of Hong Kong harbor. ⊠ *34/F, The Excelsior, 281 Gloucester Rd., Causeway Bay* ☎ *852/2837–6786.*

Tango Martini. Shaken or stirred is what this martini bar is all about. A stylish and sophisticated lounge, this joint also has an adjoining restaurant. ⊠ *3/F, Empire Land Commercial Centre, 81–85 Lockhart Rd., Wanchai* ☎ *852/2528–0855.*

V 13. Affectionately known by locals as the Vodka Bar, V 13 teems with locals and expats who enjoy hearty libations. Once the bartenders start pouring the vodka, they don't stop until they reach the rim. Then they add the tonic. ⊠ *13 Old Baily St., SoHo* ☎ *852/8208–1313.*

★ **Vong.** A small but wonderfully elegant bar with excellent service, Vong specializes in martinis. Try the lychee concoction while admiring the view of Kowloon. The popular bar is also a restaurant. ⊠ *25/F, Mandarin Oriental Hotel, 5 Connaught Rd., Central* ☎ *852/2522–0111.*

Nightclubs

★ **C Club** (⌧ 32–34 D'Aguilar St., basement, Lan Kwai Fong ☎ 852/2526–1139) is where the upwardly mobile and occasional Hong Kong minor celebrity party. There's a large dance floor, a flashy bar, and

★ plenty of nooks to lounge in. **dragon i** (⌧ Upper G/F, The Centrium, 60 Wyndham St., Central ☎ 852/3110–1222) is the the latest establishment where the glamour set prances, poses, and preens. The club's entrance is marked by an enormous birdcage (filled with real budgies and canaries) made entirely of bamboo poles. Have a drink on the wonderful alfresco deck by the doorway or step inside the rich, red playroom.

Discos

As its name suggests, **Club Ing** (⌧ Renaissance Harbour View hotel, 1 Harbour Rd., Wanchai ☎ 852/2824–0523) is about slipping into a pair of dancing shoes and hitting the floor. **Joe Bananas** (⌧ 23 Luard Rd., Wanchai ☎ 852/2529–1811) is one of the mainstays of Wanchai nightlife; its reputation for all-night partying and general good times remains unchallenged. Despite being one of the oldest discos, **Rick's Cafe** (⌧ 53–59 Kimberly Rd., Luna Ct., Tsim Sha Tsui ☎ 852/2311–2255) remains popular. If you arrive after midnight on a weekend, be prepared to stand in line.

Jazz & Folk Clubs

Ned Kelly's Last Stand (⌧ 11A Ashley Rd., Tsim Sha Tsui ☎ 852/2376–0562) is an Aussie-managed home for pub meals and Dixieland, courtesy of Ken Bennett's Kowloon Honkers. Get here early, before 10 PM, to get a comfortable seat. Wanchai's unpretentious alternative to the topless bar scene is **The Wanch** (⌧ 54 Jaffe Rd., Wanchai ☎ 852/2861–1621), providing live local folk and rock performances.

The Arts

The most comprehensive calendar of cultural events is *HK Magazine,* a free weekly newspaper distributed each Friday to many restaurants, stores, and bars. You can also read daily reviews in the City section of the *South China Morning Post.* The free monthly newspaper *City News* lists City Hall events.

Tickets

URBTIX outlets are the easiest places to buy tickets for most arts performances in the city; you'll find branches at the Hong Kong Arts Centre in addition to City Hall and the Cultural Centre. ⌧ *Hong Kong Cultural Centre, 10 Salisbury Rd., Tsim Sha Tsui* ☎ *852/2734–2009* ⌧ *Hong Kong Arts Centre, 2 Harbour Rd., Wanchai* ☎ *852/2582–0232* ⌧ *City Hall, 5 Edinburgh Pl., near the Star Ferry, Central* ☎ *852/2921–2840.*

Chinese Opera

★ There are 10 **Cantonese opera** troupes headquartered in Hong Kong, as well as many amateur singing groups. These groups perform "street opera" in, for example, the Temple Street Night Market almost every night, while others perform at temple fairs, in City Hall, or in playgrounds under the auspices of the Urban Council. Visitors unfamiliar with the form are sometimes alienated by the strange sounds of this highly complex and extremely sophisticated art form. Every gesture has its own meaning; in fact, there are 50 gestures for the hand alone. Props attached to the costumes are similarly intricate and are used in exceptional ways. For example, the principal female often has 5-foot-long pheasant-feather tails attached to her headdress; she shows anger by dropping the head and shaking it in a circular fashion so that the feathers move in a perfect circle. Surprise is shown by what's called "nodding the feathers." One can also "dance with the feathers" to show a mixture of anger and determination. Orchestral music punctuates the singing. It's best to attend with a local acquaintance, who can translate the gestures, since the stories are so complex that Wagner and Verdi librettos begin to seem basic in comparison.

The highly stylized **Peking opera** employs higher-pitched voices than Cantonese opera. Peking opera is an older form, more respected for its classical traditions; the meticulous training of the several troupes visiting Hong Kong from the People's Republic of China each year is well regarded. They perform in City Hall or at special temple ceremonies. The Hong Kong Cultural Centre provides the latest programs and flyers.

Dance

★ **City Contemporary Dance Company.** The flagship of modern dance in Hong Kong presents innovative programs with local themes at various venues both indoors and outdoors. ☎ *852/2326–8597* ⊕ *www.ccdc.com.hk.*
Hong Kong Ballet. Hong Kong's first professional ballet company and vocational ballet school is Western oriented in both its classical and its contemporary repertoires. The company performs at schools, auditoriums, and festivals. ☎ *852/2573–7398* ⊕ *www.hkballet.com.*
Hong Kong Dance Company. Since 1981, the company has been promoting the art of Chinese dance and choreographing modern works with historical themes. The 30-odd members are experts in folk and classical dance. Sponsored by the Urban Council, they perform about three times a month throughout the territory. ☎ *852/3103–1888* ⊕ *www.hkdance.com.*

Film

Hong Kong reigns as the film capital of Asian martial-arts/triad-theme movies. Unlike the shoot-'em-ups of Hollywood films, the camera work in martial-arts flicks emphasizes the ricochet choreography of physical combat. The international success of the critically acclaimed *Crouching Tiger, Hidden Dragon* and heavy influence on the more recent *Kill Bill* are testament to the industry's emerging importance in world cinema.

If you want to experience a true Hong Kong Canto-flick, you'll have plenty to choose from. If a Jackie Chan or Chow Yun-Fat film is in release, you can be sure nearly every cinema in town will be showing it. Other movies are mostly B-grade, centering on the cops-and-robbers and slapstick genres; locals love these because they star popular (and very attractive) Hong Kong actors. Wong Kar Wai, Ann Hui, John Woo, and

MARTIAL ARTS GO HOLLYWOOD

ALTHOUGH A CULT FAVORITE *around the globe, martial-arts films in Hong Kong are no less than a phenomenon—their actors no less than superstars. Walk into a Hong Kong shop, visit a tourist office, step into an office atrium, and who do you see? Jackie Chan. Not the man, but his image. A life-size, cutout figure of the humorous martial-arts superstar with a thousand-watt smile.*

Chan has been called a "physical genius" and "the world's greatest action star." After years of international fame and accolades, this ultraflexible stuntman extraordinaire finally broke into the American market with Rumble in the Bronx in the mid-1990s. Two years later, Chan solidified his fame in the West with his first exclusively U.S. production, Rush Hour.

But in Hong Kong he's been a god, a crutch during economic hard times, when he was routinely asked to step in, support, sing praise, and raise the spirits of the people, as he is at this writing in the Hong Kong Tourist Board's marketing campaign for Hong Kong. He's the man who's guaranteed to draw the crowds every time his latest movie is released. When he's on the silver screen, Hong Kongers know they can kick back and forget about their troubles for a while.

Of course Chan is not the first, or only, martial-arts golden son of Hong Kong. Recent heroes include John Woo, who created such bullet-ridden cult classics as A Better Tomorrow, The Killer, and Hard-Boiled. He was also responsible for launching Chow Yun-Fat's movie career. Chow Yun-Fat, who was born on the small island of Lamma and moved to Hong Kong in 1965, is the ultratough, muscular martial artist who worked with Woo on A Better Tomorrow, which propelled both men into the limelight of the action-movie

genre. Both men are also known for the slick Hollywood flick The Replacement Killers, which Woo produced and Chow Yun-Fat starred in; but Yun-Fat's name is now most associated with his graceful fighting prowess in the international hit Crouching Tiger, Hidden Dragon.

Although their Hollywood films do well in the United States, both Chow Yun-Fat and Jackie Chan are equally famous in the Hong Kong film industry for their locally filmed slapstick and heroic bloodshed films. Like the godfather of the genre, Bruce Lee, both are more than just hometown boys made good—they're international stars.

But it was Lee who broke the ground and still shines as the martial artist to live up to in life and on the screen. Martial artists still talk about Lee and his muscular physique and Lee and his style.

Just after moving to America in the 1960s, Lee was challenged to a fight by Cantonese experts in Oakland's Chinatown because he was teaching Chinese "secrets" to non-Chinese individuals. This was perceived as treason among some members of the martial-arts community. Lee won the challenge, and nowadays students around the world study such techniques. In part they can thank Lee for their schooling.

Unlike other areas in the region, Hong Kong isn't a city where you're likely to get into a bar fight with a local who thinks he is Jackie Chan or Bruce Lee. But you are likely to see some of the cheesiest, funniest, most artistically and athletically amazing movies here if you just pop into a local movie theater. It's a Hong Kong experience without parallel.

Ang Lee, all international award–winning filmmakers, have helped draw attention to Hong Kong film with their visionary and dynamic direction. For show times and theaters, check the listings in *HK Magazine* and the *South China Morning Post*.

★ **Broadway Cinematheque.** If you're looking for more than just a visual feast (that is, you want to see an art-house feature), visit this theater. The train-station design of this art house has won awards; the departure board displays foreign and independent films (local films are rare). Here you can read the latest reel-world magazines from around the globe in a minilibrary. A shop sells current and vintage film paraphernalia, and there's a coffee bar as well. To get here, use the Temple Street exit at the Yau Ma Tei MTR. ⊠ *Prosperous Garden, 3 Public Square St., Yau Ma Tei* ☎ *852/2388–3188 for ticket reservations* ⊕ *www.cinema. com.hk.*

Hong Kong Arts Centre Theatre. This theater screens some of the best independent, classic, documentary, animated, and short films from around the world as well as local productions, often with themes focusing on a particular country, period, or director. ⊠ *2 Harbour Rd., Wanchai* ☎ *852/2582–0200* ⊕ *www.hkac.org.hk.*

★ **Palace IFC.** Large, sink-into red leather seats and ushers in tuxedos make this brand-new boutique cinema seem more like a Broadway theater than a mini-multiplex. Five screens show new releases, foreign and independent films, as well as classic celluloid such as *Gone With the Wind* and *West Side Story*. But what really sets Palace apart from the rest is the "Shawl Loan" for those who get a little chilly—Hong Kong cinemas are notoriously frigid. There's also a bookshop and café, where visitors can discuss afterwards whether Rhett really did give a damn. ⊠ *IFC Mall, 8 Finance St., level 1, Central* ☎ *852/2388–6268* ⊕ *www.palaceifc. cinema.com.hk.*

Orchestras

Hong Kong Chinese Orchestra. Created in 1977 by the Urban Council, this orchestra performs exclusively Chinese works. It consists of bowed strings, plucked instruments, wind, and percussion. Each work is specially arranged for each concert. ☎ *852/3185–1600* ⊕ *www.hkco.org.*

★ **Hong Kong Philharmonic Orchestra.** Almost 100 musicians from Hong Kong, the United States, Australia, and Europe perform everything from classical to avant-garde to contemporary music by Chinese composers. Past soloists have included Vladimir Ashkenazy, Rudolf Firkusny, and Maureen Forrester. Performances are usually held Friday and Saturday at 8 PM in City Hall or in recital halls in the New Territories. ☎ *852/ 2721–2030* ⊕ *www.hkpo.com.*

Theater

Chung Ying Theatre Company. This professional company of Chinese actors stages plays—most of them original and written by local playwrights—mainly in Cantonese. The group also organizes exchanges with theater companies from overseas, often inviting international directors to head productions. Performance venues vary. ☎ *852/2521–6628* ⊕ *www.chungying.com.*

SPORTS & THE OUTDOORS

Beaches

Hong Kong is not known for its beaches, but it's surrounded by hundreds of them and has a thriving sunbathing culture. About 40 of the beaches around Hong Kong and its outlying islands are "gazetted"—cleaned and maintained by the government, with services that include lifeguards, floats, and swimming-zone safety markers.

The scenery is often breathtaking, but pollution is occasionally a problem, so don't swim if a red flag—indicating either pollution or an approaching storm—is hoisted. The red flag flies often at Big Wave Bay (on the south side of Hong Kong Island) because of the rough surf.

Big Wave Bay, Hong Kong's most accessible surfing beach, lives up to its name and is frequently closed for swimming as a result. The beach has kiosks, barbecue pits, a playground, changing rooms, showers, and toilets. From Shau Ki Wan, take Bus 9 to the roundabout; walk about 20 minutes along the road, which is usually lined with cars on weekends.

At **Deep Water Bay** the action starts at dawn every morning, all year long, when members of the Polar Bear Club go for a dip. The beach is packed in summer, when there are lifeguards, swimming rafts, and safety-zone markers, plus a police reporting center. Barbecue pits, showers, and restrooms are open year-round. A taxi from Central will take about 20 minutes. You can also take Bus 6A from the Exchange Square Bus Terminus; for a scenic route, take Bus 70 from Exchange Square to Aberdeen and change to Bus 73, which passes the beach en route to Stanley.

Repulse Bay has changing rooms, showers, toilets, swimming rafts, swimming safety-zone markers, and playgrounds. Several Chinese restaurants dot the beach, and kiosks serve light refreshments. The Lifesaving Club is at the east end and resembles a Chinese temple, with large statues of Tin Hau, goddess of the sea, and Kwun Yum, goddess of mercy. Take Bus 6, 6A, 64, 260, or 262 from Exchange Square, or Bus 73 from Aberdeen.

Shek O, not far from Big Wave Bay, is almost Mediterranean in aspect. A wide beach with shops and restaurants nearby, it has refreshment kiosks, barbecue pits, lifeguards, swimming rafts, playgrounds, changing rooms, showers, and toilets. The views are magnificent as the bus begins its descent toward the heart of the small village. In the center of town there are several outdoor dining areas, serving everything from Thai to Cantonese. Take the MTR from Central to Shau Ki Wan (there is a bus from Central to Shau Ki Wan, but it takes between one and two hours), then Bus 9 to the end of the line.

Stanley Main, a wide sweep of sand, is popular with the windsurfing crowd and has a refreshment kiosk, swimming rafts, changing rooms, showers, and toilets, plus a nearby market packed to the rafters, where you should bargain—in a friendly but confident manner. It also hosts the annual dragon boat races, usually held in June, in which friendly teams paddle out into the sea, turn around, and, at the sound of the gun, race ferociously back to the beach. It's a great day out, but head out early to claim a spot along the beach, as it gets chaotically crowded. There are several English pubs and Southeast Asian restaurants along the main strip. Take a taxi from Central (about 45 minutes); Bus 6, 6A, 6X or 260 from Exchange Square; or Bus 73 from Aberdeen.

Turtle Cove, isolated but scenic, has lifeguards and rafts in summer, barbecue pits, a refreshment kiosk, changing rooms, showers, and toilets. From Central take the MTR to Sai Wan Ho and change to Bus 14; get off at Tai Tam Road after passing the dam of Tai Tuk Reservoir.

Participant Sports

Golf

Locals generally head to Hong Kong's only public course at Kau Sai Chau or to nearby Shenzhen, which is across the border in mainland China, to play golf; however, you need a Chinese visa to play in Shenzhen without spending an arm and a leg. Hong Kong's top clubs will also allow you to play their courses, but don't expect much change from US$200.

Clearwater Bay Golf and Country Club in the New Territories permits overseas visitors to play golf on its 18-hole course on weekdays with tee-off times between 9:30 and 11:30 AM as long as you book three days in advance. It's best to take a taxi if you are going here. ⊠ *139 Tai Aumum Rd., Clearwater Bay* ☎ *852/2719–1595, 852/2335–3885 for booking office* ⊟ *Green fee HK$1,400 with golf cart.*

Deep Water Bay Golf Course, the most convenient course to play if you're staying on Hong Kong Island, or even Tsim Sha Tsui for that matter, can be deceptive. Though it's only 9 holes—played twice as a par 56 with two tees for each pin—it represents a tough challenge. With 16 par 3s and two par 4s, almost every shot is at the flag. As a test of your short game, with no margin for error, it can't be beaten. It's a members' club (some of Hong Kong's richest businessmen play here), owned by the Hong Kong Golf Club, but visitors with handicap cards are admitted on weekdays, and it's casual enough to allow you to play in trainers. Deep Water Bay is just 20 minutes from Central via Bus 6, 64, or 260, or you can take a taxi. ⊠ *19 Island Rd., Deep Water Bay* ☎ *852/2812–7070* ⊟ *Green fee HK$450; club rental HK$100.*

Discovery Bay Golf Club, on Lantau Island, has an 18-hole course open to visitors on Monday, Tuesday, and Friday between 7:30 and 11:45 AM. You must reserve two days in advance. Take the Discovery Bay ferry from the Star Ferry Terminal in Central, then catch the bus to the course (call the club for up-to-date bus information). ⊠ *Discovery Bay* ☎ *852/ 2987–7273* ⊟ *Green fee HK$1,400; club rental HK$160; golf-cart rental HK$190; shoe rental HK$50; ½-hr lesson HK$400.*

★ **Hong Kong Jockey Club, Kau Sai Chau,** Hong Kong's only public golf course, is by far its cheapest and most popular. Overseas visitors pay a marginal premium on green fees, but the cost is well worth it. Both the more difficult North Course and the less-taxing but still challenging South Course are superb tests of accuracy amid breathtaking scenery on an island 20 minutes by dedicated ferry from the delightful fishing port of

Sai Kung. Booking is advisable, especially on weekends, on these Gary Player–designed gems, but unbooked "walk-ons" for lone golfers are usually possible on weekdays. Take the MTR to Choi Hung and then Bus 92 or 96R, or Minibus 1 to Sai Kung Town, where you can catch the golf-course ferry to Kau Sai Chau; the ferry departs the Sai Kung waterfront every 20 minutes. ☒ *Kau Sai Chau* ☎ *852/2791–3380 automated booking line, 852/2791–3390 help line* ☒ *Combined green fee and ferry ticket: HK$550 for South Course, HK$600 for North Course; club rental HK$160; shoe rental HK$35.*

Tuen Mun Golf Centre, a public golf center in the Western New Territories, has 100 driving bays and a practice green, but there is no course. Take the MTR to Tsuen Wan station and then Bus 66M or 66P to Tuen Mun, then take a taxi to the golf course. ☒ *Lung Mun Rd., Tuen Mun* ☎ *852/2466–2600* ☒ *HK$12 per bay; HK$12 per club; HK$12 per hr per 30 balls* ☉ *Daily 8 AM–10 PM.*

Hiking

Before setting off for the wild, pick up guides such as *Hong Kong Hikes* from any bookstore. You can purchase hiking trail maps at the **Government Publications Centre** (☒ Pacific Place, Government Office, G/F, 66 Queensway, Admiralty ☎ 852/2537–1910). Ask for blueprints of the trails and the Countryside Series maps. The HM20C series comprises handsome four-color maps, but it's not very reliable.

You can hike through any of the territory's country parks and around any of the accessible outlying islands. Here are some short one-day hikes and two camping treks on the most popular trails.

★ **Dragon's Back,** one of Hong Kong's most popular trails, crosses the "rooftop" of Hong Kong Island. Take the Peak Tram from Central up to the Peak, and tackle as much or as little of the range as you feel like—there are numerous exits "downhill" to public-transport networks. Surprisingly wild country feels a world away from the urban bustle of Hong Kong below, and the panoramas of Victoria Harbour on one side, with South Island and outlying islands on the other, are the most spectacular you will find anywhere, especially on a clear day. You can follow the trail all the way to the delightful seaside village of Shek O, where you can relax over an evening dinner before returning to the city by minibus or taxi. The entire trip takes the better part of an unforgettable day.

The trail to **Lion Rock,** one of Hong Kong's most spectacular summits, is also the most convenient to access from Kowloon. The hike passes through dense woodland with bamboo groves along the Eagle's Nest Nature Trail and up open slopes to Beacon Hill for 360-degree views over hills and the city. The contrasting vistas of green hills and the city's hustle and bustle are extraordinary. There's a climb up the steep rough track to the top of Lion Rock, a superb vantage point for appreciating Kowloon's setting between hills and sea. The trail ends at Wong Tai Sin Taoist Temple, one of Hong Kong's most famous temples, where you can have your fortune told. To start, catch the MTR to Choi Hung (15 minutes from Tsim Sha Tsui) and a 10-minute taxi ride up Lion Rock. From Wong Tai Sin, return by MTR.

The **MacLehose Trail**, named after an ex-governor of Hong Kong, is the course for the annual charity MacLehose Trailwalker, a grueling 97-km (60-mi) event. Top teams finish in an astonishing 15 hours, but the average hiker can only tackle relatively short sections of the trail in one day; otherwise, allow two days from beginning to end. This splendidly isolated path through the New Territories starts at Tsak Yue Wu, beyond Sai Kung, and circles High Island Reservoir before breaking north. Climb through Sai Kung Country Park to a steep section of the trail, up the mountain called Ma On Shan. Turn south for a high-ridge view, and walk through Ma On Shan Country Park. From here you walk west along the ridges of the mountains known as the "Eight Dragons," which gave Kowloon its name. After crossing Tai Po Road, the path follows a ridge to the summit of Tai Mo Mountain, at 3,161 feet above sea level the tallest mountain in Hong Kong. Continuing west, the trail drops to Tai Lam Reservoir and Tuen Mun, where you can catch public transport back to the city. To reach Tsak Yue Wu, take the MTR to Choi Hung and then Bus 92 or 96R, or Minibus 1 to Sai Kung Town. From Sai Kung Town, take Bus 94 to the country park.

Spectator Sports

Horse Racing

Horse racing is the nearest thing in Hong Kong to a national sport. It is a multimillion-dollar-a-year business, employing thousands of people and drawing crowds that approach insanity in their eagerness to rid themselves of their hard-earned money. Even if you're not a gambler, it's worth going to one of Hong Kong's two tracks just to experience the phenomenon. The "sport of kings" is run under a monopoly by the Hong Kong Jockey Club, one of the most politically powerful entities in the territory. Profits go to charity and community organizations. The racing season runs from September through June. Some 65 races are held at one or the other of the two courses—on Saturday or Sunday afternoon at Sha Tin and Wednesday night at Happy Valley—which must rank as one of the world's great horse-racing experiences. The HKTB organizes tours to the club and track. Costs range from HK$245 to HK$490 and can include transfers, lunch, and tips on picking a winner. Alternatively, you can watch the races from the public stands, where the vibe is lively and loud—this is highly recommended for a truly local experience, and the cost is only HK$10. Both courses have huge video screens at the finish line so that gamblers can see what's happening every foot of the way.

★ **Happy Valley Racetrack** on Hong Kong Island, is one of Hong Kong's most beloved institutions. Racing is on Wednesday evenings and the atmosphere is electric. The track is a five-minute walk from the Causeway Bay MTR, or you can take a taxi. ⊠ *Hong Kong Jockey Club, 1 Sports Rd., Happy Valley* ☎ *852/2966–8111 or 852/2966–8364.*

★ **Sha Tin Racecourse**, in the New Territories, is newer than Happy Valley; in fact, it's one of the most modern racecourses in the world. Racing is on Saturday or Sunday afternoon, and it is the venue for all of Hong Kong's championship events. The easiest way to get here is by taxi, or you can catch the MTR to Kowloon Tong and transfer to the KCR train, which stops at the track on race days. A walkway from the station takes you directly to the racetrack. ✉ *Tai Po Rd., next to Racecourse KCR station, Sha Tin* ☎ *852/2966–6520.*

Rugby

★ One weekend every spring (usually in March), Hong Kong hosts **International Rugby Sevens,** more popularly known as "the Sevens," at the Hong Kong Stadium (take the MTR to Causeway Bay and then exit F, or take a taxi). The entire city, swelled with rugby supporters from across the planet, goes wild. It's a serious party event; in fact, it's one of Hong Kong's wildest parties of the year, so don't be afraid to sport fancy dress or take the kids. Purchasing tickets (around HK$550 for both days) in advance through your overseas travel agent is advisable, but you can usually acquire them at the entrance. One word of warning: if you attend the Sevens once, you might get addicted and find yourself coming back year after year. *Hong Kong Rugby Football Union* ✉ *Sports House, 1 Stadium Path, Room 2001, Causeway Bay* ☎ *852/2504–8300.*

Water Sports

Junks

Dining on the water aboard large pleasure craft—which also serve as platforms for swimmers and water-skiers—is a boating style unique to Hong Kong. Junking has become so popular that there is now a fairly large junk-building industry producing highly varnished, plushly appointed, air-conditioned junks up to 80 feet long. After a day out on a junk, sailing by the shimmering lights of Hong Kong Island on the ride back into town is spectacular.

These floating rumpus rooms serve a purpose, especially for denizens of Hong Kong Island who suffer from "rock fever" and need to escape for a day on the water. Also known as "gin junks" because so much alcohol is consumed, these junks are commanded by "weekend admirals." If anyone so much as breathes an invitation for junking, grab it.

You can also rent a junk. The pilot will take you to your choice of the following outer islands: Cheung Chau, Lamma, Lantau, Po Toi, or the islands in Port Shelter, Sai Kung.

Jubilee International Tour Centre (✉ Far East Consortium Bldg., 121 Des Vouex Rd., Central ☎ 852/2530–0530) is an established charter outfit recommended by the HKTB.

Simpson Marine Ltd. (✉ Aberdeen Marina Tower, 8 Shun Wan Rd., Aberdeen ☎ 852/2555–7349) is an established charter operator whose crewed junks can hold 35 to 45 people. Prices begin at HK$2,800 for an eight-hour day trip or a four-hour night trip during the week, HK$4,500 on summer weekends. The price goes up on holidays. You need to reserve in advance; half of the fee is required upon receipt of a signed contract, the remaining half at least five days prior to departure.

Scuba Diving

Bunn's Divers Institute (✉ 38–40 Yee Woo St., Causeway Bay ☎ 852/2574–7951) runs outings for qualified divers to areas like Sai Kung. The cost of a day trip runs HK$700 and includes two dive sessions, one in the morning and another in the afternoon. You'll need to bring your own lunch.

Waterskiing

Patrick's Waterskiing (⊠ Stanley Main Beach, Stanley ☎ 852/2813–2372) is run by the friendly, laid-back man himself. Patrick will take you to the best waters in the Stanley Beach area and give you pointers on your waterskiing or wakeboarding technique. The fee—HK$700 per hour—includes a range of equipment and life jackets. To rent a speedboat, equipment, and the services of a driver, contact the **Waterski Club** (⊠ Pier at Deep Water Bay Beach, Deep Water Bay ☎ 852/2812–0391) or ask your hotel for the names and numbers of other outfitters. The cost is usually about HK$580 per hour.

SHOPPING

Although Hong Kong is no longer the mercantile paradise it once was, many shopping aficionados still swear by it, returning year after year for such items as Chinese antiques, art from China and Southeast Asia, porcelain, tea and tea ware, pearls, watches, cameras, computers and peripherals, eyeglasses, silk sheets and kimonos, tailor-made suits, and designer clothes found in off-the-beaten-path outlets.

If you are short on time, visiting one of Hong Kong's many malls might be the answer. On Hong Kong Island, in Central District, the main ones are Landmark, Prince's Building, Shun Tak Centre, Admiralty Centre, and Pacific Place. Times Square is in Causeway Bay and Cityplaza in Quarry Bay. In Kowloon, just next to the Star Ferry, is Harbour City, encompassing the Ocean Terminal and Ocean Centre. Up the street a bit is the New World Centre and Palace Mall.

Hong Kong Island

Art & Antiques

Hollywood Road is the place to look for Chinese antiques and collectibles. **Altfield Gallery** (⊠ 248–249 Prince's Bldg., 10 Chater Rd., Central ☎ 852/2537–6370) carries furniture, fabrics, and collectibles from all over Asia. **C. L. Ma Antiques** (⊠ 43–55 Wyndham St., Central ☎ 852/2525–6665) has Ming Dynasty–style reproductions, especially large carved chests and tables made of unlacquered wood. **Eastern Dreams** (⊠ 47A Hollywood Rd., Central ☎ 852/2544–2804 ⊠ 4 Shelley St., Central ☎ 852/2524–4787) has antique and reproduction furniture, screens, and curios. **Galerie La Vong** (⊠ 13/F, 1 Lan Kwai Fong, Central ☎ 852/2869–6863) is the place to see the works of today's leading Vietnamese artists, whose creations reveal a combination of French and Chinese influences, as well as purely contemporary styles. **Honeychurch Antiques** (⊠ 29 Hollywood Rd., Central ☎ 852/2543–2433) is known especially for antique silver jewelry from Southeast Asia, China, and England. **Schoeni Art Gallery** (⊠ 27 Hollywood Rd., Central ☎ 852/2542–3143) sells Japanese, Chinese, and Thai antiques; Chinese silverware, such as opium boxes; and rare Chinese pottery. **Teresa Coleman**

(✉ 79 Wyndham St., Central ☎ 852/2526–2450) carries antique embroidered pieces and unusual Chinese collectibles.

Chinese Department Stores

Traditionally, Chinese department stores specialize in merchandise from the People's Republic of China, everything from fine silk and hand-stitched, embroidered tablecloths to porcelain and jade. Many also carry everyday goods ranging from pots and pans to school stationery.

★ **Chinese Arts & Crafts** (✉ Shop 230, Pacific Place, Admiralty ☎ 852/2827–6667 for information ✉ China Resources Bldg., 26 Harbour Rd., Wanchai ✉ Star House, 3 Salisbury Rd., Tsim Sha Tsui ✉ Nathan
★ Hotel, 378 Nathan Rd., Tsim Sha Tsui) has a number of branches. **Yue Hwa Chinese Products Emporium** (✉ 143–161 Nathan Rd., Tsim Sha Tsui ☎ 852/2739–3888 ✉ 54–64 Nathan Rd., Tsim Sha Tsui ☎ 852/2368–9165 ✉ 301–309 Nathan Rd., Yau Ma Tei ☎ 852/2384–0084 ✉ 1 Kowloon Park Dr., Tsim Sha Tsui ☎ 852/2317–5333) sells a wide selection of Chinese goods.

Clothing—Tailor Made

Ascot Chang (✉ Prince's Bldg., Central ☎ 852/2523–3663 ✉ Peninsula Hotel, Tsim Sha Tsui ☎ 852/2366–2398 ✉ Regent Hotel, Tsim Sha Tsui ☎ 852/2367–8319) has specialized in making shirts for men since 1949.
★ **Sam's Tailor** is one of the most famous of all Hong Kong's custom tailors, having outfitted everyone from European royal families to American and British politicians and, of course, your average tourist looking for a bargain. It serves women as impeccably as it serves men. ✉ *Shop K, Burlington Arcade, 94 Nathan Rd., Tsim Sha Tsui* ☎ *852/2721–8375.*

Department Stores

Blanc de Chine (✉ 12 Pedder St., Central ☎ 852/2524–7875) has beautiful Chinese clothes, in styles similar to those at the more famous Shanghai Tang, but in subtler colors, plus reproductions of antique
★ snuffboxes and silver mirrors and picture frames. **Shanghai Tang Department Store** (✉ 12 Pedder St., Central ☎ 852/2525–7333), on the ground floor of the Pedder Building, is the current retro rage in Hong Kong, selling old-fashioned Mandarin suits for men and women, either custom-made or ready-to-wear, and Chinese memorabilia, including novelty watches depicting Mao Zedong and Deng Xiaoping.

Factory Outlets

★ **The Joyce Warehouse** (✉ 21/F, Horizon Plaza, 2 Lee Wing St., Ap Lei Chau ☎ 852/2814–8313) has taken shopaholic locals by storm. This is the outlet for women's and men's fashions that are sold in the ritzy Joyce Boutiques in Central and Pacific Place, with labels by major designers. The **Pedder Building,** just a few feet from a Central MTR exit, contains five floors of small shops. The number of shops offering discounts of around 30% off retail—and sometimes more—seems now to be growing. **Blanc de Chine** (☎ 852/2524–7875) has beautiful Chinese clothes, in styles similar to those at the more famous Shanghai Tang but in subtler colors, plus reproductions of antique snuffboxes. **Labels Plus** (☎ 852/2521–8811) has some men's fashions as well as women's daytime separates. **La Place** (☎ 852/2868–3163) has youthful fashions, Prada bags, and a large selection of Chanel jackets at about 20% off retail. **Shopper's World–Safari** (☎ 852/2523–1950) has more variety than most outlets and a small upstairs department with men's fashions.

★ **Stanley Village Market** (Stanley Village; take Bus 6, 6A, or 260 from the Central Bus Terminus on Hong Kong Island, or Bus 260 from the Star Ferry; in Kowloon, take Bus 973 from Tsim Sha Tsui) is a popular haunt for designer sportswear, washable silk, and cashmere sweaters at factory outlet prices and in Western sizes. **Allan Janny Ltd.** (⊠ 17 Stanley New St.) has antique furniture and porcelain. **China Town** (⊠ 39 Stanley Main St.) has well-priced cashmere sweaters, but remember you get what you pay for as far as quality is concerned. **Sun & Moon Fashion Shop** (⊠ 18A–B Stanley Main St.) sells casual wear, with bargains on such familiar names as L. L. Bean, Yves St. Laurent, and Talbots (keep in mind that some of these are factory seconds). **Tong's Sheets & Linen Co.** (⊠ 55–57 Stanley St.) has sheets, tablecloths, and brocade pillow covers, as well as silk kimonos and pajamas. ⊠ *Stanley.*

Jewelry

Kai-Yin Lo (⊠ Pacific Place, Admiralty ☎ 852/2840–0066) has fabulous modern jewelry with an Asian influence. **K. S. Sze & Sons** (⊠ Mandarin Oriental Hotel, 5 Connaught Rd., Central ☎ 852/2524–2803) is known for its fair prices on one-of-a-kind pearl and gemstone creations. **Po Kwong** (⊠ 82 Queen's Rd., Central ☎ 852/2521–4686) is a good place to shop for South Sea Island pearls and other varieties. **The Showroom** (⊠ Room 1203, 12/F, Central Bldg., Pedder St., Central ☎ 852/2525–7085) specializes in creative pieces using diamonds and other gems.

JEWELRY FACTORY OUTLETS **TSL Jewelry Showroom** (⊠ Wah Ming Bldg., 34 Wong Chuk Hang Rd., Aberdeen ☎ 852/2873–2618) has fairly good prices on diamonds and other precious stones in unique settings, and each location has an on-premises workshop where you can watch the jewelry being made.

Kung Fu Supplies

Kung Fu Supplies Co. (⊠ 188 Johnston Rd., Wanchai ☎ 852/2891–1912) is the most convenient place to buy your drum cymbal, leather boots, sword, whip, double dagger, studded wrist bracelet, Bruce Lee *kempo* gloves, and other kung fu exotica.

Outdoor Markets

★ Hong Kong's best-known market is **Stanley Village Market** (⚓ Stanley Village; take Bus 6, 6A, or 260 from the Central Bus Terminus on Hong Kong Island, or Bus 260 from the Star Ferry; in Kowloon, take Bus 973 from Tsim Sha Tsui) a crowded haunt popular with Western residents and tourists looking for designer sportswear, washable silk, and cashmere sweaters at factory outlet prices and in Western sizes. Dozens and dozens of shops line a main street so narrow that awnings from each side meet in the middle. The stores open at about 10 and close between 5 and 6.

Photographic Equipment

Photo Scientific Appliances (⌧ 6 Stanley St., Central ☎ 852/2522–1903) has excellent prices on a wide variety of cameras and other photographic equipment.

Tea

Fook Ming Tong Tea Shop (⌧ The Landmark, Pedder St. and Des Voeux Rd., Central ☎ 852/2521–0337) is a mecca for the sophisticated tea shopper. You can get superb teas in beautifully designed tins or invest in some antique clay tea ware.

Kowloon

Art & Antiques

Charlotte Horstmann and Gerald Godfrey (⌧ Ocean Terminal, Tsim Sha Tsui ☎ 852/2735–7167) is good for wood carvings, bronze ware, and antique furniture.

Clothing—Tailor Made

Jimmy Chen Co. Ltd. (⌧ The Peninsula Hong Kong, Salisbury Rd., Tsim Sha Tsui ☎ 852/2722–1888) can make everything from a suit to a shirt
★ for a man or woman. **Sam's Tailor** (⌧ Shop K, Burlington Arcade, 94 Nathan Rd., Tsim Sha Tsui ☎ 852/2721–8375) is one of the most famous of all Hong Kong's men's and women's custom tailors, having outfitted everyone from the royal families of Europe to American and British politicians. **W. W. Chan & Sons** (⌧ Burlington House, 92–94 Nathan Rd., Tsim Sha Tsui ☎ 852/2366–9738) is known for top-quality classic cuts and has bolts and bolts of fine European fabrics from which to choose. **Irene Fashions** (⌧ Burlington House, 92–94 Nathan Rd., Tsim Sha Tsui ☎ 852/2367–5588) is the women's division of W. W. Chan.

Jewelry

China Handicrafts & Gem House (⌧ 25A Mody Rd., Tsim Sha Tsui East ☎ 852/2366–0973) sells loose gemstones. **Chow Sang Sang** (⌧ 229 Nathan Rd., Tsim Sha Tsui ☎ 852/2730–3241) has shops all over. **Chow Tai Fook** (⌧ 29 Queen's Rd., Central ☎ 852/2523–7128) is one of the biggest jewelry chains.

Outdoor Markets

The **Flower Market** (⌧ Flower St. near Prince Edward MTR station, Mong Kok) is a collection of street stalls offering cut flowers and potted plants, with a few outlets specializing in plastic plants and silk flowers. The **Kansu Street Jade Market** (⌧ Kansu St. off Nathan Rd., Yau Ma Tei) displays jade in every form, color, shape, and size. Some trinkets are reasonably priced, but unless you know a lot about jade, don't be tempted into buying expensive items. The **Ladies Market,** outside the Mong Kok MTR subway station along Mong Kok Road, has outdoor stalls full of women's clothes. If you rummage around enough, you might find a designer item or two at rock-bottom prices. **Temple Street** (⌧ Near Jordan MTR station) becomes an open-air market at night, filled with a colorful collection of clothes, handbags, electrical goods, gadgets, and all sorts of household items. The market, stretching for almost a mile, is one of Hong Kong's liveliest nighttime shopping experiences.

SIDE TRIP TO MACAU

In Chinese hands since 1999 after almost 450 years of Portuguese rule, Macau is one of the few places in the world that can legitimately lay claim to being a hybrid of East and West. It had a brief period of prosperity in the 16th century but then entered a long decline made worse by the rise of nearby Hong Kong. It is now in the midst of something like a rebirth, although it is still poorer and more traditional than its brash neighbor, and it is known within the region primarily for its good food, graceful colonial buildings, and bustling casinos. Macau's 450,000 people live squeezed into its 9-square-mi peninsula and two outlying islands, Taipa and Coloane; while most of them speak Cantonese, English is widely used in tourist areas.

Exploring Macau

★ The heart of old Macau and one of the most charming squares in Asia, the **Largo do Senado** (Senate Square) is surrounded by an exquisite collection of brilliantly colored colonial buildings. It's paved with black and white stone tiles arranged in a Portuguese-style wave pattern and furnished with benches, plants, and a fountain. Residents appropriated the space immediately, and it now functions as a town square should: as a communal meeting place where old women gather to gossip and children run free. At night the buildings are lighted by spotlights, and the square becomes even more alluring, as locals of all generations meet and socialize. ⊠ *Av. Almeida Ribeiro.*

A superb example of colonial architecture, **Leal Senado** (Loyal Senate) anchors the southern end of Largo do Senado. It was built in the late 18th century to house the Senate of leading citizens—which was, at the time, far more powerful than the governors, who usually served their appointed time and then promptly returned to Portugal. Today the Senate has both elected and appointed members and acts as the municipal government, with its president holding the same power as a mayor. Inside the building, a beautiful stone staircase leads to wrought-iron gates that open onto a charming garden. Note the blue-and-white tile work (such tiles are called *azulejos*), a typical Portuguese craft originally perfected by the Moors of North Africa. The attractive garden in the back has cast busts of two great Portuguese men of letters: the 16th-century poet Luis de Camões and the 19th-century writer João de Deus. The foyer and garden are open during business hours, and there are frequent art and historical exhibitions in the foyer and gallery.

On the second floor of the Leal Senado is the **Macau Central Library**, a superb copy of the classic Portuguese library in Mafra. It holds what may be the world's best collection of books in English about China—many were inherited from the British- and American-managed Chinese Customs House. The library also has rare books from the early days of the Portuguese empire and bound copies of old Macau newspapers. Scholars and others are welcome to browse or study; there's also a nice view of the square. ⊠ *Largo do Senado at Rua Dr. Soares, 2/F* ☎ *853/558– 049* 🖷 *853/318–756* ⊙ *Daily 2–8.*

Macau Forum is home to two museums, one devoted to cars and the other, wine. The **Grand Prix Museum** (☎ 853/798–4126 ⊕ www.macautourism. gov.mo ⊠ 10 patacas ⊙ Wed.–Sun. 10–6) tells the story of the races that were first run in Macau in 1953 and today are on par with Monaco's famed race. It's a required stop for all racing fans, with an exquisite collection of winners' cars, among which pride of place is given to Eduardo de Carvalho's gorgeous Triumph TR-2 "long door," which won the first Grand Prix. In the background you hear the suitably frenzied voices of English announcers, and around you are videos, photos, and memorabilia. The **Wine Museum** (☎ 853/798–4108 ⊕ www.macautourism. gov.mo ⊠ 15 patacas ⊙ Wed.–Mon. 10–6) lovingly illustrates the history of wine making with photographs, maps, paintings, antique wine presses, Portuguese wine fraternity costumes, and 750 different Portuguese wines. The cellar's oldest bottle is an 1815 Porto Garrafeira, and because the museum had a problem with theft when it first opened, all the valuable bottles are kept in a locked chamber. Admission includes a glass of wine in the tasting area, and there is a small shop that sells a variety of wines and port. ⊠ *Rua Luís Gonzaga Gomes.*

★ The **Maritime Museum** is ideally placed on the waterfront **Barra Square,** this gem of a museum has been a favorite since it opened in 1987. The four-story building resembles a sailing ship and contains one of the foremost maritime museums in Asia. The adjacent dock was restored as a pier for a tug, a dragon boat, a sampan, and working replicas of a South China trading junk and a 19th-century pirate-chasing *lorcha* (a wooden sailing ship). Inside the museum is a breathtaking series of detailed models of local and foreign ships, with illustrations of how each one catches fish or captures the wind. There are also light-box charts of great voyages by Portuguese and Chinese explorers, a relief model of 17th-century Macau, the story of the A-Ma Temple in slide-show style, navigational aids such as a paraffin lamp once used in the Guia Lighthouse, and all manner of interactive touch screens and videos. The museum also operates a 30-minute pleasure junk (10 patacas extra per person) around the Inner and Outer harbors daily except Tuesday and the first Sunday of the month. ⊠ *Largo do Pagode da Barra opposite A-Ma Temple* ☎ *853/595–481* ⊕ *www.museumaritimo.gov.mo* ⊠ *10 patacas* ⊙ *Wed.–Mon. 10–5:30.*

São Domingos. Following an ambitious restoration, St. Dominick's is once again the most beautiful church in Macau. The stunning cream-and-white nave leads to a filigreed altar intricately carved in the Mannerist style. São Domingos was originally a convent founded by Spanish Dominican friars in 1587, but was rebuilt as a church in the 17th century. When convents were banned in Portugal in 1834, this church became a repository for sacred art. The works are now on display in the museum on the first to third floors, accessible via a small staircase to the right of the altar. Indeed, the church itself has had a stormy history: in 1644 a Portuguese officer was murdered at the altar by a mob during mass; in

1707 the church was besieged by the governor's troops when the Dominicans sided with the pope against the Jesuits on the question of whether ancestor worship should be permitted among Chinese Christian converts. After three days the soldiers broke down the doors and briefly imprisoned the priests. ⊠ *Rua de São Domingos at Largo do Senado* 🖾 *Museum, free* ⊙ *Museum, daily 10–6.*

São Paulo. The church of St. Paul, which occupies an imposing site at the top of a long flight of steps, has long since been adopted as Macau's symbol, even though the only thing that remains of the once spectacular structure is its facade. Built under the direction of the Jesuits by exiled Japanese Christians and local craftsmen between 1602 and 1627, St. Paul's has always been tied to the struggle to preserve a Christian presence in Asia. The story of the church is told on its carved-stone facade and in the excavated crypt, which contains the tomb of the church's founder, Alessandro Valignano, and the bones of Japanese and Indo-Chinese martyrs. St. Paul's also served as part of the first Western-style university in Asia, attended by such scholars as Matteo Ricci and Adam Van Schall, who studied here before going to the emperor's court in Peking. The college, along with the body of the church and most of Monte Fort, was destroyed in the disastrous fire in 1835. Behind the facade, in an underground site beneath the onetime body of the church, is the **Museum of Sacred Art,** which holds statues, crucifixes, chalices, and other sacramental objects dating from the 17th through the 18th century and borrowed from local churches. The 17th-century paintings by exiled Japanese artists depict the crucified martyrs of Nagasaki and the Archangel Michael in the guise of a samurai. ⊠ *Rua de São Paulo at Largo da Companhia* 🕾 *853/ 358–444* ⊕ *www.macautourism.gov.mo* 🖾 *Free* ⊙ *Daily 9–6.*

Dining

WHAT IT COSTS In patacas				
$$$$	**$$$**	**$$**	**$**	**¢**
AT DINNER over 300	200–300	100–200	60–100	under 60

Prices are for a main course at dinner and do not include the customary 10% service charge.

★ **$$$–$$$$**   ✕ **Robuchon a Galera.** For a truly fine dining experience and a slice of Paris in the heart of Macau, this restaurant from French celebrity chef Joël Robuchon is a must. The luscious gold-and-royal-blue interior is exquisitely detailed. Elaborate presentations are the norm; among the signature dishes are a heavenly mille-feuille of tomato and crabmeat, duck breast with turnips and foie gras, and lamb au jus served with creamy potato puree. Finish with a choice from the sophisticated cheese trolley, or dig into the warm molten chocolate cake. The wine list is as thick as an encyclopedia and is reputed to be the most extensive in Asia. ⊠ *Hotel Lisboa, Lisboa Tower, Av. de Lisboa, 3/F* 🕾 *853/377–666* ⚏ *Reservations essential* 🖃 *AE, DC, MC, V.*

★ **$–$$**   ✕ **A Lorcha.** Ask people in town to name their favorite Portuguese restaurant, and odds are they'll mention A Lorcha. It's not a fancy place, but they get everything just right. The menu leans towards traditional stalwarts such as *bacalhau* (salt cod), grilled seafood, or meat, but the dishes are always prepared with quality ingredients and lots of care; be sure to ask what is fresh that day. This is also a good place to try typical Macanese desserts such as cool mango pudding and *serradura* (a very sweet, rich cream and biscuit pudding). ⊠ *289 Rua do Almirante Sergio* ☎ *853/313–195* ⌖ *Reservations essential* ▭ *AE, DC, MC, V* ⊘ *Closed Tues.*

★ **$–$$** ✕ **Pizzeria Toscana.** Don't be put off by the "pizzeria" or the strange location in the middle of a parking lot opposite the ferry terminal: this is one of the best restaurants in the city, owned by a Macanese family with roots in Pisa. Try the *bresaola involtini* (air-cured beef with shredded Parmesan) or the delicate salmon carpaccio to start; then move on to grilled king prawns in a garlic-and-tomato sauce or tortellini with porcini mushrooms. The owner is one of the biggest wine importers in the region, and the wine list is superb. There's also the quaint Toscana café (run by different management) in the heart of the old quarter Travessa de São Domingos, which serves a slightly smaller menu. ⊠ *Av. da Amizade opposite the ferry terminal* ☎ *853/726–637* ▭ *AE, DC, MC, V.*

★ **¢–$$** ✕ **Litoral.** One of the most popular local restaurants, Litoral serves Portuguese and Macanese dishes that are relatively humble but invariably delicious. Be warned that the Portuguese favor cuts of meat for which you need to acquire a taste: pig's ear and ox tripe, to name just two. From time to time the owner removes some dishes—such as the braised duck in a complex sweet-soy sauce—from the menu; it's worth asking if it's available. The braised pork with shrimp paste is a must. For dessert, try the *bebinca de leite,* a coconut-milk custard, or the traditional egg pudding, *pudim abade de priscos.* ⊠ *261 Rua do Almirante Sergio* ☎ *853/967–878* ▭ *AE, MC, V.*

¢–$ ✕ **Praia Grande.** The Praia Grande used to have the most lovely view of the harbor but now faces not-so-lovely reclaimed land. Nevertheless, the simple interior at this classic Portuguese restaurant—white arches, terracotta floors, and wrought-iron furniture—still makes it a pleasant place to dine. The menu presents such imaginative fare as Portuguese dim sum, African chicken (in a peppery coconut broth), mussels in white wine, and clams *cataplana* (in a stew of pork, onions, tomatoes, and wine). The esplanade, with a serving kiosk and umbrella-shaded tables, is ideal for drinks and snacks. ⊠ *10A Lobo d'Avila, at Ave. da Praia Grande* ☎ *853/973–022* ▭ *AE, MC, V.*

Lodging

WHAT IT COSTS In patacas				
	$$$$	**$$$**	**$$**	**$**	**¢**
FOR 2 PEOPLE	over 1,800	1,000–1,800	500–1,000	200–500	under 200

Prices are for two people in a standard double room on a typical Saturday night, not including 10% service charge and 5% tax.

★ **$$$$** ⌂ **Westin Resort.** The Westin is designed for those primarily interested in getting away from it all. Occupying a magnificent site on a headland overlooking the black-sand beach of Hac Sa, the resort is surrounded by open water and total silence. From the moment you enter the lobby the pace slows to that of a tropical island. The comfortable rooms are large and the terraces even larger, while the sports and recreational facilities are the best in Macau—you'll even have course and clubhouse privileges at the Macau Golf & Country Club, accessible directly from the hotel. ⊠ *Hac Sa Beach, Coloane* ☎ *853/871–111 or 2803–2002, 800/228–3000 in Hong Kong* 🖷 *853/871–122* ⊕ *www.westin-macau. com* 🖵 *200 rooms, 8 suites* ⌂ *4 restaurants, room service, in-room data ports, in-room safes, minibars, cable TV with movies, driving range, 18-hole golf course, miniature golf, 8 tennis courts, 2 pools (1 indoor), health club, 2 hot tubs (1 outdoor), massage, bicycles, badminton, squash, 2 bars, shops, baby-sitting, Internet, business services, meeting rooms, car rental, no-smoking rooms* 🖃 *AE, DC, MC, V.*

$$$ ⌂ **Hotel Lisboa.** Though hectic, the Lisboa is an unexpectedly appealing place to stay. Its exterior has become a popular symbol of Macau: a gaudy mustard-and-white confection with a roof of giant balls on spikes that is said to resemble a roulette wheel. The lobby is more tasteful, though still a little ostentatious. The rooms, especially in the Lisboa Tower, come as a delightful surprise: large, comfortable, wedge-shape spaces with opulent furnishings that have been decorated with a thoughtful and restrained hand. Geographically speaking, the Lisboa is like Rome: all roads (and many buses) lead here, making this an exceptionally convenient option. ⊠ *Av. da Amizade* ☎ *853/577–666, 853/559–1028 or 800/969–130 in Hong Kong* 🖷 *853/567–193* ⊕ *www.hotelisboa.com* 🖵 *830 rooms, 79 suites* ⌂ *18 restaurants, coffee shop, pizzeria, pool, sauna, bar, casino, theater* 🖃 *AE, DC, MC, V.*

★ **$$$** ⌂ **Pousada de São Tiago.** The São Tiago has the monopoly on charm among Macau's hotels. It was ingeniously built into a 17th-century Portuguese fortress that once guarded the southern tip of the peninsula, and the entrance alone is worth a visit, with a staircase that runs through an old lichen-covered tunnel through which water seeps in soothing trickles. Rooms are decorated with unusual mahogany furnishings and azulejos that lend atmosphere. Views from most guest rooms and dining terraces take in the harbor and mainland China beyond. The only shortcoming is that service can be a little lethargic. ⊠ *Av. da República* ☎ *853/378–111, 852/2739–1216 in Hong Kong* 🖷 *853/552–170, 852/2739–1198 in Hong Kong* ⊕ *www.saotiago.com.mo* 🖵 *20 rooms, 4 suites* ⌂ *Restaurant, room service, minibars, cable TV, pool, bar, dry cleaning, laundry service* 🖃 *AE, DC, MC, V.*

$$–$$$ ⌂ **Hotel Sintra.** This location is arguably the best of any hotel, within easy walking distance of both the old quarter and the bustling surrounding areas. In 2002 a major renovation was completed, giving all rooms a much-needed face-lift, adding large beds and comfy goose-down duvets. The hotel mainly attracts businesspeople, who don't care that the room's lake views are obstructed by ugly office blocks. The restaurant claims to serve the best steak in town. ⊠ *58–62 Av. Dom João IV* ☎ *853/710–111* 🖷 *853/510–527* ⊕ *www.hotelsintra.com* 🖵 *228 rooms, 12 suites*

⚙ *Restaurant, room service, some in-room data ports, some in-room safes, minibars, refrigerators, cable TV, sauna, shops, dry cleaning, laundry service, business services, meeting rooms, no-smoking floor* ▤ *AE, DC, MC, V.*

$$–$$$ 🏨 **Hyatt Regency & Taipa Island Resort.** The Hyatt was the originator of the resort concept in Macau, but in the last few years it has been trumped by its rivals—the newer Mandarin, which is closer to downtown, and the Westin, which is much more secluded and special. Nevertheless, the Hyatt is a pleasant place to stay, though the last major renovation was in 1997. The resort has superb facilities, including a health spa, a huge outdoor swimming pool, and a hot tub that looks like a modern take on the Turkish bath. The Hyatt is particularly popular with Hong Kong families. ✉ *2 Est. de Almirante Joaquim Marques Esparteiro, Taipa Island* ☎ *853/831–234, 852/2559–0168 in Hong Kong, 800/633–7313 in the U.S.* 📠 *853/830–195* ⊕ *www.macau.hyatt.com* 🛏 *308 rooms, 18 suites* ⚙ *3 restaurants, coffee shop, minibars, cable TV with movies, 4 tennis courts, pool, health club, hair salon, bicycles, 2 squash courts, 2 bars, casino, children's programs (ages 5–12)* ▤ *AE, DC, MC, V.*

Nightlife & Pubs

Many nightspots are staffed with hostesses from Thailand, the Philippines, or Russia and are merely thinly veiled covers for the world's oldest profession. The legitimate clubs that do exist tend not to survive for very long. Check with the Macau Government Tourist Office to find out about interesting spots that are currently open.

Pubs and music bars open and close with astonishing speed and are mostly known only to locals by word of mouth. You can inquire at the tourist office or, better still, spot the coolest-looking person on staff at your hotel and ask where they go out at night. For some time the government has been promoting the area on the reclaimed land near the Hotel Lisboa as Macau's own Lan Kwai Fong—after Hong Kong's popular nightlife district. Although the comparison to Hong Kong is still a bit of a stretch, there is finally a critical mass of bars, live music spots, and restaurants. It's somewhat desolate during the day and on most weeknights, but the area comes alive on Friday and Saturday. The main street here is Avenida Marginal Baia Nova, known as "The Docks" to expatriates, and most of the hot spots are gathered on the southwestern block. There are a few that stand out in the crowd.

Celluloid is the theme at the aptly named **Casablanca** (✉ Av. Dr. Sun Yat Sen ☎ 853/751–281), where homages are paid to Marcello Mastroianni and Hong Kong director Wong Kar Wai's *Chungking Express* via large posters. It's opulently fitted out with deep-plush red velvet curtains and chairs. **The Embassy** (✉ Mandarin Oriental, 853/956–1110 Av. da Amizade ☎ 853/567–888) bar is reminiscent of foreign correspondent clubs around the world. Portraits of ex–consuls general and indigenous souvenirs from their countries hang somberly on the walls. For live Latin American, jazz, or the occasional pop music, depending on the night, head to the **Green Spot** (✉ Emperor Hotel, Rue de Xangai, lobby ☎ 853/

788–666). The spacious mint-color lounge was opened by popular Hong Kong singer Maria Cordeiro, who is originally from Macau (she also owns the Green Spot in Hong Kong). Reservations are recommended for a table on the weekends. Evoking South American mystique is the loungy **Rio Café** (⊠ Av. Dr. Sun Yat Sen ☎ 853/751–306), fitted out with large leafy plants and fiery orange-and-red decor.

Casinos

Since the late 1950s, Stanley Ho has had a monopoly on the gambling scene in Macau—he owned *all* of Macau's casinos. However, things are on the move, as three more casino-operating concessions have been won (one by Mr. Ho himself, the other two by consortiums that have connections to Las Vegas). Plans are underway to revamp the seedy image of gambling and to create resort-style entertainment venues offering conference halls, hotels, theaters, restaurants, shopping malls, and the like. The first of these Las Vegas–style casinos, the Las Vegas Sands, opened in May 2004 next to the Mandarin Oriental; the most eagerly awaited, however, is the Venetian from the same group; it is expected to open in Cotai, a new development area between Coloane and Taipa islands, in March 2006. Las Vegas entrepreneur Steve Wynn has his own casino plans in the works, but hasn't yet broken ground on his project. The busiest and largest casino is the two-story operation in the Lisboa, where the games are roulette, blackjack, baccarat, *pacapio,* and the Chinese games called fan-tan and "big and small." There are also hundreds of slot machines, which the Chinese call "hungry tigers."

At this writing, there are a dozen casinos in Macau, and the main ones are in several major hotels, including the **Hotel Lisboa, Mandarin Oriental, New Century, Kingsway Hotel,** and **Hyatt Regency & Taipa Island Resort.** The **Las Vegas Sands** (⊠ Av. de Amizade and Av. Dr. Sun Yat Sen ☎ 853/883–388) is the first of Macau's Las Vegas–style casinos and dwarfs the adjacent Mandarin Oriental. The gold reflective windows give it a sense of glitz and glamor, long missing from the Macau gambling scene. The **Palacio de Macau** (⊠ Av. de Amizade, at the Outer Harbour ☎ 853/346–701) is more popularly known as the Floating Casino. The **Pharoah's Palace** (⊠ Landmark Plaza, Av. da Amizade ☎ 853/788–111) is an independent casino.

Macau A to Z

To research prices, get advice from other travelers, and book travel arrangements, visit www.fodors.com.

BOAT & FERRY TRAVEL

The Hong Kong–Macau route is one of the world's easiest border crossings. Ferries run every 15 minutes and take just under an hour, with no more than 5 minutes for immigration control on either side (be sure to bring your passport). Only on weekend evenings and major public holidays is it necessary to reserve in advance; at all other times, just show up and take the next boat. Of course, service can be disrupted when typhoons sweep in.

The majority of ships to Macau leave Hong Kong from the Macau Terminal in the Shun Tak Centre, which has its own marked exit from the Sheung Wan MTR station. From Macau, ferries use the modern three-story ferry terminal. There is also limited service to and from the China Hong Kong Terminal, on the Kowloon side of Hong Kong Harbour.

The Shun Tak Centre houses the Macau Government Tourist Office, booking offices for all shipping companies, and offices of most Macau hotels, travel agents, and excursions to China.

Following the merger of Far East Jetfoil Company and CTS-Parkview, there is now a unified service of turbojets, which run every 15 minutes around the clock, with slightly less frequent sailings from 3 AM to 6 AM. The turbojets are larger and more comfortable than the old jet foils and make the 64-km (40-mi) trip in about an hour. Beer, soft drinks, and snacks are available on board, as are duty-free cigarettes and Macau's instant-lottery tickets. There is no smoking on board. First-class seats are available for a small premium, but there is no discernible difference in quality save for a free box of unappetizing snacks.

First Ferry also runs service, with almost hourly round-trips daily from the China Terminal in Tsim Sha Tsui. Fares range from HK$140 on weekdays to HK$155 on weekend days, and HK$175 nights.

FARES & SCHEDULES There are three classes of tickets—economy, first, and super—as well as VIP cabins for four or six people. The prices, depending on class, are HK$130 to HK$232 on weekdays, HK$141 to HK$247 on weekends and holidays, and HK$161 to HK$260 at night (after 6 PM). The return trip from Macau is HK$1 more per ticket. Although boats are frequent, it's wise to book your return ticket if you visit on a weekend. Otherwise you'll be stuck back at the gambling tables or at a bar until the next available ferry.

Ferry Reservations and Turbojet Tickets ☎ 853/2859-3333 for schedules, 2921-6688 for bookings ⊕ www.turbojet.com.hk. **First Ferry** ✉ Shun Tak Centre, 200 Connaught Rd., Sheung Wan, Hong Kong ☎ 852/2516-9581, 853/726-301 in Macau.

CAR RENTAL

Macau is the land of counterintuitive directions, where roundabouts and detours often require you to turn left in order to go right, so you might think twice about driving yourself around. Still, you can rent *mokes,* little jeeplike vehicles that are fun to drive and ideal for touring. Unlike in Hong Kong, you drive on the *right* side of the road. International and most national driver's licenses are valid here. Rental rates are 350 patacas for 24 hours, plus a whopping 3,000-pataca deposit (credit cards accepted). The price includes third-party insurance, and the very nice staff will often give a discount if asked. Hotel packages often include special moke-rental deals. Contact Happy Mokes for rental details. Along with mokes, Avis rents cars for 450 to 600 patacas weekdays and 500 to 650 patacas weekends. Book in advance and you'll receive a discount, but as always, you must ask for it. Avis also has 15% discounts for selected frequent-flyer programs.

Rental Agencies Avis ☎ 853/336-789 in Macau, 852/2576-6831 in Hong Kong. **Happy Mokes** ☎ 852/2523-5690 in Hong Kong, 853/831-212, 853/439-393 in Macau.

MONEY MATTERS

At this writing, one U.S. dollar is worth about 8.3 Macau patacas (sometimes denoted as MOP), making the pataca marginally weaker than the Hong Kong dollar, which is pegged at 7.75 to the U.S. dollar. You'll get roughly 5.5 patacas to the Canadian dollar and 12.8 patacas to the pound sterling. The Hong Kong dollar is accepted everywhere in Macau at parity with the pataca, so it is not really necessary to change money at all for short trips. No one in Hong Kong will accept patacas, however, so be sure to change any leftover patacas back into Hong Kong dollars before you leave Macau.

PASSPORTS & VISAS

Passports are required for everyone. No visa is required for Portuguese citizens or nationals of the United States, Canada, Australia, New Zealand, any European countries, and most Asian countries for visits of up to 20 days, or for Hong Kong residents for up to 90 days. Other nationals need visas, which can be obtained on arrival: these cost 100 patacas for individuals, 200 patacas for family groups, and 50 patacas for tour group members.

TAXIS

Taxis are inexpensive and plentiful. The black cabs with cream-color roofs can be flagged on the street; the yellow cabs are radio taxis. All are metered, and most are air-conditioned and reasonably comfortable. Drivers often speak limited English and may not recognize English or Portuguese place names, so you're strongly advised to carry a bilingual map or name card for your destination in Chinese. The base charge is 10 patacas for the first 1¾ km (about 1¼ mi) and 1 pataca for each additional 250 meters. Drivers don't expect more than small change as a tip. Trips to Taipa incur a 5-pataca surcharge; trips to Coloane, 10 patacas. Expect to pay about 15 patacas for a trip from the terminal to downtown.

TOURS

Two basic tours of Macau are available. One covers mainland Macau, with stops at the Chinese border, Kun Iam Temple, St. Paul's, and Penha Hill; this lasts about 3½ hours. The other typical tour consists of a 2-hour trip across the bridge to the islands to see old Chinese villages, temples, beaches, the Jockey Club, and the international airport. Tours travel by bus or car, and prices vary between operators.

The most comfortable way to tour is by chauffeur-driven luxury car. A car with a maximum of four passengers goes for HK$200 an hour with Avis. You can also rent a regular taxi for touring, though few drivers speak English or know the place well enough to be good guides. Depending on your bargaining powers, the cost will be HK$60 or more per hour.

Most travelers going to Macau for the day book tours with travel agents in Hong Kong or before leaving home. If you prearrange in this way, you'll have transportation from Hong Kong to Macau all set, with your guide waiting in the arrival hall. There are many licensed tour operators in Macau; the ones we list focus on English-speaking visitors.

🔢 Tour Operators **Able Tours** also operates Grayline tours ✉ Room 1015, Av. da Amizade, Ferry Terminal, Macau ☎ 853/725-813. **Estoril Tours** ✉ Shop 333, Shun Tak Centre, 200 Connaught Rd., 3/F, Central, Hong Kong ☎ 852/2559-1028 🖶 852/2857-1830 ⊕ www.estoril-tours.com. **Sintra Tours** ✉ Hotel Sintra, 58-62 Av. Dom João IV, Macau ☎ 853/710-361.

TRANSPORTATION AROUND MACAU

Walking is the best method of getting around in the old parts of town and in shopping areas—the streets are narrow and crowded. You can rent a bicycle for about 10 patacas an hour at shops near the Taipa bus station. Public buses (2.50 patacas–5 patacas) are convenient. Tricycle-drawn two-seater pedicabs cluster at the ferry terminal and near hotels; be sure to bargain with the driver.

VISITOR INFORMATION

The Macau Government Tourist Office (MGTO) has an excellent Web site that provides information on the latest exhibitions and festivals, as well as cultural sights, restaurants, and hotels. The site also has an interactive city map. In 2003 the main office of the MGTO moved from the historic Largo do Senado to the modern Lam Van Lakes development area. There are information counters across Macau, and at whichever location you find them, the MGTO is exceptionally helpful and has brochures in a host of languages, on almost every aspect of Macau, as well as the usual maps and general information. They also have offices at the ferry and airport terminals.

Business visitors to Macau can get trade information from the Macau Trade and Investment Promotion Institute.

🔢 **Macau Government Tourist Office** (MGTO). ✉ Macau Ferry Terminal, Macau ☎ 853/726-416 ⊕ www.macautourism.gov.mo ✉ Macau International Airport, Arrival Hall ☎ 853/861-436 ✉ Shun Tak Centre, 200 Connaught Rd., Sheung Wan, Hong Kong ☎ 852/2857-2287 🖶 852/2559-0698 ✉ Hong Kong International Airport, Hong Kong ☎ 852/2769-7970 or 2382-7110 🖶 852/2261-2971. **Macau Trade and Investment Promotion Institute** ✉ World Trade Centre, Av. da Amizade, 5/F, Macau ☎ 853/712-660 🖶 853/590-309 ⊕ www.ipim.gov.mo/pageen/home.asp.

HONG KONG A TO Z

By Sofia A. Suárez

To research prices, get advice from other travelers, and book travel arrangements, visit www.fodors.com.

AIR TRAVEL TO & FROM HONG KONG

CARRIERS Cathay Pacific is Hong Kong's flagship carrier. It maintains high standards, with friendly service, good in-flight food, and a safe track record, all of which drive the price up slightly higher than some of the other regional carriers; there are flights from both Los Angeles and San Francisco on the west coast and from New York–JFK on the east coast, including a new nonstop flight from New York. Singapore Airlines is usually slightly less expensive and offers direct flights to San Francisco on the west coast and Newark on the east coast. Continental also frequently offers good price deals, and has a nonstop flight to Hong Kong from Newark Airport. Several other airlines offer service from the United States to Hong Kong, sometimes with connections in Asia.

Airlines & Contacts Air Canada ☎ 888/247-2262, 2867-8111 in Hong Kong ⊕ www.aircanada.com. **Asiana** ☎ 800/227-4262, 2523-8585 in Hong Kong ⊕ www.flyasiana.com. **Cathay Pacific Airways** ☎ 800/233-2742 in the U.S., 800/268-6868 in Canada, 2747-1888 in Hong Kong ⊕ www.cathay-usa.com. **China Airlines** ☎ 800/227-5118, 2868-2299 in Hong Kong ⊕ www.chinaairlines.com.hk. **Continental** ☎ 800/231-0856, 3198-5777 in Hong Kong ⊕ www.continental.com. **Korean Air** ☎ 800/438-5000, 2366-2001 in Hong Kong ⊕ www.koreanair.com. **Northwest** ☎ 800/447-4747, 2810-4288 in Hong Kong ⊕ www.nwa.com. **Qantas** ☎ 800/227-4500, 2822-9000 in Hong Kong ⊕ www.qantas.com. **Singapore Airlines** ☎ 800/742-3333, 2520-2233 in Hong Kong ⊕ www.singaporeair.com. **United Airlines** ☎ 800/241-6522, 2810-4888 in Hong Kong ⊕ www.united.com.

AIRPORTS & TRANSFERS

The gateway to Hong Kong is the mammoth Hong Kong International Airport (universally referred to as Chek Lap Kok), off Lantau. Be warned: because the arrivals hall is so vast, arriving passengers often have trouble finding those meeting them. This vastness also translates into long, long walks to or from the plane, made worse by the lack of baggage carts on the airplane side, which can mean dragging your hand luggage more than a mile in some cases. Two Hong Kong Hotels Association counters take reservations, and two Hong Kong Tourist Board counters offer assistance.

Airport Information Hong Kong International Airport ☎ 852/2181-0000 ⊕ www.hkairport.com.

AIRPORT TRANSFER

The spectacular, high-speed, high-frequency **Airport Express** service run by the MTR Corporation, which also operates Hong Kong's subway system, whisks you between the airport and Kowloon in 19 minutes via Tsing Ma Bridge, and to and from Hong Kong Island (Central) in 23 minutes between 5:50 AM and 1:15 AM. This is the most convenient and economical way to get to and from the airport. There is plenty of luggage space, legroom, and comfortable seating with television screens on the backs of the passenger seats showing tourist information and the latest news. A noteworthy feature of Airport Express is the convenient in-town check-in for most destinations (except for the United States), whereby you check your luggage, get your boarding pass, and pay departure tax while still on Hong Kong Island. To do this, you must purchase an Airport Express ticket and get to the train station anytime from one day to 90 minutes before your flight. The office is open from 6 AM to 1 AM. The Airport Express station is connected to the MTR's Central station (albeit via a long, underground walkway with no luggage carts). One-way or same-day return fare to or from Central is HK$100; from Kowloon, HK$90. Round-trip tickets valid for one month cost HK$180 for Central and HK$160 for Kowloon.

The Airport Express also runs a free shuttle bus between major hotels and its Hong Kong and Kowloon stations. To board, you must show your ticket, boarding pass, or Airport Express ticket.

Airbus has eight routes covering just about every hotel and hostel in Hong Kong, Kowloon, and the New Territories. Prices range from HK$14 to HK$45 for the one-hour trip.

A 24-hour **Airport Shuttle** bus departs major hotels every 30 minutes and costs HK$120.

A number of regular public buses—including service by **Citybus, Kowloon Motor Bus,** and **Long Wing Bus Company**—serve the airport; though cheaper (HK$23 and under), these take longer than express options.

Taxis from the airport cost up to HK$330 for Hong Kong Island destinations and up to HK$270 for Kowloon destinations, plus HK$5 per piece of luggage.

DCH Limo Service is located at counter B13 in the Arrival Hall. Depending on the zone and the type of car, limo rides from the airport range from HK$390 to HK$600. A pick-up service is available at the same rates, as is a car service at HK$320 per hour not including tolls and parking, with a minimum of three hours.

🏢 **Airbus** 🕾 852/2745-4466. **Airport Express** 🕾 852/2881-8888 for MTR hotline. **Airport Shuttle** 🕾 852/2377-0733. **Citybus** 🕾 852/2873-0818. **DCH Limo Service** 🕾 852/2262-1888 🖷 852/2753-6768. **Kowloon Motor Bus** 🕾 852/2745-4466. **Long Wing Bus Company** 🕾 852/2261-2791. **Taxis** 🕾 852/2574-7311.

BOAT & FERRY TRAVEL

Since December 1888, the Star Ferry has been running across Victoria Harbour; in fact, it is a Hong Kong landmark. Double-bowed, green-and-white vessels connect Hong Kong Island with Kowloon in just eight minutes daily from 6:30 AM to 11:30 PM; the ride costs HK$2.20 on the upper deck, HK$1.70 on the lower deck.

New World Ferry Services Ltd., better known as First Ferry, runs nine different ferry routes from Central to the outlying islands of Lantau, Cheung Chau, Lamma, and Peng Chau. Printed schedules are obtainable at the HKTB Information and gift centers at two locations: the Star Ferry Concourse, Kowloon, and the Center, 99 Queen's Road Central, Central; as well as through the HKTB Visitor Hot Line. Or, you can simply pick one up at the ferry ticket counters. Round-trip fares vary from HK$15 to HK$62.

🏢 **HKTB Visitor Hot Line** 🕾 852/2508-1234. **New World First Ferry** 🕾 852/2131-8181 ⊕ www.nwff.com.hk. **Star Ferry** 🕾 852/2367-7065.

BUS TRAVEL WITHIN HONG KONG

Double-decker buses run from 6 AM to midnight and cover most parts of Hong Kong. Bus drivers usually don't speak English, so you may have to ask other passengers for help or you must know exactly where you want to disembark.

When determining bus direction, buses ending with the letter L will eventually connect to the Kowloon–Canton Railway; buses ending with the letter M connect to an MTR station; and buses ending with the letter X are express buses.

As with other big cities, buses can be quite busy during rush hours, public holidays, and at weekends, so it's best to use them during nonpeak times.

Maxicabs and minicabs both seat 16 people. Maxicabs are cream color, with green roofs, and a route number and fixed price prominently displayed. They stop at designated spots, and you usually pay as you board. Minibuses are also cream color but have red roofs. Minibuses display both fares and destinations (albeit in very small English letters), though these can change based on demand. They stop almost anywhere, and you pay as you get off the bus. Maxicabs and minibuses are both quick, though they cost slightly more than buses.

For information, call the HKTB Visitor Hot Line or, for double-decker-bus route maps, stop in at the HKTB Information and Gift Centres at the Center, 99 Queen's Road Central in Central or at the Star Ferry Concourse in Kowloon.

FARES & SCHEDULES Double-decker bus fares range from HK$1.20 to HK$45; the fare is paid when you enter the bus. Maxicab fares range from HK$1.50 to HK$18. Similarly, you pay as you board. Minibus fares range from HK$2 to HK$20, but you pay as you exit. For all three types of transportation you must pay exact change.

🚹 **HKTB Visitor Hot Line** ☎ 852/2508-1234.

CAR RENTAL
Avoid renting a car on Hong Kong Island or Kowloon. Driving conditions, traffic jams, and limited parking are bound to make your life difficult. Public transportation is excellent here, and taxis are inexpensive. If you do decide to rent a car, you may want to hire a driver as well; this can be arranged through your hotel. The fee is HK$800 to HK$1,200 for the first four hours (depending on car model) and HK$200 to HK$300 for each subsequent hour.

Rental rates begin at HK$702 per day and HK$2,900 per week for an economy car with air-conditioning, automatic transmission, and unlimited mileage.

🚹 Major Agencies **Alamo** ☎ 800/522-9696 ⊕ www.alamo.com. **Avis** ☎ 800/331-1084, 800/879-2847 in Canada, 0870/606-0100 in the U.K., 02/9353-9000 in Australia, 09/526-2847 in New Zealand ⊕ www.avis.com. **Budget** ☎ 800/527-0700, 0870/156-5656 in the U.K. ⊕ www.budget.com. **Dollar** ☎ 800/800-6000, 0800/085-4578 in the U.K. ⊕ www.dollar.com. **Hertz** ☎ 800/654-3001, 800/263-0600 in Canada, 0870/844-8844 in the U.K., 02/9669-2444 in Australia, 09/256-8690 in New Zealand ⊕ www.hertz.com. **National Car Rental** ☎ 800/227-7368, 0870/600-6666 in the U.K. ⊕ www.nationalcar.com.

CONSULATES & COMMISSIONS
🚹 Australia **Australian Consulate** ✉ 23/F, Harbour Centre, 25 Harbour Rd., Wanchai ☎ 852/2827-8881 🖷 852/2585-4457 ⊕ www.australia.org.hk.
🚹 Canada **Canadian Consulate** ✉ 11/F-14/F, Tower 1, Exchange Sq., 8 Connaught Pl., Central ☎ 852/2810-4321 🖷 852/2810-8736 ⊕ www.dfait-maeci.gc.ca.
🚹 New Zealand **Consulate General** ✉ 18 Harbour Rd., 6508 Central Plaza, Wanchai ☎ 852/2525-5044 🖷 852/2845-2915 ⊕ www.nzembassy.com.

🖪 United Kingdom **British Consulate General** ⊠ Visa Section, 3/F, 1 Supreme Court Rd., Central ☎ 852/2901-3000 🖷 852/2901-3066 ⊕ www.britishconsulate.org.hk.
🖪 United States **U.S. Consulate General** ⊠ 26 Garden Rd., Central ☎ 852/2523-9011 🖷 852/2845-1598 ⊕ www.usconsulate.org.hk.

EMERGENCIES

Locals and police are usually quite helpful in an emergency situation. Most police officers speak some English or will contact someone who does. There are no 24-hour pharmacies; however, Fanda Perfume Co., Ltd., and Watson's both have pharmacy departments and numerous shops throughout the city; they are usually open until 9 PM.

🖪 Emergency Services **Police, fire & ambulance** ☎ 999.

🖪 Hospitals **Prince of Wales Hospital** ⊠ 30-32 Ngan Shing St., Sha Tin, New Territories ☎ 852/2632-2211. **Princess Margaret Hospital** ⊠ 2-10 Princess Margaret Hospital Rd., Lai Chi Kok ☎ 852/2990-1111. **Queen Elizabeth Hospital** ⊠ 30 Gascoigne Rd., Yau Ma Tei ☎ 852/2958-8888. **Queen Mary Hospital** ⊠ 102 Pok Fu Lam Rd., Pok Fu Lam ☎ 852/2855-3838. **Ruttonjee Hospital** ⊠ 266 Queen's Rd. East, Wanchai ☎ 852/2291-2000.

MAIL & SHIPPING

Hong Kong has an excellent reputation for its postal system. Airmail letters to any place in the world should take three to eight days. The Kowloon Central Post Office and the General Post Office in Central are open 8 AM to 6 PM Monday through Saturday.

🖪 Post Offices **General Post Office** ⊠ 2 Connaught Rd., Central ☎ 852/2921-2222 ⊕ www.hongkongpost.com. **Kowloon Central Post Office** ⊠ 10 Middle Rd., Tsim Tsa Shui.

MONEY MATTERS

The Hong Kong dollar is closely pegged to the U.S. dollar, and exchange rates don't usually vary too widely.

ATMS Reliable and safe, ATMs are widely available throughout Hong Kong. If your card was issued from a bank in an English-speaking country, the instructions on the ATM machine will appear in English.

CREDIT CARDS Major credit cards are widely accepted in Hong Kong, though they may not be accepted at small shops. However, prices are often 3% to 5% higher if you pay by credit card to compensate for the processing fees charged by the card companies.

🖪 Reporting Lost Cards **American Express** ☎ 852/2811-6122. **Diners Club** ☎ 852/2860-1888. **MasterCard** ☎ 852/800/966-677. **Visa** ☎ 852/2810-8033.

CURRENCY Units of currency are the Hong Kong dollar ($) and the cent. Bills come in denominations of 1,000, 500, 100, 50, 20, and 10 dollars. Coins are 10, 5, 2, and 1 dollar and 50, 20, and 10 cents. At this writing, the Hong Kong dollar was pegged to the U.S. dollar at approximately 7.8 Hong Kong dollars to 1 U.S. dollar, approximately 5.8 Hong Kong dollars to 1 Canadian dollar, and 14.05 Hong Kong dollars to 1 British pound. Although the image of Queen Elizabeth II does not appear on new coins, old ones bearing her image are still valid.

CURRENCY EXCHANGE There are no currency restrictions in Hong Kong. You can exchange currency at the airport, in hotels, in banks, and through private money changers scattered through the tourist areas.

For the most favorable rates, **change money through banks.** Although ATM transaction fees may be higher abroad than at home, ATM rates are excellent because they're based on wholesale rates offered only by major banks. You won't do as well at exchange booths in airports or rail and bus stations, in hotels, in restaurants, or in stores. To avoid lines at airport exchange booths, get a bit of local currency before you leave home.

PASSPORTS & VISAS

ENTERING
HONG KONG
Citizens of the United Kingdom need only a valid passport to enter Hong Kong for stays of up to six months. Australian, Canadian, New Zealand, and U.S. citizens need only a valid passport to enter Hong Kong for stays up to three months. It is best to have at least six months' validity on your passport before traveling to Asia.

🚹 **Hong Kong Immigration** ☎ 852/2824-6111 🖷 852/852/2877-7711.

SUBWAY TRAVEL

Hong The four-line Mass Transit Railway (MTR) links Hong Kong Island to Kowloon (including the shopping area Tsim Sha Tsui) and parts of the New Territories. Trains run frequently and are safe and easy to use. Station entrances are marked with a simple line symbol resembling a man with arms and legs outstretched. You buy tickets from ticket machines or from English-speaking workers at the counters by the turnstile entrances. For the machines, change is available at the stations' Hang Seng Bank counters and from the machines themselves.

FARES &
SCHEDULES
Fares range from HK$4 to HK$26. The special Tourist MTR 1-Day Pass (HK$50) allows you unlimited rides in one day. The Airport Express Tourist Octopus (HK$220/HK$300) includes single journeys from/to the airport.

🚹 Subway Information **HKTB Visitor Hot Line** ☎ 852/2508-1234. **Mass Transit Railway (MTR)** ☎ 852/2881-8888.

TAXIS

Taxis in Hong Kong and Kowloon are usually red. A taxi's roof sign lights up when the car is available. Fares in urban areas are HK$15 for the first 2 km (1 mi) and HK$1.20 for each additional ⅕ km (¹⁄₁₀ mi). There is luggage surcharge of HK$5 per large piece, and surcharges of HK$20 for the Cross-Harbour Tunnel, HK$30 for the Eastern Harbour Tunnel, and HK$45 for the Western Harbour Tunnel. The Tsing Ma Bridge surcharge is HK$30. The Aberdeen, Lion Rock, and Junk Bay tunnels also carry small surcharges (HK$3 to HK$8). Taxis cannot pick up passengers where there are double yellow lines. Note that it's hard to find a taxi around 4 PM when the drivers switch shifts. Many taxi drivers do not speak English, so you may want to ask someone at your hotel to write out your destination in Chinese.

Backseat passengers must wear a seat belt or face a HK$5,000 fine. Most locals do not tip; however, if you do—HK$5 to HK$10—you're sure to earn yourself a winning smile from your underpaid and overworked taxi driver. Outside the urban areas, taxis are green (blue on Lantau Island). Cabs in the New Territories cost less than urban taxis: HK$11.80 for the first 2 km (1 mi) and HK$1.10 for each additional ⅕ km (¹⁄₁₀ mi). Urban taxis may travel into rural zones, but rural taxis must not cross into urban zones. There are no interchange facilities for the two, so do not try to reach an urban area using a green taxi.

TELEPHONES

COUNTRY & AREA CODES

The code for Hong Kong is 852.

DIRECTORY & OPERATOR ASSISTANCE

Dial 1081 for directory assistance from English-speaking operators. If a number is constantly busy and you think it might be out of order, call 109 and the operator will check the line. The operators are very helpful, if you talk slowly and clearly. However, do not be surprised if you call a local business and they simply hang up on you; often when local, nonnative English speakers don't understand you, they simply hang up rather than stammer through a conversation and lose face.

INTERNATIONAL CALLS

You can dial direct from many hotel and business centers, but always with a hefty surcharge. Dial 10013 for international inquiries and for assistance with direct dialing. Dial 10010 for collect and operator-assisted calls to most countries, including the United States, Canada, and the United Kingdom. Dial 10011 for credit-card, collect, and international conference calls.

AT&T, Sprint, and MCI services are all available in Hong Kong.

🔲 **Access Codes AT&T Direct** ☎ 800/96-1111. **MCI WorldPhone** ☎ 800/96-1121. **Sprint International Access** ☎ 800/96-1877.

LOCAL CALLS

Given that your hotel will likely charge you for a local call, you might consider simply walking out of your hotel, stopping at the nearest shop, and asking the shopkeeper if you can use the phone. Most locals will not charge you to you use their phone for a local call since the phone company does not charge for individual local calls.

PHONE CARDS

Phone cards are available throughout Hong Kong in 7-Eleven shops. Directions are written in English on the back of the cards, and they can be used on nearly all public phones.

TIPPING

Hotels and major restaurants usually add a 10% service charge; however, in almost all cases, this money does not go to the waiters and waitresses. Proprietors will tell you it goes to the cost of replacing broken crockery, napkins, and so on. If you want to tip a waiter or waitress, be sure to give it directly to that person and no one else. It is generally not the custom to leave an additional tip in taxis and beauty salons; but, if you do choose to tip, you'll receive more attentive service and make the usually not-very-well-paid employees immensely happy. If you buy your newspaper from a corner vendor, consider searching for one of the numerous octogenarians who are sadly still working for a living—leaving your extra change with these people is also another much-appreciated tip.

TOURS

HKTB (⇨ Visitor Information, *below*) offers a variety of tours, from horse racing to a four-hour Heritage Tour.

TRAIN TRAVEL

The **Kowloon–Canton Railway** (KCR) has 13 commuter stops on its 34-km (22-mi) journey through urban Kowloon (from Kowloon to Lo Wu) and Sha Tin and Taipo on its way to the Chinese border. The main station is at Hung Hom, Kowloon, where you can catch express trains to China. Fares range from HK$7.50 to HK$40, and no reservations are required. The KCR meets the MTR at the **Kowloon Tong** station. In the New Territories, the **Light Rail Transit** connects Tuen Mun and Yuen Long.

TRAM TRAVEL

Trams run along the north shore of Hong Kong Island from Kennedy Town (in the west) all the way through Central, Wanchai, Causeway Bay, North Point, and Quarry Bay, ending in the former fishing village of Shaukeiwan. A branch line turns off in Wanchai toward Happy Valley, where horse races are held in season. Destinations are marked on the front of each tram; the fare is HK$2. Avoid trams at rush hours, which are generally weekdays from 7:30 to 9 AM and 5 to 7 PM. Trams are generally quite slow, and a great way to inhale a lung full of car fumes, but they also give you an opportunity to see the city from a slow-moving vehicle.

VISITOR INFORMATION

🖪 Web sites **Hong Kong Tourist Board** (HKTB) ⊕ www.discoverhongkong.com. **Macau Government Tourist Office** ⊕ www.macautourism.gov.mo.

🖪 Government Advisories **U.S. Department of State** ⊠ Overseas Citizens Services Office, 2100 Pennsylvania Ave. NW, 4th fl., Washington, DC 20520 ☎ 888/407-4747, 202/647-5225 interactive hotline ⊕ travel.state.gov. **Consular Affairs Bureau of Canada** ☎ 800/267-6788 or 613/944-6788 ⊕ www.voyage.gc.ca. **U.K. Foreign and Commonwealth Office** ⊠ Travel Advice Unit, Consular Division, Old Admiralty Bldg., London SW1A 2PA ☎ 0870/606-0290 or 020/7008-1500 ⊕ www.fco.gov.uk/travel. **Australian Department of Foreign Affairs and Trade** ☎ 300/139-281 travel advice, 02/6261-1299 Consular Travel Advice Faxback Service ⊕ www.dfat.gov.au. **New Zealand Ministry of Foreign Affairs and Trade** ☎ 04/439-8000 ⊕ www.mft.govt.nz.

SOUTH CENTRAL CHINA

RURAL CHINA &
THE LIMESTONE VALLEY

9

By Anya
Bernstein and
Christopher
Knowles

Updated by
Keming Liu

FROM THE LOFTY MOUNTAINS OF HUNAN to the lush scenery of Guizhou, from the river towns of Hubei to the tropical coastline of Guangxi, South Central China (the provinces of Hubei, Hunan, Guangxi, and Guizhou) is a region as varied as it is large.

Hubei and Hunan are known for their historical significance as much as for their natural beauty. It was in this region that the modern revolutionary spirit first took hold, during the Taiping Rebellion in Hubei from 1850 to 1860 and later as the site of major Communist uprisings in the 1920s. Wuhan was the base for a time of the left-leaning faction of the Nationalist Guomindang party. Today it's a port of departure for boats taking the Three Gorges river cruise. Hunan, primarily known as the province where Mao Zedong was born, is also the site of the magnificent nature reserve of Zhangjiajie, as well as Hengshang Shan, one of China's Five Holy Mountains.

In Guangxi you'll find the sublime limestone karst and river scenery of Guilin. This is one of the great natural sites of the world. It has been commercialized to exploit its beauty, and there is an atmosphere of gold fever about this town that can be disconcerting. The scenery, however, is typical of central Guangxi and can still be appreciated in smaller towns across the province. At Guangxi's southern tip lies the peaceful coastal city of Beihai.

Guizhou is the site of China's mightiest waterfall and home to a large number of colorful non-Han peoples. Many small minority villages are scattered about the province and can be visited by tour or on your own from the metropolitan city of Guiyang.

Exploring South Central China

To travel through this region, you need to be well organized. Unless you have limitless patience and time on your hands, set your priorities in advance. Hunan is rugged and deeply rural, and perhaps the best place in the region to get a sense of both imperial China (the museum at Changsha) and revolutionary China (Mao's birthplace at Shaoshan). Most of Hubei's cities of interest lie along or near the Yangzi River and can easily be reached by train or a cruise down the river. Guilin is in the heart of the tropical province of Guangxi, which borders Vietnam to the west and the South China Sea to the south. Lush and green most of the year, Guangxi unfolds south from the highlands it shares with Guizhou to a tropical coast. In Guizhou, a territory of high valleys and low mountains, you can visit the villages of the province's indigenous peoples, composed of at least nine non-Han ethnic groups, of whom 82% are farmers.

About the Restaurants

Given the region's hot weather and abundant irrigation, locals favor hot and spicy cuisine. The medicinal rationale for this is that sweating helps to cool down the body temperature. Hunan is renowned for its liberal use of fiery chili peppers, shallots, and garlic with a pungent brown sauce. Following centuries-old recipes that are closely guarded family secrets, each of the storied restaurants of the region prides itself on its inimitable signature dishes. Some famous examples include Wuchang steamed

To get the most out of this large area, a minimum stay of two weeks is recommended, three to explore it properly. However, with good planning, it would be possible to extract some of its flavor within a week or 10 days. For shorter stays you'll be limited to one or two destinations in the region.

Numbers in the margin correspond to points of interest on the South Central China, Changsha, Guilin, and Nanning maps.

9

If you have 2 days

Fly directly to **Guilin** ⑰ – ㉖ ▶ and book space on a cruise along the Li River to Yangshuo. This effectively takes up a whole day but is one of the highlights of any visit to China. On the second day either explore the town on foot or, better still, rent a bicycle and spend the day cycling around the countryside through the mountains and tropical-fruit farms, perhaps including a visit to the gaudy attractions of the **Reed Flute Cave** ㉕. At night there may be an acrobatic display, or you might join a party following a cormorant fisherman on the river.

If you have 7 days

Start with **Guilin** ⑰ – ㉖ ▶, as above, then catch a train at the end of the day to **Guiyang** ㊳. Stay overnight in Guiyang and spend the following day exploring the city. Catch a train on the same day to **Huangguoshu Pubu** ㊵. From there arrange a tour to **Kaili** ㊷ or surrounding minority villages or take a cruise down the Wuyang River. Next, fly to Zhangjiajie for the spectacular peaks and waterfalls of the **Wulingyuan Nature Reserve** ⑮.

If you have 10 days

Stay in **Guilin** ⑰ – ㉖ ▶ for three nights. Take a train to **Guiyang** ㊳ and see the waterfall and minority villages. On the fifth day fly to the town of Chongqing to take a three-day Yangzi River cruise to **Wuhan** ①. Spend the day exploring Wuhan and finish up by taking an overnight train to the holy mountain of **Wudang Shan** ⑤.

---

fish, hot and spicy chicken, steamed cured meat or sour meat, and delicacies such as steamed soft-shell turtle, oily and spicy tender bamboo shoots, and cured cabbages. If you yearn for some sweet dessert to balance the slow burn on your palate, try the tender and light honey-dipped chestnut specialty.

About the Hotels

Driven by the booming tourism industry as well as the parade of executives from multinational companies who pour into China in search of joint ventures, hotels in the region have enjoyed a dramatic upturn in quality and design. Don't be surprised if you find yourself surrounded by many of the elements of an international boutique hotel, including minimalist decor, starkly modern cocktail lounges, attentive staff decked out in chic uniforms, and gleaming, state-of-the art amenities in the bathroom.

As the international chains moved into the region, local entrepreneurs adopted international standards and copied the formula for success in an effort to compete. Even budget travelers and backpackers are finding improved conditions at hostels and dormitories that may only cost a few dollars a night. Wuhan's Holiday Inn Riverside is a shining example of recent change of hands in joint-venture efforts and the Wandai Dajiudian and Hunan Bestride Hotel in Changsha are among the top properties created by a new breed of Chinese hotelier.

WHAT IT COSTS In Yuan					
	$$$$	$$$	$$	$	¢
RESTAURANTS	over 165	100–165	50–99	25–49	under 25
HOTELS	over 1,800	1,400–1,800	1,100–1,399	700–1,099	under 700

Restaurant prices are for a main course, excluding tax and tips. Hotel prices are for a standard double room, including taxes.

Timing

The best time of year is spring, in April or early May. Winter months can be surprisingly cold (except on the south coast of Guangxi), and the heat in summer is stifling. Mid-September can also be a comfortable time to travel here. The falls at Huangguoshu are at their best in the rainy season from May through October.

Inhabitants of coastal areas celebrate the birthday of Mazu or Tianhou, goddess of the sea, on the 23rd day of the third lunar month (May or June). The minority peoples of Guizhou hold frequent festivals, particularly during the first, fourth, and sixth lunar months. For example, the *lusheng* (bamboo flute) festivals, celebrated by the Miao people, take place in January or February, when mothers trying to find a partner for their daughters present them to local boys, who play their lusheng pipes. To obtain a festival schedule, contact the local CITS or a travel agency.

HUBEI

The Yangzi River cuts lengthwise from west to east through Hubei, giving the province an age-old edge on transportation and a whole stretch of densely foliated land. Centrally located, Hubei, with more than 56.5 million people and a host of waterways, has long been one of China's most important provinces. In the mid-19th century it suffered through battles between the Taiping rebels and imperial troops. Shortly afterward, several of its cities were opened to European trade, which spread some Western influence through parts of the province. The 1911 revolution started here, toppling the already unsteady Qing Dynasty. Over the next 38 years the province hosted some of the country's leading politicians and military leaders as they vied for control of China's future. Known for both its scenery and its history, the province offers water travel, hiking, mysterious wildlife—and Mao Zedong, who lived in the city of Wuhan for a time before and during the Cultural Revolution (1966–76).

Wuhan is the port for river cruises through the Three Gorges—Qutang Gorge, Wu Gorge, and Xiling Gorge—which run from western Hubei to eastern Sichuan province. The Three Gorges, where China's longest

Art Comes To Life

The greatest highlight of a visit to this part of China is the breathtaking scenery. Most famous, of course, is the fairy-tale landscape of Guilin, in Guangxi province, with its hundreds of karst-formation mountains rising sheer out of a vast plain of streams and paddy fields. The Tang Dynasty poet Han Yu likened them to "kingfisher jade hairpins." But Guilin is far from the only possibility for lovers of natural beauty. Guizhou is home to China's highest waterfall, at Huangguoshu Pubu. In Hunan, the Wulingyuan Scenic Reserve, among the Wuling Mountains, is home to several minority peoples and the largest cave in Asia. Hunan and Hubei both have green rice-paddy fields and mountains, including Hengshang Shan in Hunan.

South Central China has been renowned for its stunning scenery since the earliest days of Chinese art. The most famous painters of the golden age (the Tang and Sung dynasties) used its hauntingly beautiful peaks as the subject for their landscapes. Even today, every Chinese schoolchild learns the old saw, "Guilin Shanshui Jia Tian Xia," or "Guilin's Landscape is the Most Lovely Under Heaven." A Li River cruise transports you into the magic of a classic scroll painting, winding its way through karst formations that are transformed, moment by moment, as you float along, viewing them from different angles.

A True Melting Pot

This region of China is unmatched for its vibrant cultural panoply of minority cultures. Some of them have been so isolated, until recently, that they retain a traditional individuality rare in today's homogeneous, globalized world. The region is home to the nation's largest indigenous minority communities, whose rituals, customs, and colorful costumes make your trip an opportunity to observe China's diverse cultural heritage. The observance of ancient rituals is one such opportunity. During the Zhuang People's Song Festival in March you can watch the splendidly dressed young men and women compete in singing contests. Young men demonstrating a strong voice and just the right tune will win beautiful brides. The Miao people's horse-racing festival in November shows off the equestrian prowess of the local riders and everyone dresses up for this colorful occasion, during which subtle courtship rites are enacted between eligible young men and women. This is China as it used to be, and standing among smiling faces and embroidered costumes, it is hard to imagine that this will be how China will remain.

river, the Yangzi, passes between soaring cliffs, has become a point of contention both domestically and internationally. The Yangzi, which runs from Tibet to the Pacific Ocean, has long been one of the most heavily populated regions in China. In summer, when torrential rain falls in this region, the Yangzi unleashes its massive current and floods the plain. The worst flooding occurred in the summer of 1998 when 3,656 lives were lost. To control flooding and increase power supply, the Chinese government has embarked on what is arguably the biggest hydroelectric facility in the world: the Three Gorges Dam. The project involves

South Central China

KEY

▶ Start of itinerary

not only the forced relocation of 1.2 million people, but also—scientists predict—a major disaster for the ecosystem. The first two phases of the project are complete, bringing the water level to 575 feet and flooding the Temple of Zhang Fei and 39 other historical sites and towns. As the project enters its third and last phase (due to be completed in 2009), tourists from far and near rush to sail down the river to get a last glimpse of China's rustic beauty and rich historical legacy.

In the west of the province, the Wudang Mountain range holds several important Taoist temples, while the Shennongjia region, in the northwest, is China's cross between the Bermuda Triangle and the abode of Bigfoot: travelers are warned of ghostly beasts of unknown origin and purpose, and rumors persist of visitors who penetrate the Shennongjia never to return. Nevertheless, the number of people around to testify to the existence of the unidentifiable animals seems surprisingly high. As long as you aren't too overwhelmed by the beauty of the place, you'll probably make it back, too.

Wuhan

❶ *13 hrs (1,225 km [760 mi]) by train south of Beijing; 6 hrs (536 km [332 mi]) by train south of Zhengzhou.*

Whether you're coming into town on a train or in a shuttle from the airport, you can't miss the water. Wuhan, capital of Hubei province, is located at the juncture of the Yangzi and Hanshui rivers and the land around the city seems permanently half submerged, a swampy marsh traversed by Yangzi tributaries. This impression does not stop when you get to the city. Various lakes, large and small, appear all around town, among which Donghu (East Lake) is often named as a sort of little sister counterpart to Hangzhou's famous Xihu (West Lake). (That the East Lake actually lies far to the west of West Lake does not faze anybody.)

Wuhan is actually a conglomerate of what used to be, until 1949, three distinct towns. Wuhan is the only city in China to lie on both sides of the Yangzi River, which separates Hankou and Hanyang towns on the west and Wuchang on the east. The waterways make Wuhan a little cumbersome to traverse. Taxi rides are always long, bus trips usually require at least one transfer, and ferry rides across the river, although fun, take a bit of planning. A two-day layover here can be broadly divided along the river: one day for the east and one for the west. Be sure to visit during the pleasant seasons of early spring and autumn: Wuhan is one of China's summer "furnaces."

The area has historically been a hotbed of revolutionary activity of one sort or another. It was a center of anti-Qing unrest during the Taiping Rebellion of 1850–60 and the cradle of the 1911 Republican revolution. During the uneasy 1920s it was the site of one of the decade's most prominent and most brutally put-down railway strikes. In 1926 it hosted an unlikely and short-lived coalition government of Guomindang (a.k.a. the Nationalist Party, which overthrew the Chinese monarchy and established the Chinese Republic in 1912) and Communist forces. An even shorter-lived right-wing Guomindang faction ran the city after the coalition with the Communists, against the wishes of Chiang Kai-shek, whose headquarters were in Nanjing. Mao Zedong ran the Peasant Movement Institute here until the city was taken by the Guomindang in 1928. During the civil war in the 1940s, the uprisings and strikes led by students and workers in the city helped to bring on the Communist victory in the area in 1949. Nowadays it is home to major iron and steel complexes, as well as such other industries as textiles, heavy machinery, glass, railroad cars, and trucks.

The **Guiyuan Buddhist Temple** (Guiyuan Si) was first built by two monks in the early Qing Dynasty (1644–1911). The existing structure was rebuilt after suffering from a number of battles so you see reconstructed points of interests, such as the Tower of Buddhist Sutra, the Main Hall, and the Arhat Hall. You can also see a white jade statue of the Buddha, another of Weito (the temple guardian) carved from oak, the 500 disciples of Buddha (Arhat) with distinctly different expressions and postures, the 1,000-hand Guanyin, and more than 7,000 volumes of Buddhist scripture presented by India, Sri Lanka, Burma, Thailand, and Japan. A number of buses run regularly between the temple and city center. ⊠ *Cuiwei Xi Lu* ☎ *027/8283–2707 or 027/8484–2298* ⊑ *Y20* ⊙ *Daily 8:30–5.*

Yellow Crane Tower (Huang He Lou) is a wooden structure on top of the Snake Hill originally built in AD 223, first serving as a military watchtower then becoming a gathering place for scholars holding farewell banquets for friends. These convivial events were often captured in the great poems and novels of the literati, including a famous poem by the Tang Dynasty poet, Cui Hao, whose masterpiece is entitled "Yellow Crane Tower." In 1981 the tower was rebuilt for historic preservation, restoring it to its original design of 10 stories inside and 5 stories outside. It offers a stunning bird's-eye view of the city. ⊠ *56 Wuchang Lu, on southern end of Yangzi River Bridge on Snake Hill, Wuchang* ☎ *027/ 8887–1394* ⊑ *Y50* ⊙ *Daily 8:30–5.*

FodorśChoice ★ The **Hubei Provincial Museum** (Hubei Sheng Bowuguan) is internationally renowned as a showcase of the province's most valuable historical relics, unearthed from the intact tomb of Marquis Yi of Zeng, from the 5th century BC. The collection has grown as archaeological discoveries have been made. One of the most exciting additions was excavated in 1978: a huge musical instrument consisting of 64 bronze chimes, known as a *Bian Zhong,* cast during the Warring States Period (476–221 BC) and occasionally played for visitors. In addition to an ensemble of ancient musical instruments, the tomb included coffins, gold and jade decorative items, weapons, and impressive bronze- and lacquer ware. With the bell performance, give yourself about two hours here. ⊠ *188 Donghu Lu, Buses No. 14 and No. 578* ⊑ *Y30* ⊙ *Tues.–Sun. 8–11:30 and 1:30–4:30.*

Mao Zedong's Private Villa (Maozedong Bieshu) is located on the scenic bank of East Lake in the suburbs of Wuchang. The house was constructed in 1958 during the early phase of Mao's reign as chairman. As one of Mao's numerous private retreats, the villa hosted important meetings of officials, including Richard Nixon in 1972 and labor activist Anna Louise Strong in 1960. An avid swimmer, Mao held his annual ritual crossing of the Yangzi River near the villa (every stroke covered by the state press as proof of the chairman's able body). An oversize swimming pool at the villa dwarfs the simple and plain separate bedrooms for him and his wife. A prolific and voluble poet, Mao nicknamed the villa "home of the white clouds and yellow cranes," a reference to Wuhan's natural scenic beauty. It was here that Mao spent many quiet and relaxing days even as the nation was engulfed in turmoil during the Cultural Revolution. The well-landscaped grounds are laced with neat footpaths among the pines, bamboo, and plum trees. ⊠ *Zhongnan Lu, Bus No. 578, 709, 14, or 701; get off at Provincial Museum and follow tree-lined drive behind old museum building* ☎ *027/8679–6106* 🖅 *Y10* ☉ *Daily 8–5.*

East Lake Park (Donghu Gongyuan) is located on the south bank of the Yangzi River and east of Wuchang. It covers 87 square km (34 square mi), surrounding the lake on three sides and making it the biggest lake within a city in China. Due to abundant rainfall and sunshine as well as a humid climate, the area is rich in flora, including 372 kinds of trees and more than 390 varieties of flowers, of which the plum blossom and lotus are most famous. Not surprisingly, China's Plum Research Center and Lotus Research Center are based here. ⊠ *Off Donghu Lu, take Bus No. 14, 63, 501, or 701* 🖅 *Y30* ☉ *Daily 8–5.*

The **Yangzi River Bridge** (Wuhan Changjiang Da Qiao) links Snake Mountain in Wuchang with Turtle Hill in Hanyang. The bridge and its approaches are 2 km (1 mi) long and comprise a six-lane highway and a two-track railway running along its eight piers and nine arches. Vehicles on the motorway travel 262 feet above the river. It is the first steel modern bridge completed after the founding of the People's Republic of China and it appears frequently in government propaganda as a symbol of Socialist achievement. ✛ *From Wuchang take Minzhu Lu; from Hanyang take Lanjiang Lu.*

The **Guiyuan Temple of Original Purity** (Guiyuan Si) is one of the four largest Buddhist meditation temples in Hubei. The temple was first built in the early Qing Dynasty (1644–1911) by two monks named Baiguang and Zhufeng. The existing structure was rebuilt after destruction by wars, including the Tower of Buddhist Sutra, the Main Hall, and the Arhat Hall. It holds more than 7,000 volumes of Buddhist scripture, including the white jade Buddhist statue and the Buddhist scriptures presented by India, Sri Lanka, Burma, Thailand, and Japan in their own languages. Surviving repeated assaults by wars and hard times, the temple never ceased to lead all the other temples in Wuhan with public worship. ⊠ *20 Cuiwei Lu, from Wuchang take Minzhu Lu; from Hanyang take Lanjiang Lu* ☎ *027/8283–2707* 🖅 *Y20* ☉ *Daily 8–4:30.*

Wuhan's main hotels and restaurants are in **Hankou**, but that section of the city also holds the fewest places of interest. The stretch of Hankou that runs along the river between the two bridges—Yanjiang Dadao as well as the street directly west of it, Shengli Jie—retains some pretty buildings from the late 19th century. The city was open then to European concessions; Chinese architects eagerly accepted the foreign influence but with their own interpretations. Several parks here make good places for a walk.

Where to Stay & Eat

For the best local cuisine head straight for **Jiqing Jie,** locally known as *Yeh shi* (night food street). All the restaurants here serve similar fare, and it's all generally good. Fish is a specialty, and one of the best is *hong-shao huangyu* (braised yellow fish)—served whole, it's only about 5 inches in length and bony, but the reward is tender tasty flakes of salt-water fish. If you can stand the heat, a local favorite is *qianbian mei* (deep-fried tofu with garlic, red pepper, and Sichuan pepper). These tender rounds of slightly fermented tofu, curled up like cinnamon rolls, are delicious. Like Sichuan cuisine, Hubei dishes incorporate a lot of pepper—but not all the dishes are fiery. *Danbai shao gupai* (pork ribs braised in egg white) are succulent and mild. A meal of six dishes easily feeds four. Add a couple large beers and the whole feast should set you back around Y80. The night food street operates daily from 6:30 PM until everyone goes home. The liveliest time is after 10. ⊠ *Jiqing Jie starting from Dazhi Jie.*

★ $-$$$$ 🏨 **Holiday Inn Riverside** (Qingchuan Holiday Inn). Located in the center of downtown Wuhan on the banks of the Yangzi River, this Holiday Inn is a glistening 20-story modern high-rise with a stunning view on a clear day and a pleasant riverbank jogging trail. Its multilingual staff can greet you in English or even French and Japanese. Rooms are bright, attractively furnished, and either smoking and no-smoking. Some rooms come with a kitchenette. A complimentary shuttle takes you to local tourist attractions and the airport. The hotel has two restaurants, one offering international and Asian buffets, the other a fine traditional Chinese restaurant. ⊠ *88 Xi Ma Chang Jie, Hanyang 430050* 🕾 *027/8471–6688* 🖷 *027/8471–6181* ⊕ *http://wuhan-cn.hotels-x.net/Holiday-inn-riverside-wuhan.html* 🛏 *336 rooms* ⌂ *2 restaurants, minibars, tennis courts, indoor pool, gym, sauna, steam room, lounge, nightclub, dry cleaning, business services, travel services* ▤ *AE, MC, V.*

$-$$$ 🏨 **Novotel.** This new addition to the high-end hotel selection in Hankou is characterized by the international chain's signature style of stark, decisively modern decor. Minimalist furniture and design and high-tech accessibility offset the small size of its cozy standard guest rooms. White-tiled bathrooms are elegantly accentuated by contrasting black marble sink tops. Centrally located with shopping, sightseeing, and transportation all within a very short distance, Novotel is ideal for a short stay in Wuhan. Inquire about promotional packages such as free gym membership during your stay. ⊠ *558 Jianshe Dadao, Hankou* 🕾 *027/8555–1188* 🖷 *027/8555–1177* ⊕ *www.accorhotels-asia.com/* 🛏 *303 rooms* ⌂ *2 restaurants, room service, in-room safes, minibars, gym, sauna, bar, dry cleaning, business services* ▤ *AE, DC, MC, V.*

$-$$ 🏨 **Wuhan Asia Hotel.** This is one of the high-end international hotels established in recent years in Wuhan. Conveniently located in Hankou on the west bank of the Yangzi River, Wuhan Asia sports quiet yet elegant

ON THE MENU

THE FAMOUSLY SPICY XIANG CUISINE of Hunan is actually a medley of regional specialties, including those of the Xiangjiang region and Dongting Lake, famous for its lotus seed confections, as well as the subtly different western Hunan taste. Although Sichuan is internationally famous for its spicy taste, Hunan chefs actually outdo their Sichuan counterparts in the liberal use of chili peppers and garlic. South Central China's eclectic cooking styles are a result of its ingenious chefs' skill in mixing and matching flavors from neighboring regions. This makes South Central a hotbed of Chinese fusion cuisine. Every restaurant has its signature dish, but you won't go wrong if you order the Dongan chicken (whose sauce is an exquisite example of the use of peppers), or the many versions of what the French call bouillabaisse, a chowder in which lake fish is slow-cooked in a fiery red brew of chili peppers, garlic, fresh vegetables, and bean curd.

The cooking of Guangxi and Guizhou tends to have strong influences from both Guangdong and the spicy dishes of Hunan and Sichuan. There is a wide range of vegetables and fruit, and a love of dishes that may seem at best exotic and at worst repellent—snake, dog, and, illegal, rare animals such as the pangolin. Guizhou in particular has a wide variety of traditional dishes, as the province is home to so many ethnic groups; bean curd is again a specialty, most famously Lian'ai Dofu, or "fall in love bean curd," which is mixed with chili sauce, wild garlic shoots, vinegar, and soy sauce. Look also for hotpot (Huo Guo or "fire pot" in Chinese), a specialty dish that involves dipping meat into a pot fondue style, and for ginkgo fruit served in beaten egg white.

---

color tones in room decor and a tranquil atmosphere. Guest rooms are spick and span with wall-to-wall carpeting and clean furniture. Floor lamps and night-lights are individually controlled. The bathrooms are roomy and water pressure just right. The hotel also features a famous revolving restaurant, which serves a variety of delicious Western cuisine. The Ming Palace can cater for up to 350 people for banquets and serves authentic Chinese cuisine. Group discounts apply and the listed prices are negotiable. ⊠ 616 Jiefang Dadao, Hankou 430030 ☎ 027/8380–7777 ⤶ 263 rooms ⚹ Restaurant, hair salon, laundry service ▤ AE, DC, MC, V.

$–$$ ▦ **Yangtze Hotel.** This is Wuhan's first joint-venture hotel, sporting a subtle blend of Western and Asian traditions and modern facilities. The highly motivated and trained staff provides fine multilingual service. Guest rooms are flooded with bright sunlight on clear days and suites are tastefully designed and well decorated. Bathrooms are outfitted with standard outlets to accommodate Western appliances. ⊠ 1131 Jiefang Dadao, Hankou 430030 ☎ 027/8363–2828 ⤶ 180 rooms ⚹ Restaurant, in-room safes, sauna, business services ▤ AE, DC, MC, V.

★ **$** ▦ **Ruiya Guoji Jiudian** (New World Courtyard Wuhan or Swiss-Belhotel on the Park Wuhan). On a small quiet street a short walk from two city parks, the inn is known for its excellent service. The accommodations are comfortable without being imposing, and the Western restaurant and the coffee shop are serious about quality. The coffee shop provides tasty snacks and Continental cuisine; the lobby lounge serves beers, cocktails, coffee, and tea as well as snacks in a relaxing environment. The Chinese restaurant, Hua Mei Garden, offers a taste of local culture and exotic Cantonese flavors, and seafood. Guest rooms are well equipped with modern facilities and top-notch comfort. Seasonal and group discounts apply. ⊠ *9 Taibei Yi Lu, Hankou 430015* ☎ *027/8578–7968* 🖷 *027/8578–9171* ⊕ *www.marriott.com* 🖅 *138 rooms* ⚭ *2 restaurants, gym, hair salon, sauna, bar, business services, meeting room* ▭ *AE, MC, V.*

★ ¢–$ 🖭 **Tian'an Holiday Inn** (Tian'an Jiari Jiudian). This is Wuhan's most upscale hotel, carefully decorated and amply staffed. It's conveniently located in the city's commercial, shopping, and entertainment district. Each guest room is equipped with electric door locks, energy-saving devices, individually controlled air-conditioning, and satellite TV. The hotel offers three elegant dining venues. Bloom's Cafe offers the best grilled steaks and seafood in town. Teng Yun Ge Chinese Restaurant, with private rooms, treats you to authentic Cantonese cuisine and a variety of fresh seafood. The Panorama Revolving Restaurant has an extravagant buffet for breakfast, lunch, and dinner. ⊠ *868 Jiefang Dadao, Hankou 430022* ☎ *027/8586–7888* 🖷 *027/8584–5353* ⊕ *www.holiday-inn. com* 🖅 *367 rooms, 17 suites, 10 apartments* ⚭ *3 restaurants, pool, gym, hair salon, bar, dance club, business services, meeting room, travel services* ▭ *AE, MC, V.*

Nightlife

If you are in Wuhan in summer, a favorite hangout is the **Jiqing Jie,** the night food street. To the Wuhanese, one way to ward off heat is to eat hot and spicy food and increase perspiration. Physiology aside, the night food street distracts you from the heat with its boisterous crowds. Locals come in groups to this newly renovated half block of outdoor restaurants and make an evening of dining and enjoying roving singers, musicians, sketch artists, flower sellers, photographers, and shoe shiners. For those who want to be serenaded there are plenty of choices, from Beijing opera to modern pop songs. Customers order from a song menu with a price list. For around Y10, a male opera singer of female roles will sing you an aria.

Shopping

The half-mile stretch of Jianghan Lu (between Jinghan Dadao and Yanjiang Dadao) is a popular place to stroll, especially on hot summer evenings, and is lined with trendy shops and boutiques sporting such internationally well-known names as Pierre Cardin and Chanel. Diamond, jade, and genuine leather goods are readily available all seasons. **Hanzheng Jie,** not far from the Wuhan Asia hotel running parallel to Yanhe Dadao along the Hanjiang River, has around 1,000 stores and stands lining the street. The **New World Department Store** (Xin Shijie Baihuo Shangchang), on Jianshe Dadao around the corner from Novotel hotel, also has a large supermarket on the basement level.

Side Trips from Wuhan

The real reason to come to Hubei is not for the capital but for the scenery nearby. Wuhan is the stopover on the way to wilder places, and many Yangzi River tours start or end here. You can buy tickets at your hotel travel desk or book them through CITS, which will also be able to arrange unusual, tailor-made packages.

EASTWARD A two-day trip down the scenic river ends at what is arguably China's most cosmopolitan city: Shanghai. The trip also provides side-trip possibilities of its own. The boat stops at Jiujiang in Jiangxi province. From here Jiangxi's Lu Shan Mountains are easily accessible. Guichi and Wuhu in Anhui province are both excellent places to start a trip to one of China's most famous, and most beautiful, mountain ranges: Huangshan. Because the mountains are not well served by railroad lines, a combined river-land approach—traveling inland by bus—is the best way to go. You can stay overnight and explore Huangshan before boarding the boat again for other cities on the river. Boats also pass the major metropolis of Nanjing and the small but attractive city of Zhenjiang, in Jiangsu province, both worth exploring if you have the time.

WESTWARD The trip upriver is slower because of the current, but it also has some of China's most fabulous scenery. A four-day trip west to Chongqing in Sichuan province will take you through a variety of sights. You'll first ② pass **Jingzhou,** in the southern part of Hubei province. This city, which still retains part of its ancient wall, was a major center during the Spring and Autumn and Warring States Period (770 BC–221 BC) and has been the site of several archaeological digs (the museum contains a 2,000-year-old preserved male body). The boat also passes the Shennong River, which flows into the Yangzi from **Shennong Mountain. Nanjin Pass** in ③ **Yichang,** western Hubei, marks the easternmost entrance point of the Three Gorges: Qutang, Wu, and Xiling.

④ **Shennongjia Nature Reserve** has the wildest scenery in Hubei, combining rolling majestic mountains with vast expanses of lush forest, exotic flowers and plants, rare birds and animals, and traces of the legendary "Bigfoot" or "wild man." The pyramid-shape **Shennong Peak** (Shennongding) is the highest peak in Central China at 10,188 feet above sea level. Clouds often nestle at the summit where ridges stretch on into the distance. But among the mountains there are many beautiful valleys, including the so-called Hongping Gallery, displaying unusual plants, flowers, trees, and birds. Caves, waterfalls, and trickling streams add to the charm of the region.

The reserve contains more than 2,000 species of wild plants, 1,000 types of trees, and 500 species of wild animals (including 20 that are officially protected by the state). The area is covered by tiers of fir, bamboo, and azalea (which blossom pink and violet in summer). Rare animals on the reserve include the golden monkey, white bear, and antelope. With enough time and the help of a travel agent or CITS, you may find this one of the most interesting trip possibilities in China.

⑤ **Wudang Shan** is a sacred mountain area in northwest Hubei. The range of 72 peaks stretches for 400 km (248 mi). At 5,250 feet, **Tianzhu Feng,** whose name means pillar to the sky, is the highest of Wudang Shan's peaks. Many of Wudang Shan's hills have Taoist temples scattered on their slopes, which date back to the Ming Dynasty (1368–1644); the area is one of the most sacred for Taoists. The Ming emperor Zhen Whu, who became a Taoist deity, lived here during the 15th century; there's a statue of him in the impressive **Taihe Temple,** which is about halfway up Tianzhu Feng. Jinding (Golden Summit) is at the top of Tianzhu Feng Peak. The climb takes about three hours. There are numerous other temples to visit in this scenic area, including the 1413 Zixiao Gong (Purple Cloud), which is northeast of Tianzhu Feng.

It's said that tai chi has its origins in Wudang Shan, based on a style of boxing developed by Zhang Sanfeng, a Taoist monk who lived in the 14th century and created a martial art from his observations of birds and animals in Wudang Shan. Monks reside here and practice martial arts at what is considered to be the highest level of the world. You've probably seen it before: it was the setting for the final scene in the 2000 Academy Award–winner, *Crouching Tiger, Hidden Dragon.*

Trains and buses from Yichang can take you to the Wudang Shan village.

Hubei A to Z

To research prices, get advice from other travelers, and book travel arrangements, visit www.fodors.com.

AIR TRAVEL

Wuhan has daily flights to Beijing, Kunming, Shanghai, Guangzhou, and Shenzhen; and service four times a week to Fuzhou, Xian, and Nanjing. Due to airline deregulation and the breakup of the government monopoly through CAAC (Air China), the domestic airline travel situation is a bit fragmented. To get from Wuhan to other major cities in China, contact your hotel or the Hubei CITS (⇨ Travel Agencies) for information.
🛧 **Wuhan Tianhe International Airport** ☎ 027/8581-8305 arrivals, 027/8581-8494 departures.

BOAT & FERRY TRAVEL

Boats run in either direction from Wuhan along the Yangzi River, going to Chongqing in the west and Shanghai in the east. A few private ferries offer first-class accommodations; these are definitely advisable for sanitation and service, but cost more. Tickets can be purchased at your hotel travel desk; check also with CITS.

Ferries cross the Yangzi between Hankou and Wuchang frequently. This is faster and more enjoyable than the bus.

BUS TRAVEL

Buses run daily from Wuhan to Xiamen and Nanchang, northern Hubei, northern Anhui, and Yichang. Planes are preferable if you are going between Wuhan and Hangzhou, Nanjing, or Xian.

Buses traverse Wuhan, but the system is a little unwieldy. You can expect to switch buses one or two times if you're crossing the river between city sections. Taxis, which are easy to flag down on any major street, and the ferry are more convenient.

EMERGENCIES
🔲 **Fire** ☎ 119. **First-Aid Center** ☎ 120. **Police** ☎ 110. **Traffic Accident** ☎ 122. **Wuhan Public Security Bureau (PSB)** ☎ 027/8271-2355.
🔲 Hospitals **Hubei Medical University Affiliated Hospital No. 1** ✉ Jiefang Lu, Wuchang ☎ 027/8884-4437. **Tongji Hospital** ✉ 1095 Jiefang Lu, Wuhan, ☎ 027/8363-8881. **Wuhan Hospital No. 1** ✉ Zhongshan Dadao, Hankou ☎ 027/8585-5900.

TOURS
CITS has the latest information on tours of northern Hubei and of the Three Gorges area. Look into tours for seeing the northwest—the region can be difficult going without a working knowledge of Chinese.

TRAIN TRAVEL
Train service to and from this region is excellent. There are varying levels of comfort depending on how much you want to pay, from "hard seat" for budget travelers to first-class sleepers. Trains from Beijing, Guangzhou, Shanghai, Guilin, and Xian arrive in the region several times a day. For information, contact the Hubei CITS.

TRAVEL AGENCIES
🔲 Local Agent Referrals **Hubei CITS** ✉ 26 Taibei Lu, Wuhan 430015 ☎ 027/8578-4117 🖷 027/8578-4096. **Wuhan Overseas Tourism Corp.** ✉ 48 Baofeng Lu, Hankou 430030 ☎ 027/8362-6473 🖷 027/8362-6601. **Wuhan Tourism Administration** ✉ 17 Hezuo Lu, Wuhan 430017 ☎ 027/8283-3107 🖷 027/8578-4096.

VISITOR INFORMATION
🔲 Tourist Information **Directory Assistance** ☎ 114. **Hubei Tourism Administration Foreign Affairs Office** ☎ 027/8271-2355. **Hubei Tourist Complaint Line** ☎ 027/8481-8760. **Time Inquiry** ☎ 117. **Weather Forecasting** ☎ 121. **Wuhan CTS** ✉ 868 Jiefang Dadao, inside Tian'an Holiday Inn, Hankou 430014 ☎ 027/8280-0940.

HUNAN

This large inland province of rural communities and thinly populated mountainous regions is particularly associated with Mao Zedong, who was born and educated here. It was his upbringing and experiences in rural Hunan that provided the impetus for his revolutionary activities.

Hunan was part of the Kingdom of Chu during the era before the unification of China, known as the Warring States Period (474–221 BC). In several waves of migration starting in the 3rd century AD, the northern Han people moved to avoid the constant threat of invasion from the steppe lands of Manchuria and Mongolia. But only in the 8th century, after heavier migrations from the north, did Hunan begin to develop. Its population increased many times up to the 11th century, the rich agricultural land proving a great attraction for settlers. During the Yuan and Ming dynasties, Hunan and its neighbor to the north, Hubei, were united to form the province of Huguang, becoming the principal source of grain and rice for the Chinese empire. In 1664 Hunan became an independent province.

In the 19th century the population outgrew its resources, a problem aggravated by constant war and corrupt government, so that the Communists found a ready supply of converts here in the early 20th century. Mao was not the only influential revolutionary from Hunan—Liu Shaoqi, China's Vice Chairman before the Cultural Revolution, was born here, and so was Hu Yaobang, a Mao-installed chairman who was stripped of power soon after Mao's death. Hunan is essentially Han China but is also home to a few non-Han minority peoples, the Miao and Yao (the original natives of the area), the Dong, and the Tujia.

Hunan (literally, South of the Lake) occupies an area of 210,000 square km (81,000 square mi) and has a population of 65 million. The flat northern part of the province falls within the catchment area of the Dongting Lake (Dongting Hu); the remaining regions are hilly or mountainous. The climate is sharply continental with short, cold, and wet winters and long, very hot summers. It is still an important agricultural region; half of the cultivated land is devoted to the production of rice.

The capital, Changsha, is a good place to visit for its excellent museum and its revolutionary sites. Mao's birthplace is in rural Hunan at Shaoshan, and Wulingyuan is beautiful.

Changsha

6 hrs (300 km [186 mi]) by train west of Nanchang; 11 hrs (675 km [419 mi]) by train north of Hong Kong; 15½ hrs (1,300 km [806 mi]) by train southwest of Beijing.

Changsha is mainly known for its links with Mao, the Chinese Communist founding father, who staged the Cultural Revolution and organized peasant uprisings in rural Hunan during the 1920s. The town was made the capital city of Hunan province in 1664 and opened to foreign trade in 1904. Today's Changsha is a city with nondescript modern concrete buildings and almost no traces of the city's history.

Changsha is the gateway to the Five Sacred Mountains of Taoism and to Wulingyuan, a gorgeous scenic area that has been designated a World Heritage site. It is also home to one of the most spectacular tomb configurations in China—the Mawangdui, which dates back to the Western Han Dynasty (206 BC–AD 9). During China's Ten Kingdoms (AD 907–960), Changsha became the capital of the Zhou Kingdom and grew into a leading commercial and cultural center through the Song Dynasty (AD 960–1126), a time of artistic and intellectual expansion in the region.

However, since that period of relative stability, repeated wars have destroyed many important architectural and artistic relics of the great age. The violent fanaticism of the Boxer Rebellion in the late 19th century and the Japanese invasion during World War II had disastrous effects on the area. Among the many cities affected, Changsha was hit hard by the destruction, which still burns in the memory of many who live here.

Changsha is known today as the birthplace of Mao's power, but he was by no means the only young Hunanese who became ruler. A number of his contemporaries also rose in the ranks of the Communist Party, including Liu Shaoqi, Mao's deputy until he became a victim of the Cul-

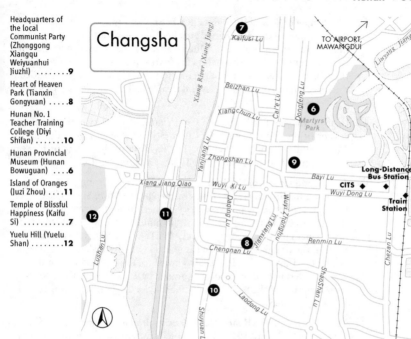

tural Revolution; four Politburo members under Deng Xiaoping, including the former Party chief, Hu Yaobang; and Hua Guofeng, Mao's look-alike and briefly empowered successor. Today, Changsha's few formal attractions are dominated by the chairman's presence, though there are also a couple of parks to wander around, and the fascinating Provincial Museum. The only real day trip from Changsha is out to Mao's birthplace at Shaoshan, 90 km (55 mi) to the southwest, a very pleasant excursion made easier by well-organized public transport.

★ ❻ The **Hunan Provincial Museum** (Hunan Bowuguan), on the banks of Lake Nianjia, contains some interesting exhibits, most notably those from the royal graves at Mawangdui. These were the family graves of the Marquis of Dai, who died in 186 BC. The bodies were in extremely good condition upon discovery, especially that of the Marquis's wife, whose body had been wrapped in 20 layers of silk and whose coffin was sealed in charcoal and white peat, which excludes moisture and air. The beautiful coffins are on display, as are many of the funerary objects, including illustrated books and documents and a silk banner depicting Han afterlife beliefs. Also exhibited here are Shang bronzes and illustrated items from the Warring States Period. ✉ *3 Dongfeng Lu* ☎ *0731/451–4629* 🚋 *Y15* ⊘ *Daily 9–noon and 2:30–5:30.*

❼ The **Temple of Blissful Happiness** (Kaifu Si) was founded in the 10th century AD, during the Five Kingdoms Period, when the Kingdom of Chu made a brief reappearance. Much added to and altered over the succeeding centuries, it received its last extension in 1923. Very much in the southern style in its rich decoration, it consists of a *pailou* (decorative, ceremonial gate) and several temple halls. ⊠ *Kaifusi Lu* ☯ *Daily 8:30–5.*

❽ **Heart of Heaven Park** (Tianxin Gongyuan), at what was the southeast corner of the old city wall, was occupied by a rebel leader during the 19th-century Taiping Rebellion. The **Pavilion of the Heart of Heaven** (Tian Xin Dian) was restored in 1759. ⊠ *Jianxiang Lu* ☯ *Daily 9–5.*

❾ The **Headquarters of the local Communist Party** (Zhonggong Xiangqu Weiyuanhui Jiuzhi) is sometimes known as the Qing Shui (Clearwater Pool), a reference to professed government transparency. It was here that the first meeting of the local Communist Party was held, under the auspices of Mao Zedong, in July 1921. Mao and his first wife, Yang Kaihui, the daughter of one of his teachers at Changsha, lived here between 1921 and 1923. It was also home to Yang's mother. On display are a conference room and the room where Mao and his wife lived, with furniture in the traditional Hunan style. ⊠ *Qingshui Tang* ▨ *Y10* ☯ *Daily 8:30–5.*

❿ Mao studied at the **Hunan No. 1 Teacher Training College** (Diyi Shifan) between 1913 and 1918, becoming "student of the year" in 1917 (though presumably not for his various political activities, which were already in full swing by this time). The original school was destroyed in 1938 during the war with the Japanese, but the buildings associated with Mao were later meticulously reconstructed, and some parts of them have been turned into a small museum. On view here are photographs, documents, and schoolbooks associated with his time here, as well as period newspaper clippings relating to revolutionary events around the world. ⊠ *Shuyuan Lu* ▨ *Y5* ☯ *Daily 8:30–5.*

⓫ The narrow 5-km (3-mi) **Island of Oranges** (Juzi Zhou), in the Xiang River, is known for its orange orchards. A park at its southern tip affords some fine views. On a tablet here is inscribed a poem written by Mao in praise of the town.

⓬ **Yuelu Hill** (Yuelu Shan) supports the lush grounds and bamboo thickets of Hunan University. Other educational establishments preceded this one, notably the 10th-century Yuelu Academy, one of the most celebrated of the Song Dynasty. Several illustrious figures, including the philosopher Zhu Xi, whose texts became the basis for the imperial examinations, studied there. Nothing is left of the academy, except a single stela, but there are still some beautiful pagodas from the Qing Dynasty, including the **Aiwan Ting**, with its severe eaves, built in 1792, and at the summit, the **Yunlu Gong**, a pavilion built in 1863. The **Lushan Si**, on the lower slopes, was originally built in AD 268 and is one of the oldest temples in the province. The doorway and a pavilion remain. ⊠ *Lushan Lu on west bank of river, Bus 12* ☯ *Daily 8–5.*

en route Just outside Changsha lie the **Han Graves** (Han Mu) (✥ Mawangdui, 4 km (2½ mi) northeast of Changsha ✎ Y10 ☉ Daily 8:30–5), discovered in 1972. The contents of these three graves, more than 2,000 years old, have provided much of the interest of Changsha's Provincial Museum. They belonged to the Marquis of Dai, Li Cang (Tomb 2), who was prime minister to the king of Changsha between 193 BC and 186 BC; his wife, To Hou (Tomb 1); and their son (Tomb 3), who died in 168. To Hou's tomb was in a pounded earth mound 65 feet high and up to 200 feet in diameter, lying about 50 feet from the top; her body lay in the innermost of several coffins, the outer ones highly decorated and covered in bamboo mats. It seems that Tomb 1, the last to be built, completely escaped the depredations of tomb robbers (the other two were less fortunate); bamboo slips listing everything that was placed in the tomb to help To Hou on her way to the underworld showed that nothing had been removed for more than 2,000 years.

Where to Stay & Eat

$$–$$$ ✕ **Changdao Restaurant** (Changdao Fandian). Centrally located, this bustling restaurant, popular with locals, serves a wide variety of Chinese dishes, from *gongpao* chicken to meat- and vegetable-filled dumplings. ⊠ *Wuyi Xi Lu* ☎ *No phone* ▤ *No credit cards.*

$$–$$$ ✕ **Changsha Restaurant** (Changsha Canting). One of the original restaurants in Changsha before private restaurants were permitted, this large upscale establishment serves good Hunanese food, such as *gualieng fen* (cold rice noodles in a hot and spicy sauce). ⊠ *116 Wuyi Dong Lu* ☎ *No phone* ▤ *No credit cards.*

$$–$$$ ✕ **Youyicun.** At this pleasant, conveniently located restaurant, with a traditionally decorated interior, you can choose from a wide variety of dishes from all over China. Try the *hongshao rou* (red cooked pork) or *mapo doufu* (peppery tofu). ⊠ *Youyicun Grand Hotel, 225 Zhongshan Lu* ☎ *No phone* ▤ *No credit cards.*

$–$$ ✕ **Kaiyulou.** In this simple restaurant the fare is snack foods such as *jiaozi* (pork and cabbage dumplings) and soups, including *niuroumian* (beef noodle soup). ⊠ *Wuyi Dong Lu* ☎ *No phone* ▤ *No credit cards.*

$ 🏨 **Dolten International Hotel.** Conveniently located in the downtown area of Changsha, Dolten is a modern building that houses spacious and pleasantly furnished rooms and tasteful bedding. Bathrooms provide soft and clean towels and shower curtains are clean. The hotel staff is professional and friendly. If you have children under 12, they can stay with you free, on cot beds. ⊠ *149 Shaoshan Bei Lu, 410011* ☎ *0731/416–8888* 🖷 *0731/416–9999* ⇄ *450 rooms* ⚁ *2 restaurants, room service, in-room safes, minibars, refrigerators, cable TV, indoor pool, gym, 3 bars, dry cleaning, business services* ▤ *AE, DC, MC, V.*

$ 🏨 **Shennong Dajiudian.** Despite a renovation in 2002, Shennong still needs some upgrading. The poorly decorated rooms are small with small bathrooms. The in-house restaurants, however, offset the shortcomings of the guest rooms. Delicious Hunan and Chaozhou cuisine are available and the City Pub serves both Chinese and Western drinks. All rooms come with satellite TV and Internet access. ⊠ *298 Furong Nan*

Lu, 410007 ☎ *0731/521–8888* 🖷 *0731/523–6112* 🛏 *375 rooms* ⚄ *3 restaurants, in-room safes, minibars, refrigerators, indoor pool, 6 bars, dry cleaning, business services* ▤ *AE, DC, MC, V.*

¢–$ 🏨 **Hunan Bestride Hotel** (Hunan Jiacheng Jiudian). This Hong Kong–managed hotel sets itself apart from other Chinese-owned hotels by its effort to make guests feel extremely welcome. Tastefully decorated rooms are outfitted with stylish furniture and kept clean. The competent staff speaks British English at a conversational level. A good Chinese restaurant on the premises serves excellent food. ✉ *386 Laodong Xi Lu, 410000* ☎ *0731/511–8888* 🖷 *0731/511–1888* 🌐 *www.hnbrhotel.com* 🛏 *238 units* ⚄ *5 restaurants, room service, in-room safes, minibars, refrigerators, spa, 2 bars, dry cleaning, business services* ▤ *AE, DC, MC, V.*

¢ 🏨 **Wandai Dajiudian.** Opened in August 2002, this hotel gives its customers a feel of exoticism. The living-room areas of the rooms are screened off from the beds by Japanese-style wooden panels. Views from the rooms are either of the indoor garden plaza, Wuyi Square, on the east side or the river. Rooms are clean and pleasantly decorated with standard amenities. Be sure to inquire about seasonal and group discounts. ✉ *101 Huangxing Zhong Lu* ☎ *0731/488-2333* 🖷 *0731/488–2111* 🛏 *321 rooms* ⚄ *2 restaurants, room service, bar, dry cleaning, business services* ▤ *AE, DC, MC, V.*

¢ 🏨 **Zidongge Huatian Hotel.** This downtown is the first Huatian Hotel chain in Changsha, and the first in the province to be rated by the Tourism Authority with four stars. The rooms are nicely furnished and come with satellite TV. Not all rooms are for nonsmokers so be sure to ask when you reserve. The hotel has three restaurants serving decent Chinese and Western dishes. The hotel coffee shop is an ideal place to chill out. In addition, the hotel also provides a gym with sauna, disco, and KTV (karaoke) rooms. ✉ *68 Bayi Xi Lu, 410001* ☎ *0731/228-8888* 🛏 *400 rooms* ⚄ *3 restaurants, in-room safes, cable TV, gym, hair salon, massage, sauna, dance club, shop, business services* ▤ *AE, DC, MC, V.*

Nightlife & the Arts

Besides local opera and acrobatics, Hunan's specialty is **shadow puppets,** and the province has its own troupe. For information ask CITS or at your hotel.

Karaoke is popular here; the best bars are in the hotels.

The Outdoors

For bicycle rentals see CITS on Wuli Dong Lu. For jogging the best place is **Martyrs' Park** (Lie Shi Gongyuan; ⊹ off Dongfeng Lu, near museum). The best places for walking and hiking are in nearby Wulingyuan; maps with trails are for sale in the area.

Shopping

Tea is a good buy in Hunan, and Changsha embroidery is some of the best known in China. The main shopping district of Changsha is Zhongshan Lu; there is also an antiques shop in the Provincial Museum.

Shaoshan

★ ⓭ *3 hrs (130 km [81 mi]) by train southwest of Changsha.*

The small town of Shaoshan, within fairly easy driving distance of Changsha, is in many ways indistinguishable from thousands of similar towns all over China. For many years, however, pilgrims came to this town every day, pouring out of the trains that arrived regularly on the railway line especially built for the purpose, eager to see Mao Zedong's birthplace. At the height of his cult, in the mid-1960s, particularly during the Cultural Revolution, some 3 million visitors came here every year—that's 8,000 a day. The numbers declined, of course, as the terrible consequences of the period became clear, but as time has passed, those consequences have come to be placed in the context of Mao's overall achievements, and a train to Shaoshan still leaves Changsha daily at 7 AM.

The older part of Shaoshan and its surrounding countryside are quite charming. The original town—about 4 km (2½ mi) away from the newer, uninspired buildings by the train station—is a farming community. It stands among reflective paddy fields and is cradled by lush green hills covered in tea plantations, orange orchards, and bamboo groves. Apart from the Mao industry, Shaoshan offers an opportunity to enjoy one of China's greatest attributes—its countryside.

Visitors are welcome to the **House Where Mao Was Born** (Mao Zedong Guju). The son of a farmer (who was better off than the poor peasant of Communist mythology), Mao was born in 1893 and lived here until 1910 when he moved to Changsha to begin college. The house, which became a museum in 1964, is surprisingly large, with a thatched roof and mud walls. It is, of course, in a better state of repair than most of its neighbors. Nonetheless, the spirit of simplicity has been retained, and it has an air of formal hominess. From the courtyard you enter a room originally devoted to the ancestral altar, then pass a kitchen, a dining room, three family bedrooms, and a guest room, all within close proximity to the livestock pens. Personal items belonging to Mao and his family are on display here, as well as photos of his parents and of him from his revolutionary days. Take a bus at Changsha South Bus Station to Shaoshan. Buses leave every half hour daily, from 8 AM to 5 PM; a one-way ticket costs around Y25. The trip takes about two hours. ⊠ *Northeastern outskirts of village which lies 90 km (55 mi) to the southwest of Changsha* 🎫 *Y5* ⊘ *Daily 8:30–5.*

The **Museum of Comrade Mao** (Mao Zedong Tongzhi Jinianguan), which opened during the Cultural Revolution, is devoted to Mao's life in its revolutionary context. Unfortunately, the exhibition, which is full of photographs, has few English captions. ⊠ *Village square* 🎫 *Y5* ⊘ *Daily 8:30–5.*

When you have had enough of Mao, you may wish to simply explore the countryside around the town. A path leads up **Shaofeng**, the hill that dominates the town. The route meanders among trees and bamboo groves past inscribed tablets up to the Taoist pavilion at the top.

en route   Dripping Water Cave (Dishuidong) is about 3 km (2 mi) from the village, close to the Mao family tombs. It's here that Mao apparently retired for 11 days of contemplation in 1966 just as the Cultural Revolution was getting under way. Daily round-trip buses leave from the Changsha South Bus Station (Y35).

Where to Stay & Eat
Simple dining is available all over Shaoshan.

¢-$ ✕⭐ **Shaoshan Guesthouse** (Shaoshan Binguan). The rooms here are comfortable, though far from luxurious. You can find something a little more sophisticated in the way of dining options at the next-door Guesthouse Restaurant ($–$$), which serves tasty Hunanese specialties. ⊠ *Village square behind statue of Mao* ☎ *0732/568–2309* ⌁ *50 rooms* ⌂ *Restaurant* ⊟ *No credit cards.*

Nightlife & the Arts
Occasional performances of traditional **opera** or of one of the more modern versions permissible during the Cultural Revolution, which are revived from time to time, take place here. Inquire with the CITS in Changsha for information.

The Outdoors
Walking on the hills around Shaoshan is enjoyable—there are paths that can be followed across and alongside fields.

Hengyang

⑭   *2½ hrs (140 km [87 mi]) by train south of Changsha.*

The second-largest city in Hunan has a few points of interest—**Mountain of the Wild Geese** (Huiyanfeng), with its temple ruins, and **Stone Drum Mountain** (Shigushan).

Fodor'sChoice   But the main reason for visiting Hengyang is to go on to the beautiful ★   4,234-foot **Hengshang Shan,** one of China's Five Holy Mountains. At the foot of the massif is the large **Nanyue Grand Temple** (Nanyue Damiao), originally built in AD 725. Covering a considerable area, it consists of an array of halls and pavilions dedicated to various aspects of Buddhism and, about 4 km (2½ mi) from the main monastery, the tomb of the monk Xi Qian, who founded the Japanese sect of Buddhism in the 8th century. ✛ *1 hr by road northeast of Hengyang.*

Wulingyuan Nature Reserve

⑮   *15 hrs (350 km [217 mi]) by train northwest of Changsha.*

This reserve in northwest Hunan comprises three areas—**Suoxiyu,** Fodor'sChoice   **Tianzishan,** and the best known, **Zhangjiajie.** A spectacular area of ★   peaks eroded into dramatic shapes, waterfalls, and caves, including the largest cavern in Asia, Zhangjiajie is a splendid place for relaxing and for walking along trails (maps are available). The natural scenery speaks for itself, but many of the rocks, pools, and caves have been given names in accordance with their perceived resemblance to buildings, animals, and so on. Train service connects Zhangjiajie with surrounding cities in Hunan.

Where to Stay

¢–$ ⊞ **Zhangjiajie Hotel** (Zhangjiajie Binguan). Among the few hotels in town, this establishment has a new wing (xin fang) with quite clean, well-appointed rooms and an old wing (lao fang) where the rooms are damp and rather shabby. List price is negotiable and seasonal promotion packages are available. ⊠ *Off main street* ☎ *0744/857–2388* ⚑ *Restaurant, shop, travel services* 🖃 *No credit cards.*

Yueyang

16 *1½ hrs (150 km [93 mi]) by train north of Changsha.*

This small town on the Yangzi has a lively port atmosphere. The **Yueyang Pavilion** (Yueyang Lou), one of the best known south of the Yangzi, is a temple set above the river that dates from the Tang Dynasty (618–970), famous as a meeting place for such great classical poets as Du Fu and Li Bai. The main tower is surrounded by pavilions, including the **Pavilion of the Three Drinking Sprees** (Sancui Ting), named in honor of the Taoist Lu Dongbin, who became drunk here on three occasions. The brick **Cishi Pagoda** (Cishi Ta) dates from 1242. Both are on the shoreline of Dongting Hu, the second-largest freshwater lake in China, with an area of 3,900 square km (1,500 square mi). On one of the islands of the lake, Junshan Dao, or silver needle tea, one of the most famous and expensive teas in China, is grown. The island can be easily reached on one of the boats that regularly depart from the town.

A good time to visit is when the town plays host to a **Dragon Boat Festival** on the fifth day of the fifth lunar month (June or July).

Where to Stay

$$ ⊞ **Yueyang Hotel.** This is your safest bet in town. It's close to Dongting Lake and serves well for a short stay, especially during the Dragon Boat Festival. Given the local climate, the hotel rooms may feel a bit damp, but this is one of the best Yueyang can offer. ⊠ *26 Dongting Bei Lu, 414000* ☎ *0730/822–3011* 🖷 *0730/822–5235* ⚑ *Restaurant* 🖃 *No credit cards.*

Hunan A to Z

To research prices, get advice from other travelers, and book travel arrangements, visit www.fodors.com.

AIR TRAVEL

The Changsha Airport is 34 km (21 miles) east of town. Destinations include Beijing (four or more flights daily), Guangzhou (four flights daily), Hong Kong (two flights daily); Kunming (four flights daily), Chengdu (four flights daily), Shanghai (four or more flights daily), and Xian (two flights daily). An airport shuttle from the Minhang Hotel (Minhang Dajiudian) at 5 Wuyi Dadao 5 and Chaoyang Lu; takes about 40 minutes and costs Y15. It departs the hotel 2½ hours before flights. A taxi to the airport is around Y100.

🚩 **Changsha CITS** ✉ 38 Zhanlanguan Lu. ☎ 0731/443-3943.

BUS TRAVEL

Changsha has three main bus stations: South Station (Qiche Nan Zhan), East Station (Qiche Dong Zhan), and West Station (Qiche Xi Zhan). Buses to Hengshang Shan, Shaoshan, Xiamen, and Guilin leave from the South Station. Buses to Hankou, Guangzhou, and Nanjing leave from the East Station. Buses to Zhangjiajie and Yichang leave from the West Station.

CAR RENTAL

Self-drive cars are out of the question, but cars with drivers can be hired through CITS.

EMERGENCIES

Known to foreigners as the **PSB** (Public Security Bureau or *gong'an ju*), the police are not always helpful. Approach your hotel for assistance first, or ask the CITS for help in an emergency.

🚩 **PSB** ✉ Huangxing Lu, in western part of Changsha ☎ 110.

MONEY MATTERS

The main Bank of China has an ATM and full foreign-exchange services Monday through Friday from 8:30 to noon and 2 to 5. It can also gives cash advances on credit cards. There's an ATM in the lobby of the Huatian Dajiudian, at 176 Wuyi Dadao, as well.

🚩 Bank **Bank of China** ✉ 127 Furong Zhong Lu, Changsha 410011 ☎ 0731/258-0703 🖷 0731/258-0707.

TRAIN TRAVEL

The Changsha Railway Station is in the eastern part of the city. Changsha is linked by direct services to Guangzhou (11 hrs, hard sleeper Y96), Guilin, Beijing (15½ hrs, hard sleeper Y345), Kunming (27 hrs, hard sleeper Y207), Lanzhou (27 hrs), Shanghai (15 hrs), and Xian (18½ hrs), as well as to Hengyang (2½ hrs), Yueyang (1 hr), and Zhangjiajie (15 hours), and to the Mao shrine at Shaoshan (3½ hrs).

🚩 Train Stations **Changsha Railway Station** (Changsha Huoche Zhan) ✉ Wuyi Dong Lu ☎ 0731/229-6421. **Zhangjiajie Train Station** ☎ 0744/561-8654.

TRANSPORTATION AROUND HUNAN

Changsha has comprehensive bus service (maps are available from the railway station and from bookshops). Taxis and pedicabs can be hailed or found at hotels and at the railway station.

Everything in Shaoshan village can be reached on foot. Pedicabs and taxis are available around the railway and bus stations to take you to the village.

VISITOR INFORMATION

🚩 Tourist Information **CITS** ✉ 38 Zhanlanguan Lu, Changsha ☎ 0731/443-3943.

GUANGXI

The Autonomous Region of Guangxi is famous for the scenery of Guilin, an oasis of fairy-tale stone peaks rising from valleys and rivers that has been celebrated by painters and poets for centuries.

Guangxi has often been the object of struggle between its indigenous peoples and the Han, who established suzerainty only in the 19th century. At the same time it drew the attention of the French and British, who were competing for trade advantages in the region. Several towns and cities were compelled eventually to open themselves up to trade with the Western powers of the era. During World War II Guangxi was occupied at various times by the Japanese. In 1958 it began to be a sop to the indigenous peoples of the region—the Dong, Gelao, Hui, Jing, Maonan, Miao, Shui, Yao, Yi, and, in particular, the Zhuang people, who constitute about a third of the Guangxi's population: the government in Beijing turned Guangxi into one of five autonomous regions, which, in theory only, have an element of self-government.

Although thoroughly assimilated into Chinese life today, there's enough archaeological evidence—including a fantastic series of prehistoric rock friezes along the Zuo River near the Vietnam border—to link the Zhuang with a Bronze Age culture of Southeast Asia. The Zhuang language is unusual in that, instead of using pinyin, it follows its own method of rendering Chinese characters into roman text. This accounts for the novel spellings you'll encounter on street signs and elsewhere: "Minzu Dadao" (Nationality Avenue), for example, becomes "Minzcuzdadau." Other areas of Guangxi, such as the northeastern hills around Sanjiang, are home to less integrated groups, such as the Dong, whose more actively traditional way of life makes for a fascinating trip (you can hop between villages on public buses). The village chief maintains his headquarters way up high in the mountains and it's only accessible by stairs. There, traditional Dong customs are preserved in forms of communal male bonding practices: dancing, singing, and land cultivation. Arranged marriages are considered the only acceptable form of matrimony for those who remain in the village. The attraction of Guangxi's cities is more ephemeral, as their characters are vanishing along with traces of their colonial heritage. Liuzhou is at the heart of Guangxi's rail network, while plenty of people pass through easterly Wuzhou, terminus for the journey up the Xi River from Guangzhou. Far fewer manage to reach the south and the tropically languid capital, Nanning, or the coastal port of Beihai. Those who do, cross a central region whose history touches on the origins of the Taiping Rebellion, 19th-century China's most widespread uprising against the rotting Qing Empire.

Guangxi is an essentially mountainous region known for its distinctive karst rock formations that have made Guilin so famous. They rise from the coastal plain in the south, by the Gulf of Tonkin, and reach a height of 7,030 feet. The climate is subtropical, affected by seasonal monsoons, with long, hot, humid, and frequently wet summers and mild winters.

Guilin

▶ *15 hrs (500 km [310 mi]) by train northwest of Hong Kong; 28 hrs (1,675 km [1,039 mi]) by train southwest of Beijing; (400 km [248 mi]) by train southwest of Changsha.*

By Chinese standards Guilin is a small town and architecturally not very distinguished at that, mostly because of the amount of bombing it suffered during the Sino-Japanese War. Yet it is plumb in the middle of some of the most beautiful scenery in the world. This landscape of limestone karst hills and mountains, rising almost sheer from the earth and clustered closely together over hundreds of square kilometers of orchards, paddy fields, and shallow streams, has a dreamy quality that is hypnotic. Formation of the hills dates back about 200 million years, to when the area was under the sea. As the land beneath began to push up, the sea receded, and the effects of the ensuing erosion over thousands of years produced this sublime scenery.

The town itself has a surprisingly long history. Its current name dates only from the Ming Dynasty; before that it was known as Shian. The first emperor of a united China, Qin Shihuang, established a garrison here when he made a military expedition to the south in 214 BC. He later built the Lingqu Canal to link the Li River (Lijiang), which flows through Guilin, with the Xiang River (Xiangjiang) to create what was for centuries the most important traffic route between central and south China and between the Pearl (Zhu) and Yangzi (Chang) rivers.

During the early years of the Ming Dynasty Guilin was the capital of a small kingdom ruled by Zhu Shouqian, a nephew of the dynasty's founder. The last of the Ming royal house took refuge here in the mid-17th century as the Manchurians seized power in the country to begin the last imperial dynasty, the Qing. The town's population grew quickly during the Sino-Japanese War, when refugees fled here from the north. Nowadays the population is swollen, indeed saturated, by a constant flow of visitors, a challenge to which local entrepreneurs have risen with alacrity.

Although the real beauty of the countryside lies outside the town and is best enjoyed by boat, there are several hills in the town itself. By means of the stairways that have been cut into their flanks, it is possible to climb them without too much trouble and enjoy wonderful views across the town to the sea of misty hills beyond.

⓱ The **Peak of Solitary Beauty** (Duxiu Feng) is about 492 feet high, the summit reached by just over 300 steps. It is within the precincts of the old Ming Palace, which was built in 1393 and of which little remains. The peak is also inside Guangxi Shifan Xueyuan (Guangxi Teachers College) and is accessible only after 2 PM, when classes end.

⓲ **Whirlpool Hill** (Fubo Shan) offers views, and at its base is a huge bell and the **Vessel of a Thousand Men** (Qian Ren Gang) from the Qing Dynasty. Here, too, is the **Cave of the Returned Pearl** (Huanzhu Dong), containing a 10-foot stalactite.

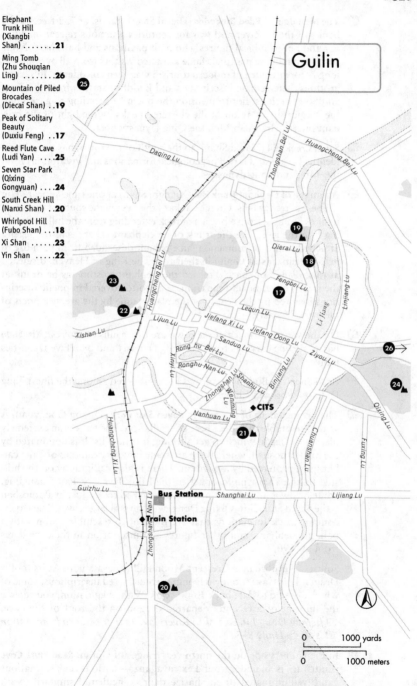

Guilin

⑲ The **Mountain of Piled Brocades** (Diecai Shan) stands, at 732 feet, on the banks of the Li River and was for centuries a famous retreat for literary and philosophical figures who built pavilions and halls here. None survive, but in the past their fame attracted visitors from all over China, long before the idea of modern tourism was even considered. In several grottoes there remain inscriptions and Buddhist statues from the Tang and Song periods, not to mention the poem "Ascending to gaze upon the magical birds amongst the clustered peaks by the light of the brilliant moon," by Yuan Mei, the Qing Dynasty poet.

⑳ **South Creek Hill** (Nanxi Shan), to the south of the town, has two almost identical peaks and is rich in geological formations and inscriptions from the Tang and Song dynasties.

㉑ An image of **Elephant Trunk Hill** (Xiangbi Shan) at one time appeared on Chinese currency bills. On the banks of the river in the south of the town, it takes its name from a branch of rock extending from the hill and arching into the river like the trunk of an elephant. There is also a legend attached to this phenomenon: an elephant descended from paradise to help the citizens of Guilin in their toil. The King of Heaven, disgusted at this display of charity, turned the elephant to stone as he drank at the river's edge. Behind the trunk is a grotto covered in poetic inscriptions inspired by the beauty of the place, some by the greatest poets of the Song Dynasty.

㉒ On the western fringes of the town are other hills of interest. **Yin Shan** has some fine carvings from the Tang Dynasty and by a Five Dynasties monk.

㉓ At **Xi Shan** the Buddhist carvings are considered among the finest Tang Dynasty works in China.

㉔ The arrangement of the hills in **Seven Star Park** (Qixing Gongyuan) is said to resemble the Great Bear constellation. The park is an extremely pleasant place in which to get a feeling for the hills. It is dominated by the hill **Putuoshan,** where there are some famous examples of Tang calligraphy, protected by a pavilion. There is also calligraphy on the hillside by the Taoist philosopher of the Ming Dynasty, Pan Changjing, while below is an array of interestingly shaped rocks. Just by Putuoshan is the **Seven Star Cliff** (Qixing Dong) with several large caves. The largest contains rock formations that are thought to resemble a lion with a ball, an elephant, and other figures. An inscription in the cave dates from AD 590.

South of Putuoshan is **Crescent Moon Hill** (Yueya Shan). At its foot is **Dragon Lair Cave** (Longyin Dong), rich in carved inscriptions, some of which are said to date back 1,600 years. With imagination, you can see the imprint of a recently departed dragon on the roof of the cave. ✉ *Jiefang Dong Lu, east of Li River; take taxi or pedicab from station* 💰 *Y40* 🕐 *Daily 8–5.*

㉕ In the countryside on the northwest fringes of Guilin, **Reed Flute Cave** (Ludi Yan) is an underground extravaganza—curious rock formations gaudily illuminated to emphasize their coincidental similarity with birds, plants, and animals—that you either love or hate. A path, a third of a mile long, threads through what is, in many ways, quite an entertaining and sometimes dramatic underground palace. Some of the formations are remarkable, but perhaps the most impressive item is the Crystal Palace of the Dragon King, where there is an area of pools and small mounds that resemble a miniature Guilin. Although the cave is illuminated, a flashlight is useful. The hawkers outside the cave can be particularly aggressive and dishonest. ✛ *Northwest edge of town; take bicycle, taxi, or pedicab from station* ▨ *Y50* ⊘ *Daily 8:30–11 and 12:30–3:30.*

㉖ A few miles east of the town is the **Ming Tomb** (Zhu Shouqian Ling), the tomb of Zhu Shouqian, the nephew of the first Ming emperor, who founded a principality here. The tomb is complete with a sacred way and makes a pleasant excursion by bicycle. ✛ *Take Jiefang Dong Lu east about 9 km (5 mi)* ▨ *Free* ⊘ *Daily 8–5.*

Where to Stay & Eat

The main streets of Guilin are lined at night with tables serving simple, flavorsome, and cheap dishes (always check the price in advance). Other restaurants serve exotic dishes like snake soup—these are easily spotted because of the snakes coiled up in cages outside.

★ **$$** ✕ **Jufulin Meishiyuan.** One of the more popular restaurants on the new Zhengyang Buxing Jie (Pedestrian Street), this well-lighted and clean restaurant offers local food, stir-fries, and dim sum on the first floor and outdoors, and Cantonese cuisine on the second floor. Local favorites include sautéed snails, Li River shrimp, steamed Li River fish, and stewed turtle. You can also order from the food on display outside the restaurant—spicy crayfish, skewered meats, tofu, and assorted vegetables—all of which can be grilled on the spot over an open fire. ▨ *10 Zhengyang Lu* ☎ *0773/280–8748* ▤ *No credit cards.*

$$ ✕ **Tailian Hotel** (Tailian Fandian). At this restaurant, well known to locals, you'll find a tasty array of Cantonese dim sum. A self-service buffet is available and the price for a "one-person meal" is about half of that of a main entrée. ▨ *102 Central Zhongshan Lu* ☎ *0773/282–2888* 🖶 *0773/282–6251* ▤ *V.*

$–$$ ✕ **Yiyuan Restaurant** (Yiyuan Fandian). At this friendly restaurant, with its all-wood exterior, the specialty is Sichuanese cooking: excellent spicy dishes, including the tear-inducing diced chicken stir-fried with chilies and garlic; the *shuizhu niurou* (tender beef slices and vegetables in a chili sauce; *tangcu cuipiyu* (crispy sweet-and-sour fish); and the famous Chinese *dandan mian* (noodles in spicy peanut sauce). ▨ *106 Nanhuan Lu* ☎ *No phone* ▤ *No credit cards.*

★ **$–$$** ✕ **Yueyalo.** This pleasant restaurant, surrounded by a park dominated by karst rocks and hills, serves local and regional dishes. Specialty dishes feature a combination of southern Guangdong flavor with local recipes, such as noodles with scallions, kale, and peanuts in a hot sauce. Sweating, red-faced locals sit together gossiping and challenging each other to hotter and hotter chili peppers. Friendly waitresses are obliged to relay to the chef your tolerance for spicy food so he can modify his generally hot recipes. ▨ *Seven Star Park* ☎ *No phone* ▤ *AE, V.*

★ **$$$**　🏨 **Sheraton Guilin** (Guilin Dayu Dafandian). This modern, comfortable, well-managed hotel overlooking the river has good facilities and rooms that are clean and spacious. The formal restaurant serves excellent Chinese cuisine. A small café attracts homesick Westerners and stylish locals with a 1950s rock-and-roll motif and eclectic snacks such as pizza, steak sandwiches, and pumpkin soup. ⊠ *Binjiang Lu on west bank of Li River, 541001* ☎ *0773/282–5588* 🖷 *0773/282–5598* ⊕ *www.sheraton.com* 🛏 *411 rooms, 19 suites* ♨ *3 restaurants, room service, in-room safes, minibars, bar, nightclub, shops, meeting rooms, travel services* ▤ *AE, MC, V.*

　　$　🏨 **Guilin Royal Garden Hotel** (Guilin Diyuan Jiudian). Overlooking the most celebrated riverscape in all China, immortalized in paintings and poems for centuries, this luxury hotel offers spacious airy rooms with breathtaking views of Guilin's famous peaks. The three restaurants serve a wide variety of foods. The Jade Garden serves Chinese cuisine: Sichuan, Cantonese, or local style dishes. For Y80 you can enjoy an unforgettable cultural show presented every night starting at 8 with cocktails and light desserts in the indoor garden. The quiet traditional design of the only Japanese restaurant in Guilin, the Ginza, attracts visitors who enjoy its authentically prepared sushi, tempura, noodle soups, and other dishes. The Marco Polo Grill offers Continental dining serving European cuisine by candlelight. ⊠ *Yanjiang Lu, 541004* ☎ *0773/581–2411* 🖷 *0773/581–5051* ⊕ *www.c-b-w.com/hotel/royalgarden/* 🛏 *335 rooms* ♨ *3 restaurants, in-room safes, minibars, tennis courts, pool, gym, sauna, bar, lounge, shops, dry cleaning, concierge* ▤ *AE, MC, V.*

★ **$**　🏨 **Holiday Inn Guilin** (Jiari Guilin Binguan). Here you'll find the chain's standard comfort and value in a pleasant location by the bamboo-lined Banyan Lake in the older part of town. ⊠ *14 Ronghu Bei Lu, 541002* ☎ *0773/282–3950* 🖷 *0773/282–2101* 🛏 *259 rooms* ♨ *2 restaurants, in-room safes, refrigerators, pool, gym, nightclub* ▤ *AE, MC, V.*

　　¢　🏨 **Lijiang Hotel** (Lijiang Fandian). For many years the main tourist hotel, the Lijiang still has one of the best locations in town, right next to the Li River. It is fairly well appointed, though it has been surpassed in quality by newer hotels in town. Rooms are clean. ⊠ *1 Shanhu Bei Lu, 541001* ☎ *0773/282–2881* 🖷 *0773/282–2891* ✉ *gllj@public.glptt.gr.cn* 🛏 *378 rooms* ♨ *8 restaurants, bar, nightclub, shops, travel services* ▤ *AE, MC, V.*

★ **¢**　🏨 **Osmanthus Hotel** (Dangui Dajiudian). This low-budget yet comfortable and pleasant hotel is staffed with bilingual employees who are efficient and professional. The room decor could use new upholstery and you may want to request fresh shower curtains at the desk. The in-house restaurants serve great Chinese cuisine, but be warned: Chinese songs are on tap on the karaoke player. ⊠ *451 Zhongshan Nan Lu, 541002* ☎ *0773/383–4300* 🖷 *0773/383–5316* ✉ *glosmh@public.glptt.gx.cn* 🛏 *362 units* ♨ *4 restaurants, refrigerators, pool, sauna, steam room, bar, nightclub, shops, laundry service* ▤ *AE, MC, V.*

Nightlife & the Arts

The best bars are in the hotels and there are plenty of karaoke options around town. Performances of **opera** or acrobatics frequently take place; to find out what's on, ask CITS or at your hotel.

The Outdoors

Taking a night excursion on the river in order to follow a cormorant fisherman at work can be an unusual diversion. Inquire at CITS, or simply head toward the congregation of boats along the Li riverbank at dusk. Watch as the slender birds plunge into the river and retrieve fish. They can't swallow the fish because their throats are bound by metal collars, and the fishermen sit in the stern of their boats to collect the catch.

Guilin is an excellent place for **bicycling,** which is the best way to appreciate the countryside. The areas between the hills are almost dead flat, and bicycles can readily be hired all over the town. You can go **jogging** around Banyan Lake, along the Li River, or in the country.

Shopping

A few items of local interest—jewelry, bamboo products, indigenous peoples' woven clothes, handwoven linen and tablecloths, and crochet work—are available. Be aware that tourists in Guilin are frequently seen as potential victims: a favorite technique at stalls is for the seller to bend down to place the chosen item in the bag and switch it for something cheaper. To browse, head toward the Li River, where many merchants display their wares, especially in the evening.

Side Trip from Guilin

Fodor'sChoice
★

The best way to absorb the beauties of Guilin's landscape is to spend a long time in the area and explore the countryside on foot. The next best thing is the **Li River Cruise,** which operates most days between Guilin and Yangshuo. The shallow and limpid Li River, overhung in many places by bamboo fronds and disturbed only by the splashing of children and water buffalo cooling themselves in the shallows, takes you through breathtaking scenery, threading its way between the mountains. Narrow flat rafts made of bamboo skim by, perhaps with cormorants, used for fishing, tethered to the prow. You will likely be on one of a fleet of boats, but you will hardly know it.

Where the route begins will depend on the level of the water. Sometimes it's not possible to start from Guilin, in which case a transfer by bus is made about 40 minutes downstream. The cruise lasts about four hours (lunch is served on board, and delights caught en route are often offered as extras), terminating in the small market town of Yangshuo, from which it's a two-hour bus journey back. The peaks that you pass en route have all acquired fantastic names—Dou Ji Shan (Cockfighting Hill), Si Hua Shan (Embroidery Hill)—conjuring something familiar out of nature. ⚓ *Boat leaves from docks on Binjiang Lu* ✉ *Approximately Y450, includes lunch and return by bus.*

Yangshuo

★ ㉗   *4 hrs (100 km [60 mi]) by boat south of Guilin.*

The boat cruise from Guilin ends at the small market town of **Yangshuo.** Most days the whole town seems to be one giant market. If you watch out for pickpockets, you'll enjoy the experience. In the immediate vicinity are a number of interesting sights, including **Green Lotus Peak** (Bil-ian Feng) and **Dragon Head Hill** (Long Tou Shan). A short bike ride away are **Black Buddha Cave** (Heifo Dong), **Moon Hill** (Yueliang Shan), a number of other caves, and an underground river. Moon Hill has breath-taking views of the surrounding countryside.

A pleasant place to relax, it's also a good base from which to explore the surrounding countryside. You can also go by boat farther down river to the village of Fuli, where indigenous people farm and live in centuries-old style.

Where to Stay & Eat

Outside the Yangshuo Paradise Resort are a number of small informal restaurants serving good coffee and Western and Chinese food. Prices are low, and there's a wide selection of dishes. Street stands sell noo-dles, wonton soup, and other delicious fare.

¢–$ **Yangshuo Paradise Resort** (Yangshuo Dujia Fandian). On a quiet patch of land away from the main road, this resort has amenities you won't find in other parts of Yangshuo, in addition to a superior bilingual staff, proximity to local markets, and authentic local food. Rooms are comfortable and some have nice views of the surrounding karst peaks. Seasonal and group discounts apply. ✉ *116 Xi Jie, 541900* ☎ *0773/ 882–2109* 🖷 *0773/882–2106* ⊕ *www.paradiseyangshuo.com* ➯ *145 rooms* ♨ *2 restaurants, minibars, pool, gym, shops, business services* ⊟ *AE, MC, V.*

Nightlife

Many restaurants double as bars in the evenings, catering to young in-dividual travelers. Karaoke is popular here.

The Outdoors

You can hike in the countryside or rent canoes to explore the river and its creeks. Hiking and biking, especially to the surrounding peaks, is pop-ular; bikes can be rented from most of the small hotels on Xi Lu. In warmer months you can go swimming in the river. As in Guilin, you can also hire boats to follow the cormorant fishers along the Li River at night. For information on rentals, contact the local CITS or the Guilin Over-seas Tourist Corporation (☎ 0773/383–4116).

Shopping

There is plenty to buy in the market—Mao paraphernalia, batiks, T-shirts, and antiques. Prices in Yangshuo are more reasonable than those in Guilin.

Longsheng

28 *3 hrs (120 km [74 mi]) by bus northwest of Guilin.*

A small town near the northern border of Guizhou, Longsheng is in the middle of a mountain area populated by several indigenous peoples, no-tably the Dong, Miao, Yao, and Zhuang. The countryside around the town, made up of steeply terraced hills and bamboo forests, is particu-larly beautiful.

North of Longsheng, the town of **Sanjiang** is close to several Dong villages. It is reached via a very bad gravel road. The Dong villages, crowded with beautifully built brown wooden houses, are extraordinary.

> **off the beaten path**
>
> **DRAGON'S BACKBONE RICE TERRACES** (Longji Titian) – Another impressive spot, about 20 km (12 mi) west of Longsheng, is this mesmerizing pattern of undulating fields that have been cut into the hills up to a height of 2,625 feet and are reachable by bus.

Where to Stay

¢ ⌂ **Longsheng Dajiudian.** One of a few hotels in Longsheng, this hotel offers small but acceptable sleeping quarters. Rooms are damp, but once you turn on the self-adjustable air-conditioner the rooms afford a restful stay. Bathrooms are small and the facilities are bare bones. While Western toilet seats are available in some bathrooms, most are equipped with squatters only. Stand-alone showers are more like an outdoor fixture, but water pressure and temperature are good. ⊠ *Zhongxin Jie* ☎ *0773/751–7718* ⇥ *36 rooms* ⌂ *Restaurant* ▭ *No credit cards.*

¢ ⌂ **Riverside Hotel** (Kaikai Lyushe). This is truly a poor man's heaven. With dormlike rooms and small narrow beds, it feels a bit like an army bunkhouse. However, the rate is under Y100 and it's still good enough to put your feet up after a long day's trekking in the rice paddies. The restaurant serves inexpensive but palatable Chinese meals. ⊠ *5 Guilong Lu* ☎ *0773/751–1335* ⇥ *17 rooms* ⌂ *Restaurant* ▭ *No credit cards.*

Liuzhou

㉙ *4 hrs (130 km [81 mi]) by train southwest of Guilin; 6 hrs (250 km [155 mi]) by train northeast of Nanning.*

Liuzhou is a major railway junction on the Liujiang (Liu River). It first attained importance at the time of the unification of China under the first emperor, Qin Shihuang. But it's primarily associated with the Tang Dynasty scholar and minister of rites, Liu Zongyuan (AD 773–819), who was exiled here in 815 after trying unsuccessfully to have government reforms enacted. Notwithstanding his banishment, in Liuzhou he rose to an eminent position and was widely respected for his good works.

Since 1949 Liuzhou has become an industrial town of considerable importance. There is little left of the handsome town described by Liu Zongyuan. The surrounding scenery is a somewhat paler version of that at Guilin, but you are unlikely to find many other foreigners in the neighborhood.

Named for the Tang Dynasty man of letters, who was dubbed a prince during the Song Dynasty, **Prince Liu Park** (Liuzhou Gongyuan), in the city center, contains his tomb and his ancestral temple, originally built in 821 and rebuilt in 1729. Inside is a stela with Liu's portrait inscribed upon it, as well as a number of others from various dynasties. The park also has caves and hills that you can climb for a panoramic view of the city. ⊠ *East of Liuzhou Guangchang* ▤ *Y2* ⊙ *Daily 8:30 AM–10 PM.*

Fishpeak Hill (Yufeng Shan) is in a park of the same name. The name comes from the reflection of its summit in the **Little Dragon Pool** (Xiaolong Tang) below, which resembles a fish jumping out of the water. The hill is also tied up with a legend, in which a girl named Liu Sanjie sang songs on the mountain, complaining of the oppressive rule of the local despots. Finally she threw herself into the pool, whereupon a fish sprang out and bore her up to heaven. To commemorate this, a song festival is held every year on the 15th day of the eighth lunar month (usually September). ☉ *Daily 8–10.*

In the south of the city, **Horse-Saddle Mountain** (Maan Shan) reaches almost 500 feet. So named because of its shape, it bears inscriptions in its praise and has a cave with interesting geological features. ⊠ *Next to Yufengshan.*

Where to Stay & Eat

¢–$ ✕⌷ **Liuzhou Hotel** (Liuzhou Fandian). The best hotel in town is not wonderful, but it is reasonably well located near Prince Liu Park. In a city not known for its cooking, the Liuzhou's restaurants are an oasis, serving varied regional and Western food. ⊠ *1 Youyi Lu, 545001* ☎ *0772/ 282–4921* 🖷 *0772/282–1443* ⇙ *251 rooms* ⚭ *6 restaurants, bar, shops, business services* ▤ *AE, MC, V.*

Nightlife & the Arts

Check with CITS for performances, such as the traditional Zhuang People's Song Festival, on the third day of the third lunar month (usually April) at which young men court young women by singing love songs to them from opposite mountaintops. When a young woman is interested in one of the men's singing, she responds with her own song; the exchange is known as *duige* (paired singing).

Apart from karaoke parlors, there are a couple of entertaining bars on **Liuzhou Square** (Liuzhou Guangchang).

The Outdoors

The chief option is to get out into the countryside and walk. Try Prince Liu Park for **jogging**.

Nanning

5 hrs (350 km [217 mi]) by train southwest of Guilin; 24 hrs (440 km [273 mi]) by train southeast of Guiyang; 16 hrs (600 km [372 mi]) by train west of Hong Kong.

In the south of Guangxi, Nanning, with a population of about 900,000, is built on the banks of the Yongjiang (Yong River), about 200 km (124 mi) north of the border with Vietnam. Now an important industrial city, 1,600 years ago it was the political and military center of the Jin Dynasty (AD 265–420), outside the rule of the Chinese emperors. Nanning, called Yong at the time, was subjugated only during the Mongolian Yuan Dynasty (1271–1368), when it received its present name.

Nanning became capital of Guangxi province in 1912, and then capital of the Zhuang National Autonomous Region of Guangxi in 1958,

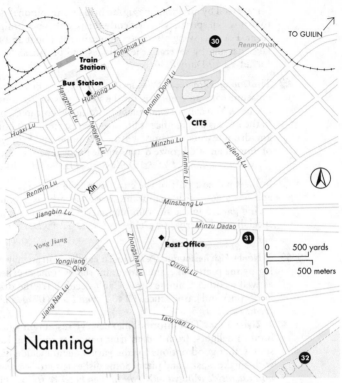

Nanning

when Guangxi became one of five autonomous regions. Like Chengdu and Kunming (although it lacks their charm), Nanning has become a busy exponent of economic policies that bear more resemblance to those of the Western democracies than to those normally associated with communism. It is not a beautiful town but has some interesting sites and lies amid attractive countryside. It has also become a transit point for travelers continuing to Vietnam. Visas can be obtained here, and although it may be necessary to change trains at the border, you should be able to reach Hanoi by rail. The link that was built after World War II was severed in 1979, but in recent years, as relations between China and Vietnam have thawed, the journey has become much easier, to the extent that Chinese travel agents host trips to Vietnam.

30 **People's/White Dragon Park** (Renminyuan/Bailong Gongyuan) is a picturesque, comparatively tranquil area of flowers and greenery, with some 200 species of rare trees and flowers. The **White Dragon Lake** (Bailong Hu) and some pagodas can be found here, as well as the remains of fortifications built by a warlord in the early part of the 20th century. Within the **old fort,** which offers attractive views of the area, is a cannon built by the German Krupp firm, placed here in 1908 as part of a defensive line against a possible French invasion from Vietnam. The lake is traversed by an attractive zigzag bridge, a traditional design intended to throw evil spirits, who evidently thrive only on a straight line, off the scent. For a relaxing afternoon you can rent a boat and float along the lake, passing by several other bridges and pagodas. ⊠ *Renmin Dong Lu* 🚇 *Y2* ⊙ *Daily 8:30–6.*

③ The **Guangxi Provincial Museum** (Guangxi Sheng Bowuguan) is a history museum with an emphasis on the numerous indigenous peoples who live here. You can see examples of traditional costumes, pots, and tools. In the back is a magnificent life-size reconstruction of houses, pagodas, and drum towers, set among attractive pools and bridges. A collection of more than 300 bronze drums made by local people is also on display. ⊠ *Minzu Dadao* 🚇 *Y5* ⊙ *Daily 8:30–11:30 and 2:30–5.*

③ In the southeast part of the city, **South Lake** (Nanhu) covers 230 acres and has a good fish restaurant, as well as a bonsai exhibition and an orchid garden in the surrounding park. Close by is a botanical garden specializing in herbs. ⊠ *Gucheng Lu* 🚇 *Y2* ⊙ *Daily 8–5.*

Where to Stay & Eat

$–$$ ✕ **Nanhu Fish Restaurant** (Nan Hu Yu Fandian). In an ugly concrete building by the pretty lake, the restaurant serves some excellent fish dishes, as well as other Chinese food. Can't decide? Try the dried scallops in hot pepper and garlic sauce. ⊠ *43 Xinhu Lu* 🕾 *0771/585–9705* 🖃 *No credit cards.*

¢ ✕ **Ziyun Xuan.** This informal inexpensive restaurant offers a smorgasbord of delights, from Indian fruit pancakes to Hong Kong–style dim sum. Other good options for the varied menu include local quail soup with gingko, sushi, and pizza. Some dishes tend to be greasy. ⊠ *38 Xinmin Lu, inside Mingyuan Xindu Jiudian hotel* 🕾 *0771/211–8290* 🖃 *No credit cards.*

★ ¢ 🏨 **Majestic Hotel** (Mingyuan Xindu Jiudian). This older luxury hotel, close to the main square and department stores, has been refurbished reasonably well and is efficiently run by its overseas Chinese management. Its low price, excellent location, and fine gym make it a top choice for Nanning. ⊠ *38 Xinmin Lu, 530012* 🕾 *0771/283–0808* 🖷 *0771/283–0811* 🛏 *298 rooms* ⌂ *3 restaurants, in-room safes, minibars, pool, gym, bar, shops* 🖃 *AE, DC, MC, V.*

¢ 🏨 **Xiang Yuan Hotel** (Xiang Yuan Dajiudian). Ignore the ugly, white-tiled, blue-glass exterior of this sprawling hotel just west of the Majestic Hotel. The guest rooms that were renovated in 2002 are considerably homier than the older ones, with new carpets, new furniture, fresh white wallpaper, and firm comfortable beds, so make sure to ask for a new room if you make a reservation. Bathrooms are clean and the service is adequate. ⊠ *59 Xinmin Lu , 530012* 🕾 *0771/282–2888* 🖷 *0771/283–3106* ✎ *xydjd@public.nn.gx.cn* 🛏 *208 rooms* ⌂ *2 restaurants, room service, minibars, gym, bar, lounge, shops, dry cleaning, concierge, business services, airport shuttle* 🖃 *AE, DC, MC, V.*

¢ 🏨 **Yongjiang Hotel** (Yongjiang Binguan). Fairly centrally located, this is a comfortable hotel on the riverside, with well-decorated rooms in a new section (xin fang) and an older part (lao fang) where the rooms are considerably cheaper and rather worn. ⊠ *41 Binjiang Dong Lu, 530012*

☎ *0771/280–8123* 🖷 *0771/280–0535* 📞 *359 rooms* 🍴 *6 restaurants,* *minibars, bar, dance club, shops* 🖃 *AE, MC, V.*

Nightlife & the Arts

The colorful **Dragon Boat Festival** (Duanwujie) takes place on the fifth day of the fifth lunar month, usually sometime in June. Oarsmen row long narrow boats, sitting low in the water, on the river, urged on by a coxswain at the back who screams encouragement as he beats out a rhythm on a drum. Other festivals include the **Zhuang People's Song Festival** (Zhuang Zou Ge Hui), on the third day of the third lunar month (usually April).

Theaters (consult CITS for information) often host performances of local opera, some of which is based on the lore of the Zhuang people.

In Nanning nightlife is concentrated in karaoke parlors and bars in the hotels.

Shopping

Nanning is a good place for crafts by the local minority peoples, including bamboo ware and traditional clothes. Try the **Arts and Crafts Store** (🖃 Xinhu Lu). There is a reasonably priced antiques store with a good selection attached to the Guangxi Provincial Museum.

Side Trips from Nanning

33 More than 700 years old, the little hamlet of **Yangmei Zhen** has the best-preserved Qing Dynasty architecture in Guangxi province. At the heart of it is the alley, with its distinctive Qing-style carved eaves. Inside, the walls are covered with frescoes of landscapes, portraits, and still-lifes, all in remarkably good condition. The outside lane is paved with ancient slates that remain cool on sweltering hot summer days.

Long favored by artists and poets, Yangmei Zhen inspired Wang Wei, one of the Tang Dynasty's greatest poets and painters, to write a quatrain, the traditional four-line lyric that is memorized by scholars and schoolchildren alike: "Indigenous are the red beans to the southern atmosphere/ Sprouting at the first sign of spring./ Come, passionate young gentlemen,/ Pick a few for your beloved." It is believed that, once showered by the red beans, beautiful young women become intoxicated with love. More recently, Yangmei Zhen has become a favorite location for contemporary Chinese filmmakers. For a day trip to the village, contact the regional tour agency: **Nanning Tourist Office** (🖃 71 Chaoyang Lu, Yangmei Zhen ☎ 0772/242–0371) or the **Nanning CITS** (🖃 14 Jiaoyu Lu ☎ 0772/532–0165). ✛ *30 km (19 mi) west of Nanning.*

34 Among the Nanning Hills, the **Yiling Cave** (Yiling Dong) is noted for its exotic and colorful arrangement of illuminated stalactites and stalagmites, through which a path threads for about 1 km (½ mi). It is said to have been the refuge of a Taoist hermit who lived here 1,500 years ago, as well as a retreat for people in difficult times. ✛ *30 km (19 mi) northwest of Nanning* 🎫 *Y10* 🕐 *Daily 9–5.*

35 **Waters of the Soul** (Ling Shui) is a 1-km-long (½-mi-long) lake close to Wuming, with clear spring-fed waters that have a temperature of

18–22°C (64–72°F) year-round. There are bathing pools and pavilions on its shores. ✚ *42 km (26 mi) north of Nanning* 🎫 *Y10* 🕐 *Daily 8:30–5.*

Hua Mountain & the Zuo River

㊱ *200 km (124 mi) southeast of Nanning.*

★ In the **Hua Mountain** (Huashan) vicinity is spectacular scenery, much like the karst formations more famously found around Guilin. Nearby are several examples of **Zhuang rock paintings** depicting very primitive sketches of hunters, animals, and local scenes, sometimes on a gigantic scale (almost 150 feet high). Several dozen sites all told, in varying states of repair, lie within a rough triangle formed by the towns of Chongzuo, Longzhou, and Ningming. They have yet to be precisely dated, though they are believed to be at least 2,000 years old. CITS runs excursions to the area from Nanning.

Beihai

㊲ *175 km (109 mi) southeast of Nanning.*

With its tree-lined streets and wide boulevards, tropical Beihai has managed to retain the peaceful and relaxing demeanor so often associated with coastal towns. The beaches here, in particular **Silver Beach** (Yin Tan), named after its white sands, are good by Chinese standards. Many Chinese tourists also pass through Beihai en route to the neighboring island of Hainan, which is accessible by overnight ferry from Beihai.

Guangxi A to Z

To research prices, get advice from other travelers, and book travel arrangements, visit www.fodors.com.

AIR TRAVEL
There are flights to Beihai from Guangzhou, Changsha, Guiyang, Guilin, Beijing, and Hong Kong. The Guilin airport, amid splendid scenery, is about a half-hour ride outside the town. Information concerning flights to and from Guilin can be obtained from the ticket office of the Guilin Aviation Tourism Company. Flights go to all main destinations in China.

Liuzhou has several flights a week to Guangzhou, Guiyang, Beijing, and Shanghai. Nanning has direct flights daily to Guangzhou and Beijing, regular flights to Kunming and Shanghai, and a weekly flight to Guilin, as well as flights to Hanoi and Hong Kong.

🏢 **Guangxi Airlines** ✉ 1 Huaqiao Lu, Guilin ✉ Chaoyang Lu, Nanning ☎ 0771/243-1459. **Guilin Aviation Tourism Company** ✉ Zhongshan Lu, Guilin ☎ 0773/383-5789.

BOAT & FERRY TRAVEL
There is boat service between Hong Kong and Wuzhou. Nightly river service operates from Liuzhou to Guangzhou (12 hours); accommodation is dormitory-style.

🏢 **China Travel Service** ✉ 10 Qiaoguang Lu, Guangzhou ☎ 020/8333-6888 Ext. 5385. **Chu Kong Passenger Transport** ☎ 0852/2859-1688.

BUS TRAVEL

From Guilin's long-distance bus station on Zhongshan Lu, you can get regular buses to Liuzhou and Nanning. There are also various types of buses (sleepers, with or without air-conditioning) to Guangzhou (16 hours) and Wuzhou (9 hours). Buses and minibuses leave regularly from the Guilin Railway Station for Yangshuo.

Daily buses link Beihai with Nanning, Guilin, and Liuzhou. From Liuzhou buses run frequently direct to Guilin (6 hrs) and once a day to Yangshuo. There is also direct service to between Beihai, Guangzhou, and Nanning, and Longsheng (4 hrs).

🚌 Bus Depots **Guilin Bus Station** ✉ North of railway station, off Zhongshan Nan Lu ☎ 0773/382-2153. **Nanning Main Bus Station** ✉ 65 Huadong Lu ☎ 0771/242-4529. **North Bus Station** ✉ Beida Lu, Nanning ☎ 0771/385-6728.

CAR RENTAL

A car with driver can be arranged through CITS in any of the cities.

CONSULATES

The nearest consulates are in Guangzhou or Hong Kong. In Nanning, visas for Vietnam can be arranged through CITS (Y700). For a Chinese visa extension, contact the Foreign Affairs Office of the Public Security Bureau (PSB) in Guilin or Nanning.

🏢 **PSB** ✉ Keyuan Dadao, Nanning ☎ 0771/289-1260.

EMERGENCIES

For emergencies contact your hotel. The Public Security Bureau, or PSB, can be reached in Guilin, Nanning, Liuzhou, and Yangshuo.

🏢 **PSB Guilin** ✉ Sanduo Lu near Banyan Lake ☎ 0771/282-4290. **PSB Liuzhou** ✉ 65 Youyi Lu ☎ 0772/282-6171. **PSB Nanning** ✉ 25 Youyi Bei Lu ☎ 0771/289-1260. **PSB Yangshuo** ✉ Chengbei Lu.

MONEY MATTERS

Money can be changed in the major hotels or at the Bank of China.

🏦 Banks **Bank of China** ✉ Shanhu Bei Lu just east of Zhongshan Lu, Guilin ✉ Feie Lu south of Liu River, Liuzhou ✉ Binjiang Lu close to river, Yangshuo.

TRAIN TRAVEL

Guilin's railway station is located in the south of the city. There is direct service to most major Chinese cities, but journey times are long. For example, to Beijing and Kunming, it's 30 hours; to Shanghai and Xian, 35 hours. Guangzhou is a bit better at 15 hours.

Liuzhou has direct service to Guangzhou (16 hrs), Changsha (12 hrs), Guilin (4 hrs), Guiyang (17 hrs), Nanning (6 hrs), Kunming (19 hrs), Beijing (24½ hrs), Shanghai (29 hrs), and Xian (31 hrs). Nanning's station is at the northwest edge of town; there are direct trains to Beihai, Guilin, Chongqing, Liuzhou (6 hrs), Beijing, Shanghai, Wuhan, Guiyang (24½ hrs), and Xian.

🚆 Train Information **Guilin Railway Station** ✉ Off Zhongshan Nan Lu ☎ 0773/383-3124. **Liuzhou Railway Tourist Information** ✉ Feie Lu ☎ 0772/361-8201. **Nanning Station** ✉ North end of Chaoyang Lu off Zhonghua Lu ☎ 0771/243-2468.

TRANSPORTATION AROUND GUANGXI

In Guilin the best way to get around, even in the heat, is by bicycle; these can be hired from several places around town. Nanning has motorbike taxis, which means riding in a sidecar. Bicycles can be rented in Yangshuo.

All cities have comprehensive public bus service, with maps available from CITS and the railway station. Otherwise, pedicabs and taxis gather at hotels and at the railway and bus stations.

VISITOR INFORMATION

Tourist Information CITS ✉ 41 Binjiang Lu, Guilin ☎ 0773/282-3518 ✉ 33-1 Dongsi Dajie, at Yaru Lu, Liuzhou ☎ 0772/281-7294 🖷 0772/282-1407 ✉ 40 Xinmin Lu, Nanning ☎ 0771/532-0165 ☎ 0773/882-7102 ✉ Xi Jie near junction with Pantao Lu, Yangshuo.

GUIZHOU

With its green terraced paddy fields, undulating mountains, and traditional villages, Guizhou is among China's most attractive provinces. Because it is also one of the least developed, however, few people pass through the region. Guizhou remains poor partly because of the unpredictable weather (often cloudy and rainy) and partly because of the difficult terrain, with its thin limestone soil.

Guizhou's ethnic groups include the Dong, Hui, Yao, Zhuang, and Miao, among whom the latter are in the majority. The history of Guizhou has been marked by the constant struggle of the native population, now dominated by the Miao, for independence from Chinese subjugation. Chinese influence was established here around 100 BC, when farms and garrisoned towns were spread along the relatively accessible and fertile Wu River, a tributary of the Yangzi which settlers followed down from southern Sichuan. Beyond the river valley, however, the Han Chinese encountered fierce opposition from the indigenous peoples they were displacing, and the empire eventually contented itself less with occupying the province than with extracting an honorary recognition from local chieftains. This did not prevent uprisings: one Miao uprising in the 16th century, near Zunyi, lasted more than two years. Full subjugation didn't come until the Qing era, after war and population growth in Central China sent waves of immigrants flooding into Guizhou's northeast. The tribes rose in rebellion but were overwhelmed, and finally retreated into remote mountain areas.

Consisting of about 30 ethnic groups and forming a quarter of Guizhou's population, these groups remain there today as farmers and woodworkers for the most part, especially the Miao and Dong in the eastern highlands; the Bouyei, a Thai people, in the humid south; and the Yi and Muslim Hui over on western Guizhou's high, cool plateaus. Currently Guizhou is increasingly influenced by Beijing, and occasional conflicts between the Han and the Hui ensue over religious beliefs and practices. The most recent incident occurred in January 2001 when six Hui people were killed by armed police officers in Luoyang, Henan province; the incident touched off a nationwide protest by the Hui people.

Guizhou's capital, Guiyang, has a few sites of interest, but the province's main attraction is Huangguoshu Pubu. The countryside surrounding Guiyang and Kaili is sprinkled with fascinating villages whose impressive wind and drum towers can be visited by tour or boat. Guizhou is one of the few provinces that has managed to preserve traditions that are rapidly disappearing throughout the rest of China.

About 85% of the province is high plateau intersected by mountains, which reach a height of 9,520 feet. It has warm, reasonably comfortable summers and fairly mild winters, the main disadvantage of which is the high volume of rain brought by monsoons.

Guiyang

38 *17 hrs (350 km [217 mi]) northwest of Guilin; 25 hrs (425 km [264 mi]) northwest of Nanning; (850 km [527 mi]) by train northwest of Hong Kong; 29 hrs (1,650 km [1,023 mi]) by train southwest of Beijing.*

The provincial capital of Guizhou, with a population of about 3 million, is noted for its mild climate and its convenience as a starting point for a visit to Huangguoshu Pubu. In the center of the province on a high plateau surrounded by mountains, the city stands on the banks of the Nanminghe (Nanming River). The town's historical name is Zhu, but not a lot is known about its history. There was a settlement here during the Han Dynasty (206 BC–AD 220), and it became a military base during the Yuan (Mongol) Dynasty in the 13th century. It was only during the following dynasty, the Ming, that the town rose to prominence. Then it acquired its city walls (parts of which still stand). It became known as Xingui and only acquired its current name in 1913.

Guiyang, with its large boulevards and metropolitan atmosphere, is a pleasant city. Although like most cities in China it is fast losing its older quarters, enough still remains to render a short stay here worthwhile. The main streets of the sprawling town are Zhonghua Lu and Yan'an Lu.

In the old quarter of the city, the **Hua Jia Pavilion** (Hua Jia Lou), an attractive Ming Dynasty pagoda, is brightly painted with dragons and phoenixes. ⊠ *Huangcheng Dong Lu off Minsheng Lu* ✆ *Free* ⊙ *Daily 9–5.*

The **Pavilion of the Erudite Man** (Jiaxiu Lou) is a collection of wood-shingled pagodas attractively located on the Zhu River in the center of the city. Built during the Ming and Qing dynasties, one pagoda has a handsome triple roof 65 feet in height. Two 18th-century iron pillars stand in the forecourt. ⊠ *East of Fushui Lu and south of river.*

Riverbank Park (Hebin Gongyuan), a pleasant spot of green on the banks of the Nanning River, is most noted for its Ferris wheel. The park has attractions for children in addition to its bamboo groves and ascending walkways. ⊠ *Huangcheng Dong Lu off Minsheng Lu* ✆ *Y2* ⊙ *Daily 6:30 AM–10:30 PM.*

The colorful Ming Dynasty **Wen Chang Pavilion** (Wen Chang Lou) is surrounded with buildings that house a collection of ancient coins and tools. ⊠ *Huangcheng Dong Lu off Minsheng Lu* 🎫 *Y2* ⊙ *Daily 9–5.*

Qianlingshan Park (Qianlingshan Gongyuan) lies just outside the city. Covering an area of about 740 acres, it has a bit of everything—thousands of different species of plants and trees, medicinal herbs, a lake and hills, and a collection of birds and monkeys. The park is dominated by 4,265-foot-high **Mt. Qianling** (Qianlingshan), which has fine views of the town from its western peak. The **Temple of Great Fortune (Hongfu Si)**, on the higher slopes of the mountain, was built in 1672. The **obelisk** on the wooded slopes behind the mountain, erected in 1949, is dedicated to those who fell in the 1946–49 civil war and in the Sino-Japanese War.

★ The **Cave of the Unicorn** (Qiling Dong), discovered in 1531, was used as a prison for the two Nationalist generals Yang Hucheng and Chang Hsueliang, who were accused by the Guomindang of collaborating with the Communists when Chiang Kai-shek was captured at Xian in 1937. ⊠ *Zhaoshan Lu, 1½ km (1 mi) northwest of city* 🎫 *Y2* ⊙ *Daily 8 AM–10 PM.*

★ **Underground Gardens** (Dixia Gongyuan) is the poetic name for a cave about 25 km (15 mi) south of the city. In the cave, at a depth of 1,925 feet, a path weaves its way through the various rock formations, which are illuminated to emphasize their similarity with animals, fruit, and other living things. 🕾 *0851/511–4014* 🎫 *Y15* ⊙ *Daily 8:30–11:30 and 2:30–5.*

en route Huaxi Park (Huaxi Gongyuan; 🎫 Y5 ⊙ Daily 8–6) is a scenic enclave about 18 km (11 mi) south of Guiyang on the banks of the Huaxi, the River of Flowers. The Huaxi Waterfall is nearby; the park itself is filled with teahouses, pavilions, and ornamental scenery.

Where to Stay & Eat

$$ ✕ **Jinqiao Restaurant** (Jinqiao Fandian). Although the decor is rather plain, the menu at this good restaurant offers regional food from Beijing and Canton. ⊠ *34 Ruijin Zhong Lu* 🕾 *0851/582–5310* ▤ *MC, V.*

$–$$ ✕ **Jue Yuan Vegetarian Restaurant** (Jue Yuan Sucaiguan). Excellent vegetarian food, featuring many tofu and eggplant dishes, is the draw here. ⊠ *51 Fushui Bei Lu* 🕾 *0851/582–9609* ▤ *No credit cards.*

★ **¢–$** ✕ **Hongfu Temple Vegetarian Restaurant** (Hongfu Si Sucaiguan). You'll find good vegetarian food here at very reasonable prices in appealing surroundings. ⊠ *Qianling Park* 🕾 *0851/682–5606* ▤ *No credit cards* ⊙ *No dinner.*

★ **¢** 🏨 **Guizhou Park Hotel** (Guizhou Fandian). The most luxurious hotel in town is a high-rise standing in the north close to Qianling Park. ⊠ *66 Beijing Lu, 550004* 🕾 *0851/682–3888* 🖷 *0851/682–4397* 🛏 *410 rooms* 🍴 *2 restaurants, in-room safes, minibars, bar, dance club, shops, business services, travel services* ▤ *AE, DC, MC, V.*

¢ 🏨 **Nenghui Jiudian.** Opened in September 2002, this handsome modern hotel delivers accommodations and facilities above its official three-star designation. Guest rooms are large and bright with high ceilings, big firm beds, modern furniture, and sparkling bathrooms. ⊠ *38 Ruijin Nan Lu, 550003* ☎ *0851/589–8888* 🖷 *0851/589–8622* 🛏 *125 units* ⚭ *Restaurant, in-room safes, minibars, gym, sauna, bar, lounge, shops, dry cleaning, concierge, business services* ▤ *AE, DC, MC, V.*

Nightlife & the Arts

Ask CITS or at your hotel about the occasional performance of **opera** or local song and dance, particularly in the village of Caiguan, near Anshun.

Nightlife is generally limited to karaoke and hotel bars.

Shopping

Crafts to buy in Guiyang and surroundings include batik, Miao and Bouyei embroidery and jewelry, Yuping flutes, lacquerware, opera masks, tea, and Jinzhu glazed pottery.

Anshun

39 *2 hrs (80 km [50 mi]) by bus southwest of Guiyang.*

The most important town in western Guizhou, with some nice old streets and wooden houses, Anshun lies in an attractive area of karst rock formations. Its Ming Dynasty **Wen Temple** (Wen Si), 30 minutes northeast of town off Hongshan Dong Lu, was built at the end of the 14th century and later refurbished. Inside the temple are four 15-foot-high exquisitely carved stone columns; the carved dragons that wind their way up the columns are considered the acme of Chinese stone carving.

Anshun is also a good base for visiting the Huangguoshu Pubu, 45 km (28 mi) to the southwest, and the **Dragon Palace Caves** (Longgong Dong), 32 km (20 mi) to the south. The caves, parts of which are adorned with spectacular rock formations, meander for some 30 km (19 mi) through a chain of mountains; part of them are visible from tin boats that can be hired here for about Y35.

Huangguoshu Pubu

40 *60 km (37 mi) south of Anshun; about 160 km (99 mi) southwest of Guiyang.*

Fodor'sChoice
★

Here the Baishuio River streams over nine sets of rocks, creating nine waterfalls over a course of 2 km (1 mi). At their highest, Huangguoshu Pubu (literally, Yellow Fruit Trees Falls) drop 230 feet and are 263 feet wide. The largest in China, they're set in lush countryside that is home to a number of minority peoples. You can enjoy the falls from afar or by wading across the **Rhinoceros Pool** (Xiniu Jian) to the **Water Curtain Cave** (Shui Lian Dong) behind the main fall. Seven kilometers (4½ mi) downstream are the **Star Bridge Falls** (Xing Qiao Pu). The falls are at their best from May through October and cost Y90.

The most populous group at Huangguoshu are the Bouyei, a Thai people who have a festival in the village at the lunar new year, during which young people sing songs and dance around bonfires in the village center. Wedding ceremonies are often scheduled around this time as it is considered auspicious. The Bouyei are known for their unique production of batik cloth, which you can buy cheaply in the area.

Xingyi

❹ *160 km (99 mi) southwest of Huangguoshu Pubu; 12 hrs (320 km [198 mi]) by bus southwest of Guiyang.*

This small town in the southwest of Guizhou has a minorities museum but is mainly notable for the **Maling Gorge** (Maling Hexiagu), which cuts deeply and impressively into the mountains for 15 km (9 mi), with a path running alongside it. The gorge lies close to the town and is best reached by taxi.

Kaili

❹ *3 hrs (about 200 km [124 mi]) by train east of Guiyang.*

Kaili, the capital of the Qian Dongnan Autonomous region, serves as the starting point for a journey into the minority cultures of the Miao and Dong nationalities that dominate eastern Guizhou. More than 65% of the Qian Dongnan population is Miao, whose villages range along the eastern and northeastern outskirts of Kaili. The villages of the Dong people are located to the southeast. To get a real flavor for these groups, try to catch a glimpse of a local festival; the entire region holds more than 100 festivals annually, many in fall or spring, good times to visit.

In the town itself are a few sights. The **Drum Tower** (Gu Lou) in Jinquanhu Park, is the Dong people's gathering place for entertainment and holiday celebrations. The **Minorities Museum** (Zhou Minzu Bowuguan; ☞ Y10 ☺ Closed Sun.) displays arts, crafts, and relics of the local indigenous peoples. There is a nice **pagoda** in Dage Park.

Outside town the local villages are of great interest. To the north is the Wuyang River, which passes by many mountains, caves, and Miao villages. At **Shibing,** you can take boat rides (contact CITS) through spectacular limestone gorges and arrange stops at these towns. South of Kaili are the Dong villages of **Leishan, Rongjiang,** and **Zhaoxing.**

Zunyi

❹ *3 hrs (160 km [99 mi]) by train north of Guiyang.*

The small town of Zunyi has associations with the Communists' Long March of 1934. Having set out from Jiangxi in October, the party members reached Zunyi in December. In January they held a conference here to analyze their position, a conference at which Mao distinguished himself, establishing a reputation that would ultimately lead him to power. West of town lies the **Zunyi Conference Center** (Zunyi Huiyi Zhi), a Western-style house built in the 1920s for a wealthy landowner. It's furnished as it would have been in the 1930s when the party members held their conference here. The **Long March Museum** (Changzheng Bowuguan) is in an old house and church built by the French in the 19th century. A huge Soviet-inspired monument to the Red Army Martyrs stands in **Phoenix Hill Park** (Fenghuang Shan Gongyuan).

Northwest of Zunyi is the town of **Maotai**, home to the distilleries that produce the liquor of the same name, considered the best in China. ✛ *100 km (62 mi) northwest of Zunyi.*

Guizhou A to Z

To research prices, get advice from other travelers, and book travel arrangements, visit www.fodors.com.

AIR TRAVEL

The Guiyang airport lies to the southwest of the city. There are direct flights between Guiyang and most of the main cities in China, including Beijing, Chengdu, Guangzhou, Guilin, Hong Kong, Shanghai, Xiamen, and Xian. The Guizhou Overseas Travel Service, a branch of CITS, can help with arrangements.

🚩 **Guizhou Overseas Travel Service** ✉ 20 Yan'an Zhong Lu, Guiyang ☎ 0851/586-4678.

BUS TRAVEL

From Guiyang's station there is regular bus service to Anshun (2 hrs), Kaili (5 hrs), Xingyi (approximately 12 hrs over very bad roads), and Zunyi (5 hrs). There are also special tour buses to Huangguoshu Pubu from the Guiyang Railway Station. From Anshun the journey to Xingyi is 8 hrs.

🚩 Bus Information **Guiyang Station** ✉ Yan'an Xi Lu ☎ 0851/685-5336.

CAR RENTAL

Cars with drivers can be hired through the CITS in Guiyang.

EMERGENCIES

🚩 **PSB** ✉ 5 Zhuxin Lu, Guiyang ☎ 0851/676-5230.

MONEY MATTERS

Change money at your hotel or at the Bank of China.

🚩 Bank **Bank of China** ✉ Ruijin Lu, Guiyang.

TRAIN TRAVEL

Direct trains link Guiyang with Chongqing (9 hrs), Guilin (16½ hrs), Kunming (10 hrs), Liuzhou (13 hrs), Nanning (24½ hrs), and Shanghai (30 hrs). The railway station is at the southern edge of the city. There is train service from Guiyang to Kaili (3 hrs) and Zunyi (3 hrs).

🚩 Train Information **Guiyang Railway Station** ☎ 0851/818-1222 ✉ Zunyi Lu.

TRANSPORTATION AROUND GUIZHOU

Maps for the comprehensive public and minibus network around Guiyang can be obtained from bookshops, bus stations, or CITS.

VISITOR INFORMATION

🚩 Tourist Information **CITS** ✉ 20 Yan'an Zhong Lu, Guiyang ☎ 0851/582-5873.

SOUTHWESTERN CHINA

THE YANGZI RIVER & THE BORDERLANDS

10

By Christopher Knowles

Updated by Richard Meyer

SEVERAL OF THE MOST BEAUTIFUL DESTINATIONS IN CHINA ARE HERE in the southwestern region. Sharing borders with Tibet, Burma, Laos, and Vietnam, Yunnan and Sichuan have each integrated influences from their neighbors in a way that has enhanced and enriched their original characters and landscapes. The Yangzi River, and especially its Three Gorges, has recently become the worldwide focus of this region as China proceeds at full throttle with its plans to complete a huge dam across the river by 2009. The first stage of the project is already finished and the water started rising in 2003. Boats must now navigate through a set of locks as they journey down the river.

Sichuan is famous for its delicious spicy cooking, its mountain landscapes, and the Yangzi River, as well as for being the principal home of the panda. In and near the province are the cities of Chengdu, the capital and these days known as the modern gateway to Tibet, and Chongqing, the Yangzi River port where most boats embark on the Three Gorges river cruise. Natural and religious sites are also significant here: Jiuzhaigou, a wonderland of waterfalls and pools that is a home to the Tibetan people; Emeishan, a sacred mountain to Buddhists; and Leshan, site of the largest Buddha in the world. A predominantly rural province whose beauty has attracted the likes of poets Li Bai and Du Fu, Sichuan has often been noted for its distinctive character and people. Beyond the modernization progressing in the cities lies a countryside of paddy fields and serene mountains.

Much of Yunnan is subtropical China, a diverse land of tepid rain forests, the colorful non-Han minority peoples, and the natural wonders of the Stone Forest and the spectacular Tiger Leaping Gorge. A bit more slowly paced than Sichuan, Yunnan brims with the influences of its 26 minority peoples, and every city, from Dali to Xishuangbanna, brings an encounter with some new minority culture. Of all regions, Yunnan seems the most unlike the rest of the China, with its distinctive Burmese, Thai, and minority influences and geographical features. Its capital, Kunming, is a big but more relaxed city. The hot and humid Southwest exudes a languor and a cheerful charm that harks back to a simpler past, far from the formal complexities of mainstream Han China.

Exploring Southwestern China

Sichuan is one of the largest provinces in the country and has the densest population. In the eastern part of the province is the rural Chuanxi plain; to the west is its mountainous border with Tibet. In the north and south are less populated areas; the north is noted particularly for its high mountain landscapes, which are still inhabited by the Tibetan people. Watered by the Yangzi, Sichuan is rich in natural resources.

Yunnan, bordering Burma, Laos, and Vietnam, is the most southwesterly of the Chinese provinces. Home to about a third of China's ethnic minorities, it is also an area of considerable physical variety, from the rain forests of the deep Southwest and the mountains in the north on the border with Tibet, to the alpine plateaus around Kunming.

You can begin your exploration of Southwestern China on a four-day cruise up the Yangzi River before disembarking at Chongqing or flying to Kunming from Chongqing to explore the rest of the region. To cover the most territory, you can start in Chongqing with a one-day excursion to Dazu; move on to Yunnan's Kunming, with its year-round comfortable temperatures, and take a day trip to the Stone Forest. If time allows, spend a few days in the remoter areas, such as Tiger Leaping Gorge and Xishuangbanna. Another alternative is to choose a particular area and go into it in as much depth as time, money, and tolerance allow.

From Chengdu you can easily plan a tour by bus to the sacred mountain Emeishan or to Leshan. Beyond these sites, still comparatively difficult to get to, are the Tibetan villages and magnificent scenery of northern Sichuan. From Kunming you can fly to Dali, Lijiang, Zhongdian, or Xishuangbanna, until recently accessible only by long road journeys.

Although surface connections between the major cities are plentiful, travel times are long and conditions can be poor, particularly on the overnight buses. Fortunately, planes also ply these routes and ticket prices are generally very low, especially on the busier segments. The 20-hour train ride between Chengdu and Kunming, for example, can be reduced to a 1-hour flight. The cost difference between the two options is about Y150 if a good discount is found. But, as with hotels in this region, travel becomes a problem during the holidays. Prices soar and seats can be impossible to reserve.

Keep in mind that everything becomes more difficult in the western part of both provinces. Even with improved infrastructure, the region is still high above sea level and the terrain mountainous. Extra time should be allotted when traveling in this region for the inevitable transportation difficulties and to allow for acclimatization at higher altitudes.

About the Restaurants

It's hard to find a bad meal on the street in any of these cities, but often it's tough to find a great meal in the nicer places. Most of the larger restaurants have become generic Chinese establishments, offering a wide variety of Chinese food and even some foreign dishes, but doing none of it particularly well. These cities are also being "redeveloped," with older establishments moving to new locations and often suffering in the transition.

Prices are very low in the region. Expect to pay under Y1 for a bowl of noodles and about Y4 for each dish at the bigger restaurants. Even the restaurants that specialize in foreign foods tend to keep their prices low, reflecting the low cost of labor and ingredients. There are, of course, exceptions, so it's good to check the menu first. Service is generally very relaxed but friendly and the restaurants extremely casual. Few places require anything more formal than the most down-to-earth travel wear.

The style of the restaurants tends to reflect the rest of the country. The tables are big and round. The furniture is basic and sometimes uncomfortable. The lighting is usually too bright. The better restaurants tend to overdo things and err on the side of too much rosewood and mar-

Any itinerary to the region should start from either Chengdu or Kunming. These two points offer frequent and easy connections to all the major scenic spots in the region. They can be used either as bases or as starting points for longer, sustained trips. When planning a trip to this region, factor inevitable setbacks into the itinerary. If no problems occur, extra sites can be visited.

Numbers in the margin correspond to points of interest on the Southwestern China, Kunming, Chengdu, and Chongqing maps.

10

If you have 4 days

Fly to the historic and growing town of **Chengdu** ㉑–㉘ 🏳 and stay for a day in the city exploring its sites, especially the **Giant Panda Breeding Research Base** ㉘. From there, fly to the natural beauty surrounding **Jiuzhaigou** for two days in the mountains. Return and take a day trip to visit old but lively **Leshan** ㉛ or up the holy mountain of **Emeishan** ㉚.

Alternatively, start in bustling **Kunming** ❶–❾ and work your way northwest. The first stop would be charming **Dali** ❿ for a day. With a short schedule, flying is recommended. After that, take the three- to four-hour bus ride to picturesque **Lijiang** ⓭, visiting the local sites before flying back to Kunming on the fourth day.

If you have 7 days

Combine the two itineraries above. Start in **Chengdu** ㉑–㉘ 🏳 and fly to **Jiuzhaigou,** spending two days there. Return to Chengdu and then fly to **Lijiang** ⓭. From there take the bus to **Dali** ❿ and then the train or plane to **Kunming** ❶–❾. If there's time, an excursion to the **Stone Forest** ❾ can be planned before returning to Chengdu. The itinerary can also be reversed, starting in Kunming rather than Chengdu.

If you have 10 days

An extra three days permits excursions beyond the sites near the major destinations. The trails of **Jiuzhaigou Natural Preserve** ㉜ can be more thoroughly explored and **Tiger Leaping Gorge** ⓯ can be hiked for a day out of **Lijiang** ⓭. You can also extend the **Kunming** ❶–❾ to Lijiang farther west by adding a day for the more rural Buddhist outpost of **Zhongdian** ⓰.

ble. But as in much of China, it is tough to judge a place by how it looks. There is often little relationship between the food and the decor.

Visitors should note that MSG is a main ingredient in most dishes. Those sensitive to the chemical may ask the restaurants to leave it out and they will usually happily comply. But often it is impossible to make a meal completely MSG free.

About the Hotels

With overbuilding, hotel rates are falling through the floor in China, and Southwestern China is no exception. There are just too many rooms and not enough visitors. At the same time, quality is inconsistent. The hotels aren't making enough money to maintain their infrastructure and are sometimes driven to cut corners. With care, however, the discerning traveler can do well. Most hotels will offer discounted prices to even walk-in guests. More generous discounts are available to visitors booking ahead over the Internet. Care should be taken, however, during holiday seasons. Hotels will sometimes charge outrageous prices for substandard accommodations. Even the guesthouses will engage in profiteering.

Western travelers should be aware of "star inflation." Although Chinese hotels utilize a government-mandated five-star rating system, adjustments must be made to the advertised score. Most hotels exist a notch or two below their star rating and there tend to be various substrata within the five-star range. Travelers must also bear in mind that construction materials are often of poor quality and hotels in China don't age well. Conversely, a brand-new three-star hotel can be a great find. It will be cheap yet still in good condition.

Guesthouses have become a bit of a commodity on the backpacker trail in Dali and Lijiang. They all offer about the same to guests, at roughly the same price. But there are subtle differences and it is worth spending a few minutes investigating. Check the water. Hot water at any hour is available at most hostels these days, but water pressure and temperature vary a lot. One hostel offered 24-hour hot water, for example, but cold water only 8 hours a day.

WHAT IT COSTS In Yuan				
$$$$	**$$$**	**$$**	**$**	**¢**
RESTAURANTS over 165	100–165	50–99	25–59	under 25
HOTELS over 1,800	1,400–1,800	1,100–1,399	700–1,099	under 700

Restaurant prices are for a main course, excluding tax and tips. Hotel prices are for a standard double room, including taxes.

Timing

In general, high summer is not the best time (the heat is intense and unrelenting, and the humidity is high)—unless you are visiting the mountainous areas, in which case summer is the best time. Lowland Yunnan is at its best in winter; the rest of the region is most comfortable in either spring or autumn.

Southwest China is festival country. The most famous is probably the mid-April **Water Splashing Festival,** in the rain forests of Xishuangbanna, the purpose of which is to wash away the sorrow of the old year and refresh you for the new. At Hidden Lake, in the area of the Stone Forest near Kunming, the people hold the June 24 **Torch Festival,** which includes, apart from singing and dancing, bullfighting and wrestling. Dali has two festivals of note—the **Third Moon Fair,** from the 15th day to the 21st day of the third lunar month (usually April), in honor of Guanyin, the bodhisattva of mercy; and the **Three Temples Festival,** from the 23rd to the 25th day of the fourth lunar month (usually May). Lijiang has a **fertility festival** on the 13th day of the third lunar month.

Calling All Savvy Shoppers

After eating, shopping may be the next favorite pastime in China. Southwestern China especially offers the visitor plenty of opportunities to splurge. The region has an abundance of cheap, made-in-China, off-the-rack clothing and other bargains for purchase. The big cities, especially Chongqing and Chengdu, are transportation hubs, so whatever is in Guangzhou or Shanghai is likely to be found in these urban centers as well. Much of what's available is counterfeit and it's up to you to sort out the authentic from the fake.

It's the local goods, however, that make Southwestern China shopping special. Walking through the bird and flower markets is always a good way to spend a few hours. Even if you don't buy anything, the atmosphere is wonderful. Serious authentic shopping should be done at the ethnic minority markets in Dali or Lijiang. Batik, bright fabrics, and leather goods are especially interesting. Unique items are there to be discovered, with shapes, styles, and colors unlike anywhere else the world. But beware, just as with the Western brand-name goods, many of the minority products can also be fake, manufactured at factories farther east.

The Hills Are Alive

Eastern Sichuan and northern Yunnan are dominated by the majestic beginnings of the high Tibetan Plateau. If the mountains are high, the gorges are deep, including the Tiger Leaping Gorge in northern Yunnan, which is among the deepest in the world. The Yangzi, the world's third-longest river, cuts across both Yunnan and Sichuan as well as five other provinces before merging with the East China Sea. The land of the Three Gorges, which slice between Chongqing and Yichang in Hubei, looms high above some of the Yangtze's most turbulent waters before flattening out into a gently sloping countryside of rice paddies and rocky shorelines. In Yunnan green hills dotted with villages that have remained unchanged for centuries stretch to the farthest horizon beyond Lijiang, while Xishuangbanna's palm trees sway over the placid Mekong River. In central Sichuan, scalloped terraces rise up hills that give way in the north to crystalline pools and daunting mountains.

If you plan to explore the natural highlights of this beautiful region, you'll need to get your bearings. A line can be drawn, north to south, across Sichuan and Yunnan. To the east there are people, lots of them. Some of the largest cities in the world lie there. On the western side are few people and some of the most beautiful terrain in the world. It is a region of alpine peaks, pristine meadows, and crystal-clear glacial streams. You could spend months exploring these regions, and it would take that long, given the topography and lack of roads, to cover much ground. Fortunately, much is within easy reach. Even in the tourist areas of Yunnan and Sichuan, the masses tend to congregate in certain areas. Walk just a few hundred yards to either side of their path or beyond the parking lot where the masses are dropped off to shop, and you'll find unspoiled nature. But take care; it's easy to get lost in rural regions and storms can come in fast. It's always a good idea to hire a local guide.

The View at 10 Miles an Hour In Yunnan you can spend a couple of days walking along Tiger Leaping Gorge, three hours to the north of Lijiang. In the southwest of Yunnan, Xishuangbanna offers numerous opportunities to explore the subtropical forest (CITS should be able to provide a guide). In Sichuan you can try the three-day pilgrimage up the holy mountain of Emeishan, or hike around Qingcheng Shan, near Chengdu. In the north of the province, in the Aba Autonomous Prefecture, you can go horse trekking in the mountains around Songpan. Beautiful Jiuzhaigou, also in the north of Sichuan, has excellent hiking trails.

If you really want to travel like a local, however, rent a bike. Given the country's poverty, it has long been necessary to pedal. Now, even with a boom in cars, biking is still a preferred form of transportation. It enables the rider to get around easily and cheaply, and avoid the traffic and one-way streets. Chongqing or Kunming are not biking cities. The former has too many hills, the latter too many cars. Chengdu is the city for bikes. It is flat and the tree-lined streets make for pleasant rides. It is also one of the few cities in China not yet so congested with traffic as to make biking unpleasant. Renmin Lu and a few other main thoroughfares do get clogged, but the bike lanes remain open. Dali is another good place for biking; most sites outside the old town are too far to walk and a bike is a fun way to get to them. Renting one and heading down to the shores of Dali's Erhai Hu to an ethnic minority village makes for a full and adventurous day. More intrepid travelers may want to consider a longer bike tour: getting up onto the Tibetan Plateau is a great challenge (with or without a group to lead you) for the fit biker.

Chinese holidays should most definitely be avoided. Costs go through the roof and casual travelers may find themselves out on the street. Chinese New Year in late January or early February (it changes every year) and the National Day Holidays in October fill hotels for about a week. Planes are also packed. Those who must travel on these dates, however, can sometimes find package tours going at low rates (just before the holiday) being sold by agents with unused flights and rooms on their hands.

YUNNAN

Bordering Burma, Laos, Vietnam, and Tibet, as well as the Chinese provinces of Sichuan, Guizhou, and Guangxi, Yunnan is a rich and picturesque province that has absorbed influences from many of its neighbors. Dali, Lijiang, and Xishuangbanna immerse you in an astounding environment of cultural and geographical diversity in a region that is both traditionally and untraditionally Chinese.

Yunnan has always been an unwilling member of the Chinese empire. Originally the home of peoples that now form ethnic minority groups, Yunnan was first absorbed into China during the Qin Dynasty, but long managed to maintain a determined, if uneasy, independence. By the 7th century, for example, the Bai people had established a considerable kingdom, Nanzhao, which by the 8th century had become sufficiently powerful to defeat the Tang armies. In the 10th century the Nanzhao was succeeded by the Dali Kingdom; it was only during the Mongol Yuan Dynasty that this area finally submitted directly to Beijing. Nonetheless, separatist movements persisted into the 20th century.

Yunnan has an area of 394,000 square km (152,000 square mi) and a population of approximately 38 million, including the Bai, Dai, Hani, Naxi, and Yi peoples. Geographically, it is characterized by high plateaus, with an average altitude of some 8,250 feet, which are part of the foothills of the Tibetan Plateau. In the northwest the average altitude reaches 16,500 feet. The climate is varied throughout the province—harsh and wintry in the north, subtropical in the south and southwest, and mild and vernal year-round in the area of Kunming. About one-third of China's minorities live here, while half of the country's plant and animal species originated here.

Kunming

11 hrs (400 km [248 mi]) by train southwest of Guiyang; 21 hrs (650 km [403 mi]) by train southwest of Chengdu; 27 hrs (1,200 km [744 mi]) by train northwest of Hong Kong; 45 hrs (2,000 km [1,240 mi]) by train southwest of Beijing.

Kunming, the capital of Yunnan, with a population of 3.5 million, is one of the more relaxed and pleasant of China's major cities. Like most cities in China, Kunming has lost much of its heritage, but here and there pockets remain. The mild climate has caused Kunming to be known as "the city of eternal spring." Both the city and the immediate area harbor places of interest. Kunming is also the jumping-off point for visits to other sites in the region.

Although there is archaeological evidence of people inhabiting this area as early as 30,000 years ago, the city of Kunming is relatively young by Chinese standards. During the 3rd century BC, the Eastern Zhou Period, General Zhuang Qiao was forced to retreat to the shores of Lake Dian Chi, where he founded Kunming. It became an important military base for subsequent dynasties and eventually became a capital of the Nanzhao Kingdom and a focal point of trade with India, Burma, Indochina, and central China. Later it briefly became the capital when the last prince of the house of Ming took refuge here to rule over the Southern Ming Kingdom. Kunming was 11 years later, in about 1660, by the invading Qing, and the prince was murdered here in 1662.

Kunming did not, however, lose its antipathy to subjugation; in 1855 the local Muslims (a couple of whose mosques still exist in the city), descended from the 13th-century Mongol conquerors, staged an uprising against the Manchurian rulers, a rebellion that was brutally put down. In 1863 a Muslim leader, Du Wenxiu, took the city and proclaimed a new kingdom. It lasted for a decade before the Qing reasserted themselves. The advent of the railways at the beginning of the 20th century turned Kunming into a modern city. Built by the French to link Kunming with Hanoi, the railway made possible the export of the region's copper and forestry resources. The process of modernization continued during the

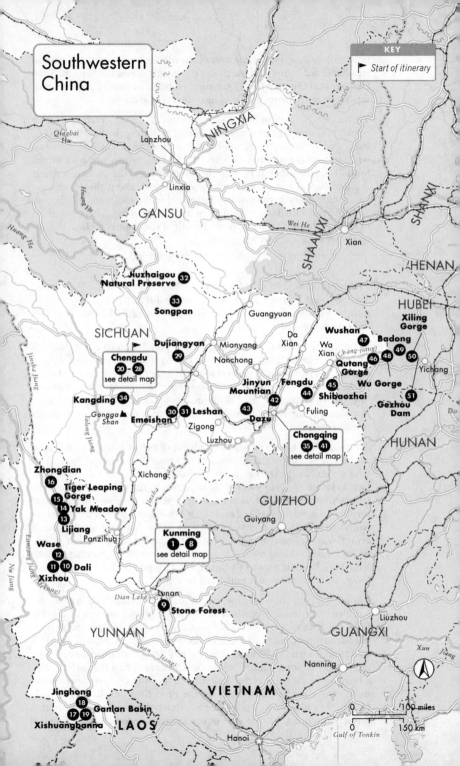

Southwestern China

KEY
▶ *Start of itinerary*

Qinghai Hu

Lanzhou

NINGXIA

Linxia

GANSU

Huang He

Huang He

Wei He

SHAANXI

Xian

HENAN

Juzhaigou Natural Preserve 32

Songpan 33

SICHUAN

Guangyuan

Dujiangyan 29

Mianyang

Da Xian

Nanchong

Chengdu 20 – 28
see detail map

Wushan 47

Wa Xian

Xiling Gorge

Badong 49

(Chang-jiang)

Qutang Gorge 46

48

50

HUBEI

Yichang

Kangding 34

Jinsha jiang

Jinyun Mountian

Fengdu 44

Wu Gorge

Shibaozhai 45

51

Gezhou Dam

Gongga Shan

Emeishan

Leshan 30 31

Zigong

Dazu 43 42

Fuling

Chongqing 35 – 41
see detail map

Dalong jiang

Yangzi

HUNAN

Luzhou

Zhongdian 16

Tiger Leaping Gorge

Yak Meadow 14 15

GUIZHOU

Xichang

Jinsha jiang

Guiyang

Lijiang 13

Panzhihua

Wase 12

Dali 10 11

Xizhou 13

Lancang jiang (Mekong)

Nu jiang

Kunming 1 – 8
see detail map

Dian Lake

Lunan

Stone Forest 9

Liuzhou

GUANGXI

YUNNAN

Yuan jiang

Nanning

Xun Jiang

Jinghong 18

Ganlan Basin

Xishuangbanna 17 19

LAOS

VIETNAM

Hanoi

Gulf of Tonkin

0   100 miles

0   150 km

Second World War, when a number of industries were transferred here to protect them from the invading Japanese. The recent growth of Kunming gradually pushed many industries to the gray outskirts of town, leaving the city center relatively open, with large parks and plazas. Today, however, traffic is becoming a problem all hours of the day. Although the city is compact, with the airport and train station both conveniently located near downtown, it can still be tough to get around.

★ ❶ **Yuantong Temple** (Yuantong Si), the largest temple in the city, dates back some 1,200 years to the Tang Dynasty. It is composed of a series of pavilions and temples partially surrounded by water. There are plenty of vantage points from which to enjoy the busy and colorful comings and goings of worshippers and pilgrims, and there are frequently displays of flowers and miniature plants here. Among the temples is a recent addition housing a statue of Sakyamuni, a gift from the king of Thailand. ⊠ *30 Yuantong Jie* 🗺 *Y4* 🕙 *Daily 8–5:30.*

❷ **Emerald Lake Park** (Cuihu Gongyuan), in the northwest part of the city next to Yunnan University, is one of the better big-city parks in China. Trees and flowers line the paths, and carp and goldfish fill the large pond surrounding the park—as in most traditionally styled Chinese parks. The grounds are immaculately kept and the crowds are at a minimum. Several nice tearooms serving various Yunnan teas are in and just outside the park. ⊠ *Cuihu Nan Lu* 🗺 *Free* 🕙 *Daily 9–9.*

❸ The **Yunnan Provincial Museum** (Yunnansheng Bowuguan) is mostly devoted to the ethnic minorities that live in the province. Although few exhibits have English captions, to a certain extent they speak for themselves, consisting of traditional costumes, photographs of people in their native environment, and the tools and artifacts they made and used. More than anything else it gives you an idea of the extraordinary ethnic diversity that thrives in this region. ⊠ *118 Wuyi Lu* 🕾 *0871/362–7718* 🗺 *Y10* 🕙 *Daily 9:30–5.*

❹ The **Kunming Museum** (Kunmingshi Bowuguan) doesn't get the traffic of the Yunnan Provincial Museum, but the modern structure may be worth a visit for its dinosaur skeletons, if nothing else, as it's a rare thing for Chinese museums. It also has bronze ware and ancient stone structures. ⊠ *71 Tuodong Lu* 🗺 *Y5* 🕙 *Daily 10–5.*

Where to Stay & Eat

Bad restaurants don't survive long in Kunming, so just about any established place in the city is going to have good food. Below are some of the best places serving cuisines hard to come by outside the province.

¢–$ ✕ **Baitadaiwei Canting.** This is the place for Dai minority–style food—including fried pork in banana leaf and black rice in pineapple—at very reasonable prices. Also consider the deep-fried goat cheese, sweetened with *rushan* (sugar). The restaurant has a different feel from most Chinese restaurants. It's less noisy and slightly, though not overly cozy. ⊠ *143 Shanyi Lu* 🕾 *0871/317–2932* ▭ *No credit cards.*

Fodor'sChoice
★

¢–$ ✕ **Guoqiao Mixianguan.** (Across-the-Bridge Noodles Restaurant). This restaurant, minimalist in terms of decor, specializes, of course, in cook-

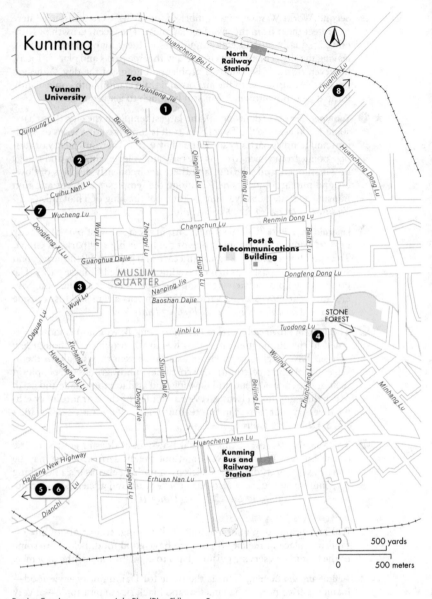

Kunming

ON THE MENU

WITH SO MANY CULTURES in the region having been cut off from the rest of China for so long, many interesting and exotic flavors remain in this part of the world. In Yunnan and, above all, in Sichuan, the food is excellent. Sichuanese-style cooking is hot, spicy, and strongly flavored, a more hearty version of traditional Chinese cooking. It is said that the use of peppers and spices, which abound in the province, came about to make people sweat in summer (in order to cool the eater in the great summer heat) and to warm them in winter. The adaptable Sichuan peppercorn, when mixed with other ingredients, produces a whole range of flavors, from the fish-based soy-and-garlic sauce to the tangy vinegar, pepper, and ginger sauce, which has a hint of sweetness.

A famous Sichuanese dish is mapo doufu (bean curd with minced pork, chili sauce, and hot peppers); its name comes from its supposed inventor, a certain pockmarked Granny Chen, who owned a restaurant in Chengdu. Dumplings are very good in Sichuan, too—for example, tangyuan, which might consist of four separate dumplings, each stuffed with a different honeyed filling. In Sichuan, dandan mian is a must. It is a basic dish of spicy noodles with a touch of garlic and some peanuts, but few do it well. Good dandan mian should have noodles just soft enough and the right balance of spices added. Chongqing's specialty is the Sichuanese huoguo (hotpot), a simmering broth flavored with hot bean paste and fermented soy beans into which raw meat, vegetables, and noodles are dipped to cook. And then there is gongbao jiding or Viceroy's Chicken, a stir-fried dish of diced chicken, peanuts, and green chilies.

Lijiang, in Yunnan, is famous for its baba (pancakes), while the minority peoples in the subtropical part of the province are liberal with coconut, fish, lemongrass, bamboo, and peanuts. Fried river moss and Burmese-style food are delicacies in the border areas. In Kunming, try guoqiao mixian (literally, "across-the-bridge-noodles"), a bowl of hot soup with a film of oil, into which raw pork or chicken, vegetables, and noodles are added to cook. The Muslim quarter also has good food, particularly the noodles and pastries.

Finding these local foods, however, becomes more difficult by the day. Progress is equated with Western food or food from the wealthier parts of the country. Food in the big cities is becoming increasingly less distinctive. To find something different and interesting, you may have to venture a bit off the beaten path, either down the side streets, into the markets, or out of town. Even then, it is a hit-and-miss game. The food of some of the ethnic minorities is heavy and bland to start and has lost much of its flavor as locally grown and raised ingredients have been replaced with the canned and processed. But great rewards come to those who are persistent. Every now and then, the odd canteen or anonymous-looking noodle stand will yield something both unusual and impressive.

it-yourself guoqiao mixian ("across-the-bridge noodles"). ✉ *148 Xichang Lu* ☎ *0871/414–4976* ▤ *No credit cards.*

¢ ✕ **Cheng Bian Xiang Restaurant.** This is a simple cafeteria-style eatery that's a favorite with locals. You can try noodles at one end, a plate of rice with your choice of three vegetables and three meats in the middle, and dumplings on the far end. This down-to-earth but clean restaurant has curt yet friendly service. There's no menu here; just point. ✉ *357 Huancheng Dong Lu* ☎ *0871/331–1323* ▤ *No credit cards.*

¢–$$$ ▦ **Golden Dragon** (Jinlong Fandian). Once a joint venture, now locally owned, this hotel offers moderately priced rooms and a reasonable standard of service. The location is very convenient to the railway and bus stations. ✉ *575 Beijing Lu, 650011* ☎ *0871/313–3015* 🖷 *0871/313–1082* ⌨ *150 rooms* ⌂ *2 restaurants, pool, hair salon, bar, shops, business services* ▤ *AE, D, MC, V.*

$ ▦ **Horizon Hotel.** This five-year-old establishment is about as good as it gets in Kunming. Staff is courteous and location central. The rooms go from standard high-end and very comfortable to tacky with overstuffed couches and too much rosewood, so ask to see the room first. ✉ *432 Qingnian Lu, 650021* ☎ *0871/316–6666* 🖷 *0871/319–2118* ⌨ *440 rooms* ⌂ *7 restaurants, coffee shop, gym* ▤ *AE, D, MC, V.*

¢–$ ▦ **Green Lake Hotel** (Cuihu Binguan). In a pleasant part of town near the university and Cuihu Park, just outside the center, the hotel has old and new sections. The lobby and coffee shop are restful, and the rooms are comfortable. The Chinese restaurant hosts performances of traditional music. Once a Hilton, it still maintains international standards. ✉ *6 Cuihu Nan Lu, 650031* ☎ *0871/515–8888* 🖷 *0871/515–3286* ⌨ *307 rooms* ⌂ *4 restaurants, bar, shops, business services* ▤ *AE, D, MC, V.*

¢ ▦ **Holiday Inn Kunming** (Yonghua Jiari Jiudian). Close to the city museum, this hotel has an inner courtyard with attractive Chinese architectural accents. The live music on weekends and Thai/Western food attract Kunming's community of expatriates. The rooms are standard and the service poor. ✉ *25 Dongfeng Dong Lu, 650011* ☎ *0871/316–5888* 🖷 *0871/313–5189* ⊕ *www.sixcontinentshotels.com/holiday-inn* ⌨ *237 rooms* ⌂ *4 restaurants, pool, bar, dance club, shops, baby-sitting, laundry service, business services* ▤ *AE, D, MC, V.*

¢ ▦ **Kunming Fandian.** The oldest of the luxury hotels in town is centrally located and has reasonably comfortable rooms. There is a pool and a practice range for golfers on the premises. ✉ *52 Dongfeng Dong Lu, 650051* ☎ *0871/316–2063* 🖷 *0871/316–3784* ⌨ *320 rooms* ⌂ *3 restaurants, driving range, pool, gym, 2 bars, business services* ▤ *AE, D, MC, V.*

Nightlife & the Arts

The main arts possibilities are minority dance performances or acrobatic displays. The **Yunnan Xiu** troupe gives performances Monday through Saturday evenings at 6:30. Tickets can be purchased at the **Kunming Art Theatre** (✉ Nianqing Lu ☎ 0871/316–5583).

In addition to the numerous karaoke bars, several Western-style bars have popped up around town. Many of these, as well as Chinese teahouses, cluster outside Cuihu Gongyuan and near Yunnan University. These tend to fill up with rowdy students in the evening. The **Bluebird** (✉ 132 Dongfeng Dong Lu ☎ 0871/531–4071) is a comfortable and relaxed café-bar that attracts mostly locals. The **Holiday Inn** (✉ 25 Dongfeng Dong Lu ☎ 0871/316–5888) has a good bar and disco.

The Outdoors

Bicycles can be rented at the **Kunming Fandian** (✉ 52 Dongfeng Dong Lu ☎ 0871/316–2063). You can jog in Cuihu Gongyuan or, even better, jog or hike around **Lake Dian**, near Kunming.

Shopping

Yunnan specialties include jade, batiks and other ethnic clothes and fabrics, embroidery, musical instruments, jewelry, marble, pottery, tea, and medicinal herbs. The main shopping streets are Zhengyi Lu, Dongfeng Dong Lu, Beijing Lu, and Jinbi Lu. The **Flower and Bird Market** on Tongdao Jie is worth a visit for the atmosphere and the array of antiques—fake and otherwise—and crafts on sale. The **Kunming Antiques and Handicrafts Shop** (Kunming Wenwu Shangdian), next to the Holiday Inn on Dongfeng Dong Lu, has items of interest. The **Yunnan Antiques Store** (Yunnan Wenwu Shangdian) on Qingnian Lu has objects from the region.

Side Trips from Kunming

Most of the reasons for coming to Kunming lie outside the city. The strangest and most compelling of the famous tourist sites is the Stone Forest (Shilin), a minimum of two hours by train from Kunming.

⑤ **Lake Dian** (Dian Chi), with a shoreline of about 150 km (93 mi), lies just south of Kunming. As it is still exploited for fishing, junks with their traditional sail and rigging can be spotted at work here (it was the model for the Kunming Lake in the Summer Palace in Beijing). Away from the industrial areas, it is a pleasant place for its scenery, sites, and general rural atmosphere.

At the lake's northern tip **Daguan Park** (Daguan Gongyuan), which was first landscaped in 1682 for a Buddhist temple, offers rowboats, pavilions, and the 1690 Daguan Tower, inscribed with a rhapsody on the lake's beauty by the Qing poet Sun Ranweng. Boats can be taken from the park's dock to **Shan Yi village** at the foot of the Western Hills.

Zheng He Park (Zheng He Gongyuan) lies near the southeastern point of the lake. It is dedicated to the admiral of the same name, a Muslim eunuch, who between 1405 and 1433 made a series of extraordinary sea voyages throughout Asia and Africa, leading to the establishment of trading links between China and large parts of the world. In a mausoleum here tablets record his life and achievements.

Near the lake's northeast end is another park, Haigeng Gongyuan, which features the **Yunnan Minorities Village** (Yunnan Minzu Cun), a sort of living ethnographic display of the architecture and ways of life of the province's various minority peoples. It has life-size replicas of the towers at Dali and Xishuangbanna—worthwhile if you don't have the chance to visit other parts of Yunnan. Buses from West Bus Station, on Renmin Zhong Lu, serve the road around lake.

★ ❻ **Western Hills Forested Park** (Xishan Senlin Gongyuan) stretches more than 40 km (25 mi) along the western shores of Lake Dian. As its name implies, it is a mostly wooded nature park, ideal for hiking or strolling. Footpaths begin at both Gaoyao and Shan Yi. It's also possible to drive to the places of interest in the park. Several temples of average interest are scattered throughout the area, mostly on mountaintops, situated for the best views of the lake.

The verdant grounds of **Huating Temple** (Huating Si), a relic from the Nanxia Kingdom dating from the 11th century, lie at the foot of the hills. Rebuilt in the 14th century, it was further embellished in the final two dynasties. Farther up is the pretty **Taihua Temple** (Taihua Si), from the Ming Dynasty. Next to the temple is the **Tomb of Nie Er.** Nie Er was the composer of the Chinese national anthem. Admission to all three is Y3 each.

Behind the tomb is a chairlift (Y10, Y15 on weekends) rising to the top of the mountain. Close to the top is the Taoist **Sanqing Temple** (Sanqing Ge), formerly the residence of a Yuan (Mongol) Dynasty prince. Finally you reach the **Dragon Gate** (Long Men), a network of narrow corridors, shrines, and grottoes dug out of the hillside by Taoist monks between 1781 and 1835 (Y10). Tremendous views open out across the lake from up here, but the rock corridors are narrow and become crowded.

❼ Northwest of Kunming is the much-restored Tang Dynasty **Bamboo Temple** (Qiongzhu Si), the birthplace of Zen Buddhism in Yunnan. It is said that as two princes of the Kingdom of Dali were hunting, they came across a horned bull, which they pursued to the hill on which the temple stands. It disappeared in a cloud of smoke, through which the princes espied a monk whose staff sprouted to become a grove of bamboo. During its last major reconstruction, between 1883 and 1890, the abbot of the day employed a lay Buddhist, a master sculptor from Sichuan, to fashion 500 *arhats* or *lohans* (life-size statues of those freed from the material shackles of earthly existence) of particular vividness. ✛ *In hills about 10 km (6 mi) northwest of city; minibus from West Bus Station on Renmin Zhong Lu* 🚌 *Y10* 🕐 *Daily 8–5.*

❽ The Taoist **Golden Temple** (Jindian Si) sits on a forested hill northeast of Kunming. Its current incarnation dates from the Ming Dynasty, after which, during the early Qing, it was enlarged when it became the residence of Wu Sangui, a general sent here to deal with the recalcitrant locals. The most interesting construction is a pavilion, built on a vast slab of Dali marble and surrounded by a crenellated wall that is much decorated with cast bronze, from which the temple acquired its name. The bronze work, which is used in many parts of the pavilion's construction, is meant to resemble timberwork; the use of real timber has been kept to a minimum. Among the many trees in the temple are two camellias thought to date from the Ming Period. There is also a large bronze bell cast in 1423. ✛ *About 10 km (6 mi) northeast of town; Bus 10 from North Railway Station at the north end of Beijing Lu* 🚌 *Y15* 🕐 *Daily 8–5.*

One of the most important sites near Kunming is a geological phenomenon known as the **Stone Forest** (Shilin). It is composed of closely knit outcrops of dark gray limestone karst that have weathered into interesting shapes since their formation beneath a sea some 270 million years ago. Many have been given names to describe their resemblances to animals (phoenixes, elephants, and turtles) and people. The journey here takes you through hilly countryside dotted with the timber-frame architecture typical of the area.

You can take walks through the forest, which is watered with small lakes and pools; you'll find plenty of Sani tribeswomen eager to act as guides and sell you their handicrafts. The area that most tourists go to has, inevitably, become rather commercialized, but there are plenty of similar formations in other parts of the park if you wander off the main trail.

There are several ways to get to Shilin from downtown Kunming. The best is by train, which leaves once a day at 8:30 AM; a return train leaves Shilin in the afternoon (two hours each way, Y30 round-trip). Many people opt for one of the cheap bus tours (Y20 round-trip), which leave each morning from the area around the train station. However, the bus trip takes twice as long as the train ride—at least four hours—as the driver makes numerous "rest" stops at souvenir stands and junk stores along the way. ⊹ *Lunan, 125 km (78 mi) southeast of Kunming* ⌷ *Y80* ⊙ *24 hrs.*

Dali

★ ⑩ *5 hrs (250 km [155 mi]) by bus northwest of Kunming; 4 hrs (140 km [87 mi]) by bus south of Lijiang.*

The charming town of Dali, at the edge of the Erhai Lake (named for its ear shape), has become something of a cult destination for independent travelers, like a miniature Katmandu. The old gate towers stand intact at either end of the town, and between them stretches a long, single main street (Fuxing Lu) intersected by smaller streets leading to the lake on one side and up to the hills behind. The most heavily frequented street, Huguo Lu, known to locals as the *Yangren Jie* (Foreigner Street), is lined with a whole variety of quaintly named cafés and restaurants that are largely aimed at the young foreigners passing through. Nearby, street markets and food stands abound among shops selling jade, clothing, and batik.

Dali is now the capital of the Bai Autonomous Region, a sop by the Beijing government to the independence aspirations of minority peoples. The Bai, a branch of the Yi people, first settled this area some 4,000 years ago. During the Tang Dynasty, with the support of the Chinese, the Nanzhao Kingdom (AD 738–902) exerted considerable influence over large parts of Yunnan province and even Burma. Dali, called Taihe at the time, was the kingdom's capital. During the Song Dynasty the independent Dali Kingdom grew up before the region finally came under the heavy hand of Beijing in the Mongol Period.

It is worth noting that there are actually *two* Dalis. One is the charming old city of Dali, Dali Gucheng; the other is an ugly, gray model of

Chinese sprawl called Dali Xiaguan. Unfortunately, most bus traffic is routed through the latter. If you find yourself in Dali Xiaguan, jump in a taxi or on the No. 4 bus, which will take you to the interesting part of town.

Walking down almost any street from Fuxing Lu will bring you, after about a half hour, to the shore of **Erhai Lake** (Erhai Hu). Here, apart from the scenery, you may catch a glimpse of fishermen with their teams of cormorants tied to their boats awaiting the chance to go fishing. The birds are used in much the same way as they are in Guangxi province— with a sort of noose about their necks that prevents them from swallowing the fish once they have caught them. There is also a temple on **Putuo Island** (Xia Putuo Dao).

Regular ferry crossings around various parts of the lake offer, in good weather, wonderful views of the lake, distant pagodas, and the surrounding mountains. The ferries usually cost between Y30 and Y70 (depending on your ability to bargain in Chinese). More interesting perhaps—and cheaper—would be to hire one of the local fisherman to paddle wherever you want to go. ✥ *Boats leave from Zhoucheng.*

The most outstanding landmarks in Dali, the **Three Pagodas** (San Ta), are used as a symbol of the town and appear on just about every calendar of Chinese scenery. The largest, 215 feet high, dates from AD 836 and is decorated on each of its 16 stories with Buddhas carved from local marble. The other two pagodas, also rich in carved decoration, are smaller and more elegantly classical in style. In moments when the water is still, you can see their reflection in a nearby pool. ✥ *Main road north of town; easy cycling distance or 20-min walk* 🎫 *Y40* ⊙ *Daily 7 AM–8 PM.*

Although its story is little more than a piece of local hokum, **Butterfly Spring** (Hudiequan), about 25 km (16 mi) north of Dali, is a beauty spot. It consists of a pool surrounded by a marble balustrade, overhung by an ancient tree whose flowers are said to resemble butterflies. Another tale holds that two lovers committed suicide here to escape the wrath of a cruel king and are among the butterflies that tend to congregate here every spring. The nearby village is made up of the indigenous, non-Han Chinese Pei tribe. ✉ *Lijiang Lu, north of town, or ferry through CITS* 🎫 *Y25.*

★ **Cangshan** (Green Mountain), whose highest peak rises to over 14,765 feet, is the mountain range that can be seen from just about any place in Dali. A 16-km (10-mi) path carved into the side of the mountain halfway between the summit and the old town of Dali offers spectacular views of town, Erhai Lake, and the surrounding villages. There are also several temples, grottoes, and waterfalls just off the main trail. If you don't want to climb several thousand feet to the path, there is a cable car (more like a ski chair, but they call it a "car") that will take you up for Y25; the ride down costs Y50. ✥ *To get to cable car entrance, follow Yuer Lu outside old town to bottom of hill.*

Where to Stay & Eat

Dali has numerous small restaurants aimed at foreign travelers. Most are around the intersection of Huguo Lu and Fuxing Lu; although the owners and the names come and go, these establishments all generally provide friendly service and a variety of local and foreign-inspired cooking, much of it quite good. You can also try some of the smaller Chinese establishments for a taste of local Bai cooking. There are many guesthouses as well around Huguo Lu, with rooms starting from Y50 and dormitory beds from Y10. Some have a certain charm, though some rooms are without bathrooms. Be sure to have a look at the facilities before money is exchanged.

★ ¢–$ ✕ **Jack's Place.** A favorite haunt for foreign travelers, the food is a big draw, especially its pizzas and desserts. But it's Jack's book collection that earns special praise. The shelves of English-language literature and pulp are the best in town and for many miles around. The books are not for sale, only barter. At least two must be left to take another away. ✉ *82 Bo'ai Lu* ☎ *0872/267–1572* ▭ *No credit cards.*

¢ ▦ **Higherland Inn.** Up in the verdant mountains behind the old town sits the Higherland Inn. At 8,500 feet, just off Cloud Road, it's the perfect place to start a hike, enjoy the view, or just get up into the thin air. Accommodations are hostel decor and prices. Food and drink are roughly the same as those in town. There is a booking office in Dali Old Town at 67 Bo'ai Lu, near Renmin Lu. ✉ *Cangshan Daorendong; a short walk after getting off cable car, 671003* ☎ *0872/266–1599* ↩ *8 rooms* ⌂ *Library* ▭ *No credit cards.*

¢ ▦ **No. 5 Guest House** (Siji Kezhan). No. 5, or Old Dali Inn, is attractively built around a wood-and-bamboo courtyard It's a comfortable hotel and a favorite with travelers. The new wing built in back has added more rooms without ruining the pleasant feel of the original structure. Plenty of DVDs are available to watch on the big communal TV and Internet is free for guests. ✉ *51 Bo'ai Lu, 671003* ☎ *0872/267–0382* 🖷 *0872/267–5360* ⊕ *www.dalitour.gov.cn/sijiinn.htm* ↩ *55 rooms* ⌂ *Restaurant, Internet* ▭ *No credit cards.*

¢ ▦ **No. 4 Guest House.** For Foreigner Street locations, this is one of the better places to stay. Located at the far end of the strip and with an extensive courtyard, it's close to the action yet still quiet. The restaurant at the guesthouse does a good job with a wide selection of local and international foods. The staff is particularly good at finding plane and train tickets, for a fee of course, when others can't. ✉ *Huguo Lu, 671003* ☎ *0872/267–2093* ↩ *50 rooms* ⌂ *Restaurant, Internet, laundry service* ▭ *No credit cards.*

¢ ▦ **Yuyuen Kezhan.** There are no restaurant, no bar, and no coffee shop, but this newly redecorated family-run guesthouse-hotel offers some of the nicest rooms in its price range. It is located close to the center of old town on a quite street. Despite its minimal offerings, the guesthouse does laundry and provides free Internet access. ✉ *8 Honglongjin, 671003* ☎ *0872/267–3267* ↩ *20 rooms* ⌂ *Laundry service, Internet* ▭ *No credit cards.*

Nightlife & the Arts

There is the occasional performance of traditional song and dance, but most entertainment is aimed at backpackers and comes in the form of small bars-cum-restaurants and cafés along Huguo Lu. An art exhibition also makes an appearance now and then.

The Outdoors

There are plenty of opportunities for hiking in the hills around Dali and biking to all the other villages in the area. Mountain bikes are available for rent at most hotels and all along Yangren Jie.

Shopping

Local shops in Dali sell marble in various forms as well as batik (mostly imported from Guizhou province), clothes, Bai minority jewelry, and local art. Clothes can be made to measure. Bargaining is expected everywhere. Don't be put off by the aggressiveness of the Bai merchants. They take pride in their negotiation skills and get pushy and loud at time. Most often it is all in fun.

Side Trips from Dali

A number of interesting villages or small towns lie fairly close to Dali. **⑪** Among the prettiest towns is **Xizhou**, which has managed to preserve a fair amount of Bai architecture. The daily morning market and occasional festivals of traditional music attract a fair number of tourists from neighboring Dali. There is also a grungy hotel, which accepts foreigners, if you happen to miss the last bus (Y4) back. ✚ *About 20 km (12 mi) north of Dali.*

The town of Shaping used to be the place to go to see a lively market. But the locals started hawking fake "authentic" ethnic goods and the visitors **⑫** stopped coming. For the time being, **Wase** is the preferred destination for traditional Bai clothing and trinkets. The market is only in full swing on the 5th, 10th, 15th, 20th, 25th, and 30th of each month. ✚ *On opposite shore of Erhai Hu from Dali Old Town. Boats can be arranged from town or by going down to shore; a car can be taken as well.*

Lijiang

★ **⑬** *4 hrs (150 km [93 mi]) by bus north of Dali; 8 hrs (320 km [198 mi]) by bus northwest of Kunming; 20 hrs (550 km [341 mi]) by bus southwest of Chengdu.*

Lijiang is the old capital of the Naxi people, kin of the Tibetans, who are traditionally matriarchal and whose music and Dongba script are unique to them. Badly damaged by an earthquake in early 1996, the delightful town sits on a plain dominated by the snowcapped Jade Dragon Snow Mountain (Yulong Xue Shan). You may have thoughts of Shangri-la when you are lost among the cobblestone streets and alleys of the small old town, with its icy, fast-flowing stream (the River Li) and charming bridges. The modern suburbs are unfortunately composed of dreary streets lined with concrete apartment blocks. Predictably, it was the old town that suffered most from the earthquake, but a serious restoration project is under way. UNESCO named it a World Cultural Heritage Site in 1997.

One of the highlights of a visit to Lijiang is attending a concert of Naxi music in the old town. Because of Lijiang's isolation, the authentic sound of ancient Chinese music—elsewhere destroyed by the Cultural Revolution—has survived here.

The town is set amid beautiful scenery, including the 18,360-foot **Jade Dragon Snow Mountain** (Yulong Xue Shan). The well-maintained road to the scenic area is a nice drive, passing numerous minority villages and offering fine valley and mountain views. The park entrance is about a 30-minute drive from the old town. Admission is Y80. In the town itself, the **Black Dragon Pool Park** (Heilong Tan Gongyuan) is home to the **Dongba Research Institute Museum** (Dongba Yanjiu Suo), a museum devoted to the study of minority cultures in the region. It also has the Ming **Deyue Pavilion** (Deyue Tian), a lovely pavilion where locals come to play cards and drink tea. ⊠ *Xinde Lu* ✆ *Y20* ⊙ *Daily 6:30 AM–8 PM.*

In the vicinity you can visit monasteries with fine frescoes at **Fuguo**, **Longquan**, and **Baisha** (the former Naxi capital). Excellent views of Jade Dragon Snow Mountain can be had from a meadow halfway up its slopes, reached by chairlift.

★ ⑭ It takes a bit of doing, but getting to **Yak Meadow** (Maoniuping) on the way up Jade Dragon Snow Mountain is worth it. The grassy plain, at a height of 12,000 feet, offers a spectacular view of Jade Dragon Snow Mountain. Yak Meadow has, you guessed it, yaks, as well as a small monastery and some local Tibetan log cabins. To get there, hire a car, pay the Y80 for admission into the Jade Dragon Snow Mountain Scenic Area and the environment tax, fork out another Y60 for a rather frightening cable car ride, and then walk past a mile of hawkers.

Nightlife & the Arts

Lijiang offers a number of ethnic minority shows, beyond the free dancing that can be enjoyed every evening in the main square. The shows are a bit expensive, for Lijiang at least, and can border at times on kitsch, but may well be worth a visit.

The **Mountain Spirit Show** offers fire eating and other extraordinary feats by the Yi shamen. The performance is just outside the old town. ⊠ *Meeting Hall of Lijiang, Minzu Lu* ✆ *Y120* ⊙ *Daily 8 PM.*

The **Nationality Culture Exchange Center Theater** is home to the Grand Dancing Epic which is, well, epic. The two evening shows, which are performed by the Yi ethnic group and include singing, dancing, and a bit of flying, are staged in the imposing theater located appropriately across from the chairman Mao statue just outside the old town. ⊠ *National Cultural Exchange Theater, Xin Dajie* ✆ *Y120* ⊙ *Daily 7:30 and 9:20.*

For the cultural glutton, there's also Naxi music to be heard at the Naxi Concert Hall. ⊠ *Naxi Concert Hall, Dong Dajie Old Town* ✆ *Y100* ⊙ *Daily 8 PM.*

Where to Stay & Eat

Long the center of Lijiang dining, Yangren Jie, off the main square, is looking a bit tired these days. The workers at the restaurants and bars are getting jaded and the food is relatively expensive and not particularly good. It's a place for a quick bite or a late-night beer, but better to venture off the road most traveled for better options.

Accommodation in Lijiang has long meant staying in a guesthouse. They are easy to find—if no one offers one just start asking—cheap, and relatively clean. Outside of national holidays, rooms are plentiful. But the hotels are worth considering as well. A room glut has forced prices at hotels down to guesthouse levels and some of the guesthouses are looking a bit shabby.

¢–$ ✕ **Lamu's House of Tibet.** The two-story structure offers a full range of Western food, from vegetarian lasagna to french fries, as well as Chinese, Tibetan, and Naxi food. The atmosphere is pleasant and the staff very helpful. ✉ *56 Xiyi Jie* ☎ *139/8704–9750* ▭ *No credit cards.*

¢–$ ✕ **Prague Café.** The top choice for good coffee, the café's food is good as well. The restaurant also has a nice book collection, free Internet, and a small store in back. ✉ *80 Mishixiang Xiyi Jie, near Old Well* ☎ *0888/512–3753* ▭ *No credit cards.*

¢–$ ✕ **Well Bistro.** Near the Old Well, this small eatery serves a nice variety of international food at reasonable prices in a pretty setting away from the Square Street touts. Its coffee is very good and it's a top choice for breakfast. ✉ *32 Mishixiang Xiyi Jie* ☎ *0888/518–6431* ▭ *No credit cards.*

¢–$$$$ ▦ **Yulong Garden Hotel.** One of the few "four-star" options in town, this hotel offers a pleasant combination of traditional architecture and modern convenience. It may not be special but is very clean and well maintained, and the water is reliable. ✉ *Dinghong Lu, 674100* ☎ *0888/518–2888* 📠 *0888/518–7999* ⇥ *150 rooms* ⚿ *Restaurant, business services* ▭ *AE, MC, V.*

¢ ▦ **Ancient Stone Bridge Inn.** Two of the rooms in this guesthouse look directly out over a brook, a small pedestrian street, and two bridges. It's the perfect Lijiang setting. It's a bit more expensive than the average guesthouse, but the setting may justify the extra few yuan. The front door locks at midnight. ✉ *71 Wuyi Jie Xingrenxia, 674100* ☎ *0888/518–4001 or 139/8882–5829* ⇥ *10 rooms* ▭ *No credit cards.*

¢ ▦ **First Bend Hotel.** Renovated after being damaged in the 1996 earthquake, this is one of the old town's most charming hotels. The building is mostly wood, replicating traditional Naxi architecture, and there is a relaxing courtyard in the center. The hotel also operates an excellent restaurant serving Naxi and Chinese dishes. ✉ *43 Mishixiang Xiyi Jie, 674100* ☎☎ *0888/518–1688* ⇥ *18 rooms* ⚿ *Restaurant* ▭ *No credit cards.*

¢ ▦ **Senlong Hotel.** Although slightly overpriced (on the high end of the budget price category) when compared with the hostel competition, this is the best and most modern of the hotels in the old town. There is a lovely garden area in the center of the hotel, and the rooms are large and nicely furnished. The restaurant serves a wide variety of local dishes. ✉ *Minzu Lu, 674100* ☎ *0888/512–0666* 📠 *0888/518–1968* ⇥ *243 rooms* ⚿ *Restaurant, sauna, bowling, business services* ▭ *No credit cards.*

Side Trips from Lijiang

⑮ A 2½-hour ride from Lijiang, **Tiger Leaping Gorge** (Hutiao Xia) is one of the great, and mostly unspoiled, scenic spots in not only Yunnan province, but surely in China as well. Here the Yangzi begins its long journey toward Shanghai, where it pours into the Pacific. The gorge,

FodorsChoice
★

one of the deepest in the world, is about 30 km (19 mi) long and can be hiked over two or three days. The trail follows the lower mountains on the northern side of the gorge, offering magnificent views of Jade Dragon Snow Mountain's alpine peaks. Another trail actually descends into the gorge and runs alongside the river. If there is any "must-visit" place in Yunnan, this is it.

Tiger Leaping Gorge can be hiked from either direction. Most trekkers choose to start from the quaint city of Daju, at the eastern end of the gorge, and finish at Qiaotou, a miserable truck stop of a town at the western end. If you plan on spending a few days in one of the villages around Tiger Leaping Gorge recuperating after your hike, start from Qiaotou. There are five guesthouses in the gorge itself, scattered at distances to accommodate hikers at any stage of their trek. All offer food, hot showers, and beds for Y10–Y20.

16 Seven hours from Lijiang on a high mountain plateau bordering Sichuan and Tibet, **Zhongdian** makes an interesting trip for those who want to see Yunnan's Tibetan and Naxi societies without the tourists and souvenir shops of Lijiang and Dali. The city, in a state of constant repair and reconstruction, is ugly and dusty, but the snowcapped mountains rising around Zhongdian make the trip worthwhile.

For those who aren't traveling as far as Tibet, **Songzanlin Temple** (Songzanlin Si), about 5 km (3 mi) outside Zhongdian's center, gives you the next best thing to the majestic temples of Lhasa. This 300-year-old Tibetan Buddhist temple is a little tattered and overrun with vermin, but it is still quite active and very different from the temples you are likely to see in other parts of China. In one of the halls an impressive Buddha statue stands 98 feet high. If your interest level is high, consider hiring a guide (Y30) to take you around to the more unusual (and often hidden) places in the temple and explain the Tibetan Buddhist iconography on the walls. ☞ *Y10.*

Xishuangbanna

17 *12 hrs (400 km [248 mi]) by bus southwest of Kunming; 16 hrs (425 km [264 mi]) by bus south of Dali.*

The subtropical plateau and rain forest of the Xishuangbanna Dai Autonomous Prefecture lies in the southern part of Yunnan, close to the borders of Burma and Laos. It is the home of the Dai people, Buddhists who are related to the Thais. The main city in the region is the capital, **18** **Jinghong**—interesting in itself and small enough to explore in an afternoon. Outside Jinghong, however, is what attracts most visitors. The rain forest and the numerous minority villages make you forget that this is still China.

On the northeast edge of Jinghong, within walking distance of the center, is **Manting Park** (Manting Gongyuan), a pleasant forested park where you can have a closer look at some of the area's indigenous plants without traveling into the rain forest. Also inside the park is a large peacock aviary. The park is especially lively in mid-April when people gather here to celebrate the Water Splashing Festival. ⊠ *Manting Lu* 🎫 *Y15* ⊙ *Daily 7:30–7:30.*

⑲ One of the most important areas of Xishuangbanna is **Ganlan Basin** (Ganlanbei), 37 km (23 mi) from Jinghong. Minority peoples still live in bamboo huts here, amid the beautiful rain forest. The area is famous in Yunnan for its tropical flowers and the millions of butterflies that inhabit this valley. If you want to spend a few days hiking and investigating the basin, you can stay at one of the many village guesthouses, most of which accept foreigners. ✛ *1 hr south of Jinghong.*

Where to Stay

¢ 🏨 **Banna Hotel.** This hotel is for the budget traveler, with beds in dormitory rooms as low as Y33. The standard rooms are clean and with working showers. However, don't expect much in the way of service or amenities. ⊠ *11 Galan Lu, 666100* ☎ *0691/212–4901* 🖷 *0691/212–2036* 🛏 *100 rooms* ⚭ *Restaurant, business services* ▤ *AE, MC, V.*

¢ 🏨 **Xinmin International Hotel** (Xinmin Guoji Dajiudian). This is the most modern hotel in Xishuangbanna, located in the center of town. A travel agency inside the hotel can arrange tours to most areas of interest outside the city. ⊠ *2 Jingde Dong Lu, 666100* ☎ *0691/212–6888* 🖷 *0691/212–9999* 🛏 *56 rooms* ⚭ *Restaurant, gym, hair salon, business services* ▤ *AE, MC, V.*

Yunnan A to Z

To research prices, get advice from other travelers, and book travel arrangements, visit www.fodors.com.

AIR TRAVEL

Yunnan is served by several branches of Air China (CAAC), Yunnan Airlines, Shanghai Airlines, and Dragonair, among other airlines. Kunming is a busy air hub with flight links all over China, as well as to Dali (Xiaguan), Lijiang, and Xishuangbanna (Jinghong). The airport is about 20 minutes by taxi from the center of town. There are weekly flights from Zhongdian to Lhasa, Tibet.

BUS TRAVEL

Kunming's long-distance bus station is in the south of the city. Buses leave for Dali (6 hours), Lijiang (15 hours), Shilin (Stone Forest; 3 hours), Xishuangbanna (26 hours), and Guiyang (13 hours).

🚏 Bus Depot **Bus and Railway Station** ⊠ Beijing Lu, Kunming ☎ 0871/534-9414 or 0871/351-1534.

CAR RENTAL

Self-drive cars cannot be rented in Kunming or Dali, but cars with drivers can be hired through CITS.

CONSULATES

🚩 **Burma (Myanmar)** ⊠ Camellia Hotel, 96 Dongfeng Lu, Kunming ☎ 0871/312-6309. **Laos** ⊠ Camellia Hotel, 96 Dongfeng Lu, Kunming ☎ 0871/317-6623.

Thailand ⊠ Golden Dragon hotel, 575 Beijing Lu, Kunming ☎ 0871/396-8916.

EMERGENCIES
The Public Security Bureau (PSB) is essentially the police. They must be contacted in the case of lost passports and may be of help to foreign visitors in need of assistance. The PSB can be reached by calling 110, the Chinese equivalent of 911.

🚩 **PSB** ✉ Beijing Lu, Kunming ✉ Huguo Lu, Dali ☎ 110.

MONEY MATTERS
Foreign cash cards on the "Cirrus" or "Plus" systems can be used at many Chinese ATMs. The Bank of China and ICBC are the best bets and will often display logos indicating the foreign banking networks to which they connect. The farther one roams from major cities in this region, the more difficult it is to make such withdrawals. When going to remote parts of the country, it is good to have a number of sources of cash on hand, including traveler's checks, credit cards, and some cash.

🚩 Banks **Bank of China** ✉ Fuxing Lu, Dali ✉ Renmin Dong Lu, Kunming. **ICBC** ✉ Huguo Lu, Dali.

TRAIN TRAVEL
Direct service links Kunming with Guangzhou (25 hrs), Chengdu (24 hrs), Chongqing (21 hrs), Emeishan (21 hrs), Guilin (23 hrs), Guiyang (13 hrs), Beijing (46 hrs), and Shanghai (60 hours). The station is on the southern edge of the city.

🚩 Train Depot **Bus and Railway Station** ✉ Beijing Lu, Kunming ☎ 0871/534-9414 or 0871/351-1534.

TRANSPORTATION AROUND YUNNAN
Kunming has no shortage of taxis, and the public bus system is comprehensive and cheap. Some taxis will take visitors around at a fixed rate for the full day. Expect to pay about Y250–Y300 for 8 to 10 hours of driving. To see things outside town you can rent a bicycle or take a minibus from the Yunnan Hotel at 128 Dongfeng Xi Lu, or one of the railway stations. The towns of Dali and Lijiang can easily be explored on foot. You can go farther afield by bicycle or ferry; both are available locally.

VISITOR INFORMATION
🚩 Tourist Information **CITS** ✉ 1–8 Wuyi Lu, 220 Huancheng Nan Lu, Kunming ☎ 0871/313-2332 ✉ Galan Zhong Lu, Jinghong ☎ 0691/213-1165 ✉ Xin Dajie, Lijiang ☎ 0888/512-3508.

SICHUAN

This beautiful province (known to the Chinese as *tian fu zhi guo*, or "heaven on earth"), with an area of 567,000 square km (219,000 square mi), is larger than France (though it forms only one-seventeenth of the whole country) and believed to be the most populous in China. Essentially Han, it is also home to a number of ethnic minorities—the Hui, Qiang, Miao, Tibetans, and Yi.

Geographically it is dominated by the Sichuan Basin, or Red Basin (because of the red sandstone that predominates here), in the east of the province, which accounts for almost half its area. On all sides it is surrounded by mountains: the Dabashan in the northeast, the Wushan in the east, the Qinghai Massif in the west, beneath which extends the fertile Chengdu Plain, and the Yunnan and Guizhou plateaus in the south. Sichuan's natural beauty is augmented by its cultural and agricultural wealth. It is home to several minority groups, and the Sichuan Valley (Sichuan Pendi) is one of China's more fertile regions.

Sichuan has a variable climate, influenced by the annual monsoons. The plains areas enjoy mild winters and long hot summers. The mountain areas of the northwest are subject to harsh conditions year-round, while the highlands of the Southwest have moderately severe winters and temperate summers.

Although the civilization of northern China reached Sichuan about 2500 BC, the province has always exhibited a character of its own, perhaps due to its strongly rural nature. Kingdoms with a distinct culture ruled the area from 1600 BC to 300 BC approximately, but by 221 BC Sichuan had become part of a united China.

After the founding of the first Republic of China in 1911, Sichuan fragmented into territories controlled by warlords and petty fiefdoms. Until the 1930s the province degenerated into poverty, massive debt, and corruption. The civil war and the threat of Japanese invasion threw the situation into relief. Many warlords sided with the Nationalists, although a large part of the Long March undertaken by the Communist troops passed through Sichuan. Then, when the Japanese took Nanking, Chongqing unexpectedly became the temporary capital of China.

Since Mao's death in 1976, Sichuan has gone from strength to strength, making the most of the economic reforms introduced by Deng Xiaoping, who came from Sichuan. Even now rumblings can be heard on the subject of an independent Sichuan, but that seems remote. The vibrant city of Chengdu, the holy mountain of Emeishan, the giant Buddha at Leshan, and the river port of Chongqing on the Yangzi are among the region's attractions.

Chengdu

▶ *4 hrs (240 km [149 mi]) by bus northwest of Chongqing; 32 hrs (1,450 km [900 mi]) by train southwest of Beijing; 40 hrs (1,300 km [806 mi]) by train northwest of Hong Kong.*

Chengdu (literally, Perfect Metropolis) has long been recognized as a significant city on the Chinese agricultural and cultural landscape. With a population of more than 9 million (including the suburbs), it has been progressive since its founding as the capital of the province of Sichuan in 1368. More recent ventures by westward-bound travelers have given Chengdu another title: the "Gateway to Tibet."

Chengdu has more than 2,500 years of recorded history. Until 316 BC it was the capital of the Zhou Shu Kingdom, before the first unification of China under the short-lived Qin Dynasty. In the centuries that followed, it never lost its importance, becoming the chief political, cultural, and economic center of Southwestern China. Indeed, because of its growing importance at the center of the silk industry, it quickly became known as Brocade City (Jin Cheng, by which it is still sometimes known today).

Its importance as a center of the arts was enhanced during the period known as the Three Kingdoms (AD 220–280), when it became capital of the state of Shu Han, its reputation for the production of brocade reaching its peak at this time. In the 8th century, during the Tang Dynasty, perhaps the greatest period of Chinese history from the point of view of culture, the arts of lacquerware and silver filigree were cultivated here as the city became a major center of trade and commerce. At the same time, it developed a reputation as a place outside the mainstream of Chinese life (partly, no doubt, due to its position in the far west of Han China), and a refuge for poets and artists. Its reputation as a cultural center, in the academic sense, persists to this day—there are 14 colleges in Chengdu, including Sichuan University.

Like many large cities, Chengdu is still negotiating its role in China's rapid economic development. As in other parts of this region, merchants toting baskets of cabbage and well-dressed bicyclists chatting on cell phones somehow manage to coexist, despite the statue of the Great Helmsman that still stands in the main square, gazing portentously along Renmin Dong Lu. Beyond the circuits of furious traffic, however, lies a city of tree-lined boulevards from which here and there radiate streets lined with traditional Chinese architecture.

It is perhaps especially interesting as an example of a great city, obscurely located as far as the rest of the world is concerned, that reflects the pace of change—and the tensions that go with it—of modern China. It is also a great center for Sichuan cooking, which many believe to be the best in China, and is one of the last bastions in China of the art of tea drinking. The places of interest for most visitors are scattered about the town at inconvenient distances. To see the city well, at least three days are necessary. Within a reasonable distance from Chengdu are Emeishan, one of China's sacred mountains; Leshan, home of the world's largest Buddha; and the beautiful landscape of the mountainous Jiuzhaigou.

20 **Du Fu's Cottage** (Du Fu Caotang) belonged to the famous poet Du Fu (712–770) of the Tang Dynasty, whose poetry continues to be read today. A Manchurian, he came to Chengdu from Xian and built a cottage or hut overlooking the bamboo and plum tree–lined Huanhua River in 759, spending four years here and writing well over 240 poems. After his death the area became a garden; a temple was added during the Northern Song Dynasty (960–1126). A replica of his cottage now stands among several other structures, all built during the Qing Dynasty. Some of Du Fu's calligraphy and poems are on display here. ⊠ *Caotang Lu off Yihuan Xi Lu* ☎ *028/8731–9258* ⌸ *Y30* ☉ *Daily 7:30–7.*

21 The four-story wooden pavilion in **Riverview Pavilion Park** (Wangjiang Lou Gongyuan), dating from the Qing Dynasty, offers splendid views of the river and the surrounding countryside. The poet Xue Tao, who lived in Chengdu during the Tang Dynasty, was said to have spent time on this site by the Fuhe (Fu River), from which she apparently drew water to make paper for her poems. The pavilion stands amid more than 120

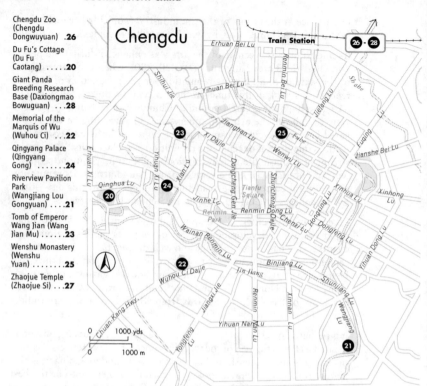

species of bamboo, a plant particularly revered by the poet. There are also several other pavilions to enjoy in the park. ⊠ *Wangjiang Lu* 🚋 *Y15* 🕙 *Daily 9–5.*

> **need a break?**
>
> One of the best places to spend a few hours in Chengdu is at a teahouse. These establishments are everywhere and come in all shapes and forms. They can be just a couple of chairs, a few tables, and a thermos of hot water. Or they can be elaborate neon-lighted structures offering all levels of service. One of the more interesting teahouses is the **Jiafu Yuen** (⊠ Yuding Qiao 🕾 026/8675–8175). It's actually a tea garden and it was partly funded by Kofu City, Chengdu's Japanese sister city. It sits on the banks of the newly reconditioned (formerly a local garbage dump) Fulan River at the Yuding Bridge.

㉒ The **Memorial of the Marquis of Wu** (Wuhou Ci), in Nanjiao Park in the southwest of the city, was built in the 6th century to commemorate the achievements of Zhuge Liang (AD 181–234), a prime minister and military strategist of the Three Kingdoms era. Of the two pavilions here, one is dedicated to Zhuge, the other to Liu Bei of the Kingdom of Shu, emperor at the time of Zhuge Liang, whose tomb is close to the Liu temple. The pleasant grounds also have a museum and tea garden. ✉ *231 Wuhou Ci Dajie* ☎ *028/8555-2397* 💰 *Y30* 🕙 *Daily 7:30-7.*

㉓ In the northwest section of Chengdu stands the 49-foot-high, 262-feet-in-diameter **Tomb of Emperor Wang Jian** (Wang Jian Mu), which honors the ruler of the Kingdom of Shu from AD 847 to 918. Made of red sandstone, it is distinguished by the male figures that support the platform for the coffin and the carvings of musicians, thought to be the best surviving record of a Tang Dynasty musical troupe. There are a lovely park and teahouse on the grounds, both quite popular among locals. ✉ *Off Fuqin Dong Lu* 💰 *Y5* 🕙 *Daily 8:30-5:30.*

> **need a break?**
>
> **Chunxi Lu,** a street running east of Tianfu Square, has been thoroughly rebuilt in recent years. Although much of the city is undergoing perpetual renovation, Chunxi Lu is currently a great area for walking and avoiding the dust and noise. It has everything from fast food to Japanese department stores, and everything in between. You can sit out at a café, try all-you-can-eat sushi, or catch a film. Shopping is, of course, an option. Few international brands are available, but local fashion is everywhere. You can also just sit for a while and watch the local Chinese enjoying their newfound prosperity. The one thing Chunxi Lu lacks is cars, except for the little trainlike vehicle that chugs around, available for people who would rather not walk.

㉔ First built during the Tang Dynasty, **Qingyang Palace** (Qingyang Gong) is the oldest Taoist temple in the city and one of the most famous in the country. Six courtyards open out onto each other before arriving at the sculptures of two goats, which represent one of the earthly incarnations of Lao Tzu (the legendary founder of Taoism). If you arrive mid-morning, you will be able to watch the day's first worshippers before the stampede of afternoon pilgrims arrives. ✉ *Yihuan Xi Lu at Xi Erduan* ☎ *028/8776-6584* 💰 *Y2* 🕙 *Daily 6 AM-8 PM.*

㉕ **Wenshu Monastery** (Wenshu Yuan), the largest in Chengdu, is in the northern suburbs of the city. It dates from the Tang Dynasty, though the current incarnation was constructed in the Qing Dynasty. Besides the small museum of calligraphy and paintings, the monastery has exquisite carving on some of the buildings. Worshippers come here in great numbers, creating the restful atmosphere special to Buddhist temples. The streets in the immediate vicinity are interesting, too, as much of the commerce is related to worship at the temple. ✉ *Wenshu Yuan Jie off Renmin Zhong Lu* 💰 *Y1* 🕙 *Daily 8:30-5.*

FodorśChoice ★

㉖ The **Chengdu Zoo** (Chengdu Dongwuyuan) wouldn't be worth mentioning were it not for the giant pandas in captivity here. However, like nearly every zoo in the Far East, the place is mostly depressing and very crowded. As well as the other animals you'd expect to find in zoos, Chengdu also exhibits some rare animals native to China, including the eccentric-looking golden-hair monkey and the red panda. The best time to view is in the early morning. ✚ *Northeastern suburbs; Bus No. 302 or No. 9 from near train station on Erhuan Bei Lu* 💰 *Y15* 🕙 *Daily 8-6.*

㉗ Founded in the Tang Dynasty, **Zhaojue Temple** (Zhaojue Si) became an important place of instruction for both Chinese and foreign (mostly Japanese) Zen (Chan) Buddhists. It has been rebuilt several times over the centuries, most recently in 1985. ✛ *Northeastern suburbs, next to zoo* ▨ *Y5* ⊙ *Daily 8–5.*

★ ☝ ㉘ For those only interested in pandas, the **Giant Panda Breeding Research Base** (Daxiongmao Bowuguan) is perhaps a better choice than the Chengdu Zoo. About a dozen giant pandas live in luxurious conditions here. There is a special breeding area and a small museum that explains the evolution and habits of pandas. As with the zoo, the best time to see the pandas in action is in the early morning. ⊠ *Jiefang Lu* ☎ *028/8350–5513* ▨ *Y30* ⊙ *Daily 8–6.*

Where to Stay & Eat

In Chengdu, hotpot is everywhere and easy to find. A walk down just about any street will yield at least one restaurant serving this local specialty. Hotpot restaurants tend to be open affairs, with big windows or actually spilling out onto the sidewalk. There are many styles and varieties, but they all share one thing in common: they are hot. Restaurants in Chengdu will often assume that foreigners can't take the spice and will make a dish mild for a non-Chinese visitor. Be warned: if you say you want more heat this may be taken as a challenge, and the dish will arrive with a bit of extra chili to test your tolerance.

¢–$$$$ ✕ **Old House** (Lao Fangzi). There's nothing old about the Old House, other than the faux-old interior. But this is a place for eating, not architecture. Big tables and a giant menu with just about everything Chinese in it, from the local to the coastal, make it a good spot for a large group. The staff is attentive to a fault, though they tend to push the overpriced seafood first. Don't be discouraged. Work through the picture menu until you spot a dish you prefer. ⊠ *289 Yangxi Jie* ☎ *028/8753–3399* ⊠ *243 Wuhou Ci Dajie* ☎ *028/8509–8822* ▤ *No credit cards.*

★ ¢–$$$$ ✕ **Paioxiang.** This restaurant is renowned for its efforts to take traditional Sichuanese dishes and make them modern, transforming down-home cooking into a cuisine. It's all ribs, stir-fry, tofu, and chili sauce, but more refined than your average street stall. ⊠ *60 Yihuan Lu Dong Sanduan* ☎ *028/8437–9999* ▤ *No credit cards.*

¢–$$$ ✕ **Grandma's.** If you're sick of hotpot and hot pepper, this is the place to go. Solid American and other foreign foods are served up at decent prices. It's an excellent choice for breakfast, but also a good standby any time of day. The Renmin Nan Lu branch is cozy (some may argue a bit too much so), but most people there are too busy enjoying their food to argue. ⊠ *73/75 Kehua Bei Lu* ☎ *028/8524–2835.* ⊠ *22 Renmin Nan Lu* ☎ *028/8555–3856* ▤ *No credit cards.*

$–$$ ✕ **Shizi Lou Dajiudian.** The specialty here is Sichuan-style hotpot—very spicy and delicious. It's more expensive than your run-of-the-mill places, but worth it. If you're lucky, your visit might coincide with evening entertainment, most often music. ⊠ *2 Mannian Lu, off Er Xi Lu at Dong Sanduan* ☎ *028/8433–3975* ▤ *No credit cards.*

¢–$$ ✕ **Chengdu Caoshou Canting.** It's a cafeteria downstairs and a restaurant up. But on all levels they serve set menus of local food and other Chinese dishes. On the ground floor, push to the counter, pick a set, take a ticket, and sit down. Soon seven or eight dishes will be served, from rice in palm leaves to wanton soup. If that's too much like fast food, the second and third levels provide better sets and full service. ⊠ *8 Chunxi Nan Lu* ☎ *028/8666–6947* ▤ *No credit cards.*

¢–$ ✕ **Chen Mapo Doufu.** This chain of restaurants has been famous for more than 100 years but infamous of late. Riding on its reputation, the quality of food and service have declined considerably. The place is still worth a try, but you can also sample their signature dish, *mapo doufu,* from a street vendor. ⊠ *197 Xi Yulong Jie* ☎ *028/8675–4512* ⊠ *145 Qingyang Zheng Jie* ☎ *028/8776–9737* ▤ *No credit cards.*

¢ ✕ **Shanbala Zangcan.** For a taste of Tibet without leaving town, this is the place. They make their own yogurt and don't use sugar. They use yak from the grasslands, not beef from the store. The tea comes in a big pot, and it's free for paying customers. Tibetan cowboys sit at tables shooting the breeze as a monk eats quietly alone in the corner. No English menus are available, but the friendly staff does its best and ordering is easy: some bread, yak noodles, and a few dumplings will do anyone right. Warning: the meat is a bit fattier and tougher than you may be used to. The restaurant sits on a street of Tibetan establishments near the ethnic minority university called Southwest Nationalities University (Xinan Minzu Daxue). ⊠ *3 Wuhou Ci Dong Jie* ☎ *028/8553–8665* ▤ *No credit cards.*

¢ ✕ **Ziyunxuan.** Locals say the food here is authentic Sichuanese. The well-translated English menu makes selecting dishes easy and the prices allow the most budget conscious to test their limits and make a few mistakes with little concern. The rice is highly recommended; it comes in a big bowl and is of the "fragrant pearl" variety that goes well with spicy foods. ⊠ *155 Zhengfu Lu, off Renmin Lu* ☎ *028/8662–1161* ▤ *No credit cards.*

¢–$ ▥ **Jinjiang Binguan.** Thoroughly refurbished in 2003, this old Soviet-inspired structure is a local establishment reaching international standards. Located on the banks of the Jinjiang River, the city's main waterway, it is in a pleasant spot in the center of town. ⊠ *80 Erduan, Renmin Nan Lu, 610012* ☎ *028/8550–6666* 🖷 *028/8550–7550* ⇖ *523 rooms* ⋄ *5 restaurants, bar, dance club, shops* ▤ *AE, MC, V.*

¢ ▥ **Chengdu Grand Hotel** (Chengdu Dajiudian). Close to the railway station in the north of the city, this old standby, although a tad tired, has reasonably commodious if overpriced (for what you get) rooms. ⊠ *29 Erduan, Renmin Bei Lu, 610041* ☎ *028/8317–3888* 🖷 *028/8317–6818* ⇖ *468 rooms* ⋄ *2 restaurants, shops, business services* ▤ *AE, D, MC, V.*

¢ ▥ **Minshan Fandian.** In a good location, this modern hotel with a grand lobby has comfortable but overpriced rooms. The Taibai Lou Restaurant inside is one of Chengdu's popular places for Sichuan cooking. ⊠ *55 Erduan, Renmin Nan Lu, 610016* ☎ *028/8558–3333* 🖷 *028/8558–2154* ⇖ *422 rooms* ⋄ *2 restaurants, bar, shops, business services* ▤ *AE, D, MC, V.*

¢ ▥ **Sim's Cozy Guest House.** Opened in 2004 by a Singaporean man and his Japanese wife, this guesthouse offers large comfortable rooms and clean common facilities. The owners, having traveled extensively in the region, along with their local staff, are very helpful in providing information about regional destinations and accommodations elsewhere. ☒ *42 Xizhushi Jie, 610017* ☏☏ *028/8691–4422* ⊕ *www.gogosc.com* ➥ *22 rooms* ⬧ *Restaurant; no room TVs* 🖮 *No credit cards.*

¢ 🖻 **Tibet Hotel** (Xizang Fandian). Near the train station, this hotel built by the Tibet Autonomous Region Government is a good option for those planning trips to Tibet. There is a tourist office in the hotel lobby specializing in travel to Tibet, though the "Tibetan" restaurant suffers from a surprising lack of Tibetan food. ☒ *10 Renmin Bei Lu, 610081* 🖀 *028/8318–3388* 🖷 *028/8318–5678* ➥ *360 rooms* ⬧ *3 restaurants, business services, travel services* 🖮 *AE, D, MC, V.*

Nightlife & the Arts

Chengdu normally has something going on somewhere. Find out about local opera performances, visiting acrobatic troupes, art exhibitions, shadow puppet shows, and other events from CITS or from your hotel. Check the **Jinjiang Theater** (☒ Huaxingzheng Jie) for performances.

Tea drinking in teahouses is a traditional pastime in Chengdu, and sometimes amateur opera performances take place in them. The best time to go is in the afternoon. Many parks have teahouses, like in **Renmin Park** (Renmin Chaguan). There is also a good teahouse at the otherwise unimpressive **Qingaong Palace,** located on Yihuan Xi Lu at Xi Erduan.

The nightlife scene has the usual karaoke parlors, but there also are private bars around Renmin Nan Lu in the area of the Jinjiang Binguan hotel. **Carol's by the River** (☒ 2 Lin Jiang Lu) is a favorite among foreign residents. It's a restaurant by day and bar at night. Located just across the bridge and down the river from the Jinjiang Binguan hotel, it is the first in a series of pubs along the water. Another old standby is the **Half Dozen Pub** (☒ 26 Fang Cao Jie). It's on the south side of town and has been going strong for more than a dozen years.

The Outdoors

Rent **bicycles** at the Traffic Hotel (☒ Off Renmin Nan Lu south of river). For **jogging** your best options are the riverbank, Renmin Park, or perhaps the park of Du Fu's Cottage. There is a **swimming pool** in the area of Mengzhuiwan (☒ Off Xinhua Dong Lu east of city).

Shopping

The main street for shopping is **Chunxi Lu,** off Tianfu Square, where there are a number of shops selling interesting items. One shop to look for is the **Arts & Crafts Service Department Store.**

Dujiangyan

29 *1 hr (55 km [34 mi]) by car northwest of Chengdu.*

The **Du River Canal Irrigation System** (Dujiangyan) has been in place for 2,200 years. In 256 BC the local governor, Li Bing, tired of seeing maidens sacrificed to placate the river gods, decided to harness the power of the Minjiang (Min River) to irrigate the Chengdu Plain. The river was divided in two and then further divided to feed 6,500 square km (2,500 square mi) of canal. If you cross the Inner and Outer rivers via the pedestrians-only **Anlan Cable Bridge,** you will reach the **Two Princes Temple** (Erwang Miao), dedicated to Li Bing and his son, who saw his father's plan to fruition. Buses (Y5–Y10) leave the Chengdu terminal about every 15 minutes for Dujiangyan. ⊠ *Lidui Park* 🎫 *Y5* 🕓 *Daily 8–6.*

Emeishan

★ ㉚ *3 hrs (100 km [62 mi]) by train southwest of Chengdu.*

One of China's holy mountains, the dwelling place of the Samantabhadra, the Buddhist Bodhisattva of Pervading Goodness, 10,000-foot-high Emeishan (literally, Lofty Eyebrow Mountain) is in the south of Sichuan. On it are some 50 km (31 mi) of paths leading to the summit; the climb can be accomplished in two or three days. No mountaineering skills are required, but be prepared for sudden weather changes, which can produce mist or rain at a moment's notice. There are several temples (with simple accommodations) and places of interest en route. You can spend the night at the summit to see the sea of clouds and the sometimes spectacular sunrise. Solid footwear with a good grip is required, and a walking stick could be useful. The mountain is known for its wily golden monkeys, who have been known to steal items (such as cameras) and hang them in trees. Too much attention has made them rather spoiled and audacious, and they should not be approached.

The government charges an outrageous Y120 admission fee entrance to the park. It's an extortionate price for a day hike on public trails and it's near impossible to get around the toll gates. Going elsewhere is a tempting option, but Emeishan is truly amazing and tough to walk away from.

For an easier pilgrimage, use the minibus service up to **Jieyin Dian** at 7,800 feet, from where the climb to the top will take about two hours. To avoid climbing altogether, ride the cable car (Y40 round-trip) to the summit from Jieyin Dian (though long queues can form for this). At the top of the mountain is the **Golden Summit Temple** (Jinding Si).

Direct bus (3 hrs) service links Chengdu with Baoguo, at the foot of the mountain and about 6 km (4 mi) from the town of Emei, where trains from Chengdu stop.

Where to Stay & Eat

★ ¢–$ ✕ **Teddy Bear Café.** A visitor arriving at the Emei bus terminal will likely be accosted by touts offering to take them to the Teddy Bear Café. It's a good idea to go with them. Despite its odd name and spartan decor, the Teddy Bear is the place to start when visiting Emeishan. The café has everything from hamburgers to pancakes, and also a good selection of Chinese dishes. The eggplant, crispy to avoid sogginess but not overcooked, must be tried. The sign outside says "local prices," and it's the truth. In an area known for the tourist-trap premium, the Teddy Bear keeps things reasonable. The owners are friendly, know the mountain well, and will cheerfully assist visitors, doing everything from loaning walking sticks to arranging guides. They even have their own hotel in back; it's exceptionally clean and comfortable. ✉ *43 Baogu-osi Lu, next to Emei Tour Passenger Transport Center* ☎ *0833/559–0135* ▭ *No credit cards.*

¢ ▣ **Baoguo Monastery.** This monastery, at the foot of the mountain, is one of the better among those offering accommodation. The monks here kindly keep all vermin that sneak inside away from the guests' belongings. ✉ *Baoguo Si , 614201* ☎ *No phone* ▭ *No credit cards.*

¢ ▣ **Emeishan Hotel** (Emeishan Dajiudian). This "luxury" hotel is at the foot of the mountain, offering good access for those going on early hikes. ✉ *Baoguo Si, 614201* ☎ *0833/552–6888* ⊟ *0833/559–1061* ⤳ *200 rooms* ⌂ *Restaurant, bar, business services* ▭ *No credit cards.*

Leshan

★ ㉛ *3 hrs (165 km [102 mi]) by bus south of Chengdu.*

In the small, swiftly changing town of Leshan a towering Buddha, carved from the rock face, sits inscrutably at the confluence of the Dadu and Min rivers. The Leshan **Grand Buddha** (Da Fo), at 233 feet, is the tallest stone Buddha and among the tallest sculptures in the world. The big toes are each 28 feet in length. The construction of the Grand Buddha was started in AD 713 by a monk who wished to placate the river waters that habitually took local fishermen's lives. Although the project took more than 90 years to complete, it had no noticeable effect on the river waters. It is possible to clamber down, by means of a cliff-hewn stairway, from the head to the platform where the feet rest; or you can take a boat ride (about Y30) to see it in all its grandeur from the river. ▨ *Y50.*

There are also several temples or pagodas in the vicinity, including **Wuyou Temple** (Wuyou Si) on Wuyou Mountain (Wuyou Shan), with its hall of recently restored statues of arhats. Right next to the Buddha on Lingyun Shan is the **Lingyun Temple** (Linguan Si), more interesting for the expansive view it offers of the Min River. ✛ *To get to Wuyou Si take boat from Leshan jetty and climb staircase* ▨ *Y2 each* ⊙ *Daily 8–5.*

The town of Leshan is quite a lively place, with some interesting old streets—Dong Dajie and Xian Jie—and a good market.

Jiuzhaigou

8–10 hrs (350 km [217 mi]) by bus north of Leshan; 4–6 hrs (225 km [140 mi]) by bus northwest of Chengdu.

High among the snowcapped peaks of the Aba Autonomous Prefecture ㉜ of northern Sichuan lies the **Jiuzhaigou Natural Preserve** (Jiuzhaigou Ziran Bao Hu Qu), a wonderland of turquoise pools and interwoven waterfalls that has long been home to the Qiang and Tibetan peoples. Jiuzhaigou provides an invaluable opportunity to observe the customs and lifestyles of people still living as they did hundreds of years ago. Reaching these places was once a matter of long bus journeys on potentially treacherous roads, but the opening of a new airport in 2002 has made the trip much easier and the preserve is very busy with tourists.

33 **Songpan** (two hours south of Jiuzhaigou by bus) is a lively market town in the midst of beautiful scenery where horse trekking on excellent hiking trails is popular.

Kangding

34 *8 hrs (215 km [133 mi]) by bus southwest of Chengdu.*

Western Sichuan, toward Tibet, has tougher terrain than other parts of the region. The scenery at Kangding is magnificent, its enormous mountains snowcapped year-round. Just south of here, **Hailougou Glacier** (Hailougou Bingchuan), part of 24,790-foot Mt. Gongga (Gongga Shan), is at the lowest altitude of any glacier in Asia. There are several Buddhist monasteries in the region, and you can go hiking and pony trekking. On the downside, Kangding is currently undergoing redevelopment and can get dusty and unpleasant at times. It can also be quite expensive during peak-season periods.

Chongqing

4 hrs (240 km [149 mi]) by bus southeast of Chengdu; 3 hrs (1,800 km [1,116 mi]) by plane southwest of Beijing; 34 hrs (1,025 km [636 mi]) by train northwest of Hong Kong.

In 1997 the Chinese separated Chongqing from Sichuan, making it one of China's four municipalities (the other three are Beijing, Tianjin, and Shanghai). Though Chongqing is technically no longer part of Sichuan, Sichuan still survives in the city's food, dialect, and culture. Built on undulating hills at the point of confluence of the Yangzi and Jialing rivers, it is one of the few cities in China where the bicycle is all but useless (in fact Chongqing is sometimes referred to as Mountain City). Chongqing is a major point of embarkation or disembarkation for the Yangzi cruise. Although gray, the city is animated and industrious. The vicinity affords fine scenery and numerous day trips.

The recorded history of Chongqing (which means "Constant Celebrations," a name conferred by the first Song emperor to celebrate his conquest of the area) goes back some 3,000 years. During the 13th century BC, before the unification of China, it was the capital of the Kingdom of Ba. Its importance has always depended on trade, which in turn has depended on the city's position on the river at the head of the Yangzi Gorges, through which the river flows to the ports of Wuhan and Shanghai. Before the arrival of the train and the airplane, nearly all of Sichuan's trade flowed through Chongqing, and yet it received the status of "city" only in 1927.

Once the Western powers established permanent footholds in China, from the mid- to the late 19th century, they showed interest in exploiting the markets of Sichuan. The first Westerners reached Chongqing by river in 1898, after the Chefoo Agreement of 1876 was amended in 1890 to allow the city to be opened to foreign trade. A regular steamer service began to ply the length of the river. By the first years of the 20th century a substantial foreign community had established itself, with offices of all the great trading companies of the day and with consulates to serve the residents.

When the Japanese took the Nationalist capital of Nanjing in 1938, the Chinese government moved to Chongqing, regarded as an impregnable fortress because of its location. The population grew quickly, particularly as it became home to the so-called united front, the temporary alliance between the Communists and the Nationalists against the Japanese. Chongqing's population swelled to 2 million, and it became a place of intrigue and desperation, where the misery of overcrowding and squalor was exacerbated by endless air raids by the Japanese, who were able to identify the city easily by following the Yangzi on moonlit nights.

What had been an attractive town of temples within a city wall, was largely destroyed by the end of the war. And yet the city still has something—there are sections where it is possible to grasp some idea of how it must once have been. It has not lost that air of activity, of arrival and departure, that characterizes any port. The spicy cooking of Sichuan is recognized by the Chinese themselves as the best in the country. It is an interesting city to stroll around—but not in high summer when it becomes unbearably hot, fully deserving of its reputation as one of the furnaces of China.

★ ㉟ Two items almost unique to Chongqing are its **cable cars.** One links the north and south shores of the Jialing River, from Canbai Lu to the Jinsha Jie station. It is a worthwhile experience for the view of the docks, the city, and the confluence of the Jialing and Yangzi rivers. The other crosses the Yangzi itself and starts close to Xinhua Lu.

㊱ There are also three bridges across the rivers—the oldest, built between 1963 and 1966, crosses the Jialing while the two newer bridges, built in 1981 and 1989, cross the Yangzi. The biggest of these is the **Great Changjiang Bridge** (Changjiang Daqiao).

㊲ Perhaps not as busy and bustling as once upon a time, **Chaotianmen Docks** (Chaotianmen Matou) still offer an opportunity to glimpse something of China at work. From here you can see the various boats departing for the Three Gorges river cruise. ⊠ *Shaanxi Lu.*

㊳ At 804 feet, **Loquat Hill** (Pipa Shan), until 1950 a private garden, is the highest point in the city. It is a good place from which to see the layout of the city and the activity on the river below or, at night, the city lights. ⊠ *Zhongshan Er Lu* 🚇 *Y10* ⏱ *Daily 7 AM–11 PM.*

㊴ Originally built about 1,000 years ago (Song Dynasty) and rebuilt in 1752 and again in 1945, the **Luohan Temple** (Luohan Si) is a popular and atmospheric place of worship. A small community of monks is still active here. The main attraction is the hall of 500 lifelike painted clay arhats, Buddhist disciples who have succeeded in freeing themselves from the earthly chains of delusion and material greed. ⊠ *Minzu Lu* 🚇 *Y2* ⏱ *Daily 8:30–5:30.*

㊵ **Red Crag Village** (Hongyancun) is where Zhou Enlai, among other luminaries of the Chinese Communist Party, lived between 1938 and 1945 and where the Chongqing office of the Chinese Eighth Route

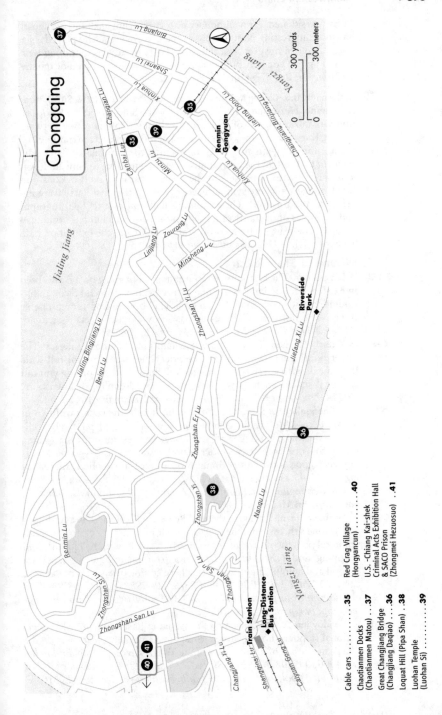

Chongqing

Jialing Jiang

Yangzi Jiang

300 yards
300 meters

Renmin Gongyuan

Riverside Park

Train Station
Long-Distance Bus Station

Army was situated. A **revolutionary history museum** (geming bowuguan) has some interesting photographs of the personalities who played a significant role in the events of the time. There is, however, nothing written in English; you may perhaps find an English-speaking guide on-site. ⊠ *Hongyan Bus Terminus* 🚊 *Y6* ⏱ *Daily 8:30–5.*

❹ In the name **U.S.-Chiang Kai-shek Criminal Acts Exhibition Hall & SACO Prison** (Zhongmei Hezuosuo), SACO stands for the Sino-American Cooperation Organization, a group developed through collaboration between Chiang Kai-shek and the U.S. government, dedicated to the training and supervision of agents for the Guomindang, the Nationalist Party government that fought the Communists before retreating to Taiwan. It was jointly run by the Chinese and the Americans, who built prisons outside Chongqing where sympathizers of the Communist Party were imprisoned and tortured. The exhibition hall houses a few photographs and examples of the hardware used on the prisoners but has nothing in English. The prisons are a considerable walk from the exhibition hall. ⚜ *Foot of Gele Hill, northwest suburbs* 🚊 *Y5* ⏱ *Daily 8:30–5.*

Where to Stay & Eat

¢–$$$ ✕ **Lao Sichuan.** The best-known restaurant in Chongqing because it's been in existence for as long as anyone can remember, the Old Sichuan has traditional and exotic food (for example, chili-braised frogs) at reasonable prices. The hot-pepper dishes are as spicy as you'll get in Sichuan. ⊠ *186 Minzu Lu* ☎ *023/6382–6644* 🔲 *AE, MC, V.*

¢–$$ ✕ **Yizhishi Fandian.** This is one of Sichuan's most famous eateries. The upper floors are upscale and can be pricey; head upstairs for full-scale local meals with specials like tea-smoked duck. In the morning you can eat local snacks such as pastries and *jiaozi* (dumplings) downstairs. ⊠ *114 Zourong Lu* ☎ *023/6384–1456* 🔲 *No credit cards.*

★ ¢ ✕🏨 **Chongqing Fandian.** This hotel is located in the center of town in an art deco–style building. It boasts low prices and relatively well-equipped rooms, making it a good value. The restaurant, Chiao Tiang Gong ($)—one of the city's older, more famous eateries—serves generally very good local and regional food in pleasant modern surroundings. ⊠ *41–43 Xinhua Lu, 630011* ☎ *023/6160–9999* 🖨 *023/6384–3085* ⊕ *www.chungkinghotel.com* 🛏 *197 rooms* ⚴ *2 restaurants, minibars, bar, shops* 🔲 *MC, V.*

¢–$$ 🏨 **Harbour Plaza.** Smack in the middle of town—if there is a middle—and a stone's throw from the Liberation Monument, this clean and modern hotel puts the visitor near a pedestrian street, with restaurants and shopping, and a short walk or cab ride from many other sites. Service is good and helpful, a plus in a city where getting oriented is not always easy. ⊠ *Wuyi Lu, 400010* ☎ *023/6370–0888* 🖨 *023/6370–0778* ⊕ *www.harbour-plaza.com/hpcp* 🛏 *390 rooms* ⚴ *2 restaurants, coffee shop, bar, gym* 🔲 *AE, MC, V.*

¢–$ 🏨 **Holiday Inn Yangzi Chongqing** (Yangzijiang Jiari Fandian). This international standard hotel is just outside the city center. The rooms on the hotel's north side offer full views of the Yangzi River. ⊠ *15 Nanping Bei Lu, 400060* ☎ *023/6280–3380* 🖨 *023/6280–0884* 🛏 *365 rooms* ⚴ *5 restaurants, pool, gym, bar, dance club, business services* 🔲 *AE, MC, V.*

¢ ⌧ **Renmin Binguan.** This grand and opulent structure, originally built in the 1950s to resemble the Temple of Heaven in Beijing, is where former president Jiang Zemin stays when he's in town. Drab and somewhat depressing, with service to match, this throwback's one redeeming quality is its price, which approaches hostel rates. ⊠ *173 Renmin Lu, 400015* ☎ *023/6385–6888* 🖷 *023/6385–2076* 🛏 *227 rooms* ⚭ *2 restaurants, bar, dance club, shops* ⊟ *AE, MC, V.*

Nightlife & the Arts

There are often performances of Sichuan opera and acrobatics—ask CITS or at your hotel for information. The square in front of the Renmin Binguan hotel usually hosts free public performances. It is worth trying to visit the **Painters Village** (Huajia Zhi Cun) at Hualongqiao. Established as a sort of collective in the 1950s, it has produced some good work.

Despite Chongqing's being a port, it has even less in the way of nightlife than most other cities in China; beyond the karaoke parlors there is little besides a few bars along Chaotianmen Dock.

Shopping

The principal shopping area is in the vicinity of the Liberation Monument in the center of town. It is a lively district of shops and restaurants where you might pick up examples of lacquerware, embroidery, and bamboo ware, as well as teas and local produce.

Side Trip from Chongqing

★ ㊷ North of the city on **Jinyun Mountain** (Jinyun Shan) are some pretty views and a smattering of pavilions from the Ming and Qing periods. Three house imposing statues of the Giant Buddha, the Amitabha Buddha, and the famous general of the Three Kingdoms Period, Guan Yu. The park also has a set of **hot springs**, where it is possible to bathe in the 30°C (86°F) water, either in a swimming pool or in the privacy of cubicles with their own baths. ⊹ *Jinyun Shan, 2 hrs (50 km [30 mi]) by bus north of city* 🎫 *Y15* ☉ *Daily 8:30–6.*

Dazu

★ ㊸ *3 hrs (160 km [99 mi]) by bus northwest of Chongqing.*

At Dazu a group of Buddhist cave sculptures that rival those at Datong, Dunhuang, and Luoyang is worth the effort to reach if you have the opportunity. The impressive sculptures, ranging from tiny to gigantic, contain unusual domestic detail in addition to the purely religious work. There are two major sites at Dazu—Bei Shan and Baoding Shan. Work at the caves began in the 9th century (during the Song and Tang dynasties) and continued for more than 250 years.

Located outside Dazu, **Baoding Shan,** where the carvings were completed according to a plan, is the more interesting site. Here you will find visions of hell reminiscent of similar scenes from medieval Europe; the Wheel of Life; a magnificent 100-foot reclining Buddha; and a gold, thousand-armed statue of the goddess of mercy. ⊹ *16 km (10 mi) east of Dazu town; take minibus* 🎫 *Y85* ☉ *Daily 8–5.*

Where to Stay

¢ ⌐ **Dazu Binguan.** Most foreign guests end up staying in this comparatively nice hotel. The on-site travel agency can help you buy bus or
train tickets. ⊠ *47 Gongnong Jie, 402360* ☎ *023/4372–2476* 🖷 *023/
4372–2967* 🖑 *132 rooms* ⌂ *Restaurant, business services* ▤ *D,
MC, V.*

Sichuan A to Z

*To research prices, get advice from other travelers, and book travel ar-
rangements, visit www.fodors.com.*

AIR TRAVEL

Chengdu has flights to and from all the major cities of China, including Beijing, Guangzhou, Chongqing, Guilin, Guiyang, Hong Kong,
Kunming, Lhasa (if you can get a visa), Nanking, and Shanghai. A bus
service links the CAAC office and the airport, which is 20 km (12 mi)
west of the city.

There are daily or regular flights between Chongqing and all the major
cities in China. The airport lies 25 km (16 mi) north of the city, and CAAC
runs shuttle buses between it and their office.

🖪 Airlines & Contacts **CAAC Chengdu** ⊠ Renmin Nan Lu across from Jinjiang Binguan hotel, Chengdu ☎ 028/8666-8080. **CAAC Chongqing** ⊠ 161 Zhongshan San Lu,
Chongqing ☎ 023/6360-3223.

BOAT & FERRY TRAVEL

Boats go on the Yangzi from Chongqing all the way to Shanghai (seven
days), but the most popular route is the cruise downstream from
Chongqing to Yichang or Wuhan (three–four days) or upstream from
Wuhan to Chongqing. Most major sights, including the Three Gorges
and Three Little Gorges, lie between Chongqing and Yichang. Tourist
boats offer air-conditioned cabins with television and private bath; the
ordinary passenger steamers used by most Chinese offer minimal comforts. Tickets can be arranged through CITS or your travel agent.

It is possible to get to Leshan by boat from Chongqing.

BUS TRAVEL

There are four bus stations in Chengdu, but figuring out which one to
go to is often a challenge. In general, Wuguiqiao is the biggest bus station and takes you to Chongqing and other points east. Xinanmen takes
you to Emeishan, Leshan, and other tourist destinations (and on weekends also offers buses to points northwest). Chadianzi takes you to points
northwest, such as Jiuzhaigou. Ximen is for closer destinations, those
within an hour or so. The best bet is to ask a travel agent for the latest
schedule. Buses leave frequently for Emeishan, Leshan, and Chongqing.
There is also service to Dazu and Kanding.

With one or two exceptions, arriving and departing Chongqing by bus
is the least practical method because of its hilly location. The bus station
offers regular departures for Chengdu (4 hrs), Dazu (3 hrs), Yibin

(5½ hrs), and Zigong (3½ hrs). The Kangfulai Passenger Transport Company runs air-conditioned buses to Chengdu, Dazu, Yibin, and Zigong.

Buses link Leshan with Chengdu (5 hrs) and Emeishan (1 hr), only 31 km (19 mi) away.

Bus Information **Chadianzi bus station** ✉ Sanhuan Lu, Chengdu. **Chongqing bus station** ✉ Off Nanqu Lu in southwest of city, close to railway station. **Kangfulai Passenger Transport Company** ✉ 223 Renmin Lu, Chongqing. **Wuguiqiao bus station** ✉ Dongguichun Sanzhu, Chengdu. **Ximen bus station** ✉ Yuejingchun Yizhu, Chengdu. **Xinanmen bus station** ✉ 57 Linjiang Lu, Chengdu.

CAR RENTAL

Self-drive cars cannot be hired in either Chengdu or Chongqing, but cars with drivers can be hired through CITS.

CONSULATE

United States **U.S. Consulate** ✉ 4 Lingshiguan Lu, Chengdu ☎ 028/8558-3992.

EMERGENCIES

PSB ✉ Wenwu Lu, part of Xinhua Dong Lu; 40 Wenmiaohou Jie, Chengdu ☎ 110 or 028/8674-4683 ✉ Linjiang Lu, Chongqing ☎ 110 or 023/6375-8200.

MONEY MATTERS

In Chengdu money can be exchanged in the major hotels and at the Bank of China. You can change money in Chongqing in the hotels or at the Bank of China.

Bank of China ✉ Renmin Nan Lu, Chengdu ✉ Minzu Lu, Chongqing.

TRAIN TRAVEL

There are services from Chengdu to Chongqing (12 hrs), Dazu (7 hrs—trains stop at Youtingpu, about 30 km [19 mi] from Dazu), Emeishan (3 hrs), Kunming (23 hrs), and Xian (16 hrs). It is also possible to get to Guangzhou (40 hrs), Lanzhou (26 hrs), Beijing (25 hrs), Shanghai (45 hrs), and Ürümqi (42 hrs).

The train station in Chongqing is in the southwest of the city. Direct trains serve Guangzhou (39 hours), Chengdu (11 hours), Kunming (23 hours), Nanning (35 hours), Beijing (32 hours), Shanghai (2 days), and Xi'an (30 hours).

Train Information **Chengdu Train Station** ✉ Erhuan Lu ☎ 028/8370-9580. **Chongqing Train Station** ✉ Off Nanqu Lu ☎ 023/6386-2607.

VISITOR INFORMATION

The chief way to visit the Three Gorges is by arranging a package tour through a travel agent in the United States or through any of the CITS offices in Chongqing, Wuhan, Chengdu, or Kunming. Depending on the itinerary, boats may stop at all or a select number of sights—ask your travel agent in advance about which destinations you will be visiting; you may be able to request some.

Tourist Information **CITS** ✉ 65 Renmin Nan Lu, Chengdu ✉ Renmin Binguan hotel, Renmin Lu, Chongqing ☎ 028/8668-7058 or 028/8665-7598. **Tibet Tourism Office** ✉ 10 Renmin Bei Lu, Chengdu ☎ 028/8161-9875.

YANGZI RIVER (CHANG JIANG)

The third-longest river in the world after the Amazon and the Nile, the Yangzi cuts across 6,380 km (3,956 mi) and seven provinces before flowing out into the East China Sea. After descending from the mountain ranges of Qinghai and Tibet, the Yangzi crosses through Yunnan to Sichuan, winding its way through the lush countryside between Sichuan and Hubei before flowing northward toward Anhui and Jiangsu. Like other civilizations that have flourished around great waterways, the Chinese are fond of calling the Yangzi, or Chang Jiang (Long River), the "cradle of ancient Chinese civilization." The river has long been a source of food and transport, as well as an inspiration to painters and poets. Before the 20th century plenty of brave boatmen lost their lives trying to pass through the fearsome stretch of water running through what is known as the Three Gorges—the complicated system of narrow cliffs between Fengjie, in Sichuan, and Yichang, in Hubei.

In 1992 the Chinese government recognized the value of harnessing the power of the river and decided to begin the construction of a huge dam, or *gezhouba*. When completed in 2009, the dam is intended to supply one-third of the nation's electrical power output, control flooding, and improve overall navigation along the river. On the downside, flooding from the construction will prompt the relocation of 1.2 million riverside residents, mostly to the already burgeoning Chongqing Municipality. More than 1,000 important cultural and archaeological sites are expected to be submerged and lost forever. Ecologists and scientists also predict dire effects from pollution and temperature changes on the river wildlife when the dam opens. Even more frightening is the location of this massive project: right on top of an earthquake fault line. Disaster scenarios abound with what may befall those living downstream should a dam of this size break during an earthquake.

The official view is that the spectacular scenery of the Three Gorges— Qutang, Wu, and Xiling—will not be submerged once the dam is completed. There is some concern, though, that the sheer cliffs and rapids may be compromised, as flooding may create a much shallower and altogether less impressive landscape. Currently, a trip through the Three Gorges offers a view of the old China that no longer exists in cities on the path to modernization. Panoramas of hills covered with rice fields; fishermen scooping the waters with large nets from the shores; cliffs and clouds parting to reveal narrow passages of water barely wide enough for two boats—these are the images that have persisted for centuries.

The cities and sights you see on a cruise on the Yangzi River depend on what type of cruise you select and the tour operator you use.

Fengdu

🚤 *193 km (120 mi) by boat northeast of Chongqing; 1,055 km (654 mi) by boat southwest of Wuhan.*

On the banks of the Yangzi, Fengdu, also known as Guicheng or the "city of devils," is filled with temples, buildings, and statues depicting demons and devils. During the Tang Dynasty, the names of two local princely families, Yin (meaning "hell") and Wang (meaning "king"), were linked through marriage, making them known as Yinwang, or the "king of hell." Ever since, people have believed that the town is populated by ghosts. You can take a series of staircases or a cable car to the top of the mountain. The bamboo-covered **Ming Hill** (Mingshan) has a Buddhist temple, a pavilion, and pagodas with brightly painted dragons and swans emanating from the eaves. The hill has a nice view of the Yangzi River.

Shibaozhai

45 *6 hrs (290 km [180 mi]) by bus northeast of Chongqing; 10 hrs (945 km [586 mi]) by bus southwest of Wuhan.*

Shibaozhai (literally, Stone Treasure Stronghold) is actually a rectangular rock with sheer cliffs, into which is built an impressive 12-story pagoda, constructed by Emperor Qianlong (1736–96) during the Qing Dynasty. Wall carvings and historical inscriptions describing the construction of the building can be seen along the circuitous stairway that leads from the center of the pagoda to the top.

Three Gorges (San Xia)

★ *475 km (295 mi) by boat northeast of Chongqing; 655 km (406 mi) by boat southwest of Wuhan.*

46 Between the cities of Fengjie, in Sichuan, and Yichang, in Hubei, lie the Three Gorges. The westernmost gorge, **Qutang Gorge** (Qutang Xia) is the shortest, at 8 km (5 mi). Although the currents are strong here, the surrounding cliffs are not very high. At the top of some of the cliffs are caves that once held coffins of officers from the Warring States Period.

47 Near **Wushan,** at the entrance to Wu Xia, you can change to a smaller boat navigated by local boatmen to the **Little Three Gorges** (Xiao San Xia). Here there are cliff formations similar, on a smaller scale, to those of the Three Gorges. Sometimes you can hear monkeys and other wildlife from your boat.

48 The impressive **Wu Gorge** (Wu Xia) is 33 km (20 mi) long. Its cliffs are so sheer and narrow that they seem to be closing in upon each other as you approach in the boat. Some of the cliff formations are noted for their resemblances to people and animals.

49 At the city of **Badong** in Hubei, just outside the eastern end of Wu Gorge, boats leave for Shennongjia on the Shennong River, one of the wildest and strangest parts of the country.

50 **Xiling Gorge** (Xiling Xia), 66 km (41 mi) long, is the longest and deepest of all the gorges, with cliffs that rise up to 4,000 feet. At the eastern
51 end of the gorge is the **Gezhou Dam** (Gezhou Ba), sometimes simply referred to as *Da Ba* (Big Dam). When completed, the 607-foot-high dam will be a total of 2 km (1¼ mi) long.

INNER MONGOLIA & THE REPUBLIC OF MONGOLIA

THE LAND OF KHAAN

11

SPIN PRAYER WHEELS WITH MONKS
at the Tibetan Gandan Monastery ⇨*p.601*

LEARN HOW TO BUILD YOUR OWN YURT
at the Inner Mongolia Museum ⇨*p.589*

TOUR THE HOME OF A LIVING BUDDHA
at the lavish Winter Palace Museum ⇨*p.603*

CHOW ON TASTY MONGOLIAN BARBECUE
in the neo-Western Modern Nomads ⇨*p.604*

DIG INTO KOREAN BARBEQUE
on the deck of the Seoul Restaurant ⇨*p.603*

STAY IN AN OLD SOVIET SANITARIUM
transformed into the Xincheng Hotel ⇨*p.594*

BUNDLE UP IN A TRADITIONAL YURT
at the cozy Karakorum Ger Camp ⇨*p.612*

By Bill Smith
Updated by
Gregor Irvine-
Halliday

THE MONGOL EMPIRE once covered most of the Eurasian landmass, stretching from the Yellow Sea in the east to Budapest in the west and from Lake Baikal in the north to Myanmar (Burma) in the south. Chinggis Khaan (also known as Genghis Khaan) united the fierce tribes of the Mongolian steppes in the early 13th century. In Mongolia, Karakorum—the site of Chinggis Khaan's capital—attracts many visitors, though little remains of the original city.

Under Kublai Khaan, Chinggis Khaan's grandson, the Mongols conquered most of China, establishing their Yuan Dynasty capital in present-day Beijing in 1272. The Great Mongol Empire disintegrated after the Yuan Dynasty collapsed in 1368. In the 17th century the Chinese Qing (Manchu) Dynasty took control of Mongolia, separating it into Inner Mongolia and Outer Mongolia. The overthrow of the Qing in 1911 brought short-lived independence to Outer Mongolia (now the Mongolian People's Republic, or more commonly, the Republic of Mongolia), which was subsequently invaded by China in 1919. With some assistance from Bolshevik Russia, the Mongolian hero Sukhbaatar drove the Chinese out of Outer Mongolia and reestablished independence.

At first a theocracy under the Living Buddha Bogd Khaan, following his death in 1924 Outer Mongolia officially became the Mongolian People's Republic, a Communist state under strong Soviet influence. Inner Mongolia was occupied by the Japanese from 1931 to 1945 and became the Inner Mongolia Autonomous Region of China in 1947 when World War II ended and the Chinese forced them out. To this day many in the Republic of Mongolia harbor fears over imperial intentions China may have regarding its northern border. As a result of both Mongolias being closed to the outside world for many years, today huge areas of countryside remain largely untouched by Western culture. Soviet and Chinese communism increased the differences between the two areas.

There are 2.7 million ethnic Mongolians in Mongolia—comprising 85% of the population (the rest are Turkic, Tungusic, Chinese, and Russian)—and over 4 million in Inner Mongolia. In its cities and southern farming areas, Inner Mongolia is dominated by Han Chinese, who constitute 80% of the region's overall population of 23.8 million. Mongolia has more wildlife and is less developed than Inner Mongolia, and the grassland is generally less populated. Residents of the Republic of Mongolia have a more traditional lifestyle. Wool, leather, meat, and dairy industries continue to form the mainstay of the rural economies. Inner Mongolia has large agriculture, coal, iron, and steel industries. The influx of Han Chinese has made Mandarin the main language of Inner Mongolia, although Mongolian and Chinese characters are found together on all official notices and street signs. In Mongolia, on the other hand, a Mongolian script based on Cyrillic has largely replaced traditional Mongolian characters. In all but the most western regions of the country everyone speaks Mongolian.

In both Mongolias you can stay in yurts (circular felt tents called *gers* in Mongolian; the word *yurt* is of Turkic origin and is not used in the Republic of Mongolia), eat mutton, drink *airag* (tangy fermented mare's milk), and watch riders use *urgas* (pole-mounted lassos) to round up horses, sheep, goats, cows, and camels. Midsummer Naadam fairs feature spectacular competitions in archery, Mongolian wrestling, and horse racing.

Exploring the Mongolias

Inner Mongolia is a crescent-shape region that stretches 2,400 km (1,500 mi) along China's northern and northeastern borders. The Gobi Desert straddles much of Inner Mongolia's long border with Mongolia to the north. Both Mongolias are landlocked, with Siberia to the north and east and China's Xinjiang province and Kazakhstan to the west.

Visiting the Republic of Mongolia has become much less difficult as government restrictions have been relaxed in the past few years. Letters of invitation and tour bookings are usually no longer required in order to obtain a Mongolian visa. Visas are issued from Mongolian embassies and at the Mongolian consulate office in the border town of Erenhot. Depending on where you apply, tourist visas are issued for either 14 or 30 days and can be extended once you are in the country. Border and visa regulations require foreign tourists to travel in both directions between Mongolia and China, including Inner Mongolia, by rail or air. So travel between rural areas of the two Mongolias is not possible. Customs and immigration formalities are conducted on the train, and there is a two-hour wait at the border while the wheels on the carriages are changed to fit the other region's track size.

Touring the Mongolian countryside is nothing less than spectacular. The difficulty is deciding where to go and how to get there, as distances are great and public transportation either slow or unavailable. You may be best off taking a tour, which can be easily arranged in both Hohhot and Ulaan Baatar. If you're traveling alone, you can cut down on costs by attaching yourself to a tour that has already been booked. Otherwise, try to meet other travelers and form your own group.

In Ulaan Baatar travel agencies will design tours to meet your specifications in terms of both duration and destination. A good method for traveling across Mongolia's varied terrain is to hire a Russian-made four-wheel-drive van or jeep. Prices vary considerably between agencies, so shop around. The no-frills companies charge a minimum of $50 a day for a van (and driver) regardless of the number of tourists piled in the back. This price usually includes all necessary transportation expenses (gasoline and road tolls), camping and cooking equipment, and food, but be sure to verify. A guide costs an additional $10 per day for someone who just speaks English (more for one who has a bit of historical knowledge). The cooking, cleaning, and tent setup is usually performed by the driver and guide no matter how often you ask to help. Hotels, if necessary, are not included in the price.

About the Restaurants

Mongolians traditionally subsist on mutton, beef, noodles, and dairy products. The main specialties are "finger" mutton (hunks of boiled or roast mutton eaten from the bone), milk tea, cheese, and airag. Less com-

If you have
2–3
days

Go to **Hohhot** ❶–❼ ▶ to explore its temples, mosque, and old town. The next day travel 87 km (54 mi) to **Xilamuren** ❽ to tour the grassland, visit *aobaos* (hilltop shrines) and local people, and try horseback riding and Mongolian wrestling. Stay one or two nights in a yurt. Return to Hohhot.

If you have
5–6
days

Take the train from Beijing to **Ulaan Baatar** ⓫–⓰ ▶. Spend the first day visiting the city, temples, and museums. Travel 360 km (223 mi) west across the grassland by four-wheel-drive vehicle to **Karakorum** ⓭. Stay two or three nights in a ger (a Mongolian yurt), spending the days touring the grassland, horseback riding, visiting historic sites and Mongolian families, and watching horses, sheep, camels, and wildlife. Drive back to Ulaan Baatar, stopping to climb sand dunes near Hogno Khaan Mountain. If time permits, add a day trip from Ulaan Baatar to **Manzshir Khiid** ⓱. Fly back to Beijing.

11

If you have
10–12
days

Starting from Hohhot, drive 250 km (155 mi) to Ejin Horo Qi, site of the **Chinggis Khaan Mausoleum** ❿. Stay in a yurt and return the next day to Hohhot. Spend a day visiting Hohhot's temples and old town. Drive 170 km (105 mi) to **Gegentala** ❾ and Xilamuren for a taste of life in the grassland; spend two nights in a yurt. Return to Hohhot before flying direct or via Beijing to Ulaan Baatar. Then visit Karakorum and the Manzshir Monastery as above, adding a day of horseback riding in **Terelj-Gorkhi** ⓲ if you have time. Return from Ulaan Baatar to Beijing by train.

---

mon in the cities, this fare is usually served at grassland yurt sites. Mutton hotpot, thin slivers of meat plunged fondue style into a circular trough of boiling water surrounding a miniature stove, is popular in Inner Mongolia. Served with bean curd, noodles, vegetables, and chili and sesame sauces, a hotpot is perfect for a group. Two of Ulaan Baatar's most popular snacks are *buuz* (mutton-filled dumplings like Chinese *baozi*) and *horshoo* (mutton fritters). Hohhot and Ulaan Baatar have restaurants serving good Chinese, Korean, Muslim, and Russian-style dishes. If you have the opportunity to try a *khorkhog* (mutton, vegetables, and spices pressure-cooked with heated rocks on an open fire) in the countryside you will experience the essence of Mongolian cuisine: rich, tasty, high in protein, and definitely not low calorie. On almost every block in Ulaan Baatar you will find several *guantz* (Mongolian restaurants), so it is not difficult to sample the traditional fare—linguistic challenges notwithstanding.

About the Hotels

Retiring to the comfort of a ger, or yurt, after watching a vivid sunset over boundless grassland, you can open the roof flap to reveal the clear, starry night sky. Gers are warm but do not have toilets or showers; the latter are usually provided in separate blocks of circular wood, concrete, or tin buildings styled to blend with the gers. Hohhot and Ulaan Baatar both have high-quality hotels. Rural hotels can be very basic, with few facilities in the rooms other than TV sets, so ger accommodation is generally more enjoyable. Some tourist yurts in Inner Mongolia have smaller tin "yurts" attached, which house en suite toilets and washbasins. When entering a ger, especially one belonging to a Mongolian family, avoid treading on the wooden threshold; many local people believe this represents stepping on the neck of the ger's owner. It is also considered polite to enter the ger in a clockwise manner.

WHAT IT COSTS In Yuan and Tugriks				
$$$$	$$$	$$	$	¢
INNER MONGOLIA				
RESTAURANTS	over 125	75–125	30–74	15–29	under 15
HOTELS	over 1,500	800–1,500	500–799	200–499	under 200
REPUBLIC OF MONGOLIA				
RESTAURANTS	over 20,000	13,000–20,000	5,000–12,999	2,000–4,999	under 2,000
HOTELS	over 110,000	65,000–110,000	30,000–64,999	15,000–29,999	under 15,000

Restaurant prices are for a main course, excluding tax and tips. Hotel prices are for a standard double room, including taxes.

Timing
The dry continental climate makes May to September the best time for temperatures and for greenery. Because most of the Mongolias occupy a plateau at an altitude of 3,250–4,900 feet, even summer evenings can be cool. Severe cold and wind make winter touring impractical. Early to late spring can be very dusty with winds sandblasting pedestrians and leaving eyes stinging with dust. Naadam fairs take place from mid-July to mid-August. As a result, this is peak tourist season when some tours and hotels may be fully booked.

INNER MONGOLIA

Inner Mongolia (Nei Menggu) is a vast area across northern China. Its borders with Soviet-influenced Mongolia and eastern Siberia made it a sensitive region during the Sino-Soviet Cold War (mainly during the 1960s). Around 70% of Inner Mongolia is arid grassland sparsely occupied by herds of sheep, horses, goats, cattle, and camels. Open steppe land occupied by nomadic yurt dwellers can be found in most parts of the region. Short trips, even day trips, are possible from Hohhot.

Hohhot

▶ *10 hrs (410 km [254 mi]) by train west of Beijing.*

In the Chinese-dominated city of Hohhot the only yurts you see are in restaurants and entertainment centers, though some of the modern white-tile office blocks are topped by yurt-style domes. Many of the more run-down areas in western parts of the city have undergone redevelopment, replacing the formerly grimy hutong-style residences with drab

11

Grassland Adventure

The spectacle of a Mongolian rider chasing galloping horses across a lush green plain or steppe is something most visitors to the Mongolias want to see. Because of the great distances involved and lack of settlements and public transport, it is best to travel by minibus, jeep, horse, or plane. Unless you are competent in Chinese or Mongolian, an English-speaking guide is essential. Before you book a tour, ensure that both the booking office and the tour guides are licensed, check the itinerary carefully, and make sure the price is agreed upon in advance. There's no better way to see the grassland than by horse; the small, sturdy Mongolian horse is amazingly well suited to the high plains—though long rides can be hard for novices. On some tours yurts or gers are carried with the group, providing a taste of real nomadic life. All tours of more than one day need to be booked in advance. Camel tours of desert areas can also be arranged. Many different tours are possible in both Mongolias, incorporating varied terrains—steppes, mountains, deserts, forests—ancient ruins, temples, traditional crafts, animal husbandry, and wildlife.

Naadam Fairs

Naadams are annual gatherings of nomadic Mongol tribes for shamanist worship, trade, and courtship, along with archery, wrestling, equestrian, and drinking competitions. Although a few fairs are now staged mainly for tourists, the games and pageants are taken seriously by local people. Events, including evening song and dance performances, usually take place in a wide arena encircled by gers, market stalls, and food tents. Archery, horse racing, and the highly ritualistic Mongolian wrestling comprise the "Three Manly Sports" that draw the greatest amount of publicity. Though it may at first confuse those unfamiliar with its elaborate rules and symbolism, Mongolian wrestling is a spectacle of color and pageantry, whatever one may think of the somewhat sedate pace at which the combat seems to progress. Naadam offers locals and foreigners alike an opportunity to celebrate at the height of summer after a long winter, while also demonstrating the essential survival skills that have permitted the Mongols to survive in an environment inhospitable to those less adaptable to its demands. Naadam fairs normally last three days and start around July 11 in Mongolia and in late July or mid-August in Inner Mongolia. Exact dates vary each year. The biggest festivities are in Ulaan Baatar, which holds grand opening ceremonies and features the best of the competition.

Temple Touring

With greater religious freedom in China (since the 1980s) and Mongolia (since the departure of the Soviets in the early '90s), many Buddhist temples have been revived. During the Stalinist purges of the 1930s, more than 500 monasteries and temples were destroyed in Mongolia alone. Only a few have been rebuilt. Temples in the Mongolias follow Lamaism, a Tibetan branch of Buddhism which belongs to the same order as the one headed by the Dalai Lama: the Yellow Hat or Gelugpa sect. Two of the best temples for Lamaist art, music, monks, and local devotees are Gandan Khiid, in Ulaan Baatar, and Xiletuzhao, in Hohhot.

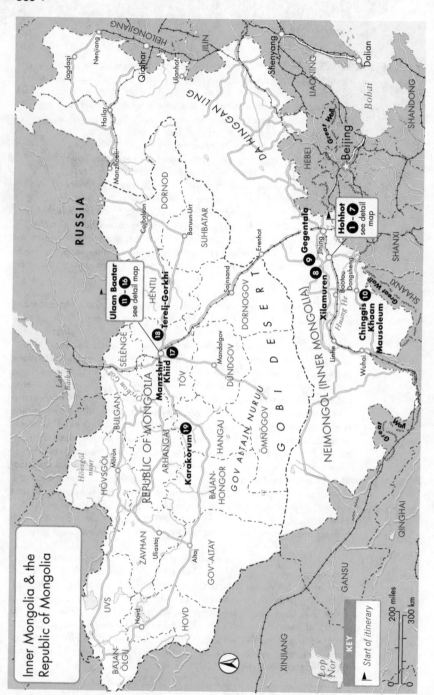

Inner Mongolia & the
Republic of Mongolia

grey six story apartment buildings. While relatively clean and orderly by Chinese standards, Hohhot remains in many respects remarkably monotone and lacks any significant character to distinguish it from similar sized cities elsewhere in China.

Hohhot is the capital of the Inner Mongolia Autonomous Region. Pronounced "Hu-he-hao-te," or "Hu-shi" in its short form, it is Mongolian for "blue city." Hui Muslims are the most prominent minority in a population of 1 million. Mongolian, Ewenki, Daur, and other minorities live in the city but rarely wear traditional dress and are relatively invisible among the large Han Chinese majority.

A trip to Inner Mongolia must include a visit to the *caoyuan* (grassland), and Hohhot is the region's main base for grassland tours. The city itself has several interesting diversions, notably the Inner Mongolia Museum, White Pagoda, and what remains of the old city section next to Dazhao Temple.

Despite the rarity of real horses and camels, other than those used as photographers' props in Xinhua Square, the city's equine symbols are outlasting newer icons. Hohhot's Mao statue, which stood outside the railway station as many others still do across China, was felled in 1987 and replaced by a rearing silver horse. Another sign of China's reforms are the thriving mosques and Lamaist temples of Hohhot's old town.

Xinhua Square is fascinating in the early morning, when it is full of people practicing *qi gong* (a breathing exercise), playing badminton, basketball, volleyball, or soccer, or just promenading. In the evening, children's rides and trampolines, food stalls, an English-language corner, photographers, and skateboarders take over. On the streets are kebab sellers, cigarette and yogurt stands, cyclists, yellow taxis, and tricycle carts carrying wardrobes and refrigerators. Restaurants are busy every evening and, as in Ulaan Baatar, many men drink heavily.

★ ☾ ❶ Visit the **Inner Mongolia Museum** (Nei Menggu Bowuguan) to find out how to build a yurt or a birch-bark tepee, or to learn how Mongolians once used boomerangs to hunt hares, marmots, and other small animals from horseback. The museum has a section devoted to fossilized remains of dinosaurs and other ancient animals. It houses Asia's largest dinosaur skeleton as well as a giant brontosaurus skeleton that fills its own room. On the other side of the museum are exhibitions of minority cultures, with items such as Mongolian bows, saddles, a ger, a Daur shaman's costume, and an Oroqen tepee. The second floor's focus is on the history of Inner Mongolia: one wing is devoted to Stone Age artifacts; another section, with photographs and war memorabilia, offers a glimpse of the region's 20th-century history—as seen through the eyes of the Chinese Communist Party. Some captions have English translations. Children will enjoy the numerous dinosaur models. ⊠ *2 Xinhua Dajie at Holon Buir Nan Lu* ☎ *0471/628–1487* 🎟 *Y10* ☉ *May–Sept., Wed.–Mon. 9–5; Oct.–Apr., Wed.–Mon. 8–6.*

★ ❷ Bare wood and subtle, faded shades of green and red make **Xiletuzhao Temple** (Xiletuzhao Si) more of a genuine throwback to the past than many

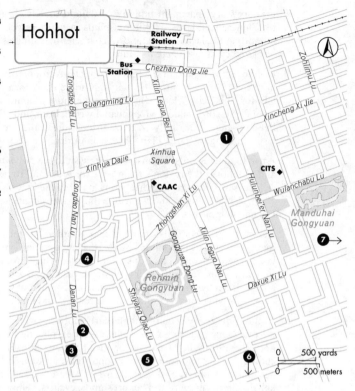

of China's more garishly renovated temples, though the plain, unadorned facade may leave some visitors disappointed. Although the temple boasts a 400-year history, the current buildings date from the 19th century, after the original structure burned down; the ruined annex opposite the temple's main entrance is undergoing a slow renovation. Duck into caverns under the temple to visit the Tibetan Buddhist vision of hell, with graphic depictions of the various tortures awaiting sinners. If you go weekdays you may meet the 11th Grand Living Buddha (now in his sixties), who runs the temple. Monks still come to pray in the mornings from 8 to 10. ⚜ Off Da Nan Jie, 5 mins north of Dazhao Temple, on east side of street 🎫 Y10 ☺ May–Sept., daily 8–6; Oct.–Apr., daily 10–4.

❸ First built in the Ming Dynasty, **Dazhao Temple** (Dazhao Si) is also known as Silver Buddha Temple, for its statue of the Sakyamuni Buddha cast mainly from silver. The temple was rebuilt in 1640, and many of the existing structures and artifacts date from then, though the result isn't awe-inspiring if you've been to other Chinese temples. Still, the temple is an active one, with several young monks in brown robes who wander hourly around the pavilions chanting. The 400-year-old Silver Buddha is housed in one of China's best-preserved Ming Dynasty wooden halls. Close to the altar is an exquisite pair of carved dragon pillars, and by the door to the hall are two cast-iron lions, with cast-iron incense burners in the courtyard outside. To the west of the temple, a street market and the cobblestone lanes of what remains of the old city section may prove more fascinating to wander through; under the sloping eaves of old wooden roofs, an older generation of Chinese live out their days as they've done for years. ⊠ *Da Zhao Qian Jie off Da Nan Jie, on west side* ☎ *0471/630–3154* ✆ *Y15* ⊗ *Daily 8–6:30.*

4 A gray medieval fortress set amid the green-trimmed walls of a Chinese courtyard, the **Great Mosque** (Qingzhen Dasi) is readily identified by its crescent-top minaret and Arabic script, and by the bearded Muslim men who congregate outside. The mosque dates mainly from the Qing Dynasty and is surrounded by the few *hutongs* (alleys) of Hui Muslim houses, shops, and restaurants that have survived recent redevelopment. Tea and snacks can be purchased at a lively street market just outside the mosque. With the surrounding buildings under reconstruction at the time of publication, access was limited to the rear courtyard. Non-Muslims are not permitted entry to the mosque. ⊠ *28 Tongdao Lu, at Zhongshan Xi Lu* ⊗ *Daily 10–4, except during prayer between noon and 2.*

5 The Indian-style **Five Pagoda Temple** (Wuta Si) was built in 1733 as a stupa. In the Qing Dynasty the temple was part of a larger complex, but little else remains. Its square base tapers upward to five glazed pagodas decorated with Buddhas and Mongolian, Tibetan, and Sanskrit script. Behind the pagoda is a carved screen that includes a Mongolian astronomical chart, purportedly the only one of its kind ever discovered. Climb the narrow stairwell up to the pagodas for a view of the surrounding neighborhoods of tile-roof adobe houses. ⊠ *Wuta Si Hou Jie off Shiyang Qiao Lu* ✆ *Y15* ⊗ *Daily 8–6:30.*

6 The **Tomb of Wang Zhaojun** (Zhaojun Mu) is one of nine such tombs spread across Inner Mongolia. Many variants of Wang Zhaojun's story are floating around, but the most intriguing one goes something like this: one of China's four historical beauties, Wang Zhaojun was a ravishing imperial concubine who lived during the Han Dynasty. Despite her beauty, she was never called by Emperor Yuandi to serve him, for the ruler used portraits of the women to decide his bed partner for the night, never realizing that his crafty court painter was beautifying the portraits of the concubines who bribed him. When Emperor Yuandi decided to appease the chief of the warring southern Hun tribes with a bride, he chose the ugliest of the concubine pictures, and discovered his mistake too late. Wang Zhaojun's "sacrifice" in 33 BC, which led to 60 years of peace, is still celebrated throughout the region. A pyramid-shape burial mound 98 feet high is topped by a small pavilion. There are good views of the surrounding park and farmland. One story says that only a pair of Wang Zhaojun's shoes was buried here. To get here, hire a taxi for about Y50–Y60 (all cabbies know the way), or hire a car through CITS. Alternatively, take Bus 1 south from the Bayantala Hotel located on Xilin Leguo Bei Lu and transfer to Bus 44 at Nanchangfang. ✛ *9 km (6 mi) south of Hohhot* ✆ *Y25* ⊗ *Daily 8–6.*

7 Few tourists visit the **White Pagoda** (Baita), but it is one of the finest brick pagodas in northern China. The 138-foot-high octagonal structure has seven stories coated in chalk. Restored in the 1990s, the pagoda was first constructed in the Liao Dynasty (916–1125) and was once a destination for pilgrims from all over Asia. Easy to get to by taxi or by a bicycle ride through flat farmland, the pagoda grounds make a good picnic spot. Note that no buses run here; a hired car with driver will run Y60–Y70. ✦ *16 km (10 mi) east of Hohhot* ✉ *Y10* ☉ *May–Sept., daily 8–6; Oct.–Apr., daily 9:30–5.*

Where to Stay & Eat

Hohhot's main specialty, Mongolian hotpot, is traditionally a group meal eaten from a large communal pot. Many of the city's best restaurants are in the best hotels; eateries outside the hotels don't usually have English-speaking staff or English menus, but it is possible to enjoy an excellent and inexpensive meal at any of the many *canting* (dining hall; pronounced "tsan-ting") if you can remember a few of your favorite Chinese dishes, or are willing to gamble a little. Casual but neat dress is the norm.

$–$$$ ✕ **Min Su Cun.** At the end of a long dark alleyway, this rustic, white, double-decker warehouse of a Chinese eatery rises into view, replete with folk touches like red lanterns, hewn wooden furniture, and banquet rooms ornamentally trimmed with tiled eaves. Popular with locals, this hotel restaurant is touted for its hotpot as well as good traditional Chinese fare served up in a cheerful atmosphere: servers in red-flowered overalls bring prompt service with a smile. ✉ *Next to Xincheng Hotel, 40 Hulunbei'er Nan Lu, Entrance is off Wulanchabu Lu, west of Inner Mongolia Hotel; look for the red Fu Li Hua sign* ☎ *0471/629–2534 or 0471/629–2533* ▤ *No credit cards.*

$–$$$ ✕ **Sorabol Korean Restaurant** (Solabuo Hanguo Canting). Located on the lower level of the Zhaojun Hotel, the Sorabol is part of a chain, with other locations in Beijing and Seoul. The environment is serene with calligraphy-adorned walls and soft classical music cascading gently down upon diners. Quality is consistent and service is attentive (at times bordering on obsessive during off-peak hours). Inexpensive favorites such as *bibimbap* (rice, vegetables, beef, hot sauce, and a fried egg on top) and spicy tofu soup are naturally accompanied by a selection of small plates of kimchi, cucumbers in chili sauces, and rice-based soups. Tabletop Korean barbecues allow for a wide selection of finely sliced meats to be cooked with the assistance of the diligent staff. A full selection of Korean, Chinese, and foreign beers and spirits is available. Ten rooms are available for private parties. ✉ *53 Xinhua Dajie, ground floor of Zhaojun Hotel* ☎ *0471/696–2211 Ext. 8158* ▤ *No credit cards.*

¢–$$ ✕ **Da Bu Tong Huo Guo.** With six outlets in Hohhot this hotpot chain offers up excellent quality food at a very modest price. Choose from a staggering number of chicken, beef, mutton, tofu, and vegetable plates (most less than Y10), then select the broths in which to cook the dishes. While the decor is decidedly minimalist, the bustling restaurant offers a glimpse of gregarious China. Local beers and Chinese *baijiu* (hard liquor) are available for Y5–Y15. ✉ *Nan Wu Lu and Zan Bei Lu* ☎ *0471/626–3898* ▤ *No credit cards.*

¢–$$ ✕ **Malaqin Fandian.** In a sunny, spacious dining room an army of waiters wearing bright pink-and-green vests serves up excellent southern Chinese cuisine and tea shooting out from a long-necked Dai brass teapot. Succulent meat, vegetable, and seafood entries are available—try the *xiangpu daieu liu* (tender deep-fried carp cutlets cooked with chili peppers, onions, and spices)—but save room for the house specialty: a delicious *yindu shoupao bing* (Indian-style naan), served in a variety of salty and sweet flavors from curried beef to apple. No English menu is available. ⊠ *122 Xincheng Xi Jie* ☎ *0471/692–6685* ▭ *No credit cards.*

$$–$$$ ✕▤ **Inner Mongolia Hotel** (Nei Menggu Fandian). Completely renovated with a smart new look, Inner Mongolia's first five-star hotel for foreign tourists has a 20-meter swimming pool, one of the best restaurants in Hohhot, and a multilingual staff. Upon entry you can pass through the palatial lobby and comfortably enjoy a coffee or aperitif in the delightful colonial-styled lounge. The hotel has always been a favorite with tour groups, and an excellent venue for conferences. The Florence restaurant ($$) succeeds in the unexpected combination of Italian and Chinese dishes complemented by a respectable selection of imported wines and several palatable Chinese reds. ⊠ *Wulanchabu Lu, 010010* ☎ *0471/693–8888* 🖷 *0471/695–2288* ✍ *nmghotel@nmghotel.com* ➘ *370 rooms, 30 suites* ⚴ *4 restaurants, cable TV, pool, massage, sauna, bar, concert hall, dance club, business services, meeting rooms, travel services* ▭ *AE, MC, V.*

★ $ ✕▤ **Zhaojun Hotel** (Zhaojun Dajiudian). This sleek but aging Hong Kong joint venture offers comfortable and spacious rooms, with touches like gold-striped comforters and pine panels. However, the bathrooms are tiny, the reception desk downstairs is often chaotic, and the elevators are slow. From the reception area, a corridor leads to a large shopping arcade, with a bank, travel center, and bowling alley. The hotel's main restaurant, the Suiqing Garden Restaurant (¢–$$), is popular with locals in search of a delicious seafood or vegetable hotpot, Cantonese dishes such as sizzling "iron plate" beef and Singapore rice noodles, and snake, frog, and crab dishes. ⊠ *53 Xinhua Dajie, 010050* ☎ *0471/696–2211* 🖷 *0471/696–8825* ➘ *247 rooms, 18 suites* ⚴ *3 restaurants, cable TV, gym, hair salon, bowling, bar, dance club, shops, business services, travel services; no a/c* ▭ *AE, MC, V.*

$$$ ▤ **Holiday Inn** (Jia Ri Jiu Dian). Opened in late 2003, the Holiday Inn is the newest addition to an already crowded market. Geared toward business travelers, the hotel features some of the most luxurious suites in a location as downtown as is possible in Hohhot. Rooms are spacious and bright, and unrivaled in functionality (with plenty of desk space, Internet connections, and new furniture). A high percentage of the knowledgeable staff speak English, a rarity in Hohhot, and a superb business center, a secretarial service, and rooms equipped with separate IDD (international direct dial), fax, and DSL lines all make the hotel a choice destination for conference attendees. The hotel is also conveniently located a block west of Hohhot's only McDonald's and KFC, for those seeking the familiar taste of fast food. ⊠ *185 Zhongshan Xi Lu* ☎ *0471/635–1888* 🖷 *0471/635–0888* ⊕ *www.holidayinn-hohhot.com* ➘ *198 rooms, 6 suites* ⚴ *4 restaurants, gym, massage, sauna, spa, business services* ▭ *AE, DC, MC, V.*

★ $$–$$$ ⊞ **Xincheng Hotel** (Xincheng Binguan). Once the only luxury hotel in Inner Mongolia, this former 1950s Soviet-style sanitarium is now a vast hotel complex surrounded by evergreens and lush gardens, and crowned by an indoor 25-meter swimming pool. A 1998 high-rise has modern, standard rooms that have some of the prettiest views in town. An older building, to the side, offers shabbier accommodation, with similar views, at much lower rates. The complex houses the three-story Xincheng Club, a conference and entertainment center that has a variety of activities from bowling to minigolf to karaoke. It's popular with locals. ⊠ *40 Hulunbei'er Nan Lu, 010010* ☎ *0471/629–2288* 🖷 *0471/629–2334* ⊕ *www.xincheng-hotel.com.cn* ⇘ *313 rooms, 45 suites* ⚙ *9 restaurants, cable TV, tennis court, pool, gym, hair salon, massage, bicycles, bowling, business services, travel services; no a/c in some rooms* 🖃 *AE, MC, V.*

$$ ⊞ **Jin Hui Hotel.** This distinctive glass-and-steel high-rise would look more at home in modern Shanghai than in dilapidated Hohhot. A high-ceilinged lobby with a glittering ballroom chandelier and white marble columns has a restaurant and money-exchange services. Although the hallways and lobby appear strangely narrow, the large-windowed rooms are spacious and have bright carpeting, wooden furniture, and floral bedspreads. The hotel is close to the railway station, restaurants, and shopping. The entrance is hidden to the left of the large Industrial and Commercial Bank of China in the same building. ⊠ *105 Xilin Leguo Bei Lu, 010010* ☎ *0471/694–0099 or 0471/694–0214* 🖷 *0471/694–0088* ⊕ *www.jh-hotel.com.cn* ⇘ *73 rooms, 30 suites* ⚙ *Restaurant, food court, cable TV, gym, massage, billiards, bar, nightclub, shops, business services, travel services* 🖃 *AE, MC, V.*

$ ⊞ **Bayantala Hotel.** Surprisingly modern, from its sloping entranceway to the bar in the brightly lighted reception area, only the pink cement floor betrays the hotel's Socialist origins. Wood and amber tones dominate the clean, standard rooms in the VIP building. Popular with Chinese travelers and conveniently located, one of the hotel's few drawbacks is how little English spoken by the staff. On the first floor is a branch of Beijing's famed roast-duck restaurant, Quanjude. ⊠ *42 Xilin Leguo Bei Lu, 010020* ☎ *0471/696–3344* 🖷 *0471/696–7390* ⇘ *122 rooms, 4 suites* ⚙ *6 restaurants, cable TV, hair salon, billiards, bar, business services, travel services* 🖃 *AE, MC, V.*

¢ ⊞ **San Yuan Da Jiu Dian.** Roughly three blocks east of the train station amid a strip of small noodle shops, the San Yuan may have worn red rugs in its corridors, but it also has spacious clean rooms with (usually) 24-hour hot water, modern bathrooms, and friendly service. ⊠ *188 Che Zhan Dong Jie, on the south side of the street, 010050* ☎ *0471/628–0423 Ext. 8666* 🖷 *0471/628–0426* ⇘ *47 rooms, 3 suites* ⚙ *Restaurant, cable TV, sauna; no a/c* 🖃 *No credit cards.*

Nightlife

All major hotels have discos and/or karaoke bars. The Xincheng Club at the Xincheng Hotel has the widest range of evening activities. Many smaller hotels and restaurants offer similar but less grandly presented options.

Resembling a Rocky Mountain cabin from the inside, the diminutive **Yesterday's Ballad Bar** (✛ 1 block north of Bayantala on east side of Xilin Leguo Bei Lu; look for Heineken sign across from Jin Hui Hotel) is a relaxing place to sip a beer or simply hear a few crooners sing along with the band. With two upper decks at each end of the stage, the atmosphere can rapidly become smoky and rowdy at the end of the week as the place gets going toward midnight.

New York Club (Niu Yue Julebu; ✉ 58 Dong Ying Nan Lu ☎ 0471/492–0022) is an ambitious attempt to provide every form of evening entertainment in a single venue. The ground floor is occupied by a large semi-circular dance floor replete with Stars-and-Stripes paraphernalia, whirling propellers and, predictably, pounding rave music at decibel levels bordering on the industrial. Upstairs, a quiet lounge is available for those seeking conversation, and no fewer than 37 private karaoke rooms.

Shopping

Prior to heading out of the city to the grassland, outdoor gear can be purchased at **Beiweixian Hu Wai** (✉ 3 Daxue Xi Lu, slightly west and north of No. 16 Middle School ☎ 0471/696–4814 or 139/4718–7540 ⊕ www.outdoorsnmg.com). It sells a variety of Gore-Tex gear, trekking poles, and hiking boots at decent prices. Staff speak some English.

The **Minorities' Department Store** (Minzu Shangchang; ✉ 69 Zhongshan Xi Lu) is the best place for cashmere clothing and souvenirs such as Mongolian robes and hats, hotpots, ornamented teapots, knives, and bowls, though you may have to hunt through the tourist kitsch. The large hotels sell similar items, but choice is more limited and prices higher. The Dazhao and Xiletuzhao temples both have shops selling Buddhist and other souvenirs.

Side Trips to the Grassland

In Hohhot tour companies compete fiercely for independent travelers to the grassland (*caoyuan*). Tourists are often assailed as soon as they arrive at the railway station and some companies even have stands at the Beijing station. Most tours will give you a wonderful experience of the grassland, but don't be rushed into booking. Check the itinerary and price carefully first, especially if you want to do some serious horseback riding. Standard packages usually allow little more than a few minutes on a horse. Major operators all offer the destinations that follow.

Most of the agencies feature similar itineraries, but are willing to customize to meet your needs. Some degree of English is spoken at most agencies. However, to avoid confusion you should verify your precise travel arrangements with your hotel's staff.

❽ At **Xilamuren** you can spend your days roaming across the carpet of green on foot or on horseback, trying Mongolian wrestling, and visiting local families, a temple, and *aobaos* (hilltop shrines). Nights involve folk songs and dancing, listening to the *matouqin* (horse-head fiddle), and eating roast mutton. Some people criticize tourist sites like Xilamuren as not being genuine, but the rolling grassland scenery, horses, sheep, temples, and aobaos are all authentic. Local people in this area mainly live in villages or isolated farmhouses, so yurts are restricted to seasonal use by herdspeople. Visitors can sleep in a traditionally constructed yurt with some modern facilities. Prices range from Y120 for lodging without self-contained washroom, to Y160 for basic accommodation (*pubao*), to Y180 for deluxe (*haobao*), the latter two including washroom facilities. If you're a first-time visitor to the grassland, you're likely to enjoy it, but return visitors may be disappointed. A Naadam fair is held for tourists in the second half of August, but at any time from mid-June to late August the land will be green and the air redolent with the smell of grass and native flowers. Horses can be hired on-site for around Y50 per hour. ✥ *Road to Bayan Aobao, 87 km (54 mi) northwest of Hohhot; book a tour, or take a bus to Zhaohe, Xilamuren (2–3 hrs, about Y20).*

❾ Gegentala has scenery and activities similar to those at Xilamuren but is better during the Naadam fair. Events at the tourist site merge with those of a larger fair nearby, and wrestling, archery, horse racing, and rodeo competitions at the tourist site are all attended enthusiastically by the locals. The men and women of the region are known for their wrestling skills; the Inner Mongolia regional team usually takes part in the local Naadam wrestling competitions. Over the hill to the south of the tourist camp, a tent-encircled Naadam arena is set up with food stalls, circus tents, and a stage for Mongolian song and dance. The lively fair lasts for about a week, immediately following the events at the tourist site. Book a tour, as Gegentala is difficult to get to independently. ✥ *Siziwang Qi, 170 km (105 mi) northeast of Hohhot.*

❿ A journey to the **Chinggis Khaan Mausoleum** (Chengjisi Han Lingyuan) involves crossing the Yellow River to the desert and grassland of the Ordos Highland, where eventually the imposing navy-and-tan ceramic domes of the mausoleum come into view. The tomb was built in 1954 and refurbished after the Cultural Revolution. In front of the central chamber stands a large golden censer between gigantic pikes topped with the nine-yak-tail banner of the Mongol armies. At the entrance a white-marble effigy of the all-conquering warrior greets visitors with a steely gaze. Rich murals decorate the interior walls, portraying the life story of Chinggis Khaan with details such as a depiction of the traditional Mongolian method of skinning a sheep. Mongolians place offerings of incense, liquor, cigarettes, sweets, and trinkets in front of a yellow-silk yurt purported to contain the great Khaan's funeral bier. From the buildings you can see open grassland grazed by sheep, horses, goats, and camels. The entire location is undergoing redevelopment that is to include a hotel, a model traditional village, a horse arts performance center, and an entirely new museum devoted to the legacy of Chinggis and the Mongolian people. The mausoleum will be accessible during the entire construction period. A trip to the Resonant Sand Gorge and Wudang Lamasery (Lamaist Monastery), near Baotou, can be combined with a visit to the mausoleum; expect to book a two-day tour, minimum, if you're visiting from Hohhot. ✥ *25 km (15 mi) from Ejin Horo Qi; from Hohhot, take a 3-hr bus ride (Y30) or the more comfortable but slower 4-hr train (Y30–Y45) to Dongsheng and then a 1½-hr bus ride from there* 🚍 *Y30* ☉ *Daily 9–5.*

Xilamuren, Gegentala, and the Chinggis Khaan Mausoleum have yurt camps for tourists. All camps have dining halls where mutton dominates the set menus, accompanied by seasonal Chinese standards such as stir-fried chicken and chili, green beans, and egg-fried rice. Vegetarian and other special meals also can be ordered. All camps have bathroom facilities, including basic showers that do not always have hot water, in communal blocks outside the yurts. Xilamuren and Gegentala also offer individual tourist yurts, which have a tiny hut attached containing a toilet and washbasin. At all sites yurts are spaced out on concrete bases. They have traditional latticed frames with birch roof struts, felt walls covered with canvas, and thick rugs and low beds on the floor. Quilts, pillows, hot-water flasks, and electric lights are standard. In summer you are unlikely to be cold in a yurt, but at other times you should take warm sleeping clothes.

Inner Mongolia A to Z

To research prices, get advice from other travelers, and book travel arrangements, visit www.fodors.com.

AIR TRAVEL TO & FROM INNER MONGOLIA

Regular flights connect Hohhot with Beijing, Guangzhou, Shenzhen, Shanghai, Xian, and Wuhan. There are flights between Ulaan Baatar and Hohhot every Monday and Thursday.

🚹 Carriers A Mongolian airline, Aero Mongolia, runs flights twice a week from Hohhot to Ulaan Baatar.

🚹 Airlines & Contacts **Aero Mongolia** ⊠ 5 Wu Lan Xiao Qu, Xin Cheng Qu (same building as Mongolian Embassy) ☎ 0471/430-2026 🖷 0471/430-2015.

AIRPORTS & TRANSFERS

Hohhot Airport is 35 km (22 mi) east of the city center. Airport buses leave from the China Air ticketing office. A taxi fare from downtown should cost no more than Y30.

🚹 Airport Information **Hohhot Airport** ☎ 0471/696-4102 or 0471/494-1122.

🚹 Taxis & Shuttles **China Air ticketing office** ⊠ Xilin Leguo Bei Lu and Wulaan Xijie, southwest catercorner to Bayantala Hotel ☎ 0471/693-3637 or 0471/693-4005.

BIKE TRAVEL

Hohhot is flat, and cycling is the best way to get around. Bicycles can be rented outside the Xincheng Hotel. You will normally be asked to deposit some form of identification. If you're fit, you can ride to the White Pagoda or the Tomb of Wang Zhaojun. Traffic is much lighter than in Beijing and other larger cities, but take care. Watch the locals, then copy their moves.

BUS TRAVEL TO & FROM INNER MONGOLIA

Modern buses, many equipped with video equipment, run daily to Datong and Beijing. These buses, some with sleepers, are quicker and cheaper than the train, but less comfortable. The Hohhot bus station is right outside the railway station, to the west of the station square.

🚹 Bus Information **Hohhot Bus Station** ⊠ Chezhan Xi Lu 🖷 No phone.

BUS TRAVEL WITHIN INNER MONGOLIA

City buses in Hohhot are crowded and relatively slow, though the fare is less than Y2. They can be useful if you're just exploring the downtown shopping area or for cutting your cab costs en route to some of the sites in the greater vicinity of Hohhot.

EMERGENCIES

There are no hospitals or clinics with English-speaking staff. If you need medical help, ask your hotel to assist. The large hotels have competent security staff and sometimes police officers on-site.

INTERNET SERVICES

Several Internet bars have sprung up around Hohhot, most of them small and crowded with teens playing video games. Many are dingy, smoke-filled places where you will want to watch your wallet. However, a couple are relatively clean with fully functional keyboards. Some establishments require a passport number and the purchase of a card for Y10. You are refunded whatever amount is left when you leave.

Note that Internet bars are often shut down for political reasons and you may have better luck asking your hotel where the nearest *shang sang ba* (Internet café) is located. If it has closed by the time you arrive, the best café is in the downtown area, at Wei Duo Li Wang Ba, with 50 computers and charging Y2 per hour for Internet use. Runners-up include Fei Yu Wang Ba and Shi Dai Wang Ba.

🔲 Internet Cafés **Fei Yu Wang Ba and Shi Dai Wang Ba** ✉ Near intersection of Renmin Lu and Dizhe Bie Jie, from Zhongshan Lu walk south on Renmin Lu 4 blocks to Dizhe Bie Jie. **Wei Duo Li Wang Ba** ✉ Roughly 1 block west of Xilin Leguo Bei Lu; on north side of Zhongshan Dong Lu; look for sign in alley adjacent to bike stand ☎ 0471/691–8305.

MAIL & SHIPPING

The Central Post Office is on Zhongshan Dong Lu at Renmin Lu. China Air Express is located next door to the China Air ticketing office.
🔲 Offices **China Air Express** ✉ South of Xinhua Sq. ☎ 0471/691–0691 ⊕ www.cae.com.cn.

MONEY MATTERS

ATMS   There are ATMs in many of the larger hotels and at all of the larger banks. Most cards permit withdrawal in local currency, but keep receipts in case there is any system problem.

CURRENCY   The main branch of the Bank of China, opposite the Zhaojun Hotel,
EXCHANGE   changes all major foreign-currency traveler's checks and cash. Smaller branch banks and larger hotels have foreign-exchange services. Note that the banks will not change Mongolian tugriks, so if you're coming from Mongolia be sure to exchange Mongolian currency before departure.
🔲 Exchange Services **Bank of China** ✉ Xinhua Dajie.

TAXIS

Taxis are plentiful and cheap in Hohhot. Metered fares begin at Y6, and most destinations within the city will cost no more than Y15.

TRAIN TRAVEL

Daily trains run from Hohhot's train station to Datong (4½ hours), Yinchuan (10 hours), Zhongwei (12 hours), Lanzhou (17½ hours), Tianjin (11 hours), and Beijing (10 hours). If you're traveling on to Mongolia, you can reach Ulaan Baatar by direct train that runs Wednesday and Sunday night (roughly 36 hours, Y500 hard sleeper, Y800 soft sleeper), or via the border town of Erlian.

To save Y150–Y200 on the trip, budget travelers can first buy a ticket from Hohhot to Erlian (or to the Mongolian border town of Zamin Uud), and then purchase the rest of the ticket to Ulaan Baatar from a train official, once customs inspections are complete. The best alternative to the two-hour (Y504) Beijing–Hohhot flight is the relatively pleasant overnight train (Y244 soft sleeper, Y159 hard sleeper). Train tickets, especially sleepers, are hard to obtain during holidays and high season; book through CITS, CTS, or hotel travel services at these times when it is worth the Y10–Y20 fee they charge. If you have the time, it may be worth comparing prices among these sources.

📋 Train Information **Hohhot Train Station** ✉ Chezhan Dong Jie ☎ 0471/224-3222.

TRAVEL AGENCIES

📋 Local Agent Referrals **CITS** ✉ Nei Menggu Lu You Ju (Inner Mongolia Tourism Bureau), 95 Yishuting Nan Jie, 3rd fl., next to the Inner Mongolia Hotel, ☎ 0471/620-3436, 0471/629-7534, or 0471/692-4494 ⊕ www.cits.com.cn. **CTS** ✉ 95 Yishuting Nan Jie, 1 fl. above CITS, ☎ 0471/696-4233 Ext. 8936. **Inner Mongolia Zhaojun Travel Service** ✉ Zhaojun Hotel lobby, 53 Xinhua Dajie ☎ 0471/691-8178, 0471/682-9948, or 139/4711-4028 🖷 0471/691-8278. **Inner Mongolia Guang Ming Travel Service Co., Ltd.** ✉ Datian Hotel, corner of Xinhua Dajie and Xilin Leguo Bei Lu ☎ 0471/226-3698 or 0471/683-6755 🖷 0471/226-3689. **Inner Mongolia Leisure Holiday Travel Service Co., Ltd.** ✉ Wang Fu Hotel, 1 Che Xhan Xi Lu, 1st fl., 1 block west of train station ☎ 0471/229-5111 or 0471/626-9618 🖷 0471/626-9618 ⊕ www.nmhhtaw.com.

VISITOR INFORMATION

Little information is available other than tour-company leaflets. Hotels and bookstores sell city maps in English and Chinese. The Foreign Languages Bookstore stocks an English-language guide to Inner Mongolia. In summer CITS and CTS have stands inside the soft-seat waiting room of the Beijing railway station. Other tour companies also have representatives at the station and most of the larger hotels offer package tour deals as well.

📋 Tourist Information **Foreign Languages Bookstore** (Xinhua Shudian) ✉ Xinhua Dajie on south side of street across from Zhaojun Hotel.

SIDE TRIP TO THE REPUBLIC OF MONGOLIA

The Republic of Mongolia, once known as Outer Mongolia, was a Soviet satellite state from the 1920s until the late 1980s. In the post-Communist era, Chinggis Khaan is once more a national hero. Mongolia is one of the world's least-developed countries but is a paradise for wildlife enthusiasts, refugees from consumerism, and anyone who likes open spaces. The country is home to snow leopards, Gobi bears, wild camels, giant sheep, wolves, falcons, golden eagles, buzzards, marmots, deer, and gazelles. The horse and the ger (yurt) remain the mainstays of life on the steppes and even on the outskirts of the capital, Ulaan Baatar. Lamaism, a Tibetan form of Buddhism that incorporates many shamanistic elements, has resumed its position as the main religion.

Ulaan Baatar

▶ *36 hrs (850 km [527 mi]) by train north of Hohhot; 30 hrs (1,120 km [694 mi]) by train northwest of Beijing.*

Grassland and forested hills surround the Russian-style capital of Ulaan Baatar, creating a frontierlike atmosphere completely different from that of any Chinese city. Alongside ice-cream-color baroque buildings, dilapidated wooden shacks, empty run-down lots, and vast Soviet-style apartment blocks, people occasionally ride horses along the busy streets while others drive shiny new luxury vehicles and SUVs. Trendy Western fashions are common, but *dhels* (long robes tied at the waist and designed for horseback riding), knee-length boots, and felt or fur hats are also widespread. The ger districts on the outskirts of the capital still house up to a third of the city's population.

In old Mongolia even the capital was nomadic. It moved more than 20 times along the Orkhon, Selenge, and Tuul river valleys before an encampment was established in 1639 at Urga, now Ulaan Baatar. After several more moves and three name changes, modern Ulaan Baatar was founded in 1924 and named after the hero of Mongolian independence, Sukhbaatar. Today the city has a population gradually approaching a million. As a result of the Communist government's promotion of population growth, more than 60% of Ulaan Baatar's—and the rest of the country's—residents are under 30, making Mongolia arguably the youngest nation in the world.

Once drab under Soviet control, Ulaan Baatar is home to a growing international development community. An influx of loans and foreign investment from institutions such as the World Bank, combined with the needs of an ever-increasing expatriate community, has led to the development of new housing complexes, stylish Western restaurants, Korean cosmetics boutiques, and improved facilities within the city limits. Though UB, as the city is known to its foreign community, is rapidly modernizing (with all the concomitant pollution, which at times casts a haze over the surrounding mountains), the metropolis continues to have a laid-back small-town atmosphere that makes it an exciting and pleasant place to while away a week.

Richly adorned museums, traditional Mongolian culture, and the Gandan Khiid Monastery are the prime attractions in the city. The Naadam fair, which begins around July 11, has horse racing, archery, and Mongolian wrestling. The city's main east–west boulevard is Enkh Tayvan Urgun Chuloo, also known as Peace Avenue, which runs past the city's center—Sukhbaatar Talbai–on the south side.

⑪ At **Gandan Monastery** (Gandan Khiid), golden roofs and Tibetan script, **Fodor'sChoice** brilliant white walls, and red-, green-, and yellow-painted woodwork **★** provide a colorful backdrop to morning worshippers who gather outside the temples. Monks dressed in red, gold, burgundy, violet, chocolate, and amber robes mingle with local people in suits, miniskirts, or traditional dhels. Built in 1840, Gandan Khiid is one of Mongolia's most important Lamaist monasteries (lamaseries). Most of the temple buildings were destroyed or ransacked in Mongolia's Stalinist purges and have been rebuilt.

Sometimes shaven-headed young monks will offer to show visitors the prayer circuit around the temples, where Buddhists turn copper- and brass-covered prayer wheels, prostrate themselves on prayer stands in front of the monastery's central white stupa, and touch the sacred temple walls, prayer flag mast, and bronze incense burners. The current Dalai Lama, head of the Yellow Hat sect of Lamaism, to which the monastery belongs, has visited several times. His picture is displayed in front of the altars. Photographs are not allowed inside the temples. ⊠ *Zanabazar Gudamj* ☎ *11/360–023* ⌚ *Free* ☺ *Mon.–Sat. 9–11, Sun. 9–1.*

⑫ Beautifully presented Buddhist art is the main treasure of the small **Zanabazar Museum of Fine Arts** (Orligiin Muzei). In this green two-story building, scowling Tsam dancing masks, delicately brushed landscape paintings, and gorgeous Tibetan-Mongolian *thangkhas* (embroidered silk scroll pictures of Buddhist deities) are the pick of the collection. The first floor houses a small collection of Stone Age petroglyphs and Bronze Age knives and pottery. A new art gallery inside the museum showcases modern Mongolian painting and sculpture, some of which are available for sale. Art works change every three weeks. ⊠ *East side of Barylgachidyin Sq. off Khuldaldaany Gudamj, 1 block west of Trade and Development Bank on Khuldaldaany Gudamj* ☎ *11/323–986* ⌚ *T2,500* ☺ *Daily 9–5.*

⑬ From naturalistic paintings of herdsmen to violent cubist and batik-inspired fantasies, the **Mongolian National Art Gallery** (Oorun Ehoorgiin Oodzehstehpen) gives an intriguing overview of the country's modern and contemporary art scene. The second floor houses rotating exhibitions, of varying quality, with occasional works by distinguished contemporary artists. The sprawling and poorly lighted third floor showcases state-honored paintings from 1950 to the present, as well as a hodge-podge of glass cases filled with ceramic figurines, chess sets, and silver bowls, among other esoterica. ⊠ *Central Cultural Palace, 3 Sukhbaatar Talbai* ☎ *11/313–191* ⌚ *T1,500* ☺ *May–Sept., daily 10–6; Oct.–Apr., Wed.–Sun. 9–5.*

⑭ Two complete dinosaur skeletons, several nests of cracked dinosaur eggs, and fossilized footprints enliven the musty and packed **Museum of Natural History** (Baigaliin Muzei). In one of the world's richest countries for dinosaur fossils, many of them from the Gobi Desert area, the museum displays some of the best finds. Three floors of exhibits also show Mongolian steppe culture, wildlife, flora, and geology: you'll pass several rooms of stuffed animals as you wind your way through colorful hallways

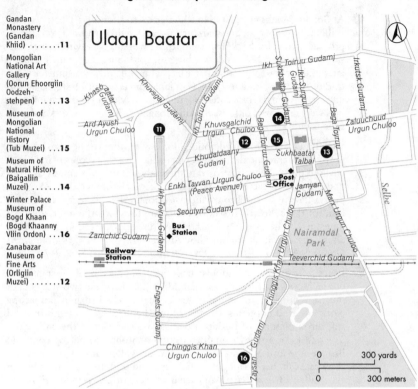

crowned by antelope heads. ✉ *Khuvsgalchid Urgun Chuloo and Sukhbaatar Gudamj* ☎ *11/318–179 or 11/315–679* 💰 *T2,000* ☉ *May–Sept., daily 10–5:30; Oct.–Apr., Wed.–Sun. 10–4:30.*

15 Traditional decorations, ethnic clothing, jewelry, and handicrafts fill the white-pillared **Museum of Mongolian National History** (Tub Muzei), which houses more than 40,000 artifacts dating from the Stone Age to the present day. The first-floor exhibition—prehistoric stone axes, bronze arrowheads, and ceramic shards—may be of interest to history buffs, but the real attraction is the sumptuous third-floor exhibition, which gives a peek at the riches of the Mongol Empire in all its glory—from carved wooden banknotes, to princely gold-threaded headdresses, to the implements of war with which the Mongols once wreaked havoc on Europe and Asia, including gold crossbows, bronze drums, a saddle-mounted cannon, and a trunk-size wooden jail cell with a tiny hole for air. ✉ *Khuldaldaany Gudamj* ☎ *11/325–656 or 11/329–102* 💰 *T2,000* ☉ *May–Sept., daily 10–4; Oct.–Apr., Thurs.–Mon. 10–4.*

16   The **Winter Palace Museum of Bogd Khaan** (Bogd Khaanny Vliin Ordon)
Fodor'sChoice   is the splendid European-style residence of the debauched and power-
★   ful Bogd Khaan, a Living Buddha who governed Ulaan Baatar's districts
of monks, nobles, merchants, artisans, and Russians and Chinese until
1924 as a god-king. The museum is worth visiting just to walk around
the courtyards and admire the faded glory of the architecture, but the
real strength of the museum lies in its resplendent collection of the
Khaan's innumerable possessions, from the silver knives that he used
to cut off people's fingers to precious Buddhist artifacts and jeweled ceremonial robes, including his winter coat made from 130 minks, a lavish ger decorated with 150 leopard skins, and a stuffed zoo of exotic
animals. Wind past the Khaan's Western luxuries, crowned by a 19th-
century London carriage, to find his bizarre collection of curios, capped
off by a nobleman's dried brain, a Buddha's tooth, and two eggs hatched
from a male hen. In other courtyards, divided by Chinese-style archways,
there are six more halls of intricate Buddhist embroideries, paintings,
and sculptures. Be sure to request an English-language tour if one isn't
offered to you. ⊠ *Chinggis Khaan Urgun Chuloo, south of Peace Bridge*
☎ *11/342–195 or 11/343–071* ⊠ *T2,500, photo permit T5,000*
◷ *Fri.–Tues. 9–4.*

Where to Stay & Eat

The variety and quality of restaurants available in Ulaan Baatar improved
considerably in the late 1990s. Outside the capital there may only be
mutton, but within the city limits you can find Italian, French, Korean,
Japanese, Czech, and an assortment of fast-food establishments. Some
restaurants in Ulaan Baatar double as bars or discos, so they may stop
serving food between 6 PM and 9 PM. It is best to dine early, like the locals, as restaurants sometimes run out of food well before they close.
Casual, neat dress is acceptable. Shorts and vest tops are rarely worn
in Mongolia and are not advised.

$$–$$$$ ✕ **Sekitei Restaurant.** From the patterned-mosaic stone floor to white paper
screens and a rock pool with lazy goldfish, Sekitei has an atmosphere
of quiet tranquillity more reminiscent of Tokyo than Ulaan Baatar. Ex-
pect to pay through the nose for the superb Japanese sushi, udon, tem-
pura, teppanyaki, and other traditional fare—virtually all ingredients
are imported from other parts of Asia. Private dining rooms are avail-
able. The Japanese-run restaurant is diagonally opposite the dilapi-
dated Flower Hotel, at the north end of the mini-mall. ⊠ *Sansar Service
Center, Bayanzurkh District* ☎ *11/458–723 or 11/451–361* 🖷 *11/451–
361* ▭ *AE, MC, V.*

★ **$–$$$**   ✕ **Seoul Restaurant.** Located in a large round edifice in the center of
Nairamdal Children's Park, the second floor of the gold-lettered Seoul
Club includes an outer deck area with a park view where waiters prepare Korean barbecue at your table. The cafeteria-style Asian eatery has
red-backed chairs, plaid tablecloths, and a central counter topped by
dozens of futuristic chrome-plated serving pots. Korean chefs are on hand
to panfry delicious marinated beef and potatoes; choose from a wide
variety of set-price buffets of Korean, Japanese, Chinese, and Western
food. Downstairs is a bakery, karaoke bar, and another restaurant.

⚜ *Nairamdal Children's Park, across from Bayan Gol hotel* ☎ *11/329–709 or 11/326–554* ▤ *AE, MC, V.*

$$ ✕ **Hazara.** Quality Indian food has made its way to Ulaan Baatar with this chain, which also has restaurants in Shanghai, Jakarta, and Singapore. Tandoori ovens bake delectable breads and a variety of meat and poultry dishes. Delicately spiced basmati rice, curries, fruit *lassis* (yogurt drinks), and a wide assortment of vegetarian dishes are also served proudly by an attentive staff. Each of the wooden tables is draped by a brightly colored cloth tent, and pleasant Indian music plays softly in the background. ✉ *16 Enkh Tayvan Urgun Chuloo (Peace Ave.), next to Negdelchin Hotel* ☎ *11/455–071 or 11/9919–5007* ⚑ *Reservations essential* ▤ *AE, MC, V.*

$–$$ ✕ **Ding Chen Hotpot Restaurant.** Spicy and flavorful Chinese hotpot is the mainstay of this small no-frills establishment. Sit at one of the three tables, underneath a poster of a turquoise sea, and cook to your liking a choice of meats, sprouts, tofus, noodles, and an assortment of seasonal vegetables. The divided hotpot allows for two levels of spiciness, and the selection of sauces provides a wide variety of flavorings. A range of other northern Chinese dishes can be ordered, though vegetable selections are limited. ✉ *Baga Toiruu Gudamj, across street (east) from State Department Store on Baruun Selbe St.* ☎ *11/321–767* ▤ *No credit cards.*

$–$$ ✕ **Los Banditos.** Vibrant colors light up the city's first Mexican restaurant, from the Crayola-color chairs to the blue-striped cloth laid over long wooden tables. Generous portions of Mexican fare—cooked up by an Indian chef—are heaped on orange-rimmed plates, from nachos and chicken wings to fajitas, enchiladas, and burritos, as well as a creative sampling of Indian fare. The restaurant may be hard to find: look for the log-cabin of an exterior, surrounded by a log-stump of a fence, just south of Peace Avenue opposite the Peace and Friendship Palace. The eatery is on a little alleyway behind the post office. ✉ *Namnansvren St., south of Enkh Tayvan Urgun Chuloo (Peace Ave.)* ☎ *11/9515–6322 or 11/9919–4618* ▤ *AE, MC, V.*

$–$$ ✕ **Millie's Espresso.** This checkerboard-floor coffee shop with superb cappuccinos and friendly service will satisfy your cravings for Western food. Spinach lasagna, chicken tacos, huevos rancheros, Cuban pork sandwiches, fruit smoothies, and lemon pie often appear on the menu board. Tables at this popular expat hangout can be hard to come by at lunch hours. A second location serving coffee and pastries is located on the ground floor of the Ulaan Baatar Hotel. ✉ *Marco Polo Pl., 5/3 Jamyan Gudamj* ☎ *11/9926–1550 or 11/9927–5808.* ✉ *Ulaan Baatar Hotel, 14 Sukhbaatar Talbai, off Enkh Tayvan Urgun Chuloo* ☎ *No phone* ▤ *No credit cards.*

$–$$ ✕ **Modern Nomads.** An essentially Westernized rendition of traditional
Fodor'sChoice Mongolian fare, this decidedly upmarket eatery has proven popular with
★ locals and tourists alike. Authentic Mongolian dishes, including *buuz* (steamed meat dumplings), *khuusshur* (fried meat dumplings), *bansch* (smaller dumplings served in soup), and *shandas* (pancakes), are supplemented with the "Mongolian barbecue" that has become so common in Western countries. A lunch-and-dinner combination is an excellent

introduction to the best Mongolian cuisine has to offer. ⊠ *Baga Toiruu Gudamj and Sukhbaatar Gudamj, across from Children's Creative Center* ☎ *11/318–744* 🖷 *11/316–819* ▤ *MC, V.*

$–$$ ✕ **Pizza della Casa.** Favorites with the expat crowd, both locations of this bistro have good, moderately priced salads, pastas, and pizzas served on blue peasant plates. The original Pizza della Casa is just east of Centrepoint on Peace Avenue; the stylish Ristorante della Casa, with flowing white curtains, large windows, and light-color tiles, is opposite the restaurant of the Ulaan Baatar Hotel, in an oval redbrick building fronted with windows. ⊠ *Enkh Tayvan Urgun Chuloo (Peace Ave.)* ☎ *11/324–114* ⊠ *Ristorante della Casa: Time Center, 2nd fl., Baga Toiruu Gudamj* ☎ *11/312–072* ▤ *AE, MC, V.*

$–$$ ✕ **Taj Mahal.** The city's second Indian restaurant, opened by the former manager of Hazara, radiates a quiet sophistication with its polished pinewood floors, lime-green and beige tablecloths, and Indian-style window facades. The eclectic menu has a dizzying array of tandoori, curries, vegetarian selections, and breads prepared by the Taj's two Indian chefs— don't miss the succulent naan. The wine list has imported French and German labels. There are also good-value lunch specials here, with a choice of one main dish served with naan, rice, salad, and pickles. The restaurant is across the road from the Ulaan Baatar Hotel; the entrance is in an interior courtyard through the archway connecting the Sports Palace and Teacher's College on Baga Toiruu Gudamj. ⊠ *Baga Toiruu Gudamj* ☎ *11/311–009 or 11/9919–5062* ▤ *AE, MC, V.*

$–$$ ✕ **UB Deli.** Importing Idaho potatoes for its American-style fries, UB Deli offers the city's broadest selection of salads and sandwiches. With hardwood floors and modern art decorating the brightly sunlighted interior, the deli is a relaxing nook in which to savor a latte and catch up on the news. For those craving a taste of home, the menu includes such favorites as grilled Reuben sandwiches, chicken Caesar salads, and Philadelphia cheesesteak. The entrepreneurial owners are also extremely knowledgeable and able to provide information on tours to the countryside, horseback riding, and apartment rentals, and they are in the process of building a resort. ⊠ *Bldg. 48, Seoul Gudamj at corner of Tserendorj Gudamj, tucked away snugly just north of the Circus, a large round building directly south of the State Department Store* ☎ *11/325–240* ⊕ *www.ubdeli-mongolia.com* ▤ *No credit cards.*

¢–$ ✕ **Chez Bernard Café.** Up a flight of russet-color stairs, this quaint backpacker's café lined with wooden tables is a homey place to stop for coffee and desserts—brownies, cheesecake, vegetable quiche, loaves of peasant bread, and other homemade goods. The message board by the door lists art events about town, and a small outdoor patio completes the setup. The café is on Peace Avenue, just west of the State Department Store and east of the Central Post Office. ⊠ *Enkh Tayvan Urgun Chuloo (Peace Ave.)* ☎ *11/324–622* ▤ *No credit cards.*

¢–$ ✕ **Indra Foodplanet.** This is the place for Mongolian fast food at a price that cannot be rivaled by any foreign venture. Bearing an uncanny resemblance to a mall food court, the cafeteria serves very cheap (but hardly memorable) fried chicken, pizza, burgers, and goulash, often with a side of potato and rice and having a consistent mutton taste. There is not much reason to hang around in terms of ambience, so takeout is a nice option; there's a small park located adjacent to the entrance. Indra tends to get busy with office workers at noon. ⊠ *Zaluuchuud Urgun Chuloo,, across from Museum of Mongolian National History, facing away (west) from Government House* ☎ *11/323–769* ▤ *No credit cards.*

¢–$ ✕ **Khaan Brau.** The Khaan Brau has a formal dining area, a relaxed bar-restaurant, and an ice-cream parlor, plus an outdoor patio in summer. Roast pork, pizza, schnitzel, and a plethora of pastas are served in your choice of dining areas. The bar-restaurant has a small dance floor in the middle and hosts live music on weekends. The locally microbrewed Khaan Brau is proudly served on tap. ⊠ *Tamian Junii Gudamj, across from Bayan Gol hotel, catercorner to Central Post Office* ☎ *11/326–626* ⊕ *www.khaanbrau.mn* ▤ *MC, V.*

$$$ ✕▨ **Bayan Gol.** Each of this centrally located hotel's two red towers has its own reception: although more services are housed in the north tower, nearer Sukhbaatar Talbai, the south tower is more aesthetically pleasing, with plush dark-green rugs and diamondback gold coverlets. All rooms in both towers have balconies, many with good views of Nairamdal Park or the mountains south of Ulaan Baatar. The hotel's main restaurant ($$–$$$), flanked by the twin towers, has a good-value, four-course, prix-fixe menu, which might feature egg with caviar, cream of chicken soup, mutton goulash, and fruit salad. ⊠ *5 Chinggis Khaan Urgun Chuloo, 49* ☎ *11/328–869* 🖷 *11/326–794* ✉ *info@bayangolhotel.mn* 🖳 *212 rooms, 31 suites* ⚭ *4 restaurants, cable TV, hair salon, massage, billiards, 3 bars, business services, travel services; no a/c* ▤ *AE, MC, V.*

$$$–$$$$ ▨ **Chinggis Khaan.** A mirrored-glass and red-concrete tiered structure on the east side of the city, the Chinggis Khaan has a huge empty foyer with a marble floor, a hanging crystal chandelier, and glass walls. The standard Western-style rooms have wooden desks, lounge areas, and IDD phones. Although singles are roomy, the standard double rooms are slightly claustrophobic, and bathrooms in both are small. A post office counter, a bank, and a doctor are also available on-site. Conveniently located on the east side of the building is the Sky Shopping Center, which includes a bakery, a supermarket, and an electronics store. ⊠ *5 Tokyo St., east of Selbe River, north of Zaluuchuud Urgun Chuloo, 49* ☎ *11/313–380* 🖷 *11/312–788* ⊕ *www.chinggis-hotel.com* 🖳 *180 rooms, 42 suites* ⚭ *2 restaurants, minibars, cable TV, gym, massage, sauna, billiards, bar, laundry service, business services, travel services* ▤ *AE, MC, V.*

$$$–$$$$ ▨ **Puma Imperial Hotel.** Its proximity to Sukhbaatar Talbai Square makes this small hotel an ideal location for visiting many of the city's downtown attractions. Rooms are spacious with modern bathrooms but lack a view of anything other than the adjacent alleyways. Still relatively unknown in Ulaan Baatar (it opened in 2002), the Puma is a relatively good value in the generally overpriced local hotel market. ⊠ *2 Amariin Urgun Chuloo, directly east of Government House on north end of Sukhbaatar Talbai* ☎ *11/313–043* 🖷 *11/319–148* ⊕ *www.puma_imperial.mn* 🖳 *31 rooms* ⚭ *2 restaurants, coffee shop, cable TV, hair salon, billiards, business services* ▤ *AE, MC, V.*

$$$ ▨ **Bishrelt Hotel.** This small, friendly establishment dominated by an elegant central white spiral staircase has many facilities and services nor-

mally found only at larger hotels. All rooms have high ceilings; smaller rooms come with balconies, while larger rooms are furnished with coffee tables, couches, and matching sofa chairs. The restaurant serves up a variety of cuisine that includes Hungarian beef goulash, fried chicken, cucumber soup, and ox tongue. A Continental breakfast is included in the rate. ⊠ *3/1 Erhk Cholori Talbai (Liberty Sq.), off Khuvsgalchid Urgun Chuloo, 43* ☎ *11/313–786* 🖷 *11/313–792* ✍ *bishrelt@magicnet.mn* ⤳ *20 rooms* ⚬ *Restaurant, sauna, bicycles, billiards, nightclub, business services, meeting room, travel services; no a/c* ▤ *AE, MC, V.*

★ **$$$** ⌘ **Ulaan Baatar Hotel.** With an unbeatable location just east of Sukhbaatar Talbai Square, the hotel has a plain, gray-concrete facade with pillars at its entrance that mask its small, homey interior. The lobby has leather settees and red wool carpets leading up a double staircase. Plush beige carpets, scarlet bed coverings, and bright jade furniture decorate the well-lighted double rooms, though space is somewhat limited in all but the deluxe suites. The first-floor restaurant serves both Mongolian and Western food and is popular with foreign travelers and expatriates. The room-service menu includes barbecued mutton and Mongolian milk tea. ⊠ *14 Sukhbaatar Talbai, off Enkh Tayvan Urgun Chuloo (Peace Ave.), 49* ☎ *11/320–620* 🖷 *11/324–485* ✍ *ub-hotel@magicnet.mn* ⤳ *165 rooms, 35 suites* ⚬ *3 restaurants, minibars, cable TV, hair salon, sauna, billiards, business services* ▤ *AE, DC, MC, V.*

$$$ ⌘ **White House Hotel.** A smiling doorman greets you as you enter a lobby decked out in red carpet, black leather sofas, and a white piano. Upstairs, the spacious rooms are decorated with gray drapes, bedspreads, and sofa covers, and have comfortable beds. The White House is one of the best choices in town for comfort and value. ⊠ *Damdinbazaryn Gudamj, 49 Amarsanaa St., southwest of Gandan Khiid, a few blocks north of Enkh Tayvan Urgun Chuloo (Peace Ave.)* ☎ *11/367–872* 🖷 *11/369–973* ⤳ *14 rooms* ⚬ *Restaurant, cable TV, billiards, nightclub, business services, travel services; no a/c* ▤ *AE, MC, V.*

$$ ⌘ **Marco Polo Hotel.** Within easy walking distance of the downtown area, the Marco Polo is a reasonable compromise of quality, location, and price. Somewhat spartan, doubles are nevertheless pristine and include a full bathroom. ⊠ *2/B Erkhuugiin St., just northeast of Chinese Embassy* ☎ *11/310–803* 🖷 *11/311–273* ✍ *gangaa27@yahoo.com* ⤳ *21 rooms* ⚬ *Cable TV* ▤ *MC, V.*

¢ ⌘ **Gana's Guest House.** If you're willing to forgo a few creature comforts, you can spend a night in a ger without leaving Ulaan Baatar. Down a residential alleyway 200 yards south of Gandan Khiid, Gana's has traditional-style gers, each outfitted with five beds, a washbasin, a table, and a wood-burning stove. Primitive outhouses and a foot-pump shower room are a few steps away. The restaurant is closed in winter. Gana also offers some of Mongolia's most reasonably priced travel services. ⊠ *House No. 22, Ondor Geegen Zanabazaryn Gudamj, 49, climb up hill toward Gandan Khiid, turn east onto unpaved alleyway flanked at the entrance by tourist stands, walk 2 mins, and look for the sign on the left-hand side* ☎ *11/367–343* ✍ *ganasger@magicnet.mn* ⤳ *5–8 gers, depending on season* ⚬ *Restaurant, travel services; no a/c, no room TV* ▤ *No credit cards.*

¢ 🏠 **Serge's Guest House.** Oriented toward backpackers and the budget-minded, Serge's can provide lodging with breakfast, showers, and laundry for well under $10 per day. Expect the most basic rooms, though there are kitchen facilities. Serge can also provide assistance in ticket booking, car rental, guide and interpreter services, and offers ultra-low cost tours of Karakorum, Khovsgol Lake, and Terelj. ✉ *Enkh Tayvan Urgun Chuloo (Peace Ave.) and Ondor Geegen Zanabazaryn Gudamj, south of Gandan Monastery* ☎ *11/320–267* ✍ *sergetour@yahoo.com* ➫ *30* ⚄ *No a/c, no TV in some rooms* ⊟ *No credit cards.*

Nightlife & the Arts

THE ARTS   For traditional Mongolian song and dance, the main venue is the **National Academic Drama Theater** (Ulsyn Dramyn Teatr; ✉ Chinggis Khaan Urgun Chuloo and Natsagdorj Urgun Chuloo ☎ 11/323–490). The **State Opera and Ballet Theater** (Duur Bujgiin Balet Teatr; ✉ Sukhbaatar Talbai, east side of street ☎ 11/320–357) stages Mongolian versions of classical ballets and operas. Ticket prices are T5,000. Fees of T3,000 for photographs and T30,000 for amateur video are charged.

NIGHTLIFE   Ulaan Baatar is home to an ever-increasing number of nightclubs, pubs, and discos. Most are safe and are happy to entertain tourists; others are dark, dangerous, and full of aggressive vodka-swigging men and prostitutes. If possible, avoid all nightclubs that aren't close to major roads: muggings (or worse) are not infrequent in unlighted alleyways. A little prudence and some local advice should steer you clear of any trouble.

Diminutive and cozy in winter, **Dave's Place** (✉ Eastern fringe of Sukhbaatar Talbai between the State Opera and Ballet Theater and Culture Palace ☎ 11/9979–8185) expands in summer from a traditional English pub to an outdoor beer terrace on the east side of Sukhbaatar Talbai Square. Quiz nights, an always-busy dartboard, and a proper English pub menu make it a pleasant place to quaff a few pints. Popular with the young and chic, **Face Club** (✉ Khuldaldaany Gudamj across from the Museum of Natural History ☎ 11/9918–2677) has cozy couches surrounding a modest-size dance floor featuring the latest in international pop and techno. There's live music from 10 PM. A slightly older crowd favors the live-music club **River Sounds** (✚ 1 alley south of Enkh Tayvan Urgun Chuloo (Peace Ave.), opposite the State Opera and Ballet Theater in Sukhbaatar Talbai ☎ 11/9915–8548). **Brauhaus** (✉ Seoul Gudamj, 2 blocks southwest of State Department Store) features an amusing beer stock exchange that is in operation several nights a week. Customers can attempt to beat the market while prices of various microbrewed beers vary according to the eternal laws of supply and demand. The dark-wood **Chinggis Club** (✉ Sukhbaatar Gudamj ☎ 11/325–820 or 11/9911–5605), with live music on weekends, is popular among pub crawlers. Located west of the city, the enormous **UB Palace** (✉ Enkh Tayvan Urgun Chuloo [Peace Ave.], west of Amarsanaa St., Bayangol District ☎ 11/682–957 or 11/114–1657) includes three large distinct discos (Laserland, Flower, and Studio 54) with cover charges ranging from free to T3,000. Pool and snooker players will enjoy the subterranean tables of **Apollon** (✉ Enkh Tayvan Urgun Chuloo [Peace Ave.], facing Russian Embassy, 1 block west of Central Post Office ☎ No phone), while couples can find candlelit privacy in the pub's lower level. Pool and snooker tables are available for T2,000 and T3,000 per hour, respectively.

Shopping

Knives, boots, traditional clothes, paintings of grassland scenes, and Buddhist art are among the items worth buying in Ulaan Baatar. Under Mongolian customs law, antiques must have an export certificate. Check that the shop can issue one before you buy.

Up a flight of pale green stairs, the **Antique Shop** (⌧ Baruun Selbe St., 1 block south of Liberty Sq. ☎ 11/317–839 or 11/9919–6825) has a small but fine collection of traditional copper-and-silver pitchers, ornamented teapots, silver jewelry, carved wooden boxes, and other objects, many of them genuine antiques. The **Fine Art Shop Antique and Art Gallery** (⌧ Enkh Tayvan Urgun Chuloo [Peace Ave.], next to Peace and Friendship Palace ☎ 11/324–234) houses a collection of traditional paintings, felt dolls and wall-hangings, souvenirs, and art books. Just beyond the southern gates of Gandan Khiid, the **Friendship Art Shop** (☎ 11/9015–1879) offers very much the same Buddhist devotional paraphernalia, including leather work and prayer beads, all at a lower price. Kiosks outside the south and east gates of **Gandan Khiid** (⌧ Zanabazar Gudamj) stock incense burners, hand-painted Buddhas, and thangkhas. **Gobi Cashmere House** (⌧ Enkh Tayvan Urgun Chuloo [Peace Ave.] facing Russian Embassy ☎ 11/326–867 or 11/9918–7837) carries a wide selection of women's and men's cashmere clothing. A small section of the shop also sells traditional Mongolian clothing and souvenirs.

The well-known local artist and newspaper cartoonist **Gulset** (⌧ Chinggis Khaan Urgun Chuloo, small cabin in front of Bayan Gol hotel) sells watercolors, oils, copper teapots, brass Buddhas, thangkhas, and masks. Some of the paintings are his own work. For a fine selection of beautiful handwoven Kazakh wall hangings, as well as ethnic clothing, carved chessboards, trinkets, woolen rugs, and leather bags, head to the small **Odyssey** (⌧ Aero Voyage Bldg., 2nd fl., Khuldaldaany Gudamj ☎ 11/312–378 office). Set up by a nongovernmental organization that works to rectify conditions in Mongolian prisons, many items in the shop were voluntarily made by prisoners participating in the program. All proceeds from the sales are used to improve their prison conditions.

Sky Shopping Center (⌧ Western side of Chinggis Khaan hotel ☎ 11/319–090) is not the most inexpensive place to purchase daily use items, but, like the State Department Store, it does offer a wide range of Western consumer goods. It's a good place to stop before heading out to the hinterland. The fourth floor of the city's largest shop, the **State Department Store** (Ikh Delgüür; ⌧ Enkh Tayvan Urgun Chuloo [Peace Ave.] ☎ 11/324–311), is good for leather boots, Mongolian dhels and headgear, and souvenirs, including Mongolian chess sets and miniature gers. A large shop inside the gate of the **Winter Palace Museum of Bogd Khaan** (⌧ Chinggis Khaan Urgun Chuloo ☎ 11/342–195) has Mongolian teapots, knives, wool and cashmere, artwork, Buddhist items, and some antiques. If you are in need of reading material, **Xanadu** (⌧ Marco Polo Plaza, next to Millie's Espresso café ☎ 11/319–748 ⊕ www.xanadu.mn) carries travel, fiction, history, and biographies in English.

Manzshir Khiid

⑰ *1 hr (46 km [29 mi]) by bus south of Ulaan Baatar.*

Manzshir Khiid is a unique combination of a ruined monastery, Mongolia's oldest nature reserve, and two small museums in a forested area among the Bogd Mountains. Founded in 1733 at the site of a healing spring, the grand monastery was once home to 20 temples and 350 lamas. Here, late-autumn Tsam mask dances that reflected the shamanist roots of Tibetan Buddhism were held once a year to drive away evil spirits. Unfortunately, the site was all but annihilated by the Stalinist purges of 1937. In the late 1990s the main temple was restored and now houses a museum with photos of Manzshir in its former glory, as well as Buddhist art and fierce-looking Tsam masks. Among the objects recovered from the ruins is an enormous bronze cooking pot, cast in 1732, large enough to boil 10 sheep and two cows. Behind the temple, you can climb up to a hilltop shrine strewn with old money, much of it from Mongolia's Communist era.

On the mountain slopes you can ride horses or hike through deer forests. Manzshir is easily accessible on a day trip: you can either book a tour through an agency or hire a vehicle to drive you there. A taxi should cost T11,000–T18,000 (U.S. dollars are also often accepted; $10–$15) one way. Minivans leave hourly each day (8–6) from the long-distance bus station for the provincial capital of Zuunmod. From here it's a beautiful, easy 5-km (3-mi) walk to the monastery. If you want to stay overnight, there are ger accommodations. ⊠ *Manzshir* 🏛 *Monastery and museums T1,000* ⊙ *May–Oct., daily 10–6.*

Terelj-Gorkhi

🐾 **⑱** *1 hr (85 km [46 mi]) by car northeast of Ulaan Baatar.*

Originally built as a retreat for the ruling party elite in the days of communism, Terelj has since become a popular destination for those seeking to escape the capital for some fresh air. There are ample opportunities for hiking, horseback riding, and nature appreciation within a rather bumpy hour's drive from the capital.

en route

Turtle Rock, visible about 15 minutes from the "main parking lot" in Terelj-Gorkhi, is a natural formation that resembles a turtle—at least from a short distance and from the right direction. It is easily spotted on the left (northwest) side of the main road between Ulaan Baatar and the main travel center in Terelj-Gorkhi and is accessible by car (a couple of bumpy minutes from the main road). It's a good place to stop for a break if the potholed road is proving to be a trial.

There are sights to see in Terelj-Gorkhi, but the real appeal is the actual horseback (or even camel) riding itself at a modest T5,500 an hour. Be sure to request a Russian or Western saddle—Mongolian saddles are constructed from wood and can be quite uncomfortable to those unaccustomed to their use. You can arrange to stay in one of the many ger camps in Terelj-Gorkhi by booking through a Ulaan Baatar travel agency or via one of the larger hotels. Gers can be rented at a rate of T5,000 per hour for meals and relaxation or T27,000 overnight. Mongolian and Russian cuisine are the main items on the menu at hotel restaurants. To reach the center of the park a taxi can be hired from Ulaan Baatar for the day at a rate of T20,000–T30,000. Otherwise contact one of the many travel agents to charter a minibus.

off the beaten path

GUNJIIN SUM MONASTERY – Largely in ruins, Gunjiin Sum is not a significant religious sight in and of itself, but is a worthy destination for a daylong riding adventure from your ger. The monastery is the grave site of the queen of the Mongolian king Dondovdorjan. An odd sight along the way is the "ghost money" of old and worthless Communist currency that has littered a hillside. The monastery is a full day's ride on horseback from the Terelj-Gorkhi travel center. You will need a guide to get there.

Where to Stay

$ ▣ **Tyrelj-Hirota.** This Japanese-owned lodge is in the center of the park and is an ideal location from which to venture out to investigate the surrounding countryside and visit local people who still practice traditional herding. While day trips are popular, there are few places where one can expect to see more stars than here, so an overnight stay—particularly in a ger—is an ideal way to appreciate the timeless peace and tranquility of the grassland. Standard and deluxe hotel rooms are also available. The restaurant is a good opportunity to try some locally made airag. ✉ ☎ 11/9919–4578 ➶ 30, plus gers available ⌂ Restaurant; no a/c, no room TV ▭ MC, V.

Karakorum

⑲ 6 hrs (360 km [223 mi]) by hired jeep southwest of Ulaan Baatar.

Chinggis Khaan's 13th-century capital, Karakorum (Kharkhorin in Mongolian) was built on one of the ancient silk roads. The crosswinds of trade brought foreign traders, missionaries, warriors, and—on a journey that took a year from Rome—even the pope's ambassador to this once-cosmopolitan city. The Franciscan monk William of Rubruk, the only Westerner to leave a contemporaneous account of the place, dismissed the capital as no bigger than the suburb of St. Denis in Paris. However, the Mongols brought the plunder of 20 kingdoms here, foreign and Mongolian currency were accepted as legal tender, and 12 religions were allowed to coexist with equal status.

The centerpiece of the city was the Khaan's 7,500-square-foot palace, which was built like a church with a Chinese-style roof and crowned by a silver fountain so ingeniously constructed by a Parisian jeweler that wine, mare's milk, and other liquors poured forth from fabulous spouts shaped like lion's and snake's heads. Surrounding the palace were canals, and alongside a thriving foreign merchants' sector, Nestorian churches, mosques, and Buddhist temples could all be found fiercely competing for Mongolian souls. Although the area is Mongolia's richest historic site, the city actually served as the imperial capital for only 40 years;

in 1264, Kublai Khaan moved the capital to Beijing. After the demise of the Mongol empire, the city was razed by the vengeful Chinese Ming Dynasty in 1388. Modern-day Karakorum is a small, modern town nearby. Of further interest may be the long-term excavation of the original site. A team of German and Mongolian researchers have been steadily unearthing the foundations of *several* preceding cities, buried under silt over thousands of years.

To get to Karakorum, hire a jeep or minivan through a tour operator or your hotel. Minibuses are available but they are uncomfortable, especially in the summer heat.

In 1586 the **Erdenezu Monastery** (Erdenezu Khiid) was built using the fallen stones of the city, leaving just a few remains such as Turtle Rock, which marked one corner of the old city walls. Mongolia's largest monastery, Erdenezu housed 1,000 monks in 60 temples at its height. It was closed and damaged during the Stalinist purges of the 1930s but now has 7 active temples in the huge compound. Topped with 108 white stupas, the walls are said to be a smaller replica of the original Karakorum city walls. The temples are a mixture of flat-roof Tibetan-style and Chinese-style wooden pillars, tiled roofs, and red walls. ✛ *2 km (1 mi) east of center of town* ✉ *T8,000, photo permit T3,000* ☉ *Daily 9–9; visitors are welcome to the temple Lavrim Sum's daily morning ceremonies (at around 11).*

Accessible on day trips from Karakorum are the ruins of an **ancient Uighur Muslim kingdom;** several **Turkish monuments** and inscriptions dating from the 8th and 9th centuries; the relaxing natural hot springs at **Khujirt;** and the **Orkhon Waterfall,** legendary birthplace of the Mongolian people. The relics are interesting if unspectacular, but on the way to them you pass beautiful unspoiled grassland scenery with marmot hunters (who use falcons), camel herds, isolated gers, falcons, foxes, and horsemen using their urgas. There are also wolves and snow leopards in the area, though you're not likely to see them unless you go on a wildlife safari. Horseback riding and visits to local families give you an even better idea of the traditional Mongolian way of life. You normally get to sample airag, cheese, and milk tea boiled on a dung-burning stove. These trips are all best taken on a tour.

en route
The **Mongol Els sand dunes,** adjacent to Hogno Khaan Mountain, are popular stops located about three-quarters of the way to Karakorum from Ulaan Baatar, on the main road of the Khustain Nuruu National Park. With a little ingenuity and a sheet of cardboard or plastic, you can clamber up the dunes and do a little Mongolian tobogganing.

Where to Stay & Eat

$$ ⚠ **Karakorum Ger Camp.** You can stay in a real ger without having to
Fodor'sChoice rough it too much at this camp, set on open grassland within sight of
★ old and new Karakorum. The gers are in traditional style, with orange-painted posts and roof slats, wool rugs on the floor, small but comfortable wooden beds, and a wood-burning stove that is kept going

for you by the staff. Each ger sleeps up to four people. Bathrooms and showers (not always hot) are in a separate block 100 yards away. A giant ger makes an evocative dining room and venue for song and dance performances. The set meals include buuz, mutton stew, and other Mongolian standards. Vegetarian or other special dishes can be ordered. The rate is for a bed (not the whole ger), as well as meals. A number of other nearby ger camps also offer similar services at lower rates, so inquire at your hotel or travel agent regarding available sites. ✧ *Look for a spread of camps available all over the area* ☎ *55/2376* ⛎ *Restaurant, horseback riding; no a/c, no room TVs* ▭ *No credit cards* ⊙ *Closed Nov.–Apr.*

Republic of Mongolia A to Z

To research prices, get advice from other travelers, and book travel arrangements, visit www.fodors.com.

AIR TRAVEL
Regular flights connect Ulaan Baatar to Beijing, Hohhot, Moscow, Irkutsk, Seoul, Osaka, and Berlin.

CARRIERS   The Mongolian airline, MIAT, and Air China run Ulaan Baatar–Beijing flights several times a week. MIAT also runs regular flights to, Moscow, Irkutsk, Seoul, Tokyo, and Berlin. Air China, Aeroflot, and Korean Airlines also have offices in Ulaan Baatar. Air Mongolia flies Monday and Thursday from Ulaan Baatar to Hohhot. Opposite the MIAT building, Exc-El & Travel International Air Ticketing Service can provide tickets for all of the above airlines. In Beijing contact the China Air ticketing office or MIAT.

🛪 Airlines & Contacts **Aero Mongolia** ✉ Exc-El & Travel ticketing office, Chingeltei District, Ulaan Baatar ☎ 11/9515-4188 🖷 11/379-616 ⊕ www.aeromongolia.mn. **Aeroflot** ✉ Seoul Gudamj, Ulaan Baatar ☎ 11/320-720. **Air China** ✉ North of Flower Hotel, across street from the NIC gas station, Sansar District, Ulaan Baatar ☎ 11/328-838 or 11/452-548 🖷 11/312-324. **Exc-El & Travel International Air Ticketing Service** ✉ Baga Toiruu Gudamj, Ulaan Baatar ☎ 11/323-364 🖷 11/328-567 🖂 Puma Imperial Hotel's ground floor, east side of Sukhbaatar Square directly across from the Parliament building, Ulaan Baatar ☎ 11/313-333. **Korean Airlines** ✉ Chinggis Khaan hotel, 5 Tokyo St., 3rd fl., Ulaan Baatar ☎ 11/326-643 🖷 11/326-712. **MIAT** ✉ 8 Baga Toiruu Gudamj, Ulaan Baatar ☎ 11/322-273 or 11/322-144.

🛪 Airlines & Contacts in China **China Air ticketing** ✉ Aviation Bldg., 15 Xi Chang'an Jie, Xidan District, Beijing ☎ 010/6656-9118 🖷 010/6601-7585. **MIAT** ✉ Sunjoy Mansion, 6 RiTan Lu, 7th fl., behind Friendship Store (CITIC Bldg.), Beijing ☎ 010/6507-9297 🖷 010/6507-7397.

AIRPORTS
Buyant Uha Airport, the country's only international airport, lies 15 km (9 mi) to the south of town, about 20 minutes or T5,000 by taxi.

🛪 Airport Information **Buyant Uha Airport** ☎ 11/320-221 or 11/313-163.

BUS TRAVEL
Buses run up to the border on both sides, but there are no direct buses from Hohhot to Ulaan Baatar. Minibuses do run between the railroad

stations of the border towns of Zamin Uud and Erlian (T8,000, plus a border tax of Y6,000), but it's easier and far more convenient to take the rail direct to Ulaan Baatar from Hohhot or Beijing.

🚌 **Bus Depot** **Long-distance bus station** ⊠ Intersection of Ikh Toiruu Gudamj and Teeverchid Gudamj, Ulaan Baatar 🕾 No phone.

FARES & SCHEDULES

Several useful routes run along Enkh Tayvan Urgun Chuloo (Peace Avenue) and past Sukhbaatar Talbai Square in Ulaan Baatar, but buses can be crowded and pickpockets abound. Mongol Teever is the main operator; a fleet of privately owned minibuses have also sprung up, following the same routes at the same T200 fare. Regular buses run to Karakorum and Manzshir. The one-hour bus to Manzshir runs hourly each day 8–6 from the long-distance bus station (T700). The eight-hour bus to Karakorum runs three times a week and is much cheaper and slower than jeep travel—but can be more of an adventure. Quicker, privately owned micro-buses also run to both places daily, for a slightly higher fee, starting from the bus station as well; signs to destinations aren't well marked, but ask individual drivers. As in China, drivers often wait for all the seats to fill up before starting on their journey.

CUSTOMS & DUTIES

Trains stop twice at the China-Mongolia border, at the Mongolian border town of Zamin Uud, and also at the Chinese border town of Erlian for immigration and customs inspections. Your passport will be taken and stamped by officials from both countries; and you may have your bags checked as well. If you're exporting any antiques, you must have a receipt and a customs certificate from the store where you bought it. Exporting fossils is illegal. Delays usually take from 3 to 6 hours, as the train wheels are also changed. The train between Hohhot and Ulaan Baatar can be delayed for up to 13 hours. Once you get your passport back, you can get off the train and wander through the border town. If you're traveling to Mongolia, you can stock up on a wide variety of food and beverages at Erlian; going the other way, the Zamin Uud station does not sell food.

EMBASSIES & CONSULATES

🚩 **Consulates** **Canada** ⊠ Diplomatic Services Corp. Bldg., Suite 56, Ulaan Baatar 🕾 11/328-285 🖷 11/328-289. **China** ⊠ Zaluuchuud Urgun Chuloo, Ulaan Baatar 🕾 11/320-955 or 11/323-940 🖷 11/311-943. **United Kingdom** ⊠ 30 Enkh Tayvan Urgun Chuloo (Peace Ave.), Ulaan Baatar 🕾 11/458-133 🖷 11/458-036. **United States** ⊠ 59/1 Ikh Toiruu Gudamj, Ulaan Baatar 🕾 11/329-095 🖷 11/320-776 ⊕ www.us-mongolia.com.

EMERGENCIES

Most hospitals and clinics in Mongolia are chronically short of medical supplies and doctors, and medical training is often inadequate. If you have a minor ailment that persists, ask your hotel to recommend a specific doctor in a hospital to visit. For more serious ailments, contact your local embassy for assistance in finding a Western doctor; you may also want to consider heading to Beijing for medical treatment. The places listed below cater to foreigners; unfortunately, English-speaking doctors are rare, and you will almost certainly have to bring your own translator. UB Assist offers intermediary services to clients with travel insurance, including English-speaking doctors and translators. Those lacking medical insurance can pay cash up front.

Hospitals & Clinics **Arono Dental Clinic** ⊠ 300 feet north of the Winter Palace Museum of Bogd Khaan, Ulaan Baatar ☎ 11/341-210. **Russian Hospital** ⊠ Enkh Tayvan Urgun Chuloo (Peace Ave.), next to U.K. Embassy, Ulaan Baatar ☎ 11/450-007. **UB Assist** ⊠ Seoul Gudamj, 1 block east of Circus, 1 block southwest of State Department Store ☎ 11/312-392 or 11/326-939 🖶 11/311-979.

Police **Emergency hotline** ☎ 102. **Bayan Gol District** ⊠ Enkh Tayvan Urgun Chuloo (Peace Ave.) ☎ 11/361-734. **Sukhbaatar District** ⊠ Negdsen Undestniy ☎ 11/332-0341.

INTERNET SERVICES

Major hotels offer Internet services at a premium price, but there is hardly a block without at least one cybercafé. The most conveniently located Web cafés are located near the State Department Store. Fast online connections at T600–T800 an hour are available at NetCentre from 8 AM to 2 AM, where printing and scanning services are also available. The smaller Mouse House has cyber access for T600 an hour from 10 to 10. It is also relatively straightforward to connect laptops by purchasing a dial-up Internet card from MiCom (⊕ www.micom.mng.net) at the Central Post Office or from the larger hotels. Another option, near the Ulaan Baatar Hotel, is iCafe.

Internet Cafés **iCafe** ⊠ Baga Toiruu Gudamj, northeast side of Ulaan Baatar Hotel, across from Mongolian Technical University ☎ 11/313-316. **Mouse House** ⊠ Baga Toiruu Gudamj, east of State Department Store ☎ No phone. **NetCentre** ⊠ Corner of Seoul and Tserendorj Gudamj, north of Circus, south of State Department Store ☎ 11/329-259 or 11/315-303.

LODGING

APARTMENT RENTALS Those seeking accommodation for a month or more may wish to contact one of the many local real estate agencies. In business in Ulaan Baatar for over five years, the reputable CTB Real Estate Agency is able to find clean, safe apartments on short-term leases year-round in any price category.

Local Agents **CTB Real Estate Agency** ☎ 9918-1786.

MAIL & SHIPPING

The Mongolian postal system is very slow but usually reliable. Allow at least a few weeks for letters and postcards mailed from Ulaan Baatar to arrive; if you're en route to Beijing, you may want to post your mail from there instead. Parcel shipping is expensive and slow. There are no mailboxes on the streets; post letters from the Central Post Office at the southwest corner of Sukhbaatar Talbai Square. For express deliveries, courier services such as DHL and TNT offer door-to-door service.

Post Offices **Central Post Office** ⊠ Enkh Tayvan Urgun Chuloo (Peace Ave.). **DHL** ⊠ Pickup outlet located at business center of Ulaan Baatar Hotel ☎ 11/310-919 🖶 11/325-772. **FedEx** ⊠ Tuvshin Hotel, Khudaldaany Gudamj, 4th fl. ☎ 11/320-591 or 11/312-092. **TNT** ☎ 11/311-655.

MONEY MATTERS

ATMS There are as of yet no standard ATMs in Mongolia. However, Visa card machines are located at the Trade and Development Bank, and at the Ulaan Baatar, Bayan Gol, and Chinggis Khaan hotels. The machines only allow cash advance on Visa cards and users must know their PIN code to withdraw cash.

CURRENCY   The unit of currency in Mongolia is the tugrik or tugrog, abbreviated "Tg." or "T." The exchange rate at press time was T1,192 to the U.S. dollar, T1,453 to the euro, T2,195 to the pound sterling, T909 to the Canadian dollar, T913 to the Australian dollar, T788 to the New Zealand dollar, and T144 to the Chinese yuan.

CURRENCY   Major hotels exchange U.S. dollars or traveler's checks. Some of the banks
EXCHANGE   exchange cash and traveler's checks or provide cash advances on major credit cards. Find out the rates and fees before initiating your transaction. The redbrick Trade and Development Bank, open weekdays 9–12:45 and 2–4, accepts traveler's checks and credit cards (American Express, MasterCard, and Visa). The entrance for currency exchange is to the left of the main entrance: look for the red Moneygram sign. The best cash exchange rates are to be found at the small exchange outlet located on the west side of Baga Toiruu Gudamj, halfway between Enkh Tayvan Urgun Chuloo (Peace Avenue) and Khuldaldaany Gudamj. Note that it is highly imprudent to carry large sums of money in Ulaan Baatar, particularly at night.

🖪 Exchange Services **Trade and Development Bank** ✉ 7 Khuldaldaany Jie 7, Baga Toiruu Gudamj, at Khuldaldaany Gudamj ☎ 11/324–690 or 11/310–665.

PASSPORTS & VISAS

ENTERING THE   In Beijing the Mongolian Embassy (open 9–11 and 2–4) issues 30-day
REPUBLIC OF   visas for US$40 (or the equivalent in yuan) plus a Y20 processing fee. It
MONGOLIA   takes four days. Next-day service is also available for US$60 and a Y25 fee. Letters of invitation or confirmation of hotel and/or tour booking are no longer required to visit Mongolia. Visas may also be obtained in Hohhot, at the consular office roughly one block south of Zhaojun Huayuan (open Monday, Tuesday, and Thursday 8:30–12:30), or at the Chinese border town of Erenhot Erlian (Erenhot in Mongolian), at the consular office in the Erlian Hotel. The Hohhot Consulate can provide a 30-day visa for Y369 in seven days or Y526 in one day. One passport-type photo is required for all visas. Note that a letter of invitation may be required if you arrive in Erlian without a visa, so at this time it is not recommended that visas be sought there; instead, plan to visit consular offices in Beijing or Hohhot for relatively speedy, problem-free services.

If you want to stay longer in Mongolia than your visa permits, you must register at the third floor of the State Centre for Civil Registration and Information. Stays of longer than 30 days may require an accompanying letter from an official tour operator or an official work unit. Tourist registration fees are around T5,000.

🖪 **Erlian Hotel** ☎ 139/0479–0825 or 139/0479–0273.

Hohhot Consulate office (Menggu Lingshiguan) ✉ 5 Wulaan Xi Jie, south of Zhaojun Huayuan, Xincheng Qu, Hohhot ☎ 0471/430–3266 or 0471/430–3254.

Mongolian Embassy (Menggu Dashiguan) ✉ 2 Xiushui Beidajie, Jianguomenwai, Beijing ☎ 010/6532–3210. **State Centre for Civil Registration and Information** ✉ Tsagdaagiin Gudamj, Ulaan Baatar ☎ 11/327–182.

TAXES

DEPARTURE TAX Departure tax is T12,500 or US$10.

TELEPHONES

AREA & The country code for Mongolia is 976. Major hotels all offer local and
COUNTRY CODES International Direct Dial (IDD) services. You can also buy a phone card
(for T5,000, 10,000, and 20,000) at the post office, and use a pay
phone. White mobile phones for public use and carried by vendors in
the streets cost T100–T200 per minute.

TRAIN TRAVEL

Although flying is much quicker, if you have the time, the 30-hour train
journey from Beijing is one-fourth of the price, and worth making on
one leg of your trip. On the way you pass the Great Wall and open grassland scenery and meet mainly Mongolian, Russian, and Chinese fellow
passengers. Both classes of sleeper offer ample comfort.

Mongolia has only one main railway line, the Beijing–Ulaan
Baatar–Irkutsk section of the trans-Siberian route. Trains run to and from
Moscow and Beijing twice a week.

RESERVATIONS In Ulaan Baatar, you can buy tickets at the International Railway Ticketing Office (weekdays 9–1 and 2–4, weekends 9–2); the two-story yellow building is a block north and then west of the train station. Bring
your passport. Reservations up to 10 days in advance can be made here,
but overbooking is common in summer months, so don't count on getting a ticket until it's in your hands. In Beijing you can buy tickets at
the international ticketing counter at the central railway station, Beijing Zhan. Otherwise, CITS can book tickets. Contact Ulaan Baatar Railway Authority or the CITS in Beijing.

🚩 **CITS** ✉ Lu You Da Sha (Tourism Bldg.), 28 Jianguomenwai Da Jie, Beijing ☎ 010/
6205-5580 ⊕ www.cits.com.cn. **International Railway Ticketing Office** ✉ Across
from railway station on Zamchid Gudamj at Magsarjav Gudamj ☎ 11/94-133 🖷 11/944-
124. **Ulaan Baatar Railway Authority** ✉ Zamchid Gudamj ☎ 11/320-332.

TRANSPORTATION AROUND THE REPUBLIC OF MONGOLIA

TAXIS Official taxis came to Ulaan Baatar in 2000, in the form of small yellow or light-blue vehicles, with a checkered "City Taxi" sign up top. If
you don't see an official taxi coming, however, any vehicle—either inside or outside Ulaan Baatar—may be a taxi in disguise. Stand on the
side of the street, wave your arm up and down, and before long someone is bound to stop. At night it is advisable to stick to the official taxis
for security reasons.

FARES & The standard rate is T250 per kilometer for local and long-distance jour-
SCHEDULES neys. Make sure the driver sets the odometer back to zero or make a
mental note of the mileage before you head off. Most cab rides within
the city shouldn't cost more than T1,500.

TRAVEL AGENCIES

In Mongolia's emerging tourism industry, at least 50 local operators are
competing or cooperating with foreign tour companies. All offer tours,
plane and train booking, and visa services. While prices vary depend-

ing on itinerary, services, and number of days, expect to pay US$300–$800 per person for a three-day trip to Karakorum, including a driver, meals, accommodation, and English-speaking guide. Longer excursions that require air transport range from $600 into the thousands of dollars. Prices go down depending on the number of people in your group; individual travelers may find it hard to join a group tour outside of high season. Going alone is possible; you'll just pay more.

🚩 Local Agent Referrals **Guchidhan** 🕮 Box 49/411, Ulaan Baatar 46 ☎ 11/456–442 ⊕ www.mol.mn/guchidhan. **Juulchin** 🕮 5B Chinggis Khaan Gudamj, Ulaan Baatar ☎ 11/328–428 🖷 11/320–246 ⊕ www.mongoljuulchin.mn. **Monkey Business** ✉ Hidden Tree Bar, 12 Dong Da Qiao Xie Jie, at Nan San Li Tun, Chao Yang District, Beijing 100027 ☎ 010/6591–6519 🖷 010/6591–6517 ⊕ www.monkeyshrine.com. **Nature Tours** 🕮 Room 106, Cho Burt Plaza, Seoul St., Ulaan Baatar ☎ 11/312–392 or 11/311–801 🖷 11/311–979 ⊕ www.naturetours.mn. **Nomin Tours** ✉ 44 Enkh Tayvan Urgun Chuloo (Peace Ave.), State Department Store, 4th fl. ☎ 11/313–232 🖷 11/314–242 ⊕ www.nomintours.com. **Sand Dune Travel** 🕮 Box 882, Ulaan Baatar 46 ☎ 11/367–343 ⊕ www.mongoltours.mn. **SSS Travel** ✉ 24 Baga Toiruu Gudamj ☎ 11/328–410 🖷 11/311–915 ⊕ www.ssstravel.mn.

VISITOR INFORMATION

The *UB Guide* is a tourism-oriented publication funded by local businesses, featuring maps and listings. The guide provides insights into recent developments and information on travel, etiquette, some very useful Mongolian vocabulary, and can be found at any of the larger hotels. MIAT sponsors a colorful tourist map in English that is indispensable for navigating Ulaan Baatar's potholed streets. Ulaan Baatar also has two weekly English-language newspapers, the *Mongol Messenger* and the *U.B. Post*. Both are stocked by many kiosks and bookstalls along Enkh Tayvan Urgun Chuloo (Peace Avenue) and west of Sukhbaatar Talbai. They are a good source of information on entertainment and cultural events in Ulaan Baatar. The government-sponsored ⊕ www.mongoliatourism.gov.mn is an excellent source of information on activities. Visitors can also consult with ⊕ www.mongolart.mn, which offers helpful listings of current cultural and arts-related events. The *Mongolian Arts Council* (⊕ www.artscouncil.mn) organizes tours of cultural sites and art exhibitions and can be reached at 11/319–015. The less-useful ⊕ www.mol.mn has more news-oriented items.

SIDE TRIP TO TIBET
ROOF OF THE WORLD

12

By Josie Taylor **THE BEGINNINGS OF THE TIBETAN PEOPLE ARE STEEPED IN MYTH.** The six ancient tribes of Tibet are said to have come from the offspring of a persuasive ogress called Sinmo and a willing monkey named Avalokiteshvara. Yet, Tibet did not become a full-fledged nation until the 7th century, when a chieftain, Songtsen Gampo, consolidated his rule by overpowering the ancient kingdom of Zhangzhung in the west. Songtsen became the first true king of the unified Tibetan Empire, making Rasa (later renamed Lhasa) the capital. Many of the great palaces—including the Potala Palace—were initially built by Songtsen.

For 200 years the Tibetan Empire prospered. It reached advantageous treaties with, or invaded, its neighbors. In 763 the Tibetans even seized the then Chinese capital of Chang-an (present-day Xian). The Chinese emperor, Hehu Ki Wang, and his ministers were reportedly so terrified that they offered a yearly tribute of 50,000 rolls of silk to prevent further land grabs. During this period of trade, knowledge was exchanged and the teachings of Buddha were brought to Tibet and received with enthusiasm by the ruling class. Elements of the shamanistic Bön faith, which the Tibetans had previously embraced, were incorporated into Buddhist practices. Still, riddled with political and religious differences, the empire disintegrated in the 9th century, the influence of Buddhism diminished, and Tibet subsided into isolation for the next four centuries. It wasn't until the Mongols swept through Central Asia in the 13th century that Buddhism experienced a rebirth in Tibet, as it did all over East Asia, becoming the country's official religion.

Tibet emerged again as an autonomous nation-state in the 15th century, when the monk Tsongkhapa (founder of the Gelugpa order) rose as the spiritual leader. He established a new Buddhist doctrine, which emphasized moral and philosophical rigors rather than mysticism, and, in 1409, he renovated and enlarged Jokhang Temple and brought the Great Prayer Festival to Lhasa. He also founded three great monasteries: Ganden, Drepung, and Sera. This building frenzy was supported by the widening acceptance of Tsongkhapa's doctrine, which later was embodied in the Gelugpa order, or Order of the Virtuous Ones.

Though political power lay in the hands of the kings of Tsang, a Tibetan tribe that ruled out of Shigatse (the country's second-largest city), the spiritual power rested with the head lama of the Gelugpa order. This leader was (and still is) chosen among newborn infants on the death of the previous head lama in the belief that the latter's spirit had entered the newborn. The third lama received the title of Dalai Lama, meaning "Ocean of Wisdom," a title held by the current and 14th Dalai Lama. Not surprisingly, the kings perceived the lamas as a threat. In 1611 the king of Tsang attacked the Drepung and Sera monasteries. Eventually the division between the spiritual lamas and the temporal kings of Tsang became untenable. The Mongols sided with the lamas in the 17th century, defeating the king of Tsang and paving the way for the 5th Dalai Lama (1617–82) to become both spiritual and temporal head of state. Lhasa was once again securely positioned as the nation's capital and a theocracy was established.

Most of the sights included in the Tibet Exploring section can be visited in under a week. This will allow plenty of rest time in the first few days as you acclimate to walking in the high altitude. However, if you only have four days you will be able to cover the most important monasteries, markets, and ethnic quarters—all excellent ways to immerse yourself in a culture that was secluded for centuries.

Numbers in the text correspond to numbers in the margin and on the Tibet and Lhasa maps.

12

If you have 4 days

Spend your time in **Lhasa** ❶–❹ ► following the Good Route described.

If you have 10 days

One you've seen the sights of Lhasa over a leisurely four or five days, head off into the countryside—the "real" Tibet. You'll visit monasteries largely untouched by the Chinese Revolution, ocher ruins, inspiring gorges, extreme climatic conditions, friendly local villages, and gob-smacking views of the worlds highest mountains. Within a couple of hours of Lhasa you can visit the off-the-beaten-path monastery of **Ganden** ❺, but with 10 days you will also be able to organize a 3-day tour through Tsang province or 5 days to the base of the Himalayan ranges at **Everest Base Camp** ❻, as outlined in the side trips.

The debauchery (wine, women, and gambling) of the 6th Dalai Lama, combined with the declining Mongol influence, gave the Manchu Qing Dynasty (1644–1912) its opportunity. Chinese troops moved into Lhasa and the Chinese emperor Kang Xi declared Tibet a protectorate. The Dalai Lama fled to British India where he become friends with Tibetan scholar and political officer Sir Charles Bell. This relationship would influence Tibetan affairs in regard to British concerns about Russia's proximity to Tibet, and the British sent an expeditionary force to the region in 1904 to deter Russian encroachment. Nevertheless, Chinese control, sometimes manifest, sometimes latent, lasted until 1912.

At the fall of the Qing Dynasty in 1912, Tibet, with British support, gladly expelled all Chinese and declared the country's total independence. The withdrawal of the British from India in 1947 made Tibet vulnerable once again, and three years later 30,000 veteran troops of the new People's Republic of China attacked a defending force of 4,000 ill-equipped soldiers. The result was slaughter on a gigantic scale, culminating in the death of 1.2 million Tibetans and the destruction of virtually every historic structure. Fearful of incurring Chinese disapproval, the newly minted United Nations did not act. Tibet became a vassal state of China once again.

In 1959, to quell a massive popular uprising in Lhasa, sparked by rumors of a planned kidnapping of the Dalai Lama, the Chinese ruthlessly shelled the Sera Monastery and both palaces of the Dalai Lamas—the

Potala and the Norbulingka. When a crowd of 10,000 sought sanctuary in Jokhang Temple, the Chinese bombarded that, too, and after three days of gunfire in the capital, some 10,000 to 15,000 Tibetan corpses littered the streets. Three days before the massacre, the present Dalai Lama had sought asylum in India, where he later set up a government-in-exile in Dharamsala. The Tibetan government was then abolished. In 1965 China formally absorbed more than two-thirds of Tibet into the People's Republic, sparking a process of dissolving monasteries and stripping Tibetans of their culture. The region was renamed the Tibet Autonomous Region (Xizang Zizhiqu) or TAR.

In 1967 the first Red Guards marched into Lhasa and over the next three years virtually every sacred and cultural monument was damaged if not destroyed outright. Monks, nuns, and Tibetan loyalists were jailed and tortured, or simply killed. The havoc abated after Mao's death but by then some 6,250 monasteries and convents had been destroyed or severely damaged, thousands of Tibetans tortured and killed, and another 100,000 herded into labor camps.

Starting in 1980, Deng Xiaoping's era of tolerance restored some religious institutions and religious practices are now permitted—notwithstanding frequent crackdowns. Talks aimed at bringing the Dalai Lama back to Tibet broke down in 1983. A year later, hundred of thousands of Han Chinese, encouraged by economic incentives, moved west. Continued immigration means Tibetans will soon become a minority in their own land. In some areas, like Lhasa, more than half the population is Chinese, and there is little integration.

Tibet again opened its doors to tourists in 1986. Foreigners got their first glimpses of the impact of assimilation on Tibet. Demonstrations still take place, and the call for Tibetan freedom is still heard. In 1988, 1989, and 1993, a series of bloody uprisings inspired by the monks challenged Chinese rule. Martial law was temporarily instituted. Discontent with the Chinese "invasion" continues, and the possibility of more demonstrations is always present. In December 1999 there were mass arrests after a boy, Urgyen Trinley Dorje, fled his monastery in Tsurphu for India; Beijing officials recognized that many Tibetan followers believe the boy to be the 17th Karmapa, the head of the Kagyu school of Tibetan Buddhism. Stepping up security following the Karmapa's escape, China also dismissed at least 29 tour guides, all of whom were educated in India, where the Tibetan government-in-exile is currently led by the Dalai Lama. Then, in May 2000, China reportedly recruited 100 Chinese tour guides who would tow the government line. The forced adoption of Chinese curriculum in schools and Beijing control of all media continues the culture-squashing assimilation. Once the railway line to the mainland is complete there may be no limit to the migration of Chinese to Tibet.

Since July 2000 all foreigners must travel with an official guide who is trained at the Government Tourist Travel Bureau's so-called guide department. Many of the old experienced guides are blacklisted and no longer allowed to work in their profession. And while the price for hiring guides

12

Bargain for Bargains

The stalls around the Barkhor circuit and lanes near the Jokhang are fun. Where else could you pick up a rainbow-hued head-dress for a horse and a coral pendant for yourself at the same stall? You'll be able to find knickknacks and clothes from across Tibet and Kathmandu that make fine gifts. The best buys are traditional jewelry, metalwork, carpets, woodwork, and textiles. Appliquéd thangkhas make superb wall hangings to take home. Tibetans love to bargain, if the negotiation is done with patience and in good humor. Visit a fixed-price souvenir store at one of the better hotels for an idea of the higher-end price. Remember that once you make an offer, you are committed to the deal. Government regulations require a permit to export antiques.

Monk See, Monk Do

If Lhasa is Tibet's heart, its monasteries are its soul. More than just a series of halls, chapels, and courtyards, they are integral to Tibetan life as lively centers of education, politics, art, and worship. Notto be missed is the Jokhang, humming with pilgrims day and night. Sera and Drepung were relatively unscathed by the Cultural Revolution. For a rural setting near Lhasa head out to the hilltops of Ganden. The Tashilhunpo Monastery in Shigatse is the largest functioning monastic institution in Tibet. If you are heading to Everest Base Camp, stop off at the remote Rongphu Monastery which is the highest house of worship in the world. Although the Chinese government has reduced the size of religious communities and many of the buildings suffered at the hands of the Red Guards, the constant buzz of Tibetans paying homage will give you the best chance to understand the guiding principles of Tibetan life.

Rocky Mountain High

Snowcapped peaks, hidden lakes, desolate gorges, and lush plateaus combined with the challenge of extreme climates attracts trekkers of all experience levels to Tibet. Leave the jeep behind and get off the beaten track. Only by exploring on foot will you wander among ruins of ancient villages and come across nomads tending to their yak herds at temporary camps. Join a small group out of Lhasa for popular treks from Mt. Qomolangma Base Camp to Tingri. You'll usually walk five to seven hours a day for up to five days. Less arduous are the koras (pilgrim circuits) around the monasteries. Those around the Potala or Drepung monasteries in Lhasa or the Ganden Monastery are standouts. Even if you travel into the Everest region by jeep, a special treat is to walk the last two hours from Rongphu Monastery to Base Camp using a trail that hugs the base of the Himalayas.

---

has increased, the guides' salaries have decreased. Still, there is no way around this policy. Some backpackers try to go at it alone, seduced by thoughts of a windswept landscape and thrilling adventures, but just remember, if you go this route, you put everyone you encounter—from the guesthouse owner who rents you a room, to the restaurateur who serves you a meal, to the pilgrim who points you in the right direction—at risk for arrest. While you may have a fascinating vacation, they may end up "reeducated." To avoid such consequences, even veteran travelers who have visited several dozen times hire official guides. If you plan to stay in heavily touristed regions and do not really wish to be guided, you should be able to find an official guide who will meet you at the airport, take you to your hotel, ask not to discuss political matters with you, leave you alone for your stay, and eventually escort you to the airport again.

Certain "closed" regions cannot be visited at all; others may be visited with a special permit, which your guide will obtain for you. Officials may suspend travel without prior notice by denying entry permits or by claiming all flights to Lhasa are "fully booked." Suspensions are most likely at politically sensitive times, such as the Tibetan New Year, the March 10 anniversary of the 1959 uprising, the anniversary of the 1989 demonstration in June, and International Human Rights Day in December. And, sadly, the slightest hint of public protest can prompt the Chinese to make a few more Tibetans disappear and deny foreigners permission to enter the TAR. To the casual observer Tibet may not seem to be a police state, but it is.

On the "Roof of the World," people live at altitudes that average between 11,500 feet and 16,400 feet. At the higher elevations vegetation is sparse. Wild grasses in the mountain wilderness are covered by a blanket of snow in winter. Narrow gorges wind between sky-scraping peaks, making billowy clouds seem within reach of the earthbound dweller. A few valleys are open to cultivation, and turquoise freshwater lakes perfectly mirror the color of the sky through the rarified air. Western sensibilities may often romanticize Tibet while also underestimating the inherent juxtaposition of a traditional culture faced with imposed modernization by the Chinese with their ugly modern buildings and the proliferation of cell phones. Still, you will no doubt feel as if you are tiptoeing along the top of the world, knocking at the doors of the deities' heavens.

Exploring Tibet

The Tibetan plateau is more than twice the size of France, sandwiched between two Himalayan ridges whose peaks reach an altitude of 8 km (5 mi). Lhasa is the best base from which to take day trips to the fertile Kyi-chu Valley or longer jaunts into the southwestern highlands of Tsang to visit Gyantse, Shigatse, and the Everest region. Most hotels or travel operators can arrange four-wheel-drive jeeps with a driver and guide. The roads are as bumpy as the mountain passes steep, but as you pass locals riding on tractors and in overcrowded buses, your jeep's suspension won't seem so bad.

About the Restaurants

With the explosion of Chinese migration and steady Western tourism to Tibet, the variety of food available in the region has bloomed. Chinese restaurants are numerous but you will need to wander around the dining room and point to order as few of them have English-language menus.

In Lhasa take advantage of the competitive market of hybrid restaurants that serve Chinese, Indian, Nepali, Tibetan, and Western fare. Most have sprung up from backpacker haunts serving perennially favorite dishes, from banana pancakes to yak burgers. The most dependable eateries are on hotel or guesthouse premises. However, a more expensive meal does not necessarily mean it's good. A handful of places have a bar area where you can enjoy a predinner tea or cocktail but there are no actual bars as such. Outside the capital, the variety of food leaves something to be desired, but in areas commonly visited by tourists you should be able to find a simple meal. You can even order a picnic from your hotel for a countryside trip.

You will be able to eat around your sightseeing schedule. Other than breakfast, there are usually no set meal times. Reservations are preferred for large groups and if you visit from November through April, telephone ahead to be sure the hotel hasn't closed for winter.

About the Hotels

As a foreigner you can only stay in certain hotels designated by the Chinese government. In Lhasa, most of these, be they large or small, offer rooms of varying quality and price. Ask and you may be shown rooms ranging from a depressing 20-person dormitory to a deluxe suite with private bath, balcony, and minibar. Some of the more expensive hotels even equip their rooms with oxygen machines to ease the effects of altitude sickness. Televisions are becoming standard, though non-Chinese-language programming is rare. Tibetan guesthouses are a warm and welcoming alternative. Staffed by locals, these lodgings are more personable but some of the shared bathing facilities at the lower end options can be archaic. In the major towns outside Lhasa there are bland Chinese hotels, about half of which have hot running water. Throughout Tibet prices are negotiable from December to March and then tend to soar in the high season.

WHAT IT COSTS In Yuan				
$$$$	**$$$**	**$$**	**$**	**¢**
RESTAURANTS over 165	100–165	50–99	25–49	under 25
HOTELS over 1,800	1,400–1,800	1,100–1,399	700–1,099	under 700

Restaurant prices are for a main course, excluding tax and tips. Hotel prices are for a standard double room, including taxes.

Timing

Consider your adaptability to extreme weather conditions and your willingness to battle throngs of tourists when choosing a time to visit Tibet. Temperatures can sink to −23°C (−10°F) from November to January. It may be frightfully cold, but the climate is dry and the skies perpetually blue. Cold weather also means fewer tourists, and travel is less restrictive as police at checkpoints are more concerned with keeping warm than turning back visitors. Many tourist sights in Lhasa shorten their opening hours in winter months, with some restaurants and hotels refurbishing or temporarily closing altogether. From June to August highs reach

27°C (80°F). Summer sees a bit of rain, and often roads will be closed to popular tourist destinations, including the Everest Base Camp. The best touring conditions occur from mid-April through August, but with pleasant weather come hordes of tourists particularly at the tail end of the season. September through mid-November, with its mild weather, is another good option.

Try to time your visit with one of the brilliantly colorful traditional Tibetan festivals. The Tibetan calendar is the same as the lunar calendar so exact dates as they relate to the Western calendar are only published a year in advance. Dancing monks whip up a frenzy to dispel the evil spirits of the previous year at the Year End Festival on the 29th day of the 12th lunar month. The 1st week of the 1st lunar month includes Losar (New Year Festival), when Lhasa is filled with Tibetan drama performances, incense offerings, and locals promenading in their finest wardrobe. Grand butter lanterns light up the Barkhor circuit during the Lantern Festival on the 15th of the 1st month. On the 7th day of the 4th month you can join the pilgrims in Lhasa or Ganden to mark the Birth of Sakyamuni (Buddha), or you may want to wait until the 15th for the celebrations of Saga Dawa (Sakyamuni's enlightenment) and join the pilgrims who climb the Drepung Monastery to burn juniper incense. Picnics at the summer palace of Norbulingka are common during the Worship of the Buddha in the 2nd week of the 5th month. During Shö-tun (Yogurt Festival) in the 1st week of the 7th month, immerse yourself in the operas, masked dances, and picnics from Drepung (7 km [4 mi] out of Lhasa) to Norbulingka. During the festival, giant thangkas of the Buddha are unveiled in Drepung Monastery and Tibetan opera troupes perform operas at Norbulingka. Lhabab Düchen (Buddha's descent from heaven) on the 22nd day of the 9th month, Palden Lhama (Jokhang's protective deity) on the 15th day of the 10th month, and the Tsongkhapa Festival on the 25th day of the 10th month, all bring pilgrim processions to Lhasa.

LHASA

▶ Once a great military power that renounced violence in favor of Buddhism, Lhasa is a treasure trove of medieval monasteries, devout pilgrims, and colorful festivals. Geographically the city is divided into western (Chinese) and eastern (Tibetan) areas. The Chinese section includes many upmarket hotels, the Nepalese embassy, and Norbulingka Palace. More colorful is the Tibetan section, full of guesthouses, laid-back restaurants, street markets, the Barkhor pilgrim circuit, and Jokhang Temple. There is also a small Muslim Quarter to the southeast of the Barkhor. The old winding lanes in and around the Barkhor are immensely walkable and a great way to rub shoulders with the locals. Don't worry about getting lost: most of the thoroughfares are circular; if you follow the pilgrims, you'll make it back to the circuit.

With a population of a little more than 200,000, the city is remarkably small, considering its long history. The major sights, both historical and architectural, fall into three eras: First, the 7th- to 9th-century building

ON THE MENU

Tibetan eating is an adventure in itself. Epicureans may be disappointed by Tibetan cooking since not much grows at 4 km (2½ mi) above sea level. The traditional staple is tsampa (roasted barley flour mixed with yak butter tea). You are likely to eat tsampa more than once only if panic hunger strikes. A more enjoyable dish is the momo, a steamed or fried dumpling filled with meat or vegetables, often served with then-thuk (noodles). Other dishes include lasha (lamb with radish), gyuma (black pudding made from dark-colored grains), thu (cheesecake; though not a version Westerners know), and dresi (sweet rice).

Tibetans drink liters of yak butter tea every day. Made of melted butter, soda, milk, hot water, tea leaves, and salt, it is an acquired taste. If offered a cup it is perfectly acceptable for you to ask for sweet milk or plain tea instead. Beer, soft drinks, and bottled water are available nearly everywhere. The local drink is chang (a fortified barley ale). Local water is not potable; it must be boiled or treated with iodine.

boom, which produced the original Potala Palace on Mt. Marpori and Buddhist-influenced Jokhang Temple; second, the 15th century, when Tsongkhapa renovated and enlarged Jokhang Temple and founded the three great monasteries: Ganden, Drepung, and Sera; and third, when Lhasa again became the capital, and the Fifth Dalai Lama rebuilt (and expanded) the Potala Palace on the foundations of the original. Over the next three centuries the lamas constructed the great Gelugpa monasteries and palaces, of which the Norbulingka Palace is the most notable.

Located in the heart of Tibet, it takes only a few hours to reach Lhasa by airplane over the impressive Himalayas. The easiest way to explore its sights is by one of the many fixed-price bicycle rickshaws (Y4 for any distance) or taxis (Y10 for any distance) that roam the streets. Ask your hotel to write down both the Tibetan and Chinese name of your destination, as many of the streets are referred to by their name in either language. To help you get your bearings, look for Dekyi Num Lam, which becomes Dekyi Shar Lam in the east of town. It's also known as Beijing Dong Lu, and runs past the Tibet Hotel, the Lhasa Hotel, the yak statues, the Potala Palace, and the main post office for the Tibetan part of town.

a good tour

The high altitude of Lhasa will tax your stamina on your first day, so take it easy. After settling into your hotel go down to the **Barkhor** ① ☞ for lunch and then spend the afternoon in the **Jokhang Temple** ②. While in old Lhasa, shop around the Barkhor or spend an hour at the **Tibetan Traditional Hospital** ③, a block west of Jokhang Temple. If there is time, you can visit the temple of **Meru Nyingba** ④ (adjoining the east wall of the Jokhang) and the **Ani Tshamkung** ⑤ nunnery, just south of the Jokhang. Nearby is the **Gyel Lhakhang** ⑥, Lhasa's mosque. Or follow smells and sounds as you wander the streets of Barkhor. North of Dekyi Shar Lam is the 15th-century **Ramoche Temple** ⑦.

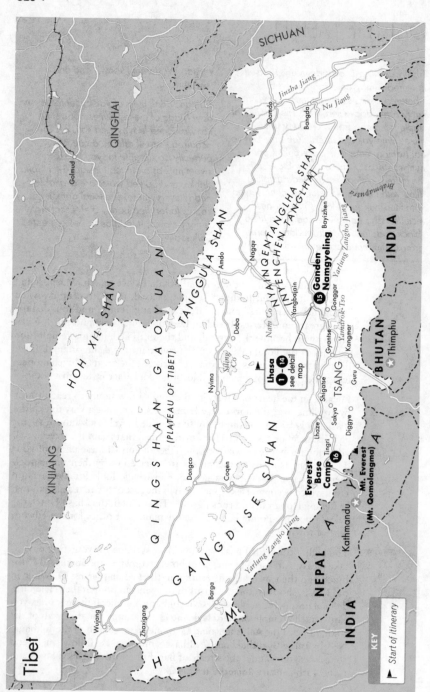

Tibet

The monumental **Potala Palace** ⑧ should be your first stop on the second day. It will take the full morning to cover both the White and Red palaces. Spend the afternoon exploring the religious cave paintings and carvings on Chakpo-Ri, being sure to visit the **Chogyel Zimuki Temple** ⑨.

On the third day go out to the **Drepung Monastery** ⑩. Give yourself at least an hour and a half to explore, then make the Drepung Linghor— the 90-minute pilgrimage walk around the monastery. The next stop is the **Nechung Monastery** ⑪, just southeast of Drepung.

For the fourth day go out to **Sera Thekchenling** ⑫, northeast of Lhasa. Return to spend an afternoon at the **Norbulingka** ⑬ complex, followed by an hour at the **Tibet Museum** ⑭. If you have more than four days in Tibet, you can head out of town, possibly to visit the enormous **Ganden Monastery** ⑮, 40 km (25 mi) from Lhasa, or simply to get the feel for rural Tibet.

What to See

⑤ **Ani Tshamkung** (Ani Sanghung). When you visit this lively nunnery, beaming nuns will encourage you to meander through their temple, listen to their chanting, and watch them make ornamental butter flowers. Their main hall was built in the early 14th century; a second story was added in the early 20th century. Considerable damage occurred during the Cultural Revolution but the nunnery was restored between 1982 and 1984 and now houses more than 60 nuns in this two-story residence. The chief pilgrimage site is the Tshamkung (meditation hollow) where Songtsen Gampo concentrated his spiritual focus on preventing the flood of the Kyi River. ⊠ *Waling Lam, southeast of Jokhang, look for a front entrance painted yellow* ☜ *Y10* ⊗ *Daily 9–6.*

▶ ① **Barkhor.** Join the pilgrims on the Barkhor circuit and step back in time. Look for the monks sitting before their alms bowls and chanting mantras while the faithful constantly spin their prayer wheels to send their orisons up to the sky. The brilliant colors of silk robes and turquoise jewelry may catch your eye, but watch your step: you may accidentally trip over pilgrims prostrating themselves toward the Jokhang Temple. The circuit is crammed with stalls where vendors sell trinkets, carpets, hats, prayer shawls, and just about anything else. The streets running north off the Barkhor walkway to Dekyi Shar Lam are shopping streets. South of the Barkhor plaza are several notable buildings, including former residences of advisers to the 14th Dalai Lama.

⑨ **Chogyel Zimuki** (Dragla Lugug). Religious rock paintings dating from as early as the 7th century can be seen at this grotto-style temple. Beyond the temple's gate is a monastic building from which you can mount the steps of the two-story grotto chapel. On the second floor you'll find the entrance to the spherical cave, which has a central rock column. Three of the cave's walls and the column bear 71 sculptures carved into the granite, probably by Nepalese artists from the 7th to 9th century. The entrance of the chapel has views of the Potala Palace. ✛ *On Iron Mountain (Chakpo-Ri) on which a large TV station antenna stands. Look for track southwards from Dekyi Num Lam or walk 20*

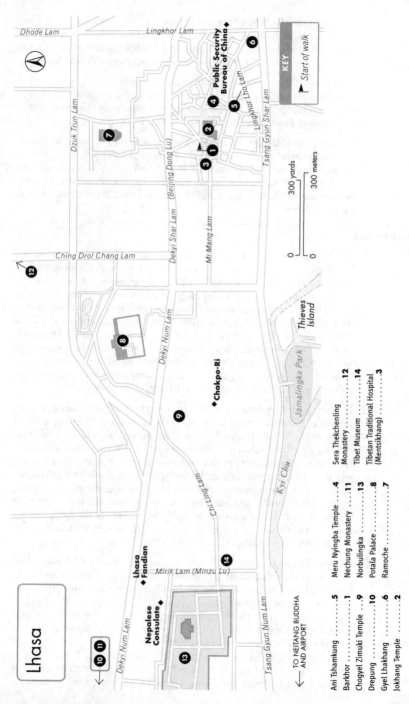

Lhasa

KEY

▲ Start of walk

Dhode Lam

Lingkhor Lam

Public Security Bureau of China ◆

Dzuk Trun Lam

(Beijing Dong Lu)

Dekyi Shar Lam

Mi Mang Lam

Lingkhor Lha Lam

Tsang Gyun Shar Lam

Ching Drol Chang Lam

Dekyi Num Lam

◆ Chakpo-Ri

Jamalingka Park

Thieves Island

Kyi Chu

Chi Ling Lam

Tsang Gyun Num Lam

Lhasa Fandian ◆

Mirik Lam (Minzu Lu)

Dekyi Num Lam

Nepalese Consulate ◆

← TO NEITANG BUDDHA
AND AIRPORT

300 yards

300 meters

mins up trail that begins opposite exit from Potala ⌦ *Free* ☉ *Daily sunrise–sunset.*

⑩ Drepung. The largest of the Gelugpa monasteries was the residence for lesser lamas. Founded in 1416, it was enlarged in the 16th century by the Second Dalai Lama. By the era of the Fifth Dalai Lama it had become the largest monastic institution in the world, with 10,000 residents. During the Cultural Revolution it suffered only minimally because the army used the building as its headquarters and therefore didn't ransack it as much as other temples. The monastery was reopened in 1980 and the number of resident monks varies (though it's currently fewer than 50), as they are often sent away by Chinese officials to be reeducated.

The monastery's most important building is the Tshomchen, whose vast assembly hall, the **Dukhang,** is noteworthy for its 183 columns, atrium ceiling, and ceremonial banners. Chapels can be found on all three floors as well as on the roof. In the two-story **Buddhas of Three Ages Chapel** (Düsum Sangye Lhakhang), at the rear of the Dukhang on the ground floor, the Buddhas of past, present, and future are each guarded by two bodhisattvas.

To set out on a pilgrimage around the monastery, the **Drepung Linghor** walking route leaves from the corner of the parking lot. The walk takes about 90 minutes. The path winds west of the perimeter wall and up-hill in the direction of the **retreat of Gephel Ritrö** and then descends in the direction of Nechung. You can also walk 3½ hours up to Gephel Ritrö. The retreat (now restored) was founded in the 14th century at the place where monks tended yak herds. The summit, **Gephel Ütse,** is another 2½ hours of steep climbing. ✛ *Off Dekyi Num Lam, 7 km (4 mi) west of Lhasa center; take bus that passes Lhasa Hotel, get off at base of Gephel Ri, and walk 1 km (½ mi) north; or hire a car or minibus taxi from town* ⌦ *Y55* ☉ *Daily 8:30–5; some chapels close noon–2.*

⑥ Gyel Lhakhang. In perhaps the most Buddhist of cities, Gyel Lhakhang is a bit of an anomaly. It is Lhasa's largest mosque and now consists of both a modern building and the original 18th-century structure. Intended for immigrants who had arrived in the 17th century from Kashmir and Ladakh, it was completed in 1716. Fresh-food market stalls are set up every day outside the decorative old entry gates. ⌧ *Linghor Lho Lam near E. Linghor Lam* ☉ *Daily 8–5, except during prayers Fri.* AM.

② Jokhang Temple. This temple is the most sacred building in all of Tibet. From the gentle flicker of a butter-lamp light dancing off antique murals, statues, tapestries, and *thangkhas* (scroll paintings), to the air thick with incense and anticipation as thousands of Tibetans pay homage day and night, it contains a plethora of sensory delights.

FodorsChoice
★

Most likely built in 647, during Songtsen Gampo's reign, Jokhang stands in the heart of the old town. The site was selected as the geomantic center of Tibet by Queen Wengcheng, a princess from China brought to Songtsen Gampo as his second wife. She also divined that before the completion of the temple, the demon ogress (of the Tibetan creation myth) needed to be pacified. This required the construction of

12 outlying temples, built on the "thighs," "knees," and other body parts of the "supine ogress" to pin her down; the design entails three successive rings of four temples around the location of Jokhang.

Songtsen's first wife, Princess Bhrikuti from Nepal, financed the building of Jokhang. In her honor and in recognition of Tibet's strong reliance on Nepal, Jokhang's main gate was designed to face west, toward Nepal. Among the few bits remaining of its 7th-century construction are the door frames of the four inner chapels, dedicated to Mahakarunika (a protector deity), Amitabha (the Buddha of perfected perception), Sakyamuni (the historical Buddha), and Maitreya (the Buddha of loving kindness).

Over the centuries renovations have enlarged the Jokhang to keep it the premier temple of Tibet. Its status was threatened in the 1950s when the Chinese Army shelled it and the Red Guards of the Cultural Revolution ransacked it. During this period of sacrilege parts of it were used as a guesthouse and as a pigsty. About a third of the damage has since been repaired, some is currently under repair, and a portion is lost forever.

The Inner Jokhang has three stories and forms a square enclosing the inner hall, Kyilkhor Thil. Encircling the Inner Jokhang is the Inner Circumambulation, known as the Nangkhor. The Outer Jokhang, sometimes referred to as the western extension and constructed in 1409, contains the lesser chapels, storerooms, kitchens, and residences. The whole complex is encircled by the Barkhor Walkway and the old city of Lhasa.

Start your visit in the Barkhor. Look for the two enclosures at the entrance to the temple and step through the tapestry hanging over the door of the small roofed building. Inside are hundreds of butter lamps removed from inside the Jokhang by the Chinese government which declared them a fire hazard. Back outside, peer through the walled structures grate for a glimpse of the stump of a willow tree planted by Queen Wengcheng. You will also see three graved pillars. One of them is inscribed with the terms of the Sino-Tibetan treaty of 822 which recognizes Tibet and China as two distinct countries.

Enter the temple through the portico supported by six fluted columns. Centuries of pilgrims prostrating themselves in the threshold courtyard have worn the flagstones smooth. Within the main courtyard is the assembly hall that Tsongkhapa had constructed for the Great Prayer Festival in 1409—an event that greatly enhanced Lhasa's position as the spiritual capital of Tibet. Along the outer walls are 19th-century murals, and in the inner hall are murals dating from 1648. On the north side is one of the residences of the Dalai Lamas.

Before entering the Inner Jokhang, you should walk the Nangkhor (Inner Circumambulation) in a clockwise direction. It's lined with prayer wheels and murals depicting a series of Buddhist images. On the north side are several chapels of minor consequence. Outside, the wall on the south side is the debating courtyard, renovated in 1986, which contains the platform where thrones for Tsongkhapa and other dignitaries were set up for the Great Prayer Festival. Enter by the **Main Gate** (Zhung-go), which has finely carved door frames from the early-Tibetan period (7th to 9th century). To the left of the door is a painting of the future Buddha, on the right a painting of the past Buddha. A footprint of the 13th Dalai Lama (1876–1933) is enshrined in a small niche. Continue on to the large Entrance Hall, whose inner chapels have murals depicting the wrathful deities responsible for protecting the temple and the city. Straight ahead is the inner sanctum, the three-story **Kyilkhor Thil,** some of whose many columns probably date from the 7th century, particularly those with short bases and round shafts.

The chapels on the ground floor of the Kyilkhor Thil are the most rewarding. In the west wing be sure to see the **Je Rinpoche Dakpa Namgye Lhakhang,** a chapel whose central image is Tsongkhapa flanked by his eight pure retainers. In the north wing, in the chapel **Mahakarunika Lhakhang,** is a reproduction of the image of the deity Mahakarunika. The most revered chapel of the inner hall is **Jowo Sakyamuni Lhakhang,** in the middle of the east wing, opposite the entrance. Here is the 5-foot statue of Jowo Rinpoche, representing the Buddha at age 12. It was brought to Tibet by Queen Wengcheng and somehow has survived, despite a history of being plastered over and buried in sand. Many of the upper-floor chapels are closed but head for the roof for sweeping views over the Barkhor, Potala Palace, and Lhasa to the snowcapped mountains. ⊠ *Barkhor* 🎫 *Y60* 🕒 *Daily 9–12:30 and 3–6.*

> **need a break?** Located two blocks south of the Jokhang, the **Phuritsang Tibetan Culture Kitchen** (⊠ Yuthok Department Store, 2nd fl., Yuthok Rd., Lhasa 850001 ☎ 0891/633–6088 ➾ No credit cards) is a good place to take a break from the Barkhor circuit area. Look for the Songtsen restaurant sign at street level and walk one floor up the worn-out-looking stairs. Sit at any of the low tables near the windows for good people-watching on one of the city's busier intersections.

❹ Meru Nyingba. The original version of this temple, built soon after the Jokhang, is where the Tibetan alphabet was finalized by the scholar Tonmi Sambhota. Within this 20th-century reconstruction are murals portraying many of the forms taken by Pehar, the chief guardian of the Gelugpa Buddhist sect. ⊠ *Eastern wall of Jokhang off northern arc of Barkhor* 🕒 *Daily sunrise–sunset.*

⓫ Nechung Monastery. From its construction in the 12th century until 1959, this monastery was home to the highly influential Nechung Oracle. Every important decision made by a Dalai Lama is done so after consulting this oracle (a medium for the protective deity Pehar). The current oracle resides in Dharamsala as an adviser to the Dalai Lama and his government-in-exile. Except for the gilded roofs and their embellishments, Nechung's buildings largely survived the Cultural Revolution. The murals on the portico depict Pehar and his retinue. In the assembly hall murals show the *Deities of the Eight Transmitted Precepts,* and in the Jordungkhang chapel on the western side you'll find more images of Pehar. There are two other chapels on the ground floor, two on the second floor, and a single chapel on the third floor. You can also visit the former residence of the Nechung Oracle, behind the main building. ⊠ *Dekyi Num Lam, 8 km (5 mi) west of Lhasa center, 1 km (½ mi) southeast of Drepung Monastery* 🚌 *Y20* ⊘ *Daily 9–noon and 2–5.*

⑬ Norbulingka. The 7th Dalai Lama (1708–57), a frail man, chose to build a palace on this site because of its medicinal spring. In 1755, not content just to have a summer home for himself, he added the **Kelzang Podrang** to the southeast, a three-story palace whose ground floor is dominated by his throne. He had his whole government moved here from the Potala Palace. The next Dalai Lama expanded the property, adding the **Tsokyil Podrang Palace**, a debating courtyard, a pavilion, and a library. The gardens were landscaped by the 13th Dalai Lama who also oversaw the construction of a new complex, **Chensel Lingka Podrang**, to the northwest, containing three small palaces. The last addition, built by the current Dalai Lama in 1954–56, was **Takten Migyur Podrang**, in the north, an ornate two-story building notable for its lion-and-tiger image, symbolic of political and religious power, which is found on alternative sides of the stairs leading to the Dalai Lama's private quarters. It turned out to be the place from which, disguised as a soldier, he fled to India on March 17, 1959, three days before the Chinese massacred thousands of Tibetans and fired artillery shells into every Norbulingka building. Only after searching through the corpses did they realize the Dalai Lama had escaped.

The work done to repair the damage in the aftermath of the March 1959 uprising is not of high caliber. The palace's 40 acres are divided into three sectors: the opera grounds (where Tibetan operatic performances are held during the Yogurt Festival, government buildings, and the palaces. The four complexes of palaces are visited by pilgrims in the following sequence: Kelzang Podrang, to the southeast; Takten Migyur Podrang, to the north; Tsokyil Podrang, in the center; and Chensel Lingka Podrang, to the northwest. ⊠ *Mirik Lam* 🚌 *Y25* ⊘ *Daily 9–5:30.*

❽ Potala Palace. Virtually nothing remains of the original 11-story Potala Palace built in 637 by King Songtsen. What you see today is a 17th-century replacement. The Fifth Dalai Lama, anxious to reestablish the importance of Lhasa as the Tibetan capital, employed 7,000 workers and 1,500 artisans to resurrect the Potala Palace on the 7th-century foundation. After 8 years the portion called the White Palace was completed, in 1653. The Red Palace, the central upper part, was not completed until 1694, 12 years after the Dalai Lama's death (which was kept secret by the regent in order to prevent interruption of the construction). The Potala has been enlarged since then and continually renovated, such as when the structural walls were strengthened in 1991. Once the headquarters of Tibet's theocracy, the vast Potala is now a museum.

Fodor's Choice
★

The Potala Palace was the world's tallest building before the advent of modern skyscrapers. Towering above the city from the slopes of Mt. Marpori, the structure is 384 feet high; its 1,000 rooms house some 200,000 images. The outer section, the White Palace, was the seat of government and the winter residence of the Dalai Lama until 1951. In it you can pass through the Dalai Lama's spartan quarters. On either side of the palace are the former offices of the government. The Red Palace, looming above the White Palace, is the spiritual part of the Potala. Murals chronicle Buddhist folklore and ancient Tibetan life. Within the four stories that make up the functional part of the Red Palace are dozens of small chapels, where often a human skull and thigh bone are the only decoration. Interspersed among the chapels are eight golden chorten containing the remains of the 5th and 7th through 13th Dalai Lamas.

The eastern gatehouse is the main entrance used by pilgrims, who climb up from Zhol Square below. Officials will try to usher you to the rear drive-in entrance on the north side (but you can also try to slip in among the pilgrims), as there is a substantial difference between tourist and local admission prices. If you enter from the north, you miss the ancillary buildings, including two printing presses dating from the 17th century.

Between the White and Red palaces is a yellow building that houses the Thangkha Rooms, where huge thangkhas are kept. Once used in the Yogurt Festival, they are no longer displayed, although one was unfurled in 1994. Underneath the 13-story, 1,000-room fortress are the dungeons. Justice could be harsh—torture and jail time were the punishments for refusing to pay taxes, displaying anger, or insulting a monk. The worst place to be sent was the Cave of Scorpions, where prisoners were the targets of stinging tails. ✉ *Zhol* 🎫 *Y100* 🕐 *Mon., Wed., and Fri. 9–noon; Tues., Thurs., and weekends 9:30–noon.*

❼ Ramoche. This temple was founded by Queen Wengcheng at the same time as the Jokhang. Its three-story structure dates from the 15th century. Despite restorations in the 1980s, it lost much of its former glory after the Chinese used it to house the Communist Labor Training Committee during the Cultural Revolution.

Ramoche was intended to house the most revered statue of Jowo Rinpoche. A threat of a Chinese invasion in the 7th century induced Queen Wengcheng to hide the statue in the Jokhang. Some 50 years later it was rediscovered and placed within the Jokhang's main chapel. As a substitute, Jokhang reciprocated with a Nepalese statue of Jowo Mikyo Dorje, which represented Buddha as an eight-year-old. It was decapitated during the Cultural Revolution and its torso "lost" in Beijing. Both head and body were later found, put back together again, and placed in a small chapel at the back of Ramoche's Inner Sanctum (Tsangkhang). ✉ *Ramoche Lam, off north side of Dekyi Shar Lam, north of Tromzikhang Market* 🎫 *Y20* 🕐 *Daily 9:30–5:30.*

★ ⑫ Sera Thekchenling Monastery. This important Gelugpa monastery, founded in 1419 on 24 acres, contains numerous chapels, with splendid murals and icons. Originally it was a hermitage for Tsongkhapa and his top students. Within a couple hundred years it housed more than 5,000 monks. The complex comprises the *tsokchen* (great assembly hall), three *tratsangs* (colleges), and 30 *klangstens* (residential units).

On the clockwise pilgrimage route, start at the two buildings that will take up most of your visit. **Sera Me Tratsang** (founded in 1419), which promotes elementary studies, has a *dukhang* (assembly hall) rebuilt in 1761 with murals depicting Buddha's life. Among the five chapels along the dukhang's north wall, the Ta-og Lhakhang is hard to forget, as its exterior is adorned with skeletons and skulls. The complex's oldest surviving structure, **Ngagpa Tratsang,** is a three-story college for tantric studies. Here you'll find statues of famous lamas and murals depicting paradise.

Continue to the four-story-high **Sera Je Tratsang,** where you can take time out in the shaded courtyard used for monastic philosophical debates. Don't be alarmed if you see children leaving this college with black ash on their noses. They have been blessed at the **Chapel of Hayagriva,** also known as the Horse Head Buddha. ✛ *5 km (3 mi) north of Lhasa at base of Mt. Phurbuchok* 🎫 *Y30* ⊙ *Daily 9:30–4.*

⓮ Tibet Museum. For the Chinese interpretation of Tibetan history, politics, and culture visit this modern museum. The free personal audio guide provides commentary on important pieces on prehistoric times, Chinese dynasties, and traditional Tibetan life. If you are a scholar of history, you may find some of the explanations intriguing. ✉ *19 Gongyan Rd.* 🎫 *Y30* ⊙ *Tues.–Sun. 9–5.*

❸ Tibetan Traditional Hospital (Mentsikhang). This may be a busy working and teaching medical center, but the hospital has a small exhibition on the history and philosophy of Tibetan medicine which doctors will gladly guide you through. Giant medical thangkhas, which are used to teach student doctors diagnosis and treatments, line the walls. Once inside the lobby take the stairs up to the upper floor and ask the nurse in the admissions room where the exhibit is. A small donation to support the hospital is appreciated. ✛ *1 block south of the Jokhang* 🎫 *Free* ⊙ *Mon.–Sat. 9–5.*

Where to Eat

$$ ✕ **Dunya.** Meaning "the world" in 10 languages, Dunya serves a melting pot of international dishes. The food here is first-rate and can be complemented by a bottle of Australian wine and real coffee—both rarities in Tibet. Try the Motuk Soup (vegetable dumplings in a tasty broth), roasted chicken leg, or Lhasa's only yak enchilada. The homemade ice cream and rich chocolate sauce is also delicious. Upstairs is a well-stocked bar complete with dartboard and balcony with a Dutch raconteur at the helm. ✉ *100 Dekyi Shar Lam, next to Yak Hotel, 850001* 🕾 *0891/633–3374* ▤ *No credit cards* ⊙ *Closed Nov.–Apr.*

$ ✕ **Makye Ame.** Ask to be seated by the second-floor windows or on the rooftop for some of the best and least-intrusive views of pilgrims on the Barkhor circuit which passes right by this corner restaurant. Try the Tibet Tucci (spinach ravioli in homemade tomato and basil sauce), chicken butter marsala, or *then-thuk* (homemade noodles in ginger tomato broth). For fun, ask the staff to explain the legend of Makye Ame. She was a mystery woman immortalized in a poem penned by the Sixth Dalai Lama who spied her in a bar where the café now stands. ✛ *Building with big mural of Makye Ame, 2nd fl., southeast corner of Barkhor circuit* 🕾 *0891/632–4455* ▤ *No credit cards.*

$ ✕ **Shangrila.** As dancers perform traditional routines, your taste buds will be treated to an 18-dish Tibetan buffet—a superb opportunity to try indigenous food such as sautéed yak lung, cheese momos, Tibetan Ginseng (wild sweet potatoes), and cold yak tongue. The colorful Tibetan thangkhas that line the dining room, dark-wood furniture, and the congenial staff who happily explain the dishes set it apart from other dinner and performance shows in the city. Call ahead and arrive by 7 PM for the best seats. Upstairs is a Western-style bar. ⊠ *12 Dekyi Shar Lam, inside Kirey Hotel courtyard* ☎ *0891/636–3800* ▤ *No credit cards.*

$ ✕ **Snowlands Restaurant.** Join aid workers, local businessmen, and small tour groups at this cozy café. You're likely to pick up some travel tips by inadvertently eavesdropping on other diners as you sit, cramped among the small tables and booths. Try the Tibetan *Gyacock* (traditional hotpot) or feast on grilled yak's fillet with pepper sauce. This place can be hugely popular so service may be a little slow. Fresh cinnamon rolls, apple pie, and croissants are also available for takeout. ⊠ *4 Mentsikhang Lam* ☎ *0891/633–7323* ▤ *No credit cards.*

$ ✕ **Yeti Café.** Curious about how Tibetan food is prepared? Then stop off at the Yeti, where you will find English menus which describe the main ingredients for each dish and how it is prepared. Find a comfy oversize couch in the dining area and lounge under the warm glow of cascading red chandeliers. The yak steak marinated in Tibetan spices is recommended. Spicy Sichuan food is also available. ⊠ *77–10 Dekyi Num Lam, north of Lhasa Hotel* ☎ *0891/681–5755* ▤ *No credit cards.*

Where to Stay

$$$ ▣ **Lhasa Hotel.** If you stay here between July and September you'll be pleased with the piped-in oxygen (to ease the effects of altitude sickness) and the swimming pool. The rest of the year you will pay premium rates for an average hotel where the building and the gardens look largely ignored. Nevertheless, rooms come equipped with comfortable sitting chairs. The gift shop on the mezzanine floor has a wide selection of fixed-price souvenirs and some excellent over-the-counter altitude-sickness remedies. The hotel was previously known as the Lhasa Fandian and before that, the Holiday Inn Lhasa. Foreign-currency-exchange services are available. ⊠ *1 Mirik Lam, 850001* ☎ *0891/683–2221* ▦ *0891/683–5796* ⏎ *468 rooms, 12 suites* ⌂ *5 restaurants, room service, minibars, cable TV, pool, hair salon, bar, laundry service, business services, meeting rooms* ▤ *AE, DC, MC, V.*

$ ▣ **Grand Hotel.** Within strolling distance of the Norbulingka, the Grand is a large complex offering a wide variety of accommodations. Floral wallpaper, brightly colored bedspreads, and Italian-made whirlpool bathtubs are standard. Ask to inspect the room before accepting it. Few of the standard rooms have external windows. Behind the thick curtains may be a window into a teahouse or office space. Foreign-currency-exchange services are available. ⊠ *1 Mirik Lam, 850001* ☎ *0891/683–2888* ▦ *0891/683–2195* ⏎ *380 rooms, 20 suites* ⌂ *6 restaurants, hair salon, laundry service, business services, travel services* ▤ *AE, DC, V.*

$ ⊞ **Tibet Hotel.** The otherwise standard rooms at this well-maintained hotel have a few nice extras for a Tibetan accommodation: hair dryers, cotton robes, plush carpets, and tea- and coffee-making facilities. Officially there are 10 restaurants serving Western and Asian food but many of these are leased to independent managers, so their opening hours are erratic (which is trying if you're hungry since you're quite a ways from downtown). Many of the staff have limited English-language skills but their enthusiasm makes it easy to bridge communication gaps. Foreign-currency-exchange services are available. ⊠ *64 Dekyi Shar Lam, 850001* ☎ *0891/683–4966* 🖷 *0891/683–6787* 🖅 *260 rooms* ⚏ *10 restaurants, hair salon, dance club, laundry service, business services, travel services* ▤ *AE, DC, MC, V.*

¢ ⊞ **Banakshol.** A popular Tibetan Quarter choice with the backpacker crowd, the bright, homey guesthouse has dormitories and doubles. Try to stay in one of the Tibetan-theme rooms with multicolor furniture and religious motifs hand-painted on the walls. The rooms are basic but clean, and the all-Tibetan staff is incredibly friendly and helpful. The restaurant, with outdoor seating, is always a popular meeting spot to relax over a meal, a beer, and conversation. A computer is available for Internet access (guests pay per minute) and you can leave your belongings in a storage room before going on long treks. ⊠ *8 Dekyi Shar Lam, 850001* 🖷🖷 *0891/633–8040* 🖅 *38 rooms, 2 dormitories* ⚏ *Restaurant, laundry service, Internet, meeting rooms, travel services; no a/c* ▤ *No credit cards.*

¢ ⊞ **Himalaya Hotel.** Sliding glass doors open onto a lavishly appointed entrance defined by four grand columns, a marble floor, and a central chandelier. The rooms range from luxury suites to budget triples, all of which are clean and comfortable. Ask for a room with a view of the Potala. On the ninth floor is a teahouse—a civilized resting place after a hard day of hectic sightseeing. The hotel stands near the Kyi River, a 10-minute walk from the Barkhor. ⊠ *6 Linghor Dong Lu, 850001* ☎ *0891/632–3888* 🖷 *0891/632–1111* 🖅 *133 rooms, 13 suites* ⚏ *3 restaurants, massage, sauna, laundry service, business services, meeting room, travel services* ▤ *AE, MC, V.*

¢ ⊞ **Kyichu Hotel.** A small, charming hotel in the heart of the Tibetan Quarter, the Kyichu veers away from the modern sterility of other hotels in its class. Hallways decorated with old black-and-white Tibetan photographs lead to rooms with hardwood floors, dark-wood furniture, and thangkhas on the walls. All the standard rooms look out onto a large garden which is a peaceful place to sit and enjoy a drink at any time of the day. On the ground floor is a small restaurant that serves tasty Indian, Chinese, Western, and Tibetan food. The lobby has a small sitting area, a book exchange, and a well-stocked art shop. ⊠ *149 Dekyi Shar Lam, 850000* ☎ *0891/633–1541* 🖷 *0891/632–0234* 🖅 *52 rooms, 4 suites* ⚏ *Restaurant, dry cleaning, laundry service, business services, travel services; no a/c* ▤ *No credit cards.*

¢ ⊞ **Pentoc Guesthouse.** Just one block north of Barkhor Square, this hotel is a clean and comfortable option for the budget-minded traveler. All rooms have bedside reading lights, colorful Tibetan-style bedcovers, and either a love seat or chair. The communal toilets and showers are immaculate and staff are always on hand if there are any problems with the hot water. Videos are shown nightly at 8 PM in the lounge and a shop offers unique handcrafted souvenirs. ✉ *5 Mentsikhang Lam, 850001* ☎ *0891/632–6686* ↩ *24 rooms* ↺ *Business services; no a/c, no room TVs* ▭ *No credit cards.*

★ ¢ 🏨 **Shangbala Hotel.** This modern Barkhor Square hotel has clean, warm rooms with big bathtubs and steaming hot water. The thick carpet is as comfortable and soft as the beds. The staff is professionally trained, giving service on par with more expensive hotels. If you are suffering slightly from the high altitude, try the Gao-Yuan-An Tibetan medicine tea offered in the minibar. It tastes like licorice and seems to work. ✉ *1 Danjelin Rd., 850000* ☎ *0891/632–3888* ⎙ *0891/632–3577* ↩ *70 rooms* ↺ *Restaurant, room service, minibars, hair salon, bar, laundry service, business services* ▭ *AE, DC, MC, V.*

¢ 🏨 **Snowland.** One of the original hotels that foreigners were permitted to stay in, this is a good budget-conscious option near the Jokhang. Enter the inner courtyard of the Snowland and you will soon forget the hustle and bustle of Lhasa's streets. Try to get a room with its own bath since the communal bathrooms are very basic (although reasonably clean). A good-natured staff is always eager to please. ✉ *4 Mentsikhang Lam, 850001* ☎ *0891/632–3687* ⎙ *0891/632–7145* ↩ *18 rooms, 2 suites, dormitory* ↺ *Restaurant, bicycles, laundry service, travel services; no a/c* ▭ *No credit cards.*

¢ 🏨 **Yak Hotel.** Once the first choice for travelers on a tight budget, the Yak has reinvented itself into a hotel with rooms ranging from dormitories to deluxe. Regardless of what kind of room you choose, it will be immaculate. Even in the most economical of rooms you will find Tibetan chests as bedside tables, colorful ceilings, and ample bedding. You can enter the popular Dunya restaurant to the right of the courtyard. ✉ *100 Dekyi Shar Lam, 850001* ☎ *0891/632–3496* ↩ *28 rooms* ↺ *Bar* ▭ *AE, DC, MC, V.*

Nightlife & the Arts

Tibetan operas are performed at the **Lhasa City Academy of Performing Arts** and the **TAR Kyormolung Operatic Company.** Your guest house will likely have notices about opera performances. Traditional Tibetan music is played at the **Shangrila restaurant.** The bar upstairs at **Dunya** is a good place for an evening drink.

Shopping

Arts & Crafts

For trinkets varying from prayer flags to jewel-encrusted horse bridles, stop by one of the hundreds of open-air stalls that line the Bhakhor circuit and the roads leading to the Jokhang. Bargain hard but in a friendly manner and stall owners may throw in extra items for luck. Many of the goods come from around Tibet and Kathmandu. For Tibetan handicrafts, visit **Dropenling** (✉ 11 Chak Tsal Gang Rd., down alley opposite mosque's old gates ☎ 0891/633–0898). All profits are returned to the Tibetan artisan community. Lhasa's first contemporary art gallery, the **Gedunchoephel Artists Guild** (⊠ Barkhor's northeast corner) sells paintings by emerging Tibetan artists. The **Kyichu Guesthouse** (⊠149 Dekyi Shar Lam) has a good selection of silver jewelry, miniature prayer-wheel pendants, and door hangings—all great gifts at reasonable prices. If you are looking for high-quality, award-winning Tibetan carpets and a guarantee that child labor wasn't employed in their making, consider the **Snow Leopard Carpet Industries** (⊠ 2 E. Zang Yi Yuan Rd.), northwest of the Bhakhor circuit. The **Thangkha Mandala Gallery & Workshop** (⊠ Barkhor circuit, south side, Door 32) has a wide assortment of traditional-style Tibetan paintings. Bargain hard here: this shop caters to tourists with big bucks.

Outdoor Equipment

North Col Mountaineering Shop (⊠ West side of Potala Sq. ☎ 0891/633–1111) has the best collection of outdoor equipment.

en route	On the road between Lhasa and the airport you can stop at **Neitang Buddha,** (⊠, 40 km (25 mi) southwest of Lhasa on the airport road ☉ Daily 9–5) the largest stone carving of a Buddha image in Tibet, engraved on a roadside cliff and freshly painted each year. It's an easy stroll to help you acclimate if you've just flown in.

Side Trip to Ganden Namgyeling

⑮ *2 hrs (45 km [28 mi]) by jeep southeast of Lhasa.*

Fodor's Choice
★

If you only have time for one day trip out of Lhasa, this rambling monastery is your best bet. Established by Tsongkhapa, the founder of the Gelugpa sect, in 1409, its abbot is chosen on merit rather than heredity. Its rich ocher-color walls are striking backdrops for pictures. The 90-minute jeep ride from Lhasa will also give you a glimpse of life in rural Tibet—where more than 80% of Tibetans live.

Of the six great Gelugpa monasteries, Ganden was the most seriously desecrated and damaged by Chinese using artillery and dynamite during the Cultural Revolution. Since the early 1980s Tibetans have put tremendous effort into rebuilding the complex. Some 400 monks are now in residence; the Ganden community once numbered around 3,300 monks. Pilgrims come daily from Lhasa (buses leave the Jokhang at 6:30 AM) to pay homage to the sacred sites and relics.

The monastery comprises eight major buildings on either side of the dirt road. The most impressive structure is the **Gold Tomb of Tsongkhapa** (Serdhung Lhakhang) in the heart of the complex, easily recognized by the recently built white chorten before the red building. On the second floor is the chapel of **Yangchen Khang,** with the new golden chorten of Tsongkhapa. The original (1629), made of silver, later gilded, was the most sacred object in the land. In 1959 the Chinese destroyed it, although brave monks saved some of the holy relics of Tsongkhapa, which are now in the new gold-covered chorten. Be careful walking around this shrine: the buttery wax on the floor is thick and slippery. If you wish to take photos here it will cost Y20; video costs a whopping Y1,500 for foreigners.

The **Assembly Hall** was repainted in 2001, so the murals are bright and shiny, but the old Assembly Hall exhibits more charm. From the second-floor balcony you can look down onto the two-story-tall Buddha statues. Walk downstairs to the main floor to see the old dark murals. Be sure to climb up the particularly rickety ladder stairs to see the ruling abbot's throne between the Buddha statues. At this shrine, you can admire the shoes of the 13th Dalai Lama. ✥ *36 km (22 mi) southeast on main Tibet–Sichuan Hwy., then right onto winding road 9 km (5½ mi)* ☉ *Daily sunrise–sunset.*

Side Trip Through Tsang Province

10 hrs (500-km [300-mi] route) by jeep, starting and finishing in Lhasa.

The traditional Tibetan province of Tsang includes some of the region's most important historical sites outside of Lhasa, but it's also rich in stunning scenery and dotted with small villages and makeshift nomad camps complete with brightly decorated yaks.

Head south out of Lhasa early in the morning and crawl through the **Kamba-la Pass** that soars to almost 5 km (3 mi) and down to the brilliant blue waters of the **Yamdrok-Tso,** one of the holiest lakes in Tibet. Devout pilgrims walk around the lake in seven days but depending on when you travel, it can be a challenge to tramp through the bog between the road and water's edge. Alternatively, you can stop near one of the small villages where the land is firmer.

Pass the ruins of old fortresses and small villages of flat-roof houses with outdoor billiard tables, and marvel at the jagged peaks of the mountains on either side of the road en route to **Gyantse,** one of the least-Chinese-influenced towns in Tibet. Wandering the winding lanes and markets that make up the old town is an unbeatable way to see the delicate balance between modernization and tradition in Tibetan life.

In the 14th and 15th centuries, the town rose to political power in tandem with the rise of the Sakyapa monastic order. To get an idea of the breadth of the construction during this period take the alley on the left of the eastern road from the central roundabout and make the 20-minute walk up to **Gyantse Dzong,** the old fort. Here you'll be treated to staggering views of the town and surrounding Nyang Chu Valley. It is possible to explore some of the buildings inside the fort but be prepared to climb well-worn wooden ladders that look like they are held together by woven yak hair. It is worth a quick visit to the **Anti-British Imperialist Museum** within the complex for a creative version of the 1904 British invasion of the area. The **Pelkhor Chode Monastery** in Gyantse is one of the few multidenominational monastic complexes in Tibet, housing Gelugpa, Sakyapa, and Bupa monks. The highlight inside is the **Gyantse Kumbum,** with its glittering golden dome rising over four floors, with four sets of spellbinding eyes peering out over the town. Inside there are six floors, each a labyrinth of small chapels adorned with Nepalese-influenced murals and statues. You can access the roof from a steep ladder at the rear of the fifth floor.

Tibet's second-largest city, **Shigatse,** is the traditional capital of Tsang and home to the **Tashilhunpo Monastery,** the seat of the Panchen Lama and one of the few religious sites not to be destroyed during the Cultural Revolution. Most impressive is the Chapel of Maitreya, the Future Buddha. It houses an 85-foot-high statue of Maitreya that is covered in more than 600 pounds of gold. More than a thousand more images of the god are painted on the surrounding walls. You will also be able to visit the Panchen Lama tombs, many of which are lined with photos of their later reincarnations.

The small monastic town of **Sakya** is 25 km (15 mi) from Shigatse. Notice the change in the color of the buildings. Unlike the whitewash effect that predominates in the region, houses in the Sakya area are painted in gray, white, and red stripes (for either political or religious purposes; the origin is disputed). The key attraction here is exploring the **Sakya Monastery** and its peaceful ruins. Founded in 1073, it became an important scholastic and spiritual center in the early 13th century and a center of political power when Kublai Khan made its abbot the head of state.

Hiring a jeep with a driver and guide or going on an organized tour from Lhasa are the easiest ways to visit the area. Public transport is patchy at best and prayer seems to be the most popular safety strategy for passengers in the minibuses that hug the edges of the steep roads. Your guide should be up to date on the latest permit requirements and which hotels are open to foreigners in Shigatse and Gyantse.

Side Trip to Everest Base Camp

16 *4 days (508 km [314 mi]) by jeep southwest from Lhasa.*

"Because it's there," mountaineer George Mallory quipped in 1922 when asked why he wanted to climb the tallest mountain on the planet.

The fabled peak is located in the world's highest national park, Sagarmatha National Park, which is a visual delight that alone is worth the trek from Lhasa. After the monsoon rains in June the hillsides become green and light up in varieties of blooming flowers and butterflies. Even from April to June the light snow blanketing the rugged ground and along babbling brooks is striking.

To get there, head from Lhasa to the town of Tingri. En route you'll pass a marker showing the 5,000-km (3,000-mi) spot from Beijing, just before your jeep snakes up three mountain passes littered with brightly colored prayer flags. On a clear day some 20 km (10 mi) after Gyatso pass you'll see Mt. Everest and an eyeful of the Himalaya Range.

Tingri, also known as Shegar, is a tiny village but it's important to stop and rest here before moving to the **Mt. Qomolangma (Everest) Base Camp** as a precaution against altitude sickness. Numerous unmarked walks and ruins crisscross the gentle slopes around the town and the local children are keen to point you in the right direction. Unless you have arranged to sleep under canvas at Base Camp, book into a hotel for two nights in Tingri.

You can also visit the world's highest monastery, **Ronguk Monastery** on your way to Base Camp. There were once 500 monks living here but now there are only 20, along with 10 nuns who delight in the company of visitors. Take it easy climbing the entrance to the main chapel that sits at 5 km (3 mi) above sea level—you will be breathless. It is 8 km (5 mi) from the monastery to Base Camp. It will take you about 15 minutes to drive but it's more thrilling to make the two-hour walk—even if it is just to say that you trekked the Everest region. Base Camp is a simple plateau where climbing groups have color-coded tents, yaks wonder through the camp, and the Tibetan mountaineering station has a permanent hut. Have your photo taken in front of the "Mt. Qomolangma Base Camp" sign and climb the small rise festooned with prayer flags for a better view of Everest.

Almost all travel agents in Lhasa arrange tours to Everest Base Camp that include jeep, driver, guide, accommodation at assigned hotels in Tingri, entry fees to Sagarmatha National Park, and government permits. During very heavy rains the rising rivers make driving on the low roads difficult. You may need to be flexible on departure dates on advice from your guide, so book this trip first and fit the Lhasa sights around it.

TIBET A TO Z

To research prices, get advice from other travelers, and book travel arrangements, visit www.fodors.com.

AIR TRAVEL

🚄 Carriers **China Southwest Airlines** covers all points of entry into China. The easiest direct route is one of the four daily flights from Chengdu for about $250 one way. There are also flights from Chongqing (three times a week); from Shanghai, Xinhang, Xian, and Dinqing (twice a week); and from Beijing (daily). If you are coming from Kathmandu, the nonstop flights made twice a week will give you fantastic views of the Himalayas, including Everest. You must show your Tibet permit upon check-in.

🚄 Airlines & Contacts **China Southwest Airlines** ☎ 86/2866–68080 🖷 86/2867–10992 🌐 www.cswa.com.

AIRPORTS

🚄 Airport Information **Gongka Airport (LXA)** is the only Tibetan airport that foreigners can fly into. Jeep transfers to Lhasa will take about 90 minutes and cost Y400. The local bus is much cheaper (Y25) but takes considerably longer. A new road to Lhasa is still under construction but if it opens before you arrive, your travel time should be cut in half. Remember to have Y90 for departure tax. There is a small café that serves Chinese and Tibetan food adjacent to the departure gates.

🚄 Airport Contact **Gongka Airport** ✉ Airport Rd. ☎ No phone.

CAR TRAVEL

By road from Kathmandu, you can (usually) cross the border at Kodari. The Tibetan border guards have been known to grant individuals a permit at the border, though the law is for groups to enter on a prearranged tour. The 900-km (560-mi) route from Kathmandu to Lhasa takes two or more days to travel, traversing passes as high as 16,400 feet. Overnight stops are in Zhangmu and Shigatse. Minivans are available to shuttle you across the 8-km (5-mi) stretch between the two border posts—Kodari in Nepal and Zhangmu in Tibet. The cost from Zhangmu to Lhasa is about $60 in a minibus. Hiring your own four-wheel-drive vehicle with driver and unlimited passengers costs about $200. Exiting Tibet from Lhasa to Kathmandu is easier. The police do not stop you; the Nepalese frontier is always open, and a Nepalese visa is granted at the border.

Road travel from China into Tibet is tough. The inexpensive way most likely to meet with success is to cross the frontier by bus from Golmud, a sprawling town in Qinghai, at the end of the railway line from Xining. The distance is 1,115 km (691 mi), and the trip takes up to 50 hours by bus (Y200); it can get very bleak and cold at night.

RULES OF THE ROAD Foreigners are not permitted to drive in Tibet. All cars are hired with a driver and tour guide (Chinese law requires both). Rates depend on mileage, with a daily charge if the mileage is low. Daily rates start at $90 for a Landcruiser or Y5 per kilometer (plus permits), but will vary from agent to agent. Try a local agent to check rates and service. There is a jeep station two blocks south of the Jokhang where you can negotiate directly with owners. A jeep to and from Ganden hired here should cost you Y350. Older jeeps are cheaper.

CONSULATES
🇳 Nepal **Nepalese Consulate** ✉ 13 Norbulingka Lu, Lhasa ☎ 0891/632-2881.

EMERGENCIES
The People's Hospital is open 24 hours a day.
🇳 The**People's Hospital** ✉ Linghor Lam ☎ 0891/632-2200.

HEALTH
ALTITUDE ALERT At the 12,000-foot altitude (Lhasa is at 12,138 feet), shortness of breath is common. You may experience mild discomfort—perhaps a headache, minor chest pains, or waking in the morning with a dry mouth. These can be managed by an aspirin or two. Avoid exertion and drink plenty of nonalcoholic fluids, especially water. If you travel outside of Lhasa towards Everest, always sleep at an altitude lower than the highest point you traveled that day. Severe altitude sickness should be immediately brought to the attention of a physician. If you have high blood pressure, heart ailments, or respiratory problems, you may want to reconsider your route and consult a doctor first.

HOLIDAYS
Tibet has two sets of holidays: events observed by the People's Republic of China, which shuts down businesses and government offices on these holidays, and Tibetan Buddhist festivals, the celebrations of which are often shut down by the government. The lunar calendar determines the timing of many events.

MONEY MATTERS
CURRENCY EXCHANGE The larger hotels all offer foreign-exchange service for cash but cannot process credit card advances. Only the Bank of China, open weekdays 9–1 and 3:30–6:30, weekends 10:30–3, can facilitate cash advances and only for Visa and MasterCard. The exchange rates for traveler's checks

or cash is slightly better than the hotels. Outside Lhasa, try the Bank of China branches in Shigatse, Zhangmu, and Shiquanbe.

🔃 Exchange Services **Bank of China** ⊠ Dekyi Linghor Lam ⊠ Dekyi Shar Lam.

PASSPORTS & VISAS

ENTERING TIBET A visa valid for the People's Republic of China is required. When you apply for a visa, do not share your Tibet travel plans with consulate officials. There have been reports of visa applications being denied because of an impending visit to Tibet. The PRC embassy in Kathmandu will not issue these visas: you need to obtain one elsewhere—such as New Delhi, Bangkok, or your home country. You will also need to get a Tibet travel permit which is usually arranged by the travel agent who books your flights to Lhasa.

The Chinese government would prefer that you join a group with a guide. Groups find it easier to get the Tibet travel permit as well as permits to visit sites outside of Lhasa. You can, however, be a group of one person. Travel agents in the Chinese cities with direct flights to Lhasa can help arrange this. A typical package includes flights to Lhasa and a guide to pick you up at the airport and take you to a hotel. You will then be on your own until your departure when the guide will take you back to the airport.

SAFETY

Don't openly talk politics with Tibetans. If they speak out against the government they may be charged with treason and receive a 20-year jail term.

Public Security Bureau (PSB) personnel are everywhere, sometimes in uniform, sometimes in civilian clothes, and even in monks' robes. The PSB monitors civil unrest, visa extensions, crime, and traffic. Beware the charming Tibetan who may be a secret policeman trying to entrap you into giving him a photograph of the Dalai Lama. You could be detained, deported and even risk being beaten. PSB offices are in all towns and many of the smaller townships.

TIME

Tibet observes Beijing standard time, which is 8 hours ahead of Greenwich mean time and 13 hours ahead of U.S. eastern standard time.

TOURS

BOOKING WITH Arranging a tour before arriving in Tibet will save you time that can
AN AGENT be used to lap up Tibet. There are a growing number of tours that can be arranged via the Internet. However, be sure to travel only with reputable firms. If you choose to find one in Lhasa, plan to spend a couple of days meeting with different agents and processing any permit requirements.

Typically the cost of an organized tour for a week runs $1,000–$2,000, plus airfare. When booking a tour, be sure to get confirmation in writing that details your hotel and meal arrangements. Some local agents have part ownership of certain Chinese restaurants and will try to take you to the same place every day. Often the only significant difference between travel agents is the quality of the guide in Lhasa, which, unfortunately, is hard to control.

Agents should be able to advise you on the latest changes to travel restrictions and permit requirements. Speak with a couple of travel agents around town to compare prices and itineraries. You hotel will be able to help. Most tour companies will tailor a trip to meet your needs and budget.

🚩 Tour-Operator Recommendations **CITS** ✉ Dekyi Num Lam, Lhasa ☎ 0891/633-6626 ✉ 208 Dekyi Shar Lam ☎ 0891/683-5046. **Tibet International Sports Travel** (TIST) ✉ Himalaya Hotel, Shar Linghor Lam, Lhasa ☎ 0891/633-4082. **WildChina** ⊕ www.wildchina.com. **Wind Horse Adventure** ✉ 1 Mirik Lam, Lhasa ☎ 0891/683-3009.

TRANSPORTATION AROUND TIBET

Taxis are plentiful in Lhasa. Hailing one on the street is quicker than trying to call for one. A set fare of Y10 will get you anywhere within the city limits. Minibuses ply a fixed route with fares of Y2 or less. Bicycle rickshaws are also available for short trips and normally cost Y3.
🚩 **Taxi** ☎ 8091/683-4105.

VISITOR INFORMATION

🚩 Tourist Information **Tibet Tourism Bureau** ✉ 18 Yuanlin Lam, Lhasa ☎ 0891/683-4315 information, 0891/683-4193 to register a complaint.

UNDERSTANDING CHINA

CHINA AT A GLANCE

Fast Facts

Capital: Beijing
National anthem: *March of the Volunteers*
Type of government: Communist
Administrative divisions: 23 provinces (including Taiwan), 5 autonomous regions, 4 municipalities, 2 special administrative regions (Hong Kong and Macau)
Independence: October 1, 1949
Constitution: December 4, 1982
Legal system: A mix of custom and statute, largely criminal law, with rudimentary civil code
Suffrage: 18 years of age
Legislature: Unicameral National People's Congress; 2,985 members elected by municipal, regional, and provincial people's congresses to serve five-year terms; next elections scheduled for late 2007 or early February 2008
Population: 1.3 billion; the largest in the world
Population density: 138 people per square km (361 people per square mi)

Median age: Female 31.7, male 31.2
Life expectancy: Female 74.3, male 70.3
Infant mortality rate: 25.3 deaths per 1,000 live births
Literacy: 86%
Language: Standard Chinese or Mandarin (official), Yue (Cantonese), Wu (Shanghainese), Minbei (Fuzhou), Minnan (Hokkien-Taiwanese), Xiang, Gan, Hakka dialects
Ethnic groups: Han Chinese 92%; Zhuang, Uygur, Hui, Yi, Tibetan, Miao, Manchu, Mongol, Buyi, Korean, and other nationalities 8%
Religion: Officially atheist but Taoism, Buddhism, Christianity, and Islam are practiced.
Discoveries & Inventions: Decimal system (1400 BC), paper (100 BC), seismograph (AD 100), compass (200), matches (577), gunpowder (700), paper money (800), movable type (1045)

Geography & Environment

Land area: 9.3 million square km (3.6 million square mi), the fourth-largest country in the world, and slightly smaller than the United States
Coastline: 14,500 km (9,010 mi) on the Yellow Sea, the East China Sea, and the South China Sea
Terrain: Mostly mountains, high plateaus, deserts in west; plains, deltas, and hills in east
Islands: Hainan, Taiwan, many smaller islands along the coast
Natural resources: Aluminum, antimony, coal, hydropower, iron ore, lead, magnetite, manganese, mercury, molybdenum, natural gas, petroleum, tin, tungsten, uranium, vanadium, zinc
Natural hazards: Droughts, earthquakes, floods, land subsidence, tsunamis, typhoons

Environmental issues: Air pollution (greenhouse gases, sulfur dioxide particulates), especially from China's reliance on coal, which is used to generate 70% of the country's electric power. Acid rain is also a consequence of the burning of China's high-sulfur coal, particularly in the north; deforestation; soil erosion and economic development have destroyed one-fifth of agricultural land since 1949; desertification; trade in endangered species; water pollution from untreated wastes; water shortages

China is an attractive piece of meat coveted by all . . . but very tough, and for years no one has been able to bite into it.

— Zhou Enlai,
Chinese Premier, 1973

Economy

Currency: Yuan
Exchange rate: Y8.28 = $1
GDP: $6 trillion
Inflation: −0.4%
Per capita income: Y4,329 ($523)
Unemployment: 9%
Workforce: 744 million; agriculture 50%; industry 22%; services 28%
Debt: $149.4 billion
Major industries: Armaments, automobiles, cement, chemical fertilizers, coal, consumer electronics, food processing, footwear, iron and steel, machine building, petroleum, telecommunications, textiles and apparel, toys

Agricultural products: Barley, cotton, fish, millet, oilseed, peanuts, pork, potatoes, rice, sorghum, tea, wheat
Exports: $325.6 billion
Major export products: Footwear, machinery and equipment, mineral fuels, sporting goods, textiles and clothing, toys
Export partners: U.S. 21.5%; Hong Kong 18%; Japan 14.9%; South Korea 4.8%
Imports: $295.3 billion
Major import products: Chemicals, iron and steel, machinery and equipment, mineral fuels, plastics
Import partners: Japan 18%; Taiwan 11%; South Korea 10%; U.S. 9%; Germany 6%

Political Climate

Since the Chinese Communist Party (CCP) took control of the government in 1949, it has shown little tolerance for outside views. Other major political parties are banned and the government is quick to crack down on movements that it doesn't approve of, most recently the Falun Gong. China's size and diversity complicate national politics, with party control weaker in rural areas, where most of the population lives. Successful politicians have sought support from local and regional leaders and must work to keep influential nonparty members from creating a stir. The decade-long struggle for democracy, which ended in the bloody Tiananmen Square protests of 1989, has fragmented and lost much of its power. The party blamed its rise on foreign agitators and reminds the population that political stability is essential for China's economic growth. The poor handling of the SARS outbreak in early 2003 prompted new calls for government reform.

Did You Know?

• China has nearly 13 million more boys than girls, leading demographers to fear that 40 million Chinese men will remain single in the 21st century.

• The country dropped its Soviet-style centralized economy for a more market-oriented system in 1978. As a result, its GDP had quadrupled by 1998.

• China is the world's largest producer of red meat and rice.

• One out of every three cigarettes in the world is smoked in China.

The nation consumes more than three times the cigarettes puffed away by U.S. smokers.

• Since the revolution, China has had four constitutions in less than 60 years. The first three couldn't keep up with the rapid pace of change, particularly during the Cultural Revolution.

• China executed more than 17,500 people between 1990 and 1999, more than the rest of the world put together.

CHINA'S DANCE

TAPED TO AN OLD SHOP WINDOW in Suzhou, a city more than 2,500 years old with its walls still intact, is an advertisement for cellular phones: a young Chinese woman holds a phone to her ear as she stands on the Great Wall, the long structure twisting off into the distance behind her. "Get connected," says the ad. "This is the new China."

Bamboo scaffolding and gleaming department stores, construction cranes looming over wooden villages, KFC and chopsticks, yak herders and cell-phone abusers within miles of each other, communism and capitalism coexisting—China has more paradoxes than it has dialects. To visit China now is to witness a country revolutionizing itself in the cities and struggling to stay alive in the countryside.

The fourth-largest country in the world, holding the world's largest population, China is chiefly challenged by questions of cohesiveness—how to bring a country speaking hundreds of different dialects together under one rule. Beginning with the Zhou Dynasty (1100–771 BC), Chinese governors held the country together not only by force but by claiming a heaven-sent legitimacy known as the Mandate of Heaven. The mandate was a convenient claim of legitimacy, as anyone who led a successful rebellion could assert his victory was predicated upon the support of the gods. The traditional belief was that heaven would demonstrate disapproval of evil rulers through natural disasters like droughts and earthquakes, disease, and floods.

Today, as China's mesh of socialist and capitalist policies brings instability to the country, it is becoming unclear who holds the mandate. Are the heirs to Mao's revolution the conservative members of the Communist Party, or are President Hu Jintao and other reformers intent on imbuing the national economy with a capitalist bent? Whatever the case, it's clear that as the country continues to modernize, especially with Hong Kong under its belt, communism appears to be taking the backseat to a still undefined front seat, neither capitalism in a Western sense nor communism as in the years of Mao. The Chinese government has found itself in an awkward situation. If it tries to clamp down, it will surely lose in the race for modernization. If it allows modernization to continue, its control is inevitably weakened.

Ranging from the Three Gorges Dam, a colossal project that is uprooting 2 million people, to the perpetual construction of skyscrapers crowding the cities' skylines, the Chinese landscape is quickly changing. In some respects it's as if the people had been plucked from their traditional homes and transported 100 years into a future. Foreign companies and joint ventures have demanded that single men and women climb a corporate ladder at an accelerated pace; eating habits have changed from family style to a quick bite at McDonald's; grocery stores have begun to replace outdoor markets; bars and discos stay open all night. The country has become more modern, but what does that mean to a nation that looks back on more than 5,000 years of history?

THE ANCIENT PHILOSOPHY OF Confucianism laid a foundation for Chinese ethics and morals that still survives today, teaching respect, selflessness, obedience, and a sense of community. Unlike Americans, who prize their individuality and independence, the Chinese believe it is important to stay within and abide by a community. Shame is considered a much graver emotion than guilt: the Chinese judge themselves according to how they believe they are perceived by those whom they love and respect.

The Chinese believe that, no matter where you were born, where you live, or what your native tongue, if you have Chinese ancestry, you are still Chinese. Their sense of pride about emerging as a colossal force in the global economy is combined with a deep sense of race that holds the country tentatively together. Paradoxically, China is busy buying up Western products, from french fries to Hollywood action movies. Nike is cool. Celine Dion is hip. This external desire for Western style co-exists comfortably, though ironically, with a perennial internal nationalism. The Chinese have so internalized their landscape that, for example, the TV tower in Shanghai is for them comparable to the Jade Buddha Temple down the street as a sight not to be missed; advertisements in subway stations are celebrated as a new form of artistic expression; the elderly happily practice tai chi to the beat of rock music.

More than 70% of the mainland population lives along the eastern seaboard, leaving the westernmost provinces barren and nearly vacant, in part because only 20% of China's land is arable. In the 1970s peasants' lifestyles improved as a result of Deng Xiaoping's policy of allowing profit after government quotas had been met, but small plots of land and an ever-increasing population meant the new policy only provided limited relief. People still flock to the cities, creating a large homeless population. Although China appears to be overhauling itself, many residents of the smaller cities and villages are still living the way they did 100 years ago. As in other countries experiencing rapid development, there is a profound division between the growing middle class and unemployed farmworkers.

Excursions to small towns reveal just how much China relies on basic human power. Farm laborers stand up with their tools and wave as a train passes, a girl wearing a Nike jacket carries buckets swinging from a yoke over her shoulders, herds of sheep carry goods down dirt roads into the village center, local buses are crowded full of men and women carrying raw animal furs, and everywhere cycles of every description carry people and goods. Even in the cities, a surplus of men work with hammer and nail to build a skyscraper. Perhaps these images will disappear in a few years, but for now they reveal a country in the throes of revolution still holding on quite tightly to tradition.

During a visit to China, often the best moments are the ones you invent on your own, not what the hotel or the China International Travel Service (CITS) recommends. In this way you can enjoy China's hidden secrets—nature walks, bustling markets, small villages. Of course, the consequence of making up your own itinerary is having to follow a very cryptic and archaic route, one where the roads may not be paved, the train does not show up, hotels are not where they are supposed to be, and People's Liberation Army officers creep up out of nowhere. There is little peace, little comfort, and incredible markups for foreigners; keep an open mind and an adventurous spirit.

— Angela Yuan

RELIGION IN CHINA

ALTHOUGH CHINA IS OFFICIALLY ATHEIST, it has historically adopted a pragmatic and eclectic attitude toward belief systems, and it has incorporated Taoism, Buddhism, Islam, and Christianity into its societal fabric. Indeed, the typical Chinese philosophy is a rich tapestry of Confucianism, Taoism, and Buddhism. In theory, Chinese have the freedom of religious belief, and their religious activities are protected by the Constitution. However, there are only two government-sanctioned sects of Christianity—the Catholic church without ties to Rome and the "Three-Self-Patriotic" Protestant church. Other "unauthorized" churches exist in many parts of China, where the local governments may tolerate them, attempt outright to control them, or offer them treatment that falls somewhere between the two.

Because of the hodgepodge of beliefs, it is difficult to pigeonhole people as belonging to any one religion. However, official figures put Buddhism in the forefront, with an estimated 100 million adherents. Traditional Taoism also is practiced. Official figures indicate there are 18 million Muslims, 10 million Protestants, and 4 million Catholics; unofficial estimates are much higher.

Religion often follows ethnic divisions. Hui, Uygur, Kazak, Kirgiz, Tatar, Ozbek, Tajik, Dongxiang, Salar, and Bonan, for example, follow Islam. Tibetans, Mongolians, Lhobas, Moinbas, Tus, and Yugurs subscribe to Lamaism (Mahayana Buddhism practiced in Tibet), while Dai, Blang, and Deang are largely Theravada Buddhist. Many Miao, Yao, and Yi are Catholic or Protestant; Han are mainly divided among Buddhism, Protestantism, Catholicism, or Taoism.

Taoism

Taoism developed from the philosophical and naturalist text, the *Tao Te Ching*, believed to have been written by Lao Tzu, a contemporary of Confucius in the 1st century BC. Taking form in the 2nd century, Taoism is one of two belief systems indigenous to China. Lao Tzu and his followers emphasized individual freedom, laissez-faire government, human spontaneity, and mystical experience. The goal of Taoism is to attain balance and harmony with nature and spiritual forces, as well as within oneself. Tao, the Way, is the journey to understanding the unseen reality behind appearances.

Confucianism

Confucianism, the other indigenous Chinese belief system, provided a large part of the foundation of the Chinese society and culture. Confucius (K'ung Fu-tzu) was a philosopher who lived from 551 BC to 479 BC. His philosophies shaped the mores and behaviors of the Chinese for nearly 2,000 years. Confucius believed that moral behavior stemmed from the fulfillment of traditional roles and hierarchies. He defined five basic relationships, which he called *wu lun*. Each relationship represents a reciprocal obligation.

• Emperor to Subject—An emperor must show his subjects kindness; a subject must be loyal.

• Father to Son—A father must provide protection and favor to his son; the son reciprocates with respect and obedience.

• Husband to Wife—A husband has the obligation to provide for his wife; a wife respectfully submits.

• Older Brother to Younger Brother—The older brother cares for his younger brother; the younger brother models himself after his older brother.

• Friend to Friend—The relationship between friends is one of mutual trust.

From this basic framework come ideas of hierarchy, group orientation, and respect for age and tradition. It's important to remember that the basis of this system is not the subjugation of one person by another. It is concern for one person by another. According to Confucian thought, when one's basic motivation is the well-being of another person, then one's behavior is moral.

Buddhism

Buddhism was begun in India by Siddhartha Gautama, a prince turned teacher and philosopher. The name Buddha means "awakened." The ideals of Buddhism focus on achieving freedom from the cycle of death and rebirth and thereby entering into Nirvana, perfect and total peace and enlightenment.

The centerpiece of Buddhism is the Four Noble Truths:

• Life is suffering.

• Desire is the cause of suffering.

• When you cease to desire, you eliminate suffering.

• Desire, and thus suffering, can be eliminated by following the Middle Way and the Eightfold Noble Path.

The Middle Way is exactly that: a way of life that exists between the wanton sating of desire and zealous self-denial. The Eightfold Noble Truths consist of right views, intention, speech, conduct, livelihood, effort, attention, and meditation.

Buddhism reached China via foreign merchants on the trade routes to the West. By AD 166, Buddhism had a presence in the imperial court, although it remained primarily a religion practiced by foreigners until the beginning of the 4th century. By the end of the 5th century, it had swept across China. In Tibet, Buddhism evolved into Lamaism, also known as Tibetan Buddhism.

Islam

China was introduced to Islam by Arab and Persian merchants, probably during the 8th century. The Muslim God is Allah, and their prophet is Muhammad, who was born in Mecca around AD 570. The revelations of Muhammad were compiled in the Koran, which sets forth the four principle tenets of Islam:

• Faith in the absolute unity of Allah

• Belief in angels as messengers of Allah

• Belief in prophetic messengers (Muhammad being the last of these, following Jesus and the Old Testament prophets)

• Belief in a final judgment which will reward the faithful

Salvation is achieved through the Five Acts of Worship, or the Pillars of Islam:

• Physical and spiritual purification

• Prayer

• Giving of alms

• Fasting during the holy month of Ramadan

• The hajj, or pilgrimage to Mecca

SOCIAL ETIQUETTE IN CHINA

IF YOU ARE INTRODUCED TO A GROUP OF **PEOPLE** (for example, if you tour a factory), you may be greeted with applause. You should also clap in greeting. Although bows are the standard greeting, you may see handshakes, especially with foreigners. When greeting someone, follow his or her lead. Men can wait for a Chinese to offer his hand for a handshake or bow in reply to his bow. Women who want to shake hands will generally have to offer their hand first. A Chinese handshake is generally quite soft; don't use your power handshake or pump the other person's hand. You will not see people kissing hello or good-bye.

You may see people of the same gender holding hands; this is merely a sign of close friendship. However, it's unlikely that your Chinese friends will do this with you. Queuing is not common; be prepared to assert yourself in stores, at bus stops, and in post offices.

Expect to be stared at when you are out and about. Most Chinese are extremely curious about Westerners and staring is not considered rude. Privacy and personal space are not held sacred. If your Chinese counterpart stands closer to you than is comfortable, try not to back away, since doing so will send a negative signal.

On a personal level, physical contact between strangers is not appreciated. Don't try to pat someone on the back, or casually touch someone's arm. On an impersonal level, such as in crowded subways, buses, or trains, contact with others cannot be avoided and there is much pushing and shoving. No apology is necessary in these instances. Because it is forbidden for monks and Buddhist priests to have any physical contact with women, women should take care not to bump into or accidentally brush against them.

The Chinese prefer not to display their emotions in public, either verbally or non-verbally. If you are prone to animated gesturing and facial expressions, try to minimize them when speaking with Chinese.

It's considered unclean to put your fingers in your mouth for any reason, so don't lick your fingers! When visiting someone, keep your feet on the floor and off desks, tables, and other furniture.

Your posture is a reflection of your upbringing and education. Don't slouch and keep both feet on the floor; don't cross your legs. If you need to point, use your open hand, not one finger, which is rude. Never use your head or foot to point out a person. Don't offend by beckoning someone with one finger. Use your whole hand, palm down, and make a scratching motion with your fingers. Don't use your foot to move objects.

Spitting on the sidewalk is common in some parts of China, but it is definitely not good manners. You will also see people blowing their noses (without a tissue) onto the street.

"Going Dutch" does not translate into Chinese. If a colleague or friend pays for a meal or even a subway ride, try to pick up the tab the next time.

Ask for permission before taking pictures of a person. Respect your surroundings in terms of dress, decorum, and photography.

Chinese names have the family name first, the given names second. Therefore, Kai Chong Chen's family name is "Kai" and his given name is "Chong Chen." Given names are used only by family and close friends. Always address people by their family names and courtesy title (Miss Xie, Mr. Man, etc.). Use professional titles, such as Doctor, if you know it. Doctor, Mayor, Lawyer, and Professor are professional titles often heard. You will also hear business titles, such as General Manager, Manager, and Engineer. The title can be used without a family name.

Women do not take their husband's name when they marry. Refer to married women by Madam and their own last name.

Don't be surprised if you are asked questions you wouldn't be asked at home, such as "How old are you?," "Are you married?," and even "How much money do you make?" Don't be offended by these questions. If you do not wish to answer, just decline in a friendly tone with humor. For example, to the question about your income, you might say "Just enough to pay the bills, I'm afraid." Do not say how much you make without also mentioning the cost of living in your home country. A salary in the United States is generally several times that of a Chinese salary, and you run the risk of alienating coworkers if they perceive only the difference in salary without appreciating the difference in the cost of living.

There are many things that you will enjoy discussing with Chinese, such as travel, cuisine, art, and family. However, some topics are better left alone, such as politics and government (including the situation with Taiwan), and human rights. Other sensitive issues, such as the 1999 U.S. bombing of the Chinese embassy in Belgrade or the charges of espionage on the part of China, are perhaps best left unaddressed. Avoid negative comments about China and its history. No one likes to have his or her country criticized by outsiders.

Certain gestures and other forms of nonverbal communication are important to know. For example, a laugh or smile is often used to indicate embarrassment or nervousness rather than amusement. A typical expression of displeasure is a quick sucking of air between the teeth. A nod does not always signal agreement. It can be a confirmation that the person has understood you or even a polite gesture if the person has not.

You will have to learn to read between the lines. Chinese are generally uncomfortable communicating negatives, and may respond with a positive to maintain harmony. Negatives might also be communicated in a jesting manner. Humility, patience, and an easygoing nature are all important qualities. Using these skills will ensure harmony, the goal of most interactions. Don't forget the all-important concept of face (not embarrassing another person in public)!

Jokes do not travel well. Puns and double entendres don't translate and references to events or icons of one's home country are often not understood. Avoid sexual or political jokes especially. Avoid the American propensity to jump-start conversation with a joke to break the ice.

F YOU'RE A BUSINESS TRAVELER IN CHINA, you probably still feel like a pioneer, even though it's been almost 20 years since former leader Deng Xiaoping launched the "open-door" policy and started inviting foreign investment into the previously isolated country. "We are learning how to compete in the market economy, and we need foreign expertise," a Chinese official or enterprise manager might tell you. But don't be misled into believing that you can come in with a plan this week and sign a contract next week, or that Western-style efficiency will be welcome in a joint venture with a Chinese company.

The Chinese, as every foreign business traveler quickly learns, have an elaborate unwritten code of rules that apply to every aspect of business, from negotiating the contract to selling the product. A good way to prepare yourself is to read Sun Tze's *The Art of War*. The true author of this Chinese classic is unknown, but the best guess is that it was written by a brilliant military strategist who lived sometime around the 4th century BC. Sun Tze's basic principle held that moral strength and intellectual faculty were the decisive factors in battle, and today these are the guiding factors in negotiating business deals. Not that you're dealing with adversaries. But from the days when the first foreign firms began to eye China's vast potential market of 1.2 billion consumers, the Chinese quickly realized that they had something the world wanted, so why not assure themselves a share in the capital that foreign ventures were sure to generate?

Upon joining the World Trade Organization in January 2002, China agreed to gradually open the financial services industry within the country to foreign competition by 2007. In January 2004, Citibank and HSBC became the first foreign banks to get permission for issuing credit cards in China. The move comes as part of a package of reforms China is undertaking to meet its WTO obligations. But foreign businesses can't expect to expand into China without a hitch. The Japanese carmaker Toyota ran into serious problems with Chinese state-run newspapers in late 2003 when it put out two ads: one featured a Toyota vehicle towing a truck that resembled a Chinese military vehicle, and the other showed a stone lion—a traditional Chinese symbol of authority—saluting a Toyota truck. Both ads were considered to imply the superiority of Japanese products over Chinese products. Toyota immediately apologized for the oversight, stating that the two ads were solely commercial and contained no other intention.

According to *The Art of War,* you sometimes have to yield a city or give up ground in order to gain a more valuable objective. Although it might seem a good idea in the short run to bow to ideological pressure from China, it is probably best for a company's long-term goals and international image to hold out. There is dissension today within the ranks of China's government, and attempts to appease the authorities who make demands today may backfire if these people fall out of favor domestically, or if America's political relations with China deteriorate.

Furthermore, though the Chinese authorities may insist that their politics are none of our business, the lack of a clear rule of law in China can work against conducting business here. On a number of occasions businesspeople have found themselves arrested and detained on trumped-up or nonexistent charges following a disagreement with a local partner or government authority over terms. Often the disagreement has to do with a city or provincial ministry's wanting an unreasonable share in the company. It is to the advantage of all foreigners living or spending time in China to push for political reforms that would incorporate due process of law.

This is all part of pioneering. In a country that had almost no modern roads 20 years ago, there are now huge swathes of concrete everywhere—and vehicles to run on them. From being a country with virtually no capital, China has moved to among the top six nations in the world in terms of foreign-exchange reserves. The people in the cities wear designer fashions, and construction cranes loom above almost every city or village street. Some observers think that as the market economy grows, a measure of democratic reform will come. The Chinese people themselves are likely to demand a freer flow of information, if only to help them make financial decisions. With the Internet more and more accessible to the masses, the Chinese government is having a harder time censoring communications. Nevertheless, China has the most extensive Internet censorship regulations of any nation. In January 2004, Amnesty International urged China to free 54 people jailed for expressing opinions on the Internet, citing a sharp rise in the number of people detained for anything from political speech to spreading news about SARS. Specialists maintain that China must reform its current political system to keep pace with its fast-growing economy. In spite of the economic reforms, this is still a centrally planned system called "socialism with Chinese characteristics." It is still a society with a thousand years of practice at handling foreign traders. Here are some fundamentals you should know before you go:

Your team: If you're new to the place, retain the services of a China consultant who knows the language and has a strong track record. The nonprofit United States–China Business Council (✉ 1818 N St. NW, Suite 200, Washington, DC 20036 ☎ 202/429–0340 🖷 202/775–2476 ⊕ www.uschina.org), which has additional offices in Hong Kong, Beijing, and Shanghai, is a good source for consulting services, referrals, and other information. Choose your own translator who will look out for your interests.

Know who you'll be meeting with in China, and send people with corresponding titles. The Chinese are very hierarchical and will be offended if you send a low-level manager to meet a minister. All of this ties into the all-important and intricate concept of "face," which can best be explained as the need to preserve dignity and standing.

Don't bring your spouse on the trip, unless he or she is involved in the business. Otherwise the Chinese will think your trip is really a vacation.

Attitudes toward women: The Chinese will take a woman seriously if she has an elevated title and acts serious. Women will find themselves under less pressure than men to hang out at the karaoke until the wee hours. This is partly because the party list might include prostitutes. (A woman will also avoid the trap that Chinese local partners sometimes lay to get rid of an out-of-favor foreign manager. They'll have a prostitute pick him up, then get the police to catch him so that he can be banished from the country for a sexual offense.)

Business cards: Bring more than you ever thought you'd need. Consult a translator before you go and have cards made with your name and the name of your company in Chinese characters on the reverse side.

The greeting: When you are introduced to someone in China, immediately bow your head slightly and offer your business card, with two hands. In the same ceremonious fashion accept your colleague's business card, which will likely be turned up to show an Anglicized name.

Promptness: Be there on time. The Chinese are very punctual. When you are hosting a banquet, arrive at the restaurant at least 30 minutes before your guests.

The meeting: Don't make plans for the rest of the day, or evening, or tomorrow, or the next day. And don't be in a rush to get home. Meetings can go on for days, weeks, whatever it takes to win concessions. Meetings will continue over a lavish lunch, a lavish dinner that includes many toasts with *mao tai* (a local, and potent spirit), and a long night at a karaoke, consuming XO cognac from a showy bottle. To keep in shape for the lengthy meetings, learn the art of throwing a shot of mao tai onto the floor behind you instead of drinking it down when your host says "ganbei." (Chances are he is not really drinking either.)

Gifts and bribes: Yes, a local official might ask you to get his child into a foreign university or buy your venture partner a fleet of BMWs. A few years ago a survey by the Independent Commission Against Corruption in Hong Kong found that corrupt business practices may represent 3%–5% of the cost of doing business in China, a factor that respondents (Hong Kong firms) claimed was bearable and not a disincentive. However, the Chinese government has been campaigning against corruption and business fraud. American companies have the added constraint of the Foreign Corrupt Practices Act, which prohibits offering or making payments to officials of foreign countries. The law can be a good excuse for not paying bribes. However, you may find yourself faced with a great many arbitrary fees to be paid to the city and county for everything from your business license to garbage collection. It is hard to avoid paying these.

To win friends in a small but legal way, give small gifts to the people you meet. Bring a shipment of such items as pens, paperweights, and T-shirts emblazoned with your company logo. And, before you leave town, host a banquet for all of the people who have entertained you.

Communication: Gestures that seem insignificant on the surface will help make or break your efforts to gain entry into China. Escort a departing visitor to the elevator as a way of giving him face, for example. To make a visitor feel particularly esteemed, walk him all the way to the front door of the building. And don't "have other plans" when your Chinese associates invite you out. As in many Asian countries, personal relationships are more important than the contract. The people you are dealing with may not tell you what they really want from a partnership with you until you're out eating and drinking.

There are many ways of saying "no" that may sound like "yes" to foreigners. If you hear that your proposal "is under study" or has arrived at "an inconvenient time," start preparing a new one.

A manager of a local factory in search of a foreign venture partner might tell you that the deal can be done, but that doesn't mean it will be. Make sure you meet with the officials in charge of your sector in the city, those who have the authority to approve the deal. If someone says he has to get the boss's approval, you should have a hearing with the boss—even if it means getting your boss there on the next flight to meet with his counterpart.

Early on, you may be asked to sign a "letter of intent." This document is not legally binding; it serves more as an expression of seriousness. But the principles in the letter, which look like ritual statements to the Westerner because they lack specific detail, may be invoked later if your Chinese partner has a grudge against you. He'll say you have not lived up to the spirit of mutual cooperation and benefit initially agreed upon.

How to compromise: You will have to give your Chinese partner something he wants. He might, for instance, want your capital to go into lines of business other than what you had in mind. You might have to agree to this if establishing a presence in China is important to your business. Know when to be flexible, but for important details such as who actually has control of the venture and its operations, hold out, even if it takes a year or more. There are ways to make sure of who is really in charge of a joint venture, even though for matters of face and power the Chinese partner will probably want to provide the person with the loftiest title. You will also want to own the controlling share, because it means quality control, profitability, and decision-making power over matters for which your company is legally liable. Often an inside deal is worked out, whereby the foreign party provides the general manager, who actually is in charge of day-to-day operations, while the Chinese partner brings in the chairman, who works with a board of directors and has authority only over broad policy issues.

Don't go to China and tell your prospective partner you want to start production by a certain date. Expect your Chinese associates to drive their hardest bargain just when you thought it was safe to go home. They know that once rumors of a concluded negotiation become public, you will not be able to back down from the deal without having to make difficult explanations to your investors and headquarters.

Demand that your contract include an arbitration clause, which stipulates that if a dispute arises the matter will be tried by an arbitrator, preferably in the United States or a third country. However, even in China, there are arbitration centers that comply with international standards and are well ahead of the court system.

The law in China: China works on civil law—that is, laws are passed by the National People's Congress and implemented. Quickly. Hong Kong's legal structure is based on common law (the same as Britain's and the United States'), which develops through judicial decisions (case law). The heart of Hong Kong's existence, "One Country, Two Systems," is that both judicial systems exist side by side. But sometimes they clash, particularly when it comes to business. China lacks predictability in its business environment because its laws aren't all consistent. The government has made a partial transition to a market economy but some laws still protect local firms and state-owned firms from imports, while encouraging exports. There are still remnants of a planned economy, prone to overinvestment and overproduction, unrelated to supply and demand.

Will feng shui help your prospects?: The 7,000-year-old art of placing objects in harmony with the environment and the elements is virtually mandatory in Hong Kong and Taiwan—it always had a stronger influence in southern China. In other areas, it's officially considered feudalist superstitious nonsense, but of course, if it facilitates business. . . . If there's any doubt in your mind, by all means call a geomancer.

While China speeds along toward overtaking the United States as the world's largest economy—the World Bank forecasts that will happen in the year 2020—any number of factors may make or break your efforts to reap some of the benefits of this dizzying growth. Barring serious political upheaval, you'll probably want to stay here and make constant—i.e., day-to-day—adaptations to the changing demands of the market. Like armies, companies in China have to figure out when to advance their presence, when to scale back, when to retreat to another location. And with each new strategy, be prepared to negotiate, feast, and sing karaoke songs.

— By Jan Alexander
Updated by Keming Liu

UNDERSTANDING THE VISUAL ARTS IN CHINA

THE MOST IMPORTANT ARTIST IN CHINESE HISTORY was "anonymous." Much ancient art consists of durable objects—jades, ceramics, bronzes, stone carvings, and the like—and for all but recent periods the authorship of these works is simply unknown. Even when history is well documented, material culture emanated from workshops staffed with artisans whose names were rarely recorded. These workshops were often established for the imperial institution, and their quality standards were extraordinarily high. Only in the final century of the Eastern Han Dynasty (2nd century AD) do we start to have names of scholar-officials who were master calligraphers; famous-name painters are known from a slightly later period. Outside the realm of calligraphy and painting, however, the makers of buildings, sculpture, and objects remained anonymous. It was not until the 17th and 18th centuries that the court began to recognize renowned ceramic masters, such as Liu Yuan from Henan, and Tang Ying from Shenyang. Thus, unlike the history of recent Western art with its emphasis on famous masters, for much of Chinese art history attention is focused on long-lasting artistic traditions and on the particular periods when they flourished.

The "Son of Heaven," the emperor, was the most important patron in Chinese history. From the time of the Qin First Emperor (circa 221 BC) onwards, the imperial institution was responsible for almost all of the great public works and artistic monuments of China: from the Great Wall to imperial palaces, from Buddhist cave-chapels to pagodas. The emperors, through their court staff, dictated the designs of these sites, and officials charged with carrying out such projects could be held accountable with their life if they failed to satisfy their ruler's demands. In a very real sense, a tour of China becomes an overview of the remains of those strong, long-lasting dynasties—the Han (206 BC–AD 220) and Tang (618–906), the Ming (1368–1644) and Qing (1644–1911)—that left behind notable monuments. Imperial projects are characterized by their scale (the vastness of a Tang tomb), by their quantity (the myriad furnishings of the Forbidden City), by the quality of their materials and work (the images of the Great Buddha niche at the Dragon Gate Grottoes, near Luoyang), and by their symbols of imperial power (most typically, dragons and phoenixes). No other institution or segment of the population in premodern China could challenge the imperial institution in the realm of art production and patronage.

Among the earliest arts to flourish in China were jade carving and pottery. These traditions have roots in Neolithic cultures of the 5th through 3rd millennia BC; jade, for example, was especially notable in the Hongshan Culture of modern-day Inner Mongolia and Liaoning and in the Liangzhu Culture of modern-day Shanghai, Jiangsu, and Zhejiang. The minute designs worked on the surfaces of these stones seem impossible in an age before sophisticated magnification and power tools. The high volume and high quality of imperial kilns anticipates the achievements of sophisticated modern-day production. With both jade and ceramics there is a living connection to the remote past: the materials and processes of modern Chinese workshops and factories (often a part of tours) are not fundamentally different from their premodern antecedents. Jade carving continues to flourish in China today, using a great variety of hard stones and other attractive minerals. Many celadons offered for sale today—including Longquan, Guan, and Yaozhou wares—use the same clay sources and glaze recipes as their imperial-era prototypes. Although excavated artifacts are not for sale and true antiques are very pricey, affordable replicas of both hard stones and ceramics are widely available.

The worlds of ancient and medieval China may be lost, but they are not utterly beyond our experience. Tombs from the Han Dynasty (206 BC–AD 220) were made mainly of brick and stone, and were buried very deeply; they are thus very well preserved. To date, more than 40 Han mausoleums have been unearthed, of which the Tomb of the Southern Yue Kings in Guangzhou (Guangdong) remains one of the few sites intact. A visit to a tomb or the Forbidden City in Beijing affords the visitor an experience akin to time travel. At such sites you can begin to appreciate the setting and context for objects now displayed in museum cases. Dragon robes take on new meaning once you have stood in the vast courtyard before the Hall of Supreme Harmony within the Forbidden City, where the Ming and Qing emperors presided over predawn court gatherings. There you can begin to understand the role of the dragon as a symbol for the unity of the Chinese people. Tombs, temples, and cave-chapels offer the richest experiences of art in context for ancient and medieval times, while the former imperial palaces at Beijing, Chengde (Hebei), and Shenyang (Liaoning) are the most complete repositories for many of the arts of late imperial eras, after the 15th century.

In late medieval times, with the Northern Song Period (10th–12th century), scholar-officials came to dominate Chinese society through their unique social status and the perquisites of rank they enjoyed. They created their own arts for personal expression and relaxation. Calligraphy was preeminent, but painting, garden design, and the collecting of antiquities and of objects for the scholar's studio were also significant. Modern-day museums display much calligraphy and painting by scholar-artists ("literati," *wenren*)—men like Ni Zan, Shen Zhou, or Dong Qichang who were self-styled amateurs in the sense that they did not obtain their social identity through their artistic skills. Garden design of the Ming and Qing is also largely a scholar's taste, designed to engage all the senses and to be savored in different ways at all times of the day and year. The many fine gardens in cities like Suzhou, Yangzhou, Nanjing, Hangzhou, and Shanghai were aped by imperial patrons in Beijing (as at Bei Hai and the Summer Palace). Idealized views of the Chinese past derived from the exquisitely harmonized settings of scholars' gardens (as in the 18th-century novel, *The Dream of the Red Chamber*) should be taken with the proverbial grain of salt. Only a small percentage of the population actually lived in such idyllic precincts.

* * *

EVOCATIONS OF THE NATURAL WORLD, especially the "mountains and waters" (*shan shui*) of the diverse Chinese continent, played an exceptionally large role in later Chinese arts. Paintings, garden design, porcelain decoration, and scholars' objects all took the eternal and ever-changing natural environment as their theme. This does not mean that Chinese artists or scholar-amateurs actually lived in nature or were devoted to the great outdoors. It does suggest the importance of the natural world as a source of Taoist and Buddhist imagery about life and the human condition. And because it can be appreciated without a specialist's knowledge of history or literature, landscape—both the real and the artistic—offers many rewards for the traveler. A tour of the Huangshan Mountains (Anhui) or Li River (Guilin) is a quintessential artistic experience as well as a nature lover's delight. The images of the natural world that you see from your train window are evoked in the gardens or museums you visit.

Because calligraphy and paintings were mounted as scrolls that were rolled up when not on view, it is very difficult to see the great works of the most acclaimed

Chinese artists. Unlike the Mona Lisa, which is dependably on view in the Louvre, Chinese paintings are shown for limited periods only once or twice a year. The superb Shanghai Museum, with its modern galleries and strong holdings in painting and calligraphy, is something of an exception. Painters of the Southern Song (1127–1279), Yuan (1279–1368), Ming, and Qing dominate Chinese museum holdings. If you are a fan of Ma Yuan's "one-corner" compositions (Ma was the scion of a whole family of Southern Song court painters), you will be able to see works of his period and style, if not necessarily works of his hand. Your chances to see the great names of later dynasties will increase considerably. The "Four Great Masters" of the Yuan, of the Ming, and of the Qing—artists who constitute one of the backbones of scholar painting—are regularly on display because they produced large numbers of works that in turn were collected avidly in later periods. With an artist like Shen Zhou (1427–1509) the lifetime output was so great and so diverse that, with diligent looking in museums, you can probably encounter the master repeatedly. Many literati works are ink monochrome and something of an acquired taste, like prints and drawings. Brilliantly colored works on silk produced for the Qing court—such as a large impressive portrait of the Qianlong emperor (18th century) in armor on horseback—are well represented in Chinese museums. Until lately these were scorned by Western art historians.

For the last thousand years or more, rulers and scholars in China have collected certain objects primarily for their historical value. The most prized objects, such as bronze ritual vessels and stone monuments, could be compared with the received historical record and Confucian classics because they carried inscriptions. Antiquarian study of relics preoccupied collectors, leading to the compilation of extensive illustrated catalogs of their holdings, and, not surprisingly, to a flourishing art market as well as considerable fakery. The collections of the Palace Museum (within the Forbidden City, Beijing) reflect these traditional interests and practices. Rich in archaic bronzes and jades, but poor in sculpture, the Palace collection was amassed by art-loving emperors starting in the Northern Song Period (10th–12th century). Today it is not only one of the world's strongest collections of calligraphy and painting, it also houses the extensive furnishings of the Qing imperial court, from dragon robes to cloisonné and mechanical clocks sent as gifts by European powers. A fraction of the collections was moved to the island of Taiwan in 1949, but the bulk of its holdings remains intact and has been augmented by donations and discoveries in the 1990s. Visiting the Palace Museum can serve as a quick introduction to the kinds of things regarded as art in premodern China, as well as an immersion in the luxurious lifestyle of the ruling class.

A wider range of objects fills the many other museums in China. Most museums focus on history, using objects to tell the story of Chinese civilization from prehistory to modern times (circa 1840). These displays generally bring to mind exhibits in natural history and science museums, with their educational graphics, dioramas, models, and reproductions. Original works, including ancient jades, bronzes, ceramics, and other art, are installed amid these pedagogical aids. (Such display practices horrify some non-Chinese art curators, who place great weight on the unencumbered aesthetic experience of authentic art objects.) The preeminent example of this kind of presentation is the Museum of Chinese History, on Tiananmen Square in Beijing. The museum staff has gathered together many important new acquisitions, such as a blue glazed lamp of the Six Dynasties Period (222–589), Tang stone figurines, and a Ming embroidered silk portrait of the Heavenly Kings. The exhibits interpret the objects, which is useful both for the local population and for viewers who cannot read labels written in Chinese. Thus a visit to the Museum of Chinese History can provide a useful overview of Chinese civilization, albeit with history diced into neat dynastic segments under an overall Marxist framework ("primitive society, slave society, feudal society"). Most city and provincial museums depict the history of their own region, so the periods emphasized and the material displayed reflect the strengths and weaknesses of each area. The Shaanxi History Museum in Xian, an imperial capital for many dynasties, is thus correspondingly rich in tomb treasures and luxury goods from those epochs, and has some of the most modern facilities in all of China. Similarly, the Yunnan Provincial Museum in Kunming reflects the ethnic diversity of its peoples, both historically and in the present day.

Since 1950, the national government has made a notable commitment to archaeology, rescuing sites and artifacts from the path of bulldozers and carrying out extensive surveys and excavations in every province and region. The artistic and artifactual heritage as it is known today, a half century later, has caused scholars to rewrite the history of China from earliest times to the early imperial periods (beginning 221 BC). Virtually any volume written prior to the 1970s has been seriously compromised by information gathered in more recent decades. Books and journals can be found in museums and bookstores, but most of them are in Chinese. Many of the finest discoveries are, however, presented comprehensively through site museums—such as the Banpo Neolithic Village and the Qin First Emperor's Terra-cotta Army, both a short drive east of Xian, or the tombs of the Southern Yue Kings in downtown Canton (Guangzhou). In these you can actually walk into an ancient site and see the artifacts in place, much as the archaeologists first encountered them. Many museums have galleries devoted exclusively to important local discoveries, such as the chime of 65 musical bells in the Hubei Provincial Museum (Wuhan) or the desiccated corpses in the Xinjiang Museum (Ürümqi). Don't be surprised if the most famous objects from a particular museum are not on display; they may be on loan to Beijing or abroad in a traveling exhibition.

Many fine art titles are now available at Chinese museums, sites, and bookstores, generally at bargain prices, although only a small fraction have English texts. Recent archaeology and expanding definitions of what constitutes serious topics for study have greatly enlarged the purview of "Chinese art history," and no one can command it all. Some of the most useful guides to discoveries of the late 20th century are exhibition catalogs: *The Golden Age of Chinese Archaeology: Celebrated Discoveries from the People's Republic of China* (National Gallery of Art, 1999), *The Great Bronze Age of China* (Metropolitan Museum of Art, 1980), *The Quest for Eternity* (Los Angeles County Museum, 1987), *Son of Heaven: Imperial Arts of China* (Seattle, 1988), *Mysteries of Ancient China* (British Museum, 1996), *China: Five Thousand Years* (Guggenheim Museum, 1997), and *The Golden Age of Archaeology* (National Gallery, 1999). Two recent volumes also make good use of art and archaeology to introduce Chinese history and culture: *The Cambridge Illustrated History of China* (Patricia Buckley Ebrey, Cambridge, 1996), and *Cradles of Civilization: China* (Robert E. Murowchick, editor, University of Oklahoma, 1994). *The Art and Architecture of China* (Laurence Sickman and Alexander C. Soper, Pelican History of Art, Yale University Press, many editions) remains the best one-volume text, but covers only architecture, painting, and sculpture. *The British Museum Book of Chinese Art* (Jessica Rawson, editor, British Museum, 1992) is especially broad in its coverage.

BOOKS & MOVIES

Books

History: For general overviews of Chinese history from the 1600s to the present, start with *Modern China: A Guide to a Century of Change* (Graham Hutchings, Harvard University Press, 2000) or *The Search for Modern China* (Jonathan Spence, Norton, New York, 1990). To explore deeper roots, with essays on specific cultural topics, read *An Introduction to Chinese Civilization* (John Meskill, editor, D. C. Heath, 1973) or *Anglo-China: Chinese People and British Rule in Hong Kong 1841–1880* (Christopher Munn, Curzon Press, 2001). To get a better understanding of the rise of Mao and his archrival, Chiang Kai-shek, pick up *Before Mao* (Patrick Lescot, Ecco, 2004) or *Chiang Kai-Shek* (Jonathan Fenby, Carroll & Graf, 2004). *Chinese Lives: An Oral History of Contemporary China* (W. J. F. Jenner and Delia Davin, editors, Pantheon, 1987), by the Chinese journalists Sang Ye and Zhang Xinxin, though dated makes an interesting read. *One China, Many Paths* (Chaohua Wang, Verso Books, 2003) is a collection of essays that paint a vibrant panorama of the contemporary intellectual scene in the People's Republic.

Excellent books on Tibet include *High Peaks, Pure Earth: Collected Writings on Tibetan History and Culture* (Hugh Richardson, Serindia, 1998) and *Amdo Tibetans in Transition: Society and Culture in the Post-Mao Era* (Toni Huber, Brill Academic Publishers, 2002).

Memoir: A number of memoirs provide not only personal stories, but also intimate windows on China's vast socioeconomic changes. *The Lost Daughters of China: Abandoned Girls, Their Journey to America, and the Search for a Missing Past* (Karin Evans, J. P. Tarcher, 2001) is part memoir, part travelogue, part East–West cultural commentary that weaves the author's experience of adopting a Chinese infant with observations about Chinese women's history and that country's restrictive reproductive policies. *The Private Life of Mao Zedong: The Memoirs of Mao's Personal Physician* (Zhisui Li, with Anne Thurston, Random House, 1994) combines the doctor's personal history and an intimate, controversial focus on the PRC's founding father. For a portrait of modern China, try *Behind the Wall* (Colin Thubron, Penguin Books, 1989) and *China Wakes* (Nicholas D. Kristof and Sheryl Wudunn, Vintage Press, 1995). For light reading about the Chinese techno generation, *Shanghai Baby* (Weihui Zhou, Simon & Schuster, 2001) is a Chinese version of *Bright Lights, Big City*. It portrays a young urban woman, Coco, who explores the intoxicating but at times cruel underbelly of China's most Westernized city, Shanghai. Coco represents a new generation in China whose search for moral grounding in a country of shifting values is complicated by issues of sexuality, feminism, and material desire.

Fiction: For a taste of historical Chinese literature, spend some time with *Story of the Stone*; it's also known as *The Dream of the Red Chamber* (Xueqin Cao, translated by David Hawkes, Penguin Books, 1973). Any book or essay by author Lu Xun will give you a taste of China's painful path from dynastic rule through early Communist rule; try *Diary of a Madman and Other Stories* (William Lyell, translator, University of Hawaii Press, 1990). *Bolshevik Salute* (Meng Wang, University of Washington Press, 1989) is one of China's first modern novels translated into English. Of the collections of Chinese literature and poetry both ancient and modern, check out *An Anthology of Chinese Literature: Beginnings to 1911* (Stephen Owen, editor and translator, Norton, 1996) and *From May Fourth to June Fourth: Twentieth Century Chinese Fiction and Film* (David D. W. Wang and Ellen Widmer, editors, Cambridge University Press, 1993).

A number of the works of Gao Xianjian, the Nobel Laureate for Literature, have been translated into English, including *Buying a Fishing Rod for My Grandfather* (HarperCollins, 2004), a collection of short stories that depict the fragility of love and life, and the haunting power of memory. Anchee Min, known for her best-selling memoir, *Red Azalea* (Berkley Books, 1995), has since published several novels, including *Wild Ginger* (Houghton Mifflin, 2002) and *Empress Orchid* (Houghton Mifflin, 2004). The novel *Waiting* (Ha Jin, Vintage Books, 2000) won the 1999 National Book Award and the 2000 PEN/Faulkner Award for Fiction. The story tells of one man's frustration at the hands of the bureaucracy as he tries to marry the woman he loves.

Movies

Among Chinese directors, Chen Kaige captures the beauty of the Chinese countryside in his mysterious, striking *Life on a String* (1991). He also directed an epic story of the artistic and personal commitment of two Peking opera stars, *Farewell, My Concubine* (1993) and *Temptress Moon* (1997). Tian Zhuangzhuang directed the controversial *The Blue Kite* (1994), a story of the travails of a young schoolteacher under communism in the 1950s and '60s. (It is currently not allowed to be shown in China.) The outstanding films of director Zhang Yimou, such as *Red Sorghum* (1987), *Ju-Dou* (1990), *Raise the Red Lantern* (1991), *Shanghai Triad* (1995), *The Story of Qiu Ju* (1992), and *To Live* (1994), all star the excellent actress Gong Li, whose roles range from a glamorous mob mistress in 1930s Shanghai to a rural worker.

The director Ang Lee was celebrated for his 2001 *Crouching Tiger, Hidden Dragon,* which won four Academy Awards. Lee's earlier films are also worth seeing; *Eat Drink Man Woman* and *The Wedding Banquet* are amusing looks into modern-day Chinese relationships.

An American filmmaker of Chinese descent, Peter Wang, looks wryly at contemporary China in *A Great Wall* (1986). Director Ann Hui's *Song of the Exile* (1990) follows a young woman returning home to Hong Kong after graduating from a British university.

A Western take on Chinese history is presented in Bernardo Bertolucci's *The Last Emperor,* filmed in China. Three documentary films by Ambrica Productions (New York), *China in Revolution 1911–1949* (1989), *The Mao Years 1949–1976* (1994), and *Born under the Red Flag 1976–1997* (1997), depict the political and social upheavals that followed the death of the last emperor. They are available from Zeitgeist Films (☎ 800/255-9424). The Long Bow Group (Boston) has produced *The Gate of Heavenly Peace* (1996), a documentary film about the Tiananmen Square protests; it is available from Naata (☎ 415/552-9550).

CHINA: A CHRONOLOGY

400,000–200,000 years ago	Early Paleolithic age: fossil remains date Peking Man, which exhibits characteristics of modern Mongoloids. Evidence of use of stone tools.
8000 BC–5000 BC	Neolithic age: beginnings of agriculture.
2205 BC–1766 BC	Purported reign of Xia Dynasty; no archaeological proof of its existence. Noted for use of fire, houses, and silk.
1766 BC–1122 BC	Shang Dynasty: beginnings of concept of "mandate of heaven," emphasizing good conduct of government and right of the populace to rebel against wicked leaders. Noted for highly developed bronze castings, carved jade ritual objects, and oracle bones.
1027 BC–770 BC	Zhou Dynasty establishes capital near present-day Xian. Development of the feudal system. Writing used to keep records and for history and poetry books. Usage of coin currency.
607 BC–487 BC	Lifetime of Lao Tzu, philosopher who sought truth (tao) and utmost virtue in political relations and human nature, believing power should be in hands of people. Advisor to emperor. Purported author of *Tao Te Ching*. Founder of Taoism.
551 BC–479 BC	Lifetime of K'ung Fu-tzu (Confucius), teacher of moral principles of conduct and princely rule. Author of the *I Ching,* or Book of Changes. Stressed importance of humanity, courtesy, uprightness, honesty, and knowledge. Beginnings of Iron Age.
476 BC–221 BC	Warring States Period.
220 BC–206 BC	Despotic Qin Shi Huang Di (self-named "First Emperor") unites China and divides country into present-day 48 commanderies. Establishes capital and underground tomb with terra-cotta soldiers at Changan (Xian). Work begun on Great Wall to keep out nomadic tribes of north. Civil service exams instituted. Script, weights and measures, and coinage standardized. Books burned and Confucian scholars persecuted. Beginning of overland trade with Roman Empire.
206 BC–AD 220	Han Dynasty. Gao-zu (202–195 BC) prevents attack from Huns by marrying daughter to Hun emperor. Wu Di (141–87 BC) encourages revival of Confucian studies; expands Chinese power to almost present-day position. Beginnings of papermaking. Collapse of Han Dynasty and dissolution of the empire.
AD 25–AD 220	Introduction of Buddhism from India. Silk Route developed.
265–420	Xin Dynasty.
420–589	Division of China into Northern and Southern dynasties.
589–618	Empire reunified under the Sui Dynasty. Grand Canal constructed, connecting northern and southern China. Development of gentry class. Reinstatement of civil service exams.

618–907   Tang Dynasty. China's "Golden Age"; great flowering of arts and sciences under Xuan Zong (712–756). Notable poets: Du Fu, Wang Wei, Gao Shi, Bo Juyi, and Yuan Zhen. Coexistence of foreign religions. Rise of scholar-officials. Expansion of Buddhism and Confucian ethics. Paper and printing exported to West. Expansion of Buddhism and Confucian ethics. Only empress ever to rule China, Empress Wu (627–705), concubine to previous emperors, declares herself emperor in 690, orders ruthless persecution of opponents.

907–960   Instability following collapse of Tang Dynasty leads to division of rule into Five Dynasties in north and Ten Kingdoms in south. Empire collapses and Barbarians invade north China. Beginnings of urban life and neo-Confucianism. Paper money and a primitive printing press are introduced, as well as the foot binding of women. First military use of gunpowder.

960–1280   China reunited under Song Dynasty, capital established at Kaifeng. Coexistence with Jurchen, Khitan, and Jin rule. Flourishing of landscape painting. Genghis Khan defeats Jin in northwestern China in 1215.

1260   Mongol leader Kublai Khan, grandson of Genghis Khan, establishes Peking as his capital.

1279–1368   Mongol conquest of all of China and Tibet; founding of Yuan (Original) Dynasty under "foreign" rule. Marco Polo reputed to visit China; serves under Kublai Khan (1275–92). Rebellion instigated by White Lotus and Red Turbans groups leads to collapse of empire.

1368–1644   Ming (Brilliant) Dynasty is marked by consolidation of power and institutional foundations of Chinese state. Capital moved to Nanjing until 1403. Beijing becomes capital again and Forbidden City constructed in 1421. Maritime expeditions across Indian Ocean.

1550   Europeans come to China seeking trade and Christian converts; Macau established as first European settlement in 1553.

1644   Manchu (Jurchen) conquest and founding of Qing Dynasty. Capital returns to Peking. Pigtail forced on Chinese as sign of submission.

1662–1722   Kangxi Emperor, strong supporter of Confucian morality, consolidates the dynasty militarily. Taiwan reclaimed by China from Dutch.

1773   To offset growing British demand for tea, and in response to restrictions on foreign trade, British begin exporting opium to Canton.

1839–42   Opium War. China orders complete halt of opium trade. British naval forces capture Fujian and Zhejiang.

1842   Qing emperor is forced to sign Treaty of Nanjing, which permits full resumption of British drug trade and exacts payments of indemnities from China.

1843   Hong Kong ceded to Great Britain and China opened to Christian missionaries.

1853   Taiping Rebellion. The Taipings (Heavenly Kingdom of Great Peace), a peasant organization founded on Christian beliefs, take Nanjing and declare it their capital.

1856–60   Second Opium War. In retaliation against Chinese acts of protest against British and French, Treaty of Tianjin opens additional ports to foreign traders and grants extraterritorial privileges to foreigners.

1860   Chinese refuse ratification of Treaty of Tianjin. Anglo-French troops enter Peking and destroy Old Summer Palace.

1864   Final defeat of Taipings by combined Chinese and European forces.

1883–85   Sino-French War, resulting in French control of Vietnam. Extravagant Empress Dowager Cixi (1835–1908), mother of the successor to the Qing throne, advises and exploits following three emperors. Under her direction, naval funds are squandered on reconstruction of Summer Palace.

1893   Birth of Mao Zedong to upper-level peasants in Hunan.

1894–95   China loses Korea, Taiwan, and Pescadores Islands in Sino-Japanese War.

1898   Hundred Days Reform seeks to remake the examination system, the administration, and government institutions in order to inaugurate a system of modern government.

1900–01   Boxer Rebellion, led by fanatical peasant secret societies, suppressed by Eight-Power allied invasion (English, French, American, Japanese, Russian, and other forces). The Empress Dowager forced to flee, palace occupied. Russia invades Manchuria.

1901–11   Qing reforms: establishment of college system, introduction of modern government departments, and abolition of old examination system.

1908   Death of Empress Dowager Cixi. Her son, two-year-old Emperor Pu Yi, inherits the throne.

1911   Republican revolution led by Sun Yat-sen (1866–1925) leads to fall of the Qing Dynasty.

1912   Nationalist party (Guomindang; GMD) is formed. Yuan Shikai becomes president of the Republic and Beijing is declared capital.

1916   Death of Yuan Shikai. Beginnings of Warlord Era, during which Japanese, military commanders, and Communists compete in seeking to reform China.

1917   China declares war on Germany.

1919   China refuses to sign Treaty of Versailles, which cedes former German territories in Shandong province to Japan. Anti-imperialist sentiments give way to the May Fourth Movement, characterized by liberal thinking reflected in literature, political participation by women, and educational reform.

1921   Chinese Communist Party (CCP) founded in Shanghai.

1925   Death of Sun Yat-sen. May 30th Movement marked by anti-imperialist student demonstrations in Shanghai.

1926   GMD armies in the Northern Expedition, from Guangzhou to Yangzi Valley, defeat warlord forces, including Japanese, in south China.

1927   GMD turns against CCP. Chiang Kai-shek establishes GMD capital in Nanjing.

1928   U.S. recognizes government of Chiang Kai-shek in Nanjing.

1931   Japan occupies Manchuria.

1934   Communists driven out of base in Jiangxi province by GMD and begin Long March, arriving in Yanan, Shaanxi province, some 9,600 km (6,000 mi) and one year later. Only one-fourth of the 90,000 people survive the cross-country expedition.

1935   Mao Zedong becomes chairman and undisputed leader of CCP at Zunyi Conference.

1936   With encouragement from some Communist officers, Chiang Kai-shek is kidnapped by one of his generals in the Xian Incident and is released only when GMD agrees to cooperate with Communists against Japanese.

1937–45   Sino-Japanese War. GMD and CCP join forces against Japanese, but alliance ends by 1941.

1945   U.S. General George Marshall arrives in China to try to put together a coalition government between Communists and Nationalists.

1946   Full-scale civil war between GMD and CCP breaks out.

1949   People's Republic of China is established under Mao Zedong in Beijing. Nationalists, led by Chiang Kai-shek, flee with national treasures and entire gold reserves to Taiwan, leaving China bankrupt.

1950   China enters Korean War against United States. Marriage and agrarian reform laws passed. Sino-Soviet Treaty of Friendship, Alliance, and Mutual Assistance is signed.

1951–52   Three Antis Campaign against corruption, waste, and bureaucratism and the Five Antis Campaign against bribery, tax evasion, theft of state assets, cheating, and stealing of economic intelligence.

1952   Land Reform completed. Violent measures against landlords and local despots.

1953   Korean armistice. Beginning of First Five-Year Plan inaugurating transition to socialism by subordinating agriculture to industry.

1954   First National People's Congress adopts PRC state constitution. U.S. signs Mutual Defense Treaty with Nationalist government on Taiwan.

1955   Setting up of agricultural producers' cooperatives begins, in which peasants cultivate land together and share a common product in proportion to their pooled contributions.

1956 Mao Zedong makes Hundred Flowers speech inviting criticisms of cadres and the bureaucracy.

1957 Anti-Rightist Campaign purging erstwhile critics of regime who dared to speak out during Hundred Flowers Period.

1958 Commune system established by amalgamating former agricultural producers' cooperatives. Great Leap Forward aimed at economic transformation in industry and agriculture. Chinese shell Nationalist offshore islands of Quemoy and Matsu.

1959 Resistance to occupation of Tibet suppressed. Dalai Lama flees to India. Chinese Defense Minister is dismissed for speaking out against Great Leap Forward.

1960 Soviet withdrawal of experts. Overambitious and misguided industrial targets of Great Leap result in devastating famine with an estimated 30 million deaths.

1960–62 Three years of natural disasters.

1962 Sino-Indian border war.

1964 China's first nuclear explosion.

1965 First signs of Cultural Revolution erupt in literary sphere in nationwide criticism of play, *Hai Rui Dismissed from Office*.

1966 Eleventh Plenum of Eleventh Central Committee formalizes the Cultural Revolution in move against Mao's critics, which leads to ousting of head of state Liu Shaoqi and general secretary of party Deng Xiaoping. Reign of terror and massive destruction ensue.

1967 Military is called in to restore order.

1968 Millions of urban youth sent to countryside to learn from peasants.

1969 Border clashes with Soviet Union. Ninth Party Congress names Defense Minister Lin Biao as Mao Zedong's closest comrade-in-arms and successor.

1971 Head of a powerful military faction, Lin Biao dies in mysterious plane crash over Mongolia. U.S. State Department abolishes travel restrictions to China, and U.S. table tennis team visits Beijing. Taiwan is expelled from UN, and China takes its seat on UN Security Council.

1972 President Nixon and Prime Minister Tanaka of Japan visit China. Shanghai communiqué is signed beginning process of normalization of relations between China and United States.

1975 Premier Zhou Enlai outlines program of four modernizations in agriculture, industry, science and technology, and national defense. Death of Chiang Kai-shek in Taiwan.

1976 Death of Zhou Enlai. First Tiananmen demonstrations against radical political line of Cultural Revolution. Severe earthquake measuring 7.5 demolishes city of Tangshan. Death of Mao Zedong is followed by arrest of Cultural Revolution protagonists, the "Gang of Four," led by Mao's wife.

1977   Deng Xiaoping returns to power.

1978   Sino-Japanese Treaty of Peace and Friendship is signed. Third Plenum of Eleventh Central Committee inaugurates socialist modernization and liberalized agricultural policies.

1978–79   Wall poster movement attacking Cultural Revolution and Mao Zedong evolves into Democracy Wall Movement.

1979   Resumption of formal diplomatic relations with United States. Deng Xiaoping visits United States. Sino-Vietnamese war. Democracy Wall is closed down and leading dissident Wei Jingsheng is arrested and sentenced to 15 years' imprisonment.

1980   Trial of "Gang of Four" and former military figures associated with Lin Biao. Opening of four special economic zones.

1981   Campaign against spiritual pollution and Western influences.

1983   Anti-crime campaign resulting in thousands of executions and deportations to countryside.

1984   Third Plenum of Twelfth Central Committee endorses broad economic and urban reforms.

1986   Student demonstrations begin in Hefei, Anhui province, and spread to Shanghai, Beijing, and 17 other cities.

1987   Party General Secretary Hu Yaobang is dismissed for failure to crack down on students. Anti-bourgeois liberalization campaign ensues against Western values and institutions.

1989   Death of Hu Yaobang leads to massive demonstrations in Beijing on Tiananmen Square for six weeks. Declaration of martial law does not quell crowds in Square. Military is brought in on June 4, resulting in thousands of deaths. General Secretary Zhao Ziyang is dismissed from office.

1992   Fourteenth Party Congress endorses concept of socialist market economy. First free elections in China.

1995   Chinese test-fire missiles off northern coast of Taiwan.

1997   Paramount leader Deng Xiaoping dies. Upon expiration of 99-year lease, sovereignty over Hong Kong reverts to China. Jiang Zemin becomes chairman of the Republic.

2000   China attains "normal" trade status with the United States.

2001   Beijing is chosen as the site of the 2008 Olympic Games. China officially joins the World Trade Organization.

2002   President Jiang Zemin gives up the top spot in the Communist Party to Hu Jintao; five months later Hu ascends to the presidency.

2003   China's first manned space mission is completed successfully.

— Mielikki Org

LANGUAGE NOTES

PRONUNCIATION & VOCABULARY

CHINESE PLACE NAMES

PRONUNCIATION & VOCABULARY

	Chinese	English Equivalent	Chinese	English Equivalent
Consonants				
	b	boat	p	pass
	m	mouse	f	flag
	d	dock	t	tongue
	n	nest	l	life
	g	goat	k	keep
	h	house	j	and yet
	q	chicken	x	short
	zh	judge	ch	church
	sh	sheep	r*	read
	z	seeds	c	dots
	s	seed		
Vowels				
	ü	you	ia	yard
	üe	you + e	ian	yen
	a	father	iang	young
	ai	kite	ie	yet
	ao	now	o	all
	e	earn	ou	go
	ei	day	u	wood
	er	curve	ua	waft
	i	yield	uo	wall
	i (after z, c, s, zh, ch, sh)	thunder		

Word Order

The basic Chinese sentence structure is the same as in English, following the pattern of subject-verb-object:

He took my pen.	Tā ná le wǒ de bǐ.
s v o	s v o

Nouns

There are no articles in Chinese, although there are many "counters," which are used when a certain number of a given noun is specified. Various attributes of a noun—such as size, shape, or use—determine which counter is used with that noun. Chinese does not distinguish between singular and plural.

a pen	yìzhī bǐ
a book	yìběn shū

Verbs

Chinese verbs are not conjugated, and they do not have tenses. Instead, a system of word order, word repetition, and the addition of a number of adverbs serves to indicate the tense of a verb, whether the verb is a suggestion or an order, or even whether the verb is part of a question. *Tāzài ná wǒ de bǐ.* (He is taking my pen.) *Tā ná le wǒ de bǐ.* (He took my pen.) *Tā you méi you ná wǒ de bǐ?* (Did he take my pen?) *Tā yào ná wǒ de bǐ.* (He will take my pen.)

Tones

In English, intonation patterns can indicate whether a sentence is a statement (He's hungry.), a question (He's hungry?), or an exclamation (He's hungry!). Entire sentences carry particular "tones," but individual words do not. In Chinese, words have a particular tone value, and these tones are important in determining the meaning of a word. Observe the meanings of the following examples, each said with one of the four tones found in standard Chinese: *mā* (high, steady tone): mother; *má* (rising tone, like a question): fiber; *mǎ* (dipping tone): horse; and *mà* (dropping tone): swear.

Phrases

You don't need to master the entire Chinese language to spend a week in China, but taking charge of a few key phrases in the language can aid you in just getting by. The following supplement will allow you to get a hotel room, get around town, order a drink at the end of the day, and get help in case of an emergency.

Listen to the phrase and repeat what you hear in the space provided.

Common Greetings

Hello/Good morning.	Nǐ hǎo/Zǎoshàng hǎo.
Good evening.	Wǎnshàng hǎo.
Good-bye.	Zàijiàn.
Title for a married woman or an older unmarried woman	Tàitai/Fūrén
Title for a young and unmarried woman	Xiǎojiě
Title for a man	Xiānshēng
How are you?	Nǐ hǎo ma?
Fine, thanks. And you?	Hěn hǎo. Xièxie. Nǐ ne?
What is your name?	Nǐ jiào shénme míngzi?
My name is . . .	Wǒ jiào . . .

| Nice to meet you. | Hěn gāoxìng rènshì nǐ. |
| I'll see you later. | Huítóu jiàn. |

Polite Expressions

Please.	Qǐng.
Thank you.	Xièxiè.
Thank you very much.	Fēicháng gǎnxiè.
You're welcome.	Bú yòng xiè.
Yes, thank you.	Shì de, xièxiè.
No, thank you.	Bù, xièxiè.
I beg your pardon.	Qǐng yuánliàng.
I'm sorry.	Hěn baòqiàn.
Pardon me.	Dùibùqǐ.
That's okay.	Méi shénme.
It doesn't matter.	Méi guānxi.
Do you speak English?	Nǐ shuō Yīngyǔ ma?
Yes.	Shì de.
No.	Bù.
Maybe.	Huòxǔ.
I can speak a little.	Wǒ néng shūo yī diǎnr.
I understand a little.	Wǒ dǒng yì diǎnr.
I don't understand.	Wǒ bù dǒng.
I don't speak Chinese very well.	Wǒ Zhōngwén shūo de bù haǒ.
Would you repeat that, please?	Qǐng zài shūo yíbiàn?
I don't know.	Wǒ bù zhīdaò.
No problem.	Méi wèntí.
It's my pleasure.	Lèyì er wéi.

Needs and Question words

I'd like . . .	Wǒ xiǎng . . .
I need . . .	Wǒ xūyào . . .
What would you like?	Nǐ yaò shénme?
Please bring me . . .	Qǐng gěi wǒ . . .
I'm looking for . . .	Wǒ zài zhǎo . . .
I'm hungry.	Wǒ è le.
I'm thirsty.	Wǒ kǒukě.
It's important.	Hěn zhòngyào.
It's urgent.	Hěn jǐnjí.
How?	Zěnmeyàng?

How much?	Duōshǎo?
How many?	Duōshǎo gè?
Which?	Nǎ yí gè?
What?	Shénme?
What kind of?	Shénme yàng de?
Who?	Shuí?
Where?	Nǎli?
When?	Shénme shíhòu?
What does this mean?	Zhè shì shénme yìsi?
What does that mean?	Nà shì shénme yìsi?
How do you say . . . in Chinese?	. . . yòng Zhōngwén zěnme shūo?

At the Airport

Where is . . .	. . . zài nǎr?
customs?	Hǎigūan
passport control?	Hùzhào jiǎnyàn
the information booth?	Wènxùntái
the ticketing counter?	Shòupiàochù
the baggage claim?	Xínglǐchù
the ground transportation?	Dìmìan jiāotōng
Is there a bus service to the city?	Yǒu qù chéng lǐ de gōnggòng qìchē ma?
Where are . . .	. . . zài nǎr?
the international departures?	Guójì hángbān chūfā diǎn
the international arrivals?	Guójì hángbān dàodá diǎn
What is your nationality?	Nǐ shì něi guó rén?
I am an American.	Wǒ shì Měiguó rén.
I am Canadian.	Wǒ shì Jiānádà rén.

At the Hotel, Reserving a Room

I would like a room . . .	Wǒ yào yí ge fángjiān.
for one person	dānrén fáng
for two people	shuāngrén fāng
for tonight	jīntīan wǎnshàng
for two nights	liǎng gè wǎnshàng
for a week	yí ge xīngqī
Do you have a different room?	Nǐ hái yǒu bié de fángjiān ma?
with a bath	dài yùshì de fángjiān
with a shower	dài línyù de fángjiān
with a toilet	dài cèsuǒ de fángjiān
with air-conditioning	yǒu kōngtiáo de fángjiān

| How much is it? | Duōshǎo qián? |
| My bill, please. | Qǐng jiézhàng. |

At the Restaurant

Where can we find a good restaurant?	Zài nǎr kěyǐ zhǎodào yìjiā hǎo cānguǎn?
We'd like a(n) . . . restaurant.	Wǒmen xiǎng qù yì gè . . . cānguǎn.
elegant	gāo jí
fast-food	kuàicān
inexpensive	piányì de
seafood	hǎixiān
vegetarian	sùshí
Café	Kāfeī diàn
A table for two	Liǎng wèi
Waiter, a menu please.	Fúwùyuán, qǐng gěi wǒmen càidān.
The wine list, please.	Qǐng gěi wǒmen jiǔdān.
Appetizers	Kāiwèi shíwù
Main course	Zhǔ cài
Dessert	Tiándiǎn
What would you like?	Nǐ yào shénme cài?
What would you like to drink?	Nǐ yào hē shénme yǐnliào?
Can you recommend a good wine?	Nǐ néng tūijiàn yí ge hǎo jiǔ ma?
Wine, please.	Qǐng lǎi diǎn jiǔ.
Beer, please.	Qǐng lǎi diǎn píjiǔ.
I didn't order this.	Wǒ méiyǒu diǎn zhè gè.
That's all, thanks.	Jiù zhèxie, xièxiè.
The check, please.	Qǐng jiézhàng.
Cheers!/Bottoms Up! To your health!	Gānbēi! Zhù nǐ shēntì jiànkāng.

Out on the Town

Where can I find . . .	Nǎr yǒu . . .
an art museum?	yìshù bówùguǎn?
a museum of natural history?	zìránlìshǐ bówùguǎn?
a history museum?	lìshǐ bówugǔan?
a gallery?	huàláng?
interesting architecture?	yǒuqù de jiànzhùwù?
a church?	jiàotáng?
the zoo?	dòngwùyuán?

I'd like . . .	Wǒ xiǎng . . .
to see a play.	kàn xì.
to see a movie.	kàn diànyǐng.
to see a concert.	qù yīnyuèhuì.
to see the opera.	kàn gējù.
to go sightseeing.	qù guānguāng.
to go on a bike ride.	qí dānchē.

Shopping

Where is the best place to go shopping for . . .	Mǎi . . . zuì hǎo qù nǎr?
clothes?	yīfu
food?	shíwù
souvenirs?	jìniànpǐn
furniture?	jiājù
fabric?	bùliào
antiques?	gǔdǒng
books?	shūjí
sporting goods?	yùndòng wùpǐn
electronics?	diànqì
computers?	diànnǎo

Directions

Excuse me. Where is . . .	Duìbùqǐ . . . zài nǎr?
the bus stop?	Qìchēzhàn
the subway station?	Dìtiězhàn
the rest room?	Xǐshǒujiān
the taxi stand?	Chūzū chēzhàn
the nearest bank?	Zùijìn de yínháng
the hotel?	Lǚguǎn

To the right	Zài yòubiān.
To the left.	Zài zuǒbiān.
Straight ahead.	Wǎng qián zhízǒu.
It's near here.	Jiuzài zhè fùjìn.
Go back.	Wǎng húi zǒu.
Next to . . .	Jǐnkào . . .

Numbers

Cardinal

0	Líng	5	Wǔ
1	Yī	6	Lìu
2	Er	7	Qī
3	Sān	8	Bā

4	Sì	9	Jǐu
10	Shí	30	Sānshí
11	Shíyī	40	Sìshí
12	Shí'èr	50	Wǔshí
13	Shísān	60	Lìushí
14	Shísì	70	Qīshí
15	Shíwǔ	80	Bāshí
16	Shílìu	90	Jǐushí
17	Shíqī	100	Yìbǎi
18	Shíbā	1,000	Yìqiān
19	Shíjǐu	1,100	Yìqiān yìbǎi
20	Ershí	2,000	Liǎngqiān
21	Ershíyī	10,000	Yíwàn
22	Ershí'èr	100,000	Shíwàn
23	Eshísān	1,000,000	Bǎiwàn

Time

What time is it?	Xiànzài shénme shíjiān?
It is noon.	Zhōngwǔ.
It is midnight.	Bànyè.
It is 9:00 A.M.	Shàngwǔ jǐu diǎn.
It is 1:00 P.M.	Xiàwǔ yì diǎn.
It is 3 o'clock.	Sān diǎn (zhōng).
5:15	Wǔ diǎn shíwǔ fēn.
7:30	Qī diǎn sānshí (bàn).
9:45	Jǐu diǎn sìshíwǔ.
Now	Xiànzài
Later	Wǎn yì diǎnr
Immediately	Mǎshàng
Soon	Hěn kuài

Days of the Week

Monday	Xīngqī yī
Tuesday	Xīngqī èr
Wednesday	Xīngqī sān
Thursday	Xīngqī sì
Friday	Xīngqī wǔ
Saturday	Xīngqī lìu
Sunday	Xīngqī rì (tiān)

Modern Connections

Where can I find . . .	Zài nǎr kěyǐ shǐ yòng . . .
a telephone?	diànhuà?
a fax machine?	chuánzhēnjī?
an Internet connection?	guójì wǎnglù?
How do I call the United States?	Gěi Měiguó dǎ diànhuà zěnme dǎ?
I need . . .	Wǒ xūyào . . .
a fax sent.	fā chuánzhēn.
a hookup to the Internet.	yǔ guójì wǎnglù liánjiē.
a computer.	diànnǎo.
a package sent overnight.	liányè bǎ bāoguǒ jìchū.
some copies made.	fùyìn yìxiē wénjiàn.
a VCR and monitor.	lùyǐngjī he xiǎnshìqì.
an overhead projector and markers.	huàndēngjī he biāoshìqì.

Emergencies and Safety

Help!	Jiùmìng a!
Fire!	Jiùhuǒ a!
I need a doctor.	Wǒ yào kàn yīshēng.
Call an ambulance!	Mǎshàng jiào jiùhùchē!
What happened?	Fāshēng le shénme shì?
I am/My wife is/My husband is/ My friend is/Someone is . . .	Wǒ/Wǒ qīzi/Wǒ Zhàngfu/ Wǒ péngyǒu/Yǒu rén . . .
very sick.	bìng de hěn lìhài.
having a heart attack.	xīnzàngbìng fāzuò le.
choking.	yēzhù le.
losing consciousness.	yūndǎo le.
about to vomit.	yào ǒutù le.
having a seizure.	yòu fābìng le.
stuck.	bèi kǎ zhù le.
I can't breathe.	Wǒ bù néng hūxī.
I tripped and fell.	Wǒ bàn dǎo le.
I cut myself.	Wǒ gē shāng le.
I drank too much.	Wǒ jiǔ hē de tài duō le.
I don't know.	Wǒ bù zhīdào.
I've injured my . . .	Wǒ de . . . shòushāng le.
head	tóu
neck	bózi
back	bèi
arm	shǒubèi
leg	tuǐ
foot	jiǎo
eye(s)	yǎnjīng
I've been robbed.	Wǒ bèi qiǎng le.

CHINESE PLACE NAMES

Pinyin	English	Chinese Character

Chapter 1, Beijing

Pinyin	English	Chinese Character
Běijīng	Beijing	北京
Bādálǐng Chángchéng	Badaling Great Wall	八达岭长城
Gùgōng	Forbidden City	故宫
Jiètāisì	Temple of the Altar	戒台寺
Lúgōuqiáo	Lugouqiao (Marco Polo Bridge)	芦沟桥
Míng Shísānlíng	Ming Tombs	明十三陵
Mùtiányù Chángchéng	Mutianyu Great Wall	慕田峪长城
Qīngdōnglíng	Eastern Qing Tombs	清东陵
Sīmǎtái Chángchéng	Simatai Great Wall	司马台长城
Tiānānmén Guǎngchǎng	Tiananmen Square	天安门广场
Yíhéyuán	Summer Palace	颐和园
Yúnjūsì	Yunju Temple	云居寺
Zhōukǒudiàn Běijīng Yuánrén Yízhǐ	Zhoukoudian Peking Man Site	周口店北京猿人遗址

Chapter 2, North Central China

Pinyin	English	Chinese Character
Tiānjīn	Tianjin	天津
Dū Lè Sì	Du Le Temple	都乐寺
Pānshān	Pan Mountain	攀山
Héběi	Hebei	河北
Běidàihé	Beidaihe	北戴河
Chéngdé	Chengde	承德
Shānhǎiguān	Shanhaiguan	山海关
Shānxī	Shanxi	山西
Dàtóng	Datong	大同
Xuánkōng Sì	Hanging Monastery	悬空寺
Yīngxiàn Mùtǎ	Yingxian Timber Pagoda	应县木塔
Yúngāng Shíkū	Yungang Grottoes	云冈石窟
Hénán	Henan	河南
Huáng Hé Youlan Qu	Yellow River Park	黄河公园
Luòyáng	Luoyang	洛阳

Shàolín Sì	Shaolin Monastery	少林寺
Zhèngzhōu	Zhengzhou	郑州
Zhōngyuè Sì	Temple of the Central Peak	中岳寺
Shāndōng	Shandong	山东
Jǐnán	Jinan	济南
Láoshān	Mt. Lao	崂山
Qīngdǎo	Qingdao	青岛
Tàishān	Mt. Tai	泰山

Chapter 3, Northeastern China

Heilongjiang	Heilongjiang	黑龙江
Hārbīn	Harbin	哈尔滨
Jílín	Jilin	吉林
Běidàhú Huáxuě Chǎng	Beidahu Ski Resort	北大湖滑雪场
Chángbáishān	Changbaishan Nature Reserve	长白山
Chángchūn	Changchun	长春
Sōng Huā Hú	Song Hua Lake	松花湖
Liáoníng	Liaoning	辽宁
Dàlián	Dalian	大连
Jīn Shī Tān	Golden Stone Beach	金石滩
Shěnyáng	Shenyang	沈阳

Chapter 4, Northwestern China

Shǎnxī	Shaanxi	陕西
Gùyuán	GuYuan	咕原
Gǔzhōngkoǔ	Guzhongkou	滚钟口
Huáshān	Huashan	华山
Níngxià	Ningxia	宁夏
Qīngtóngxiá Zhen	Old Qingtonxia	青铜峡
Tóngxīn	Tongxin	同心
Xīān	Xian	西安
Xīxià Wánglíng	Western Xia Tombs	西夏王陵
Yínchuān	Yinchuan	银川
Zhōngweì	Zhongwei	中卫
Gānsù	Gansu	甘肃
Bǐnglíng Sì Shíkū	Thousand Buddha Temple and Caves	炳陵寺石窟

Dūnhuáng	Dunhuang	敦煌
Jiāyùguān	Jiayuguan	嘉峪关
Lánzhōu	Lanzhou	兰州
Maìjīshān Shíkū	Maijishan Grottoes	麦积山石窟
Xiàhé	Xiahe	下河
Yáng Guān	Southern Pass	阳关
Yùmén	Jade Gate	玉门
Qīnghǎi	Qinghai	青海
Géěrmù	Golmud	格尔木
Hóngaízǐgoū	Dek Tser	红崖子沟
Niǎo Dǎo	Bird Island	鸟岛
Qīnghǎi Hú	Qinghai Lake	青海湖
Rìyuè Shān	Sun Moon Mountain	日月山
Tǎ'Ěr Sì	Ta'Er Monastery	塔尔寺
Tánggǔlā Shānkoǔ	Tanggula Mountain Pass	唐古拉山口
Xīníng	Xining	西宁
Xīnjìāng	Xinjiang	新疆
Āsītǎnà Gǔmù	Atsana-Karakhoja Tombs	阿斯塔那古墓
Bózīkèlǐkè Qiānfó Dòng	Bezeklik Thousand Buddha Caves	柏孜克里克千佛洞
Gaōchāng Gǔchéng	Ancient city of Gaochang	高昌古城
Jiaōhé Gùchéng	Ancient city of Jiaohe	交河故城
Kāshí	Kashgar	喀什
Pàmǐ'ěr	Pamir Mountains	帕米尔
Pútáo Goū	Grape Valley	葡萄沟
Saì Lǐ Mù Hú	Sayram Lake	赛里木湖
Tiānchí Hú	Heavenly Lake	天池
Tǎshíkùěrgān	Tashkurgan	塔什库尔干
Tǔlǔfān	Turpan	土鲁番
Wūlǔmùqí	Ürümqi	乌鲁木齐
Yīníng	Yining	伊宁

Chapter 5, Shanghai

| Dàjìng Gé | Old City Wall | 大境路老城墙 |
| Dōngtaí Lù Gudaì Chǎng | Dongtai Road Antiques Market | 东台路古代场 |

Shànghǎi Pǔdōng Fázhǎn Yínháng	Former Hongkong & Shanghai Bank	上海浦东发展银行
Fúyóu Lù Gudài Chǎng	Fuyou Road Antiques Market	富有路古代场
Hépíng Fàndiàn	Peace Hotel	和平饭店
Waì Tān	The Bund	外滩
Yùyuán	Yu Garden	豫园
Zhōngguo Yínháng	Bank of China	中国银行
Dà Jù Yuàn	Grand Theatre	上海大剧院
Dà Shìjiè	Great World	大世界
Guójī Fàndiàn	Park Hotel	国际饭店
Huā Niǎo Shìchǎng	Bird and Flower Market	花鸟市场
Jǐngān Gu Sì	Jingan Temple	静安古寺
Rénmín Gōngyuán	People's Park	人民公园
Rénmín Guáng Chang	People's Square	人民广场
Shànghǎi Bówùguǎn	Shanghai Museum	上海博物馆
Shànghǎi Meǐshūguǎn	Shanghai Art Museum	上海美术馆
Shànghǎi Zhánlán Zhōngxīn	Shanghai Exhibition Center	上海展览中心
Yúfó Sì	Jade Buddha Temple	玉佛寺
Fúxīng Gōngyuán	Fuxing Park	复兴公园
Lónghuá Gu Sì	Longhua Temple	龙华古寺
Lánxīng	Lyceum Theatre	兰心大剧院
Shànghǎi Gōngyì Meǐshù Yànjiūsuǒ	Shanghai Arts and Crafts Research Institute	上海工艺美术研究所
Sóng Qìnglíng Gùjū	Soong Chingling's Former Residence	宋庆龄故居
Sūn Zhōngshān Gùjū	Song Yat-sen's Former Residence	孙中山故居
Yàndàng Lù	Yandan Lu Pedestrian Street	雁荡路
Xújiāhuì Dàjiàotǎng	Xujiahui Cathedral	徐家汇教堂
Zhōnggòng Yīdàhuìzhi	Site of the First National Congress	中共一大会址
Bīngjiāng Dà Dào	Riverside Promenade	冰江大道
Dōngfāng Míngzhū	Oriental Pearl TV Tower	东方明珠
Jīnmào Dàshà	Jinmao Building	金茂大厦

Pudōng Mătóu	Pudong Ferry Terminal	浦东码头
Shànghǎi Lìshǐ Bówùguǎn	Shanghai History Museum	上海历史博物馆
Shànghǎi Zhèngquàn Jiāoyìsuo	Shanghai Securities Exchange Building	上海证券交易所
Lu Xùn Gōngyuán	Lu Xun Park	鲁迅公园
Móxī Huìtáng	Moshe Synagogue	摩西会堂
Huǒshān Gōngyuán	Huoshan Park	火山公园

Chapter 6, Eastern China

Jiāngsū	Jiangsu	江苏
Nánjīng	Nanjing	南京
Sūzhōu	Suzhou	苏州
Wúxī	Wuxi	无锡
Zhènjiāng	Zhenjiang	镇江
Ānhuī	Anhui	安徽
Héféi	Hefei	合肥
Huángshān	Huangshan	黄山
Zhèjiāng	Zhejiang	浙江
Hángzhōu	Hangzhou	杭州
Fújiàn	Fujian	福建
Fúzhōu	Fuzhou	福州
Méizhōu	Meizhou	湄洲
Quánzhōu	Quanzhou	泉州
Wǔyí Shān Fēngjǐngqū	Wuyi Mountain Nature Reserve	武夷山风景区
Xiàmén	Xiamen	厦门
Jiāngxī	Jiangxi	江西
Jǐngdézhèn	Jingdezhen	景德镇
Jiǔjiāng	Jiujiang	九江
Lúshān	Lushan	庐山
Nánchāng	Nanchang	南昌

Chapter 7, Southeastern China

Guǎngdōng	Guangdong	广东
Cháozhōu	Chaozhou	潮州
Cuìhēng	Cuiheng	翠亨
Fóshān	Foshan	佛山
Guǎngzhōu	Guangzhou	广州

Jǐn Xiù Zhōng Huá	Splendid China	锦绣中华
Shàntóu	Shantou	汕头
Shékǒu	Shekou	蛇口
Shēnzhèn	Shenzhen	深圳
Zhōng Huá Mínzú Wén Huà Cūn	China Folk Culture Villages	中华民族文化村
Zhōngshān Shì	Zhongshan Shi	中山市
Zhūhǎi	Zhuhai	珠海
Hǎinán	Hainan	海南
Hǎikǒu	Haikou	海口
Sānyà Shì	Sanya	三亚市
Tōngzhá	Tongzha	通什市

Chapter 9, South Central China

Húběi	Hubei	湖北
Shénnǒngjià	Shennongjia	神农架
Wǔhàn	Wuhan	武汉
Yíchāng	Yichang	宜昌
Húnán	Hunan	湖南
Chángshā	Changsha	长沙
Héngyáng	Hengyang	衡阳
Sháoshān	Shaoshan	韶山
Wǔlíngyúan	Wulingyuan	武陵源
Yuèyáng	Yueyang	岳阳
Guǎngxī	Guangxi	广西
Guìlín	Guilin	桂林
Liǔzhōu	Liuzhou	柳州
Lóngshèng	Longsheng	龙胜
Nǎnníng	Nanning	南宁
Wúzhōu	Wuzhou	梧州
Yángshuò	Yangshuo	阳朔
Zǔojiāng	Zuo River	左江
Guìzhōu	Guizhou	贵州
Ānshùn	Anshun	安顺
Guìyáng	Guiyang	贵阳
Huángguǒshù Pùbù	Huangguoshu Falls	黄果树瀑布
Kǎilǐ	Kaili	凯里
Xīngyì	Xingyi	兴义
Zūnyì	Zunyi	遵义

Chapter 10, Southwestern China

Yúnnán	Yunnan	云南
Dàlǐ	Dali	大理
Hǔtiaò Xía	Tiger Leaping Gorge	虎跳峡
Jǐnghóng	Jinghong	景洪
Kūnmíng	Kunming	昆明
Lìjiáng	Lijiang	丽江
Shāpíng	Shaping	沙坪
Shí Lín	Stone Forest	石林
Xīshuāngbǎnnà	Xishuangbanna	西双版纳
Xǐzhōu	Xizhou	西州
Yuán Shǐ Yǔ Lín Gōngyuán	Primitive Rain Forest Park	原始雨林公园
Zhōngdiàn	Zhongdian	中甸
Zhōuchéng	Zhoucheng	周城
Sìchūan	Sichuan	四川
Bādōng	Badong	巴东
Chéngdū	Chéngdū	成都
Chóngqìng	Chongqing	重庆
Dàzú	Dazu	大足
Dūjiāngyàn	Dujiangyan	都江堰
Éméishān	Emeishan	峨眉山
Fēngdū	Fengdu	丰都
Gězhōu Bà	Gezhou Dam	葛州坝
Jiǔzhaìgōu	Jiuzhaigou	九寨沟
Kāngdìng	Kangding	康定
Lèshán	Leshan	乐山
Qútáng Xiá	Qutang Gorge	瞿塘峡
Shíbaǒzhài	Stone Treasure Stronghold	石宝寨
Sōngpān	Songpan	松潘
Wū Shān	Wu Mountain	巫山
Wū Xiá	Wu Gorge	巫峡
Xīlíng Xiá	Xiling Gorge	西陵峡

Chapter 11, Inner Mongolia and the Republic of Mongolia

Nèi Méng Gǔ	Inner Mongolia	内蒙古
Hū Hé Hào Té	Hohhot	呼和浩特

INDEX